INTERNATI

D1187814

International Trade
Theory, Strategies, and Evidence

LUIS A. RIVERA-BATIZ
AND
MARIA-A. OLIVA

OXFORD
UNIVERSITY PRESS

OXFORD
UNIVERSITY PRESS

Great Clarendon Street, Oxford OX2 6DP

Oxford University Press is a department of the University of Oxford.
It furthers the University's objective of excellence in research, scholarship,
and education by publishing worldwide in

Oxford New York

Auckland Bangkok Buenos Aires Cape Town Chennai
Dar es Salaam Delhi Hong Kong Istanbul Karachi Kolkata
Kuala Lumpur Madrid Melbourne Mexico City Mumbai Nairobi
São Paulo Shanghai Taipei Tokyo Toronto

Oxford is a registered trade mark of Oxford University Press
in the UK and in certain other countries

Published in the United States
by Oxford University Press Inc., New York

British Library Cataloguing in Publication Data

Data available

Library of Congress Cataloging in Publication Data

Data available

ISBN 0-19-829711-4

1 3 5 7 9 10 8 6 4 2

Typeset by Newgen Imaging Systems (P) Ltd., Chennai, India
Printed in Great Britain
on acid-free paper by
Biddles Ltd., Guildford and King's Lynn

To our parents
Conchita and José
Ada and Luis

To the memory of the late
Harry Gordon Johnson

Contents

Part II. Strategic Trade, Competition, and Environment

Part III. Innovation, Skills, and Contracts

Part IV. Liberalization, Protection, and Sanctions

Part V. Trade Politics and Regionalism

Part VI. WTO and International Cooperation

Figures

Tables

Preface

International Trade: Theory, Strategies, and Evidence presents a self-contained treatment of the main strands of trade analysis. It examines the latest theoretical and empirical research in the area as well as a wide array of policy issues. Policy coverage includes the latest research on openness and trade restrictions, anti-dumping and other contingent interventions, noncooperative and cooperative policy formulation, preferential trade arrangements and the World Trade Organization.

Our intended audience includes policymakers, professionals and students in economics and business who wish to examine international interactions. The discussions are self-contained and chapters are written so that they can be read independently of each other. General equilibrium modeling, game theory, and the econometric tools required to understand the themes studied are thoroughly reviewed in the text. The material is suitable for advanced undergraduates and graduate courses in economics and business. Most chapters have been successfully used in undergraduate and postgraduate courses.

The progressive integration of economies at a worldwide level has proved to be a formidable force. International trade and foreign investment (FDI) have been growing strikingly fast. The growth rate of trade exceeded 6 per cent per year during the past two decades, doubling average GDP growth rates during the same period. FDI has increased even faster than trade, reaching a record of $1.3 trillion in 2000. The pervasiveness of globalizing forces calls attention to the importance of understanding their rationales and consequences.

Interest in the analytics and empirical evidence relating to all forms of international exchange has experienced a veritable boost. Major concerns include the effect of trade, migration and foreign investment on wages and unemployment, the role of agglomeration, scale and externalities in the location of economic activities, the relation between trade, technology and growth, the political economy of trade policy, the global spread of multinational operations and the effects of rules guiding international competition.

One of the major developments in the field is the revival of research focusing on the determinants and effects of countries' comparative advantages and availability of human and other resources. In the early nineties, traditional approaches based on comparative advantages and the availability of productive resources were deemed to have failed empirically on the grounds that were unable to explain the structure of trade. The so-called traditional trade analysis appeared bound to be replaced by new trade theories stressing increasing returns, imperfect competition, product differentiation and strategic interactions. The modification of traditional frameworks to produce much better fit with the data has renewed the interest in the theoretical implications and empirical counterparts of alternative approaches to trade.

Strategic thinking has emerged as a main instrument of trade analysis. Modern industrial organization and game theory now provide main tools and a new language to tackle issues involving strategic interactions and oligopolistic markets. A wide array of policy measures and business initiatives have strategic content. Strategic behavior underlies firms' globalization strategies, interest group lobbying, international negotiations, and the formulation of industrial, competition and environmental policies. These themes lie at the core of international economics, business, and political economy.

PREVIEW

The exposition is divided into six parts. The first part covers the theory and empirical evidence on the determinants of trade patterns, economic geography and location, multinational corporations, and the interaction between trade and economic growth. The second part deals with strategic trade policy formulation, covering strategic policy interventions such as subsidies to exports, research, and firms' capacities. The third part deals with research and development, skills and contracts. The fourth part examines trade restrictions, sanctions and competition policy. The fifth part tackles the political economy of trade policy, that is, the endogenous formation of policy through the interaction between interest groups and the government. The interactive policy formation process helps to explain bloc formation and a host of coexisting trade-restricting and trade-promoting practices that are difficult to rationalize in traditional frameworks. The sixth part focuses on the global trading system and the economics of the World Trade Organization. It examines multilateral negotiations, cooperative agreements, and their sustainability.

ACKNOWLEDGMENTS

This book is multinational by birth and breeding. It evolved from our lectures on international trade issues at Universitat Pompeu Fabra in Barcelona, University of Florida at Gainesville, University of California at San Diego and ESCP-EAP (European School of Management) in Paris. It was partly written while we held positions at McGill University, Columbia University and MIT. We are thankful for numerous suggestions by students, colleagues and anonymous referees who helped to improve the exposition and encouraged us to expand the original coverage of the book, which focused on strategic issues, into a comprehensive treatment.

Luis A. Rivera-Batiz would like to acknowledge the influence of the works, discussions and expositions received from the late Harry G. Johnson, Rachel McCulloch, Jacob Frenkel, Michael Mussa, Robert Lucas, Paul Romer, In-Koo-Cho, Lester Telser and Ariel Rubinstein at the University of Chicago; Robert Staiger, Robert Wilson, Ennio Stacchetti, Mordecai Kurz and Dilip Abreu during a stay at Stanford; Elias Dinopoulos at the University of Florida at Gainesville; Carlos Asilis at the International Monetary Fund; Gabriel Sánchez at Universitat Pompeu Fabra, and Michel Robe at McGill University. The fuel provided by discussions with Francisco Rivera-Batiz has been inexhaustible.

Maria A. Oliva would like to thank Timothy Bresnaham, Jordi Caballé, Timothy Kehoe, Howard Petith and Xavier Vives at Universitat Autònoma de Barcelona; Antonio Cabrales and Andreu Mas Colell at Universitat Pompeu Fabra; Kyle Bagwell and Francisco L. Rivera-Batiz at Columbia University; Leonard Dudley at Université de Montréal; Zubair Iqbal at the International Monetary Fund; and Susan Athey, Abhijit Banerjee, Glenn Ellison, Bengt Holmström and Paul Krugman at MIT. The opportunity to attend Eric Maskin lectures at Harvard University was a pleasant and rewarding intellectual experience.

We are most grateful to the team at Oxford University Press and especially to Stuart Fowkes, Andrew Schuller, and Sarah Dobson, our editors, for encouragement and remarkable patience during the elaboration of the manuscript. Their advice helped us to improve product quality and successfully complete the project.

Luis A. Rivera-Batiz
Maria A. Oliva
Paris and Montreal

PART I

INTERNATIONAL TRADE MODELING

PART II

INTERNATIONAL TRADE MODELING

1

The Volume and Structure of Trade

What determines international trade patterns? David Ricardo's theory of comparative advantage states that production specialization and international trade patterns are determined by relative factor productivities. This theory predicts that exporters of manufactures will display higher labor productivity in manufacturing, relative to labor productivity in other industries, than importers of manufactures. These ideas are useful in rationalizing trade in different products, such as manufactures and food, between countries displaying different technologies. However, the Ricardian model does not explain the sources of cross-country productivity differentials.

The framework developed by Eli Heckscher and Bertil Ohlin assumes that countries have the same technologies. Specialization and trade are determined by relative factor abundances. Consider two countries trading capital intensive and labor intensive manufactures. The country that is relatively more capital abundant, in the sense of featuring a greater endowment of capital per worker, is predicted to export capital-intensive manufactures and import labor-intensive manufactures. The idea is that, in a scenario with no trade, the relatively abundant factor earns a low rental rate in relation to other factor. There are thus incentives to specialize and export the product that uses the relatively abundant factor more intensively while importing the product that uses the relatively scarce factor more intensively. The relative factor abundance theory, or simply the factor abundance theory, is useful in explaining a significant part of word trade. For instance, the exchange of US manufactures for Venezuelan oil can be explained by the fact that skilled labor is relatively abundant in the United States while oil is relatively abundant in Venezuela.

Sections 1.1 and 1.2 develop the Ricardian comparative advantage model in the two-good and continuum of goods settings. Sections 1.3 and 1.4 examine the factor abundance trade framework developed by Heckscher and Ohlin. Section 1.5 shows that, when factor endowments do not differ 'too much' in a Heckscher–Ohlin (HO) global economy, free trade with no labor mobility achieves the same global resource allocation and sustains the same factor prices as an integrated equilibrium featuring full factor mobility. Sections 1.6–1.8 discuss the duality theory approach. Section 1.9 develops Stolper–Samuelson and comparative advantage theorems applying when there are many goods and factors.

1.1. RICARDIAN COMPARATIVE ADVANTAGE

The Ricardian model assumes that countries display exogenously given differences in production costs. The simplest Ricardian model considers only one factor of production, labor, and assumes that labor is fully mobile across sectors but immobile internationally. Countries tend to specialize in the good in which they enjoy a relative comparative advantage. This section reviews the determination of wages, relative prices, resource allocation, and trade patterns in a static Ricardian framework. Cordella and Gabszewicz (1997) examine the Ricardian model with oligopolistic markets and show that comparative advantages and mutually beneficial exchanges can be wasted due to imperfect competition.

1.1.1. Comparative Advantage and Demand

Consider a two–sector Ricardian model with one input, labor. Two economies, domestic and foreign (denoted by an asterisk) have labor endowments L and L^* potentially employed in sectors I and II. Each sector's output $Q_j, j \in \{I, II\}$ is a function of the amount of labor used L_j and a sectorial productivity parameters A_j

$$Q_I = A_I L_I, \quad Q_{II} = A_{II} L_{II}, \quad Q_I^* = A_I^* L_I^*, \quad Q_{II}^* = A_{II}^* L_{II}^*,$$

where full employment requires

$$L = L_I + L_{II}, \qquad L^* = L_I^* + L_{II}^*.$$

The analysis assumes that the domestic economy enjoys a comparative advantage in the production of good I, meaning that the domestic economy is relatively more efficient than the foreign economy in producing good I,

$$\frac{A_I}{A_{II}} > \frac{A_I^*}{A_{II}^*} \iff \frac{A_{II}}{A_I} < \frac{A_{II}^*}{A_I^*}. \tag{1.1}$$

In a two-sector framework, if the domestic economy enjoys a comparative advantage in good I, the foreign economy must enjoy a comparative advantage in the production of good II. To show this, just take the reciprocal on the left–hand side inequality in (1.1) and recall that the inequality is reversed when reciprocals are obtained.

Comparative advantage refers to labor productivity in one industry relative to productivity in the other industry. It does not refer to absolute productivities. For instance, even if the domestic economy enjoys an absolute advantage in both sectors, $A_I > A_I^*$ and $A_{II} > A_{II}^*$, a comparative advantage can be enjoyed in only one sector. The previous comparative advantage condition is often expressed in terms of lower relative unit labor costs as measured by the input–output ratios $a_{Lj} \equiv L_j / Q_j = 1/A_j$ indicating the amount of labor used per unit of output

$$\frac{a_{LII}}{a_{LI}} < \frac{a_{LII}^*}{a_{LI}^*} \iff \frac{a_{LI}}{a_{LII}} > \frac{a_{LI}^*}{a_{LII}^*}.$$

Both countries share the same Cobb–Douglas utility functions

$$U(D_I, D_{II}) = D_I^\mu D_{II}^{1-\mu}, \qquad U(D_I, D_{II}) = D_I^{*\mu} D_{II}^{*(1-\mu)}, \tag{1.2}$$

where D_I and D_{II} represent consumption and $\mu > 0.5$ is a parameter of preferences.

The assumptions $\mu > 0.5$ and $A_I/A_{II} > A_I^*/A_{II}^*$ imply that the domestic economy specializes and employs its whole labor endowment in good I. Depending on whether or not the foreign economy specializes, we have two possible specialization patterns in equilibrium.

1. *Full global specialization.* In this case the foreign country fully specializes and employs its entire labor endowment in industry II so that both countries are fully specialized.
2. *Partial global specialization.* The foreign economy is not specialized but rather produces both goods while the domestic economy fully specializes in good I.

In both cases, the home country exports good I and the foreign country exports good II.

1.1.2. Full Specialization: Wages, Prices, and Trade

Consider first the case in which the domestic country specializes in product I (i.e. $L_I = L$), and the foreign country specializes in product II (i.e. $L_{II}^* = L$). The resulting trade pattern is trivial. The domestic country must export good I and the foreign country must export good II.

Under full specialization, (1) there is an equality of the domestic wage bill, the value of domestic good I output and world spending on good I, (2) there is an equality of the foreign wage bill, the value of foreign good II output, and world spending on good II

$$wL = p_I Q_I = p_I(D_I + D_I^*) = \mu E^W \rightarrow p_I = \frac{\mu E^W}{Q_I},$$

$$w^* L^* = p_{II} Q_{II} = p_{II}(D_{II} + D_{II}^*) = (1-\mu)E^W \rightarrow p_{II} = \frac{(1-\mu)E^W}{Q_{II}},$$

where E^W denotes world nominal expenditure, p_I and p_{II} denote prices. The appendix shows that the identical Cobb–Douglas utility functions in (1.2) imply that a constant share μ of domestic, foreign and world's total expenditure falls on good I (and a constant share $1 - \mu$ falls on good II).

The domestic-to-foreign country wage ratio w/w^* is equal to the ratio of the shares of good I and good II in total expenditure times the foreign-to-domestic labor endowment

$$\frac{w}{w^*} = \frac{\mu}{1-\mu}\frac{L^*}{L} > 1, \quad \mu > 0.5. \tag{1.3}$$

Under full specialization, relative country wages are pinned down by the preference function parameter μ and relative labor endowments and do not vary with the productivity of labor A and A^*. The domestic economy has a higher wage the larger the spending share of the good in which it enjoys a comparative advantage and the lower its labor supply relative to its trading partner's labor supply.

The equilibrium relative price of good I in terms of good II is determined by the condition that the global supply of each good is equal to its global demand, $Q_I = \mu E^W / p_I$ and $Q_{II} = \mu E^W / p_{II}$, which implies

$$p \equiv \frac{p_I}{p_{II}} = \frac{\mu}{1-\mu} \frac{Q_{II}}{Q_I} = \frac{\mu}{1-\mu} \frac{A_{II} L_{II}}{A_I L_I} = \frac{\mu}{1-\mu} \frac{A_{II} L^*}{A_I L}, \tag{1.4}$$

where $Q_I = A_I L_I = A_I L$ and $Q_{II} = A_{II} L_{II} = A_{II} L^*$. The equilibrium relative price turns out to be a function of the relative labor endowment and preference and technology parameters. Good II is taken as the numeraire of the system so that its price can be defined to be equal to one.

1.1.3. Partial Specialization: Wages, Prices, and Trade

If the foreign economy does not specialize, intersectoral labor mobility implies that a single nominal wage rate w^* must prevail in both active sectors,

$$w^* = A_I^* p_I = A_{II}^* p_{II}. \tag{1.5}$$

Because $w = A_I p_I$, the domestic-to-foreign relative wage rate under partial specialization is

$$\frac{w}{w^*} = \frac{A_I}{A_I^*} > 1. \tag{1.6}$$

The intersectoral wage condition $w^* = A_I^* p_I = A_{II}^* p_{II}$ also implies

$$p \equiv \frac{p_I}{p_{II}} = \frac{A_{II}^*}{A_I^*}.$$

An intuitive condition for partial specialization arises in the special case in which countries have the same labor endowments, $L = L^*$. World nominal expenditure is equal to world nominal income

$$E^W = wL + w^* L^* = (w + w^*)L \quad \rightarrow \quad \frac{E^W}{w^*} = \left(\frac{w}{w^*} + 1\right) L.$$

Because the whole income generated in industry II is paid to labor, $w^* L_{II}^* = p_{II}(D_{II} + D_{II}^*) = (1 - \mu)E^W$,

$$L_{II}^* = (1 - \mu)\frac{E^W}{w^*} = (1 - \mu)\left(\frac{w}{w^*} + 1\right)L = (1 - \mu)\left(\frac{A_I}{A_I^*} + 1\right)L,$$

where the last step utilizes the equality $w/w^* = A_I/A_I^*$ holding under partial specialization.

The conditions for partial specialization ($L_{II}^* < L$) when trading partners have identical labor endowments are: (1) a high enough share of good I in total spending (high μ), and (2) a low enough value of the ratio of home to foreign country productivity. Under these conditions, the global demand for good I is high enough and the home country supply is low enough to justify some foreign production of good I even if labor endowments are the same.

1.2. RICARDIAN MODEL: CONTINUUM OF GOODS

The single-input version of the Ricardian model can be generalized in many directions. For instance, the development of a two-factor model with fixed input–output coefficients is straightforward. This section examines the popular generalization of the Ricardian framework to encompass a continuum of goods, due to Dornbusch *et al.* (1977*a*).

1.2.1. Productivity Differentials, Specialization, and Trade

Consider a two-country model with a continuum of goods z defined on the interval $z \in [0, 1]$. There is only one input, labor. Domestic and foreign labor endowments are L and L^* and there is no international labor mobility. The full employment condition is

$$L = \int_0^1 l(z)\, dz = \int_0^1 a(z) q(z)\, dz = \int_0^1 a(z)\, d(z)\, dz, \quad a(z) \equiv \frac{l(z)}{q(z)},$$

where $l(z)$ denotes the amount of labor devoted to produce z. Market clearing implies that the output of good z, $q(z)$, is equal to the amount demanded $d(z)$. A similar full-employment equation holds for the foreign country.

Domestic and foreign prices correspond to unit labor costs,

$$p(z) = \frac{l(z) w}{q(z)} = a(z) w, \qquad p^*(z^*) = \frac{l^*(z^*) w^*}{q^*(z^*)} = a^*(z^*) w^*,$$

where the domestic and foreign input–output coefficients for goods z and z^*, $a(z)$ and $a^*(z^*)$ are assumed to be constant. Home country labor productivity in the production of good $z \in [0, 1]$, relative to foreign country productivity, is

$$\frac{A(z)}{A^*(z)} = \frac{a^*(z)}{a(z)}, \quad a(z) \equiv \frac{l(z)}{q(z)}, \quad a^*(z) \equiv \frac{l^*(z)}{q^*(z)},$$

where $l(z)$ and $q(z)$ denote labor use and output.

Goods are ranked in such a way that a lower value of z corresponds to higher home country's relative productivity. Specifically, for any pair of goods z_1 and $z_2 \in [0, 1]$,

$$z_1 < z_2 \quad \Leftrightarrow \quad \frac{A(z_2)}{A^*(z_2)} < \frac{A(z_1)}{A^*(z_1)} \quad \Leftrightarrow \quad \frac{A^*(z_1)}{A^*(z_2)} < \frac{A(z_1)}{A(z_2)}.$$

In other words, goods are ordered according to diminishing home country relative comparative advantage.

What is the pattern of specialization and trade? Conditional on given domestic and foreign wages, the pattern of trade is determined by relative productivities. The home country is the sole producer of all goods carrying indexes lower than threshold index $\bar{z}$, that is, all goods for which $z < \bar{z}$. Accordingly, the home country exports all goods for which $z < \bar{z}$. By the same token, the foreign country produces and exports all goods for which $\bar{z} < z$. At the borderline product, both countries are equally efficient and trade is indeterminate. These rules are just a generalization of the specialization and trade rules in the two–good Ricardian framework.

The borderline commodity index, $\bar{z} \in [0, 1]$, corresponds to the fraction of the total number of goods produced in the home country. The value of $\bar{z}$ is determined by the condition that home and foreign per unit labor costs are the same, $wa(\bar{z}) = w^*a^*(\bar{z})$, or

$$\frac{w}{w^*} = \frac{a^*(\bar{z})}{a(\bar{z})} = \frac{A(\bar{z})}{A^*(\bar{z})} \equiv \hat{A}(\bar{z}). \tag{1.7}$$

The function $\hat{A}(\bar{z})$ is the ratio of home to foreign country productivity in the borderline good. It is assumed to be a smooth function with no flat segments that declines with z by construction. Therefore, (1.7) establishes a negative relation $w/w^* = \hat{A}(\bar{z})$ between the home country relative wage, w/w^*, and the fraction of the total number of goods produced in the home country, $\bar{z}$.

1.2.2. Ricardian Equilibrium

In order to obtain the equilibrium relative wage rate w/w^* and borderline product $\bar{z}$ demand conditions must be considered. Both countries are assumed to have identical homothetic preferences. Total home country expenditure on all goods in $[0, 1]$ is equal to income wL

$$wL = \int_0^1 p(z)d(z)\,dz,$$

where $d(z)$ represents an infinitesimal demand for product z. In the continuum of goods framework examined, the contribution of any individual product z to total spending is negligible (i.e. infinitesimal, essentially zero). By contrast, the share in total spending of any continuous interval of products in $[0,1]$ is nonnegligible (i.e. a positive number).

Let us define $v(z_1)$ as the share in total spending of the products in set $[0, z_1]$

$$v(z_1) \equiv \frac{\int_0^{z_1} p(z)d(z)\,dz}{wL}.$$

Domestic income wL equals the sum of the local and foreign demands for domestic products

$$wL = v(\bar{z})wL + v(\bar{z})w^*L^*, \quad v(\bar{z}) = \frac{\int_0^{\bar{z}} p(z)d(z)\,dz}{wL},$$

where identical homothetic preferences imply that $v(\bar{z})$ is the share of domestic products in both domestic and foreign income (or spending). The following positive relation between w/w^* and $\bar{z}$ obtains

$$\frac{w}{w^*} = \frac{v(\bar{z})}{1 - v(\bar{z})} \frac{L^*}{L} \equiv B(\bar{z}; L, L^*), \tag{1.8}$$

where $v(\bar{z})$ is the fraction of home and foreign income spent on home goods and the function $B(\cdot)$ is introduced for notational convenience.

What determines the equilibrium relative wage rate w/w^* and the borderline product $\bar{z}$? Equations (1.7) and (1.8) define a two-equation system in the variables w/w^* and $\bar{z}$. Equating their right-hand sides pins down the borderline product $\bar{z}$ satisfying both relations simultaneously

$$\frac{A(\bar{z}^R)}{A^*(\bar{z}^R)} = \frac{v(\bar{z}^R)}{1 - v(\bar{z}^R)} \frac{L^*}{L}, \tag{1.9}$$

where the superscript R indicates Ricardian equilibrium. Substituting the equilibrium relative productivity into the relative wage equation (1.7) yields

$$\left(\frac{w}{w^*}\right)^R = \frac{A(\bar{z}^R)}{A^*(\bar{z}^R)}. \tag{1.10}$$

Uniqueness of equilibrium can be verified by depicting the equilibrium as the intersection of curves $w/w^* = \hat{A}(\bar{z})$ and $w/w^* = B(\bar{z}; L, L^*)$ on the $(\bar{z}, w/w^*)$ plane. Because $\hat{A}(\bar{z})$ defines a downward-sloping function of $\bar{z} \in [0, 1]$, and $B(\bar{z}; L, L^*)$ defines an upward-sloping function of $\bar{z}$ that starts at $B(0; L, L^*) = 0$, the borderline product and the relative cross-country wage rate are unique.

1.2.3. Migration and Integrated Equilibrium

What determines factor movements (i.e. migration) and what are their effects in this framework? For given factor endowments, a Ricardian global economy generates migration incentives because relative cross-country wages are not equalized. If there are no barriers to migration, labor moves toward the higher wage location, which is the one with greater labor productivity in the borderline product.

Suppose that the home economy is initially the most productive. The effect of migration, an increase in L and corresponding decline in L^*, can be determined from (1.9). Migration toward the home economy raises the borderline product index and thus the fraction of the products elaborated in the home economy. Moreover, the new equilibrium borderline product features a lower ratio of home to foreign labor productivity. Therefore, migration reduces wages in the host economy relative to wages in the source economy. The migration process stops when the borderline product is the one at which relative productivities and wages are equalized. If the home economy happens to be more productive in all products, then the whole population agglomerates there.

The equilibrium resource allocation that would occur under perfect labor mobility is called an integrated equilibrium. In the Ricardian setup, the integrated equilibrium differs drastically from the free trade equilibrium with no migration. Specifically, wages equalize in the integrated equilibrium while the free trade equilibrium with no labor mobility features a wage gap.

In the Ricardian environment, current residents of the more productive economy have incentives to prevent migration. However, there are world gains from migration as labor always migrates to the more productive economy at the margin, which generates efficiency gains at a global scale. It is globally more efficient to allocate labor to the most efficient rather than the less efficient economy. The Ricardian model captures a fundamental trade-off involving migration. It illustrates a clear conflict between reduced national welfare and increased global welfare. Higher global welfare is associated with higher wages for migrants and remaining source country workers, but lower host country wages.

1.3. PRODUCTION AND FACTOR REWARDS

The factor abundance model of trade developed by Eli Heckscher, Bertil Ohlin, Paul Samuelson, Jaroslav Vanek, and Ronald Jones, among others, is one of the major tools of international trade analysis and policy formulation. Economist Bertil Ohlin won a Nobel prize in economics for the early development of this general equilibrium trade framework (Ohlin, 1933).

The basic version of the HO model of trade focuses on a $2 \times 2 \times 2$ world consisting of two countries, two goods I and II, and two homogeneous factors of production, capital K and labor L. The reader can verify that the following assumptions are used at some step of the ensuing trade analysis based on the two–sector general equilibrium model.

1. Consumers have identical homothetic preferences. Therefore, for any given relative price p, both countries consume goods in the same proportion

$$\frac{D_{II}}{D_I}(p) = \frac{D_{II}^*}{D_I^*}(p), \quad p = \frac{p_I}{p_{II}} = p_I,$$

   where good II is chosen as the numeraire ($p_{II} \equiv 1$).

2. Countries share identical constant returns to scale production functions for each sector

$$Q_I = F_I(K_I, L_I), \qquad Q_I^* = F_I(K_I^*, L_I^*),$$
$$Q_{II} = F_{II}(K_{II}, L_{II}), \qquad Q_{II}^* = F_{II}(K_{II}^*, L_{II}^*).$$

   The constant returns to scale assumption means that production functions are homogeneous of degree one in the inputs K and L, that is, if both inputs are multiplied by an arbitrary constant c, the resulting level of output is also multiplied by c

$$cQ_J = F_j(cK_j, cL_j), \quad j \in \{I, II\}.$$

The homogeneity of degree one property can be used to express the production function in per worker terms. This is accomplished by substituting $c = 1/L_j$ into the previous production function

$$\frac{Q_j}{L_j} = F_j\left(\frac{1}{L_j}K_j, \frac{1}{L_j}L_j\right) = F_j(k_j, 1) = f_j(k_j),$$

where $k_j = K_j/L_j$ is defined in per unit of employment terms.

3. There are no factor intensity reversals, that is, the ordering of the sectorial capital–labor ratios is invariant to changes in the ratio of wages w to the rent r on the use of capital services. The discussion assumes that, for any given wage–rental ratio $\omega = w/r$, good I is capital intensive and good II labor intensive. Formally, the following factor intensity inequality holds for all ω

$$k_I(\omega) = \frac{K_I}{L_I}(\omega) \; > \; k_{II}(\omega) = \frac{K_{II}}{L_{II}}(\omega), \quad \omega \equiv \frac{w}{r}.$$

The absence of factor intensity reversals permits defining industries' relative factor intensities unambiguously, independently of the value of the wage–rental ratio.

4. Factors are inelastically supplied in each country, are perfectly mobile across industries but immobile across countries, and are fully employed. The full employment of labor is given by equality of the economy wide supply of labor, L, and the sum of the labor used in both sectors, $a_{LI}Q_I + a_{LII}Q_{II}$. By the same token, full employment of capital is given by equality of the economywide supply of capital, K, and the capital input used in both sectors, $a_{KI}Q_I + a_{KII}Q_{II}$. Formally, the full employment conditions are:

$$L = L_I + L_{II} = a_{LI}(\omega)Q_I + a_{LII}(\omega)Q_{II},$$
$$K = K_I + K_{II} = a_{KI}(\omega)Q_I + a_{KII}(\omega)Q_{II},$$

where, contrary to the Ricardian model, the input–output coefficients a_{ij} are functions of the wage to rental ratio.

5. Perfect competition prevails in all goods and factors markets.
6. There are no taxes, subsidies, or trade barriers such as tariffs and transport costs.
7. Welfare analysis assumes that aggregate preferences can be represented by a representative consumer or by a social indifference curve.

The assumptions of the HO model serve to bypass behavioral complexities and highlight the key production elements determining international trade. The assumption that consumers have the same homothetic utility functions is unrealistic in that it precludes superior goods but is useful analytically in focusing on the role of the production sector. The assumption that countries are identical ex ante except for factor endowments permits isolating the role of factor abundances in international trade patterns. International factor immobility provides a benchmark that can be extended to cover international factor mobility. Moreover, under the conditions giving rise to factor price equalization, resource allocation under free trade and factor immobility is exactly the same as under perfect factor mobility (see below). The assumption of frictionless and instantaneous factor mobility across industries is not realistic in the short run but is used to focus on longer term general equilibrium effects of policies and changes in the economic environment.

A large literature examines what happens when the assumptions of the basic HO model are relaxed. Key results hold when there are many goods and productive factors, as long as the number of goods is equal or greater than the number of factors (Ethier, 1984). The model can be extended to tackle issues relating to international factor mobility (see chapter on migration), interindustry immobility of factors that are specific to a particular sector (see chapter on political economy), noncompetitive market structures, and others.

1.3.1. Core Theorems

The basic properties of the HO model are captured in four major theorems:

1. The Stolper–Samuelson theorem is a comparative static result relating factor and product prices, holding factor endowments fixed (Stolper and Samuelson, 1941). If the relative domestic price of the labor-intensive commodity is raised, then labor unambiguously benefits and capital loses. If the relative domestic price of the capital-intensive commodity is raised, then capital unambiguously benefits and labor loses.

   The theorem also states that a higher price of the factor employed relatively intensively in sector II relative to the price of the factor intensively used in sector I implies a higher relative price of good II. In other words, the higher the wage–rental ratio w/r, the greater the relative price of the good produced with the higher labor-to-capital ratio. This theorem shows that the HO model assumptions establish a one-to-one relationship between relative and absolute factor rewards on one side and relative goods prices on the other.

2. The factor price equalization theorem states that, when two countries satisfying the HO assumptions freely trade with each other and their factor endowments do not differ 'too much', factor prices will be equalized across countries even if there is no factor mobility. The factor-price equalization theorem gives conditions under which trade in goods makes factor mobility unnecessary for the equalization of factor returns. The meaning of factor-price equalization is that the trade in factor services implicit in trade in goods can substitute for trade in the factors themselves (Samuelson, 1948, 1949; Mundell, 1957).

3. The Rybczynski theorem is a comparative static result relating the endowments of a given factor and output levels, holding factor rewards fixed (and thus relative prices fixed according to the Stolper–Samuelson theorem). The theorem states that, if

there is an increase in a factor's endowment, the output of the good that uses that factor relatively more intensively will increase. Also, the output of the good that uses that factor relatively less intensively will decline (Rybczynski, 1955).

4. The HO theorem, also called the factor abundance theorem, states that a country will export the good that employs more intensively the country's relatively abundant factor. This theorem and its generalizations embody a key testable prediction relating factor endowments and trade patterns.

We proceed to review the two-sector general equilibrium model and present the demonstrations of the core theorems related to the HO model. The mathematical proofs are standard and appear in Jones (1965), Wong (1995), Bhagwati *et al.* (1998), and Bowen *et al.* (1998). Dornbusch, *et al.* (1977*b*) examine the HO model with a continuum of goods.

1.3.2. Optimal Factor Utilization and Product Exhaustion

Factors' marginal productivities in a given industry are given by

$$\frac{\partial F(K,L)}{\partial K} = \frac{\partial (Lf(k))}{\partial K} = Lf'(k)\frac{1}{L} = f'(k),$$

$$\frac{\partial F(K,L)}{\partial L} = \frac{\partial (Lf(k))}{\partial L} = f(k) + Lf'(k)\left(\frac{-K}{L^2}\right) = f(k) - kf'(k),$$

where the prime stands for a derivative. All marginal products are a function of a single variable: the capital–labor ratio. Marginal products are assumed to be positive and to decrease with the capital–labor ratio, that is, $f'(k) \equiv \partial f/\partial k > 0$ and $f''(k) \equiv \partial^2 f/\partial k^2 < 0$.

The condition for optimal factor utilization in the production of commodities I and II is that the price of each factor is equal to the value of its marginal productivity, that is,

$$r = \frac{\partial F_I}{\partial K} = p_I f'_I = p_{II} f'_{II},$$

$$w = \frac{\partial F_I}{\partial L} = p_I (f_I - k_I f'_I) = p_{II}(f_{II} - k_{II} f'_{II}).$$

The wage–rental ratio ω is thus equal to

$$\omega = \frac{w}{r} = \frac{f_I}{f'_I} - k_I = \frac{f_{II}}{f'_{II}} - k_{II}.$$

The slope of $\omega_j(k_j)$ is given by

$$\omega'_{k_j}(k_j) = \frac{f'_j(k_j)}{f''_j(k_j)} - 1 < 0,$$

where we use the assumptions $f'_j(k_j) > 0$ and $f''_j(k_j) < 0$. Because a homogeneous of degree one production function is homothetic, the capital-labor ratio is a one-to-one function of the wage–rental rate. This means that, once the wage-rental ratio is determined, each industry's capital-labor ratio is also specified. Moreover, the capital–labor ratio uniquely determines the wage–rental ratio.

A homogeneous of degree one function $F(K, L)$ displays the following property

$$F(K, L) = \frac{dF(K, L)}{dK} K + \frac{dF(K, L)}{dL} L,$$

meaning that the total level of output can be decomposed into the sum of the amount of each factor used multiplied by the marginal productivities of each factor. The previous property is called product exhaustion because it implies that, if factor markets are competitive so that the wage rate w and the rental rate on capital r are equal to the marginal products of labor and capital, total factor rewards are equal to the output level

$$F_I(K_I, L_I) = wK_I + rL_I, \qquad F_{II}(K_{II}, L_{II}) = wK_{II} + rL_{II}.$$

1.3.3. Unit Costs, Wage–Rental Ratios, and Prices

The constant returns to scale assumption implies that total costs C_j can be expressed as the average (i.e. unit) cost c_j times the output level Q_j,

$$C_j = c_j(w, r, Q_j)Q_j, \quad j \in \{I, II\}.$$

A competitive equilibrium sustains the output level Q_j that maximizes sector $j \in \{I, II\}$ profits, $\Pi_j(p_j, w, r) = p_j Q_j - c_j(p_j, w, r)Q_j$ for given goods and factor prices. In the two-sector model, constant returns to scale implies that average costs are equal to marginal costs and depend on the wage rate w and the rental rate on capital r but do not change with the level of output.

The competitive zero profit condition $0 = \Pi_j = p_j Q_j - c_j Q_j$ is assumed to hold in both industries so that goods prices $p = p_I / p_{II} = p_I (p_{II} \equiv 1)$ are equal to the average production costs c_I and c_{II}

$$p \equiv p_I = c_I = a_{LI} w + a_{KI} r, \quad a_{LI} \equiv \frac{L_I}{Q_I}, \quad a_{KI} \equiv \frac{K_I}{Q_I},$$

$$p_{II} \equiv 1 = c_{II} = a_{LII} w + a_{KII} r, \quad a_{LII} \equiv \frac{L_{II}}{Q_{II}}, \quad a_{KII} \equiv \frac{K_{II}}{Q_{II}}.$$

$$(1.11)$$

Goods prices are equal to the sum of average labor costs and average capital costs. The labor cost per unit of output equals the amount of labor used per unit of output a_{LI} or a_{LII} times the wage rate w. By the same token, the capital cost per unit of output is equal to the input–output ratio a_{KI} or a_{KII} times the rental rate r on the use of capital.

Solving for w in each sector's zero profit condition yields

$$w = \frac{1}{a_{LII}} p - \frac{a_{KII}}{a_{LII}} r, \quad w = \frac{1}{a_{LI}} - \frac{a_{KI}}{a_{LI}} r,$$

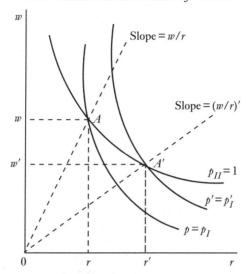

Figure 1.1. *Good prices and factor rewards*

where all the input–output coefficients are functions of the wage rate w and the rental rate on the use of capital r, but not of the output level, which implies that an economy is characterized by a single relation between factor and goods prices.

Figure 1.1 illustrates the determination of the wage–rental ratio as a function of the relative price p. Good I is assumed to be capital intensive and good II labor intensive. The curves labeled $p_I = p$ and $p_{II} = 1$ depict the combination of wage w and rents r keeping average costs and goods' prices constant in sectors I and II. The intersection of the two curves at point A pins down the economies' equilibrium wage–rental ratio. The assumption of no factor intensity reversals ensures that the isoprice curves intersect only once. The curves are convex due to the way in which factor proportions change when factor prices change. For instance, consider increases in the wage rate and the required reduction in the rental rate on capital so as to keep average costs constant. As the wage rate increases, the use of labor declines relative to the use of capital. This feature implies that additional increases in wages have a smaller impact on labor costs while reductions in the rental on capital have a greater cost-reduction impact. Therefore, as we move up the curve representing (r, w) combinations consistent with a given price, wage increases require smaller and smaller reductions in the rental rate to keep average costs constant.

1.3.4. Stolper–Samuelson Theorem: Product and Factor Prices

The Stolper–Samuelson theorem characterizes the mapping from goods prices factor rewards, holding factor endowments fixed. The theorem states that there is a one-to-one association between relative prices and absolute and relative factor rewards.

Specifically, if the relative domestic price of the labor-intensive commodity is raised, then labor unambiguously benefits (wages go up) and capital unambiguously loses (its rental rate declines). Therefore, the wage–rental ratio increases. If the relative domestic price of the capital-intensive commodity is raised, then capital unambiguously benefits and labor ambiguously loses so that the wage–rental ratio declines. These relations can be viewed as comparative static results relating changes in products prices determined in global markets to internal factor prices in the presence of factor immobility.

Figure 1.1 illustrates the Stolper–Samuelson theorem stating that an increase in the relative price of a good raises the rental price of the factor used relatively more intensively in that good and lowers the rental price of the other factor. Given the assumption that good I is capital intensive and good II is labor intensive, a higher relative price $p' > p$ of good I requires a higher r, a lower w and a lower wage–rental ratio $(w/r)' < w/r$. This reflects the assumption that, for a given (r, w), the slope of the isoprice curve for good I is greater than the slope of the isoprice curve for good II. This slope condition in turn reflects the assumption that good I is relatively more intensive in the use of capital and good II is relatively more intensive in the use of labor.

The Stolper–Samuelson theorem also contains a proposition about a factor price magnification effect. The factor price magnification effect of a change in the relative price $p = p_I/p_{II}$ states that the percentage increase in the wage rate exceeds the percentage increase in the good price p

$$\hat{r} > \hat{p} > 0 > \hat{w},$$

with the 'hat' symbol denoting percentage change. Notice that constant returns to scale implies that an equiproportional increase in w and r entails the same proportional increase in p. Therefore, movements along the ray w/r are associated with $\hat{w} = \hat{p} = \hat{r}$. The shift to the ray $(w/r)' < w/r$ must thus imply $\hat{r} > \hat{p}$.

1.3.5. Factor Price Equalization

The factor price equalization theorem states conditions under which free trade leads to the international equalization of trading partners' absolute and relative factor prices. Under these conditions, the free trade equilibrium sustains the same wage rates and the same rental on capital even if trading partners differ in their factor endowments and there is no trade in factors. Factor equalization derives from the Stolper–Samuelson theorem establishing that there is a one-to-one relation between prices of goods and the prices of the factors that produce them. The one-to-one relationship means that the knowledge of goods prices pins down factor prices uniquely. Because international trade causes goods prices to be equalized across countries factor rewards must also be equalized.

The meaning of the factor price equalization theorem is that, from the perspective of potentially migrating factors, trade in goods can substitute for trade in factors. If commodity prices are equalized through free trade between two countries, then factor prices will also be equalized and the incentives to migrate disappear. Factor price equalization contrasts with the factor reward differentials obtained in the Ricardian model.

The equalization of factor prices can be obtained from Fig. 1.1 by incorporating the corresponding analysis for the foreign country. Observe that, as long as both countries produce both goods in the trading equilibrium, Fig. 1.1 can be used to represent factor market equilibrium in both countries because they have the same production function and production is diversified in both countries. These conditions mean that both countries feature the same isoprice map and face the same production relation between the local relative price p and factor rewards. Therefore, both countries must have the same factor prices w and r and the same wage–rental ratio.

Factor price equalization fails, in the sense that trade in goods does not entail international equalization of factor prices, when cross-country differences in factor endowments are so large as the lead to full specialization even if the basic assumptions of the HO framework hold. Lack of factor-price equalization also results when the HO assumptions do not hold, namely: (1) countries' production functions are not the same so that product price equalization does not translate into equal factor prices, (2) transport costs prevent price equalization and thus factor price equalization, (3) nonhomothetic demands or demands that differ across countries lead to production specialization, and (4) other factors breaking the HO assumptions, such as different technologies across countries or the existence of joint production technologies.

1.3.6. Rybczynski Theorem, Endowments, and Output

The Rybczynski theorem specifies how an exogenous change in factor supplies affects the structure of production for given product prices. It states that, for given product prices, the increase in the endowment of a factor will cause an expansion in the production of the good that uses that factor relatively more intensively and a reduction of the output of the good that uses this factor relatively less intensively.

Figure 1.2 uses the Edgeworth box depicting factor use to illustrate the Rybczynski theorem. Initial factor endowments are K and L. The isoquants depicting the combinations of capital and labor that produce a given level of output are labeled Q_I and Q_{II}. The origin of the isoquant map for good II is point O_{II} and production increases as one moves on the southwest direction. The contract curve joining the origins O_I and O_{II} (not shown) traces the points at which there is full employment and production is efficient. The isocost line $K = C/r - (w/r)L$ depicts the combinations of K and L that entail the same total cost C. For any given wage-rental ratio, efficiency requires the tangency between isoquants Q_I and Q_{II} and the isocost line, as shown in the figure.

Consider now an increase in the endowment of capital and examine how factor allocation changes while maintaining the relative price p constant at an arbitrary level. The Stolper–Samuelson theorem implies that a constant relative price p is associated with a constant wage–rental ratio. Production under constant returns to scale implies that a constant wage–rental ratio is associated with a constant capital–labor ratio. This means that a change in the endowment of capital, at a given relative price, affects the scale of production of each industry but not the optimal input mix.

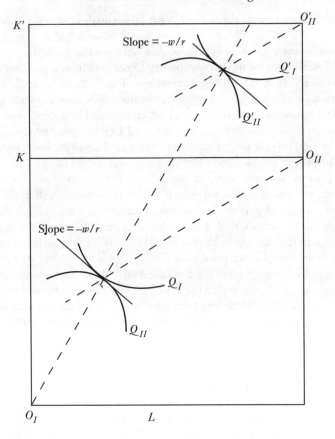

Figure 1.2. *Capital endowment and Rybczynski theorem*

The new efficient point involves greater production of capital intensive good I and a reduced output of labor intensive good II. The reason is that the additional capital must be absorbed by the sector that uses capital intensively. The absorption of capital requires obtaining labor previously employed in the labor intensive industry, which must contract to release enough labor to absorb the additional capital employed in the capital intensive industry. A similar analysis applies to an increase in the endowment of labor. Labor intensive industry II expands while capital intensive industry I must contract.

The Rybczynski theorem also contains a proposition about an output magnification effect. The output magnification effect of a change in endowments states that the percentage increase in the output of the good intensive in the augmented factor exceeds the percentage increase in the augmented factor. Given the assumption that good I is capital intensive and good II labor intensive

$$\hat{Q}_I > \hat{K} > 0 > \hat{Q}_{II}, \qquad \hat{Q}_{II} > \hat{L} > 0 > \hat{Q}_I.$$

The magnification effect follows from the assumption of constant returns to scale and the fact that the contracting industry must leave free both the augmented factor and the other factor. By leaving free the augmenting factor it generates the magnification effect because the expanding industry ends up employing more than the increase in the endowment of the factor it uses intensively.

1.4. FACTOR ABUNDANCE AND TRADE

The HO factor proportions theory offers an explanation for relative comparative advantage that is not captured by the Ricardian model of exogenous labor productivities. According to the two-good HO framework with two factors, a country exports the good that uses relatively more intensively the factor that is relatively more abundant in the country. The idea is that, in the absence of trade (i.e. in autarky), the relatively abundant factor receives a low rental price relative to the other factor. If there is no home demand bias favoring the good that utilizes the abundant factor more intensively, its price will be lower at home than abroad. If free trade ensues, there are incentives to export the low price product that utilizes the abundant factor more intensively while importing the product that utilizes the scarce factor more intensively.

Figure 1.3 illustrates the HO theorem. The production possibility frontier or transformation curve $Q_{II} = T(Q_I)$ describes the maximum output of good II that can be produced for each feasible level of output of good I. The transformation curve can be derived from the production functions, $Q_I = F_I(K_I, L_I)$ and $Q_{II} = F_{II}(K_{II}, L_{II})$, given capital and labor endowments and the full employment conditions $K = K_I + K_{II}$ and $L = L_I + L_{II}$. Constant returns to scale implies that the transformation curve is concave. The concave foreign transformation curve $Q_{II}^* = T^*(Q_I^*)$ can be derived in a similar manner.

Under free trade with perfect competition and no trade barriers, home and foreign agents take world prices as given

$$\frac{p_I^W}{p_{II}^W} = \frac{p_I}{p_{II}} = \frac{p_I^*}{p_{II}^*}.$$

The figure assumes that (1) the domestic country is capital abundant and the foreign country is labor abundant, and (2) good I is capital intensive while good II is labor intensive. The production structure differs across countries because they have different factor endowments. Under constant returns to scale, if good I is capital intensive and II is labor intensive, the Rybczynski theorem implies that the ratio of the output of good I to the output of good II is greater for the capital abundant domestic economy than for the labor abundant foreign economy. This relation is illustrated by the production points Q and Q^*

$$\frac{K^*}{L^*} < \frac{K}{L} \rightarrow \frac{Q_I^*}{Q_{II}^*} < \frac{Q_I}{Q_{II}}.$$

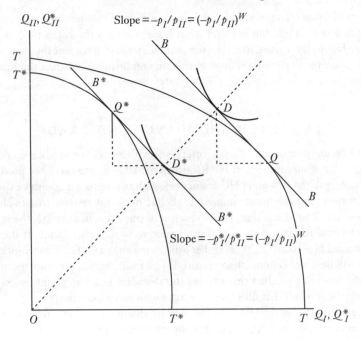

Figure 1.3. *Heckscher–Ohlin factor abundance theorem*

Each country's equilibrium requires, as depicted in Fig. 1.3,

1. National utility maximization, as depicted by the tangency of each country's indifference curve to the national budget line implied by world prices. The consumption choice tangency is depicted by consumption points D and D^*.
2. Maximization of national income, as depicted by the tangency of each country's transformation curve to the relative price line implied by world prices. The production choice tangency is depicted by production points Q and Q^*.
3. Balanced trade, as depicted by the equality of the two trade triangles.

The so-called double tangency condition, the tangency of the budget line to both the aggregate indifference curve and the transformation curve, reflects the maximization of consumer utility and profits. Balanced trade ensures world market clearing. If both countries have the same homothetic utility functions, demand biases favoring one good over another cannot arise. At equilibrium world prices, both countries consume goods in the same proportion. Moreover, this proportion does not change with the level of income. Therefore, the consumption points must be on the consumption expansion line OD^*D.

The HO theorem follows directly from the Rybczynski theorem given the assumption on relative factor abundances and the assumption that the trading partners have the same homothetic utility functions. Because consumption patterns are the same across countries, demand patterns are the same in both countries. If domestic production is biased toward the capital intensive good and foreign production is biased toward the labor intensive good, equilibrium requires that the capital abundant country exports the capital intensive good and the labor abundant country exports the labor intensive good. This is the proposition stated by the HO theorem and illustrated in Fig. 1.3.

The factor abundance theory of trade patterns goes beyond Ricardo's theory of comparative advantage because the HO model of trade does not depend on exogenous relative productivity levels. Instead, the HO model assumes that countries have the same production functions, posits endogenous factor productivities and explains pre-trade comparative advantages on the basis of relative factor abundances. This framework is consistent with an equilibrium displaying similar post-trade labor productivities and no measurable post-trade comparative productivity advantages across freely trading countries.

1.4.1. Welfare: Free Trade vs Autarky

The competitive free trade equilibrium is welfare-improving relative to autarky. The reason is that free trade expands the consumption possibility set relative to that available under autarky. Consider the two-country free trade equilibrium depicted in Fig. 1.3. For each country, the consumption possibility set under autarky is given by its transformation curve (TT or T^*T^*). The consumption possibility set under free trade is depicted by the national budget line (BB or B^*B^*).

Each country's consumption possibility set under free trade is greater than the consumption possibility set under autarky. Therefore, assuming that national utility can be represented by a community indifference curve, welfare must be greater under free trade than under autarky.

Observe that the welfare analysis bypasses the distributional issues involved. The Stolper–Samuelson theorem specifies that changes in relative prices cause one factor to win and the other to lose. Therefore, if opening increases the relative price of, say, the capital intensive good, capital wins and labor loses. Because a move to free trade always causes one factor to lose and another to win, a political scenario raising the possibility of lobbying and compensation naturally emerges. These issues are examined in the chapters dealing with liberalization, restrictions and politics.

Finally, the reader can verify that all the previously mentioned HO framework assumptions have been utilized at some step of the analysis. It is instructive to find out at which specific steps each assumption was utilized.

1.5. FACTOR CONTENT AND GLOBAL EQUILIBRIUM

International trade can be viewed as implicit or indirect trade in the factor services used to produce the amounts exchanged. The world trade equilibrium can thus be represented in terms of the factor content of the goods exchanged. Figure 1.4 assumes a factor content perspective to illustrate the two-country free trade competitive equilibrium. Sector I is capital intensive and sector II is labor intensive. The home country

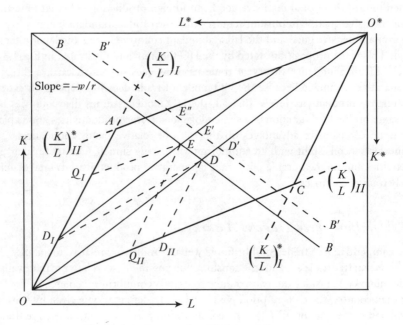

Figure 1.4. *Integrated equilibrium and factor content*

is assumed to be capital abundant while the foreign country is assumed to be labor abundant. There is no factor mobility.

The global factor use box indicates the factor contents of goods produced and consumed. The factor use box consists of two so-called Lerner diagrams, one for each country, depicting the capital-labor ratios for both industries given each country's endowment. The box origins O and O^* refer to countries and the box size indicates global endowments $(K^W, L^W) = (K + K^*, L + L^*)$. Factor use is read on the axes starting from origins O and O^*. Domestic and foreign endowments are given by point E. The global factor use box differs from the previously featured Edgeworth box depicting national factor use in Fig. 1.2, where the origins indicate sectors rather than countries and the size of the box indicates national rather than global endowments.

Output quantities are measured by the *length* of the capital–labor rays emanating from the origins. Under constant returns to scale, the length of the distance from the origin to any isoquant along the ray depicting a product's capital–labor ratio can be used to measure the output level. The production points along the capital–labor ratios are found by ensuring that full employment is achieved, that is, total factor use must correspond to the global endowment E. Graphically, the output of each good produced by the home country is found by completing the parallelogram with vertices at O and E and sides given by the capital–labor ratio rays. This procedure ensures that total factor use corresponds to country endowments. A similar procedure applies to the foreign country.

The home country isoincome line BB must pass through the global endowment point E and has a slope equal to the negative of the wage-rental ratio, $-w/r$. Point D indicates the total factor content of the goods consumed by each country. Graphically, the factor content of each good consumed by the home country is found by completing the parallelogram with vertexes at O and D and sides given by the capital–labor ratio rays. This procedure ensures that the total factor content of consumption corresponds to country consumption. A similar procedure applies to the foreign country. The home country is an exporter of product I and an importer of product II. The factor content of exports is indicated by the factor content of production point Q_I minus the factor content of consumption point D_I.

The equilibrium depicted in Fig. 1.4 neatly illustrates the HO factor abundance theorem. The capital abundant home country is a net exporter of the capital intensive good and a net importer of the labor intensive good.

1.5.1. Replication of Integrated Equilibrium

The factor price equalization theorem specifies conditions under which international trade leads to the equalization of the rental prices of labor and capital, even when these factors are prevented from migrating across countries. This theorem can be better understood by imagining a shift from an integrated world economy exhibiting perfect factor mobility to a world economy in which nations bar factor migration. An integrated equilibrium is the resource allocation in a world economy without barriers to factor movements. If there are no costs or barriers to factor mobility across countries, labor and capital migration cause factor prices to equalize. If the equilibrium with immobile factors can replicate the equilibrium with perfect factor movements, factor price equalization must hold. The notion of replicating an integrated equilibrium by an economy with factor immobility was devised by Paul Samuelson to clarify why the factor price equalization theorem holds.

Figure 1.4 depicts the replication of the integrated equilibrium. Observe that countries are not completely specialized and produce both types of goods. The equilibrium price of good I relative to good II determines the unique factor price ratio w/r supporting diversified production. Formally, production diversification arises because each country's endowment lies within the cone of diversification. The economy lies within the diversification cone when the aggregate capital–labor ratio indicated by endowment point E lies within the area delimited by the optimal capital–labor ratio in each sector. These are the areas between $(K/L)_I$ and $(K/L)_{II}$ in the home country's Lerner diagram and between $(K/L)_I^*$ and $(K/L)_{II}^*$ in the foreign country's Lerner diagram.

In general, only a subset of the partitions of global factor endowments can sustain an equilibrium with no factor mobility that replicates the integrated equilibrium. The factor price equalization (FPE) set is defined as the set of distributions of global endowments across countries consistent with replicating the integrated equilibrium. Because factor price equalization requires the endowment point E to lie within both countries' diversification cones, the FPE set is delimited by the domestic and foreign countries capital–labor ratio lines in Fig. 1.4. When factor endowments lie within this set, countries produce both types of goods in equilibrium.

The factor price equalization set is the set of points OAO^*C in Fig. 1.4. Inside this set, international trade can be viewed as a perfect substitute for factor mobility in the sense that trade in goods completely eliminates international differences in factor rentals. For instance, any shift of the endowment point along the isoincome line BB within the factor price equalization set affects trade while leaving global resource allocation and prices unchanged.

1.5.2. Factor Price Insensitivity

An insightful way to look at the factor price equalization theorem is to treat it as a factor price insensitivity theorem. Holding product prices fixed, a change in factor endowments does not alter factor prices. The insensitivity of factor prices to changes in factor endowments is due to general equilibrium changes in relative sectorial production altering factor demands so as to keep factor markets in equilibrium. Observe the implication that trade, relative factor rewards and factor movements, if they do not affect relative product prices as determined in world markets, cannot affect factor rewards. The empirical evidence on this result will be examined in the chapters focusing on trade empirics and factor mobility.

In the two–sector model considered, the free trade equilibrium with factor immobility replicates the integrated equilibrium in the sense that outputs, demands and factor prices are the same as in a perfectly integrated world with full factor mobility. The key conditions for factor price equalization in a model with multiple goods satisfying the HO assumptions are:

1. The number of goods must be equal to or exceed the number of factors. Indeed, trade analysts often proceed on the presumption that a limited set of factors can be used to produce multiple goods so that the number of goods exceeds the number of factors.
2. Countries' factor endowments should not differ 'too much' in the sense that each country's factor endowments must lie within the cone of diversification defined by each country's equilibrium capital–labor ratios. The set of capital and labor endowments lying in both countries' cones of diversification defines the factor price equalization set.

1.5.3. Trade Effects of Relative Size and Factor Abundance

What are the trade effects of relative country size? A shift of the endowment point from E to E' means that the home country becomes larger relative to the foreign country. This movement is associated with a change in the factor content of consumption from points D to D' where D' lies along the isoincome line $B'B'$ determined by endowment point E'. However, the move from BB to $B'B'$ does not affect the volume of trade. The reason is that the factor content of trade is measured by the difference in factor use between the endowment and the consumption points. But the factor use (i.e. factor content) gap between points E and D is exactly the same as that between points E' and D'. In fact, the level of trade remains constant along the line passing through E and E'.

It is easy to see that wider differences in factor endowment ratios lead to larger trade volumes. The curve showing the endowment points (within the factor price equalization set) that keeps the volume of trade constant is called a level line for total volume of trade. By construction, a change in relative country size taking place along a trade level line does not affect the volume of trade. In the $2 \times 2 \times 2$ HO model, the sets of factor endowments leading to constant trade defines a map of trade level lines standing parallel to the diagonal.

Observe that, if the endowment point lies on the diagonal line DD', relative factor endowments are the same and the volume of trade is zero. By contrast, the line passing through E and E' indicates a set of endowments leading to a constant positive level of trade. The farther away a level line lies from the diagonal DD', the larger the volume of trade. Therefore, a greater difference in factor endowment ratios, as indicated by a global endowment point lying on a level line located farther away from the diagonal, entails a larger trade volume. This feature can be seen by drawing the triangles indicating the factor content of trade. Endowment point E'' generates a greater volume of trade than endowment point E' because the consumption point D' does not change with a shift of the endowment along a given isoincome line $B'B'$.

1.6. OPTIMIZATION, DUALITY, AND CONSUMPTION

The theory of duality provides a unified framework to develop the properties of demand and supply functions, solve general equilibrium models and analyze international trade patterns. It is used in many parts of this book. Dixit and Norman (1980), Woodland (1982), and Kohli (1991) offer extensive coverage of the duality approach to general equilibrium trade analysis.

Duality is a relationship between two constrained optimization problems, each of which is said to be the dual of the other. The structures of dual problems are closely related and the solution to one problem can be used to infer the solution to the other. In practice, the solution to the easier problem is used to obtain the solution to the tougher problem. The dual problem that one focuses upon is called the 'primal' while the other is called the 'dual'. A property of dual problems is that if the primal entails constrained maximization the dual entails constrained minimization, and vice versa. Which problem is called the primal is arbitrary as the label merely serves to avoid confusion about which of the two problems we are referring to.

This section uses the duality approach to develop the theory of consumer's budget allocation. Let the primal be the standard utility maximization problem subject to a budget (i.e. expenditure) constraint. The dual problem entails minimizing the amount of consumer expenditure that achieves a given level of utility. It is clear that maximizing utility subject to a budget constraint and minimizing expenditure subject to a utility level constraint are two alternative ways of looking at the same consumer choice problem. Therefore, the budget allocation problem can be solved using either the primal or the dual.

1.6.1. Utility Maximization and Demand

Assume that individual preferences can be aggregated so that the economy's preferences can be expressed in terms of the preferences of a representative consumer and can be depicted by a social indifference curve. If goods are sold in competitive markets, consumers and producers take prices as given. The maximization of a strictly concave utility function U subject to (s.t.) a linear budget constraint can be written as

$$\max_{D} U(D) \quad \text{s.t.} \quad Y - p'D = Y - (p_1, \ldots, p_J) \begin{pmatrix} D_1 \\ \vdots \\ D_J \end{pmatrix}$$

$$= Y - \sum_{j=1}^{J} p_i D_i \geq 0,$$

where the prime symbol stands for the transposition operator transforming a column vector into a row vector, p' is a $1 \times J$ row vector of product prices, D is a $J \times 1$ column vector of consumption demands, Y is a scalar denoting income, and the linear constraint $Y - p'D \geq 0$ defines a compact and convex set.

A linear budget constraint set defines a convex set. A convex set $\mathcal{D}$ is one in which, if D_0 and D_1 are elements of $\mathcal{D}$, then $\lambda D_0 + (1 - \lambda)D_1$ is also element of $\mathcal{D}$ for all $\lambda \in (0, 1)$. A function $U(D)$ is said to be concave on a convex set $\mathcal{D}$ if $\lambda U(D_0) + (1 - \lambda)U(D_1) \leq U(\lambda D_0 + (1-\lambda)D_1)$ for all $\lambda \in (0, 1)$. Strict concavity of the function means that the inequality holds as a strict inequality. Well-behaved utility functions displaying decreasing marginal rate of substitution of one good for another are strictly concave functions. Optimization theory shows that, if the maximization of a strictly concave function subject to a convex constraint set admits a solution, that solution is unique and can be obtained by maximizing the problem's Lagrangian (Sundaram, 1996).

Let us obtain the solution to the budget allocation problem by maximizing the Lagrangian function $\mathcal{L}$ with respect to the demand vector D and the Lagrange multiplier λ

$$\max_{\{D,\lambda\}} \mathcal{L}(D, \lambda; p, Y) \equiv U(D) - \lambda(Y - p'D). \tag{1.12}$$

The first order conditions for the demand vector D and the Lagrange multiplier λ are

$$\frac{\partial \mathcal{L}}{\partial D} = \frac{\partial U(D)}{\partial D} + \lambda p \equiv U_D + \lambda p = 0, \qquad \frac{\partial \mathcal{L}}{\partial \lambda} = Y - p'D = 0,$$

where the budget constraint is binding since more is better (i.e. nonsatiation). The $\mathcal{J}$ first order conditions (one for each good) plus the budget constraint can be solved to obtain the demand vector $D(p, Y)$ for the $\mathcal{J}$ goods and the Lagrange multiplier $\lambda(p, Y)$ as functions of prices and income.

As an illustration, consider a consumer allocating the budget among goods I and II. Utility maximization implies that the relative price is equal to the marginal rate of substitution $\text{MRS}(D_I, D_{II})$ of good I for good II

$$\frac{\partial U(D)}{\partial D_i} = -\lambda p_i \quad \rightarrow \quad \frac{p_I}{p_{II}} = \frac{\partial U(D)}{\partial D_I} \Big/ \frac{\partial U(D)}{\partial D_{II}} \equiv \text{MRS}(D_I, D_{II}).$$

The optimal consumption point is determined at the point of tangency of the budget line and an indifference curve. The slope of the budget line $p_I D_I + p_{II} D_{II} = Y$ is the relative price ratio

$$\frac{dD_{II}}{dD_I} = -\frac{p_I}{p_{II}}.$$

The slope of the indifference curve $U(D) = U_0$ is given by the negative of the marginal rate of substitution of good I for good II

$$0 = dU(D) = \frac{\partial U(D)}{\partial D_I} dD_I + \frac{\partial U(D)}{\partial D_{II}} dD_{II}$$

$$\rightarrow \quad \frac{dD_{II}}{dD_I} = -\frac{\partial U(D)}{\partial D_I} \Big/ \frac{\partial U(D)}{\partial D_{II}} \equiv \text{MRS}(D_I, D_{II}).$$

Figure 1.3 illustrates the tangency of the budget line and the indifference curve in the open economy, as indicated by the equality of minus the relative price $-p_I/p_{II}$ and the marginal rate of substitution in consumption.

Value of Utility Maximization Problem: Indirect Utility Function

Any problem entailing the optimization (i.e. maximization or minimization) of a function $f(x; \alpha)$ with respect to x for a given vector of parameters and exogenous variables α, produces a function specifying the maximized value of f as a function of the exogenous vector α. In the jargon of optimization theory, the function giving the optimized value of $f(x; \alpha)$ as a function of α is called the value function $V(\alpha)$ of the optimization problem

$$V(\alpha) \equiv \max_x f(x; \alpha).$$

The value function $V(p, Y)$ of the standard utility maximization problem, called the indirect utility function, specifies the maximized value of utility $U(D)$ as a function of prices and income. It is obtained by substituting the demand function vector $D(p, Y)$ into the utility function

$$U(D(p, Y)) = V(p, Y).$$

Observe that the consumer's maximization problem maximizes utility subject to a budget constraint. By contrast, in the indirect utility function V, utility has already been maximized and is expressed as a function of exogenous prices and income (rather than as a function of endogenous quantities of goods D as in the usual utility function).

Mas-Colell *et al.* (1995) show that the value function of the utility maximization problem is continuous, increasing in Y, nonincreasing in p_j, and quasiconvex (meaning that the set $V(p, Y) \leq V_0$ is convex for any V_0). Convex functions are quasiconvex but quasiconvex functions might not be convex.

Indirect Utility Function, Roy's Identity and Demand

Let us recall the envelop theorem (proved in Mas-Colell *et al.*, 1995). Consider the maximization of differentiable concave function $f(x; \alpha)$ subject to (s.t.) the binding convex constraint $g(x, \alpha)$

$$\max_x f(x; \alpha) \quad \text{s.t. } g(x, \alpha) = 0,$$

where $g(x, \alpha)$ is a differentiable concave function of α and $g(x, \alpha) \leq 0$ defines a convex set in the parameter or exogenous variable vector α.

The envelope theorem states that the partial derivative of the associated Lagrangian $\mathcal{L} = f(x; \alpha) + \lambda g(x, \alpha)$ with respect to α is equal to the derivative of the value function $V(\alpha)$ with respect to α (assume that V is differentiable)

$$\max_\alpha \mathcal{L}(x, \lambda; \alpha) = f(x(\alpha)) + \lambda g(x, \alpha) \quad \rightarrow \quad \frac{\partial \mathcal{L}(\bar{x}, \bar{\lambda}; \alpha)}{\partial \alpha} = \frac{\partial V(\alpha)}{\partial \alpha} \equiv V_\alpha,$$

where x and λ are evaluated at their optimal values $\bar{x}$ and $\bar{\lambda}$ given α. A similar envelope theorem holds for the minimization of a differentiable convex function $f(x; \alpha)$ subject to a convex constraint set $g(x, \alpha) \leq 0$.

The envelope theorem leads to Roy's identity, which tells us how to obtain product demand functions from the indirect utility function. Define the Lagrangian $\mathcal{L} = u(D) + \lambda(Y - p'D)$, with $f(x) = u(D)$ and $g(x, \alpha) = Y - p'D$. Obtaining the first order conditions and using the envelope theorem yields, for $j \in \{1, \ldots, \mathcal{J}\}$,

$$\frac{\partial \mathcal{L}(\bar{D}, \bar{\lambda}; p, Y)}{\partial p_j} = -\lambda D_j(p, Y) = V_{p_j} \equiv \frac{\partial V(p, Y)}{\partial p_j} < 0,$$

$$\frac{\partial \mathcal{L}(\bar{D}, \bar{\lambda}; p, Y)}{\partial Y} = \lambda = V_Y \equiv \frac{\partial V(p, Y)}{\partial Y} > 0.$$

The partial derivatives of the indirect utility function V with respect to prices yield the demand functions multiplied by $-\lambda$. By the same token, the partial derivative of the indirect utility function with respect to income is equal to the Lagrange multiplier λ, implying that λ can be interpreted as the marginal utility of income. The demand functions are obtained by dividing $-V_{p_j}$ by V_Y

$$\frac{-V_{p_i}}{V_Y} \equiv \frac{-\partial V(p, Y)/\partial p_j}{\partial V(p, Y)/\partial Y} = \frac{\lambda D_j(p, Y)}{\lambda} = D_j(p, Y). \tag{1.13}$$

The previous result telling us how to derive the demand functions from the indirect utility function is called Roy's identity in honor of René Roy.

1.6.2. Dual Problem: Expenditure Minimization

The dual of the utility maximization problem is the expenditure (consumer's cost) minimization problem subject to a given utility level u

$$\min_{D} E \equiv p'D \quad \text{s.t. } u \leq U(D),$$

where $p'D$ represents expenditure on the $\mathcal{J} \times 1$ goods vector D at given prices p. The indifference function $U(D)$ is concave, which means that the set $u \leq U(D)$ is convex. In other words, the set $\mathcal{D}$ of utilities greater than a given utility $u, u \leq U(D)$, defines a convex set.

Expenditure $E \equiv p'D$ is a linear function of prices and quantities demanded and is a convex C^1 function of exogenous prices. A function $f(D)$ is said to be convex on a convex set $\mathcal{D}$ if $f(\lambda D_0 + (1 - \lambda)D_1) \leq \lambda f(D_0) + (1 - \lambda)f(D_1)$ for all $\lambda \in (0, 1)$. Strict convexity means that the inequality holds as a strict inequality. A C^1 function is defined as a continuous and differentiable function. The solutions to the minimization of a convex C^1 function on a convex set can be obtained from the first order conditions of the problem's Lagrangian.

The solution to the expenditure minimization problem can be found by minimizing the associated Lagrangian $\mathcal{L}$

$$\min_{\{D,\lambda\}} \mathcal{L}(D, \lambda; p, u) \equiv p'D + \lambda(u - U(D)).$$

The first order conditions with respect to demands and the Lagrange multiplier λ are

$$\frac{\partial \mathcal{L}}{\partial D_j} = p' - \lambda \frac{dU}{dD_j} = 0, \qquad \frac{\partial \mathcal{L}}{\partial \lambda} = u - U(D) = 0.$$

These $\mathcal{J} + 1$ equations yield the $\mathcal{J} \times 1$ vector of demands $D(p, u)$ and the Lagrange multiplier. Observe that $D(p, u)$ depends on prices and utility while the standard demand function $D(p, Y)$ depends on prices and income.

Value of Expenditure Minimization: Expenditure Function
The value function for the expenditure minimization problem is the expenditure function $E(p, u)$ indicating the minimum expenditure level needed to achieve utility level u for given goods' prices

$$E(p, u) \equiv p'D(p, u).$$

Suppose that we are given the expenditure function $E(p, u)$, that is, the value function of the expenditure minimization problem. How can we determine the demand functions $D(p, u)$? Using the first order conditions of the minimization problem and the envelope theorem gives

$$\frac{\partial \mathcal{L}(\bar{D}, \bar{\lambda}; p, u)}{\partial p} = D(p, u) = \frac{\partial E(p, u)}{\partial p} = E_p, \qquad \frac{\partial \mathcal{L}(\bar{D}, \bar{\lambda}; p, u)}{\partial u} = \lambda.$$

The amounts of each good purchased can be specified as the gradient (vector of derivatives) of the expenditure function E with respect to p

$$D(p, u) \equiv \begin{pmatrix} D_1(p, u) \\ \vdots \\ D_{\mathcal{J}}(p, u) \end{pmatrix} = \begin{pmatrix} \dfrac{\partial E(p, u)}{\partial p_1} \\ \vdots \\ \dfrac{\partial E(p, u)}{\partial p_{\mathcal{J}}} \end{pmatrix} \equiv E_p(p, u).$$

The aggregate expenditure of a small open economy that faces given world prices p^W is thus given by $E(p^W, u) = p^{W'} E_p(p^W, u)$.

Recapping, the utility maximization problem yields the demand for each product as a function of prices and income, $D(p, Y)$. Its dual problem, the expenditure minimization problem, yields the demand for each good as a function of prices and the utility level, $D(p, u)$. The value function for the utility maximization problem is the indirect utility function $V(p, Y)$ specifying the maximum value of utility as a function of prices and income. The product demand functions $D(p, Y)$ can be obtained by differentiating the indirect utility function (Roy's identity, envelope theorem). The value function for the expenditure minimization problem is the expenditure function $E(p, u)$ specifying the minimum expenditure needed to reach utility level u at given prices p. In short, indirect utility functions and expenditure functions are the value functions of the dual utility maximization and expenditure minimization problems.

1.7. MINIMUM COST FUNCTION AND FACTOR DEMAND

The determination of factor demands in competitive factor markets and associated output levels can be examined using duality theorems. A firm's factor allocation choice can be thought of as either (1) maximizing output subject to a cost constraint or (2) minimizing the cost of producing a given level of output. Under appropriate conditions the production function and the minimum cost function are dual in the sense that each can be derived from the other.

Consider a representative firm with production function $Q_j = F_j(l_j)$, specifying sector j's output as a function of the vector of inputs $l_j = (l_{1j}, \ldots, l_{Ij}), i \in \{1, \ldots, I\}$. The minimum cost $C_j(w), j \in (1, \ldots, \mathcal{J})$, as a function of the factor reward vector w is

$$C_j(w) \equiv \min_{l_j} w l_j = (w_1 \ldots w_I) \begin{pmatrix} l_{1j} \\ \vdots \\ l_{Ij} \end{pmatrix}, \qquad 0 \leq l_j.$$

The first order conditions for the minimization of $\mathcal{L}(l_j; w, Q_j) \equiv w l_j + \lambda(Q_j - F_j(l_j))$ are (ignoring the j subscript) obtained using Shepard's lemma. This lemma establishes that the firm's total factor demand function $l_j(w, Q_j)$, conditional on output Q_j, is given by the partial derivative of the total cost function with respect to the vector w of input rental prices

$$\frac{\partial \mathcal{L}(l_j; w, Q_j)}{\partial w} = l_j(w, Q_j) = \frac{\partial C_j(w, Q_j)}{\partial w} \equiv C_{j,w}(w, Q_j).$$

A similar argument applies to the minimization of the unit cost function. The unit factor demand function $a_j(w, Q_j) \equiv l_j(w, Q_j)/Q_j$, conditional on output level Q_j, is given by the partial derivative of the unit cost with respect to the wage rate. Recalling that constant returns to scale implies that the unit cost function is not a function of the level of output

$$c_j(w) \equiv \min_{a_j} w a_j(w, Q_j) \equiv w \frac{l_j(w, Q_j)}{Q_j}$$

$$\rightarrow \frac{\partial \mathcal{L}(a_j; w, Q_j)}{\partial w} = a_j(w, Q_j)$$

$$= \frac{\partial c_j(w, Q_j)}{\partial w} \equiv c_{j,w}(w, Q_j).$$

Recapping, the analysis has shown how to use the minimum total and unit cost functions $C(w, Q)$ and $c(w)$, the value functions of the producer's total cost and unit cost minimization problems, to derive total and unit factor demand functions $l(w, Q) = C_w(w, Q)$ and $a(w, Q) = c_w(w, Q)$.

If the production function exhibits constant returns to scale then total costs can be expressed as output Q_j times a unit cost function $c_j(w)$ that does not depend on output, $C_j(w) = Q_j c_j(w)$. The unit cost function equals the factor rewards vector times the vector of input–output coefficients a_j

$$c_j(w) \equiv \min_{a_j} w a_j(w) = (w_1 \ldots w_I) \begin{pmatrix} a_{1j} \\ \vdots \\ a_{Ij} \end{pmatrix}, \quad 0 \le a_{ij},$$

where $a_{ij} = a_{ij}(w)$ indicates the amounts of factor $i \in \{1, \ldots, I\}$ used per unit of sector j output.

1.8. REVENUE FUNCTION AND GLOBAL EQUILIBRIUM

This section examines the economy's revenue function $R(p, FE)$, the value function of the economy's revenue maximization problem as a function of prices p and factor endowment vector FE. The revenue function, also called the GNP function, represents a key relationship between income, product prices, and factor endowments in an economy. It can be estimated empirically as for instance in Kohli (1991). Because aggregate revenue from productive activities is equal to aggregate expenditure on consumption, revenue maximization implies that an undistorted economy chooses the output point at the production possibility frontier that maximizes the consumption possibility set at given prices. A competitive equilibrium results from demand and supply choices, full employment of factors and the assumption of free entry. Global equilibrium requires that countries' trade balances cancel each other out in the aggregate for each good.

Consider an economy utilizing I productive factors to produce J goods under constant returns to scale technologies. The endowment of each factor is exogenously given. Goods are sold and factors are rented in competitive markets. The determination of aggregate factor demands and aggregate production levels can be examined using duality theorems.

An economy's production choice can be formalized as either (1) maximizing the value of aggregate output subject to a factor endowment constraint, and (2) minimizing the factor cost of producing a given output vector.

Equilibrium outputs maximize the value of output $p'Q$, taking as given the economy's price vector. The maximized value of the output vector for given prices and endowments, $R = R(p, FE)$, is called the revenue function or the gross national product (GNP) function. Formally, the revenue function maximizes a linear function subject to (s.t.) a convex constraint set $Q(FE)$

$$R(p, FE) \equiv \max_Q p'Q = \sum_{j=1}^{J} p_j Q_j \quad \text{s.t. } Q \in Q(FE),$$

where p, Q, and FE are $J \times 1, J \times 1$ and $I \times 1$ vectors of prices, outputs, and factor endowments, respectively, and $Q(FE)$ is the convex production set for a given endowment vector FE.

Assume that the revenue function is twice differentiable. This requires (1) smooth substitutability among factors, and (2) at least as many factors as goods, that is, $I \geq J$. Using the envelop theorem, the output vector that maximizes the revenue function at given prices can be shown to be equal to the gradient of $R = R(p, FE)$ with respect to p (often written $\nabla_p R(p, FE)$). Formally,

$$Q(p, FE) \equiv \begin{pmatrix} Q_1(p, FE) \\ \vdots \\ Q_J(p, FE) \end{pmatrix} = \begin{pmatrix} \dfrac{\partial R(p, FE)}{\partial p_1} \\ \vdots \\ \dfrac{\partial R(p, FE)}{\partial p_J} \end{pmatrix} \equiv R_p(p, FE),$$

where $Q \in \text{argmax } p'Q$. The previous result indicating optimal production choices in terms of the revenue function's gradient (i.e. the vector of price derivatives R_p) is called Hotelling's lemma.

As an illustration, consider an economy that produces two goods in amounts Q_I and Q_{II}. Hotelling's lemma implies that the optimal outputs are determined at the point of tangency of the transformation curve and the economy's consumption possibilities frontier (i.e. the equality of the slope of the production possibility frontier and minus the relative price ratio)

$$Q_J = \frac{\partial R(p, FE)}{\partial p_I} = \frac{\partial (p_I Q_J(p) + p_{II} Q_{II}(p))}{\partial p_I} = p_I \frac{\partial Q_J}{\partial p_I} + Q_J + p_{II} \frac{\partial Q_{II}}{\partial p_I}$$

$$\rightarrow \frac{\partial Q_{II}}{\partial Q_J} = -\frac{p_I}{p_{II}}.$$

The revenue-maximizing output vector for a small economy facing price vector p^W, is given by the gradient $R_p(p, FE)$ evaluated at the price vector p^W, that is, by $R_p(p^W, FE)$. The value of output is given by $p^W R_p(p^W, FE)$.

Using the envelope theorem, the gradient of $R = R(p, FE)$ with respect to FE, that is, the vector of partial derivatives $R_{FE}(p, FE)$, can be shown to be equal to the rental vector that maximizes the revenue function at given product prices. Formally,

$$w(p, FE) \equiv \begin{pmatrix} w_1(p, FE) \\ \vdots \\ w_I(p, FE) \end{pmatrix} = \begin{pmatrix} \dfrac{\partial R(p, FE)}{\partial FE_1} \\ \vdots \\ \dfrac{\partial R(p, FE)}{\partial FE_I} \end{pmatrix} \equiv R_{FE}(p, FE).$$

In short, the revenue function indicates the maximum value of an economy's output obtainable from a vector of factor endowments at given product prices. The optimal output levels (i.e. the supply of output) are given by the derivatives of the revenue function with respect to goods prices, $Q(p, FE) = R_p(p, FE)$. This result is called Hotelling's lemma and implies the tangency of the transformation curve and the aggregate budget line. The derivatives of the revenue function with respect to factor endowments give the factor reward functions, $w(p, FE) = R_{FE}(p, FE)$.

1.8.1. Global Competitive Equilibrium

A competitive equilibrium in a two-country world in which all domestic consumers have the same tastes and domestic firms have the same cost functions requires that (similar conditions apply to the foreign country)

1. Consumers maximize utility or minimize expenditure given goods prices and income.
2. Each firm in industries $j \in \{1, \ldots, J\}$ maximizes profits Π_j for given product price and factor reward vectors p and w. Sectorial profits Π_j are

$$\Pi_j(p_j, w) \equiv \max_{Q_j}[p_j - c_j(w)]Q_j, \quad Q_j \geq 0 \rightarrow p_j - c_j(w) \geq 0.$$

3. Long run profits are equal to zero (due to free entry)

$$p_j Q_j - C_j(w, q) = [p_j - c_j(w)]Q_j = 0$$

$$\rightarrow \sum_{j=1}^{J} p_j Q_j = \sum_{j=1}^{J} c_j(w)Q_j.$$

4. The economy achieves full employment of all factors of production. Full-employment equilibrium requires that the sum of the demand for each factor i over all sectors does not exceed the factor endowment FE_i

$$a_i Q = \sum_{j=1}^{J} a_{ij} Q_j = \sum_{j=1}^{J} \frac{\partial c_j(w)}{\partial w_i} Q_j = \frac{\partial c(w, q)}{\partial w_i} Q \leq FE_i,$$

or, making the vectors explicit

$$(a_{i1} \ldots a_{iJ}) \begin{pmatrix} Q_1 \\ \vdots \\ Q_J \end{pmatrix} = \left(\frac{\partial c_1(w)}{\partial w_i} \cdots \frac{\partial c_J(w)}{\partial w_i} \right) \begin{pmatrix} Q_1 \\ \vdots \\ Q_J \end{pmatrix} \leq FE_i,$$

where a_{ij} is the input–output coefficient indicating the use of input i per unit of output of sector j and a_i is the vector of all sectorial uses of factor i.

5. Global goods market equilibrium requires the equality of global supply $Q^W = Q + Q^*$, and global demand $D^W = D + D^*$. In a two-country setting, the global equilibrium condition is

$$Q^W \equiv Q(p, FE) + Q^*(p, FE^*) = D(p, R) + D^*(p, R^*) \equiv D^W.$$

This global condition can be also expressed in terms of the vector of physical trade balances $X \equiv Q - D$ and $X^* \equiv Q^* - D^*$

$$X(p, FE) \equiv Q(p, FE) - D(p, R) = D^*(p, R^*) - Q^*(p, FE^*)$$
$$\equiv -X^*(p, FE^*).$$

The global market equilibrium condition permits determining the free trade price vector p.

1.9. TRADE WITH MANY GOODS AND FACTORS

This section uses duality to prove generalized comparative advantage theorem that applies when there are many but finite goods and factors. A generalized Stolper–Samuelson theorem for many goods and factors is also proved. The analysis of comparative advantage and trade with a continuum of goods was previously undertaken for the special case of a Ricardian fixed input–output coefficient model.

1.9.1. Comparative Advantage

First, notice that the maximized value of output under autarky $R(p^A, FE)$ must be at least as large as the value of free trade output evaluated at autarky prices p^A

$$[p^A]'Q(p^{FT}, FE) = [p^A]'R_p(p^{FT}, FE) \leq R(p^A, FE),$$

where the $Q(p^{FT}, FE) = R_p(p^{FT}, FE)$ vector represents optimal production choices under the free trade price vector p^{FT}. The reasoning behind this inequality is that the production point prevailing in the open economy can be chosen under autarky. If the free trade point is not chosen under autarky, it must be because its value at autarky prices is smaller than the value of the optimal production point under autarky evaluated at autarky prices.

Second, the minimum expenditure needed to achieve free trade utility u^{FT} at autarky prices must exceed the minimum expenditure needed to achieve autarkic utility u^A

$$E(p^A, u^A) \leq E(p^A, u^{FT}).$$

If the purchases made in an open economy could be realized under autarky, then it would be better to consume in autarky the same amounts as in the open economy (because $u^A \leq u^{FT}$).

The previous two equations imply

$$[p^A]'R_p(p^{FT}, FE) - E(p^A, u^{FT}) \leq R(p^A, FE) - E(p^A, u^A). \tag{1.14}$$

Now, notice that the value at autarky prices of the commodities purchased under free trade, $[p^A]'D(p^{FT}, u^{FT})$, must exceed the minimum expenditure (at autarky prices) needed to attain the open economy utility level

$$E(p^A, u^{FT}) \leq [p^A]'D(p^{FT}, u^{FT}) = [p^A]'E_p(p^{FT}, u^{FT}).$$

This result derives directly from the definition of the expenditure function $E(p^A, u^{FT})$ as the minimum expenditure that achieves utility level u^{FT} at prices p^A. It must thus be lower or equal than the expenditure $[p^A]'D(p^{FT}, u^{FT}) = [p^A]'E_p(p^{FT}, u^{FT})$ achieving the same utility level at the same prices. Substituting the right-hand side of this equation for the term $E(p^A, u^{FT})$ in (1.14) implies

$$[p^A]'[R_p(p^{FT}, FE) - E_p(p^{FT}, u^{FT})] \leq R(p^A, FE) - E(p^A, u^A) = 0.$$

The equality is obtained using the identity between revenue (i.e. income) and expenditure at the economy-wide level, $R(p^A, FE) = E(p^A, u^A)$.

Recapping, we have obtained an equation indicating that the aggregate value of net exports X^{FT} evaluated at autarky prices is less than zero. In other words, the sum of free trade production minus domestic spending on each good, evaluated at autarky prices, is negative. A similar equation holds for the foreign country. Formally,

$$p^{A\prime}X^{FT} \equiv p^{A\prime}Q^{FT} - p^{A\prime}D^{FT} = p^{A\prime}R_p^{FT} - p^{A\prime}E_p^{FT} \leq 0,$$

$$p^{*A\prime}X^{*FT} \equiv p^{*A\prime}Q^{*FT} - p^{*A\prime}D^{*FT} = p^{*A\prime}R_p^{*FT} - p^{*A\prime}E_p^{*FT} \leq 0,$$

where the asterisk $*$ represents the foreign country. The price and net export vectors $p^{A\prime}$ and X^{FT} have dimensions $1 \times \mathcal{J}$ and $\mathcal{J} \times 1$. Adding both equations and recalling the global market equilibrium condition $X^{FT} = -X^{*FT}$ yields

$$(p^{A\prime} - p^{*A\prime})X^{FT} \equiv \sum_{j=1}^{\mathcal{J}}(p_j^A - p_j^{A*})X_j^{FT} \le 0.$$

The previous equations tell us that an economy will tend to export those goods in which it has comparative advantages in the sense that the autarky price is smaller than the foreign country's autarky price. Notice that for any particular good j, we do not obtain that a lower domestic autarky price, $p_j^A - p_j^{A*} < 0$, means that the good will be exported, $X_j^{FT} > 0$. The comparative advantage equation applies to the sum over all goods, and does not say that $(p_j^{A\prime} - p_j^{A*\prime})X_j^{FT} \le 0$ for each good $j \in \{1, 2, \ldots, \mathcal{J}\}$. More precisely, there is a positive correlation between the domestic-to-foreign autarky price gap and net exports.

This result presents a form of the theory of comparative advantage that applies to the case of many goods and factors. Specializing to the two-good case we do obtain the Ricardian two-good result establishing that the good with a lower autarky price will be exported ($X^{FT} > 0$) and the good with a higher autarky price will be imported ($X^{FT} < 0$).

An empirical difficulty with the general theory of comparative advantage is that it is based on autarky prices, which are unobservable because economies trade with each other (Deardorff, 1979, 1980). Bernhofen and Brown (2001) conduct an empirical test of a general formulation of comparative advantage. They focus on Japan, which was a completely closed economy before 1854 but underwent a liberalization process that transformed it into a relatively open economy by the late 1860s. Because Japan was a closed economy at the time, the authors are able to find data on autarky prices. Their results show that the structure of Japan's post-liberalization trade could have been predicted from comparative advantage theory.

1.9.2. Stolper–Samuelson Theorem

A general but weaker version of the Stolper–Samuelson theorem can be derived from the price equals average cost condition $p = w'A(w)$, where w' is a $1 \times I$ vector, $A(w)$ is the $I \times \mathcal{J}$ input–output matrix and p is a $\mathcal{J} \times 1$ vector. Differentiating $p = w'A(w)$ with respect to the reward vector w yields

$$dp = [dw]'A(w) + w'dA(w) = [dw]'A(w) \rightarrow [dp]'dp = [dw]'A(w)dp > 0.$$

Recall that cost minimization implies $w'dA(w) = 0$ and observe that $[dp]'dp = \sum dp_j^2 > 0$. The previous inequality implies that there is a correlation between changes in prices, weighted by the input–output matrix, and changes in factor prices.

Restating, small changes in goods prices are associated on average with greater (or lower) rewards for the factors they employ relatively more (or less) intensively. The general result applies for the general case of I factors and J goods and does not embody particular factor intensity assumptions. It is an average relationship across goods and factors but does not allow predicting the relationship between any given good's price and any given factor's reward.

1.10. CONCLUSIONS

We have reviewed the comparative advantage and factor abundance models of international trade. The Ricardian theory of comparative advantage stresses the role of exogenously given factor productivities and shows that production specialization and trade patterns are determined by relative rather than absolute cross-country factor productivities. The HO model focuses on relative factor abundances and predicts that countries tend to export the goods that utilize relatively more intensively the factors that are relatively abundant in the country.

Until the late 1970s, most trade analyses were based on perfect competition or monopoly market structures in Ricardian and HO models. At that time, the monopolistic competition modeling was advanced as an alternative benchmark explaining how intra-industry trade emerges from a taste for product variety and production specialization to exploit decreasing costs. This approach, which combines the tools of competitive equilibrium and monopoly analysis, assumes that each firm has a monopoly in a variety (e.g. an auto brand) but competes with a large number of rival firms producing competing varieties (e.g. competing auto brands). The varieties framework and alternative approaches rationalize trade classified as intra-industry trade, which constitutes a large component of international trade.

1.11. APPENDIX

1.11.1. Derivation of Constant Share Demand Functions

Utility functions U and U^* are identical Cobb–Douglas functions of the aggregate consumption of goods I and II, D_I and D_{II}. The home country demand functions are found by solving the consumer's utility maximization problem,

$$\max_{D_I, D_{II}} U(D_I, D_{II}) = D_I^\mu D_{II}^{1-\mu},$$

subject to the budget constraint $E = p_I D_I + p_{II} D_{II}$. The Lagrangian and first order conditions are

$$\mathcal{L} \equiv D_I^\mu D_{II}^{1-\mu} + \lambda(p_I D_I + p_{II} D_{II} - E),$$

$$\frac{\partial \mathcal{L}}{\partial D_I} = \mu D_I^{\mu-1} D_{II}^{1-\mu} + \lambda p_I, \qquad \frac{\partial \mathcal{L}}{\partial D_{II}} = (1-\mu) D_I^\mu D_{II}^{-\mu} + \lambda p_{II}$$

$$\rightarrow \frac{p_I}{p_{II}} = \frac{\mu}{1-\mu} \frac{D_{II}}{D_I}.$$

The previous formula gives us the relative demand function. To get the demand function for good II, substitute $p_I D_I = \mu p_{II} D_{II}/(1 - \mu)$ into the budget constraint

$$E \equiv p_I D_I + p_{II} D_{II} = \frac{\mu}{1 - \mu} p_{II} D_{II} + p_{II} D_{II} = \frac{1}{1 - \mu} p_{II} D_{II}$$

$$\rightarrow D_{II} = (1 - \mu)\frac{E}{p_{II}} \rightarrow \frac{p_{II} D_{II}}{E} = 1 - \mu.$$

The demand function for good II implies that its share in expenditure is constant and equal to $1 - \mu$. Because there are two goods, the remaining spending goes to good I so that $\mu = p_I D_I/E$ and the demand function for good I is the constant share demand function $D_I = E/\mu p_I$.

Using $E = p_{II} D_{II}/(1 - \mu)$, and noticing that the same argument implies $E^* = p_{II} D_{II}^*/(1 - \mu)$, we have that $E^W = E + E^*$ is equal to

$$E^W = \frac{1}{1 - \mu} p_{II} D_{II} + \frac{1}{1 - \mu} p_{II} D_{II}^* = \frac{1}{1 - \mu} p_{II}(D_{II} + D_{II}^*)$$

$$= \frac{1}{1 - \mu} p_{II} D_{II}^W \rightarrow \frac{p_{II} D_{II}^W}{E^W} = 1 - \mu.$$

The remaining world expenditure goes to good I, $p_I D_I^W/E^W = \mu$.

Recapping, the appendix has shown the following two properties used throughout the book. First, a Cobb–Douglas utility function of two goods implies that a share μ of a country's total expenditure E falls on good I, and a share $1 - \mu$ falls on good II. Second, if there are two countries with identical Cobb–Douglas utility functions, a share μ of world expenditure E^W falls on good I and a share $1 - \mu$ falls on good II.

2

Intra-industry Trade

A large share of world trade consists of intra-industry trade. This type of trade takes place when traders both import and export goods that have similar characteristics. Wine producing regions import wines produced from the same varieties grown in competing regions. The United States imports Japanese and European autos while exporting American autos to Japan and Europe. These exchanges represent simultaneous imports and exports of different varieties of the same product.

Table 2.1 shows the values of the Grubel and Lloyd (1975) index of bilateral intra-industry trade between the United States and several developed countries. The values of the index, shown in the column labeled 'trade', are quite high. The Grubel–Lloyd index of intra-industry trade (IIT) in industry i is defined as the fraction of total trade in industry i, $X_i + M_i$, that is accounted for by intra-industry trade

$$IIT = \frac{X_i + M_i - |X_i - M_i|}{X_i + M_i}.$$

Observe that $|X_i - M_i|$ measures the amount of trade that does not involve intra-industry trade. Therefore, $X_i + M_i - |X_i - M_i|$ is the amount of intra-industry trade. If there is no trade overlap in industry i, so that either X_i or M_i is positive, but not both, the value of the index is equal to zero. For instance, if $X_i > 0$ and $M_i = 0$, the index's numerator is $X_i - |X_i| = 0$. By the same token, if $M_i > 0$ and $X_i = 0$, the numerator is also equal to zero. By contrast, if there is complete trade overlap, so that $X_i = M_i$, the index is equal to 1 (or 100 if the index is expressed as a percentage by multiplying by 100). The table also shows that intra-industry foreign direct investment (FDI) measured by a similar index is as important as intra-industry trade.

There are two types of intra-industry trade: horizontal and vertical. Horizontal intra-industry trade is the exchange of differentiated products produced with

Table 2.1. *Intra-industry trade and FDI, 1992–4 average*

	Trade	FDI
US–Germany	0.67	0.64
US–UK	0.66	0.58
US–France	0.50	0.44
US–Canada	0.37	0.45

Source: Greenaway *et al.* (1998).

identical factor intensities, featuring the same product quality and carrying the same price. Vertical intra-industry trade alludes to quality-differentiated products utilizing different factor intensities and sold at different prices.

Vertical intra-industry trade is a major component of global trade and dominates intra-industry trade. It represents about 80 percent of total intra-industry trade among the major global traders. The determination of which type of trade is classed as vertical intra-industry trade is based on the differences of the qualities of imports and exports. The quality distinction is established by comparing prices (if available) or unit values. A standard rule is to compute the ratio of the unit value of exports to the unit value of imports in a bilateral trade relationship for a given product variety. If the unit value ratio differs from one by more than a threshold of 15 or 20 percent, trade is classified as vertical intra-industry trade. If the unit value ratio falls within the range established by the chosen threshold, trade is classified as horizontal intra-industry trade.

The importance of horizontal intra-industry trade among developed countries does not easily fit into a theory of specialization based on relative factor abundances. In the Heckscher–Ohlin (HO) model, it is superfluous to engage in the activity of exporting a product to pay for the imports of a product that could be produced locally with identical resources. Moreover, the explanation of vertical intra-industry trade requires incorporating the choice of product qualities.

This chapter focuses on a line of theoretical and empirical analyses aiming to explain why most trade among developed countries consists of intra-industry trade and other stylized facts about trade that are not explained by the comparative advantage and factor abundance approaches. First, higher income countries trade a greater number of varieties. Second, higher income countries secure a higher price for their exports than lower income countries. Third, the increase of the trade to income ratio over time seems greater than what can be accounted for by reduced trade barriers. Trade models with differentiated products, endogenous quality and trading costs help rationalizing these stylized facts.

Section 2.1 reviews the theories of horizontal and vertical intra-industry trade. Section 2.2 develops the monopolistic competition model of intra-industry trade in varieties produced with decreasing costs. Section 2.3 discusses intra-industry trade with transport costs. Section 2.4 examines a general equilibrium model with intra-industry trade in varieties and inter-industry trade based on factor abundances. Section 2.5 combines HO and Ricardian economics to develop the HO–Ricardo approach to intra-industry trade. Sections 2.6 and 2.7 discuss the nature of trade in products differentiated by characteristics, quality and production origin. Section 2.8 contrasts the empirical performance of alternative intra-industry trade models.

2.1. EXPLAINING INTRA-INDUSTRY TRADE

The simplest way to introduce intra-industry trade is to adopt Armington's (1969) assumption that products are differentiated by production location. Armington's preferences embody the assumption that consumers perceive goods produced in different countries to be different even if they differ only in the place of production. These consumers' perceptions rationalize intra-industry trade of products differentiated by production location. Examples include different perceptions of sparkling wines such as French champagne and Catalonian cava. The Armington assumption can be incorporated into models with either horizontal or vertical intra-industry trade (as in Section 2.7). From a theoretical perspective, this convenient assumption works by imposing an *ad hoc* preference map that generates intra-industry trade because products are differentiated on the basis of their nationality by sheer assumption.

The main approaches to horizontal intra-industry trade include:

1. Taste for variety approach to trade of differentiated products subject to decreasing costs (Krugman, 1979; Helpman and Krugman, 1985). In this setting, consumers are endowed with a love for variety. Consumers exploit their taste for variety by consuming a set of differentiated products displaying similar qualities and carrying the same price. Differentiated products include clothing, wines, restaurants, pharmaceuticals, electronics, autos, and others. Each variety requires a fixed production cost, which gives rise to decreasing average production costs, and is produced by a single firm in order to exploit decreasing costs. Therefore, each variety is produced in a different country.

   The 'new trade theory' offers a theory of trade in differentiated products elaborated under increasing returns to scale that is not based on comparative advantages and factor abundances. Producers do not enjoy comparative advantages because trading partners are assumed to share the same technologies. Factor intensities and abundances do not play a role because traders exchange varieties that are produced with the same factor intensities. Horizontal intra-industry trade is based on (1) taste for variety, which generates a demand for other countries' products, and (2) decreasing costs arising from the presence of fixed costs, which sustain trade with the single source country per variety. Horizontal intra-industry trade is beneficial because it offers consumption variety and enables producers to spread fixed production costs over larger markets. Observe that the assumption that varieties are produced with the same technologies and factor intensities has the limitation that the model does not allow determining which specific variety is produced in which specific location. In other words, consumption patterns are determinate but 'who produces what' is indeterminate in the model.

2. HO–Ricardo approach in which horizontal intra-industry trade in goods produced with the same factor intensities arises from the interaction of comparative advantages and factor abundances. This approach to horizontal intra-industry trade, developed by Donald Davis (1995), explains who imports what, and vindicates traditional trade theory by showing that, even if the standard HO model does not provide a rationale for intra-industry trade, an extension of that model does generate intra-industry trade. A HO framework with more goods than factors is modified to incorporate exogenous comparative advantages à la David Ricardo. The combination of exogenous comparative advantages and the HO factor abundance model can induce both inter-industry trade à la HO and intra-industry trade. Intra-industry trade between similar countries can arise because arbitrarily small comparative advantages lead to

specialization under constant returns to scale and perfect competition. A country benefitting from a comparative advantage in a variety will become the sole producer of that variety and, depending on relative endowments, might import other goods produced with identical factor intensities.

3. Reciprocal dumping model (Brander, 1981; Brander and Krugman, 1983). Two-way trade in identical products (i.e. reciprocal dumping) arises in oligopolistic market structures exhibiting market segmentation. This type of trade pattern is discussed in the chapter on dumping.

Vertical differentiation can be rationalized in terms of products incorporating differentiated characteristics or ranked by quality, namely:

1. Product characteristics approach based on a demand for product characteristics. The characteristics approach, developed by Kelvin Lancaster (1979), considers consumers that vary in their preferences for specific product characteristics (such as car quality, size, power, gadgets). Given income and the prices of different characteristics, each consumer purchases a product incorporating the characteristics that approximate the most-preferred variety. Vertical intra-industry trade seeks to obtain the most preferred package of product characteristics. This approach is particularly useful in rationalizing the demand for different product features.

2. Vertical intra-industry trade approach to exchanges of products of varying qualities. In the models developed by Falvey and Kierzkowski (1987) and Flam and Helpman (1987), consumers differing in income levels demand different product quality levels and countries produce different qualities. Intra-industry trade in quality-differentiated products produced using different factor intensities arises from within country income inequality, which generates demands for locally available qualities as well as for the qualities offered by trading partners.

2.2. TRADE, VARIETIES, AND DECREASING COSTS

The model of trade in symmetric differentiated products displaying decreasing average costs, developed by Krugman (1979) and others, is one of the basic frameworks for trade analysis. This framework, inspired in the model of optimum product diversity under monopolistic competition developed by Dixit and Stiglitz (1977), provides a coherent explanation for the large amount of intra-industry trade among industrial economies. Moreover, the framework explains the economics of trade in products requiring substantial fixed costs of research, product design, and advertisement.

2.2.1. Monopolistic Competition Equilibrium

Product differentiation can be achieved by incurring a fixed cost of designing a new model or creating a new variety that sustains a monopoly. This scenario entails an endogenous number of varieties and thus differs from the standard general equilibrium analysis with a fixed number of goods. Moreover, if varieties display identical constant marginal costs of production, the fixed cost element creates an inconsistency with perfect competition. The equality of price and marginal costs under perfect competition does not permit generating the revenues required to pay for the fixed costs. A perfectly competitive industry would incur losses in such case.

In the presence of fixed costs leading to decreasing average costs, trade in differentiated products can be modeled using a monopolistic competition market structure. This modeling approach moves away from perfect competition and the condition that marginal cost equals price. It combines two features, monopoly and zero profits, which seem paradoxical at first sight. The trick that solves the paradox is endogenizing the number of commodities. The equilibrium number of varieties, and firms monopolizing individual varieties, is determined through free entry. New monopolized varieties are created up to the point at which the competitive zero profit condition holds due to free entry into competing varieties.

The conditions for a monopolistic competition equilibrium are:

1. Each firm holds a monopoly position in the variety it produces, and thus sets quantities using the standard monopoly condition equating marginal revenue MR and marginal costs MC

$$MR = MC. \tag{2.1}$$

As in the case of pure monopoly, price exceeds marginal costs so that operating profits gross of fixed costs are positive.

2. The possibility of entry to produce competing differentiated goods implies that the number of varieties and firms are not given in advance but are rather endogenous to the analysis. Free entry to produce new competing varieties takes place up to the point at which the competitive zero profits condition (net of fixed costs) holds for all varieties. In equilibrium, the product price p (average revenue AR) equals average cost AC inclusive of the fixed costs of creating a variety

$$p \equiv AR = AC \equiv C/q. \tag{2.2}$$

The idea behind the zero profit condition is as follows. Consider a situation in which the net profits from producing differentiated goods are positive. This situation is not an equilibrium. If there are profits to be earned, entry into competing varieties takes place. Because the consumer has a given budget to spend among varieties, an increase in the number of available varieties represents a downward shift in the demand curve for each variety. The equilibrium number of varieties has to be large enough to lower the demand for each variety and sustain the zero profits condition.

Declining average cost is a crucial feature of the model for two reasons. First, if firms share the same technologies and marginal costs are constant, production efficiency under decreasing average cost requires that each differentiated good should be produced by a single firm. Monopolized production requires a single fixed cost while producing at the same constant marginal cost as a market structure with many firms, each of which must incur a fixed cost. In fact, decreasing costs explains why a monopoly in each variety is sustained in equilibrium.

Second, declining average cost implies that selling in a larger market will reduce average costs. Because international trade creates a larger market, it allows firms to spread costs over a larger sales base. The exploitation of economies of scale related to fixed costs creates a motive for trade that is different from the motive for trade in the Ricardian model (exploitation of differences in relative industrial productivities) and the HO model (different factor abundances across countries).

2.2.2. Free Trade: Consumption, Production, and Entry

In Krugman's (1979) model of trade in varieties, the shift from autarky to an open economy expands the range of varieties consumed by agents to incorporate those produced abroad. The analysis proceeds from an additive utility function of the consumption of n differentiated domestic varieties and n^* differentiated foreign varieties

$$U(d_1, \ldots, d_n, d_{n+1}, \ldots, d_{n+n^*}) = \sum_{i=1}^{n} u(d_i) + \sum_{i=n+1}^{n+n^*} u(d_i), \quad u' > 0, \quad u'' < 0.$$

Foreign varieties are ordered to carry indexes from $n+1$ to $n+n^*$.

The representative domestic consumer maximizes utility subject to a binding budget constraint equating total income to total spending

$$\mathcal{L} = \sum_{i=1}^{n} u(d_i) + \sum_{i=n+1}^{n+n^*} u(d_i) + \lambda \left(y - \sum_{i=1}^{n} p_i d_i - \sum_{i=n+1}^{n+n^*} p_i d_i \right),$$

where d_i and p_i denote the demand and price of i and y represents the representative consumer's income. The domestic consumer's first-order conditions are given by maximizing the Lagrangian with respect to d_i

$$u'(d_i) - \lambda p_i = 0 \quad \rightarrow \quad p_i = \lambda^{-1} u'(d_i), \quad i \in \{1, \ldots, n+n^*\}.$$

The marginal utility of an additional unit of income spent on each variety is equal to $\lambda = u'(d_i)/p_i$, $i \in \{1, \ldots, n+n^*\}$. The first-order conditions imply that the utility of each additional unit of income spent must be the same for all varieties purchased. Similar conditions characterize the foreign country's representative consumer.

Consider a production process involving a single factor of production, labor. Assume that the fixed cost of producing a variety consists of f units of a labor while variable costs consist of aq_i units of labor. The total cost function C_i is

$$C_i = w l_i = w(f + aq_i) = F + cq_i, \tag{2.3}$$

where w is the wage rate, l_i represents labor use and q_i is the level of firm output. The total cost function exhibits constant marginal cost wa. The fixed cost can be viewed as the annualization of a once and for all sunk cost or as a recurrent fixed cost that is independent of the output level.

The presence of a fixed cost implies that average costs, $C_i/q_i = wf/q_i + wa$, decrease with the level of output. This scale effect is internal to the producer because it can be exploited by any individual producer no matter what others do. Internal economies contrast with external economies deriving from other producers' actions (such as inter-firm spillovers) or from the aggregate behavior of an industry or nation (such as learning-by-doing at the industry or national levels).

Fixed costs and a single world market imply that the production of each variety is concentrated on a single firm. Decreasing costs cause firms to prefer producing a differentiated product over sharing the world market for a variety. Consequently, foreign and domestic firms produce different varieties when their economies are open. Domestic and foreign monopolistically competitive firms maximize profits Π_i

$$\max_{q_i} \pi_i = p_i q_i - F - c q_i = p_i q_i - (f + a q_i)w.$$

The equilibrium price satisfies the first-order condition $\partial \pi_i / \partial q_i = p_i + q_i \partial p_i / \partial q_i - c = 0$, or

$$p_i \left(1 + \frac{\partial p_i}{\partial q_i} \frac{q_i}{p_i}\right) = p_i \left(1 - \frac{1}{\varepsilon(D_i^W)}\right) = p_i \frac{\varepsilon(D_i^W) - 1}{\varepsilon(D_i^W)} = c,$$

where

$$\varepsilon(D_i^W) \equiv -\frac{\partial D_i^W}{\partial p_i} \frac{p_i}{D_i^W} = -\frac{\partial q_i}{\partial p_i} \frac{p_i}{q_i} > 0.$$

At equilibrium, q_i is equal to the world demand for a given variety,

$$q_i = D^W = Ld + L^* d^*,$$

where L and L^* are the domestic and foreign labor endowments.

The model of varieties is symmetric in the sense that all differentiated products enter symmetrically in the utility function (i.e. they have the same share in total spending) and are produced with identical cost functions and factor intensities. The symmetric treatment in demand and supply implies that, in equilibrium, all firms produce the same amount of each differentiated good, $d_i = d$, and charge the same price, $p_i = p$. Imposing symmetry, we obtain that the elasticity of global demand $\varepsilon(D^W)$ is equal to the elasticity of individual consumer demand $\varepsilon(d) = -(\partial d/\partial p)(p/d)$

$$\varepsilon(D^W) \equiv -\frac{\partial[(L + L^*)d]}{\partial p} \frac{p}{(L + L^*)d} = -\frac{\partial d}{\partial p} \frac{p}{d} \equiv \varepsilon(d) > 1.$$

The value of the own price elasticity of demand is greater than one because a monopolist always operates on the elastic segment of its product demand function.

Pricing takes the form of a markup over marginal costs, where symmetry allows writing the markup as a function of the elasticity of individual demand,

$$p(d) = \frac{\varepsilon(d)}{\varepsilon(d) - 1}c = \frac{\varepsilon(d)}{\varepsilon(d) - 1}aw > aw, \quad \varepsilon(d) = -\frac{\partial d}{\partial p}\frac{p}{d} > 1. \tag{2.4}$$

The price markup provides the revenues paying for the fixed production costs.

Free entry into new competing varieties takes place up to the point at which the competitive zero profits condition holds for all varieties. The zero profit condition $\pi = pq - (f + aq)w = 0$, implies a positive relation between prices and wages

$$\frac{p}{w} = a + \frac{f}{q} = a + \frac{f}{(L + L^*)d} = \frac{p^*}{w^*}. \tag{2.5}$$

In a global economy, symmetry implies that the price-wage ratio and the output of varieties are the same in both economies. Moreover, because trade equalizes the price of symmetric varieties, wages are the same across countries. Factor price equalization holds in this setting.

2.2.3. Autarky vs Free Trade

International trade plays basic roles in the supply and the demand sides. First, trade represents a channel for increasing the number of product varieties consumed. Symbolically, domestic agents consume domestic varieties $(d_1, \ldots, d_n)$ and import foreign varieties $(d_{n+1}, \ldots, d_{n+n^*})$. Second, trade permits exploiting decreasing production costs that are internal to firms.

Figure 2.1 depicts the autarkic and free trade equilibria on the $(d, p/w)$ plane. The price-wage ratio p/w in (2.4) increases with the level of individual demand because the elasticity $\varepsilon(d)$ is assumed to decline with the level of individual consumption d. A less elastic demand sustains a higher monopoly price markup.

The price-wage markup obtained from the zero profit condition (2.5) is depicted as a rectangular hyperbola. Recall that a rectangular hyperbola is a set of points $(y, x) =$ such that $yx = k$, where k is a constant. In the monopolistic competition setup, operating profits measured in labor units, $(p/w - a)d$ must be equal to fixed labor costs per global worker $f/(L + L^*)$. Intuitively, the price markup over marginal costs needed to cover fixed costs declines with market size as measured by the level of individual demand d (the size of the world labor supply $L + L^*$ is taken as given).

What are the differences between the resource allocations under autarky and free trade? The free trade equilibrium FT entails a lower variety demand per worker, and thus a smaller price markup, than the autarkic equilibrium A. The markup pricing equation (2.4) and the zero profit condition (2.5) pin down individual consumption (and the equilibrium price markup)

$$d^{FT} = \frac{f}{L + L^*}\frac{\varepsilon(d^{FT}) - 1}{a} < d^A = \frac{f}{L}\frac{\varepsilon(d^A) - 1}{a}, \tag{2.6}$$

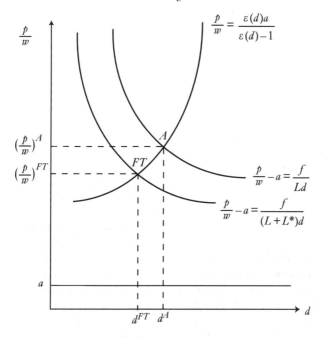

Figure 2.1. *Monopolistic competition equilibrium*

where $\varepsilon(d^A) < \varepsilon(d^{FT})$. The autarkic equilibrium demand d^A is obtained by utilizing L (or L^* for the foreign country) instead of $L + L^*$. Because the analysis does not impose a specific utility function $u(d)$, the elasticity $\varepsilon(d)$ and the value of consumption per variety must be given in implicit form.

What is the effect of trade on the output of each variety and the number of varieties? Economic integration in the form of free trade creates a larger market that reduces per worker consumption of each variety but increases the number of consumers of each variety. If the elasticity of demand declines with the level of individual consumption, the global output of each variety will be greater in the open economy than in the close economy. Because $d^{FT} < d^A$ in (2.6), the relation between autarkic output $q^A = Ld^A$ (or $L^* d^{*A}$) and free trade output $q^{FT} = (L + L^*)d^{FT}$ is

$$q^A = (\varepsilon(d^A) - 1)\frac{f}{a} < q^{FT} = \left(\varepsilon(d^{FT}) - 1\right)\frac{f}{a}, \quad \varepsilon(d^A) < \varepsilon(d^{FT}). \tag{2.7}$$

The number of varieties produced in each country is determined by the full-employment conditions

$$L = nl = n(f + aq), \qquad L^* = n^*l = n^*(f + aq),$$

where q may denote autarky or free trade global output. Solving from n yields the equilibrium number of varieties for each economy and the world

$$n^{FT} = \frac{L}{f + aq^{FT}} = \frac{L}{f + aLd^{FT}} < n^A = \frac{L}{f + aq^A} = \frac{L}{f + aLd^A}, \qquad (2.8)$$

and

$$n^A = \frac{1}{f/L + ad^A} < n^{FT} + n^{*FT} = \frac{L^W}{f + aL^W d^{FT}} = \frac{1}{f/L^W + ad^{FT}}, \qquad (2.9)$$

where $q^A = Ld^A < q^{FT} = (L + L^*)d^{FT}, d^{FT} < d^A$ and $L^W = L + L^*$.

Because equilibrium free trade output exceeds autarkic output, $q^A < q^{FT}$, the number of varieties produced in each economy is less under free trade than under autarky, $n^{FT} < n^A$. However, free trade permits purchasing foreign produced varieties, which are not available in a closed economy trade regime. The greater availability of varieties implies that free trade welfare exceeds close economy welfare.

How does the equilibrium of two freely trading economies compare with the fully integrated equilibrium involving full labor mobility (or a single country with a labor force equal to $L^W = L + L^*$)? Individual variety demand and price, global output, number of varieties, and the wage rate are the same in the fully integrated equilibrium and free trade conditions. This allocation equivalence relates to the fact that the free values of demand and the number of varieties, d^{FT} and n^{FT}, depend on model parameters and the size of the global labor supply, $L + L^*$. In this setup, free trade entails wage equalization and replicates the integrated equilibrium with free labor mobility.

If the demand elasticity ε is constant, p/w has the constant value $\varepsilon/(\varepsilon - 1)$ under free trade and autarky. Setting a constant elasticity $\varepsilon = \varepsilon(d^A) = \varepsilon(d^{FT})$ in (2.6) and (2.7) implies that individual demand d is smaller under free trade than under autarky while global output q is the same under both trade regimes. For instance, if $L = L^*$, sales are equally divided across markets and $d^{FT} = d^A/2$. Because $n = L/(f + aq)$, the number of varieties n (or n^*) produced in each country will be the same under autarky and free trade. The welfare gain from free trade derives exclusively from the availability of foreign varieties. Moreover, observe that free trade prevents an overlap between the varieties produced in different countries (there is the possibility that two isolated economies produce the same differentiated good).

2.2.4. Export Volume and Indeterminate Trade Pattern

The value of intra-industry exports (or imports) between the two countries considered is easily determined. Recall that under free trade, both countries produce the same amounts of each differentiated good while the number of varieties produced depends on the level of the local labor supply. The values of domestic and foreign exports are equal,

$$pX = pnL^*d = pn^*Ld = pX^*,$$

and are given by the sum of the values of foreign consumptions of all domestically produced varieties (or by the sum of the values of the domestic consumptions of all varieties produced abroad). Expression (2.8) for the equilibrium number of varieties n and n^* yields the trade volume equation

$$pX = p\frac{LL^*}{f + aq}\frac{q}{L + L^*} = \frac{LL^*}{L + L^*}w = pX^*,$$

where (2.5) implies that $pq/(f + aq) = w$.

The nature of the solution for the volume of international trade as measured by exports is clear from the condition $nL^* = n^*L$. Suppose that $L > L^*$. Because the domestic country has the largest labor supply, it will produce and export the greater number of varieties (i.e. $n > n^*$). Consumption per worker is the same in both countries, $d = d^*$. A larger labor force means that the domestic economy displays greater total consumption of each variety, $L^*d < Ld$, and will sell a smaller amount of each variety abroad. In other words, compared with the smaller country, the larger country sells a smaller amount of a greater number of varieties.

A limitation of the monopolistic competition model of trade in symmetric varieties is that it offers a theory of the volume of trade but not of the structure of trade. The direction of trade is indeterminate because all varieties are consumed in each country, but which country produces any specific variety remains indeterminate. The assumption that all varieties are produced with identical factor intensities, have identical production costs, and are treated symmetrically by consumers does not permit explaining the structure of trade in the sense of determining who imports what.

2.2.5. CES Varieties' Utility Function

The behavior implied by complex economic models is often studied through simulation techniques. Obtaining numerical solutions in computable general equilibrium models requires imposing a specific utility function. The ensuing analysis is conducted at the level of a fully integrated economy but, because the free trade equilibrium replicates a fully integrated economy, the extension to a freely trading global economy merely involves reinterpreting the formulas.

The model has two sectors, manufacturing and agriculture but it does not allow for intersectoral mobility. Agricultural labor is assumed to be attached to land and its wage rate (the numeraire) can thus differ from the manufacturing labor wage. Because all demands are identical and homothetic, the distribution of income between manufacturing and agricultural labor does not affect the aggregate demand for any product. A case in which there is intersectoral mobility, agricultural labor is endogenously determined, and intersectoral wage equalization holds is examined in Asilis and Rivera-Batiz (2002).

Consumers are assumed to share identical Cobb–Douglas utility function defined over two types of goods, differentiated manufacturing products M and a homogeneous agricultural product A

$$U(D_M, D_A) = D_M^\mu D_A^{1-\mu}. \tag{2.10}$$

The quantity of manufactures D_M is a quantity index and can be viewed as a sub-utility function defined over the whole continuous set of differentiated manufactures $d_i, i \in [o, n]$

$$D_M \equiv \left(\int_0^n d_i^\rho \, di \right)^{1/\rho} = \left(\int_0^n d_i^{(\sigma-1)/\sigma} \, di \right)^{\sigma/(\sigma-1)}, \quad 0 < \rho \equiv \frac{\sigma-1}{\sigma} < 1,$$

(2.11)

where $1 < \sigma \equiv 1/(1-\rho)$ is the constant elasticity of substitution (CES) between any two varieties. Observe that if all varieties have the same demand d, $D_M = n^{\sigma/(\sigma-1)}d$. Because there is a continuum of differentiated goods, the equations are expressed in terms of integrals. Formulas and derivations are similar if there is a discrete number n of differentiated goods and the equations are expressed in terms of summations rather than integrals.

Utility maximization is subject to a budget constraint equating total income Y to total spending E on manufactures and agricultural products

$$Y = E = E_M + E_A = \int_0^n p_i d_i di + p_A A,$$

where $p_i, i \in [o, n]$, represents the price of differentiated manufacture i. Agricultural products are homogeneous and are sold at price p_A. Recall from the appendix of Chapter 1 that, with a Cobb–Douglas utility function such as (2.10), the shares of manufacturing and agriculture in total income are given by parameters μ and $1 - \mu$. Therefore, $E_M = \mu Y$ and $E_A = p_A D_A = (1 - \mu) Y$.

The aggregate demand function for variety j is (see appendix)

$$D_j = \left(\frac{p_j}{p_M} \right)^{-\sigma} D_M = \frac{p_j^{-\sigma}}{p_M^{1-\sigma}} \mu Y,$$

(2.12)

where μ is the share of manufacturing spending in total spending and Y is aggregate income. The appendix shows that $E_M = p_M D_M = \mu Y$, where the price of manufactures P_M is defined as

$$p_M \equiv \left(\int_0^n p_i^{1-\sigma} \, di \right)^{1/(1-\sigma)} = \left(\int_0^n p_i^{-\rho/(1-\rho)} \, di \right)^{(\rho-1)/\rho}, \quad 1 < \sigma, \ 0 < \rho < 1.$$

If all manufactures are sold at a common price $p_i = p$ and have the same demand $d = d_i$, we obtain

$$p_M = n^{1/(1-\sigma)} p = n^{-1/(\sigma-1)} p \rightarrow E_M = p_M D_M = n^{-1/(\sigma-1)} p n^{\sigma/(\sigma-1)} d = npd,$$

which explains why the seemingly contrived definitions given for p_M and D_M turn out to be quite natural.

Under symmetry, the demand for a differentiated manufacture can be expressed as

$$D = \frac{p^{-\sigma}}{p_M^{1-\sigma}} \mu Y = p^{-\sigma} p_M^{\sigma-1} \mu Y, \quad p_M = n^{1/(1-\sigma)} p = \frac{p}{n^{1/(\sigma-1)}}. \tag{2.13}$$

The representative individual consumer treats prices and individual income as given and the resulting aggregate demand (the sum of individual demands) is thus conceived as treating p, Y, n and the value of the price index $p_M = n^{1/(1-\sigma)} p$ as exogenously given. The aggregate demand for a variety:

1. Increases with the aggregate level of consumer's income, which raises the demand for all varieties proportionately.
2. Declines with the number of available varieties n. Formally, a greater number of varieties lowers the price of manufactures. This raises the relative price of any variety in terms of the aggregate of manufactures, which reduces the demand for each variety. Intuitively, a greater number of varieties entails intensified competition for attracting consumer's spending among related products.
3. Declines with a greater value of the elasticity of substitution $\sigma > 1$. The greater the substitutability between varieties, the lower the demand for any of them at given prices.

Production of q units of a differentiable product requires a fixed amount of labor f and aq units of labor. The fixed cost per period is $F = wf$ and variable costs are waq

$$C = wl = w(f + aq),$$

where w is the wage rate, q is the output of a differentiated good and l represents total labor use. Equating price to average cost C/q and dividing by w yields

$$\frac{p}{w} = a + \frac{f}{q} = a + \frac{f}{Ld} = a + \frac{f}{D}. \tag{2.14}$$

Under monopolistic competition, a consumer purchasing variety j takes income and the price index of manufactures as given. Therefore, the elasticity of substitution σ corresponds to the elasticity of demand, $1 < \varepsilon \equiv -\partial \ln d_j / \partial \ln p_j = \sigma$ for all j. The markup price function is thus given by imposing $\varepsilon = \sigma$ in (2.4)

$$p = \frac{\varepsilon}{\varepsilon - 1} aw = \frac{\sigma}{\sigma - 1} aw > aw, \quad 1 < \sigma. \tag{2.15}$$

The price declines with a higher elasticity of substitution σ, increases with marginal costs $c = aw$ and is independent of the fixed cost f (which affects the equilibrium number of varieties). The real wage w/p is pinned down by the elasticity of demand and the marginal cost coefficient a and will thus be the same under autarky and free trade.

Substituting the markup price function (2.15) into the zero profit condition (2.14), $p = C/q = F/q + c$, yields the levels of output ($q = Ld = D$) and labor use l per variety

$$q = D = (\sigma - 1)\frac{F}{c} = (\sigma - 1)\frac{f}{a}, \quad l = f + aq = \sigma f.$$

The equilibrium number of differentiated products is

$$n = \frac{L_M}{l} = \frac{L - L_A}{\sigma f},$$

where L_M is labor in manufacturing and agricultural labor is assumed to be attached to land so that it can be treated as a constant. Calculating $d = q/L$ yields the equilibrium individual demand for a variety

$$d = \frac{q}{L} = \frac{\sigma - 1}{L} \frac{f}{a}.$$

Because free trade replicates the integrated equilibrium, the previous equations can be used to contrast autarky (L) and free trade $(L + L^*)$. The individual demand for a variety is smaller under free trade than under autarky. The number of varieties produced in each country, $n = (L - L_A)/\sigma f$, and the total output of a variety, $q = (\sigma - 1)f/a$, are the same in a close and an open regime. The markup function (2.15) implies that the real manufacturing wage rate is the same in both regimes. The welfare gains of free trade are due to the access to a greater number of varieties, which allows each consumer to exploit taste for variety by consuming less units of more varieties.

2.3. INTRA-INDUSTRY TRADE WITH TRANSPORT COSTS

This section introduces transport costs, which have a determinant effect on trade patterns and resource allocation. Moreover, the introduction of transport costs causes the cross-country manufacturing wage equalization property of the varieties model with zero transport cost to break down. The extension of the monopolistic competition model to comprise transport costs follows Fujita *et al.* (1999) and Neary (2001). Amiti (1998a) offers a generalization to two countries of unequal size with nonidentical consumer tastes featuring two monopolistic competition industries differing in trade costs and factor intensities.

Consumer preferences are described by identical Cobb–Douglas utility functions defined over differentiated manufactures M and a homogeneous agricultural product A. Varieties enter symmetrically in the utility function and have the same cost function. The subutility function for manufactures has constant elasticity of substitution between varieties. Production requires a fixed labor cost and takes place at constant marginal costs. The analysis comprises only one factor, labor. Agricultural labor is attached to land and the wage rate in agriculture is taken to be the numeraire.

Two countries trade in the presence of 'iceberg-type' transport costs that reduce a shipment of $T = 1 + t$ units sent abroad to one unit on arrival. The analysis resembles the previous section analysis except that total production is devoted to:

1. Local consumption $d(p)$.
2. Foreign consumption net of transport costs $d^*(pT)$, which is a function of the price of one unit inclusive of transport costs, $pT = p(1 + t)$.

Intra-industry Trade 53

3. Transport costs $td^*(pT)$ in the form of production lost in transit to a foreign location. Formally,

$$q = d(p) + Td^*(Tp) = \frac{p^{-\sigma}}{p_M^{1-\sigma}}\mu Y + T\frac{(pT)^{-\sigma}}{p_M^{*1-\sigma}}\mu Y^*$$

$$= p^{-\sigma}\left[\frac{\mu Y}{p_M^{1-\sigma}} + \frac{T^{1-\sigma}\mu Y^*}{p_M^{*1-\sigma}}\right], \tag{2.16}$$

where the term $Td^* = (1+t)d^*$ includes real transportation costs and

$$p_M^{1-\sigma} = np^{1-\sigma} + n^*(pT)^{1-\sigma}, \qquad p_M^{*(1-\sigma)} = n(pT)^{1-\sigma} + n^*p^{1-\sigma}. \tag{2.17}$$

How does the demand function change when transport costs are introduced? First, the pricing and demand symmetries of home and foreign varieties are lost because exports are subject to transport costs and the product's price is greater in an importing location. Second, because the demand function derived from atomistic consumers is conceived as taking income and prices as given, the transport cost factor affects the level of demand but not the demand elasticity, which is equal to the elasticity of substitution σ.

2.3.1. Price and Home Market Effects

The price index equation shows that residents of a larger country, which in equilibrium produces a larger number of varieties, face a lower price index than residents of a small country, who must import a greater number of varieties. This effect is called the price index effect of a larger market in the presence of transport costs. For given variety prices, the cost of living is lower in a larger market because imports require transport costs but locally produced varieties do not.

In order to formally demonstrate the existence of a price index effect in manufacturing, assume that manufacturing transport costs are constant at t and ignore the transport cost of agricultural goods so that $(1 + t_A)p_A = p_A \equiv 1$. Let us differentiate the manufacturing price index equation (2.17) around the symmetric equilibrium in which both locations have equal prices, incomes and number of varieties. Moreover, $dn = -dn^*$ so that the change refers to the number of local versus imported varieties involving transport costs. The percentage change in the manufacturing price index p_M due to a change in the number of varieties n and the variety price p is (see appendix)

$$\frac{dp_M}{p_M} = -\frac{Z}{\sigma - 1}\frac{dn}{n} + \frac{dp}{p}, \qquad Z \equiv \frac{1 - T^{1-\sigma}}{1 + T^{1-\sigma}} = \frac{1 - 1/T^{\sigma-1}}{1 + 1/T^{\sigma-1}} < 1, \tag{2.18}$$

where Z is an index of trade costs with the property that $Z = 0$ for zero transport costs ($Z = 0$, $T = 1$, $t = 0$) and rises to $Z = 1$ as T and t approach infinity (infinitely large transport costs).

An increase in the number of local varieties n (taking place jointly with a reduction in the number of imported varieties n^*) lowers that manufacturing price index because $\sigma - 1 > 0$. An increase in the net of transport costs price of manufactures p, raises the manufacturing price index. A larger country produces more varieties and thus faces a lower manufacturing price index (i.e. the price index effect). In a setup with alternative locations and transport costs, residents of agglomerated locations producing a greater number of amenities sold at the local price p (i.e. a large n relative to $n + n^*$) face a lower price index than residents of locations where imports and transport costs play a greater role. An increase in the home price of varieties increases the price index of manufactures proportionately.

The percentage change in the total demand $D^W = q$ for the product of an individual manufacturing firm is obtained in the appendix by differentiating the global demand function (2.16)

$$\frac{dq}{q} = Z\left[\frac{dY}{Y} + (\sigma - 1)\frac{dp_M}{p_M}\right] - \sigma\frac{dp}{p}, \quad Z \equiv \frac{1 - T^{1-\sigma}}{1 + T^{1-\sigma}} < 1. \tag{2.19}$$

Keeping the quantity and variety price fixed, $dq/q = dp/p = 0$, implies that an increase in income (or demand) is associated with a fall of the manufacturing price index. In turn, (2.18) implies that a fall of the manufacturing price index, $dp_M/p_M < 0$, is associated with an increase in the number of varieties, $dn/n > 0$.

An expression for the percentage change in the number of varieties n as a function of the percentage change in the level of income obtains from (2.18) and (2.19). Taking the varieties' output and price as fixed (setting $dq/q = dp/p = 0$), solving for dp_M/p_M in (2.19) and inserting the resulting expression into (2.18) yields

$$\frac{dn}{n} = \frac{1}{Z}\frac{dY}{Y}, \quad Z \equiv \frac{1 - T^{1-\sigma}}{1 + T^{1-\sigma}} < 1.$$

The previous equation reflects a home market effect that disappears only if transport costs are very high (i.e. $Z = 1$). An increase in income (or demand) results in a more than proportional increase in product variety ($1/Z > 1$). The home market effect implies that, ceteris paribus, larger countries export a larger share of manufactures. The home market effect rationalizes the prediction that countries tend to export products for which they have a relatively large local sector.

The analysis in this section assumes factor immobility across locations even if, in the presence of transport costs, real wages are not equalized across locations. If labor mobility prevailed, the variety effect would contribute to attract mobile human resources toward the agglomerated high-wage location, as discussed in the chapter on geography and location.

2.4. FACTOR ABUNDANCE AND IIT

The HO factor abundance model and the monopolistic competition approach for intra-industry trade (IIT) can be combined in a general equilibrium model. The book *Market*

Structure and Foreign Trade: Increasing Returns, Imperfect Competition, and the International Economy, by Helpman and Krugman (1985) integrates both approaches and contains a detailed exploration of diverse aspects of this type of equilibrium.

Figure 2.2 illustrates a two–country equilibrium with two factors, labor and capital, and two sectors, a differentiated goods sector labeled I and a competitive homogeneous good sector labeled II. The monopolistically competitive sector I produces differentiated goods with capital intensive techniques. Varieties are assumed to be symmetric in terms of demand and production costs and their number is exogenously given at $n + n^*$ (i.e. there is no entry). Home produced varieties are labeled $1, \ldots, n$ and foreign varieties are labeled $n + 1, \ldots, n^*$. Fixed costs and transport costs are ignored.

The home country is assumed to be capital abundant while the foreign country is assumed to be labor abundant. The global endowments of capital and labor are $(K^W, L^W) = (K + K^*, L + L^*)$. There is no factor mobility. The factor use box indicates the factor contents of goods produced and consumed. Factor use is read on the axes. Output produced and quantities consumed are indicated by the *length* of the capital–labor rays emanating from the origin. Differentiated goods' isoquants are placed on top of each other. The length of the segment joining the isoquants, measured along the equilibrium capital–labor ratio, indicates each variety's factor use and production level.

Domestic and foreign endowments are given by point E and are read starting from their respective origins O and O^*. The isoincome line BB (a budget line in the input space) has a slope equal to the negative of the wage–rental ratio, $-w/r$, and passes through the global endowment and consumption points E and D. The production

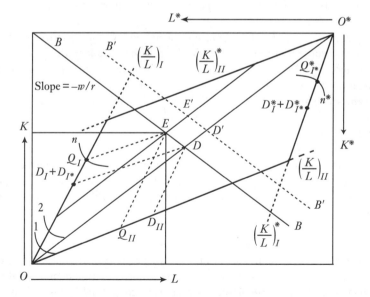

Figure 2.2. *Integrated equilibrium with differentiated products*

points along the capital–labor ratios are found by completing the parallelogram so that full employment is achieved.

Equilibrium in the market for home country varieties requires that the excessive home supply is sold abroad. In equilibrium, each variety's output is equal to the sum of local demand and exports (i.e. its global demand). Formally,

$$Q_I = D_I + D_I^*, \qquad Q_{I*}^* = D_{I*} + D_{I*}^*,$$

where D_I and D_I^* represent home and foreign demands for domestically produced varieties while D_{I*} and D_{I*}^* represent domestic and foreign demand for foreign varieties.

The home country is a net exporter of differentiated goods (sector I) and an importer of homogeneous good II. The equilibrium output of each variety is just sectorial output Q_I divided by the number of locally produced varieties n (and Q_{I*}^* divided by n^*). Production per home variety exceeds home consumption per variety, which is given by home consumption of all varieties $D_I + D_{I*}$ divided by the total number of varieties consumed $n + n^*$.

The factor content of home country exports of varieties is equal to the factor content of the output Q_I of home produced varieties minus the factor content of home consumption D_I of home-produced varieties. This factor content corresponds to the factor content of the sum of the imports of differentiated goods and homogeneous product II.

The factor content of *net* exports of varieties is equal to (1) the factor content of home output Q_I minus the factor content of total home consumption of varieties produced at home and abroad, $D_I + D_{I*}$, and (2) the factor content of homogeneous product II imports, $D_{II} - Q_{II}$.

A difference between the HO model and the mixed HO and varieties model is that zero net factor content of trade can be identified with no trade in the HO model, but not in the model with varieties. For instance, if the endowment point coincides with the consumption point at D, there is intra-industry trade in varieties but intra-industry exports and imports are equal, $Q_I - D_I = D_I^*$ and there is no trade in product II. Because all trade consists of intra-industry trade in varieties produced using identical factor intensities, the net factor content of trade is zero.

The equilibrium associated with endowment and consumption points E and D lies in the factor price equalization (FPE) set and thus replicates the integrated equilibrium featuring perfect international mobility of capital and labor. The equilibrium price of a variety relative to good II determines the unique factor price ratio w/r supporting diversified inter-industry production. Inter-industry production diversification arises because each country's endowment lies within its cone of diversification.

Figure 2.2 illustrates how the HO factor abundance theorem and the intra-industry trade model based on taste for variety fit into a single general equilibrium framework. First, the capital abundant home country is a net exporter of capital intensive differentiated goods and a net importer of the labor intensive good. Inter-industry trade is thus governed by the HO factor abundance theorem. Second, there is intra-industry trade within the differentiated goods sector I consisting of varieties produced with similar factor intensities. The reason is that each variety is produced by a single firm. The home and foreign outputs of varieties, Q_I and Q_{I*}^*, are sold in both countries.

2.4.1. Interindusty Trade: Size and Abundance Effects

What are the inter-industry trade effects of relative country size and relative factor abundances? Let us keep the endowments within the factor price equalization set. Consider an increase in the home country's relative size, depicted by a shift from endowment and consumption points E and D on isoincome line BB to points E' and D' on isoincome line $B'B'$. This shift neither affects the net factor content of trade (the length of ED is the same as the length of $E'D'$) nor the associated volume of inter-industry trade. If relative size is altered while keeping the endowment points on the same trade level line (e.g. on line EE'), inter-industry trade volume is unaffected.

The inter-industry trade effect of a change in relative factor abundances (a shift of the endowment point along a given isoincome line) stands in contrast with the effect of a change in relative size (a shift of isoincome line). A greater difference in factor endowments as indicated by a shift of the endowment point along a given isoincome line raises the net factor content of trade and leads to greater inter-industry trade volume. Formally, a greater difference in relative factor endowments means that the endowment point is on a trade level line standing farther away from the diagonal. For instance, the pure intra-industry trade case arises when the endowment point lies on the diagonal and thus coincides with consumption point D. At this point, there is no exchange of net factor content, as $Q_I = D_I + D_I^*$ and $Q_{II} = D_{II}$. A movement of the endowment point from D to E increases the net factor content of inter-industry trade and thus of total trade (as intra-industry trade generates a zero net factor content of trade).

The inter-industry trade and net factor content effects of relative size and relative factor abundances are the same characterizing the HO model with two homogeneous goods. But recall that net factor content does not correspond to total trade in the presence of both inter-industry and intra-industry trade. In order to clarify the effects on total trade one must clarify the behavior of intra-industry trade.

2.4.2. Intra-industry Trade: Size and Abundance Effects

What are the effects of relative size and relative factor abundances on the level of intra-industry trade? An increase in the home country's relative size (shift from E to E') increases home country demand for varieties by the same amount that it reduces foreign country demand. This is a consequence of sharing identical constant returns to scale utility functions. But the shift from E to E' increases home country production of varieties by the same amount that it raises home country demand. Graphically, the distance between E and E' is the same as the distance between D and D'. Therefore, inter-industry trade, trade in varieties and total trade remain unaffected by changes in relative size along the trade level line passing through E and E'.

A change in factor endowments to the right (or left) of the diagonal increases intra-industry trade. The reason is that both countries' demand for varieties remain unaffected but the total quantity of varieties produced by the home country changes. Home country intra-industry exports increase as the endowment point moves to the left of the diagonal line, which represents the minimum level of intra-industry trade. Home country intra-industry imports increase as the endowment point moves to the right of the diagonal line. Therefore, inter-industry trade, intra-industry trade and total trade increase as the endowment point moves farther away from the diagonal, that is, as relative factor endowments become more heterogeneous.

2.5. INTRA-INDUSTRY TRADE: HO–RICARDO VIEW

Intra-industry trade takes place when countries exchange products that, if factor costs are the same, use similar factor intensities. When two products use identical factor intensities for all common factor prices, they are called 'perfectly intra-industry' products. In the HO model with homogeneous products there is no product differentiation based on taste for variety, production location or quality. Trade in perfectly intra-industry products is superfluous because it entails devoting resources to produce exports in order to import products that can be produced at home with the same resources. An infinitesimally small transport cost eliminates this superfluous trade pattern.

Is intra-industry trade consistent with the factor abundance theory of trade based on perfect competition and constant returns to scale? A positive answer emerges if the HO model is modified to comprise Ricardian comparative advantage. The HO–Ricardo approach, developed by Davis (1995), offers a unified account of intra-industry and inter-industry trade in a setting with constant returns to scale and perfect competition. He develops a model with more goods than factors in which infinitesimally small comparative advantages can generate different trade patterns, including patterns with both intra-industry and inter-industry trade.

Consider a HO–Ricardo model with three goods, labeled I, II (the numeraire), and III. There are two productive factors, capital and labor. Sectors I and II produce perfectly intra-industry goods in the sense that, for all possible wage–rental ratios, factor intensities are identical. Goods I and II are produced with a greater capital intensive technique than good III.

The key challenge, generating intra-industry trade without recourse to Armington preferences, a taste for variety or quality differentiation, is met by introducing exogenous Ricardian comparative advantages. Production functions are the same in both countries except for good I, which features small Hicks-neutral technological differences across countries. Specifically, the home country produces good I more efficiently than the foreign country as captured by the technology parameter $A > 1$,

$$Q_I = AF_I(K_I, L_I), \quad Q_I^* = F_I^*(K_I^*, L_I^*), \qquad A > 1.$$

Because goods *I* and *II* are produced with the same factor intensities, the relative price of *I* in terms of *II*, $p_I/p_{II} = p_I = 1/A$, is given by relative country productivities as in the Ricardian model. The relative price can be infinitesimally close to one if *A* is also infinitesimally close to one. A key property of the model is that an infinitesimally small comparative advantage induces the home country to be the sole producer of good *I* in equilibrium (as long as it has enough resources to supply the whole global demand for good *I*).

Figure 2.3 illustrates a trade pattern characterized by both intra-industry and inter-industry trade. The home and foreign countries have identical homothetic preferences. The equilibrium relative price of good *III* is such that the implied equilibrium wage–rental ratio leads to optimal capital–labor ratios sustaining full employment with

$$k_I = k_{II} > k_{III}.$$

The home country exports good *I* and imports good *II* (giving rise to intra-industry trade) and good *III* (giving rise to inter-industry trade). The total factor content of good *I* production becomes the origin $O' = Q_I$ for an interior factor use box for goods *II* and *III*.

The home country generates a surplus $Q_I - D_I$ in good *I*, which corresponds to a trade deficit in goods *II* and *III* together. Therefore, the length of factor use segment

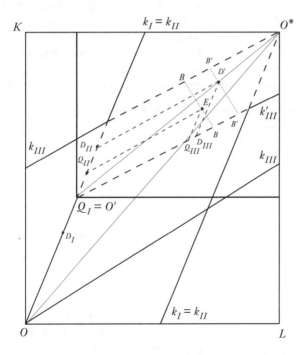

Figure 2.3. *Intra-industry trade, technology, and factor abundance*

$Q_J D_I$ is the same as the distance separating BB and $B'B'$ (measured along a line with the same slope as OQ_J). By the same token, the foreign country generates a trade surplus in goods II and III together, which is used to pay for its imports of good I.

The factors used to produce goods II and III in each country are obtained by completing the parallelogram with vertex at endowment point E in the interior box originating at O'. Consumptions of goods II and III, D_{II} and D_{III}, are read from the origin at point $O' = Q_J$. The factor content of the consumption of goods II and III is given by the intersection of the interior box diagonal and the home country isoincome line $B'B'$. The consumption of goods II and III is determined by completing the parallelogram with vertexes at O' and consumption point D'.

The HO–Ricardo trade pattern generates intra-industry trade exhibiting simultaneous exportation and importation of goods with identical factor intensities. Specifically, the sole producer and exporter of intra-industry product I simultaneously imports product II featuring identical factor intensities.

The perfectly competitive model with constant returns to scale and more goods than factors can explain intra-industry trade because:

1. A small Hicks-neutral cross-country technological gap generates a Ricardian comparative advantage in one of two perfectly intra-industry products. The country benefitting from a comparative advantage becomes the sole supplier of that product. Observe that generating a relative comparative advantage requires a country's technological advantages to be nonuniform across products. Because the Hicks-neutral technological shift indicated by A applies to good I only, the home country enjoys both an absolute and a relative comparative advantage in producing good I.
2. The HO factor abundance theory of production with homothetic preferences explains the trade pattern of the remaining goods and particularly why the sole supplier of a product might import another product with a similar factor intensity.

Why is it that the capital-abundant home country imports a capital intensive good? Why is it that the labor-abundant foreign country exports a capital intensive good even if it does not have a comparative advantage in that good? These paradoxes are explained by the combination of two elements observable in Fig. 2.3.

First, the home country is capital abundant from the perspective of the exterior box but is labor abundant from the perspective of the interior box determining the production and consumption of goods II and III. The slope of the home country's capital to labor endowment line (the slope of $O'E$) is less pronounced than the slope of the diagonal $O'O^*$ depicting the aggregate capital–labor ratio of the interior factor use box. According to the HO framework, a labor abundant economy would export the labor intensive product III and import the capital intensive product II.

Second, the additional demand for capital intensive good II, corresponding to part of the trade surplus in good I, reinforces the relative factor abundance effect. Observe that the capital abundant home country imports the capital intensive good II in equilibrium, $Q_{II} < D_{II}$, because demand outstrips supply. Therefore, if the additional demand for good II accounted for by the surplus generated in good I is strong enough, the home country would import the capital intensive good II in equilibrium even if it remains

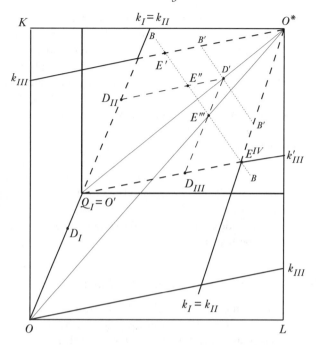

Figure 2.4. *The pattern and volume of trade*

capital abundant from the perspective of the interior box. This possibility is illustrated in Fig. 2.4 by any point on the segment joining endowment point E'' and the interior box diagonal $O'O^*$.

2.5.1. Explaining the Pattern of Trade

Let us review how different factor endowments points (within the factor price equalization set) generate (1) a HO–Ricardo pattern of simultaneous inter- and intra-industry trade (heterogeneous trade), (2) a HO pattern of pure inter-industry trade and, (3) a pattern of pure intra-industry trade.

Figure 2.4 depicts how the trade pattern varies with different possible endowments along line BB. In all cases, the home country is the sole producer of good I and there is trade in either good II or good III, or both. The factor content of consumption of goods II and III is given by the intersection of diagonal $O'O^*$ and the isoincome line $B'B'$ and does not depend on the endowment point along BB.

First, if the endowment point falls on the line segment connecting points E' and E'', the foreign country exports good III and imports goods I and II. In this case, there is no intra-industry trade. This trade pattern corresponds to the HO model of pure inter-industry trade.

Second, if the endowment point falls on the line segment connecting endowment points E'' and E''', the foreign country exports both goods II and III and there is simultaneous intra- and inter-industry trade (heterogeneous trade).

Third, if the endowment point is E''' on diagonal OO^*, countries have identical endowment ratios (given by the slope of OO^*). The domestic country's consumption and production of good III are equal and there is no trade in this good. This feature can be seen by completing the parallelogram with vertex at point E'''. Therefore, trade involves only goods I and II. In other words, all trade is pure intra-industry trade because the factor content of the surplus $Q_I - D_I$ corresponds to the factor content of the excess demand for good II (the length of $Q_I - D_I$ is equal to the length of $D' - E'''$).

Fourth, if the endowment point corresponds to points between E''' and E^{IV}, the foreign country exports good II and imports goods I and III. In this case, there is both intra-industry and inter-industry trade. Observe that this case represents a different pattern of heterogeneous trade compared with the second case discussed, in which the foreign country exports both goods II and III.

2.5.2. Volume of Inter-industry and Intra-industry Trade

What determines the volume of trade in the HO–Ricardo framework? Let us define the total volume of trade VT as the sum of the values of trading partners' exports. This definition corresponds to twice the total exports of either country with balanced overall trade.

Consider a trade pattern in which the home country exports good I and the foreign country exports goods II and III (e.g. segment $E''E'''$ in Fig. 2.4). The total volume of trade is

$$VT = p_I(Q_I - sQ_I^W) + (Q_{II}^* - s^*Q_{II}^W) + p_{III}(Q_{III}^* - s^*Q_{III}^W)$$
$$= 2p_I(Q_I - sQ_I^W), \qquad (2.20)$$

where good II is the numeraire so that $p_{II} = 1$ and trade balance implies that countries exports have the same value. The relative size of countries, s and s^*, are measured by the ratio of national GDP to global GDP and are linear functions of each country's endowments

$$s = \frac{wL + rK}{wL^W + rK^W}, \qquad s^* = \frac{wL^* + rK^*}{wL^W + rK^W}, \qquad s + s^* = 1.$$

Relative size explains the share of world production Q_i^W, $i \in \{I, II, III\}$, demanded by each country, that is, $D_I = sQ_I^W$, $D_{II}^* = s^*Q_{II}^W$ and $D_{III}^* = s^*Q_{III}^W$.

Consider the trade pattern illustrated in segment $E^{III}E^{IV}$ of Fig. 2.4, in which the foreign country exports numeraire good II. Balanced trade implies that the value of the foreign country's exports of good II, $Q_{II}^* - s^* Q_{II}^W$, is equal to the value of its imports of goods I and III, which is equal to the value of home country exports of goods I and III, $p_I(Q_I - sQ_I^W) + p_{III}(Q_{III} - sQ_{III}^W)$. Therefore, the total volume of trade can be expressed as

$$VT = 2(Q_{II}^* - s^*Q_{II}^W). \tag{2.21}$$

For the particular trade pattern considered, the total volume of trade corresponds to twice the foreign country surplus obtained from its exports of good II. Within the price equalization set, the global production Q_{II}^W of good II is given. Moreover, under constant returns to scale and for given factor prices, Q_{II}^* and s^* are linear functions of the endowments.

Recall the derivation of the level curves indicating a constant value of inter-industry trade. Any endowment point lying along the diagonal OO^* while staying within the factor price equalization set, such as endowment point E''' in Fig. 2.4, does not generate trade in good III and represents pure intra-industry trade. This feature can be seen by completing the parallelogram for the production point for alternative endowment points along diagonal OO^*. In other words, the diagonal OO^* is the level curve for no inter-industry trade.

How does the level of intra-industry trade behave as the endowment point moves along the diagonal OO^*? Intra-industry trade, and thus total trade, contracts as the endowment shifts up the diagonal and expands as the endowment shifts down the diagonal. To see why, observe that the home country surplus generated by good I, and thus intra-industry trade, is smaller as the endowment moves up diagonal OO^*. The reason is that $Q_I = Q_I^W$ remains the same (global production patterns are not altered within the factor price equalization set) and D_I increases because the home country is larger in relative terms. Observe that, as the endowment point moves along the diagonal, it causes a parallel shift of the line $D'ED_{III}$ so that the home country remains self-sufficient in good III.

The previous considerations provide the main intuition about the determinants of the volume of trade. As in the HO model, inter-industry trade is higher the farther apart the trade level curve (the line showing a constant factor content of trade) is from the diagonal. Observe that inter-industry trade level lines have the same slope as diagonal OO^*.

The level of intra-industry trade is characterized by examining how it changes with different endowment points along isoincome line BB and for different isoincome lines. Davis (1995) offers a detailed analysis of these relations.

1. There is no intra-industry trade for endowment points lying along the inter-industry trade level curves passing through points on the E' to E'' segment (Fig. 2.4). In this region, the foreign country exports good III and imports I and III. The volume of trade as measured by the sum of all exports is equal to two times the exports of good III

$$VT = 2(Q_{III}^* - s^*Q_{III}^W).$$

2. Intra-industry trade increases as the inter-industry trade level line on which the endowment point lies approaches diagonal OO^* from the left. Specifically, there is

no intra-industry trade in endowment points lying on or to the left of the inter-industry trade level line passing through point E''. Intra-industry trade levels increase monotonically as the endowment point approaches point E''' on diagonal OO^* (the zero inter-industry trade line). Observe that, as the endowment point approaches point E''', trade in good III declines toward zero while trade in perfectly intra-industry good II increases. Intra-industry trade is constant along a given inter-industry trade level line in this region.

3. Intra-industry trade is highest at diagonal point E''' on diagonal OO^* and declines as the endowment point shifts along isoincome line BB from point E''' to point E^{IV}. The reason for this decline is that, as the endowment point approaches E^{IV}, the home country becomes more and more specialized in good III and imports more and more perfectly intra-industry good II. In this region, intra-industry trade increases as the endowment point on diagonal OO^* shifts closer to origin O (the home country becomes smaller and its demand for good I declines so that $Q_I - D_I$ increases). Intra-industry trade declines as the endowment point moves closer to origin O^* (the home country becomes larger and its demand for good I increases so that $Q_I - D_I$ declines).

2.5.3. *Contrasts with Alternative Frameworks*

Intra-industry trade, in the sense of trade in products requiring the same factor intensities in production, has been shown to arise in a setting with competitive markets and constant returns to scale. The previous approach is known as the HO–Ricardo approach because trade patterns are explained by the interaction of (1) the factor proportions, relative abundance relations and demand patterns stressed by Eli Heckscher and Bertil Ohlin, and (2) the type of technological differences across countries stressed by David Ricardo.

What are the differences with the predictions of the HO model? In the HO–Ricardo approach, key results of the HO model can break down. The HO theorem can fail because a capital abundant country might import a capital intensive good, relative size can matter for the volume of intra-industry trade and thus total trade within the factor price equalization set, and trade volumes might fail to increase with greater differences in factor endowments because changes in inter- and intra-industry trade offset each other. Let us illustrate the conditions giving rise to these breakdowns.

1. The HO framework predicts that a country exports the good that uses relatively more intensively the factor that is relatively more abundant in the country. By contrast, Fig. 2.3 shows a case in which the capital abundant home country imports the capital intensive perfectly intra-industry good II in equilibrium.

2. In the HO framework, relative country size does not necessarily affect the total volume of trade (given that the economy is in the factor price equalization set). If a country becomes larger in such a way that it increases the production and the consumption of goods by the same amount, the gap between production and consumption will be kept constant and the volume of trade will not change.

By contrast, relative country size can matter in the HO–Ricardo model. To see why country size can matter, consider the case in which the home country exports good I in exchange for imports of goods II and III (i.e. the heterogeneous trade segment joining E'' and E'''). The total volume of trade is two times the value of home country exports, $2p_I(Q_J - sQ_I^W)$, which is the same as twice the value of foreign country imports of good I, $2p_Is^*Q_I^W$,

$$VT = 2p_I(Q_J - sQ_I^W) = 2s^*p_IQ_I^W. \qquad (2.22)$$

Formally, if the global economy lies within the factor price equalization set, a change in relative country size s^* does not affect the relative price p_I and production Q_I^W. Therefore, the total trade volume equation implies that total trade volume is affected. Intuitively, trade declines with a relatively smaller foreign country (a lower s^*) because the size redistribution shifts demand for good I toward the home country and away from the foreign country, and the only motivation for trade is to satisfy foreign country demand for good I.

3. In the HO framework, greater differences in factor endowment ratios induce a higher volume of trade. In the HO–Ricardo framework, the effect of endowments in the total volume of trade (inclusive of intra-industry trade) hinges on the region in which endowment E lies. For instance, refer to total trade volume equation (2.22) for the case in which home country exports good I in exchange for imports of goods II and III (the heterogeneous trade segment joining E'' and E'''). The trade volume remains constant as the endowment point moves along isoincome line BB because $Q_J - D_I$ is unaffected by those shifts. The relative size s^* (i.e. relative income) is kept constant along segment $E''E'''$ of isoincome line BB and world production is unchanged for any endowment that lies in the factor price equalization set. Intuitively, a move away from the diagonal along isoincome line BB increases inter-industry trade, as in the HO model, but reduces intra-industry trade. One effect must exactly offset the other so that there is no net change in the volume of trade.

How does the HO–Ricardo intra-industry trade environment contrast with models of intra-industry trade with imperfect competition, increasing returns and taste for variety? The major distinction is that the HO–Ricardo approach has enough structure to be able to determine a trade pattern specifying who exports what from whom. By contrast, in the symmetric varieties model it is not possible to determine which country produces each specific differentiated good.

2.6. CHARACTERISTICS AND VERTICAL IIT

This section focuses on the characteristics approach and the quality-differentiated product approach to vertical intra-industry trade. Differentiation by quality provides an explanation for why richer countries' exports command higher prices than poorer country exports in the market.

2.6.1. Characteristics Approach

The characteristics approach to intra-industry trade developed by Lancaster (1979, 1984) moves away from the symmetry assumption of the monopolistic competition model. In this setup, products feature different characteristics and consumers attach different values to them. The idea is that, given the prices of product characteristics, the individual consumer has an ideal combination of characteristics that he or she would like to have in a product. The market provides products that offer alternative packages of desired characteristics. For instance, some people prefer large automobiles while others prefer small cars. Also, buyers differ in whether or not they consider air conditioning and automatic gears important. Because different countries produce different packages, there are simultaneous exports and imports of goods' varieties differing in specific characteristics.

Stokey (1991) utilizes the Lancaster framework to explain why developing countries often produce lower quality goods for their own local consumption while exporting higher quality goods to developed countries. The explanation hinges on a key feature of demand. The range of characteristics that a consumer can buy depends on her income. Therefore, low income countries tend to purchase lower quality goods than high income countries even if higher quality goods are available.

2.6.2. Vertical Intra-industry Trade

Formal modeling of vertical intra-industry trade was introduced by Falvey (1981). His analysis was expanded to incorporate an appropriate demand side and other factors in Falvey and Kierzkowski (1987), Flam and Helpman (1987), and subsequent work.

Let us sketch how models of vertical integration determine who produces what and who trades what. Consider two countries that can produce different qualities of a given product. A higher quality product is assumed to be produced using a higher capital–labor ratio. Factor abundances and technological differences lead to different specialization patterns. If factor endowments are dissimilar and technologies are shared, the capital abundant and labor scarce country specializes in high quality products even if there is factor price equalization à la HO. If factor endowments are similar but there are technological differences that generate cross-country gaps in factor rewards, the high wage country specializes in the capital intensive high-quality product.

Vertical intra-industry trade arises because of within-country income inequality. An unequal distribution of income within countries implies that there is a demand for different product qualities in both countries. Low income consumers demand lower quality products and high income consumers demand higher quality products. If the trading partners' income distributions overlap, trade in quality differentiated products emerges.

A trade pattern prediction of the vertical intra-industry model that is validated by empirical evidence is that richer, capital abundant countries export higher quality products than poorer, labor abundant countries. Observe, however, that this prediction is often contradicted by foreign direct investment seeking low wage production locations to export to high-income markets.

2.7. QUALITY DIFFERENTIATION BY NATIONAL ORIGIN

Making quality choice endogenous permits reconciling larger relative country size and greater trade with improved terms of trade due to a greater quality of exports. This response to greater relative size and trade contrasts with the constant terms of trade prediction of the symmetric varieties model and with the terms of trade deterioration prediction of the fixed quality Armington model.

A simple Armington model incorporating endogenous quality choice is presented in Hummels and Klenow (2002). They consider two trading partners each of which produces a single variety. The model satisfies the Armington assumption as varieties display quality differentiation across national lines. The home country's representative consumer allocates his income y to consumption d_I and d_{II} of home and foreign country products I and II. The utility maximization problem is

$$\max_{d_I, d_{II}} U = Q_I(d_I)^{1-1/\sigma} + Q_{II}(d_{II})^{1-1/\sigma} \quad \text{s.t.} \quad p_I d_I + p_{II} d_{II} \leq y,$$

where Q_I and Q_{II} represent home and foreign quality levels and $\sigma > 1$ is the consumption elasticity of substitution.

Defining the Lagrangian $\mathcal{L} = U + \lambda(y - p_I d_I - p_{II} d_{II})$ and computing the first-order maximization conditions yields

$$\frac{\partial U}{\partial d_I} = \left(1 - \frac{1}{\sigma}\right) Q_I(d_I)^{-1/\sigma} = \lambda p_I,$$

$$\frac{\partial U}{\partial d_{II}} = \left(1 - \frac{1}{\sigma}\right) Q_{II}(d_{II})^{-1/\sigma} = \lambda p_{II}.$$

The implied relative price as a function of qualities and quantities demanded is

$$\frac{p_I}{p_{II}} = \frac{(1 - \frac{1}{\sigma})Q_I(d_I)^{-1/\sigma}}{(1 - \frac{1}{\sigma})Q_{II}(d_{II})^{-1/\sigma}} = \frac{Q_I(d_I)^{-1/\sigma}}{Q_{II}(d_{II})^{-1/\sigma}}. \tag{2.23}$$

Relative demands d_I/d_{II} and d_I^*/d_{II}^* are given by

$$\frac{d_I}{d_{II}} = \left(\frac{p_I/Q_I}{p_{II}/Q_{II}}\right)^{-\sigma} = \frac{d_I^*}{d_{II}^*}. \tag{2.24}$$

The relative quantities demanded decline with the quality-adjusted relative price.

Each variety is produced by a single firm and its output q is sold in a monopolistically competitive global market (Helguera and Lutz, 1998 examine quality models in oligopolistic markets). Because the number of goods is fixed, firms earn positive profits in equilibrium. The home firm's profit maximization problem is

$$\max_{q_I,L} p_I q_I - wL \quad \text{s.t.} \quad q_I = F(L, Q_I; A_I, Z_I) = A_I e^{-Q_I/Z_I} L,$$

where $q_I = Ld_I + L^* d_{II}$, L and L^* stand for number of workers and A_I is a Hicks-neutral productivity parameter. Z_I denotes quality productivity, that is, home country productivity in producing quality. For a given quality level, higher quality productivity Z_I implies a lower Q_I/Z_I and a higher e^{-Q_I/Z_I}. Therefore, output q_I is also higher. Observe that a greater quality level Q_I implies that a greater Z_I results in a larger increase of q_I. In other words, the marginal output effect of quality productivity Z_I increases with the level of quality.

The first-order profit maximization condition for quality Q_I and labor use L yield the solution for equilibrium quality Q_I and a condition for the labor use L. Equilibrium quality is

$$Q_I = \frac{\sigma}{\sigma - 1} Z_I \quad \rightarrow \quad \frac{Q_I}{Q_{II}^*} = \frac{Z_I}{Z_{II}^*}. \tag{2.25}$$

Higher quality productivity Z_I translates into better product quality Q_I. The relation $Q_I/Q_{II}^* = Z_I/Z_{II}^*$ implies that $Q_I/Z_I = Q_{II}^*/Z_{II}^*$, which allows solving for the output ratio in terms of the productivity ratio and the labor ratio

$$\frac{q_I}{q_{II}^*} = \frac{A_I e^{-Q_I/Z_I} L}{A_{II}^* e^{-Q_{II}^*/Z_{II}^*} L^*} = \frac{A_I L}{A_{II}^* L^*}. \tag{2.26}$$

Profit maximization implies that labor use L/L^* can be expressed as

$$\frac{L}{L^*} = \left(\frac{Z_I/w}{Z_{II}^*/w^*} \right)^{\sigma} \left(\frac{A_I}{A_{II}^*} \right)^{\sigma - 1}. \tag{2.27}$$

The ratio of home to foreign labor use L/L^* increases with relative quality productivity Z_I/Z_{II}^* and with relative Hicks-neutral productivity A_I/A_{II}^*. The labor use ratio decreases with the relative labor cost w/w^*. The labor use equation permits solving for the relative cross-country wage rate as a function of labor endowments and productivity parameters

$$\frac{w}{w^*} = \left(\frac{L}{L^*} \right)^{-1/\sigma} \frac{Z_I}{Z_{II}^*} \left(\frac{A_I}{A_{II}^*} \right)^{(\sigma-1)/\sigma}.$$

The equilibrium relative price derived from $q_I/q_I^* = d_I/d_{II} = d_I^*/d_{II}^*$

$$\frac{q_I}{q_{II}^*} = \frac{Ld_I + L^* d_I^*}{Ld_{II} + L^* d_{II}^*} = \frac{Ld_I + L^*(d_I/d_{II})d_{II}^*}{Ld_I/(d_I/d_{II}) + L^* d_{II}^*} = \frac{d_I}{d_{II}} = \frac{d_I^*}{d_{II}^*}.$$

The equilibrium price ratio p_I/p_{II} and the quality-adjusted relative price are obtained from (2.23) and (2.26)

$$
\frac{p_I}{p_{II}} = \frac{Q_I}{Q_{II}^*}\left(\frac{d_I}{d_{II}}\right)^{-1/\sigma} = \frac{Q_I}{Q_{II}^*}\left(\frac{q_I}{q_{II}^*}\right)^{-1/\sigma} = \frac{Z_I}{Z_{II}^*}\left(\frac{A_I L}{A_{II}^* L^*}\right)^{-1/\sigma},
$$

$$
\frac{p_I/Z_I}{p_{II}/Z_{II}^*} = \left(\frac{A_I L}{A_{II}^* L^*}\right)^{-1/\sigma}.
$$

(2.28)

Equilibrium relative income Y/Y^* and relative income per capita are

$$
\frac{Y}{Y^*} = \frac{p_I q_I}{p_{II} q_{II}^*} = \frac{Z_I}{Z_{II}^*}\left(\frac{A_I L}{A_{II}^* L^*}\right)^{1-1/\sigma}, \qquad \frac{Y/L}{Y^*/L^*} = \frac{Z_I A_I}{Z_{II}^* A_{II}^*}\left(\frac{A_I L}{A_{II}^* L^*}\right)^{-1/\sigma}.
$$

Recapping, the endogenous quality Armington model exhibits the following properties

1. A larger relative size Y/Y^* due to a relatively larger labor supply L/L^* or a higher productivity ratio A_I/A_{II}^* is associated with a lower relative price of exports p_I/p_{II} (i.e. deteriorated terms of trade).
2. A larger relative size due to greater relative quality productivity Z_I/Z_{II}^* improves the terms of trade p_I/p_{II} and leaves the quality-adjusted price unchanged. Endogenizing quality choice reconciles larger relative size with improved terms of trade and unchanged quality-adjusted relative prices. This terms of trade response to greater relative country size contrasts with the constant terms of trade prediction of the symmetric varieties model and with the terms of trade deterioration prediction of the fixed quality Armington model.
3. Endogenizing quality choice reconciles larger relative per capita income with improved terms of trade and unchanged quality-adjusted price.
4. The relation $q_I/q_{II}^* = A_I L/A_{II}^* L^*$ implies that greater relative quality productivity does not affect relative production. Greater size due to a higher relative productivity ratio A_I/A_{II}^* or to a greater relative labor endowment L/L^* increases relative output.

2.8. TRADE EMPIRICS: QUANTITY, VARIETY, AND QUALITY

Empirical trade analysis aims to explain not only why most trade among developed countries consist of intra-industry trade but also several stylized facts about trade. First, the actual increase of the trade to income ratio over time seems greater than what can be accounted for by reduced trade barriers. Second, higher income results in trading a greater number of varieties. Third, higher income countries secure a higher price for their exports than lower income countries.

What are the predictions of alternative models of intra-industry trade about the trade to income ratio and about the extent to which trade takes the form of exchanges in quantities, varieties and qualities? Which models' predictions show greater consistency with the behavior of the relative price of exports (terms of trade)? Hummels and Klenow (2002) confirm the finding that larger countries tend to trade more than smaller countries. They contrast the predictions of models about the extent to which greater trade takes the form of trading larger quantities of a common set of goods (the intensive margin), a larger set of goods (the extensive margin) and higher qualities.

The models examined by Hummels and Klenow (2002) are as follows.

1. Armington differentiation based on production nationality. This model predicts that greater trade takes the form of trade in larger quantities of a common set of goods (intensive margin to the exclusion of the extensive margin). Furthermore, greater trade causes a deterioration of exporters' terms of trade as they move down the world demand curve for their nationally differentiated exports. Estimated welfare effects based on computable general equilibrium models are often dominated by these terms of trade effects.
2. Armington preferences with an endogenous number of varieties and terms of trade effects (Acemoglu and Ventura, 2002). This model predicts that greater trade is associated with a terms of trade deterioration. The details and empirical evidence on the growth model developed by Acemoglu and Ventura (2002) are discussed in the chapter examining growth and trade.
3. Taste for variety with increasing returns and monopolistic competition. This model predicts that greater exports take the form of exporting a larger set of differentiated products (the extensive margin for exports), which can be accompanied by larger quantities of the same goods (intensive margin) if the elasticity of demand varies with the level of real income. The terms of trade are not altered by greater trade.
4. Armington preferences with quality differentiation. This model predicts that greater trade takes the form of higher quality goods, which thus command higher prices, with no terms of trade deterioration in quality-adjusted prices.
5. Specialized imported intermediate inputs used to produce final goods. These imports require incurring a fixed cost, such as setting up a service and parts supply network (Romer, 1994). Imported varieties are symmetric, have the same demand and are sold at the same price so that the extensive margin for imports corresponds to the number of imported goods. This model predicts that greater trade takes the form of a wider diversity of imports, that is, a greater number of imported goods (extensive margin for imports). Romer's (1994) analysis of imports, fixed costs of importing and trade restrictions is discussed in the chapter on trade restrictions.

The empirical analysis uses: (1) 1995 data on shipments by 110 exporters to 59 importers in 5000 6-digit product categories and (2) US 1995 imports from 119 countries in over 13,000 10-digit product categories. The results indicate that the extensive margin accounts for two-thirds of the greater exports and one-third of the greater imports of larger economies. Moreover, richer countries export more high price units, which is interpreted as meaning that they export higher quality goods. The authors cannot find terms of trade deterioration effects.

A model of varieties matches the results that the extensive margin accounts for a substantial part of greater exports, a model of quality differentiation accounts for the higher prices of richer countries' exports, and a model with fixed costs of trading explains the results that the extensive margin accounts for a substantial part of greater imports. The authors conclude that a model incorporating product differentiation, quality and fixed costs of importing matches the data better than models based on Armington preferences and terms of trade effects. Quality differences are estimated to account for about twenty-five percent of country differences in real income per worker.

2.9. CONCLUSIONS

Until the late 1970s, most trade analyses were based on either perfect competition or monopoly market structures. At that time, the monopolistic competition model-ing was advanced as an alternative benchmark explaining how intra-industry trade emerges from a taste for product variety and production specialization to exploit decreasing costs. This approach combines the tools of competitive equilibrium and monopoly analysis, assuming that each firm has a monopoly in a variety (e.g. an auto brand) but competes with a large number of rival firms producing competing varieties (e.g. competing auto brands).

Can horizontal intra-industry trade be consistent with the HO factor abundance model, perfect competition and constant returns to scale? A positive answer hinges on modifying the HO framework to incorporate exogenous comparative advantages à la David Ricardo. Intra-industry trade between similar countries can arise because arbitrarily small comparative advantages lead to specialization under constant returns to scale and perfect competition.

A large share of intra-industry trade is quality differentiated (i.e. vertically differ-entiated). Contrary to the symmetric varieties and Armington models, an endogenous quality model predicts that a large country (i.e. high income country) can increase the volume of exports without experiencing a terms of trade deterioration.

Greater trade takes the form of exchange of greater quantities, a greater number of varieties and goods with different qualities. Tests of alternative models' predictions suggest that a model incorporating product differentiation, quality and fixed costs of importing matches the quantity, quality and variety of actual trade patterns.

The next task is to confront the basic theories of trade patterns with additional data. The next chapter focuses on the empirical validity of alternative trade models predictions of the net factor content of trade, production patterns and other variables.

2.10. APPENDIX

2.10.1. Derivation of (2.12)

In order to obtain the demand function for variety j, observe that (2.11) implies that the marginal utility of differentiated product i is $(1/\rho)(\int_0^n d_i^\rho \, di)^{(1/\rho)-1} \rho d_i^{\rho-1}$. Recall that the first-order utility maximization condition equates the marginal rate of substitution between any two differentiated products i and j to their relative price, $d_i^{\rho-1}/d_j^{\rho-1} = p_i/p_j$. Substituting $d_i = d_j p_i^{1/(\rho-1)}/p_j^{1/(\rho-1)}$ into the quantity index D_M yields

$$D_M = \left(\int_0^n d_i^\rho \, di \right)^{1/\rho} = d_j p_j^{-1/(\rho-1)} \left(\int_0^n p_i^{\rho/(\rho-1)} \, di \right)^{1/\rho}.$$

Solving for d_j yields (2.12)

$$d_j = \frac{p_j^{1/(\rho-1)}}{\left(\int_0^n p_i^{\rho/(\rho-1)} \, di \right)^{1/\rho}} D_M = \frac{p_j^{-\sigma}}{\left(\int_0^n p_i^{1-\sigma} \, di \right)^{-\sigma/(1-\sigma)}} D_M$$

$$= \frac{p_j^{-\sigma}}{P_M^{-\sigma}} D_M = \frac{p_j^{-\sigma}}{p_M^{1-\sigma}} \mu Y,$$

where $\sigma > 1$ is the elasticity of substitution between varieties and

$$p_M \equiv \left(\int_0^n p_i^{1-\sigma} \, di \right)^{1/(1-\sigma)} \qquad \sigma = \frac{1}{1-\rho}, \quad \rho = \frac{\sigma-1}{\sigma}.$$

The price p_M of a basket composed of n symmetric manufactured products is defined as an index aggregating the prices of individual varieties. The rationale for the definition of p_M and D_M can be seen by substituting the solution for d_i into total expenditure on manufactures

$$E_M \equiv \int_0^n p_i d_i \, di = \frac{\left(\int_0^n p_i^{1-\sigma} \, di \right)}{\left(\int_0^n p_i^{1-\sigma} \, di \right)^{-\sigma/(1-\sigma)}} D_M$$

$$= \left[\left(\int_0^n p_i^{1-\sigma} \, di \right)^{1/(1-\sigma)} \right] D_M \equiv p_M D_M.$$

In other words, the previous definitions of p_M and D_M permit us to express spending on manufacturing as $E_M = p_M D_M$, that is, total spending on manufactures is the product of an appropriately defined price index and an appropriately defined quality index.

2.10.2. Derivation of (2.18)

Assuming that $n = n^*$, (2.17) becomes

$$p_M^{1-\sigma} = n p^{1-\sigma} + n^* (pT)^{1-\sigma} = n p^{1-\sigma} (1 + T^{1-\sigma}). \tag{2.29}$$

To obtain (2.18), let us totally differentiate (2.29)

$$(1-\sigma)p_M^{-\sigma}\,dp_M$$
$$= p^{1-\sigma}\,dn + n(1-\sigma)p^{-\sigma}\,dp + (pT)^{1-\sigma}\,dn^* + n(1-\sigma)T^{1-\sigma}p^{-\sigma}\,dp$$
$$= (1-T^{1-\sigma})p^{1-\sigma}\,dn + (1+T^{1-\sigma})(1-\sigma)np^{-\sigma}\,dp,$$

where we have used $n = n^*$ and $dn = -dn^*$. Simplifying yields

$$(1-\sigma)p_M^{1-\sigma}\frac{dp_M}{p_M} = (1-T^{1-\sigma})np^{1-\sigma}\frac{dn}{n} + (1+T^{1-\sigma})(1-\sigma)np^{1-\sigma}\frac{dp}{p},$$

$$(1-\sigma)p_M^{1-\sigma}\frac{dp_M}{p_M} = \frac{1-T^{1-\sigma}}{1+T^{1-\sigma}}p_M^{1-\sigma}\frac{dn}{n} + p_M^{1-\sigma}(1-\sigma)\frac{dp}{p},$$

$$\frac{dp_M}{p_M} = \frac{1}{1-\sigma}\frac{1-T^{1-\sigma}}{1+T^{1-\sigma}}\frac{dn}{n} + \frac{dp}{p}.$$

2.10.3. *Derivation of (2.19)*

In order to obtain dq/q in (2.19) let us first totally differentiate expression

$$q = p^{-\sigma}\left[\frac{\mu Y}{p_M^{1-\sigma}} + \frac{T^{1-\sigma}\mu Y^*}{p_M^{*1-\sigma}}\right].$$

The exposition is less cumbersome if the derivation is divided into three parts

$$\frac{dq}{q} = \frac{\Lambda_p + \Lambda_Y + \Lambda_{p_M}}{q}. \tag{2.30}$$

Part 1. Totally differentiate with respect to p

$$\Lambda_p = (-\sigma)p^{-\sigma-1}\left[\frac{\mu dY}{p_M^{1-\sigma}} + \frac{T^{1-\sigma}\mu dY^*}{p_M^{*1-\sigma}}\right]dp$$
$$= (-\sigma)p^{-\sigma}\left[\frac{\mu dY}{p_M^{1-\sigma}} + \frac{T^{1-\sigma}\mu dY^*}{p_M^{*1-\sigma}}\right]\frac{dp}{p},$$

dividing the resulting expression by q and simplifying terms yields

$$\frac{\Lambda_p}{q} = (-\sigma)p^{-\sigma}\left[\frac{\mu dY}{p_M^{1-\sigma}} + \frac{T^{1-\sigma}\mu dY^*}{p_M^{*1-\sigma}}\right]\frac{dp}{p}\Big/\left(p^{-\sigma}\left[\frac{\mu Y}{p_M^{1-\sigma}} + \frac{T^{1-\sigma}\mu Y^*}{p_M^{*1-\sigma}}\right]\right)$$

$$= -\sigma\frac{dp}{p}. \tag{2.31}$$

Part 2. Let us first compute the component dependent on Y. Totally differentiating q with respect to Y

$$\Lambda_Y = p^{-\sigma} \left[\frac{\mu dY}{p_M^{1-\sigma}} + \frac{T^{1-\sigma} \mu dY^*}{p_M^{*1-\sigma}} \right],$$

Dividing the resulting expression by q and simplifying terms yields

$$\frac{\Lambda_Y}{q} = p^{-\sigma} \left[\frac{\mu dY}{p_M^{1-\sigma}} + \frac{T^{1-\sigma} \mu dY^*}{p_M^{*1-\sigma}} \right] \bigg/ \left(p^{-\sigma} \left[\frac{\mu Y}{p_M^{1-\sigma}} + \frac{T^{1-\sigma} \mu Y^*}{p_M^{*1-\sigma}} \right] \right)$$

$$= \left[\frac{dY}{p_M^{1-\sigma}} - \frac{T^{1-\sigma} dY}{p_M^{*1-\sigma}} \right] \bigg/ \left[\frac{Y}{p_M^{1-\sigma}} + \frac{T^{1-\sigma} Y}{p_M^{*1-\sigma}} \right]$$

$$= \left[\frac{1}{p_M^{1-\sigma}} - \frac{T^{1-\sigma}}{p_M^{*1-\sigma}} \right] dY \bigg/ \left[\frac{1}{p_M^{1-\sigma}} + \frac{T^{1-\sigma}}{p_M^{*1-\sigma}} \right] Y$$

$$= \frac{(1 - T^{1-\sigma})/p_M^{1-\sigma}}{(1 + T^{1-\sigma})/p_M^{1-\sigma}} \frac{dY}{Y} = \frac{1 - T^{1-\sigma}}{1 + T^{1-\sigma}} \frac{dY}{Y}, \tag{2.32}$$

where we have used $dY = -dY^*$ and $Y = Y^*$ in the second equality. The fourth equality uses the index price, obtained from (2.17) and $n = n^*$

$$p_M^{1-\sigma} = np^{1-\sigma} + n^*(pT)^{1-\sigma} = n(pT)^{1-\sigma} + n^*(p)^{1-\sigma} = p_M^{*(1-\sigma)}$$

$$\rightarrow p_M^{1-\sigma} = p_M^{*(1-\sigma)} = np^{1-\sigma}(1 + T^{1-\sigma}).$$

Part 3. Let us first compute the component dependent on p_M. Totally differentiating q with respect to p_M

$$q = p^{-\sigma} \left[\frac{\mu Y}{p_M^{1-\sigma}} + \frac{T^{1-\sigma} \mu Y^*}{p_M^{*1-\sigma}} \right].$$

$$\Lambda_{p_M} = -(1-\sigma)p_M^{-\sigma} p^{-\sigma} \frac{\mu Y}{(p_M^{1-\sigma})^2} dp_M - (1-\sigma)p_M^{*(-\sigma)} p^{-\sigma} \frac{T^{1-\sigma} \mu Y^*}{(p_M^{*1-\sigma})^2} dp_M^*$$

$$= -(1-\sigma)p_M^{-\sigma} p^{-\sigma} \frac{\mu Y}{(p_M^{1-\sigma})^2} dp_M - (1-\sigma)p_M^{-\sigma} p^{-\sigma} \frac{T^{1-\sigma} \mu Y^*}{(p_M^{*1-\sigma})^2} dp_M$$

$$= -(1-\sigma)p_M^{-\sigma} p^{-\sigma} \frac{\mu Y}{(p_M^{1-\sigma})^2} dp_M + (1-\sigma)p_M^{-\sigma} p^{-\sigma} \frac{T^{1-\sigma} \mu Y}{(p_M^{*1-\sigma})^2} dp_M$$

$$= -(1 - \sigma) p_M^{-\sigma} p^{-\sigma} \frac{\mu Y - T^{1-\sigma} \mu Y}{(p_M^{1-\sigma})^2} dp_M$$

$$= -(1 - \sigma) p_M^{-\sigma} p^{-\sigma} \frac{(1 - T^{1-\sigma}) \mu Y}{(p_M^{1-\sigma})^2} dp_M,$$

where $p_M = p_M^*$. Dividing the resulting expression by q and simplifying terms yields

$$\frac{\Lambda_{p_M}}{q} = -(1 - \sigma) p_M^{-\sigma} p^{-\sigma} \frac{(1 - T^{1-\sigma}) \mu Y}{(p_M^{1-\sigma})^2} \Big/ \left(p^{-\sigma} \frac{\mu Y + T^{1-\sigma} \mu Y^*}{p_M^{1-\sigma}} \right) dp_M$$

$$= -(1 - \sigma) p_M^{-\sigma} p^{-\sigma} \frac{(1 - T^{1-\sigma}) \mu Y}{(p_M^{1-\sigma})^2} \Big/ \left(p^{-\sigma} \frac{(1 + T^{1-\sigma}) \mu Y^*}{p_M^{1-\sigma}} \right) dp_M$$

$$= -(1 - \sigma) p_M^{-\sigma} \frac{1 - T^{1-\sigma}}{p_M^{1-\sigma}} \Big/ (1 + T^{1-\sigma}) dp_M,$$

where we use $Y = Y^*$ to obtain the second equality. The third equality results from simplifying terms.

Simplifying and rearranging terms yields

$$\frac{\Lambda_{p_M}}{q} = \frac{-(1 - \sigma)(1 - T^{1-\sigma})/p_M}{1 + T^{1-\sigma}} dp_M = \frac{(\sigma - 1)(1 - T^{1-\sigma})}{1 + T^{1-\sigma}} \frac{dp_M}{p_M}. \qquad (2.33)$$

The percentage change $dq/q = (\Lambda_p + \Lambda_Y + \Lambda_{p_M})/q$ is obtained substituting (2.31), (2.32), (2.33) into (2.30)

$$\frac{dq}{q} = \frac{1 - T^{1-\sigma}}{1 + T^{1-\sigma}} \frac{dY}{Y} + \frac{(\sigma - 1)(1 - T^{1-\sigma})}{1 + T^{1-\sigma}} \frac{dp_M}{p_M} + -\sigma \frac{dp}{p}$$

$$= \frac{1 - T^{1-\sigma}}{1 + T^{1-\sigma}} \left[\frac{dY}{Y} + (\sigma - 1) \frac{dp_M}{p_M} \right] - \sigma \frac{dp}{p}.$$

3

Trade Empirics

This chapter introduces the rich body of empirical work on the determinants and effects of trade. Do countries' relative factor endowments determine international trade patterns? What is the role of distance, transport costs and national borders in international trade? Do countries trade more with their neighbors? Is it true that greater trade with Southern countries brings down Northern countries' unskilled labor wages? The answers to these and many related questions are key to the assessment of alternative views about trade and policy formulation.

The Heckscher–Ohlin (HO) model was generalized by Jaroslav Vanek (1968) into a theory of the factor content of trade. It is called the Heckscher–Ohlin–Vanek (HOV) model in this context. The HO–HOV framework offers testable predictions about who exports what, who imports what and the factor content of trade. Incorporating some additional assumptions produces testable predictions about international factor rewards. The framework has naturally become, for many years, the support of a large body of empirical work on the determinants and effects of international trade. The evidence about international trade patterns shows, though, that the HOV model predictions about the factor content of trade are frequently at odds with the data. In the early nineties, the HOV model seemed to be on the way out as an empirical tool.

The millennium renewal of empirical trade analysis has been fueled by several complementary lines of research. First, a major conclusion stemming from extensive empirical testing is that traditional trade models require modifications in order to fit trade data. Several reformulations embodied in 'modified' HOV models display consistency with trade data. These modifications include: (1) relaxing the assumption that all countries have the same technologies and allowing for international productivity differences, (2) introducing a demand function that permits home biases in consumption, (3) incorporating trade costs and distance, and (4) introducing intermediate inputs and distinguishing between tradeable and nontradeable goods. The modified HOV models substantially improve the performance of the standard HOV model in predicting the factor content of trade flows.

Second, in order to explain intra-industry trade among countries with similar factor endowments, which represents a major part of global exchange, a line of empirical studies has focused on trade models incorporating product variety, some form of increasing returns, and imperfect competition. Third, the gravity approach focuses on the role of distance and transport costs in determining the volume of trading partners' bilateral trade. Gravity models provide a benchmark for empirical analyses related to the volume of trade. They are used to examine policy-related issues such as the volume of trade within and among regional trading groups and the effects of currency unions on trade volumes. Fourth, parallel research has focused on issues of practical interest such as the determinants of exports, foreign direct investment (FDI), labor wages, and many others. Feenstra (2003) and Helpman (1998a,b) thoroughly examine empirical modeling.

Section 3.1 reviews factor content theory. Section 3.2 focuses on productivity differentials and home biases. Sections 3.3 and 3.4 examine the evidence on multicone models, factor price equalization and factor price insensitivity. Section 3.5 focuses on the empirical relation between trade and wages. Sections 3.6 and 3.7 introduce the gravity approach and examine market integration and trade barriers. Section 3.8 looks at empirical tests of alternative trade models. Sections 3.9 and 3.10 focus on exportation, product cycles, patents and productivity. Section 3.11 assesses the quantitative importance of terms of trade effects.

3.1. FACTOR CONTENT AND THE LEONTIEF PARADOX

The standard 2 good-2 factor-2 country ($2 \times 2 \times 2$) model of trade under constant returns to scale predicts that a country:

(1) Exports the good that uses more intensively the factor that is relatively abundant in the country;
(2) Imports the commodity that uses more intensively the factor that is relatively scarce in the country.

For empirical testing purposes, this prediction must be generalized to the case of many factors, products and countries. What emerges is a theory of the factor content of traded goods.

3.1.1. *Equilibrium in Factor and Good Markets*

The full-employment condition means that all factor endowments are fully used in the production of goods. If FE^c denotes country c's vector of factor endowments and Q^c denotes its production vector, the full employment condition can be expressed as

$$
\begin{pmatrix} FE_1^c \\ \vdots \\ FE_I^c \end{pmatrix} = \begin{pmatrix} a_{11}^c & \cdots & a_{1J}^c \\ \vdots & \ddots & \vdots \\ a_{I1}^c & \cdots & a_{IJ}^c \end{pmatrix} \begin{pmatrix} Q_1^c \\ \vdots \\ Q_J^c \end{pmatrix} = \begin{pmatrix} \sum_{j=1}^{J} a_{1j}^c Q_j^c \\ \vdots \\ \sum_{j=1}^{J} a_{Ij}^c Q_j^c \end{pmatrix}.
$$

The typical element a_{ij}^c of the input–output matrix is the coefficient indicating the number of units of factor i used in the production of a unit of good j. In other words, a_{ij}^c is an input–output coefficient indicating the technique of production as a unit input requirement.

The typical element of the endowment vector FE^c is

$$FE_i^c = [a_i^c]'Q^c = \sum_{j=1}^{J} a_{ij}^c Q_j^c, \tag{3.1}$$

where $i \in \{1, 2, \ldots, I\}$, the prime symbol denotes the transposition of a column vector into a row vector, and $[a_i^c]'$ is the ith row of the input–output matrix. The endowment of factor i is equal to the sum of the amounts used in the production of goods $1, 2, \ldots$, and J.

In short-hand matrix notation

$$FE^c = A^c Q^c \iff Q^c = [A^c]^{-1} FE^c, \tag{3.2}$$

where FE^c and Q^c are the $I \times 1$ and $J \times 1$ column vectors of factor endowments and outputs while A^c is the $I \times J$ matrix of input–output coefficients. The second equation expresses the output vector in terms of factor endowments and combinations of input–output coefficients. The $J \times I$ matrix $[A^c]^{-1}$ is the inverse of the input–output matrix, which is assumed to be invertible.

If a production function is homothetic, the factor reward vector $w = [w_1, \ldots, w_I]$ uniquely determines both the input–output coefficient matrix $A^c = A^c(w)$ and factor intensities. In the HO model with capital and labor inputs, unit input requirements can be expressed as functions of either the wage-rental ratio or the capital–labor ratio.

Demand with Identical Homothetic Preferences
Assume that preferences are homothetic and identical across countries. The appendix of Chapter 1 shows that the demand vector D^c representing country c's demand for each good can be expressed as country c's share in world income, s^c, times world output for each good. Formally

$$D^c = s^c Q^W = s^c \sum_{k=1}^{C} Q^k = s^c \sum_{k=1}^{C} [A^k]^{-1} FE^k, \tag{3.3}$$

where D^c, Q^W, and Q^k are the $J \times 1$ vectors. The world output vector Q^W is obtained as the summation of output vectors over the C countries in the world. The last step merely substitutes for Q^k using the inverted form of the full-employment condition (3.2). The share of country c's income Y^c in world income Y^W is

$$s^c = \frac{Y^c}{Y^W} = \frac{[w^c]'FE^c}{\sum_{k=1}^{C}[w^k]'FE^k}, \quad k \in \{1, \ldots, C\},$$

where $[w^k]' = [w_1^k, \ldots, w_I^k]$ is the $1 \times I$ row vector representing country k's factor rewards.

3.1.2. The Factor Content Equation

The exports and imports of traded goods correspond to the gap between production and consumption. Let $T^c = Q^c - D^c$ represent the $\mathcal{J} \times 1$ vector of country c's *net exports* of goods $j \in \{1, \ldots, \mathcal{J}\}$. The value of net exports $T^c_j = Q^c_j - D^c_j$ is positive if good j is exported and negative if good j is imported. Accordingly, in developing the factor content equation for trade we are going to assign a positive value to the amount of each factor used in an export and a negative value to the amount of each factor used in an import. These factor amounts are added up over all exports and imports to obtain the content of each factor in a country's trade. Notice that the content of a factor that is used only in exportables will be positive while the content of a factor that is used only in importables will be negative by definition.

Formally, the content of each factor $i \in \{1, \ldots, I\}$ in the vector of goods $j \in \{1, \ldots, \mathcal{J}\}$ is given by the corresponding element of the $I \times 1$ vector FC^c

$$FC^c \equiv A^c T^c = A^c(Q^c - D^c) = FE^c - A^c D^c,$$

$$= FE^c - A^c s^c \sum_{k=1}^{C} [A^k]^{-1} FE^k. \tag{3.4}$$

In deriving this result, recall the full-employment condition $FE^c = A^c Q^c$ and the homothetic preferences condition (3.3).

How is the factor content of imports measured? The HO model assumes that the input–output matrix is the same in country c and all its trading partners, $A^c = A^k$ for all trading partners $c \neq k$. If this assumption is valid, empirical tests can safely use the input–output coefficients of the import competing industries at home as a proxy for the input–output coefficients of imported goods production.

Jaroslav Vanek's factor content matrix equation is obtained observing that the equality $A^c = A^k, k \neq c$, implies that $A^c[A^k]^{-1} = I$ for all k. Therefore,

$$FC^c \equiv A^c T^c = FE^c - s^c \sum_{k=1}^{C} FE^k = FE^c - s^c FE^W. \tag{3.5}$$

Factor Content Equation: Interpretation

The typical element of the factor content matrix equation is

$$FC^c_i \equiv [a^c_i]' T^c \equiv \sum_{j=1}^{\mathcal{J}} a^c_{ij} T^c_j = FE^c_i - s^c FE^W_i,$$

where $[a^c_i]'$ and T^c are the $1 \times \mathcal{J}$ and $\mathcal{J} \times 1$ vectors so that FC^c_i is a number indicating the net content of factor i in all the goods traded by country c. The computation of the content of each factor i in trade simply adds up, over all traded goods, the factor content implicit in the trade of each product j.

The factor content equation views a country as implicitly exporting or importing factor services through the factor content of the goods traded. The key idea is that international trade represents implicit trade in the factor services used to produce the exports sold abroad and the products imported from abroad. The factor content equation generalizes the HO theorem, which in this incarnation is called the HOV theorem, as a theorem of the implicit factor content of trade for the case of many goods and factors. First, the measured content of factor i in trade, $FC_i^c \equiv [a_i^c]'T^c$, is positive if the factor tends to be used more intensively in exports and negative if it tends to be used more intensively in imports. Second, the predicted factor content of trade, $FE_i^c - s^c FE_i^W$, is equal to factor i's endowment, FE_i^c, minus the product of country c's share s^c in world income (and consumption) times the world factor endowment FE_i^W.

In a nutshell, if a factor is abundant relative to the endowment that would correspond to a country's share in world income, that factor is predicted to have a positive factor content in a country's net exports. This means that the abundant factors tend to be used more intensively in exports than in imports. In the aggregate, a capital-abundant country implicitly exports capital by exporting capital-intensive goods. By the same token, a labor-scarce country implicitly imports labor by importing labor-intensive goods.

Factor Content Equation: Testing

The factor content equation with identical technologies and identical homothetic preferences can be implemented empirically as a test of the HOV model. Formally, the measured factor content of trade is computed from the left-hand side of (3.5), $FC^c \equiv A^c T^c$, which is called the measured factor content of trade. The data used to compute FC^c consists only of trade data and traded goods' input–output coefficients. In particular, no information about factor endowments is used in the computation of FC^c.

Given the information about factor contents, the theory's predictions are embodied on the right-hand side of (3.5), $FE_i^c - s^c FE_i^W$, which is called the predicted factor content of trade. This equation predicts that the content of factor i in the vector of country c's net exports is positive if and only if country c's endowment of factor i, FE_i^c, exceeds the proportion s^c of factor i's world factor endowment FE_i^W. The model is empirically implementable because information about the factor endowments of country c and the world as a whole, is available at various levels of disaggregation of productive factors.

Summarizing, the factor content model predicts that factor i has a positive content in country c's net exports if and only if country c's factor endowment of i is larger than the component of the world factor endowment of i that corresponds to the share of country c in world income (i.e. $FE_i^c > s^c FE_i^W = (Y^c/Y^W)FE_i^W$). In other words, when country c's factor endowment of i is 'large enough' relative to the world endowment of i, so that we can interpret that the country is relatively abundant in that factor, the factor content of i in net exports should be positive

$$FC_i^c > 0 \quad \Leftrightarrow \quad FE_i^c - s^c FE_i^W > 0.$$

Two popular tests of the HOV model, which are not passed by the model, are the sign and the correlation tests. The prediction that the signs of each side of the factor content equation will match provides a popular test of the HOV hypothesis expressed in terms of the exports of services that are implicit in trade. A country should export (implicitly through a positive factor content in trade, $FC_i^c > 0$) the factor services offered by its abundant factors, where any given factor is considered abundant if $FE_i^c - s^c FE_i^W > 0$. By the same token, a country imports the factor services of relatively scarce factors. In other words, both sides of the factor content equation should have the same sign empirically. The sign test is quite popular in the literature but notice that it does not incorporate a null hypothesis, explicit statistical hypothesis testing or factor content magnitudes. The sign test is a weak test based on the notion that, if a factor is relatively abundant in a country, the least that we could expect is that the country is not a net importer of that factor implicitly through trade.

The raw correlation test considers the measured and predicted factor content as an observation and computes the correlation between the measured and the predicted factor content of trade. The rank correlation test orders the measured and predicted contents according to their values and then computes the correlation between these ranks. If the HOV model holds, the raw and rank correlations should be near one. The correlation tests indicate the consistency of the model with the data but do not test a null hypothesis.

Leontief (1953) launched a long-lasting controversy when he produced evidence documenting what has come to be known as the Leontief paradox. He found that the United States exported labor-intensive goods and imported capital-intensive goods, which is the opposite of the factor endowment model's predictions. A long line of studies continued to cast doubt over the empirical validity of the factor endowments model. An important study by Bowen *et al.* (1987) found that exports of net factor services are predicted as well by a random process similar to flipping a coin as by the factor endowments model.

3.2. PRODUCTIVITY DIFFERENTIALS AND HOME BIAS

Leontief's (1953) suggested explanation for the failure of the HOV model in the tests he conducted was that countries' productivities differ. This explanation suggests a modification of the standard model, which indeed assumes all countries have the same technologies. In a widely cited empirical study, Trefler (1993*a*) took Leontief's sugges-tion seriously and empirically tested a 'modified' model that allows for cross-country productivity differences. Technologies are assumed to differ by a country-specific term that can be thought of as measuring Hicks-neutral technological differences. Trefler tested for whether or not the data rejected the 'modified' model. He found that Leontief was right in the sense that modifying the framework to encompass factor-augmenting international productivity differences could substantially improve the model's factor content of trade prediction.

3.2.1. *Factor Content with Productivity Differentials*

Country c's effective labor endowment FE_L^{c*}, measured in productivity-equivalent units, is equal to the usual labor endowment measure FE_L^c (say, the number of person-years) times a factor π_L^c reflecting the productivity of each unit of labor. Formally,

$$FE_L^{c*} = \pi_L^c FE_L^c,$$

where we follow Trefler in using an asterisk to represent the productivity-adjusted labor endowment (and not foreign variables as usual). The multiplication by the productivity factor π_L^c accounts for the fact that each unit of labor in vector FE_L^c provides π_L^c units of productivity-equivalent units of service. With this notation, Leontief's claim is equivalent to arguing that π_L^c is larger for the United States than for its trading partners.

In the case of I productive factors, the $I \times 1$ vector of productive-equivalent factor endowments (effective factor endowments) can be expressed as

$$FE^{c*} = \pi^c FE^c,$$

where π^c is an $I \times I$ diagonal matrix consisting of diagonal elements $\pi_1^c, \ldots, \pi_I^c$ and zeros elsewhere.

The utilization of productivity-equivalent factor units affects the measurement of inputs and input–output coefficients. The matrix of input–output coefficients in terms of productivity equivalent units is called A^{c*}, $a_{ij}^{c*} = \pi_i^c a_{ij}^c$.

The derivation of a factor content equation when inputs are measured in productivity equivalent units follows the same procedure as the derivation of the standard factor content equation. Let FC^{c*} be the $I \times 1$ vector indicating the effective content of each factor $i \in \{1, \ldots, I\}$ in the trade vector for goods $j \in \{1, \ldots, \mathcal{J}\}$. We have,

$$FC^{c*} \equiv A^{c*} T^c = A^{c*}(Q^c - D^c) = FE^{c*} - A^{c*} D^c$$

$$= FE^{c*} - s^c \sum_{k=1}^{C} FE^{k*} = \pi^c FE^c - s^c \sum_{k=1}^{C} \pi^k FE^k,$$

where $D^c = s^c Q^W = s^c \sum_k [A^{k*}]^{-1} FE^{k*}$ and A^{c*} is assumed to be equal to A^{k*} for all $k \neq c$. The typical element of FC^{c*} is a number indicating the productivity-equivalent content of a given productive factor i in the goods traded by country c

$$FC_i^{c*} \equiv \sum_{j=1}^{\mathcal{J}} a_{ij}^{c*} T_j^c = FE_i^{c*} - s^c \sum_{k=1}^{C} FE_i^{k*}$$

$$= \pi_i^c FE_i^c - s^c \sum_{k=1}^{C} \pi_i^k FE_i^k,$$

where FC_i^{c*}, FE_i^{c*}, and FE_i^{k*} are the numbers representing magnitudes of effective factor contents and endowments, FE_i^k denotes actual endowments and π_i^k is the productivity–equivalent adjustment parameter.

3.2.2. Testing the Effective Factor Content Equation

From a statistical estimation perspective, the productivity-equivalent factor content equation differs from the standard factor content equation used by Bowen *et al.* (1987). By introducing the unobserved productivity factors π_i^c, the factor content equation can be made to fit exactly. In other words, if there are no independent measures of the π_i^c factors, they can be defined in such a way as to make equal the right-hand and left-hand sides of the equation. There is a perfect fit because there are I factor content equations to fit, one for each factor, and I free productivity parameters ($\pi_i^c, i = 1, \ldots, I$) to generate the fit.

How can we get a test out of the factor content equation with unobserved factor productivities? One test consists of examining the estimated π_i^c factors to see if they have unrealistic values. For instance, the estimated π_i^c factors would have unrealistic values if they exhibited the following features:

1. Estimates have a negative sign.
2. Estimated values are too large or too small to be consistent with a priori notions about cross–country productivity differentials.
3. Estimated values contradict independent estimates of productivity differentials.

In other words, if we must use utterly unrealistic values for the productivity factors π_i^c to make the factor content equation fit, this can be interpreted to mean that factor abundances fail to predict the factor content of trade.

Trefler (1993*a*) examined 1983 data for thirty-three countries accounting for about 75 and 80 percent of world exports and GNP, respectively. Productivity estimates pass the tests but only in a weak sense. Namely:

1. There are only ten negative values of π_i^c out of a total of 384 estimates.
2. There are indeed outliers in the quantitative estimates, but the estimates are in the right direction. For instance, countries with unrealistically high estimated productivity factors are high productivity countries like Japan (but with an unrealistic $\pi_i^c = 15.56$!), the Netherlands, Denmark, Switzerland, and Belgium. Unrealistically low productivity estimates occur in countries with low agricultural productivity.
3. The productivity estimates are generally reasonable and consistent with other available data. For instance, all countries have lower estimated productivities than the United States, especially in agriculture. Also, a higher per capita GNP is positively correlated with the productivity differential estimated from the content equation.

A second test conducted by Trefler (1993*a*) consists of using the cross–country estimated productivity factors to account for cross–country wage differentials. The United States is assigned a value of $\pi_i^{US} = 1$. The estimated value of $\pi_i^{Britain}$ is 0.66

for Britain. This means that British productivity is estimated to be 66 percent of US productivity. A testable implication is that British wages should be near 66 percent of US wages, as they actually are in the sample studied. This test is discussed in detail below in relation to the controversy about cross-country factor price equalization.

3.2.3. Home Biases in Consumption and Missing Trade

A major stylized fact of international trade is that consumers display a bias for home products. In other words, countries' utility functions seem to value domestic products more than foreign products.

In Trefler (1995), the HOV model is modified to incorporate

1. International technology differences across countries, which were previously incorporated in Trefler (1993*a*). Taking productivity differentials into account helps to tackle the so-called 'endowments paradox'. This paradox arises because poor countries are found to be abundant in all factors and rich countries are found to be scarce in almost all factors. In other words, poor countries have greater factor endowments than those corresponding to their share in the world economy. Adjusting for productivities serves to increase the factor supplies of rich countries relative to those of poor countries and generates measured scarcities in poor countries and abundances in rich countries. Cross-country gaps in productivities imply that factor price equalization fails to hold even if product prices are equalized through trade. If productivity differentials are Hicks–neutral, though, countries use the same techniques of production (i.e. the same input–output coefficients).
2. Home biases in consumption. Home biases can arise from nationalistic Armington preferences in which products are differentiated by production location, as in Armington's (1969), and consumers are assumed to prefer domestic products to foreign products. Indeed, most countries appear to trade less than implied by trade theories. In particular, the predicted factor content of trade tends to be empirically greater than the measured content of trade. The prediction of greater trade than is actually observed was labeled the 'mystery of the missing trade' by Trefler.

Allowing for home biases in consumption helps tackling the missing trade puzzle as incorporating a home bias assumption improves the empirical results. The data utilized is the same as in Trefler's (1993*a*) paper, but in the 1995 paper the author tests different hypotheses to identify how alternative premises lead to systematic sources of deviations from the HOV model. The assumptions tested include cross-country endowment's differences, technology differences (neutral and nonneutral), consumption differences, and a combination of technology and consumption differences.

3.2.4. A Modified-HOV Account of Global Trade

Trefler tests lead to a rejection of the standard HOV model (which assumes equal cross-country technologies) but advance a simple modification allowing for international productivity differences. Subsequent research has provided even greater support for a modified HOV model and has helped to re-establish the framework, which in the late eighties was viewed by many as plainly rejected by empirical evidence. Another contribution of this literature is that it provides measures of the productivity variable and thus of international productivity differentials. Productivity variables are key elements for understanding development gaps and differing growth experiences.

In general, unit input requirements vary according with each country's capital–labor endowment and technology. If the country that is relatively more capital abundant has a lower price of capital services, different techniques of production can be sustained in a two country equilibrium. Substitution toward more capital intensive techniques implies that the capital abundant country uses relatively more capital-intensive techniques in all industries. Even if the price of capital services is the same across countries, technology differences can lead to different techniques of productions.

If the assumption that $A^c = A^k$ for all k is relaxed one must take into account that the unit input requirements of imports are not the same as for domestic production. The analogous to factor content expression (3.4) is

$$FC^c = A^c Q^c - A^c D^{cc} - \sum_{k=1, k \neq c}^{C} A^k M^{ck},$$

$$D^c = D^{cc} + \sum_{k=1, k \neq c}^{C} M^{ck},$$

(3.6)

where net exports are calculated as $T^c = Q^c - D^c = Q^c - D^{cc} - \sum M^{ck}, k \neq c$. The vector D^{cc} is the component of demand that is met by local production and M^{ck} is the vector of imports from countries $k \in \{1, \ldots, C\}$. The matrix A^k specifying the unit input requirements of imports from country k is specific to the country. The content of each factor $i \in \{1, \ldots, I\}$ in the vector of goods $j \in \{1, \ldots, J\}$ is given by the corresponding element of the $I \times 1$ vector FC^c. Estimating the previous relation requires knowing the input–output matrix of each trading partner but these data were not available in the past.

Davis and Weinstein (2001) offer a general account of global factor trade. They utilize country-specific unit input requirements for imports (i.e. take into account different techniques of production), allow for international productivity differentials and the failure of factor price equalization, introduce gravity (i.e. distance, cost of trading) into their empirical testing, and take into account the presence of nontraded goods.

The data set used provides information about the elements of the A^k matrix for several countries, which permits estimating the structural parameters of the modified HOV model.

The empirical testing of factor content predictions is based on an HOV theory modified to:

1. Measure the factor content of absorption using the producer country's input–output coefficient rather than a US matrix based on import-competing industry coefficients. The component of total demand filled by domestic demand, D^{cc}, is

produced using the domestic input–output matrix A^c. The imports in the set of vectors M^{ck} are produced using the source country k input–output matrix A^k. The data set permits measuring country-specific input–output matrices for imports.

2. Measure the factor content of production in productivity-adjusted terms, $A^{c*}Q^c = FE^{c*}$.

3. Incorporate nontraded goods and the costs of trade.

Once the model modifications are factored in, the HOV model is found to hold fairly well for ten OECD countries and an aggregate of the rest of the world. Countries are found to export their abundant factors in approximately the right magnitudes according to the modified HOV model.

3.2.5. Production, Spending, and Trade

Contrary to the usual emphasis in trade literature, which is concerned with predicting the factor content of trade, Davis *et al.* (1997) center their attention on predictions about the factor content of production and the pattern of absorption. In other words, the authors test standard HOV model predictions about production, the pattern of absorption and trade. The aim is to explore the consistency between data and theory at various levels and to identify which specific elements might be causing failures in the performance of the HOV model.

The data set includes a cross-section of twenty-one countries and ten Japanese regions. The utilization of regional data on production and consumption provides a benchmark in which there are no important trade barriers across areas and there is almost perfect factor mobility. The production tests focus on whether the factor content equation $A^J Q^c = FE^c$ holds for twenty-one countries c and a gross output vector Q^c containing thirty sectors. Notice that the tests assume that all countries share the Japanese direct input requirements matrix, labeled A^J. This assumption is valid if all countries examined share the same constant returns to scale technology and factor price equalization holds, technological gaps are Hicks-neutral or input requirements are fixed.

The cross-section tests are based on either (1) measures of a set three productive factors, unskilled labor, skilled labor, and capital or (2) a set of ten productive factors. The tests are not passed. For instance, the correlation between the predicted (obtained from $A^J Q^c$) and actual (obtained from FE^c) use of people that have not gone to college is less than 30 percent. If the United States (an extreme value) is dropped from the sample, the correlations between predicted and actual use of college graduates and capital are 27 and 63 percent.

Do the HO factor use predictions hold for Japanese regions' production? A set of empirical tests focus on whether the factor content equation $A^J Q^r = FE^r$ holds for ten Japanese regions indexed by r. The tests assume that all regions share the Japanese direct input requirements matrix A^J but can differ in terms of factor endowments. If Japanese regions have the same constant returns to scale technologies and factor price equalization holds within Japan, the factor content equation holds at the regional level.

The reason is that, within the factor price equalization set, the HOV theory holds at any level, country or regional. The tests conducted at the regional level were passed using both three productive factors and a more detailed decomposition using ten factors. The authors conclude that the HOV theory of regional location of production is validated for regions sharing the same technologies, displaying factor price equalization and using similar techniques of production A^r.

What is the performance of the HOV model when absorption is taken into account? The homothetic preferences assumption implies the absorption equations $D^c = s^c Q^J$ and $D^c = s^c Q^W$. Indeed, Japanese regional absorption (consumption plus investment) is found to be proportional both to aggregate Japanese absorption and to world absorption. These findings suggest that failures of the HOV model predictions might not arise from nonhomotheticity of preferences.

Paradoxically, even though the production and absorption elements of the HOV model are consistent with the data, $A^J Q^r = FE^r, D^r = s^r Q^J$ and $D^r = s^r Q^W$ perform well, the HOV model as embodied in the factor content of trade equation

$$A^J T^r = FE^r - s^r A^J Q^W = FE^r - s^r FE^W$$

is not validated by the data. The questions raised concern why the empirical failure takes place and whether additional extensions can improve performance.

Factor Content with Intermediate Inputs

Let us incorporate intermediate inputs into the analysis and specify factor content equations for production, absorption and trade that take intermediate inputs into account. The first step is to distinguish between direct factors of production, such as labor and capital, and inputs such as automobile motors, which are manufactured using other inputs and productive factors. The matrix B^c includes the productive factor requirements per unit of output (B^c is analogous to the previous A^c). The production equation with intermediate inputs is thus

$$B^c Q^c = FE^c. \tag{3.7}$$

In order to derive an absorption equation for the intermediate inputs case, one must distinguish between the gross output vector Q^c and the net output vector Q^{netc},

$$Q^{netc} = (I - A^c) Q^c \iff Q^c = (I - A^c)^{-1} Q^{netc}, \tag{3.8}$$

where the matrix A^c is made up of the input–output coefficients for final good production, including intermediate inputs. $I - A^c$ simply takes out the intermediate inputs used in the production of final goods.

The absorption equation for factors in the presence of intermediates is derived in two steps. The first step states the absorption equation for products in the presence of intermediate inputs. Assuming homothetic preferences and equal good prices across locations, so that demand D^c is a constant share s^c of world net output Q^{netW}, yields

$$D^c = s^c Q^{netW}.$$

The second step transforms the previous equation for absorption of goods (expressed in terms of goods) into an equation for absorption of factors (expressed in terms of factor content). Both sides of the absorption equation for products are pre-multiplied by $(I - A^c)^{-1}$ to transform it into gross output and the resulting expression is pre-multiplied by B^c to obtain the direct factor content vector. Formally,

$$B^c (I - A^c)^{-1} D^c = B^c (I - A^c)^{-1} s^c Q^{netW} = s^c B^c Q^W. \tag{3.9}$$

The trade equation with intermediate inputs for country c is

$$T^c = (I - A^c) Q^c - D^c = Q^{netc} - D^c, \tag{3.10}$$

where I is the identity matrix, A^c is an intermediate input–output matrix, and $A^c Q^c$ is a vector of quantities of intermediate inputs acquired by industries from other industries to produce the gross output vector Q^c. The trade vector T^c is thus defined by net output $(I - A^c) Q^c$ minus consumption D^c. In order to obtain the factor content of the trade equation in the presence of intermediate goods, let us pre-multiply the trade equation by B^c

$$FC^c \equiv B^c (I - A^c)^{-1} T^c = B^c (I - A^c)^{-1} [(I - A^c) Q^c - D^c]$$

$$= B^c Q^c - B^c (I - A^c)^{-1} D^c = B^c Q^c - B^c s^c (I - A^c)^{-1} Q^{netW}.$$

where $D^c = s^c Q^{netW}$ and Q^{netW} is net world output. Using $B^c Q^c = FE^c, Q^W = (I - A^c)^{-1} Q^{netW}$ and $B^c Q^W = FE^W$ yields the factor content equation with intermediate inputs

$$FC^c \equiv B^c (I - A^c)^{-1} T^c = FE^c - s^c FE^W.$$

Davis *et al.* (1997) estimate the following regional factor content equation with intermediate goods for ten Japanese regions

$$FC^r \equiv B^J (I - A^r)^{-1} [Q^{netr} - D^r] = FE^r - s^r FE^W, \tag{3.11}$$

where $T^r = Q^{netr} - D^r$. Regions are allowed to differ in the input–output coefficients A^r but not in the direct factor unit requirements B^J. A region's trade is defined as trade with the rest of the world (not just trade with other Japanese regions).

The version of the HOV model embodied in the regional net factor content of trade equation (3.11) fails to agree with cross-country data and with Japanese regional data. The nature of the failure is the phenomenon of the 'missing trade' mystery. The actual factor content of trade as measured on the left-hand side of the equation is less, often markedly, than the predicted net factor content of trade from the right-hand side of the equation. The HOV model is found to perform well as a theory of regional production location and regional absorption but not as a theory of the net factor content of trade for Japanese regions.

Why is it that the factor content theory fails as a model for regional data in Japan while the production and consumption components of the theory are accepted at the regional level? In order to find out the culprit, the error vector of the estimated factor content equation (3.11), ε_T, can be decomposed into a component ε_Q arising from the production model and a component ε_D arising from the absorption equation

$$\varepsilon_T = \varepsilon_Q + \varepsilon_D = B^J (I - A^r)^{-1} Q^{netr} - FE^r$$
$$+ B^J (I - A^r)^{-1} D^r - s^r FE^W.$$

The key finding is that the absorption component of the factor content of trade equation is the one that accounts for the errors of the trade model. Because the absorption equation for products works well, the element making the trade models fail empirically is the assumption $B^r = B^W$ in $B^r Q^r = FE^r$. This assumption is used in the second step taken to transform the absorption equation for products into an absorption for factors (see derivation). The derivation of the factor content of absorption assumed universal price equalization and universal production techniques, which do not hold empirically as production techniques differ across countries. The estimation of a factor content equation taking into account the differences in techniques of production ($B^r \neq B^W$) should reduce measured missing trade (but the data was not available at the time).

What can we conclude from these findings? First, the assumption of unit factor requirements, $B^c = B^k$ for all k, is found to be at odds with cross-country data, $B^r \neq B^W$, but not with regional data, $B^r = B^J$. This result suggests that Japanese regions utilize the same techniques of production but countries differ in production techniques. The cross-country divergences in techniques of production might reflect nonneutral differences in productivities, observed factor reward differentials or both.

Second, the assumption of homothetic preferences is supported by the data examined. Several tests performed cannot reject the hypothesis that Japanese regions' preferences are homothetic. Japanese regions' absorption is found to be proportional to national absorption and national Japanese absorption is in turn found to be proportional to world absorption.

3.2.6. Trade and Consumption Nonhomotheticity

The predictions of the HOV factor abundance model are based on the assumption that consumption exhibits homotheticity. In other words, countries facing identical goods prices exhibit the same allocation of spending across goods. The literature on the empirical performance of trade models overwhelmingly relies on this assumption.

Empirical evidence is not always consistent with the consumption homotheticity assumption. For instance, low income countries devote a greater share of their income to food than higher income countries. Hunter and Markusen (1998) and Hunter (1991) examine trade in the presence of consumption nonhomotheticity and present evidence showing that homotheticity does not hold in practice. Because trade can be motivated by cross-country differences in demand patterns as well as factor abundances, the question that arises is what is the proportion of trade that is accounted for by the demand side of trade. Hunter (1991) estimates that consumption nonhomotheticity accounts for about 25 percent of total trade.

3.3. TESTING WEAK FACTOR CONTENT RESTRICTIONS

Helpman (1984*a*) develops a test of the factor content of trade that relies on very weak restrictions in the sense that the test neither imposes factor price equalization nor demand function homotheticity. The idea is that if factors are immobile, countries differ in factor endowments, and there are multiple goods, countries will not produce the same tradables. Therefore, the link between tradable good prices and factor prices is broken, even if countries have access to the same technology. Compared with a relatively capital-poor trading partner, a relatively more capital-rich country produces goods that are more capital-intensive and sustains a greater wage–rental ratio, which in turn induces the choice of more capital intensive techniques. Therefore, the exports of the relatively capital-rich country will necessarily embody a higher capital–labor ratio than the exports of a relatively labor-rich country.

The previous argument arrives at a key HOV framework prediction about the factor content of trade without assuming homothetic demand functions and factor price equalization (even if countries have access to the same technology). The weak factor content result hinges on lack of factor price equalization and the choice of different techniques of production (i.e. capital–labor ratios) in a multicone model in which countries share identical technologies but choose different sets of diversified production because they have different diversification cones.

Figure 3.1. depicts the case of two factors, capital and labor, and six goods represented by isoquants numbered 1–6. The Lerner diagram is the same for the three

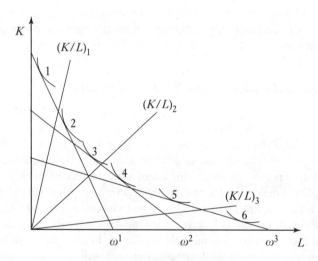

Figure 3.1. *Factor content*

trading partners considered because technologies are assumed to be identical and to exhibit constant returns to scale. Country 1 displays the highest capital–labor ratio and specializes in goods 1 and 2, the more capital intensive goods. By the same token, country 2 specializes in goods 3 and 4, produced with intermediate capital–labor ratios. Country 3 specializes in goods 5 and 6, produced with the lowest capital–labor ratios. Given this production diversification specialization pattern (and multiple cones of diversification) country 1 must export a more capital intensive good and must import a less capital intensive good than either partner.

The notion of multiple cones of diversification has been validated empirically by Dollar *et al.* (1989), who find that there is a high correlation between country capital–labor endowments and (1) industry capital–labor ratios, (2) output per worker. Further evidence of multiple cones of diversification based on different methodologies is offered by Leamer (1987, 1995), Schott (1999) and Davis and Weinstein (2001).

Consider the trade equation with intermediate inputs for country c

$$T^c = (I - A^c)Q^c - D^c,$$

where I is the identity matrix, A^c is the input–output matrix, and $A^c Q^c$ represents the quantity of intermediate inputs each industry acquires from other industries to produce final goods Q^c. The corresponding factor content equation for country c in the presence of intermediate goods is

$$FC^c = B^c(I - A^c)^{-1}T^c = B^c(I - A^c)^{-1}[(I - A^c)Q^c - D^c]$$
$$= B^c Q^c - B^c(I - A^c)^{-1}D^c$$

obtained by pre-multiplying the trade equation by the technology matrix $B^c(I - A^c)^{-1}$ accounting for inputs and direct productive factors.

The overall factor content of trade equation can be translated into a bilateral factor content equation relating country k's gross import vector of factor content FC^{kc} from country c to the vector of country k gross imports T^{kc} from country c. Formally,

$$FC^{kc} = B^c(I - A^c)^{-1}T^{kc} = B^c Q^c - B^c(I - A^c)^{-1}D^{kc}. \qquad (3.12)$$

Combining (3.12) with the revenue function $R(p, FE) = p'Q^c$, where p is the vector of commodity prices and $R(p, FE)$ is concave in FE, produces two testable restrictions on the factor content of trade. For country k and country c imports respectively (see appendix)

$$(w^k - w^c)FC^{kc} \geq 0, \quad (w^k - w^c)FC^{ck} \leq 0. \qquad (3.13)$$

The previous factor content inequalities can be combined into a single restriction

$$(w^k - w^c)(FC^{kc} - FC^{ck}) \geq 0, \qquad (3.14)$$

where factor contents are estimated using (3.12).

Inequality (3.14) means that, on average, country k is a net importer from country c of the content of the factors of production that are cheaper in c relative to k. The idea is that a relatively more capital rich country chooses a greater capital to labor ratio in all industries and sustains a greater wage–rental ratio. Therefore, the exports of the relatively capital-rich country embody a higher capital–labor ratio than the exports of a relatively labor-rich country. This result hinges on different techniques of production and holds even if technologies are not the same and factor price equalization fails. The whole system can be generalized to comprise Hicks-neutral differences in factor productivities by expressing factor amounts and rewards in productivity terms relative to a benchmark country.

Are weak factor content restrictions validated by the data? Choi and Krishna (2001) test the factor content equations, (3.13) and (3.12), for bilateral trade patterns between Canada, Denmark, France, Germany, Korea, the Netherlands, United Kingdom, and the United States. The analysis is extended to allow for cross-country Hicks-neutral factor efficiency differences, and to control for domestically produced intermediate goods (and exclude those produced abroad). Estimates, however, do not validate the factor content theory. Only 55 percent of the bilateral trade flows are consistent with (3.13) and (3.12) implied by the theory. If Hicks-neutral adjustments are allowed, results slightly improve as the consistency of trade flows with the theory increases from 55 to 59 percent.

3.4. INTERNATIONAL FACTOR PRICES

The hypothesis that factor prices equalize internationally is inconsistent with the observed wide and persistent divergences in factor rewards across countries. Factor price equalization does not hold. This fact is now widely accepted. Wages among OECD countries differ by a factor of five. Between developed and developing or emerging countries wages differ by a factor of between five and thirty or more. Economists attribute these large wage disparities to different factor endowments, education and quality of labor and productivity gaps.

The failure of factor price equalization raises the issue of how to account for it. Recent empirical work has presented opposing views on the subject. Trefler (1993*a*, 1995) found that a modified model that controlled for international productivity differentials could explain most cross-country variations in factor prices.

3.4.1. The Failure of Factor Price Equalization

Historically, the factor price equalization theorem is closely identified with the HOV framework. The theorem was first derived by Paul Samuelson from the HOV model supplemented by extra assumptions. Furthermore, most attempts to account for international factor price divergences are based on joint tests of a modified version of the HOV model and cross-country factor price equalization. Accordingly, the rejection of factor price equalization has been branded as a rejection of the HOV framework by many critics. Strictly speaking, this is not a correct inference because the model does not predict that factor price equalization will hold except under special circumstances.

Let us review the conditions underlying the HOV model and factor price equalization. The HOV model assumes two goods, two factors and two countries, constant returns to scale production functions, homothetic preferences that are identical across countries and the absence of factor mobility. The factor price equalization theorem can be derived from the HOV model by adding the following stringent assumptions. First, there are no factor intensity reversals. Second, countries diversify their production in equilibrium, which means that there are no large differences in countries factor endowments. The need to impose stringent assumptions implies that tests of cross-country factor price equalization are not direct tests of the trade model.

3.4.2. *Conditional Factor Price Equalization*

A key idea of Trefler's (1993*a*) paper is that international factor price equalization is not observed but holds conditionally after adjusting for international productivity gaps. Trefler does not provide a theory of divergence in productivities but shows that salaries do equalize after correcting them to eliminate the effects of international differences in productivities. This result is known as conditional factor price equalization in the sense that adjusted wages equalize internationally after controlling for international differences in productivities by utilizing the salary divided by the productivity level.

Let us formalize the notion of conditional factor price equalization. Because one unit of FE_i^c provides π_i^c units of service, $1/\pi_i^c$ units of FE_i^c provide one productivity-equivalent unit of service. If the wage rate for FE_i^c is w_i^c, the wage rate w_i^{c*} per productivity-adjusted unit of labor input is equal to $1/\pi_i^c$ times the wage rate w_i^c

$$w_i^{c*} = \frac{w_i^c}{\pi_i^c}.$$

If international productivity differs across countries, factor price equalization fails but there is conditional factor price equalization in the sense that factor prices divided by productivity levels equalize across countries, that is, $w_i^{1*} = \cdots = w_i^{C*}$, or,

$$\frac{w_i^1}{\pi_i^1} = \frac{w_i^2}{\pi_i^2} = \cdots = \frac{w_i^C}{\pi_i^C}$$

for all factors $i \in \{1, 2, \ldots, I\}$. The previous equation embodies the hypothesis that factor prices per efficiency unit, w_i^c/π_i^c, equalize internationally. Conditional factor price equalization can be expressed using the United States as a benchmark

$$\frac{w_i^c}{w_i^{US}} = \frac{\pi_i^c}{\pi_i^{US}}, \quad i \in \{1, \ldots I\}, \ c \in \{1, \ldots, C\}.$$

3.4.3. Statistical Results

We proceed to review empirical tests of conditional factor price equalization using the United States as reference country. The productivity levels are the values of π_i^c that make the factor content equation fit

$$FC_i^{c*} = \pi_i^c FE_i^c - s^c \sum_{k=1}^{C} \pi_i^k FE_i^k.$$

The empirical testing methodology utilized is the following. Trefler (1993*a*) presumes that the HOV model holds and then tests for whether or not the factor price equalization (FPE) hypothesis holds. In other words, the author jointly tests the hypotheses of factor price equalization and the HOV model. The analysis used 1983 data for thirty-three countries which account for about 75 percent and close to 80 percent of world exports and GNP, respectively.

The paper tests whether or not the ratio of the productivity for factor i (say, labor L or capital K) in country c and the United States, is equal to the ratio of factor prices. Formally, the null hypothesis H_0 states that the ratio π_i^c/π_i^{US} is equal to the ratio of factor prices, w_i^c/w_i^{US} while the alternative hypothesis H_A states the ratios differ

$$H_0 : \frac{\pi_i^c}{\pi_i^{US}} = \frac{w_i^c}{w_i^{US}},$$

$$H_A : \frac{\pi_i^c}{\pi_i^{US}} \neq \frac{w_i^c}{w_i^{US}}.$$

As a first step, the author finds a strong correlation between productivity parameters and factor price differentials for labor, w_L, and capital, w_K,

$$corr\left(\frac{\pi_L^c}{\pi_L^{US}}, \frac{w_L^c}{w_L^{US}}\right) = 0.90,$$

$$corr\left(\frac{\pi_K^c}{\pi_K^{US}}, \frac{w_K^c}{w_K^{US}}\right) = 0.68.$$

If the joint hypothesis putting together the HOV model and conditional factor price equalization is correct, we should conclude that the productivity and factor price series π_i^c/π_i^{US} and w_i^c/w_i^{US} are equal, and the correlations should be close to 1. The reported correlation is close to 1 in the case of labor but not in the case of capital.

In a second step, Trefler estimates regression equations relating (1) wage rates to the labor productivity factors, and (2) the price of capital services to the capital productivity factor. If there is conditional factor price equalization the constant term should be statistically close to zero, and the coefficient of the productivity factor should be statistically close to 1.

The wage equation is

$$\log(w_L^c) = \underset{(0.061)}{-0.180} + \underset{(0.042)}{0.678} \log(\pi_L^c), \qquad R^2 = 0.90,$$

where standard errors are reported in parenthesis. In this case, the hypothesis that the estimated coefficient, $\hat{\beta}_L = 0.678$, is statistically close to one, is rejected. Further analysis led the author to conclude that biases are due to data errors.

With respect to capital, results are shown to hold well. There are no systematic biases in the capital series. Results are reported in the following regression

$$\log w_K^c = \underset{(0.038)}{-0.004} + \underset{(0.094)}{0.816} \log \pi_K^c, \qquad R^2 = 0.72,$$

where $\hat{\beta}_L = 0.816$ is statistically close to unity.

The author concludes that there is strong evidence to accept the joint hypothesis of a modified version of the HOV model and factor price equalization across countries in the conditional sense (i.e. after controlling for factor-augmenting international productivity differentials).

3.4.4. Factor Price Insensitivity Hypothesis

The surveys of empirical evidence on international trade by Leamer and Levinsohn (1995) and Leamer (1995) define factor price insensitivity as 'within a country, factor prices are altogether insensitive to changes in factor supplies, holding product prices fixed'. They argue that factor-augmenting productivity differentials across countries might not fully explain factor price differentials so that factor prices might not be related to changes in factor supplies. A direct consequence of this hypothesis is that, if output prices remain fixed, large migratory movements across frontiers or even changes in internal factor accumulation rates would not translate into changes in wages.

Repetto and Ventura (1998) examine factor prices in cross-sections for 1970 (sixteen countries), 1975 (thirty-one countries), 1980 (fifty-one countries) and 1985 (fifty countries). Except for the case of the European Union, they reject the Leontief–Trefler hypothesis that factor-augmenting international productivity differences explain most of the cross-country variation in factor prices. This result suggests that there is a need for searching for determinants of factor prices other than the productivity differences stressed by Trefler. Moreover, they test the Leamer–Levinsohn hypothesis that wage-rental ratios are not related to measures of factor endowments in open economies. By regressing productivity-adjusted wage-rental ratios (obtained from the tests of the Leontief–Trefler hypothesis) on measures of factor abundances and other factors, they fail to find a significant relation in open economies. The authors conclude that theoretical models should feature the factor-price insensitivity property stressed by Leamer and Levinsohn.

3.5. TRADE, FACTOR CONTENT, AND WAGES

The wage gap between skilled and unskilled US workers substantially increased from the 1970s to the 1990s. The real wage of workers with 16 or more years of education increased by about 3.4 percent between 1979 and 1995 while the real wage for those workers with less than 12 years of education fell by 20 percent (Katz and Autor, 1999). The drop of unskilled worker wages relative to skilled wages was also experienced in the United Kingdom and to lesser extent in other industrialized economies such as Australia, Canada, Japan, and Sweden.

What are the factors accounting for the drop in real unskilled wages and the rising gap in wage inequality? Unskilled real wage decline and the rise of the skilled premium have been attributed to rapid and biased technological change, heavy deindustrialization and declining employment in manufacturing, globalization as indicated by greater trade and foreign direct investment, and migration of unskilled workers (discussed in the chapter on migration). With so many suspects, it is not surprising that the debate about the extent to which trade, FDI, technological change and other factors explain rising wage inequality remains unsettled and heated.

3.5.1. Does Trade Push Wages Down?

Trade with developing countries and the global dispersion of production activities have been blamed for pushing wages down in developed countries. Labor unions and many government officials have attributed the decline on skilled labor wages to increased trade with developing countries. The share of developing countries in US imports of manufactures rose from 29 percent in 1978 to 36.4 percent in 1990. This phenomenon justifies raising a question about whether greater trade with developing countries has pushed US unskilled wages down.

Are unskilled labor wages in the United States and the European Union determined in China, the awakened trading giant? Trade economists have tried to draw conclusions about the effect of trade on wages and wage inequalities by examining the effects of trade on product prices. According to the Stolper–Samuelson theorem, changes in goods prices have magnified effects in factor prices.

One view stresses that international trade does not appear to be large enough to explain factor prices and labor market changes in major developed countries. Two trade-related arguments are used to sustain this position. First, the small amount of trade with developing countries cannot generate the product price changes necessary to explain observed changes in factor rewards. If factor rewards are a function of product prices, international trade can be exonerated.

Second, trade with developing countries has not generated large enough changes in factor content to explain observed changes in factor rewards. The reason is that the importance of developed country trade with developing countries is quite small when measured in relation to developed countries' GDP. Imports of manufactures from developing countries represent a mere 2 percent of the combined GDP of OECD countries. Despite rapid growth in trade, large developed economies do not generally trade much and most of it takes place with other developed countries. Changes in the factor content of trade are small and cannot generate large changes in relative factor rewards.

Leamer (2000) argues that trade might contribute to explain changes in wage inequality but the small factor content argument is irrelevant because the factor content of trade does not determine factor rewards (see the debate in same volume).

What are the difficulties arising in linking factor content with wages? The zero profit equations state that, for each country c, the price vector is equal to factor costs

$$p^c = \begin{pmatrix} p_1^c \\ \vdots \\ p_J^c \end{pmatrix} = A^{c\prime} w^c = \begin{pmatrix} a_{11}^c & \cdots & a_{1I}^c \\ \vdots & \ddots & \vdots \\ a_{J1}^c & \cdots & a_{JI}^c \end{pmatrix} \begin{pmatrix} w_1^c \\ \vdots \\ w_I^c \end{pmatrix}.$$

This equation system links the price and factor reward vectors. In order to be able to invert this system of equations, the number of tradable products J cannot be less than the number of factors I, $I \leq J$. If the system is invertible, factor prices can be uniquely determined from the vector of tradable good prices

$$w^c = S(p^c), \tag{3.15}$$

where the function S behaves according to the Stolper–Samuelson theorem.

Let us relate the factor content of imports and factor rewards. First, observe that (3.4), $FC^c \equiv A^c T^c = FE^c - A^c D^c$, implies

$$p^c = p(A^c D^c) = p(FE^c - FC^c).$$

Second, use the Stolper–Samuelson relation (3.15) to express product prices as a function of the factor content of imports and factor endowments

$$w^c = S(p^c) = w^c(p(FE^c - FC^c)).$$

This equation implies that greater factor content affects factor rewards in the same manner as emigration (i.e. a reduction of factor endowments) would affect factor rewards in a closed economy. Observe that setting the factor content of imports equal to zero yields the relation between factor endowments and factor rewards in a closed economy.

Many observers argue that trade and trade barriers do not greatly affect relative labor market rewards in the United States. The reason is that the net import of labor services embodied in US trade has been historically small and relatively stable.

Can we conclude that, if the import of labor services embodied in trade is a small share of total labor supply, then trade does not impinge greatly on labor rewards? The answer is yes if the following assumptions happen to hold. First, the autarkic factor demand vector $w^c = w^c(p(FE^c))$ must not be too elastic. This assumption does not generally hold because the demand for any given factor can exhibit high elasticity.

Second, the vector mapping factor endowments into factor rewards must be such that the abundance of one factor does not greatly affect the rewards of other factors. This assumption does not generally hold in a multifactor setting. For instance, changing the supplies of land and capital can affect the wage rate under autarky. By the same token, the compensation of labor can change even though the imports of labor services implicit in international trade are small. These considerations imply but do not prove that trade in labor services could explain factor rewards disparities even if trade in labor services is small.

3.5.2. Wage and Employment Effects of FDI

Outsourcing and global production sharing, resulting in international trade in intermediate inputs, can be as important as technological change in explaining the wage gap. The argument is that the geographic separation of production stages increases trade in intermediate goods, shifting the demand away from local unskilled labor and prompting the increase of relative skilled wages.

Feenstra and Hanson (2002) examine the relation between changes in the share of skilled labor s_{Hm} (proxied by nonproduction labor) and total wages per industry. Data on 447 US manufacturing industries show that the nonproduction wage share moved up from 35 to 42 percent between 1979 and 1990. The increase in the nonproduction wage share s_{Hm} for $m = 1, \ldots, M$ industries is explained by annual changes in capital K_m, output Y_m and a set of structural variables included in vector z_m

$$\Delta s_{Hm} = \phi_0 + \phi_K \Delta \ln K_m + \phi_Y \Delta \ln Y_m + \phi_X \Delta z_m.$$

Outsourcing, defined as imported intermediate inputs as a share of total materials purchases, accounts for 15–24 percent of the increase of the nonproduction wage share. The share of computer spending in total capital, used as proxy for technological change, accounts for 8–30 percent of the nonproduction wage share increase. The conclusion is that both technological change, as measured by computers expenditures, and trade, as measured by outsourcing, are important in explaining a wider wage gap.

3.5.3. Biased Technological Change

The observed decline in the wage of unskilled relative to skilled workers might be due to technological change rather than trade, foreign investment and migration. The rise of the skill premium is often attributed to biased technological change, which has raised skilled labor productivity to a greater extent than unskilled labor productivity. Biased technolgical change helps to explain why the share of college-educated workers in employment has increased in most industries while the skilled wage premium has also increased. Labor supply effects in the presence of neutral technological change would have called for a lower skilled wage premium.

In order to determine the skilled wage premium, one must consider labor demand and supply effects. Recent experience involves two opposite labor market effects. On one hand, technological change biased toward skilled labor increases the demand for skilled labor, which tends to raise skilled wages. On the other hand, a larger supply of skilled labor tends to reduce relative skilled wages. Which of these effects dominate, and specifically whether the bias in technological change has been strong enough to generate observed factor reward changes, is an empirical question that remains on the table.

An increasing supply of skilled labor can be made consistent with a higher skilled premium if skilled labor generates biased technological change. Acemoglu (1998, 1999) presents a theoretical model in which wage inequality favoring skilled labor is the result of the increased supply of skilled labor relative to unskilled labor. The increase of skilled labor induces sustained skilled-biased technological change consisting of qualitative change in production techniques, modifications in the organization of work or the introduction of new technologies. These changes would lead to a higher demand for skills and to a greater gap in wage inequality.

3.6. THE GRAVITY THEORY OF BILATERAL TRADE

The theory of gravitational forces in physics tells us that the gravitational attraction exerted on an object by a body, such as the earth, declines with the distance between the object attracted and the center of the attracting body. We also learn that gravitational attraction increases with the mass of the attracting body. Furthermore, the theory tells us that gravitational forces act on both bodies involved. For instance, the earth attracts the moon, but the moon also attracts the earth. These considerations have been enshrined in Isaac Newton's famous law of universal gravitation. Newton's gravity law states that every particle in the universe attracts every other particle with a force that is proportional to the product of their masses, and inversely proportional to the square of the distance between the particles.

Economists have found an analog to gravitational forces in the volumes of international trade between two countries, that is, bilateral trade. The gravity model of trade states that the volume of bilateral trade is positively related to countries' size as measured by their income levels, and negatively related to the distance between them. Gravity theory provides an estimate of the volume of bilateral trade between any two countries i and j. The gravity equation posits that the value of the volume of trade between country i and country j is

1. Positively related to both countries' size as measured by income levels Y^i and Y^j (income per capita is also often used), and
2. Negatively related to the distance D^{ij} between the trading partners, which serves as a proxy for transport and communication costs.

The previous relations can be summarized through the so-called gravity equation of bilateral trade T^{ij} between countries i and j. The 'gravity' terminology derives from the following formula's resemblance to Newton's law

$$T^{ij} = A \frac{Y^i Y^j}{D^{ij}}, \tag{3.16}$$

where A is a constant, Y^i and Y^j are the income levels of countries i and j, and D^{ij} is the distance between the countries. T^{ij} is a measure of bilateral trade, such as the exports from country i to country j (which is also the value of country j imports from i). Because the exports from country i to country j generally have a different value than the exports from j to i, the definition of the volume of bilateral trade is ambiguous. Alternative definitions include the sum or average of the bilateral exports of the two countries involved.

3.6.1. The Gravity Equation

What are the theoretical foundations supporting the gravity equation? Let us derive a gravity equation for the case of zero transport costs. Consider a world economy consisting of two countries i and j producing many symmetric differentiated varieties of two goods, I and II. The technology used to produce these varieties displays increasing returns to scale, which ensures perfect specialization in each variety. Recall that each country produces a different number of varieties of each good but, if varieties are symmetric in demand and cost, the output of each variety is the same in both countries. For instance, $n_I^i \neq n_I^j$ but $Q_I = Q_I^i = Q_I^j$.

Consumers in each country value product variety. Recall that homothetic preferences imply that the demand for foreign varieties depends on the share $s^i = Y^i / Y^W$ of a country's *GDP* on world *GDP*. The value M^{ij} of country i's imports from country j is

$$M^{ij} = s^i [p_I n_I^j Q_I + p_{II} n_{II}^j Q_{II}] = \frac{Y^i Y^j}{Y^W},$$

$$Y^j = p_I n_I^j Q_I + p_{II} n_{II}^j Q_{II},$$

(3.17)

where p_I is the price of the varieties of good I, Q_I is the output of I, n_I^j is the number of varieties of good I produced in country j, and so on. By the same token, the volume of country j's imports M^{ji} from country i is

$$M^{ji} = s^j [p_I n_I^i Q_I + p_{II} n_{II}^i Q_{II}] = \frac{Y^j Y^i}{Y^W},$$

$$Y^i = p_I n_I^i Q_I + p_{II} n_{II}^i Q_{II}.$$

(3.18)

Defining trade T^{ij} as the value of bilateral imports yields

$$T^{ij} \equiv M^{ij} = AY^i Y^j = M^{ji} \equiv T^{ji},$$

where $A = 1/Y^W$.

How can we modify the gravity model to take distance into account? The role of distance can be easily understood in terms of transportation costs that operate as a barrier to trade and increase with distance. Therefore, trade should tend to decline with the distance between the trading countries as reflected in higher transport costs.

A gravity equation with transport costs can be derived in a monopolistically competitive model of varieties. Assume symmetry in demand and costs and a constant elasticity of substitution in consumption σ. The price faced by country c consumers on their imports of products from country k is equal to the exporter's market price p^k adjusted for the trade cost $T^{ck} = 1 + t^{ck}$ faced by the importer

$$p^c = T^{ck} p^k.$$

The bilateral trade equation specifies country c's purchases of goods from source k, M^{ck}, as a function of their output levels Y^c and Y^k, good j price $p^k T^{ck}$ (inclusive of all *ad valorem* transaction costs T^{ck}), and a price index p^c_{index} of all the goods available in country c

$$M^{kc} = AY^c Y^k \frac{(p^k T^{ck})^{-\sigma}}{p^c_{index}}. \tag{3.19}$$

The value of the elasticity of substitution σ has been estimated to range between 5 and 8 (Acemoglu and Ventura, 2002).

The notion that trade increases with trading partners' income is in tune with appealing notions of the relation between the volume of trade and country size. Intuitively, one might expect that larger trading partners (measured by income) tend to engage in greater bilateral trade among themselves. Despite its intuitive appeal, the gravity equation has been often criticized for lacking an analytical framework. For instance, observe that the bilateral trade import equation was derived under the assumption of complete specialization in production. The notion that the volume of trade must depend positively on trading partners' size stands in contradiction to the basic $2 \times 2 \times 2$ HO framework when there is production diversification. Indeed, the simple vision of gravity does not rely on the analysis of preferences, technologies, factor endowments, government regulation, strategies, and other factors that constitute the bread and butter of trade analysis.

The gravity approach was vindicated when several authors showed that gravity equations can be derived in different types of models. Anderson (1979) and Bergstrand (1985) develop gravity models based on the Armington assumption of product differentiation by national origin. Bergstrand (1989) develops gravity in a model with monopolist competition and Deardorff (1998) shows that gravity equations can be derived in a very general setting that is independent of any particular trade model. Harrigan (2002) reviews the literature on gravity and the volume of trade.

3.6.2. Is Trade Affected by Gravity Forces?

The simple notion of gravity in trade can be implemented empirically utilizing measures of bilateral trade, countries' incomes and the distance between countries, frequently measured by the distance between the countries' capitals. A long line of empirical studies have found that the gravity model performs well as a description of bilateral trade patterns.

Substantial evidence indicates that:

1. Higher trading partners' income and income per capita levels are associated with greater bilateral trade. In other words, larger and richer countries trade more with each other than small and poorer countries.
2. Bilateral trade flows decline with distance and increase with geographic adjacency. This result is consistent with the notion that transport costs are lower and communications are greater when trading partners are closer to each other. For instance, Canada and the United States are the main trading partners of each other. The effect of the variable distance is also evident in the trade relation between the Netherlands and Germany as well as Brazil and Argentina. The North American Free Trade Agreement (NAFTA) is based on the historically close trade relations between Canada, the United States and Mexico. A similar point applies to the European Union.

Some stylized facts derived from gravity models are that nearness and common language encourage trade while national borders, nonoverlapping preferential trading arrangements, different national monies and poor institutions act as trade barriers and discourage trade.

Middle Eastern countries' trade patterns represent a partial exception and a partial confirmation of stylized facts derived from gravity modeling. Al-Atrash and Yousef (1999) present evidence that, at the group level, Middle East and North African (MENA) countries intra-regional trade is too low compared with the level of trade predicted by the gravity model of trade. Moreover, membership in regional groups (such as Gulf Cooperation Council (GCC) and Arab Maghreb Union (AMU)) does not necessarily imply member countries trade more among themselves. Policy-induced trade restrictions and factors such as similar comparative advantages, high trade costs, and different levels of income per capita are cited as the major impediments to trade liberalization in the region. Trade is greater with the European Union than with regional partners despite the short distance between any two partners (a gravity force), membership in regional trade agreements, common borders and related languages. At the same time, the size and relative close location of the European Union operates as a magnet for international exchange.

Can the gravity model account for bilateral trade deficits such as the high deficit sustained by the US economy *vis-à-vis* Japan and China? These controversial deficits are often attributed to excessive protectionism in these countries. The gravity model appears to be unsuccessful in explaining bilateral trade imbalances. Davis and Weinstein (2002c) examine the mystery of the excess trade imbalances. They find that the gravity model fails to explain observed bilateral trade imbalances even after controlling for macroeconomic imbalances and 'triangular trade' effects. The so-called 'triangular trade' effects refer to idiosyncrasies in supply and demand such as running large bilateral deficits with countries that are important suppliers of a good that is strongly demanded in a country (e.g. deficits with Middle Eastern oil producers). The authors point to the need to consider protection and other potential explanations.

3.7. TRADE BARRIERS, HOME BIAS, AND INTEGRATION

Formal trade barriers have declined significantly over time. Tariff rates are at single-digit levels among industrial countries and many nontariff barriers have been eliminated. In the past decades, developing countries have joined the trade liberalization trend. Informal trade barriers, closed networks and market-share arrangements still play a significant role in limiting imports in Japan and other countries, but generally less and less so. Knowledge-related (informational) barriers to trade are presumed to decline in an era of increased communications. Under globalization, lax contract enforcement is difficult to hide.

Paradoxically, despite the many factors facilitating international trade, a home bias persists. There are several proposed explanations for the local concentration of trade. First, some argue that shipping costs remain relatively high because they have declined significantly on a secular basis, but not so in recent years. Second, a high elasticity of substitution in consumption can help to explain why not-so-high transport costs might be consistent with a substantial home bias. Third, nontariff barriers such as antidumping measures and other forms of contingent protection have become more popular (see chapter on antidumping and sanctions). Fourth, there is a continuing controversy on the role of informal trade barriers such as the weak enforcement of international contracts and participant lack of information.

3.7.1. Bilateral Trade, Transport Costs, and Consumption Elasticities

Do transport costs impose a higher or a lower trade barrier than tariffs? Hummel's (1999a) cross-country study utilizes 1994 transport cost data for the United States, New Zealand, and five Latin American countries. Available transport cost data allow computing an *ad valorem* freight rate, F_j^{ck}/V_j^{ck}, where F_j^{ck} represents transportation expenditures in country c's imports of product j from k and V_j^{ck} is the value of the corresponding imports exclusive of transportation expenditures.

Transport costs, measured by an unweighted average of exporters' freight costs, appear to pose larger trade barriers than tariffs. Appearances can be deceiving, though, as this result hinges on how the average is computed. Transport costs measured as a trade-weighted average of exporters freight rates are lower than tariff rates and tend to vary less across products. For instance, the weighted average freight cost of US imports was less than 4 percent of the import value in 1994 and did not vary greatly across products. The weighted average is pretty low because importers minimize transport costs by selecting the cheapest exporters.

Do low transport costs imply that they do not play a significant role in explaining bilateral variation in trade flows? An answer is that, if the consumption elasticity of substitution is high enough, low transport costs can have a significant effect on trade and can help explaining phenomena such as the home bias of trade.

In order to extricate the effect of transport costs from the effect of substitution elasticities, Hummels (1999a) presents an estimation procedure that allows isolating the channels through which trade barriers affect trade volumes and estimating the implied substitution elasticities. The relationship between *ad valorem* freight rates F_j^{ck}/V_j^{ck} and distance $DIST^{ck}$, controlling for goods' transportability by using the weight-to-value ratio of shipments WGT_j^{ck}/V_j^{ck} as a regressor, is

$$\ln \frac{F_j^{ck}}{V_j^{ck}} = a_j + \gamma_1 \ln \frac{WGT_j^{ck}}{V_j^{ck}} + \gamma_2 \ln DIST^{ck} + \eta_j^{ck},$$

where η is the error term. The estimated transport cost distance elasticities $\hat{\gamma}_2$ lie in the 0.2–0.3 range, which are close to previous estimates. This regression yields distance- and weight-corrected measures of *ad valorem* freight rates. The distance elasticities obtained from different data sets are utilized to measure the elasticity of substitution σ in gravity equations.

The relationship trade costs, $T^{ck} = 1 + t^{ck}$, to distance $DIST$ proxy variables measuring trade costs of the t^{ck}, $T^{ck} = 1 + t^{ck}$, to distance $DIST$ and the savings in *ad valorem* trade costs derived from a common language $LANG$, geographic adjacency ADJ and home trade $HOME$ (in the sense of not crossing national boundaries) is assumed to be (LANE, ADJ and HOME are 0-1 dummies)

$$T^{ck} = (DIST^{ck})^{\delta_1} \exp\{\delta_2 LANG^{ck} + \delta_3 ADJ^{ck} + \delta_4 HOME^{ck}\}.$$

Incorporating the previous equation into gravity equation (3.19), $M^{ck} = AY^c Y^k (T^{ck})^{-\sigma} (p^k)^{-\sigma}/p^c$, expressing the resulting relation in terms of logs, ignoring the price term, and adding an error term, yields the import demand regression equation

$$\ln M^{ck} = \alpha_0 + \alpha_1 \ln Y^c Y^k + \beta_1 DIST^{ck} + \beta_2 LANG^{ck} + \beta_3 ADJ^{ck}$$

$$+ \beta_4 HOME^{ck} + \varepsilon^{ck}, \quad \beta_n = -\sigma \delta_n.$$

The trade barrier coefficients are interpreted as the negative of the product of the elasticity of substitution σ and the elasticity δ_n of each factor determining transport costs. Estimates of the elasticity of substitution, $\hat{\sigma} = -\hat{\beta}_1/\hat{\delta}_1$, are within the range $\hat{\sigma} = 2$ to $\hat{\sigma} = 5.26$. The implied price markups $\hat{\sigma}/(\hat{\sigma} - 1)$ lie within the range of 23 percent ($\hat{\sigma} = 5.26$) to 100 percent ($\hat{\sigma} = 2$). Estimates $\hat{\delta}_1$ derive from $\hat{\gamma}_2$.

The consumption elasticities of substitution affect both the impact of trade barriers on trade volumes and the monopoly markup. Invisible trade barrier estimates $\hat{\delta}_1 = \hat{\beta}_i/\sigma$ are relatively high, perhaps because the estimated elasticities of substitution are too low. The implicit trade barriers of not speaking a common language, nonadjacency, and borders exceed 100 percent.

3.7.2. The Home Bias Effect

International trade is less than predicted by trade models after controlling for transport costs, distance and other factors. Most countries trade with themselves to a much greater extent than they trade with other countries.

Why is it that trade is characterized by a strong home bias? Proposed explanations include:

1. Home biases in consumer preferences (Armington preferences and consumption elasticities).
2. Transport costs (Hummels, 1999*a,b*).
3. Tariffs and a variety of formal and informal nontariff barriers to trade, including the sunk costs on exportation (Roberts and Tybout, 1997*a*).
4. Unidentified factors incorporated in the existence of large border costs after controlling for distance, transport costs and other trade barriers (McCallum, 1995).
5. The decision of intermediate input producers to locate near their downstream costumers (Hillbery and Hummels, 2000).
6. National currencies (Frankel and Rose, 2002).
7. Imperfect contracts and patent right enforcement at the international level (Anderson and Marcouiller, 2002).

Let us briefly examine the explanations for the home bias. Armington preferences can account for home biases although many observers argue that this is largely an *ad hoc* explanation. The role of distance and transport costs is supported by a large literature validating the gravity approach to trade. Moreover, gravity equations provide a benchmark for evaluating whether preferential trading arrangements, different national monies, poor institutions and other factors discourage international trade. Gravity tests estimate versions of bilateral import equations, such as those developed by Anderson (1979) and others, augmented to include the variables of interest. The findings deriving from gravity equations suggest that several factors discourage trade and thus help to explain the 'home bias' of trade and the mystery of the 'missing trade' as measured by the factor services embodied in trade. These factors can be viewed as barriers to trade causing deviations from frictionless bilateral free trade.

Share arrangements play a role in limiting importation in Japan and other countries. This applies to both close and distant partners. Informational barriers and institutional factors such as the strength of the enforcement of contracts and intellectual property rights limit trade. Despite a growing body of evidence documenting diverse barriers to trade, there is little evidence yet about the relative importance of these factors.

Evidence on the role of trade barriers is provided by a large literature on trade barriers and preferential trade arrangements. What are the effects of regional agreements on the volume of international trade? A regional trade agreement is deemed to encourage trade between two members of the agreement if bilateral trade under the agreement is greater than the predictions from the gravity equation. Gravity model estimations reviewed in the chapter on preferential trading arrangements suggest that regional agreements shift trade toward members and away from the rest of the world. However, this effect can partly be explained by the fact that preferential agreements tend to join countries that are geographically close to each other. These countries are natural trade partners that tend to trade more with themselves due to gravity considerations.

McCallum (1995) examines the border effect in the context of regional trading patterns in Canada and the United States. He estimates regressions incorporating a gravity factor (i.e. distance), treating domestic sales as a bilateral trade option along with bilateral international trade. A dummy variable indicates domestic purchases and measures the strength of the domestic purchase vs foreign purchase effect. The procedure permits estimating the role of borders. The study finds important and puzzling border effects. Domestic purchases greatly exceed foreign purchases and this excess can not be explained by distance (gravity) and the other variables included in the model. In other words, the dummy variable representing domestic sales has a large and statistically significant positive effect on regional trade.

The dramatic border effect puzzle has been confirmed in a score of studies. Engel and Roger's (1996) study 'How wide is the border' finds similar effects. Helliwell's (1998) book on the role of national borders contains detailed tests and a survey of the large literature on the subject. Eaton and Kortum (2002) estimate that, in the absence of geographic barriers to trade (zero gravity), worldwide trade would increase fivefold. Haveman and Hummels (2001) find that the observed ratios of internal to external prices range between 13 and 2000 in a sample of nineteen countries.

Do national monies represent a barrier to international trade? Rose (2000) finds that, for a sample of 186 countries for 1970–90, bilateral trade was higher for a pair of countries using the same currency than for a pair of countries with different currencies. In other words, belonging to a common currency union leads to greater bilateral trade. Rose and van Wincoop (2001) estimate that trade barriers associated with national borders are halved when countries join a union. This result suggests that national currencies help to explain the home bias effect and that the euro will substantially increase trade among monetary area members. Glick and Rose (2001) utilize the gravity model estimated for a sample of 217 countries from 1948 to 1997 to examine whether belonging to a currency union expands trade and whether leaving a currency union reduces trade. Countries leaving currency unions are found to experience declines in bilateral trade after controlling for other factors. Using data for over 200 countries and dependencies, Frankel and Rose (2002) find that belonging to a currency union or a currency board triples trade with other currency union members. Moreover, they estimate that a 1 percent increase in the overall trade per GDP ratio rises per capita income by more than 0.33 percent.

Can poor institutions prevent trade? Anderson and Marcouiller (2002) utilize a gravity model of bilateral trade to examine whether corruption and imperfect contract enforcement constitute a hidden tax that discourages international trade. They find support for the hypotheses that less corruption and imperfect contract enforcement reduce trade and contribute to generate a disproportionately high volume of trade among high income countries. The World Economic Forum data on institutional quality supports the following hypotheses

1. Greater transparency, better enforceability of commercial contracts, and a higher value of a measure of relative composite security raise the demand for imports. Because institutional quality is positively associated with per capita income, institutional effects contribute to explain why a disproportionately high volume of trade takes place among high income countries.

2. Home bias of trade emerges as a consumption phenomenon based on nonhomotheticity of preferences in the sense that the share of expenditures devoted to nontraded goods rises with the level of per capita income. Excluding institutional variables as regressors generates an omitted variable problem because the positive trade effect of better institutions is incorporated in the estimated coefficient of per capita income. As a result, the nonhomotheticity of preferences is obscured.

3.7.3. Has Commerce Become More Integrated?

A large body of evidence suggests that visible trade barriers have declined substantially over time. The trade negotiation rounds conducted under the sponsorship of the General Agreement on Tariffs and Trade (GATT) and the World Trade Organization (WTO) have caused average tariffs to decline to single-digit levels in industrial countries and close to that in many developing countries. The data in Feenstra (1996) show that average US tariff rates went down from over 8 percent in the mid-1970s to less than 5 percent in the mid-1990s. Quotas and other nontariff barriers to trade have been gradually dismantled although the use of antidumping investigations and duties has increased.

Transport costs declined dramatically over the past 150 years. Have international transportation costs continued to decline during the past decades? Hummels (1999*b*) examines the behavior of transportation costs from the early 1950s to the mid-1990s. The GDP deflator is used to adjust cost indexes (air, ocean, and overland freight rates) for inflation. The resulting price series are deflated by the relevant export or import price index so that costs represent *ad valorem* trade barriers. Hummels finds that:

1. The cost of ocean transport rose or remained constant over time. These costs apply to most of world trade. Two-thirds to three-quarters of the value of world trade is transported via ocean liners.
2. The costs of air transport declined, which helps to explain the shift toward air transport in the United States.
3. The costs of distant transport declined relative to the cost of proximate transport, which helps to explain the shift toward distant partners.
4. The quality of transportation services has improved due to increased ocean liner speed and the shift to air transport, a faster means of shipping.
5. Overland transport costs declined relative to ocean transport.

Have the measured reductions in visible trade barriers led to greater market integration? The reduction in visible barriers to trade facilitates the movement of goods across frontiers as well as trade in services. However, the evidence does not indicate rapid market integration along all dimensions.

3.8. WHICH TRADE MODEL PERFORMS BEST?

The challenges posed by the Leontief paradox and a long line of subsequent studies fueled skepticism about the empirical relevance of the simple HOV model. The
controversy has been bypassed by modifying the HOV model.

First, allowing for international technique differences increases substantially the
correlation between measured and predicted factor content. This correlation rises
from 28 percent using the standard HOV model to 59 percent in Davis and Weinstein
(2001) and 74 percent in Trefler and Zhu (2000).

Second, incorporating the gravity model into the HOV framework helps to increase
explanatory power (Davis and Weinstein, 2001). Countries with higher per capita
income levels tend to trade more among themselves. This effect prevails even after
controlling for variables suggested by the gravity model, which relates intra-industry
bilateral trade with per capita income, population, and distance, or other benchmark
models. Moreover, the gravity model has been shown to be consistent with all the
standard trade models so that it neither offers a direct confirmation nor a challenge to
them.

The revival of the HOV model raises the query of how well it performs compared to
analytical trade frameworks stressing different empirical determinants of the volume
and composition of trade. Two continuing challenges to the HOV model concern
the observation of large volumes of intra-industry trade and evidence suggesting the
presence of some form of increasing returns to scale in major industries. The empirical
importance of intra-industry trade depends on the level of aggregation. For instance,
trade in different electronics products are classified as intra-industry trade if the data is
gathered at a high level of aggregation. This trade becomes trade in entirely different
products (i.e. inter-industry trade) if industries are disaggregated into finer categories.
The determination of the right aggregation level is crucial as the relative importance
of intra- and inter-industry trade depends on that decision. We proceed to review the
evidence on alternative trade frameworks and the debate over the empirical support
for trade models featuring increasing returns and monopolistic competition.

3.8.1. Intra-industry Trade and Gravity

What is the empirical support for monopolistic competition models in international
trade? Helpman (1987) utilizes the positive gravity relationship between trade and
incomes to show that greater income similarity leads to greater trade. If preferences
are identical and homothetic and trade is balanced, the share of total trade among
group G members relative to group GDP, VT^G/Y^G, is (see the appendix)

$$\frac{V^G}{GDP^W} = s^G \left[1 - \sum_{c \in G} \left(s_c^G \right)^2 \right], \tag{3.20}$$

where $s^G = Y^G/Y^W$ is group G's share of world output and the similarity index
$1 - \sum (Y^c/Y^G)^2$ is higher when countries have similar incomes.

The volume of total intra-group trade in terms of the group's total output, VT^G/Y^G, provides a clue about the importance of intra-industry trade under monopolistic competition. Helpman's cross-section analysis of fourteen OECD countries for the 1956–81 period suggests that there is a negative correlation between total intra group trade measured in relation to group GDP and countries' size disparities as measured by income shares. This result is consistent with the IIT monopolistic competition model notion that the volume of trade between countries increases with greater similarity in incomes.

An empirical model embodying the relationship between factor differences and intra-industry trade relates the Grubel–Lloyd index of bilateral intra-industry trade between countries c and k, IIT^{ck}, to factor differences and size effects. Formally,

$$IIT^{ck} = \alpha_0 + \alpha_1 \log \left| \frac{GDP^c}{L^c} - \frac{GDP^k}{L^k} \right| + \alpha_2 \min(\log GDP^c, \log GDP^k)$$

$$+ \alpha_3 \max(\log GDP^c, \log GDP^k) + \varepsilon^{jk}.$$

The differential $GDP^c/L^c - GDP^k/L^k$ stands for country factor differences and L^c stands for country c population. The third and fourth terms, $\min(\cdot)$ and $\max(\cdot)$ are used to control for relative country size effects.

Helpman finds that intra-industry trade as a share of bilateral flows is (1) negatively and significantly (for the first seven years in the sample) correlated with dissimilarity in country-pairs per capital incomes (i.e. $\alpha_1 < 0$), (2) positively correlated with the size of the small country (i.e. $\alpha_2 > 0$), and (3) negatively correlated with the size of the large country (i.e. $\alpha_3 < 0$). These results are interpreted as evidence that size convergence over time explains the increasing trade volumes among OECD countries.

Hummels and Levinsohn (1995) contest the interpretation of Helpman's findings. They confirm the evidence presented in support of the IIT monopolistic competition model but claim that the correlations appear in alternative models. Both OECD data for ninety-one country-pairs during 1962–83 and non-OECD data show a negative correlation between the trade to income ratio and income disparities, even though IIT is small for non-OECD countries (non-OECD IIT regressions are not performed.)

Result robustness is tested using different econometric methods such as OLS regression, country-pair fixed and random effects estimation as well as instrumental variables analysis. Hummels and Levinsohn find that Helpman's result can be replicated, even though it imposes unrealistic assumptions such as the assumption that each good is produced in only one country and countries display homothetic preferences, in statistical analyses restricted to low income non-OECD countries. Moreover, the IIT regressions offer evidence indicating that intra-industry trade is specific to country pairs and that distance seems to play an important role. These results shade doubts over the hypothesis that a good fit of the gravity-based equation is necessarily due to trade in differentiated products.

The empirical results obtained by Hummels and Levinsohn (1995) suggest that the gravity equation does not hinge on product differentiation and that estimates of this equation might not be able to discriminate between alternative frameworks. This view is reinforced by the theoretical work of Deardorff (1998), who derives the gravity equation in a setup based on general assumptions that do not depend on any particular trade framework as long as large differences in factor endowments lead to production specialization. The reason is that gravity forces apply no matter what determines trade.

3.8.2. Increasing Returns vs Factor Proportions

The link between product differentiation and gravity equations is revisited by Evenett and Keller (2002) and Feenstra *et al.* (2001). They recognize that the gravity approach is consistent with alternative trade models but argue that modified gravity equations can discriminate between alternative frameworks. The reason is that alternative frameworks imply differences in theoretical parameter values and these differences can be empirically tested.

Evenett and Keller (2002) present evidence supporting the claim that increasing returns and product differentiation help to explain trade patterns among OECD countries while factor endowment divergences provide a rationale for non-OECD countries' trade patterns. The results are thus consistent with the scale economies explanation of OECD countries' trade patterns stressed by Helpman (1987) and with Hummels and Levinsohn's (1995) intriguing funding for non-OECD countries. Endowment divergencies explain large trade among similar countries.

The increasing returns and factor proportions rationales can be made compatibles by the following argument. If the empirical validity of the gravity equation reflects trade in different brands, then gravity equations for bilateral trade should work better for countries with larger shares of intra-industry trade. Gravity performs better when intra-industry trade is greater because product differentiation leads to specialization. Intra-industry trade diminishes with the higher trade costs generated by greater distance separating specialized trading partners. In other words, the coefficients of gravity equations vary depending on the production shares of different goods, which allows discriminating among alternative frameworks.

The empirical tests are based on gravity equations that differentiate between homogeneous and differentiated products. The Grubel–Lloyd index measures intra-industry trade. Country pairs are split into six broad classes. In one class, bilateral trade is dominated by factor proportions in the operational sense that bilateral intra-industry trade is less than 5 percent of total bilateral trade. The other five classes have a larger than 5 percent share of intra-industry trade and differ in the degree of intra-industry trade. The estimated equations condition the coefficients on the group to which a country pair belongs.

The estimates:

1. Reject the perfect specialization versions of the HO and increasing returns models.
2. Support imperfect specialization model in which trade is due to both factor endowments and increasing returns for countries with over 5 percent IIT share.

3. Support the imperfect specialization model relying solely on differences in factor endowments and trade in two constant returns to scale homogeneous goods.

How are these results obtained. The perfect specialization gravity model is

$$T_v^{ij} = \alpha_v \frac{Y_v^i Y_v^j}{YW} + \epsilon_v^{ij},$$

where ϵ_v^{ij} is a shock, countries i and j are capital and labor abundant, and v controls for the degree of IIT. The Grubel–Lloyd index, or factor proportions differences, are lowest for $v = 1$ and highest for $v = 5$.

A test is conducted for the five classes that have a larger than 5 percent share of intra-industry trade but differ in the degree of intra-industry trade. Gravity theory implies that the estimated coefficient should be equal to one but this is not confirmed by the data.

A separate test is performed for the subsample of country pairs with less than 5 percent of intra-industry trade, so that trade in homogeneous products strongly dominate. If intra-industry trade is small and trade is explained by relative factor abundances, the parameters of gravity equations hinge on whether divergences in countries' factor abundances are large enough to induce specialization. Specifically, greater factor divergences lead to specialization and greater correspondence with the gravity theory (i.e. the estimated coefficient is closer to one).

The test for the low Grubel–Lloyd subsample of country pairs with less than 5 percent of intra-industry trade (so that most trade is in homogeneous products) is performed as follows. Country pairs within this subsample are split into five classes according to divergences in factor endowments. The five classes $v \in \{1, \ldots, 5\}$ are constructed by assuming that the calculated value of the factor proportion differences (i.e. capital–labor ratios) between two partners, $FDIF^{ij}$, determines the share v of bilateral trade that is based on product specialization. Actual factor proportion differences $FDIF^{ij}$ are assumed to be given by their true value plus an error term θ^{ij}

$$FDIF^{ij} = FDIF^{ij,true} + \theta^{ij}, \quad \theta^{ij} \sim N(0, \sigma_\theta^2).$$

As in the multicone models discussed above, factor proportion differences indicate the true share of perfectly specialized goods trade. This relation justifies using $FDIF^{ij}$ to determine the five factor proportions subclasses v.

Gravity theory implies that the estimated coefficient should be closer to one the greater the difference in factor endowments. However, the estimated coefficients for the low Grubel–Lloyd subsample were below the theoretical implication of a unity coefficient. The theoretical predictions for the value of coefficients were not confirmed because they were smaller the greater the measured bilateral divergence in factor endowments. These findings suggest a rejection of both the perfect specialization version of the HOV and increasing returns models.

Empirical tests provide support for an imperfect specialization framework in which trade is due to both factor endowments and increasing returns. The model correctly predicts greater production of differentiated goods when the level of intra-industry trade is greater. The estimated equations, based on the high Grubel–Lloyd sample, condition the coefficients on the intra-industry trade group to a which country pair belongs. In other words, there is a separate estimate γ_v^i for each group

$$T_v^{ij} = (1 - \gamma_v^i)\frac{Y_v^i Y_v^j}{YW} + \epsilon_v^{ij}, \quad \gamma_v^i = \frac{Q_I^i}{P_{II}Q_{II}^i + Q_I^i},$$

where γ_v^i is the share of good I in country i's GDP. Estimated $1 - \gamma_v^i$ coefficients are closer to one the larger the group's Grubel–Lloyd ITT index, which is consistent with the model. Labor abundant country j exports labour intensive homogeneous good I, produced under constant returns to scale. It imports capital intensive differentiated goods from the increasing returns to scale sector II. With balanced trade, $T^{ji} = T^{ij} = s^j p_{II} Q_{II}^i = s^j(1 - \gamma^i)Y^i = (1 - \gamma^i)Y^i Y^j / Y^W$.

Finally, estimates support the imperfect specialization model relying solely on differences in factor endowments and trade in two homogeneous goods produced under constant returns to scale. The bilateral trade equation is

$$T^{ij} = (\gamma_v^j - \gamma_v^i)\frac{Y_v^i Y_v^j}{YW} + \epsilon_v^{ij}, \quad \gamma_v^c = \frac{Q_I^c}{P_{II}Q_{II}^c + Q_I^c}, \quad c \in \{i,j\},$$

where good I is the numeraire and γ_v^c is the share of the labor intensive good I in country c's GDP. Countries i and j are capital and labor abundant, respectively.

Ceteris paribus, a larger gap $\gamma_v^j - \gamma_v^i$ between the shares of the countries' labor intensive sectors is associated with greater trade. This test is constructed for the subsample of country pairs with less than 5 percent of intra-industry trade so that most trade is in homogeneous products. The authors estimate a modified gravity equation for each of the five subclasses displaying a low Grubel–Lloyd index for the case in which there is both production specialization and production diversification. The estimated coefficients are larger the greater the divergence in factor endowments, confirming the theoretical predictions. This test is interpreted as rejecting Deardorff's (1998) argument stressing that the gravity equation does not rely on any particular trade framework but is rather driven by specialization arising from divergences in relative factor endowments or product differentiation.

Evenett and Keller (2002) conclude that factor endowments and increasing returns help to explain different components of the international variation of production patterns and trade volumes.

Feenstra *et al.* (2001) report that empirical work for differentiated products is consistent with the predictions of the monopolistic competition model or a reciprocal dumping model with free entry. They use Rauch (1999) index to measure intra-industry trade.

The Level of Aggregation and Intra-industry Trade

There are two types of models of intra-industry trade: trade in horizontally differenti-ated products and trade in vertically differentiated products. In both the monopolistic competition models of Krugman (1979) and the characteristic approach of Lancaster (1980), intra-industry trade involves the exchange of goods that are differentiated hori-zontally. In Krugman's benchmark model, products exchanged are symmetric in the sense of displaying similar qualities and being produced by similar factor intensities. In Lancaster approach, products are not symmetric and are differentiated by character-istics. An alternative approach to product differentiation is developed by Falvey (1981). Intra-industry trade represents vertically differentiated products displaying different qualities and being produced with different factor intensities.

The empirical determination of what constitutes intra-industry trade depends on the level of aggregation undertaken in the analysis. Exchanging Mercedes for Volvos appears superfluous and inconsistent with comparative advantage if the level of aggreg-ation is high. If the level of aggregation is minimized, though, Mercedes and Volvos will be classified as distinct commodities and the paradox disappears.

Empirical studies present evidence that both horizontal and vertical differentiation are important in trade. Greenaway *et al.* (1994) define goods as vertically differentiated if their unit values at the 5-digit level differ by more than 15 percent. According to this definition, about seventy percent of UK intra-industry trade is vertical. Aturupane *et al.* (1997) find even higher proportions of vertically differentiated goods in intra-industry trade.

3.8.3. In Search of Economies of Scale

Can we detect scale economies at the national, industry or plant levels? Harrigan (1999) provides independent measures of total factor productivity for several industries in ten OECD countries during the 1980s. The US productivity for 1987 is used as the benchmark. He finds that there are large total factor productivity differentials across developed countries, including cases in which total factor productivity is often half the US level (office and compute equipment) and cases in which productivity is often two times the US level (electrical machinery). The analysis explores whether the estimated productivity gaps are due to industry-level scale economies or to country-specific technological differences with constant returns to scale production functions. The findings support the notion that there are technology differences and constant returns to scale.

In Helpman and Krugman (1985) model, the factor content of trade depends on each industry's economies of scale. Scale matters because it determines the trade pattern and the amount of factors used to produce exportables. Antweiler and Trefler (2002) use Helpman and Krugman (1985) factor content equations to estimate returns to scale at the industry level for thirty-four industries, three types of land and eleven factors for seventy-one countries during 1972, 1977, 1982, 1987 and 1992. Measured increasing returns combine plant scale economies, industry externalities, and scale-biased technical change. Econometric testing offers evidence that these 'scale economies and all that' help to explain the sources of comparative advantage. Productivity is found to be higher the higher the level of output. A one percent increase in output causes costs to decline about 0.05 percent on average. About a third of all goods-producing industries feature scale economies, displaying scale elasticities ranging between 1.10 to 1.20. The economy-wide scale elasticity is 1.05 and the scale coefficients are significantly greater than zero. These results suggest that "scale economies must figure prominently for any understanding of the factor content of trade," and are a source of comparative advantage.

The empirical methodology takes into account inter-country productivity gaps and the possibility of increasing returns to scale. The input–output ratio $a_{ij}^c = a_{ij}^{US}$, which is invariant across countries, is adjusted for the productivity level π_i^c and scale $\phi_j^c(Q_j^C) = (Q_j^C)^{-\alpha_{ij}^c}$ divided by the US scale factor

$$a_{ij}^{c*} = \frac{\phi_j^c/\phi_j^{US}}{\pi_i^c} a_{ij}^{US} = \frac{(Q_j^c)^{-\alpha_{ij}^c}/(Q_j^{US})^{-\alpha_{ij}^{US}}}{\pi_i^c} a_{ij}^{US}.$$

First, static inter-country productivity gaps are accounted for by the productivity adjustment parameter π_i^c, which is higher the greater the productivity of factor i in country c. Recall that this procedure gives rise to an adjusted input–output matrix A^{c*}, with input–output coefficients $a_{ij}^{c*} = \pi_i^c a_{ij}^c$. Second, increasing returns are taken into account by introducing a country-specific scale function $(Q_i^c)^{\alpha_{ij}^c}$ for each input i used to produce good j. For any given $\alpha_{ij}^c > 0$, a greater output requires a smaller input–output ratio. In other words, the model incorporates a scale effect.

Recall (3.6) stating that the content of each factor $i \in \{1, \ldots, I\}$ in the vector of goods $j \in \{1, \ldots, J\}$ is given by the corresponding element of the $I \times 1$ factor content vector FC^{c*} (the authors add intermediate inputs and a consumption residual)

$$FC^{c*} = A^{c*}X^c - \sum_{k=1,k\neq c}^{C} A^{k*}M^{ck}, \qquad D^c = D^{cc} + \sum_{k=1,k\neq c}^{C} M^{ck}.$$

Exports equal excess local production, $X^c = Q^c - D^c = Q^c - D^{cc} - \sum M^{ck}, k \neq c$, where D^{cc} is the vector of demand that is satisfied by local production and $\sum M^{ck}$ is the sum of the demand for imports from countries $k \in \{1, \ldots, C\}, k \neq c$. The unit input requirement matrix A^{k*} specifying the unit input requirements of imports from country k is specific to the exporting country.

This model has implications for the debate on trade and wages. Specifically, introducing nonhomotheticity in production implies that output expansion shifts production techniques. Moreover, skill based scale effects raise the demand for skilled labor relative to unskilled labor.

3.9. EXPORTATION, PRODUCT CYCLES, AND PATENTS

What determines exports? Who is likely to become a successful exporter? The question about the determinants of exports and who is likely to be able to export has given rise to a long line of research. Some dynamic approaches have stressed that there is a cycle that products follow and that the exporting country changes over time depending on the ability of low cost potential exporters to imitate innovative products. Other research focuses on the cost of exporting, exchange rates, and policy factors such as state export promotion.

3.9.1. *Who Exports?*

What determines whether firms are able to break into foreign markets? Bernard and Jensen (2001*a*) undertake a dynamic econometric analysis benefiting from the availability of data at the plant level. The study uses a panel of 13,550 US manufacturing plants that operated continuously during the export growth period 1984–92. The plants in the sample were a small percentage of the almost 200,000 plants surveyed in the Census of Manufactures in 1987 but accounted for 41 percent of total manufacturing employment and 70 percent of total manufacturing exports in that year. About 48 percent of the plants in the sample exported in 1984 and 54 percent in 1992.

The econometric analysis tests for the effects of entry costs, exchange rates, plant characteristics, state export promotion, and other factors, on the probability of exporting. Entry costs discourage exporting, a finding that is also reported by Roberts and Tybout (1997*a*) for Colombia. Favorable exchange rate shocks and plant characteristics indicative of past successes are found to significantly increase the probability of exporting. Export promotion by the states is found to have positive but statistically insignificant effects on exporting probabilities. However, the authors indicate that the evidence is subject to the caveat that the study focuses on a sample of large firms but state export promotion—which mounted to $96 million in 1992—often targets small and medium enterprises.

3.9.2. *Product Cycle Dynamics*

Why is it that innovative goods production initially takes place in innovating countries but is eventually shifted to developing countries which end up exporting the goods to the innovating countries? Vernon (1966) stresses that the entrepreneurship resources necessary to develop and market new products are concentrated in innovating countries. His product cycle hypothesis suggests a sequential process going from product development to exportation and importation. In the first stage of the product cycle, a new product is introduced. It is initially sold only in the innovating country but the product gradually builds up an export market abroad. In the second stage, innovating country exports decline as production shifts overseas to take advantage of low-cost production. In the third and final stage of the product cycle, the innovating good technology is standardized and diffuses to developing countries, which become the only exporters of the good.

Grossman and Helpman (1991*a,c*) develop models in which an innovative product is initially produced in the innovating country but there is a positive probability that a lower cost foreign competitor will successfully copy the technology in any given period. When imitation is accomplished, production shifts to the low wage developing country imitator (i.e. the South) and production in the innovating country (i.e. the North) ceases. A version of this imitation model introduces the notion of quality ladders entailing discrete qualitative improvements that continue forever over time. Each improvement takes place in the North and is eventually cloned by the South. But when a new generation of better quality products is developed in the North, production shifts back to the North until the South is able to imitate. The process of innovation and subsequent cloning results in a cyclical pattern of innovation and exportation in the North followed by exportation by the South. The rise of Korea as a leading computer industry exporter corresponds to this pattern of cloning technological improvements. Grossman and Helpman (1991*a*) contains a full discussion of these models and we refer the reader to the excellent exposition.

What is the evidence on the product cycle hypothesis? The product cycle hypothesis suggests two orderings. First, more advanced countries are able to begin exporting earlier than developing countries. Second, less advanced products are developed and exported earlier. In general, advanced countries are expected to begin exporting more advanced products earlier than less advanced countries.

Feenstra and Rose (2000) use these intuitions from the product cycle model to produce a ranking of products and a ranking of country sophistication. The product and country rankings are based on the product cycle notion that all goods are not exported by most countries and that countries tend to export goods to the United States in a sequential order. First, the ranking of unobserved product sophistication is constructed according to the first year of exportation. A product is deemed less advanced if it begins to be exported earlier to the United States. Second, the ranking of country sophistication is constructed according to the first year in which a country exported each commodity to the United States. A country is considered more advanced if it begins to export commodities earlier to the United States.

Empirical analysis shows that countries ranked as more advanced, in the sense that they tend to export sooner to the United States, tend to grow faster and to display higher levels of economic activity and of total factor productivity than countries ranked as less advanced. The top more sophisticated countries, according to a ranking based on the exports of manufacturing goods, are Japan, Germany, Canada, the United Kingdom, France, Italy, Switzerland, the Netherlands, and Mexico. Notice that the ranking is affected by trade relations with the United States, which explains why Mexico is number nine among 160 countries.

3.9.3. Do Weak Patent Rights Restrict Exporting?

The strength of intellectual property rights (IPRs) protection varies widely across countries. In particular, patents, copyrights, trademarks, and trade secrets are subject to weak protection in many developing countries.

Whether or not stronger IPRs help to expand exports is an empirical issue. In theory, stronger IPRs have ambiguous effects on exports as they exert a market power effect that restricts exports and a market expansion effect that expands exports. First, stronger IPRs protection restricts imitation and sustains greater market power. In turn, greater monopolistic power creates incentives to restrict export sales in order to increase prices. Second, stronger IPRs support exportation because better enforcement reduces the proliferation of low-price sales by local firms that mimick rivals. Third, stronger IPRs could shift the mode of supplying foreign markets towards FDI or licensing, although this effect is ambiguous. If exporting, FDI and licensing are substitute modes of supplying foreign markets, stronger IPRs tend to favor licensing. If exports and FDI are complementary and licensing is not important, though, stronger IPRs favor both FDI and exportation.

Is exportation actually discouraged by weak IPRs protection abroad? Maskus and Penubarti (1995) examine the relationship between the manufacturing exports of twenty-two OECD countries and the enforcement of patent rights in sixty-one countries (including OECD and developing countries). The estimated bilateral trade equations for twenty-eight 3-digit ISIC sectors in 1984 are based on an augmented version of the monopolistic competition model. Maskus and Penubarti develop an index of patent strength which corrects the property rights index of Rapp and Rozek (1990) for measurement error and endogeneity. The index of Rapp and Rozek measures the conformity of countries' national patent laws in 1984 with the standards proposed by the US Chamber of Commerce in 1987. The reduced form bilateral trade equation estimates imply that IPRs are trade-related. There is a strong positive relationship between the strength of patent protection and OECD manufacturing exports. In other words, countries with stronger IPRs tend to produce greater manufacturing exports.

The US government and US firms have often claimed that weak patent rights represent a barrier to US exports. Smith (1999) examines this question by utilizing the global patent protection index of Ginarte and Park (1997) and the property rights index of Rapp and Rozek (1990). The cross-section analysis for 1992 estimates bilateral trade equations based on the monopolistic competition and gravity models. The exporters are the fifty US states and Washington, DC while the importers are a group of ninety-six countries. Weak patent rights are found to restrict US exports only to countries heavily engaged in imitation, such as China. Paradoxically, stronger patent rights in countries that do not pose a threat of imitation reduce US exports to these markets. The proposed explanation is that stronger patent rights reinforce US monopoly power. The beneficiaries from patent rights gain greater monopoly power, which they can exploit by reducing the amount of production allocated to the market with stronger patent rights.

Does stronger protection favor high-tech exports? At first sight it would seem so but the answer is complex. First, stronger IPRs protection increases market power, which can offset the market expansion effects of stronger protection, and may induce high-tech firms to serve foreign markets by FDI, partially replacing exports. Second, the exportation of knowledge intensive goods can be based on the exploitation of learning economies (i.e. movements down the learning curve) or first-mover advantages. In these cases, exporters can appropriate the benefits from investments in R&D independently of the IPRs regime abroad. Third, empirical analyses might mask a true relationship if explanatory variables are omitted or the protection index does not fully capture the effects of IPRs protection.

Fink and Primo Braga (1999) use a gravity model of bilateral trade flows to estimate the effects of IPRs on high-tech product trade. They find a positive relationship between IPRs protection and trade flows for the total nonfuel trade aggregate, but do not find IPRs to be significant in explaining high-tech trade flows.

3.10. EXPORTS AND PRODUCTIVITY

Exporting plants have been found to exhibit greater productivity than nonexporting plants. However, this fact does not permit inferring that exporting causes superior performance. The question that is raised concerns the direction of causality. Does exporting induce productivity improvements or is it the other way around, that is, greater productivity leads to exporting?

3.10.1. *Why Are Exporters More Productive?*

Bernard and Jensen (1995) report that exports typically represent a small percentage of a plant's output and that exporters tend to grow faster than nonexporters in terms of shipments and employment. Moreover, US exporting plants display greater productivity and are more technologically sophisticated than nonexporting plants in the same industry. Bernard and Jensen (1999) report labor productivity differentials of 16–19 percent and TFP differentials of 13–16 percent favoring exporting plants over nonexporting plants in the same 4-digit industry.

Why is it that US exporting plants display greater productivity than nonexporting plants in the same industry? Complementary explanations focus on selection biases due to sunk costs, reallocation of resources toward more efficient plants induced by openness, the exploitation of economies of scale, and learning by exporting effects.

The presence of sunk costs can generate a positive relationship between productivity and exportation. The reason is that only the most efficient plants in an industry will find it profitable to pay the sunk costs of entering into foreign markets (Roberts and Tybout, 1997a). In this case, the causality goes from high productivity levels to exporting rather than the other way around.

A second explanation for why exporting firms display greater productivity than non-exporting firms is that exporting is associated with the reallocation of resources from less to more efficient plants. This productivity effect is not due to enhanced intrafirm productivity of exporting plants but rather to ex ante productivity differentials that determine exportation efforts and production reallocation.

Let us examine why trade can increase productivity without generating intrafirm productivity improvements. Consider a reduction in trade barriers in a setup in which firms are heterogeneous and differ in productivity levels. Bernard *et al.* (2000) develop a model in which protection shelters inefficient firms. Lower trade barriers serve to filter out low productivity plants while permitting high productivity plants to export. The productivity-enhancing reallocation effect of opening produces a positive relationship between exportation and productivity. Melitz (2002) develops a dynamic monopolistic competition model in which firms differ in terms of productivity. Trade contributes to the Darwinian evolution of industries forcing least efficient firms to contract or exit while promoting the growth of the more efficient firms. Trade liberalization leads to inter-firm reallocations toward more productive firms.

Let us examine the evidence supporting the trade-driven reallocation effect. Improvements in the efficiency of factor use can be measured by changes in total factor productivity (TFP). Growth in total factor productivity is measured as the component of changes in output that is not accounted for by changes in factor use. Suppose that output Q is a function of labor L, capital K, and technology A

$$Q = F(L, K, A) \quad \rightarrow \quad \Delta Q = F_L \Delta L + F_K \Delta K + \Delta TFP,$$

where the change in *TFP* is the residual term representing the change of technology or productivity change. Assuming that the marginal productivity of labor and capital are equal to the wage rate w and the rental on capital r, $F_L = w$ and $F_K = r$, yields

$$\Delta TFP = \Delta Q - w \Delta L - r \Delta K.$$

In words, the change in *TFP* in relation to output is the residual computed as the change of output Q minus the component of this change that is explained by changes in the use of factors.

The change in aggregate total factor productivity TFP_A of all plants can be decomposed into (1) an own (or within plant) productivity effect measured as the change in plant i productivity, ΔTFP_i, times the average output share $\overline{SH_i}$ (the share of plant i output in total output), plus (2) a reallocation effect measured as the change in the output share of plant i from years $t - 1$ to t, ΔSH_i, times the average total factor productivity $\overline{TFP_i}$

$$\Delta TFP_A = \sum_{i=1}^{I} \Delta TFP_i \cdot \overline{SH_i} + \sum_{i=1}^{I} \Delta SH_i \cdot \overline{TFP_i}.$$

The productivity effect derived from resource reallocations has been detected by several researchers. Bernard and Jensen (2001*b*) find that 58 percent of the change in TFP in a sample of US firms can be explained by own productivity effects (the change in *TFP* times the average output share) while 42 percent can be explained by reallocation effects measuring increasing output shares at more productive plants (the change in the output share times the average *TFP*).

3.10.2. Scale Economies, Productivity, and Liberalization

In the presence of increasing returns, an output expansion lowers the average cost of production. An explanation for exporters' superior productivity is that exportation expands the size of the market, induces an expansion in output and permits exploiting economies of scale.

The Mexican trade liberalization of the 1980s offers evidence of productivity gains. Tybout and Westbrook (1995) plant-level study shows that average cost fell in most industries and that tradeable goods industries experienced the greatest cost reductions. Open sectors successfully shifted market share toward more productive plants and benefited from lower intermediate good prices. However, productivity gains due to the exploitation of scale economies were minor and were not correlated with increases in foreign competition. The authors conclude that their study casts doubts on simulation studies of trade liberalization focusing on scale effects as a major source of efficiency gains. Head and Ries (1999) and Trefler (2001) find limited scale economies due to the trade liberalization produced by the Canada–US Free Trade Agreement implemented in 1989.

3.10.3. Does Exporting Raise Total Factor Productivity?

An explanation for the greater productivity of exporting relative to nonexporting firms stresses the influence of exporting in productivity rather than the other way around. The key idea is that exporters are more productive because exporting generates increases in productivity. A main factor alleged to increase exporters productivity is the so-called learning-by-exporting effect. Notice that openness on the import side can increase the productivity of both exporters and import-competing plants. First, foreign competitive pressures cause previously sheltered inefficient plants to shut down and induce firms to organize production more efficiently. Second, trade makes available lower priced high quality equipment and intermediate inputs.

Does empirical evidence support the claim that firms (plants) learn by exporting in the sense that they become more efficient after becoming exporters? The productivity and growth superiority of exporting plants is not direct evidence indicating that exports increase plant productivity growth rates. Exporters will exhibit high productivity relative to nonexporters if there is a self-selection bias in the sample of exporters.

Clerides *et al.* (1998) examine export market participation and production costs for a sample consisting of all Colombian plants with at least ten workers (1981–91), 2800 large Mexican firms (1986–90) and most Moroccan firms with at least ten workers (1984–90). They search for evidence that plants' stochastic cost processes shift when they break into foreign markets. The key finding is that relatively efficient plants become exporters but that plants' unit costs are not affected by previous export market participation. They conclude that the efficiency gap between exporters and non-exporters is due to self-selection. More efficient firms are able to break into export markets but there is no evidence that they 'learn-by-exporting'.

Bernard and Jensen (2001*b*) do not find evidence that exporting leads to greater *TFP* growth. They examine the impact of exports on the total factor productivity growth rate of individual plants in the US manufacturing sector. A plant with exporter status in any given year is found to have 0.72 percent lower productivity growth rate in the subsequent year than a similar firm producing only for the domestic market. That is, the exporting status of a plant at a given year is negatively correlated with following year's productivity growth.

One possible explanation of the poor productivity performance of exporting status is that the sample combines firms that continue exporting and those that stop exporting. Indeed, exporting plants that do not continue to export tend to have less productivity growth in the subsequent period. However, exporting plants that continue to export and nonexporting plants have the same productivity trajectory. In other words, the productivity trajectory of a firm depends on the controlling variables rather than on whether it is a continuous exporter or not.

Were there plant productivity improvements attributable to Chilean trade liberaliz-ation during 1979–86? Pavcnik (2002) focuses on whether producers of exportables and import-competing products experienced productivity gains, controlling for self-selection due to plant exit of less productive firms. On one hand, the analysis does not indicate that exporters exhibited productivity improvements attributable to trade liberalization. In fact, exporters did not exhibit productivity improvements relative to the nontraded goods sector. On the other hand, plants in import-competing sectors became more productive than plants in the nontraded goods sector (during 1981–86). The differences in import-competing industries' productivity increases attributable to trade liberalization were estimated to range from 3 to 10.4 percent. The details of Pavcnik's econometric analysis are presented in the chapter on trade liberalization.

3.11. ARE TERMS OF TRADE EFFECTS SIGNIFICANT?

A country's terms of trade, that is, the price of a country's exports relative to its imports, is a key determinant of the standard of living and welfare. Large countries' ability to alter their terms of trade often underlies trade policies while exogenous terms of trade changes can have substantial welfare and allocation effects in small countries.

Terms of trade effects underlie diverse economic theories and calculations. First, the welfare effects of computable general equilibrium models rely in significant terms of trade effects. Second, the theory of the role of the WTO is based on the need to counteract large countries' incentives to set tariffs as a mechanism to affect their terms of trade. Third, the theory of regionalism is partly based on the notion that preferential arrangements are formed to exploit terms of trade effects. Fourth, immiserizing growth theories explaining why a larger size and growth can adversely affect a country rely on adverse terms of trade effects due to a larger supply of goods (Bhagwati, 1958). Acemoglu and Ventura (2002) rely on a deterioration of the terms of trade to explain income convergence and a relatively stable world income distribution in the presence of richer countries exhibiting higher investment rates relative to poorer countries. Davis and Weinstein (2002e) argue that migration creates an excess supply of host country production in world markets causing a deterioration of the terms of trade and an income loss from immigration. Fifth, theories explaining slow growth in developing countries stress that secular adverse terms of trade effects hinder the development efforts of primary sector exporters.

Are terms of trade effects significant in practice? The practical importance of terms of trade effects remains a contested issue. On one side, many economists reject the notion that terms of trade effects are important in practice, except for monopoly exports of coffee, oil and other products. Hummels and Klenow (2002) do not find terms of trade deterioration effects from greater trade by richer countries.

On the other side, several studies offer evidence of either substantial terms of trade effects in different situations. Goldberg and Knetter (1997) find that the degree of exchange rate passthrough is about sixty percent on average. That is, a 10 percent change in the exchange rate results in a 4 percent change in the terms of trade.

Preferential trading arrangements offer evidence of trade of terms effects. Kreinin (1961) finds that one-third of US tariff reductions negotiated under the GATT Kennedy Round were passed on to US consumers and two-thirds benefitted foreign exporters as terms of trade improvements for their exports. Winters and Chang (2000) examine how the relative tariff-inclusive prices of United States and Japanese sales in Spain respond to changes in relative costs and tariffs between EU member and non-member countries. Using data for 1980–93, they estimate an elasticity of 0.4–0.8 for the United States and 0.6–0.9 for Japan, meaning that a 10 percent preference offered to members of the European Community (EC) cause the United States and Japan pre-tariff prices to fall relative to EC pre-tariff prices by about 2–6 and 1–4 percent. Winters and Chang (1999) find that regional liberalization under Mercosur entailed substantial terms of trade effects. They utilize data of nonMercosur country exports to Brazil during the 1990s and report that nonmember countries substantially cut their prices in favor of Brazil to maintain their competitiveness *vis-à-vis* Mercosur country members. This evidence suggests that the formation of a preferential arrangement such as Mercosur entails changes of the terms of trade.

Acemoglu and Ventura (2002) examine the elasticity of substitution in consumption as an indicator of the demand impact of given terms of trade changes. The estimated elasticity of substitution in consumption through which terms of trade operate are substantial. Moreover, they confirm the prediction that greater exporter investment rates, and associated higher income levels, lead to exporter terms of trade deterioration.

3.12. CONCLUSIONS

The controversy on the empirical relevance of alternative trade approaches has been and continues to be a powerful source of empirical and theoretical work in the field. The ongoing revival of empirical trade analysis has provided modification of standard models that perform well and offer a detail account of the determinants of international trade. Several modifications of the HOV model achieve high correlations between measured and predicted factor contents. A most important element of this revival is the elaboration and public diffusion of new data sets by Leamer, Feenstra, the OECD, and others.

The simple HOV model has died as a general empirical tool but it has been successfully replaced by several closely related spinoffs. Daniel Trefler uncovers two simple modifications of the HOV model that greatly improve model performance. The first modification relaxes the assumption that all countries have the same technologies and allows for international productivity differences. The second modification introduces a demand function that permits home biases in consumption. The modified models improve the performance of the standard model in predicting the factor content of trade flows.

Subsequent research along alternative lines has renewed empirical trade analysis. In order to explain intra-industry trade among countries with similar factor endowments, a major part of global exchange, a line of empirical studies has focused on models incorporating product variety, some form of increasing returns and imperfect competition. Bilateral trade flows behave according to the gravity model in the sense that they tend to increase with income levels and decline with the distance between the trading partners. A long line of studies suggest that tariffs and transport costs do not represent a major trade barrier in industrial countries and that many forms of transport costs have declined over time. However, a home market bias remains detectable both across nations and on the subnational level (Wolf, 2000).

3.13. APPENDIX

3.13.1. Testing Weak Factor Content Restrictions

Recall the bilateral factor content equation relating country k's gross import vector of factor content FC^{kc} from country c to the vector of country k imports from country c, T^{kc}

$$FC^{kc} = B^c (I - A^c)^{-1} T^{kc} = B^c Q^c - B^c (I - A^c)^{-1} D^{kc}$$

obtained by pre-multiplying the trade equation by the technology matrix $B^c (I - A^c)^{-1}$ accounting for inputs and direct productive factors.

Country c's revenue function is

$$p'Q^c = R(p, FE^c).$$

Suppose that country k receives a supplementary endowment, over and above its own endowment, equal to its gross import of factor content FC^{kc} from country c, $FE^{kc} = FC^{kc}$. Because the additional production equals at least the value of gross imports of $p'T^{kc}$ and Π is concave the revenue function is

$$p'(Q^c + T^{kc}) \le R(p, FE^c + FE^{kc})$$
$$\le R(p, FE^c) + R_{FE}(p, FE^c)FE^{kc}$$
$$= p'Q^c + w^k FE^{kc}$$
$$\rightarrow p'T^{kc} \le w^k FE^{kc}.$$

Subtracting country c's perfect competition relation $p'T^{kc} = w^c FE^{kc}$ from the last inequality yields

$$0 \le (w^k - w^c)FE^{kc}.$$

A similar equation holds for country c

$$0 \le (w^k - w^c)FE^{ck}.$$

The previous inequalities are the ones appearing in (3.13).

3.13.2. Derivation of (3.20)

If preferences are identical and homothetic and countries are specialized, expression (3.17) implies that the total volume of trade between members c and g of group G is $VT = s^c Y^g + s^g Y^c$. Balance trade implies $2s^c Y^g = 2s^c s^g Y^W$, which achieves a maximum if $s^c = s^k$ and approaches zero if s^c or s^g approach zero.

The ratio of the total volume of trade between all members of group of countries G divided by group income is.

$$VT^G = \sum_{c \in G} \sum_{g \in G, g \ne c} s^c Y^g = Y^G \sum_{c \in G} s^c \left(\sum_{g \in G, g \ne c} \frac{Y^c}{Y^G} \right) = Y^G \sum_{c \in G} s^c \left(1 - \frac{Y^c}{Y^G} \right),$$

where $s^c = Y^c/Y^W$. Dividing by Y^G

$$\frac{VT^G}{Y^G} = \frac{Y^G}{Y^W} \sum_{c \in G} \frac{Y^c}{Y^G} \left(1 - \frac{Y^c}{Y^G}\right) = \frac{Y^G}{Y^W} \left[\sum_{c \in G} \frac{Y^c}{Y^G} - \sum_{c \in G} \left(\frac{Y^c}{Y^G}\right)^2\right]$$

$$= \frac{Y^G}{Y^W} \left[1 - \sum_{c \in G} \left(\frac{Y^c}{Y^G}\right)^2\right],$$

which achieves a maximum when countries' shares in group income are similar and $1 - \sum(Y^c/Y^G)^2$ is interpreted as a size similarity index.

4

Geography and Location

How does globalization, in the sense of lower barriers to trade, affect the location of economic activity and countries' real national incomes? What determines whether a particular location constitutes a magnet for capital and labor? What determines specialization and trade patterns in the presence of capital and labor mobility? These questions require changing the scenario from one with given factor endowments to one admitting factor mobility. They also require developing a theory of dynamic economic geography, which seeks to explain why economic activities are concentrated in particular countries, regions, and cities and how activity clustering develops over time.

The ample evidence of concentration of economic activity presents unmistakable geographical imprints. The shift from rural to industrial and subsequently service economies is mirrored by the development of large metropolitan areas and cities that attract a large proportion of countries' population. London, Paris, New York, Chicago, Los Angeles, Barcelona, Buenos Aires, and other city clusters developed in locations providing access to trade routes and transportation through harbors, rivers, and channels. Canadian manufacturing is heavily concentrated in Ontario. In fact, most of Canada's population and economic activity concentrates near the US border. The US concentration magnets include the East Coast, the West Coast, and the Great Lakes in the Midwest. The Ruhr region is Germany's industrial backbone. The concentration of economic activity and income per capita in 'northern' countries stands in contrast with 'southern' countries development plights.

In many cases, industrial regions spread across national borders. The US manufacturing belt extends to include the Ontario manufacturing region in Canada. The region encompassing the Ruhr, Belgium, and Northern France constitutes an international manufacturing triangle. These cross-national clusters show that agglomeration forces can be stronger than the barriers implicit in national borders, including different political, regulatory, and judicial regimes.

What determines the pattern of location and the growth of economic clusters such as cities, regions, and countries? The historical development of population and industrial clusters reflects the key role of physical geography. However, physical geography often becomes a past history factor that fails to explain cluster longevity by itself. Moreover, trade and other policies can have substantial regional effects, depending on regional characteristics. An interesting case to follow is the impact of China's 2002 WTO accession on Hong Kong. About 40 percent of China's current trade is routed through Hong Kong, a large international financial center that plays an intermediary role between China and the rest of the world. China's WTO accession might induce foreign investment and services already established in Hong Kong to move to Shanghai or other mainland centers. However, this move might be discouraged by corporate taxes, which are higher in Shanghai than in Hong Kong, and by the current sophistication of markets and governance variables, which work in favor of Hong Kong.

Once we move to the municipal and intracountry spheres, the power of international trade analysis weakens. Explanations based on given national policies, factor endowments, and comparative advantages must be reinforced with further considerations. A policy rationale must consider regional policies and explain why national policies might have different cross-regional impact. Factor endowments cannot be taken as given in a regional context. There are few limitations on internal migration of human and physical capital across regions and cities, especially in the long term. It is quite easy for New York firms to hire a Californian with the right skills and the candidate faces no restrictions on migration. Regional endowments become endogenous variables to be explained by the analysis. By the same token, the comparative advantage of regions and cities become variables to be explained.

Models of economic geography tend to produce core-periphery structures if trading costs are low enough. A key element of the explanation of the location of activities involves finding out what are the incentives triggering sustained migration to particular clusters. Large migratory pressures and movements of capital across frontiers take place despite a host of international hiring and investment restrictions imposed by both source and host countries.

The spatial location of production raises a host of questions relating to the growth processes of regions (cities, nations). The following questions guide our exposition.

1. Why do economic activities agglomerate in particular locations?
2. What motivates labor and capital to migrate to particular metropolitan areas, regional magnets and Northern countries rather than Southern countries?
3. Why do real wages vary within countries and across countries and what are the resulting migration patterns?
4. What are the growth consequences of location decisions, why do regions grow at divergent rates and why do they settle at different per capita incomes?
5. How do regions interact and what patterns of agglomeration, production specialization and trade emerge?
6. To what extent is production location largely arbitrary, dependent on history or based on fundamental economic factors?
7. How do clusters affect the competitive advantage of nations?

Sections 4.1 and 4.2 examine the causes of agglomeration. Section 4.3 explores regional dynamics. Sections 4.4 and 4.5 discuss the impact of preferential agreements and the choice between North–South and South–South integration. Sections 4.6 and 4.7 examine the empirical evidence on agglomeration and location.

4.1. WHAT CAUSES AGGLOMERATION?

Geographic concentration of people and industry is extensive. Porter (1990) documents clustering in many internationally competitive industries. Krugman (1991c) reports that about half of the three-digit manufacturing industries examined had a higher Gini concentration coefficient than the US auto industry, which concentrates half of its US employment in Michigan, Indiana, and Ohio. The fact that the auto industry's Gini coefficient was slightly above median indicates substantial geographic concentration in many other industries. The locational Gini coefficient, G, provides a measure of the geographic concentration of an industry. It is half of the sum (over all regions) of the absolute values of the differences between (1) the share of region k in national employment in industry i, s_i^k, and (2) the share of region k in national manufacturing employment, s^k,

$$ G = \frac{1}{2} \sum_{k=1}^{K} \left| s_i^k - s^k \right| = \frac{1}{2} \sum_{k=1}^{K} \left| s_i^k - \sum_i s_i^k \right|. $$

If industry i is equally dispersed across all regions, $s_i^k = s^k$, the index is equal to zero. If the industry is concentrated in a single small region k', the index is equal to $\frac{1}{2}\left(1 - s^{k'} + \sum_{k \neq k'} s^k\right) \approx (1/2)2 = 1$, where $s^{k'} \approx 0$ and $\sum_{k \neq k'} \approx 1$.

Economists have focused on several broad approaches to the link between geographic industrial concentration, regional specialization and regional growth. Let us review them. Detailed analyses can be found in Fujita (1988) Fujita *et al.* (1999) and Fujita and Thisse (2002).

4.1.1. Localized External Economies

Marshall (1920), Henderson (1974, 1988), and others establish a link between agglomeration and localized economies that are external to the firm. Increasing returns to scale deriving from positive Marshallian externalities between firms and workers concentrated in the same location make them more productive. For instance, localized knowledge spillovers expand the exchange of ideas and enhance learning, which in turn trigger further clustering of activities. Another localized externality is labor market pooling, referring to the timely and low cost availability of resources (i.e. skilled technicians, specialists) serving a localized industry but not a dispersed industry.

4.1.2. Internal Increasing Returns and Market Access

The internal increasing returns approach to location in geographic space focuses on agglomeration forces attracting consumers and firms producing at decreasing average costs to particular locations in the presence of costs of accessing final goods and inputs.

First of all, observe that this framework combines increasing returns at the firm level (i.e. internal to the firm) and transport costs. Internal increasing returns stemming from concentrating production facilities in a single location do not necessarily generate agglomeration. The reason is that internal returns from production concentration can be exploited at any location.

Second, the costs of accessing goods and services give a role for spacial proximity and regional concentration in the presence of internal returns. Transport costs create cost advantages of proximity to specialized input suppliers and consumers. Transport cost savings when utilizing the services of locally available specialized inputs (cost linkages) and selling differentiated inputs and final goods (demand linkages) lead to agglomeration economies even if increasing returns are internal to firms. For instance, the availability of specialized labor at low cost helps to explain why the car industry is concentrated in Detroit, the aerospace industry is concentrated in the Toulouse area, and high-tech firms are agglomerated in California Silicon Valley.

There are several variants of the framework with internal increasing returns and cost of accessing goods and services. Rivera–Batiz (1988) develops a monopolistically competitive model in which consumers are endowed with love of variety, firms utilize differentiated nontraded inputs and production takes place at decreasing average costs due to fixed costs. He examines locational clustering in the presence of economies of scale and nontradeable intermediate inputs, that is, inputs subject to infinite transport costs (e.g. services). Firms gain from being close to markets featuring a large demand and supply because of nontradeability. Krugman (1991*d*) examines the case in which agglomeration is justified as a means to exploit large market benefits while minimizing fixed production costs per unit and finite transportation costs. Firms gain from being close to markets featuring a large demand and supply due to transport costs. Venables (1996) examines the interdependence of demand and supplier decisions in the presence of vertical linkages and transport costs.

4.1.3. Fundamentals and Random Shocks

A limitation of geography models based on externalities and internal returns in the presence of transport costs is that they explain agglomeration but not the specific location where activity agglomerates. It is clear that economic fundamentals, including physical geography traits, help to explain why major magnets developed. But, it is often difficult to explain why a specific magnet specialized in a specific activity. Many experts take the position that random and arbitrary historical elements must be included in a full theory of agglomeration. For instance, a Silicon Valley could have developed around the MIT, Harvard and Boston University network rather than around Stanford University.

The theory of locational fundamentals developed by Krugman (1996) asserts that location is based on economic fundamentals that in turn contain random elements. This approach predicts that, as long as fundamentals are unchanged, agglomeration patterns are maintained after temporary shocks. Long term changes in regional location patterns are explained by random and sustainable shifts in economic fundamentals.

The random growth approach states that the size distribution of cities emerges from stochastic processes. This approach explains Zipf's Law, also called rank–size rule, about the distribution of city sizes. This law or rule, discovered by George Kingsley Zipf states that the log of size of a city as measured by its population (or the log if its population relative to country population) is a negatively sloping linear function of the log of the rank of the city in its country according to population size. Gabaix (1999) explains this intriguing regularity by using a model in which both the growth rate and the variance of the growth rate of a city's population are independent of city size.

4.2. MODELING AGGLOMERATION AND LOCATION

A revival of studies on geography, location and trade took place in the nineties as economists and business researchers focused on optimal location choices and the general equilibrium effects of these decisions (Krugman, 1991c). Location choices can generate agglomeration economies benefiting those firms coinciding in choosing to produce in a given location.

The Competitive Advantage of Nations (1990) by Michael Porter, presented influential evidence suggesting that comparative advantages, including natural resource endowments and pools of labor resources, were not anymore the key to the competitive advantages of nations or locations in global competition. The analysis of ten leading exporting countries suggested that companies' competitive advantages (rather than countries comparative advantages) derive from firm productivity as determined by innovation.

Porter stresses that a country's capacity to innovate depends on a 'diamond' of four elements: factor conditions, demand conditions, supporting industries, and firm strategy, structure and rivalry. These elements are embodied in 'clusters' or groups of firms, suppliers, industries, and institutions that agglomerate in a location. The concept of 'competitive advantage' and the analysis of clusters, agglomeration, productivity and innovation have been embraced by businesspersons and policymakers, who have translated these ideas into cluster promotion projects.

In the 1970s, many critics of globalization asserted that the South (i.e. periphery) was bearing the costs of globalization and recommended some form of delinking from the developed world. The irony of the policy recommendation was that the South was being harmed by delinking caused by economic factors pulling resources toward the North. Specifically, most trade and foreign direct investment took place among developed countries not between developed and developing countries.

Lucas (1990) pointed out that agglomeration effects help explain why it is that capital does not flow from rich to poor countries. The law of diminishing returns suggests that the marginal product of capital should be smaller in capital-abundant rich countries than in labor-abundant poor countries. Therefore, capital should flow to the South. In practice, this migration of capital is not observed. In fact, foreign direct investment tends to concentrate in the North rather than the South. An explanation hinges on agglomeration effects that increase Northern productivity.

By the 2000s, development thinking had taken a turn away from North-bashing. Many thought that the North (i.e. the core) was bearing globalization costs due to the rise of Asian economies and the shift of production to low wage locations.

4.2.1. Globalization and Linkages: No Interregional Labor Mobility

Is globalization a win-win strategy for both the North and the South? Or does one of the parties inevitably lose? Krugman and Venables (1995) develop a North–South, core-periphery general equilibrium model of location in which who wins and who loses from globalization depends on the phase of the globalization process. The model assumes perfect intersectoral mobility within a region but no interregional mobility. This case is akin to the labor mobility situation within the European Union. Because labor mobility is low (in the 1990s, only one percent of a country's workers were born in another European Union country), an expansion of a country's manufacturing sector must draw its labor force from national agriculture.

Let us characterize globalization as a continuous decline in transport costs and examine how this decline affects real national incomes, the location of manufacturing and the gains from trade. The impact of globalization can be described by an inverted U-shaped process in which the real income gap initially increases (i.e. divergence) and subsequently declines (i.e. convergence).

The North and the South are assumed to have similar preferences and endowments. Moreover, they use the same technology to produce manufactures and agricultural goods. Countries do differ ex post but income and location effects are not determined by ex ante differences in countries' characteristics. There is free entry and exit of manufacturing firms and free mobility of labor across sectors but not locations.

Manufacturing M produces differentiated goods and intermediate inputs and has a monopolistically competitive market structure. The agriculture sector A is assumed to be perfectly competitive and agricultural goods are used as numeraire so that $p_A = 1$. Manufactures carry transport costs while agricultural goods are assumed not to entail transport costs. Observe that the assumption that transport costs are lower in agriculture applies to some but not all manufactures. Bulldozers and grand pianos are not easily transportable but low weight manufactures such as CDs entail lower transport costs than agricultural perishables.

Consumers' preferences can be represented by the expenditure function

$$E = V p_A^{1-\gamma} p_M^{\gamma}, \tag{4.1}$$

where p_A is the price of agricultural goods and p_M is the manufacturing sector price index. The consumer's budget constraint $E = wL$ indicates that expenditure must be equal to the value of labor services wL, where w denotes the wage rate and L represents units of labor. $V = wL/p_A^{1-\gamma} p_M^{\gamma}$ denotes the real wage bill.

The price of manufactures is (see Chapter 2)

$$p_M = [np^{1-\sigma} + n^*(p^*T)^{1-\sigma}]^{1/(1-\sigma)}$$

depends on the number n of varieties made and sold in the North at price p, the n^* varieties produced in the South and sold at price p^*T (inclusive of the Samuelson's iceberg-type transport cost T) in the North and the demand elasticity $\sigma > 1$ for a single variety.

Agricultural output Q_A is produced with only labor and exhibits constant returns to scale, $Q_A = L_A$. For simplicity, let us assume that manufacturing uses its own output as input. The total cost function TC of a representative manufacturing firm that sells q^{local} units in the domestic market and exports q^{exp} units is

$$TC = w^{1-\mu} p_M^{\mu} [f + a(q^{local} + q^{exp})], \tag{4.2}$$

where w stands for the wage rate, μ is the share of intermediates in production costs, f is the fixed cost and a is per-unit marginal output cost. Fixed and variable costs are assumed to require labor and intermediates in the same proportions so that fixed costs are $w^{1-\mu} p_M^{\mu} f$ and marginal costs are $w^{1-\mu} p_M^{\mu} a$.

Manufacturing firm profits are given by

$$\pi = pq^{local} + p(T)q^{exp} - w^{1-\mu} p_M^{\mu} (f + aq), \tag{4.3}$$

where local consumers do not pay transport costs for locally produced goods.

Intermediates generate forward and backward linkages. Both of these linkages among firms are stronger the higher the value of μ in (4.2). Forward and backward linkages in the monopolistically competitive manufacturing sector are modeled by introducing transport costs à la Krugman (1980) into a differentiated inputs setup à la Ethier (1982*a*). The resulting linkages represent centripetal forces in the sense of creating incentives inducing firms to move to more agglomerated locations.

Forward or cost linkages refer to the reduction in the cost of producing final and intermediate goods due to greater local input availability. A region offering a wider range of intermediate goods generates savings in transport costs to local users, thus providing cheaper access to inputs. Cost-reducing forward linkages among firms in one location arise because abundant locally produced input varieties entail a lower price index for intermediates. *Ceteris paribus*, less costly inputs lower the average and marginal production costs of firms using these inputs, including both final goods and intermediate goods producers. Lower production costs raise short-run firm profitability in regions with a larger number of firms thus inducing additional firm entry and intersectorial mobility (interregional labor migration triggered by higher real wages is ignored) and further agglomeration.

Backward or demand linkages refer to the greater demand due to the lower prices implied by savings in transport costs when a higher number of firms produce in a given location. These linkages arise because the agglomeration of manufacturing firms increases local demand for locally produced differentiated inputs and final goods, which can be bought at zero transport cost. *Ceteris paribus*, these demand linkages cause the demand and marginal revenue curves facing intermediate and final goods producers to shift upward. A region featuring greater input and final good demand due to availability at a zero trading cost is more attractive to input and final good producers than a region with a smaller manufacturing sector. Greater demand and marginal revenue raise short-run firm profitability in regions with a larger number of firms, thus inducing further entry of firms into the region (and workers if real wages were higher and interregional mobility were allowed).

The cumulative causation process triggered by demand and cost linkages can explain regional inequalities. Greater and greater agglomeration based on linkages leads to a core-periphery structure in equilibrium.

Linkages constitute centripetal forces that can be offset by two different types of centrifugal forces. These so-called neoclassical forces, known as centrifugal forces because they oppose spacial agglomeration and encourage dispersion of activity, include product and factor market competition effects. The procompetitive or product market competition effect arises because additional firms lower the manufacturing industry price index, the demand facing each existing producer of varieties and the price of each variety. This price competition effect reduces profits and thus discourages agglomeration. Smith and Venables (1988) show that greater market size has a procompetitive effect in an oligopolistic market composed of firms that behave strategically *vis-à-vis* each other. The procompetitive effect arises under either Cournot or Bertrand conjectures (see the chapters on rivalry and mode of competition).

The factor market competition effect refers to the positive impact on wages of an increase in the number of firms in a region. In other words, industry agglomeration increases wages and thus reduces the profits of the producers of varieties.

In short, the spacial concentration of producers offers 'large market advantages' through forward and backward linkages. These agglomeration effects, arising in the presence of scale economies and transport costs, tend to be persistent and can build up a circular process favoring further agglomeration. This feature explains why an initial small difference between two almost equal locations can cause them to diverge over time. Agglomeration also creates centrifugal forces opposing further agglomeration. Centrifugal effects derive from a lower demand per variety as the number of varieties increase and the positive effect of agglomeration on real wages and firms' costs.

Whether centripetal or centrifugal effects dominate determines the equilibrium pattern and dynamics of agglomeration when there is intersectoral but no interregional mobility. There is a critical value of the transport cost level T^{Break} at levels below which the stability of the symmetric regional equilibrium is broken and a core-periphery structure emerges as a stable equilibrium. Krugman and Venables (1995) and Puga (1999) show that the value of T^{Break} is

$$T^{Break} = \left[\frac{1 + \mu \; \sigma(1+\mu) - 1}{1 - \mu \; \sigma(1-\mu) - 1} \right]^{1/(\sigma-1)} = \left[\frac{(1+\mu)(\rho+\mu)}{(1-\mu)(\rho-\mu)} \right]^{-\rho/(1-\rho)},$$

where $\rho = (\sigma - 1)/\sigma$ and $1 < \sigma$. In other words, if transport costs fall below T^{Break}, a core-periphery structure develops. Moreover, Puga (1999) shows that if transport costs fall enough, the real wage differential increases to a point at which polarization is reversed as firms move to the South in search of low wages.

4.3. DYNAMICS OF CORE-PERIPHERY STRUCTURES

A basic objective of the theory of regional development is to explain the pattern and dynamics of agglomeration. Industrial concentration patterns are stable in the short run but undergo changes over decades-long time spans. Witness the rise of the South in the United States in the past decades and the development of the United States–Mexico border area following the implementation of the maquiladora program. Economic geography models often imply that a core-periphery structure emerges if trading costs are low enough and do not emerge if transport costs are high enough.

A simple version of the dynamics of a core-periphery model can be developed by focusing on a two-region economy that produces differentiated manufactures (or services) and a homogeneous agricultural good. Farmers are assumed to be attached to land so that they do not move or change activity. By contrast, labor employed in manufacturing is fully mobile across the two regions considered. In other words, this setting allows interregional manufacturing labor mobility but neither intersectoral nor interregional farmer mobility. This labor mobility pattern differs from Krugman and Venables (1995) analysis with perfect intersectoral mobility but no interregional mobility.

Agricultural activities are evenly distributed across the land. The key question concerns the allocation of manufacturing production across the two regions. Manufactures carry transport costs while agricultural goods are assumed not to entail transport costs.

A key element of the explanation of agglomeration is to find out why productive factors move to particular locations. If labor is the only productive factor, one must specify the dynamics of interregional labor migration. The engine of migration is the level of real wages. Workers move towards locations showing agglomeration because they offer a higher real wage rate. Agglomeration generates local pecuniary externalities.

If workers maximize the lifetime expected utility of the income earned from working at different locations, they will migrate toward locations offering high real wages. Baldwin (1999) examines forward-looking workers who formulate migration decisions by evaluating their entire future income stream. He considers the case in which (1) migration costs are quadratic in the flow of migration per unit of time and (2) workers have static expectations in the sense that they anticipate that the current real wage gap will persist forever. The rate of change in the share of Northern labor employed in manufacturing to the global amount of labor devoted to manufacturing, $s_{LM} = L_M/L_M^W$, is shown to be equal to

$$\dot{s}_{LM} \equiv \frac{ds_{LM}}{dt} = \left(\frac{w}{p} - \frac{w^*}{p^*}\right) s_{LM},$$

where w/p and w^*/p^* represent Northern and Southern real wages. Migration flows are a function of the current real wage gap and the Northern share s_{LM} in global manufacturing labor. In other words, migrants move towards locations currently offering high real wages in manufacturing and featuring a larger size of the manufacturing sector relative to alternative locations.

Figures 4.1–4.3 depict three different real wage dynamic patterns as a function of the share of the North in global manufacturing labor and output. Each dynamic pattern corresponds to a different level of transport costs. A comparison of the figures provides a graphic illustration of the relation between transport costs and the behavior of real

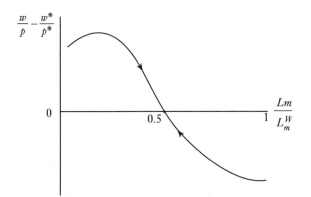

Figure 4.1. *Real wage dynamics with high transport costs*

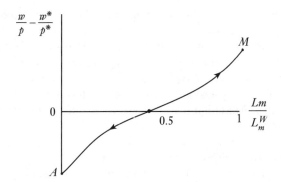

Figure 4.2. *Real wage dynamics with low transport costs*

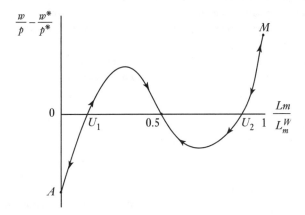

Figure 4.3. *Real wage dynamics with intermediate transport costs*

wage differentials. The formal dynamic analysis can be found in Fujita *et al.* (1999) and Baldwin (1999).

What is the outcome of agglomeration processes driven by migration dynamics and local pecuniary externalities? Consider a two-region economy. The equilibrium pattern of agglomeration depends on how the level of transport costs affects the balance between agglomeration and dispersion forces.

1. Figure 4.1 depicts a stable symmetric equilibrium in which both regions have the same size and income per capita in the long term. This pattern evolves if there is a negative relation between the share in global manufacturing labor and real wage differentials near the symmetric equilibrium with $s_{LM} = 0.5$. A high initial real wage differential favoring the North will attract migrants, increase the share of the North in manufacturing, and thus reduce real wages. As a result, there is convergence to the symmetric equilibrium in which real wages are equalized.
2. Figure 4.2 depicts a core-periphery equilibrium, in which one core region concentrates the whole manufacturing sector and the other region becomes a periphery fully specialized in agriculture. The manufacturing region is identified with the North and the periphery with the South. This pattern evolves if there is a positive relation between the share of manufacturing and real wage differentials. A high initial real wage differential favoring the North attracts migrants and increases the share of the North in global manufacturing, which results in an even higher real wage differential. Migration dynamics creates greater and greater incentives for the migration of manufacturing labor to the North. Because agricultural labor is immobile (say, farmers are attached to their land), the core region features higher real wages than the agriculture-based periphery.
3. Figure 4.3 depicts a path-dependent equilibrium. This is the case in which the evolution of the system depends on the initial point. If the initial global share of manufacturing is close enough to the $s_{LM} = 0.5$ symmetric equilibrium, there is convergence to that equilibrium. If an economy starts with the global share of manufacturing labor near to the 0–1 core-periphery structure, it converges to the asymmetric core-periphery equilibrium. Observe that the path-dependent case has two unstable asymmetric equilibria, labeled U_1 and U_2, that do not involve agglomeration in a single manufacturing region. Asymmetric equilibrium points U_1 and U_2 are unstable because, if these equilibria are disturbed, the economy does not come back to them.

Figure 4.4 neatly summarizes the discussion of core-periphery structures. It depicts how the equilibrium Northern manufacturing share s_{LM} changes with the level of manufactures transport costs T. The continuous lines depict stable equilibria while the dashed segments depict unstable equilibria.

The symmetric distribution of activity is always an equilibrium but whether or not it is stable depends on the level of transport costs. Let us define T^{Break} as the critical value of the transport cost level at which the stability of the symmetry regional equilibrium

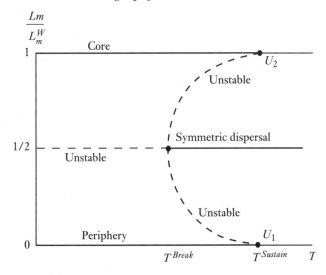

Figure 4.4. *Trade costs and agglomeration*

is broken. Puga (1999) shows that

$$T^{Break} = \left(\frac{1+\mu}{1-\mu}\right)^{1/(\sigma-1)} \left(\frac{\sigma(1+\mu)-1}{\sigma(1-\mu)-1}\right)^{1/(\sigma-1)}, \tag{4.4}$$

which depends on the elasticity of demand σ and the share μ of intermediate goods in production costs given a Cobb–Douglas technology. The parameter μ of costs spent on intermediates controls for backward and forward linkages. Observe that this formula is the same as the no interregional mobility case of Krugman and Venables (1995).

The symmetric equilibrium is a stable equilibrium only if $T \geq T^{Break}$. If transport costs are smaller than the break transport cost, $T < T^{Break}$, the stability of the symmetric regional equilibrium is broken. By contrast, the core-periphery equilibrium is stable in this region.

In the core-periphery structure, the North becomes an industrialized region while the South becomes a deindustrialized region specialized in agriculture. The South (i.e. periphery) inevitably loses as measured in real income terms. The reason is that manufacturing firms locate in the North, which means the North needs to import a narrower range of manufactures and thus incurs in less transport costs. The opposite holds for the deindustrialized South.

What determines the transport cost region in which a core-periphery-structure represents a stable equilibrium? The critical transport cost $T^{Sustain} > T^{Break}$ determines the region at which an established core-periphery pattern can be sustained, that is, the core-periphery structure represents a stable equilibrium (although not necessarily unique). If transport costs fall below the sustain transport cost $T < T^{Sustain}$, then the model generates multiple equilibria (symmetric and core periphery). Moreover, the core-periphery pattern is stable in this region. By contrast, if transport costs exceed the sustain transport cost, $T^{Sustain} < T$, the core-periphery structure is not an equilibrium. In this region, there is a unique and stable symmetric regional equilibrium.

What happens if transports are at an intermediate level, $T^{Break} < T < T^{Sustain}$. In this case, there are multiple equilibria (symmetric and core-periphery equilibria). Moreover, regional development patterns exhibit path dependence. The symmetric equilibrium is locally stable but not globally stable. In other words, if the initial regional distribution of manufacturing activity is close enough to the symmetric distribution, the regional distribution of manufacturing will eventually converge to it. If the initial distribution of manufacturing activity is far enough from the symmetric case, however, a locally stable core-periphery structure emerges.

Recapping, let us describe the circular economic processes sustaining strong agglomeration. A large number of companies producing differentiated products in a given location allow residents to purchase a larger number of differentiated products locally. Local purchases save on transport costs. Real wages are higher than in less agglomerated locations because residents obtain a higher utility from any given nominal wage rate due to a lower price of differentiated products. A higher real wage attracts immigration, which in turn increases the number of consumers in the target location. A larger local market attracts new firms because it facilitates spreading out fixed costs and supports more specialized inputs. Because greater demand and input availability attract new consumers and firms, the circular process continues.

4.4. PREFERENTIAL AGREEMENTS AND LOCATION

How do firms' location decisions change with the formation of preferential trade arrangements (PTAs)? Puga and Venables (1997) build on the analysis of Krugman and Venables (1995) to examine the location impact of (1) global free trade, (2) a free trade area, and (3) a hub-and-spoke trade arrangement in which the hub (an active business activity center like the European Union) liberalizes bilaterally with the spokes (regions trading with the hub, say, two Central and Eastern European countries) while the spokes fail to liberalize their mutual trade relations.

Despite the complex structure of the model some general results can be obtained. First, in the presence of economies of scale and transport costs, liberalization favors the liberalizing regions, possibly but not necessarily at the expense of the nonliberalizing regions. Second, a preferential arrangement could trigger a core-periphery structure with manufacturing agglomerated in the free trade area or hub even if the starting equilibrium is symmetric. Also, the formation of a free trade area does not necessarily imply the convergence of members' productive structures and income levels.

Consider a $K > 2$ country variant of Krugman and Venables (1995). A multicountry model is required in order to capture the discriminatory nature of preferential trade arrangements. There are two sectors, a homogeneous commodity sector, which we label agriculture A, and manufacturing M. There is only one factor of production, labor, which is immobile across sectors. Agricultural labor is not allowed to migrate while manufacturing labor is mobile across regions.

Agricultural products are sold in competitive markets and are produced under constant returns to scale using only labor. The manufacturing sector is a monopolistically competitive industry producing differentiated goods. Total cost and profit functions are given by (4.2) and (4.3). Increasing returns derive from fixed production costs. Transport costs are zero in agriculture but positive in manufacturing.

Each firm's output can be consumed as a final good or used as an intermediate good. Such feature permits controlling for forward and backward linkages, as in Krugman and Venables (1995), and generates centripetal forces favoring agglomeration. The greater price competition and greater real wage effects due to larger markets represent centrifugal forces favoring dispersed production.

4.4.1. Multicountry Global Free Trade

Let us examine first global free trade in a world of K countries. The equilibrium pattern of location is characterized by a symmetric equilibrium with intra-industry trade. This symmetric equilibrium is stable if trade barriers T exceed the critical value T^{Break} (see Puga, 1999)

$$T^{Break} = \left(1 + \frac{\mu}{1 - \mu} \frac{K(2\sigma - 1)}{\sigma(1 - \mu) - 1}\right)^{1/(\sigma-1)},$$

which depends on the elasticity of demand σ, the share μ of intermediate goods in production costs, and the number of countries K in the world trading system. For $T < T^{Break}$, the model's solution is characterized by an unstable symmetric equilibrium and by multiple stable asymmetric equilibria. Countries specializing in industrial production sustain higher wages than other countries.

4.4.2. Free Trade Area

Consider three countries, an initial equilibrium that is symmetric and stable ($T > T^{Break}$) and assume that two countries form a free trade area. The two members cut the tariffs applied to each other's imports to zero while maintaining their tariffs *vis-à-vis* the third (nonmember) country.

What is the effect of the formation of a free trade area? Let us focus first on the case in which the PTA does not elicit a core-periphery equilibrium. The presence of a free trade area pulls firms toward the integrating countries. Firms operating within the preferential arrangement benefit from an expansion of their production volumes and from the increase in the size of the industry at the expense of the nonmember firms. As a result, the number of firms operating in each member country increases while the number of firms operating in the nonmember country declines. This firm relocation effect represents production shifting toward the free trade area. The welfare levels of the member countries increase due to tariff declines and to the larger number of varieties available in their markets. Welfare declines in nonmember countries.

The formation of a free trade area starting from a stable symmetric equilibrium can lead to a core-periphery structure. Agglomeration takes place if transport costs are below a critical value and is favored by stronger input–output linkages (a higher μ).

4.4.3. Hub-and-Spoke Liberalization

Consider a set of preferential arrangements in which a hub country 1 (e.g. the United States) bilaterally reduces trade barriers between country 1 and spoke countries 2 and 3. Trade barriers between countries 2 and 3 are kept unchanged. This is the case of the United States–Mexico and United States–Israel free trade areas and the case of the European Union and the associated Central and Eastern European countries (CEECs). Hub-and-spoke trading arrangements give the hub better access to each spoke than the spokes have to each other.

The hub-and-spoke arrangement induces a greater number of firms to locate in the hub and raises hub welfare. This effect takes place even in the absence of input–output links between firms because firms locating in the hub sell to firms located in the spokes at a lower trade costs than firms exporting from one spoke to the other. The hub effect is a centripetal force arising because firms located in the hub benefit from better access to spoke countries than firms located in the spokes. Input–output linkages imply that spoke firms are penalized by higher costs and a smaller demand from both consumers and intermediate input users located in the other spoke. This effect accentuates the agglomeration consequences of the hub effect.

Both hub and spoke firms face lower trade barriers in trading with each other so that, ceteris paribus, production costs decline, profits increase and industry size expands in both the hub and the spokes. Hub welfare unambiguously increases. Spoke welfare might increase or decline depending on parameter values and initial conditions.

In short, welfare and the number of firms operating in a region unambiguously increase in the hub and could rise or fall in the spokes depending on model parameters.

Finally, the formation of a hub-and-spoke arrangement starting from a stable symmetric equilibrium can lead to a core-periphery structure and can generate divergence between the spokes. Hub welfare increases and spoke welfare is ambiguous.

4.5. NORTH–SOUTH VS SOUTH–SOUTH INTEGRATION

Let us start from a situation in which all manufacturing is produced in the North. What is the impact of multilateral, unilateral, and preferential tariff cuts on the dynamics of location? How do trade liberalization through North–South and South–South preferential tariff cuts contrast? These issues are important in deciding whether and with whom enter into a preferential trading arrangement.

Puga and Venables (1998) compare North–South and South–South trade liberalization in a model with four countries and two sectors, agriculture A and manufacturing M. North and South have identical technologies, relative endowments and labor skills. Initially, there is a core-periphery structure in which two

Northern countries have developed manufacturing industries and two Southern countries lack manufacturing industries. The complex model is solved by numerical simulation methods. In order to focus on Southern countries, the numerical simulations assume that Northern countries have the same economic structures and follow the same trade policy.

Labor is assumed to be mobile across sectors but is immobile between countries. This pattern of labor mobility implies that an expanding manufacturing region can attract labor from agriculture but not from other countries.

Agricultural output in country c, Q_A^c, is produced utilizing land T_A^c (which is sector specific) and labor L_A^c

$$Q_A^c = (T_A^c)^\alpha (L_A^c)^{1-\alpha},$$

where α is the land's share in production costs. Agricultural products are sold in competitive markets.

The industrial sector is a monopolistically competitive industry producing differentiated goods. Each manufacturing firm's output has two uses: final good and intermediate good. For simplicity, each sector is assumed to use its own output as input. The production of variety i entails firm level costs C_i inclusive of tariffs paid and transport costs

$$C_i = (w^c)^{1-\mu}(p_M^c)^\mu \left[f + a q_i^c \right],$$

$$(p_M^c)^\mu = \left(\sum_{k=1}^{4} \left[\int_{h=0}^{h=N^c} \left(p_h^{ck} T^{ck} T \right)^{1-\sigma} dh \right] \right)^{\mu/(1-\sigma)},$$

where N^c is the set of varieties produced in country c, p_h^{ck} is the free on board (fob) price of variety h shipped from country c to country k, and q_i^c is the volume of production of variety i in country c.

Trade policy is identified with tariff setting on imports of manufacturing goods (trade restrictions on agricultural products are assumed away). The policy variable $T^{ck} = 1 + t^{ck} > 1$ is the ad valorem tariff applied in country c on industrial goods exported to k. $T = 1 + tc > 1$ stands for Samuelson's iceberg-type real trade costs on industrial goods exports. A shipment of $T = 1 + tc$ units is reduced to one unit on arrival in the importing country because $T - 1 = tc$ units are lost in transit.

Firms exit or enter into the manufacturing industry according to calculations of short-run profit opportunities. In the long run, firm entry ensures that profits are equal to zero. The procompetitive effect of industry agglomeration, on one hand, reduces product prices and thus profits. On the other hand, agglomeration pushes the level of wages up, which negatively affect profits. In equilibrium, wages increase and prices fall up to the point at which profit opportunities disappear.

4.5.1. *Multilateral and Unilateral Liberalization*

If centripetal forces dominate centrifugal forces in the status quo, can multilateral and unilateral tariff reductions reverse such dominance? The numerical simulations conducted in Puga and Venables (1998) show that reversion can take place.

How does trade liberalization affect firms' location decisions? Multilateral trade liberalization makes firms more sensitive to factor price differences. Wage gaps between the North and the South induce firms to relocate in the South because the gains in terms of lower production costs exceed transport costs.

In the numerical exercise conducted in Puga and Venables (1998), assuming that manufacturing is initially concentrated in the North, 15 percent tariffs applied to North–South and South–South exchanges imply that equilibrium real wages in the South correspond to 65 percent of Northern real wages.

If multilateral liberalization reduces all tariffs by one percent (to 14 percent), firms located in the North find incentives to move to the South. This relocation of firms is justified by greater short-run profits in the South. Such profits result from the intermediate imports prices reduction and the major access to Northern countries after the tariff cutting. At equilibrium, these effects offset the heated competition resulting from trade liberalization, a force working against relocation to the South. Moreover, after a firm operating in the North decides to move to the South, then followers will also move to the same Southern country.

The reason why industrialization takes place in just one of the Southern countries hinges on the agglomeration forces derived from the backward and forward linkages. This result holds for intermediate tariff levels (i.e. tariffs ranging between 10 and 14 percent). For larger tariff cuts, there is also relocation to the second Southern country.

What are the relocations taking place when a Southern country unilaterally decides to reduce tariffs on imports? Numerical exercises show that relocation from the North to that country can take place. The reason is that the combination of a cost-reduction effect derived from lower-price intermediate imports and lower wages in the South may generate enough benefits to justify such move.

4.5.2. *North–South vs South–South PTAS*

Do Southern countries gain more from North–South trade liberalization than from South–South liberalization? What are the effects of North–South trade liberalization and South–South liberalization on Northern countries? The answer is that Southern and Northern countries prefer North–South agreements. Let us examine why.

Consider the case of a South–South preferential arrangement in which both Southern parties cut their tariffs to zero while maintaining their tariffs *vis-à-vis* the North. The South–South preferential arrangement creates a larger market and raises the profitability of producing in the South. The access to a larger market could attract to the South firms once operating in the North.

Consider the case in which a single Southern country enters into a PTA with both Northern countries (assumed to follow a single policy). North–South trading arrangements provide greater market access to developed country markets and offer lower prices of intermediate goods. As a result, the North–South arrangement can break down agglomeration in the North. Firms reallocate to the Southern country member because the benefits from lower wages, access to the North intermediates at lower prices and access to the Northern market, exceed the costs derived from keener competition.

Numerical simulations show that North–South agreements are better than South–South agreements. From a Southern perspective, the North–South integration arrangement might be better than South–South integration because the former opens the door for Southern exports to the Northern market.

From the Northern country perspective, North–South integration might also be better than South–South integration. There are three reasons sustaining such result. First, if disparities between the North and the South are not too large in the sense that unit labor costs differentials between the North and the South are moderate enough and the South is 'sufficiently' developed *vis-à-vis* the North, then real wages in the North might increase rather than decline. Second, the costs for the North of remaining closed when a South–South arrangement takes place exceed the costs of opening to the South in a North–South arrangement. Third, closing the gap between real wages in the North and the South might discourage migratory flows to the North. When integration leads to convergence, trade in goods under North–South regionalism can replace factor mobility. Indeed, regionalism can take place to replace factor mobility for trade in goods. A case in point is NAFTA.

4.6. GEOGRAPHICAL EMPIRICS

What is the importance of scale economies, externalities, fundamental economic factors, and random processes in explaining the spatial configuration of economic activity? How do we measure the extent of agglomeration, regional specialization, and industrial concentration? Is there evidence indicating that regional concentration increased during the past century in the United States and Europe? Geographical empirics focus on explaining the trends and sources of agglomeration, regional specialization, industrial concentration, regional polarization, and inequality.

What are the economic forces behind agglomeration? The ensuing discussion distinguishes between

(1) agglomeration of economic activity as measured by size and population density;
(2) regional specialization in particular activities;
(3) industrial geographic concentration, which is consistent with both regional specialization and regional diversification (because an industry might be concentrated in diversified regions);
(4) regional polarization in the sense of cross regional inequalities in real incomes and the ability to create and maintain employment.

The relations between economic geography and externalities, regional linkages involving demand and costs, fundamentals and random elements are difficult to tackle empirically. Technical econometric problems limiting the clear identification of the sources and impact of agglomeration effects include unobserved regional characteristics, simultaneity problems in regional data, and multiple sources of externalities. For instance, it is difficult to separate the effects of externalities and linkages if regional linkages generate externalities (Krugman, 1991*d*). Moreover, externalities might be short-run rather than permanent phenomena and they might be transmitted at different rates across space.

4.6.1. Explaining Agglomeration

Davis and Weinstein (2002*d*) examination of the time series behavior of agglomeration during 8000 years of Japanese history offers a test of the increasing returns, random growth and locational fundamentals models of agglomeration. Agglomeration is measured by variations in population densities.

The data suggest that increasing returns help to account for the increase in agglomeration that took place during the last century in Japan. This explanation is based on the premise that increasing returns are stronger in a modern knowledge-based economy. At the same time, random effects are important as evidenced by substantial variations in densities over time. In other words, there are forces apart from increasing returns in explaining concentration.

Why is it that the identities of the most populated regions are stable over time? The theory of locational fundamentals developed by Krugman (1996) predicts that agglomeration patterns are maintained after temporary shocks that do not affect the fundamentals. The substantial degree of historical persistence in the identity of the most densely populated regions can be explained by the forces stressed by the locational fundamentals theory.

A prediction derived from the locational fundamentals model is that the sizes of locations are maintained after temporary shocks. A piece of evidence in support of this prediction is that the Allied forces bombing of Japan during Second World War disrupted the relative size of cities, but only temporarily. Within 15 years, most cities had gone back to their previous relative position in the distribution of city size.

4.6.2. Regional Specialization and Industrial Concentration Trends

Kim (1995) examines the trends in the degree of regions' specialization and the concentration of industries. The description of regional specialization trends builds up on Krugman's (1991*c*) regional specialization index (*SI*)

$$SI^{jk} = \sum_{i=1}^{n} \left| \frac{E_i^j}{E^j} - \frac{E_i^k}{E^k} \right|,$$

where E^j_i and E^k_i are the industry i employment in regions j and k while E^j and E^k denote total employment in regions j and k. The index of regional specialization provides information about regional developments in manufacturing geographic concentration. If regions are completely specialized the value of the index is $SI^{jk} = 2$ and if regions are completely despecialized the value of the index is $SI^{jk} = 0$.

The conjecture that US regional concentration has increased in the past decades is not supported by the data. Historical evidence indicates that US regional specialization has gone through different phases. It slightly declined during 1860–90, increased substantially from the late 1890s to the early 1900s (the period of great improvement in means of transport), flattened in the interwar period, and substantially declined between 1930 and 1987. Specifically, data for nine census divisions and manufacturing employment at the two-digit SIC industry level indicates that, between 1947 and 1987, the two-digit (three digit) index of regional specialization declined by 47 percent (about 32 percent).

The period of deepening US regional specialization, from the late 1890s to the early 1900s coincides with a period during which the American economy integrated economically, improved its transportation infrastructure and lowered freight rates. This pattern is consistent with the notion that lower transport costs can trigger a process of regional specialization.

The analysis of industrial concentration trends shows that United States industries became more localized when regions specialized and became more dispersed as regions despecialized. Industrial concentration is measured by the Hoover's localization coefficient

$$L^j_i = \frac{E^j_i}{E^{US}_i} \bigg/ \frac{E^j}{E^{US}} ,$$

which gives information on each industry's evolution. A region j has a higher share of industry i than the other regions if coefficient $L^j_i > 1$. If $L^j_i = 0$, then the industry is completely dispersed across regions. The localization curve (similar to Lorenz curve) is constructed from industry i's location quotient for all regions, ranking the regions by their location quotients in descending order and calculating the cumulative percentage of employment in industry i over the regions (y-axis). The cumulative percentage of employment in total manufacturing over the regions is graphed along the x-axis. If the industry is evenly distributed across regions, the location quotient will be equal to one for all regions and the localization curve corresponds to the 45-degree line. If the industry is more regionally concentrated, then the localization curve will be more concave (more convex with descending order ranking). The Gini coefficient G (coefficient of localization) is the area between the 45-degree line and the localization curve divided by the entire triangular area between the 45-degree line and the axes.

Hoover's location index declined from about 0.27 in 1950 to less than 0.2 in 1987. At the industry level, changes in location long run trends are driven by industries such as lumber and wood, rubber and plastic, electrical machinery, and transportation equipment among others. The locational index first increased and subsequently declined in these industries. Among the remaining industries, tobacco displayed increased geographic concentration through the whole period. Dispersion remained stable in food and chemicals during 1947–87.

What is the relation between the behavior of the regional specialization and the industrial concentration indexes? The two indexes are complementary as they measure different phenomena. The specialization index provides data on the development of regional industrial structure as measured by differences in industrial structures for any pair of regions at different times. The localization index provides data about any given industry's regional concentration across time.

The evidence indicates that US industries became more localized when regions became more specialized and industries became more dispersed as regions despecialized. As regional specialization deepened in the nineteenth century and early twentieth century industrial regional concentration also deepened. As regional specialization fell since the 1930s the measure of industrial concentration declined (industries dispersed geographically).

4.6.3. Industrial Concentration: Externalities, Resources, and Scale

Kim (1995, 1999) examines the empirical relevance of three sources of regional specialization—external economies, scale economies, and resources—in explaining industry concentration across US regions. The external economies rationale for industrial concentration is rejected. By contrast, industrial concentration patterns are found to be consistent with both the Heckscher–Ohlin resource-based framework and the production scale economy framework. The major regional reallocations of production, the shift from agriculture to manufacturing and the subsequent shift from manufacturing to services are attributed to comparative advantages.

Because externalities are difficult to measure, the role of externalities is indirectly tested by examining the industrial concentration of high-tech industries compared with other industries. If localization is caused by external economies, then high-tech industries (as identified by a high proportion of engineers and scientists relative to industry employment) are predicted to be more localized than low-tech industries. The evidence, however, does not corroborate this prediction. For instance, localization levels for high-tech industries were similar to low-tech industries such as tobacco and textiles in 1987. In other words, Kim does not find evidence of a positive relation between the strength of Marshallian externalities and US industry's geographic concentration patterns.

The role of scale economies and resources in explaining industrial concentration is exploited by examining how the value of the localization coefficient for different industries is explained by variables standing for scale and resources. The empirical model consists of a localization equation with fixed-effects estimated using data for five years (1880, 1914, 1947, 1967, and 1987) and twenty US industries. The estimated relation between location patterns L (measured by the Hoover localization index), scale economies SC (proxied by average plant size), and resources RES (proxied by the cost of raw materials relative to value added) is given by

$$L_{it} = \beta + \underset{(0.24)}{0.66\,SC} + \underset{(0.02)}{0.05\,RES} + \alpha_i + v_t + \varepsilon_{it},$$

where α_i is the industry i specific effect, v_t is the year t specific effect and ε_{it} is the Gaussian error. The figures in parentheses report the standard errors. The regression equation offers evidence of a positive relation between industrial concentration and both scale economies and resources.

4.6.4. Localized Externalities and Spillovers

A tough empirical problem facing theories of localized externalities is measuring spillovers or obtaining adequate proxies. However, the predictions of these theories can be tested to establish whether or not they are consistent with the theory. Hanson (2001) review of the growing empirical evidence on the geographic concentration of economic activity concludes that there is evidence of:

1. Localized human capital externalities since there is a positive relation between workers' level of education and individual wages.
2. Long-run industry growth rate increases in regions supporting a wider range of industrial activities.

Models featuring localized external economies suggest that higher local knowledge stocks lead to agglomeration. Glaeser *et al.* (1995) and Black and Henderson (1999) find that US metropolitan areas starting with a more educated population tend to grow faster than those starting with lower educational levels. These findings are consistent with a positive association between localized human capital spillovers and spatial concentration. Localized human capital spillovers cause the social returns to higher education to exceed private returns.

Does firm productivity benefit from diversified agglomeration and from agglomeration in its own industry? Glaeser *et al.* (1992) examine the behavior of industry employment in US metropolitan areas from 1956 to 1987. The empirical testing controls for initial relative establishment size, initial relative industry size and initial wage levels. There is a positive association between employment growth in a city's industry and the initial diversity of industry employment in that city. These results suggest that firms benefit from diversified agglomeration due to interaction with firms in different industries. An industry's employment growth is not clearly associated with initial own industry employment, suggesting that there might not be permanent agglomeration benefits from firms in the own industry. Observe that, despite controlling for several variables, these associations are subject to identification difficulties.

The models of localized human capital spillovers developed by Eaton and Eckstein (1997), Black and Henderson (1999), and others predict a positive relation between the regional stock of public knowledge (as measured by average regional education) and regional wages and land rents. These results are consistent with the notion that localized externalities help to explain the positive association between geographic concentration and the level of wages and housing prices.

4.6.5. Regional Demand Linkages, Concentration, and Location

What is the evidence supporting the hypothesis that regional demand linkages induce spatial agglomeration? Justman (1994) regresses demand and supply correlations with industry characteristics on the notion that industries in which demand plays a greater role should exhibit greater correlation between demand and supply. He finds a major role for demand in location and industrial concentration in the United States. Davis and Weinstein (1999) focus on magnitudes of demand and supply relations rather than correlations. They interpret Linder's hypothesis, that unusually high demand for a product in a region can make it an export, as requiring demand deviations to lead to more-than-proportionately supply responses. Recall that this is the case in Krugman's (1980) monopolistic competition model with decreasing average costs and transport costs. High demand has a magnification effect in production because of large market advantages. The empirical evidence shows that greater regional absorption of an industry's output is associated with a more than one for one increase in Japanese prefectures' industrial production. International evidence on demand effects is presented in Davis and Weinstein (2002b). This evidence suggests that regions featuring high demand for a product exhibit a greater concentration of production.

The determinants of European economic geography are studied by Haaland *et al.* (1999), who examine the factors explaining relative and absolute concentration for thirty-five industries in thirteen European countries in 1985 and 1992. Relative industrial concentration (RC) measures the degree to which an industry is geographically concentrated relative to the average concentration of activities in a group of regions or countries. An industry exhibits high relative concentration when its output shows less geographical dispersion than the average industry in a group of regions or countries. Absolute industrial concentration (AC) measures whether most of the activities take place in a few countries

$$RC_i = \sqrt{\frac{1}{K} \sum_{k=1}^{K} (s_i^k - s^k)^2}, \qquad AC_i = \sqrt{\frac{1}{K} \sum_{k=1}^{K} (s_i^k)^2},$$

where s_i^k is the share of production in industry i carried out in country k, s^k is country k's share in total production, and K is the number of countries in the sample.

The cross-section analysis for the years 1985 and 1992 indicate that the concentration of demand variable stressed by new economic geography is the most important variable explaining both relative and absolute concentration. The greater relative concentration of industries based on skill intensity in countries with a high proportion of skilled labor is attributed to specialization based on resource endowments and comparative advantages. The greater absolute concentration of industries featuring more links between firms is attributed to intra-industry linkages measured by input–output linkages within industries.

The demand linkage or market access hypothesis can be indirectly tested by examining whether there is a positive correlation between Mexican states' wages and proximity to large urban markets (Hanson, 1997) and between US countries' wages and proximity to large US markets during 1970–90 (Hanson, 2001). The regression equation relates wages to the market potential, which measures proximity to large markets, controlling for regional characteristics such as education levels. The market potential function MP^j states that the demand for goods produced in location j is the sum of purchasing power across locations Y^k, weighted by the reciprocal of the distance d^{jk} between j and other locations. Formally,

$$MP^j = \sum_{k=1}^{K} \frac{Y^k}{d^{jk}}.$$

Purchasing power Y^k can be viewed as standing for the concentration of demand in location k while d^{jk} can be viewed as standing for transport costs between locations j and k. Locations standing closer to large consumer markets are found to offer higher wages. These results provide indirect evidence consistent with the hypothesis that demand linkages between firms create location-specific externalities contributing to spacial agglomeration.

4.6.6. Home Market Effects and Transport Costs

The home market effect implies that regions or countries with a larger home market (1) have a larger share of manufacturing than smaller markets, and (2) tend to export manufactures that benefit from agglomeration. Locations near large markets provide zero transport costs access to a large set of locally produced goods and services. If transport costs in manufacturing are higher than in agriculture, the larger market tends to specialize in differentiated manufactures and the smaller market in agriculture.

Davis (1998) presents a two-country model with a differentiated manufactures sector and a homogeneous good sector (labeled agriculture) in which international migration does not take place. In this setup, the home market effect disappears if agriculture and manufacturing have similar transport costs. In fact, the evidence on transport costs (insurance and freight) gathered by Rauch (1999) suggests that differentiated goods have far lower transport costs (less than half) than homogeneous or near-homogeneous goods. Moreover, Davis correlates trading costs (including both transport costs and tariffs) with several variables often used as proxy for scale economies (R&D, Grubel–Lloyd index, and measures of concentration). The correlations are usually negative contradicting the notion that products featuring economies of scale require relatively high transport costs.

The conclusion is that there is no compelling argument for the idea that market size and agglomeration influence industrial structure through a transport-cost driven home market effect. Common fears that integration will cause some regions to deindustrialize, due to the presence of a home market effect favoring the location of manufacturing in larger markets, might be unwarranted. However, recall that Davis and Weinstein (1999) report evidence supporting the existence of home market effects in the regional production structure of Japanese prefectures.

4.6.7. Persistence of Regional Specialization and Agglomeration

Are regional specialization and agglomeration forces persistent or temporary? Kim (1995) does not find evidence of a continuing trend towards increasing regional specialization in the United States. A possible explanation for this phenomenon is the conjecture that increased agglomeration, which is observed mostly in young growing industries, stops after firms reach their optimal size.

Evidence supporting the notion that agglomeration effects are not persistent is provided by Dekle and Eaton (1999), who give estimates of the rate at which agglomeration effects decay over time in Japanese prefectures, and Dumais *et al.* (1997), who find that own-industry agglomeration effects are temporary.

4.6.8. Integration, Specialization, and Polarization

Has European integration promoted agglomeration? Amiti (1998*b*) finds that European economic activity exhibited increased geographic concentration and increased industrial concentration during the 1968–90 period. During this period trading costs declined due to the fall of transport costs, tariffs and nontariff barriers. Combes and Lafourcade (2001) study of seventy-one industrial sectors finds that a reduction of road transport costs is associated with greater specialization and regional inequality in France.

Does regional experience support the inverted U-shaped relationship in which concentration and the real income gap initially increases and subsequently declines? Using European data, Brülhart and Torstensson (1996) find evidence supporting an inverted U-shaped relationship associated with greater regional integration. Industries generating large scale economies tended to cluster near the core EU members in the initial stages of EU formation. In the 1980s, though, clustering had slowed down. This evidence supports the view that the forces accentuating regional concentration might not be persistent.

Does regional specialization lead to regional polarization? A polarization outcome divides an area into advanced regions featuring high incomes and employment and depressed regions featuring low incomes and employment. A key concern among EU countries has to do with the means of avoiding regional polarization.

Braunerhjelm *et al.* (2000) differentiate between agglomeration, regional specialization, and polarization. For instance, the United States exhibits greater regional specialization but less polarization than European countries. The authors argue that the right policies can advance integration among the regions of Europe while preventing polarization.

4.7. CONCLUSIONS

Economic geography is the latest newcomer to the international trade field. Regional development and trade flows are influenced by agglomeration, regional specialization, and induced factor movements. There is evidence of agglomeration effects in the sense that existing agglomeration induces human and physical capital migration to urban and regional clusters. Agglomeration works through externalities and industrial linkages. First, a region with a larger manufacturing sector provides access to more intermediate varieties at zero transport cost. These forward or cost linkages raise short-term profits, inducing entry and further agglomeration. Second, a larger region supports greater demand for differentiated inputs and consumer varieties, which entails a higher marginal revenue curve. Demand linkages raising short-run firm profitability in regions with a larger number of firms encourage firm entry and worker migration.

How is the geographic analysis affected by the rise of the Internet and business-to-business? The geographic analysis applies to the case of those services that tend to be subject to high transport costs such as haircutting services. However, services provided through the internet entail lower transport costs than other products, which represents a force for dispersion.

In general, the equilibrium pattern of location hinges on the strength of trade barriers reduction (transport costs, tariff) and on whether centripetal forces offset or are offset by centrifugal forces. For instance, if forward and backward linkages (centripetal forces), dominate factor market competition and product market competition (centrifugal forces tending to break agglomeration), the equilibrium pattern of location entails a cumulative process of industrial agglomeration. Models of economic geography tend to produce core-periphery structures if trading costs represents a relevant variable creating linkages but are not so high as to create a strong motive for location near existing markets, and thus for dispersion.

Models based on exogenously given country size do not explain international differences in country size because they do not encompass factor migration due to the benefits from agglomeration. Because larger countries exploiting increasing returns offer greater wages, they are a magnet for migrants and thus tend to become even larger in equilibrium.

Agricultural production by nature spreads geographically depending on land availability, soil quality and another natural factors. There are advantages from concentrating manufacturing near the final market (the home market effect) for manufacturing goods.

Agglomeration offers a market large enough to pay for the cost of introducing new differentiated products and thus provides greater variety in consumption. Forces precluding complete agglomeration are congestion, housing costs, pollution, difficulties in enforcing security and other negative externalities deriving from agglomeration. Notice that these effects reinforce each other. For instance, migration flows due to higher wages create larger markets that in turn exploits increasing returns and expands product variety, pushing real wages up and thus inducing more migration.

The Gini coefficient across US states was calculated for the variable $s_i^k / \sum_k s_i^k$, where s_i^k denotes the share of region k in industry i employment and the sum over all regions indicates the national manufacturing employment share of region k.

5

Migration and Foreign Investment

This chapter focuses on the economics of factor mobility. The growing role of labor migration and the rise of foreign direct investment and multinational operations have broken down frontiers and legal restrictions. These forms of factor mobility generate policy initiatives to either attract or limit the flows.

The large and growing share of the foreign-born population in industrialized countries has triggered a heated debate on the determinants and impact of immigration. In many OECD countries, foreign-born workers exceed 5 percent of the labor force and this level has been increasing (OECD, 1999). A large earnings gap between developed and developing countries, demographic factors such as low fertility and shrinking developed country population, low transportation costs and porous borders suggest that immigration pressures are likely to remain high. An enlarging European Union faces immigration from Central and Eastern European countries joining the European Union in stages. Despite the large earnings gap between developed and developing countries at all skill levels, migration has not been massive due to immigration quotas, the cost of migration and preferences for living in the source country.

According to the US census, the foreign-born US work force represented 6.4 percent of the country's total work force in 1980, 9.7 in 1994 and 11.7 percent in 2000. In terms of population, the share of the foreign-born increased from 7.9 in 1990 to 11.1 in 2000, the fastest growth rate in the past 150 years. The foreign-born population share, though, still falls short of the peak share of 14.8 percent of the total population in 1890.

Immigration quotas constitute the major policy tool restricting migration to high-income countries. Great Britain passed its first quota law in 1905, France in 1932 and the United States in 1921. Quality-selective immigration policies are being used as a screening device in several countries. Australia and Canada have adopted a migration policy featuring a high skill bias, resulting in an increased share of highly educated migrants. In EU countries, migration policy stresses refugee status and family ties. However, in 2002 Germany passed a quality-selective migration law skewed toward high-skill migrants and limiting refugee status migration. A proposal to cap the foreign-born population at 18 percent of the total population was rejected by Swiss voters in a 2000 national referendum.

In the European Union, the fiscal impact of immigration is a major argument in favor of large migration flows. A demand for immigrants arises from their positive financial impact on the current pay-as-you-go pension system. A shrinking population, low fertility and an expected reduction in the size of the labor forces imply that, unless immigration continues, pension systems will require higher taxes and grant lower benefits in the coming decades.

The role of capital mobility has turned out to be as controversial as migratory pressures. In the past decades, the growth in FDI has exceeded the rate of growth of trade and GDP. The worldwide stock of FDI exceeded $6.8 trillion in 2002. FDI inflows were $735 billion, down from $1,492 billion in 2001. Over 93 percent of outward FDI is undertaken by developed countries, led by the United States, the European Union and Japan. Over 68 percent of inward FDI goes to developed countries, especially the United States and the European Union. There is much two-way FDI between bilateral trading partners, including large two-way FDI in the same industry.

The international mobility of capital, and organizational skill and technology transfer through FDI are major elements of globalization. The choice of conducting multinational operations and FDI is based on multinational advantages derived from ownership, localization, and internalization factors (i.e. the OLI framework). Firm-specific assets such as firm-specific knowledge, other intangible assets such as brand recognition and company reputation, and a single set of common headquarter facilities give advantages to multinationals because they can be used in multiple locations.

Horizontally integrated multinationals consisting of plants producing the same commodity in different countries arise to minimize trade costs. Horizontal FDI dominates exportation when trade costs are large, foreign markets are large and the economies of scale gained by concentrating production in a single plant are not too large. Vertical FDI takes place to locate each stage of production in the location that permits exploiting comparative advantages and factor abundances or international factor price differentials. The choice between FDI and licensing hinges on the trade off between internalization and the development of inter-firm networks. Licensing can be viewed as an arm's-length relationship that generates contractual costs due to uncertainties about the true value of an invention and the costs of monitoring and disciplining the licensee.

Sections 5.1 and 5.2 examine the determinants and effects of migration and migrant characteristics. Section 5.3 estimates the host country losses from migration due to terms of trade deterioration. Section 5.4 examines the economics of the brain drain. Sections 5.5–5.8 focus on the rationales and impact of FDI and alternative modes of entry to foreign markets. Section 5.9 examines the complementary and substitutability between FDI and exports. Section 5.10 examines intra-industry FDI. Sections 5.10 and 5.11 focus on mergers and acquisitions (M&As), competition and M&A evaluation in the open economy.

5.1. MIGRATION AND MIGRANT CHARACTERISTICS

The core of the immigration debate has to do with the assessment of the impact of immigration on host and source countries. A major factor fueling the controversy over migration is that estimates of the costs, benefits, and welfare gains or losses from immigration differ, sometimes sharply. Calculating the net gain or loss to the host-country economy is a complex matter. It involves adding up gains and losses for different local factors, determining the extent to which migrants cause natives to relocate, and assessing fiscal impacts, externalities due to immigration and the possibility of return migration. Similar difficulties apply to estimates of source country impact.

The Ricardian model discussed in Chapter 1 rationalizes migration due to technology differentials that generates cross-country wage differentials. The Heckscher–Ohlin trade literature on international factor flows focuses on a situation in which migration is motivated by cross-country factor reward differentials. In that general equilibrium framework, cross-country divergences in factor rewards can be sustained if countries' factor endowments lie outside the factor price equalization set and labor mobility is absent or limited. Factor reward differentials create sustained migration pressures arising from relative factor abundances.

Wage differentials have been found to motivate legal migration as well as illegal migration in the face of migration quotas. Hanson and Spilimbergo (1999) find that illegal migration from Mexico to the United States is highly responsive to changes in Mexican wages relative to those prevailing in the United States. An apprehension equation relates the number of individuals caught while crossing the US border illegally and real wages in the United States and Mexico. A 10 percent decrease in Mexico's real wages corresponds to a 7.5–9 percent increase in apprehensions at the US border. Moreover, apprehensions tend to be larger in the aftermath of an important devaluation of the peso. The growing gap between rising US wages and stagnant wages in Mexico during the debt crisis of the 1980s and its aftermath might have encouraged Mexico–United States integration as a mechanism to stem growing illegal migration to the United States. Greater trade and foreign investment flows represent an indirect migration policy because they create or sustain jobs, raise source country wages, and reduce migration incentives.

A second determinant of migration has to do with demographic factors and supply and demand gaps closed by migration. Low population growth in developed countries has resulted in a lower share of the working age population (18–65 years) in total population. The combination of a large supply of young workers willing to incur the costs of migration and excess demand for labor in industrialized countries results in large migratory flows.

5.1.1. *Migration as Human Capital Investment*

The human capital migration model views migration as a costly human capital investment that generates wage benefits over an extended period of time (Sjaastad, 1962; Becker, 1964; Chiswick, 1999). Consider a perfect information framework in which workers and employees are able to observe workers' characteristics. The human capital of investment and migration considers two types of migration costs: forgone earnings C_f, such as what the migrant would have earned at home during the time spent relocating and searching for a job abroad, and direct costs C_d such as airfare. The benefits of migration correspond to the differential between the host and source country wages, $w_1 - w_0$. The rate r of return of migration is thus

$$r = \frac{w_1 - w_0}{C_d + C_f}.$$

Suppose that there are two types of potential migrants, high skill and low skill. The high skill wage in the source country is k_0 percent greater than the source country low skill wage. The high skill wage in the host country is k_1 percent greater than the host country low skill wage. Formally, the host and home country wages and forgone earnings are

$$w_0^H = (1 + k_0)w_0^L, \qquad w_1^H = (1 + k_1)w_1^L,$$
$$C_f^H = (1 + k_0)C_f^L.$$

The rate of return on migration is thus

$$r^i = \frac{(1 + k_1)w_1^L - (1 + k_0)w_0^L}{C_d + (1 + k_0)C_f^L},$$

If the skill wage differential is the same in the source and host economies, $k_1 = k_0$, the rate of return on migration is

$$C_f^L, r^L = \frac{w_1 - w_0}{C_d/(1 + k)}.$$

The human capital migration investment model yields several predictions. First, younger potential migrants have greater incentives to migrate than older potential migrants. The reason is that the cost of migration is similar to a fixed cost while the benefits from receiving a higher wage abroad are accrued over a longer period for the young than for the old. In other words, cost and benefit considerations explain why migrants tend to be young.

Second, a high skill potential migrant is more likely to migrate than a low skill migrant because the high skill brings a larger rate of return from migration investments than a low skill migrant can expect. In other words, self-selection tends to cause high skill workers to migrate. This is clear in the case in which the skilled wage differential is the same in both locations, $k_1 = k_0$. Negative self-selection can arise, though, if the skilled differential is lower abroad than at home.

How does asymmetric information affect migration? Asymmetric information arises because potential migrants and employers at the origin know migrants' productivity, but employers at destination do not observe migrant productivity. If employers at destination are not able to distinguish between high and low skill workers, there is a 'pooling' equilibrium in that all workers receive the same wages at destination, $w_1^H = w_1^L$ while $w_0^H > w_0^L$ (Katz and Stark, 1987). Adverse selection induces low skill workers who are indistinguishable from high skill workers to migrate. When there are many types of workers, highly skilled workers will not migrate if their skill is recognized at home but not at the potential destination. This is a case of negative self-selection.

5.1.2. *Unobserved Characteristics and Self-selection*

What determines who migrates when workers have observable and unobservable characteristics? Borjas (1987) develops a self-selection model in which earnings are related to individual characteristics that have a random element. Individuals have two types of characteristics: (1) observed human capital such as education and training and (2) unobserved human capital such as ability, entrepreneurship, and other personal characteristics. The equilibrium type (quality) of migrants is determined by the distributions of unobservable human capital at origin and destination. These distributions determine whether an individual achieves above or below average earnings in the origin and destination countries.

The earnings w of immigrants in the origin and destination location can be decomposed into an observed characteristic μ determining immigrants mean income and an unobserved characteristic ε determining actual earnings

$$\ln w_0 = \mu_0 + \varepsilon_0, \qquad \ln w_1 = \mu_1 + \varepsilon_1,$$

where subscript '0' denotes origin, '1' stands for destination country, and the random shock ε_i has a zero mean normal distribution $N(0, \sigma_i^2)$ with variance σ_i^2. Immigration takes place if indicator I is positive, meaning that destination earnings exceed the sum of earnings at origin plus mobility costs C. Using $\ln(1 + \pi) \approx \pi$ yields

$$I = \ln\left(\frac{w_1}{w_0 + C}\right) \approx (\mu_1 - \mu_0 - \pi) + (\varepsilon_1 - \varepsilon_0) > 0,$$

where $\pi = C/w_0$ is the cost of mobility measured as a proportion of earnings at origin.

The rate of immigration is equal to the probability that the benefits from migration exceed the costs of emigration, that is, the probability of immigration P

$$P(I > 0) = P(\varepsilon_1 - \varepsilon_0 > -(\mu_1 - \mu_0 - \pi))$$

$$= P\left(\frac{\varepsilon_1 - \varepsilon_0}{\sigma_{\varepsilon_1 - \varepsilon_0}} > -\frac{\mu_1 - \mu_0 - \pi}{\sigma_{\varepsilon_1 - \varepsilon_0}}\right) = \Phi\left(-\frac{\mu_1 - \mu_0 - \pi}{\sigma_{\varepsilon_1 - \varepsilon_0}}\right)$$

$$= 1 - \Phi\left(\frac{\mu_1 - \mu_0 - \pi}{\sigma_{\varepsilon_1 - \varepsilon_0}}\right) = 1 - \Phi(z_0),$$

where the distribution of $\varepsilon_1 - \varepsilon_0$ is a zero mean normal with variance $\sigma_{\varepsilon_1 - \varepsilon_0}^2$, $z = (\mu_1 - \mu_0 - \pi)/\sigma_{\varepsilon_1 - \varepsilon_0}$ is a standardized normal $N(0, 1)$ and $\Phi(z_0 < 0)$ is the probability that z is less than z_0.

In order to control for the effects of observable human capital, consider that $\mu_1 = \mu_0$ and focus on the random terms. The characteristics of migrants are determined by three parameters. These are the transferability of unobserved skills across locations, as measured by the correlation $\rho(\varepsilon_0, \varepsilon_1)$ between the unobserved components at origin and at destination, and the distribution of opportunities at origin and destination, $\sigma(\varepsilon_0)$ and $\sigma(\varepsilon_1)$.

Migration can be subject to positive, negative, and refugee sorting selection:

1. Positive selection takes place if unobservable human capital has a greater effect on destination than on origin earnings

   $$E(\ln w_1 | I > 0) > E(\ln w_0 | I > 0).$$

   Immigration tends to be biased toward individuals with a large stock of unobservable human capital, who tend to achieve above average earnings both at the origin and at destination. Positive selection takes place if country of origin skills are easily transferable, $0 < \rho(\varepsilon_0, \varepsilon_1)$, and the distribution of opportunities at destination has greater dispersion than at the origin, $\sigma_{\varepsilon_0} < \sigma_{\varepsilon_1}$. These conditions resemble those characterizing migrants coming from more equalitarian societies that have transferable skills, such as Western European migration to the United States.

2. Negative selection takes place if unobservable human capital has a greater effect at the origin than at destination. Immigration is biased toward individuals with a relatively small stock of unobservable human capital and below average earnings in the origin and destination countries. Negative selection takes place if country of origin skills are easily transferable, $0 < \rho(\varepsilon_0, \varepsilon_1)$, and the distribution of opportunities at destination has lower dispersion than at the origin, $\sigma_{\varepsilon_1} < \sigma_{\varepsilon_0}$. These conditions match the characteristics of migrants coming from highly unequal societies that have transferable skills, such as Latin American migrants to the United States.

3. Refugee sorting takes place if there is a low or negative correlation between the earnings attributable to unobservable human capital at origin and at destination, that is, $\rho(\varepsilon_0, \varepsilon_1)$ is low or negative. For instance, if $\rho(\varepsilon_0, \varepsilon_1) < 0$, individuals achieving above average earnings in the origin country have smaller benefits from migration than those with below average earnings. Therefore, migrants achieving below average earnings at origin have incentives to migrate and tend to achieve above average earnings in the destination country. This is the case of workers endowed with unobservable skills that are relatively undervalued at home. For instance, if entrepreneurship is not valued at the country of origin, entrepreneurial people would tend to migrate to locations attaching a greater value to entrepreneurship. These conditions resemble political refugees burdened by a hostile political regime at home.

5.1.3. Evidence on Skills, Selectivity, and Catch-up

What is the experience of immigrants in host countries? The experience of migrants depends on personal characteristics such as

1. The initial skill composition of immigrants relative to host country natives;
2. The selectivity of migrants due to either migration policies or self-selection, the ability to catch up with native population, and the motivation to invest in human capital.

How do immigrant education levels compare with host country natives? This varies across host and source countries. Davis and Weinstein (2002*e*) point out that the proportion of US foreign-born workers with college degrees was 29 percent in 1994 compared with 32 percent for US born workers. Poor education is more frequent among immigrants than among natives legal and illegal. (Rivera–Batiz (1999)).

What is the evidence on the selectivity of migrants? Selectivity can be gauged by examining whether migrants do well in the host country. If immigrants are positively selected, they will be able to close the earnings gap with host country natives relatively easily. Do migrants catch up with natives? Chiswick (1978) cross-section estimates of earning functions show that the age–earnings profile of immigrants is steeper than that of the native-born. As a result, migrants catch up with the native-born and overtake them after 10 to 15 years. Chiswick concludes that migrants are favorably selected. He argues that immigrants self-select themselves positively in terms of ability and motivation and invest in human capital after migration.

The proposition that migrants tend to self-select positively, and the empirical finding of earnings overtaking, are questioned by Borjas on statistical grounds (1987, 1999). He argues that a single cross-section analysis cannot distinguish between the effects of (1) labor market experience and assimilation, and (2) the characteristics of migration cohorts. A rapidly growing earning profile in a single cross-section can either reflect a positive assimilation effect or a reduced quality of new cohorts. In order to separate age and generation, a longitudinal analysis focusing on cohort data is necessary. The empirical analysis of US earnings of immigrants from forty-one countries using cross-sections from the 1970 and 1980 census controls for changing conditions by focusing on the behavior of immigrants' earnings relative to the native population. The rate of assimilation is defined as the rate of earnings growth of an immigrant cohort (relative to natives) ten years after immigration.

Borjas (1987, 1999) finds that younger migrants, those coming from countries with lower English proficiency, and those coming from politically freer countries have lower assimilation rates than older migrants, those from countries with repressive regimes or recent loss of political freedoms, and those coming from countries with higher English proficiency. The proposed interpretation is that the incentives to assimilate rapidly are less for the young and those facing lower costs of return migration. Immigrants from countries featuring less English proficiency have greater costs of adjustment.

In fact, newer US migrants are less educated than older migrants. These considerations suggest that the appearance of improvement derived from a single cross-section equation pooling different cohorts is misleading. The appearance of improvement over time is due to the fact that new immigrant cohorts have lower-quality than previous cohorts. Pooling higher-quality older cohorts with lower-quality with recent cohorts produces a sample in which migrants with a greater time in the country (i.e. earlier migrants) perform well due to their higher quality and not necessarily because they adapt and perform better over time. Moreover, migrants with a shorter time in the country perform badly because they feature a lower quality rather than because they are starting their adaptation. The positive relation between time in the country and performance (partly due to the better quality of earlier migrants) gives an upward bias to the measure of the extent to which performance improves with the time after immigration for a given quality level.

An explanation offered for the lower skills of migrants to the United States has to do with the lifting of national-origin quotas in 1965. The composition of the foreign born has shifted drastically since that time. In 1970, Europeans were the major immigrant force but in 2000 they represented only 15.8 percent of the total foreign born, compared with 26.4 of foreign born in Asia and 51.7 percent of foreign born in Latin America. This change in composition of the 31.1 million foreign-born US residents in 2000 has led to claims that the educational level of migrants is excessively low.

The finding that some immigrant groups do not catch up with the native-born population suggests the policy implication that migration policies should be selective across migrant groups. A counter position claims that the US economy has been able to absorb all educational levels.

What is the human capital investment pattern of immigrants? A series of studies testing the human capital investment model with the US immigrant data is reviewed in Duleep and Regets (1999). Control for the initial level of human capital is realized by including age and education as explanatory variables. The authors find that migrants and low-skill immigrants display a steeper earnings profile than natives and high-skill migrants, due to human capital investments. School attendance is greater for Indo-Chinese, Central and South American immigrants than for immigrants from Western Europe. The slow growth rate of earnings and the fall in entry wages experienced by Mexican migrants is attributed to the low costs of return migration. The authors suggest that the dummy variables used by Borjas do not effectively control for cohort effects because entry earnings and earnings growth are negatively related.

A lively and increasingly sophisticated debate about empirical findings and their policy implications has emerged between Borjas and critics. A final resolution of the disagreements remains ahead of us.

5.2. MODELING THE EFFECTS OF MIGRATION AND QUOTAS

What are the effects of immigration? It is not possible to provide an unambiguous answer on the basis of theoretical considerations alone. Recall the analysis of migration in the Ricardian model examined in Chapter 1. Immigration raises labor supply in the host economy causing a move down the factor marginal product curve. Relative abundance effects suggest that, if there are different types of labor, migration causes a loss to host country workers in the same skill class as the migrant worker. Also, increasing the number of migrants in a given skill class tends to raise the marginal productivity (and thus market rewards) of other skill classes and factors of production.

In the absence of externality effects, positive effects from migration arise from the impact on the nontraded services sector. The key idea is that migration substitutes for the absence of trade in nontraded services and thus generates benefits similar to the gains from trade (Rivera-Batiz, 1982, 1983). In the presence of positive scale and agglomeration effects due to externalities, immigration also produces positive welfare effects in the host country. For instance, immigration increases the variety of nontraded services sold at a price (and thus marginal value) in excess of marginal costs.

What determines the post-immigration human capital accumulation behavior? Immigrant human capital investments depend on return and cost factors. On the return side, if the skills acquired in the destination are transferable to the source country, greater human capital investments at destination have a normal return in the destination plus an immigrant specific return that raises labor–market value in the source country. On the cost side, if the source country human capital of immigrants is only partially transferable to the destination, the opportunity cost of post-immigration human capital investments (the potential wages and salaries at destination) is lower for immigrants than for natives. Moreover, opportunity costs will be lower for low-skill immigrants than for high-skill immigrants. The combination of high demand and low-cost factors leads to greater human capital investment by immigrants.

What are the growth effects of immigration quotas? Lundborg and Segerstrom (2002) examine the effects of immigration quotas in a North–South quality ladders model of economic growth, similar to the quality ladders model examined in the chapter on growth. Workers in the North can engage in both low-tech and high-tech R&D, while workers in the South can engage only in low-tech R&D. Because of these asymmetries, Northern workers have higher real wages in equilibrium and there are incentives for migration. Under free trade, the South exports low-tech goods to the North.

Immigration and a higher quota result in faster economic growth, but lower wages and the static utility level and discounted welfare of Northern workers. If Northern, asset owners' discounted welfare falls. Therefore, the North loses from immigration. Immigrants and remaining workers in the South gain.

5.2.1. Labor Market Effects

What is the economic impact of immigration? The welfare impact of immigration flows on the host country depends on the characteristics of immigrants and their labor market effects.

A key issue concerns whether migration lowers the wages of the native born. The study by Altonji and Card (1991) finds that immigration has no significant effect on less-skilled native wages. Inflows equivalent to 1 percent of the population in a standard metropolitan statistical area (SMSA) result in a weekly earnings reduction for less skilled natives of a mere 1.2 percent. Gang and Rivera–Batiz (1994) find that the impact of migration at the US national level, at the state level, and for particular ethnic groups (blacks, white, hispanics), is small.

The previous analyses neglect that native-born population location decisions are affected by incoming migrants. One reason why native salaries are not greatly reduced is that downward wage pressures might induce natives to move to work in alternative locations. Because immigration increases the host country labor supply, immigration flows can be fully offset by outflows of equivalent-skilled native-born workers. Borjas *et al.* (1996) estimate that 1980–90 immigration and labor supplied through imports caused an earnings decline of -0.08 logarithm points for high-school dropouts relative to other workers and -0.18 for the case of high school to college graduates.

What is the evidence supporting the displacement effect? Card and DiNardo (2000) develop a general equilibrium model that allows workers to move across locations. They test for the reaction of natives to changes in the supply of immigrants with similar skills. The analysis employs US census data for years 1970, 1980, and 1990 and for the 119 larger metropolitan statistical areas (MSA). They find evidence that, within the same skilled group, native-born population increases rather than declines as a response to immigration (although the effect is weak). These results contradict the argument that native outflows increase with inflows. The authors conclude that there is little evidence supporting the displacement effect.

New York, Los Angeles, Chicago, and Miami have been greatly affected by migration. Card (2001) presents evidence indicating that the immigrant inflows of the 1980s had a modest impact on native out-migration in these cities. However, low skill wages and the employment rates of natives are found to be lower in cities with higher relative supplies of workers in a given occupation. He concludes that immigration lowered wages by 1–3 percentage points in Miami and Los Angeles.

Why is it that migration fails to substantially reduce native wages and induce large displacements? One possible explanation is that migration takes place to close structural disequilibria so that they fill an existing excess demand for labor.

5.3. TECHNOLOGY, MIGRATION, AND TERMS OF TRADE

A potentially substantial effect of immigration is that it could result in terms of trade deterioration. Migrants increase host country production levels which result in a terms of trade deterioration for the host country. The possibility that terms of trade deterioration leads to lower income and welfare has been demonstrated by Bhagwati (1958). An increase in the size of an open economy that is large in the sense that its trading can affect its terms of trade, can cause what Bhagwati calls immiserizing growth. This possibility arises, though, only if a greater size causes a large enough deterioration in the country's terms of trade.

Davis and Weinstein (2002e) calculate the income losses from immigration due to terms of trade effects derived from labor and capital migration. The income loss figures derived from the analysis differ sharpy from calculations that neglect the terms of trade. The analytical framework used to study the impact of immigration in the US economy is based on the Ricardian model with a continuum of goods developed in Dornbusch *et al.* (1977a). Immigration is motivated by technology gaps. In this framework, immigration towards a more productive economy hurts the host economy relative to the free trade benchmark. By contrast, the source country gains. Immigration does not generate incentives for emigration of adversely affected host country factor owners because it is driven by technological differences that sustain high rewards for all host country factors.

The US economy is among the world's most productive economies. As such, it attracts skilled labor, unskilled labor, and capital seeking to be employed in a high productivity environment. Increases in US labor force and capital skills are estimated to translate into a 12 percent increase in US output and, at initial prices, an equivalent excess supply of US products in world markets. As a result, the terms of trade deteriorate and the US economy suffers income and welfare losses.

The size of the income losses depends on the elasticity of the terms of trade with respect to *GDP*. This elasticity is estimated to be about $\varepsilon^{TOT} = -0.6$ in Acemoglu and Ventura (2002). Using this elasticity implies that the terms of trade *TOT* deteriorate by -7.2 percent due to net factor inflows

$$\frac{\Delta TOT}{TOT} = \varepsilon^{TOT} \frac{\Delta GDP}{GDP} = (-0.6)(0.12) = -0.072.$$

The estimated lost income to *GDP* ratio, *L/GDP*, depends on the percentage *GDP* change due to factor inflows, the elasticity of the terms of trade with respect to *GDP*, and the ratio of total trade $M + X$ to *GDP*,

$$\frac{L}{GDP} = \frac{1}{2} \frac{M + X}{GDP} \varepsilon^{TOT} \frac{\Delta GDP}{GDP} = \tfrac{1}{2}(0.19)(-0.6)(0.12) \approx -0.007.$$

The estimated income loss due to terms of trade deterioration mounts to about $80 billion for the year 1998 in terms of trade losses. Of this amount, $70 billion are borne by US natives. These losses plus additional estimated losses due to lower output abroad, which in turn lowers US terms of trade by an estimated additional 1 percent, represent about 8 percent of annual *GDP*.

The authors urge caution on generalizing the results. These apply to a large country that influences its terms of trade and to the distributional effects of migration (as world income increases due to immigration and the gains to migrants offset the losses to native workers). Moreover, the analysis ignores externalities such as potentially positive agglomeration effects and other channels through which migration might benefit native workers. The authors stress that the assessment of the effects of factor migration should incorporate the terms of trade effects of such migration.

5.4. BRAIN DRAIN AND SOURCE COUNTRY IMPACT

What is the impact of immigration on the source country? Emigration has source country benefits deriving from alleviation of local labor market pressures as source and host countries' labor markets become interlinked. Moreover, international remittances from migrants established in high-income countries represent a substantial source of income in their home countries.

US immigrant earnings are about 25 percent less than the earnings of US native-born population. This observation applies to most source countries of US immigration, implying that cross-country differences in unobserved skills are much smaller than the income gap relative to the United States. Despite the earnings gap in the host country, immigrants earn more in the host than in the source country. The explanation hinges on the fact that immigrants seek locations with better technologies.

The brain drain is the major source of negative effects on source countries due to emigration. Scientists, engineers, physicians, information technology experts, and many others have better opportunities in high-income countries and are often favored by these countries' immigration policies. The concept of a brain drain admits a strong definition alluding to a stream of highly skilled and qualified workers migration and a weaker definition focusing on relatively highly skilled workers. Under both definitions, the brain drain can be viewed as positive selection based on observable variables such as education.

The so-called reverse transfer of human capital towards a few human capital abundant developed countries (Australia, Canada, the United States, and the European Union) entails the loss of developing country human capital. Migrating human capital is often either educated in the source country or educated abroad benefitting from source country financing. Human capital outflows toward developed countries can render source countries' investments in education ineffective.

Bhagwati and Rodriguez (1975) examine the economics of brain drain. If the migrant's contribution to the source economy exceeds its marginal product, the welfare of those left behind in the source country falls. For instance, if the social return to education exceeds its private return, and if education is partially financed by the migrant's source country government, emigration reduces source country welfare. The notion that the brain drain must negatively affect the source country might not hold if prospects of migration, validated by the brain drain, encourage human capital investment at the source country (Mountford, 1997; Stark *et al.*, 1998).

Is the brain drain quantitatively important? Carrington and Detragiache (1998) use data for sixty-one developing countries, representing nearly 70 percent of total population in developing countries, to measure the extent of brain drain from developing countries to the United States, the European Union, and other OECD countries in 1990. Inflows to the United States, which represent over 50 percent of total inflows in the sample, are characterized by

1. Seven percent of US immigrants have only primary education. This figure covers illegal immigrants (US census questionnaires are kept confidential) but does not control for legal and illegal immigrants that do not file census questionnaires.
2. Over 50 percent of all immigrants (3.7 million out of 7 million) have secondary schooling education. The most important group of migrants with secondary education comes from Mexico and the Caribbean. The second largest group comes from Asia and the Pacific (including Philippines and China).
3. From the source country's perspective, migration to the United States is skewed toward the professions characterized by greater education. High-skill migration to the United States are substantial for Latin American and Caribbean countries. Seventy percent of Guyana's individuals with tertiary education had migrated to the United States. Aggregate figures do not reflect this dramatic pattern as the greatest source of migrants, Mexico, constitutes an exception to the rule.

5.5. FDI AND MULTINATIONALS

Multinational enterprises and foreign direct investment (FDI) represent an increasingly important element of global commerce and factor mobility. During the past decades, the growth of FDI has surpassed the growth of exports. By the late nineties, global sales of foreign affiliates had surpassed the value of exports. Moreover, many countries have dismantled long-standing restrictions on FDI and have shifted strategies toward policies designed to attract FDI. Moran (1998) reports that the number of countries with a more proactive stance toward FDI doubled from 60 to 118 between 1991 and 1998.

A multinational enterprise (MNE) is a firm that owns and controls productive assets located in more than one country. Multinationals engage in FDI by acquiring or augmenting control over host country firms. There are two forms of FDI, namely,

1. Location of new or expanded production facilities (greenfield investments), research and development activities, and managerial resources in a 'host' country. This type of FDI requires physical investment abroad;
2. Merger with and acquisition of existing 'host' country firms (M&As) to secure partial or absolute control of a 'source' country firm. M&As do not require committing new physical investment to the host country but often generate physical investment for upgrading and expansion purposes.

FDI is different from portfolio investment, that is, the acquisition of firm share without securing control over company decisions. In practice, there is no clear-cut distinction between the ownership of company assets (i.e. owning equity shares) and holding control over its decision making. The line between direct and portfolio investment is thus blurry and definitions vary somewhat from country to country. Equity ownership in excess of 10 percent of the outstanding shares of a foreign company is often considered the threshold above which a degree of effective control is deemed to exist and investments are classed as FDI.

There are three types of FDI: horizontal, vertical, and conglomerate. Horizontal FDI entails setting up production or marketing facilities in the same industry at home and abroad. Vertical FDI involves a supplier and its customer in different stages of the production process. Backward FDI takes place when a company acquires an input provider and forward FDI takes place when an input producer acquires an input user or when a company acquires a distributor. Conglomerate FDI involves companies operating in different businesses.

What are the rationales for multinationals and FDI? What are their roles in international trade? The ensuing discussion is cast in terms of the establishment of facilities abroad but its applicability extends to FDI through mergers and acquisitions. The chapter on networks, contracts and outsourcing expands the discussion of the geographical fragmentation of production processes and global spread of foreign investment characterizing multinational operations. Markusen (2002) and Caves (1996) contain detailed expositions of the economics of the multinational enterprise.

5.5.1. *Advantage-based FDI*

Why do multinationals exist? Dunning (1977) presents a general framework, appropriately called the OLI framework or eclectic approach, explaining multinationalization and FDI in terms of advantages concerning ownership, location, and internalization. These advantages must be large enough to offset the initial disadvantages of operating abroad, such as language barriers, lack of familiarity with local markets and regulations, and the costs of coordinating activities taking place in different countries. The OLI framework focuses on.

1. Ownership advantages, meaning those advantages that are exclusive to the investing firm. Ownership advantages arise from the presence of firm-level assets as opposed to plant-level assets. Firm-specific assets include good reputation, marketing advantages, intellectual property, organizational skills, and entrepreneurial ability. To a large extent, ownership advantages are knowledge-based assets that can be transferred at a low cost within a firm.

    Multinationals benefit from sharing a single set of headquarter facilities among many subsidiaries, which is considered an ownership advantage. Headquarter services (e.g. central administration) can be provided at a common cost for the firm as a whole thus achieving savings compared to the cost of providing the services to each individual plant. This cost advantage does not arise in a two-firm ownership structure entailing two-headquarters and potential duplication of costs.
2. Location advantages favoring in-country production over exportation include proximity to the target market, availability of low input costs and low taxes benefitting FDI. The sources of location advantages differ depending on whether the multinational investment is horizontal or vertically-oriented. Horizontal foreign investment to produce abroad is encouraged when the host country market is large enough and transportation costs are high enough to discourage exportation. By contrast, vertical FDI spreading out the location of different stages of production (e.g. component production and component assembly) is preferred if trade costs are low enough to permit the exploitation of cross-country factor-price differentials arising from differences in relative factor endowments.
3. Internalization refers to the decision to keep activities within the domain of the firm. Internalization advantages such as avoiding complex licensing contracts or keeping secrets and know-how from diffusing to rivals make it beneficial to produce within the boundary of the firm rather than dealing with foreign partners who might be more familiar with the local environment (Buckley and Casson, 1976).

The ownership aspect of the OLI approach is often qualified on two accounts. First, ownership advantages can be considered an element of internalization advantages. Second, firm-level assets such as possession of a patent can be exploited by a firm that exports from a single location or licenses the rights of production. In other words, ownership advantages provide an explanation for why a multinational might produce at lower costs than local firms but do not explain by themselves why these advantages are not exploited by alternative modes of penetration into foreign markets.

It is often stated that FDI serves to exploit brand recognition or monopoly power. In fact, the products of well-known multinationals, such as Microsoft and Coca-Cola, have brand name recognition advantages and often hold monopoly power. Brand recognition advantages and the ability to exploit monopoly power can be viewed as intangible assets that can be used in one location with no negative effects on the profits of subsidiaries in other locations. These assets provide advantages over local firms but do not require multinationalization because they can also be exploited via exports. Moreover, if quality control and contract enforcement are adequate, the exploitation of brand name, and monopoly power are consistent with licensing production rights in the target markets. Indeed, neither brand name recognition nor market power involve advantages requiring direct control over production decisions abroad (such as keeping secrecy about production methods).

5.6. TYPES OF FDI AND MODES OF ENTRY

There are several modes of entry into a foreign market. These include international trade (exporting and importing), establishing a wholly-owned foreign subsidiary, and inter-firm relationships such as licensing, franchising, joint-venturing, and the establishment of alliances such as a strategic partnerships.

The paradigmatic form of foreign investment takes the form of a wholly-owned foreign subsidiary. In this case, a parent company holds the ultimate control over operations, secures financing and carries project risks. In an international joint venture, a firm commits capital abroad and participates in running a foreign project. If the capital committed by a firm entering into a joint venture is large enough, so that the investing firm keeps a degree of operating control, a joint venture project would be classified as FDI. Contrary to a joint venture, which creates a separate legal entity, a strategic alliance joins two partners without establishing a new entity.

Licensing is an arrangement in which the owner (licensor) of some product or service grants the right to use the resource to another firm (licensee). Patents, copyrights, trademarks, and technologies are often licensed. In a franchising arrangement, the franchisor provides a package of support services to a franchisee, who produces or markets the good or service within an agreed geographic area. Support packages can include input supplies, equipment, management services, advertisement, and others including financing. McDonalds has achieved globalization through a system of franchises. In franchising and licensing agreements, the licensee or franchisee pays royalties and fees to the licensor or franchisor for the rights granted or the support services provided.

What determines whether a firm chooses to export, set up a wholly-owned foreign subsidiary, license rights to foreign firms, franchise operations abroad, or establish joint ventures or strategic partnerships? A growing body of work focuses on the choice between alternative modes of supplying foreign markets and the potential substitutabilities and complementarities between them. The ensuing analysis focuses on the export vs FDI and licensing vs FDI decisions.

Why do firms choose to penetrate markets through foreign investment rather than through exportation or licensing of production rights to local firms? In order to determine the preferred mode of entry and explain the geographical separation of activities, we must develop frameworks in which there are explicit decisions among location of activities and alternative modes of foreign market entry.

5.6.1. Horizontal and Vertical FDI

Multinationals engage in horizontal and vertical FDI. Horizontal FDI takes place when a company manufactures the same product in different countries. Vertical FDI performs different stages of the production process in different countries and generates intrafirm trade. In practice, large multinationals from developed countries tend to undertake horizontal FDI and vertical FDI involving sophisticated stages in other developed economies. Vertical FDI takes place in particular stages of the production process such as assembly in developing economies.

Horizontal FDI vs Exporting
The choice between exporting and horizontal investing can be viewed as an aspect of the economics of location and optimal production decisions. The key decision is whether to locate production at home, shift all activities to some target market, or produce in both locations (multinational). The export vs foreign invest decision is taken on the basis of location advantages. Ownership and internalization advantages are not a sufficient condition for choosing horizontal FDI over exportation. First, ownership advantages such as common headquarters can be exploited by either foreign investing or exporting. Second, both exporting and FDI entail full internalization of decisions.

Consider the standard HO models with two countries, two factors and two sectors subject to constant returns to scale. If factor price equalization holds, there are no taxes, and the costs of trading are zero, there are no location advantages. In this instance, multinationals do not arise because they do not accomplish anything that exporting cannot equally accomplish.

Which conditions pose a choice between serving a foreign market by exporting or investing to produce in the target market? The integration of trade analysis and models of endogenous multiplant multinationals is developed by Markusen (1984), Horstmann and Markusen (1992), Brainard (1993), and Markusen and Venables (1998). In Helpman *et al.* (2002), greater firm productivity heterogeneity leads to more FDI.

In the presence of trade costs, location advantages such as proximity to the target market to minimize trade costs call for servicing each market with separate facilities and favor FDI over exports. On the other hand, in the presence of economies of scale, production costs are lower if production is concentrated in a single location and other markets are served by exportation. The choice between FDI and exporting is determined by which factor dominates the trade off between proximity to market to minimize trade costs and production concentration to exploit scale economies.

The endogenous formation of horizontal multinationals can be formalized by considering a firm facing the choice between (1) exporting from a single plant established at home, and (2) establishing two plants, one in each of two target markets.

Markusen and Venables (1998) utilize the following two–country model with two sectors. Marginal production costs are constant in both sectors. The two countries are similar in terms of factor costs so that marginal costs are the same in both alternative locations. Sector *I* is subject to constant returns to scale and offers a product that can be traded without transport costs. Sector *II* can breed multinationals because it requires fixed costs for setting up a plant (which favors concentration in one plant) but generates trade costs (which favors multinationalization).

The decision to set up one or two plants to produce good *II* is a function of whether the benefits from concentrating production in one plant dominate or are dominated by the trade costs of exportation. First, high trade costs (or trade barriers) favor proximity to the target market and create a motive for the existence of multinationals. Second, setting up a plant requires a plant-specific fixed cost. The presence of plant-specific fixed costs favors exporting because fixed costs are minimized by setting up a single plant. There is a cost reduction benefit from concentrating production in a given location. Horizontally integrated multinationals arise endogenously if trade costs are large enough and the fixed costs of setting up a plant are small enough.

A difficulty with a trade cost explanation of FDI is that the boom of multinational operations in recent decades coincides with a period of declining trade costs as well as other barriers such as tariffs. A response is that other variables have favored FDI. Higher world income encourages FDI because it entails greater sales and facilitates paying the fixed costs of setting up a plant in each target market. Moreover, the liberalization of FDI flows has led countries into a path of aggressive FDI promotion policies and strategic tax competition by offering tax breaks. Gropp and Kostial (2001) report that during 1997 and 1998 the OECD average statutory corporate tax rate declined from 44 to 36 percent and the standard deviation around this average fell from 8 to 5 percent. Moreover, the average value and dispersion of the effective corporate tax rate also went down. A possible explanation for this decline is that tax competition has surged. In fact, OECD countries featuring high corporate tax rates have experienced both high net FDI outflows and a decline in corporate tax revenue. The perception of a casual link between high taxes, capital outflows, and reduced corporate tax revenues has led EU countries to call for tax harmonization to alleviate tax competition.

Vertical FDI

The endogenous formation of multinationals engaged in vertical FDI can be rationalized using standard trade theories focusing on differences in factor abundances, different sectorial factor intensities, and the notion of specialization. It is optimal to place a stage of production in the location that has a comparative advantage in that activity (the relative cost factor) or in the location that is relatively abundant in the factor used intensively in the stage (perhaps because this factor will be less expensive in this location).

Firm-level costs related to firm-specific assets can also motivate vertical FDI. Suppose that a fixed cost is required to provide services such as company administration and product marketing or to create firm-level assets such as brand name. The required fixed costs are incurred only once but the resulting firm assets can be used in multiple locations. The parent company provides services to subsidiaries, possesses firm specific-knowledge, and holds intangible assets such as brand recognition and company reputation, which give cost advantages to the firm and its subsidiaries (if any).

Research and development (R&D) can be viewed as a fixed cost of creating new products, designing better quality products or lowering production costs (process innovation). Cantwell and Mudambi (2001) find that R&D intensity differs across subsidiaries depending on which one achieves a competence-creating output mandate. Traditionally, subsidiary R&D sought to adapt company products to local tastes and production conditions. Recently a closer integration of subsidiaries in international R&D networks within a multinational has led to a change from competency-exploiting to a competency-creating subsidiary. This change has encouraged greater R&D at the subsidiary level as part of firm research networks.

Helpman (1984b) models multinationalization as a channel to exploit firm-specific assets. The framework can generate inter-industry, intra-industry, and intra-firm trade. Sector I produces a homogeneous good under competitive conditions so that price (normalized to one, $p = 1$) is equal to marginal cost c_I. Sector II produces differentiated goods at a fixed design cost. The product is sold under monopolistically competitive conditions and price is set as a markup over marginal cost c_{II}. The competitive sector I is assumed to be labor intensive relative to the monopolistically competitive sector II.

The two-country global equilibrium can be determined by combining the analysis of the Heckscher-Ohlin and monopolistic competition models. If the two countries are symmetric and there are no trade costs, all prices are the same in both countries and multinationals do not arise. If countries differ in relative factor endowments, inter-industry trade is explained by the Heckscher-Ohlin framework and intra-industry trade is explained by trading in varieties. The motive for the existence of multinational corporations is to shift productive activities to lower cost locations. If the conditions for factor price equalization hold, multinationals' decentralization will be such that they are consistent with it. Specifically, country A specializes in differentiated products and is the source country of the multinational. Country B specializes in the homogeneous good and is the host country. The profits obtained by the multinational in the host country finance the fixed cost. Intra-firm trade consists of the exchange of the services of firm specific assets to the subsidiary abroad. In other words, the profits that the parent company obtains from its subsidiary finance the fixed costs of producing services that benefit the subsidiary.

Consider now a setting with two productive stages: administration and final good production. If administrative work is intensive in the use of skilled labor, headquarters will be set up in the location, that is, abundant in skilled labor while production will take place in locations that are abundant in unskilled labor. Specialization leads to a form of vertical FDI and the geographic fragmentation of production and administrative activities.

5.6.2. Licensing and Other Types of Alliances

What determines the choice between market penetration through FDI and by licensing production rights to local firms? This question can be approached as an aspect of a broader question concerning the decision between foreign investing and entering into alliances such as licensing arrangements and joint ventures. The choice is rationalized by weighting the internalization benefits of FDI against the benefits from establishing arm's-length relationships through inter-firm networks. FDI is preferred over licensing if arm's-length contracts are too complex, agency costs too high and learning externalities benefitting potential rivals abroad are high enough.

Costs of Complex Arm's Length Contracts

Large enough costs deriving from contract incompleteness favor FDI vs licensing. A contract is incomplete when it cannot specify (i.e. write in a document) how to act under each possible situation that could conceivably arise. Multinationals internalize complex contractual arrangements and avoid the costs arising when complete contracts cannot be fully specified. Ethier (1986) stresses that the internalization view of multinationals is an application of the theory of the firm, which explains which activities are realized within the boundaries of the firm and which ones are outsourced or realized by other firms. In order to prevail, arm's length contracts should be simple because complex arrangements induce internalization.

Agency Costs

If the agency costs of enforcing licensing contracts are large enough as to offset any cost advantage possessed by a potential host country licensee, FDI will be preferred over licensing. Licensing is a type of principal–agent relationship in which the host-country licensee acts as an agent on behalf of the source country firm (i.e. the principal). Agency relationships give rise to agency costs related to contract enforcement. Complete contracts (those covering all possible contingencies) are less than fully enforced if parties do not have the right incentives to fulfill them.

A potential licensee seeking to reduce costs might have strong enough incentives to produce low-quality goods and thus squander the reputation of the licensor and the brand name of its product. Agency costs generate a trade off. On one hand, the potential licensee beats the source country in some aspect such as lower costs of producing in the local market or better knowledge about local demand conditions (i.e. the size of the local market). On the other hand, FDI allows the source country firm to avoid the agency costs of either nonenforcement or costly contract enforcement.

In Horstmann and Markusen (1987), source-country firms have access to the technologies needed to produce a high or a low quality product. The potential licensee has access only to the technology to produce a low quality good. The low quality market is competitive and the host country firm can produce low quality products at the same cost as the source-country firm. Under these conditions, there are no incentives to produce a low quality product by direct investment or licensing. FDI or licensing take place only to produce a high quality product.

Licensing entails transferring to the local licensee the source-country firm's reputation and brand name associated with a high quality product. The licensing contract (F, S) requires the licensee to pay a nonrefundable fixed amount F to obtain the license and a per period payment S if the license continues over time. The license can potentially last for an infinite number of discrete periods but can be annulled at the end of any period $t \in \{1, 2, \ldots\}$, in which case the payment of S is terminated. If product quality cannot be verified before quality choice and sale take place, the licensor can choose to produce a low or a high quality product. In making the quality and pricing decision (p, q), the licensee maximizes profits taking into account the licensing contract (F, S) and that the license can be cancelled at the end of the period due to verification of poor quality sales.

If the licensee has incentives to produce a low quality product, the reputation of the licensor will be squandered. Therefore, licensing requires designing a contract providing the licensee with high enough profits as to create incentives for high quality production and render low quality production unprofitable. From the perspective of the source-country firm, enforcing high quality in a licensing arrangement is costly because it requires transferring rents to the licensee. The decision of whether to foreign invest or license takes into account the profit maximization process of the licensee, the design of the licensing contract and the implied agency costs. In the symmetric case in which all firms have the same cost functions, agency costs imply that it is better to foreign invest than to license. Licensing takes place only if the licensee enjoys large enough cost advantages.

Licensing represents an arm's length agreement serving to exploit the superior information about local markets possessed by the local licensee. Horstmann and Markusen (1998) develop an agency cost model in which the host country firm is assumed to know the potential customer pool (i.e. the size of the local market) while the source country firm lacks access to this information. Therefore, a licensing agreement provides the foreign investor with information about market conditions. A trade off arises because there are agency costs and the licensee is able to extract some of the rents. FDI is preferred if the agency costs offset the benefits from superior knowledge about market conditions.

Learning-by-Doing and Defection

Licensees benefiting from learning-by-doing effects might be tempted to deviate and challenge the licensor. FDI prevents a potential licensee from learning-by-doing and acquiring incentives to defect and offer the product on its own. Ethier and Markusen (1996) develop a model in which potential licensors aim to prevent the licensee from becoming a local rival. Observe that FDI solves this problem only partially because the local manager or employees of a subsidiary might have incentives to defect.

5.7. MODELING FDI VS EXPORTATION

The model of multinationals developed in Baldwin *et al.* (2001) extends the differentiated products model with transport costs appearing in the chapter on intra-industry trade to consider the decision to become a multinational. The two-country model assumes symmetry in demand and all cost functions. Specifically, the transport costs of manufacturing exports and the fixed cost of becoming a multinational firm (i.e. the additional fixed cost of operating abroad) are identical across firms.

5.7.1. Demand for Varieties and Production Costs

The representative consumer's utility function is

$$U(D_A, D_M) = \ln(D_A^{1-\mu}, D_M^{\mu}),$$

where D_A denotes the consumption of agricultural product A and D_M is a constant elasticity of substitution composite of N^W varieties, where N^W is the number of varieties N and N^* sold in the domestic and foreign markets. Formally,

$$D_M = \left(\int_0^{N^W} d_i^\rho \, di \right)^{1/\rho} = \left(\int_0^{N^W} d_i^{(\sigma-1)/\sigma} \, di \right)^{\sigma/(\sigma-1)}, \quad 0 < \rho = \frac{\sigma-1}{\sigma} < 1,$$

where $1 < \sigma = 1/(1-\rho)$ is the consumption elasticity of substitution between two varieties. The quantity of manufactures is a quantity index and can be viewed as a sub-utility function defined over the whole continuous set of differentiated manufactures $d_i, i \in (0, N^W)$.

Spending on variety j, $p_j d_j$, is a constant fraction μ of total income Y (or expenditure $E = Y$). Recall that the demand function for j is

$$d_j = s_j \frac{\mu Y}{p_j} = \frac{p_j^{-\sigma}}{p_M^{1-\sigma}} \mu Y, \qquad s_j = \frac{p_j d_j}{\mu E} = p_j \frac{p_j^{-\sigma}}{p_M^{1-\sigma}} = \frac{p_j^{1-\sigma}}{p_M^{1-\sigma}},$$

$$p_M = \left(\int_0^{N^W} p_i^{1-\sigma} \, di \right)^{1/(1-\sigma)}, \quad \sigma > 1,$$

where s_j is the share of variety j in total spending and p_M is a perfect price index. Foreign demands are similar. Both agriculture and manufacturing goods are tradeable but trade in manufactures is subject to iceberg transport cost $T = 1 + t$, while trade in A is free of charge.

The model distinguishes between two types of firms: local firms (labeled n-firms) and multinationals (labelled m-firms). There are n domestic firms and n^* foreign firms producing differentiated products only in their home market. Also, there are m domestic multinationals and m^* foreign multinationals, each of which produces a differentiated product that is sold both in the home market and abroad. The total number N^W of varieties offered in the market is equal to $n + n^* + m + m^*$. The model is symmetric so that the total number of goods produced and consumed in both countries, N and N^*, is equal to $N = n + m^* = n^* + m = N^*$.

Sectorial mobility is assumed, so that real wages equalize across sectors in each country. This setup differs from the case of agriculture examined previously, which assumed that agricultural labor was attached to land and could not move to the manu-facturing sector. Units of product A and labor are chosen to satisfy $p_A = w = w^* = 1$. Real wages equalize internationally. If production of good A is positive in both coun-tries, because there are no transport costs in agriculture, there is a single world price of agricultural goods and agricultural productivity is the same across countries. Sectorial mobility ensures that industrial wages also equalize internationally.

Domestic production of q units of a differentiable product requires a fixed amount of labor f and aq units of labor. With wage rate $w = 1$, the variable costs are $cq = waq = aq$ and the marginal cost are $c = wa = a$. The fixed labor cost per period is $F = wf = f$ and represents the cost of designing a product. It permits pro-ducing one unit of knowledge–capital K, which can be interpreted as secrets involving industrial knowledge that cannot be protected through patenting. A unit of knowledge-capital is produced by using f units of labor. Knowledge-capital is sold under perfectly competitive conditions so that it is priced at marginal cost.

A nonmultinational's total cost function is

$$C^n = F + wl = F + cq = w(f + aq) = f + aq,$$

where l represents total labor use and q is output of a differentiated good.

The total amounts of labor and knowledge-capital are given. They are owned by a representative agent that receives an income equal to labor revenue $wL = L$ plus capital revenue πK. The reward to capital π is the Ricardian profit (operating profit) obtained by using owned industrial secrets to produce and sell a variety. Labor is immobile internationally but not knowledge capital. Moreover, knowledge capital (i.e. a product design) cannot be traded in arms–length transactions, that is, it cannot be licensed. Exploitation of knowledge capital can only be done by exportation or by incurring the additional costs of establishing a plant abroad.

A multinational enterprise produces at home and abroad and supplies each market by means of local production. Establishing a multinational requires an additional fixed cost Γ of operating abroad. This fixed cost is assumed to be proportional to the domestic fixed cost F, that is, a multinational's total fixed cost is $F(1 + \Gamma)$.

The multinational total cost function C^m is

$$C^m = (1 + \Gamma)F + wl = (1 + \Gamma)F + cq = (1 + \Gamma)f + aq.$$

5.7.2. Monopolistic Pricing and Mode of Entry

The location decision entails two sequential stages. The first stage involves deciding whether to be an exporter or a multinational. The key parameters determining this decision are transport costs and the fixed cost of becoming a multinational. Transport costs can be interpreted as trade barriers, generally including tariffs and nontariff barriers. The second stage is the pricing choice. The model is solved by backward induction.

The second stage entails making a pricing decision in the domestic and foreign markets. The domestic market monopolistic pricing condition for the local and multinational firms is (pricing is not affected by fixed costs)

$$p_j = \frac{\sigma - 1}{\sigma} c = \frac{\sigma - 1}{\sigma} aw = 1,$$

where $w = 1$ and units are chosen to make the domestic consumer price to be equal to one (i.e. $a = \sigma/(\sigma - 1)$). Because the multinational produces in the foreign market, it charges a price equal to 1 abroad. However, an exporter will charge a price equal to the iceberg-cost T

$$p_j^{\text{exports}} = \frac{\sigma - 1}{\sigma} Tc = \frac{\sigma - 1}{\sigma} Taw = T,$$

with $a = \sigma/(\sigma - 1)$ and $w = 1$.

The first stage involves manufacturers' decision to either become an exporter or invest abroad. The Ricardian surpluses left over to pay capital (operating profits) vary according to whether a firm is local or multinational (see appendix)

$$\pi^n = \frac{(1 + \phi)\mu E/\sigma N}{2s_m + (1 - s_m)(1 + \phi)}, \qquad \pi^m = \frac{2\mu E/\sigma N}{2s_m + (1 - s_m)(1 + \phi)},$$

where $s_m = m/N$ is the share of m-type firms, and $N = n + m$ is the total number of varieties produced by each country. The transport cost parameter $\phi = T^{1-\sigma} = (1+t)^{1-\sigma}$ is smaller than one (because σ is greater than one) and has a negative relation with transport costs. Observe that prohibitive transport costs imply that $\phi = 0$ and zero transport costs implies that $\phi = 1$.

The foreign investment decision hinges on the balance between transport costs and the cost of multinationalization. On one hand, the effect of the cost parameter $\phi = T^{1-\sigma}$ is to reduce local firms' operating profits from exports relative to multinationals' operating profits. Transport costs create a motive for proximity to the market. On the other hand, the multinational faces an additional fixed multinationalization cost (but does not face transport costs). The presence of this fixed cost of multinationalization favors the concentration of production in a single location.

In short, the foreign investment decision hinges on the balance between proximity to market through direct investment and concentration of production in the home market to exploit decreasing average costs. Because multinational fixed costs are proportional to local fixed costs, the foreign investment decision compares the Ricardian surpluses per unit of fixed costs of (1) producing locally and (2) producing locally and abroad. The indifference condition is (using expressions and simplifying terms)

$$\frac{\pi^n}{F} = \frac{\pi^m}{F(1 + \Gamma)} \quad \rightarrow \quad \frac{\pi^n}{\pi^m} = \frac{1 + \phi}{2} = \frac{1}{1 + \Gamma},$$

$$1 + \Gamma + \phi + \phi\Gamma = 2 \quad \rightarrow \quad -1 + \phi + \Gamma(1 + \phi) = 0,$$

$$\Gamma = Z \equiv \frac{1 - T^{1-\sigma}}{1 + T^{1-\sigma}} = \frac{1 - \phi}{1 + \phi}.$$

Foreign investment takes place if

$$\Gamma < Z \equiv \frac{1 - T^{1-\sigma}}{1 + T^{1-\sigma}} = \frac{1 - T^{-(\sigma-1)}}{1 + T^{-(\sigma-1)}}.$$

The decision to foreign invest balances the cost of multinationalization and the transport costs of exportation. Foreign investment will take place if the cost of multinationalization is low enough (the concentration of production motive is not strong enough) or transport costs are high enough (strong enough proximity to market motive).

The condition for foreign investment can also be expressed in terms of the complementary slackness condition

$$s_m(1 - s_m)\left[\frac{\pi^n}{F} - \frac{\pi^m}{F(1+\Gamma)}\right] = 0.$$

This condition says that there are three possible equilibria:

1. No firm becomes a multinational: $s_m = 0$ and $1 - s_m = 1$;
2. All firms are multinationals: $s_m = 1$ and $1 - s_m = 0$;
3. All firms are indifferent between exportation and foreign direct investing: $\pi^n/F = \pi^n/F(1+\Gamma)$.

The knife edge result is due to assumed symmetry in all costs and demands. It can be easily relaxed by introducing asymmetries (say, home country m-firms face low costs of multinationalization and foreign country m-firms face high costs). The equilibrium number of varieties depends on whether firms are multinationals or local. Because each variety is assumed to require a unit of capital, if all firms are local, $N = K$. When all firms are multinationals, $N = K/(1+\Gamma)$. When both types of firm exist, $\Gamma = (1-\phi)/(1+\phi)$ and the full employment condition is $K = n + (1+\Gamma)m$, or, $K/N = 1 + s_m\Gamma$ (but s_m is indeterminate).

5.8. FDI: MOTIVES AND ACCOMPLISHMENTS

What are the determinants of the volume and location of FDI and M&As? The wide range of factors includes multinationals characteristics, host country policies, and others. Markusen (1995) presents the major stylized facts about FDI. Multinationals are important in industries offering products that are innovative, sophisticated, and differentiated. These industries display high levels of R&D relative to sales, show a high value of intangible assets relative to firm market value, hire a large share of professional and technical workers, and engage on high levels of product advertising. Indicators of scale economies at the plant level are often negatively related to multinationalization. Firm age is positively related to multinationalization.

An intriguing finding is that many studies do not find clear evidence relating FDI to a number of factors that would appear to be natural determinants. FDI is not related to cross-country differences in factor endowments. Notwithstanding the substantial wage gaps, FDI does not flow from rich to poor countries. It rather flows from a developed country to a roughly similar developed country. FDI is not always closely associated to differences in the rates of return on capital or to risk diversification motives. The evidence about whether the level of FDI is related to transport costs and trade barriers is mixed. Once a size threshold is exceeded, FDI is not related to firm size.

5.8.1. Location and FDI

Industrial externalities and linkages contribute to attract foreign investment, although it is difficult to pin down the specific source of the agglomeration effect. Mayer and Mucchielli (1998) study the determinants of the choice of Japanese FDI location between the United Kingdom, France, Germany, Italy, and Spain from 1984 to 1994. They find evidence of agglomeration effects in the sense that, controlling for other factors, Japanese firms tend to be attracted to countries with a higher number of European firms of the same industry and a larger number of previous Japanese investments.

5.8.2. Do Weak IPRs Deter FDI?

Stronger intellectual property rights (IPRs) eliminate inefficient imitators and expand the residual size of foreign markets. This tends to increase FDI. Moreover, stronger IPRs shift the mode of supplying foreign markets from exports towards FDI, although it might also shift the mode of supplying toward licensing. Lee and Mansfield (1996) perform regressions of the volume of US direct investment is several locations over 1990–92. They find a significant impact of weak IPRs protection in a particular location on both the volume and the quality of FDI in that location.

5.8.3. Japanese FDI, R&D, Advantages, and Host Country Protection

Belderbos and Sleuwaegen (1996) find that Japanese trading houses in South Asian countries provide Japanese firms with market intelligence advantages. By contrast, Japanese FDI in western markets does not enjoy the same market intelligence advantages. These informational advantages explain why Japanese investments are heavily concentrated in Asia. Authors examine the determinants of the probability that a Japanese firm remains local, foreign invests in Asia and foreign invests in the West. They find that the higher labor cost of nonfactory employees over total labor cost, used as a proxy for a supply of expatriated staff that facilitates the transfer of organizational skills, increases the probability of foreign investment in Asia. The probability of foreign investment in Western countries increases with (1) R&D intensity, (2) the relative importance of the sales force and advertising spending expressed as a fraction of sales, which serves as a proxy for marketing advantages, and (3) the above-mentioned proxy for the ability to transfer organization skills.

The internationalization of Japanese electronics firms was based on an export penetration strategy complemented by the establishment of production facilities worldwide, especially after 1985. Belderbos (1997*a*) studies at the micro-level how internationalization through exporting and foreign investment was shaped by a complex set of forces comprising technological advantages, managerial capabilities, inter-firm linkages within industrial groups (keiretsu), and United States and European trade policies and barriers. European antidumping measures and local content rules targeting Japanese electronics firms encouraged FDI. Paradoxically, EU trade barriers turned out to promote the expansion of Japan electronics manufacturing rather than protect European industry.

5.8.4. Effects of Inward and Outward FDI

When the effects of FDI come into play the subject becomes controversial. FDI has been blamed for reducing employment and wages in their home markets. Hosts often argue that foreign investors monopolize local markets. On the other hand, FDI is said to increase employment, to generate transfers of technologies, to lead to faster productivity growth and encourage growth in host countries. Let us explore these turbulent waters.

Spillover Effects

There is no scarcity of spillover effects attributable to FDI. It brings managerial talent, generates technological spillovers, raises the marginal productivity of labor to a greater extent than it lowers the productivity of capital in a varieties model (Rivera-Batiz and Rivera-Batiz, 1990), features more advanced technologies than those available to local firms and can serve as a catalyst for development (Markusen and Venables, 1999).

There are two major types of dynamic externalities (i.e. spillovers). One externality arises from communication among firms within a sector. Variants of this type of externality appear in Paul Romer's (1990) model of research spillovers and Michael Porter's (1990) model of agglomeration externalities related to cluster location. The second type of externalities, often called Jacobian spillovers, derive from the accumulation of knowledge associated with diversity and therefore involves learning across sectors. In other words, firms in one sector learn from the activities in other sectors. There is evidence that both intra-sectorial and inter-sectorial spillovers are highly localized (Glaeser *et al.*, 1992).

The substantial evidence indicating that multinational corporations have positive spillover effects on home countries and that technology transfer is a major channel for these effects is surveyed by Blomström and Kokko (1998). Rhee and Belot (1989) offer evidence of technology transfer to domestic textile firms in Bangladesh and Blomström (1989) finds that Mexican sectors featuring greater foreign ownership experience faster productivity growth and faster convergence to US productivity levels.

Several case studies find limited or no spillovers. Mansfield and Romeo (1980) fail to find evidence of local technology spillovers. Aitken and Harrison (1999) report that the technology gains from foreign investment in Venezuela are captured by joint ventures rather than FDI. Moreover, they offer evidence suggesting that foreign investment negatively affects the productivity of domestically owned plants with no foreign investment.

Employment Effects of Outward FDI

What is the effect of outward FDI on source country employment and wages? Groups and political leaders in developed countries sourcing FDI have argued that it reduces source country employment and wages. The notion that FDI reduces wages has an analog in the notion that FDI reduces the demand for labor and employment. In the cases of Japan and Sweden, Lipsey *et al.* (2000) detect a positive correlation between the foreign affiliates' volume of production and parent's employment levels. Moreover, Swedish firms are found to allocate more capital-intensive production in foreign affiliates located in high-wage countries. In the US case, though, the allocation of labor-intensive production to foreign affiliates located in developing countries results in lower employment at the US parent.

5.9. ARE EXPORTS AND FDI SUBSTITUTES OR COMPLEMENTS?

Intra-firm trade, that is, trade between different subsidiaries of a multinational, accounts for a large share of global international trade. About 30 percent of world trade is made up of intra-firm trade. This fact suggests that FDI generates trade, although the interpretation of intra-firm trade is unclear because accounting data does not separate trade in intermediate products and trade in final products (Feenstra, 1998). Part of the measured increase in the share of intra-firm trade in aggregate trade represents double-counting in the sense that it is due to the same value added being moved across borders more frequently and does not represent an increase in the amount of value added entering into intra-firm trade. Consolidation of global production and income at the level of the multinational firm would eliminate double counting but this consolidation is not realized by statistical data sources.

In principle, FDI can be either trade creating or trade replacing. Trade creation takes place if FDI opens up a new market and facilitates exports from the home country to the host country. FDI can be realized to establish marketing and distribution channels that in turn facilitate exportation of final goods and services to the host country. This beachhead effect implies that FDI and exports are complementary modes of penetration. Trade diversion takes place if (1) trade and FDI are substitute modes of supplying a foreign market so that previous exports of final products from the home country are displaced by local production (as in the case of tariff jumping or when FDI seeks to obtain managerial control in a location previously supplied by exports), or (2) home country exports to third countries are replaced by a foreign affiliate's exports (Svensson, 1996).

Does available empirical evidence validate the conjecture that FDI and exports are complementary or substitute modes of penetration? A growing body of evidence suggests that FDI and exports are complements at some level of aggregation. Buigues and Jacquemin (1994) conduct a pooled cross-section analysis to examine the character of Japanese and US exports and FDI to the European Community. FDI and exports are found to be complementary, after controlling for intra-EC nontariff barriers, final demand growth rate, and sectorial specialization in the EC.

Brainard (1997) examines the relationship between exports and FDI. The empirical analysis tests the proximity-concentration hypothesis, captured by a firm's choice of selling abroad through foreign investment and exporting. The dependent variable is foreign investment measured as the share of US foreign affiliates sales relative to total sales. The explanatory variables include freight costs, barriers to trade and investment, economies of scale in plant production, and foreign production firm-specific advantages. The share of total sales accounted for by foreign sales is positively correlated with freight costs and trade barriers but negatively correlated with plant scale economies and barriers to investment. Inward and outward net affiliate sales elasticity with respect to tariffs is about 0.45 and 0.17 if measured with respect to NTBs. The import and export elasticity measured in terms of transportation costs is -1.

Brainard detects complementarity between trade and affiliate sales when relative income and intellectual property increases, but a relation of substitution when advertising increases. The complementary result hinges on multinational firms' intellectual property advantages (such as technologies and trademarks). Internationalization advantages permit capturing more market share abroad, and simultaneously increase both trade and foreign investment. The substitution effect is used as evidence of the importance of a presence for advertising-intensive goods.

Lipsey *et al.* (2000) find a positive relationship between exports to a region and affiliates production there. *Ceteris paribus*, greater production by affiliates in a region is associated with higher multinational parent companies exports from their home country to that region. Moreover, a Japanese parent's worldwide exports tend to be larger, relative to its output, the larger the firm's overseas production. This result has also been found to hold for US multinationals.

Head and Ries (2001) analysis of 932 Japanese manufacturing firms between 1966 and 1990 shows that firms first overseas investment raises exports by over 16 percent for distribution and over 11 percent for manufacturing. Norbäck (2001) develops a model in which the monopolist selects the technology by choosing the level of R&D and then decides whether to use the selected technology in the domestic plant (i.e. export) or foreign plant (i.e. FDI). The level of output depends on these technology choices.

The decision between exporting and producing abroad is determined by the level of technology transfer costs. If these are high (low) enough exporting (FDI) dominates. When transfer of technology is less costly, high-tech firms (firms in knowledge intensive industries with a relatively high return to R&D) tend to locate production abroad, while low-tech firms prefer exporting. When transfer of technology costs are high, high-tech firms tend to export while low-tech firms choose FDI. The reason is that high tech firms gain more by avoiding technology transfer costs than by avoiding transport costs. These hypotheses are tested using a database on Swedish multinationals.

The dependent variable is the share of foreign sales accounted for by the affiliates. The explanatory variables are: R&D intensity defined as R&D spending over total sales transport cost defined as the share of transport and packing costs in total variable costs the geographical distance between Sweden and the trading partner, a scale variable, and technology transport costs measured by the experience in foreign production as captured by a weighted average or the mean age of the affiliates in a particular country, the effects of R&D conducted abroad (indicated by a dummy variable that takes a value of one if the firm performs any R&D abroad), and another dummy variable that takes a value of 1 if the firm performs any R&D in the country in question. Experience in foreign production increases the probability of producing abroad. Establishing R&D laboratories in a host country, which facilitates transfer of technology, increases the probability of producing abroad. Economies of scale reduce the probability of producing abroad. These results confirm the predictions of the model.

5.10. INTRA-INDUSTRY FDI

One of the key stylized facts about FDI is the importance of intra-industry FDI, which is comparable to the importance of intra-industry trade. Greenaway *et al.* (1998) construct measures of intra-industry FDI utilizing the Grubel–Lloyd index of IIT. The Grubel–Lloyd index of intra-industry FDI, is defined in terms of outward FDI (OFDI) and inward FDI (IFDI) as follows

$$IIFDI = \frac{OFDI_i + IFDI_i - |OFDI_i - IFDI_i|}{OFDI_i + IFDI_i} \times 100.$$

Table 2.1 shows that the indexes of intra-industry FDI are as high as the indexes of intra-industry trade. The importance of intra-industry FDI poses a puzzle to theories of multinationals based on advantages over local firms. If FDI would be based only on multinational advantages over local firms, we would not expect that intra-industry FDI would be an important phenomenon.

One explanation for the intra-industry FDI puzzle is based on the proximity vs scale model. This approach stresses that single-product firms must choose between reducing trade costs by producing near their customer and exploiting scale economies by concentrating production at home and exporting. Horstmann and Markusen (1992) and Brainard (1993) develop imperfect competition models in which intra-industry FDI can take place between identical countries. Under imperfect competition, intra-industry FDI between identical nations takes place when the importance of proximity dominates the importance of scale. The idea is that trade in varieties under monopolistic competition is realized through FDI to be near the final market.

The proximity to market vs economies of scale approach poses the puzzle of what explains the simultaneity of exportation and FDI. Models that focus on the choice between exporting and FDI conclude that, depending on which factor dominates, firms either export or engage in FDI in the same product or variety. However, these models do not explain why exportation and FDI take place simultaneously. An exception is Markusen and Venables' (1998) model of firms that simultaneously export and foreign invest.

Baldwin and Ottaviano (2001) develop a model in which final good firms simultaneously engage in intra-industry FDI and intra-industry trade. Multiproduct firms produce differentiated varieties which are sold in all markets. Producers reduce competition among varieties by placing production of some varieties abroad. Producing abroad displaces some exports but creates trade via reversed imports. The economic mechanisms behind two-way FDI and two-way trade hinge on the presence of imperfect competition and are similar to the reciprocal dumping model developed by James Brander and Paul Krugman (1983). This model, examined in the chapter on dumping, utilizes oligopoly theory and a form of market segmentation to explain why the same type of good is imported from and exported to another country. In other words, intra-industry FDI can be viewed as reciprocal-FDI dumping.

5.11. CROSS-BORDER M&As AND COMPETITION

A substantial share of foreign investment takes the form of mergers with and acquisitions of foreign firms rather than greenfield investments. Domestic and cross-border mergers and acquisitions (M&As) are subject to competition policy. Mergers often affect firm efficiency, the degree of competition in a market, or both. The efficiency effects from mergers take place by generating reductions of fixed costs and marginal costs (usually called synergistic effects) and by expanding product pipelines.

M&As are often viewed as a mechanism to (1) impose market discipline by replacing bad managers, (2) exploit potential synergies among existing companies, (3) acquire knowledge or intangible assets, and (4) gain monopoly power.

The approach to takeovers as a market for managers acting under imperfect information has been extensively explored in the finance and corporate governance literature. Rossi and Volpin (2001) find a significant governance motive in cross-border mergers and acquisitions. Takeovers of companies displaying poor governance produce efficiency gains and can improve company performance and profits. The extent to which takeovers are productive and there are thus incentives for undertaking them hinges on the institutional and policy environments of the target country.

Kang and Johansson (2000) stress that the main reason why firms choose M&As instead of greenfield investment is the need to acquire complementary intangible assets such as technology, human resources, brand names, etc. The synergy view of M&As in research-oriented industries is formalized by Oliva and Rivera-Batiz (2002), who develop a model in which M&As arise endogenously to exploit knowledge synergies. International M&As represent a channel to establish multi-country research facilities that facilitate the appropriation and exploitation of technologies developed abroad. Moreover, M&As represent a strategy to respond to other firms cross-border M&As. They change the ownership of rival firms but do not necessarily change market concentration.

The model is consistent with stylized foreign investment facts. First, inward and outward foreign investments occur mostly among industrialized countries. In 1996, 70 and 91 percent of the stock of inward and outward foreign direct investment, respectively, was concentrated in the most industrialized countries. Second, M&As

dominate, for some industries overwhelmingly, foreign investment in the United States. Third, research-based manufacturing companies frequently conduct research in facilities spread at strategic locations, especially in the United States, the United Kingdom, France, and Germany.

5.11.1. Mergers and Strategic Trade Policy

Merger-antitrust policies are defined analytically in terms of the number of domestic firms, which is assumed to be a function of competition policy and partially controllable by the regulator. The extent of competition increases with the number of domestic firms. Notice that this formulation captures the concept of competition policy but is not fine enough to distinguish between merger policies and antitrust policies. For simplicity, the exposition is cast in terms of merger policies.

Mergers can involve domestic firms, domestic and foreign firms (cross-border mergers) and foreign firms. Domestic mergers reduce the number of firms operating in the domestic markets and thus have a direct effect on competition (that could be offset by foreign producers). By contrast, cross-border acquisitions alter ownership but do not directly reduce the number of firms operating in a market. Mergers between foreign firms affect market concentration abroad and have effects on domestic producers and welfare.

Dixit (1984) examines how optimal tax and subsidy policies depend on the number of home and foreign firms. The analysis does not treat the number of firms as an endogenous variable but rather as a variable subject to policy.

Merger and trade policies can be used as alternative or complementary instruments to attain national goals. Let us focus on export promotion. Paul Krugman (1984) shows that, when the total cost function $C_i(q_i)$ exhibits declining marginal costs, protection can work as an export-promotion policy. Tariff protection discourages imports and encourages domestic production for the local market, which in turn reduces marginal costs. If the marginal cost reduction due to tariff protection is strong enough and production expands enough, the country will become an exporter. This rationale is called the import protection as export promotion argument.

Is there a competition policy that promotes exports by promoting the home market? This question is examined by Bliss (1996) and Rysman (2000). Rysman utilizes Brander and Spencer's third-market model to show that merger-divestiture policies can be viewed as a substitute for a strategic export subsidy. A merger-divestiture policy used to control the number of firms can be used as a substitute for a domestic production subsidy in a free trade situation. The optimal merger policy is to promote divestitures and thus increase the number of domestic firms and domestic industry production. This policy allows domestic industry to establish a Stackelberg leadership position and shift profits toward domestic firms in a Cournot competition model.

Bliss (1996) argues that it is not possible to generally specify a priori which type of competition policy actually promotes exports. Bliss uses a reciprocal dumping model in which two countries dump goods on each other (reciprocal dumping is studied in the chapter on dumping) to show that competition policy entails two conflicting effects.

On one hand, a lax policy that reduces the number of producers in the home market allows surviving firms to exploit economies of scale (say, falling marginal costs) by increasing production, which in turn promotes exports. On the other hand, *ceteris paribus*, the smaller the number of producers, the lower the level of exports. Specifically, keeping constant marginal costs, a competition policy that increases the number of firms helps to promote exports. The net effect of a lax competition policy, which allows exploiting economies of scale while lowering the number of potential exporters, is ambiguous in the presence of economies of scale. Therefore, it is not possible to generally specify whether a lax or a strict competition policy will promote exports.

The policy analysis is quite different under declining and constant marginal costs. When marginal costs are declining, firms have incentives to merge voluntarily. A lax competition policy will lead to mergers. When marginal costs are constant, there are no general incentives to merge or divest because profits may increase or decrease after either operation.

5.12. MERGER EVALUATION IN AN OPEN ECONOMY

How are M&As and antitrust policies formulated in an open economy? In a close economy, conventional welfare analysis of mergers compares the sum of domestic consumer surplus and producer's profits in the pre-merger and post-merger situations. In an open economy, the nationalistic welfare criterion includes nationals and ignores foreign agents. As such, welfare assessments must take into account the division of surplus generated by the merger between participating domestic and foreign firms. The incentives and effects of mergers among an exogenously chosen group of firms are examined in Barros and Cabral (1994) and Long and Vousden (1995).

What criteria should authorities use to decide whether or not to approve domestic and cross-border mergers in an open economy? Cabral and Barros (1994) provide an open economy rule for the approval of horizontal mergers. The analysis extends the pioneering work on domestic merger evaluation undertaken by Farrell and Shapiro (1990) in a closed economy context to control for the impact of mergers on foreign firms and foreign consumers in the evaluation of a merger proposal.

Consider an open economy model with M foreign firms and $N = I + O$ domestic firms, where I (for inside) denotes domestic firms participating in a merger and O (for outside) stands for the rest of domestic firms. Firms interact in a Cournot market structure. Consumer demand is denoted by $p(Q)$. Firms produce an homogenous good with cost function $C_i(q_i)$ so that firm profits are given by $\pi_i = p(Q)q_i - C_i(q_i)$.

Two alternative systems of merger evaluation are considered. Under independent national policies, each country has a national merger authority maximizing domestic welfare. Under an harmonized system, a supra-national merger authority maximizes total welfare.

The optimal merger policy differs depending on the perspective adopted. Farrell and Shapiro (1990) derived a formula from a closed economy perspective. They notice that a merger would not take place unless it increases the profits of the merging firms. They thus focus on what are usually called the 'external' or 'spillover' effects of mergers on consumers and nonmerging firms. If these 'external' effects are positive, the mergers are welfare-enhancing. In other words, a sufficient condition for a merger to enhance welfare is that the merger produces a positive effect on the sum of consumer surplus plus the profits of the firms that do not form part of the merger.

Farrell and Shapiro's (1990) sufficient condition for a welfare-enhancing merger effect is that the industry production share of the merging firms does not exceed the weighted share of the firms outside the merger (denoted by O) after the merger takes place. Formally, a proposed merger would be approved, because it produces positive external spillover effects, if (Barros and Cabral, 1994, contains detailed derivations)

$$s_I - \sum_{j \in O} \lambda_j s_j < 0,$$

where I (for inside) denotes the merging firms, $s_I = \sum_{i \in I} s_i = \sum_{i \in I} q_i / Q$ is the post-merger share of domestic merging firms in total supply, and $\lambda_j = -dq_j/dQ > 0$.

In an open economy, the rules for merger approval take into account that national regulators are concerned with domestic welfare and ignore the effects of mergers on foreign firms and foreign consumers. A merger is approved if domestic external effects are positive, which happens if and only if (see Barros and Cabral, 1994)

$$s_I + s_F - \sum_{j \in O} \lambda_j s_j < 0,$$

where $s_F = \sum_{j \in F} s_j$ is the post-merger domestic production share of merging foreign firms and nonmerging foreign firms operating in the domestic market. This rule applies to mergers between domestic firms, cross-border mergers between domestic and foreign firms (in which case s_I refers only to the production share of merging domestic firms), and mergers between foreign firms (in which case $s_I = 0$). Other things equal, the smaller the extent of foreign penetration in the domestic market as measured by the share of foreign firms production, the easier it would be to satisfy the approval of a merger. This feature reflects the property that foreign producers get positive external effects from a merger's anticompetitive impact but profits received by foreign firms are not taken into account by the domestic regulator.

Adopting a European Union perspective, let us compute the difference between the rule applying to a supra-national authority and the rule applying to a national authority (country k) in a system of decentralized national merger policies. From the perspective of country k, the external effect of a merger involving country k's I firms is positive if (see Barros and Cabral, 1994)

$$d^k - s^k + s_I^k - \sum_{j \in O^k} \lambda_j^k s_j^k < 0, \tag{5.1}$$

where $d^k = D^k/D$ represents each country's share in total demand, s^k is each country's share in total supply (Q^k/Q), $s_I^k = \sum_{i \in I} s_i^k = \sum_{i \in I} q_i^k / Q$, and $\lambda_j = -dq_j^k/dQ$. The close economy formula developed by Farrell and Shapiro is a particular case of condition (5.1) with $d^k = 1$, $s^k = 1$, and $O^k = O$ (the complement set of O^k is a null set because there is no foreign country). The open economy formula obtains if $d^k = 1$ and $S^k = 1 - SF$. Condition (5.1) also applies for the external effect of a cross-border merger to be positive with the caveat that s_f^k refers only to domestic firms in the mergers and does not include foreign firms participating in the merger.

A supranational regulator would assume a community perspective and thus utilize a formula similar to the closed economy formula. In general, the supranational regulator will reach different decisions from national authorities. However, the community regulator might possess less information about λ_j^k than a national regulator. There is thus a trade off between acting on behalf of the overall community and the information requirements for efficient community welfare maximization.

Horn and Persson (2001) derive the patterns of merger endogenously, determine whether domestic or cross-border mergers are likely to take place, and assess the welfare effects of these mergers. Specifically, the authors address the following issues: (1) how domestic or international merger decisions vary with trade costs if there are no synergies, (2) policies toward mergers that save fixed costs such as administrative costs, and (3) policies toward mergers that generate synergies in the sense that they reduce merging firms marginal costs.

The endogenous merger structure approach takes into account that foreign firms will have the same incentives as foreign firms. A domestic merger might then induce a foreign merger. A cross-border merger might also induce a response in the form of another cross-border merger. In these cases, marginal cost reductions do not automatically generate positive market share effects for the merging firms (see also Oliva and Rivera-Batiz, 2002).

5.13. CONCLUSIONS

Factor mobility has exploded in the past decades. Increased migration reflects a large supply of migrants due to large cross-country wage differentials as well as demand factors arising from labor scarcity in host countries and structural changes in labor markets. The proliferation of FDI reflects the globalization of production as well as liberal policies toward capital flows. Even though migration and FDI have always been and continue to be highly controversial, evidence shows that they fulfill an economic role. With the possible exception of adverse selection in some migrant groups, induced terms of trade deterioration in host countries, and potential income distribution effects in host and source countries, factor mobility represents an efficient channel for the global allocation of resources.

5.14. APPENDIX

The operating profits of an n-firm type are given by (see Chapter 2)

$$\pi^n = \frac{p_j d_j}{\sigma} = \frac{1}{\sigma} \left[p_j \frac{p_j^{-\sigma}}{p_M^{1-\sigma}} \mu E + p_k \frac{p_k^{-\sigma}}{p_M^{1-\sigma}} \mu E \right],$$

which assumes the local firm sells good j at home and exports good k abroad

$$\pi^n = \frac{1}{\sigma}\left[\frac{1}{p_M^{1-\sigma}}\mu E + \frac{T^{1-\sigma}}{p_M^{1-\sigma}}\mu E\right] = \frac{1}{\sigma}\frac{\mu E + T^{1-\sigma}\mu E}{2m + n(1+T^{1-\sigma})},$$

where we have used $p_j = 1$ and $p_k = T$.

The price index can be decomposed into the following three integrals: (1) goods sold by a multinational producing in each location, (2) goods n^* exported, and (3) goods n sold locally

$$p_M^{1-\sigma} = \int_0^{m+m^*} 1^{1-\sigma}\,di + \int_{m+m^*+n}^{N^W} T^{1-\sigma}\,di + \int_{m+m^*+n^*}^{N^W} 1^{1-\sigma}\,di$$

$$= i\,|_0^{m+m^*}\,(T^{1-\sigma})i\,|_{m+m^*+n}^{N^W} + i\,|_{m+m^*+n^*}^{N^W}$$

$$= m + m^* + n^*T^{1-\sigma} + n = 2m + (T^{1-\sigma} + 1)n.$$

Dividing numerator and denominator of π^n by N and rearranging terms yields

$$\pi^n = \frac{1}{\sigma}\left[\frac{\mu E/N}{2m/N + n/N(1+T^{1-\sigma})} + \frac{T^{1-\sigma}\mu E/N}{2m/N + n/N(1+T^{1-\sigma})}\right]$$

$$= \frac{(1+T^{1-\sigma})\mu E/\sigma N}{2s_m + (1-s_m)(1+T^{1-\sigma})}.$$

The operating profits of a multinational are

$$\pi^m = \frac{2\mu E/\sigma N}{2s_m + (1-s_m)(1+\phi)}.$$

The reason is that a multinational produces in both markets (so there are no exports), which implies

$$\pi^m = \frac{p_k d_k}{\sigma} = \frac{1}{\sigma}\left[p_j\frac{p_j^{-\sigma}}{p_M^{1-\sigma}}\mu E + p_k\frac{p_k^{-\sigma}}{p_M^{1-\sigma}}\mu E\right]$$

$$= \frac{1}{\sigma}\left[\frac{1}{p_M^{1-\sigma}}\mu E + \frac{1}{p_M^{1-\sigma}}\mu E\right]$$

$$= \frac{1}{\sigma}\frac{2\mu E}{2m + n(1+T^{1-\sigma})} = \frac{1}{\sigma}\frac{2\mu E/N}{2m/N + n/N(1+T^{1-\sigma})}$$

$$= \frac{2\mu E/\sigma N}{2s_m + (1-s_m)(1+\phi)}.$$

6

Growth, Trade, and FDI

The miraculous performance of outward-oriented East Asian economies in the post-Second World War period fueled a search for explanations of how they came to grow so fast for so long. Static trade theories predict that greater specialization leads to higher income measured at international prices but do not offer an explanation for sustained growth.

Can international trade promote growth? The endogenous growth literature implies that trade and technology diffusion can generate growth effects by increasing the size of the economy's research sector. The empirical evidence on the relation between trade and growth has become a controversial subject.

What determines whether a country becomes a technological leader or a follower? Technological change, that is, the development of new technologies, alters the competitive conditions of firms, regions, and countries. The availability of new technologies causes some traders to gain competitive advantage, while others lose them. A dominant industrial position can be lost due to the inability or unwillingness to adopt or develop new technologies.

A major part of the action in the international competition game takes place in the quality and productivity improvement arenas. Producers invest in research and development in order to upgrade product quality. Winners gain a temporary leader position that allows them to reap monopoly profits. In turn, the diffusion of the new technology and the monopoly profit potential induce followers to conduct research to better the product quality offered by the incumbent. Rivalry for monopoly profits generates a quality ladder of ever improving qualities.

Technological leadership is often gained by adopting productivity-increasing technological breakthroughs. A key point is that current industry leaders are not always the first to adopt new technologies. For instance, learning-by-doing implies that the productivity of existing and new technologies depends on the accumulated experience in using them. New, untried technologies might thus be less productive initially than old but well-understood technologies. In fact, nations that have established an industrial lead, and have acquired a large enough accumulated experience in using a particular technology, will find out that new technologies can be initially worse than older alternatives. Producers will stick to an old technology if cumulative learning-by-doing productivity improvements from using the old technology are large enough and new technologies are initially less productive than the old.

New leaders arise when they develop or adopt new technologies that improve their competitive position by a large enough margin. Learning-by-doing productivity gains resulting from using a new technology dominate the old technology once users acquire experience with it. Leapfrogging is a process allowing a lagging region or country to become a leader following the adoption of new technologies that the current leader fails to adopt. The implementation of new technologies enables the lagging region or country to eventually achieve lower costs of production than the current leader. This process generates a cycle of alternating technology leaders.

The emergence of England as the leader of the industrial revolution illustrates leapfrogging. In the eighteenth century, Holland had established a lead in shipping, banking, and trading. Its income per capita and wage levels were higher than in England, other European economies, and the United States. However, Holland stayed within the scope of its leading sectors and did not exploit new technologies such as that for cotton spinning. In contrast, the poorer English rapidly exploited the new technologies arising at the onset of the industrial revolution. Eventually, England surpassed the Dutch in technology leadership and income per capita. A similar process underlies the rise of the United States as the industrial leader of the twentieth century and the rise of Japan to become a formidable US rival in the 1980s.

Section 6.1 develops a model of trade and growth driven by a research sector and research spillovers. Section 6.2 presents a model of cyclical leadership proceeding along increasing quality ladders and policy responses to loss of technological supremacy. Section 6.3 examines international competition affected by learning-by-doing effects in manufacturing but exhibiting no leapfrogging. Section 6.4 develops the dynamics of leapfrogging based on adoption of technological breakthroughs as a channel that, in combination with learning-by-doing, can induce the replacement of an industrial leader. Section 6.5 reviews the controversy on the empirical relation between trade and growth. Section 6.6 examines convergence across countries and regions, poverty and inequality. Section 6.7 explores the relation between growth and foreign direct investment.

6.1. ENDOGENOUS GROWTH THROUGH R&D

Endogenous growth theory explains the growth residual, that is, that part of growth that is not explainable by growth in factors of production (e.g. capital accumulation, population growth). This approach aims to provide explanations for the observed differences in growth rates across countries. The voluminous literature on endogenous growth is discussed in the books by Grossman and Helpman (1991a), Aghion and Howitt (1998) and Barro and Sala-i-Martin (1998).

In Romer (1990), the engine of growth is technological change. The representative consumer's utility function is given by the discounted value of consumption D_t over an infinite lifetime

$$U = \int_{t=0}^{t=\infty} e^{-\rho t} \frac{D_t^{1-\sigma}}{1-\sigma},$$

where the rate of discount $\rho > 0$ (i.e. the rate of time preference) and the intertemporal elasticity of substitution in consumption $\sigma > 0$ are assumed to be constant. Maximizing utility subject to a lifetime budget constraint yields a relationship between the rate of growth of consumption and the rate of interest

$$\frac{\dot{D}_t}{D_t} = \frac{r - \rho}{\sigma} \iff r = \rho + \sigma \frac{\dot{D}_t}{D_t}.$$

A higher interest rate r, a lower the rate of time preference ρ, and a lower the intertemporal elasticity of substitution σ encourage savings causing consumption to rise faster.

The productive side of the economy consists of two sectors: research and manufacturing. The research sector is devoted to produce new technologies and is the engine of growth in the model. The rate of change $\dot{A}$ of the level of technology A is taken to increase with the amount of human capital H_A devoted to research (i.e. engaged in technology creation) and with the current level of technology A

$$\dot{A} = \delta H_A A,$$

where δ is a research productivity parameter, assumed to be constant. The previous technological change function reflects the idea that technology advances faster the greater the volume of resources devoted to it and the more advanced current technologies are.

The manufacturing sector produces two types of goods: homogeneous consumption goods and capital goods consisting of differentiated inputs. In order for a differentiated input to be produced, however, it must have been previously invented or designed. In this model, new intermediate inputs (i.e. machines) are invented or designed through research efforts.

The manufacturing production function utilizes human capital H_m, unskilled labor L and a set of intermediate inputs x_i, $i \in \{0, A\}$, à la Ethier (1982)

$$Y = H_m^\alpha L^\beta \int_0^A x_i^{1-\alpha-\beta} \, di = H_m^\alpha L^\beta \int_0^A \bar{x}^{1-\alpha-\beta} \, di = A H_m^\alpha L^\beta \bar{x}^{1-\alpha-\beta}.$$

Observe that a more advanced technology (i.e. a higher value of A), is reflected in a greater number of currently available intermediate inputs. Intermediate inputs are assumed to cost the same to produce and to enter symmetrically in the manufacturing production function. Therefore, the amount of each intermediate input used in manufacturing is the same for all existing inputs ($x_i = \bar{x}$) at equilibrium. The manufacturing production function embodies a form of increasing returns. If all inputs, including technology A, are increased proportionately, output increases more than proportionately.

The previous model of a research sector and a sector producing differentiated intermediate goods can be solved for the steady state growth rate of output g. The steady state is characterized by the equality of the growth rates of output g, technology $\dot{A}/A$ and consumption $\dot{D}/D$

$$g = \frac{\dot{A}}{A} = \delta H_A = \frac{\dot{D}}{D} = \frac{r - \rho}{\sigma}.$$

The closed economy or autarky solution is

$$g^{autarky} = \frac{\delta H - \Lambda\rho}{\Lambda\sigma + 1}, \quad \Lambda = \frac{\alpha}{(1 - \alpha - \beta)(\alpha + \beta)}. \tag{6.1}$$

This solution implies that the steady state growth rate g is

(1) an increasing function of human capital $H = H_A + H_M$ and the productivity δ of human capital devoted to research;
(2) a decreasing function of the rate of discount ρ and the intertemporal elasticity of substitution in consumption σ.

6.1.1. Trade and Growth

What is the effect of greater international trade on income and economic growth? The general intuition explaining the relation between trade, income and growth is that greater openness leads to higher income or faster growth if it expands sectors generating technological change and encourages activities that produce learning-by-doing productivity gains (Young, 1991). Greater trade leads to slower growth if it expands sectors that do not generate new technologies or produce learning-by-doing gains.

A takeoff effect leading to sustained income growth can arise if trade has an enlarged market effect that (1) leads to exploitation of economies of scale in the presence of increasing returns to scale, (2) encourages the diffusion of ideas, (3) induces the elimination of duplication in research, and (4) strengthens creative destruction. If these effects lead to sustained improvements in manufacturing and R&D productivity, technological change will proceed at a faster rate resulting in faster growth. These positive growth effects are explicitly modeled in Segerstrom *et al.* (1990), Grossman and Helpman (1990, 1991*a*), Rivera-Batiz and Romer (1991*a*,*b*), and Aghion and Howitt (1992).

Let us contrast two polar cases in the open economy model of Rivera-Batiz and Romer (1991*a*): trade in technology only and trade in goods only. Trade in technology refers to trade in ideas leading to diffusion of technology with no trade in intermediates goods. Trade in goods refers to trade in intermediate goods and no diffusion of technology.

When there is trade in ideas only, the growth rate becomes

$$g^{ideas} = \frac{2\delta H - \Lambda\rho}{\Lambda\sigma + 1} > g^{autarky} = \frac{\delta H - \Lambda\rho}{\Lambda\sigma + 1}. \tag{6.2}$$

This formula can be heuristically derived from its closed economy analog by recognizing that trade in ideas effectively doubles the productivity of research in this setup and is equivalent to doubling δ. The growth rate in an economy that is open to trade in ideas is higher than the growth rate in a closed economy. This result illustrates the growth-promoting role of technology diffusion. The intuition is that technology diffusion makes the research sector more productive for both economies.

What happens if there is only trade in goods with no trade in technology and growth is driven by endogenous technology creation? In this case, trade in goods is counterproductive in terms of economic growth. The growth case when there is trade in inputs but no trade in ideas is given by (Barreto and Kobayashi)

$$g^{inputs} = \frac{\delta H - 2\Lambda\rho}{2\Lambda\sigma + 1} < g^{autarky} = \frac{\delta H - \Lambda\rho}{\Lambda\sigma + 1}. \tag{6.3}$$

This formula is heuristically derived by replacing Λ for 2Λ in the formula, which takes into account that expanding the range of available intermediate inputs increases the productivity of human capital in the manufacturing sector. Trade makes the manufacturing sector more productive. In turn, a more productive manufacturing sector shifts resources away from the growth-creating research sector.

The previous example illustrates a case in which opening trade in goods is counterproductive in terms of the growth rate. The reason is that it shifts resources away from the sector that generates growth. A policy of trade liberalization turns out to be growth-reducing.

What happens if there is trade in intermediates and trade in ideas? The knowledge-driven model with trade in intermediates plus trade in ideas incorporates growth effects through both the manufacturing and research sectors. The growth rate is given by

$$g^{ideas+inputs} = \frac{2\delta H - 2\Lambda\rho}{2\Lambda\sigma + 1} = \frac{\delta H - \Lambda\rho}{\Lambda\sigma + \frac{1}{2}} > g^{autarky} = \frac{\delta H - \Lambda\rho}{\Lambda\sigma + 1}. \tag{6.4}$$

The formula can be heuristically derived from Romer's (1990) model by

1. Replacing δ by 2δ. This takes into account the greater productivity of human capital devoted to research (due to trade in ideas);
2. Replacing Λ by 2Λ. This takes into account that expanding the range of available intermediates increases the productivity of human capital in the manufacturing sector.

The greater productivity of research resulting from trade in ideas shifts resources toward the research sector and reinstates a positive growth effect from trade. The combination of trade liberalization and policies to promote the diffusion of technology increases growth even if trade liberalization alone would slow down growth in this setting.

What are the lessons from these growth experiments? The key idea is that the growth effect of trade depends on whether it shifts resources toward or away from the sector that represents the economy's engine of growth. International technology diffusion makes the innovative research sector more productive and *ceteris paribus*, induces a shift of resources toward research. In turn, the growth rate increases. In general, there is no presumption that trade in goods must increase the growth rate. It could very well shift resources toward activities that do not generate growth (manufacturing or natural resources), reducing the size of the growth-generating sector. If this happens, greater trade leads to slower economic growth. Both cases, growth acceleration and growth deceleration, can be derived from alternative frameworks.

6.2. QUALITY LADDERS

Consider the two–country model with one factor, two sectors and international quality competition developed by Grossman and Helpman (1991*b,d*). Domestic innovation leads to product varieties upgrading that permit domestic firms to lead in a quality competition race against their foreign rivals. The current invention race's winner obtains an edge in the market, holds a temporary monopoly position and recovers the costs of innovation. The loser in the innovation game experiences losses. Eventually, rivals succeed in improving quality and the former winner loses the monopolist position. The model generates a cycle of technological leadership.

6.2.1. *Demand and Spending*

Infinitely lived households are assumed to maximize intertemporal utility

$$U = \int_0^\infty e^{-\rho t} \ln u(t)\, dt.$$

Instantaneous utility at time t, $\ln u(t)$, depends on component goods ω indexed by quality j

$$\ln u(t) = \int_0^1 \ln \left[\sum_j q_j(\omega) d_{jt}(\omega) \right] d\omega,$$

where $q_j(\omega)$ is the quality of good ω after j improvements and $d_{jt}(\omega)$ represents consumption of good ω (improved j times) at time t. Total spending $E(t)$ at time t is

$$E(t) = \int_0^1 \left[\sum_j p_{jt}(\omega) d_{jt}(\omega) \right] d\omega,$$

where $p_{jt}(\omega)$ is the price of good ω after j improvements. The consumer maximizes lifetime utility subject to the lifetime budget constraint indicating that the discounted value of spending is equal to initial wealth W_0

$$\int_0^\infty e^{-R(t)} E(t)\, dt = W_0,$$

where $R(t)$ is the cumulative interest factor up to time t.

Utility maximization is achieved in two stages: (1) allocation of current consumption across available goods, and (2) intertemporal allocation of spending. A maximum is attained when the consumer

1. Allocates the same expenditure to each product of type ω;
2. Chooses the variety that features the lowest quality-adjusted price $p_{jt}(\omega)/q_j(\omega)$, which corresponds to the highest available quality of good ω.

Static demand functions are ($d_{jt}(\omega) \cdot p_{jt}(\omega)$ does not depend on ω or j) given by

$$
d_{jt}(\omega) = \begin{cases} \dfrac{E(t)}{p_{jt}(\omega)}, & j = \mathcal{J}_t(\omega), \\ 0, & j < \mathcal{J}_t(\omega), \end{cases}
$$

where $\mathcal{J}_t(\omega)$ is the quality of the good with the lowest quality-adjusted price. Substituting these demand functions into $u(t)$ and the result into U yields, if $q_{jt}(\omega) = q_t(\omega)$,

$$
U = \int_0^\infty e^{-\rho t} \left\{ \ln E(t) + \int_0^1 [\ln q_t(\omega) - \ln p_t(\omega)] \, d\omega \right\} dt.
$$

Maximizing utility function U subject to the lifetime budget constraint yields that the rate of change of spending is

$$
\frac{\dot{E}}{E} = \dot{R} - \rho.
$$

6.2.2. Producers' Problem

Each firm utilizes one unit of labor to produce a unit of good ω of any available quality. The marginal cost faced by each firm is the same c and is normalized to $c = 1$. Markets are assumed to be oligopolistic and firms to compete in prices. At equilibrium, prices and output levels vary depending on the level of competition for a given quality level. Consider the following two alternative cases.

1. A group of firms in the industry produce a good with the same quality. In this case, all firms will charge the same price, which coincides with the unit cost $c = 1$. Therefore, profits are zero. For a given quality level, price competition converges to the well-known homogeneous goods equilibrium in which Bertrand prices are equal to marginal cost: $p = c = 1$.
2. A firm holds a monopoly position because it is able to produce a good of higher quality than its rivals. In this case, the leader charges the price resulting from the limit-pricing strategy, an entry deterrence strategy that leaves no scope for the rivals to make positive profits.

Under the limit pricing strategy, the adjusted-quality price is set to be slightly lower to the rivals' marginal cost. The limit-pricing for all goods ω is

$$
p = q_t(\omega)c = \lambda,
$$

where $c = 1$ and quality $q_t(\omega) = \lambda$ is assumed to be the same for every ω. The demand for a product of quality λ sold at price $p = \lambda$ is equal to $d(\omega) = E/p = E/\lambda$. Gross profits π are equal to the price markup over marginal cost times the amount sold

$$\pi = (p-1)\frac{E}{\lambda} = \frac{\lambda - 1}{\lambda}E = \left(1 - \frac{1}{\lambda}\right)E. \tag{6.5}$$

6.2.3. Rate of Innovation

Firms undertake research in order to reach the next higher step in the quality ladder. Research effort intensity I during time interval dt requires $aI\,dt$ units of labor and has a probability of success equal to Idt, where a measures the research labor requirement. Innovation is assumed to take place simultaneously in the continuum of available products, $j \in (0, 1)$.

E/λ is equal to the world labor force L^W minus labor in research aI. Also, $\pi = E - \frac{E}{\lambda} = (\rho + I)a$ implies $E = L^W - aI + (\rho + I)a = L^W + a\rho$

$$E = \lambda L^W - \lambda aI = L^W + a\rho.$$

The equilibrium rate of innovation is

$$I = \left(1 - \frac{1}{\lambda}\right)\frac{L^W}{a} - \frac{\rho}{\lambda}.$$

Innovation grows faster with a higher product quality and labor force and with a lower research labor requirement and rate of discount.

6.2.4. Licensing vs FDI

What determines the choice between foreign direct investment (FDI) and licensing in a dynamic model of endogenous quality innovation? Glass and Saggi (2002) examine the FDI vs licensing choice (exporting is not considered). Firms compete in prices and the leader adopts an entry deterrence strategy. Multinationals operating abroad have a cost disadvantage that increases marginal costs from $c_{LIC} = 1$ for licensing to $c = 1 + c_{FDI}/2$ for multinationals. Licensing is costly because licensees retain part of the profits generated by innovation. If licensees keep a fraction θ of the profits generated abroad, the profits from FDI and licensing are ($p = \lambda$)

$$\pi_{LIC} = \left(1 - \frac{\theta}{2}\right)(p-1)\frac{E}{\lambda} = \left(1 - \frac{\theta}{2}\right)\left(1 - \frac{1}{\lambda}\right)E,$$

$$\pi_{FDI} = \left(p - \left(1 + \frac{c_{FDI}}{2}\right)\right)\frac{E}{\lambda} = \left(1 - \frac{1}{\lambda}\left(1 + \frac{c_{FDI}}{2}\right)\right)E,$$

where we have used (6.5).

The profit retention effect alters the choice between FDI and licensing as well as the rate of innovation. Specifically, high profit retention abroad (1) reduces the incentives to innovate and the equilibrium rate of innovation, and (2) favors FDI over licensing. If licensees' profit retention is large enough to offset multinationals' cost disadvantage, FDI beats licensing as a mode of entry.

6.2.5. Technological Supremacy and Protection

How do countries react to the loss of technological leadership? What is the best trade policy in support of domestic firms being overtaken by rivals and facing the loss of technological leadership? In many instances, governments react by implementing protectionist measures in the form of import tariffs, countervailing duties or antidumping investigations (see chapters on trade restrictions and dumping). In other cases, like the Airbus and Boeing, large-scale subsidization dominates.

Dinopoulos and Segerstrom (1999) examine the dynamic effects associated with the protection of followers in a technology race. They consider a variant of the two-country quality ladders growth model à la Grossman and Helpman (1991). There is a continuum of final goods industries. In each industry, firms' production differs in quality. Competing firms suffer from random shifts in competitiveness as a consequence of the global technological race they are involved in. This means that at some point some firms in an industry produce a state-of-the art quality product and go ahead in the race to become the leaders. If domestic leading firms lose their position to other domestic rivals, the government maintains free trade conditions.

What is the role of contingent import tariffs when foreign rivals become technological leaders that surpass domestic firms' technological capability? The analysis focuses on two types of contingent *ad valorem* tariffs on imports (1) small rent-extracting tariffs allowing foreign leaders to keep domestic firms out of the market, and (2) large protective tariffs driving foreign leaders out of the domestic market.

The establishment of small contingent tariffs, aiming to extract rents from foreign quality leaders and transfer them to the domestic government, makes innovation more attractive in exporting industries than in importing industries. Indeed, a permanent increase in rent-extracting contingent tariff results in a permanent increase in exporting industries' R&D intensity, but in a permanent decline in importing industries' R&D intensity. Diminishing returns to R&D imply, that rent-extracting tariffs have a negative impact on the rate of global technological change in the short run and no impact on the long run growth rate (as an R&D scale effect is not present).

When domestic firms lose a position of technological leadership, tariff protection allows them to charge higher prices and shift resources from the manufacturing to the R&D sector. This represents a policy of protection contingent on the loss of leadership in a global technological race. In contrast to the rent-extracting contingent tariff case, the establishment of high contingent tariffs protecting domestic firms against foreign competitors and facilitating catching up with foreign rivals results in permanent increases in import-oriented industries' R&D intensity and in permanent reductions in export-oriented industries' R&D intensity. Protective contingent tariffs have a positive short run impact on the global rate of technological change, but no effect in the long run growth rate (as in the rent-extracting tariff case).

6.3. COMPARATIVE ADVANTAGE AND LEARNING

This section discusses a two-country model of international competition that endogenizes comparative advantage by introducing learning-by-doing effects that generate productivity improvements. The model introduces learning-by-doing into the static Ricardian model studied in Chapter 1. The dynamics endogenize the rate of technological change in sector I, which is identified with manufacturing, and assumes no technological change in sector II, identified with the food sector (the biotechnology revolution might call for a revision of this traditional view). The analysis specifies the dynamics of resource allocation, the price of manufactures relative to food, wages, and the trade pattern implied by international competition. Findlay (1995) contains an analysis of learning, innovation and growth in a generalized factor abundance model.

6.3.1. Factor Endowments and Demand

The domestic and foreign economies have the same endowments of labor L and L^*

$$L = L^*,$$

so that factor endowment differences do not play any role in the analysis. Labor is employed in two industries, called I and II. The Cobb–Douglas utility functions are

$$U(D_I, D_{II}) = D_I^\mu D_{II}^{1-\mu}, \quad U(D_I, D_{II}) = D_I^\mu D_{II}^{1-\mu}, \qquad \mu > 0.5,$$

where D_I and D_{II} represent consumption of goods I and II, respectively, and μ is a parameter of preferences.

6.3.2. Technologically Stagnant Sector

The sector producing good II is assumed to be technologically stagnant in the sense that it does not experience any sort of productivity improvement. The food production functions of the domestic and foreign countries are identical and are given by a linear function

$$Q_{II}(L_{II}) = A_{II} L_{II} = L_{II} \quad \text{and} \quad Q_{II}^*(L_{II}^*) = A_{II}^* L_{II}^* = L_{II}^*,$$

where Q_{II} and L_{II} represent production and employment in industry II, respectively. Labor productivity is normalized to be one ($A_{II} = A_{II}^*$). Because labor productivity in sector II is the same in both countries, this is a valid procedure accomplished by appropriately defining the units of output II.

6.3.3. Incremental Sectorial Learning-by-doing

Output in sector I at time T, $Q_I(T)$, is produced by

$$Q_I(T) = A_I(K(T))L_I,$$

where $A_I(K(T))$ represents labor productivity at time T, and L_I is the amount of labor devoted to good I. The productivity level is assumed to be a function of knowledge capital accumulated up to time T, which is labelled $K(T)$.

What determines the level of knowledge capital? Knowledge capital $K(T)$ is assumed to represent a learning-by-doing process, that is, it increases with the cumulative production of good I up to time T

$$K(T) = \int_{-\infty}^{T} Q_I(t)\, dt.$$

As an illustration, if good I is produced at the constant rate Q_I over times 0 to T, the previous integral yields $K(T) = TQ_I$. In this example knowledge capital increases linearly with time.

The previous formulation embodies the notion that learning-by-doing improves labor productivity over time. The productivity level at time T, $A_I(K(T)) = Q_I(T)/L_I$, is a function of knowledge capital $K(T)$, which is in turn assumed to depend on the accumulated experience in using the technology. Labor productivity $A_I(K)$ is assumed to be strictly increasing in knowledge capital (i.e. $A_I'(K) > 0$), but at a declining rate (i.e. $A_I''(K) < 0$). In other words, technology is subject to diminishing returns to learning-by-doing.

The rate of change of knowledge capital is the time derivative of $K(T)$

$$\frac{dK(T)}{dT} = \frac{d\left[\int_{-\infty}^{T} Q_I(t)\, dt\right]}{dT} = Q_I(T),$$

for any time $T \in (-\infty, \infty)$.

The foreign country's production function for good I at period T is

$$Q_I^*(T) = A_I(K^*(T))L_I^*,$$

with foreign knowledge capital

$$K^*(T) = \int_{-\infty}^{T} Q_I^*(t)\, dt.$$

Notice that the domestic and foreign countries have the same function $A_I(\cdot)$, but productivity levels can vary depending on the accumulated experience $K(T)$ and $K^*(T)$.

6.3.4. Comparative Advantage

The model that we have described is a dynamic version of the standard Ricardian model. There are two sectors and only one physical input (labor). Natural resources and physical capital are not explicitly treated. Good II is produced subject to unitary input–output coefficients. Because $K(T)$ and $K^*(T)$ are given at time T, the domestic and foreign input–output coefficients in good I, $\alpha_I(T) = 1/A_I(T)$ and $\alpha_I^*(T) = 1/A_I^*(T)$, are also given at T

$$\alpha_I(T) = \frac{L_I}{Q_I(T)} = \frac{1}{A_I(T)}, \qquad \alpha_I^*(T) = \frac{L_I^*}{Q_I^*(T)} = \frac{1}{A_I^*(T)}.$$

Therefore, at any given time T, the model is exactly the standard Ricardian model.

The only modification made to the standard Ricardian model is that we allow the input–output coefficients in good I to decline over time as the experience in the production of good I expands. Relative comparative advantage is thus determined by learning-by-doing in industry I. Knowledge capital increases incrementally in the sense that it is accumulated gradually over time and there are no jumps in knowledge capital. A country has a relative comparative advantage in industry I if it has accumulated greater experience than its rival in that sector.

6.3.5. Technological Change and Technological Leadership

What is the rate of technological change? Does the model exhibit leapfrogging? What are the dynamics of relative country wages? What are the dynamics of the relative price of manufacturing goods in terms of food?

Consider the domestic economy in the full specialization case. The rate of technological change through learning-by-doing can be easily computed by differentiating the labor productivity function $A_I(K(T))$ with respect to time

$$\dot{A}_I(K(T)) \equiv \frac{dA_I(K(T))}{dT} = \frac{dA_I(K(T))}{dK(T)}\frac{dK(T)}{dT} = \frac{dA_I(K(T))}{dK(T)}Q_I$$

$$= \frac{dA_I(K(T))}{dK(T)}LA_I(K(T)),$$

where we recall the previously derived formula for the rate of growth of knowledge capital, $dK(T)/dT = Q_I$, and use $Q_I(T) = Q_I = L_I A_I = L A_I$. In shorthand, the rate of growth of domestic labor productivity is

$$\frac{\dot{A}_I}{A_I} = A_I'L, \quad \dot{A}_I = \frac{dA_I(K(T))}{dT}, \quad A_I' = \frac{dA_I(K)}{dK}.$$

The assumption that $A_I' > 0$ implies that productivity growth is always positive. Diminishing returns to knowledge capital, $A_I''(K) < 0$, implies that additional experience leads to a declining rate of productivity growth.

In the Ricardian model with full specialization, domestic productivity, that is, productivity in sector I, grows at a rate $A_I'(K)L$ that declines as K increases. Because the foreign economy does not experience technological change, the leader consolidates its command over good I as time passes. Leapfrogging does not arise in this setting.

Notice that if the size of the economy as measured by the labor endowment L would increase, the rate of technological change would, *ceteris paribus*, also increase. This is a common questionable feature of many growth models, suggesting that a larger population would tend to accelerate technological change, and thus economic growth.

What happens if the foreign economy also produces good I? In the partial specialization case, $Q_I^* = A_I^* L_I^*$ and the foreign rate of technological change is

$$\frac{\dot{A}_I^*}{A_I^*} = A_I' L_I^*.$$

Because there are decreasing returns to learning-by-doing ($A_I'' < 0$), the foreign rate of technological change will exceed the domestic rate if L_I^* is close enough to L (i.e. if world demand for good I is high enough). However, the domestic lead will be maintained in all cases. The reason is that both countries have the same $A_I(\cdot)$ function, so that the foreign economy follows the same productivity path as the domestic economy, but with a lag in terms of learning-by-doing. The domestic technological lead declines over time but is never eliminated.

6.3.6. *Dynamics with Learning-by-Doing*

The dynamics of relative wages under the full specialization case in which the foreign country does not produce good I is given by (see Chapter 1)

$$\frac{A}{A^*} > \frac{w}{w^*} = \frac{\mu}{1 - \mu} > 1.$$

The domestic-to-foreign country wage ratio w/w^* is equal to the ratio of the expenditure shares of manufactures and food. Relative country wages under full specialization are pinned down by the preferences parameter μ, and do not vary with the productivity of labor A_I and A_I^*. This condition implies that relative wages will be constant over time, even if the domestic economy continuously improves its labor productivity and there is no productivity improvement whatsoever in the foreign economy. The constancy of relative country wages in the presence of diverging productivity change raises a paradox. It is not immediately apparent why the productivity-improving domestic economy does not experience an increase in income relative to the technologically stagnant foreign economy.

How can relative wages remain constant while one country consolidates its lead over technology? The answer is that the growing productivity in good I leads to a continuously declining relative price of good I, as shown by the relative price condition (see Chapter 1). The equilibrium price of manufactures relative to the price of food is then (under full specialization $L_I = L_{II} = L$)

$$\frac{p_I}{p_{II}} = \frac{\mu}{1 - \mu} \frac{Q_{II}}{Q_I} = \frac{\mu}{1 - \mu} \frac{L_{II}}{A_I L_I} = \frac{\mu}{1 - \mu} \frac{1}{A_I},$$

where we use the production functions $Q_{II} = L_{II}$ and $Q_I = A_I L_I$. The relation $p_I/p_{II} = [\mu/(1 - \mu)][1/A_I]$ implies that the relative price of manufacturing declines over time. In the real-world, a declining price experience can be found in industries, such as the computer industry, that are subject to continuous technological change.

Under partial specialization (the foreign economy does not specialize), intersectoral labor mobility implies that nominal wages received in the food and manufacturing sectors are the same

$$w^* = p_{II} = p_I A_I^* \quad \rightarrow \quad \frac{w}{w^*} = \frac{A_I}{A_I^*} > 1,$$

where $w = p_I A_I$. The domestic-to-foreign relative wage rate under partial specialization is given by $w/w^* = A_I/A_I^* > 1$. If technological change through learning tapers off as knowledge capital increases, relative wages will approach an asymptote of $w/w^* = 1$. In this case, there will be long-term international wage convergence. Also, $p_I/p_{II} = 1/A_I^*$ will unambiguously decline over time as the intersectoral wage condition $w^* = p_{II} = p_I A_I^*$ implies

$$\frac{p_I}{p_{II}} = \frac{1}{A_I^*}.$$

6.4. LEAPFROGGING THROUGH BREAKTHROUGHS

Why do leaders and followers change positions in the international competition game? Learning-by-doing raises productivity and generates technological change. These effects alone, though, do not explain why some followers are able to become technological leaders. The process through which lagging firms or countries gain industrial leadership is picturesquely called leapfrogging. This section examines leapfrogging by adopting technological breakthroughs that introduce new generations of technology. The interaction of learning-by-doing and technological breakthroughs is able to produce leapfrogging. The analysis follows the leapfrogging model developed by Brezis et al. (1993) in the paper 'Leapfrogging in International Competition: A Theory of Cycles in National Technological Leadership'.

Technological leapfrogging can be explained by the failure of leading countries to implement breakthrough technologies that are in turn adopted by lagging countries. This pattern of technology adoption is the result of combining the following.

1. Cost and productivity factors that result in new technologies not being adopted by the leader. In particular, if there are significant learning-by-doing effects, leading countries will have incentives to retain the current technology in which they have acquired experience.

2. The presence of localized non-pecuniary externalities arising from the use of a given technology. These localized externalities benefit lagging countries that adopt a new technology, allowing them to eventually surpass the leader. The localized feature of non-pecuniary externalities contributes to produce leapfrogging because localization means that the leader does not benefit from the experience acquired by a lagging country that adopts a new technology.

6.4.1. To Adopt or Not to Adopt

Consider the appearance of a technological breakthrough that is incompatible with the current technology generation. This incompatibility forces a decision as to whether to adopt or not adopt the new technology. The fact that a new technology generation is available at time T does not mean that it will be adopted at time T by all agents.

What determines whether agents adopt a new technology or keep the older one? Leaders will fail to adopt a new technology if the accumulated learning-by-doing productivity gains from using the old technology are large enough. For that reason, the new technology is initially less productive than the old, although it would dominate the old technology once users acquire experience with it. On the other hand, the lagging country does not have as much experience with the old technology, and the new one is thus initially more productive. The lagging country adopts the new technology and eventually gains enough experience using it to be able to surpass the previous leader. Leapfrogging has taken place!

Once a new leader is entrenched and accumulates experience in the most recent generation of technology, it is in the same position and faces the same incentives as the previous leader. When the next breakthrough arises, the current leader will not adopt the technology, paving the way for its replacement by an emerging new leader. The model thus generates cycles of technological leadership. Also, the model explains the simultaneous use of old and new technologies.

Because a leader that fails to adopt a new technology eventually loses its dominant position, the failure to take advantage of new technologies appears short-sighted. In this model, however, the failure to adopt is a rational decision from the point of view of individual entrepreneurs (although not necessarily from the point of view of the country). As shown above, a country with an established lead will be a high-wage nation (i.e. $w/w^* > 1$). From the leader's standpoint, new technologies or industries that are initially less productive than the old might be unprofitable in international competition. It is in the interest of any individual domestic firm to wait until the new technology becomes more productive and then adopt it. The situation for the lagging nation is quite different, because it has lower wages and adopting the new technology is more efficient for them.

6.4.2. Technological Breakthroughs in Manufacturing

Industry II is assumed to have no technological change ($A_{II} = A_{II}^* = 1$). By contrast, manufacturing is subject to (1) productivity-increasing learning by doing effects, and, (2) exogenous technological change that takes the form of breakthroughs. A technological breakthrough inaugurates a new generation of technologies.

The domestic and foreign manufacturing production functions depend on the technology A_i possessed by generation i. The labor productivity function $A_i(\cdot)$ is assumed to be the same in both economies. However, the value of $A_i(\cdot)$ will vary across countries, depending on the experience capital K_i and K_i^* accumulated up to time T. Algebraically,

$$Q_i(T) = A_i(K_i(T))L_i,$$
$$Q_i^*(T) = A_i(K_i^*(T))L_i^*,$$

where L_i and L_i^* represent employment utilizing technology generation i.

Knowledge capital in generation i technology is assumed to depend on the cumulative production of manufacturing goods using technology generation i

$$K_i(T) = \int_{-\infty}^{T} Q_i(t)\, dt,$$

$$K_i^*(T) = \int_{-\infty}^{T} Q_i^*(t)\, dt.$$

Notice that the per-worker level of output of generation i at time T is given by $Q_i(T)/L_i = A_i(K_i(T))$, which increases with both i and K.

6.4.3. *Learning Effects*

Learning effects $A_i(K)$ are assumed to be strictly increasing in knowledge capital (i.e. $A_i' > 0$), but at a decreasing rate, $A_i''(K) < 0$. In other words, each generation of technology is subject to diminishing returns to learning-by-doing. Also, for any given level of knowledge K, the technology generation $i + 1$ is considered to be better than the previous generation of technology i

$$A_{i+1}(K) > A_i(K).$$

If the experience in using the technologies is the same, breakthrough technologies are superior to the old. However, we will assume two features that are key to the results.

1. New technologies are inferior initially, when there is no experience with the new technology

$$A_{i+1}(0) < A_i(K).$$

The previous equation implies that countries with a large enough experience using the old technology will find it to be more productive than the newly introduced technology generation. This produces a key feature of leapfrogging, causing the leading country to prefer the old technology in which it has a large accumulated experience over the new breakthrough technology. On the other hand, new technologies will be chosen by countries with no or little enough experience with the old technology, because $A_{i+1}(0) > A_i(0)$.

2. Productivity improvements due to learning-by-doing will cause the new technology generation to eventually surpass the productivity of the previous technology generation. This feature allows leapfrogging to take place.

6.4.4. Leapfrogging Equilibrium

Assume that the condition $w/w^* = \mu/(1 - \mu) < A/A^*$ holds initially, so that there is full specialization. The current generation of technology is labeled '1'. Consider a breakthrough that takes place in period T_2, introducing a technology generation '2'.

We assume that the domestic economy leads in manufacturing and that

$$A_2(0) < A_1(K_1(T_2)).$$

This implies that domestic producers will not adopt the breakthrough and the manufacturing production will thus be

$$Q_1(T) = A_1(K_1(T))L.$$

The foreign country prefers the new technology because $A_1(0) < A_2(0)$. The breakthrough is profitable to the foreign country, and it will produce good I if

$$\frac{\mu}{1 - \mu} > \frac{A_1(K_1(T_2))}{A_2(0)} \quad \rightarrow \quad \frac{1 - \mu}{\mu} < \frac{A_2(0)}{A_1(K_1(T_2))}.$$

If the previous condition holds, the full specialization equilibrium breaks down. The world economy moves into a partial specialization equilibrium in which the domestic economy specializes in manufacturing and the foreign produces both manufacturing and food. Foreign food production is given by

$$L_{II}^* = (1 - \mu)L\left(\frac{A_1}{A_2^*} + 1\right).$$

If A_1/A_2^* declines over time, so will L_{II}^*.

Real wages in the foreign economy are $(\omega^* = p_2 = p_1 A_2^*)$

$$\omega^* = \frac{w^*}{p} = \gamma \frac{p_1 A_2^*}{p_1^\mu p_2^{1-\mu}} = \gamma(A_2^*)^\mu,$$

and increase over time because A_2^* grows. Domestic real wages could decline over time as

$$\omega = \frac{w}{p} = \gamma A_1(A_2^*)^{-(1-\mu)}, \quad \gamma = \mu^\mu(1 - \mu)^{1-\mu},$$

where the price level P_I is defined as

$$P_I = \left(\frac{p_I}{\mu}\right)^{\mu} \left[\frac{p_{II}}{1-\mu}\right]^{1-\mu}.$$

The failure of the leader to adopt the new technology and the implementation of the breakthrough by the lagging country implies that eventually $A_1(K_1(\cdot)) < A_2(K_2^*(\cdot))$. In this case, the foreign country has become the new leader and trade reversal takes place because the foreign country specializes and becomes an exporter of good I. The partial specialization condition is (home country producers I and II, exports I)

$$\frac{\mu}{1-\mu} > \frac{A_2^*(t)}{A_1(t)} > 1.$$

Full specialization eventually occurs as the technological gap between the foreign and the domestic economies widens (ω/ω^* is constant as p_I/p_{II} decline)

$$\frac{A_2^*(t)}{A_1(t)} > \frac{\mu}{1-\mu} > 1.$$

When the previous condition holds, there is an abrupt change in leadership and in production patterns associated with the emergence of a new leader.

Let us now summarize the stages of leapfrogging dynamics.

1. Stage (T_1, T_2): full specialization with domestic economy leading. The relative wage condition is

   $$w/w^* = \mu/(1-\mu) \leq A_1/A_2^*.$$

2. Stage (T_2, T_3): partial specialization with domestic economy leading. The relative wage condition is

   $$w/w^* = A_1/A_2^* < \mu/(1-\mu).$$

   The domestic economy does not adopt generation A_2 that appears at T_2 because $A_2(0) < A_1(K_1(T_2))$. The foreign economy adopts A_2 because $A_1(0) < A_2(0)$.

3. Stage (T_3, T_4): partial specialization with foreign economy leading. The relative wage condition is

   $$w/w^* = A_1/A_2^* < 1.$$

   The foreign economy leads because $A_1(K_1(\cdot)) < A_2(K_2^*(\cdot))$, but $\mu/(1-\mu) > A_2(K_2^*(\cdot))/A_1(K_1(\cdot)) > 1$. There is trade reversal as the foreign economy specializes and becomes an exporter of manufactures.

4. Stage (T_4, T_5): full specialization with foreign economy leading. The relative wage condition is

   $$1 < w/w^* = \mu/(1-\mu) \leq A_2(K_2^*(\cdot))/A_1(K_1(\cdot)).$$

6.5. DOES GREATER TRADE LEAD TO FASTER GROWTH?

The discussion of the impact of trade and trade policies on growth, productivity, and global competition is part of the broader debate on the factors determining economic success. Lucas (1993) stresses the role of human capital and externalities. Young (1995) finds that productivity growth, entry of women into the labor force and demographic factors were quite important in explaining per capita growth in Hong Kong. By contrast, high investment rates drove Singaporean growth, which was characterized by slow productivity growth. Rodrik (1995a) comparison of Korea and Taiwan stresses the role of selective and market oriented industrial polices but does not assign an important role for openness. The stagnation of Japan throughout the 1990s and the interruption of fast growth in East Asia in 1997 has shed doubts over many proposed explanations of their past successes and has led to an ongoing reexamination of the growth and productivity debate. This debate can only be refueled by the sudden slowdown or stop of growth in Argentina (1998–2002) and other paradigmatic economies.

6.5.1. The Controversy over Trade and Growth

Research on trade and growth is largely based on explaining the growth rate g of (1) real per capita income, (2) labor productivity, or (3) total factor productivity. The relation between trade and growth is tested by performing cross country regressions of country i growth rate g_i on initial income y_0, human capital H, a vector X representing additional control variables, and some measure of trade T. Formally, the standard growth equation is

$$g_{it} = a_0 + a_1 y_0 + a_2 H_{it} + a_3 I_{it} + a_4 X_{it} + a_5 T_{it} + u_{it},$$

where g refers to real income or productivity, and u is an error term.

Because investment is thought to be an endogenous variable that is jointly determined with the growth rate and is affected by growth, some authors correct using some statistical method while others report growth equations without the domestic investment variable. Because trade affects growth but growth impacts on trade, a simple ordinary least squares regression of growth on a trade measure and some control variables might yield biased estimates. Growth researchers use several methods to control for the simultaneous determination of trade and growth—instrumental variables methods, three stage least squares, and other methods.

The empirical role of trade on growth has been a subject of controversy. Sachs and Warner (1995) find evidence that thirteen developing countries opened to trade grew at 4.5 percent annual rate while seventy-four developing countries with closed economies grew by a mere 0.7 percent annual rate between 1970 and 1990. Openness is measured by the Sachs–Warner index, which is zero for a closed economy and one for an open economy. Openness increases if the average tariff is below 40 percent, nontariff barriers are low, the economy is not socialist, there is no state monopoly of major exports, and the black market premium in the 1970s or 1980s was small or zero.

Trade skeptics like Rodrik and Rodriguez (2001) question the link between freer trade and faster growth reported in cross-sectional analyses on the grounds that the openness measure of trade used in the literature is a poor indicator of trade policy. Their study suggests that the reported linkage between trade openness and growth, captured in previous analyses, is the result of a spurious correlation between the openness measure and growth. Questioning the openness explanation, Rodrik and Rodriguez (2001) suggest that the weak performance displayed by the closed developing countries in Sachs and Warner (1995) sample corresponds to African countries with poor macroeconomic performance and high levels of corruption. Moreover, most of the explanatory power of the Sachs–Warner index of openness hinges on black market premium and the state monopolization of exports, two policy variables with diverse effects, which makes difficult attributing the growth effect indicated by the index to trade.

A key issue in this discussion concerns choosing the appropriate measure of openness and whether the effect of trade on growth is robust to the indicator. Sebastian Edwards (1998) factor productivity regressions, using data for ninety-three countries between 1980 and 1990 and nine different indicators of trade openness and trade distortions, offer robust evidence of a positive impact of trade on growth. Edwards finds that lower trade distortions and greater openness result in higher total factor productivity growth.

Frankel and Romer (1999) tackle the issue of how to treat the causality between trade and income when analyzing the effects of trade on income. They propose the use of countries' geographic characteristics as instrumental variables for trade because geographic characteristics are highly correlated with trade but not with income. The effect of trade on income is found to be quantitatively large and robust, though moderately statistically significant. If the trade to GDP ratio increases by 1 percentage point, per capita income increases by 0.5–2 percentage points.

An important body of evidence on the impact of trade and growth does not derive from growth regressions but rather from case studies. Srinivasan and Bhagwati (1999) review the large body of case studies of country experiences produced at the OECD, the World Bank and the National Bureau of Economic Research (NBER) on the effects of trade liberalization during the 1960s and 1970s. They conclude that this body of evidence, which takes into account numerous country-specific factors, offers plausible evidence of a positive impact of trade on growth.

6.6. CONVERGENCE, POVERTY, AND INEQUALITY

Convergence across countries or nations can be looked at from the point of view of (1) real income per capita, (2) productivity growth, and (3) poverty reduction.

The idea behind real income per capita convergence is that, conditional on a set of control variables, such as education and investment, the poorer countries should grow faster than the richer countries (i.e. the coefficient β is negative). The simplest type of convergence analysis looks at the behavior of a single variable, income per capita, and examines whether there is long-term convergence among countries or regions. This analysis is called unconditional convergence because it does not control for other variables. Evidence on unconditional convergence shows that wealthier and newly industrialized countries tend to exhibit per capita income convergence while many poorer countries do not. An unconditional convergence regression relates the annualized growth g_y in income per capita during the period studied to initial income y_0

$$g_y = \alpha_0 + \beta y_0 + \varepsilon,$$

where ε is the error term. Convergence implies that countries with low initial incomes should grow faster than countries with high initial incomes. In other words, estimates of β should be negative. However, estimates of β are often small or statistically insignificant in relation to the null hypothesis that β is equal to zero.

What explains the lack of unconditional convergence? The key explanation is that unconditional convergence analyses do not control for human capital, government policies, and other variables that affect growth. Studies that do control for these variables evidence conditional convergence in the sense that countries tend to converge to per capita income levels that depend on the conditioning variables. A paradigmatic conditional convergence regression relates the annualized growth in income per capita g_y to initial income y_0 and the set of conditioning variables included in vector x

$$g_y = \alpha_0 + \beta y_0 + \gamma' x + \varepsilon,$$

where ε is the error term. Estimates of β tend to be negative and statistically significant.

6.6.1. Trade and Cross-country Convergence

A series of studies focus on the effect of international trade on income and total factor productivity (TFP) convergence across countries.

Do major trading partners tend to display income convergence to common income per capita levels? Close trading relations can be indicated by participation in a trade agreement or by the actual values of imports and exports. Ben-David (1996) examines a group of twenty-five countries with per capita income exceeding 25 percent of the US 1960 level. Close relations are indicated by imports and exports (there is no requirement to belong to a trading arrangement). Convergence is measured by relating the current deviation of the logarithm of countries' real per capita income from the group's average, $\ln y_t^c - \ln \bar{y}_t$, to the previous period deviation

$$\ln y_t^c - \ln \bar{y}_t = \phi(\ln y_{t-1}^c - \ln \bar{y}_{t-1}) + \epsilon_t^c.$$

Countries within a group are pooled together.

Convergence within a group is indicated by a below–unity estimated group coefficient ϕ, which indicates that deviations tend to diminish over time. The results offer evidence of convergence clubs based on trade relations. There is significant income convergence within groups of countries made up of major trading partners as measured by imports, exports or their sum. Moreover, income convergence is more likely to take place within trade-based groups than among (1) randomly-chosen groupings,

(2) groups based on geographic proximity in the sense of sharing a common border or being the closest neighbor across water, and (3) groupings based on a common language. In fact, a random grouping was likely to produce an estimated ϕ coefficient above unity, indicating divergence during the sample period. These results suggest that trade leads to convergence.

Further evidence relating to trade liberalization and convergence is examined in the chapter on trade liberalization.

6.6.2. Regional Convergence

US states display income per capita convergence to the national average. In other words, poorer states tend to grow faster than richer states. A remarkable feature of this convergence is that rapid national growth has induced a reduction in regional inequalities. Another remarkable fact is that East Asian economies grew for decades at superior growth rates while there was no tendency for reduction in the rate of returns to capital or the economies' growth rates. The East Asian experience is inconsistent with the closed-economy neoclassical growth model driven by physical or human capital accumulation. In a closed economy, neoclassical growth through capital accumulation gradually raises the capital–labor ratio and induces a reduction in the marginal productivity of capital.

In the open economy with free trade and factor immobility, the nature of the growth path is quite different. Ventura (1997) develops a growth framework for integrated economies that captures the type of regional convergence in which diminishing returns to capital do not take place and the evolution of national variables affects regional convergence dynamics. Consider the growth path exhibited by a small region (or country) facing given world relative prices. The final good (say, services) is nontraded but intermediate inputs are traded. Regions are linked through participation in a common market.

Recall that the Stolper–Samuelson model implies that (inside the cone of diversification) factor rewards and marginal productivities depend on relative prices, but not on factor endowments. An increase in the capital–labor ratio makes labor more scarce and capital more abundant. But this change in relative factor abundances does not lead to a change in techniques of production but rather to a change in the structure of production. According to the Heckscher–Ohlin (HO) framework, growth taking place by factor accumulation moves the economy along the Rybczynski line. For given relative prices, the economy absorbs the additional capital by expanding the capital-intensive sector and reducing the labor-intensive sector. An implication is that the economy will capture larger shares of national (or global) production and trade.

In the small open economy HO model, the dynamics of growth through capital accumulation displays two features (1) growth neither entails declining marginal productivity of capital nor reduced returns to capital, (2) growth induces structural transformation consisting of greater and greater specialization in the good that is capital intensive. Observe that, contrary to the closed economy, continuous growth becomes compatible with the constancy of the marginal productivity of capital. In other words, growth behaves 'as if' the technology is linear even if it exhibits diminishing returns. The paradox is solved by noticing that diminishing returns are national (or global) and that regional factor returns are not affected by regional growth. Small country growth through exportation explains why East Asian economies were able to beat diminishing returns to capital.

Do countries that rapidly accumulate a factor systematically shift their production and exports towards industries that use that factor intensively? Do countries capture larger shares of global output and trade of products that use more intensively the factor that they accumulate faster than the rest of the world? Romalis (2002*a*) presents evidence showing that the rapid accumulation of a factor affects the pattern of trade and that exports systematically shift toward industries that use the abundant factor.

6.6.3. National Poverty

What is the relationship between growth and poverty and between trade and poverty? These relationships can be examined for income groups at the national level and for countries at the global level.

What is the effect of growth and trade on poverty and inequality within countries? Dollar and Kraay (2002) utilize a panel data set covering a sample of ninety two countries during 1950–1999 to examine how average real per capita income relates to poverty in developing countries. Their interest focuses on the poor as defined by the poorest fifth percentile of the population. They conduct regressions of the logarithm of per capita income of the poor, y^{poor}, on the logarithm of average real per capita country income y and a vector of control variables X

$$y_{it}^{poor} = \alpha_0 + \alpha_1 y_{it} + \alpha_2' X_{it} + \mu_i + \varepsilon_{it},$$

where α_1 measures the elasticity of income of the poor with respect to the average income. The equation can be transformed into a regression of the log of the first quintile share on average income and the control variables included in X. Moreover, these regressions can be interpreted as relating income inequality to average income. The reason is that the first quintile share is empirically a linear function of the Gini coefficient of inequality.

In the ninety-two country sample for the past four decades, the share of income accruing to the lowest fifth percentile of the population does not vary with the average level of income as measured by the real per capita GDP. Openness to trade, good rule of law and developed financial markets are positively associated with growth but do not have a systematic effect on the share of income accruing to the lowest quintile. In other words, openness to trade neither shifts income against or in favor of the poor.

They find that poverty declines with growth. Specifically, the logarithm of the per capita income of the bottom fifth of the population (i.e. the relatively poor) rises one-for-one with the logarithm of average income per capita, after controling for several variables. They also find a fair amount of variation around this general relationship.

The paper results debunk a number of popular views about the poverty–growth relationship, namely,

1. The effect of growth on income of the poor is found to be similar in poor and rich countries.
2. Contrary to a common claim, the incomes of the poor are not found to fall more than proportionately during economic crises.
3. The poverty–growth relationship has not changed in recent years.
4. Policy-induced growth in the form of greater openness to foreign trade, good rule of law and fiscal discipline benefits the poor to the same extent that it benefits the whole economy.
5. Avoidance of high inflation is found to be 'super-pro-poor' in the sense that high inflation erodes more the income of the poor than overall GDP.
6. The econometric results do not offer evidence confirming the common view that formal democratic institutions or public spending on health and education have systematic effects on the incomes of the poor.

These authors recognize that their findings, which generated much debate, question widely held views. They conclude that 'These findings leave plenty of room for further work, because they emphasize the fact that we know very little about what systematically causes changes in the distribution of income'.

Did recent opening lead to less or more national poverty? The case study undertaken by Dollar and Kraay (2001) presents evidence showing that a post-1980 cohort of six globalizing countries—China, India, Brazil, Thailand, Argentina, and Bangladesh—experienced both accelerated growth and poverty reductions. These countries account for well over half of developing countries' worldwide population. They were chosen because they featured (1) deep reductions in average tariff rates and (2) large increases in trade as a percentage of GDP. These features create confidence that greater openness was policy induced. The new cohort of globalization led to accelerations of growth as well as reductions in poverty (but not in post-sample Argentinean data).

6.6.4. Global Inequality

The subject of global cross-country inequality is a matter of great concern. Acemoglu and Ventura (2002) depart from the traditional assumptions of technology spillovers and diminishing returns in production in explaining the large income differentials among countries and the relative stability of world income distribution between 1960 and 1990. They argue that trade can lead to stable world income distributions levels even if relaxing both assumptions. Their explanation hinges on the strength of terms of trade effects as a determinant of world income distribution. Terms of trade effects are determined by specialization in production and openness to trade, which generate de facto diminishing returns to capital accumulation at the country level.

Using data for 1965–1985, Acemoglu and Ventura (2002) run cross-sectional regressions of the growth rate of terms of trade π—measured as the annual differential between export prices and import prices growth rates—on growth rate g of GDP as well as other control variables summarized in vector X such as 1965-average years of schooling in population with ages exceeding 25 years old, life expectancy, investment rate, government consumption, and an oil producer dummy to control for oil price increases.

The main estimated equation relates the growth of the terms of trade π to the growth rate g of GDP and a vector of control variables X'

$$\pi_t = \alpha g_t + X_t'\hat{\omega} = -0.73 g_t + X_t'\hat{\omega},$$

where the coefficient of g is statistically significant (the t-student statistic is 2.4). *Ceteris paribus*, if a country's GDP growth rate increases by 1 percentage point due to accumulation, its terms of trade deteriorate by a 0.73 percentage point. The relation $\alpha = -0.73 = -1/(\varepsilon - 1)$ implies that the elasticity of export demand is $\varepsilon = 2.37$.

Estimates are obtained using two-stage least squares (2SLS) estimation procedures and by instrumenting the annual growth rate of income g_t using Barro and Sala-i-Martin (1998) conditional convergence process

$$g_t = -2\ln y_{t-1} + X_t'\hat{\theta},$$

where y_{t-1} accounts for initial level of income and the coefficient $\beta = -2$ refers to the speed of conditional convergence (amounts to 2 percent per year as in Barro and Sala-i-Martin analyses).

6.7. THE LINKAGES BETWEEN FDI AND GROWTH

FDI can affect growth if it results in increased physical investment, plant, and equipment upgrading and greater transfer of technologies to host country firms. Studies using the growth regression methodology find that FDI has significant positive growth effects, at least for countries surpassing a threshold schooling level, and that this growth effect is greater than that of domestic investment. A well cited result in the FDI and growth literature is that the productivity of FDI in Latin America is three times that of domestic investment (De Gregorio, 1992). This result was obtained comparing the growth effects of domestic investment and FDI in a sample of twelve Latin American countries, after controlling for economic and institutional variables that have been found to have an effect on growth rates.

Borenszstein *et al.* (1998) find a positive growth effect of FDI but only if the host country has surpassed a threshold schooling level. This result is derived from a sample of sixty-nine developing countries during the decades 1970–79 and 1980–89. The study performs cross-country regressions of the growth rate of per capita income g on human capital H, FDI from OECD countries as a proportion of GDP, the interaction between the FDI ratio and human capital H, and a vector X representing additional variables such as the regression constant, initial income, domestic investment, and others. The authors obtain a negative coefficient from FDI and a positive coefficient from the interaction between FDI and schooling. Putting these estimates together means that the effect of FDI on growth becomes positive only if the schooling level is high enough.

Oliva and Rivera-Batiz (2002*a*) consider a sample of 120 developing for 1970–94. They confirm the positive effects of FDI and the superiority of FDI over domestic investment and find that non-FDI capital flows did not exert a significant growth effect.

6.8. CONCLUSIONS

This chapter has examined models of growth based on technological change and endogenous dynamic comparative advantage. Producers adopting technological break-throughs are able to leapfrog over producers sticking to old technologies to become technological leaders. Alternatively, producers invest in research and development (R&D) in order to upgrade product quality and gain a temporary leadership position in a rivalry game proceeding along a ladder of ever improving qualities.

The model of international competition examined showed that the presence of learning-by-doing effects is not enough to generate the replacement of an industrial leader. In fact, learning-by-doing productivity improvements consolidate the leader's position under full specialization. In the partial specialization case, the leader's position could be undermined but can not be completely eliminated. The interaction between learning-by-doing effects and technology breakthroughs, however, was enough to gen-erate leapfrogging. A necessary condition for leapfrogging is that the current industry leader should not be the first to adopt a breakthrough that opens a new generation of technology.

The economics of endogenous technological change, quality competition and leapfrogging captures many aspects of growth and the dynamics of international com-petition in the real world. The leapfrogging framework generates technological change in which old and new technologies are simultaneously used. Industrial leaders are even-tually replaced. Learning-by-doing has a well-defined productivity role. Comparative advantage is not exogenous but is rather dynamically determined by agents' decisions, initial conditions, and the models' parameters.

PART II

STRATEGIC TRADE, COMPETITION, AND ENVIRONMENT

7

Competition and Rivalry

This chapter examines competition policy and strategic policy formulation in oligopolistic world markets. Strategic trade analysis extends the basic models of international trade by providing a set of tools for understanding market practices and policy formulation in the presence of a small number of interacting agents. It focuses on oligopolistic markets and governments that behave strategically *vis-à-vis* firms and other policymakers. Governments subject to political influence have incentives to interact strategically when they formulate export policies toward competitive industries such as agriculture. Therefore, the notion that strategic analysis does not apply to competitive markets is misleading.

The design of strategic trade policies is guided by the following broad questions. First, what is the best strategic use of trade intervention instruments? Second, what are the welfare effects of trade policies in a strategic setting? Third, how does retaliation by foreign countries affect policy determination and welfare? Explicit consideration should be given to the response of foreign governments. Strategic interactions are prone to generating responses that nullify the pluses of policies that would be beneficial, from a national perspective, in the absence of a foreign reaction.

If domestic and foreign firms compete in oligopolistic markets, export subsidization can serve to shift profits from foreign to domestic firms. The profit-shifting motive, formalized by Brander and Spencer (1985), has become a main element of policy discussions because it provides a rationale for trade intervention through the use of export subsidies. This prescription differs both from the traditional preference for *laissez-faire* and from the trade restriction rule based on the optimal tariff argument. In contrast, the subsidization of exports is a policy of trade promotion based on encouraging exports.

The consequences of government policies depend on how agents interact and the type of market imperfections faced. Specifically, the benefits from export subsidization in oligopolistic markets hinge on the response of foreign governments. If the rival country responds to subsidization by engaging in subsidization, a prisoner's dilemma situation arises and both countries lose unless one of them produces at low enough costs relative to the rival. For instance, two similar subsidized firms competing in a third market as duopolists will increase output but will be unable to increase market share in the third market. Export subsidies end up benefiting third market consumers at the expense of subsidizing countries.

The export subsidy prescription is not robust. It can be nullified or reversed by the presence of domestic distortions, new entrants, and other factors. If the financing of the subsidies requires increasing distorting taxes, the induced distortions can very well nullify the positive effects of export subsidies. Horstman and Markusen (1986) examine the role of firm entry. They show that, in the presence of decreasing average costs, new entrants work to nullify the benefits from export subsidization. The reason is that firm entry seeking to share in the gains from subsidization reduces each firm's output level and thus pushes rivals up along the decreasing average cost curve.

Competitive industries with political muscle, such as primary products, are actively engaged in political influence activities. Interest groups seeking subsidies can lead governments to act strategically and fall into a prisoner's dilemma in which low prices benefit foreign consumers at the expense of exporting country producers. Excessive subsidization due to a prisoners' dilemma situation creates incentives for either a movement toward free trade or toward the formation of a cartel that maximizes profits at the expense of global welfare.

This chapter focuses on rivalry and competition policy. Sections 7.1 and 7.2 examines European Union, United States, and Japan's competition policies. Section 7.3 shows that, if firms compete in quantities in third markets abroad, export subsidizing is best when one government intervenes unilaterally while the other remains passive. Section 7.4 demonstrates that the equilibrium subsidy induces domestic firms to act like the leader in a Stackelberg leader–follower equilibrium. Sections 7.5 and 7.6 extend the analysis to consider bilateral strategic intervention, the tax distortion created by the financing of the subsidies. Section 7.7 assesses export promotion. Section 7.8 discusses the role of political influence in designing export promotion policies. Sections 7.9 and 7.10 discuss environmental policies as a competition policy instrument. Section 7.11 discusses alternative frameworks and implied industrial policy prescriptions.

7.1. HOW DO COMPETITION POLICIES DIFFER?

How do competition policies in the European Union, United States, and Japan differ? International divergences in competition policies reflect conflicting concerns, institutional diversity and different legislation. European Union and United States market practices, competition laws, and their application by regulators, have converged in recent decades even though divergences remain. For instance, sales limitations—such as limits on price discounts, restrictive night hours and requiring store closings on Sundays—are prevalent throughout Europe but have died out in the United States.

American and European competition policies differ both in the process followed and the criteria used to reach decisions. Dissimilar processes and approaches explain why the United States and the European Union often reach quite different decisions in competition policy cases. However, a tendency for cooperation has been encouraged in recent years in gathering data and case analysis.

Major differences include the following.

1. In Washington, DC, competition cases go through an administrative process at the antitrust agency—the Federal Trade Commission—and the Department of Justice that is ultimately settled in the courts. In Brussels, the European Commission decides on competition cases based on European law. The EU competition

commissioner has the upper hand but the courts have played a role when European Commission decisions have been challenged.

2. The European Commission lacks the power to break up a company even if it finds evidence of anticompetitive practices. The types of remedy imposed by the Commission include fines, cease and desist orders, and pressuring companies to agree to a settlement. For instance, in 1984 the Commission forced IBM to license interface information to European rivals enabling them to market products displaying full compatibility with then dominant IBM products.

3. The EU system is preemptive while the US system corrects malfunctioning after the fact.

4. The relative importance given to consumer interests *vis-à-vis* the interests of rival competitors is greater in the United States than in Europe. Specifically, European views tend to stress fairness in business competition and the effects of market practices on rival competitors while the Americans stress the effects on consumers and the need to protect the consumers. The Microsoft case illustrates the consolidation of the technology criterion in the United States, namely, the effects of dominant firm practices on industry's innovative activity.

5. The formulation of European competition policies, as defined in the 1957 Treaty of Rome, contains general guidelines but does not offer details such as what is a market or the profile of merger policy. Article 85 of the Treaty of Rome addresses horizontal arrangements. It prohibits horizontal agreements between firms that restrict competition and which aim to prevent, restrict or distort competition. The application of Article 85 is dissimilar to that of section 1 of the Sherman Act. On one hand, practices such as fixing technological development are classed as illegal in Europe but might be legal in the United States. On the other hand, practices such as price fixing are considered illegal in the United States but might be exempted in the European Union.

6. Violations of section 2 of the Sherman Act violate Article 86, which addresses abusive practices in vertical arrangements, but the reverse is not true. The concept of 'abusive conduct' in the EU sense might not be 'unlawful monopolization' according to the Sherman Act.

7.1.1. Market Access in Japan

Japanese competition policies have traditionally been quite different from that of their European and American counterparts. For instance, antimonopoly regulation was lax and collusive agreements were tolerated. Foreign firms were excluded from local markets and international mergers and acquisitions were severely restricted.

The European Union and the United States have targeted Japanese competition policies for their alleged exclusion of foreign firms through both government-imposed and private firm practices. A common complaint concerns the numerous forms of restrictions on market access experienced by foreign firms. Despite very low tariff rates, Japan has traditionally featured one of the lowest imports-to-output and foreign investment-to-output ratios among industrial economies.

Until relaxed in the 1990s, government-imposed restrictions on large retailers hurt large foreign firms aiming to sell in Japan. Horizontal keiretsu involving close linkages among firms and the vertical keiretsu system involving hierarchical long-term subcontracting networks (such as auto parts subcontracting) are deemed to restrict foreign market access.

A highly publicized case of Japanese market restraint related to government practices and vertical keiretsu was raised in 1996, when US authorities presented to the World Trade Organization (WTO) a section 301 petition initiated by Eastman Kodak Company, alleging Japanese authorities were limiting Kodak market share in Japan by granting exclusive dealership arrangements to Fuji Photo Film. Nagaoka (2000) examines several procompetitive measures introduced in the 1990s. These include stronger enforcement of antimonopoly legislation against cartels and limitations on the types of cartels exempted from the application of antimonopoly law (so-called recession and rationalization cartels are not exempted from antimonopoly law).

7.2. INTERNATIONAL COMPETITION POLICY

International trade analysis has focused on the following aspects of competition policy

1. Promoting market access. This aspect includes securing openness toward exporters and foreign investment, negotiating openness and transparency of foreign government procurement practices, and avoiding product standard laws that restrict market access or increase costs to foreigners. These concerns are embodied in WTO rules and are often settled through WTO proceedings.
2. Preventing price setting entailing higher prices than under perfect competition (such as under cartels) or excessively low prices (due to dumping of excess production or predatory dumping behavior seeking to induce rival exit). Alleged foreign dumping practices are offset by imposing antidumping duties and voluntary export restraints (VERs) on the part of foreign countries. The Uruguay Round of trade negotiations prohibited VERs.
3. Limiting the concentration of market power. Policies relating to market concentration include the prevention and regulation of monopolies and merger policy—in the sense of policies toward the number of firms in a market and the assessment of the trade off between concentration and efficiency consequences of mergers and acquisitions. Investigation and approval of mergers between US and EU parties is in charge of both the US Federal Trade Commission and the Competition Directorate of the European Commission.
4. Prevention of a wide array of firm practices and relationships that limit competition. These practices include horizontal market sharing arrangements, exclusionary contracts, collusion, cooperation among firms under strategic alliances and cooperative R&D activities, and cartelization. Domestic antitrust monitoring and enforcement address these practices.

5. Limiting export and other types of subsidies that alter the competitive position of firms.
6. The elimination of anticompetitive practices, such as international cartelization, that lead to excessively high prices.

Two examples illustrate how different institutional setups and notions of cooperation and competition have placed Japan, the United States, and Europe face to face with each other.

1. Keen competition in high-tech sectors and limited market access facing US and European firms attempting to break into Japanese markets have generated bitter conflicts. But the divergences also reflect important institutional differences such as the traditional predominance of cooperative arrangements and inter-firm networks in Japan in contrast with US and European practices.
2. The United States favors legal processes while Asian and European countries favor administrative processes. The United States has traditionally stressed the need to support competition even at the expense of productive cooperation among firms. In contrast, Japan has traditionally promoted many forms of firm cooperation, including cartelization, even when competition and market access are at stake. European Union policies represent a complex package that combines pro-competitive elements with the promotion of cooperation, particularly in research, and government support to enterprises.

7.3. STRATEGIC EXPORT SUBSIDIZATION

Why do governments use costly export subsidies to influence international competition? In pioneering work, Brander and Spencer (1985) developed a model in which it is optimal for a government to subsidize domestic exports. They studied the impact of export subsidies on a firm's net profits and on the welfare level of the subsidizing country. A major finding is that unilateral export subsidies that are not matched by rival governments (1) benefit subsidized domestic firms, and (2) increase national welfare. The key mechanism is that the subsidies shift profits toward domestic producers.

The profit-shifting motive helps understand governments' incentives to promote exports and the actual strategies followed. Subsidization gives advantages to local firms against foreign competitors. The role of the government is to make it possible for domestic firms to compete with lower marginal costs than foreign firms. Subsidies allow firms to credibly commit to an aggressive production strategy, forcing rivals to respond with a follower's lower production strategy. This strategy profile derives in lower profits for foreign firms and larger profits for domestic firms.

7.3.1. Two-stage Cournot Equilibrium in the Third Market Model

This section develops a linear version of Brander and Spencer's model in the unilateral subsidization case in which only the home government intervenes. The foreign government is assumed not to have the ability or willingness to intervene. Government actions are assumed to be undertaken in a perfect information setting in which relevant variables are perfectly observable.

The game involves three active players—the domestic government, a domestic firm, and a foreign firm. The foreign government is a passive player. Home consumption is ignored in both countries so that the two firms operate only in third markets, where they are assumed to compete as duopolists. Firms' private decisions consist of choosing the volumes of production q and q^* of a homogeneous good that is entirely exported to a third country.

A setup in which domestic and foreign firms compete in third markets, but not in their home markets, is called the 'third market' model. This framework stresses international competition and export rivalry in global markets. It is most relevant when oligopolistic firms are oriented toward exports rather than toward the local market.

The behavior of domestic firms and the government is formulated as a sequential move two-stage game. In the first stage, the home government chooses the export subsidy (export taxes are shown not to be optimal). The foreign government is assumed to be passive and not to intervene. In the second stage of the game, firms take the export subsidy as given and decide the output quantities that will be entirely exported to a third country. Notice that export and output subsidies are equivalent in the third market model.

The unique subgame perfect equilibrium in pure strategies, nonrandom strategies as opposed to mixed strategies entailing random decisions, is computed using backward induction. The first step of the backward induction procedure is to solve the last stage of the game. In other words, the firm's quantity-setting stage is solved first for given arbitrary values of the government subsidy. The second step of the procedure is to solve the first stage of the sequential game, that is, the government's subsidy-setting stage. The subsidy is chosen taking into account how the subsidized firm will react to it. When the game is played out, firms choose output levels taking the specific subsidy as a commitment previously made by the government.

7.3.2. Setting Output Quantities Strategically

The world's (i.e. third market) inverse demand function is given by

$$p(Q) = a - bQ = a - b(q + q^*), \quad a, b > 0, \tag{7.1}$$

where p is the price in the third market, q and q^* are the outputs of the local and foreign firms, and $Q = q + q^*$ denotes the aggregate production level. The demand expression (7.1) expresses the market price as a linear function of total quantity and indicates that a higher output is associated with a lower price (i.e. demand is downward sloping).

The home firm's after-subsidy profit function π is defined by export revenues, $pq = [a - b(q + q^*)]q$, minus variable production costs cq, plus the total export subsidy sq received from the local government. Algebraically, profits inclusive of subsidies are

$$\pi(q, q^*; s) = (p - c + s)q = [a - b(q + q^*)]q - cq + sq, \tag{7.2}$$

where c denotes the constant marginal cost parameter and s is a flat subsidy per unit produced and exported. Expression (7.2) implies that the isoprofit equation for $\pi = \pi^0$ is given by a quadratic equation

$$\pi^0 = (a - bq - bq^*)q - (c - s)q \rightarrow q^* = \frac{-bq^2 + (a - c + s)q - \pi^0}{bq}. \quad (7.3)$$

The foreign firm's profits are given by

$$\pi^*(q, q^*) = (p - c^*)q^* = [a - b(q + q^*)]q^* - c^*q^*, \quad (7.4)$$

where the foreign country is assumed to abstain from subsidizing exports.

We focus on oligopolistic firms competing in quantities (i.e. competition à la Cournot) in international markets. This means that the strategic variable set by firms is the quantity of output, in contrast with the case in which firms use the product price as the variable to be set strategically (Chapter 8 compares both settings).

To obtain the Cournot–Nash noncooperative equilibrium, we first need to find each firm's best output response to the rival's decision, taking the per unit subsidy as given. From (7.2) and (7.4), the first order necessary conditions are

(i) $\quad \dfrac{\partial \pi(q, q^*; s)}{\partial q} = a - 2bq - bq^* - c + s = 0,$

$\qquad\qquad\qquad\qquad\qquad\qquad\qquad\qquad\qquad\qquad\qquad (7.5)$

(ii) $\quad \dfrac{\partial \pi^*(q, q^*)}{\partial q^*} = a - 2bq^* - bq - c^* = 0.$

Second order conditions are satisfied since

$$\frac{\partial^2 \pi(q, q^*; s)}{\partial q^2} = -2b, \qquad \frac{\partial^2 \pi^*(q, q^*)}{\partial q^{*2}} = -2b.$$

The reaction functions expressing each firm's output as a function of the other firm's output and the government-determined per unit subsidy s are obtained by solving (i) for $q(q^*; s)$ and (ii) for $q^*(q)$

$$q^R(q^*; s) = \frac{a - bq^* - c + s}{2b},$$

$$\rightarrow q^* = (q^R)^{-1}(q; s) = \frac{a - 2bq - c + s}{b},$$

$$q^{*R}(q) = \frac{a - bq - c^*}{2b}, \quad (7.6)$$

where the relations $\partial q^R(q^*; s)/\partial q^* = \partial q^{*R}(q)/\partial q = -1/2 < 0$ imply that firms' reaction functions are downward sloping. In other words, if the foreign firm (or domestic firm) increases the level of production, the domestic firm (or foreign firm) best response is to reduce its level of output.

The Cournot–Nash levels of output are obtained by solving for q and q^* as a function of the specific subsidy s (see appendix)

$$q(s) = \frac{a + c^* - 2c + 2s}{3b}, \qquad q^*(s) = \frac{a + c - 2c^* - s}{3b}. \tag{7.7}$$

After-subsidy profits as a function of the subsidy are

$$\pi(s) = \frac{(a + c^* - 2c + 2s)^2}{9b}, \qquad \pi^*(s) = \frac{(a + c - 2c^* - s)^2}{9b}. \tag{7.8}$$

The output and profit equations indicate the profit-shifting effect of export subsidies in a strategic setup. If the domestic government unilaterally raises the per unit export subsidy s, the domestic firm's output and profits increase while the foreign firm's output and profits decline.

Figure 7.1 illustrates the effect of export subsidies. Free trade equilibrium quantities (q^{FT}, q^{*FT}) are determined by the intersection of the domestic and foreign firms' reaction curves RR and R^*R^* at point a. These curves depict the zero subsidy case in which $s = 0$. Notice that RR does not depict $q = q^R(q^*)$ but rather its *inverse* $q^* = (q^R)^{-1}(q)$ in (7.6). The foreign firm reaction curve R^*R^* depicts $q^* = q^{*R}(q)$. The domestic reaction curve RR has a slope of -2 and is steeper than the foreign reaction curve, which has a slope equal to $-1/2$.

If the domestic government unilaterally raises the per unit export subsidy from $s = 0$ to $s > 0$, the reaction curve RR shifts to $R^U R^U$ while the foreign reaction curve

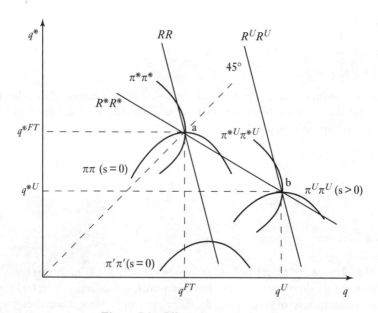

Figure 7.1. *Effects of an export subsidy*

remains the same. In equilibrium, the domestic firm's output increases and the foreign firm's output level declines. This is represented by the shift from point a to point b in Fig. 7.1.

The isoprofit curves $\pi\pi$ and $\pi^U\pi^U$ illustrate the locus of points (q, q^*) yielding constant profits π^{FT} and π^U in the free trade and unilateral subsidy cases, respectively. The isoprofit map is a function of the specific subsidy. Equation (7.3) shows that there is a set of isoprofit curves in the zero subsidy case and a different set of isoprofit curves in the positive subsidy case. For any given specific subsidy, profits are higher the lower the height of the isoprofit curve. For instance, in the zero subsidy case, $\pi\pi < \pi'\pi'$. The reason is that, for any level of domestic output, the market price is higher if the level of foreign production is lower.

Because the reaction curves depict the locus of points at which profits are maximized for a given rival's output, the slope of the domestic country's isoprofit curve is equal to zero at the point of intersection with the domestic reaction curve. By the same token, the foreign country's isoprofit curve has an infinite slope at the point of intersection with the foreign reaction curve.

7.3.3. Welfare Effects and Unilateral Subsidization

Export subsidization has a profit-shifting effect favoring the domestic firm, but also entails subsidy costs. Let us assume that export subsidies are financed by nondistorting lump-sum taxes and that the government's redistributive policy is welfare neutral. Export subsidies are viewed as a redistribution of resources whereby local consumers pay taxes sq that are then given to domestic firms as export subsidies.

Next result shows that the domestic subsidy maximizing welfare (profits net of subsidy costs) is positive. Domestic welfare $W(s)$ is defined as the difference between domestic after-subsidy profits, $\pi(s)$ in (7.8), and the costs of the subsidy, sq, where q is given by (7.7)

$$W(s) = \pi - sq = \frac{(a + c^* - 2c + 2s)(a + c^* - 2c - s)}{9b}. \tag{7.9}$$

If local firms are not subsidized (i.e. $s = 0$), domestic welfare is

$$W^{FT} = \frac{(a + c^* - 2c)^2}{9b}. \tag{7.10}$$

The question that remains to be answered is: what is the equilibrium unilateral specific subsidy s^U? The subsidy is set by the government to maximize domestic welfare. The first order condition of the welfare maximization problem is

$$\frac{dW(s)}{ds} = \frac{2(a + c^* - 2c - s) - (a + c^* - 2c + 2s)}{9b}$$

$$= \frac{a + c^* - 2c - 4s}{9b} = 0.$$

Solving for the equilibrium unilateral subsidy s^U, we obtain

$$s^U = \frac{a + c^* - 2c}{4} > 0, \tag{7.11}$$

where the positive output condition $a + c^* - 2c > 0$ implies $s^U > 0$.

The equilibrium subsidy to the local firm increases with the rival's marginal costs c^* and goes down with the domestic cost parameter c. Therefore, a more cost-competitive local firm should receive a larger subsidy (i.e. $\partial s^U / \partial c = -1/2 < 0$). The intervention policy is welfare increasing compared with free trade by construction, so that unilateral export promotion beats free trade and export taxes.

Substituting the subsidy in (7.11) into (7.7), yields equilibrium output

$$q^U = \frac{a + c^* - 2c + 2s^U}{3b}$$

$$= \frac{a + c^* - 2c + 2\frac{a+c^*-2c}{4}}{3b} = \frac{a + c^* - 2c}{2b}. \tag{7.12}$$

A positive output level requires $a + c^* - 2c > 0$. If $a + c^* - 2c < 0$, costs are too high relative to demand and production would require a subsidy. However, the subsidy equation shows that it is not optimal to subsidize. As a result, the local firm does not enter into the third market.

7.4. SUBSIDIES SUSTAIN THE STACKELBERG OUTCOME

A duopoly game in which one player is the leader and the other behaves as follower is called a Stackelberg game. In the two-firm Stackelberg game, the leader-firm plays first and the follower-firm plays second. This section shows that the equilibrium export subsidy in the third market game induces the home firm to act as if it were the leader in a related Stackelberg game in which there is no government, and thus no subsidy. In other words, unilateral export subsidization benefits the home firm by implementing the Stackelberg duopoly solution.

Unilateral export promotion constitutes an optimal strategy because it represents a government subsidization commitment that in turn allows the domestic firm to commit to an aggressive production strategy. A credibly higher production level forces the rival to respond with a follower's lower production strategy. This strategy profile derives in lower profits for the foreign firm and larger profits for the domestic firm.

The proof that the equilibrium export subsidy implements the Stackelberg equilibrium is established as follows. First, compute the leader's output in the Stackelberg duopoly game, q^S. Second, observe that it is the same as equilibrium output q^U in Brander and Spencer's unilateral subsidization game. The Stackelberg leader chooses the best strategy taking as given the whole follower's reaction function $q^{*R}(q)$ defined in (7.6). Formally, the leader maximizes total revenues $pq = [a - b(q + q^{*R})]q$ minus variable production costs cq

$$q^S = \arg\max_q \pi(q, q^{*R}(q)) = \left[a - b\left(q + \frac{a - bq - c^*}{2b}\right)\right]q - cq$$

$$= \left[a - \frac{a + bq - c^*}{2}\right]q - cq,$$

where the arg max of the profit function is the value of the argument that maximizes the function.

The first order conditions are

$$0 = \frac{\partial\pi(q, q^{*R}(q))}{\partial q} = a - \frac{a + bq - c^*}{2} - \frac{b}{2}q - c$$

$$= a - \frac{a + 2bq - c^*}{2} - c.$$

Solving for q^S, we obtain the leader's output level

$$q^S = q^U = \frac{a + c^* - 2c}{2b} > q^{FT} = \frac{a + c^* - 2c}{3b}, \tag{7.13}$$

where the free trade solution is obtained by setting $s = 0$ in (7.7).

The nonintervention Stackelberg leader's output is the same as the equilibrium output of the subsidized firm in the Cournot–Nash game, q^U in (7.12). This means that the strategic export subsidy in Brander and Spencer's game can be viewed as a way to push the local firm toward the Stackelberg solution for a leader-firm. The Stackelberg leader's output is found through a profit maximization problem that takes as given the whole *reaction function* $q^{*R}(q)$ of the follower firm. This solution method differs from the methodology used to obtain the Cournot–Nash output solution in (7.5), where the maximization was performed taking as given the rival's *output* q^*.

7.4.1. Interpretation

Figure 7.2 describes the government's strategic behavior engineering a shift to the Stackelberg outcome at point b. The Stackelberg equilibrium is characterized by the tangency of the isoprofit curve $\pi^S\pi^S(s = 0)$ to the rival's reaction curve R^*R^*. The reason is that the equilibrium point maximizes leader profits given the whole reaction function of the follower firm. Recall that domestic isoprofit curves must be flat when they intersect the domestic country reaction curve RR but the Stackelberg solution does not lie on the domestic reaction curve RR.

In a Cournot–Nash game, the domestic firm maximizes profits taking as given the foreign output q^*. The free trade Cournot–Nash equilibrium at point a is characterized by a flat isoprofit curve at the point of intersection with the foreign reaction curve. Point b is implemented as a Cournot–Nash equilibrium point because (1) it lies on the

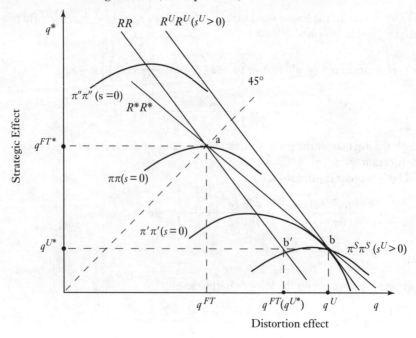

Figure 7.2. *Strategy and distortion effects of export subsidies*

foreign reaction function R^*R^* and, (2) the subsidized firm's isoprofit curve $\pi^S \pi^S$ ($s > 0$) is flat at b. The after-subsidy profit function thus achieves a maximum at point b where the reaction curve under subsidization $R^U R^U$ intersects R^*R^*.

An export subsidy has a strategic and a production distortion effect. The subsidy's strategic effect induces the rival to reduce volume of production and relates to the shift from point a to point b' along RR. Notice that profits at point b are greater than at point a: $\pi'\pi'(s = 0) > \pi\pi(s = 0)$.

The production distortion effect, depicted by the horizontal movement from point b' to point b in Fig. 7.2, takes place because the subsidy shifts the domestic firm's reaction function from RR to $R^U R^U$, generating an increase in exports. The production distortion effect means that the local firm produces excessively from the government's perspective. The government would prefer to restrict domestic exports in order to increase prices and reduce subsidy costs. Profits are higher and subsidy costs would be lower at b' than at point b: $\pi'\pi'(s = 0) > \pi^U \pi^U (s = 0)$ and $sq' < sq^U$.

7.5. BILATERAL EXPORT SUBSIDIZATION

Let us now examine what happens when both governments subsidize exports, which we call bilateral intervention. In this case, firms can end up in a prisoner's dilemma situation. The prisoner's dilemma takes its name from the plight of two crime suspects who are interrogated independently and end up accusing each other to obtain a lighter sentence, but could have gone free if they had shut up their mouths.

In the symmetric bilateral intervention game, welfare falls below the free trade welfare level. Both countries are hurt when they establish subsidies maximizing their own welfare noncooperatively, but could have gained by abstaining from intervention or by behaving cooperatively. The welfare loss from bilateral intervention compared with free trade contrasts with the positive welfare effect of unilateral intervention.

In a bilateral intervention game with asymmetric costs, free trade is best if the cost asymmetry is not too large. If the cost asymmetry is relatively large, the low-cost country's welfare surpasses the free trade welfare level. If the cost asymmetry is high enough, a subsidy by the low-cost country can drive the high-cost country out of the market (see Fig. 7.4).

7.5.1. Equilibrium for Given Subsidies

How does the game's outcome change when there is bilateral intervention? Consider domestic and foreign profits inclusive of subsidies

$$\pi(q, q^*; s) = (a - b(q + q^*))q - cq + sq,$$
$$\pi^*(q, q^*; s^*) = (a - b(q + q^*))q^* - c^*q^* + sq^* \tag{7.14}$$

and solve for output levels and equilibrium subsidies. Derivations follow the same procedures applied in the unilateral intervention case. The first order conditions associated with (7.14) yield the following bilateral intervention reaction functions

$$q^R(q^*; s) = \frac{a - bq^* - c + s}{2b}, \qquad q^{*R}(q; s^*) = \frac{a - bq - c^* + s^*}{2b}. \tag{7.15}$$

Equilibrium domestic output q and aggregate output Q are given by

$$q(s, s^*) = \frac{a + (-2c + c^*) + (2s - s^*)}{3b},$$
$$Q(s, s^*) = \frac{2a - (c + c^*) + (s + s^*)}{3b}. \tag{7.16}$$

Domestic profits are obtained by substituting q and Q into profit equation (7.14)

$$\pi(s, s^*) = \frac{[a + (-2c + c^*) + (2s - s^*)]^2}{9b}. \tag{7.17}$$

Similar equations $q^*(s, s^*)$ and $\pi^*(s, s^*)$ hold for the foreign country with appropriate change of notation.

7.5.2. Welfare Analysis

Is bilateral subsidization welfare maximizing from a societal perspective? Countries maximize welfare functions

$$W(s, s^*) = \pi(s, s^*) - sq(s, s^*), \qquad W^*(s, s^*) = \pi^*(s, s^*) - sq^*(s, s^*). \qquad (7.18)$$

Given the per unit subsidies s and s^*, the welfare level under bilateral intervention is obtained by substituting (7.16) and (7.17) into (7.18)

$$W(s, s^*) = \frac{[a - 2c + c^* - (s + s^*)][a - 2c + c^* + 2s - s^*]}{9b}. \qquad (7.19)$$

A similar equation holds for the foreign country with the appropriate change of notation.

When both governments noncooperatively choose the specific subsidy that maximizes their country's welfare, the equilibrium export subsidies are

$$s^{Bil} = \frac{a - 3c + 2c^*}{5}, \qquad s^{*Bil} = \frac{a - 3c^* + 2c}{5}. \qquad (7.20)$$

The equilibrium welfare levels W^{Bil} and W^{*Bil} under bilateral intervention are

$$W^{Bil} = \frac{2(a - 3c + 2c^*)^2}{25b}, \qquad W^{*Bil} = \frac{2(a - 3c^* + 2c)^2}{25b}. \qquad (7.21)$$

7.5.3. Symmetric Bilateral Intervention

In the symmetric linear case in which countries have the same cost function parameter c, firms' profits are always greater than under free trade

$$\pi(s, s) = \frac{(a - c + s)^2}{9b} > \frac{(a - c)^2}{9b} = \pi^{FT}. \qquad (7.22)$$

From a firm's perspective, the establishment of subsidies is a beneficial policy. But what about societal welfare? The subsidy and welfare levels under bilateral intervention are

$$0 < s^{Bil} = s^{*Bil} = \frac{a - c}{5} < s^U = \frac{a - c}{4}, \qquad (7.23)$$

$$W^{Bil} = W^{*Bil} = \frac{2}{25} \frac{(a - c)^2}{b} < W^{FT} = \frac{1}{9} \frac{(a - c)^2}{b},$$

where the bilateral subsidy is lower than the unilateral subsidy $(a - c)/4$ from (7.11) and the free trade welfare level is obtained from (7.10). The welfare level is found to be lower under bilateral intervention than under free trade. Bilateral intervention pushes authorities into a prisoner's dilemma and generates welfare losses for both symmetric countries.

Imposing $c = c^*$ in (7.16) yields

$$q^{Bil} = \frac{a - c + s^{Bil}}{3b} = \frac{a - c + \frac{a-c}{5}}{3b} = \frac{2}{5}\frac{a - c}{b}.$$

In the symmetric bilateral intervention case, domestic firm's output falls below the level of output under unilateral intervention but exceeds the production level under free trade

$$q^{U} = \frac{1}{2}\frac{a - c}{b} > q^{Bil} = \frac{2}{5}\frac{a - c}{b} > q^{FT} = \frac{1}{3}\frac{a - c}{b}.$$

Figure 7.3 illustrates the bilateral intervention exercise. The Cournot–Nash equilibrium under no intervention is given by the intersection of the reaction curves RR and R^*R^* at point a. If the domestic and foreign governments raise the per unit export subsidy from $s = 0$ to $s^{Bil} = s^{*Bil} > 0$, firms' reaction curves shift from RR to $R^{Bil}R^{Bil}$ and from R^*R^* to $R^{*Bil}R^{*Bil}$. The bilateral intervention equilibrium is depicted by point c. If there is unilateral domestic intervention, the domestic reaction curve shifts while the foreign curve remains the same and the equilibrium is represented by point b.

At the bilateral intervention equilibrium at point c, the domestic firm's output q^{Bil} is larger than the level of output q^{FT} under nonintervention but is smaller than the output

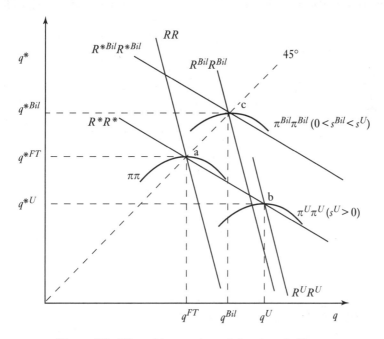

Figure 7.3. *Bilateral intervention and the prisoner's dilemma*

level q^U under unilateral domestic intervention: $q^{FT} < q^{Bil} < q^U$. Foreign production q^{*Bil} exceeds the free trade production level q^{*FT} as well as the output q^{*U} under unilateral intervention by *domestic* authorities: $q^{*U} (s > 0, s^* = 0) < q^{*FT} < q^{*Bil}$.

7.5.4. Asymmetric Bilateral Intervention

Figure 7.4 compares welfare as a function of c^* under bilateral intervention and free trade when countries have asymmetric costs. We assume that $a = 10, b = 1$ and $c = 0$. Bilateral and free trade welfare levels W^{Bil} and W^{FT} are computed from (7.21) and (7.10).

The nonnegative output conditions imply that the foreign firm does not produce for $c^* \geq 3.3$. Observe that (7.20) shows that the domestic specific subsidy increases with the level of foreign costs c^*. In terms of Fig. 7.4, the domestic specific subsidy is higher as we move upward along the curve showing the welfare differential.

Welfare under free trade exceeds welfare under bilateral intervention when the asymmetries are not too large ($W^{Bil} < W^{FT}$ when $c^* < 2.1$). With large asymmetries, subsidizing exports will push domestic welfare over the free trade benchmark. In fact, if the cost differential is high enough, the equilibrium domestic subsidy will force the foreign firm to exit the market. As a result, the domestic firm will monopolize the third market.

The consideration of the asymmetric case suggests the following rule: when costs asymmetries are not large, free trade is best. If the cost asymmetries are high enough,

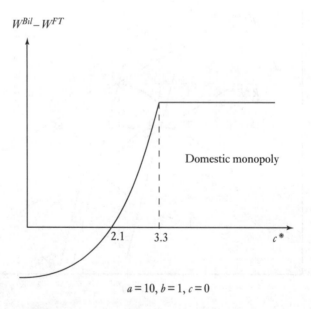

Figure 7.4. *Bilateral intervention with cost asymmetry*

subsidizing exports will be optimal for the low-cost country even if the other country also subsidizes.

Who Should Benefit from the Use of Public Funds?

Who should get higher subsidies, the high-cost firm or the low-cost firm? If firms exhibit cost heterogeneity, the bilateral intervention model provides a clear prescription. More efficient firms should receive larger subsidies than less efficient firms.

The subsidy differential is obtained from (7.20)

$$s^{Bil} - s^{*Bil} = \frac{a - 3c + 2c^*}{5} - \frac{a - 3c^* + 2c}{5} = c^* - c.$$

The domestic subsidy exceeds the foreign subsidy, $s^{Bil} > s^{*Bil}$, if the domestic firm produces at lower marginal costs than the foreign firm, $c^* > c$. The more efficient the domestic firm (i.e. the lower the cost c), the greater the subsidy differential.

By subsidizing more heavily a more efficient firm, domestic authorities maximize the revenues extracted from rivals, and thus the profit-shifting effect and domestic welfare. The argument is based on the idea that greater subsidies should be given to the firm having stronger competitive advantage in reaping gains from the rival's output reduction. The subsidy prescription allows the government to maximize the welfare impact of the domestic funds used to pay for the subsidies. This is the same prescription described in the unilateral intervention framework.

7.6. DISTORTING EXPORT SUBSIDY FINANCING

Brander and Spencer (1985) assume that export subsidies are financed by nondistorting lump-sum taxes. In practice, collecting funds to subsidize domestic exports entails taxing other sectors or activities, which gives rise to economic distortions. Taxpayers' welfare losses are not necessarily matched by the increased utility of subsidy recipients. Governments are forced to balance opposite interests coexisting in society. The presence of distortions can reverse the export subsidy prescription.

7.6.1. Export Policy and Tax Distortions

What are the equilibrium trade policies in the presence of distortions? Neary (1994) extends the government's unilateral export policy problem described in Brander and Spencer (1985) to account for tax distortions. He finds that the sign of the equilibrium export policy (subsidies or taxes) depends on the magnitudes of the distortions introduced by raising public funds. The distortion is not modeled explicitly but is rather represented by a distortion cost parameter $d \geq 0$. Ballard *et al.* (1985) quantify the costs of the distortions associated with raising public funds. They find that cost figures range between \$1.17 and \$1.56 per dollar raised.

Unilateral Trade Intervention

The domestic social welfare function is given by exporters' after-subsidy profits π minus the sum of (1) the financial cost of the subsidies, sq, and (2) the cost of the distortions created by the taxes used to finance the subsidies, dsq

$$W(q, s) = \pi - sq - dsq = \pi - (1 + d)sq = \pi - \delta sq, \tag{7.24}$$

where $\delta = 1 + d \geq 1$ embodies the subsidy transfer and the associated distortion. In this game, authorities face the following dilemma. On one hand, they wish to enhance domestic firms' strategic export market position and thus firms' profits. On the other hand, they wish to minimize the sum of the subsidy costs and domestic distortions created by raising the public funds used to subsidize exports. When exports are taxed, $s < 0$ and the $-\delta sq$ term becomes positive. Taxing entails a social benefit due to the tariff revenues and the use of the revenues gathered to reduce the cost of pre-existing domestic distortions.

Social welfare as a function of the specific subsidy s is obtained by substituting q and π from (7.7) and (7.8) into (7.24)

$$\begin{aligned} W(s) &= \frac{(a + c^* - 2c + 2s)^2}{9b} - \delta s \frac{a + c^* - 2c + 2s}{3b} \\ &= \frac{[a + c^* + 2(s - c)][a + c^* - 2c + (2 - 3\delta)s]}{9b}. \end{aligned} \tag{7.25}$$

The first order condition $\partial W(s)/\partial s = [(4 - 3\delta)(a + c^* - 2c) - 4(3\delta - 2)s]/9b = 0$ yields the equilibrium subsidy

$$s^U = \frac{(4 - 3\delta)(a + c^* - 2c)}{4(3\delta - 2)}, \tag{7.26}$$

where $\delta = 1 + d \geq 1$ implies that the second order conditions are satisfied because $\partial^2 W(s)/\partial s^2 = (-4(3\delta - 2))/9 < 0$ if $\delta > 2/3$ (i.e. the distortion index satisfies $\delta > 2/3$).

The expression for the unilateral subsidy illustrates the relationship between the equilibrium subsidy and the distortion index. Imposing the positive output condition $a > 2c - c^*$ implies that when there is no distortion (i.e. $\delta = 1 + d = 1$) the unilateral subsidy is strictly positive. If there are financing distortions, the subsidy is positive only for small enough costs $1 \leq \delta < 4/3 = \bar{\delta}$. The subsidy s^U goes down with the distortion index δ and becomes negative when $4/3 < \delta$. The introduction of strong enough distortions can justify a negative subsidy, that is, an export tax.

Intuitively, the threshold value $\bar{\delta}$ results from equating the domestic revenue gains due to the rival's output decline and the increased deadweight loss generated by imposing the distorting subsidy s. To compute the revenue gains, take q as given and recall from (7.7) that the foreign firm's output when the foreign government is passive $(s^* = 0)$ is $q^* = (a + c - 2c^* - s)/3b$. If the subsidy s increases, the strategic effect implies that the change in rival's production q^* is equal to $\partial q^*/\partial s = -1/(3b)$

per unit increase in the subsidy. The product price $p = a - b(q + q^*)$ increases by $1/3$. Taking q as given, an increase in the subsidy s increases domestic firm revenues $R = pq = [a - b(q + q^*)]q$ by $-bq(\partial q^*/\partial s) = q/3$. Also, the deadweight loss from raising funds to subsidize the domestic firm is equal to $dsq = (\delta - 1)sq$. Therefore, increasing s by one unit implies that the deadweight loss increases by $(\delta - 1)q$. The revenue gains and deadweight losses from increasing the subsidy are equalized when $q/3 = (\delta - 1)q$, which implies that $\bar{\delta} = 4/3$ in Fig. 7.5.

The equilibrium subsidy is negative when there are large distortions associated with raising funds. It is optimal to tax exports in order to obtain revenues that reduce the costs of pre-existing distortions. When the government taxes exports, $\delta > 4/3$ in (7.26), a more efficient firm should suffer a larger export tax in order to maximize government's revenues and reduce preexisting distortions.

The maximized value of welfare is obtained by substituting the subsidy (7.26) into (7.25)

$$W^U = \frac{\delta^2(a + c^* - 2c)^2}{8b(3\delta - 2)} > W^{FT} = \frac{(a + c^* - 2c)^2}{9b}, \tag{7.27}$$

where $\delta = 1 + d \geq 1$. The appendix verifies that welfare under unilateral intervention exceeds welfare attainable under free trade as given by (7.10).

A basic property of the maximized welfare function W^U is that it decreases with the level of the distortion index $\delta = 1 + d$ when $1 \leq \delta < 4/3 = \bar{\delta}$ and increases with the distortion index when $\delta > 4/3 = \bar{\delta}$

$$\frac{\partial W^U}{\partial \delta} = \frac{\delta(3\delta - 4)(a + c^* - 2c)^2}{8b(3\delta - 2)^2}.$$

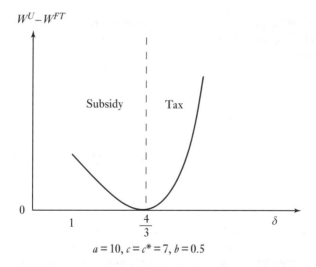

$a = 10$, $c = c^* = 7$, $b = 0.5$

Figure 7.5. *Distortions, equilibrium policy, and welfare*

7.6.2. Symmetric Bilateral Intervention with Distortions

Consider the case in which both the domestic and the foreign governments subsidize exports. Raising funds is assumed to create the same distortion d in the foreign country as in the domestic country. The foreign government's welfare function is analogous to (7.24).

In the symmetric case in which costs are equal, $c^* = c$, the equilibrium subsidy and the intervention vs free trade welfare differential have a simple relation to the distortion index value. The equilibrium subsidy is (see appendix)

$$s^{Bil} = \frac{(4 - 3\delta)(a - c)}{9\delta - 4},$$
(7.28)

with $s^{Bil} > 0$ if $\delta < 4/3$. It is easy to see that the bilateral subsidy declines with the value of the distortion index $\delta = 1 + d$,

$$\frac{\partial s^{Bil}}{\partial \delta} = \frac{-24(a - c)}{(9\delta - 4)^2} < 0.$$

Welfare in each country is obtained by setting $c^* = c$ in (7.17) and (7.16),

$$
\begin{aligned}
W^{Bil} &= \pi^{Bil} - \delta s^{Bil} q^{Bil} \\
&= \frac{(a - c + 2s^{Bil} - s^{*Bil})^2}{9b} - \delta s^{Bil} \frac{a - c + 2s^{Bil} - s^{*Bil}}{3b} \\
&= \frac{2\delta^2(3\delta - 2)(a - c)^2}{b(9\delta - 4)^2} > 0, \quad \delta \geq 1.
\end{aligned}
$$
(7.29)

Equation (7.29) implies that countries' welfares increase with the distortion index $\delta = 1 + d$. The appendix shows that, for high enough values of δ, bilateral intervention turns out to exceed the level of welfare achieved under free trade. This paradoxical result arises because large distortions discourage welfare-reducing bilateral subsidization and sustain bilateral export taxation, which serves to reduce the cost of preexisting distortions. The implication is that the export subsidy prescription is not robust to the presence of large domestic distortions.

7.7. HAS EXPORT PROMOTION WORKED?

Export promotion policies represent a major element of developed countries strategies to foster trade, penetrate markets abroad and grow. Japan, the European Union, and the United States have introduced multiple promotion programs based on direct and indirect subsidization. Since the 1960s, developing countries have gradually scaled down import substitution policies in favor of export promotion. The policy shift from import substitution development to export-led growth was supported by a wide array of export incentives. Two widely cited examples of successful outward orientation through export subsidization are the Korean case—based on subsidization contingent on performance—and the Brazilian case—with multiple export subsidy programs and subsidization of exporting multinationals.

Export subsidization should be understood in broad terms as comprising domestic policies entailing direct or implicit subsidies to exporters. These include financial, tax relief, technology, and trading measures. Financial measures include government provision of low-cost insurance to exporters, the establishment of financing lines to facilitate exports and export credit subsidies. The Export–Import Bank of the United States (Eximbank) was established in 1934 as an independent federal corporation. It offers export credit insurance protecting US exporters and their lenders against political and commercial risks of nonpayment by foreign buyers. It also provides direct loans and loan guarantees benefiting US exporters and foreign buyers. The Eximbank plays a competitive role by countering subsidized foreign export financing.

Tax measures include tax reliefs and reimbursements, temporary admissions, and investment and other tax credits. For instance, export processing zones attract firms by granting duty drawbacks. A duty drawback is a rebate of all or part of a duty on goods imported for processing and subsequent reexportation. Technology measures include financial support to innovation and technology transfers. Subsidies to research and development can also be viewed as a particular form of indirect export subsidy.

Production and trading measures include the promotion of general trading companies and the establishment of free trade zones. The general trading company (*sogo shosha*) system is a peculiar Japanese institution that has been adopted in Korea, Thailand, and other countries. It provides distribution channels and facilitates the penetration of foreign markets. Free trade zones have proliferated in developing countries partly to promote exports by exploiting trade preferences granted by developed countries. General trading companies and free trade zones represent two examples of mechanisms that have been successfully used for export promotion.

7.7.1. Pros and Cons

Active export promotion schemes can be viewed as

(1) a form of strategic trade policy in oligopolistic markets. The other side of the coin is that rival countries' strategic responses include subsidization or the imposition of trade-restricting measures—such as countervailing duties—that do not entail budgetary costs. The World Trade Organization permits imposing countervailing duties on imports from countries that subsidize their exports. For instance, Brazil's substantial export promotion efforts since the seventies have been partly nullified by US countervailing duties;
(2) an economic response to the persistence of market failures and a host of factors limiting exportation. These include imperfections in financial markets (especially as concerns large investments that do not produce benefits in the near future), lack of customer information on product quality, limited producer information about foreign markets, and high costs of entering into new markets. On the other side, policy targeting considerations suggest that it might be better to address financial and informational distortions directly rather than indirectly through

export promotion. Furthermore, in many situations private markets can attenuate market inefficiencies more effectively than public intervention;

(3) an economic, political, and social response to large terms of trade fluctuations due to lack of production diversification. Lack of export diversification and attendant large economic fluctuations can encourage output diversification policies supported by export subsidization, free trade zones, and other forms of export promotion;

(4) a form of protection to special interests. The GATT opened a loophole for food and agricultural products. As a result, agricultural export subsidies and other incentives proliferated. In fact, 90 percent of pre-WTO complains concerned agricultural and food industries and many of them focused on export subsidies.

What is effect of export subsidies for a small country that does not have market power in global markets? In this case, there are neither terms of trade not profit shifting effects from export subsidization. Export subsidies induce production above marginal costs, which is inefficient. Moreover, domestic consumers are hurt because the domestic price of subsidized exportables will rise above the marginal cost and will be higher than the price paid by foreign exporters. The reason is that, in equilibrium, the home price of exportables must be large enough to offset the subsidy received from exportation. Otherwise, producers export the goods in order to receive the subsidy and lack incentives to sell locally.

A case for export subsidization by a small country can be made as a mechanism to offset a foreign rival's tariff. According to the Lerner symmetry theorem, if all imports are subject to tariffs at a uniform rate, then the distortion can be neutralized by export subsidies. Panagariya (2000*a*) counters that this mechanism can be efficient if the administration of the subsidy is costless but not if the financing of the subsidy requires imposing a distorting tax. Moreover, the mechanism will generate inefficiencies if exporters overstate claims in order to obtain greater subsidies, as is the case in many developing countries. Also, exports subsidies fail to correct the distortions arising if the preexisting tariff structure gives rise to costly smuggling activities.

A major difficulty raised by export promotion is how to select the industries that will be favored by subsidization. The art of picking infant exporters with market potential has not yet reached its maturity. Industry or firm selection is a risky undertaking and represents an acute problem in countries facing budget difficulties. For instance, bad timing, changing market conditions, and unpredictable government policies can turn a good prospect into a lemon project burdened with large sunk costs. Moreover, selective subsidization generates distortions and inequities due to differential subsidization of industries and firms. Even worse, many countries lack the resources or political will to evaluate projects thoroughly and hand out funds on the basis of political influence rather than economic assessments.

There are two polar approaches to the selection problem. One approach is to target industries and firms. This was the route taken by Korea in the 1960s. Industries and local conglomerates were targeted for subsidization contingent on successful export performance. The overall Korean experience represents a prominent example of successful targeting and export promotion through direct and credit subsidies, duty exemptions, and tax exemptions. Dollar and Sokoloff (1990) and Pack (2000) find that Korea experienced rapid total factor productivity (TFP) growth in many sectors, including promoted ones, during the takeoff of the 1960s and 1970s. However, the effects of export promotion should not be exaggerated. TFP often grew faster in sectors that were not subject to active export promotion. Dollar and Sokoloff (1990) find that TFP growth in the heavily-promoted capital intensive sector was generally less than half the TFP growth in labor-intensive sectors. Sector displaying above average TFP growth included clothing and footwear, leather and plastic products, rubber, furniture, and electrical goods. Moreover, the promotion of chemicals, steel, autos and other heavy industries during 1973–78 did not work as planned leading to strategic retreat due to high costs, premature launching, and the oil crises of the 1970s. Pack (2000) results, however, are more favorable to the heavy and chemical industry Korean drive.

The Costa Rican strategy of facilitating large foreign investments by Intel in the 1990s also fits the targeting mold. This industrial strategy is credited for contributing to generate an export and economic boom in the late 1990s. This boom explains why the country experienced continued growth even while most Latin American countries succumbed to the East Asian crisis of 1997 and 1998 and beyond.

A second approach is to promote exports in a nondiscriminatory manner by adopting policies that facilitate exportation. Taiwan's export promotion provides an example of a relatively nondiscriminatory export promotion program in the sense that there was no favoritism toward particular industries. Instead of targeted subsidization, exports were supported through rebates of import duties and other indirect taxes on inputs used in the production of manufactured exports. Exporters and firms supplying imports to exporters benefited from the rebates while other firms were subject to duties on their imported inputs. This type of export promotion system was initiated in the mid-1950s. Its operation during the 1980s is described in Wade (1988) and Thomas and Nash (1991). A partial exception involving targeting concerns three export processing zones set up in 1965 favoring the electronics industry.

The changing structure of Taiwanese exports illustrates the fallacies of attributing observed export structures to particular targeting schemes. Since 1960, the structure of Taiwan's exports to the United States shifted from one dominated by apparel, which represented 30 percent of total 1960 exports, to one dominated by apparel, consumer products, and electrical and electronic products. The new export industries represented 0 percent of total 1960 exports. Apparel diminished in relative importance as Taiwan became a newly industrializing economy. These structural changes are in many ways similar to those experienced by other newly industrialized economies. In the case of Taiwan, though, blooming industries did not exhibit an infant industry stage, were not targeted by the government and did not benefit from discriminatory export subsidization.

7.7.2. Has Export Promotion Worked?

What does empirical evidence tells us about the performance of export promotion in practice? Despite the appeal of export subsidies as a policy to facilitate entry and successful competition abroad, there is no body of consistent statistical evidence confirming that export promotion has generally worked, or failed for that matter. Our assessment of the evidence to date suggests that this evaluation must be conducted on a case by case basis and that the reported successes in Korea, Taiwan, and other countries do not automatically extend to other countries. Country, industry, and beneficiary firms' specific conditions appear to be key in determining (1) whether active promotion of export growth and diversification are appropriate goals, (2) what is the best way to achieve these goals, and, (3) how to distinguish between the effects of different policies and alternative forms of export promotion such as credit subsidization, free trade zones, and institutional improvement.

Latin American export promotion has been investigated by Nogués (1990). While most Latin American countries have subsidized exports, the only successful export diversification program in his sample took place in Brazil in the 1970s and 1980s. Brazil actively promoted and subsidized exports during these decades. Persistent export promotion efforts in Argentina were plagued by wasteful rent-seeking activity, regional and product discrimination, and US countervailing actions. The country remained largely a close economy during the sample period. By contrast, Mexico diversified its exports of manufactures in the 1980s but did not sustain an export subsidization program. The comparative study by Rodrik (1995b) documents heterogeneous experiences. The study contrasts successful export subsidization in Korea and Brazil, failed episodes in Kenya and Bolivia, and mixed experiences in Turkey and India.

The Indian export promotion experience does not receive a mixed review in the hands of Arvind Panagariya (2000a). He recounts multiple schemes, many of them existing in some form for decades. They include export credit guarantees and insurance, export financing at below market interest rate, assistance in marketing and quality standard improvement, help in upgrading technology, and research into raw materials for the packing industry. In addition, he mentions the existence of seven export processing zones (EPZs), export-oriented units (EOUs) established outside the EPZs, seven software technology parks and an electronic hardware technology park. Despite strenuous promotion efforts, the 1990 exports to GDP ratio was a low 5 percent. This figure stood right at the bottom of the world openness ranking. By 1997, this openness ratio had risen to 10 percent. But the rise is attributed to import liberalization, successful exchange rate management and other measures that did not involve greater export promotion.

The evidence on credit subsidies is examined by Thomas and Nash (1991) and Fitzgerald and Monson (1989). They conclude that credit subsidies have not been generally effective and that the successes counted with special conditions that are not likely to be replicated elsewhere.

What are the general lessons derived from an examination of export promotion experiences? Rodrik (1995b) argues that the cases studied suggest that export policies work best when two features are present. One is substantial state autonomy in the sense that the bureaucracy is insulated from private interests. A substantial degree of state autonomy permits establishing discipline over the private sector and controlling rent-seeking behavior (Amsden, 1989; Thomas and Nash, 1991). The second condition is policy coherence in the sense that policy priorities are clearly articulated, stable, and are not in mutual conflict.

A key precondition for export promotion is the access to adequate or preferential markets for exports (Baldwin *et al.*, 1995). Many free trade zones and export promotion efforts by developing countries have been based on preferential access such as the United States' Caribbean Basin Initiative (CBI) and the North American Free Trade Agreement (NAFTA).

Promotion policies work better when they are market oriented than when they are based on strict planning, burdensome regulation, and direct state exporting. Successful private sector-oriented export promotion programs contrast with many failed initiatives based on state ownership. Porter *et al.* (2000) question the common assertion that a wide array of promotion mechanisms, protective barriers and regulations contributed to Japan's remarkable export success in the post second World War era. They present quantitative evidence showing that Japanese products became highly competitive and challenged US high-technology leadership in export sectors, such as automobile and semiconductors, that were subject to intense rivalry. Sony, Nintendo, Honda, and other winners operated in sectors that were relatively free of government controls and faced competition abroad. By contrast, highly regulated and protected sectors became uncompetitive.

7.8. POLITICS, COMPETITION, AND POLICY COLLUSION

Negotiations to reduce agricultural subsidies are at the center of the trade liberalization agenda. Dismantling the vast array of agricultural trade subsidization (and protection) schemes, though, has proved to be an arduous task. Moreover, government policies engineered to promote politically powerful producers often fall into prisoner's dilemma traps. Authorities' attempts to increase market share lead to low prices for all, rendering strategic moves counterproductive.

The United States and the Cairns group of agricultural exporters—Argentina, Australia, Brazil, Canada, Chile, Colombia, Hungary, Indonesia, Malaysia, New Zealand, the Philippines, Thailand, Uruguay, and others—have endorsed a phase out of agricultural export subsidies. The European Union has argued for a progressive reduction but not a phase out of agricultural support. Even though countries agreed in the benefits from cutting agricultural subsidies, only a moderate reduction could be achieved in the Uruguay Round. Developed countries agreed to cut 36 percent of the value of agricultural export subsidies over a 6-year period.

Bagwell and Staiger (2001*a*) examine a set up in which two governments subsidize their competitive agricultural industries to help them compete in third markets. The strategic analysis of government behavior differs from strategic trade theory à la Brander and Spencer (1985) in two elements. First, the export market is viewed as perfectly competitive. Second, governments are subject to political pressures exercised by exporters. The model is applied to agriculture but is also applicable to other competitive industries with political muscle.

Consider two perfectly competitive industries—labeled domestic and foreign—that export all their output of a homogeneous commodity to a third market, which is denoted by a double asterisk (**). Export supplies are given by

$$q = \frac{p}{2} = \frac{p^{**} + s}{2}, \qquad q^* = \frac{p^*}{2} = \frac{p^{**} + s^*}{2},$$

where p and p^* are the prices received by domestic and foreign subsidized firms on their third-market sales and p^{**} is the price paid by third market consumers. The linear third market demand function is $Q^{**} = 1 - p^{**}$.

7.8.1. Bilateral Intervention, Collusion, and Welfare

The domestic government maximizes a welfare function that assigns a political weight of ϕ to domestic exporters' after-subsidy or after-tax profits π and values negatively the financial cost of the subsidies. The higher the value of ϕ the greater the political influence of agricultural groups. Domestic welfare W is given by (see appendix)

$$W = \phi\pi - sq = \phi\frac{(2 + 3s - s^*)^2}{64} - s\left(\frac{2 + 3s - s^*}{8}\right). \tag{7.30}$$

What is the equilibrium export policy under noncooperative bilateral intervention? Calculating the first order conditions and imposing symmetry yields

$$\frac{\partial W}{\partial s} = 0: \quad s(s^*) = \frac{(3\phi - 4)(2 - s^*)}{3(8 - 3\phi)} \quad \rightarrow \quad s^{Bil} = s^{*Bil} = \frac{3\phi - 4}{10 - 3\phi}.$$

Free trade is an equilibrium if $\phi = 4/3$. Exports are subsidized, $s^{Bil} = s^{*Bil} > 0$, if $\phi \in (4/3, 8/3)$ and exports are taxed, $s^{Bil} = s^{*Bil} < 0$, if $\phi < 4/3$.

Governments have incentives to collude and design policies together to exploit market power and extract rents from third market consumers. The reason is that neither noncooperative intervention nor free trade among competitive firms maximize joint exporters' welfare. Collusion can be viewed as a means to correct the terms of trade distortion faced by noncooperating countries.

Suppose that the domestic and foreign governments collude to implement a cartel by cooperatively formulating trade policies. The equilibrium subsidy in the symmetric country case is obtained by maximizing cartel welfare (see appendix)

$$s^{Collusion} = s^{*Collusion} = \frac{\phi - 2}{4 - \phi}.$$

Observe that the parameter region supporting an export subsidy is smaller under governments collusion than under bilateral intervention. From the viewpoint of the exporting countries, free trade is best only if $\phi = 2$. If ϕ is less than 2, the equilibrium collusive policy is to impose an export tax in order to exploit the cartel's monopoly power. The collusive solution allows setting the terms of trade that better exploit monopoly power even though firms' after-tax profits suffer. If ϕ lies in the interval $(2, 8/3)$, producer after-tax profits are valued highly relative to subsidy costs and the equilibrium policy is to subsidize exports even if terms of trade effects are unfavorable.

The differential between the total welfare levels achieved by governments that behave noncooperatively and as a cartel is (see appendix)

$$2W(s^{Bil}) - 2W(s^{Collusion}) = \frac{2}{(3\phi - 10)^2(\phi - 4)},$$

where $W(s^{Bil}) + W^*(s^{*Bil}) - W(s^{Collusion}) - W^*(s^{Collusion}) = 2W(s^{Bil}) - 2W(s^{Collusion}) < 0$. The negative sign follows from the second order condition of the maximization problem, which requires that $\phi < 8/3$. This welfare result confirms that—for the intervening countries—the cartel dominates bilateral intervention. Bilateral intervention generates a prisoners' dilemma for the intervening countries and results in a lower price, which benefits third-market consumers. By contrast, a cartel maximizes benefits by extracting income from third market consumers.

What is the global welfare—including third country consumer welfare—under bilateral intervention and under a cartel? Global welfare is defined as the sum of exporting country before-tax profits (producers' surplus) and third-country consumers' surplus $W^{**}(s)$. Consumer surplus is given by

$$W^{**}(s) = \int_{p^{**}(s)}^{1} (1 - p^{**})dp^{**} = \frac{1}{2} - p^{**}(s) + \frac{[p^{**}(s)]^2}{2}$$

$$= \frac{1}{2} - \left(\frac{1}{2} - \frac{s + s^*}{4}\right) + \frac{1}{2}\left(\frac{1}{2} - \frac{s + s^*}{4}\right)^2$$

$$= \tfrac{1}{8}(s + 1)^2,$$

where the last equality uses $s = s^*$ at equilibrium. Global welfare is greater under bilateral intervention than under authorities' collusion (see appendix)

$$W^W(s^{Bil}) - W^W(s^{Collusion}) = \frac{328 - 288\phi + 87\phi^2 - 9\phi^3}{2(3\phi - 10)^2(\phi - 4)^2},$$

which is positive for $\phi < 8/3$.

The finding that bilateral subsidization is better than a cartel from a global perspective does not mean that bilateral intervention is the best global policy. Global welfare under free trade is

$$W^W(s = 0) = \frac{6 + 8\phi}{48}.$$

If firms' profits are assigned the same weight $\phi = 1$ as third country consumer's surplus, free trade dominates. The dominance of free trade points toward the positive global role of restricting export subsidies. Despite political influence, countries that intervene noncooperatively on behalf of their producers have incentives to design mechanisms to cooperate and achieve free trade. However, this is not the case for enforceable collusive agreements.

7.9. ENVIRONMENTAL REGULATION: A PRIMER

Environmental regulation plays a dual role in countries' welfare. First, regulatory restrictions improve domestic consumer's welfare by reducing pollution and by inducing environmental-friendly innovation. Second, regulatory restrictions increase firm's costs and raise the prices of affected consumer goods. Setting environmental taxes, emission standards, and other regulations imposing costs on domestic firms in order to improve the environment establishes a close link between a healthy environment, innovation, and international cost competitiveness (Carraro and Galeotti, 1997).

7.9.1. Optimal Intervention with Externalities

Economically, environmental policy concerns the problem of managing negative externalities (i.e. third party effects) under conditions in which property rights are not well-defined and agreements are difficult to enforce. In principle, firms and nations should carry the costs of the environmental externalities they generate. Unfortunately, it is easier to formulate solutions than to implement them. There are no markets and property rights on pollution and regulation. The solutions entail domestic regulation, the negotiation of self-enforcing agreements, and the establishment of markets that internalize the costs of environmental degradation.

The policy targeting framework (Bhagwati, 1971) prescripts a corrective tax addressed to the environmental externality that is source of the distortion. The optimal environmental policy for an open economy does not entail trade intervention. It rather involves free trade combined with appropriately set taxes, licenses or standards (Markusen, 1975). In general, globally optimal environmental taxes, standards, and pollution licenses vary across countries depending on how important countries are as a source of global pollution.

The optimal level of environmental degradation in perfectly competitive markets can be attained by

1. The imposition of taxes affecting the activity that degrades the environment. The optimal emissions tax (Pigovian tax) imposes a cost on firms equivalent to the marginal damage caused by the polluting effects of their production activities. Depending on whether authorities have a nationalistic or global perspective, the optimal pollution tax is set to be equal to the marginal domestic or global social cost of emissions.
2. The imposition of emission standards on polluting firms and governments. The total amount of licenses to pollute (i.e. emit) issued to firms and governments puts a cap on pollution. Permitting trade in licenses allows the reallocation of the licenses toward more productive firms, which improves the domestic or global allocation of resources.
3. The issuance of licenses to pollute. The optimal emission standard equates the marginal costs of satisfying the emission requirements to the marginal damage to the domestic or global environment.

The optimal tax (or other form of regulation) depends on market structure. The principle behind Pigovian taxes, that environmental damages should be fully internalized, does not hold under monopoly. The optimal degree of internalization is less than full under monopoly. A monopolist reaps profits by artificially restricting production to raise market prices. Emission taxes internalize environmental damages but also accentuate the low output distortion created by a monopolist's behavior.

What is the second-best environmental policy consisting of an emissions tax on a monopolist? The right social welfare balance between environmental protection and keeping monopoly prices low is struck with an emission tax that leads to less than full internalization. The first-best policy entails an emission tax that fully internalizes the marginal damages from environmental pollution and an output subsidy that leads the monopolist toward the competitive output level. A fee or lump sum tax can be used to extract the monopoly rent.

7.10. CORRECTIVE AND STRATEGIC ENVIRONMENTAL PROTECTION

A domestic and a foreign firm compete as duopolists using technologies that generate pollution. If domestic pollution does not diffuse across borders, optimal environmental taxes are set at a level that balances two opposing goals. First, corrective tax setting improves consumer's welfare by reducing pollution externalities. Second, strategic tax setting avoids raising firm's costs, reducing domestic firm's output and shifting market share toward the rival. The optimal environmental tax balances corrective and strategic goals. The equilibrium and optimal tax level depends on (1) the mode of competition, that is, on whether the domestic and foreign firms compete by setting quantities or prices, and (2) whether or not environmental policies induce innovation.

7.10.1. *Noncooperative Equilibrium in a Tax–Output Game*

Consider two rival firms, labeled I and II, located in different countries that export and compete in quantities as duopolists in a third market (i.e. the third market model). In the absence of pollution abatement, each unit of output is assumed to produce one unit of pollution. On the other hand, pollution abatement reduces emissions and thus taxes on emissions. Therefore, a tax on emissions constitutes a tax on quantity produced net of abatement.

In the second stage, the firm decides on the amount e of pollution abated, taking the emission tax t as given. On one hand, in order to abate an amount e of pollution, the firm faces the cost function $C(e) = e^2$. On the other hand, abatement e reduces emissions. Emission taxes are thus reduced from tq to $t(q - e)$. Therefore, firm i profits are

$$\pi_i = (a - q_i - q_j)q_i - cq_i - e_i^2 - t_i(q_i - e_i), \quad i \in \{I, II\}.$$

The first order necessary condition for emissions implies that the optimal level of emissions is an increasing function of the tax on emissions.

$$\frac{\partial \pi_i}{\partial e_i} = 0 \quad \rightarrow \quad e_i = \frac{t_i}{2}.$$

The first order conditions for quantities, $\partial \pi_i / \partial q_i = 0$, yield downward sloping output reaction functions

$$q_i = q_i^R(q_j, t_i) = \frac{a - q_j - c - t_i}{2}, \tag{7.31}$$

where output declines with tax emissions. The optimal level of production as a function of tax emissions is derived solving the system $q_i = q_i^R(q_j, t_i), i \in \{I, II\}$

$$q_i = \frac{a - c - 2t_i + t_j}{3}, \qquad q_j = \frac{a - c - 2t_j + t_i}{3}. \tag{7.32}$$

The level of output declines with the domestic emissions' tax but increases with the rival's emission tax.

In the first stage, each government chooses noncooperatively the tax level t_i that maximizes domestic welfare, given by the domestic firm's revenues minus the sum of production costs cq_i, the costs e_i^2 borne by firms to protect the environment (i.e. reduce emissions by e_i), and the damage $d_i(q_i - e_i)$ to the environment

$$W_i = (a - q_i - q_j)q_i - cq_i - e_i^2 - d_i(q_i - e_i), \tag{7.33}$$

where d denotes the marginal social value of the damage caused by pollution, and e_i represents reductions in emissions (i.e. abatement).

Substituting e_i defined in above, and q_i and q_j given by (7.32) into (7.33), and using the resulting expression to compute the first order necessary condition $\partial W_i / \partial t_i = 0$, yields an expression for the gap between the tax t_i and the marginal social value d_i of the damage caused by greater pollution

$$t_i - d_i = -\frac{2(a - c - d_i) + 2(t_j - t_i)}{17},$$

where $a > c + d_i$ (autonomous demand exceeds total social costs).

The previous equation is the government reaction function showing the level of domestic taxes for any given level of foreign taxes. A symmetric model (i.e. $d_i = d_j$) has a symmetric equilibrium (i.e. $t_i = t_j$)

$$t = d - \frac{2(a - c - d)}{17}.$$

In the strategic game between firms and the government, the equilibrium tax is smaller than the marginal value of the damage caused by the emissions. Therefore, the equilibrium tax is smaller than the optimal tax. In noncooperative equilibrium, both governments relax environmental policies. There are incentives to relax environmental protection in order to increase the competitive position of the domestic firm. Each government's commitment to lower emission taxes in the first stage leads to an increase of its country's output for any given level of the rival's output (i.e. the output reaction function shifts outwards). Given the foreign firm's reaction function, output is shifted toward the domestic firm. This strategy increases market share, if the rival government does not intervene.

Plugging the equilibrium tax rate into welfare function W_i shows that, when governments follow lax environmental policies, there is a prisoner's dilemma situation in which firms' profits decline and pollution increases in both countries. Both economies end up losing compared to the first-best cooperative policy that maximizes joint country welfare. The cooperative solution is not achieved because each country has incentives to deviate from it. The issue that arises is how to achieve cooperation in this type of scenario.

7.10.2. *Environmental Policy, Price Competition, and Induced Innovation*

The analysis suggesting that authorities implement lax environmental policies to promote local firms engaged in quantity competition in international markets can be reversed if firms compete in prices and if environmental policies induce emission-reducing innovation (Barret, 1994; Ulph and Ulph, 1996; Ulph, 1997).

When firms compete in prices (i.e. Bertrand competition), governments would tend to set tougher environmental policies than when firms compete in quantities. In price competition, firms set their prices taking as given their rival's price. Because reaction functions are upward sloping, when a firm raises its price the rival raises its price too. Governments increase the domestic firms cost by setting tougher than first-best environmental policies, in order to induce domestic firms to raise their prices and thus their rival's prices. These policies facilitate exploiting firms' monopoly power.

Innovation induced by environmental regulation reduces emissions per unit of output. Innovation takes place to avoid reducing output or to reduce the cost to purchasing pollution licences and can lead to a race for environmental innovation. If firms invest excessively in response to environmental regulation, as in Laffont and Tirole (1996), a second-best policy involving lax policy can improve social welfare relative to tough regulation.

7.11. INDUSTRIAL POLICY IN ALTERNATIVE FRAMEWORKS

The analysis based on Brander and Spencer (1985) offers clear policy prescriptions to intervening countries. The prescriptions favor unilateral strategic export subsidization and reject bilateral subsidization in the symmetric country case. However, the analysis implies that bilateral subsidization can be counterproductive. The prescriptions and related incentives contribute to explain the presence of aggressive direct and indirect export subsidization as well as the success of export-led industrialization in Asia during the post-second World War period.

Generally speaking, the equilibrium strategic trade intervention hinges on the specific details of supply, demand, market structure, induced distortions, and mode of competition—whether firms compete by setting quantities or prices (see next chapter). In particular, the export subsidy prescription is not robust in the sense that it does not equally apply in different economic environments. We selectively review the large literature examining how different frameworks lead to alternative policy prescriptions. Subsequent chapters cover recent research efforts aiming to define a robust strategic trade policy.

7.11.1. Multiple Instruments and Oligopoly

Dixit (1984) studies the role of export subsidies, antitrust policies determining the number of firms, import tariffs, and production subsidies. He considers an oligopolistic equilibrium of a homogeneous good traded in two segmented markets. There are n domestic and N foreign firms, each of which sells in each market. Each firm treats the output of all other firms as constant when it sets its output level. Technologies are described by a fixed (but not sunk) cost and a constant marginal cost, $C_i(q_i) = c_0 + cq_i$, $i \in \{1, \ldots, n\}$ and $C_i^*(q_i^*) = c_0^* + c^*q_i^*$, $i \in \{1, \ldots, N\}$. Domestic and foreign inverse demand functions are $p = p(D)$ and $p^* = p^*(D^*)$, where D and D^* represent total sales in each market.

In this setup, a unilateral specific export subsidy has two opposite effects. The subsidy shifts profits toward domestic firms (i.e. the strategic effect) but leads to an increase in exports that can result in a deterioration of the country's terms of trade. In other words, the production distortion effect discussed above leads to lower prices and benefits the competing country's consumers. If the number of domestic firms is small enough, the strategic effect dominates and the optimal export subsidy is positive. This is the result obtained in the single domestic firm model of Brander and Spencer (1985). If the number of domestic firms is large enough, though, the negative terms of trade effect associated with expanded production offsets the positive profit-shifting effect. In that case, it is optimal to impose an export tax. An alternative option is to reduce the number of domestic firms by adopting a lax antitrust policy promoting domestic mergers and acquisitions.

Dixit also examines the domestic tariff response to a foreign subsidy, showing that it is optimal to impose a countervailing duty in response to a foreign export subsidy. The positive countervailing duty result arises in an oligopolistic setting but not in a competitive international setting. Strong foreign competition renders antitrust policies unnecessary.

7.11.2. Free Entry and Increasing Costs

Horstman and Markusen (1986) develop a two-country model in which each country produces one good under increasing returns to scale. The domestic and foreign goods might or might not be perfect substitutes. International markets are assumed to be fully integrated. The model differs from standard oligopoly models in that free entry of firms is allowed, making the equilibrium number of firms endogenous. Profits are driven to zero because positive profits induce firm entry.

Ad valorem output or export subsidies cause inefficient entry of new firms that seek to benefit from subsidies. This leads to an increase in domestic output, but reduces output per firm. Entry is inefficient because, in the presence of sunk costs, the fall in per firm output pushes firms up the average cost curve, profits are driven down to zero, and welfare goes down. Import tariffs also entail inefficient entry and welfare losses. When the domestic and foreign goods are perfect substitutes, free trade is best.

7.11.3. Research and Development

Brander and Spencer (1983) considered a three-stage game consisting of policy, research and development (R&D), and output setting stages. In the first stage, the domestic government unilaterally sets a policy package combining taxes or subsidies to exports and R&D. In the second stage, a domestic and a foreign firm choose the levels of R&D spending. In the third stage, firms determine the levels of production.

R&D spending represents a firms' cost-reducing commitment that benefits them by affecting strategic behavior in the output stage. The equilibrium unilateral policy package combines R&D taxes and export subsidies. R&D taxes serve to offset the overinvestment in cost reduction generated by duopolistic competition.

Restrictions imposed by the WTO and other international agreements restrict the use of export subsidies. These restrictions raise the question of what is the equilibrium strategic research policy when an export subsidy policy is not feasible. If export subsidies are banned, unilateral R&D subsidies can substitute for them and are able to sustain the same Stackelberg-type equilibrium as unilateral export subsidization. By design, this type of unilateral policy is welfare increasing with respect to nonintervention. Bilateral R&D subsidization, however, generates a prisoner's dilemma situation that makes both countries worse off.

Leahy and Neary (1997) develop a two-sector, two-period oligopoly model of firms that export to a third market. Firms generate three types of R&D spillovers (1) local spillovers to domestic firms in the same industry, (2) local cross-industry spillovers, and (3) international spillovers. R&D subsidies are justified due to the externalities benefitting home firms but the presence of international spillovers can justify a tax to domestic R&D activities. The purpose of the domestic tax is to limit international spillovers, reduce foreign output, and shift rents toward the home country. Furthermore, when local firms cooperate they typically overinternalize the externalities due to the presence of local spillovers. This effect can also justify a tax on R&D.

7.11.4. General Equilibrium

Dixit and Grossman (1986) consider a targeted export firm and the effects of an export subsidy on other domestic firms. They take into account that, in general equilibrium, exports can increase only by extracting resources, say scientists, out of other industries. Because an export subsidy lowers marginal costs in the targeted industry while raising marginal costs in other sectors, the net welfare effect is ambiguous. The ambiguities in policy formulation arising from the competition for scarce resources are made particularly acute when there is limited information about industries. Dixit and Grossman show that, in order to determine whether or not an export subsidy is optimal, the policymaker must have knowledge about details relating to the targeted firms as well as other domestic and foreign firms.

7.11.5. Asset Markets, Privatization, and Lobbying

Cross-national firm ownership reduces the incentives for strategic trade policy aiming to shift profits toward domestic firms. The reason is that when domestic residents hold diversified portfolios welfare-maximizing governments take into account the profits from both domestic and foreign firms. Lee (1990) and Dick (1993) show that the strategic trade subsidy goes down with a higher degree of cross-national ownership.

Feeney and Hillman (2001) examine unilateral subsidization in an infinite horizon third market duopoly model with lobbying. Profits are stochastic due to domestic and foreign cost shocks, which are assumed to be perfectly negatively correlated for illustrative purposes. The pattern of asset ownership is endogenized by allowing investors to choose portfolios. Investors exhibit constant relative risk aversion, which implies that the share of their wealth invested in a risky asset increases with their wealth level. Asset portfolios are chosen before the realization of the cost shock while the subsidy (politically determined through lobbying) and outputs are set in sequence after the shock realization. Shocks are independent across time and there is no connection between periods so that agents do not reallocate diversified portfolios and the model solution is not time dependent.

If all firms are private and equity trades globally, each agent diversifies. A country symmetry assumption implies that home and foreign investors have the same ex ante wealth and hold half of their portfolios in home firm shares and half in foreign firm shares. This portfolio allocation pattern makes agents indifferent to profit shifting, which merely reallocates profits within a portfolio. The equilibrium level of lobbying is zero and strategic trade policy is not implemented.

Incentives to engage in strategic subsidization remain if:

1. Either the home or the foreign firm is state-owned and profits accrue to firm insiders (managers, employees). For instance, suppose that the foreign firm is state-owned and profits accrue to firm insiders that do not diversify (say, workers). In this case, the domestic wealth will exceed the wealth of that part of the foreign population that diversifies. In equilibrium, domestic investors will retain more than half of the home firm generating a motive for export subsidization.

2. There is a home bias in portfolio allocation due to factors such as barriers to international asset trade.

Privatization under cross-national ownership reduces lobbying activity and the incentives for strategic trade policy. If partial privatization of Airbus precludes United States from becoming stakeholders in Airbus, the US interests will fail to internalize Airbus profits and the motives for strategic behavior in the United States will remain. To the extent that US investors hold Airbus shares, the incentives for strategic intervention decline.

7.12. CONCLUSIONS

Until the 1980s, the traditional benchmark market structures for trade analysis were perfect competition and monopoly. In the late 1970s, a nonstrategic approach based on monopolistically competitive market structures became a standard benchmark. Strategic trade theory opened the field to consider oligopolistic structures and game-theoretic approaches. Strategic trade policy examines trade intervention incentives when countries' governments behave strategically *vis-à-vis* each other.

The reexamination of trade policy shows that incentives and outcomes in oligopolistic market structures are different from incentives and outcomes under perfect competition, monopoly, and monopolistic competition. With competition à la Cournot, export subsidies have the effect of establishing the subsidizing country as the leader in the strategic game being played (i.e. the unilateral export subsidy implements the Stackelberg outcome). In this setting, unilateral trade promotion has a profit-shifting effect that is welfare enhancing for the intervening country.

Bilateral export subsidization reduces intervening countries' welfare compared with free trade (if costs are symmetric or cost asymmetries are small enough). However, export subsidies can increase the low-cost country welfare if the international cost asymmetry is large enough. Finally, the implementation of export subsidies should take into account the distorting effects arising from the taxes imposed to finance the subsidies and the details of the economic-politico environment. Because the analysis of export subsidies hinges on cost asymmetries, it is crucial to examine how cost differentials are influenced by learning-by-doing and R&D spending.

A number of features of the strategic analysis discussed here have been a subject of much controversy. The analysis does not produce robust results or robust policy recommendations. For instance, whether the best strategic policy involves trade promotion or trade restriction hinges on the details of the model. Furthermore, governments face informational constraints when they have to choose what policy to implement. There is also the issue of how to formulate strategic analysis in an environment in which trade intervention measures, such as tariffs and trade subsidies, are limited by both regional trade agreements and the WTO. In this environment, many countries have recurred to contingent protection, as well as to indirect forms of protection such as local content laws and stringent product standards. These issues are addressed in subsequent chapters.

7.13. APPENDIX

7.13.1. Derivation of (7.7) and (7.8)

The Cournot–Nash noncooperative output response to the rival's quantity choice, taking the per unit subsidy as given is,

$$q(s) = \frac{a - bq^* - c + s}{2b} = \frac{2(a - c + s) - (a - bq - c^*)}{4b}$$

$$= \frac{a + c^* - 2c + 2s + bq}{4b},$$

where $q^*(q) = (a - bq - c^*)/2b$. Solving for q yields $q(s) = (a + c^* - 2c + 2s)/3b$. Substituting q into $q^*(q)$, we obtain

$$q^*(s) = \frac{a - bq - c^*}{2b} = \frac{3(a - c^*) - (a + c^* - 2c + 2s)}{6b}$$

$$= \frac{a + c - 2c^* - s}{3b}.$$

World production Q is obtained from $q(s)$ and $q^*(s)$

$$Q(s) = \frac{a + c^* - 2c + 2s}{3b} + \frac{a + c - 2c^* - s}{3b}$$

$$= \frac{2a - (c + c^*) + s}{3b}.$$

Aggregate output increases with the value of the specific subsidy s. This implies that the increase in domestic output more than compensates for the foreign firm's output reduction. The equilibrium market price is obtained by substituting Q into $p = a - bQ$,

$$p(s) = a - b\frac{2a - (c + c^*) + s}{3b} = \frac{a + c + c^* - s}{3}.$$

The world price declines with larger per unit export subsidies.

Profits $\pi = (p - c + s)q$ and $\pi^* = (p - c^*)q^*$ are obtained by substituting expressions $q(s), q^*(s)$, and $p(s)$ into π and π^*

$$\pi(s) = \frac{a + c + c^* - s - 3c + 3s}{3} \frac{a + c^* - 2c + 2s}{3b}$$

$$= \frac{(a + c^* - 2c + 2s)^2}{9b},$$

and

$$\pi^*(s) = \frac{a + c + c^* - s - 3c^*}{3} \frac{a + c - 2c^* - s}{3b}$$

$$= \frac{(a + c - 2c^* - s)^2}{9b}.$$

7.13.2. Welfare Effects Under Unilateral Intervention

Domestic welfare $W(s)$ is computed as after-subsidy domestic profits, $\pi(s)$ in (7.8), minus the costs of the subsidy, sq, where q is given by (7.7). Calling $A \equiv a + c^* - 2c + 2s$ yields

$$W(s) = \pi(s) - sq = \frac{A^2}{9b} - s\frac{A}{3b} = \frac{A}{3b}\left(\frac{A-s}{3}\right)$$

$$= \frac{(a + c^* - 2c + 2s)(a + c^* - 2c - s)}{9b}.$$

The differential between welfare under subsidization and free trade welfare is ($N \equiv a + c^* - 2c$)

$$W(s) - W^{FT}$$

$$= \frac{(a + c^* - 2c + 2s)(a + c^* - 2c - s)}{9b} - \frac{(a + c^* - 2c)^2}{9b}$$

$$= \frac{(N + 2s)(N - s)}{9b} - \frac{N^2}{9b} = \frac{N^2 + sN - 2s^2}{9b} - \frac{N^2}{9b}$$

$$= \frac{s(N - 2s)}{9b} = \frac{s(a + c^* - 2c - 2s)}{9b}.$$

If per unit subsidies are not too high, $0 < s < (a + c^* - 2c)/2$, then subsidization achieves greater domestic welfare than free trade, net of the costs of the subsidy. Export subsidies permit domestic firms to gain a greater share in international markets, which can result in welfare gains from the domestic country's viewpoint.

It is easy to verify that the equilibrium unilateral subsidy is in the range within which a subsidy is welfare increasing compared with nonintervention. Formally, $0 < s^U = (a + c^* - 2c)/4 < (a + c^* - 2c)/2$.

7.13.3. Asymmetric Bilateral Intervention

The equilibrium levels of output q^{Bil} and q^{*Bil} are obtained by substituting (7.20) into (7.16),

$$q^{Bil} = \frac{a + (-2c + c^*) + (2(a - 3c + 2c^*)/5 - (a - 3c^* + 2c)/5)}{3b}$$

$$= \frac{2}{5}\frac{a - 3c + 2c^*}{b},$$

$$q^{*Bil} = \frac{2}{5}\frac{a - 3c^* + 2c}{b}.$$

If $c = 0$, $q^{Bil} > 0$ and foreign production q^{*Bil} is positive only if $a - 3c^* > 0$.

7.13.4. Unilateral Export Policy and Tax Distortions

Differentiating s^U in (7.26) with respect to the distortion cost parameter δ yields

$$\frac{\partial s^U}{\partial \delta} = \frac{-3(a + c^* - 2c)}{2(3\delta - 2)^2} < 0.$$

The welfare differential in the presence of distortions is obtained from (7.27)

$$W^U - W^{FT} = \frac{\delta^2 (a + c^* - 2c)^2}{8b(3\delta - 2)} - \frac{(a + c^* - 2c)^2}{9b}$$

$$= \frac{(8\delta - 4)^2 (a + c^* - 2c)^2}{72b(3\delta - 2)},$$

which has a positive sign because $\delta \geq 1$.

7.13.5. Symmetric Bilateral Intervention with Distortions

The subsidy in (7.28) is derived as follows. Make $c = c^*$ in the profit equation (7.17) and use the output equation (7.16) to obtain

$$W(s, s^*) = \pi(s, s^*) - \delta sq(s, s^*)$$

$$= \frac{[a - c + 2s - s^*]^2}{9b} - \delta s \frac{a - c + 2s - s^*}{3b}.$$

Solving for s from the first order maximization condition yields

$$\frac{\partial W(s, s^*)}{\partial s} = 0 \quad \rightarrow \quad s = \frac{(4 - 3\delta)(a - c - s^*)}{4(3\delta - 2)}.$$

The equilibrium subsidy s^{Bil} is obtained by solving the previous equation for $s = s^*$.
The welfare differential with cost symmetry, $c = c^*$, is

$$W^{Bil} - W^{FT} = \frac{2\delta^2 (3\delta - 2)(a - c)^2}{b(9\delta - 4)^2} - \frac{(a - c)^2}{9b}$$

$$= \frac{(3\delta - 4)(18\delta^2 - 15\delta + 4)(a - c)^2}{9b(9\delta - 4)^2}.$$

This differential is positive for large enough values of δ, meaning that bilateral intervention turns out to exceed the level of welfare achieved under free trade.

7.13.6. Politics, Competition, and Policy Collusion

Domestic and foreign supply is given by

$$q = \frac{p}{2} = \frac{p^{**} + s}{2}, \qquad q^* = \frac{p^*}{2} = \frac{p^{**} + s^*}{2},$$

where p and p^* are producer prices and p^{**} is the consumer's price. The market-clearing condition equates total supply $Q = q + q^*$ and third-market demand $D^{**} = 1 - p^{**}$. Formally,

$$Q = q + q^* = \frac{p^{**} + s}{2} + \frac{p^{**} + s^*}{2} = 1 - p^{**} = D^{**}$$

$$\rightarrow p^{**} = \frac{1}{2} - \frac{s + s^*}{4}, \qquad Q^{**} = 1 - p^{**} = \frac{1}{2} + \frac{s + s^*}{4}.$$

Prices received, quantities, and profits are

$$p = p^{**} + s = \frac{1}{2} + \frac{3s - s^*}{4}, \qquad p^* = p^{**} + s^* = \frac{1}{2} + \frac{3s^* - s}{4},$$

$$q = \frac{p}{2} = \frac{1}{4} + \frac{3s - s^*}{8}, \qquad q^* = \frac{p^*}{2} = \frac{1}{4} + \frac{3s^* - s}{8},$$

$$\pi = \left(\frac{p}{2}\right)^2 = \frac{(2 + 3s - s^*)^2}{64}, \qquad \pi^* = \left(\frac{p^*}{2}\right)^2 = \frac{(2 + 3s^* - s)^2}{64},$$

where positive outputs imply the restrictions $2 + 3s - s^* > 0$ and $2 + 3s^* - s > 0$. Evaluating these restrictions at s^{Bil} and s^{*Bil} implies that

$$2 + 3s^{Bil} - s^{*Bil} = 2 + 3s^{*Bil} - s^{Bil}$$

$$= 2 + 2\frac{3\phi - 4}{10 - 3\phi} = \frac{12}{10 - 3\phi},$$

which is positive because the second order condition of the welfare maximization problem requires $\phi < 8/3$.

Domestic noncooperative welfare as a function of s is given by (7.30) in the text. Evaluated at $s^{Bil} = s^{*Bil} = (3\phi - 4)/(10 - 3\phi)$ yields

$$W(s^{Bil}) = W^*(s^{Bil})$$

$$= \phi\frac{(2 + 2(3\phi - 4/10 - 3\phi))^2}{64} - \frac{3\phi - 4}{10 - 3\phi}\frac{2 + 2(3\phi - 4/10 - 3\phi)}{8}$$

$$= \frac{3(8 - 3\phi)}{4(3\phi - 10)^2},$$

where $\phi < 8/3$. Exporting countries total welfare is two times $W(s^{Bil})$.

The total welfare of colluding countries is

$$W + W^* = \phi\pi - sq + \phi^*\pi^* - s^*q^*$$

$$= \phi\left[\frac{(2 + 3s - s^*)^2}{64} + \frac{(2 + 3s^* - s)^2}{64}\right]$$

$$- s\frac{2 + 3s - s^*}{8} - s\frac{2 + 3s^* - s}{8}.$$

The first order conditions imply the equilibrium collusion subsidy

$$\frac{\partial (W + W^*)}{\partial s} = 0 : \quad s(s^*) = \frac{s^*(3\phi - 4) + (2 - \phi)}{5\phi - 12}$$

$$\rightarrow \quad s^{Collusion} = s^{*Collusion} = \frac{\phi - 2}{4 - \phi}.$$

Total domestic and foreign welfare is

$$W^{Collusion}(s^{Collusion}) = W(s^{Collusion}) + W^*(s^{Collusion})$$

$$= \frac{2\phi \, (2 + 2(\phi - 2/4 - \phi))^2}{64}$$

$$- 2\frac{\phi - 2}{4 - \phi} \left(\frac{2 + 2(\phi - 2/4 - \phi)}{8} \right)$$

$$= \frac{1}{2(4 - \phi)}.$$

Comparing the sum of domestic and foreign welfare levels under bilateral intervention and policy collusion yields

$$W(s^{Bil}) + W^*(s^{*Bil}) - W(s^{Collusion}) - W^*(s^{Collusion})$$

$$= \frac{3(8 - 3\phi)}{2(3\phi - 10)^2} - \frac{1}{2(4 - \phi)} = \frac{2}{(-10 + 3\phi)^2(-4 + \phi)},$$

where $W(s^{Bil}) + W^*(s^{*Bil}) - W(s^{Collusion}) - W^*(s^{Collusion}) < 0$ because $\phi < 8/3$.
Global welfare under bilateral intervention is

$$W^W(s^{Bil}) = W(s^{Bil}) + W^*(s^{Bil}) + W^{**}(s^{Bil})$$

$$= \phi\frac{(1 + s^{Bil})^2}{6} - s^{Bil}\left(\frac{1 + s^{Bil}}{4} \right) + \frac{1}{8}(s^{Bil} + 1)^2$$

$$= \frac{3(8 - 3\phi)}{2(3\phi - 10)^2} + \frac{9}{2(-10 + 3\phi)^2} = \frac{3(11 - 3\phi)}{2(3\phi - 10)^2},$$

where

$$W^{**}(s^{Bil}) = \int_{p^{**}(s)}^{1} (1 - p)dp = \frac{1}{2} - p^{**}(s) + \frac{[p^{**}(s)]^2}{2}$$

$$= \frac{1}{2} - \left(\frac{1}{2} - \frac{s + s^*}{4} \right) + \frac{1}{2}\left(\frac{1}{2} - \frac{s + s^*}{4} \right)^2$$

$$= \frac{1}{8}(s^{Bil} + 1)^2 = \frac{1}{8}\left(\frac{3\phi - 4}{10 - 3\phi} + 1 \right)^2 = \frac{9}{2(-10 + 3\phi)^2}.$$

Global welfare under collusion is

$$W^W(s^{Collusion})$$

$$= W(s^{Collusion}) + W^*(s^{Collusion}) + W^{**}(s^{Collusion})$$

$$= \frac{\phi(1 + s^{Collusion})^2}{6} - s^{Collusion}\left(\frac{1 + s^{Collusion}}{4}\right) + \frac{1}{8}(s^{Collusion} + 1)^2$$

$$= \frac{1}{24}(s + 1)(4\phi(1 + s) + 3(1 - s))$$

$$= \frac{1}{2(4 - \phi)} + \frac{1}{2(\phi - 4)^2} = \frac{1}{(\phi - 4)^2},$$

where

$$W^{**}(s^{Collusion}) = \frac{(s^{Collusion} + 1)^2}{8} = \frac{1}{8}\left(\frac{\phi - 2}{4 - \phi} + 1\right)^2 = \frac{1}{2(\phi - 4)^2}.$$

Global free trade welfare is

$$W^W(s = 0) = W(s = 0) + W^*(s = 0) + W^{**}(s = 0)$$

$$= \frac{\phi}{6} + \frac{1}{8} = \frac{6 + 8\phi}{48}.$$

Comparing global welfare under bilateral intervention and collusion

$$W^W(s^{Bil}) - W^W(s^{Collusion})$$

$$= \frac{3(11 - 3\phi)}{2(3\phi - 10)^2} - \frac{1}{(\phi - 4)^2} = \frac{328 - 288\phi + 87\phi^2 - 9\phi^3}{2(3\phi - 10)^2(\phi - 4)^2},$$

which is positive for $\phi < 8/3$. Comparing global welfare under free trade $W^{W,FT}$, bilateral intervention and collusion

$$W^{W,FT} - W^W(s^{Bil})$$

$$= \frac{6 + 8\phi}{48} - \frac{3(11 - 3\phi)}{2(3\phi - 10)^2} = \frac{328\phi - 213\phi^2 + 36\phi^3 - 96}{24(3\phi - 10)^2},$$

$$W^{W,FT} - W^W(s^{Collusion}) = \frac{6 + 8\phi}{48} - \frac{1}{(\phi - 4)^2} = \frac{40\phi - 29\phi^2 + 4\phi^3 + 24}{24(\phi - 4)^2}.$$

If firms' profits are given the same weight as third country consumers, $\phi = 1$, free trade dominates.

8

Strategies and the Mode
of Competition

One of the most cited results of strategic trade theory is that equilibrim trade policies vary with the mode of competition, that is, whether firms compete in quantities or compete in prices. Brander and Spencer's (1985) demonstration that the optimal unilateral intervention policy involves export subsidization assumes Cournot competition. Competition à la Cournot means that firms compete in quantities, setting output levels as a function of the rival's output.

The Cournot model of quantity competition has been criticized on the grounds that firms compete by setting prices, not quantities. Cournot competition assumes that firms choose quantities produced and deliver the production to the market, where an auctioneer specifies a market-clearing price. However, except in a few auction markets, real-world markets do not have an auctioneer. In practice, oligopolistic firms compete by setting prices strategically, which is called competition à la Bertrand.

When firms compete à la Bertrand by setting prices as a function of the rival's price level, however, the export subsidy prescription ceases to be valid. Instead, unilateral export *taxes* tend to be optimal (Eaton and Grossman, 1986). Moreover, the welfare effects of bilateral government intervention are different in quantity and price competition models. Under price competition, noncooperative bilateral intervention entails setting an export tax. The tax pushes the exporter closer to the monopoly equilibrium, generates government revenues, and is welfare-increasing for both countries. This result is the opposite of the Cournot case in which equilibrium with bilateral intervention involves subsidization that turns out to be welfare-reducing for both countries.

Because the mode of competition affects the results of strategic interactions and policy prescriptions, it has become standard to test for robustness by examining if a model's results work under Cournot competition and Bertrand competition. Empirical trade models with oligopolistic markets encompass both modes of competition as a way to examine the robustness of predictions and prescriptions.

Section 8.1 compares Cournot and Bertrand modes of competition when rivals produce differentiated goods and there is no government intervention. Section 8.2 shows that, under price competition, it is optimal to tax exports. Section 8.3 introduces the concepts of strategic complements and substitutes and examines the effects of unilateral intervention under price and quantity competition. Section 8.4 shows that bilateral intervention is welfare-improving under Bertrand competition. Section 8.5 discusses multiple instruments and the targeting principle. Section 8.6 examines a setting in which firms move before the government intervenes. Section 8.7 examines endogenous modes of competition. The appendix contains results about the conjectural variations approach, the isoprofit function and ex post intervention.

8.1. BERTRAND vs COURNOT EQUILIBRIA

Consider a duopoly Bertrand competition model in which a domestic and a foreign firm produce differentiated commodities I and II, respectively. When the strategic choice variable is the price set by a firm, it is useful to work with direct demands expressing quantity demanded as a function of prices. Solving the two-equation system of inverse demand functions, $p_I = a - b_1 q_I - b_2 q_{II}$ and $p_{II} = a - b_1 q_{II} - b_2 q_I$, yields the following direct demand functions

$$
\begin{aligned}
q_I(p_I, p_{II}) &= \frac{a}{b_1 + b_2} - \frac{b_1}{b_1^2 - b_2^2} p_I + \frac{b_2}{b_1^2 - b_2^2} p_{II} \\
&= \alpha - \beta_1 p_I + \beta_2 p_{II}, \\
q_{II}(p_I, p_{II}) &= \frac{a}{b_1 + b_2} - \frac{b_1}{b_1^2 - b_2^2} p_{II} + \frac{b_2}{b_1^2 - b_2^2} p_I \\
&= \alpha - \beta_1 p_{II} + \beta_2 p_I,
\end{aligned}
\tag{8.1}
$$

with $a = \alpha/(\beta_1 - \beta_2), b_1 = \beta_1/(\beta_1^2 - \beta_2^2)$, and $b_2 = \beta_2/(\beta_1^2 - \beta_2^2)$. Notice that to get the usual signs for the demand coefficients we need to impose $b_1 > b_2 > 0$, which implies that $\beta_1 > \beta_2 > 0$. This assumption means that the demand effect of an increase in a firm's price is greater than the demand effect of an increase in the rival's price.

Domestic and foreign firms' profits are

$$
\pi_I(p_I, p_{II}) = (p_I - c)q_I(p_I, p_{II}) = (p_I - c)(\alpha - \beta_1 p_I + \beta_2 p_{II}),
$$

$$
\pi_{II}(p_I, p_{II}) = (p_{II} - c)q_{II}(p_I, p_{II}) = (p_{II} - c)(\alpha - \beta_1 p_{II} + \beta_2 p_I),
$$

where c denotes constant marginal costs.

The previous setup is a differentiated product version (i.e. $p_I \neq p_{II}$) of the duopoly model with homogeneous commodities (i.e. $p_I \equiv p_{II}$) studied in last chapter. Cost functions are assumed to be the same in both countries (i.e. $c = c_I = c_{II}$).

8.1.1. *Conjectural Variations and Bertrand Competition*

The conjectural variations approach assumes that each firm formulates conjectures about how its actions will modify the behavior of its rival. The conjectural variations approach serves as an umbrella that covers different modes of competition, but does not explain where the conjectures that support each mode of competition come from. Cournot and Bertrand modes of competition arise from different conjectures about a rival's responses.

Under quantity competition, also called competition à la Cournot, firms compete in quantities by setting output levels on the so-called Cournot conjecture that other firms keep their quantities fixed. Let $v_{II}(q_I)$ and $v_I(q_{II})$ represent firms' I and II conjectures about rival's quantity response. Setting quantities on the Cournot conjecture that the rival's output level will be kept constant means $dv_{II}(q_I)/dq_I = 0$ and $dv_I(q_{II})/dq_{II} = 0$. The chapter's appendix discusses the details of the conjectural variations approach. Further discussion appears in Helpman and Krugman (1989).

Under price competition, also called Bertrand competition, firms set their product prices on the conjecture that their rivals keep their prices fixed (i.e. Bertrand conjectures). A duopoly firm sets its product price and formulates a conjecture about its rival's response to the price chosen. Firms' beliefs about the rival's response to their price decision can be summarized by conjectured responses

$$p_{II} = \psi_{II}(p_I), \qquad p_I = \psi_I(p_{II}),$$

where $\psi_{II}(p_I)$ and $\psi_I(p_{II})$ are the conjectures made by firms producing I and II, respectively.

The Bertrand competition conjecture is that firms I and II set their prices taking as given the rivals' price. This hypothesis means that a firm changes its price on the conjecture that the rival will not change its price in response

$$\frac{d\psi_{II}(p_I)}{dp_I} = 0, \qquad \frac{d\psi_I(p_{II})}{dp_{II}} = 0.$$

The Bertrand conjecture is the analog in the space of prices of the Cournot assumption in the space of quantities.

Maximizing profits with respect to each country's choice variable p_I and p_{II}, taking as given the rival's price, yields price reaction functions under Bertrand competition

$$p_I(p_{II}) = \frac{a(b_1 - b_2) + b_2 p_{II} + b_1 c}{2b_1}$$

$$\rightarrow p_{II} = p_I^{-I}(p_I) = \frac{-a(b_1 - b_2) + 2b_1 p_I - b_1 c}{b_2}, \qquad (8.2)$$

$$p_{II}(p_I) = \frac{a(b_1 - b_2) + b_2 p_I + b_1 c}{2b_1}.$$

When firms compete à la Bertrand, price reaction functions are upward sloping. The best response to a firm that increases its product price is also to set higher prices. Also, condition $b_1 > b_2 > 0$ implies that $dp_I(p_{II})/dp_{II} = dp_{II}(p_I)/dp_I = b_2/(2b_1) < 1$. This means that when a firm sets a higher price, the rival's reaction function implies that the rival will increase its price by a lesser amount. This property comes from the assumption that the demand effect of an increase in a firm's price is greater than the demand effect of an increase in the rival's price.

Solving the previous system of reaction functions yields the symmetric equilibrium

$$p^B = p_I^B = p_{II}^B = \frac{a(b_1 - b_2) + b_1 c}{2b_1 - b_2} < p^C = \frac{(a + c)b_1 + b_2 c}{2b_1 + b_2},$$

where the Cournot price p^C in the two differentiated goods model is computed in the appendix. The Bertrand price is lower than the Cournot equilibrium price but higher than marginal costs. Given that $b_1 > b_2$, there is a degree of exploitable monopoly power in each market. Therefore, equilibrium Bertrand prices exceed marginal costs, $p^B > c$, even if the equilibrium is symmetric.

Consider the special case in which both firms produce a homogeneous good (i.e. goods are perfect substitutes). Price competition converges to the well-known homogeneous goods equilibrium in which Bertrand prices are equal to marginal costs: $p^B = c$. To see why, suppose that both firms price above marginal cost and $p_I > p_{II} > c$. If goods are homogeneous, there will be no demand for I but its producer could capture the whole market by setting a price $p_I = p_{II} - \varepsilon$, which is smaller than p_{II} by the infinitesimal amount $\varepsilon > 0$. But then, the producer of II has incentives to capture the whole market by underpricing the seller of I. This process can go on until prices equal marginal cost. Observe that no firm will incur losses by setting a price below marginal cost. Therefore, the equilibrium price is $p^B = c$.

The result that two firms producing perfect substitutes under the same technology and competing in prices converge to marginal cost pricing is known as the Bertrand paradox. The perfect competition outcome is replicated even if there are only two competitors in the market.

8.1.2. *Bertrand vs Cournot Equilibria*

Figures 8.1 and 8.2 compare the results of the Bertrand and Cournot competition models when countries are symmetric in terms of demand and costs. Figure 8.1 shows the Bertrand and Cournot equilibria in the price plane. Bertrand prices, depicted by point B, are lower than Cournot prices, depicted by point C. The Bertrand equilibrium takes place at point B depicting the intersection of the upward-sloping reaction curves $R_I^B R_I^B$ and $R_{II}^B R_{II}^B$ (see (8.2)). Notice that $R_I^B R_I^B$ illustrates the *inverse* of $p_I(p_{II})$ in (8.2), that is, $p_{II} = p_I^{-1}(p_I)$. $R_{II}^B R_{II}^B$ depicts $p_{II}(p_I)$. The slope of the domestic firm's reaction curve $R_I R_I$, $2b_1/b_2$ from $p_{II} = p_I^{-1}(p_I)$, is larger than 1 because $b_2 < b_1$. The slope of the foreign firm's reaction curve $R_{II} R_{II}$, $b_2/2b_1$ from (8.2), is lower than 1.

The isoprofit curves $\pi_I \pi_I$ and $\pi_{II} \pi_{II}$ depict the locus of points (p_I, p_{II}) that yield constant profit levels π_I and π_{II} in the nonintervention case. Higher isoprofit curves represent higher profits for country I, $\pi_I < \pi_I'$. Country II's profits are higher for isoprofit curves located further to the right. In general, for any given firm's price, a firm will sell more and obtain greater profits if the rival sets a higher price. A reaction curve under Bertrand competition illustrates the locus of points at which profits are maximized for a given rival's price. Therefore, the slope of each country's isoprofit curve must be equal to zero at the point of intersection with the country's reaction curve (see proof in the appendix). At point B, countries isoprofit curves $\pi_I \pi_I$ and $\pi_{II} \pi_{II}$ achieve a maximum—are flat—in terms of each country's choice variable—its product price.

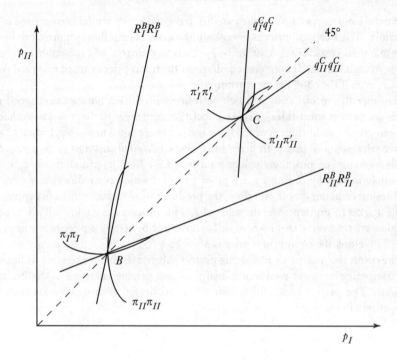

Figure 8.1. *Bertrand vs Cournot prices*

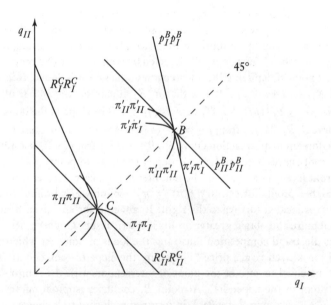

Figure 8.2. *Bertrand vs Cournot quantities*

The Cournot solution is derived taking the rival's quantity as given. Country I maximizes profits taking as given the quantity produced by country II. In the price plane, a given quantity q_{II}^C is represented by the line $q_{II}^C q_{II}^C$ depicting all price pairs that are consistent with that quantity. Therefore, in equilibrium, country I's highest attainable isoprofit curve $\pi_I' \pi_I'$ must be tangent to the line $q_{II}^C q_{II}^C$ showing the pair of prices that yield country II's equilibrium quantity in the Cournot game. The equation for $q_{II}^C q_{II}^C$ is obtained from q_{II} in (8.1)

$$ p_{II} = \frac{\alpha}{\beta_1} + \frac{\beta_2}{\beta_1} p_I - \frac{1}{\beta_1} q_{II}^C. $$

Similarly, country II's quantity choice entails the tangency of the isoprofit curve $\pi_{II}' \pi_{II}'$ with the line describing the price pairs sustaining country I's Cournot equilibrium output q_I^C. The equation for $q_I^C q_I^C$ is

$$ p_{II} = -\frac{\alpha}{\beta_2} + \frac{\beta_1}{\beta_2} p_I + \frac{1}{\beta_2} q_I^C, $$

obtained from q_I in (8.1).

Figure 8.2 shows the results of the Bertrand and Cournot models in the quantity plane. Bertrand quantities are higher than Cournot quantities. The Cournot equilibrium takes place at the intersection of the countries' reaction curves $R_I^C R_I^C$ and $R_{II}^C R_{II}^C$. At the intersection at point C, countries' I and II isoprofit curves $\pi_I \pi_I$ and $\pi_{II} \pi_{II}$ achieve a maximum (i.e. are flat) with respect to each country's choice variable (i.e. its own output). The Bertrand solution is derived taking as given the rival's price. In the quantity plane, a given rival's price p_{II} is represented as the combinations of quantities that are consistent with that price. Country I's price choice involves the tangency of country I's isoprofit curve $\pi_I' \pi_I'$ to the line $p_{II}^B p_{II}^B$ showing the combination of quantities that are consistent with the equilibrium rival's price in the Bertrand game $(a - b_1 q_{II} - b_2 q_I = p_{II}^B)$. Similarly, country II's price choice entails the tangency of the isoprofit curve $\pi_{II}' \pi_{II}'$ with the line $p_I^B p_I^B$ showing the quantity pairs sustaining the price chosen by country I in the Bertrand game $(a - b_1 q_I - b_2 q_{II} = p_I^B)$.

In the symmetric case depicted in Figs 8.1 and 8.2, both firms set the same price and produce the same quantity in equilibrium. The Bertrand equilibrium entails lower prices and higher quantities—and thus lower profits—than the Cournot equilibrium.

8.2. EXPORT TAXES UNDER PRICE COMPETITION

The Bertrand price competition assumption corresponds to the strategic framework examined by Eaton and Grossman (1986). They find that intervention under price competition leads to an export tax rather than a subsidy as in the quantity competition case. This is a key finding in strategic trade theory. Let us derive this result in a two-country linear model with unilateral intervention. The model is solved by backward induction to get the unique subgame perfect equilibrium in pure strategies.

Under unilateral intervention by the domestic government, firms' after-subsidy profit functions $\pi_I(p_I, p_{II}; s)$ and $\pi_{II}(p_I, p_{II})$ are

$$\pi_I(p_I, p_{II}; s) = p_I q_I(p_I, p_{II}) - [c q_I(p_I, p_{II}) - s q_I(p_I, p_{II})]$$

$$= (p_I - c + s)\left(\frac{a}{b_1 + b_2} - \frac{b_1}{b_1^2 - b_2^2}p_I + \frac{b_2}{b_1^2 - b_2^2}p_{II}\right), \qquad (8.3)$$

$$\pi_{II}(p_I, p_{II}) = p_{II} q_{II}(p_I, p_{II}) - c q_{II}(p_I, p_{II})$$

$$= (p_{II} - c)\left(\frac{a}{b_1 + b_2} - \frac{b_1}{b_1^2 - b_2^2}p_{II} + \frac{b_2}{b_1^2 - b_2^2}p_I\right), \qquad (8.4)$$

where $s \in (-\infty, +\infty)$ is a specific export subsidy or tax and we have used the demand functions in (8.1).

The first order conditions $\partial \pi_I(p_I, p_{II}; s)/\partial p_I = \partial \pi_{II}(p_I, p_{II})/\partial p_{II} = 0$ imply that firms' reaction functions are

$$p_I(p_{II}; s) = \frac{a(b_1 - b_2) + b_2 p_{II} + b_1(c - s)}{2b_1}$$

$$\rightarrow p_{II} = p_I^{-1}(p_I) = \frac{-a(b_1 - b_2) + 2b_1 p_I - b_1(c - s)}{b_2}, \qquad (8.5)$$

$$p_{II}(p_I; s) = \frac{a(b_1 - b_2) + b_2 p_I + b_1 c}{2b_1}.$$

Prices $p_I(s)$ and $p_{II}(s)$ for a given per unit subsidy are obtained by solving the first order conditions system (8.5)

$$p_I(s) = \frac{(2b_1 + b_2)[(b_1 - b_2)a + b_1 c] - 2b_1^2 s}{4b_1^2 - b_2^2},$$

$$p_{II}(s) = \frac{(2b_1 + b_2)[(b_1 - b_2)a + b_1 c] - 2b_1 b_2 s}{4b_1^2 - b_2^2}, \qquad (8.6)$$

where $b_1 > b_2$ implies that $p_I(s) < p_{II}(s)$.

If the domestic government unilaterally raises the per unit export tax (the absolute value of $s < 0$ increases), the price of export goods $p_I(s)$ and $p_{II}(s)$ will go up. For a given tax s, outputs are obtained by substituting (8.6) into $q_I(p_I, p_{II})$ and $q_{II}(p_I, p_{II})$ in (8.1). After-tax profits are obtained by substituting (8.6) into (8.3)

$$\pi_I(s) = \frac{b_1[(2b_1 + b_2)(b_1 - b_2)(a - c) + s(2b_1^2 - b_2^2)]^2}{(4b_1^2 - b_2^2)^2 (b_1^2 - b_2^2)}. \qquad (8.7)$$

Notice that $d\pi_I(s)/ds > 0$, implying that export tax $s < 0$ reduces domestic after-tax profits below the free trade profit level. On the other hand, foreign profits increase with the domestic tax because both $p_{II}(s)$ and $q_{II}(s)$ increase with the tax (see appendix).

8.2.1. Domestic Welfare and Export Taxes

Domestic welfare $W_I(s) = \pi_I(s) - sq_I(s)$ is defined as firm I's before export-tax profits (or before export-subsidy profits). This is computed as the sum of after export-tax profits (or after export-subsidy profits), $\pi_I(s)$ in (8.7), plus tax revenues (or minus subsidy spending) $-sq_I(s)$

$$W_I(s) = \frac{b_1[(2b_1 + b_2)(b_1 - b_2)(a - c) + s(2b_1^2 - b_2^2)]^2}{(4b_1^2 - b_2^2)(b_1^2 - b_2^2)}$$

$$- s\frac{b_1[(2b_1 + b_2)(b_1 - b_2)(a - c) + s(2b_1^2 - b_2^2)]}{(4b_1^2 - b_2^2)(b_1^2 - b_2^2)}. \tag{8.8}$$

What is the equilibrium trade policy when firms engage in price competition? Unilateral intervention entails a trade tax: $s^U < 0$. From (8.8)

$$\frac{\partial W_I(s)}{\partial s} = 0 \;\rightarrow\; s^U = \frac{-b_2^2(b_1 - b_2)(2b_1 + b_2)(a - c)}{4b_1^2(2b_1^2 - b_2^2)} < 0. \tag{8.9}$$

The assumption $b_1 > b_2$ implies that the export subsidy granted to the domestic firm is negative.

Figure 8.3 illustrates the nonintervention Bertrand equilibrium, which is specified by the intersection of the domestic and foreign firms' reaction curves at point B. Recall that $R_I^B R_I^B$ depicts the *inverse* of $p_I(p_{II})$ in (8.5), that is, $p_{II} = p_I^{-I}(p_I)$. $R_{II}^B R_{II}^B$ depicts $p_{II}(p_I)$. The slope of $R_I^B R_I^B$, $2b_1/b_2$ from $p_{II} = p_I^{-I}(p_I)$, is larger than 1 because $b_1 > b_2$. The slope of the foreign firm's reaction curve $R_{II}^B R_{II}^B$ is $b_2/2b_1 < 1$.

The export tax $s^U < 0$ causes a shift of the domestic country's reaction curve to the right—from $R_I^B R_I^B$ to $R_I^{B'} R_I^{B'}$—but does not affect the foreign country's reaction curve (see (8.5)). The new equilibrium is represented by point B'. Because the reaction curves depict the locus of points at which profits are maximized for a given rival's price, the slopes of the domestic country's isoprofit curves $\pi_I \pi_I$ and $\pi_I' \pi_I'$ are equal to zero at the point of intersection with the domestic reaction curves.

8.2.2. Export Taxation: Intuition

What is the economic intuition behind the export tax result? In a nonintervention Bertrand equilibrium both firms would benefit if they could find a way to reduce production. In particular, the domestic firm would benefit from a reduction in its rival's level of production. Under Bertrand competition, however, this can only be achieved through a price strategy that is not feasible without the intervention of the domestic government. In fact, assume the domestic firm departs from equilibrium and announces that it will increase its price and hence reduce its output. From the rival's viewpoint, such announcement does not represent a credible commitment to increase prices because the new proposed price does not belong to firm I's reaction function

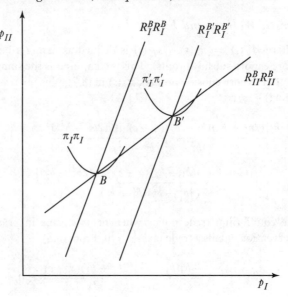

Figure 8.3. *Equilibrium under Bertrand competition*

$R_I^B R_I^B$. Therefore, firm I's announcement does not induce the rival to set a higher price.

A way to make firm I's precommitment credible, and thus induce the rival to raise its price, is by imposing an export tax to augment firm I's marginal cost. In such event, foreign firm II realizes that firm I is forced to increase its price to cover larger costs consisting of the original marginal costs c plus the tax $s < 0$. The announcement of a price increase becomes credible and the rival is driven to set higher prices and hence contract the level of output.

8.3. STRATEGIC COMPLEMENTS AND SUBSTITUTES

This section introduces the notions of strategic complements and strategic substitutes (Fudenberg and Tirole, 1984; Bulow *et al.*, 1985). These concepts help understand the contrasts between price and quantity competition. Choice variables are called strategic complements and strategic substitutes depending on whether a firm's marginal profits are positively or negatively affected by the rival's choices.

When choice variables are strategic complements, the reaction function is positively sloped and aggressive behavior elicits the response to a rival's choice is more 'aggressive'. In the third market export game, prices are strategic complements. Recall that a reaction function indicates how a firm would react if it were to learn of a change in its rival's action. If a firm were to learn that its rival behaves aggressively by setting a lower price, the marginal profit from cutting its own price would rise and the firm would also cut the price. Therefore, aggressive price setting elicits aggressive price behavior. By the same token, if a firm were to learn that the rival sets a higher price it would respond with a similar move.

When firms' choice variables are strategic substitutes, the reaction function is negatively sloped and the response to a rival's aggressive choice is not 'aggressive'. In the third market export game, quantities are strategic substitutes. If a firm were to learn that its rival behaves aggressively by increasing output, the marginal profit from increasing output is reduced and the firm would lower its output.

8.3.1. *The Slope of the Reaction Function*

Let us denote firm i's profits by $\pi_i(a_i, a_j)$ where a_i is firm i's strategic variable and a_j is the rival's strategic variable. Firm i's reaction function is given by

$$a_i = a_i(a_j), \tag{8.10}$$

and is obtained from the first order conditions $\partial \pi_i(a_i, a_j)/\partial a_i = 0$. Substituting (8.10) into $\pi_i(a_i, a_j)$, and totally differentiating $\partial \pi_i(a_i(a_j), a_j)/\partial a_i = 0$ with respect to a_j, yields the total effect of the rival's choice on a firm's marginal profits

$$\frac{d\left(\partial \pi_i(a_i(a_j), a_j)/\partial a_i\right)}{da_j} = \frac{\partial^2 \pi_i(a_i(a_j), a_j)}{\partial a_i^2} \frac{da_i(a_j)}{da_j} + \frac{\partial^2 \pi_i(a_i(a_j), a_j)}{\partial a_i \partial a_j} = 0.$$

The slope of firm i's reaction function is given by

$$\frac{da_i(a_j)}{da_j} = -\frac{\partial^2 \pi_i(\cdot)/\partial a_i \partial a_j}{\partial^2 \pi_i(\cdot)/\partial a_i^2} = -\frac{\pi_{ij}}{\pi_{ii}}$$

$$\rightarrow \text{sign}\left(\frac{da_i(a_j)}{da_j}\right) = \text{sign}\left(\frac{\partial^2 \pi_i(\cdot)}{\partial a_i \partial a_j}\right) = \text{sign } \pi_{ij},$$

where the implication is obtained by using the second order condition $\partial^2 \pi_i(\cdot)/\partial a_i^2 = \pi_{ii} < 0$ (i.e. profits are concave in the firm's actions).

When choice variables are strategic complements the cross-partial derivative is positive, $\partial^2 \pi_i(\cdot)/\partial a_i \partial a_j > 0$, and the reaction function is upward sloping, $da_i(a_j)/da_j > 0$. Under price competition, prices are strategic complements if the reaction function in the price space is upward sloping. The Bertrand competition model with differentiated products exhibits this feature.

The notion of strategic complements has an everyday life informal interpretation. When choice variables are strategic complements, firms react to more aggressive behavior with more aggressive behavior. If a firm's marginal profits decline with a rival's action a_j, the rival is said to engage in aggressive behavior

$$\frac{\partial \pi_i(a_i, a_j)}{\partial a_j} < 0.$$

Aggressive competitive behavior takes place when a firm lowers prices in price competition (increases $a = 1/p$) or produces a higher quantity under quantity competition (increases $a = q$). When prices are strategic complements under price competition, if the rival shows aggressive behavior by lowering prices, the firm responds with aggressive behavior by lowering prices too.

When choice variables are strategic substitutes, $\partial^2 \pi_i(\cdot)/\partial a_i \partial a_j < 0$, the reaction function is downward sloping, $da_i(a_j)/da_j < 0$. This means that firms react to more aggressive behavior with less aggressive behavior. For instance, recall that in the Cournot competition model, quantities are strategic substitutes. If the rival shows more aggressive behavior by increasing quantities, the firm responds with less aggressive behavior by reducing quantities.

8.3.2. Bertrand vs Cournot Equilibria with Intervention: A Comparison

Figure 8.4 utilizes the price plane to depict the results of unilateral intervention when firms compete à la Bertrand and à la Cournot. In both cases, intervention breaks the symmetry of equilibrium.

With intervention, Bertrand prices are lower than Cournot prices. The establishment of a unilateral tax shifts the domestic country's reaction curve $R_I^B R_I^B$ to $R_I^{B'} R_I^{B'}$. The intervention equilibrium occurs at the intersection of curves $R_I^{B'} R_I^{B'}$ and $R_{II}^B R_{II}^B$ depicted as point B'. This result coincides with Fig. 8.3.

The nonintervention Cournot solution is obtained by maximizing profits taking as given the rival's output level. The Cournot competition equilibrium is depicted as the intersection of lines $q_I^C q_I^C$ and $q_{II}^C q_{II}^C$. The introduction of a unilateral subsidy leads to a higher domestic output that shifts line $q_I^C q_I^C$ upward to $q_I^{C'} q_I^{C'}$ as indicated by $p_{II} = -\alpha/\beta_2 + \beta_1/\beta_2 p_I + 1/\beta_2 q_I^C$ from (8.1). Because the rival's output best response declines with the subsidy and associated domestic output increase, the $q_{II}^C q_{II}^C$ line shifts upward to $q_{II}^{C'} q_{II}^{C'}$ as indicated by $p_{II} = \alpha/\beta_1 + \beta_2/\beta_1 p_I - 1/\beta_1 q_{II}^C$ from (8.1). The appendix shows that both Cournot equilibrium prices are lower than free trade prices while $p_{II} > p_I$ as shown in Fig. 8.4.

Contrasting Bertrand and Cournot equilibria under unilateral intervention shows that:

1. Compared with free trade, the domestic government's export subsidy in the Cournot case encourages an increase in domestic output to induce a decline in foreign output. In the Bertrand case, the domestic government export tax leads to a price increase that induces a price increase by the rival.

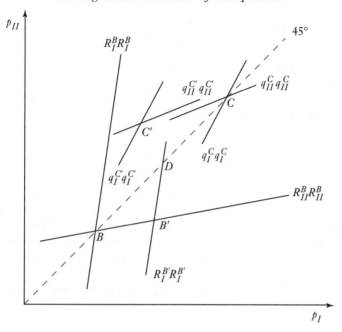

Figure 8.4. *Unilateral intervention and the mode of competition*

2. The imposition of an export subsidy in the Cournot case shifts market share toward the domestic firm and reduces foreign profits while increasing domestic net-of-tax profits. The Bertrand domestic export tax actually lowers domestic net-of-tax profits and increases foreign profits. Why is it that a policy that places domestic firms at a disadvantage when facing competitors in international markets increases welfare? The source of the domestic welfare increase is the government tax revenue from the export tax.

8.3.3. The Lack of Information Problem

Eaton and Grossman's (1986) key finding establishes that strategic-trade policy prescriptions dramatically change with the assumption concerning firms' strategic decisions. This conclusion has generated much criticism of the theory of strategic trade policy itself. Let us take for granted that the best policy is to subsidize exports if domestic firms compete in quantities but to tax them if they compete in prices. One of the main concerns is: what form of trade intervention should be followed by a government that lacks information about the mode of competition? Should the government subsidize exports or, on the contrary, tax them? Policy formulation becomes difficult when alternative policies are so much apart from each other in terms of welfare. The consequences of making the wrong decision will reduce welfare.

8.4. BILATERAL INTERVENTION WITH PRICE COMPETITION

Symmetric bilateral export taxation in the Bertrand case leads to higher domestic and foreign welfare levels than with free trade while third market consumers lose. Moreover, the Bertrand bilateral equilibrium is closer to the monopoly equilibrium (the equilibrium under joint profit maximization) than the unilateral equilibrium. Before-tax profits (welfare inclusive of government export tax revenues) increase even if after-tax profits decline.

By contrast, recall that in the Cournot case bilateral intervention leads to a prisoners' dilemma. The game's outcome implies a decline in welfare for both countries in comparison with free trade while third market consumers gain. The reason is that, under Cournot competition, joint government subsidization shifts firms toward the competitive outcome in comparison with the free trade duopoly solution. The previous chapter examined a symmetric linear case in which export subsidies cause after-subsidy profits to increase. However, before-subsidy profits (i.e. welfare) are lower under bilateral subsidization than under free trade.

Bilateral intervention by symmetric countries entails taxing exports and is welfare-improving for both countries. Observe that after-export-tax profits π go up with a subsidy and down with tax $s < 0$ (see appendix)

$$\pi(s) = \pi^*(s) = \frac{b_1(b_1 - b_2)(a - c + s)^2}{(2b_1 - b_2)^2(b_1 + b_2)}. \tag{8.11}$$

Domestic country's welfare $W(s) = \pi(s) - sq(s)$ is defined as the sum of the exporter's after-tax profits $\pi(s)$ in (8.11) and tax revenues—$sq(s)$. Welfare gains $W(s) = W^*(s)$ are

$$W(s) = \frac{b_1(b_1 - b_2)(a - c + s)^2}{(2b_1 - b_2)^2(b_1 + b_2)} - s\frac{b_1(a - c + s)}{(2b_1 - b_2)(b_1 + b_2)}. \tag{8.12}$$

What is the equilibrium trade policy when both governments intervene? Maximizing the welfare function in (8.12) yields intervention in the form of an export tax

$$\frac{\partial W(s)}{\partial s} = 0 \quad \rightarrow \quad s^{Bil} = \frac{-b_2(a - c)}{2b_1} < 0, \tag{8.13}$$

with $a > c$ and $b_1 > b_2 > 0$. Substituting (8.13) into (8.12) yields total welfare.

Bilateral intervention is welfare-increasing in relation to free trade

$$W^{Bil} - W^{FT} = \frac{(a-c)^2}{4(b_1+b_2)} - \frac{b_1(b_1-b_2)(a-c)^2}{(2b_1-b_2)^2(b_1+b_2)} = \frac{b_2^2(a-c)^2}{(2b_1-b_2)^2(b_1+b_2)} > 0,$$

where W^{FT} is obtained by setting $s = 0$ in (8.12).

We have shown that under price competition bilateral intervention is welfare-increasing compared with free trade: $W^{Bil} > W^{FT}$. The reason is that, under Bertrand competition, joint government intervention shifts firms toward the monopoly solution and increases the domestic and foreign firms' before-export-tax profits. Equation (8.11) shows that bilateral export taxation ($s < 0$) reduces after-tax profits but this loss is more than offset by the government revenues.

8.5. MULTIPLE INSTRUMENTS AND TARGETING

A widely accepted principle in international economics is that distortions that are not trade-related should be addressed with domestic policies rather than with trade policies (Bhagwati, 1971). According to this principle, trade policies should be used only to address trade-related strategic distortions and terms of trade distortions. A country's terms of trade p_X/p_M are defined as the relative price of exports (X) in terms of the price of imports (M).

Strategic trade distortions due to the inability to precommit in international inter-actions arise in the third market model and other settings. A terms of trade distortion does not arise in the third market duopoly game under free trade. The reason is that a single domestic firm internalizes all terms of trade effects. From a country's per-spective, terms of trade distortions arise when the country as a whole has monopoly or monopsony power in international markets but domestic firms or consumers behave noncooperatively. Domestic firms fail to exploit market power because they do not internalize the terms of trade effects. A terms of trade distortion constitutes the basis of the optimal tariff argument. Atomistic domestic consumers hold monopsony power as a group but are not able to exploit it to reduce prices. The government offsets the terms of trade distortion by setting an optimal tariff that reduces the global demand for imports, lowers p_M and improves the terms of trade.

Optimal policy packages combine multiple instruments and avoid too much reli-ance upon trade policies. Production and consumption distortions are addressed by appropriate domestic policies, not by trade policies. In practice, actual policies often deviate from this fundamental theorem but these deviations do not represent optimal behavior. Trade policies are rather used to benefit interest groups or as a second-best policy instrument when first-best policy tools are not available.

Krishna and Thursby (1991) examine multiple policies in a three market model in which there are domestic, foreign, and third market consumers. Conjectural variations are used to parameterize the nature of third market competition and cover both com-petition in quantities and competition in prices. Optimal tax or subsidy policies are shown to depend on the presence of other distortions and regulations, and on the assumptions made about market segmentation. Optimal policy formulation in strategic settings applies the principles of optimal policy targeting used in nonstrategic frameworks. Domestic policy targets the domestic distortion while trade policy targets the strategic distortion.

When firms are *monopolists* in their *home* markets (i.e. markets are segmented), but compete as *duopolists* in a *third* market, policy targeting entails combining two different policies. The optimal policy package consists of a consumption subsidy aiming to correct the domestic monopoly distortion and a trade policy addressing the strategic distortion in the third market. When there is a single domestic firm, the firm fully internalizes the effect of its output decisions on the price in the third market. There is thus no terms of trade distortion to justify trade policy but there is a strategic trade distortion due to the inability to precommit.

How do policy prescriptions vary with the number of firms in a multifirm oligopolistic framework? Consider segmented domestic and foreign markets with many domestic and foreign firms. These firms sell as oligopolists in a third market. When there are many domestic firms, the domestic consumption distortion disappears and the optimal consumption tax is zero. However, a terms of trade distortion appears. The reason is that when firms choose their optimal levels of output unilaterally they do not consider the impact of their decisions on other local firms' production levels. Because these effects are not internalized, there is a terms of trade distortion. This is the case of multiple firms that hold monopoly or oligopolistic power in international markets as a group but do not exploit it when they compete noncooperatively. Recall that this type of terms of trade distortion does not arise in the third market duopoly game under free trade because a single domestic firm internalizes all terms of trade effects.

If the number of domestic firms is very large so that they perfectly compete with each other, but they would be able to exploit market power in the third market if they colluded, the terms of trade distortion becomes the only first-best motive for trade policy. In fact, if the number of domestic firms is large enough, export subsidies lead to a reduction of domestic welfare both under quantity and price competition. The reason is that domestic firms fail to internalize the impact of subsidized production decisions on other local firms. As a consequence, correcting the strategic distortion through an export subsidy accentuates the terms of trade distortion that justifies an optimal tariff. When the number of domestic firms is large enough, profit shifting does not justify the terms of trade costs of implementing the export subsidy and an export tax is optimal. The terms of trade motive for intervention dominates the strategic motive and the argument for an optimal tax becomes stronger than the argument for strategic subsidization. In general, the optimal policy depends on the number of domestic and foreign firms.

8.6. INTERVENTION WHEN FIRMS MOVE FIRST

The sequencing of actions between firms and the government influences their strategic interaction. When firms move first, governments take firms' actions as given in the subsequent intervention stage. A first-mover advantage allows firms to set prices in such a way as to induce favorable behavior by the government. We proceed to show that when firms move first, it is in their advantage to set high prices and induce the government to subsidize them, reversing the export tax prescription obtained under Bertrand competition when the government moves first. This result has been obtained in different frameworks by Carmichael (1987), Gruenspecht (1988), and Neary (1994).

8.6.1. *Unilateral Intervention in the Price Game*

Consider unilateral intervention in a two-stage third market game in which firms have a first-mover advantage. The foreign government is assumed not to intervene. In the first stage, the domestic and foreign firms set the prices of differentiated commodities I and II, respectively. In the second stage, the domestic government chooses the welfare-maximizing trade intervention. The game in which firms move first is called an ex post or price-intervention game to distinguish it from the ex ante or intervention-price game in which the government acts first.

Suppose that there is unilateral intervention in the market for product I. This intervention is implemented in terms of a price subsidy that reduces the price paid by consumers below the price charged by the seller. The demand for I can be expressed in terms of the demand price $p_I^D = p_I^S - s$ paid by third market buyers, $q_I(p_I^D, p_{II}^D) = \alpha - \beta_1 p_I^D + \beta_2 p_{II}$, or in terms of the supply price $p^S = p^D + s$ received by the seller of good I

$$q_I(p_I^S, p_{II}; s) = \alpha - \beta_1(p_I^S - s) + \beta_2 p_{II},$$
$$q_{II}(p_I^S, p_{II}; s) = \alpha - \beta_1 p_{II} + \beta_2(p_I^S - s). \tag{8.14}$$

Product II is not subsidized so that the demand and supply prices are the same ($p_{II} = p_{II}^D = p_{II}^S$). Utilizing the supply price p_I^S in the domestic after-subsidy profit function $\pi_I = (p_I^D - c + s)q_I$ and in $\pi_{II} = (p_{II} - c)q_{II}$ yields

$$\pi_I(p_I^S, p_{II}; s) = (p_I^S - c)q_I(p_I^S, p_{II}; s), \tag{8.15}$$
$$\pi_{II}(p_I^S, p_{II}; s) = (p_{II} - c)q_{II}(p_I^S, p_{II}; s).$$

The model is solved by backward induction to get a subgame perfect equilibrium. At stage two, the government sets the welfare-maximizing subsidy. When there are domestic distortions, domestic welfare is defined as after-subsidy profits π_I minus the total costs of financing the subsidies $\delta s q_I$

$$W_I = (p_I^D - c + s)q_I - \delta s q_I = (p_I^S - c - \delta s)(\alpha - (p_I^S - s) + \beta_2 p_{II}),$$

where it is assumed that $\beta_1 = 1 > \beta_2 > 0$. The parameter $\delta = 1 + d > 1$ captures the amount of the subsidy and the distortion costs associated with the financing of a subsidy (or tax revenues plus the gains from reduced distortions when an export tax is imposed).

The first order condition $\partial W_I/\partial s = 0$ yields the optimum subsidy or tax as a function of the prices set by firms in the first stage

$$s(p_I^S, p_{II}) = -\frac{\alpha\delta + c}{2\delta} + \frac{1 + \delta}{2\delta}p_I^S - \frac{\delta\beta_2}{2\delta}p_{II}. \tag{8.16}$$

The domestic subsidy rises with the domestic firm's supply price and declines with the rival's price. When firms have a first-mover advantage the source of the subsidy is not purely strategic, as it is in the Cournot model, but arises as authority's response to rent-seeking behavior. Equation (8.16) shows that, for any given foreign price p_{II}, a higher domestic supply price p_I^S induces the government to set a larger price subsidy in the second stage of the game.

In the first stage, firms choose prices as a best response to each other. The optimum unilateral subsidy is obtained by substituting the prices determined in the first stage into (8.16). The appendix shows that

$$s^U = \frac{(4 + 2\beta_2 - \beta_2^2)(3 - \delta)(\alpha - c(1 - \beta_2))}{2(\delta - 1)(8 - 5\beta_2^2)}, \tag{8.17}$$

where $\beta_2 < 1$, and $\alpha > c(1 - \beta_2)$. Notice that the optimum subsidy is positive if distortions are not too large, $1 < \delta < 3$. If $\delta > 3$ the optimum unilateral subsidy is negative and if $\delta = 3$ free trade is best.

8.6.2. Unilateral Intervention Might Not Improve Welfare When Firms Move First

Are unilateral subsidies welfare-improving in the price-intervention game with distortions? When firms move first, they can precommit to a price strategy and act like a leader in relation to the government. When the government moves in the second turn, the welfare properties of ex ante unilateral intervention are altered. The possibility of reduced welfare arises under ex post unilateral intervention but not in the case of ex ante unilateral intervention. When the government acts first, the welfare level under unilateral intervention always exceeds the welfare level under free trade. Because the government can choose free trade if it desires to do so, it intervenes only to improve welfare. When the government acts second, though, firms' manipulation can lead to a reduction of welfare.

Let us compare ex post intervention and free trade welfare levels. The appendix shows that, if the distortion coefficient δ is low enough, welfare W^U in the price-intervention game falls below free trade welfare: $W^{FT} > W^U$. Figure 8.5 depicts the difference $W^U - W^{FT}$ between unilateral intervention and free trade welfares as a function of the distortion parameter δ. The figure is constructed on the assumption that $\alpha = 10, c = 7$, and $\beta_2 = 0.5$. The unilateral intervention welfare level falls below the free trade level whenever a subsidy policy is followed. The domestic firm price commitment allows increasing after-subsidy profits by extracting public subsidies, which results in lower welfare under price competition. When export taxes are imposed,

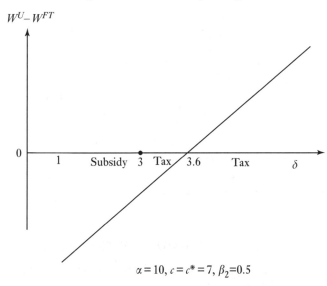

$W^U - W^{FT}$

0

1 Subsidy 3 Tax 3.6 Tax δ

$\alpha = 10,\ c = c^* = 7,\ \beta_2 = 0.5$

Figure 8.5. *Unilateral intervention can result in welfare losses*

the unilateral intervention welfare level exceeds the free trade level only when distortions are large enough. If the distortion coefficient δ is high enough, intervention is welfare-improving because export tax revenues contribute to reduce large preexisting distortions.

8.6.3. Boeing's Eximbank Credits: First Mover Advantage

The Export–Import Bank of the United States (Eximbank) is a self-sufficient organization that provides export credits to American exporters on the basis of an application in which exporters state their product price and other relevant information. These procedures illustrate a case in which firms state their product price before the government sets the subsidy.

Eximbank's export credits to Boeing provide an empirical illustration of a price-subsidy game in which firms act first. In the 1970s, Eximbank granted substantial credits to Boeing. It was intended to counteract the competitive threat posed by Airbus A-300 aircraft, produced by Airbus Industrie, which was in turn subsidized by Banque Française du Commerce Extérieur. Until April 1980, Eximbank had wide discretion over credits granted and there is evidence that, by raising the price in the credit application, Boeing was able to get a higher subsidy.

During 1980 and 1981, a series of measures were taken aiming to restrict the volume of credit granted by Eximbank and to limit Eximbank's discretion. In April 1980, interest rates on credits for aircraft exports were raised and a subsidy rate ceiling was established. In September 1980, a maximum cover on credit for short-range and medium-range aircraft was introduced, and long-range aircraft was made ineligible for receiving credit. In 1981, only new-generation aircraft became eligible to receive credit.

Carmichael (1991) estimates price and subsidy equations derived from a two-stage Bertrand duopoly model. He uses data on 30 credits approved by Eximbank for exports of Boeing 737-200 aircraft during 1977–81. He finds evidence of a structural shift in the estimated equations after the April 1980 policy shift limiting Eximbank discretion and setting a ceiling for the subsidy rate. The estimated coefficient measuring the effect of the firm's price on the government subsidy went down. This result is consistent with the effect of a subsidy rate ceiling in a duopoly price-subsidy game. Carmichael (1987) shows that, when the government establishes a rate ceiling, firms price goods closer to marginal costs and the government subsidy becomes less responsive to firms' price setting.

8.7. ENDOGENOUS MODE OF COMPETITION

This section examines two approaches in which the mode of competition is endogenously determined, in the sense that the frameworks can generate both the quantity and price competition outcomes.

The first approach, advanced by Giovanni Maggi (1996), is based on the presence of capacity constraints that are flexible in the sense that the constraints can be relaxed at a cost. A key result is that a unilateral single-rate small capacity subsidy emerges as a robust policy. By robust policy we mean that the subsidy will increase or leave unaffected domestic welfare regardless of the value of cost and demand parameters. In particular, the result that small capacity subsidies are welfare-improving does not depend on information requirements about the value of the cost parameter determining whether firms behave as quantity or price competitors in this setup. The implication is that governments have incentives to grant small capacity subsidies or follow equivalent policies even if they do not have complete information about cost and demand. Also, trade policy restrictions such as an export subsidy ban can be bypassed by domestic capacity policies that alter competitive conditions.

The second approach endogenizing the mode of competition is presented by Laussel (1992), who applies the supply function competition model of Klemperer and Meyer (1989). Each firm strategically chooses the whole supply function $q = S(p)$ before observing a demand shock. After observing the demand shock, the firm specifies a price-output point $(p_0, S(p_0))$ on the supply curve. The approach differs from the standard literature because single-rate taxes or subsidies have no impact on equilibrium prices and quantities. Optimal policies rather entail setting subsidies or taxes that are nonlinear functions of output. These nonlinear interventions change the slope of the marginal cost curve and thus equilibrium output.

The Bertrand and Cournot cases arise when the marginal cost curve—as affected by a nonlinear tax or subsidy function—becomes flat enough and steep enough, respectively. In general, the steepness of the supply function balances the gains from softening price competition and the losses from lack of adaptation to demand uncertainty. For instance, a unilateral nonlinear subsidy function that induces the domestic firm to select a vertical Cournot supply function is optimal when the variance of the demand shock is low enough. A low shock variance allows a vertical supply function to soften price competition while keeping small the ex post losses from failing to adjust production to the value of the demand shock.

8.8. CONCLUSIONS

This chapter examined how the formulation of strategic trade policies is affected by (1) the mode of competition among firms and related firms' conjectures about rivals' responses, and (2) whether the government or the private sector has a first-mover advantage. A main result applies when firms compete in prices, the government moves first making a commitment to grant an export tax at a subsequent stage, and there are no distortions. In this situation, the best unilateral intervention policy is to tax exports. This result contrasts with the unilateral export subsidy prescription applying when firms compete in quantities. Moreover, bilateral export taxes set noncooperatively are welfare-improving under price competition. This reverses the result that bilateral export subsidies set noncooperatively are welfare-reducing under quantity competition.

The sequencing of the moves made by firms and governments change their strategic interaction. When firms move first, there is the possibility of manipulating the government. In a Bertrand competition setup, a domestic firm holding a first-mover advantage sets higher prices than it would set under free trade in order to induce the government to grant greater export subsidies. Ex post intervention subsidies embody a response to the previous firm action. This induced response is not present when a government intervenes ex ante by formulating policy before the firm acts. In a Bertrand setting, ex ante intervention is centered on taxing exports to reduce output and restrict price competition.

Standard policy prescriptions are not robust to the mode of competition and the sequencing of moves. This conclusion has been obtained under the assumption that the mode of competition and firms' conjectures about rival's responses are exogenously given. This chapter examines strategic interaction when the mode of competition is endogenous and proposes a robust intervention prescription involving capacity subsidies (see also Grant and Quiggin, 1997).

8.9. APPENDIX

8.9.1. *Conjectural Variations and Cournot Equilibrium with Differentiated Goods*

This section applies the conjectural variations approach to Cournot equilibrium with differentiated commodities and symmetric costs in a two-country setup.

Reaction Functions with Conjectural Variations

The inverse demand functions for differentiated commodities I and II express product prices p_I and p_{II} in terms of output levels q_I and q_{II}

$$p_I(q_I, q_{II}) = a - b_1 q_I - b_2 q_{II}, \qquad p_{II}(q_I, q_{II}) = a - b_1 q_{II} - b_2 q_I, \qquad (8.18)$$

where $a, b_1, b_2 > 0$.

Firms' beliefs about their rival's response to their output decision can be summarized by conjectured reaction functions

$$q_{II} = v_{II}(q_I), \qquad q_I = v_I(q_{II}).$$

The derivatives of the reaction functions, $dv_{II}(q_I)/dq_I$ and $dv_I(q_{II})/dq_{II}$, indicate how the rival is conjectured to respond to each firm's output choices. These derivatives are known as the conjectural variation parameters because they are assumed to be constants. This assumption is particular of the conjectural variations approach and captures how firm I thinks that firm II would react to its decision, and similarly, firm II's conjecture about how firm I would react to its choice.

Introducing the conjecture assumption into firms' profit functions, yields conjectured profit functions $\pi_I(q_I, v_{II}(q_I))$ and $\pi_{II}(v_I(q_{II}), q_{II})$

$$\pi_I(q_I, v_{II}(q_I)) = [a - b_1 q_I - b_2 v_{II}(q_I)]q_I - cq_I + sq_I,$$
$$\pi_{II}(v_I(q_{II}), q_{II}) = [a - b_1 q_{II} - b_2 v_I(q_{II})]q_{II} - cq_{II} + sq_{II}.$$

First order necessary (and sufficient) conditions are

$$\frac{d\pi_I}{dq_I} = a - 2b_1 q_I - b_2 q_{II} - b_2 \frac{dv_{II}(q_I)}{dq_I} q_I - c + s = 0,$$
$$\frac{d\pi_{II}}{dq_{II}} = a - 2b_1 q_{II} - b_2 q_I - b_2 \frac{dv_I(q_{II})}{dq_{II}} q_{II} - c + s = 0.$$

Firms' reaction functions with conjectural variations are given by

$$q_I\left(q_{II}, s, \frac{dv_{II}(q_I)}{dq_I}\right) = \frac{a - b_2 q_{II} - c + s}{2b_1 + b_2(dv_{II}(q_I)/dq_I)},$$
$$q_{II}\left(q_I, \frac{dv_I(q_{II})}{dq_{II}}\right) = \frac{a - b_2 q_I - c + s}{2b_1 + b_2(dv_I(q_{II})/dq_{II})},$$

$$(8.19)$$

where $dv_{II}(q_I)/dq_I$ and $dv_I(q_{II})/dq_{II}$ are conjectural variation response parameters. Policy prescriptions are made contingent on exogenously-given conjectural variations parameters.

Cournot Conjectures

Under Cournot competition, each player sets its production level taking as given the rival's production level. This hypothesis means that a firm conjectures that its rival does not respond to its quantity decision. Algebraically,

$$\frac{dv_{II}(q_I)}{dq_I} = 0, \qquad \frac{dv_I(q_{II})}{dq_{II}} = 0. \tag{8.20}$$

Substituting (8.20) into the system of reaction functions (8.19), and solving for q_I and q_{II} yields

$$q_I^C = q_{II}^C = \frac{a - c}{2b_1 + b_2}, \tag{8.21}$$

where the C superscript indicates Cournot.

Let us substitute the Cournot conjectures $dv_{II}(q_I)/dq_I = dv_I(q_{II})/dq_{II} = 0$ into reaction functions (8.19). The absolute values of the slopes of $R_I^C R_I^C$ and $R_{II}^C R_{II}^C$ are $|-2b_1/b_2| = |1/(dq_I(q_{II})/dq_{II})|$ and $|-b_2/b_1|$, respectively, where $|-2b_1/b_2| > |-b_2/b_1|$.

Equilibrium Cournot prices are obtained by substituting (8.21) into the inverse demand functions (8.18)

$$p^C = p_I^C = p_{II}^C = \frac{(a + c)b_1 + b_2 c}{2b_1 + b_2}.$$

Comparing p^C and p^B yields

$$p^C - p^B = \frac{(a + c)b_1 + b_2 c}{2b_1 + b_2} - \frac{a(b_1 - b_2) + b_1 c}{2b_1 - b_2}$$

$$= \frac{(a - c)b_2^2}{(2b_1 + b_2)(2b_1 - b_2)} > 0.$$

Consistent Conjectural Variations

By consistent conjectural variations (see Bresnaham, 1981) we mean a set of conjectures that are consistent with the model's equilibrium responses, that is,

$$\frac{dv_{II}(q_I)}{dq_I} = \frac{dq_{II}}{dq_I} = -1, \qquad \frac{dv_I(q_{II})}{dq_{II}} = \frac{dq_I}{dq_{II}} = -1. \tag{8.22}$$

Under consistent conjectural variations, the firm conjectures that if it increases its output by one unit the rival will also reduce its production level by one unit, $dq_{II}/dq_I = dq_I/dq_{II} = -1$.

Substituting (8.22) into (8.19) and adding up q_I and q_{II} yields total production

$$q_I + q_{II} = \frac{a - bq_{II} - c + s}{b} + \frac{a - bq_I - c}{b} = \frac{2(a - c) + s}{b} - (q_I + q_{II}) \tag{8.23}$$

or

$$Q^{CCV} = q_I^{CCV} + q_{II}^{CCV} = \frac{a-c}{b} + \frac{s}{2b},$$

where Q^{CCV} denotes consistent conjectural variations levels of output. If $s = 0$, consistent conjectures yield the perfect competition output level $(a-c)/b$. The equilibrium subsidy level under consistent conjectures is $s = 0$, that is, free trade is best.

Cournot Equilibrium with Differentiated Goods

Obtaining the quantity reaction functions under unilateral intervention, and solving the resulting reaction function system, yields the equilibrium level of output under unilateral intervention for any given subsidy

$$q_I(s) = \frac{(\beta_1 + \beta_2)[2\beta_1 s(\beta_1 - \beta_2) + (2\beta_1 - \beta_2)(\alpha - c(\beta_1 - \beta_2))]}{4\beta_1^2 - \beta_2^2},$$

$$q_{II}(s) = \frac{(\beta_1 + \beta_2)[(2\beta_1 - \beta_2)(\alpha - c(\beta_1 - \beta_2)) - \beta_2 s(\beta_1 - \beta_2)]}{4\beta_1^2 - \beta_2^2}.$$

Substituting quantities into the demand system and solving for prices yields equilibrium prices under unilateral intervention for any given subsidy

$$p_I(s) = \frac{(2\beta_1 - \beta_2)[\alpha\beta_1 + c(\beta_1^2 - \beta_2^2)] - s(\beta_1 - \beta_2)(2\beta_1^2 - \beta_2^2)}{(4\beta_1^2 - \beta_2^2)(\beta_1 - \beta_2)},$$

$$p_{II}(s) = \frac{(2\beta_1 - \beta_2)[\alpha\beta_1 + c(\beta_1^2 - \beta_2^2)] - s(\beta_1 - \beta_2)\beta_1\beta_2}{(4\beta_1^2 - \beta_2^2)(\beta_1 - \beta_2)}.$$

8.9.2. Isoprofit Function in the Price Plane

The domestic isoprofit function is defined by

$$\pi_I^0 = \pi_I(p_I, p_{II}) = (p_I - c + s)\left(\frac{a}{b_1 + b_2} - \frac{b_1}{b_1^2 - b_2^2}p_I + \frac{b_2}{b_1^2 - b_2^2}p_{II}\right).$$

Solving for p_{II} in terms of p_I yields

$$p_{II} = \frac{b_1 p_I^2 - p_I[a(b_1 - b_2) + b_1(c - s)] + (b_1 - b_2)[a(c - s) + \pi_I^0(b_1 - b_2)]}{b_2(q_I - c + s)}.$$

The domestic country's isoprofit curves are flat when intersecting the domestic country's reaction curve. In other words, if we evaluate domestic profits at the profit maximizing value of p_I (for any given value of p_{II}), we obtain

$$\frac{dp_{II}(p_I)}{dp_I} = \frac{b_1}{b_2} - \frac{(b_1^2 - b_2^2)\pi_I^0}{b_2(p_I - c + s)^2}$$

$$= \frac{b_1}{b_2} - \frac{(b_1^2 - b_2^2)b_1(p_I - c + s)^2/(b_1^2 - b_2^2)}{(b_2(p_I - c + s)^2)} = 0.$$

The second equality is obtained by substituting the inverse of $p_I(p_{II}), p_{II} = p_I^{-I}(p_I)$ into profits $\pi_I(p_I, p_{II}; s)$ in (8.3)

$$\pi_I(p_I, p_I^{-I}(p_I); s) = \pi_I(p_I; s) = \frac{b_1(p_I - c + s)^2}{b_1^2 - b_2^2}.$$

The convexity of the isoprofit curve $\pi_1\pi_I = \pi_I^0$ when it cuts the reaction function (for any given s) is found by computing the second order condition

$$\frac{d^2 p_{II}(p_I)}{dp_I^2} = \frac{2\pi_I^0(b_1^2 - b_2^2)}{b_2(p_I - (c - s))^3} > 0,$$

where $\pi_I^0 > 0$ implies $p_I > c - s$.

8.9.3. Output under Price Competition

Using (8.3) and (8.4), the first order conditions $\partial \pi_I(p_I, p_{II}; s)/\partial p_I = \partial \pi_{II}(p_I, p_{II})/\partial p_{II} = 0$ imply that firms' reaction functions under unilateral intervention are

$$p_I(p_{II}; s) = \frac{a(b_1 - b_2) + b_2 p_{II} + b_1(c - s)}{2b_1},$$

$$p_{II}(p_I) = \frac{a(b_1 - b_2) + b_2 p_I + b_1 c}{2b_1}.$$

(8.24)

First order conditions taking the rival's price as given are

$$\frac{\partial \pi_I(p_I, p_{II}; s)}{\partial p_I} = \frac{a}{b_1 + b_2} - \frac{2b_1}{b_1^2 - b_2^2}p_I + \frac{b_2}{b_1^2 - b_2^2}p_{II} + \frac{b_1(c - s)}{b_1^2 - b_2^2} = 0,$$

$$\frac{\partial \pi_{II}(p_I, p_{II})}{\partial p_{II}} = \frac{a}{b_1 + b_2} - \frac{2b_1}{b_1^2 - b_2^2}p_{II} + \frac{b_2}{b_1^2 - b_2^2}p_I + \frac{b_1 c}{b_1^2 - b_2^2} = 0.$$

These conditions yield firms' best responses in terms of prices, $p_I(p_{II})$ and $p_{II}(p_I)$. The assumption $b_1 > b_2 > 0$ implies that the second order conditions are fulfilled

$$\frac{\partial^2 \pi_I(p_I, p_{II})}{\partial p_I^2} = \frac{\partial^2 \pi_{II}(p_I, p_{II})}{\partial p_{II}^2} = -\frac{2b_1}{b_1^2 - b_2^2} < 0.$$

For a given subsidy s, country I and II's outputs are obtained by substituting $p_I(s)$ and $p_{II}(s)$ into $q_I(p_I, p_{II})$ and $q_{II}(p_I, p_{II})$ in equations (8.1)

$$q_I(s) = \frac{b_1[(2b_1 + b_2)(b_1 - b_2)(a - c) + s(2b_1^2 - b_2^2)]}{(4b_1^2 - b_2^2)(b_1^2 - b_2^2)},$$

$$q_{II}(s) = \frac{b_1[(2b_1 + b_2)(b_1 - b_2)(a - c) - sb_1b_2]}{(4b_1^2 - b_2^2)(b_1^2 - b_2^2)},$$

(8.25)

The export tax $s < 0$ reduces $q_I(s)$ below its free trade level and raises $q_{II}(s)$ above its free level. Equilibrium outputs can be obtained substituting the unilateral subsidy s^U from (8.9) in the text.

8.9.4. Bilateral Intervention under Price Competition

Substituting the demand function into profit function $\pi_i(p_I, p_{II}; s) = (p_i - c + s)$ $q_i(p_I, p_{II}), i \in \{I, II\}$, gives

$$\pi_i(p_I, p_{II}; s) = (p_i - c + s)\left(\frac{a}{b_1 + b_2} - \frac{b_1}{b_1^2 - b_2^2}p_i + \frac{b_2}{b_1^2 - b_2^2}p_j\right).$$

(8.26)

The first order condition for firm i is obtained taking as given the rival's price

$$\frac{\partial \pi_i(p_I, p_{II}; s)}{\partial p_i} = \frac{a}{b_1 + b_2} - \frac{2b_1}{b_1^2 - b_2^2}p_i + \frac{b_2}{b_1^2 - b_2^2}p_j + \frac{b_1}{b_1^2 - b_2^2}(c - s) = 0.$$

This equation yields firm's i best response to its rival's price, $p_i(p_j)$. Assumption $b_1 > b_2 > 0$ implies that second order conditions are fulfilled because

$$\frac{\partial^2 \pi_i(p_I, p_{II})}{\partial p_i^2} = -\frac{2b_1}{b_1^2 - b_2^2} < 0.$$

The first order necessary condition, $\partial \pi_i(p_I, p_{II}; s)/\partial p_i = 0$, implies that firm i's reaction function is

$$p_i(p_j; s) = \frac{a(b_1 - b_2) + b_2p_j + b_1(c - s)}{2b_1}.$$

(8.27)

Given model symmetry, the price $p(s)$ as a function of subsidy s is obtained by imposing $p_i = p_j = p$ in (8.27) and solving for $p(s)$.

The price $p(s)$ as a function of subsidy s is obtained using the firm's first order necessary conditions, $\partial \pi_i(p_I, p_{II}; s)/\partial p_i = 0, i \in \{I, II\}$

$$p(s) = p_I(s) = p_{II}(s) = \frac{a(b_1 - b_2) + b_1(c - s)}{2b_1 - b_2}.$$

(8.28)

Country i's output is obtained by substituting (8.28) into $q_i(p_I, p_{II})$ in (8.1)

$$q_i(s) = \frac{b_1(a - c + s)}{(2b_1 - b_2)(b_1 + b_2)}.\tag{8.29}$$

A larger per unit export tax (recall that a tax means that $s < 0$), implies a higher price $p(s)$ and lower output levels. After-export-tax profits are obtained by substituting expressions (8.28) and $q_i(s)$ into $\pi_i = (p(s) - c + s)q_i(s)$

$$\pi_i(s) = \frac{b_1(b_1 - b_2)(a - c + s)^2}{(2b_1 - b_2)^2(b_1 + b_2)}.$$

8.9.5. Price–Intervention Game (Ex Post Intervention)

Recall the demand functions in expression (8.14)

$$(i)\ q_I = \alpha - (p_I^S - s) + \beta_2 p_{II}, \qquad (ii)\ q_{II} = \alpha - p_{II} + \beta_2(p_I^S - s).$$

Solving for p_{II} from (i), we obtain

$$p_{II} = \frac{\alpha - (p_I^S - s) - q_I}{-\beta_2}.$$

Substituting p_{II} into (ii), solving for p_I and simplifying terms yields

$$p_I^S - s = \frac{\alpha}{1 - \beta_2} - \frac{q_I + \beta_2 q_{II}}{(1 - \beta_2)(1 + \beta_2)} = a - b_1 q_I - b_2 q_{II},$$

$$p_{II} = \frac{\alpha}{1 - \beta_2} - \frac{q_{II} + \beta_2 q_I}{(1 - \beta_2)(1 + \beta_2)} = a - b_1 q_{II} - b_2 q_I.$$

At the first stage, domestic and foreign firms choose prices. Substituting $s(p_I, p_{II})$ from (8.16) into firms' after-subsidy profits $\pi_I(p_I^S, p_{II})$ and $\pi_{II}(p_I^S, p_{II})$ yields

$$\pi_I = (p_I^S - c)(\alpha - (p_I^S - s) + \beta_2 p_{II})$$

$$= (p_I^S - c)\left(\alpha - \left(p_I^S - \frac{-\alpha\delta - c + p_I^S(1 + \delta) - \delta\beta_2 p_{II}}{2\delta}\right) + \beta_2 p_{II}\right)$$

$$= \frac{1}{2\delta}(p_I^S - c)(\alpha\delta - c + (\delta - 1)p_I^S + \delta\beta_2 p_{II}),\tag{8.30}$$

and

$$\pi_{II} = (p_{II} - c)(\alpha - \beta_1 p_{II} + \beta_2(p_I^S - s))$$

$$= (p_{II} - c)\left(\alpha - \beta_1 p_{II} + \beta_2\left(p_I^S - \frac{-\alpha\delta - c + p_I^S(1 + \delta) - \delta\beta_2 p_{II}}{2\delta}\right)\right)$$

$$= (p_{II} - c)\left(\frac{3\alpha\delta + c - (1 - \delta)p_I^S - (2 - \beta_2)p_{II}\delta}{\delta}\right).$$

First order conditions, $\partial \pi_I(p_I^S, p_{II}, \delta)/\partial p_I^S = 0$ and $\partial \pi_{II} \; (p_I^S, p_{II}, \delta)/\partial p_{II} = 0$, yield the following equilibrium prices

$$p_I^U(\delta) = \frac{\alpha\delta(4 + 2\beta_2 - \beta_2^2) - c(8 - 5\beta_2^2 - \delta(\beta_2 + 2)(2 - \beta_2^2))}{(\delta - 1)(8 - 5\beta_2^2)},$$

$$p_{II}^U(\delta) = \frac{\alpha(3\beta_2 + \beta_2) + c(4 + \beta_2 - 2\beta_2^2)}{8 - 5\beta_2^2}. \tag{8.31}$$

The unilateral subsidy in (8.17) is obtained by substituting p_I^U and p_{II}^U into (8.16).

The domestic firm's profits are obtained by substituting the equilibrium prices and (8.17) into (8.30)

$$\pi_I^U(\delta) = \frac{\delta(4 + 2\beta_2 - \beta_2^2)^2(\alpha - c(1 - \beta_2))^2}{2(\delta - 1)(8 - 5\beta_2^2)^2}. \tag{8.32}$$

Welfare $W_I(s^U)$ as a function of the unilateral government subsidy is obtained by substituting equilibrium prices p_I^U and p_{II}^U and (8.17) into W_I

$$W_I(s^U) = \frac{\delta(4 + 2\beta_2 - \beta_2^2)^2(\alpha - c(1 - \beta_2))^2}{4(8 - 5\beta_2^2)^2}.$$

The unilateral intervention vs free trade welfare differential is

$$W_I(s^U) - W_I^{FT}$$
$$= \frac{\delta(4 + 2\beta_2 - \beta_2^2)^2(\alpha - c(1 - \beta_2))^2}{4(8 - 5\beta_2^2)^2} - \frac{(\alpha - c(1 - \beta_2))^2}{(2 - \beta_2)^2},$$

where the free trade welfare level $W_I^{FT} = \pi^{FT}$ is computed setting $s = 0$ in W_I and solving a standard two-firm maximization problem.

9

Trade under Asymmetric Information

This chapter examines trade and policy formulation when there is asymmetric information about firm costs and the level of demand. Asymmetric information raises the issue of how to convey or extract unobserved information. For instance, which mechanisms induce type revelation by a firm holding private information about whether it is a low- or a high-cost type? Types can be revealed by screening and signaling. In a screening game, the government designs a mechanism inducing firms to reveal their type. In signaling games, firms take the initiative and make a costly choice, such as increasing research spending or incurring the costs of developing an infrastructure for exporting (Shy, 2000), to signal their type to the government, rival firms or consumers.

In practice, authorities must design policies under conditions of asymmetric information about players' types or payoffs—called incomplete information—or their strategic moves—called imperfect information. A government makes decisions under incomplete information when a subsidized firm can either be a low-cost or a high-cost type, with different payoffs for each type, but the type and payoffs are not known to the government in advance. Incomplete information can give rise to an adverse selection problem in which a high-cost firm holding private information about its type passes itself for a low-cost firm to get higher subsidies. Imperfect information means a player does not know other players' current or past choices, such as when firms choose product quality but consumers do not observe it. Imperfect information gives rise to a moral hazard problem if firms choose to produce low-quality products because high-quality is not recognized in the market.

What is the optimal policy design when the government does not directly observe domestic firms' true costs? The answer depends on the mode of competition, the size of the tax distortions associated with subsidy financing, the sequential structure of the game, market structure, and other factors.

The role of the mode of competition can be illustrated in a duopoly model in which a domestic and a foreign firm compete in a third market as in Qiu (1994). The domestic government unilaterally sets subsidy rates before the domestic firm makes production decisions. Subsidy financing is assumed not to entail tax distortions. In a setting with price competition and two differentiated goods, the government sets a uniform export tax rate and there is no revelation of firm type. In a setting with quantity competition and a homogeneous good, the government designs a policy menu offering alternative policy packages. Each package consists of a subsidy enhancing a firm's competitive position in the third market and a lump-sum tax extracting firm rents. If a technical sorting condition (i.e. the single-crossing property) holds and the menu of policy packages is appropriately designed, a firm's choice of a particular package reveals its true type. The optimal menu features a high subsidy rate packaged together with a high lump-sum tax and a low subsidy rate packaged together with a low lump-sum tax. A low-cost firm chooses the high subsidy rate cum high lump-sum tax package while a high-cost firm chooses the low subsidy-low tax package. The choice of package thus reveals the firm's type. The subsidy rate applicable to each cost type is the same as under complete information.

The policy formulation process should take into account that subsidy financing entails distortionary taxes. Brainard and Martimort (1997) tackle this issue by introducing a coefficient capturing tax distortions in a duopoly model with quantity competition and a continuum of cost types. When the social costs implied by distortionary taxes are factored in, the equilibrium subsidy under incomplete information is smaller than the equilibrium subsidy under complete information with a similar tax distortion coefficient. If the coefficient measuring tax distortions is large enough, the incomplete information trade subsidy could be zero—a free trade policy—or negative—a trade tax policy.

The role of game staging can be illustrated by examining policy formulation when firms play before the subsidy is determined. What is the equilibrium unilateral intervention policy when there is quantity competition between a foreign firm and a domestic firm that chooses the level of R&D spending *before* its government sets the output subsidy rate? A low-cost domestic firm that moves first can choose the level of R&D spending to (1) indirectly manipulate the government into granting higher export subsidies, and (2) signal its type to the government and to the foreign rival. The possibility that a subsidized firm indirectly manipulates the government by overinvesting in cost-reducing R&D modifies the policy formulation process. Specifically, free trade might be optimal even in settings in which strategic policies would generate gains from profit shifting. The unilateral adoption of a free trade program can be viewed as a mechanism to prevent private sector manipulation of the policymaking process. This is accomplished by announcing a credible commitment to free trade before firms make their moves. Manipulation through overinvestment in R&D 'gets worse' when there is asymmetric information. The reason is that a low-cost firm utilizes R&D spending to signal its type. Therefore, the parameter area leading to free trade is larger when the government faces asymmetric information about a firm's true costs than under complete information (Grossman and Maggi, 1998).

Asymmetric information can arise from the demand side. What is the equilibrium strategic trade policy in the third market duopoly setup with quantity competition when firms' costs are publicly known and (1) firms know the level of industry demand but intervening governments do not directly observe demand, and (2) subsidy policies are allowed to be nonlinear functions of output? If quadratic subsidies are allowed, linear subsidies will not arise in equilibrium. Maggi (1999a) shows that the equilibrium subsidy has a positive quadratic term indicating subsidy progressivity. The marginal subsidy is greater under bilateral than under unilateral intervention, which implies that bilateral intervention exacerbates the prisoner's dilemma faced by subsidizing governments.

Sections 9.1–9.4 examine screening and signaling under quantity and price competition. Section 9.5 shows that free trade can be optimal when firms manipulate the government and signal their type with costly R&D spending. Section 9.6 considers continuous cost-types and distorting taxes in settings with complete and private information. Section 9.7 explores nonlinear policies.

9.1. INCOMPLETELY INFORMED POLICYMAKER

Consider a two-country game, drawn from Qiu (1994), involving a domestic and a foreign rival competing in a third market to which they devote all their production of a homogeneous good. This good is consumed only in the third market, which means that consumption in the exporting countries can be altogether ignored. The domestic government intervenes on behalf of the domestic firm but the foreign government is assumed to abstain from intervention. The foreign firm cost c^* is public information, meaning that it is known by all agents, and is normalized to $c^* = 0$ for simplicity. This is a case in which the foreign firm has been widely researched and its production efficiency is well known in the market.

9.1.1. Stages, Uniform Subsidy, and Policy Menu

The analysis focuses on a screening-signaling game in which neither the government nor the rival foreign firm knows the domestic firm type ex ante. Consider a two-type case in which the domestic firm can produce at either high-cost c_H or at low-cost $c_L < c_H$. All agents are assumed to know the probabilities μ and $1 - \mu$ that the domestic firm has costs c_L or c_H

$$ P(c = c_L) = \mu, \qquad P(c = c_H) = 1 - \mu, $$

where P represents probability. Notice that the domestic firm's cost is private information, but the associated probabilities are public knowledge.

The government has two options to address the informational problem due to the lack of direct information about the domestic firm's cost. It can offer a single (i.e. uniform) policy package that applies to any firm no matter its cost. The uniform policy does not allow identification of the firm's cost type. Alternatively, the government can offer a menu of policies to the domestic exporter. The menu consists of alternative combinations of export subsidies and lump-sum taxes. Each combination is designed to cater to a particular firm type (high cost or low cost). If the menu is appropriately designed, each cost type would have incentives to select a different policy package in the menu. The package choice serves as a screening mechanism inducing the firm to reveal its cost type.

The incomplete information problem is solved in two stages. Stage 1, called the screening-signaling stage, comprises a screening mechanism and firm's signaling. The domestic government's welfare maximizing problem is solved under conditions of incomplete information about the domestic firm's cost. The government chooses a welfare-maximizing uniform policy or designs a menu of policies that acts as a screening device inducing cost-type revelation. The policy decision entails comparing the gains offered by a uniform policy and an appropriately designed menu. Signaling takes place when the domestic firm's choice of a policy package reveals its type to the intervening government and an incompletely informed foreign rival.

In stage 2, called the output stage, the foreign and domestic firms engage in quantity (i.e. Cournot) competition and choose the level of production. In a separating equilibrium of the screening-signaling game there is no asymmetric information at the output stage. The foreign rival knows the domestic firm's true cost, which is inferred from the first stage choice of a policy package.

9.1.2. Output Stage in a Separating Equilibrium

For any given government policy menu, what is the output stage solution? We solve explicitly for the output stage when the domestic firm has high costs c_H. The procedure and solution for the low–cost firm is the same with the appropriate choice of subindex (L instead of H).

The second stage involves setting output for a given policy package and is solved in a complete information setting. This procedure is valid in a separating equilibrium in which the government induces revelation of the domestic firm's type in the first stage. The output stage of a pooling equilibrium, in which neither the government nor the foreign rival knows the domestic firm's cost, is solved below.

Let us focus on the linear demand function case. High-cost firm profits, after the export subsidy and the lump sum tax, are

$$\pi_H(q_H, q^*; s_H, c_H) - T_H = [a - (q_H + q^*) - c_H + s_H]q_H - T_H, \tag{9.1}$$

where π_H represents before-tax and after-subsidy profits, q_H denotes the output of a high-cost firm, q^* is the foreign firm's production level, s is the subsidy rate, and T is the lump–sum tax. The foreign firm's profits are

$$\pi^*(q_H, q^*) = [a - (q_H + q^*)]q^*, \tag{9.2}$$

where the foreign government does not intervene in favor of the foreign firm. The foreign firm's cost is public information and is normalized to zero.

In the last stage of the game firms compete à la Cournot and determine the profit-maximizing levels of q_H and q^*. The first order necessary (and sufficient) conditions, $\partial \pi_H / \partial q_H = 0$ and $\partial \pi^* / \partial q^* = 0$, can be solved for q_H and q^*, to yield the reaction functions

$$q_H(q^*) = \frac{a - c_H - q^* + s_H}{2}, \qquad q^*(q_H) = \frac{a - q_H}{2}.$$

The first order necessary conditions are also sufficient because the profit functions are concave: $\partial^2 \pi_H / \partial q_H^2 = \partial^2 \pi^* / \partial q^{*2} = -2$. Notice that outputs are strategic substitutes: $\partial q_H(q^*)/\partial q^* = \partial q^*(q_H)/\partial q_H = -1/2 < 0$. The reaction functions imply that the equilibrium output levels as a function of s_H are

$$q_H(s_H, c_H) = \frac{a - 2c_H + 2s_H}{3}, \qquad q^*(s_H, c_H) = \frac{a + c_H - s_H}{3}. \tag{9.3}$$

Domestic and foreign firms' profits are obtained by substituting the output levels in (9.3) into (9.1) and (9.2)

$$\pi_H(s_H, c_H) - T_H = [q_H(s_H, c_H)]^2 - T_H = \left[\frac{a - 2c_H + 2s_H}{3}\right]^2 - T_H,$$

$$\pi^*(s_H, c_H) = [q^*(s_H, c_H)]^2 = \left[\frac{a + c_H - s_H}{3}\right]^2. \tag{9.4}$$

9.2. TRADE POLICY IN A SEPARATING EQUILIBRIUM

A separation-inducing policy menu offers two alternative policy packages, each consisting of a constant subsidy rate (i.e. a linear subsidy) and a lump-sum tax with the following properties:

(1) $\{s_L, T_L\}$ is chosen if the domestic firm has low costs c_L;
(2) $\{s_H, T_H\}$ is chosen if the domestic firm has high costs c_H.

What is the form of a separation-inducing menu? A separation-inducing menu consists of

(1) two alternative subsidies $s_H < s_L$, where the *lower* subsidy s_H is intended for a *high*-cost firm and the *higher* subsidy s_L is intended for a *low-cost* firm;
(2) lump-sum taxes $T_H < T_L$, where the *lower* lump-sum tax T_H is intended for a *high-cost* firm and the *higher* lump-sum tax T_L caters to a *low-cost* firm.

Notice that the subscripts of the policy package $\{s_i, T_i\}$ refer to the subsidized firm type, not to whether the subsidy or tax is low or high.

When the government offers a separation-inducing menu, the low-cost firm produces more than the high-cost firm. Using the output equation in (9.3) yields ($s_L > s_H$)

$$q_L - q_H = \tfrac{2}{3}[(c_H - c_L) + (s_L - s_H)] > 0. \tag{9.5}$$

The intuition is clear. The combination of a lower marginal cost and the associated larger subsidy induces higher low-cost firm production.

9.2.1. Expected Welfare and the Policy Menu

The government does not know the cost ex ante, but knows that the domestic firm produces at low-cost c_L with probability μ or at high-cost c_H with probability $1 - \mu$. Because the firm's type is not known yet in the first stage, policy menus are chosen on the basis of expected value maximization to induce revelation and ensure that firms participate in the game.

The policymaker chooses the policy menu $\{(s_L, T_L), (s_H, T_H)\}$ that maximizes expected national welfare EW. Expected national welfare is defined as expected profits after subsidies and taxes, $E\pi(\cdot) - T$, minus expected net transfers from the government to the firm, $E[sq - T]$, where sq and T are the expected subsidy costs and lump-sum tax revenues. Formally,

$$
\begin{aligned}
\max_{\{s_L, s_H\}} EW &= \mu[\pi_L(s_L, c_L) - T_L - (s_L q_L - T_L)] \\
&\quad + (1 - \mu)[\pi_H(s_H, c_H) - T_H - (s_H q_H - T_H)] \\
&= \mu[\pi_L(s_L, c_L) - s_L q_L] + (1 - \mu)[\pi_H(s_H, c_H) - s_H q_H],
\end{aligned} \tag{9.6}
$$

where $\pi(\cdot) = [a - (q + q^*) - c + s]q$. Because the lump-sum taxes are transfers from the firm to the government and do not affect the exporter's decision, they cancel out for the country as a whole. The government maximizes welfare with respect to the subsidy rates and sets lump-sum taxes to satisfy the participation and incentive compatibility constraints discussed next.

The government's welfare maximization problem is subject to two restrictions:

1. The individual rationality constraints—also called participation constraints—requiring the domestic firm to be willing to participate in the proposed game. A firm's decision is drawn by comparing the profits it could get in the game with the firm's opportunity costs given by the profits obtainable in the status quo in which the game is not played. The analysis assumes that the best outside alternative offers zero profits. In order to induce the domestic firm to play, the game should offer nonnegative profits (after tax and subsidy) to both possible cost types for at least one policy package in the menu. Formally, the preferred policy package should offer nonnegative profits

$$
\begin{aligned}
&\max[\pi_L(s_L, c_L) - T_L, \pi_L(s_H, c_L) - T_H] \geq 0, \\
&\max[\pi_H(s_H, c_H) - T_H, \pi_H(s_L, c_H) - T_L] \geq 0.
\end{aligned} \tag{9.7}
$$

2. The incentive compatibility constraints requiring that (i) a high-cost firm should not prefer the policy package designed for a low-cost firm, and (ii) a low-cost firm should not prefer the package designed for a high-cost firm. In other words, the package designed for a high-cost firm (or low-cost firm) is required to be profit-maximizing

for a high-cost firm (or low-cost firm). Algebraically,

$$\text{(i)} \quad \pi_H(s_H, c_H) - T_H \geq \pi_H(s_L, c_H) - T_L,$$
$$\text{(ii)} \quad \pi_L(s_L, c_L) - T_L \geq \pi_L(s_H, c_L) - T_H, \tag{9.8}$$

where $s_L > s_H$ and $T_L > T_H$.

The incentive compatibility constraints, comprising one separate constraint for each possible firm type, indicate the requirement that a firm would not lie about its type when offered a policy menu. These constraints are also called self-selection or truth-telling constraints. The incentive compatibility constraints constitute a personal no-arbitrage condition in the sense that, for each type, there is no positive gain from choosing the policy package not intended for that type.

If the incentive compatibility constraints (9.8) hold as strict inequalities, a firm's choice reveals whether it has low or high costs and makes credible the screening involved in the mechanism. The choice of a menu item constitutes a self-selection mechanism giving rise to an association between the policy package chosen and the firm's type. If the government sets a uniform policy, the incentive compatibility constraints are trivially satisfied as equalities and there is no revelation.

Separating Subsidies

What are the alternative subsidy rate and tax level packages offered by the government to the domestic firm? From the discussion of (9.6), recall that the optimum subsidy can be determined independently of the lump-sum tax. This feature allows maximizing expected welfare while ignoring the participation and incentive compatibility constraints. Given the subsidy rates, lump-sum taxes intended for a high- and a low-cost firm are chosen to make the participation and incentive compatibility constraints hold. The choice of lump-sum taxes is the policy tool that induces separation in this model.

The first order conditions $\partial EW/\partial s_L = 0$ and $\partial EW/\partial s_H = 0$ are used to determine the subsidies s_L^{Sep} and s_H^{Sep} granted to a low-cost and a high-cost firm in a separating equilibrium

$$s_L^{Sep} = \frac{a - 2c_L}{4}, \qquad s_H^{Sep} = \frac{a - 2c_H}{4}, \tag{9.9}$$

which are linear decreasing functions of the corresponding cost type. The relation $c_L < c_H$ implies that the low-cost firm subsidy *exceeds* the high-cost firm subsidy. Algebraically,

$$c_H > c_L \quad \rightarrow \quad s_L^{Sep} > s_H^{Sep}. \tag{9.10}$$

The equilibrium subsidies in (9.9) display the following features. First, they correspond to the complete information equilibrium solution for each type. Second, conditions (9.10) mean that the more efficient firm should receive the higher subsidy and the least efficient the lower subsidy.

Domestic exporters' profits, after subsidies and lump–sum taxes, are obtained by substituting (9.9) into (9.4)

$$\pi_H(s_H, c_H) - T_H = \frac{(a - 2c_H)^2}{4} - T_H,$$

$$\pi_L(s_L, c_L) - T_L = \frac{(a - 2c_L)^2}{4} - T_L. \tag{9.11}$$

From the perspective of the first stage, expected welfare under a separating menu is (using (9.6), (9.9), and $q_i = (a - 2c_i)/2$ obtained from (9.3) and (9.9))

$$EW^{Sep}(\mu, c_L, c_H) = \mu \left[\frac{(a - 2c_L)^2}{4} - \frac{a - 2c_L}{4} \frac{a - 2c_L}{2} \right]$$

$$+ (1 - \mu) \left[\frac{(a - 2c_H)^2}{4} - \frac{a - 2c_H}{4} \frac{a - 2c_H}{2} \right]$$

$$= \mu \frac{(a - 2c_L)^2}{8} + (1 - \mu) \frac{(a - 2c_H)^2}{8}. \tag{9.12}$$

Separation-inducing lump-sum taxes

The separating equilibrium subsidy rates do not ensure true type revelation. In fact, both firms have incentives to choose the higher subsidy. In order to ensure that the incentive compatibility constraints are satisfied, the domestic government must attach a higher lump-sum tax to the higher subsidy rate.

Policies $\{s_i^{Sep}, T_i^{Sep}\}, i \in \{H, L\}$ are items of a separating inducing menu satisfying the incentive compatibility constraints if and only if (see appendix)

$$-\frac{(c_H - c_L)^2}{4} \leq T_L - T_H - \frac{(c_H - c_L)(a - c_H - c_L)}{2} \leq \frac{(c_H - c_L)^2}{4}. \tag{9.13}$$

Because $c_H - c_L > 0$, the incentive compatibility condition (9.13) is satisfied if

$$T_L - T_H = \frac{(c_H - c_L)(a - c_H - c_L)}{2}.$$

There are multiple lump-sum tax pairs satisfying the incentive compatibility and participation constraints. For instance, let us verify that the pair $T_H = 0$ and $T_L = (c_H - c_L)(a - c_H - c_L)/2$ satisfy the participation constraints (9.7). The high-cost firm participation constraint is trivially satisfied if $T_H = 0$. The low-cost firm participation constraint is also satisfied provided that $a > 2c_H$, which implies the condition $a > 2c_L$

ensuring a positive output level in the absence of a subsidy as implied by the low-cost firm analog of (9.3). Formally,

$$
\begin{aligned}
\pi_L - T_L &= \frac{(a - 2c_L)^2}{4} - \frac{(c_H - c_L)(a - c_H - c_L)}{2} \\
&\geq \frac{(a - 2c_L)^2}{4} - \frac{(c_H - c_L)(a - 2c_L)}{2} \\
&= \frac{a - 2c_L}{2} \frac{a - 2c_L - 2(c_H - c_L)}{2} = \frac{a - 2c_L}{2} \frac{a - 2c_H}{2} > 0.
\end{aligned}
$$

Because both firms receive rents under this lump-sum tax scheme, there are multiple ways to increase lump-sum taxes and still maximize national welfare, which does not depend on lump-sum taxes, while satisfying the participation and incentive-compatibility constraints.

9.3. SINGLE-CROSSING PROPERTY CONDITION

Figure 9.1 illustrates the screening-signaling equilibrium. The isoprofit curves are positively sloped because after-tax profits $\pi[s, c] - T$ increase with higher subsidy

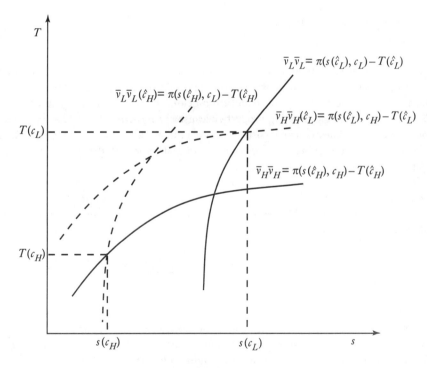

Figure 9.1. *Single-crossing property*

rates and lower lump–sum taxes. The after-tax isoprofit curves $\overline{v}\overline{v}$ vary according to cost-type and whether or not firms report their true costs. Recall that the incentive compatibility constraints embody the requirement that firms do not report a false cost type.

A separation-inducing menu of (s, T) packages induces firms to abide by the incentive compatibility constraints requiring true reporting by a high-cost and a low-cost firm

$$
\begin{aligned}
v_L(s(\hat{c}_L), T(\hat{c}_L)) &= \pi_L[s(\hat{c}_L), c_L] - T(\hat{c}_L) \\
&> v_L(s(\hat{c}_H), T(\hat{c}_H)) = \pi_L[s(\hat{c}_H), c_L] - T(\hat{c}_H), \\
v_H(s(\hat{c}_H), T(\hat{c}_H)) &= \pi_H[s(\hat{c}_H), c_H] - T(\hat{c}_H) \\
&> v_H(s(\hat{c}_L), T(\hat{c}_L)) = \pi_H[s(\hat{c}_L), c_H] - T(\hat{c}_L),
\end{aligned}
$$

where v represents profits after taxes and subsidies, $\hat{c}_L$ and $\hat{c}_H$ denote a firm's low-cost and high-cost report while the second argument in $\pi(s, \cdot)$ refers to true type.

What condition ensures that the menu presented by the government to the domestic firm works as a screening-signaling mechanism? A sufficient condition for a separating equilibrium is the single-crossing property of profit functions

$$
\frac{\partial^2 v}{\partial s \partial c} = \frac{\partial^2 \pi}{\partial s \partial c} = \frac{\partial[\partial \pi(s, c)/\partial s]}{\partial c} < 0 \tag{9.14}
$$

together with the condition $\partial \pi/\partial c < 0$ meaning that the higher the costs the lower the firm's marginal benefits from subsidies. In terms of the plane (s, π), the curve $\pi_L(s, c_L)$ must cut the curve $\pi_H(s, c_H)$ once and from below. The domestic profit function in (9.4) satisfies the single-crossing property because $\partial^2 \pi_H/\partial s_H \partial c = -8/9 < 0$, that is, the greater the domestic firm's costs, the lower the marginal benefit from subsidies. The property that marginal benefits from subsidies decline with the cost level ensures that a separating equilibrium exists.

The single-crossing property of profit functions, holding when the marginal benefits from subsidies are larger for a lower-cost firm than for a higher-cost firm, is also known as the sorting or Spence–Mirlees condition. Athey (2001) examines the role of this condition in general settings. The discrete version of (9.14) is ($s_L - s_H > 0$)

$$
\frac{\Delta[\Delta \pi(\cdot)/\Delta s]}{\Delta c} = \frac{\pi_H(s_L, c_H) - \pi_H(s_H, c_H)}{s_L - s_H} - \frac{\pi_L(s_L, c_L) - \pi_L(s_H, c_L)}{s_L - s_H} < 0.
$$

Figure 9.1 illustrates the incentive compatibility constraints and the necessary condition (9.14) requiring that, at any point, the slope of the profit function is smaller for a high-cost firm than for a low-cost firm. In terms of the isoprofit curves on the (s, T) plane, the single crossing property condition (9.14) states that the $\overline{v}_L \overline{v}_L$ curve must cut the curve $\overline{v}_H \overline{v}_H$ only once and from below. That this property is the same as condition (9.14) can be seen by totally differentiating $v(s, T) = \pi(s) - T$

$$dv(s, T) = \frac{\partial v}{\partial s} ds + \frac{\partial v}{\partial T} dT = 0$$

$$\rightarrow \frac{dT}{ds} = -\frac{\partial v/\partial s}{\partial v/\partial T} = \frac{\partial v}{\partial s} = \frac{\partial \pi}{\partial s} - \frac{\partial T}{\partial s} = \frac{\partial \pi}{\partial s},$$

where $dv = 0$ along a given isoprofit curve, $\partial v/\partial T = -1$, and $\partial T/\partial s = 0$.

9.4. UNIFORM POLICY vs POLICY MENUS

This section examines the choice between a policy menu and a uniform policy in which the government proposes a single (i.e. uniform) trade policy to the domestic firm. The decision to offer a menu or a uniform policy hinges on a comparison between the welfare levels achieved under separating and pooling equilibria. When firms compete in quantities, the government designs and offers a menu of policies inducing the domestic firm to disclose its private information. In other words, when firms compete in quantities, the uniform subsidy-cum-tax policy does not maximize government welfare in the third market model with incomplete information. When firms compete in prices, a uniform trade policy is welfare-maximizing and dominates a menu policy.

9.4.1. Pooling Equilibrium

Let us conjecture that the revelation of the firm's identity is not in the domestic government's best interest. In this case, the government proposes a uniform trade policy and the firm does not disclose any information about its true costs. An immediate consequence is that, at the output competition stage, the foreign firm will not possess information about its rival's cost, and must henceforth take its decisions on expected value grounds—instead of maximizing profits given the domestic firm's type.

Foreign firm's expected profits depend on the domestic firm's expected output Eq

$$E\pi^* = [a - (Eq + q^*)]q^*, \tag{9.15}$$

where expected domestic firm output is

$$Eq = P(c = c_L)q_L + P(c = c_H)q_H = \mu q_L + (1 - \mu)q_H.$$

Uniform Subsidy
The domestic authority chooses the subsidy level by maximizing expected domestic welfare

$$\max_s EW = E\pi - sEq = \mu[\pi_L(s) - sq_L] + (1 - \mu)[\pi_H(s) - sq_H].$$

The welfare-maximizing subsidy s^{Pool} is given by (see appendix)

$$s^{Pool} = \frac{a - 2Ec}{4}. \tag{9.16}$$

The optimal uniform subsidy is a linear decreasing function of expected costs. Let us compare the subsidy levels in the separating-inducing menu (9.9) and the uniform scheme (9.16). Since $c_L \leq Ec \leq c_H$, and the menu subsidies decline with the cost type, the uniform subsidy lies between the subsidies intended for a low-cost and a high-cost firm in a separating equilibrium.

Equilibrium expected welfare under pooling, EW^{Pool}, is

$$EW^{Pool} = \mu \frac{(a - 2c_L)(a - c_L - Ec)}{8} + (1 - \mu)\frac{(a - 2c_H)(a - c_H - Ec)}{8}.$$

$$(9.17)$$

Comparing welfare expressions (9.12) and (9.17) shows that, when firms compete in quantities, it is optimal to offer a subsidy-cum lump-sum tax menu serving as a screening mechanism inducing the domestic firm to reveal its cost-type (see appendix).

9.4.2. Uniform Policy under Price Competition

Qiu (1994) shows that, if two firms producing imperfect substitutes compete in prices, a uniform policy dominates a menu policy. Therefore, the unobserved cost-type will not be revealed in equilibrium. Why is it that quantity competition with homogeneous goods leads to a separating equilibrium while price competition with differentiated goods leads to a pooling equilibrium? In order to answer this question we must consider the basic trade off faced by the domestic government in setting its trade policy.

Let us examine the quantity competition case and the benefits and costs of type revelation. On one hand, there are benefits from identifying the domestic firm's type and setting a policy package that shifts competitive advantages and before-tax profits toward the domestic firm. On the other hand, revelation is costly because there are gains if the high-cost firm sends out a low-cost signal to the foreign rival. The reason is that, under quantity competition, quantities are strategic substitutes so that an untruthful low-cost signal induces a reduction of foreign output thus shifting profits toward the domestic firm. In the quantity competition setup, the benefits from screening exceed the costs of making public the private information about the domestic firm's true cost. For this reason, the menu policy dominates a uniform policy scheme under quantity competition.

Consider the case of price competition with two differentiated goods. The direct demand functions are

$$q_I(p_I, p_{II}) = \alpha - \beta_1 p_I + \beta_2 p_{II}, \qquad q_{II}(p_I, p_{II}) = \alpha - \beta_1 p_{II} + \beta_2 p_I, \qquad (9.18)$$

where $\beta_1 > \beta_2$ so that the demand effect of an increase in a firm's price is greater than the demand effect of an increase in the rival's price.

Paradoxically, under Bertrand competition, the welfare of maintaining incomplete information in equilibrium exceeds the welfare obtained under full information. On one hand, as with quantity competition, there are benefits from identifying the domestic firm type and setting the policy package that is appropriate for the firm true type.

On the other hand, if there is price competition, there is a gain if the *low*-cost firm sends out a *high*-cost signal to the foreign rival. The reason is that prices are strategic complements so that a high-cost signal induces an increase in the foreign firm *price*. Ceteris paribus, the price increase yields benefits to both rivals, as it implies that duopoly power is exploited to a greater extent. In the price competition setup, the benefits from nonrevelation exceed the benefits from making public the private information about the domestic firm's true costs. Revelation is not encouraged as keeping the rival firm in the dark leads to a favorable result from the domestic country's perspective.

9.5. FREE vs STRATEGIC TRADE

Should countries renounce to strategic intervention and commit to free trade even if they would be able to formulate optimal strategic trade policies? The puzzle is why choose free trade if the optimal strategic policy entails export subsidies (or taxes). An answer is that abstaining from intervention eliminates government's vulnerability to manipulation by the private sector and firms' cost of signaling their type to the government under incomplete information.

Government policy commitments affect firms' actions, but the formulation of these commitments is also influenced by firms' decisions. Vulnerability to private influence is possible when the government maximizes a welfare function that includes domestic firms' profits as a positive argument. Research-oriented firms have incentives to commit to a level of research spending that induces the government to grant higher research subsidies. A welfare-maximizing government will anticipate that intervening strategically will make it vulnerable to private sector manipulation. Free trade will be chosen if it yields greater welfare than strategic policy subject to manipulation as examined next. Vulnerability to private influence can also take place when private pressure groups make contributions to the government or political parties. The insights obtained by examining political pressures are discussed in later chapters.

This section examines the manipulation-signaling game developed by Grossman and Maggi (1998). A single domestic firm and a single foreign firm compete in an export market for a homogeneous good. The foreign firm has a constant publicly known marginal cost c^*. The domestic firm holds private information about its marginal cost but can use cost-reducing R&D expenditures for two purposes. First, R&D expenditures can signal a firm's true cost type to the government (the rival is assumed to know the domestic firm cost). Second, firm research spending can be used to manipulate domestic authorities and influence export subsidy or tax policies (research subsidies are not considered).

If the domestic exporter moves first by choosing research spending before the government moves, the policy making authority has two starkly opposed courses of action. It can either respond to manipulation when formulating trade policies or commit to a free trade policy as a mechanism to avoid firm maneuvering and costly signaling by firms. Depending on the region of the parameter space, free trade policies can dominate intervention in a game with complete information. With asymmetric information, a free trade program is optimal in environments in which, under complete information, it would be optimal to adopt an strategic trade program. The basic intuition is that more efficient firms overinvest in R&D to signal their true type and extract larger subsidies from the government. Manipulation through overinvestment 'gets worse' when there is asymmetric information. Therefore, the parameter area leading to free trade is larger when the government faces asymmetric information about firms' true costs than under complete information.

9.5.1. Stage Game, Information, and Output

Consider the following four-stage game consisting of (1) a trade program stage in which the domestic government decides between free trade and intervention, (2) a domestic firm R&D spending stage, (3) a trade policy stage in which the domestic government sets the subsidy rate, and (4) an output stage involving a domestic and a foreign firm. The game is solved using backward induction. The foreign government is assumed to be passive. The foreign firm does not engage in research and is assumed not to hold private information about its cost c^*, which is normalized to zero to facilitate the exposition.

At stage 1, the authority chooses between establishing a strategic trade program and abstaining from trade intervention. At this stage, the authority does not know the domestic firm's cost type but knows the probabilities μ and $1 - \mu$ of a low-cost type c_L and a high-cost type c_H. In stage 2, the domestic firm chooses the volume of research spending taking as given the government trade program decision at the previous stage. When choosing their R&D investments firms know their true type. At stage 3, the domestic government chooses the policy level (i.e. it fixes s). Finally, firms engage in Cournot competition at stage 4.

The analysis focuses on two intervention environments. In the symmetric information case, nature is assumed to reveal the domestic firm type before the subsidy is set in stage 3. In the asymmetric information case, the government can engineer an intervention scheme inducing the domestic firm to disclose its private information through its research decision in stage 2. The signaling model contrasts with Qiu (1994) in that (1) the domestic firm signals its type through R&D investment rather than through a choice of a policy package from a government policy menu, and (2) the domestic firm signals its type before rather than after the government sets the level of the policy variable.

With the previous staging, the information possessed by an intervening government is greater in stage 3 than in stage 1. At stage 1, the government lacks information about the domestic firm type. However, if there is either symmetric information or asymmetric information with a separating equilibrium, authorities can strategically set the level of the policy instrument after observing the cost type or indirectly inferring it from the previous R&D spending decision. The government sets a subsidy rate s_H to a high-cost firm and a subsidy rate s_L to a low cost firm.

Domestic firm profits contingent on its true type are

$$\pi_H(q_H, x_H, s_H) = [p(q_H, q^*) - (c_H - x_H) + s_H]q_H - \gamma x_H^2,$$

$$\pi_L(q_L, x_L, s_L) = [p(q_L, q^*) - (c_L - x_L) + s_L]q_L - \gamma x_L^2, \tag{9.19}$$

where c_H and c_L denote high and low production marginal costs, x_H is the cost-reducing R&D spending undertaken by the high-cost firm, x_L is the R&D spending of the low-cost firm, and γx_H^2 and γx_L^2 are the total R&D costs of the high- and low-cost firms. Foreign firm profits are $\pi^* = p(q, q^*)q^*$.

Output Stage
At stage 4, there is complete information and firms choose the Cournot–Nash output solution taking research spending and the subsidy rate as given. Profit maximization taking as given the level of research spending and the subsidy rate yields outputs q_H and q_L

$$q_H = \frac{a - 2(c_H - x_H - s_H)}{3}, \qquad q_L = \frac{a - 2(c_L - x_L - s_L)}{3}. \tag{9.20}$$

Output increases with research spending and the subsidy rate. The formula relating output to research and the subsidy rate is the same under free trade and under strategic intervention.

At this point, it is necessary to distinguish and analyze separately the alternative policy programs: the commitment to free trade vs the decision to establish a strategic trade policy program. The values of research spending and the subsidy rate differ across programs and also depend on whether information is symmetric or asymmetric.

9.5.2. Free Trade Program

At stage 2, research spending under free trade ($s_H = s_L = 0$) is computed by substituting (9.20) into (9.19), and using the first order necessary and sufficient condition $d\pi_L(x_L)/dx_L = 0$. Solving for x_L yields the low-cost firm equilibrium research spending

$$x_L^{FT}(\gamma \geq \bar{\gamma}_L^{FT}) = \frac{2(a - 2c_L)}{9\gamma - 4}, \qquad x_L^{FT}(\gamma < \bar{\gamma}_L^{FT}) = c_L, \tag{9.21}$$

where a positive cost $c_L - x_L > 0$ requires $\gamma > 4/9$ and $\bar{\gamma}_L^{FT} = 2a/(9c_L)$ satisfies $x_L^{FT}(\bar{\gamma}_L^{FT}) = c_L$. The expression for the high-cost firm R&D spending has the same form as (9.21), except that subscript H is used instead of subscript L. Because $c_L < c_H$, a low-cost firm would invest more in R&D than a high-cost firm. Low-cost firm profits are

$$\pi_L^{FT}(\gamma \geq \bar{\gamma}_L^{FT}) = \frac{\gamma(a - 2c_L)^2}{9\gamma - 4}, \qquad \pi_L^{FT}(\gamma < \bar{\gamma}_L^{FT}) = \frac{a^2}{9} - \gamma c_L^2, \tag{9.22}$$

and similarly for a high-cost firm.

Under free trade, subsidies are set equal to zero and the domestic firm does not have incentives to incur in costly signaling. When firms hold private information under free trade, social welfare is defined in terms of expected free trade profits. Using (9.22) for $\gamma \geq \bar{\gamma}_L^{FT}$ yields expected social welfare

$$EW^{FT} = \mu W_L^{FT} + (1 - \mu)W_H^{FT}$$

$$= \mu \frac{\gamma(a - 2c_L)^2}{9\gamma - 4} + (1 - \mu)\frac{\gamma(a - 2c_H)^2}{9\gamma - 4},$$

where $W_L^{FT} = \pi_L^{FT}, W_H^{FT} = \pi_H^{FT}$, and μ is the probability of a low-cost type. Expected welfare depends positively on the probability μ the government assigns to the low-cost type firm (i.e. $\partial W^{FT}/\partial\mu > 0$).

9.5.3. Manipulation with Symmetric Information

In the benchmark case, the true type is not known when the government decides to intervene in the first stage but is revealed by nature before the level of the policy variable—subsidy rate—is determined in the third stage. This setup implies there is symmetric information when the level of the policy variable is set. Therefore, the government does not need to design a subsidy policy to induce type revelation. The domestic firm does not utilize research spending as a signaling device but uses research spending in stage 2 to manipulate the government into granting greater subsidies.

At stage 3, the domestic authority sets the export subsidy rate granted to domestic exporters. The strategic trade policy program sets the subsidy rate to maximize firm's profits net of subsidy costs. The low- and high-cost firm subsidies are obtained by substituting (9.20) into the welfare function, $W = \pi(x, s) - sq(x, s)$, computing the first order necessary (and sufficient) condition $\partial W(x, s)/\partial s = 0$ for each type, and solving for s

$$s_L(x_L) = \frac{a - 2(c_L - x_L)}{4}, \qquad s_H(x_H) = \frac{a - 2(c_H - x_H)}{4}, \qquad (9.23)$$

where positive variable costs require $c_L > x_L$ and $c_H > x_H$.

The government sets the subsidy as a function of the observed level of research. Firms anticipate that the subsidy rate granted is positively related to the level of research. Therefore, there are incentives to increase research spending at stage 2 in order to manipulate the government into granting higher subsidy rates in the subsequent stage 3. Notice also that, for any given level of research spending $x = x_L = x_H, s_L(x) > s_H(x)$, meaning that the low-cost firm receives larger subsidies than the high-cost firm. A consequence of this result is that, in the asymmetric information setting discussed next, the low-cost firm will have incentives to signal its true type.

At stage 2, the domestic firm chooses R&D expenditures taking as given the anticipated subsidy function set by authorities in the next stage. Substituting the subsidy function $s_i(x_i)$ into the profit function and maximizing with respect to research spending yields the equilibrium level of subsidized research

$$x_L = \frac{a - 2c_L}{2(\gamma - 1)}, \qquad x_H = \frac{a - 2c_H}{2(\gamma - 1)}, \tag{9.24}$$

where $\gamma > 1$. The low-cost firm invests more in research than the high-cost firm ($x_L > x_H$).

Substituting the level of research in (9.24) into (9.23) yields the equilibrium subsidy granted to each type

$$s_L = \frac{\gamma}{2}x_L = \frac{a - 2c_L}{4(\gamma - 1)}\gamma, \qquad s_H = \frac{\gamma}{2}x_H = \frac{a - 2c_H}{4(\gamma - 1)}\gamma.$$

Profits under unilateral intervention with symmetric information are

$$\pi_L = \frac{\gamma(a - 2c_L)^2}{4(\gamma - 1)}, \qquad \pi_H = \frac{\gamma(a - 2c_H)^2}{4(\gamma - 1)}. \tag{9.25}$$

The decision between free trade and strategic intervention with symmetric information is made by comparing the welfare level under both regimes. Expected social welfare $\mu W_L + (1 - \mu)W_H$ under an interventionist program is given by the difference between expected profits and expected subsidy costs

$$\begin{aligned} EW &= \mu[\pi_L - s_L q_L] + (1 - \mu)[\pi_H - s_H q_H] \\ &= \mu\frac{\gamma(\gamma - 2)(a - c_L)^2}{8(\gamma - 1)^2} + (1 - \mu)\frac{\gamma(\gamma - 2)(a - c_H)^2}{8(\gamma - 1)^2} \\ &= \frac{\gamma(\gamma - 2)}{8(\gamma - 1)^2}[\mu(a - 2c_L)^2 + (1 - \mu)(a - 2c_H)^2], \end{aligned}$$

where W_L and W_H are obtained using (9.20), (9.23), and (9.25).

9.5.4. Intervention under Asymmetric Information

Consider the asymmetric information case in which authorities must design a subsidy policy to induce type revelation. In this case, firms engage in signaling through R&D spending in anticipation of the subsidy rate determination stage. The signaling and manipulation effects of stage 2 research spending influence the determination of the subsidy rate in stage 3. In the presence of asymmetric information the efficient firm will overinvest in research—in relation to the benchmark case—as a mechanism to disclose its low-cost attribute. To make the signal worthwhile, the low-cost firm must overinvest in R&D to levels that a high-cost firm would not undertake.

Separating Perfect Bayesian Equilibrium
The concept of perfect Bayesian equilibria (PBE) is based on Bayes' rule for updating prior or initial probabilities to form posterior probabilities. Suppose player i (the sender

of a signal) holds private information about its type and selects an action (which depends on the type) before agent j (the receiver of the signal) plays. Player j is assumed to observe i's action and utilize this information to update beliefs before making a move.

A PBE equilibrium consists of a set of strategies and beliefs such that, at any stage of the game, beliefs and strategies are consistent with each other. In a two-player game

1. beliefs are obtained from equilibrium strategies and observed actions using Bayes' rule. Beliefs must be consistent with equilibrium strategies in the sense that beliefs are updated according to Bayes rules along the equilibrium path;
2. strategies are optimal given beliefs. Each player equilibrium strategy, given his or her beliefs, is a best response to the other player equilibrium strategy.

The PBE concept does not impose restrictions on off-the-equilibrium posterior beliefs, that is, beliefs given the observation of an action with zero probability. If the conditional probability of player i's action is zero, the way player j updates the posterior beliefs about player i's type is unrestricted.

The asymmetric information game in which R&D spending serves as signal is solved by restricting attention to separating perfect Bayesian equilibria (SPBE). The set of SPBE is a set of R&D investment pairs $\{x_H^{SPB}, x_L^{SPB}\}$ such that the low-cost firm's research x_L satisfies two incentive compatibility constraints:

$IC1$—Research x_L is set at a high enough level to make it worthless for a high-cost firm to mimic a low-cost firm. Formally, equilibrium high-cost firm profits $\pi_H^{SPB}(x_H^{SPB}, s_H^{SPB})$ must exceed profits $\pi_H(x_L, s_L(x_L))$ obtained when a high-cost firm overinvests in R&D by mimicking a low-cost firm

$$\pi_H^{SPB}(x_H^{SPB}, s_H^{SPB}) > \pi_H(x_L, s_L(x_L)).$$

For the set of x_L values satisfying this constraint, a high-cost firm is inhibited from sending the untruthful signal that it is a low-cost firm in order to obtain the larger subsidy $s_L(x_L)$.

$IC2$—The level of research x_L is set to ensure that the low-cost firm signals its true type by choosing a low-cost level of research (thus obtaining the higher subsidies intended for a low-cost firm)

$$\pi_L(x_L, s_L(x_L)) > \pi_L(\bar{x}, s_H(\bar{x})) = \max_x \pi_L(x, s_H(x)),$$

where $\bar{x}$ is the research level that maximizes $\pi_L(x, s_H(x))$. For the set of x_L values satisfying this constraint the low-cost firm is inhibited from sending an untruthful signal by mimicking the high-cost firm. Profits $\pi_L(x_L, s_L(x_L))$ obtained by a low-cost firm that signals its true type and gets subsidy $s_L(x_L)$ must exceed the maximum profits $\pi_L(\bar{x}, s_H(\bar{x}))$ obtainable by a low-cost firm signaling that it has high costs and thus receiving $s_H(\bar{x})$. The government assumes that if a firm research is out-of-equilibrium the firm is a high-cost type and grants the subsidy corresponding to it.

At the set SPBE, the domestic firm chooses research spending to reveal its true type and the policymaker is able to offer a subsidy rate corresponding to the firm's true efficiency attributes. The set of separating equilibria entails overinvestment in research—relative to the benchmark symmetric information equilibrium with manipulation—by the low-cost firm. The high-cost firm does not gain from overinvestment in research. Research spending x_H^{SPB} is thus set at the level undertaken by the high-cost firm when the interventionist government is fully informed (i.e. benchmark case).

Signaling Through Overinvesting

The incentive compatibility constraints $IC1$ and $IC2$ can be used to characterize the research investment undertaken by a low-cost firm under separation. From (9.25) we have that the high-cost firm's equilibrium profits are $\pi_H^{SPB}(x_H^{SPB}, s_H^{SPB})$. High-cost firm profits $\pi_H(x_L, s_L(x_L))$ are evaluated at the low-cost firm research and subsidy— obtained from (9.23), (9.20), and (9.19). Condition $IC1$ is

$$\pi_H^{SPB}(x_H^{SPB}, s_H^{SPB}) = \frac{\gamma(a - 2c_H)^2}{4(\gamma - 1)} > \frac{(3a - 2(2c_H + c_L) + 6x_L)^2}{36},$$

$$-\gamma(x_L)^2 = \pi_H(x_L, s_L(x_L)) \rightarrow x_L > x_L^S, \tag{9.26}$$

where x_L^S is the positive root of the quadratic equation in x_L implied by (9.26). For R&D investments larger than x_L^S, the high-cost firm will not find it profitable to follow the low-cost firm's behavior. In this case, signaling will be a useful mechanism to reveal the domestic firm's true identity. The unique level that satisfies the intuitive criterion of Cho and Kreps (1987) is the least-cost R&D signal x_L^S.

The incentive compatibility condition $IC2$ requires that the low-cost firm finds it profitable to signal its true type

$$\pi_L(x_L, s_L(x_L)) = \frac{(a - 2c_L + 2x_L)^2}{4} - \gamma(x_L)^2$$

$$> \frac{\gamma(3a - 2(2c_L + c_H))^2}{36(\gamma - 1)^2} = \pi_L(\bar{x}, s_H(\bar{x})) \rightarrow x_L' < x_L < x_L'', \tag{9.27}$$

where x_L' and x_L'' represent the positive roots of the equation derived from (9.27). Profits $\pi_L(\bar{x}, s_H(\bar{x}))$ are obtained from (9.19) and $s_H(x_H)$ in (9.23), while profits $\pi_L(x_L, s_L(x_L))$ are obtained using (9.19), (9.20), and (9.23).

Combining the incentive compatibility conditions, we obtain that the research spending of a low-cost firm in a separating equilibrium must lie between x_L^S and x_L''. The property that x_L^S is greater than the full-information level implies that signaling entails overinvestment in research.

When the policymaker is incompletely informed about the firm's cost parameter, a program of strategic intervention may give a low-cost firm an incentive to signal its true type to the policymaker. If a low-cost firm invests more in R&D than a high-cost firm, then a low-cost firm can distinguish itself by investing in research even more than it would do otherwise. This overinvestment in research is costly for the firm to undertake, but would be even more costly for a high-cost firm to carry out. Consequently, the policymaker can infer that only a low–cost type firm would be willing to send this signal.

Free Trade or Interventionism under Uncertainty?

How does asymmetric information about firms' costs affect the desirability of an ex ante commitment to free trade? First of all, a free trade program does not eliminate over-investment taking place under free trade with oligopolistic markets in order to reduce costs and exploit the profit-shifting effect (see chapter on innovation). A free trade program does eliminate two sources of overinvestment in research. First, it pre-cludes export subsidization, which in turn induces overinvestment in cost-reducing research under symmetric information. Second, it precludes the use of overinvestment in research as a signaling device when there is asymmetric information.

The range of γ values for which free trade is socially preferable to strategic trade intervention is larger under asymmetric information than under complete information. The proof of this result can be sketched as follows (see Grossman and Maggi, 1998). First, the free trade outcome remains the same independently of the existence of symmetric or asymmetric information. Furthermore, a *high–cost* firm undertakes the same volume of research in the symmetric information with manipulation benchmark and the SPBE (asymmetric information). The *low–cost* firm overinvests in order to signal its type in the SPBE. Henceforth, the low–cost firm's profits and welfare levels will be lower than those achieved under the symmetric-information benchmark. Lower welfare levels under asymmetric information reduce the size of the parameter region associated with strategic trade policy.

Summing up, when firms play first, there are incentives to manipulate the govern-ment to obtain higher subsidies. A credible commitment to a free trade program can be optimal as an institutional barrier against excessive manipulation. This result embod-ies the notion that strategic intervention might not be optimal when the government can be manipulated by firms. The existence of incomplete information increases—in relation to the symmetric information benchmark—the parameter set under which free trade is preferred to strategic trade intervention. This result embodies the com-mon idea that authorities have less incentive to engage in trade policy when they lack information about domestic firms. In short, manipulation and limited information might cause strategic trade policy to open a Pandora's box.

9.6. TAX DISTORTIONS AND CONTINUOUS TYPES

This section extends the analysis of strategic intervention under incomplete informa-tion to account for (1) tax distortions, and (2) a continuum of cost-types. The analysis, based on Brainard and Martimort (1997), considers a government that offers either a menu of export subsidies and lump-sum taxes or a uniform subsidy and lump–sum tax package. Under asymmetric information, the lump-sum taxes utilized in a screening mechanism do not have to produce enough revenues to balance the government budget. Lump-sum taxes are used to induce firms to make decisions that satisfy the incentive compatibility constraints, not to balance the budget. A third instrument is needed to balance the budget. The residual financing of export subsidies is taken care of by taxes, such as consumption taxes, that do not affect a subsidized firm's behavior. However, a welfare-maximizing government must take into account the social costs of the attached tax distortions.

9.6.1. Demand, Firms, and Government

Consider a domestic and a foreign firm that export all their output of a homogeneous product to a third market where they compete in quantities as duopolists. The linear demand function is $p(q, q^*) = D^{-1}(Q) = a - (q + q^*)$, where $a > 0$ and p, q, and Q represent product price, firm output and aggregate production.

Firms' marginal costs c are random variables distributed uniformly over a positive support $[\underline{c}, \bar{c}]$ with density $f(c) = 1/(\bar{c} - \underline{c})$ and distribution function $F(c) = (c - \bar{c})/(\bar{c} - \underline{c})$. In a complete information setting, costs are publicly observed and verifiable. In the presence of asymmetric information, firms know the realization of their costs but domestic authorities are assumed to know only the cost distribution function $F(c)$ and to decide their best policy given firms' reports about their costs.

In the complete information setup, the domestic firm's costs are public knowledge, and the pretax profit function of the subsidized domestic firm is: $\pi(q, q^*, s, c) = [p(q, q^*) + s - c]q$. The output reaction functions, obtained from the first order conditions associated with firms' profit maximization problem are downward sloping, $\partial q(q^*)/\partial q^* < 0$. This means that if the rival increases its output, a firm's best response is to reduce its production. When the reaction function is negatively-sloped, quantities (q, q^*) are said to be strategic substitutes (Bulow *et al.*, 1985).

9.6.2. Combining Rent-shifting and Screening Policies

Under complete information, lump-sum taxes are used as a nondistorting method to finance export subsidies. The imposition of lump sum taxes ensures that the intervening government keeps a balanced budget. The public finance problem is more complex when asymmetric information is considered.

A policymaker facing asymmetric information designs a menu of contracts consisting of a subsidy rate s and a lump-sum tax T. The subsidy plays a precommitment role intended to lead the domestic firm to act like a Stackelberg leader. Under asymmetric information, the lump-sum tax plays dual rent-extracting and screening roles. First, it is used to leave the subsidized firm indifferent between participating and not participating in the game. The lump-sum tax allows the government to fully extract the surplus reaped by the subsidized firm. Second, the tax operates as part of a screening mechanism applied to the subsidized firm.

The lump-sum tax component of a policy package does not necessarily ensure that the budget is balanced or at a surplus. If the best alternative to accepting the menu offered by the government is one yielding zero profits, the binding participation constraint equating after subsidy profits to the lump-sum tax, $\pi - T = 0$, implies that the policy menu generates a surplus. The reason is that after subsidy profits exceed sq and therefore $sq < \pi = T$. If the best alternative to accepting the government menu yields high enough profits U, the binding participation constrain $\pi - T = U$ does not guarantee a balanced budget or a surplus. Indeed, the participation constraint is compatible with a budget deficit

$$sq < \pi = T + U, \quad T < sq.$$

In principle, the government could balance the budget by means of nondistorting taxes on agents other than the subsidized firm. In practice, though, distortionary taxation might be required to balance the budget under incomplete information.

In the presence of asymmetric information, the domestic authority utilizes three instruments to maximize expected welfare: (1) an export subsidy, (2) a lump-sum tax, and (3) a distorting tax that provides the resources to balance the budget. Securing the resources used to subsidize domestic exports generates a positive cost $\delta = 1 + d, d \geq 0$. The parameter d captures the administrative and distortion costs of the taxes securing the public funds allocated to subsidize exports.

The equilibrium unilateral subsidy in an incomplete information setting is (see appendix)

$$s^U(c) = \frac{a - c}{4} - \frac{d(c - \underline{c})}{1 + d}. \tag{9.28}$$

The first part of expression s^U corresponds to the optimal unilateral subsidy $s^U = (a - c)/4$ in a setting with complete information and no tax distortion. The second part is a negative term related to the distortion coefficient d and the cost gap $c - \underline{c}$.

The unilateral subsidy selected under incomplete information is smaller than the subsidy selected in a complete information setting. The reason is that, under incomplete information, a subsidy is assumed to require imposing a distortionary tax, whereas a nondistortionary lump-sum tax balances the government budget under complete information. Domestic production under incomplete information and subsidization is greater than under free trade, but falls below the full information output with intervention. Foreign production is lower than under free trade, but larger than under complete information.

If there is no distortion—d is equal to zero—the unilateral subsidy under incomplete information is the same as with unilateral intervention under complete information. If there is a positive distortion, the optimal subsidy is lower under incomplete information than when policymakers have complete information with the same distortion coefficient. If the distortion coefficient is sufficiently large, that is, if $d = (a - c)/(4(c - \underline{c}) + a - c)$, the optimal subsidy is zero.

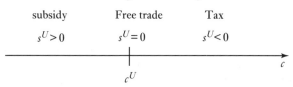

Figure 9.2. *Optimal unilateral policy scheme*

9.6.3. Screening and Precommitment Effects

Figure 9.2 depicts the pattern of trade policy as a function of the domestic firm's true cost. To clarify the figure, consider the cost level c^U under which free trade is an equilibrium. The cost level supporting free trade is obtained by imposing $s^U = 0$ on (9.28)

$$c^U = \left\{ c | c - \underline{c} = \frac{a - c}{4} \frac{1 + d}{d} \right\}. \tag{9.29}$$

Assume that $\underline{c} < c^U < \bar{c}$ so that the cost level supporting free trade belongs to the support $[\underline{c}, \bar{c}]$.

If the true cost c is below c^U, the unilateral intervention subsidy is positive. This result can be seen by observing that $c - \underline{c} < (a - c)(1 + d)/(4d)$ corresponds to $s^U > 0$ in (9.28). If $c^U < c$, s^U is negative because

$$c - \underline{c} > \frac{a - c}{4} \frac{1 + d}{d}$$

corresponds to $s^U < 0$ in (9.28).

By *taxing* the exports of a high-cost firm, domestic production becomes smaller than under free trade. If the true cost c is large enough, the export tax effect (i.e. the screening effect) dominates the subsidy effect (i.e. the precommitment effect), and domestic authorities end up hurting the domestic *firm* and benefiting foreign competitors. However, government income is higher and *social* welfare is maximized by the export tax.

9.7. NONLINEAR SUBSIDIES

Up to now, we have focused on linear subsidy functions (i.e. the subsidy rate is constant). What is the equilibrium policy when the government is allowed to set subsidies that are a nonlinear function of output? Maggi (1999*a*) examines this question in a model in which firms have better information than governments about industry demand. A domestic and a foreign firm compete in quantities as duopolists in a third market. Firms produce at a constant unit cost c and face a linear inverse demand function $p = a - b(q + q^*)$, where a and b are positive constants and the industry demand parameter $a > 0$ is known by both firms but not by governments. The level of demand a is distributed according to the density function $f(a)$ on the continuous interval (a_0, a_1). There is a continuum of firm types defined by the demand level a.

The stage model has the following four stages (1) governments choose and announce trade policy schemes that maximize firm profits (before subsidies and taxes) minus the distortion costs of subsidy financing, (2) firms decide whether to accept their corresponding government's proposal (this stage corresponds to the participation decision requiring a nonnegative expected payoff), (3) firms observe the demand parameter a, which is private information to them, and (4) firms compete in quantities and determine the level of output by noncooperatively maximizing profits gross of subsidies.

Firms observe the demand parameter after the policy formulation and participation stages but before they enter into the output choice stage. The government observes output and designs a subsidy function $s(q)$ but faces an information problem because it does not observe the level of demand a and therefore neither price nor profits. Attaching higher lump-sum taxes to larger subsidies induces firm self selection according to the level of demand faced. A firm facing a higher (lower) demand chooses a larger (smaller) output level thus getting a higher (lower) subsidy.

Governments maximize expected national welfare subject to participation and incentive compatibility constraints. The values of subsidies and taxes represent transfers that cancel out for the economy as a whole. Therefore, welfare can be defined as (1) profits (after subsidies and lump-sum taxes) minus the opportunity cost of distortionary subsidy financing, or (2) profits (before subsidies and taxes) minus the distortion costs of subsidy financing

$$W = \pi(q, q^*; a) + s(q) - T - (1 + d)(s(q) - T)$$
$$= \pi(q, q^*; a) - d(s(q) - T),$$

where $\delta = 1 + d$ measures the opportunity costs of funds and d measures distortion costs.

The subsidy schedule $s(q)$ maximizing the expected value of domestic welfare subject to the incentive compatibility constraints is the solution to

$$\max_{s(q)} E[\pi(q, q^*; a) - d(s(q) - T)] = E[\pi(q, q^*; a) - d(-\pi(q, q^*; a))]$$

$$= (1 + d)E[\pi(q, q^*; a)],$$

where the equality follows from the binding participation constraint, $E\pi = T - Es(q)$, discussed below. Profits π are defined *before* subsidies and lump-sum taxes and d captures the distortion costs of raising funds.

The foreign country can either remain passive or intervene. The maximization problem of an intervening foreign government is

$$\max_{s^*(q^*)} E[\pi^*(q, q^*; a) - d(s^*(q^*) - T^*)] = (1 + d)E[\pi^*(q, q^*; a)],$$

subject to incentive compatibility constraints.

Expected domestic welfare maximization is subject to a participation constraint, which is defined in expected terms because a firm must accept the government's proposal before it observes the demand parameter a (R means reaction function)

$$E\{\pi[q(a), R^*(q(a), a), a] + s(q(a)) - T\} \geq 0,$$

where $q^*(a) = R^*(q(a), a)$. Because public funds are costly, the domestic government chooses subsidy-tax combinations in such a way as to make the participation constraint binding. Specifically, the lump–sum taxes under unilateral and bilateral intervention, T_0^U and T_0^{Bil}, are chosen to eliminate firm net-of-tax rents in equilibrium. The binding participation constraints are

$$T^U = E\left[\pi^U + s^U(q)\right] \quad \rightarrow \quad T^U - E\left[s^U(q)\right] = E\left[\pi^U\right],$$

$$T^{Bil} = E\left[\pi^{Bil} + s^{Bil}(q)\right] \quad \rightarrow \quad T^{Bil} - E\left[s^{Bil}(q)\right] = E\left[\pi^{Bil}\right].$$

The two parts of the domestic incentive compatibility constraint are

$$\frac{\partial \pi[q(a), R^*(q(a), a), a]}{\partial q}\frac{dq}{da} + \frac{ds}{da} = 0,$$

$$\rightarrow \frac{ds(a)}{da} = -\frac{\partial \pi[q(a), R^*(q(a), a), a]}{\partial q}\frac{dq}{da},$$

which means that the first order condition should be satisfied at the true a, and (see derivation in appendix)

$$\left[\frac{\partial^2 \pi[q(a), R^*(q(a), a), a]}{\partial q \partial a} + \frac{\partial^2 \pi[q(a), R^*(q(a), a), a]}{\partial q \partial q^*}\frac{\partial R^*(\cdot)}{\partial a}\right]\frac{dq}{da} \geq 0.$$

When the foreign government intervenes, a similar incentive compatibility constraint applies to the foreign country.

When the demand is linear and marginal costs are constant, there is a unique separating equilibrium consisting of output functions of the demand level and policy menus offering combinations of lump–sum taxes and subsidy functions of observed output. The equilibrium output functions under intervention are the Stackelberg leader output functions when rival costs are symmetric

$$q^U(a) = q^{Bil}(a) = q^{*Bil}(a) = \frac{a - c}{2b} > q^{*U}(a) \rightarrow \pi^U > \pi^{Bil} = 0.$$

The unilaterally intervening government implements the Stackelberg output. Bilateral intervention implements the Bertrand $\pi = 0$ outputs.

The equilibrium output function with unilateral intervention coincides with the Stackelberg solution obtained in the chapter on Cournot competition when costs are symmetric. The bilateral intervention result is similar to the previous result that bilateral intervention through linear subsidies reduces both countries' welfare—defined to include profits $\pi = [a - b(q + q^*) - c]q$ but not consumer utility—below non-intervention. The Bertrand-like equilibrium obtained under incomplete information when there is bilateral intervention through nonlinear subsidy functions exacerbate the prisoner's dilemma from the perspective of firms. However, the unobserved demand scenario comprises the third market demand. Incorporating consumer utility into the welfare function implies that bilateral intervention can improve world welfare.

The equilibrium unilateral and bilateral subsidy functions are nonlinear convex functions of output. The output-dependent components of the subsidies are

$$s^U(q) = \frac{b}{4}q^2, \qquad s^{Bil}(q) = \frac{b}{2}q^2,$$

where the marginal subsidy $ds(q)/dq$ is positive. Because the rival firm is more aggressive under bilateral than under unilateral intervention, achieving the Stackelberg output under bilateral intervention requires a higher marginal subsidy than under unilateral intervention. The subsidy functions are obtained using the incentive compatibility constraint to find $s(a)$ and substituting for a from the demand function $p = a - b(q + q^*)$.

The unilateral and bilateral marginal subsidies $bq/2$ and bq are increasing functions of the equilibrium level of production. The marginal subsidy is greater under bilateral than under unilateral intervention, which implies that bilateral intervention exacerbates the prisoner's dilemma faced by governments that do not value consumers' utility. The convex subsidy induces a firm to self select because a firm facing a higher a produces more and chooses a higher marginal subsidy.

9.8. CONCLUSIONS

This chapter examined trade and policy when there is asymmetric information about firm cost types and the level of demand. Lack of information can hurt domestic interests if the chosen policy does not match players' types or gives rise to adverse selection. Such possibility reinforces the need for (1) using a robust instrument that works well no matter what firms' types are, or (2) devising a mechanism leading to the revelation of firms' types. If these conditions are not satisfied, and if signaling is costly, financing generates distortions and lobbying activity leads to inefficiencies, opting for nonintervention might be the best alternative.

9.9. APPENDIX

9.9.1. Condition for a Separation-Inducing Menu

A condition ensuring that $\{s, T\}$ is a separation-inducing menu is found substituting $s_i = (a - 2c_i)/4, i \in \{H, L\}$, and $\pi_H(s_H, c_H) - T_H$ and $\pi_H(s_L, c_H) - T_L$ into the high-cost type incentive compatibility constraint (9.8)

$$\frac{(a - 2c_H)^2}{4} - T_H \geq \left(\frac{2a - 3c_H - c_L + 4((a - 2c_L)/4)}{6}\right)^2 - T_L$$

$$= \frac{(a - c_H - c_L)^2}{4} - T_L,$$

which implies that $T_L - T_H$ is equal or greater than

$$\frac{(a - c_H - c_L)^2}{4} - \frac{(a - 2c_H)^2}{4} = -\frac{(c_H - c_L)^2}{4} + \frac{(c_H - c_L)(a - c_H - c_L)}{2}.$$

The low-cost type *IC* condition implies that $T_L - T_H$ is lower or equal than

$$\frac{(a - 2c_L)^2}{4} - \frac{(a - c_H - c_L)^2}{4} = \frac{(c_H - c_L)^2}{4} + \frac{(c_H - c_L)(a - c_H - c_L)}{2}.$$

The high-cost and low-cost inequalities for $T_L - T_H$ become expression (9.13)

$$-\frac{(c_H - c_L)^2}{4} \leq T_L - T_H - \frac{(c_H - c_L)(a - c_H - c_L)}{2} \leq \frac{(c_H - c_L)^2}{4}.$$

9.9.2. *Quantity Competition: Uniform Subsidy and Pooling*

High-cost firm's profits are

$$\pi_H(s) = [a - (q_H + q^*) - c_H + s]q_H, \tag{9.30}$$

where q_H and q^* represent domestic output. Foreign firm profits depend on the domestic firm's expected output Eq

$$E\pi^* = [a - (Eq + q^*)]q^*, \qquad Eq = \mu q_L + (1 - \mu)q_H. \tag{9.31}$$

The first order necessary (and sufficient) conditions $\partial\pi_H(s)/\partial q_H = 0$ and $\partial E\pi^*/\partial q^* = 0$ imply reaction functions

$$q_H = \frac{a - c_H - q^* + s}{2}, \quad q^* = \frac{a - Eq}{2},$$

which imply that

$$Eq = \frac{a - q^* + s - Ec}{2}, \tag{9.32}$$

where $Ec = \mu c_L + (1 - \mu)c_H$ is the expected marginal cost. Substituting (9.32) into q^* and the resulting expression into q_H produces

$$q_H = \frac{2a - 3c_H - Ec + 4s}{6}, \quad q^* = \frac{a - (s - Ec)}{3}. \tag{9.33}$$

The high–cost firm's profits are

$$\pi_H(s) = q_H^2 = \left[\frac{2a - 3c_H - Ec + 4s}{6}\right]^2. \tag{9.34}$$

The uniform subsidy is obtained by maximizing expected welfare

$$EW = E\pi - sEq = \mu[\pi_L(s) - sq_L] + (1 - \mu)[\pi_H(s) - sq_H]. \tag{9.35}$$

Substituting q_H in (9.33), π_H in (9.34), q_L and π_L into (9.35) yields

$$EW = \mu\frac{[2a - 3c_L - Ec - 2s][2a - 3c_L - Ec + 4s]}{36}$$
$$+ (1 - \mu)\frac{[2a - 3c_H - Ec - 2s][2a - 3c_H - Ec + 4s]}{36}. \tag{9.36}$$

Solving for s from the first order necessary condition $\partial EW/\partial s = 0$ obtains

$$s^{Pool} = \frac{a - 2Ec}{4}, \qquad q_H^{Pool} = \frac{a - (c_H + Ec)}{2}, \qquad Eq^{*Pool} = \frac{a + 2Ec}{4}. \tag{9.37}$$

The first order condition is also sufficient because $\partial^2 EW/\partial s^2 = -4/9 < 0$.
   Domestic firm profits are (substitute (9.37) into (9.34))

$$\pi_H^{Pool} = \left[q_H^{Pool}\right]^2 = \left[\frac{a - (c_H + Ec)}{2}\right]^2.$$

Total expected welfare is obtained using (9.36) and (9.37) and similar expressions for
the low type

$$EW^{Pool} = \frac{\mu(a - c_L)(a - c_L - Ec)}{8} + \frac{(1 - \mu)(a - c_H)(a - c_H - Ec)}{8}. \tag{9.38}$$

9.9.3. Quantity Competition: Separation Dominates Pooling

Expected welfare is

$$EW = \mu[\pi_L - T_L - (s_L q_L - T_L)] + (1 - \mu)[\pi_H - T_H - (s_H q_H - T_H)]$$
$$= \mu[(p_L - c_L + s_L)q_L - s_L q_L] + (1 - \mu)[(p_H - c_H + s_H)q_H - s_H q_H]$$
$$= \mu(p_L - c_L)q_L + (1 - \mu)(p_H - c_H)q_H = E\pi_{Net}.$$

The welfare differential $EW^{Sep} - EW^{Pool}$ is

$$
E\pi_{Net}^{Sep} - E\pi_{Net}^{Pool}
$$

$$
= \mu \left(p_L^{Sep} - c_L \right) q_L^{Sep} + (1 - \mu) \left(p_H^{Sep} - c_H \right) q_H^{Sep}
$$

$$
- \mu \left(p_L^{Pool} - c_L \right) q_L^{Pool} - (1 - \mu) \left(p_H^{Pool} - c_H \right) q_H^{Pool}
$$

$$
= \mu (p_L - c_L) \left(q_L^{Sep} - q_L^{Pool} \right) + (1 - \mu)(p_H - c_H) \left(q_H^{Sep} - q_H^{Pool} \right)
$$

$$
= \mu (p_L - c_L) \left(q_L^{Sep} - q_L^{Pool} \right) - \mu(p_H - c_H) \left(q_L^{Sep} - q_L^{Pool} \right) + (p_H - c_H)
$$

$$
\left[\mu \left(q_L^{Sep} - q_L^{Pool} \right) + (1 - \mu) \left(q_H^{Sep} - q_H^{Pool} \right) \right]
$$

$$
= \mu [p_L - c_L - p_H + c_H] \left(q_L^{Sep} - q_L^{Pool} \right) + (p_H - c_H)E \left(q^{Sep} - q^{Pool} \right)
$$

$$
= \mu \left[(p_L - c_L) - (p_H - c_H) \right] \left(q_L^{Sep} - q_L^{Pool} \right) > 0. \qquad (9.39)
$$

The equalities $p_H = p_H^{Pool} = p_H^{Sep}$ and $p_L = p_L^{Pool} = p_L^{Sep}$ hold because

$$
p_H = p_H^{Pool} = a - \left(q_H^{Pool} + q^* \right) = \frac{a + 2c_H}{4} = p_H^{Sep},
$$

and similarly for p_L. The third equality adds the terms $-\mu(p_H - c_H)(q_L^{Sep} - q_L^{Pool}) + \mu(p_H - c_H)(q_L^{Sep} - q_L^{Pool})$ into the previous expression. The last equality was obtained using $Eq^{Sep} = Eq^{Pool}$. Substituting q_H^{Sep}, (9.37) and the corresponding expressions for the low-cost type into (9.31)

$$
Eq^{Sep} = \mu q_L^{Sep} + (1 - \mu)q_H^{Sep} = \frac{a - 2Ec}{4} = \mu q_L^{Pool} + (1 - \mu)q_H^{Pool} = Eq^{Pool}.
$$

Using $p_i = (a + 2c_i)/2$ and $q_L^{Sep} - q_L^{Pool} > 0$ implies that $EW^{Sep} - EW^{Pool} > 0$ in (9.39)

$$
(p_L - c_L) - (p_H - c_H) = \left(\frac{a + 2c_L}{4} - c_L \right) - \left(\frac{a + 2c_H}{4} - c_H \right) = \frac{c_H - c_L}{2} > 0.
$$

9.9.4. Unilateral Subsidy with Continuous Types

In Brainard and Martimort (1997), the government maximizes welfare

$$
\max_{s(\hat{c}), U(c)} EW(\hat{c}, c) \equiv E \left[U(\hat{c}, c) - \delta \left[s(\hat{c})q(\cdot) - T(\hat{c}) \right] \right], \qquad (9.40)
$$

where $\delta = 1 + d$, $s(\hat{c})$ is a function of reported cost, and $U(c) = U(\hat{c} = c, c)$ in

$$U(\hat{c}, c) = \pi(s(\hat{c}), s^*(c), c) - T(\hat{c}),$$

subject to the individual rationality constraint (*IR*) and the incentive compatibility constraint (*IC*)

$$IR: \ U(\hat{c}, c) = \pi(s(\hat{c}), s^*(c), c) - T(\hat{c}) \geq 0,$$

and

$$IC: \ c = \arg\max_{\hat{c}} U(\hat{c}|c) = \arg\max_{\hat{c}} \pi(s(\hat{c}), s^*(c), c) - T(\hat{c}).$$

The individual rationality constraint is binding. Since firms tend to over-report their costs, we know that if the individual rationality constraint (participation constraint) would be binding for a less efficient firm reporting net profits equal to zero, then the *IR* constraint would also bind for some more efficient firms.

Substituting the *IR* into the government objective function yields

$$EW(\hat{c}, c) = E\{U(\hat{c}, c) - \delta\{s(\hat{c})q(\cdot) - [\pi(s(\hat{c}), s^*(c), c) - U(\hat{c}, c)]\}\}$$

$$= E\{(1 - \delta)U(\hat{c}, c) - \delta[s(\hat{c})q(\cdot) - \pi(s(\hat{c}), s^*(c), c)]\}.$$

Dividing the whole expression by δ and rearranging terms transforms the government maximization problem into

$$\max_{s(\hat{c}), U(c)} E\left[\pi(s(\hat{c}), s^*(c), c) - s(\hat{c})q(\cdot) + \frac{1 - \delta}{\delta} U(\hat{c}, c)\right]$$

subject to the *IC*.

The government's problem can also be written as ($s^*(c)$ is the foreign policy)

$$\max_{s(\hat{c}), U(c)} \int_{\underline{c}}^{\bar{c}} \left[\pi(s(\hat{c}), s^*(c), c) - s(\hat{c})q(\cdot) + \frac{1 - \delta}{\delta} U(\hat{c}, c)\right] f(c) \, dc,$$

subject to the *IC*. Given $s(\hat{c})$ and *IC*, choosing after tax profits U determines the tax T.

Incentive Compatibility Constraint
The incentive compatibility constraint is

$$c = \arg\max_{\hat{c}} U(\hat{c}|c) = \arg\max_{\hat{c}} \pi(s(\hat{c}), s^*(c), c) - T(\hat{c}).$$

Let us now apply the constraint reduction theorem, which states that the menu $\{s(c), T(c)\}$ satisfies the incentive compatibility constraint iff

(i) $\dfrac{ds(c)}{dc} \leq 0,$

(ii) $\dfrac{d}{dc} U(c|c) = \dfrac{\partial U(c)}{\partial c}, \ U(c/c) = \max_{\hat{c}} U(\hat{c}/c),$

almost everywhere. Condition (i) means that the subsidy s is nonincreasing in the firm's type c. If the single crossing property holds, this condition is satisfied. Condition (ii) is a local incentive compatibility constraint.

Using the fundamental theorem of calculus and the constraint reduction theorem we have

$$\int_{\underline{c}}^{\bar{c}} U(\hat{c}|c) f(c) \, dc = U(\underline{c}|\underline{c}) + \int_{\underline{c}}^{\bar{c}} \frac{\partial U(c)}{\partial c} F(c) \, dc = \int_{\underline{c}}^{\bar{c}} \frac{\partial U(c)}{\partial c} F(c) \, dc$$

$$\rightarrow \int_{\underline{c}}^{\bar{c}} U(\hat{c}|c) f(c) \, dc = \int_{\underline{c}}^{\bar{c}} \frac{\partial U(c)}{\partial c} \frac{F(c)}{f(c)} f(c) \, dc$$

$$\rightarrow \int_{\underline{c}}^{\bar{c}} U(\hat{c}|c) f(c) \, dc = E \left[\frac{\partial U(c)}{\partial c} \frac{F(c)}{f(c)} \right].$$

The second equality is obtained imposing $U(\underline{c}|\underline{c}) = 0$.

Substituting the previous result into the government's maximization problem yields

$$\max_{s(\hat{c}), U(c)} E \left[\pi(s(\hat{c}), s^*(c), c) - s(\hat{c}) q(\cdot) + \frac{(1-\delta)}{\delta} \frac{\partial U(c)}{\partial c} \frac{F(c)}{f(c)} \right].$$

Pointwise Maximization and the Optimal Subsidy / Tax
For each c, the government maximizes the function

$$H(c) = \pi(s(\hat{c}), s^*(c), c) - s(\hat{c}) q(\cdot) + \frac{1-\delta}{\delta} \frac{\partial U(c)}{\partial c} \frac{F(c)}{f(c)}.$$

(1) Differentiating expression $U(\hat{c}, c) = \pi(s(\hat{c}), s^*(c), c) - T(\hat{c})$ with respect to c (which corresponds to condition (ii) in the constraint reduction theorem) yields

$$\frac{\partial U(c)}{\partial c} \Big|_{c=\hat{c}} = \frac{\partial \pi(s(c), s^*(c), c)}{\partial c} = \frac{-2}{3} \left(\frac{a - c + 2s - s^*}{3} \right), \tag{9.42}$$

obtained from $\pi(s(c), s^*(c), c) = (a - c + 2s - s^*)^2/9$.

(2) The density function $f(c)$ is continuous and uniformly distributed with support $[\underline{c}, \bar{c}]$. Henceforth, the probability density function is $1/(\bar{c} - \underline{c})$ and the associated distribution function $F(c)$ is $(c - \underline{c})/(\bar{c} - \underline{c})$. Thus,

$$\frac{F(c)}{f(c)} = \frac{(c - \underline{c})/(\bar{c} - \underline{c})}{1/(\bar{c} - \underline{c})} = c - \underline{c}.$$

Plugging (1) and (2) into H (and expressing H as a function of s and s^*)

$$H(s, s^*) = \left[\frac{a - c + 2s - s^*}{3} \right]^2 - s(\hat{c}) \frac{a - c + 2s - s^*}{3}$$

$$- 2 \frac{1 - \delta}{\delta} \frac{a - c + 2s - s^*}{9} (c - \underline{c}). \tag{9.43}$$

Unilateral intervention means that $s^* = 0$. Therefore

$$H(s) = \left[\frac{a - c + 2s}{3}\right]^2 - s\frac{a - c + 2s}{3} - 2\frac{1 - \delta}{\delta}\frac{a - c + 2s}{9}(c - \underline{c}).$$

The first order condition $\partial H(\cdot)/\partial s = 0$ for the subsidy granted under unilateral intervention is

$$\frac{4}{3}\frac{a - c + 2s}{3} - \frac{a - c + 4s}{3} - \frac{4(1 - \delta)}{9\delta}(c - \underline{c}) = 0$$

$$\rightarrow s^U(c) = \frac{a - c}{4} - \frac{(1 - \delta)(c - \underline{c})}{\delta}.$$

9.9.5. *Nonlinear Subsidies*

Maggi (1999a) considers the profit function π (before subsidies and taxes),

$$\Pi(\cdot) = \pi[q(\hat{a}), q^*, a] + s(\hat{a}) - T,$$

where $\hat{a}$ is the demand parameter reported by the firms to the government. The level of $\hat{a}$ maximizing domestic firm profits is

$$\frac{d(\pi + s)}{d\hat{a}} = \frac{\partial\pi[q(\hat{a}), q^*, a]}{\partial q}\frac{dq}{d\hat{a}} + \frac{ds}{d\hat{a}} = 0. \tag{9.44}$$

This first order necessary condition is given by

$$\frac{\partial^2(\pi + s)}{\partial\hat{a}^2} = \frac{\partial\pi[q(\hat{a}), q^*, a]}{\partial q^2}\left(\frac{dq}{d\hat{a}}\right)^2 + \frac{\partial\pi[q(\hat{a}), q^*, a]}{\partial q}\frac{d^2q}{d\hat{a}^2} + \frac{d^2s}{d\hat{a}^2} \le 0.$$

At the Nash equilibrium: $q^*(a) = R^*(q(a), a)$. If the domestic firm reports the truth, $\hat{a} = a$, the following incentive compatibility constraint has to hold for all parameters a at equilibrium. One part of the incentive compatibility condition is

$$0 = \frac{\partial\pi[q(a), R^*(q(a), a), a]}{\partial q}\frac{dq}{da} + \frac{ds}{da}$$

$$\rightarrow \frac{ds(a)}{da} = -\frac{\partial\pi[q(a), R^*(q(a), a), a]}{\partial q}\frac{dq}{da},$$

which means that the first order condition should be satisfied at the true a. The other part of the incentive compatibility constraint (corresponding to condition (a) in Brainard and Martimort) is given by

$$\frac{ds(a)}{da} = \frac{d(\partial s/\partial a)}{da} = \frac{d[-((\partial\pi[q(a), q^*, a])/\partial q)(dq/da)]}{da} \ge 0.$$

Differentiating the first order condition (9.44) with respect to the true demand parameter a yields

$$0 = \frac{\partial^2 \pi}{\partial q^2} \left(\frac{dq}{da}\right)^2 + \frac{\partial^2 \pi}{\partial q \partial a} \frac{dq}{da} + \frac{\partial \pi}{\partial q} \left(\frac{dq}{da}\right)^2 + \frac{\partial^2 \pi}{\partial q \partial q^*} \frac{\partial R^*}{\partial a} \left(\frac{dq}{da}\right)^2$$
$$+ \frac{\partial^2 \pi}{\partial q \partial q^*} \frac{\partial R^*}{\partial a} \frac{\partial q}{\partial a} + \frac{d^2 s}{da^2}.$$

Rearranging terms,

$$-\frac{\partial^2 s}{\partial a^2} = \left[\frac{\partial^2 \pi}{\partial q^2} + \frac{\partial^2 \pi}{\partial q \partial q^*} \frac{\partial R^*(\cdot)}{\partial q}\right] \left(\frac{dq}{da}\right)^2$$
$$+ \frac{\partial \pi}{\partial q} \frac{d^2 q}{da^2} + \left[\frac{\partial^2 \pi}{\partial q \partial a} + \frac{\partial^2 \pi}{\partial q \partial q^*} \frac{\partial R^*(\cdot)}{\partial a}\right] \frac{dq}{da}.$$

Substituting $\partial^2 s / \partial a^2$ into the second order condition evaluated at $\hat{a} = a$ yields

$$0 \geq \frac{\partial \pi}{\partial q^2} \left(\frac{dq}{da}\right)^2 + \frac{\partial \pi}{\partial q} \frac{d^2 q}{d\hat{a}^2} - \left[\frac{\partial^2 \pi}{\partial q^2} + \frac{\partial^2 \pi}{\partial q \partial q^*} \frac{\partial R^*(\cdot)}{\partial q}\right] \left(\frac{dq}{da}\right)^2 - \frac{\partial \pi}{\partial q} \frac{d^2 q}{\partial a^2}$$
$$- \left[\frac{\partial^2 \pi}{\partial q \partial a} + \frac{\partial^2 \pi}{\partial q \partial q^*} \frac{dR^*(\cdot)}{da}\right] \frac{dq}{da},$$

which implies

$$\frac{\partial^2 \pi[q(a), R^*(q(a), a), a]}{\partial q \partial q^*} \frac{\partial R^*(\cdot)}{\partial q} \left(\frac{dq}{da}\right)^2$$
$$+ \left[\frac{\partial^2 \pi[q(a), R^*(q(a), a), a]}{\partial q \partial a} + \frac{\partial^2 \pi[q(a), R^*(q(a), a), a]}{\partial q \partial q^*} \frac{\partial R^*(\cdot)}{\partial a}\right] \frac{dq}{da} \geq 0.$$

From

$$\frac{\partial R^*(q(a), a)}{\partial a} = \frac{\partial R^*(q(a), a)}{\partial q} \frac{dq}{da} + \frac{\partial R^*(q(a), a)}{\partial a},$$

we obtain the form of the incentive compatibility constraint

$$\left[\frac{\partial^2 \pi[q(a), R^*(q(a), a), a]}{\partial q \partial a} + \frac{\partial^2 \pi[q(a), R^*(q(a), a), a]}{\partial q \partial q^*} \frac{\partial R^*(\cdot)}{\partial a}\right] \frac{dq}{da} \geq 0.$$

PART III

INNOVATION, SKILLS, AND
CONTRACTS

10

Innovation, Research, and Learning

What determines the level of technological sophistication and the rate of technological change in an economy? A more advanced technology can be developed by research and development spending and evolve by learning-by-doing productivity gains. Research and development (R&D) refers to investments in the production of new scientific knowledge and knowledge directed towards a practical application or commercial objective. R&D can lead to the production of new and better products and the development of new and improved production processes. Learning-by-doing is new knowledge and improvement of skills acquired through repeated experience in the production process. Technologies developed by others can be transferred by purchase or licensing. They can also generate externalities (spillovers) resulting from the interaction between innovators and noninnovators and from copying and adaptation of existing technologies.

This chapter looks at innovative activity in open economies and the formulation of policies toward trade, R&D, learning-by-doing, and education. Previous discussion examined export markets and rivalry abroad taking firms technologies as given. In this chapter, technologies are made endogenous and the subject shifts to productivity, innovation, and how to promote world class firms. The analysis focuses on three broad categories of innovation. Process innovation refers to productivity improvements leading to cost reductions. Product innovation involves the development of new products. Quality innovation makes possible the production of higher quality products.

In the United States, R&D spending has been about 2–3 percent of GDP since the 1960s. Governments are major investors in innovation. They directly participate in innovative efforts and fund private innovation activities. Direct participation includes research conducted at government research institutions and public universities while funding includes research spending subsidies, low-interest loans, credit guarantees, and others. In 1995, direct funding in the United States, France, Germany, Japan, and the United Kingdom mounted to $70b, $17b, $22b, $27b, and $9b. Government R&D spending represents a substantial fraction of innovating countries' national R&D spending. Its participation accounts for 20 to over 40 percent of total research spending in innovating countries. In the United States, the federal government has consistently accounted for 33–66 percent of total R&D spending.

The proportion of industry's R&D spending funded by the government displays wide variations across countries. Japan's funding of 3 percent of industry R&D spending pales in comparison with a 20 percent funding participation in the United States.

The US government finances a substantial portion of research spending in the defense, aircraft, electronics, and nuclear industries.

R&D policies operate through the demand and the supply side. Direct R&D spending and research subsidies encourage the demand for research. Spending on scientific and engineering education augments the supply of researchers. Romer (2000) points out that if the supply of research is limited on the supply side by scarcity of scientists and engineers research subsidies might be unproductive relative to investments in education and training. Goolsbee (1998) argues that greater R&D subsidies and direct public R&D provision might reward scientists' human capital more than they encourage innovation. He estimates that studies focusing exclusively on total R&D spending overstate the effects of R&D spending by as much as 30–50 percent.

A body of evidence supports the notion that trade, international patenting, and foreign investment results in the international diffusion of technology. In the context of the international competition game, the policy implications are dual in nature. On one hand, research subsidies offset the domestic distortion due to the local externalities generated by research. On the other hand, taxes on research might be justified on the grounds that the international diffusion of technology generates externalities to foreign countries. These different perspectives create a policy dilemma whenever it is difficult to separate domestic and international externalities in practice.

Sections 10.1 and 10.2 examine strategic and corrective R&D policies under conditions of certainty and uncertainty. Sections 10.3–10.5 examine several channels of technology transmission and the formulation of optimal government strategies in the presence of technology externalities and learning-by-doing. Section 10.6 discusses the Airbus vs Boeing saga. Section 10.7 examines the strategic allocation of resources between research and development and its effects on international competition. Section 10.8 discusses the Sematech case.

10.1. INTERNATIONAL R&D RIVALRY

What is the strategic role of research investments in the international competition game? The competitive role of research spending is made clear by focusing on process innovation in a world without externalities. Cost-reducing research spending enhances a firm's competitive position in world markets leading to a larger market share and higher profits (Spencer and Brander, 1983).

Is there a role for the subsidization of cost-reducing research spending? In the two-country case in which one country subsidizes research and the other does not intervene, research subsidization represents an optimal strategy. A domestic firm benefiting from research subsidies is induced to act like a leader in export markets. As a result, it obtains higher profits abroad. However, this type of intervention accentuates an inefficiency. In the absence of research subsidies an oligopolist invests more than the efficient level of R&D spending. Because optimal strategic R&D policies entail subsidizing research, the inefficiently high level of research is exacerbated under intervention. Despite the research inefficiency, unilateral intervention increases the intervening country's welfare in a duopoly third-market setup. Bilateral intervention by two symmetric countries, however, results in losses for both of them. In turn, this prisoner's dilemma situation benefits third-country consumers.

10.1.1. Game Staging and Profit Functions

We consider a three-stage game between two competing firms, located in countries labeled 'domestic' and 'foreign'. Authorities act as credible leaders in the sense that they can credibly commit to R&D subsidies before firms choose their levels of research spending.

At stage 1, each government establishes a subsidy on R&D expenditures. Stages 2 and 3 entail a Cournot–Nash game determining research spending (x, x^*) and final output production (q, q^*). To capture the rent-seeking effects of government R&D policies, assume that output is undertaken only for export purposes. Firms' behavior is modeled as a sequential move game and equilibrium is computed using backward induction. The analysis focuses on equilibria with pure strategies.

A firm's profit function π is given by total revenues pq minus total costs inclusive of research costs, $C = (c - x)q + (x - s)x$, where c is a constant marginal cost and s is the R&D subsidy. Larger research spending x reduces marginal costs $\partial C(q, x)/\partial q = c - x$. In the linear demand case $p = a - q - q^*$, profits are (if both governments subsidize research)

$$\pi(q, q^*, x; s) = (a - q - q^*)q - (c - x)q - (x - s)x,$$
$$\pi^*(q^*, q, x^*; s^*) = (a - q^* - q)q^* - (c - x^*)q^* - (x^* - s^*)x^*. \tag{10.1}$$

10.1.2. Output Decision

At the last stage of the game, firms choose quantities q and q^* to maximize profits for any given technology level (x, x^*). Differentiating (10.1) with respect to q and q^* we obtain the first order necessary conditions, $\partial \pi/\partial q = \partial \pi^*/\partial q^* = 0$, which are also sufficient. Solving the resulting equation system for q and q^*, yields firms' reaction functions

$$q = q^R(q^*) = \frac{a - q^* - (c - x)}{2}, \qquad q^* = q^{*R}(q) = \frac{a - q - (c - x^*)}{2}. \tag{10.2}$$

For any given values of research spending, the reaction functions $q^R(q^*)$ and $q^{*R}(q)$ are downward sloping with respect to the rival's output.

Solving the system of reaction functions (10.2) we obtain outputs as a function of the levels of research

$$q(x, x^*) = \frac{a - c + 2x - x^*}{3}, \qquad q^*(x, x^*) = \frac{a - c + 2x^* - x}{3}. \tag{10.3}$$

Given the rival's research spending, greater R&D spending x reduces variable costs, shifts the firm's reaction function, and increases the volume of final output q. The firm's market share unambiguously increases because the rival's output declines.

10.1.3. Overinvestment in Research

At the second stage of the game, firms choose the level of research. Substituting (10.3) into (10.1), profits become a function of research spending and the research subsidy, $\pi(q(x, x^*), q^*(x, x^*), x; s) = \pi(x, x^*; s)$

$$\pi(x, x^*; s) = R(q(x, x^*), q^*(x, x^*)) - (c - x)q(x, x^*) - (x - s)x,$$

where $R = pq$ denotes revenues. A similar formula applies for the foreign firm.

Totally differentiating the function profit $\pi(\cdot)$ yields

$$\frac{d\pi(x, x^*; s)}{dx} = \frac{\partial R}{\partial q}\frac{dq}{dx} + \frac{\partial R}{\partial q^*}\frac{dq^*}{dx} + q - (c - x)\frac{dq}{dx} - (2x - s)$$

$$= \frac{\partial R}{\partial q^*}\frac{dq^*}{dx} + q - (2x - s) = 0, \tag{10.4}$$

where the last step uses the output first order condition $\partial\pi/\partial q = \partial R/\partial q - \partial C/\partial q = \partial R/\partial q - (c - x) = 0$. By the same token

$$\frac{d\pi^*(x^*, x; s^*)}{dx^*} = \frac{\partial R^*}{\partial q}\frac{dq}{dx^*} + q^* - (2x^* - s^*) = 0. \tag{10.5}$$

It is easy to show that noncooperative firms overinvest in R&D relative to the competitive solution for any given level of subsidies. A competitive firm faces given prices and research spending does not affect revenues. Therefore, profit maximization entails minimizing total costs $C = (c - x)q + (x - s)x$ with respect to the level of R&D spending

$$\frac{\partial C}{\partial x} = -q + 2x - s = 0, \qquad \frac{\partial C^*}{\partial x^*} = -q^* + 2x^* - s^* = 0.$$

Total costs are convex with respect to x, $\partial^2 TC/\partial x^2 = 2 > 0$, so that the $C(x)$ function is U-shaped.

By contrast, the Nash equilibrium solution fails to minimize total costs and involves overinvestment in research. To see why, assume that commodities are substitutes, $\partial R/\partial q^* = \partial[p(q + q^*)q]/\partial q^* < 0$ and $\partial R^*/\partial q = \partial[p(q + q^*)q^*]/\partial q < 0$. Moreover, (10.3) implies that $dq/dx^* < 0$ and $dq^*/dx < 0$. Therefore, the impact of additional research on total costs is positive in a Nash equilibrium

$$\frac{\partial C(q, x; s)}{\partial x} = -q + 2x - s = \frac{\partial R}{\partial q^*}\frac{dq^*}{dx} > 0,$$

$$\frac{\partial C^*(q^*, x^*; s^*)}{\partial x^*} = -q^* + 2x^* - s^* = \frac{\partial R^*}{\partial q}\frac{dq}{dx^*} > 0.$$

Recall that total cost is a convex function of research. Therefore, a positive marginal cost with respect to research implies that research spending is greater than the minimizing level of spending.

In the noncooperative duopoly equilibrium, research spending is excessive. Total costs inclusive of research are higher than the efficient level for any given level of output. This feature derives from the drive to reduce costs in order to increase market share. Overspending relative to the competitive solution takes place under free trade ($s = s^* = 0$), unilateral intervention and bilateral intervention.

10.1.4. Strategic R&D Subsidization

The optimal strategic R&D spending as a function of R&D subsidies is (see appendix)

$$x(s, s^*) = \frac{4(a - c) + 15s - 6s^*}{14}, \qquad x^*(s, s^*) = \frac{4(a - c) - 6s + 15s^*}{14}.$$

Notice that a domestic R&D subsidy leads to higher domestic research expenditure x and induces lower foreign research investment x^*.

Each government chooses the R&D subsidy rate by maximizing after-subsidy firm profits minus government subsidy costs (i.e. firm gross profits net of government subsidy costs)

$$W(s, s^*) = \pi(x(s, s^*), x^*(s, s^*), s) - sx(s, s^*),$$
$$W^*(s, s^*) = \pi^*(x(s, s^*), x^*(s, s^*), s^*) - s^* x^*(s, s^*),$$

where (s, s^*) denote subsidies per unit of research expenditures.

Under unilateral intervention by the domestic country ($s^* = 0$), the first order condition $\partial W(s, s^* = 0)/\partial s = 0$ yields a positive optimal strategic subsidy s^U

$$s^U = \frac{4(a - c)}{27} > 0.$$

The equilibrium unilateral R&D subsidy can be shown to induce domestic firms to achieve the Stackelberg leader equilibrium.

Under bilateral intervention, $s > 0$ and $s^* > 0$, the equilibrium subsidy level is strictly positive and smaller than the unilateral subsidy s^U

$$s^{Bil} = s^{*Bil} = \frac{4(a - c)}{33} < \frac{4(a - c)}{27} = s^U.$$

Substituting these bilateral subsidies and the implied research and output quantities into the government welfare functions shows that noncooperative subsidy policies make both countries worse off. In other words, intervening governments fall into a prisoner's dilemma outcome. The importing country (i.e. the third country) is better off since subsidies induce higher production levels and lower prices.

Let us compare the Nash equilibrium level of research spending under intervention with the level of research spending under a competitive equilibrium with no research subsidies. The competitive equilibrium is an appropriate benchmark because it identifies the world social optimum in a setting with neither learning-by-doing effects nor technological spillovers. From the previous discussion, recall that in the absence of subsidies ($s = s^* = 0$), firms strategically invest more than the efficient (i.e. first-best) level of R&D spending. Because noncooperative unilateral and bilateral R&D policies entail subsidizing research, the spending inefficiency is exacerbated under intervention. In their drive for increasing market share, governments grant positive subsidies even though these accentuate the inefficiency of research spending.

10.2. STRATEGIC AND CORRECTIVE R&D POLICIES

The previous section presented a model in which, in the absence of government intervention, firms interacting noncooperatively invest excessively in research compared with the competitive equilibrium. Unilateral and bilateral intervention lead to positive subsidies. Strategic R&D subsidization reinforces firms' excessive research spending.

The result that governments engage in strategic subsidization was derived in a framework in which (1) governments abstain from subsidizing exports and choose R&D subsidies as an alternative mechanism to support domestic firms competing in third markets, (2) the outcome of the game is certain, (3) there are no externalities from research, and (4) firms and governments interact sequentially but there are no explicit dynamics and thus no consideration is given to dynamic issues involving learning-by-doing, infant industries, and technological leadership. The ensuing discussion successively relaxes these assumptions.

What is the best strategic trade and research policy package aiming to enhance the domestic firm's position in a third market? When research and export policies are used simultaneously and there is perfect information, the optimal strategic export subsidy is positive but the optimal strategic R&D subsidy turns out to be negative. By taxing R&D spending, the welfare maximizing level of production can be achieved (Spencer and Brander, 1983) because taxation offsets R&D overinvestment.

10.2.1. *Uncertainty and Stochastic Dominance*

How does the presence of uncertainty affect the formulation of strategic research policies? This section focuses on strategic and corrective research policies when there is uncertainty about research outcomes. When the cost-reduction effects of different levels of R&D spending are uncertain, the impact of R&D spending is found by comparing the distributions of cost outcomes. This comparison requires setting a criterion establishing whether a cost distribution is in some sense 'better' than another.

Cumulative distribution functions can be compared by using the first-order stochastic dominance criterion. Consider cost distribution functions $F(c)$ and $G(c)$, where c represents production costs and F is associated with a higher level of research than G. A cumulative cost distribution $F(c)$ first order stochastically dominates $G(c)$ if, for any nonincreasing profit function $\pi(c)$, distribution F yields higher profits than

G on average

$$E[\pi(F)] = \int \pi(c)\,dF(c) \geq E[\pi(G)] = \int \pi(c)\,dG(c).$$

First order stochastic dominance can also be defined using the equivalent condition that F places the bulk of its probability mass at a lower cost than G. Formally, a distribution of costs F can be said to first-order stochastically dominate distribution G if F places the bulk of its probability mass at a lower cost than G. In other words, $F(c)$ shifts the density of costs toward lower costs relative to cost distribution $G(c)$

$$F(c) \geq G(c) \quad \forall c.$$

It is easy to see that both first order stochastic dominance definitions are equivalent. Let us show that $G(c) \leq F(c)$ implies the first order stochastic dominance criterion $E[\pi(F)] \geq E[\pi(G)]$ for every nonincreasing function $\pi : R \to R$. Formally,

$$
\begin{aligned}
E[\pi(F)] - E[\pi(G)] &= \int \pi(c)\,dF(c) - \int \pi(c)\,dG(c) \\
&= \pi(c)F(c)|_0^\infty - \int \pi'(c)F(c)\,dc - \pi(c)G(c)|_0^\infty \\
&\quad + \int \pi'(c)G(c)\,dc \\
&= \int \pi'(c)(G(c) - F(c)) \geq 0,
\end{aligned}
$$

where the second equality uses integration by parts, $F(0) = G(0) = 0$, $F(\infty) = G(\infty) = 1$, $G(c) \leq F(c)$ due to the first order stochastic dominance condition, and $\pi'(c) \leq 0$ (profits are assumed to be differentiable). It can also be shown that $E[\pi(F)] \geq E[\pi(G)]$ implies $G(c) \leq F(c)$ so that the first order stochastic dominance conditions are equivalent.

10.2.2. Strategic Research Policy under Uncertainty

Bagwell and Staiger (1994) develop a stochastic version of the Spencer and Brander (1983) R&D model that captures the inherent uncertainty and risk properties characterizing research investments. Let us now focus on how the cost distribution function changes when research is changed by small amounts. To formalize this exercise, we consider the conditional distribution function $F(c; x)$ as a function of the level of research spending and assume that the first derivative $\partial F(c; x)/\partial x$ is well defined. Hadar and Russell (1969) show that the first order stochastic dominance criterion can be expressed as

$$0 < \frac{\partial F(c; x)}{\partial x}.$$

This equation tells us that an infinitesimal increase in the level of research shifts the cost density function $f(c; x) = \partial F(c; x)/\partial c$ toward lower costs. R&D spending can be said to result in unambiguously lower costs if the new firm's cost distribution function lies below the old cost distribution function. Then, expected profits $\pi(c; x)$ are greater under distribution $F(c; x_1)$ than under distribution $F(c; x_0)$, $x_0 < x_1$, precisely because greater research shifts the density toward lower costs.

Consider a domestic and a foreign monopolist that compete in a third market. Trade taxes and subsidies are forbidden, say, by international agreements. The analysis focuses on R&D policies and firms are assumed to compete in quantities.

Both countries' governments choose the R&D subsidy rate that maximize expected firm after-subsidy profits π minus government subsidy costs (firms expected gross profits minus government subsidy costs)

$$EW(s, s^*) = E[\pi(x(s, s^*), x^*(s, s^*), s)] - sx(s, s^*)$$

$$= E\left[\pi(x(r^P, r^{*P}), x^*(r^P, r^{*P}), r^P)\right] - (r^S - r^P)x(r^P, r^{*P}), \quad (10.6)$$

where $(s, s^*) = (r^S - r^P, r^{*S} - r^{*P})$ denote subsidies per unit of research expenditures, r^S is the deterministic social cost of research (assumed to be constant) and $r^P = r^S - s$ is the deterministic private cost of investment net of subsidies. Similar equations apply to the foreign country.

Suppose that research lowers the firm's mean cost distribution in a first order stochastic shift manner (first order stochastic shift). The optimal bilateral research policy for the domestic country is given by (see appendix)

$$s^{Bil} = r^S - r^P = -\frac{\partial E\pi}{\partial x^*} \frac{\partial^2 E\pi^*}{\partial x \partial x^*} \bigg/ \frac{\partial^2 E\pi^*}{\partial x^{*2}},$$

where the second order conditions imply that $\partial^2 E\pi^*/\partial x^{*2} < 0$.

If the numerator $[\partial E\pi/\partial x^*][\partial^2 E\pi^*/(\partial x \partial x^*)]$ has a positive (negative) sign, the best noncooperative policy is to subsidize (tax) research. Therefore, research is subsidized whenever both factors have the same sign. For instance, if foreign research reduces expected foreign costs and expected domestic profits decline when foreign costs fall, greater foreign research reduces expected domestic profits, that is, $\partial E\pi/\partial x^* < 0$. If in addition $\partial^2 E\pi^*/(\partial x \partial x^*) = \partial[\partial E\pi^*/\partial x]/\partial x^* < 0$, the best strategic research policy entails subsidization. This additional condition will hold whenever a reduction in expected foreign costs due to higher foreign research lowers the gain in expected foreign profits that would result from a reduction in domestic costs due to higher domestic research. Notice that if $\partial^2 E\pi^*/(\partial x \partial x^*) > 0$, then the best strategy is to tax research.

The formulation of strategic research policies changes when domestic markets are oligopolistic and some domestic firms are not exporters. The reason is that an R&D subsidy to domestic exporters may introduce distortions affecting nonexporting domestic firms (this is due to the first order stochastic shift assumption).

In the presence of domestic distortions, the optimal strategic policy is shown to depend on whether or not the gains created by granting R&D subsidies to domestic exporters offset the distortions created in the domestic market to producers not involved in foreign markets. If the distortions exceed the benefits obtained by subsidizing the research undertaken by domestic exporters, the best strategy is to establish corrective domestic taxes to R&D expenditures. On the contrary, if the benefits from greater competitiveness exceed distortion costs, the best strategy is to grant subsidies to R&D.

10.2.3. Joint Corrective Policies

If bilateral research subsidization entails excessive or deficient R&D spending relative to the socially optimal level, there is room for R&D policies directed to offset the research spending distortion. The corrective policy would maximize the joint domestic and foreign welfare. Notice that these corrective policies are defined from a joint country (i.e. world) welfare point of view rather than from a national perspective (as in the previous section).

Given symmetric countries, joint welfare maximization entails setting a single corrective subsidy or tax s^C that applies to both countries. The corrective private cost of research, $r^{PC} = r^S - s^C$, is the unit cost based on the corrective subsidy s^C that maximizes joint welfare. The constant and exogenously given social cost r^S corresponds to the private cost before the receipt of the subsidies.

Formally, the corrective subsidy maximizes joint expected welfare $EW + EW^*$

$$\max_{r^P} EW(r^P, r^{*P}) + EW^*(r^P, r^{*P}).$$

Total differentiation of (10.6) yields

$$\frac{\partial E\pi(x, x^*)}{\partial x} \frac{\partial x}{\partial r^P} + \frac{\partial E\pi(x, x^*)}{\partial x^*} \frac{\partial x^*}{\partial r^P} - (r^S - r^P) \frac{\partial x}{\partial r^P}$$
$$= \left(\frac{\partial E\pi(x(r^P, r^{*P}), x^*(r^P, r^{*P}), r^P)}{\partial x^*} - s \right) \frac{\partial x(r^P, r^{*P})}{\partial r^P} = 0,$$

where we use $\partial E\pi(x, x^*)/\partial x = 0$, $\partial x(r^P, r^{*P})/\partial r^P = \partial x^*(r^P, r^{*P})/\partial r^P$ by symmetry and $r^S - r^P = s$.

The maximization yields the solution for the corrective subsidy $s^C = r^S - r^{PC}$. The sign of the corrective policy depends on the effect of foreign research spending on expected profits and could be positive or negative

$$s^C = r^S - r^{PC} = \frac{\partial E\pi(x(r^{PC}, r^{*PC}), x^*(r^{PC}, r^{*PC}), r^{PC})/\partial x^*}{\partial x(r^{PC}, r^{*PC})/\partial r^{PC}}.$$

10.3. R&D POLICIES WHEN THERE ARE SPILLOVERS

The output of R&D is characterized by its public good nature. This feature implies that benefits are not fully appropriable by the investor. R&D activities generate domestic (i.e. local) and international (i.e. foreign) positive externalities (i.e. spillovers) because competitors benefit from R&D efforts even if they do not pay for the attached costs. Domestic spillovers are externalities between two different entities (i.e. firms) operating in the same country. International spillovers are technological externalities arising when two entities are located in different countries. These spillovers are generated by competitors who involuntarily afford rivals the opportunity to acquire technologies at less than the cost of creation.

How are externalities transmitted across economic agents? A remarkable web of channels for technology transmission develops in agglomerated technology-creating regions. For instance, the Silicon Valley region in California is characterized by a substantial degree of mobility of skilled labor between firms in related industries clustered in the same area. The mobility of skilled labor facilitates the spillover of knowledge across firms. Another common mechanism generating externalities is the copying and imitation of products designed by rival firms. In many cases, the externalities are transmitted through exchange and cooperation between firms. These free-rider type effects are also known in the literature as 'Silicon Valley' effects.

Economic incentives do not generally lead firms to undertake the first-best level of R&D spending. An objective justifying government intervention in research activities is to establish efficiency. Because some motives for intervention call for R&D subsidies and others for R&D taxes, it is not possible to formulate general rules applying to all industries and circumstances.

10.3.1. Domestic Spillovers

Which criteria serve to determine whether R&D should or should not be subsidized in particular industries? The answer to this question hinges on the mechanisms for technology creation and transmission. Spence (1984) considered investments in process innovation that decrease firms' costs. He showed that, when a firm's R&D generates positive spillover effects on other domestic firms, the private incentives to invest in R&D are reduced.

Consider R&D leading to process innovation generating domestic technological spillovers and lowering rival firms' average costs. Domestic cost-reducing spillovers allow rivals to reduce costs without having to afford the full cost of technology development. Formally, the cost function $C(\cdot)$ of a firm benefiting from cost-reducing technology spillovers can be represented as follows

$$C(q, x, x^*) = (A - x - \beta x^*)q + \Psi(x),$$

where q and x denote production and research spending. This cost function embodies the idea that a producer benefits from the rival's R&D x^* spending even if it does not pay for it. The coefficient $\beta > 0$ denotes the domestic spillover coefficient, and $\Psi(x)$ is the cost of conducting research. Typically, the literature utilizes the quadratic function $\Psi(x) = \gamma x^2$ to represent increasing costs of research.

In the absence of intraindustry spillovers across countries, policy must balance two opposing forces affecting an exporting industry. R&D should be

(1) subsidized to compensate domestic firms for the domestic externalities they generate (Pigouvian motive for subsidization);
(2) taxed to correct for the overinvestment in R&D that takes place when intraindustry spillovers do not have an international dimension. This refers to the overinvestment tax to correct the strategic research distortion examined by Spencer and Brander.

The optimal research strategy varies according to the policy instrument available. If output subsidies are not available—because they are forbidden by the World Trade Organization (WTO)—then R&D subsidies—which are allowed by the WTO—can be used to induce rent shifting (the second-best profit shifting motive).

Subsidization of research can be avoided if firms cooperate in their research endeavors. D'Aspremont and Jacquemin (1988) compare R&D cooperation and non-cooperation among duopoly firms, showing that cooperation can internalize the research spillover externality. If firm cooperation is not legally allowed, or cannot be sustained because firms have incentives to free ride on rivals' research spending, R&D subsidies can be rationalized as an alternative mechanism to correct the distortions due to the presence of positive externalities.

Leahy and Neary (1997) consider a three stage game in which the government plays first and is able to commit to the chosen policy. In the first stage, the government simultaneously chooses R&D and output subsidies. Firms invest in R&D in the second stage and decide their production levels in the third stage. R&D subsidies are justified when (1) spillovers are high enough, and (2) firms' actions are strategic complements.

10.3.2. International Spillovers

International spillovers work as an externality generated by foreign rivals or to foreign rivals. The research activities of a country's firm contribute to reduce a foreign rival's production costs but the rival is saved from having to pay for the true costs of the innovation.

What is the optimal research policy in the presence of international externalities that diffuse technology gains across borders? Leahy and Neary (1997, 1999a,b) have shown that the appropriate policy responses to foreign externalities are quite different from the responses to domestic externalities.

In the presence of international externalities, R&D should be

(1) taxed to reduce the positive effect on foreign production caused by the international externalities and induce rent-shifting toward domestic firms (international externalities rent-shifting tax motive);
(2) subsidized to correct for the underinvestment that takes place when there are international intraindustry spillovers benefiting foreign firms;

(3) subsidized if the externalities conferred abroad increase foreign R&D and the benefits of it spill back into the domestic country (spillback motive for subsidization).

When there are international externalities, foreign countries can free ride on the rival's investment without having to afford the associated R&D costs. The externalities conferred to foreign countries reduce the incentives to invest in R&D in a noncooperative equilibrium. From a global perspective, however, the positive externalities from R&D mean that benefits are greater at the global than at the domestic level. This feature implies that there are greater global than local incentives to invest in R&D. In a cooperative equilibrium, R&D subsidies reemerge.

10.4. DIFFUSION OF KNOWLEDGE: THE EVIDENCE

Are there international spillovers? How important are they relative to domestic spillovers? There are several channels accounting for the diffusion of technology across borders. These include international trade, foreign investment, patenting, and international spillovers such as when a local firm reverse engineers a foreign product and copies it. A growing body of work examines the empirical importance of these channels but their relative role and the importance of international spillovers remains an open question.

10.4.1. Technology Spillovers Through Trade

The importance of trade as a channel for the transmission of knowledge among developed countries has been examined by Coe and Helpman (1995). They quantify the estimated average long run rate of return on research and development to be 120 percent for the G-7 countries, which accounted for over 90 percent of total R&D spending in OECD countries in 1991. An additional 30 percent accrued to the other fifteen countries in the sample of twenty-one OECD countries plus Israel.

R&D spillover regressions relate total factor productivity in country i at time t (TFP_{it}) to the domestic and foreign stocks of R&D capital, S_{it}^d and S_{it}^f. Estimated slopes are positive except α_{i2} (G7 is a dummy for G7 countries)

$$\log TFP_{it} = \alpha_{i0} + \alpha_{i1} \log S_{it}^d + \alpha_{i2} \log S_{it}^f + \alpha_{i3} m_{it} \log S_{it}^f \alpha_{i4} G7 \log S_{it}^d + \epsilon_{it},$$

where ϵ_{it} is the error term and there are specifications with and without the interaction between foreign R&D and the import propensity m_{it}. The foreign R&D stock is defined as a weighted average of the trading partners' domestic R&D stocks. Coe and Helpman utilize R&D capital stock indexes with $1985 = 1$ and use the bilateral import shares as weights. Lichtenberg and van Pottelsberghe de la Potterie (1998) point out that the use of capital stock indexes with S_{i1985} 1, so that $S^f_{i1985} = 0$, creates a difficulty for equations that include an interaction effect. This procedure implies that the estimated elasticity of total factor productivity with respect to the import share might be equal to zero.

The previous work on R&D spillovers was extended in Coe *et al.* (1997), who measure the value of R&D spillovers disseminated through trade from twenty-two developed to seventy-seven developing countries, defined as countries with a low measured stock of R&D capital between 1971 and 1990. They estimated the total impact of research spillovers from developed to developing countries in 1991 to represent the equivalent of about 44 percent of official development aid via multilateral and bilateral agreements.

Keller (1998) questions the previous results using 2-digit industry data from eight countries. He conducts a Monte Carlo study that uses random bilateral import shares rather than actual import shares. He finds that in most cases the regressions with random bilateral weights often explain a greater fraction of the variance than the regressions using the true bilateral import shares. He concludes that the random weight model performs as well or better than Coe and Helpman (1995), which shades doubts over the said results. The explanation of Keller results offered by Coe and Hoffmaister (1999) is that the way the random samples of bilateral import shares are constructed leads to a concentration of import shares around the equal share case. This procedure corresponds to a regression in which foreign R&D capital is defined as the equally weighted trading partner R&D capital stocks. Bayoumi *et al.* (1999) estimate a fully specified endogenous multi-country growth model and examine the growth-promoting role of R&D spending, international R&D spillovers, and trade. They conclude that R&D linkages and trade are important growth promoting factors.

Is there evidence of asymmetric spillovers? Bernstein and Mohnen (1998) rely on United States and Japan's stock of R&D capital to assess the magnitude and impact of international spillovers between the United States and Japan on their total factor productivity growth and variable factor intensity levels. The authors cannot reject the hypothesis that there are no spillovers from Japan to the United States but they do reject the hypothesis of no spillovers from the United States to Japan. The US factor intensities and productivity growth are not significantly affected by Japanese R&D spending but Japanese factor intensities and productivity growth do benefit from US R&D spending. US spillovers explain 46 per cent of Japanese productivity growth. The analysis also examines the long run and short run effects resulting from international spillovers. In the short run, they find that greater US R&D capital induces higher R&D intensity levels and lower labor intensity in Japan. In the long run, the decline of Japanese labor intensity intensifies.

The controversy on the relative importance of intranational and international knowledge spillovers is fueled by the results of Branstetter (2001), who finds that spillovers are primarily intranational in scope. He focuses on the extent to which knowledge that diffuses abroad generates further innovation abroad. The sample consists of firm level data on publicly traded United States and Japanese firms for 1983–89 rather than industry data as used in previous studies. Japan and the United States are chosen as they are the major innovators and account for more than 60 percent of the world's scientists and engineers. Patents per firm are related to the log of the firm's own R&D, the logs of domestic and foreign spillovers, and dummy variables for the five industries in the sample. The coefficient of the domestic spillover variable is positive and significant but the foreign spillover variable has the wrong sign (it is negative). These results can be due to a high correlation between domestic and foreign spillovers, which generates unstable coefficients that can have the wrong sign. The paper finds no evidence of positive international spillovers (see also Keller (2002)).

10.4.2. Spillovers from FDI

Theoretical considerations suggest that there are several mechanisms though which Foreign Direct Investment (FDI) can result in technology transfers. Outsourcing, mergers and acquisitions, licensing, training, and stronger intellectual property rights can result in greater technological transfer.

Pack and Saggi (2001) develop a model in which international outsourcing leads to transfer of technology independently of whether firms compete in quantities or prices. For instance, Radio Shack and Texas instruments commission developing country firms to produce components and products that are sold in oligopolistic world markets using the retailer's name. Fosfuri *et al.* (2001) examine how FDI can transfer technology by training local workers that later move to work in another local firm. Oliva and Rivera-Batiz (2002*b*) present a model in which simultaneous cross-borders merger and acquisitions (M&A) generate cost-reducing synergies but push output levels toward the competitive solution, which in turn reduces merging firms' profits. In other words, simultaneous M&As in a given industry generate a prisoners' dilemma situation that lowers profits for all merging firms. This process offers a rationale for the so-called synergy trap in which firms lose from presumably synergistic M&As.

The role of intellectual property rights in encouraging or discouraging technology transfer has been a most controversial issue. Maskus (2000) offers a detailed treatment of the theory and evidence on the role of intellectual property rights.

Yang and Maskus (2001) reexamine the controversy over whether intellectual property rights (IPRs) encourage developed countries to innovate and stimulate developing countries to gain access to these innovations. They develop a product cycle model in which stronger IPRs reduce the cost of licensing contracts and increase the licensor's share of rents. As a result, additional resources are available for R&D encouraging innovation and technology transfer.

Do inward and outward FDI actually contribute to technology transfer? The survey by Blömstrom and Kokko (1998) reviews a wide array of evidence suggesting that FDI generates spillover effects. Lichtenberg and van Pottelsberghe de la Potterie (1998) extend Coe and Helpman's work to examine whether inward and outward foreign investment as well as trade flows are sources of technology transmission. They use the same data set as Coe and Helpman (1995) but a different functional formula to compute the relation between foreign R&D spending and productivity increases through imports. R&D capital stocks are not converted into indexes. The evidence supports the widely spread idea that foreign investment is associated with sourcing. The authors confirm the hypothesis that technology transfer is enhanced by trade flows and technology sourcing associated with multinationals' activities abroad. They reject the hypothesis that inward foreign investment is a major mechanism of technology transmission to the host economies.

The development of specialized technology suppliers in leading innovating countries has international spillovers benefiting developing countries. A greater number of leading country technology suppliers improve the access to technology and lowers the investment costs of users of technology in developing countries. Arora *et al.* (2001) develop a model in which specialized engineering firms in the input-producing upstream sector engage in technology development and design. Technology development is modeled as a fixed cost activity. The exogenously given number of technology suppliers in leading countries sell technologies to users in developing countries' downstream sector. The key idea is that greater technological development in one market generates technological benefits in other markets. The model predicts that a higher (exogenously given) number of developed countries' technology suppliers will be associated with (1) greater chemical plant investment in developing countries, (2) a greater number of developing country plants acquiring engineering services from developed countries, and (3) a smaller number of developing country plants featuring in-house engineering services.

In the chemical industry, upstream firms specialize in the design and engineering of chemical process sold to downstream chemical producers. Historically, the growth of the innovating countries' chemical industries gave rise to an upstream sector that created new technologies. This upstream sector generated international spillovers and stimulated the growth of developing countries' chemical industries.

The empirical analysis utilizes a sample of thirty-eight developing countries and 136 chemical process technologies to test for international technological spillovers affecting a set of more than 20,000 plants. The sample covers all investments in chemical plants in developed countries during the 1980s. The evidence of developing countries' chemical industry suggests that the greater the number of technology suppliers in leading countries (1) the more attractive the terms at which technology was supplied to developing countries, and (2) the more likely buyers in the downstream sector were to invest in chemical plants in developing countries.

10.4.3. Patenting, International Diffusion of Ideas, and Productivity

International patenting plays a key role in technology creation and diffusion. Any given invention can be patented in several countries. However, the cost of patenting usually limits the number of applications to a small set of countries or to the home country. In each country where an invention is patented, the inventor is protected from imitators producing or selling in that country.

Where does technological change originate and how does it spread across countries? Eaton and Kortum (1996) estimate regression equations explaining OECD countries' inventive output as a function of various variables including a specification for technology diffusion probabilities. Research output is measured by data on patents, which offer indirect evidence on research output. Japanese patent applications (about 300,000 per year) have been estimated to include less inventive claims than Japanese patents granted to foreigners. The number of patents is adjusted so that 4.9 Japanese domestic patent applications correspond to one patent application in other countries.

Let us define P_{ni} as one plus the number of patent applications from source country i for protection in destination country n. The logarithm $\ln P_{ni}/L_{ni}$ of patenting in country n, expressed per worker in source country i, is

$$\ln \frac{P_{ni}}{L_{ni}} = \ln \alpha + \ln \epsilon_{ni} + \beta \ln \frac{R_i}{L_i} - \psi_{ni} \frac{c_{ni}}{Y_n} + \omega^* \ln \frac{y_i}{y_n} + u_{ni},$$

where u_{ni} is the error in the patenting decision and the coefficients have an elasticity interpretation. Actual applications plus one is used to avoid the possibility that the logarithm is minus infinity when patents are zero. Patenting is regressed against the following variables affecting technology creation, the returns from patenting and diffusion. First, the logarithm of the probability of technology diffusion from country i to county n, $\ln \epsilon_{ni}$. Second, inventive inputs and the location of inventive activity as measured by the number of business researchers and engineers per worker in the source country, R_i/L_i. Third, the cost of applying for a patent in relation to output, c_{ni}/Y_n. Fourth, the productivity (GDP per worker) of the source country relative to the destination country, y_i/y_n, indicating the source country ability to use technology.

Technology diffusion from country i to country n is defined as the probability that an invention in country i is adopted in country n. A technology diffusion equation is formulated in terms of the logarithm of the probability of technology diffusion from i to n

$$\ln \epsilon_{ni} = \epsilon_{HOM} DH_{ni} + \epsilon_{KM} KM_{ni} + \epsilon_{KM^2} KM_{ni}^2 - \epsilon_{HK} \frac{1}{HK_n} + \epsilon_{IMP} \ln IM_{ni}.$$

As the probability of diffusion ϵ_{ni} approaches zero (or one), its logarithm $\ln \epsilon_{ni}$ approaches minus infinity (or zero). The dummy variable DH_{ni}, $DH_{ni} = 1$ if country $n = i$ but 0 otherwise, allows technology to flow more freely within than across countries. KM_{ni} stands for the distance between n and i and KM_{ni}^2 is the squared distance term. The distance variable reflects geographical impediments to the free flow of ideas. HK_n denotes human capital measured in terms of number of schooling years in country n. If human capital captures the ability to absorb new technologies, a higher level of human capital augments technology diffusion (as HK_n increases, $\ln \epsilon_{ni}$ also increases). IM_{ni} measures the imports of country n from country i relative to country n's GDP. If imported goods are a vehicle for the diffusion of technology, this variable will be positively related to the probability of diffusion. This variable is arbitrarily normalized to one for home countries ($n = i$).

The equation specifying technology diffusion is substituted into the logarithmic patent equation, which is estimated as a single equation by least squares. Depending on the estimation technique, the elasticity of idea production (as measured by patenting) with respect to research employment per worker is found to be 0.9 and 0.6. Greater source country productivity relative to destination country productivity has a positive effect on patenting.

The coefficient ψ_{ni} is defined as a function of dummy variables indicating (1) whether or not the destination country provides high intellectual protection and (2) imitation hazards captured by the interaction effect between the dummy indicating whether or not intellectual protection is high and a dummy variable indicating whether or not $n = i$. Countries offering stronger patent protection are found to be more attractive destination for foreign patents.

What determines diffusion of ideas? Diffusion is found to be stronger domestically than internationally. Greater human capital is estimated to enhance the spread of ideas, distance inhibits it and imports are not related to it.

How well do countries exploit their own and other countries' inventions? Eaton and Kortum's model implies that all countries eventually grow at the same rate. The impact of the spread of ideas is reflected in relative levels of country productivities rather than growth rates. In other words, the model implies that countries' possessing greater abilities to use new inventions display greater productivity levels. The ability to exploit inventions can be examined by estimating the patent equation jointly with an equation explaining productivity levels relative to US productivity. A country's productivity level $y_n^* = y_n e^v$ refers to real GDP per worker and is measured with a multiplicative error indicated by random variable v. Estimated relative productivity levels vary from 0.46 for Greece to 0.94 for Canada (US $\equiv 1$).

Which countries represent the major sources of productivity growth? Productivity growth in destination country n can be decomposed into technological change deriving from ideas generated in source countries $i \in \{1, \dots, N\}$. Defining A_i is an index of aggregate technology in country i, we can pose the following relation of productivity growth in country n as a function of the level of technology around the world relative to country n technology level A_n

$$g_n = \frac{1}{\mathcal{J}\theta} \sum_{i=1}^{N} \epsilon_{ni}\alpha_i \left(\frac{A_i}{A_n}\right)^\omega = \sum_{i=1}^{N} g_{ni} \to \widehat{g}_{ni} = \frac{\widehat{\epsilon}_{ni}\widehat{\alpha}_i}{\widehat{\theta}_{ni}\widehat{\mathcal{J}}}.$$

The size of an invention adopted by destination country n from source country i is drawn from exponential distribution $\theta_{ni} = \theta(A_i/A_n)^{-\omega}$, $\omega > 0$. $\mathcal{J}$ is a productivity parameter, α_i denotes the flow of inventions from source country i and ϵ_{ni} is the probability of diffusion from i to n.

The variable g_{ni} refers to productivity growth in country n deriving from ideas generated in i. Except for the United States, over 50 percent of productivity growth in the sample countries is estimated to derive from ideas originating abroad. The figure rises to over 90 percent for all OECD countries except the United States, Japan, Germany, France, and the United Kingdom.

Eaton and Kortum (1999) develop and estimate a model that endogenizes research effort. R&D spending is a measure of the input to the inventive process that is often used an indicator of research output. The relative productivity of researchers is assumed to be proportional to the country's technology level relative to world average technology. The hypothesis that there is substantial but not perfect international sharing of ideas is confirmed in a sample consisting of the five innovating economies: France, Germany, Japan, United Kingdom, and United States. These countries lie about two thirds of the way from autarky in ideas to free trade in ideas, in the sense that R&D performed abroad is about two thirds as effective in terms of its contribution to productivity growth as domestic research.

10.5. THE ECONOMICS OF LEARNING-BY-DOING

This section assesses the infant-industry argument in the presence of learning-by-doing. A dynamic setting with learning-by-doing economies is used to (1) examine the impact of costly public funds on the design of an strategic export policy, and (2) characterize the cost-type of firms to whom strategic policies should be addressed.

10.5.1. The Infant-Industry Argument

The traditional infant-industry argument prescribes the subsidization of currently less efficient firms that are expected to improve in the future. The idea behind infant industry protection is that less efficient firms engaged in a cost-reducing learning-by-doing process should be stimulated through subsidies or protected by tariffs. Baldwin (1969), Corden (1997), and others have examined whether dynamic scale economies can justify infant industry protection in nonoligopolistic markets. They find that infant industry protection does not correct the market distortions at their source and conclude that it is best to address distortions at their source than indirectly through trade policies. These arguments match the general theory of distortions. Optimal policies should target the sources of economic distortions rather than trade.

Can the dynamic infant-industry argument prescription be salvaged in a framework with imperfect competition, learning-by-doing distortions, and asymmetric information? The answer to this question is that the benefits of protection as a second-best instrument are ambiguous in sign and that alternative policies addressing the source of the dynamic distortion beat infant industry protection.

When the financing of subsidies generates tax and other distortions, the export subsidy prescription can be invalidated. Also, when the distorting effects of raising public funds are sufficiently large, there is a clear prescription: the more efficient firms should receive larger subsidies than less efficient firms (Neary, 1994). With such strategy, the government optimizes the use of the funds required to subsidize exports in order to shift profits towards the domestic firm and improve domestic welfare. Dinopoulos *et al.* (1995) find, that when authorities face asymmetric information about the firm's cost type, more efficient firms merit larger subsidies. These conclusions contradict the traditional infant-industry argument stating that governments should provide help to the weaker firms in the economy to protect them from foreign competition and permit their development. The prescription to protect or give greater subsidies to more efficient firms can be shown to be robust in the sense that it holds both when firms compete in quantities (competition à la Cournot) and when firms compete in prices (competition à la Bertrand).

10.5.2. *Learning-by-Doing with Cost Asymmetries*

In order to model the process of learning-by-doing, the framework developed in previous chapters is extended to include some dynamics (see Neary, 1994). The most basic intertemporal setting incorporating the dynamic features underlying the notion of learning-by-doing we could think off is a 2-period (i.e. t and $t + 1$) unilateral intervention model with two firms: a domestic and a foreign firm.

The domestic firm is assumed to learn from the past, and apply its new knowledge to reduce costs in future periods (specifically at period $t + 1$). The foreign firm is assumed not to participate in this learning-by-doing process. The domestic firm learning process is given by a cost-reduction function of the quantity produced in the first period

$$c_t = c \quad \text{and} \quad c_{t+1} = c - \lambda q_t,$$

where c_t and c_{t+1} denote marginal costs in periods t and $t + 1$, respectively, $c > 0$ is the constant marginal cost, q_t denotes the volume of output in period t, and $\lambda \in [0, 1]$ is the learning rate.

The 2-period sequential game studied is defined as follows. In period t, the domestic government unilaterally commits to the establishment of a subsidy on a period by period basis (without any precommitments before the period starts). Then, firms choose output levels by maximizing total discounted profits, taking into account the government's action and the intertemporal nature of the production function. Algebraically, the domestic firm problem is

$$\max_{\{q_t, q_{t+1}\}} \pi_t + \rho \pi_{t+1}, \tag{10.7}$$

where $\rho \in (0, 1)$ is the discount factor and subscripts refer to periods t and $t + 1$. In period $t + 1$, agents' strategies are analogous to the ones faced in the previous period, but taking as given the decisions made at t. The model is solved by backward induction. Mathematical derivations are contained in the appendix.

The domestic authority maximizes the discounted domestic social welfare function $W(\cdot)$

$$\max_{\{s_t, s_{t+1}\}} W(\cdot) = W_t + \rho W_{t+1} = (\pi_t - \delta s_t q_t) + \rho(\pi_{t+1} - \delta s_{t+1} q_{t+1}), \tag{10.8}$$

where the coefficient $\delta \equiv 1 + d$ is used to account for the direct subsidy cost plus the distortion coefficient d representing the additional social cost resulting from the financing of the subsidy. The government and the private firm are assumed to have the same discount factor ρ.

10.5.3. Infant-Industry Arguments: Production Patterns and Optimal Subsidy

At period $t + 1$ firms choose the level of output taking q_t as given. Recalling (10.7), computing first order conditions and solving for q_{t+1}, we get the domestic output at period $t + 1$

$$q_{t+1} = \frac{\delta(a + c_{t+1}^* - 2c_{t+1})}{2(3\delta - 2)} = \frac{\delta[a + c^* - 2(c - \lambda q_t)]}{2(3\delta - 2)}, \tag{10.9}$$

where $c_{t+1} = c - \lambda q_t$ and $c_{t+1}^* = c^*$. *Ceteris paribus*, a higher learning economy coefficient λ is associated with lower second period marginal costs c_{t+1} and greater production levels at $t + 1$, $\partial q_{t+1}/\partial \lambda > 0$. Moreover, domestic output declines with domestic firm's marginal costs and with the distortion parameter δ (i.e. $\partial q_{t+1}/\partial \delta = -(a + c - 2c_{t+1})/(3\delta - 2) < 0$).

The best unilateral output subsidy at t is

$$s_t^U = \Lambda(\delta, \lambda, \rho)(a - 2c + c^*) \gtreqless 0,$$

where $\Lambda(\delta, \lambda, \rho)$ is defined in the appendix. The sign of s_t^U depends on the specific parameters of the model and the sign of $\Lambda(\delta, \lambda, \rho)$. If $\Lambda(\delta, \lambda, \rho) > 0$, then the result obtained in previous sections prevails: the more efficient firm should benefit from larger subsidies. Whether or not s_t^U increases with the rate of learning λ is not clear from the model. If there is no discounting (i.e. $\rho = 0$) or there is no learning (i.e. $\lambda = 0$), the subsidy s_t^U coincides with the subsidy derived for the static model discussed in the chapter devoted to Brander and Spencer's profit shifting motive.

10.6. AIRBUS vs BOEING

The aircraft industry has been the arena of one of the major rivalries for supremacy. The industry is characterized by the following:

1 Oligopolistic market structure, essentially a duopoly.
2 The presence of large economies of scale and large learning by doing effects. Benkard (2000) finds that doubling cumulative output reduces labor requirements by 35–40 percent or more. For instance, the first L-1011 jet Lockheed produced required 1.5 million man-hours to build. By contrast, the 100th plane produced four years later required only 220,000 man-hours. This dramatic reduction in man-hours represents savings of 85 percent and reflects strong learning-by-doing effects. There are thus incentives to induce cost-reduction by subsidizing production.
3 Organizational forgetting. Benkard (2000) shows that commercial aircraft industry production experience depreciates over time and that knowledge gained from building one product does not necessarily spill over to the next generation. High forgetting rates in commercial aircraft construction are reflected in the finding that firms might keep only 60 percent of their experience from one year to the next. Moreover,

forgetting is an endogenous variable. Industry characteristics that are likely to result in higher rates of forgetting include high labor turnover, high labor intensity, and learning that is thought to be important at the individual worker level.

Both the European and the US governments have routinely subsidized their aircraft industries. Export subsidies have been a key rivalry tool in the ongoing market share contest between Airbus and Boeing. The evidence gathered by Baldwin and Flam (1989) and others suggests that these subsidies have affected industries competitive positions. The emergence of Airbus as a formidable rival points toward the role of subsidies in encouraging learning-by-doing and exploiting economies of scale. During 1970–90, Airbus received over $10 billion in subsidies from European governments to finance start-up investments and the development of a new aircraft. The costly European project was widely criticized at the time. However, Airbus did penetrate world markets. In 1994, it surpassed Boeing for the first time, selling more commercial aircraft than Boeing.

10.6.1. Economic Effects of Aircraft Industry Rivalry

What were the price effects of Airbus entry? Baldwin and Krugman (1988*b*), Klepper (1990), and Neven and Seabright (1995) estimate that the entry of Airbus led to lower prices although Neven and Seabright argue that the neglect of the effect on a third competitor, McDonnell-Douglas, leads to the overstatements of consumer benefits from lower prices.

In 1992, the United States and the EU signed an agreement limiting civil aircraft subsidies. Irwin and Pavcnik (2001) estimate that the subsidy agreement resulted in a 7 percent after-subsidy marginal cost increase and a 3 percent price increase. The longer-term effect of Airbus has been to reduce prices. The Lerner index (the markup of price over marginal cost divided by the price) declined from 1969 to 1998. In other words, despite higher market concentration and the bilateral subsidy agreement, competition has apparently increased over time.

The US response to Airbus rivalry included the Boeing–McDonnell-Douglas merger of December 1996. The $48 billion revenues of the 200,000-employee new giant, was projected to account for 65 percent of the world airline market. This share represented two times the share of Airbus Industrie, the leading rival in the civil aircraft market. In 2001, Boeing built 611 aircraft almost doubling Airbus's 311 production. The Europeans responded to the US consolidation process by restructuring and privatizing Airbus. In 2000, Airbus transformed itself from an aircraft-making consortium of four companies into an integrated company, the Airbus Integrated Company (AIC).

The European Aeronautic Defence and Space Company (EADS) owns about 80 percent of AIC. BAE Systems, a UK holding, owns the remaining 20 percent. DaimlerChrysler, holding 32 percent of the shares, became the largest shareholder of EADS. It was followed by the French government and the French media group Lagardère (16 and 14.8 percent of the shares) and the Spanish governmental consortium (5.5 percent of the shares). About 30 percent of EADS shares were sold to the public in an initial public offering (IPO) that took place in July 2000.

In 2000, Airbus represented 60 and 75 percent of EADS sales and profits. EADS aims to penetrate the market for the jumbo jet, which Boeing has controlled as a monopolist since its conception in 1970. The restructuring of Airbus manufacturing operations, which were spread among four companies, into a single company was expected to generate about Euro 350 million in cost savings by 2004. The restructuring and cost savings aimed to help Airbus compete more effectively with Boeing and to expand the liquidity reserves needed to finance the new jumbo aircraft, the 550-seat A380. This project carries estimated development cost of $12 billion—a third of which is expected to be financed by reimbursable launch-aid subsidies.

EU support for the development of the new jumbo aircraft generated controversy. Americans argued that the EU violated the 1992 US–EU bilateral agreement limiting subsidies as well as the multilateral obligation under the WTO subsidy agreement. Meanwhile, the A380 jumbo aircraft rapidly accumulated orders. There are no deliveries yet, the first deliveries are expected to take place in 2006, but the aircraft is predicted to gain a 50 percent market share.

As a response to A380, Boeing offered a stretch version of Boeing 747 but the project collapsed in 2001. Boeing also offered provision of e-mail and Internet access to several large airline companies including United, Delta, and American Airlines. Airbus's matching strategy moved the competition into the new economy arena. The new systems link satellites with aircraft antennas that send and receive data while planes cruise at high-speed around the globe.

The world economic slowdown accompanying the new millennium slapped cancelled orders on Boeing and Airbus. Competition is fueled by new projects. The A380 project stands ready to launch a tough challenge to Boeing's 747 jumbo, which has accounted for about one third of Boeing profits recently. Irwin and Pavcnik (2001) estimate that the launching of the A380 model will reduce the demand and have adverse effects on the price and market shares of existing wide-bodied aircraft produced by Airbus (A-330 and A-340). In other words, the A380 project will lead Airbus to compete against itself.

For many years after its inception, the ambitious Airbus project was widely mentioned as a paradigm of costly subsidies in ineffective projects. Decades later, the perspective has changed. Counting with almost 3000 aircraft delivered and over 4000 ordered, Airbus has become a leading competitor in the civil air transport market. The end of the Boeing-Airbus story is yet to be written.

10.7. RESEARCH vs DEVELOPMENT

How do national technological investments affect domestic firms' competitive positions in a globalized environment? In order to answer this question, it is convenient to distinguish between investments in research and firms' development activities. This is an important issue in Europe, where many experts attribute the inability of transforming technological expertise into commercial research to the limited interaction between research centers and industry.

10.7.1. R&D in OECD Countries

The term R&D hides the important distinction between research and development. According to The Measurement of Scientific and Technical Activities, Frascati Manual 1980 (Paris: OECD, 1980), the term R&D accounts for the following three concepts.

1. Basic research refers to theoretical and experimental work aiming to produce new knowledge without any particular application or use in view.
2. Applied research means original investigation undertaken to acquire new knowledge primarily directed towards a practical aim or objective.
3. Developmental research (also called experimental research) is systematic research that draws on existing knowledge gained from basic or applied research and intends to produce new materials, products or devices and install new processes, systems, and services, or improve them.

There are important differences between the level of R&D spending across the OECD countries. Table 10.1 contains the ratio of development to research spending for selected OECD countries. Notice that the share of development research in the United States is high relative to European countries, and notoriously so in comparison with Britain.

An important part of industrial countries technological change success, specifically American success, is linked to science developments and the complementarity between research conducted in universities and in industries. The institutionalization of organized research in the industries allowed research labs to apply the scientific knowledge to product and process innovation. Scientific research developed in universities was utilized to solve the problems firms found in their activities.

Table 10.1. *R&D spending in OECD countries*

	Development/Research		
	1981	1990	1994
United States	1.73	1.70	1.57
Japan	1.52	1.64*	1.54
Sweden	1.41	1.83*	NA
France	NA	0.95	0.95
Italy	0.65	0.62	0.58**
United Kingdom	NA	0.60***	0.48***
Spain	0.82	0.89	0.73**

Note: Symbol (*) stands for 1991 data, (**) for 1993, and (***) refers to data drawn from net government R&D Expenditure by Frascati type of Activity.

Source: OECD, Basic Science and Technology. Editions 1991, 1993, and 1997, Table 3 and Department of Trade and Industry, Office of Science and Technology. Science, Engineering, and Technology. London: HMSO. 1996. Table 3.5, pp. 19. Also vol. 1998. Table 3.4, p. 22.

The analyses of policies affecting science and technology creation have become particularly relevant in the current international environment. First, international competition in knowledge-based economies relies heavily on scientific developments and firms' R&D activities. Second, R&D policies are not effectively limited by the WTO rules. In contrast, current WTO rules severely limit both protectionist policies and trade subsidies. In spite of these rules, most analyses of strategic trade policies focus on trade restrictions and export subsidies (i.e. strategic trade policy).

10.7.2. Patent Races, Market Size, Research and Development

An unbalanced distribution of resources between basic R&D spending can help to explain divergent market performance across countries. Cadot and Desruelle (1998) develop a model with two asymmetric countries in which firms keep separate R&D facilities. The proportion of development to research spending increases with country size. The relatively small size of European countries can help explain the relatively small share of development spending.

Consider two firms, a domestic and a foreign rival, engaged in an R&D race. Countries differ in size but all firms are symmetric, facing the same marginal production costs, and the same per-period costs of conducting R&D in a given race. R&D costs might differ between patent races.

Exportation entails transportation and tariff costs (if facing trade barriers abroad). These barriers generate partial market segmentation in the sense that there is a wedge between the domestic price in the importing country and the free on board (f.o.b.) price in the exporting country. This partial market segmentation implies that market size matters for R&D, because firms located in a larger market anticipate larger rents and hence a greater reward for their R&D spending.

When research (R) and development (D) activities are viewed as closely linked processes in the early stages of the product's life cycle, the assumption of market segmentation implies that firms established in larger markets will obtain larger rewards for their production and their R&D spending. On the contrary, we can view R&D as separate processes in a good's product cycle. Research is an upstream-type activity, and development is viewed as a downstream activity. As long as downstream activities depend on market characteristics and markets are segmented, the larger the market size the greater the opportunities to conduct development.

10.7.3. Patent Race When Research and Development are Closely Related

The analysis examines an international patent rate when R&D activities are closely interdependent activities. The R&D model sketched in this section adopts some features of Choi's (1991) international patent race model. Choi proposes a dynamic setup in which firms invest in R&D, but have incomplete information about the true productivity associated with the R&D process.

Dynamic Staging and Preemption

Consider a dynamic three-stage framework that distinguishes between basic research and product development. In the first stage (research stage), firms choose whether or not to start a new research project. The probability $\lambda \in \{0, \lambda^{max}\}$ that the research project is successful within a given period is unknown. In probability jargon, this probability is called a hazard rate, although here it represents the probability of discovery. Firms have an a priori probability q that the project is successful (i.e. $\lambda > 0$). If the research project is successful, the firm moves to the second stage (development stage). There is a known conditional probability μ of success in the development stage (given that the research project was successful). The third stage is the production stage. Production can only take place after a firm has been successful in completing the development stage.

Firms are assumed to observe whether or not other firms' research projects are successful. The success of a firm's research project has two opposite effects on its rivals. On one hand, the success reduces the rival's expectation that it will win the technological race. This effect increases the rival's incentives to drop the race. On the other hand, it increases the probability that the rival's research projects will be successful. This effect increases the rival's incentives to continue in the race rather than abandoning it. If time passes without getting a research success, the unsuccessful firm's patience is assumed to decline and its probability of research success is revised downwards in a Bayesian manner.

Depending on the patent race outcome either a single firm monopolizes the market or firms compete in quantities as duopolists. The patent race winner benefits from a worldwide monopoly position. In case of a tie, both firms compete as duopolists worldwide in a reciprocal-dumping trade game as in Brander (1981).

The characteristics of firms' international technology race, and countries' market size, determine whether or not the equilibrium entails preemption. Preemption takes place when a country chooses to abandon a research project before being concluded, once the rival has successfully completed its own project. The analysis restricts attention to the preemption equilibrium, and to Markov strategies. Markov strategies map the game state space into a binary choice of whether or not to stay in the game. Markovian strategies consist of decision rules in which the players' current action depends on current time t and state vector x_t. In this situation, the history of the game is not directly relevant for the choice of an action at time t. History is relevant only in so far as it is reflected in the current value of the state vector. With Markovian strategies players react only to factors that are payoff relevant, that is, the state vector. The Nash equilibrium of a game in which players use Markovian strategies is called a Markovian Nash equilibrium.

Equilibrium, Market Size, Costs, and Risks in the Patent Race

Firms' incentives to remain in the patent race, in spite of the success of the rivals' research project depend on market size asymmetries, patenting race costs, and firms' risk characteristics. Domestic market size helps to explain why a country can choose to cancel its research project before its completion given that the rival has been successful and has completed its own research project. When the foreign country's market size is larger than the domestic market, the domestic firm will respond to the rival's success by canceling its research project if:

(1) Markets are segmented by tariffs or transport costs that raise trade barriers among both countries (so that size matters);
(2) the research project is feasible with an ex ante probability close to one;
(3) The cost of conducting research is low enough to facilitate R&D, but large enough to induce lagging firms that have not concluded their research project to abandon the patent race.

The intuition behind the importance of market size differences is the presumption that, when markets are protected against foreign competitors, one may expect that the larger the market the larger firms' rents, the greater the compensation for conducting research, and thus the greater the stimulus to conduct research.

The risk characteristics variable plays an important role in firms' decisions (as in Choi, 1991). If the rival completes its research project, the observed success provides (*a*) information to the domestic firm that the project is feasible, but (*b*) implies that the firm is lagging relative to its rival in the race. Whether or not the demonstration effect (*a*) prevails over the discouraging effect (*b*) depends on the probability firms assigned in advance to the project's feasibility. If firms assigned a probability close to one, the discouraging effect can be shown to prevail over the demonstration effect as the information gain from observing the rival's success is small. (see Cadot and Desruelle, 1998).

10.7.4. Resource Allocation When R&D are Not Closely Linked

Do initial country endowments matter for the allocation of resources between R&D activities? Let us focus on a situation in which R&D are separate processes, in the sense that they are conducted simultaneously, and research is not an input into the development process in the product cycle.

Patent Race Stages
Suppose that the domestic country is better endowed than the foreign country in terms of R&D resources, such as scientists. Resources are mobile between R&D activities within the R&D sector, but not across borders.

Firms conducting R&D are risk neutral, and maximize future expected discounted profits. The volumes of R&D spending are chosen simultaneously in the first period, and are adjusted in future periods depending on the success or failure of the program. Research activities in sector R are assumed to be less sensitive to their commercial value than development activities conducted in sector D.

The size x_i of a research project in country i is defined as the number of researchers engaged in a representative project. The optimal size x_i maximizes the project's net present value v_i (discovery times are exponentially distributed)

$$= \int_0^\infty e^{-rt}[\lambda(x_i)z_i - w_i x_i]e^{-[\lambda(x_i)t + \lambda(x_j)t]}dt = \frac{\lambda(x_i)z_i - w_i x_i}{r + \lambda(x_i) + \lambda(x_j)}, \qquad (10.10)$$

where $\lambda(\cdot)$ is the hazard rate of discovery, r denotes the discount rate, and w_i is the scientists' wage rate. The variable z_i denotes the research payoff and can be interpreted as either the commercial value of discoveries when referring to applied research or the access to future funding when referring to basic research. The optimal research project size is obtained maximizing v_i with respect to $x_i (\lambda' > 0, \lambda'' < 0)$

$$w_i = \frac{\lambda'(x_i)z_i[r + \lambda(x_j)]}{r + \lambda(x_i) + \lambda(x_j) - x_i\lambda'(x_i)} = \lambda'(x_i)(z_i - v_i).$$

Let π_i denote the net present value of a development project in country i. The hazard rate of discovery μ is a random variable with distribution F (known before the project starts and assumed to be the same across countries) and support $[0, m]$. Each active development project employs one scientist, has size 1, and will be undertaken if the flow benefits $\mu\pi_i$ of running the project exceed the flow cost w_i consisting of the wage rate of a researcher (i.e. $\mu\pi_i \geq w_i$ or $\mu \geq w_i/\pi_i$).

The demand for labor (i.e. scientists) in the development sector, is given by

$$D_i \int_{w_i/\pi_i}^m f(\mu)\, d\mu = D_i\left[1 - F\left(\frac{w_i}{\pi_i}\right)\right].$$

The total number of scientists n_i in the economy is obtained from the resource allocation constraint

$$n_i = Rx_i + D_i\left[1 - F\left(\frac{w_i}{\pi_i}\right)\right],$$

where R is the initial global stock of research projects, D_i is the initial stock of development projects, and $[1 - F(w_i/\pi_i)]$ is the probability of conducting development activities, which have size 1. The inverse demand for labor is

$$w_i = \pi_i F^{-1}\left(1 - \frac{n_i - Rx_i}{D_i}\right)$$

obtained from the labor demand in the research and development sectors and the resource allocation constraint.

Allocating R&D Activities: Large and Small Country
The optimal size of a representative research project is obtained from the R&D demand functions and the resource allocation constraint

$$\frac{\lambda'(x_i)z_i[r + \lambda(x_j)]}{r + \lambda(x_i) + \lambda(x_j) - x_i\lambda'(x_i)} = \pi_i F^{-1}\left(1 - \frac{n_i - Rx_i}{D_i}\right).$$

The answer to the resource allocation question depends on the relative strengths of two effects: a resource-allocation effect and a strategic effect. The resource-allocation effect refers to the impact of market size on the allocation of resources to R&D activities. A larger country will devote more scientists to work in the research sector (see proof in Cadot and Desruelle, 1998). However, the difference in the number of scientists is less than proportional to the difference in total resources. Therefore, the ratio of scientists in the research sector to total scientists declines with market size. The intuition is the following. A proportional increase in the number of scientists employed in the R&D sectors will drive down the marginal product of research labor, but will leave it constant in the development sector.

The strategic effect refers to the impact of the allocation of a country's resources between R&D activities on the rival's decisions. The strategic research externality effect means that the proportion of country 2 scientists devoted to research increases with country 1 market size. The strategic effect captures the strategic complementarity of research intensities, in the sense that greater country 1 efforts in winning the race lower the chances that the smallar rival country 2 will win the race. As a result v_2 falls, which raises the capital gain $z_2 - v_2$ and increases x_2, the optimal size of country 2 representative research project. However, for given resources, the greater the amount of resources devoted to research, the smaller the remaining resources the country can use in the development sector.

Cadot and Desruelle find that the ratio of the number of scientists conducting product development to those conducting research is greater in a large country than in a small country. Hence, the small country exhibits greater concentration conducting research than in product development activities.

10.8. R&D AND GROWTH POLICIES

What are the appropriate policies toward R&D? The demand for research activities can be stimulated by direct spending on R&D and by subsidizing research spending. Alternatively, policies can operate through the supply of research by increasing spending on scientific and engineering education. Romer (2000) stresses that, if the amount of research is limited on the supply side by scarcity of scientists and engineers, research subsidies might be unproductive relative to investments in education and training.

Goolsbee (1998) points out that R&D spending consists mostly of R&D workers and that the supply of scientific and engineering talent is quite inelastic. Therefore, greater R&D spending through subsidies or through direct provision might have a price effect resulting in higher wages rather than exerting a quality effect by increasing the supply of talent and inventive activity. In other words, the effect of R&D policy might be to reward scientists' human capital more than encouraging innovation. He estimates that studies that focus exclusively on total R&D spending overstate the effects of government R&D policies spending by as much as 30–50 percent. Moreover, R&D policies crowd out private inventive activity insofar as they have the indirect effect of increasing wages of scientists and engineers hired by firms that do not benefit from public suppport. From a dynamic perspective, though, the evidence in Murphy *et al.*

(1991) suggests that encouraging engineering as opposed to law studies increases the supply of human capital involved in innovative activities. Endogenous growth theory suggest that the acquisition of inventive human capital leads to faster growth.

10.8.1. R&D Subsidies in Semiconductors: Sematech

Integrated circuits (ICs) are composed of multiple electronic transistors combined on a small silicon chip that does not require wiring. This device, called semiconductor or microchip, was invented in 1959. It was to become the heart of the new information economy.

The semiconductor industry (SIC 3674), forms part of the electronics components industry (SIC 367). It is an important element supporting US technological leadership. It is one of the largest high-technology industries and its output serves as an input to other high-tech industries such as telecommunications. AT&T Microelectronics, Digital Equipment, Hewlett-Packard, Motorola, and Texas Instruments are just a few examples of US leading semiconductor manufacturers.

Global Competition and Sematech
In the early 1980s, the Japanese semiconductor industry's world market share soared from 33 percent in 1982 to 46 percent in 1986. At the same time, the US share declined from 57 percent to 42 percent. In a few years, the United States fell from a dominant position to second place.

The US government responded by a series of measures. Intellectual property rights in the industry were protected by means of the Semiconductor Chip Protection Act of 1984. The National Cooperative Research Act of 1984 exempted joint R&D projects from treble damage and *per se* rules of antitrust law. This Act relaxed long-standing antitrust restrictions on R&D cooperation (Browning and Shetler, 2000).

In August 1987, the US government joined 14 leading US semiconductor manufacturers representing about 80 percent of the semiconductor manufacturing industry to form Sematech (Semiconductor Manufacturing Technology). Sematech was organized as an R&D consortium of manufacturing technology. It was limited to US firm membership although joint ventures with foreign firms were allowed. Member companies shared the expenses and risks of cooperative precompetitive research. Its original budget mounted to $200 million per year, half of it financed by industry and half by the government. Sematech spending added up to $900 million over the 5-year duration of the first charter. Government funding was renewed in 1993. Sematech and the government agreed to end its direct dependence on government funding in 1997 so that Sematech would have to apply to competitive grants from the National Science Foundation and other government agencies.

The government-industry consortium and associated government subsidization of producers were intended to reinvigorate US semiconductor industry by fostering the innovative and competitive efforts of the industry and by increasing the effectiveness of members' R&D investments. The main goals were the creation of a network of technology spillovers whose appropriability was limited to the consortium members and the coordination of members' research agendas limiting overlapping and redundant duplications. By encouraging the development of new technologies, authorities aimed to enhance the industry relative competitiveness in foreign markets. Over time, Sematech moved away from its original objective to develop processes for more advanced chips in its Austin facilities toward a policy of conceding cash grants to equipment companies. Firm experience with Sematech was generally good although several firms left Sematech in the 1990s.

The creation of Sematech was associated with a strong United States rebound that is partly attributed to Sematech. The US market share of the global semiconductor market increased from 37 percent in 1988 to 43 percent in 1993, when it recovered the leader position, and 51 percent in 1999. In turn, Japan's market share shrunk from 51 percent in 1988 to 42 percent in 1993 and 29 percent in 1999. In his proposal for the creation of industry technology boards to finance high-spillover R&D, Romer (1993) cited Sematech as a prototype.

In 1999, Sematech merged with International Sematech (ISMT), an international consortium that began operations in April 1998 to form ISMT. The new global consortium puts together fourteen manufacturers from seven countries—AMD, Digital, Rockwell (Conexant), Hewlett-Packard, Hyundai, Siemens (Infineon Technologies), IBM, Intel, Lucent Technologies, Motorola, Philips, SGS-Thomsom (STMicroelectronics), TSMC, and Texas Instruments. National Semiconductor left the consortium in December 1998 due to financial reasons.

ISMT works with the US Semiconductor Research Corporation (SRC), US universities, and United States, European and Asian equipment suppliers. It also established consensus on the direction of the industry with the Japanese consortium Selete. In July 2000, ISMT signed a joint R&D agreement with IMEC—a 1000 employee Belgium-based research center considered the leading independent European research center in microelectronics and integrated circuit technologies—to advance the International Technology Roadmap for Semiconductors. The agreement aims to develop a new gate stack process for sub-100 nm semiconductor devices. The shrinking semiconductor means that the processes and material used to make it have approached their physical limits. The industry is moving toward thinner effective gate dielectrics for sub-70 nm devices. Silicon dioxide, the heart of the MOS transistor since 1959, cannot perform at or below the 1.5–2 nm mode and seems bound for replacement.

What Were the Effects of Creating Sematech?

Did the consortium lower R&D spending in aggregate terms? Irwin and Klenow (1996) present empirical evidence on R&D spending levels, profitability, and productivity effects of Sematech. Their study is conducted using data from Compustat on seventy-one US firms belonging to the semiconductor industry between 1970–93. The hypotheses studied are: (1) the commitment hypothesis asserting that firms belonging to the consortium engaged in more high-spillover research than nonmembers, and (2) the sharing hypothesis asserting that the consortium reduces the duplication of R&D spending and thus promotes efficiency. On one hand, by committing firms to engage in greater high-spillover research, Sematech would accomplish something that firms would not accomplish by themselves. On the other hand, the benefits from sharing can be achieved by forming joint ventures and do not require government intervention.

Because R&D spending in the absence of Sematech is not observed, Irwin and Klenow (1996) compare member and nonmember R&D. The ratio of R&D to sales is estimated as a function of lagged R&D/Sales, a dummy variable (Sematech) that is set equal to one if a firm is a member and zero otherwise, and dummies for firm age (A). The weighted least square estimation for 1970–93 is

$$\left(\frac{R\&D}{Sales}\right)_t = \beta_1 Sematech + \beta_2 \left(\frac{R\&D}{Sales}\right)_{t-1} + \beta_3 A_1 + \beta_4 A_2 + \beta_5 A_3$$

$$= \underset{(0.33)}{-1.02} Sematech + \underset{(0.05)}{0.57} \left(\frac{R\&D}{Sales}\right)_{t-1}$$

$$+ \underset{(2.4)}{3.6} A_1 + \underset{(1.9)}{5.8} A_2 + \underset{(1.9)}{6.5} A_3,$$

where A_1 represents an age that is less than or equal to two years, A_2 an age greater than 2 and less than or equal to 5 years, and A_3 an age less or equal to 6 years. Standard errors appear in parenthesis. The R^2 is 0.78 and the number of observations is 689.

The evidence suggests that the formation of Sematech induced a decline of R&D investments by 9 percent of the sample firms' sales (i.e. about $300 million R&D spending) per year when compared to the research spending levels undertaken by independent, noncooperative firms. The authors argue that the firms belonging to the consortium benefited from joint R&D efforts and spent fewer resources. There is weak evidence that Sematech helped to improve member profitability but there is no evidence supporting the hypothesis that Sematech induced changes in the investment patterns of the industry. The large volatility of productivity at the firm level does not allow a firm conclusion about whether productivity levels of consortium members were significantly increased.

10.8.2. *Estimating learning-by-doing in semiconductors*

A stylized fact in the semiconductor industry is that the unit production cost in the semiconductor industry has declined by an estimated 28 percent when cumulative output—a proxy variable measuring experience in the production process—has doubled (Baldwin and Krugman, 1988*a*; Office of Technology Assessment, 1983; US Department of Commerce 1979). These data comprises the period 1960s and 1970s in the United States. More recent studies by Irwin and Klenow (1994) and others present updated estimates of the learning rate in the semiconductor industry, confirming the nonnegligible relevance of learning gains.

Given the widely accepted existence of learning-by-doing effects, the following questions arise. Are learning-by-doing effects internal to the firm? or, are there significant domestic or international spillovers in the semiconductor industry? Irwin and Klenow (1994) quantify the importance of learning-by-doing spillovers in the semiconductor industry between 1974 and 1992. The study focuses on United States and Japan-based firms, and uses quarterly data on the average market price of the goods and shipments by thirty-two merchant firms for the seven generations of dynamic random access memory (DRAM) chips: 4 K, 16 K, 64 K, 256 K, 1 M, 4 M, and 16 M.

The Empirical Model Specification and the Null Hypothesis
Firms are assumed to compete in quantities and produce homogeneous goods. Each firm i's objective function is given by the expected discounted value at period 0 of its profits $\pi_{it} = P(Q_t)q_{it} - C_{it}(q_{it})$

$$E_0 \sum_{t=0}^{\infty} \delta^t \pi_{it} = E_0 \sum_{t=0}^{\infty} \delta^t [P(Q_t)q_{it} - C_{it}(q_{it})],$$

where δ is the discount factor, $P(Q_t)$ is the price, Q_t is aggregate output, q_{it} denotes firm i's production level at period t, and C_{it} denotes total costs defined as: $C_{it}(q_{it}) = c_{it}(\cdot)q_{it}$ and E is the expectation operator.

Firm i's first order maximization conditions imply the following expression

$$p_0 \left(1 + \frac{s_{i0}}{\eta} \right) = c_{i0} + E_0 \left\{ \sum_{t=0}^{\infty} \delta^t q_{it} \frac{\partial c_{it}(\cdot)}{\partial q_{i0}} \right\}, \tag{10.11}$$

where $s_{i0} = q_{i0}/Q_o$ is firm i's market share and η is the price elasticity of demand in the semiconductor industry.

Firm i's dynamic marginal cost c_i against the firm's cumulative experience E_i is

$$c_i = vE_i^\beta e^{u_i}, \tag{10.12}$$

where v is a constant. Firm i's cumulative experience E_i is a function of its cumulative output Q_i, its cumulative output Q_C in the firm's home country, and the world cumulative output Q_W

$$E_i = Q_i + \alpha(Q_C - Q_i) + \gamma(Q_W - Q_C). \tag{10.13}$$

The error term u_i is defined as a stationary process

$$u_{it} = \mu + \alpha t + \rho u_{i,t-1} + \varepsilon_{it}, \quad |\rho| < 1. \tag{10.14}$$

Following earlier studies, the authors define the learning rate concept as the rate at which costs decline when doubling cumulative output. Formally, the learning rate estimates are obtained (1) using expression: learning rate $= 1 - 2^\beta$, where β is obtained from (10.12), or (2) by regressing price on cumulative output.

The null hypotheses tested are: (1) $\alpha = \gamma = 0$ indicative that learning-by-doing is internal to the firm, (2) $\alpha = 1$ and $\gamma = 0$ indicative that learning is external to the firm boundaries but internal to the country, and finally (3) $\alpha = \gamma = 1$, learning-by-doing economies are external to the firm and the country (i.e. borders do not matter).

Null Hypothesis and Empirical Results

Table 10.2 contains the results of the nonlinear square estimation of parameters α, γ, and the learning rate for each generation from equations (10.11)–(10.14).

Semiconductor firms' learning rates for eight generations range between 14 and 29 percent. US learning rates average 20 percent. The analysis sheds no evidence that Japanese firms' learning rates differ substantially from other countries' learning rates. Moreover, authors reject the nulls (at critical values smaller than 1 percent) that learning-by-doing economies are only internal to the firm ($\alpha = \gamma = 0$) or external to the firm but internal to the country ($\alpha = 1, \gamma = 0$) using the likelihood ratio test. The null hypothesis $\alpha = \gamma = 1$, stating that learning economies are external to the firm and the country, was rejected in six out of eight cases.

The hypothesis that within-country learning spillovers are stronger than between-country spillovers is tested by finding the smallest value of $\alpha - j = k$ that cannot be rejected at the 5 percent level (i.e. test $\alpha - \gamma = k > 0$). The authors do not reject the null in six out of eight cases, but only for sufficiently small k-values.

Irvin and Klenow find evidence that most of learning-by-doing gains remain within the firm. On average, estimates α and γ are about 0.3, which is interpreted as evidence that a firm learns three times more from its cumulative output process than from rivals (domestic or foreign). In absolute terms, though, national and international spillovers are not negligible. The absolute contribution of world cumulative production to a firm's experience is more than three times the absolute contribution of each firm's cumulative production to its experience. Authors conclude that absolute learning-by-doing spillovers are substantially international in scope even though marginal learning is mostly internal to the firm.

Table 10.2. *Learning-by-doing in the semiconductor industry*

Generation	α	γ	$\alpha - \gamma$	Learning rate
4 K	0.3	0.310	0.037	21.5
16 K	0.176	0.238	0.002	28.7
16 K-5	0.263	0.241	0.201	16.0
64 K	0.335	0.425	0.036	22.9
256 K	0.328	0.369	0.044	19.8
1 M	0.130	0.247	−0.033	18.4
4 M	0.450	0.465	0.102	18.7
16 M	0.233	0.274	0.010	16.0

Source: Adapted from Irwin and Klenow, 1994.

10.9. CONCLUSIONS

The level and rate of change of technology depend on a wide array of factors leading to innovative production, faster learning-by-doing, organizational improvements
and better quality institutions. What is the role of better technologies on international competition and what are the best policies toward R&D and international trade
in innovating open economies? Public policies aim to enhance welfare by supporting
cost-effective process innovation, the development of new products and the production
of better quality goods. R&D subsidies aim to correct the economic distortions arising
from the public character of new technologies. Strategic R&D policies aim to maximize
a country's benefits derived from foreign trade taking place in imperfectly competitive markets. Unilateral R&D subsidization enables local firms to capture the largest
possible international market share at the expense of foreign firms. This objective
leads to granting higher subsidy rates to those firms undertaking greater research. In
turn, this rule induces greater subsidization to low-cost firms' R&D than to high-cost
firms' R&D.

R&D subsidizations might or might not be optimal depending on a number of
factors. First, international competition through R&D subsidization might entail a
prisoner's dilemma situation resulting in lower welfare for all competitors. Second,
international externalities from domestic R&D can offset the competitive benefits from
cost-reduction. Third, if the amount of research is limited by scarcity of scientists
and engineers, research subsidies might be unproductive relative to investments in
education and training. Fourth, the chapter on incomplete information shows that
firms might spend excessively on R&D to signal that they are low-cost type firms to
induce the government to grant higher subsidies.

Does cooperation boost R&D? Evidence on Sematech suggests that the US consortium resulted in lower R&D levels than under a noncooperative investment policy or
under a standard R&D subsidy, raising questions about the boosting effects of cooperative R&D policies. Do R&D play different roles in international competition? The
dominance of US relative to European Union in technological competition might hinge
on the fact the investment in development is relatively more important in the United
States than in the European Union.

10.10. APPENDIX

10.10.1. Overinvestment in Research

Firms' profits are a function of research spending and government subsidies

$$\pi(q(x, x^*), q^*(x, x^*), x; s)$$
$$= R(q(x, x^*), q^*(x, x^*)) - C(q(x, x^*), x) - (x - s)x$$
$$= R(q(x, x^*), q^*(x, x^*)) - (c - x)q(x, x^*) - (x - s)x,$$

and similarly for the foreign firm. Totally differentiating profit function $\pi(\cdot)$ yields

$$
\begin{aligned}
\frac{d\pi(x, x^*, s)}{dx} &= \left[\frac{\partial R}{\partial q} - \frac{\partial C}{\partial q}\right]\frac{dq}{dx} + \frac{\partial R}{\partial q^*}\frac{dq^*}{dx} - \frac{\partial C}{\partial x} - (2x - s) \\
&= \left[\frac{\partial R}{\partial q} - (c - x)\right]\frac{dq}{dx} + \frac{\partial R}{\partial q^*}\frac{dq^*}{dx} + q - (2x - s) \\
&= \frac{\partial R}{\partial q^*}\frac{dq^*}{dx} + q - (2x - s) = 0,
\end{aligned}
$$

where $R = pq$ represents revenues. The last step uses the first order output condition $\partial\pi/\partial q = \partial R/\partial q - \partial C/\partial q = \partial R/\partial q - (c - x) = 0$. By the same token

$$
\frac{d\pi^*(x^*, x, s^*)}{dx^*} = \frac{\partial R^*}{\partial q}\frac{dq}{dx^*} + q^* - (2x^* - s^*) = 0.
$$

10.10.2. Strategic Research Policy under Uncertainty

$$
\begin{aligned}
W(s, s^*) &= E[\pi(x(s, s^*), x^*(s, s^*), s)] - sx(s, s^*) \\
&= E[\pi(x(r^P, r^{*P}), x^*(r^P, r^{*P}), r^P)] - (r^S - r^P)x(r^P, r^{*P}).
\end{aligned}
$$

Totally differentiating expression $W(\cdot)$ with respect to r^P yields

$$
\begin{aligned}
\frac{dW(s, s^*)}{dr^P} &= \frac{\partial E\pi}{\partial x}\frac{\partial x}{\partial r^P} + \frac{\partial E\pi}{\partial x^*}\frac{\partial x^*}{\partial r^P} + \frac{\partial E\pi}{\partial r^P} - (r^S - r^P)\frac{\partial x}{\partial r^P} + x \\
&= \frac{\partial E\pi}{\partial x^*}\frac{\partial x^*}{\partial r^P} - (r^S - r^P)\frac{\partial x}{\partial r^P},
\end{aligned}
$$

where $\partial E\pi/\partial x = 0$ from first order conditions and $\partial E\pi/\partial r^P = -x$.
R&D first order conditions are

$$
\frac{dE\pi(x(r^P, r^{*P}), x^*(r^P, r^{*P}), r^P)}{dx} = 0,
$$

$$
\frac{dE\pi^*(x(r^P, r^{*P}), x^*(r^P, r^{*P}), r^{*P})}{dx^*} = 0.
$$

Totally differentiating the first order conditions with respect to the private cost of investment yields

$$
\frac{\partial^2 E\pi}{\partial x^2}\frac{\partial x}{\partial r^P} + \frac{\partial^2 E\pi}{\partial x\partial x^*}\frac{\partial x^*}{\partial r^P} + \frac{\partial^2 E\pi(\cdot)}{\partial x\partial r^P} = 0,
$$

$$
\frac{\partial^2 E\pi^*(\cdot)}{\partial x^*\partial x}\frac{\partial x}{\partial r^P} + \frac{\partial^2 E\pi^*(\cdot)}{\partial x^{*2}}\frac{\partial x^*}{\partial r^P} + \frac{\partial^2 E\pi^*(\cdot)}{\partial x^*\partial r^P} = 0,
$$

which can be re-written in matrix terms as

$$\begin{pmatrix} \dfrac{\partial^2 E\pi}{\partial x^2} & \dfrac{\partial^2 E\pi}{\partial x \partial x^*} \\[3mm] \dfrac{\partial^2 E\pi^*(\cdot)}{\partial x^* \partial x} & \dfrac{\partial^2 E\pi^*(\cdot)}{\partial x^{*2}} \end{pmatrix} \begin{pmatrix} \dfrac{\partial x}{\partial r^P} \\[3mm] \dfrac{\partial x^*}{\partial r^P} \end{pmatrix} + \begin{pmatrix} \dfrac{\partial^2 E\pi(\cdot)}{\partial x \partial r^P} \\[3mm] \dfrac{\partial^2 E\pi^*(\cdot)}{\partial x^* \partial r^P} \end{pmatrix} = \begin{pmatrix} 0 \\ 0 \end{pmatrix}.$$

Imposing

$$\begin{pmatrix} \dfrac{\partial^2 E\pi}{\partial x^2} & \dfrac{\partial^2 E\pi}{\partial x \partial x^*} \\[3mm] \dfrac{\partial^2 E\pi^*(\cdot)}{\partial x^* \partial x} & \dfrac{\partial^2 E\pi^*(\cdot)}{\partial x^{*2}} \end{pmatrix}^{-1} > 0,$$

implies that

$$\begin{pmatrix} \dfrac{\partial x}{\partial r^P} \\[3mm] \dfrac{\partial x^*}{\partial r^P} \end{pmatrix} = - \begin{pmatrix} \dfrac{\partial^2 E\pi}{\partial x^2} & \dfrac{\partial^2 E\pi}{\partial x \partial x^*} \\[3mm] \dfrac{\partial^2 E\pi^*(\cdot)}{\partial x^* \partial x} & \dfrac{\partial^2 E\pi^*(\cdot)}{\partial x^{*2}} \end{pmatrix}^{-1} \begin{pmatrix} \dfrac{\partial^2 E\pi(\cdot)}{\partial x \partial r^P} \\[3mm] \dfrac{\partial^2 E\pi^*(\cdot)}{\partial x^* \partial r^P} \end{pmatrix},$$

or,

$$\frac{\partial x}{\partial r^P} = - \frac{\partial^2 E\pi(\cdot)}{\partial x \partial r^P} \Bigg/ \frac{\partial^2 E\pi}{\partial x^2} \frac{\partial^2 E\pi^*(\cdot)}{\partial x^{*2}} - \frac{\partial^2 E\pi}{\partial x \partial x^*} \frac{\partial^2 E\pi^*(\cdot)}{\partial x^* \partial x},$$

$$\frac{\partial x^*}{\partial r^P} = - \frac{\partial^2 E\pi^*(\cdot)}{\partial x^* \partial r^P} \Bigg/ \frac{\partial^2 E\pi}{\partial x^2} \frac{\partial^2 E\pi^*(\cdot)}{\partial x^{*2}} - \frac{\partial^2 E\pi}{\partial x \partial x^*} \frac{\partial^2 E\pi^*(\cdot)}{\partial x^* \partial x}.$$

Substituting $\partial x / \partial r^P$ and $\partial x^* / \partial r^P$ into $dW(s, s^*)/dr^P = 0$ and solving for $(r^S - r^P)$ yields

$$\frac{\partial W(s, s^*)}{\partial r^P} = \frac{\partial E\pi}{\partial x^*} \frac{\partial x^*}{\partial r^P} - (r^S - r^P) \frac{\partial x}{\partial r^P} = 0,$$

$$r^S - r^P = \frac{\partial E\pi}{\partial x^*} \frac{\partial x^*}{\partial r^P} \Bigg/ \frac{\partial x}{\partial r^P} = \frac{\partial E\pi}{\partial x^*} \frac{\partial^2 E\pi(\cdot)}{\partial x \partial r^P} \Bigg/ \frac{\partial^2 E\pi^*(\cdot)}{\partial x^* \partial r^P}.$$

10.10.3. *The Economics of Learning-by-doing*

The domestic firm's profit function is

$$\pi = \pi_t + \rho \pi_{t+1} = (p_t - c_t + s_t) q_t + \rho (q_{t+1})^2$$

$$= (p_t - c_t + s_t) q_t + \rho \frac{\delta^2 [a + c^* - 2(c - \lambda q_t)]^2}{4(3\delta - 2)^2}, \tag{10.15}$$

and the profit-maximizing production level q_t^{learn} is

$$q_t^{learn} = \frac{2s_t\kappa + (\kappa + 2\delta^2\lambda\rho)(a - 2c + c^*)}{3\kappa - 4\delta^2\lambda^2\rho},\tag{10.16}$$

where $\kappa = (9\delta^2 - 12\delta + 4)$. A larger learning rate λ, induces greater production levels, for a given subsidy s_t. Total profits π_t^{learn} are obtained from substituting (10.16) into (10.15).

Optimal Subsidy and Infant-Industry Argument
Welfare levels at period $t + 1$ are

$$W_{t+1} = \pi_{t+1} - \delta s_{t+1} q_{t+1} = \frac{3\delta - 2}{2}\pi_{t+1}.\tag{10.17}$$

Domestic welfare W_{t+1} goes down with δ if $\delta < 4/3$

$$\frac{\partial W_{t+1}}{\partial \delta} = \frac{\delta(3\delta - 4)(a + c_{t+1}^* - 2c_{t+1})}{8(3\delta - 2)^2} < 0.$$

This intuitive result is directly derived by noticing that profits decline with the size of distortions, $\partial \pi_{t+1}/\partial \delta < 0$.

The optimal export subsidy at time t is obtained substituting equilibrium profits π into the welfare definition $W_t + \rho W_{t+1}$ given in (10.8), using expressions q_t and q_{t+1}, and computing $\partial W/\partial s_t = 0$.

$$s_t = \Lambda(\delta, \lambda, \rho)(a - 2c + c^*) \gtreqless 0,$$

where

$$\Lambda(\delta, \lambda, \rho) = \frac{\left[2(3\delta - 2)^4 + \delta^2\lambda\rho(3\delta - 2)^2(1 - 4\lambda) - 4\delta^4\lambda^3\rho^2\right]}{4\left[2\delta^2\lambda^2\rho - (9\delta^2 - 12\delta + 4)\right](9\delta^2 - 12\delta + 4)}.$$

11

Information and Moral Hazard

This chapter examines trade and policy in the presence of informational barriers. A country's exports are driven by existing exporting ventures but also by new exporters that are not well-known in foreign markets and face informational barriers already surpassed by incumbents. Roberts and Tybout (1997b) found that industrial export booms in Columbia, Mexico, and Morocco were partly accounted for by increased exports from existing exporters and partly by a greater number of new exporting firms. Successful participation in international trade hinges on the manner in which firms and policymakers address informational barriers giving rise to adverse selection and moral hazard. For instance, whether a firm is able to convey information about the quality of new products in a cost-efficient manner determines whether entry takes place or is blocked.

Potential entrants and new exporters often introduce vertically differentiated products providing better quality than rival offerings. Products or brands are said to be vertically differentiated when they can be ranked by quality, that is, consumers agree as to which product or brand is preferred. Vertical differentiation by quality is distinct from horizontal differentiation by attributes. Products or brands displaying attributes that are valued differently by heterogeneous consumers cannot be unambiguously ranked.

The lack of market reputation is a major entry barrier. The reason is that potential buyers are unable to accurately assess product quality before actual purchase and consumption. Lack of information about player's types—incomplete information—gives rise to adverse selection such as when a high-cost producer pretends to be low cost to get higher subsidies. Lack of information about player's moves—imperfect information—gives rise to moral hazard such as when firms choose to produce low-quality products because high quality is not recognized in the market. Adverse selection and moral hazard impose entry barriers on new firms and can block entry altogether.

Can trade policies targeting new firms or infant industries be justified as a means to offset informational barriers to entry? Paradoxically, infant industry protection can actually exacerbate the information problem by attracting inefficient producers or by making quality signaling more expensive (Grossman and Horn, 1988).

What is the optimal infant exporter policy? Export subsidies are inefficient if they encourage excessive entry of inefficient firms or induce costly signaling. However, blocked entry due to the inability to sell at prices reflecting a product's quality might call for export subsidies, as in the potential monopoly exporter cases examined by Bagwell and Staiger (1989) and Bagwell (1991). If the government can precommit to a future subsidy, then entry barriers can be overcome by a performance-based subsidy to be paid in the mature phase (contingent on observed future quality). If the government cannot credibly precommit to grant a future subsidy, then an introductory period subsidy can be used to overcome informational entry barriers.

In a duopoly setting in which a foreign incumbent and a new domestic firm compete in prices abroad, as in Raff and Kim (1999), the optimal policy hinges on which of two opposing forces dominates. Temporary signaling difficulties call for an export subsidy. The profit gain from restricting competition and output calls for a strategic export tax. If the strategic element dominates over the temporary signaling effect, the optimal dynamic trade policy involves a rising export tax. The rising tax strikes a balance between the benefits from taxing exports to lessen price competition abroad and the need to address the temporary signaling problem, which moderates the tax.

Section 11.1 reviews the concept of sequential equilibrium. Section 11.2 focuses on tariff protection when there are informational barriers. Sections 11.3–11.5 examine the economics of infant exportation in the presence of informational barriers. Section 11.6 reviews alternative private, public, and institutional mechanisms for export promotion.

11.1. SEQUENTIAL EQUILIBRIUM

Dynamic games of incomplete information can be solved using the sequential equilibrium concept developed by Kreps and Wilson (1982). A sequential equilibrium of an n-player game is an assessment pair (σ, b) consisting of a strategy profile σ together with a system of beliefs b. The strategy profile $\sigma = (\sigma_1, \sigma_2, \ldots, \sigma_n)$ consists of a strategy σ_i for each player $i \in \{1, \ldots, n\}$. The system of beliefs or beliefs profile $b = (b_1, b_2, \ldots, b_n)$ specifies the probability of each information node (i.e. decision point) in the game. The equilibrium strategy and belief profiles satisfy the following conditions:

1. The strategy profile is sequentially rational for all information sets given beliefs, in the sense that each player's strategies are best-replies relative to his or her beliefs. In other words, each player moves optimally at every information set given his or her beliefs and other players' strategies.
2. Beliefs at every information set reached on the equilibrium path are derived from the strategy profile according to Bayes' rule. In other words, beliefs and strategies are consistent in the sense that beliefs along the dynamic equilibrium path are formed according to Bayes' rule.
3. There exists a sequence $\{\sigma(k)\}$ of completely mixed strategies (k is the index of the sequence), the limit of which is equal to equilibrium strategy profile σ with accompanying sequence of consistent beliefs $\{b(k)\}$ such that $\{b(k)\}$ converges to the equilibrium belief profile b. A player follows a completely mixed strategy if the player assigns a positive probability to each possible action at each of his or her information sets. If all players follow completely mixed strategies, then all information sets in the game are reached with positive probability and Bayes' rule can be applied.

Conditions 1 and 2 of the previous characterization of sequential equilibria (SE) are the same as the characterization of perfect Bayesian equilibria (PBE). In fact, a sequential equilibrium is a perfect Bayesian equilibrium that satisfies additional consistency requirement 3.

The set of sequentially rational strategies and supporting Bayesian beliefs in a sequential equilibrium must be the limit of a sequence of sets of strategies and accompanying beliefs such that strategies are totally mixed and beliefs are consistent with strategies and Bayes' rule. According to consistency requirement 3, the strategies need not be optimal, given beliefs, along the converging sequence but must be optimal in the limit. This means that equilibrium beliefs can be derived from totally mixed strategies and accompanying supporting beliefs that are 'close' to equilibrium beliefs in the mathematical sense of convergence to equilibrium beliefs. In simple games, the previous consistency requirement has no bite and PBE and SE coincide.

Bayes' rule does not apply to zero probability events. Therefore, just as with perfect Bayesian equilibrium, the sequential equilibrium concept does not impose any restriction on beliefs off-the-equilibrium path. These beliefs establish how the consumer would respond to a deviation from equilibrium and their specification is key to the determination of the game's solution. The indetermination of disequilibrium beliefs can lead to multiple equilibria. Refinements of PBE and SE have been developed to eliminate multiplicity by restricting the off-the-equilibrium path beliefs.

11.2. DO INFORMATION BARRIERS JUSTIFY PROTECTION?

Established firms benefit from a market reputation about the quality of their products. Repeated purchases allow consumers to assess a product's quality and ensure a tight relationship between market price and quality. By contrast, newcomers into an established market face informational barriers that put them at a competitive disadvantage in relation to existing firms. Informational barriers exist because inspection and careful examination of product specifications do not enable consumers to accurately assess the true quality of new products. The role of repeat purchases is decisive in the case of experience products such as customs services and sophisticated consumer goods. The qualities of experience products cannot be assessed by inspection and are revealed only after they have been purchased and consumed.

Informational barriers can be surpassed when a seller of a product of unknown quality takes the initiative and makes a costly choice to signal its type to consumers. Incurring the fixed costs of increasing capacity can be used as a signal. The producer of a high-quality local product can also use the decision to export as a signal for quality. By incurring the costs of developing the infrastructure needed to enter into foreign markets, the producer signals product quality to consumers (Shy, 2000). Alternatively or complementarily, governments can design policies addressing informational barriers.

11.2.1. Competition and Infant Industries

Can trade policies targeting new firms or infant industries be justified as a means to off-set informational barriers to entry? Consider a model of competitive markets, free entry, and endogenous product quality determination. Firms are heterogeneous, differing in the marginal cost of producing a given quality level. Paradoxically, infant-industry protection of import-competing goods can exacerbate the welfare loss associated with informational barriers. The reason is that protection accentuates adverse selection problems. Protection encourages excessive entry of inefficient firms offering low-quality products in a pooling equilibrium with fixed capacity. If capacity can be used as a signal, protection exacerbates costly signaling of a low-cost firm type in a separating equilibrium.

Grossman and Horn (1988) examine the impact of tariff protection in a two-period model of a competitive market for an experience good or service. Each domestic firm can produce at most a single unit of output per period. Total demand is equal to N and the representative consumer demands a unit of the product in each period. Entry is free but limited to N firms in each period.

The domestic market is initially dominated by foreign incumbents, who sell a product of known quality and thus enjoy an informational advantage over potential domestic entrants. The introductory period represents the infancy of those potential domestic entrants who actually choose to enter the domestic market to compete against established foreign exporters.

Domestic product quality is selected in the introductory period. Consumers are able to recognize and reject qualities below a minimum level q_0. Therefore, the equilibrium can sustain only sellers offering qualities above q_0. When they make their introductory period buying decisions, consumers are not able to determine the quality of products featuring above-minimum quality $q > q_0$. Before the mature period starts, word of mouth fully reveals product quality. At that point, firms operating in the introductory period must decide whether to continue operating in the mature period or withdraw from the market at a zero exit cost.

Product quality is endogenously determined as a function of the privately observed firm technology type determining the marginal cost of producing any given quality level. There is a continuum of firms' technology types indicated by cost index θ, which varies between θ_{min} and θ_{max} and has a cumulative distribution $F(\theta)$. Formally, a type-θ firm produces a unit of output of endogenously chosen quality q with unit cost function C

$$C(q;\theta) = \theta c(q), \quad c'(q) > 0, \quad c''(q) > 0.$$

Unit production costs C increase with the quality level and with the value of the cost index θ, where a higher θ represents a less-advanced technology. There are no sunk design or research and development costs.

11.2.2. *Quality and Pricing in Pooling Equilibria*

Equilibria with domestic firm production can be either separating or pooling. In a separating equilibrium, domestic firms successfully signal product quality and high-quality products receive a higher price than low-quality products. In the specific setup examined, however, no firm has incentives to incur costs to make a signaling claim. Therefore, there is no separating equilibrium. First, quantity cannot be used to signal quality as each firm operates at full capacity, which is taken as given. Second, product price cannot serve as a signal either. Suppose that there is a pooling equilibrium with a single market price and that a high-quality firm deviates from that equilibrium by setting a higher price in order to signal its quality. This price signaling mechanism cannot work because the cost of setting a higher price is the same for a low- and a high-quality firm. Therefore, setting a high price reduces sales to zero and fails to signal better quality. Moreover, no firm has an incentive to signal its type by setting a low price in the first period. A low price cannot expand sales and will lower profits in the first period while leaving profits unaffected in the second period as true quality will be known by then.

In a pooling equilibrium, high- and low-quality domestic products command the same price in the introductory period. The equilibrium price must be low enough to limit production to N units. This production level is achieved by generating losses for domestic and foreign firms characterized by a high enough value of the cost parameter θ.

Given that buyers do not observe domestic quality in the first period, purchase decisions are made on the basis of expected consumer surplus. If the average quality of domestic products is $\bar{q}$, a consumer whose taste for quality is measured by parameter γ obtains an expected consumer surplus CS of

$$E[CS(q)] = E[U] - p_1 = \gamma\bar{q} - p_1,$$

where U is utility per unit consumed.

A domestic product is purchased at price p_1 as long as the expected surplus $\gamma\bar{q} - p_1$ exceeds the consumer surplus $U^* - (p^* + t_1)$ obtainable from an import, where U^* represents total utility obtainable from an imported unit, p^* is world or offshore price of that import, and t_1 is the specific tariff set in period 1. The quality of each foreign product is assumed to be observed so that a rational consumer equates its surplus across alternative foreign products.

If expectations are rational and out-of-equilibrium beliefs satisfy reasonable constraints (Cho and Kreps, 1987), the equilibrium expected consumer surplus obtainable from purchasing a domestic product will be equal to the consumer surplus obtainable from an import

$$\gamma\bar{q} - p_1 = U^* - p^* - t_1$$
$$p_1 = \gamma\bar{q} - [U^* - (p^* + t_1)].$$

In a 0–1 setting in which a consumer buys a unit of either a domestic product or an import, but not both, the equilibrium domestic price makes a consumer just willing to replace an import by a local product. The domestic product price is equal to expected utility per unit $\gamma \bar{q}$ minus the surplus obtainable from an import.

11.2.3. Adverse Selection and Moral Hazard

Pooling equilibria entails two types of problems: (1) an adverse selection problem among potential entrants into the industry, and (2) a moral hazard problem affects firms' choice of product quality.

Adverse selection and moral hazard distortions arise because the previous game features both incomplete information and imperfect information. Incomplete information means that players are not sure about what other players in the game are like as defined by their payoffs. In this setup, firms are heterogeneous and the cost type θ is not directly observed. Moreover, word of mouth operates with a delay. Therefore, first period quality is unobserved and lower quality products receive the same price as higher quality products in a pooling equilibrium, inducing entry of firms producing lower-quality products misrepresented as higher-quality products in the first period. These firms—called fly-by-nights—would not be able to enter the market if the qualities of their products were known. Under private information, fly-by-nights sell for one period and exit the market at a zero exit cost when qualities become known in the mature period.

In the first period, the marginal firm sells at the price corresponding to the average quality, which is greater than the price corresponding to the marginal quality. Therefore, if $t_1 > t_2$, the marginal firm must receive a higher price in the first period, when quality is unobserved and there is greater protection, than in the second period, when quality is observed and there is less protection. In other words, $t_1 > t_2$ implies that introductory period profits must exceed mature period profits, $\pi_1 > \pi_2$. Because free exit implies that mature period profits must be nonnegative, $\pi_2 \geq 0$, the first period profits of the marginal firm must be nonnegative too

$$t_1 > t_2 \quad \rightarrow \quad \pi_1 > \pi_2 \quad \rightarrow \quad \pi_1 \geq 0.$$

Under free entry, the number of domestic producers in the introductory period must be such that the marginal domestic firm—the one producing the lowest quality—makes zero discounted profits, $\pi_1 + \rho \pi_2 = 0$, where ρ is the discount factor. Because a firm can avoid second period losses by just exiting, zero discounted profits imply that the marginal firm must be a fly-by-night producing the minimum quality q_0. This firm obtains zero profits in the first period after which it exits. Formally, if $t_1 > t_2$, then the discounted profits of the marginal domestic firm are

$$\tilde{\pi}_1 + \rho \tilde{\pi}_2 = \tilde{\pi}_1 = p_1 - \tilde{\theta} c(q_0) = 0, \tag{11.1}$$

where the marginal firm is a fly-by-night and is denoted by a wiggle, ρ is the discount factor and q_0 denotes the minimum quality. Positive profits would create incentives for entry of fly-by-nights producing the minimum quality.

Domestic firms with cost factor θ exceeding the marginal firm cost factor $\tilde{\theta}$ are kept out of the market in equilibrium. Fly-by-nights—firms producing the minimum quality q_0 and exiting after one period—temporarily replace a number of foreign incumbents. Foreign incumbents and domestic firms with low enough cost parameter remain in the market in both periods. Foreign incumbents with intermediate cost parameters exit in the first period but can reenter in the mature period. Foreign incumbents with high enough cost parameter are crowded out of the market permanently.

Games played under imperfect information, in the sense that at least one player does not know all the moves other players have made in past or current periods, can give rise to moral hazard distortions. A moral hazard problem takes place when a full warranty, such as insurance, induces an agent to misuse or fail to take proper care of a product. Moral hazard can also arise because product quality is chosen by firms but consumers do not observe it.

In a pooling equilibrium in which products with unknown qualities receive the same price in the first period, firms have incentives to save costs and increase profits by lowering the quality bar. Unknown quality implies that the price $p_1(\bar{q})$ is a function of average quality rather than a function $p_1(q)$ of individual quality as it would be under full information. All firms face a moral hazard problem and have incentives to produce low-quality products because high quality is not recognized in the market. In fact, if $t_1 > t_2$, then the marginal firm in the first period will be a fly-by-night that chooses to produce the minimum unobservable quality q_0.

11.2.4. Temporary and Permanent Protection

What is the role of temporary protection when there are information barriers? Assume that the government does not observe product quality when policy is formulated. Menu policies aiming to induce separation (screening) do not work in this setup for the same reasons that signaling fails. Reputable domestic firms—those offering products featuring a quality exceeding the minimum quality q_0—sell to capacity in both periods. When all reputable firms have the same sales level (one unit), output cannot be adjusted to serve as a signal of quality and a policy menu does not generate any information. Specifically, a tariff increases the domestic product price and firms' profits by the same amount no matter firm cost type or product quality. A lump sum tax also reduces all firms' profits by the same amount. Therefore, all firms would prefer the same menu item among a set of tariff-tax combinations, which precludes the signaling effect.

Paradoxically, protection by means of a uniform specific tariff turns out to be welfare-reducing. First, tariffs hurt consumers by increasing the price paid for imported products. Second, infant-industry protection exacerbates the adverse selection distortion arising from informational barriers and thus augments the welfare loss suffered when consumers lack information about product quality. Third, protection does not influence quality decisions and thus fails to correct the moral hazard problem.

In a pooling equilibrium, temporary protection (i.e. introductory period protection) fails to correct the consumer information distortion. It rather sustains a higher domestic price in the first period leading to greater profits for all domestic firms. Higher profits promote the entry of technologically less-advanced domestic firms that produce low-quality products and would not enter the market if their quality was known. Condition (11.1) determining the marginal firm's cost factor $\tilde{\theta}$ as a function of the first period price p_1 and the given minimum quality q_0 implies that a higher price p_1 sustains a higher cost $\tilde{\theta}$. The entry of lower-quality firms exacerbates the adverse selection problem and leads to lower average domestic quality.

Temporary protection fails to alleviate the moral hazard problem. The reason is that introductory period protection applies equally to all firms and does not provide greater incentives for high-quality firms to choose better quality products. To see this, notice that the first order condition for quality choice is not affected by the value of the specific tariff t_1

$$\max_q \pi_1 + \rho\pi_2 = p_1 - \theta c(q) + \rho \max_q\{0, p_2(q) - \theta c(q)\},$$

$$-\theta c'(q) + \rho\frac{dp_2}{dq} - \rho\theta c'(q) = 0 \;\; \rightarrow \;\; \rho\frac{dp_2}{dq} = \rho\gamma = (1+\rho)\,\theta c'(q),$$

where $p_1 = \gamma\bar{q} - U^* + t_1$ and $p_2(q) = \gamma q - U^* + t_2$. In short, when the consumer price distortion, adverse selection effect and moral hazard impact are taken into account, temporary protection is shown to unambiguously worsen domestic welfare.

What about permanent protection defined as protection in the introductory period followed by promised protection in the mature period? This form of protection acts like temporary protection—in that it fails to break up the informational barriers in the first period—and adds up a credibility problem. Promised permanent protection is time inconsistent in the sense that it is no longer optimal when quality becomes known in the mature phase. The implication is that, if government cannot commit to a future tariff, firms correctly anticipate that $t_2 = 0$ and promised permanent protection lacks credibility.

If authorities can credibly commit to mature period protection by levying specific tariff t_2, the moral hazard problem can be ameliorated. To see why, let us go back to the maximization problem determining quality choice. First, notice that the quality choice of reputable firms—those firms producing above the minimum quality q_0—is not affected by t_2, which does not appear in the first order condition. Second, observe that a mature period tariff directly benefits only those firms that are active in the mature period and thus affects the choice between remaining a fly-by-night and becoming a reputable firm. Specifically, the tariff heightens the reward from choosing a higher quality in the first period and building up a reputation relative to remaining a fly-by-night firm. This leads some fly-by-nights—firms producing the minimum acceptable quality level q_0 for one period and exiting afterwards—to become reputable and produce high-quality products. As a result domestic products' average quality $\bar{q}$ improves. In short, by rewarding only those firms that behave reputable in the first period, credible mature period protection ameliorates the moral hazard distortion.

11.2.5. Protection in a Signaling Equilibrium

What are the effects of protection when firms can alter capacity k? Suppose that capacity k requires a once-and-for-all investment in capital equipment at cost $F(k)$, with $F' > 0, F'' > 0$. Installed capacity is durable so that it can be used in both the introductory and the mature periods.

Grossman and Horn (1988) examine the case in which there are two cost types and two qualities

$$\theta_R < \theta_F \quad \rightarrow \quad q_F < q_R,$$

where R and F stand for reputable and fly-by-night. Reputable firms face a low cost of producing quality and will choose to offer the high-quality product in either a pooling or a separating equilibrium. It is assumed that fly-by-night firms choosing to offer quality q_F would not be able to make any sales in a separating equilibrium.

Changing capacity is less costly for reputable (low-θ) firms than for fly-by-nights (high-θ). Reputable firms remain in the market in the mature period and can thus amortize sunk capacity costs over two periods. Fly-by-nights are forced to amortize sunk capacity costs over one period. The difference in capacity costs permits the appropriate sorting condition to hold. Low-θ firms can increase productive capacity to successfully signal their type. A firm installing large capacity makes a partial commitment to remain in the market, which serves to indicate that the firm is reputable rather than a fly-by-night.

The two-period model has a sequential equilibrium in which consumers associate high capacity investments to high product quality and low investments to low quality. Sequential equilibrium beliefs about quality, denoted q^{SE}, are given by

$$q^{SE} = \begin{cases} q^H, & \bar{k} \leq k, \\ q^L, & k < \bar{k}. \end{cases}$$

The threshold capacity level $\bar{k}$ can be shown to exceed the capacity a firm producing a high-quality product would install under full information.

The previous beliefs support a separating equilibrium in which a firm's output level signals product quality and a high-quality product would command a higher price than a low-quality product. For any given quality level, the marginal cost of supplying better quality products is lower for low-θ firms implying that they will produce better quality products than high-θ firms in equilibrium.

Consider tariff protection by means of a uniform specific tariff. The government does not observe domestic firms' cost types or product qualities when it formulates policy prior to the introductory period. In the separating introductory period equilibrium with endogenous capacity, greater transitory tariffs and credibly permanent tariffs always reduce welfare. Protection increases profits for all firms, which in turn increases the capacity $k(\theta_R)$ required to signal high quality. In equilibrium, the cost of additional capacity dissipates the subsidy implicit in the tariff.

The intuition explaining why tariff protection increases the cost of signaling and is counterproductive relates to the presence of high-θ firms offering low-quality products under asymmetric information. This creates a negative externality on low-θ firms offering high-quality products. Low-cost firms are forced to incur additional costs in order to credibly signal the high-quality of their products. By increasing the cost of signaling tariff protection exacerbates the social loss from informational barriers and is welfare-reducing.

11.3. INFANT EXPORTER AND ADVERSE SELECTION

Trade expansion through the penetration of markets abroad is plagued with difficulties. If the market price does not reflect quality, exportation of high-quality production can be blocked or require costly signaling. For instance, entry might require a low introductory price signal that cuts down on initial profits. If the required price cut is low enough, entry will not be worthwhile.

Information barriers can lead to insufficient entry even under favorable conditions such as the absence of potential competitors and no fixed costs of exporting. Bagwell and Staiger (1989) examine a potential monopoly exporter facing informational barriers but not costs of exporting. The potential monopolist can be thought of as an innovator introducing a new product. Product quality is determined exogenously and thus serves to identify the monopolist type. For any price not exceeding a critical level, demand is inelastic at one unit demanded by a single potential buyer. Demand disappears for prices exceeding the critical level. The new-product monopoly devotes its production exclusively to exporting to a market in which it faces no competitors. Exporting does not require fixed costs.

The two-player, two-period game has the following staging. In the introductory phase, product quality is exogenously determined from a discrete probability distribution assigning probabilities $P(q_L)$ and $P(q_H)$ to low- and high-qualities q_L and q_H. These initial probabilities are known to all players but the quality type drawn from the distribution is known only to the exporter, who moves first setting an introductory price given knowledge of its quality type. The consumer moves next and decides whether or not to buy. The exporter's potential client does not observe product quality but utilizes Bayes' rule and the observed introductory price to formulate beliefs about product quality.

Exogenously given quality precludes a quality choice decision and thus eliminates the possibility of a moral hazard problem. An adverse selection problem might arise due to incomplete information resulting from privately observed quality types. The possibility of low quality sales either blocks high-quality production or pushes down the introductory price of high-quality products.

In the mature phase—which takes place only if there is a sale in the introductory period—quality is revealed. The monopoly exporter sets a price knowing that quality is observed. After observing price and quality, the consumer decides whether or not to make a repeat purchase.

Assume that (1) the utility U of a high-quality product exceeds its cost but the utility of a low-quality product is less than its cost, and (2) a high-quality product is more expensive to produce than a low-quality product. Symbolically,

$$U(q_L) < c_L < c_H < U(q_H),$$

where $U(q_H)$ is the monopoly price charged when high quality is observable. An exporter producing a low-quality good is unable to earn positive profits after quality is revealed but might be active in the introductory phase as a fly-by-night firm if its true quality is unknown.

11.3.1. Free Trade with Adverse Selection

A sequential equilibrium for the monopoly exporter game with exogenous qualities is a set of price strategies (p_1, p_2) and consumer beliefs $(b_1(p_1), b_2(p_1, p_2))$ specifying the probability of a high quality product as a function of observed prices. The equilibrium price strategy must be sequentially rational for all information sets given beliefs, beliefs about quality must be formed according to Bayes' rule and a consistent requirement must be satisfied. The perfect sequential equilibrium concept of Grossman and Perry (1986), which provides a refinement of the sequential equilibrium concept by imposing 'reasonable' beliefs restricting off-the-equilibrium path beliefs, is used to obtain a unique equilibrium. Specifically, the assumption that beliefs in a disequilibrium pooling situation are given by the true probability, $b_1(p_1) = P(q_H)$, can be derived from this refinement.

Under free trade and complete information, a high-quality firm is able to export while a low-quality firm is unable to do so (given the previous utility and cost assumptions). Under incomplete information, three cases can arise. Exportation takes place under a pooling or separating equilibrium. Alternatively, exportation can be blocked altogether.

A pooling equilibrium is sustained if and only if (1) equilibrium beliefs about quality are optimistic enough to support a price equal to or exceeding c_L, and (2) a high-quality exporter obtains nonnegative discounted profits. The equilibrium introductory period price is equal to the conditional expected utility per unit consumed. Symbolically,

$$p_1^{Pool} = P(q_H \mid p_1^{Pool}) U(q_H) + P(q_L \mid p_1^{Pool}) U(q_L)$$
$$= P(q_H) U(q_H) + P(q_L) U(q_L) > c_L,$$

where the consumer's posterior probabilities $P(\cdot \mid \cdot)$ given the observation of price p_1^{Pool} are equal to the true probabilities (i.e. the prior probabilities). The equilibrium price under pooling does not introduce new information about quality so that beliefs are unchanged and posterior probabilities coincide with true probabilities. In a pooling equilibrium in which $c_L < p_1^{Pool} < c_H$, a high-quality exporter experiences losses in the introductory period. Nonnegative discounted profits imply that the initial losses of a high-quality producer are recovered by selling at the monopoly price $U(q_H)$ in the mature period

$$p_1^{Pool} U(q_H) - c_H + \rho[U(q_H) - c_H] \geq 0,$$

where ρ is the discount factor.

In a pooling equilibrium, both qualities can be exported but the equilibrium price fails to reflect the true value of the high-quality product. Given inelastic demand, setting a higher price as a signal of high-quality can be costlessly mimicked by a low-quality producer and will fail to attract sales. Moreover, a high-quality exporter lacks incentives to deviate by setting a lower introductory price to signal quality. Recall that off-the-equilibrium beliefs about quality are required to coincide with the true probabilities. Therefore, a reduction in the introductory period price lowers first period's profits and keeps the same profits in the mature period, thus leading to lower discounted profits than at equilibrium.

In a separating equilibrium, a low-quality firm does not enter so that $p_1 < c_L$ must hold. A high-quality exporter fails to reap profits in the introductory period but losses are recovered by selling at the monopoly price $U(q_H)$ in the mature period. Separation holds in the absence of intervention if a high-quality exporter can effectively signal its quality by a low introductory price strategy and has incentives to do so. In order for the low price to be a good signal of quality, it must fall below c_L so as to be low enough to preclude mimicry by a low-quality exporter. Signaling has a cost given by the gap between the monopoly price charged under complete information and the lower introductory price charged with quality revelation. The high-quality firm obtains positive discounted profits at any price $c_L - \varepsilon$ infinitesimally lower than c_L. Moreover, if the price under the true probabilities falls below c_L deviation to pooling is not possible. A separating sequential equilibrium takes place at price $p_1 = c_L$, which corresponds to the price entailing the lowest signaling cost. The reason is that a deviation away from separation is unimproving at $p_1 = c_L$, in the sense that a player's deviation does not generate a greater payoff.

Exports are blocked when a firm producing a high-quality product faces informational barriers that impede profitably distinguishing itself from a low-quality firm. In other words, the cost of signaling is so high that signaling is not worthwhile. Blocking arises if (1) 'reasonable' consumer beliefs $b(p_1) = P(q_H)$ would support a pooling price below c_L and the high-quality firm gets negative discounted profits at any price below c_L, or (2) 'reasonable' consumer beliefs would support a pooling price falling between the low- and high-cost values,

$$c_L \leq P(q_H)U(q_H) + P(q_L)U(q_L) < c_H,$$

but a high-quality firm would obtain negative discounted profits at this price. In case (1), no firm would have incentives to export. In case (2), a low-quality firm would not lose from exportation. However, negative discounted profits for a high-quality product—which would not be exported—allows identification of a low-quality firm attempting to export. Therefore, equilibrium breaks down and exportation is blocked.

The potential high-quality exporter is not able to export and the country experiences a welfare loss relative to the full information benchmark.

11.3.2. Entry and Separation Sustained by Subsidization

If the market price is high enough in a free trade equilibrium, a pooling equilibrium obtains in which both low- and high-quality firms are able to export. For instance, this happens if the market believes that average quality is close enough to high quality. The pooling free trade equilibrium generates an inefficiency from the exporting country's perspective. The reason is that a high-quality firm would not able to sell at a price that reflects its quality.

How can governments intervene to help an infant exporter offering a high-quality product overcome informational barriers? Suppose that the government, who does not observe introductory period quality, can precommit to grant a future subsidy. The optimal policy is to impose an specific export tax in the introductory period—when the government does not observe quality—combined with a precommitment to grant a specific subsidy in the mature period contingent on high-quality exportation. The mature period subsidy makes up for the introductory period tax. This dynamic performance-based policy turns out to increase welfare (relative to nonintervention) under pooling, separation, and blocked exports.

If the free trade equilibrium is a pooling equilibrium, the combination of a first period export tax and a mature period subsidy contingent on observed high-quality induces separation. The export tax would push a low-quality monopolist out of the market by causing a high-quality monopolist to get such a low after-tax price, $p_1 - t_1$, that mimicking is no longer profitable for a low-quality firm. Moreover, the tax shifts introductory period income from importing country consumers, who pay higher prices incorporating the tax, to the exporting firm's government who collects the taxes. As a result, the tax is welfare-improving. By a similar reasoning, an export tax combined with a performance-based mature period subsidy breaks a blocked equilibrium, makes possible exportation of a high-quality product and increases welfare relative to nonintervention.

Suppose that there is a separating equilibrium in the absence of government intervention but the government does not observe quality when setting specific taxes or subsidies in the introductory period. In a separating equilibrium in which only high-quality products are exported under free trade, a uniform export tax can be shown to increase welfare. The optimal policy requires taxing first period exports because a low free trade price entails a transfer of social surplus from the exporting country toward importing country consumers. The tax artificially increases the costs of an exporter who signals quality by setting a price below the full information monopoly price. The tax revenues allow the exporting country tax authorities to capture part of the surplus. The optimal mature period policy is nonintervention in this case. A subsidy would transfer income to importing consumers and there is no need to incur such cost because there is separation in the introductory period.

What is the optimal policy when exports are blocked and the government cannot credibly commit to a mature period subsidy? If precommitment is not feasible, then an introductory period subsidy can overcome a situation of blocked exports, support a pooling equilibrium, and increase welfare. Consider the case in which the high-quality firm loses under pooling and nonintervention, so that it does not produce, and the low-quality firm gains under said conditions but is identified and is not able to produce. Suppose that expected welfare is positive ex ante (calculated before quality is revealed). The first period subsidy enables the high-quality firm to produce and supports pooling, which in turn allows capturing low-quality product profits.

11.4. INFORMATIONAL BARRIERS AND MARKET POWER

This section focuses on adverse selection and moral hazard when an exporter holds market power as a monopolist. If quality is endogenous and demand is downward sloping, then a high introductory price signal can be used to reveal high-quality.

Do sellers of high-quality products set high introductory prices to signal quality? The high-price, low sales strategy is commonly used to introduce high-quality products. The strategy makes sense when low-quality producers would make greater profits by selling more products at a low price than by setting a high-price and accepting low sales to misrepresent themselves as high-quality. Evidence on the plausibility of this signaling mechanism includes, among others, a longitudinal study by Curry and Riesz (1988) and the introduction of car wax and fountain-pen ink at high prices to signal quality (Gabor and Granger, 1965).

11.4.1. Monopoly, Adverse Selection, and Moral Hazard

Bagwell (1991) presents a model featuring downward-sloping demand, perfectly elastic supply and endogenous quality. An export monopolist makes a once-and-for-all choice between high and low product qualities q_H and q_L. Unit costs $c(q_H)$ and $c(q_L)$ are constant, but quality is costly so that unit costs are higher for a higher-quality product, $c(q_H) > c(q_L)$. There are no sunk costs so that a higher quality is viewed as a function of better workmanship and more inputs devoted to production rather than a function of sunk product design or research and development costs.

Introductory phase profits $\pi_1(p, c(q_i); b)$ are given by

$$\pi_1(p, c(q_i); b) = [p - c(q_i)]D_1(p, b) > 0, \tag{11.2}$$

where $i \in \{L, H\}$ and b denotes consumers' beliefs defined as the likelihood that product quality is high. Introductory period demand D_1 is assumed to decline with the observed product price and increase with b. All firm types are assumed to obtain positive profits $\pi_1 > 0$ and are thus able to subsist as exporters no matter how low their product quality is.

In this setup there are no fly-by-night firms. The reason is that market price is assumed to exceed costs and consumers are not assumed to impose a minimum acceptable quality standard, which would eliminate all below-standard qualities. By contrast, in Grossman and Horn (1988) very low-quality firms are recognizable and make no sales in a pooling equilibrium. In the separating equilibrium with capacity signal studied by Grossman and Horn (1988) and in the separating equilibrium with low price signal studied in Bagwell and Staiger (1989), a firm offering a product of known low-quality is assumed to be unprofitable and makes no sales.

Mature phase profits $\pi_2(q, x)$ are a function of observed quality and the value of a stochastic shock X, which is defined on a support interval $[\underline{x}, \bar{x}]$ and is characterized by the cumulative distribution $F(x) = P(X \leq x)$. The random variable X captures a firm-specific future variable, such as level of future demand or costs, and denotes the firm type. For instance, a higher value of x might represent a firm facing greater future demand.

In the introductory period, the potential monopoly observes its type x (e.g. it is able to assess future demand) and formulates strategies as a function of its type. Consumers

(1) do not observe the firm type in the introductory period but know the value of x by the start of the mature period. Incomplete information gives rise to an adverse selection problem in which a low-type firm might have incentives to attempt to pass itself for a high-type firm (e.g. a firm facing high future demand);
(2) lack information about product quality choice in the introductory phase—giving rise to a moral hazard problem in the choice of quality—but learn the level of quality before the start of the mature phase.

A sequential equilibrium is a collection of (1) strategies $(p^{SE}(x), q^{SE}(x))$, consisting of an introductory price function and a quality function of the exogenous future shock x, and (2) Bayesian beliefs $b^{SE}(p)$ as a function of observed price p, where strategies and beliefs are consistent with each other. Equilibrium price and quality strategies maximize the undiscounted sum of introductory and mature period profits

$$\left\{ p^{SE}(x), q^{SE}(x) \right\} \in \underset{(p,q)}{\arg\max} \left\{ \pi_1\left(p, c(q); b^{SE}(p) \right) + \pi_2(q, x) \right\},$$

where the future is undiscounted and equilibrium beliefs $b^{SE}(p)$ represent the likelihood that product quality is high given the observation of introductory price p. Equilibrium outputs in the introductory and mature periods are given by $D_1(p^{SE}(x), b^{SE}(p^{SE}))$ and $D_2(q^{SE}(x), x)$. The introductory period monopoly profit of a firm offering a publicly known high-quality product is assumed to exceed the monopoly profits of a firm offering a publicly known low-quality product.

Let $\hat{x}$ represent the critical value of x separating the interval $x_1 < \hat{x}$ generating a low-quality choice and the interval $x_2 > \hat{x}$ generating a high-quality choice. $F(\hat{x})$ is the probability of a low-quality product and $1 - F(\hat{x})$ is the probability of a high-quality product. Equilibrium Bayesian beliefs in a pooling equilibrium are given by ($x_1 < \hat{x} < x_2$)

$$b^{SE}\left(p^{SE}(x_1)\right) = b^{SE}\left(p^{SE}(x_2)\right) = 1 - F(\hat{x}) \quad \text{if } p^{SE}(x_1) = p^{SE}(x_2).$$

Equilibrium Bayesian beliefs in a separating equilibrium are

$$b^{SE}\left(p^{SE}(x_1)\right) = 0 < 1 = b^{SE}\left(p^{SE}(x_2)\right) \quad \text{if } p^{SE}(x_1) \neq p^{SE}(x_2).$$

In a separating sequential equilibrium, a low-type firm producing a low-quality product, $x_1 < \hat{x}$ and $q^{SE} = q_L$, sets a price $p^{SE}\left(c(q_L), b^{SE}(p^{SE})\right) = p^{SE}\left(c(q_L), 0\right)$ generating the equilibrium belief that it offers a low-quality product ($b^{SE} = 0$). In other words, a type-x_1 firm does not have incentives to set a high-quality product price $p^{SE}(x_2)$ in order to augment profits by creating the false belief it offers a high-quality product.

11.4.2. Supramonopoly Price Signaling

Figure 11.1 illustrates the signaling equilibrium. In order to ensure separation, a high-quality product exporter must set a price p that works as a signal and precludes mimicking by a seller of low-quality products. Mimicking is precluded as long as a low-quality producer obtains lower profits setting a high-quality price p—which generates the false belief that a high-quality product is being offered—than setting the equilibrium low-quality price. The condition under which a low-quality product exporter would be indifferent between the equilibrium low-quality price and high-quality price p is

$$\pi_1\left[p^{SE}(c(q_L), 0), c(q_L), 0\right] = \pi_1[p, c(q_L), 1].$$

Profits in (11.2) are a quadratic function of price p so that two candidate high-quality price signals satisfy the indifference condition. One candidate high-quality price is so low that it reduces profits from mimicking to zero; the other is high enough to accomplish the same. The lower price signal is denoted $\underline{p}$ and the higher price signal is denoted $\bar{p}$. The bars distinguish low and high prices and are not being used to delimit a probability function's support interval.

It is easy to show that a high-quality producer prefers the high price signal $\bar{p}$ to $\underline{p}$. The reason is that candidate price $\bar{p}$ yields a higher profit to a high-quality producer. Using the increasing cost of quality relation $c(q_H) > c(q_L)$ and the downward-sloping demand condition $D(\underline{p}, 1) > D(\bar{p}, 1)$, we have

$$\pi_1(\bar{p}, c(q_H), 1) - \pi_1(\underline{p}, c(q_H), 1)$$

$$= (c(q_H) - c(q_L))[D(\underline{p}, 1) - D(\bar{p}, 1)] > 0.$$

This inequality is obtained by adding $\pi_1(\bar{p}, c(q_L), 1) - \pi_1(\underline{p}, c(q_L), 1) = 0$ to the profit differential, using the definition of profits in (11.2), and simplifying terms.

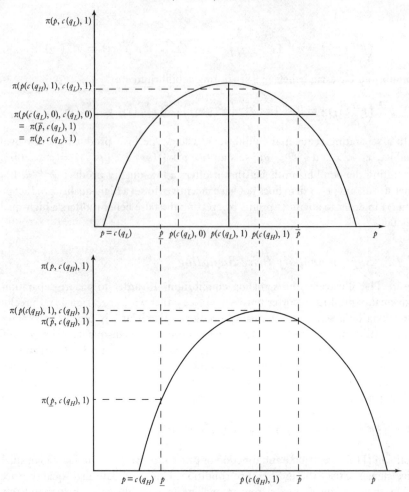

Figure 11.1. *Signaling exportation equilibrium*

Suppose that a low-quality product exporter would be able to increase profits if it could misrepresent itself as an exporter of high-quality products by pricing at the monopoly price of a high-quality product under full information. Formally, suppose that

$$\pi_1[p(c(q_H), 1), c(q_L), 1] > \pi_1[p^{SE}(c(q_L), 0), c(q_L), 0].$$

As illustrated in Fig. 11.1, the previous inequality and the concavity of the profit function $\pi_1[p, c(q_L), 1]$ imply that the monopoly price $p(c(q_H), 1)$ must lie below the equilibrium high-quality product price $\bar{p}$. In other words, signaling high product quality requires setting a price $\bar{p}$ exceeding the monopoly price $p(c(q_H), 1)$ that would prevail in the absence of asymmetric information.

The profit argument for a supramonopoly signaling price does not work in the inelastic demand models previously examined. First, setting a high price is an ineffective signaling device in Grossman and Horn's (1988) inelastic demand model with free entry and fixed capacity. A high price signal can be mimicked costlessly by a low-quality firm so that equilibrium features pooling. Second, a supramonopoly price fails in a situation in which demand is inelastic for any price below the monopoly price $U(q_H)$ but demand is null for $p > U(q_H)$. A supramonopoly price signaling strategy is ineffective because it drives demand to zero. This is the reason why signaling requires a low introductory price in Bagwell and Staiger's (1989) monopoly model. By contrast, when higher quality products require higher marginal costs and demand is downward sloping, using a low price signal is unattractive to an exporter of high-quality products.

Recapping, in order for price to signal quality, the high-quality price must be sufficiently high to preclude mimicry by a low-quality exporter. The equilibrium high-quality product price $\bar{p}$ under asymmetric information is set above the monopoly price $p(c(q_H), 1)$ that would prevail under no information asymmetries. Signaling through a distorted high-quality price reduces the volume of high-quality exports below the full information level. Moreover, the supramonopoly price $\bar{p}$ can be shown to be high enough to cause the high-quality type to produce less than the low-quality type in equilibrium. In other words, the volume of first period exports is smaller the higher their quality. Observe that the profits obtained by a high-x type in the mature period serve to eliminate the incentives to set a high introductory price as a signal of high-quality and then proceed to surprise consumers by producing a low-quality product in order to reduce costs.

11.4.3. Precluding Deviations from Separation

Let us examine how to eliminate deviations from the supramonopoly high-quality price $\bar{p}$. The intuitive equilibria of Cho and Kreps (1987) eliminates all strategies (p, q) for which (1) p is off-the-equilibrium path and, (2) strategy pair (p, q) yields lower undiscounted sum of profits than the equilibrium strategy no matter the off-the-equilibrium beliefs considered and the value of x. In other words, the intuitive criterion assigns the value $b(p) = 0$ to all off-the-equilibrium strategies that are equilibrium-dominated for all possible values of x and b. The Cho–Kreps refinement of sequential equilibrium is used to generate a unique sequential equilibrium, called 'intuitive equilibrium'.

We have already shown that price $\underline{p}$ is unattractive to a high-quality product exporter. Moreover, a high-quality producer will not choose a price p between $\underline{p}$ and $\bar{p}$ because mimicking by a low-quality producer would then be profitable. The concavity of the profit function of a low-quality product exporter imitating a high-quality pricing policy to pass itself as a high-quality exporter implies that, for $\underline{p} < p < \bar{p}$,

$$\pi_1(\underline{p}, c(q_L), 1) = \pi_1(\bar{p}, c(q_L), 1) < \pi_1(p, c(q_L), 1).$$

Off-the-equilibrium strategies in which the high-quality firm sets a price greater than $\bar{p}$ are eliminated using the intuitive criterion. To see this consider a conjectured equilibrium in which a firm with high-type $x > \hat{x}$, where $\hat{x}$ represents the threshold between a low and a high quality product decision, offers a high-quality product and sets price $p > \bar{p}$. A deviation from this conjectured equilibrium to strategy $(\bar{p}+\varepsilon, q_H)$, where $\bar{p} < \bar{p} + \varepsilon < p$, is not equilibrium-dominated for $x > \hat{x}$ because it yields higher profits than the conjectured equilibrium. Moreover, the off-the-equilibrium strategy $(\bar{p} + \varepsilon, q_L)$ is equilibrium-dominated for $x > \hat{x}$ because it yields less profits than the separating equilibrium profits of a firm producing a low quality product (this feature precludes mimicking). Therefore, the off-the-equilibrium strategy involving price $(\bar{p} + \varepsilon, q_H)$ beats strategy (p, q_H) for all possible beliefs, which eliminates a deviation to (p, q_H).

Is the low-quality price distorted in a separating equilibrium? In contrast with a high-quality producer, a low quality exporter selects the undistorted low-quality monopoly price that would prevail under complete and perfect information. The reason is that signaling is costly and a low-quality exporter does not benefit from distorting its price to signal low quality.

The producer of a low quality product maximizes profits by choosing $p^{SE}(c(q_L), 0)$ because there is no price that yields a higher profit. First, recall that if $b(\bar{p}) = 1$ the low-quality producer is indifferent between setting price $\bar{p}$ and $p^{SE}(c(q_L), 0)$. However, a pooling equilibrium in which a low-quality producer sets a price $\bar{p}$ does not subsist because the generated pooling beliefs would be $b(\bar{p}) = 1 - F(\hat{x})$. Given those beliefs, the undistorted monopoly price $p^{SE}(c(q_L), 0)$ maximizes the profits of a low-quality exporter.

Second, conjecture that the low-quality producer sets a price p, where $\underline{p} < p < \bar{p}$. This deviation cannot be eliminated by the definition of sequential equilibrium, as off-the-equilibrium beliefs $b(\underline{p}) = b(\bar{p}) = 1$ imply

$$\pi_1(\underline{p}, c(q_L), 1) = \pi_1(\bar{p}, c(q_L), 1) < \pi_1(p, c(q_L), 1).$$

However, the deviation to p can be eliminated by the following dominance argument, presented as a dialogue between a low-quality exporter setting price p and its customer:

Exporter speech: I have set a price that yields higher profits than the equilibrium price set by a low-quality producer and you should believe that I offer a high-quality product.

Customer speech: My intuition tells me that you might not really offer a high-quality product. If you were a high-quality producer you would do better by setting price $\bar{p} > p$. For that reason I believe you are a low-quality producer and will set $b(p) = 0$ for any price between $\underline{p}$ and $\bar{p}$.

Exporter speech: Given these beliefs about quality I will not set price p. The undistorted monopoly price $p(c(q_L), 0)$ maximizes the profits of a low-quality exporter when $b(p) = 0$ as $\pi_1(p, c(q_L), 0) < \pi_1(p^{SE}, c(q_L), 0)$.

The dominance argument eliminates all deviations except the deviation to $\bar{p}$, which is the best deviation. But the separating equilibrium is immune to this potential deviation because it would be an unimproving deviation, that is, $\pi_1(\bar{p}, c(q_L), 1) = \pi_1(p(c(q_L), 0), c(q_L), 0)$. Also, it is easy to see that a pooling equilibrium with price $\bar{p}$ is not immune to deviations and does not subsist. The reason is that a pooling equilibrium at $\bar{p}$ would generate beliefs $b(\bar{p}) = 1 - F(\hat{x})$. The monopoly price $p(c(q_L), 0)$ maximizes the profits of a low-quality exporter when $b(p) = 0$, which means that $\pi_1(p, c(q_L), 1 - F(\hat{x})) < \pi_1(p(c(q_L), 0), c(q_L), 0)$. We have just shown that, when the demand function is downward sloping, a single-crossing property holds and pooling equilibria based on the fixed inelastic demand assumption made by Grossman and Horn (1988) and Bagwell and Staiger (1989) do not subsist.

Export Subsidization

Let us consider intervention in the form of a specific export subsidy or tax. The non-intervention equilibrium is separating but the government does not observe product quality q or firm type x when policy is formulated. The presence of market imperfections allows welfare-improving policy intervention even though the government does not observe firm type or product quality when policy is formulated. If precommitment to a mature period policy is feasible, then the best export policy would be a mature period subsidy contingent on quality performance.

If precommitment to a mature period policy is infeasible then the government sets the uniform subsidy s maximizing expected welfare, that is, expected undiscounted unsubsidized profits (expected undiscounted after-subsidy profits plus subsidy spending). What is the optimal introductory period export policy? The best policy consists of an introductory period subsidy reducing perceived costs to $c_H(q) - s_1$ and $c_L(q) - s_1$. This prescription coincides with the no-precommitment prescription in the inelastic demand model of Bagwell and Staiger (1989).

A specific introductory period export subsidy lowers a new products's price and raises its quantity demanded. On one hand, the policy subsidizes importing country consumers by shifting the export price below the low-quality monopoly price. This effect represents a distortion in the price of low-quality exports and reduces welfare. On the other hand, the subsidy sustains the rational perception that a high-quality export can be provided at a relatively low price. This price effect increases welfare (unsubsidized profits) by enabling high-quality exports to be sold at a less distorted price. The government subsidy does not change the unsubsidized high-quality profit function but causes a change in perceived marginal costs, which lowers the price toward the monopoly price: $\bar{p}(s > 0) < \bar{p}(s = 0)$ in Fig. 11.1.

The reduction of the distortion in the high-quality market entails a first-order effect—a move toward the high-quality monopoly price with associated profit increase. The creation of a distortion in the low-quality market entails a second-order effect—a move away from the low-quality monopoly price. The feature that the price of the low-quality export is initially undistorted implies that there is a small enough export subsidy such that the distortion in the low-quality price is less than the welfare gain from the high-quality export subsidy.

An interesting situation arises from the subsidization of both quality types and the property that low quality sales exceed high quality sales. Paradoxically, an export subsidy reduces the probability that a high quality good will be exported. To see why, recall that prior beliefs about the probability of high quality are given by $1 - F(\hat{x}(s))$, where F is the distribution function of the firm type x and $\hat{x}$ is the critical value of x separating the low- and high-quality regions. The subsidy s operates by raising the critical value $\hat{x}$ and thus reducing the probability of high quality. The fact that low-quality exports exceed high-quality exports means that total specific subsidies are greater when an exporter follows a low-quality strategy. Therefore, the subsidy is especially attractive to an exporter of low-quality products, causing some firm types x to shift toward low-quality production. As a result the critical value of the shock is increased. Formally,

$$\frac{d\hat{x}(s)}{ds} > 0 \;\; \rightarrow \;\; \frac{d(1 - F(\hat{x}(s)))}{ds} = -f(\hat{x}(s))\frac{d\hat{x}(s)}{ds} < 0,$$

where the distribution function F and the density f are evaluated at the critical value $\hat{x}(s)$.

The conclusion is that an export subsidy works by reducing the distortion attached to a supramonopoly price, $d\bar{p}(s)/ds < 0$, not by encouraging the exportation of high-quality goods. The intuition is that the subsidy benefits an exporter of low-quality products disproportionately and distorts the price of low-quality exports by shifting it below the low-quality monopoly price. As a result, the subsidy diminishes the incentives to mimic a high-quality exporter, which in turn ameliorates the distortion of the high-quality price.

11.5. PRICE COMPETITION AND QUALITY CHOICE

We have examined a potential infant exporter who would hold a monopoly in the export market. If the government cannot precommit, the policy prescription is to grant an introductory period subsidy.

Does the analysis change if the exporter sells in a duopolistic market? Raff and Kim (1999) show that the introductory period subsidy prescription can be reversed. An export tax might be better when firms compete in prices. Consider an exporter entering into a market dominated by a local incumbent offering a product of known quality. In the resulting duopoly, the entrant and the local incumbent produce vertically differentiated products and compete in prices. A moral hazard problem arises because consumers, the incumbent, and the intervening government do not observe the quality of the entrant offering in the first period. An entrant might thus be tempted to cheat on quality choice. Quality is revealed to all in the mature period.

Consider a continuum of consumers, each of whom demands one unit per period and is willing to pay more the greater the perceived product quality. Consumers are indexed by parameter γ, which measures taste for quality and is uniformly distributed over interval $[0, 1]$. The net utility or surplus obtained by a consumer with taste γ is $CS(q) = U(q) - p_1 = \gamma q - p_1$. The resulting market demand function can be shown to be linear and downward sloping as a lower price attracts lower-γ consumers. The downward-sloping demand supports separation as in Bagwell (1991).

The exporter must make a once-and-for-all discrete choice between low and high qualities $q_L < q_H$. The marginal cost of production is strictly increasing in quality and constant in output. As in Bagwell (1991), the supply of output is infinitely elastic and both qualities would be produced in a full information equilibrium. Incumbent's quality q_I is exogenous, known by all, and can exceed, fall below or lie between q_L and q_H. The analysis here focuses on the case in which incumbent quality is lower than both possible domestic qualities. The incumbent does not observe introductory period domestic prices and cannot update prior beliefs about entrant's quality.

The principle of maximal product differentiation states that, if firms compete in prices and quality is endogenous, then firms do not want to locate at the same place in the product space. Instead, they choose to locate as far away as possible from each other. The maximal differentiation strategy establishes a market niche, which lessens competition allowing each firm to exploit market power. Specifically, the conditions (1) $q_I < q_L < q_H$, and (2) $q_L - q_H$ is large enough in relation to $c(q_L) - c(q_H)$, imply that the exporter's mature period profits are larger if quality is high than if quality is low. Mature period entrant quality choice (the incumbent quality is exogenous) leads to maximal vertical differentiation when firms compete in prices. The product quality decision must take into account that quality is observed in the mature period but there is asymmetric information when it is chosen in the introductory period. Therefore, high quality does not necessarily dominate.

The domestic exporter maximizes discounted profits $\pi_1 + \rho\pi_2$, where the discount factor $\rho \in (0, 1]$ is private information and defines the firm type. If the discount factor exceeds a critical value $\hat{\rho}$ product quality is chosen to be high, but is chosen to be low if $\rho < \hat{\rho}$. An adverse selection problem arises because consumers neither observe product quality nor the exporter's discount factor. Prior beliefs are endogenous and are given by the probability of high quality, $1 - F(\hat{\rho})$, where F is the distribution function of discount factor ρ. There is a separating equilibrium in which an exporter of high-quality products signals its type and quality choice through a high introductory price.

The exporter country's government maximizes welfare in the sense of unsubsidized output. Authorities do not know the quality of exports when they formulate introductory period policy and cannot commit to future trade policies. Moreover, the policy is chosen after the entrant's quality decision so that, in contrast to Bagwell (1991), policy does not affect quality choice (i.e. the critical value $\hat{\rho}$).

Trade policy works through the product price and must balance two opposite effects: a signaling and a strategic effect. A specific export subsidy can address the signaling difficulty while a specific export tax represents strategic trade policy aiming to restrict output and increase profits. The balance between the signaling and strategic effects determines whether exports are taxed or subsidized. Suppose that the benefits from restricting competition between the incumbent and the exporter dominate the benefits from signaling. In this case, a dynamic policy involving a rising export tax is optimal. The benefits from restricting price competition call for an export tax in both periods. However, transitory signaling problems moderate the first period uniform tax (the government does not observe quality in the first period). The gain from restricting competition calls for a higher tax when consumers and the government learn about the quality of the export and the signaling distortion disappears. Mature period exports are subject to an export tax that increases with observed product quality: $t(q_L) < t(q_H)$.

11.6. WHAT IS THE OPTIMAL INFANT EXPORT POLICY?

Let us recap and extend the whole discussion about the optimal infant exporter policy when neither the government nor customers directly observe quality. The optimal policy depends on the scenario considered:

1. Export subsidies are inefficient if they encourage excessive entry of inefficient firms when prices are uninformative or if they increase the costs of signaling through costly capacity investments in the presence of adverse selection (Grossman and Horn, 1988).
2. Export subsidies address the problem of insufficient entry due to the inability to sell at prices reflecting a product's quality. Such is the plight of a potential monopoly exporter facing a brand-specific reputation problem. If the government can precommit to future subsidies, maturity period subsidies contingent on observed high-quality performance can address the informational barrier, as in Bagwell and Staiger (1989) model of exogenous qualities, inelastic demand and low-price signal. If the government cannot precommit, subsidies can be granted in the introductory period to reduce the signaling costs from setting a supramonopoly price in a separating equilibrium, as in Bagwell's (1991) model of endogenous qualities, downward-sloping demand and high-price signal.

Export subsidies can also be rationalized in a setting with country-specific reputation and externalities in the sense that high-quality exports by one sector positively affects the reputation of other sectors (Mayer, 1984*a*).

1. Export taxes can be used by a country holding monopoly power to extract income from importing country consumers and transfer it to the taxing government (Bagwell and Staiger, 1989) or to restrict competition when there is excessive export market competition because sellers of differentiated products compete in prices (Raff and Kim, 1999).
2. Legal limitations exist because both export subsidies and taxes are severely restricted by the World Trade Organization (WTO). These restrictions can be bypassed by avoiding direct subsidization or taxation of trade. Alternative policies include subsidizing high-quality firms through their research spending.

Firms and national authorities have devised numerous mechanisms that bypass costly export and research subsidies. These mechanisms, which often address informational distortions directly rather than indirectly through trade and research policies, are particularly relevant for infant exporters but also apply to established firms.

Introductory phase pricing strategies do not preclude complementary welfare-increasing intervention but can break informational barriers in the absence of intervention. A high price, low sales strategy is best when quality is anticipated to become publicly known soon, quality production is expensive, and low-quality producers get higher profits from a large sales volume than by misrepresenting themselves as high-quality. If demand is inelastic, though, an exporter of low-quality products has an incentive to mimic the high product quality exporter. A high price introductory strategy fails as a signaling mechanism but the infant exporter can still formulate a low introductory price signaling strategy (Bagwell and Staiger, 1989). A low introductory price strategy also works if repeated sampling over time is necessary to accurately assess product quality. A low price leads consumers to engage in experimental buying of new products. Product sampling enhances the acquisition of product information and generates a learning-by-doing effect on the consumer side, which helps to overcome informational barriers.

Advertisement, securing a reputable distributor and the adoption of total quality management methods (TQM) to boost product quality serve to offer assurance to quality-conscious consumers. TQM is a popular management technique used to improve or ensure quality processes and products.

Firm associations and government authorities often certify or signal quality. An attached institutional certification establishes attributes and quality. The Appellation d'Origine Contrôlée (AOC) serves to officially establish the regional origin, attributes and quality of wines, cheeses and other French offerings. A product must satisfy product attribute and quality requirements to be allowed to utilize an AOC and participation is voluntary. Countries' authorities frequently launch campaigns to advertise national products internationally. These campaigns contribute to consolidate the association of a country's name and its high-quality offerings.

The evolution of international standards, is another method for minimum quality certification. In order to secure access to its markets, the European Union (EU) requires certification of a firm's manufacturing process and product under the ISO 9000 quality standard. ISO standards have two sides in that they impose a costly bureaucratic process to firms attempting to enter EU markets and can be used as a protectionist device.

11.7. CONCLUSIONS

The presence of an informational barrier to exports due to privately observed quality can be addressed by granting subsidies to high-quality firms. The subsidization prescription, though, is subject to several caveats. First, subsidies are counterproductive if they lead to adverse selection by attracting low-quality firms in a competitive equilibrium with free entry. Second, firms and national authorities have devised numerous mechanisms that bypass costly export subsidies and address informational distortions directly rather than through trade policies. These devices include signaling through research spending and advertisement, the establishment of local and international quality standards, and the subsidization of high-quality firm research spending. Finally, both export subsidies and taxes are restricted by the WTO. These legal limitations can be rationalized as an institutional mechanism to avoid prisoner dilemma situations due to subsidy competition among WTO members.

12

Networks and Outsourcing

This chapter examines the role of networks, contracts, and outsourcing in international trade. Successful participation in global markets hinges on the manner in which firms (1) participate in productive networks and joint ventures, (2) efficiently allocate observed and unobserved talents (i.e. human capital, skills, abilities) across activities, (3) address contractual imperfections potentially leading to inefficient labor hiring, and (4) efficiently combine outsourcing and internal production.

International networks such as business and social groups facilitate information sharing and help to overcome informational trade barriers. They can also act to partially correct contract imperfections due to weak contract enforcement at the international level. Better information and stronger contract enforcement in turn improve efficiency and promote trade. A downside is that economic groups can sustain collusive activities that reduce competition and divert business toward members. Moreover, networks that do not produce significant spillovers on nonmembers can have distributive effects hurting nonmembers even while benefiting members or the aggregate of members and nonmembers.

The shift from in-house production to outsourcing is a key element of the new economy. Outsourcing offers lower-cost specialized production and avoids the corporate governance costs attached to vertical integration. However, when quality is not verifiable, suppliers have incentives to save costs by lowering quality. Moreover, specialized component suppliers face a 'hold-up' problem as clients have incentives to lower prices after the supplier realizes relation-specific sunk investments. The outsourcing decision depends on the balance of these factors. In a world where intermediate input trade has so greatly expanded that products have multiple nationalities, firms must decide where to outsource. The outsourcing location decision hinges on the costs of searching for a partner abroad, the 'thickness' of the foreign market, and the quality of the foreign legal system (Grossman and Helpman, 2002a).

How is optimal matching of diverse talent accomplished? Technology factors direct more talented workers toward submodular technologies, meaning those exhibiting input substitutability or relying on the task performed by the most talented workers (i.e. product design). Less talented workers are directed into supermodular technologies, meaning those exhibiting input complementarity or relying on the task performed by the least talented workers (i.e. assembly). Cross-country differences in the diversity of talent can explain key features of observed specialization and trade patterns. A country with a more diverse labor force exports products hinging on input substitutability or the strongest input (e.g. the United States). A country with a more homogeneous labor force exports products hinging on complementarity or the weakest input (e.g. Japan). This pattern holds when talent is readily identifiable and is reinforced when talent is unobserved by all, including the worker (Grossman and Maggi, 2000).

What are the trade effects of imperfect contracting? If there is asymmetric information about worker talents and contracts are imperfect, more talented workers select activities that allow capturing rents from individual talent. Less talented workers join teams that blur individual contribution and pay a salary based on average worker talent. Accordingly, a country with a more diverse labor force specializes in activities allowing the appropriation of the rents from talent. A country with a less diverse labor force specializes in team activities in which individual contributions are unobserved and full individual appropriation of rents is not possible (Grossman, 1999).

The importance of products requiring great individual talent in US exports, and the importance of team work in Japan and Germany's exports, can be explained by greater labor diversity in the US relative to Japan and Germany. High talent is attracted toward submodular production functions or those industries rewarding individual talent and minimizing labor contracting imperfections.

Sections 12.1 and 12.2 review the theory and evidence on domestic and international networks. Sections 12.3 and 12.4 deal with the economics of outsourcing. Section 12.5 discusses submodularity, supermodularity, and the matching of tasks and labor talents. Section 12.6 explains how cross-country differences in talent diversity rationalize key features of observed specialization and trade patterns and Section 12.7 deals with incomplete contracting.

12.1. BUSINESS GROUPS AND SOCIAL NETWORKS

Markets operate through occasional and repeated interactions among a large number of agents. Networks are relations involving repeated exchanges among a limited number of business firms or individuals who engage in some form of cooperative behavior within the group. Production networks include business groups—such as Japanese keiretsu, Korean chaebol, Spanish, and Latin American grupos económicos—and social groups—such as those based on shared ethnic origin or religion. The linkages among the members of these groups range from common ownership or central control as in a holding company, supplier–procurer relationships as in Japanese vertical keiretsu, and common marketing facilities as in a trading group.

A growing body of theoretical reasoning and empirical evidence suggests that the operation of networks influences international trade, market access, productive efficiency, and technology transfer, as well as product variety and quality. Rauch's (2001) survey of networks focuses on the forces behind the demand for and supply of networks. He concludes that technological and contractual innovations can reduce the future demand for networks as informational and contractual instruments but this effect can be offset by factors expanding the supply of networks. These include better communications, lower transportation costs, the expansion of multinationals, and continuous human migration.

12.1.1. Do Networks Overcome Invisible Trade Barriers?

Do networks tend to reduce informational, contractual, and other barriers to trade or rather create informal trade barriers? In practice, both trade-promoting and trade reducing effects take place. Usually, transnational networks are deemed to be trade-promoting while domestic networks are claimed to limit market access and trade.

International networks promote trade by exploiting the familiarity of members with business opportunities in foreign countries. Members diffuse information about foreign demand and supply conditions and facilitate the search for appropriate partners abroad. These mechanisms contribute to break down informational barriers to trade.

Networks that extend across countries can also offset the negative trade effects arising from the weaker enforcement of international contracts relative to national contracts. Their presence restricts opportunistic behavior and supports trust and exchange. Indeed, networks can informally enforce contracts at the international level by providing for a multilateral punishment mechanism that would not be available otherwise. Lacking group action or effective international arbitrage by legal means, conflict resolution hinges on bilateral punishment based on retaliatory actions initiated by the party hurt by another party's opportunistic behavior.

What does the empirical evidence tell us? Keiretsu membership and the extent of keiretsu foreign activity are associated with higher exports. Belderbos and Sleuwaegen (1998) find that being a keiretsu member positively affected the 1988 intensity of the exports made by eighty-six electronics or precision machinery Japanese firms to the European Community. Head and Ries (2001) examine vertical keiretsu (in the automobile and electronics industry) constituted by an assembler and its component suppliers. They find that the 1966–90 exports of a sample of ninety-six keiretsu suppliers were positively affected by the count of foreign manufacturing investments realized by the assembler of the supplier's keiretsu.

Ample evidence shows that a larger stock of immigrants from a particular country is associated to greater trade with the country of origin, a finding that reflects the positive role of familiarity and old-country networks. The bilateral trade-promotion effect is detected using a variant of the gravity trade model to control for the distance between trading partners (the gravity effect) and other determinants of trade volumes. Gould (1994) estimates that the stock of US immigrants from forty-seven trading partners have positive and statistically significant effects on bilateral exports to and imports from the country of origin. Head and Ries (1998) find that, in Canada, the stock of immigrants during 1982–92 elicits a positive response of bilateral exports to and imports from 136 trading partners.

Overseas Chinese networks tend to increase bilateral trade volumes. Rauch and Trindade (2002) operationally define the importance of Chinese networks in bilateral trade as the product of the ethnic Chinese population shares in the two countries. The study distinguishes between trade in commodities that have a reference price and those that do not have a reference price. A commodity has a reference price when a price is quoted without reference to a brand name or producer identification. The existence of a reference price is interpreted as an indication of substantial product homogeneity. A positive trade effect is found to take place both in commodities that have a reference price and in those that do not have a reference price. However, ethnic Chinese networks are found to have a greater impact on bilateral trade in commodities without reference prices (i.e. differentiated commodities) than on bilateral trade in commodities with reference prices (i.e. homogeneous commodities). The authors argue that the larger effect of Chinese networks on trade in differentiated commodities (which requires acquiring information about product characteristics) suggests that networks provide information about business opportunities in addition to enforcing contracts and supporting trust-based exchanges.

The argument that networks facilitate search when there is trade in differentiated products is developed in Rauch (1999). Homogeneous products' prices convey the relevant information needed for buying and selling decisions. In contrast, trade in differentiated products requires familiarity in order to match the characteristics demanded and offered. It is thus more difficult to find a trading partner when there is trade in differentiated products than when there is trade in homogeneous products. This means that the role of familiarity and networks providing greater information in matching buyers and sellers is greater with differentiated products than with homogeneous products. The empirical findings—using a sample of sixty-three countries in 1970, 1980, and 1990—support this view in the sense that proximity, common language, and colonial ties are found to affect bilateral trade in differentiated products more than bilateral trade in homogeneous products. Network strength is viewed as inversely related to distance according to the notion that networks require personal contacts that are discouraged by distance.

Greif (1994) documents the use of networks to suppress opportunistic behavior and argues that this mechanism can be statically efficient while displaying dynamic inefficiencies. Dynamic inefficiencies can arise if networks discourage trade relations outside the group and limit the search for alternative ways to solve enforcement and opportunistic behavior problems.

12.1.2. Is Import Competition Reduced by Keiretsu?

Why is it that Japan remains a relatively close economy despite displaying low tariff levels and few visible nontariff barriers to trade? Many observers claim that low import penetration levels are explained by informal trade barriers. Business groups (keiretsu) become entrenched in local markets, limiting market access to foreign exporters and thus exerting a trade-reducing effect.

There are two types of Japanese business groups (keiretsu): horizontal (or intermarket) and vertical keiretsu. The ownership of intermarket groups—Mitsubishi, Mitsui, Simitomo, Fuyo, Ikkan, and Sanwa—extends over several unrelated industries and each group has an associated trading company. These groups are also called 'main bank groups' because each is organized around a main bank that provides financing. The ownership structure of vertical keiretsu—Tokai Bank, IBJ, Nippon Steel, Hitachi, Nissan, Toyota, Matsushita, Toshiba-IHI, Yokyu, and Seiba—consists of links between independent members. Suppliers and assemblers are integrated into a production process coordinated by the larger assembler members purchasing the inputs provided by suppliers.

Local business groups exert trade-reducing effects in the model developed by Spencer and Qiu (2001). They examine a market in which suppliers of interme-diate inputs (e.g. subcontractors producing auto parts) make relationship-specific investments in the sense that they benefit particular clients. These specific invest-ments are protected by means of long-term arrangements setting the terms of the supplier–assembler interaction. Otherwise, the suppliers' clients would have excessive bargaining power at the post-investment stage. In the absence of a pre-agreed arrange-ment, suppliers who have already made specific investments become captive sellers with no profitable alternative clients. This is the so-called 'hold-up' problem affect-ing specific investments. A solution is to enter into long-term contracts and repeated interactions providing security to suppliers participating in networks. As a result, the demand for imported intermediate inputs is reduced or eliminated even if inputs can be produced at a lower cost abroad. The authors point out that business groups and relationship-specific investments that serve to improve efficiency do not give rise to an 'unfair' trade barrier.

Fung (1991) finds that in 1980 the industry sales shares and the employment shares of keiretsu-affiliated firms had a negative effect on US net exports to Japan in a sample of twenty-two industries. Lawrence (1991) confirms the finding that keiretsu dis-couraged import penetration in thirty-seven industries for the year 1985. The share of keiretsu in industry sales does not have a statistically significant effect on Japan's worldwide market share, as might be expected if the greater efficiency hypothesis held. Lawrence concludes that keiretsu imposed a limited barrier to entry and rejects the hypothesis that keiretsu reduced imports by generating efficiency gains. Saxonhouse (1993) counters arguing that the composition of keiretsu was not constant and that changing membership raises questions about the entry barrier conclusion.

12.1.3. How Does Trade and Technology Affect Networks?

There is mutual feedback between networks, on one side, and technology and trade, on the other side. Just as networks influence trade activity and technology transfer, international trade and technological developments impinge on existing networks and create new networks.

Does the expansion of trade, new technologies facilitating international communica-tions and cheaper transportation encourage or discourage networks? On one hand, growing trade and improved technologies entail greater interaction and continuous learning about international business opportunities. These factors reduce the demand for networks as a mechanism to surpass informational barriers.

On the other hand, technology improvements facilitating the formation of networks, the global spread of multinationals and human migration are factors contributing to expand the supply of international networks. Also, greater business complexity, the expansion of the geographic scope of deals, and the need to evaluate vast amounts of information, require personal or close communications (i.e. face-to-face, handshake relationships). Impersonal or long-distance interactions (i.e. contracts, arms-length relationships) alone cannot fulfill all the interactive requirements of complex global deals. Finally, larger markets create a 'thickness' externality that facilitates outsourcing (and potentially the formation of networks).

12.1.4. Endogenous Relations: Handshake Deals vs Contracts

International trade can affect the type of business relationships that firms engage in. McLaren (1999) develops a theoretical model endogenizing the type of business relationship between an assembler and a component supplier. The business deal can take place either through a fixed-price contract, which creates incentives for autonomous cost-reducing investments, or through a handshake arrangement, which creates incentives for joint cost-reducing investments. Because deals closed by handshakes require personal and repeated interaction they are viewed as a network relationship.

International trade expands the number of alternative input buyers, enhances the incentives to undertake autonomous investments as opposed to joint-investments, and reduces the role of fixed-price contracts. Trade encourages interfirm relations based on handshake arrangements (bargaining) rather than on fixed-price contracts because more potential buyers raise suppliers' bargaining power.

12.2. NETWORKS AND INFORMATIONAL BARRIERS

This section presents a formal model of international networks, informational barriers, and wage costs. An instance of the role of international networks is the transformation of the Korean and Taiwanese apparel industries, both of which moved offshore in the late 1980s and early 1990s. The Korean industry moved to Latin America to benefit from low wages. By contrast, the Taiwanese industry moved to other parts of East Asia where Chinese networks are well established.

The behavior of Taiwanese firms reflects the role of familiarity and the remarkable success of Chinese networks in East Asia. According to the April 2001 *Economist* survey of Asian business (Kluth, 2001), overseas Chinese are reported to own 73 percent of market capitalization in Indonesia (where they constitute 3–4 percent of the population), 5–6 percent in Philippines (2 percent of the population) and 81 percent in Thailand (14 percent of the population).

12.2.1. International Partnerships

Rauch and Casella (2002) develop a model of networks as a mechanism to overcome informational barriers. Producers must find a matching partner, viewed as a joint venture partner, in order to be able to produce. Producer networks have two opposite effects on welfare. First, tied producers efficiently arbitrage international cost differentials, which is welfare-increasing. Second, networks can lead to welfare-reducing trade diversion.

Consider a scenario with two countries (called home and foreign), two productive service sectors, and a single factor (labor) which is inelastically supplied and internationally immobile. Workers are homogeneous in the sense that they have the same skills and talents. Both countries have access to the same technologies but differ in factor endowments. The home country is labor scarce, the foreign country is labor abundant ($L < L^*$) and domestic wages exceed foreign wages ($w^* < w$). Trade takes the form of exchanges of factor services. The international wage differential serves as a price signal used by producers in the labor-scarce country to seek matches in the labor-abundant country.

Output q_{ij} is produced by a joint venture between producers of types i and j

$$q_{ij} = F(l_{ij}, z_{ij}) = z_{ij} f(l_{ij}/z_{ij}),$$

where F exhibits constant returns to scale and l_{ij} represents the amount of homogeneous labor used by the partnership. The variable z_{ij} represents the 'distance' between the two joint venture partners and is distributed uniformly on the interval $[0, 1/2]$. The quality of the match is assumed to increase with the 'distance' measure. Joint venture profits Π_{ij} are given by the match quality times a decreasing and convex profit function π of the wage rate w determining l_{ij}/z_{ij} (l_{ij} is maximized out)

$$\Pi_{ij}(w, z_{ij}) = \max_{l_{ij}}[z_{ij} f(l_{ij}/z_{ij}) - w z_{ij}(l_{ij}/z_{ij})] = z_{ij} \pi(w).$$

Observe that the quality of the match z_{ij} does not enter into $\pi(w)$.

Recall the discussion of duality and Shepard's lemma. The firm's factor demand function $a(w, q)$ per unit of output is given by the partial derivative of the average cost function $c(w, q)$ with respect to the vector w of input rental prices

$$a(w, q) = \frac{\partial c(w, q)}{\partial w}.$$

The total demand for labor $l(w, q) = qa(w, q)$, conditional on firm output, is given by the partial derivative of the total cost function $C(w, q) = qc(w, q)$ with respect to w.

The demand for labor l_{ij} generated by partnership ij is given by

$$l_{ij}(w) = \frac{\partial C_{ij}(w, q_{ij}^{\text{opt}})}{\partial w} = -\frac{\partial \Pi_{ij}(w, q_{ij}^{\text{opt}})}{\partial w} = -z_{ij} \frac{\partial \pi(w)}{\partial w},$$

where $\Pi_{ij}(w, q_{ij}^{\text{opt}}) = pq_{ij}^{\text{opt}} - C_{ij}(w, q_{ij}^{\text{opt}}) = z_{ij} \pi(w)$ and $\partial \pi(w)/\partial w < 0$.

In each country, there is a continuum of producers uniformly distributed around the unit circle (a circle with circumference equal to 1). The distribution of potential partner types has its median at the producer's opposite side.

Each producer, assumed to have a unit mass, must find a matching partner. Partnerships can be domestic or international. Joint venture partners divide the surplus, equal to the value of the match, on the basis of Nash bargaining. Assuming that both partners have the same bargaining power, the joint surplus is divided equally between them.

Let us examine domestic matching. Each producer selects a partner and proposes to form a joint venture. The threat point of the domestic matching and bargaining game is zero because each producer gets zero profit if the potential partner rejects the proposed matching and bargaining breaks down. The threat point is never reached because there is complete information about potential domestic partner types so that all home country producers know the best domestic partner. Because all producers know the location of their best domestic partners and the quality of the match increases with distance, the best domestic match is the one on the opposite location across the circle. The optimal match with a domestic partner corresponds to $z_{ih} = 1/2$, where i and h are domestic firms. The close economy wage is obtained from $L = (1/2)(\partial \pi(w)/\partial w)$.

The quality of equilibrium two-member domestic partnerships equals $1/2$. Therefore, each partnership generates profits $\pi(w)/2$. The domestic joint venture surplus $\pi(w)/2$ is divided equally so that a firm's profits from a domestic partnership are equal to $\pi(w)/4$, which is the threat point in the international bargaining game. By the same token, the threat point for a foreign producer j is $\pi(w^*)/4$, where f represents the best foreign partner.

A system of international partnerships in which each domestic firm seeks a foreign partner to produce abroad is beneficial because it allows low-wage production ($w^* < w$). If a producer seeking a matching partner is rejected by a potential foreign partner, he or she simply returns to the home market to join the best domestic partner. Given the assumption that firms can go back to their home markets, there are incentives to search for a partner abroad. However, only a fraction m of domestic producers is assumed to be tied in the sense of knowing the location of the best foreign partner. For all other domestic producers there is incomplete information about potential foreign partners' types. A fraction $1 - m$ of every type knows the distribution of the types but not their exact location.

An international joint venture improves the matching process by leading to type revelation at the level of the partnership (but not for nonmembers). The international partnership has the option of locating in either country but the benefits from access to both countries' labor forces entails a cost of managing an international venture. This cost can be viewed as a transportation cost or trade tax causing the joint venture to lose a fraction t or t^* of its profits.

A partnership between a home and a foreign firm is formed if each partner's after transport cost surplus exceeds its threat point

$$\frac{\pi(w)}{4} \leq \frac{z_{ij}\pi(w^*)}{2}(1 - t), \qquad \frac{\pi(w^*)}{4} \leq \frac{z_{ij}\pi(w^*)}{2}.$$

Dividing the home country partner in quality by $(1 - t)$ and summing up the resulting restrictions yields

$$\frac{\pi(w)}{4(1 - t)} + \frac{\pi(w^*)}{4} \leq z_{ij}\pi(w^*).$$

The condition ensuring that an international partnership is formed is

$$\frac{\pi(w^*)}{4} \leq -\frac{\pi(w)}{4(1 - t)} + z_{ij}\pi(w^*) \rightarrow z_{ij} \geq \frac{1}{4} + \frac{1}{4(1 - t)}\frac{\pi(w)}{\pi(w^*)}, \tag{12.1}$$

where a lower wage w^* implies $l_{fj} > l_{ij}$ and thus $\pi(w^*) > \pi(w)$.

If the condition $1 - t < \pi(w)/\pi(w^*)$ holds, a profitable partnership would require $z_{ij} \geq 1/2$. Because the critical value of z_{ij} cannot exceed $1/2$ in this setup, the partnership formation condition (12.1) is violated. The net benefits from the match would not be large enough to justify the partnership. This situation happens either if t is large enough or if endowment ratios and thus relative wages are similar.

If $\pi(w)/\pi(w^*) < 1 - t$, a positive measure of international matches between producers that are not perfect complements takes place (because the critical value of z_{ij} is less than $1/2$). This type of equilibrium emerges if labor endowments and thus international wage rates differ to a large enough degree. In the intermediate case in which $\pi(w)/\pi(w^*) = 1 - t$, a positive measure of international matches in which producers match with their perfect complements is confirmed. In this case, the critical value of z_{ij} is equal to $1/2$ and only perfect matches can satisfy the partnership formation condition (12.1).

When the difference between the factor endowments of the home and foreign countries is large enough, $L/L^* < 1$ differs from unity by a large enough degree, countries become partially insulated from each other. Wages become more responsive to changes in domestic supply than to changes in foreign supply and factor prices do not converge. If the differences in factor endowments are small enough relative to the share of producers that is tied, the standard classical results hold. Wages are determined by global labor rather than domestic labor and wages converge.

In a two-country world, price signals (i.e. wages) and networks work together efficiently to transfer labor demand from the labor scarce to the labor abundant country. But in a three-country world, networks and price signals can work at cross purposes. Specifically, if ties are denser between countries with small wage differences than between countries with large wage differences, networks can worsen the allocation of resources and reduce global welfare. This negative outcome results if the effect of trade creation between the joint venturing countries is dominated by trade diversion *vis-à-vis* the country that is not part of the joint venture.

12.2.2. The Role of Familiarity in Partnership Formation

Rauch and Trindade (2000) extend the Rauch and Casella (2002) model by introducing a parameter k measuring familiarity in the matching process between domestic and foreign firms. Each domestic producer draws a potential partner from a uniform distribution of types along the unit circle. The distribution of types has support with length $k \in (0, 1)$, where k serves as an uncertainty index or an inverse index of familiarity so that a lower k indicates greater familiarity. There is no international factor mobility.

A reduction in trade barriers is modeled as an increase in the familiarity with the set of potential partners in a labor-abundant foreign economy (i.e. a reduction in k). They find that if k declines (1) countries' labor markets become more integrated in the sense that the effect of relative factor supplies on countries' relative wages declines and wages in different countries tend to move together to a greater extent, (2) the elasticity of the home demand for labor increases, and (3) changes in trade taxes have a greater effect on countries' relative wages. In particular, a reduction in trade taxes leads to greater wage equalization while full trade liberalization leads to full wage equalization. As familiarity becomes perfect (k approaches 0), trade liberalization affects relative wages in the same manner as in the Heckscher–Ohlin (HO) model.

12.3. ENDOGENOUS OUTSOURCING

Up to now, the analysis has focused on the role of networks in facilitating the matching of final goods producers (i.e. procurers) and input suppliers. The degree of vertical specialization has been taken as exogenously given.

What determines whether a production stage is realized within the firm (i.e. vertical integration) or outside the boundaries of the firm (i.e. outsourcing)? In general, the degree of vertical integration depends on the costs of corporate governance, the degree of monopolization in the input market, the extent to which input quality is verifiable in courts, and other variables such as the degree of openness to trade. For instance, international trade opening effectively increases market size and generates a 'market thickness' externality that facilitates outsourcing and creates incentives for less vertical specialization. In general, greater outsourcing can encourage the formation of producer–supplier networks but can also lead to a procurement strategy sustained by market search for a high quality-to-price ratio (i.e. the network supplier mechanism vs the market choice mechanism).

12.3.1. Governance Costs vs Nil Input Markups and Group Reputation

Business groups can be viewed as a multiproduct company rather than as a network. The distinction is that networks are interpersonal channels of communication with no head or well-defined hierarchy while a multidivisional firm has a head and a well-defined hierarchical structure.

Feenstra, Hamilton and Huang (2001) develop a model with monopolistic competition and associated price markups in both the intermediate goods market (upstream) and the final goods market (downstream). The formation of a business group that jointly maximizes member profits and has common ownership has two effects on profits. First, it leads to cost internalization and raises profits by eliminating the markup in the intermediate goods sector. Second, corporate governance costs are larger for business groups than for a single firm.

Endogenous Groups, Product Variety, and Quality
A multiproduct business group has less incentives to develop new product varieties than a single-product firm. The reason is that the introduction of a new variety by a member requires fixed costs and reduces the sales of other group members. In other words, greater product variety generates a negative externality on group members.

The endogenous group model produces multiple equilibria involving two types of market structures. One equilibrium sustains a large number of groups that feature high internalization and sell at high markups. This equilibrium can be sustained because the incentives to vertically integrate are stronger if there is a high markup in the intermediate goods sector, which in turn can be high if there is a large number of vertically integrated business groups and a small number of independent input suppliers. High-internalization groups produce at higher fixed costs and offer less product variety than low-internalization firms.

The other equilibrium sustains a large number of low-internalization groups selling at low markups and featuring smaller fixed costs and greater product variety than firms featuring high internalization. This equilibrium can be sustained because the incentives to vertically integrate are smaller the lower the markup in the intermediate goods sector, which in turn is lower if there is a small number of vertically integrated business groups and a large number of independent input suppliers.

South Korean market organization is characterized by a relatively small number of large vertically integrated business groups (chaebol) owned by families and displaying mutual shareholding among members. The five largest groups control a significant part of the Korean economy. By contrast, Taiwanese groups are smaller and more specialized in intermediate input production. Hamilton and Feenstra (2001) examine how Korean groups became large and vertically integrated (high internalization) historically while Taiwanese business groups evolved into low-internalization groups.

Differences in market structure create different incentives affecting production decisions and trade behavior. First, recall that a multiproduct business group has less incentives to develop new product varieties than single-product firms due to the negative externality caused on group members. Second, there are incentives to increase quality because this increases the reputation of high-quality output for the group as a whole. Rodrik (1993) has stressed the role of this type of intragroup reputational externality on quality perceptions of Korean products.

Feenstra *et al.* (1999) use data on exports to the United States to test the hypothesis that a greater presence of business groups encourages less product variety and higher quality products. The authors construct indexes of product variety at the 5-digit industry level and measure quality by an index indicating whether a country tends to export high-price or low-price products. The empirical analysis confirms the null hypothesis in the sense that the greater presence of business groups in Korea relative to Taiwan is associated to less product variety and greater quality of the exports to the United States. For instance, Korea specializes in high-volume products such as Hyundai cars and microwave ovens. This finding is interpreted as indicating the role of market structure rather than factor endowments, which are similar in both countries.

Japanese groups are larger, more specialized and less integrated than Korean chaebol. Moreover, Japanese production often relies heavily on competing independent suppliers. In Japan, banks can own up to 5 percent of the shares of any company. By contrast, Korean banks cannot form part of a chaebol. The hypothesis that larger market size sustains greater product variety is tested by examining Japanese exports to the United States. The results show that Japanese exports exhibit greater product variety than both Korea and Taiwan.

12.3.2. Vertical Structure and the Thickness Externality

What are the effects of greater openness on vertical integration? McLaren (2000) shows that vertical integration can confer a negative externality by thinning the market for inputs requiring junk costs and thus worsening opportunistic pricing by fewer input buyers. This situation induces complementarity and multiple equilibria in the integration decision and can support excessive integration and multiple equilibria, thus providing a theory of different industrial systems or industrial cultures in ex ante identical countries.

International openness confers a positive externality. It thickens the market and supports leaner and less integrated firms thus providing gains from international openness quite different from those that are familiar from trade theories based on Ricardian comparative advantage, factor abundance and product variety motives. The market thickness effect provides a theory of outsourcing, downsizing, and 'Japanization' as consequences of globalization.

12.3.3. Corporate Governance and Less Specialization vs Unverifiability and Hold-up

The decision between making a component (or realizing a service internally) and buying it externally hinges on the trade off between potential lower production costs and market imperfections. On one hand, corporate governance costs and loss of specialization efficiencies work against vertical specialization. On the other hand, input quality verification difficulties facing the procurer plus a hold-up investment problem confronting specialized suppliers work against outsourcing (Grossman and Helpman, 2002*a*).

Vertical integration augments an organization's complexity and entails higher costs of corporate governance. Moreover, internal production precludes reaping the gains from production specialization as reflected in the lower production costs achievable by specialized suppliers.

The outsourcing alternative offers lower production costs but presents problems for both the final product producer and the specialized supplier. First, the producer (i.e. procurer) faces economic and legal barriers because specialized components' quality cannot be verified by outsiders (i.e. the courts). If quality unverifiability means that contracts cannot specify product quality, the specialized supplier has incentives to produce a lower quality input in order to save costs. Second, the specialized supplier faces a hold-up problem due to the specialized nature of the intermediate product or service supplied. Once investments are in place or the input has been produced, a specialized intermediate product has limited value in alternative uses. The procurer has incentives to take advantage and lower the price paid for the input.

The decision to purchase externally from specialized producers rather than to produce internally is undertaken when there are net gains from doing so despite the costs generated by the quality verification and hold-up problems. This decision hinges on comparing the higher costs due to corporate governance and less specialization under vertical integration with the inefficiency costs arising from quality unverifiability and the weak ex post bargaining position of specialized input suppliers that have few alternative uses for their specialized products.

12.4. GLOBAL vs DOMESTIC OUTSOURCING

What we call globalization is the mixture of information diffusion, economic integration through trade and capital flows, and geographic dispersion of productive activities. In order to stress particular features, the global dispersion of productive activities is called outsourcing by Feenstra (1998), fragmentation by Deardorff (2001), production sharing by Hummels *et al.* (2001), and vertical specialization by Yeats (2001).

Campa and Goldberg (1997), Hummels *et al.* (2001), and Yeats (2001) document the growth in international outsourcing as reflected in the expansion of intermediate input trade. Manufacturing has been transformed so much that products have multiple nationalities. A US auto can embody Canadian and Japanese components and technology, Korean assembly, European advertisement and data processing, as well as US value added.

The shift from in-house production to outsourcing is a major element of the new economy. The subcontracting of multiple activities that were previously performed within firms and government units has proliferated. Outsourcing comprises the whole productive process including R&D, product design, assembly, marketing, post-sale servicing, accounting, and financing. The economics of outsourcing deals with the factors encouraging vertical specialization and the associated vertical disintegration of productive units.

12.4.1. Where to Outsource

The outsourcing decision entails deciding whether and where to outsource. The outsourcing alternative requires deciding where to buy. In an open economy a key decision involves choosing between a domestic and a foreign specialized supplier. Grossman and Helpman (2002*b*) examine a world of two countries (North and South). There are two industries, a homogeneous good z and a differentiated good y, which can only be produced in the North. The fixed cost of designing good y is equal to $w^N l_j^N$, where w^N is the Northern country's wage and l_j^N indicates the fixed labor requirement of good $j \in \{1, \ldots, \mathcal{J}\}$. The fixed cost represents the cost of entry determining the equilibrium number of producers of final goods, each of which utilizes a Northern or Southern supplier for components.

Intermediate input suppliers have a fixed entry cost of $w^i l_m^i, i \in (N, S)$, where w^i is country i's wage and l_m^i indicates the fixed labor requirement of intermediate product $m \in \{1, \ldots, M^i\}$. The fixed entry cost determines the equilibrium number M^i of intermediate product producers in country i. A market is said to be 'thicker' than another if it has the greatest number of suppliers.

The locations of suppliers are unknown to the Northern firm. It is thus necessary to devote Northern labor to search for partners whose expertise is close to the input requirement so that the cost of customization will be low. Both the cost of search and the cost of customization are assumed to increase with the distance x^i between the Northern country producer and its supplier in country $i \in \{N, S\}$. In fact, the distance between a producer and a given supplier is defined to be equal to the intensity of the search that would lead the producer to that supplier. Therefore, x^i stands for both producer–supplier distance and search intensity. The outcome of a search process is uncertain because the searching firm does not know in advance whether it will be able to find a supplier or whether the supplier will be in a nearby location or far away.

12.4.2. Bilateral Matching and Customization

The search for a supplier ends up with a bilateral match to produce a customized product. The partners bargain bilaterally in two stages: the investment negotiation stage and the subsequent order negotiation stage.

The investment negotiation determines the price p^i of the customized prototype developed by the supplier by dividing the total rewards from the bilateral relation. Both partners are assumed to have the same bargaining power so that total rewards are divided equally. The investment contract specifies the supplier's investment in customization I^i and the amount of compensation for the prototype, which is assumed to be valuable only inside the partnership. The investment can be observed by the producer and supplier but is only partly verifiable to third parties, who can verify a fraction $\gamma^i < 1/2$ of the supplier's investment. Imperfect verifiability in turn constraints contracting possibilities so that the investment contract is an incomplete contract. The value of parameter γ^i can be interpreted as a measure of the quality of country i's legal system.

In the order negotiation stage, partners negotiate an order contract specifying the quantity and price of an input order. The order contract is a complete contract because both quantity and prices can be verified by third parties. Quantity and price are negotiated second because otherwise the input supplier would have incentives to avoid investing in customization while demanding payment for noncustomized inputs. The order negotiation divides the verifiable surplus S^i from the subsequent sale of the product. Both partners are assumed to have the same bargaining power so that half of the surplus goes to each party.

The negotiated investment contract $(I^i(x^i), p^i(x^i))$ specifies the investment I^i and price of the prototype $p^i(x^i)$ in country $i \in \{N, S\}$. The payment from the downstream firm (i.e. the final goods producer) to the upstream firm (i.e. the supplier) is an increasing linear function of the distance x^i between the supplier's expertise and the buyer's input needs. Specifically, $p^i(x^i)$ is equal to one-half of the linear labor costs $w^i \mu^i x^i$ of developing the prototype, where w^i is the wage rate in the supplier's location and μ^i is a prototype cost parameter.

Formally,

$$p^i(x^i) = \frac{I^i(x^i)}{2} = \frac{w^i \mu^i x^i}{2}, \qquad (1 - \gamma^i)w^i \mu^i x^i \leq \frac{S^i}{2} < w^i \mu^i x^i,$$

where a positive price requires x^i to satisfy two constraints. The constraint $S^i/2 < w^i \mu^i x^i$ states that the supplier's surplus from the subsequent sale of the product fails to cover the prototype costs, which makes the investment agreement a precondition required to induce the supplier to produce the prototype. If the linear prototype cost $w^i \mu^i x^i$ is less than the supplier's surplus $S^i/2$, the investment agreement is not needed and the associated stage turns out to be irrelevant. The constraint $(1 - \gamma^i)w^i \mu^i x^i \leq S^i/2$ requires the surplus $S^i/2$ to exceed or be equal to the unverifiable component of the investment so that the supplier has incentives to realize the full prototype investment $0 < I^i(x^i) = w^i \mu^i x^i$ even if the investment is unverifiable.

The order contract $(p^i(w^i), y^i(w^i))$ as a function of the wage rate in country $i \in \{N, S\}$ is obtained utilizing the markup pricing formula under monopolistic competition, $(p^i - w^i)/p^i = 1/\varepsilon$, substituting the resulting pricing formula into the constant elasticity demand for the final product y^i, and using $w^i = \alpha p^i$

$$p^i = \frac{\varepsilon w^i}{\varepsilon - 1} = \frac{w^i}{\alpha}, \qquad y^i = A(p^i)^{-\varepsilon} = A\left(\frac{w^i}{\alpha}\right)^{-\varepsilon}$$

$$\rightarrow S^i = (1 - \alpha)p^i y^i = (1 - \alpha) A \left(\frac{w^i}{\alpha}\right)^{1-\varepsilon},$$

where price p^i is a markup over wages, $\varepsilon = 1/(1 - \alpha) > 0$ is the elasticity of demand for variety y^i and $0 < \alpha < 1$ is a demand parameter. The total surplus S^i (joint profits) is positively related to country i's wage rate and $w^i \mu^i x^i < (w^i \mu^i x^i/2) + (S^i/2)$.

12.4.3. Searching for a Supplier

There are M^i potential suppliers in country i, which are assumed to be evenly distributed along the edge of a circle with circumference equal to one. Suppliers stand at a distance $1/M^i$ from each other along the circle. In other words, the greater the number of suppliers, the closer they are to each other. The density function of suppliers along the circle edge is uniform and equal to M^i. The probability that a supplier is found is equal to $2x^i M^i = 2x/(M^i)^{-1}$, because a search of intensity x^i is assumed to cover an arc of length $2x^i$ with uniform supplier density $(M^i)^{-1}$. If the search intensity x^i is equal to $1/(2M^i)$, the probability of finding a partner is equal to one.

A final producer is assumed to search in only one country. Confining search to a single market can be rationalized if the fixed cost of searching a market is large enough. Northern firm n is indifferent between searching for a supplier in the Northern or the Southern country only if expected profits are the same in equilibrium: $E[\pi_n^N(x^N)] = E[\pi_n^S(x^S)]$. Otherwise, outsourcing is concentrated in the country promising the greatest expected profits.

The search intensity x^i in country $i \in \{N, S\}$ is defined as the amount of Northern labor devoted to searching a partner. The equilibrium search intensity maximizes the expected operating profits obtained from the relation with the supplier in country i. The calculation of expected profits considers all suppliers that a firm might find at distances $q \in (0, x)$

$$\max_{x^i} E[\pi_n^i(x^i)] = E\left(\frac{S^i}{2} - p^i(q)\right) - w^N \eta^i(x^i)^2$$

$$= 2M^i \int_0^x \left(\frac{S^i}{2} - p^i(q)\right) dq - w^N \eta^i(x^i)^2,$$

s.t.

$$x^i \leq \frac{1}{2M^i}, \qquad (1 - \gamma^i)\, w^i \mu^i x^i \leq \frac{S^i}{2},$$

where q is a dummy variable. The final producer is assumed to know the number M^i of input suppliers in country i. Search costs $w^N \eta^i(x^i)^2$ are a quadratic function of search intensity x^i, where w^N is the wage rate in the North and η^i is a search cost parameter.

Profit maximization is subject to two constraints. First, because a firm enters into a single bilateral relationship there is no benefit from searching for a second partner. Therefore, the intensity x^i must be no greater than $1/(2M^i)$, which ensures that a partner will be found. Second, the surplus $S^i/2$ exceeds the unverifiable component of the investment so that the supplier realizes investments even if they are not verifiable. Notice that search must take place even if an investment contract is unnecessary so that there is no constraint ensuring that an investment contract is signed.

Country i's equilibrium search intensity $\hat{x}^i$ is the value of x^i that maximizes profits and depends on which constraints are binding. For instance, we obtain

$$(1 - \gamma^i)\, w^i \mu^i x^i = w^i \mu^i x^i = \frac{S^i}{2} \quad \rightarrow \quad \hat{x}^i = \frac{S^i}{2w^i \mu^i}$$

in the special case in which (1) the supplier's investment is altogether unverifiable, $\gamma^i = 0$, (2) $\hat{x}^i$ satisfies the constraint $\hat{x}^i \leq 1/(2M^i)$, which implies $M^i \leq (w^i \mu^i)/S^i$, and (3) $M^i \geq (w^N \eta^i)/(w^i \mu^i)$, obtained from the maximization problem.

Finally, the Southern and Northern equilibrium wage rates, assumed to satisfy $w^S < w^N$, are determined by the full employment of labor supplies L^S and L^N among their diverse uses.

What determines the location of outsourcing? The profits from searching in a given country increase with the number of input suppliers M^i. The number of suppliers M^i that are active in a market is known as the 'thickness' of that market. Market thickness can generate an externality because the profits from searching are greater the larger the number of firms in country i while a supplier's profits increase with the number of Northern customers. The thick-market externality, which can be viewed as a type of network externality, has been studied by McLaren (2001), who finds that this externality can give rise to multiple equilibria in the choice between outsourcing and production inside the firm's boundaries. In the present setup, multiple equilibrium might include specialization of input production in one country.

The profits from searching are greater the lower the value of the search cost parameter η^i. The quality of a country's legal system γ^i does not affect outsourcing decisions through expected profits but enters indirectly through the constraint indicating that the supplier is induced to undertake the unverifiable component of the investment.

12.5. SUBMODULARITY AND SUPERMODULARITY

The optimal allocation of talent across activities hinges on the technologies determining the optimal matching of heterogeneous workers. Efficiency motives direct more talented workers toward technologies in which production depends on the strongest input links—called submodular technologies. Less talented workers are directed into technologies in which production hinges on the weakest links—called supermodular technologies.

12.5.1. Matching under Submodularity

In some activities, like research in pursuit of a discovery, the most productive task is the major determinant of output. The remaining workers are either dispensable or supporting staff. In these activities, the productive process is as strong as its strongest link, which favors talented individuals working with less talented support staff. In other activities, like automobile production, tasks are complementary in the sense that a flaw in one employee's task performance causes a disproportionate reduction in output. Activities in which the productive process is as strong as its weakest link favor team work.

The distinction between a production process based on the tasks performed by the most talented worker and one based on skill complementarity can be formalized utilizing the mathematical properties of the production function. The submodularity property corresponds to processes that exhibit task substitutability or are largely dependent on the most talented workers. By contrast, the supermodularity property corresponds to processes that exhibit task complementarity or in which least talented workers play an important role.

Submodular Production Function
Consider a production process involving two indivisible tasks A and B, each of which must be performed by exactly one worker. The production function is $F(t_A, t_B)$, where t_A and t_B represent the talents of workers performing tasks A and B.

Production processes in which two tasks are substitutable or one is dispensable in producing output can be represented by a submodular production function. A two-task production function $F(t_A, t_B)$ is submodular if, for all (t_A, t_B) and (t'_A, t'_B) belonging to the set T of paired tasks

$$F(t_A, t_B) + F(t'_A, t'_B)$$
$$\geq F(\min\{t_A, t'_A\}, \min\{t_B, t'_B\}) + F(\max\{t_A, t'_A\}, \max\{t_B, t'_B\}). \tag{12.2}$$

Topkis (1978) shows that, under weak conditions, submodularity is equivalent to the condition that the marginal product of talent in each task is nonincreasing in the amount of talent used to perform the other task

$$F_{AB} \equiv \frac{\partial^2 F(t_A, t_B)}{\partial t_A \partial t_B} = \partial \left(\frac{\partial F(t_A, t_B)}{\partial t_A} \right) \bigg/ \partial t_B = \partial \left(\frac{\partial F(t_A, t_B)}{\partial t_B} \right) \bigg/ \partial t_A$$
$$= F_{BA} \leq 0.$$

Consider a production function F exhibiting constant returns to talent for the firm as a whole. Euler's theorem for homogeneous of degree one functions applies so that $t_A F_A + t_B F_B = 0$. If condition $F_{AB} = F_{BA} \leq 0$ holds, the marginal product of individual talent within a firm is nondecreasing

$$t_A F_{AA} + t_B F_{BA} = 0 \quad \rightarrow \quad 0 \leq F_{AA} = \frac{-t_B F_{BA}}{t_A}.$$

By the same token, if $F_{AB} = F_{BA} < 0$, the marginal product of individual talent is increasing.

Example. What is the optimal matching of workers when the production function exhibits submodularity? Expression (12.2) implies that it is better to combine dissimilar talents. As an illustration, consider the submodular production function $F(t_A, t_B) = \max(t_A, t_B)$. The constant marginal product of talent is equal to one for the most talented worker and zero for the least talented worker. Moreover, $F_{AB} = F_{BA} = 0$. The max production function exhibits constant returns to talent for the firm as a whole as $\max\{k t_A, k t_B\} = k \max\{t_A, t_B\}$.

If $t_B < t'_A < t_A < t'_B$

$$\max(t_A, t_B) + \max(t'_A, t'_B) = t_A + t'_B$$
$$> \max(t'_A, t_B) + \max(t_A, t'_B) = t'_A + t'_B.$$

In this case, it is better to combine dissimilar talent pairs (t_A, t_B) and (t'_A, t'_B) than similar talent pairs (t'_A, t_B) and (t_A, t'_B). A simple example takes place when two firms match four workers into two pairs. Two workers have higher talent t_H and two have lower talent t_L. It is optimal to pair together the most and least talented workers as $\max\{t_L, t_L\} + \max\{t_H, t_H\} = t_L + t_H < 2 \max\{t_L, t_H\} = 2 t_H$.

Firms have incentives to achieve the matching pattern that maximizes the value of their production. Therefore, self-sorting achieves optimal matching.

12.5.2. *Matching with a Supermodular Production Function*

Production processes in which two tasks are complementary or essential in producing output can be represented by a supermodular production function. A two-task production function $F(t_A, t_B)$ is supermodular if, for all (t_A, t_B) and (t'_A, t'_B) belonging to the set T of paired tasks,

$$F(t_A, t_B) + F(t'_A, t'_B)$$

$$\leq F(\min\{t_A, t'_A\}, \min\{t_B, t'_B\}) + F(\max\{t_A, t'_A\}, \max\{t_B, t'_B\}). \tag{12.3}$$

Topkis (1978) shows that, under weak conditions, supermodularity is equivalent to the condition that the marginal product of talent in each task is nondecreasing in the amount of talent used to perform the other task

$$F_{AB} \equiv \frac{\partial^2 F(t_A, t_B)}{\partial t_A \partial t_B} = \partial \left(\frac{\partial F(t_A, t_B)}{\partial t_A} \right) \Big/ \partial t_B$$

$$= \partial \left(\frac{\partial F(t_A, t_B)}{\partial t_B} \right) \Big/ \partial t_A = F_{BA} \geq 0.$$

If F exhibits constant returns to talent and $0 \leq F_{AB} = F_{BA}$, the marginal product of individual talent within a firm is nonincreasing

$$t_A F_{AA} + t_B F_{BA} = 0 \quad \rightarrow \quad F_{AA} = \frac{-t_B F_{BA}}{t_A} \leq 0.$$

By the same token, if $0 < F_{AB} = F_{BA}$, the marginal product of individual talent is decreasing.

Example. What is the optimal matching of workers when the production function exhibits supermodularity? Expression (12.3) implies that it is optimal to pair together the two most talented workers and the two least talented. As an illustration consider the supermodular production function $F(t_A, t_B) = \min(t_A, t_B)$. The constant marginal product of talent is equal to one for the least talented worker and zero for the most talented worker. Moreover, $F_{AB} = F_{BA} = 0$. The min production function exhibits constant returns to talent for the firm as a whole as $\min\{kt_A, kt_B\} = k \min\{t_A, t_B\}$.

If $t_B < t'_A < t_A < t'_B$, we have

$$\min(t_A, t_B) + \min(t'_A, t'_B) = t_B + t'_A < \min(t'_A, t_B)$$

$$+ \min(t_A, t'_B) = t_B + t_A. \tag{12.4}$$

In this case, maximizing aggregate output requires combining similar talents (t'_A, t_B) and (t_A, t'_B) rather than dissimilar talents (t_A, t_B) and (t'_A, t'_B). A simple takes place when two firms match two workers displaying high talent t_H and two with lower talent t_L. Self-sorting will pair together the two most talented workers and the two least talented because $2 \min\{t_L, t_H\} = 2t_L < \min\{t_L, t_L\} + \min\{t_H, t_H\} = t_L + t_H$.

12.6. TRADE AND THE ALLOCATION OF
DIVERSE TALENTS

Developed countries have access to similar technologies, display similar relative factor endowments and trade products with similar factor intensities. Therefore, observed exchanges cannot be explained by exogenous Ricardian comparative advantages and differences in relative factor endowments—stressed in the HO framework. Increasing return models rationalize specialization but do not pin down the specific goods exported.

What determines developed countries' trade patterns and the specific goods exported? Consider two countries featuring the same average level of talent (i.e. human capital, skills) but varying in the diversity of their labor forces, that is, varying in the spread of talent as opposed to the average talent level. Cross-country divergences in the diversity of talent can be viewed as the outcome of different educational and social systems that are exogenous from the perspective of trade structure analysis. In the presence of talent diversity, technological differences in worker interaction across sectors affect the matching of workers to firms and determines the pattern of international trade.

12.6.1. The Spread of Talent

Grossman and Maggi (2000) develop a two-sector competitive model of trade between two countries that have access to the same technologies and feature the same average talent level. The two countries are assumed to differ in the spread of talent, defined as the spread of the distribution of human capital (e.g. abilities, skills) across a country's population. Individual talent is public information such as when talent is perfectly measured by years of schooling or some test. The distributions of domestic and foreign abilities are exogenously given by the cumulative distributions $\Phi(t)$ and $\Phi^*(t)$. These cumulative distributions, defined on a common support $[t_{min}, t_{max}]$, represent the fraction of the labor forces L and L^* consisting of workers with ability less or equal to t. The distribution of talent $\Phi(t)$ is called more diverse than distribution $\Phi^*(t)$ if, for some $t_0 > t_{min}$,

$$\Phi(t) < \Phi^*(t), \quad t < t_0, \qquad \Phi^*(t) < \Phi(t), \quad t > t_0.$$

This definition corresponds to what it is technically known as simple (or elementary) increase in risk (see Mas-Colell *et al.*, 1995; Meyer and Ormiston, 1989).

The distribution Φ^* represents a simple increase in risk from Φ if Φ^* is generated from Φ taking all the mass that Φ assigns to an interval $[t', t'']$ and moving it away to the endpoints t' and t'' while keeping the same mean Et, where $t' < Et < t''$. This procedure takes the probability mass which Φ assigns to the center of the distribution and moves it away to the tails of the distribution. Suppose that the distributions cross at a single point corresponding to the mean Et of both distributions. The assumption of single-crossing distributions ensures that the generated distribution function Φ^* has uniformly fatter tails than Φ. If the mean is preserved but the generated distribution Φ^* has greater spread than Φ, the distribution Φ is said to be less risky than Φ^*.

Consider two economies engaged in two productive activities, I and II, each of which requires two tasks A and B. There is a continuum of workers of size L and L^*. The number of workers with talent less than or equal to t are $\Phi(t)L$ and $\Phi^*(t^*)L^*$. Sectorial outputs $q_i, i \in \{I, II\}$ are given by the following constant returns to talent production functions

$$q_I = F_I(t_{AI}, t_{BI}), \qquad q_{II} = F_{II}(t_{AII}, t_{BII}),$$

and similarly for q_i^*. Assume that tasks are symmetric, meaning that $F(t_A, t_B) = F(t_B, t_A)$.

What is the optimal sorting of talent and the resulting trade pattern? The analysis focuses on two scenarios both involving production functions exhibiting constant returns to talent and leading to a competitive equilibrium that maximizes the value of output at given prices and is technically efficient. One scenario examined concerns two supermodular functions that imply a linear production possibility frontier. If countries have the same homothetic utility function, trade does not arise because the production possibility frontier is linear and any desired consumption level can be achieved at a constant relative cost by just moving along the national production frontier. The other scenario consists of an economy with one supermodular and one submodular production function, which implies a nonlinear production possibility frontier. If the distributions of talents and the homothetic production functions are the same, there are no incentives for trade because the two economies are different-sized replicas of each other. If the diversity of talent varies across nations, $\Phi(t) \neq \Phi^*$, the autarkic patterns of production and consumption differ and there are gains from trade. The country featuring greater diversity in talent exports goods with submodular (i.e. substitutable) technologies while the more homogeneous country exports goods with supermodular (i.e. complementary) technologies.

12.6.2. Matching and Trade: Two Supermodular Functions

Consider two supermodular production functions exhibiting constant returns to talent. If individual abilities are observable, the optimal allocation of talent is characterized by $t_i = t_{Ai} = t_{Bi}, i \in \{I, II\}$, for all firms in both countries. Constant returns to talent implies that firm output is proportional to the talent t employed

$$q_i(t_i) = F_i(t_i, t_i) = t_i F_i(1, 1).$$

The wage rate $w_i(t)$ of a worker with talent t is equalized across sectors $i \in \{I, II\}$. Formally,

$$w_I(t) = p \frac{t F_I(1, 1)}{2} = w_{II}(t) = \frac{t F_{II}(1, 1)}{2}, \quad p = \frac{p_I}{p_{II}},$$

where we divide by 2 because each firm hires two workers of the same talent level so that q_i is produced with $2t$ and the output of a worker with talent t is $q_i(t)/2$. Constant returns to talent implies that workers performing tasks A and B exhaust the value of outputs q_I and pq_{II}. Labor market equilibrium requires full employment

$$T_I + T_{II} = T = L \int_{t_{\min}}^{t_{\max}} t \, d\Phi.$$

Aggregate sectorial output $Y_i, i \in \{I, II\}$ is proportional to the amount of talent T_i allocated to sector i. Formally,

$$Y_i = L \int \frac{t F_i(1,1)}{2} d\Phi(t) = \frac{F_i(1,1)}{2} L \int t \phi(t) \, dt = \frac{F_i(1,1)}{2} T_i,$$

where $\phi(t)$ denotes the density function of talent associated with Φ and ϕ is assumed to be symmetric. The inferior and superior limits of the integral depend on sectorial demands, which determine the range of talents allocated to sector i. Because production and wages are linear in talent, the specific talents used in i do not matter as long as the demand for i is fulfilled.

The assumption that both countries have access to the same linear technologies implies that both production possibility frontiers are linear and have the same slope

$$-\frac{dY_{II}}{dY_I} = -\frac{F_{II}(1,1)/2}{F_I(1,1)/2} \frac{dT_{II}}{dT_I} = \frac{F_{II}(1,1)}{F_I(1,1)} = \frac{F_{II}^*(1,1)}{F_I^*(1,1)} = -\frac{dY_{II}^*}{dY_I^*},$$

where $dT_{II}/dT_I = -1$ as $T_I + T_{II} = T$.

If both countries have identical homothetic preferences, they will consume and produce both goods in the same ratios under autarky no matter the distribution of talents ϕ and ϕ^*. In fact, any desired consumption level can be achieved at the same constant relative cost as the potential trading partner by just moving along the national production frontier. Therefore, trade will not take place even if the distributions of talent differ in both countries.

12.6.3. Matching and Trade: A Supermodular and a Submodular Function

Suppose that sector I is supermodular, sector II is submodular and both exhibit constant returns to talent. Labor matching in the supermodular sector is given by $t_I = t_{AI} = t_{BI}$.

Labor matching within the submodular sector II is realized as follows. The highest and lowest skill workers are matched to utilize submodular technologies producing pair $(t_{\min}, t_{\max})$. The next-to-highest and next-to-lowest talents are matched to produce submodular technologies, and so on. In general, a worker of talent t is paired with a matching worker of talent $m(t) > t$, where $\Phi(m) = 1 - \Phi(t)$. The symmetry of density ϕ implies that the gap between average talent $\bar{t} = T/L$ and any given talent t

assigned to the supermodular sector is equal to the gap between the matching talent $m(t)$ and the average talent, $\bar{t} - t = m(t) - \bar{t}$, or $m(t) = 2\bar{t} - t$. Cross-matching workers in this way goes on up to critical low and high skill levels $\hat{t}$ and $m(\hat{t}) = 2\bar{t} - \hat{t}$. All intermediate skills between these two levels are allocated to the supermodular sector and are self-matched, that is, matching involves workers of similar skills.

The production functions in the supermodular and submodular sectors are

$$Y_I = \frac{F(1,1)}{2} L \int_{\hat{t}}^{2\bar{t}-\hat{t}} t\phi(t)\,dt = \frac{F(1,1)}{2} L\bar{t}[\Phi(2\bar{t}-\hat{t}) - \Phi(\hat{t})],$$

$$Y_{II} = L \int_{t_{min}}^{\hat{t}} F_{II}(t, m(t))\phi(t)\,dt = L \int_{t_{min}}^{\hat{t}} F_{II}(t, 2\bar{t}-t)\phi(t)\,dt.$$

The expression for Y_I is derived observing that the truncated distribution of talents between $\hat{t}$ and $2\bar{t} - \hat{t}$ has density $\phi(t)/[\Phi(2\bar{t} - \hat{t}) - \Phi(\hat{t})]$. Therefore, the mean of the truncated talent distribution is given by

$$\bar{t} = \int_{\hat{t}}^{2\bar{t}-\hat{t}} t\frac{\phi(t)}{\Phi(2\bar{t} - \hat{t}) - \Phi(\hat{t})}\,dt$$

$$\rightarrow \int_{\hat{t}}^{2\bar{t}-\hat{t}} t\phi(t)\,dt = \bar{t}[\Phi(2\bar{t} - \hat{t}) - \Phi(\hat{t})].$$

The production possibility frontier is nonlinear because the least talented worker in the supermodular sector, $\hat{t}$, is a variable that depends on the production pattern. Formally,

$$-\frac{dY_{II}}{dY_I} = -\frac{dY_{II}/d\hat{t}}{dY_I/d\hat{t}} = -\frac{LF_{II}(\hat{t}, 2\bar{t} - \hat{t})}{LF_I(1,1)\bar{t}/2} \frac{\phi(\hat{t})}{-2\phi(\hat{t})} = \frac{F_{II}(\hat{t}, 2\bar{t} - \hat{t})}{F_I(1,1)\bar{t}},$$

where the symmetry of ϕ implies

$$\frac{d[\Phi(2\bar{t} - \hat{t}) - \Phi(\hat{t})]}{d\hat{t}} = \phi(2\bar{t} - \hat{t})(-1) - \phi(\hat{t}) = -2\phi(\hat{t}).$$

If the distribution of talent is the same in both countries, $\phi = \phi^*$, the mean talent levels are the same in both countries. If tastes are homothetic, consumption patterns are the same and the autarky levels of the critical talents $\hat{t}$ and $\hat{t}^*$ are also the same. There is no trade even if factor endowments, the diversity of talent and countries' sizes differ. This result arises because talent is observable so that self-sorting works perfectly and the two economies are essentially identical except in size (returns to talent are constant so that size does not affect the production patterns for a given relative price).

If the distribution of talent is not the same in both countries, $\phi \neq \phi^*$, the economies are no longer identical and there are opportunities for trade. Comparative advantage considerations determine specialization along the nonlinear production frontier and the associated trade pattern. Specifically, the pattern of trade reflects the distribution of labor force talents. The country with a more diverse labor force has a comparative advantage in the sector with substitutable tasks, which favors talented individuals working with a less talented support staff. The country with a less diverse labor force has a comparative advantage in sectors requiring complementary tasks, which favors working in teams. Therefore, the country with a more diverse labor force specializes in and exports goods produced with substitutable tasks (i.e. a submodular production function). The country with a homogeneous labor force specializes in and exports goods requiring task complementarity (supermodular production function).

The specialization pattern due to divergences in talent spread mirrors trade between the United States and Japan or Germany. The United States has a diverse and unequal labor force and specializes in activities such as software and sophisticated services—financial, consulting, acting, musical—that hinge on individual talent. Japan and Germany exhibit less labor force inequality and specialize in activities utilizing complementary skills such as the production of automobiles and electronics.

What are the effects of trade on income distribution and the composition of firms in each industry? If trade leads to specialization in goods in which individual talent prevails, the skilled–unskilled reward differential will expand. This effect is consistent with greater wage inequality in the United States, viewed as a country that specializes in goods produced with high-talent, than in Europe, viewed as a region that specializes in team goods. In other words, specialization patterns increase skilled–unskilled wage gaps in the United States and reduce them in Japan and Germany.

12.6.4. *Unobservable Talent and Imperfect Matching*

Suppose that talent $t_i = q_i e_i$ is made up of an observable factor q_i and a factor e_i, which is assumed to be unobservable to the employer and the worker. Because the worker does not know her or his talent, this is not a setting with asymmetric information. The distributions of observable and unobservable talent are assumed to be independent.

What type of trade patterns emerge when productivity is not observable? Imperfect observability of talent strengthens the forces of comparative advantage and accentuates the trade patterns emerging when talent is observable and diverse. The country with a more diverse work force exports the good for which individual success is more important. The country with a relatively homogeneous population exports the good produced by a technology with task complementarity.

12.7. INCOMPLETE INFORMATION AND IMPERFECT CONTRACTS

How are trade volumes and patterns affected by imperfect contracting? Informational asymmetries and the costliness of verifying the multiple contingencies that may appear in contract specifications give rise to contract imperfections. Lax contract enforcement can reduce trade linkages among countries (Anderson and Young, 2002). Imperfect labor contracts due to asymmetric information about worker talent induce more talented workers to go into activities that allow capturing rents from their talents while less talented workers have incentives to work in teams that blur individual contribution (Grossman, 2002).

12.7.1. Imperfect Labor Contracts

Suppose that worker ability is private information and the value of team output is not verifiable in court by employers and workers. Because labor contracts cannot distinguish between workers, firms pay uniform wages corresponding to average employee productivity. A uniform compensation scheme is unattractive to high-productivity workers and generates adverse selection by attracting low-productivity workers. This type of contract is imperfect because it cannot generate efficient worker matches in teams.

Grossman (2002) considers an economy with one sector in which output is produced by a two-worker team and a second sector in which individuals work alone

$$q_I = F_I(t_A, t_B), \qquad q_{II} = F_{II}(t_{II}) = \lambda t_{II},$$

where F_I is supermodular so that it is better to pair workers with similar skills, output is measured in quality terms, and t_A and t_B represent the skills of the workers performing tasks A and B. Output q_I is a joint product of the workers and there is no identifiable output of individual contributors. By contrast, individual contribution is identifiable in sector II so that the productivity of worker with skill t_{II} is perfectly identifiable. The distribution of domestic abilities is exogenously given by the cumulative distribution $\Phi(t)$ representing the fraction of the labor force of L workers with ability less or equal to t. Similar definitions apply to the foreign country.

The allocation of talent across activities hinges on the contractual factors determining worker rents. In the presence of talent diversity and unverifiable output, imperfect labor contracts fail to efficiently match workers with teams and affect the allocation of labor across sectors. Because individual productivity is not observable and group output is costly to verify, least talented workers have incentives to enter into the team sector. The most talented workers prefer activities that permit measuring their individual contribution and avoid sharing rents with less productive workers. They keep rents by either working alone or becoming entrepreneurs who hire teams and receive the residual claim on team output. For instance, talented workers have incentives to work in the software, research, and art industries, which reward individual talent, rather than in teams producing automobiles.

Cross-country differences in the distribution of talent are a source of comparative advantage and affect trade patterns when labor contracts are imperfect. Consider two countries featuring similar average worker talent but differing in the spread of talent. Greater talent diversity favors specialization in sectors rewarding individual talent, such as software, relative to specialization in sectors rewarding team production, such as automobiles. Therefore, a country displaying greater inequality in labor skills exports products rewarding individual contribution and imports team products. This comparative advantage effect hinges on incomplete information precluding full compensation of talented workers in the team sector. A comparative advantage does not exist if contracts reward talent because worker productivity is known and both countries have the same average worker productivity, even if they differ in the spread of talent.

Trade opening and globalization exacerbate the specialization pattern caused by unobservable productivity and imperfect contracts. In countries with more diverse talent, opening leads to a contraction of the team sector and a reduction in the wage of less talented workers relative to the wage of more talented workers. These labor market effects help to understand why globalization has widened the skilled–unskilled wage differential in the United States, which displays greater labor market inequalities relative to developed trading partners. If inefficient allocation and distributional effects result from imperfect contracting, there might be scope for welfare-improving policies inducing an expansion of the team sector in the country importing team goods.

12.8. CONCLUSIONS

Production efficiency and competitiveness are improved when networks are utilized effectively, workers are appropriately matched, unusual talent is recognized in the market and the benefits from outsourcing are appropriately exploited. Networks such as business groups help to match productive activities and economic agents. The multiple issues concerning the trade effects of international and domestic networks have been enmeshed in controversy as networks have trade-creating and trade-reducing effects. Moreover, repeated interaction can facilitate cooperation and productive efficiency as well as collusion. Participation in groups can open up trade opportunities or sustain collusive arrangements limiting rivals' market access.

Outsourcing takes place when the input markets are 'thick' enough and the costs of vertical integration due to higher governance costs and less production specialization exceed the costs of external supply arising from bad matches, input price markups due to imperfect competition, input quality unverifiability, and the specific-investment hold-up problem. Outsourcing abroad takes place when the costs of searching for a foreign partner are low enough and a foreign market features a quality legal system and enough 'thickness'.

What determines the pattern of trade in a world in which worker talent is diverse? Cross-country differences in the diversity of talents represent a source of comparative advantage and can explain features of trade patterns that are not easily rationalized by standard theories stressing comparative advantages due to exogenous sectorial productivity divergences, relative factor abundances, and increasing returns to scale. In particular, countries with large diversity tend to export products made by highly talented individuals while countries with less talent diversity tend to export products made in teams. One reason is that self-sorting directs talented individuals toward submodular sectors relying on high talent and featuring high input substitutability.

Imperfect labor contracts affect the relative importance of sectors and associated trade patterns. In the presence of talent diversity and unverifiable output, imperfect labor contracts might fail to efficiently match workers with teams and influence the allocation of labor across sectors. Workers with unobserved large productivity have incentives to work in industries rewarding individual talent and permitting measuring individual contribution rather than industries relying on team work. A more heterogeneous labor force leads to greater specialization in products and sectors rewarding the contribution of talented individuals. If contractual features affecting worker rents cannot accommodate the diversity in worker talent, occupational choices and the sectorial allocation of labor can be distorted. There might thus be room for policies increasing the share of the team sector in more diverse countries and reducing it in less diverse countries.

Recent work stresses the relationship between contracts and trade. Antràs (2002) develops an incomplete contract model that explains why the share of intra-firm imports in total US imports increases with (1) the capital intensity of the importing industry, and (2) the capital to labor ratio of the importing country. Yi (2003) develops and tests a model of vertical specialization that contributes to explain why world trade has rapidly increased in the past decades despite a mere eleven percent reduction in tariffs.

PART IV

LIBERALIZATION, PROTECTION,
AND SANCTIONS

13

Trade Liberalization and Protection

Tariff barriers have declined dramatically since the Second World War. Developed countries' average tariff rates are now at single digit levels. The dismantling of tariff barriers under the sponsorship of the General Agreement on Tariffs and Trade (GATT) and the World Trade Organization (WTO) has not meant the end of protection. Instead, it has led to other forms of protection. Nowadays, protection takes two broad forms. First, high tariff rates continue to prevail in many developing countries. Second, nontariff barriers to trade have become a major protective device in both industrial and developing countries.

A host of trade restrictions often limit trade between natural partners. For instance, trade restrictions explain why Middle Eastern and North African countries do not trade much among themselves despite the short distance between them (a gravity force) and related languages and cultures. Oliva (2001) finds that high tariff rates coupled with abundant nontariff barriers in key sectors and high tariff dispersion represent an impediment to regional trade. In the late 1990s, nonoil exporting countries such as Egypt, Morocco, Pakistan, and Tunisia featured tariff rates well over 20 percent. Moreover, Middle East and North African countries often rely heavily on nontariff barriers, especially quantitative restrictions and technical requirements.

Trade reform can substantially create trade and expand a country's participation in world markets. Yam (2001) estimates that China's 2002 accession to the WTO could double China's trade volumes by year 2005. In terms of export share in world exports the figures are estimated to jump from 3.7 to 7.3 percent, and for imports from 3.4 to 7.2 percent.

Is free trade best? When perfect competition prevails, and there are no externalities or preexisting distortions, free trade is the best policy. But when international trade takes place in imperfectly competitive markets and there are externalities, appropriately imposed trade restrictions can in principle, but not necessarily, improve social welfare. The ambiguous effects of trade restrictions and their distributional impact gave rise to heated controversies between mercantilists and free traders in the seventeenth century. The intellectual descendants of mercantilists and free traders have continued to argue the cases for protection and free trade ever since.

Sections 13.1–13.3 provide an overview of overall measures of protection, the classical theory of distortions, and estimates of welfare costs in static and dynamic settings. Sections 13.4 and 13.5 examine the theory and empirical evidence on trade liberalization. Section 13.6 discusses the impact of liberalization on the environment and Section 13.7 reviews the pros and cons of specific protection devices. Section 13.8

shows that when the source of a country's imports is a monopolist exporter, import tariffs can be used to extract part of the monopoly rents. Section 13.9 explains why countries discriminate in tariff setting, and the role of GATT's nondiscrimination principles. Section 13.10 assesses available evidence on whether import protection has promoted exports in practice. Section 13.11 explains why protection can delay the adoption of foreign technologies. Sections 13.12–13.14 focus on import quotas and voluntary export restraints. Sections 13.15–13.17 review the Multifiber Agreement, local content laws, and tariff jumping.

13.1. MEASURING TRADE BARRIERS

A tariff is a tax levied at the border. It is calculated as either a percentage of the value of the imported goods (i.e. *ad valorem* tariff) or as a fixed monetary amount per imported unit (i.e. a specific tariff). Tariffs raise the consumer price of imports making them less competitive relative to import-competing products.

A popular method of calculating an average tariff rate is to divide total tariff revenues by the total value of imports. The method only requires data that is regularly reported by countries. There are several alternative procedures to measure an average tariff rate (simple average rate, weighted average rate). However, each method might lead to very different conclusions in terms of the protection levels of a country. The simple or unweighted average tariff rate is obtained by adding up all tariff rates within each heading line and dividing the resulting number by the total number of import categories. If there are many high tariff peaks with few imports, the simple average overstates the degree of protection in the economy. A trade (or import weighted) tariff average weights each tariff by its share of total imports. Import categories with high tariffs but few imports are appropriately assigned a low weight.

The trade-weighted tariff gives a misleading impression of protection when tariffs are set so high as to eliminate imports (prohibitive tariffs) so that the category has a zero weight. This problem also plagues the average tariff obtained by dividing total tariff revenues by the total value of imports. If tariffs are so high that revenues are very low, the index inappropriately reports a low average tariff for a highly protectionist country. In this case, the simple average might be a more accurate indicator.

The most-favored-nation (MFN) tariff rate is the rate agreed to in the negotiating rounds sponsored by the WTO and before 1995 by the GATT. Formally, it is the statutory tariff rate applied to all WTO members in the absence of exemptions or participation in a preferential agreement that sets lower rates for participants. The cumulative effect of WTO/GATT negotiation rounds has reduced the developed countries average MFN tariff rate on nonagricultural goods from around 40 percent to less than 5 percent. These reductions are applied on a MFN basis to all WTO members.

The WTO distinguishes between bound and applied rates. A binding is a WTO member country legal obligation not to raise tariffs on a particular product above a negotiated level. If a member country breaks a binding, it is required to compensate affected WTO members. Tariff bindings remove the maximum tariff uncertainty faced by exporters. Tariff bindings are often negotiated at a higher level than the current applied rate. For example, a country may choose to bind a tariff at 20 percent but actually apply a tariff rate of 15 percent. This gap provides the flexibility to increase the applied rate up to the bound rate without breaching WTO obligations.

Observe that the bound rates are top rates. First, participants in a preferential trading arrangements such as EU members, can be allowed to set lower rates among themselves. Second, developing countries can be granted tariff preferences (lower rates than other members) under the Generalized System of Preferences.

13.1.1. Nontariff Barriers

A major inaccuracy from using average tariff rates to measure the degree of protection is that average tariff rates ignore nontariff barriers to trade such as import quotas and licenses, voluntary export restraints (VERS), export taxes, nationalistic government procurement policies, domestic content rules, and others. The rising relative importance of nontariff barriers means that tariff measures do not fully capture trade restrictiveness. The WTO encourages the transformation of quotas and other nontariff barriers into tariffs. This transformation is called tariffication and might entail increasing tariffs while reducing de facto protection levels.

Nontariff barriers are particularly difficult to measure. Detailed discussions of measuring trade barriers are contained in Deardorff and Stern (1998) and Laird and Yeats (1990). The most frequent measures are as follows.

1. The frequency ratio and the coverage ratio. The frequency ratio is the number of tariff lines affected by a nontariff measure divided by the total number of tariff lines. This measure of nontariff barriers does not capture the intensity of the nontariff measures set by the country. The import coverage ratio is an import-weighted frequency ratio. It indicates the proportion of a country's import values (rather than the proportion of tariff lines) subject to nontariff barriers. Because the coverage ratio accounts for the value of imports subject to nontariff barriers, product lines subject to prohibitive nontariff barriers (i.e. imports are zero) are not controlled by this measure.

2. The price-comparison measure (price-gap measure, implicit tariff rate). This measure indicates the extent to which domestic prices depart from free trade prices and entails computing the tariff equivalents of nontariff barriers at the product level. Price-gaps are defined as the difference between the price of a good produced domestically and the price of imported perfect substitute goods. This measure assumes that (1) domestic and imported goods are perfect substitutes and differences are negligible in terms of their economic value, (2) prices are comparable at the time and location dimension, and (3) prices are obtained for each distribution stage. The assumptions can be quite stringent in practice. For instance, assumption (1) is usually violated when country-of-origin plays a role in signaling product quality.

13.1.2. Overall Measures of Protection

Measuring overall trade restrictiveness is a delicate task. First, trade liberalization is not applied uniformly to all sectors and products. Second, openness entails dismantling quantitative and qualitative barriers to trade, such as nonobjective tools that are very difficult to verify. Third, de facto liberalization heavily relies on how it is administered on a daily basis. Fourth, a country's openness as measured by the ratios of exports to GDP or GNP, imports to GDP or GNP, or the sum of exports and imports divided by GDP or GNP (the trade intensity ratio TIR) are not necessarily closely related to protection. Trade liberalization and trade openness are related but are not the same thing. These factors explain the absence of a widely accepted overall indicator of protection that would permit an unambiguous ranking of countries in terms of their trade restrictiveness.

An ideal measure should control for restrictiveness induced by the level of tariffs, tariff dispersion and the application of multiple nontariff barriers currently in place. On many occasions, there is conflicting behavior in the design of these protectionist tools (tariffs, tariff dispersion, and nontariff barriers). A country might sustain low tariffs while applying highly dispersed tariff schemes and recurring to nontariff barriers. Using the TRAINs (TRade Analysis and INformation system) database developed by the UNCTAD, Oliva (2001) finds evidence that Middle East and North African countries utilized tariff rates and nontariff barriers as substitute instruments of protection in the late 1990s.

There are numerous indexes of overall protection. The most commonly used indexes in the literature to rank countries' openness are as follows.

1. The nominal rate of protection (NRP) is the premium paid by domestic importers due to the presence of import barriers. In other words, it refers to the protection level granted to domestic producers with the imposition of an import tariff on competing products. Formally,

$$NRP = \frac{p}{p^W} - 1,$$

where the world price p^W is expressed in domestic units and adjusted for transport costs and quality differences between the domestic and imported items. This measure assumes that domestic and imported goods are perfect substitutes or differences are negligible in terms of their economic value and that prices are comparable at the time and location dimensions. Notice that the index requires obtaining prices for different distribution stages.

2. The effective rate of protection (ERP) was developed by Balassa (1965), Johnson (1965), and Corden (1966). The ERP captures the rate of protection conferred to the value added (VA) in a given industry i. Formally,

$$ERP_i = \frac{VA_i - VA_i^*}{VA_i^*},$$

where VA_i and VA_i^* denote domestic and world value added, respectively. These measures serve as a proxy for the most efficient way of production in a given industry i.

In practice, the effective rate of protection measures effective tariff protection rather than overall protection. If the input–output relation is linear and tariffs are the only trade restrictions, the ERP can be written as follows

$$ERP_i = \frac{t_i - \sum_k \phi_{ik} t_k}{1 - \sum_k \phi_{ik}},$$

where t_i is the nominal tariff rate on final good i and t_k is the nominal tariff rate levied on input k. The input–output coefficient ϕ_{ik} is the share of intermediate good k in one unit of final good i (measured at free trade prices). If tariffs on final and intermediate inputs are the same, $t_i = t_k$ the effective rate of protection will also coincide with the final good tariff level. However, if the tariff rate t_i of final goods exceeds (is lower than) the tariff rate t_k on intermediate inputs then the effective rate of protection will be larger (lower) than the final good tariff. Indeed, the effective rate of protection might be negative, that is, the tariff on intermediate stages might substantially exceed the tariff on the final good. Lower tariffs on imported inputs raise the ERP (given t_i).

The effective tariff rate is an adjusted tariff rate that takes into account the tariff rates applied on imported inputs and tends to imply higher levels of protection on value added than the applied MFN rates levied on finished imported goods. A specific example concerns the European Union tariffs on coffee. In the 1990s, these ranged from 4 per cent on raw green coffee to 13.8 percent on toasted coffee, and to 16.5 on decaffeinated coffee. The progressivity of taxation with the degree of transformation of coffee substantially restricted imports of toasted coffee giving heavy protection to European coffee makers which transform imported raw coffee. Tariffs on coffee substantially affected Brazil, Mexico, Indonesia, and Vietnam, because other large producers such as Colombia and El Salvador are exempted from tariffs on coffee. Under the Agricultural Agreement of the Uruguay Round of trade negotiations, the European Union agreed to reduce tariffs on raw, toasted, and decaffeinated coffee to 4, 7.5, and 9 percent, respectively, by year 2000. Data limitations justify the use of the applied MFN rate as the standard notion of tariff rate.

The practice of setting higher tariffs on goods by degree of processing, called tariff escalation, is one of the major sources of high effective rates of protection for final goods. For instance, a schedule in which the tariff on imported cotton is 10 percent and the tariff on finished shirts is 20 percent exhibits tariff escalation.

3. The trade restrictiveness index (TRI), due to Anderson and Neary (1994, 1996, 2003), is the scaling factor by which period-1 prices must be deflated to maintain utility when trade restrictions and domestic prices change (relative to period-0) in a small economy. Consider the traded goods spending function, B, equal to the net value of expenditure on traded goods, E, minus net tariff revenues

$$B(p^{tariff}, u) = E(p^{tariff}, u) - (p^{tariff} - p^W)m(p^{tariff}, u) = E - tp^W E_p,$$

where $p^{tariff} = (1 + t)p^W$ is the domestic price vector inclusive of tariffs, p^W is the given world price vector, and u is the representative consumer's utility level. Net tariff revenues are $(p^{tariff} - p^W)E_p$, with $p^{tariff} = (1 + t)p^W$. Using Shepard's lemma, the price derivative of the spending on traded goods function E, $E_p = \partial E/\partial p$, is the economy's general equilibrium utility-compensated (or Hicksian) import demand vector $m(p^{tariff}, u)$. Let us see how to calculate the welfare-based trade restrictiveness index (TRI), and the associated uniform tariff, using a computable general equilibrium model.

Consider an equilibrium utility level in period-1 such that traded goods spending B is equal to a given initial level B_0

$$B(p_1^{tariff}, u_1) = B(p_0^{tariff}, u_0) = B_0.$$

The TRI is the uniform deflator of period-1 prices that maintains welfare and the trade balance if prices change from p_0^{tariff} to p_1^{tariff}. The uniform tariff τ^Δ is a general equilibrium measure of the average tariff. A higher TRI denotes greater restrictions. If $p_0^{tariff} < p_1^{tariff}$, TRI > 1. If $p_1^{tariff} = p^W$, TRI < 1

$$B\left(\frac{p^W}{TRI}, u_0\right) = B((1 + \tau^\Delta)p^W, u_0) = B(p_0^{tariff}, u_0),$$

where $B(\cdot)$ is traded goods spending net of tariff revenues and u_0 denotes period-0 utility. The uniform tariff, $t^\Delta = (1/TRI) - 1$ and the restrictiveness index, $TRI = 1/(1 + t^\Delta)$ are such that the trade balance is maintained for a given utility level.

In a partial economy setup with linear demand functions, the welfare equivalent uniform tariff index is obtained from (see Anderson and Neary, 2003)

$$\sum (t^\Delta p_i^W)^2 \gamma_i = \sum (t_i p_i^W)^2 \gamma_i,$$

where γ_i is the price-responsiveness of imports of product i.

The mercantilist trade restrictiveness index (MTRI) is the scaling factor (deflator) measuring the uniform tariff, $t^\mu = (1/MTRI) - 1$, that makes the volume of imports equal to the import volume under the tariff vector p_0^{tariff}

$$M\left(\frac{p^W}{MTRI}, B_0\right) = M((1 + t^\mu)p^W, B_0) = M(p_0^{tariff}, B_0),$$

where $M = p^W m$ is the import volume function. Anderson and Neary (2003) show that the MTRI, which maintains import volume rather than welfare, implies a uniform tariff t^μ cannot exceed the welfare-based tariff t^Δ. These indexes can be extended to comprise NTBs.

4. The Index of Aggregate Trade Restrictiveness developed by Sharer *et al.* (1998) at the International Monetary Fund (IMF) provides a measure of protectionism that combines the unweighted average tariff rate and a ranking of nontariff barriers. In a first step, countries are classified in five categories (ranging from open to restrictive) according to the level of tariffs. For instance, a country with tariff rates ranging between

0 and 10 percent is considered open, but a country with tariff rates exceeding 25 percent is rated as restrictive. In a second step, countries are classified in three categories (open, moderate, and restrictive) according to the use of nontariff barriers. The classification is based on data on the share of imports and production, the number of tariff lines subject to nontariff barriers, and the share of trade subject to nontariff measures (depending on the availability of data). In the third and last step, the ratings given to a country for the use of tariff and nontariff barriers are mapped into a classification scheme providing a unique measure for overall trade restrictiveness.

13.2. THE CLASSICAL THEORY OF DISTORTIONS

The results obtained by the classical (i.e. nonstrategic) theory of international trade distortions constitutes a main frame of reference for trade policy analysis. The classical theory states the specific nature of optimal intervention (or lack of it) under different conditions when there are no strategic interactions. Game-theoretic models feature strategic effects, but do not dissipate the effects stressed by the classical theory of distortions. This theory serves both as a reference and as a reminder that there are additional aspects frequently bypassed in strategic analyses.

The classical theory of distortions yields clear trade intervention prescriptions. Let us present the main prescriptions in a nutshell. Free trade is found to be optimal for a small country. If there are pre-existing distortions and externalities, the prescription is to set a policy addressed to the specific market affected. For instance, a production distortion should be addressed by a production tax or subsidy, not by trade policy. For a large country, export subsidies are always welfare reducing, because they create domestic distortions and entail government spending that implicitly subsidizes foreign buyers. On the other hand, a large country can impose an optimal tariff that improves welfare by reducing the world market prices of imported goods, and generating government revenues paid by foreigners.

13.2.1. Terms of Trade of Small and Large Countries

Trade policy is analyzed without recourse to strategic analysis by considering: (1) a small country that cannot affect the terms at which it trades with other countries, and (2) a large country that holds a degree of monopoly power in world markets, and can thus affect its terms of trade.

We define a country's terms of trade (TOT) as the country's external relative price, that is, the price of its exports p_X over the price of imports p_M, evaluated at the prices prevailing in the rest of the world (ROW). Symbolically,

$$TOT \equiv \left(\frac{p_X}{p_M}\right)^{ROW}.$$

The small country assumption means that trade intervention by one country does not exert any influence whatsoever over its terms of trade in world markets. On the other hand, trade intervention by a large country's government can affect the country's terms of trade (i.e. the prices prevailing when trading with the rest of the world).

13.2.2. Perfect Competition and the Optimality of Free Trade

Consider a small country that produces an exportable and an importable good. An export subsidy raises the domestic price of the exportable good relative to the imported good (because subsidized exporters will only sell locally if the domestic price is high enough to compensate for the forgone export subsidy). The artificial domestic price increase: (1) induces a reduction of exportables' consumption, causing a loss of consumer surplus, and (2) leads to inefficiently high production of export-ables (at marginal costs that exceed the free trade price). The losses of consumer and producer surplus mean that the society as a whole suffers a welfare loss. A similar argument implies that a tariff-induced increase in the domestic relative price of import-ables causes a welfare loss (by reducing importables' consumption and inefficiently protecting domestic producers of importables).

The optimality of free trade under perfect competition (in a no-externalities set-ting with no domestic distortions), underlies that drive for the elimination of trade barriers through bilateral and multilateral trade negotiations that has taken place in the world economy since the 1940s. In practice, though, many countries keep utilizing trade subsidies and protective measures to favor their domestic industries. With perfect competition, one factor explaining trade intervention is that it provides gains to par-ticular groups. For instance, domestic firms benefit when exports are subsidized (i.e. their profits increase). However, these profit gains come out of government subsidies and consumers' pockets, so that the increase in firms' profits is cancelled out for the nation as a whole.

The previous discussion has a clear lesson. A small country can affect internal prices but not foreign prices, and can thus neither alter its terms of trade nor have an impact on the rest of the world's welfare. The only effect of establishing an export subsidy or import tariff is to hurt the country at the national level.

13.2.3. Large Country Optimal Tariff Argument

The optimality of free trade ceases to be valid, from a nationalistic perspective, if we consider a country holding a degree of monopoly power in world markets. Specifically, a large trader in a particular good can affect prices in the rest of the world and can thus modify its terms of trade in a favorable direction. Improved domestic welfare can be achieved by imposing a trade-restricting tariff t that reduces the demand for imports (i.e. foreign goods). The tariff-induced reduction in the price of imports, increases the price of exports relative to imports over the free trade price prevailing before the imposition of the tariff: $(p_X/p_M)^{ROW}(t > 0) > (p_X/p_M)^{FT}$.

Consider a per unit import tariff $t = p_M(t) - p_M^{ROW}(t)$, where $p_M(t)$ and $p_M^{ROW}(t)$ stand for the price of the importable good in the domestic market and in the 'rest of the world'. The tariff creates domestic consumption and production distortions no matter if imposed by a small or a large country. However, in the case of a large country, the tariff generates government revenues partly paid by foreigners. Let us see why.

Tariff revenues are

$$tM(t) = [p_M(t) - p_M^{ROW}(t)]M(t)$$
$$= [p_M(t) - p_M^{FT}]M(t) + [p_M^{FT} - p_M^{ROW}(t)]M(t),$$

where $M(t)$ represents post-tariff imports and p_M^{FT} is the importables' free trade price. The previous equation shows that tariff revenues are paid by domestic consumers and foreign exporters. Domestic consumers sustain a domestic price increase over the free trade price ($p_M(t) > p_M^{FT}$), and suffer a loss of $[p_M(t) - p_M^{FT}]M(t)$ due to the tariff payments. Foreign exporters sustain a decline in the world price of the goods they sell in the domestic market ($p_M^{FT} > p_M^{ROW}(t)$). Therefore, exporters lose $[p^{FT} - p^{ROW}(t)]M(t)$ in revenues, corresponding to that part of tariff collections that represent exporters' revenues under free trade.

Figure 13.1 illustrates the optimal tariff argument. The part of tariff revenues $[p_M^{FT} - p_M^{ROW}(t)]M(t)$ paid by foreigners is depicted by the rectangle c (with base equal to the total amount of imports M and height equal to $p_M^{FT} - p_M^{ROW}(t)$). On the other hand, the size of the domestic distortion is given by the triangles a and b (with base equal to the change in consumption and production caused by the tariff, and height equal to $p_M(t) - p_M^{FT}$). It can be shown that, by choosing a small enough tariff, the size of the distortion triangles can be reduced to make their sum smaller than the size of the revenue rectangle. For that reason, there is always a small enough positive tariff that has

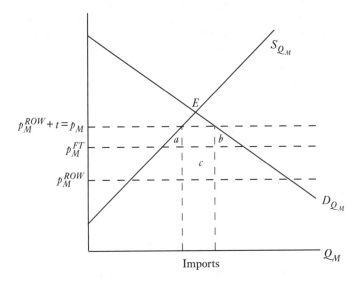

Figure 13.1. *Optimal tariff argument*

a positive impact on domestic welfare in the large country case despite the deadweight losses (triangles *a* and *b*).

Why is it that a large country requires the intervention of the government to exploit its monopsony power in world markets? The reason is that we are considering a perfectly competitive market structure in which domestic firms act as if they cannot affect world prices, even if they can do so by acting collectively. The government tariff drives perfectly competitive firms to the optimal position they can achieve as a group, but not as perfect competitors. Notice that the optimal tariff argument requires that other countries do not get together to retaliate.

13.2.4. Large Country: The Inefficiency of Export Subsidies

Export subsidies are welfare-reducing in the large country case (as well as in the small country case). The artificially increased domestic relative price of exportables causes a loss of consumer's surplus, and inefficiently high production of exportables. Furthermore, export subsidies represent an implicit subsidy to foreign consumers, who are able to buy at below-marginal-cost prices at the expense of the domestic government. Because export subsidies cause inefficiencies and entail subsidizing foreigners, they are not optimal policies for large countries (in contrast to optimal tariffs).

13.2.5. The Targeting Principle

The results of the classical theory of distortions are embodied in the targeting principle (Bhagwati and Ramaswami, 1963; Bhagwati, 1971). The principle states that policies should be targeted to address the market in which the distortion arises. In particular, trade policy instruments should be targeted to offset external distortions, while domestic policy instruments should be targeted to offset domestic distortions.

Trade intervention can only be justified to offset an external distortion. An external distortion arises when the country as a whole holds monopoly power in a given market, but it is not able to exploit it because its productive sector is composed of perfectly competitive firms that do not have monopoly power by themselves. In this case, the relative price of the foreign good is set at a suboptimally high level. There is a terms of trade distortion, and the optimal policy is to offset it by an optimal tariff. In other words, authorities should target trade policy to offset the external distortion.

When distortions are domestic, authorities should target policies to offset domestic distortions. For instance, a production distortion should be addressed by a production tax or subsidy, and a consumption distortion should be addressed by a consumption tax or subsidy. It is not optimal to target trade policies to offset domestic distortions. As a corollary, if there are no domestic distortions, free trade is best.

13.3. WELFARE EFFECTS OF TRADE RESTRICTIONS

The cost of distortions depends on (1) the square of the gap between price and marginal cost due to trade restrictions (e.g. tariff rates), (2) the elasticities of demand and supply, and (3) the volume of trade. Most triangle estimates of the welfare costs of trade restrictions represent a relatively small fraction of GDP. The pioneering empirical work on the cost of trade restrictions in Chile by Harberger (1959) estimated a cost of about 2.5 percent of GDP.

A series of studies on the costs of trade protection sponsored by the Institute for International Economics, a Washington, DC, think tank, have found that the costs of protection vary substantially among countries. Messerlin (2001) estimates that the trade barriers prevailing in European countries in 1990 had a cost of 92 billion euros (about 6–7 percent of GDP) to European consumers. Sazanami *et al.* (1995) estimate that 1989 barriers cost $105 billion to Japanese consumers (3.6 percent GNP) and that their removal would imply increasing Japanese imports by $47 billion. Hufbauer and Elliot (1994) estimate that 1990 US trade barriers cost $70 billion to US consumers (over 1 percent of GDP) and estimate net US welfare losses of $11 billion. Shuguang *et al.* (1998) estimate substantial short term costs as percent of GDP and in terms of jobs but estimate long-term benefits of $35billion for consumers.

Static measures of the welfare costs of trade restrictions focus on the resource allocation cost of trade distortions. A dynamic measure of welfare costs would take into account the effects of distortions on the adoption of new technologies, products, and specialized inputs.

Incorporating the possibility of creation and importing new inputs substantially changes the estimated welfare cost of trade restrictions. Romer (1994) developed a model with specialized imported inputs that are used to produce final goods. Imported inputs are symmetric, have the same demand and are sold at the same price so that the extensive margin for imports corresponds to the number of imported goods. Imports require incurring a fixed cost, such as setting up a service and parts supply network. Higher import tariffs reduces the demand for foreign differentiated products, which reduces the number of imported products that are able to sell enough units locally to cover the fixed costs of importing. Therefore, tariffs reduce the number of products that are imported.

The estimated welfare cost of tariffs in a setting with an endogenous number of available import varieties is far greater than the estimated welfare cost of tariffs when the number of goods imported is exogenously given. Estimates of the welfare and productivity losses from a 10 percent tariff on all imports is 10 percent of GDP compared with 1 percent in a model with an exogenously given number of goods.

13.4. WHY ARE TRADE LIBERALIZATIONS GRADUAL?

The shift from protection to openness in major industrial countries has taken place gradually over time through GATT-sponsored rounds of trade liberalization and individual country trade reform programs. The explanation of gradualism in trade liberalization has focused on the costs of adjustment, avoiding a sudden deterioration of income distribution, governments inability to credibly commit to temporary protection, and the self-enforceability of agreements.

13.4.1. Liberalization and Adjustment Costs

Mussa (1986) examines unilateral trade liberalization by a small country when unemployment is the source of adjustment costs. He finds that the effects of gradual liberalization differ from those of abrupt liberalization. Gradual liberalization limits the income and wealth losses sustained by the owners of resources initially employed in the protected sector undergoing liberalization. If adjustment costs are convex, optimal unilateral liberalization would be gradual. Observe that this argument implies that shock liberalization might be unsustainable on political grounds.

13.4.2. Self-Enforceable Gradual Liberalization

Is gradual liberalization self-enforceable when import competing workers have rent-earning skills specific to that sector? In exploring the enforcement question, Staiger (1995) assumes that workers reallocation entails a cost of adjustment because reallocating workers stand to lose their sector specific skills. Temporary unemployment of displaced workers and the retraining costs caused by trade liberalization are not explicitly considered. The enforcement problem associated with the costs of adjustment diminishes over time because liberalization induces some workers to reallocate out of the import-competing sector. The possibility of stronger enforcement, in turn, makes possible additional rounds of liberalization.

What is the role of adjustment assistance to reallocating workers? Furusawa and Lai (1999) analyze dynamic bilateral trade liberalization between two large countries. The contraction of importable sectors requires labor reallocation across sectors and imposes fixed adjustment costs on reallocating workers. Total adjustment costs are linear in the amount of reallocated workers. Trade liberalization is self-enforced by threats of reversion to protection if liberalizing countries deviate from the trade liberalization path. Specifically, if a country deviates from the trade liberalization agreement, a trade war ensues and both countries shift to the optimum tariff for an infinite period.

The most cooperative liberalization path is generally gradual for a wide range of parametric values. Liberalization can be accelerated by adjustment assistance compensating workers who reallocate away from the protected sector. Greater trade adjustment assistance reduces the distortion in the importable sector due to adjustment costs and raises the benefits from cooperation.

13.4.3. Technology Adoption and the Credibility of Liberalization

Why is it that temporary protection tends to become long-lived? Matsuyama (1990) explores the relation between technology adoption and the long-lasting nature of protective measures. Protection is modeled as a temporary trade measure granted on the condition that a protected firm must adopt technologies while protection lasts. However, suppose that the protected firm fails to innovate during the assigned period of protection. If this happens, the government will be in the same situation as when it granted the temporary protective measures. The same conditions that led to protection maintain the incentives for protective measures.

The tendency of protection to remain alive for a long time, would disappear if the government could credibly commit to temporary protection to begin with. In practice, though, governments cannot credibly commit to temporary protection and protection that is intended to be temporary tends to last a long time.

13.5. WHAT IS THE IMPACT OF TRADE LIBERALIZATION?

In the 1970s and 1980s, a large literature offered case studies evidence supporting the notion that trade liberalization experiences have produced positive long-term effects on liberalizing countries. Choksi and Papageorgiou (1986) details the large evidence gathered. Issues concerning the effects of trade liberalization, however, remain contentious. Recent studies have often focused on selected countries or the general relation between trade and growth rather than on the systematic study of trade liberalization experiences. Iqbal and Khan (1998) contains a set of studies examining the role of trade reform and liberalization in promoting growth in Africa.

13.5.1. Trade Liberalization and Income Convergence

What is the impact of trade liberalization reforms on the real income convergence process? Taking trade liberalization as exogenous, Ben-David (1993) shows that tariff barrier cuts result in a reduction of income differentials among those countries that have displayed for decades relatively stable income differentials. Moreover, in the aftermath of the liberalization process, income differentials remain lower than those prevailing in the prereform stage. In other words, trade liberalization induces income convergence.

Because the trade reform programs examined in Ben-David (1993) took place according to specific timetables and convergence took place following the implementation of the reforms, opening led to convergence rather than convergence to opening. These results shade light on the important question concerning the causality of the trade and convergence relation. The positive relation between closer trade and convergence raises a question about the direction of causality. In order to attribute convergence to trade, one must distinguish between the hypothesis that trading partners tend to converge and the alternative hypothesis that similar countries trade more among themselves than dissimilar ones so that convergence leads to greater trade. Linder (1961) argued that similar countries tend to trade more, which suggests that the causality might go from income convergence to greater trade rather than the other way around.

The application of a new medical procedure, the establishment of minimum wages and trade liberalizations can be viewed and studied as 'treatments' or 'programs'. The effect of the treatment on each agent subject to it can be assessed by comparing the outcome before and after application. The estimation of the effect of applying the treatment can be made through either a single-difference or a difference-in-differences approach.

In the trade liberalization case, a single-difference approach estimates income per capita (or per worker income) for country i as a function of dummy variable d_t which is equal to 1 after the treatment (i.e. at $t = 1$) and 0 before the treatment (i.e. at $t = 0$)

$$y_{it} = \alpha + \beta d_t + \varepsilon_{it}.$$

The econometric assumption allowing interpreting β as the causal effect of the treatment is that in its absence all agents are comparable over time, $E[\varepsilon_{it}|d_t] = 0$, so that β would be estimated to be equal to zero if there was no treatment.

Slaughter (2001) utilizes the difference-in-differences approach to assess the impact of trade liberalization viewed as a 'treatment'. The difference-in-differences approach indexes the agent according to whether or not it belongs to the control group. The index $j = 1$ if agent i belongs to the treatment group and $j = 0$ if agent i belongs to the control (i.e. untreated) group

$$y_{it}^j = \alpha + \alpha_1 d_t + \alpha^1 d^j + \beta d_t^j + \varepsilon_{it}^j.$$

The difference-in-differences regression estimates income y_{it}^j per capita of an indexed agent as a function of:

1. A dummy variable d_t indicating whether the treatment is being applied at time t ($d_t = 1$ after treatment). The parameter α_1 measures how treated and untreated groups are effected by elements that do not depend on the treatment.
2. A dummy variable d^j indicating whether the agent is part of the treatment group ($d^j = 1$) or not. The parameter α^1 indicates time invariant differences between the treated and untreated groups.
3. A dummy variable d_t^j indicating whether the agent is part of the treatment group at time t ($d_t^j = 1$ if $j = 1$ and $t = 1$ and $d_t^j = 0$ otherwise).

The difference-in-differences estimate $\widehat{\beta}$ indicates the effectiveness of the program after controlling for factors that would affect the behavior of agents in the absence of the program.

Slaughter does not find evidence of a convergence effect among members of trading groups. Ben–David (2001) points out the difficulties in pinpointing out the appropriate treated group and treatment period for the interpretation of the results. For instance, Slaughter's analysis is based on membership in formal preference groups even if trade did not substantially increase. Convergence among group members that do not trade much among themselves tells about the effect of the preferential arrangement but not about the convergence effects of international trade.

13.5.2. *Liberalization, Growth, and Poverty*

The debt crisis of the 1980s and subsequent recovery prompted a wave of trade liberalizations in developing countries. There is currently no systematic body of case studies dealing with the effects of these liberalizations on growth and poverty. However, detailed studies on selected countries are available.

The relation of post-1980s tariff liberalization and greater openness with growth and national poverty is studied by Dollar and Kraay (2001) in a sample of six global-izing countries accounting for over half of developing countries' population. China, India, Brazil, Thailand, Argentina, and Bangladesh sharply reduced tariff rates in the 1990s and increased trade in relation to GDP, which suggests that greater openness was induced by policy. Trade liberalization was associated to accelerated growth and poverty reduction in the 1990s (although Argentina stopped growing and experienced a large increase in poverty in the post-sample period 1999–2002).

The relation between growth and trade on one side, and within country poverty and inequality, on the other side, is examined in Dollar and Kraay (2002). A developing country sample for 1950–99 shows that trade openness (as well as good rule of law and developed financial markets) are positively associated with growth but do not have a systematic effect on the share of income accruing to the lowest quintile of the population. In other words, trade openness benefits the poor to the same extent that it benefits the whole economy. These results contradict the common antiglobalization argument that greater openness breeds poverty. Although the subject of the study is not the impact of trade liberalization experiences, the results are quite suggestive of the potential growth and poverty effects of policy-induced trade liberalizations.

13.5.3. Productivity and Firm Exit in Chilean Liberalization

Chile engaged in deep trade liberalization during 1974–9. Plant exit played a major role in the resulting reallocation of resources. In a sample of all Chilean manufacturing plants with ten or more employees, 35 percent of active plants in 1979 had ceased their production by 1986. Within this set of exiting plants, 13 percent belonged to export-oriented sectors, 40 percent to import-competing sectors and the rest to nontraded goods sectors. Exiting plants were on average 8 percent less productive than those continuing to produce, indicating a reallocation effect. Plants in export-oriented sectors were about 11 percent more productive than producers of nontraded goods.

A key question is whether producers of exportable and import-competing products experienced productivity gains. After controlling for self-selection due to plant exit of less productive firms, Pavcnik (2001) examines plant productivity improvements attributable to trade liberalization during 1979–86. A plant's productivity improve-ments are measured as the individual plant productivity measure for a given year minus the productivity of a reference plant in base year 1979.

Consider a regression of plant i productivity index pr_{it} at time t on a vector t of time indicators (standing for macroeconomic factors), dummy variables D_{it}^M and D_{it}^X that are equal to one if the plant is import-oriented or export-oriented, and the interactions $t_{it}D_{it}^M$ and $t_{it}D_{it}^X$ between time and the trade orientation dummies

$$pr_{it} = \alpha_0 + \alpha_1 t_{it} + \alpha_2^M D_{it}^M + \alpha_2^X D_{it}^X + \alpha_{3t}^M t_{it} D_{it}^M + \alpha_{3t}^X t_{it} D_{it}^X + \alpha_4' X_{it} + \epsilon_{it}.$$

The explanatory variables in vector X_{it} include plant characteristics such as industry affiliation and whether a plant ceases to exist in a given year.

The coefficients α_{3t}^M and α_{3t}^X attached to the interaction between time and the trade orientation vector are 'difference-in-differences' estimates of the effects of trade. These estimates are used as indicators of the productivity differential for traded goods (compared to the nontraded goods sector) attributable to a change in the trade regime (i.e. liberalized trade). The analysis offers no evidence indicating that producers of exportable products exhibited productivity improvements relative to the nontraded goods sector. These results suggest that exporters did not experience productivity increases attributable to trade liberalization. Plants in import-competing sectors, though, became more productive than plants in the nontraded goods sector (during 1981–6). The differences in import-competing industries' productivity increases attributable to trade liberalization were found to range from 3 to 10.4 percent.

13.6. IS FREE TRADE GOOD OR BAD FOR THE ENVIRONMENT?

Will trade liberalization result in polluting competition or can liberalization induce countries to embrace environmentally friendly production techniques? The question is especially relevant to developing countries undergoing trade liberalization.

There are two opposed views on the trade and environment subject. As a normal good, environmental quality responds positively to greater real income. If international trade raises real incomes, the richer population will adopt less pollution-intensive production techniques and enforce higher environmental standards. The notion that higher income promotes technology changes is not universally applauded. Skeptics argue that countries becoming richer due to trade can keep polluting production techniques. In this case, trade generates more pollution and might support the use of pollution-intensive production methods.

Copeland and Taylor (1994) examine the determinants of the level of pollution and its international impact in a two-country, many goods general equilibrium setup à la Dornbusch *et al.* (1977). The analysis focuses on the differences in pollution policies between the South and North regions, and assumes (1) ample income disparities between the North and the South based on different per capita human capital levels, and (2) domestic authorities design their tax pollution policies to ensure efficiency both under autarky and under trade. Environmental policies are treated as a local public good and pollution-related damages are faced by the emitting country alone.

Copeland and Taylor find that the effects of real incomes on the level of pollution depend on whether the trade regime is autarkic or open. Under autarky, higher real incomes due to increased trade may encourage the adoption of cleaner techniques of production. This result hinges on the independence between human capital endowments and the levels of pollution. Results change in the open economy setup. There is a direct link between income and pollution: world pollution increases with rich countries' wealth increases, but declines when poor countries become less poor. The paper's corollary is that larger differences in human capital endowments between the North and the South imply that increased trade results in greater pollution levels.

How does the analysis change if global environmental quality is treated as a pure public bad (transboundary pollution) rather than a local public bad? In the presence of transboundary pollution, noncooperative domestic pollution policies are suboptimal since policymaking does not internalize all the externalities. Copeland and Taylor (1995) examine, in the presence of a large number of countries, the noncooperative outcomes of countries holding a pollution quota. Under factor price equalization, trade raises pollution generated by Southern countries and lowers pollution generated by Northern countries. These effects offset each other so that world pollution remains the same. In the presence of large human-capital initial endowment gaps, a move to free trade accentuates global pollution. The reason is that, under large disparities in initial endowments, factor price equalization fails and trade encourages producing in 'pollution havens'.

13.6.1. Is Trade Openness Bad or Good for the Environment?

The empirical evidence on the impact of trade on environment is examined by Antweiler *et al.* (2001). They investigate how trade openness affects the concentration of sulfur dioxide, which is highly correlated with other types of airbone emissions. The sample consists of 108 cities representing forty-three countries for the period 1971–96.

The effect of international trade can be decomposed into three types of effects: output scale effect, production technique effect, and national output composition effect.

1. The output scale effect refers to the increase of pollution due to a higher level of production. Scale is measured by GDP per square kilometer for each city examined.
2. The production technique effect arises because increases in income encourages the use of environmentally friendly techniques.
3. The composition effect has to do with the pollution intensity of activities. The composition of output influences pollution intensity because polluting industries happen to be capital-intensive. If relative factor abundances mean that trade shifts the composition of output toward polluting industries, average pollution intensity will increase.

The empirical results suggest that production technique effects offset output scale effects. Moreover, the combination of these effects and the output composition effects implies that trade liberalization is good for the environment. If trade liberalization raises GDP per capita by 1 percent, pollution concentration falls by about 1 percent.

13.7. PROTECTION: PROS AND CONS

Let us review the pros and cons of protection and some protective policies. There are several general arguments against protection. It artificially raises the prices faced by consumers, induces domestic producers to overextend production, shifts resources toward import-competing industries and limits exporter gains from exploiting economies of scale, and reduces the gains from access to greater product and input variety.

Can trade restrictions improve countries' welfare? Trade literature advances a major argument for protection. The optimal restrictive tariff argument applies to a large country that holds monopoly power as a buyer (i.e. holds monopsony power) in the world market for a particular good. If consumers behave atomistically, though, they will not be able to exploit the monopsony power by themselves. It is then optimal to impose a tariff that restricts imports, reduces the world demand for the imported good, and lowers its world price. The reduction in the price received by foreign exporters represents a net loss for them, and generates a net gain for the importing economy. The extent to which countries affect their terms of trade is a contentious issue that we encountered and will continue to encounter throughout the book.

The range of observed protective measures and strategies go well beyond an optimal restrictive tariff imposed on foreign suppliers by a monopsonist country that can affect its terms of trade. Several arguments are often branded on behalf of protective measures.

Trade restrictions can be approached from the perspective of the regulation of a foreign monopolist. When the sole source of a country's imports is a foreign monopolist, the domestic country gains by imposing a tariff as a means of extracting a portion of the monopoly rents. This situation provides an interesting example of a case in which it is optimal for a small country to impose trade restrictions. A small country's optimal restrictive tariff policy exploits the market imperfection generated by the foreign monopolist.

Do importing countries have incentives to discriminate among trading partners when specifying import tariffs? The answer depends on whether the government imposing the tariffs has complete or incomplete information about foreign exporters' costs. Under complete information, there are strategic incentives to discriminate by subjecting more efficient exporters to higher tariffs in order to maximize rent extraction from them.

Tariff discrimination assumes that the tariff authority is able to determine which foreign suppliers produce at low cost and which produce at high cost. Under incomplete information about exporters' costs, it might not be cost-efficient for the authority to screen producers to determine which ones are low- and high-cost producers, and it might not be possible for producers to send a credible signal about their true costs. Tariff discrimination breaks down when a government voluntarily chooses to impose uniform tariffs to avoid high costs of screening under incomplete information.

A main principle of trade policy is that a restriction that appears beneficial from an individual country's perspective might not be so when many countries follow the same strategy. Tariff discrimination provides an example of a restriction that creates inefficiencies when many countries apply it even if it appears to be beneficial for a country that acts unilaterally. The MFN principle of the WTO establishes that countries must apply the same tariffs (called nondiscriminatory tariffs) to all member countries that supply a given commodity. This principle can be viewed as a mechanism to achieve global production efficiency by enforcing uniform tariffs while discouraging discriminatory tariffs that distort production efficiency by penalizing low-cost producers.

A major argument for import protection is that it can promote exports. Let us examine the pros and cons. Reduced costs due to productivity improvements generated by learning-by-doing in a protected industry can induce exportation. Baldwin and Krugman (1988*a,b*), Venables and Smith (1986), and other researchers have presented evidence that import protection has had an export promotion effect in semiconductors, wide-bodied commercial aircraft, refrigerators, footwear, and other industries.

In practice, protection aiming to promote exportation can be counterproductive. Trade barriers can reduce the incentives to invest in productivity improvements and keep inefficient domestic firms operating when they would otherwise exit the market. Dick (1994) failed to detect the export promotion effect of import protection in 200 US industries in 1970. On the contrary, he found evidence of the presence of export deterrence. Overall, the export promotion question is an empirical issue that remains unsettled and must be examined on a case-by-case basis.

The infant industry argument states that temporary protection can lead to improved international competitiveness. One line of argument is that protection can offset informational barriers facing new products, although it can also promote entry of inefficient firms and encourage production of less-quality products. Another line of argument is that protection buys time for technological advancement. This raises the policy-oriented question of whether trade protection accelerates or delays technology adoption. By increasing the profits obtainable from technology adoption, tariff protection that is credibly permanent—in the sense that firms are convinced that it will not be dismantled soon—can speed up adoption of foreign technologies. Short-lived transitory protection does not advance the adoption of technology. Therefore, temporary protection based on the notion that an infant or lagging industry should buy time for technology adoption can be ineffectual while distorting consumption.

13.8. RENT EXTRACTION

When the source of a country's imports is a foreign monopolist, the domestic country gains by imposing a tariff as a means of extracting a portion of the monopoly rents. The rent extraction motive illustrates a case in which it is optimal for a small country to impose trade restrictions. A small country's optimal rent-extracting tariff policy exploits a market imperfection generated by the foreign monopolist. The theory of rent-extracting tariffs has been developed by Katrak (1977), Svedverg (1979), and Brander and Spencer (1984*a,b*).

Suppose that the domestic market is served exclusively by a foreign monopolist. The domestic market inverse demand function is $p = p(q)$. The foreign monopolist's profits π^* resulting from sales to the domestic market are given by

$$\pi^* = [p(q) - c^* - t]q,$$

where c^* denotes a constant foreign marginal cost and t is the specific tariff imposed by the domestic country. The first order condition of the firm's profit maximization problem is

$$\frac{d\pi^*}{dq} = p(q) + q\frac{dp(q)}{dq} - c^* - t = 0,$$

which implies

$$\frac{p}{c^* + t} = \frac{1}{1 + (q/p)dp(q)/dq} = \frac{1}{1 - \frac{1}{\eta}} = \frac{\eta}{\eta - 1} > 1, \quad \eta = -\frac{p}{q}\frac{dq}{dp} > 0.$$

The elasticity of the demand for exports exceeds unity, $\eta > 1$, because a monopolist is always in the range of the demand function where the elasticity is greater than unity.

The monopolist foreign exporter price is determined as a markup over the sum of marginal costs and the specific tariff. The price declines with the elasticity of demand for imports η and increases with the tariff rate t: $dp/d\eta < 0$ and $dp/dt > 0$.

The domestic government chooses the specific tariff that maximizes welfare defined as the sum of consumer's surplus—total consumer's utility minus the import bill—plus government's tariff revenues

$$W(t) = U(q(t)) - p(q(t))q(t) + tq(t)$$

$$= \int_0^{q(t)} p(q)\,dq - p(q(t))q(t) + tq(t).$$

Total utility U is obtained as the area under the demand curve up to the quantity consumed.

Figure 13.2 depicts consumer's surplus and tariff revenues. The change in utility due to a small increase in the specific tariff rate is equal to the change in the area under the demand curve. The change in utility is approximately equal to the shaded area $p\Delta q$ depicting the equilibrium price times the change in demand due to the tariff change. The rectangle $p\Delta q$ entails a small approximation error to the change in utility.

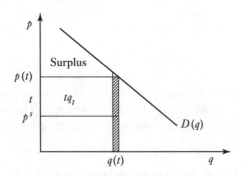

Figure 13.2. *Consumer surplus and revenues*

The reason is that it neglects the small unshaded triangle area, which is negligible for an infinitesimally small tariff change.

The change in total utility due to an *infinitesimally* small change in the tariff level corresponds to the derivative of the total utility integral with respect to the tariff. A tariff change alters the quantity demanded q and thus the limit superior of the integral. The change in utility is computed as the equilibrium price times the derivative of the quantity demanded with respect to the tariff

$$\frac{dU(q(t))}{dt} = \frac{dU(q)}{dq}\frac{dq(t)}{dt} = \frac{d\left[\int_0^{q(t)} p(q)dq\right]}{dq}\frac{dq(t)}{dt}$$

$$= p(q(t))\frac{dq(t)}{dt},$$

where $dU(q)/dq = p(q)$.

Differentiating the welfare function with respect to the specific tariff t yields the first-order condition

$$\frac{dW}{dt} = p\frac{dq}{dt} - q\frac{dp}{dt} - p\frac{dq}{dt} + t\frac{dq}{dt} + q = -q\frac{dp}{dt} + t\frac{dq}{dt} + q = 0.$$

The optimal rent-extracting specific tariff t is given by

$$t^{Optimal} = \frac{dp/dt - 1}{dq/dt} q,$$

where $dq/dt < 0$ and the markup pricing equation implies that $dp/dt > 0$.

The optimal rent-extracting tariff is positive whenever $dp/dt < 1$, that is, when a higher tariff is not fully matched by a price increase. In this case, the tariff extracts rents from the monopolist. Import subsidies can only be sustained in the extreme case in which the demand function is highly convex so that the price goes up more than the tariff increase (i.e. $(dp/dt) > 1$). For instance, if the elasticity of import demand $\eta > 1$ is constant the markup factor is also constant. The price equation implies that a specific tariff increase results in an even greater domestic price increase

$$p = \frac{\eta}{\eta - 1}(c^* + t) \quad \rightarrow \quad dp/dt > 1.$$

In this case, it is optimal to subsidize imports.

Finally, recall that the producer price p^S is equal to the demand price p minus the specific tariff, $p^S = p - t$. We can also express the tariff condition in terms of the producer price p^S

$$t^{Optimal} = \frac{dp^S/dt}{dq/dt} q.$$

13.9. TARIFF DISCRIMINATION AND MFN CLAUSE

Do importing countries prefer to impose uniform or discriminatory tariffs to different foreign countries? The answer varies depending on market structure and whether the government imposing the tariffs has complete or incomplete information about foreign exporters' costs (see Gatsios, 1990; Hwang and Mai, 1991). Under complete information, there are strategic incentives to discriminate in order to maximize rent extraction from oligopolistic foreign exporters. Under incomplete information, though, the incentives to discriminate can break down.

13.9.1. Uniform vs Discriminating Tariffs

Gatsios (1990) develops a model in which two exporting countries—who sell a homogeneous good to a third country—engage in strategic trade policy while the importing country (i.e. the third market) imposes an optimal rent extracting tariff. Exporters produce at constant but different marginal cost levels. Each exporting country follows a strategic trade policy and grants an optimal export subsidy à la Brander and Spencer (1985). Because the importing country purchases from duopolists that hold a degree of monopoly power, it gains from following a rent extraction policy. The importing country's government knows that exporters have different costs, which creates incentives to discriminate in setting tariffs. The general intuition explaining tariff discrimination when exporters differ in costs is that utilizing multiple tariff instruments—discriminatory tariffs—allows greater rent-extraction than possible with a single tariff instrument—nondiscriminatory tariffs.

What is the best specific tariff policy? If exporters have the same cost function, uniform tariffs represent the best strategy. If there is a cost differential, subjecting the most cost-efficient exporter to a higher tariff allows extracting greater rents from the exporting duopolists than under a single tariff. The logic behind tariff discrimination can be seen by considering an initial situation in which there is no discrimination. In that situation, the low-cost exporter will hold a larger market share than the high-cost exporter. What happens if the importing nation increases at the margin the tariff on the low-cost producer while reducing the tariff on the high-cost producer? *Ceteris paribus*, that is, keeping the same import levels (and thus consumer surplus), total revenues will increase. The reason is that the tariff increase applies to the firm with a larger tax base while the tariff reduction applies to a lower tax base.

The revenue effect of tariff discrimination has a positive impact on the importing country welfare, defined as the sum of government revenues and consumers' surplus, but there is also a cost-increasing effect. The shift from equal to unequal tariffs lowers the production of the low-cost firm and increases the production of the high-cost firm. This diversion of production from the low-cost to the high-cost exporter has a cost-increasing effect and leads to lower imports. However, there is always a small enough degree of tariff discrimination that makes the cost-increasing effects of the production changes negligible relative to the positive revenue effect of tariff discrimination. The reason is that the production effects generate second order welfare changes (i.e. relatively small triangles) while the revenue effects are first order welfare changes (i.e. relatively large rectangles).

In the noncooperative Nash equilibrium, exporting countries' will subsidize their exports following the strategic third market model popularized by Brander and Spencer (1985). A low-cost exporter is promoted by receiving a higher subsidy than a high-cost exporter. Consider a linear demand function $p = a - bQ$ and constant marginal exporters' cost functions (with $c^* > c$). The Nash equilibrium subsidy s partially compensates for the discriminatory tariff t^D imposed by the importing country

$$s = \frac{bq}{2} < bq = t^D,$$

where q represents both production and exports. In the uniform tariff case, the solution would be: $s = bq/2 < b(q + q^*)/2 = t^{Uniform}$. This uniform tariff solution is based on the average production level of the exporters to which it applies. It is thus greater than the discriminatory tariff applied to the country with low costs and high production and lower than the tariff applied to the country with high costs and low production.

The Nash equilibrium tariffs $t^* = bq^* < t = bq$ entail discrimination against the low-cost producer, which in turn receives a larger strategic export subsidy than its high-cost rival. The relation between the tariff and subsidy results is that the discriminatory tariff result is formulated from the viewpoint of the third market that seeks to extract rents from exporters (recall that the third market is the *importing* country in strategic export promotion models). The strategic subsidy result is formulated from the different viewpoint of an *exporting* country.

13.9.2. MFN Clause: Goals and Enforcement

Discriminatory policies give preferential treatment to high-cost producers and penalize low-cost foreign producers by subjecting them to higher tariffs. As such, tariff discrimination generates an inefficient global production pattern compared with nondiscrimination (i.e. applying uniform tariffs to all foreign exporters).

The MFN principle of the WTO specifies conditions under which countries must apply the same tariffs to all WTO members. This principle works as a mechanism to enforce world production efficiency. The efficiency goal is achieved by sustaining a nondiscriminatory import tariff regime in an environment in which countries have noncooperative discrimination incentives that are welfare-reducing from a joint or global perspective.

The application of the nondiscriminatory tariff regime implied by the MFN clause of GATT/WTO is not free of problems. First, the nondiscriminatory tariff regime faces resistance from authorities imposing noncooperative tariffs as a source of rents. The solution to this problem lies in implementing a cooperative process that presents an alternative to noncooperative behavior. Cooperation can be sustained through WTO-sponsored international negotiations leading to an enforceable agreement.

Second, the shift from a discriminatory to a uniform international tariff regime has income distribution effects that favor developed countries and harm developing exporting countries. This happens because the more developed exporters are the more cost-efficient and are thus subject to higher discriminatory tariffs.

Acceptance of the MFN clause requires compensation. Developed countries compensate developing countries by means of various types of side-payments. International transfers such as foreign aid compensate losing countries in order to ensure their acceptance of a more efficient global regime.

13.9.3. Incomplete Information

Tariff discrimination can break down under incomplete information. Even if a government could induce exporters to signal their cost-type through an appropriate discriminatory tariff policy, it might not be optimal to screen exporters' types. The reason is that signaling takes place when high-cost producers lower output (and thus trade) to signal their cost in order to receive a lower tariff. Because signaling reduces trade and is thus costly to the importing country, the government might choose not to induce disclosure of firm's types. When a nondiscriminatory tariff policy is chosen, the equilibrium entails pooling.

Kolev and Prusa (1999) develop a signaling model in which tariff discrimination can break down under asymmetric information. The signaling problem is developed in the context of a government that faces a multinational monopolist serving the domestic market for an infinite number of periods. The monopolist has private information over its marginal cost (assumed to be constant). The government can either renounce to discriminate or devise a screening mechanism to determine the cost-type and be able to discriminate.

In the first period, the monopolist chooses the volume of exports under free trade conditions. In the second period, the domestic government selects the optimal per-unit tariff that will be kept in place for the remainder of the infinite period game.

The tariff choice is made after observing the volume of free trade imports from the monopolist and using Bayes' rule to form the government's posterior beliefs about the monopolist's costs. Private information allows the foreign producer to act strategically in the first period in order to influence the government's posterior beliefs and the subsequent tariff choice.

Sequential Equilibria
Consider an infinite-horizon signaling game with continuous strategies and incomplete information about a monopolist's cost type. The game is played out sequentially in discrete-time. This type of game can be solved using the concept of sequential equilibrium (Kreps and Wilson, 1982; Kreps and Sobel, 1994). Sequential equilibrium imposes sequential rationality and two consistency requirements on beliefs:

1. players maximize their payoff functions given the dynamic strategies and rationally formed beliefs of the other players. This is called the sequential rationality requirement;

2. the set of players' posterior beliefs is consistent with Bayes' rule for forming posterior beliefs at nonnull events;
3. there exists a sequence of completely mixed strategies—meaning strategies in which a player assigns a positive probability to each possible action at each information set—the limit of which is equal to an equilibrium strategy profile and system of beliefs. Intuitively, equilibrium beliefs can be derived from totally mixed strategies that are mathematically close to equilibrium beliefs in the sense of convergence.

A well-known problem with the sequential equilibrium concept is that there are multiple sequential equilibrium paths. The solution of a dynamic game must consider all possible messages, including those that will not take place in equilibrium, and the beliefs that would be generated. A dynamic signaling game encompasses a wide range of permissible beliefs in response to out-of-equilibrium messages, which in turn supports multiple equilibria (pooling, semi-pooling, and separating). In order to restrict the equilibrium set, several criteria have been proposed to eliminate unreasonable systems of beliefs in response to out-of-equilibrium messages. The solution concepts arising from alternative criteria are called refinements of sequential equilibrium.

When focusing on behavior off-the-sequential equilibrium path, a government might entertain different beliefs about the cost-type of the monopolist it faces. Kolev and Prusa (1999) rely on the so-called Intuitive Criterion proposed by Cho and Kreps (1987) to obtain a single separating equilibrium.

If the discount rate is low enough (i.e. it is below a threshold level), there is a separating equilibrium in the sense that a high-cost monopoly exporter would be subject to a different tariff rate than a low-cost monopoly exporter. With a low enough discount rate, it is worthwhile for a high-cost monopolist to reduce the level of output below the profit-maximizing level in the free trade period to signal its high-cost type and benefit from a lower tariff in the future.

Given that a high-cost exporter would signal its type by reducing output, it is not worthwhile for a low-cost firm to mimic a high-cost firm by reducing output to the level of a high-cost firm and thus receive a lower tariff in the future. The reason is that a low-cost firm's monopoly output is higher than a high-cost firm's monopoly output under free trade. When mimicking a high-cost firm, a low-cost firm must experience a reduction in output that is larger and thus more costly than the output reduction of a high-cost firm. Therefore, the incentive compatibility constraint is satisfied and there is no mimicking by a low-cost firm. A separating equilibrium ensues.

In a separating equilibrium, the ex ante expected value of trade is reduced relative to the complete information case. This happens because (1) a high-cost firm reduces output to credibly signal its true type and qualify for a lower tariff, and (2) a low-cost firm's output is the same as under complete information.

If the discount rate exceeds a threshold level, the optimal policy is to set uniform tariffs (i.e. an optimal MFN-tariff). Because inducing signaling is costly to the importing country in terms of reduced high-cost exporter's output (and thus trade), it might not be worthwhile to discriminate. A pooling sequential equilibrium results.

13.10. CAN PROTECTION PROMOTE EXPORTS?

A major argument for import protection is that it can indirectly promote exports. This possibility arises when production costs decline with the current or the accumulated level of production. The increased domestic output due to protection reduces domestic marginal and average costs. In turn, the cost-reducing effect allows enhancing the export share in markets abroad (Krugman, 1984). The downside of protection as an export promotion strategy is that protection might lead to an inefficiently large firm scale, entry of inefficient firms into the protected industry, and delayed technology adoption.

There is ample evidence supporting the hypothesis that protection has promoted exports in major industries but not of large positive welfare effects. Successful export promotion is illustrated by Japan, Korea and other countries, who have penetrated foreign export markets while continuing to protect local markets purportedly to exploit economies of scale and encourage learning-by-doing. Venables and Smith (1986) provide evidence of export promotion arising from the refrigerators and foot-wear industries. Baldwin and Krugman (1988*a*,*b*) offer evidence of export promotion in semiconductors and the wide-bodied commercial aircraft industry. Baldwin and Krugman (1988*a*) conclude that Japanese protection contributed to the development of the semiconductor industry but did not increase overall welfare. Head (1994) finds that US steel rail industry protection encouraged strong learning effects but hurt rail users in the short and long run. The welfare effects of protection are estimated to be positive but small. Head also points out that the remarkable growth of the US steel industry in the late nineteenth century can be explained by new discoveries (iron ore and coal) and the development of infrastructure (railroads and canals) that shifted US comparative advantage toward metal production.

Despite heated controversies, systematic evidence on the role of protection as export-promotion is scarce. The empirical basis for the protection–export promotion link has been examined by Dick (1994). The econometric analysis uses cross section data on exports and other variables for 200 US industries in 1970. The question raised is whether import protection might have acted to promote US exports. The study finds evidence of export deterrence effects associated with (1) higher targeted nontariff barriers, and (2) a larger international market share of the protected US market. Moreover, the export-deterring effects of these variables were largest in the subgroup of industries with strongest increasing returns to scale.

The empirical analysis relates US export market share in industry i to several variables

$$\frac{X_i}{\sum_{j=1}^{N} X_{ij}} = F(CA_i, t_i, NTB_i, S_i),$$

where $X_i / \sum X_{ij}$ represents the share of US industry i exports in the combined industry i exports of ten sample countries ($N = 10$). The explanatory variables are (1) a measure of the free trade comparative advantage CA_i of industry i, (2) the industry's effective relative tariff rate t_i, (3) the industry's nontariff barrier index (NTB_i) calculated by the US International Trade Commission, and (4) the US relative domestic market size S_i measured as the ratio of US consumption to total consumption of the other countries included in the sample.

In order to obtain a measure of free trade comparative advantage, revealed comparative advantage is adjusted for the estimated effect of trade policy on comparative advantage. The study also controls for the political economic endogeneity of trade barriers by adjusting the tariff rate to eliminate the estimated political economy component incorporated in the observed tariff rate.

An export share equation involving linear and quadratic terms is estimated for 1970 US exports to Belgium, Canada, France, West Germany, Italy, Japan, the Netherlands, Sweden, and the United Kingdom

$$\frac{X_i}{\sum_{j=1}^{N} X_{ij}} = \underset{(8.57)}{28.24} + \underset{(2.63)}{1.92\,CA_i} - \underset{(-1.03)}{0.13\ t_i} + \underset{(0.65)}{0.00 t_i^2} - \underset{(-2.06)}{3.17\ NTB_i}$$

$$+ \underset{(1.51)}{0.34\,NTB_i^2} - \underset{(-6.02)}{18.22\,S_i} + \underset{(5.34)}{2.03\,S_i^2} + \varepsilon_i,$$

where ε_i is the error term and the numbers between parentheses denote the White-corrected t-statistics (White, 1980). The inclusion of the squared explanatory variables t_i^2, NTB_i^2, and S_i^2 in the econometric specification increases the R^2 to 18 percent (compared to 11 percent for the corresponding linear regression).

The cross-section analysis is consistent with the notion that import protection was deterring US exports in 1970. The tariff rate, the index of nontariff restrictions, and relative domestic market size turns out to be negatively associated with export shares. The nontariff barriers index and market size were statistically significant at the 5 percent significance level. The tariff rate was not statistically significant (in 1970 tariff rates were generally quite low in the United States and other OECD countries). Notice that the International Trade Commission nontariff barriers index seemed to be a better indicator of trade restrictions than the effective tariff rate.

When the econometric analysis is restricted to those US industries with the strongest increasing returns to scale (as indicated by measured static economies of scale, the steepness of learning curves, and research intensities) the export deterring effect of protection becomes stronger. These results are interesting because the export promotion effect of protection is presumed to be more relevant for those industries with stronger increasing returns to scale.

In short, there is conflicting evidence on the export promotion effects of import protection. Evidence suggests that the magnitude of the export expansion effect and the sign of the welfare impact inclusive of consumption distortions are industry- and country-specific.

13.11. TECHNOLOGY ADOPTION UNDER PROTECTION

The loss of market share to Japan in autos, steel and other products has been a source of serious concern in the United States and Europe. Japan's successes have been often driven by efforts to move first in the commercial introduction of new and existing technologies. Rival countries with lagging technologies have turned to trade protection as a means to buy time to adopt new technologies. For instance, Japan introduced robots in the auto industry in the 1970s. By the 1980s, robots had replaced human labor in painting, steel sheet stamping, and other tasks. At that time, it took less than 19 h to assemble a vehicle in Japan while it took about 27 h in the United States (Dertouzos *et al.*, 1989). The United States and European countries responded by using protection on grounds that it would buy time for local firms to adopt the new technologies.

13.11.1. Can Protection Buy Time for Technology Adoption?

Can tariff protection accelerate the adoption of technologies? The answer depends on whether tariff protection is viewed as permanent or transitory. Miyagiwa and Ohno (1995) find that permanent protection can speed up technology adoption relative to adoption under free trade. In practice, though, protection is a temporary phenomenon. Long-lasting transitory protection leads to the same adoption date as permanent protection. Protection maintained over a short enough period delays adoption relative to permanent protection and is akin to adoption under free trade. This feature implies that public announcements of permanent protection or long-lasting transitory protection will turn out to be ineffectual if they are not credible. Moreover, permanent protection is undermined by the rules of the WTO, hurts welfare by creating permanent consumer distortions and might not be a time consistent policy.

The finding that temporary protection for a short enough period does not affect technology adoption implies that common protection policies used as a means to buy time for technology adoption can be ineffectual. For instance, the infant industry argument stresses that temporary protection will allow new industries to achieve learning-by-doing gains and become competitive internationally. The technology adoption analysis does not negate the presence of dynamic learning-by-doing effects. But it brings home the point that infant industry protection might be required to be long-lasting to advance retarding the adoption of foreign technologies.

Permanent and Transitory Protection
Technology adoption at time T requires incurring a once and for all fixed cost k to shift from old technology $\underline{\theta}$ to new technology $\bar{\theta}$. The adoption of $\bar{\theta}$ represents a cost-reducing innovation lowering variable costs and thus profits π (gross of the fixed adoption cost k).

The optimal time T to adopt a new technology is the point in time maximizing the discounted present value of the sum of the profits obtained before and after selecting the new technology net of the discounted value of the costs of adopting the new technology

$$\int_0^T e^{-rv} \pi(\underline{\theta}, t)\, dv + \int_T^\infty e^{-rv} \pi(\bar{\theta}, t)\, dv - e^{-rT} k(T),$$

where $\pi(\underline{\theta}, t)$ and $\pi(\bar{\theta}, t)$ are the home firm's momentary profits before and after technology adoption, t is a given tariff rate, and r is the constant interest rate.

The trade off between adopting technology today and postponing it for a short period is balanced at time T if

$$\pi(\bar{\theta}, t) - \pi(\underline{\theta}, t) = rk(T) - \frac{dk(T)}{dT}.$$

Adopting technology at time T will increase profits immediately. The gap $\pi(\bar{\theta}, t) - \pi(\underline{\theta}, t)$ denotes the marginal value of technology adoption. This marginal value does not depend on the timing of the adoption but will be affected by the imposition of a tariff (or the establishment of a quota).

The marginal cost of adopting technology at time T corresponds to the benefits $rk(T) - dk(T)/dT$ from postponing the investment in technology adoption for a short period. A postponement of adoption saves interest payments on the amount of $rk(T)$. Furthermore, ongoing basic research implies that the cost of adopting technology will fall over time at the rate $dk(T)/dT < 0$. This implies that postponement will reduce adoption costs by $-dk(T)/dT > 0$.

Figure 13.3 illustrates the determination of the optimal adoption date. The marginal benefit of adoption is the profit differential that is assumed to be constant over time. The marginal costs of adoption at time T, $rk(T) - dk(T)/dT$ are assumed to decline over time. First, the fixed costs $k(T)$ are taken to decline over time due to technological change. Second, the assumption that $d^2k(T)/dT^2 \geq 0$ implies that the fall in fixed costs does not accelerate over time, that is, the postponement benefit $-dk(T)/dT$ either remains constant or slows down over time.

Under free trade ($t = 0$), the optimal time to adopt the new technology is $T(t = 0)$. The effect of setting a permanent tariff t is to increase the marginal value of adopting

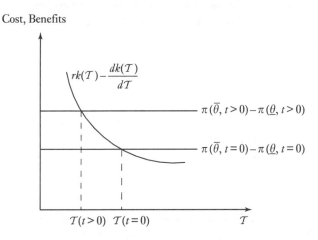

Figure 13.3. *Optimal adoption date*

technology $\bar{\theta}$ and therefore accelerate the adoption of technology. In other words: $T(t > 0) < T(t = 0)$.

The effect of an adjustment of the tariff rate on the marginal benefit from technology adoption is given by

$$\frac{d}{dt}[\pi(\bar{\theta}, t) - \pi(\underline{\theta}, t)] = \frac{d}{dt}\left(\int_{\underline{\theta}}^{\bar{\theta}} \pi_\theta(\theta, t)d\theta\right)$$

$$= \int_{\underline{\theta}}^{\bar{\theta}} \pi_{\theta t}(\theta, t)d\theta > 0,$$

where $\pi_{\theta t}(\theta, t) > 0$. The assumption $\pi_{\theta t} > 0$ means that the higher the tariff t the greater the profit increase that would result from a shift from $\underline{\theta}$ to $\bar{\theta}$. In other words, the profitability of lower production costs due to technology adoption increases with a higher tariff. Notice that technology θ is treated as a continuous variable even though only discrete values $\bar{\theta}$ and $\underline{\theta}$ are considered.

It is easy to see that there is an early technology adoption argument for permanent protection. The intuition for this result is that new technology increases firms' momentary profits and raises consumer surplus, but the consumer effect is neglected by the home firm which only cares about profit maximization. Therefore, the socially optimal date of technology adoption precedes the date chosen by the domestic firm. If the permanent consumer distortion caused by permanent protection is small enough, the optimal rate of permanent tariff protection is positive.

The effect of transitory protection on the timing of technology adoption depends on the period of transitory protection (Miyagiwa and Ohno, 1995). Consider transitory protection until date T_0, treated as exogenous, where the period of protection is shorter than the time to adoption $T(t > 0)$ under permanent protection and the time to adoption $T(t = 0)$ under free trade. In this case, transitory protection can be shown to delay the adoption of technology relative to permanent protection. The optimal time to adopt under transitory protection for a short period is the same as under free trade

$$T_0 < T(t > 0) < T(t = 0) = T(t^{transitory} > 0).$$

If accelerating adoption through permanent protection can beat free trade, transitory protection during period $(0, T_0)$ reduces welfare relative to free trade.

Sufficiently long transitory protection will cause the firm to adopt at the same date as under permanent protection. If the period of transitory protection lasts at least until the date of adoption under free trade, $T_0 \geq T(t = 0)$, the optimal date of adoption can be shown to be the same as under permanent protection. This result implies that transitory protection can dominate permanent protection. The reason is that transitory protection has lower consumption distortion costs and the same adoption date as permanent protection.

Different forms of protection have different effects on the timing of technology adoption. Short-lived transitory tariffs and quotas delay adoption compared to permanent tariffs. Permanent tariff protection can speed up technology adoption but, under the same assumptions, a permanent quota delays adoption (unless the quota is highly restrictive). Notice we are alluding to the effects of a quota on the importing country imposing the quota. What is the effect of the quota on exporters? Quotas are usually thought to increase exporters' product quality as a means to circumvent them.

13.12. IMPORT QUOTAS

An import quota is a restriction limiting the quantity of a good that can be imported into a country. Quantitative restrictions are frequently set for a fixed period of time but they are routinely extended. Because quotas lack transparency, and consumers are frequently unaware that they exist, they are attractive from the perspective of political acceptance. Quotas are enforced by issuing import licenses specifying the maximum quantities of the good subject to the quota that can be imported into a country. The US sugar and apparel quotas allocate to exporting countries' governments the right to sell these products in the United States.

13.12.1. Import Quotas vs Tariffs

Because quotas raise domestic prices above world market levels, they generate rents to domestic producers and to the holders of import licenses. Hufbauer and Elliot (1994) estimate that the US sugar quota, restricting imports to about 2 million tons of sugar, increased the US price of sugar more than 40 percent above world prices.

Just as in the case of a tariff, when a large country imposes an import quota, the consequent reduction of demand reduces world prices. In contrast to the case of a tariff, though, a government does not necessarily get any revenue from import quotas. The allocation of rents depends on the system adopted by the government to allocate import rights. If licenses conferring the right to sell are issued free of cost, the quota rents go to the foreign exporters. If licenses are sold in an auction, the government can grab part of the quota rents.

Can quotas and an equivalent tariff (a tariff that sustains the same volume of imports) generate the same government revenue and have the same welfare effects? The classic work of Bhagwati demonstrated that tariffs and quotas are equivalent in terms of prices, production, and welfare effects under perfect competition, but differ in the presence of monopoly power. A quota and a tariff that sustain the same level of imports produce the same effects if (1) there is perfect competition among foreign suppliers and domestic producers, and (2) the quota is allocated to ensure perfect competition among quota holders. Auctioning quota rights to the importer that offers the greater amount of money for them allows the government to extract the full quota rents. The auctioned import quotas yield the same revenue and welfare effects as an equivalent tariff.

If the domestic producer is a monopolist (in the sense that it is the only domestic firm in the industry), Bhagwati (1969) shows that domestic welfare under a quota is lower than under an equivalent tariff. The presence of a quota restriction enhances the power of the monopolist because it makes demand less elastic for an increase in the price charged. First, a tariff reduces the quantity demanded, increases domestic output and reduces imports. The monopolist's domestic sales increase at the expense of imports. Second, because a binding quota means that imports are given, an increase in domestic sales can only come from an increase in quantity demanded. Therefore, the marginal revenue evaluated at any given level of domestic output is lower under the quota than under an equivalent tariff. In equilibrium, a quota that produces the same level of imports as a tariff yields a lower domestic level of output and a higher domestic price than the equivalent tariff.

The general intuition of why the price under a quota is higher than under an equivalent tariff is that the binding quota does not allow further entry while the equivalent tariff permits entry. The possibility of entry under an equivalent tariff poses an entry threat that is not present under a binding quota. The possibility of entry limits the domestic monopolist's ability to increase the price charged.

Consider a domestic monopolist (in the sense that it is the only domestic producer) who faces competition from foreign exporters. If the supply of foreign exporters is elastic at the world price p^W, the tariff will increase the domestic price to $p^t = p^W + t$. The domestic producer will equate marginal costs to the tariff-adjusted price. If it is subject to increasing marginal costs, the price increase allows an expansion of output. Note that the domestic monopolist will not be able to fully exploit its local monopoly power. The possibility of entry by foreign exporters effectively limits the price increase to $p^W + t$.

A quota that yields the same level of imports as the equivalent tariff would place the domestic monopolist at a more advantageous position than under the tariff. The reason is that the quota allows the monopolist to restrict output below the level prevailing under the equivalent tariff and charge a higher price p^Q without any threat of entry. In short,

$$p^t = p^W + t < p^Q < p^M,$$

where the monopoly price p^M is the highest price because it is determined under no foreign entry at all.

13.13. VOLUNTARY EXPORT RESTRICTIONS

Quantity restrictions include import quotas and VERs (voluntary export restraints, voluntary export restrictions). Both types of quantitative restrictions represent a form of protection enhancing domestic firms' profitability by restricting foreign exports.

A Voluntary Export Restriction (VER) is an import quota that is set on the exports of a foreign country and is administered by the exporting country. The restraints are 'voluntary' because they are requested by the importing country and are accepted by the exporter. The term 'voluntary' often signifies that the discriminated exporter agrees under the threat of alternative more painful trade restrictions.

VERs come in a variety of guises and names and have been quite common in international trade. They can be divided into bilateral and multilateral VERs. Bilateral VERs involving two countries include several US–Japan agreements affecting

Japanese exports of automobiles (negotiated in 1981 and extended until 1985, after which the VERs were unilaterally kept by Japan), steel (1984, 1885, and 1989), and machine tools (1986, 1987). In 1992, several European countries' steel quotas and bilateral VERs involving Japan were replaced by a European Union VER that would expire in December 1999.

Multilateral VERs involve many countries. The most important multilateral VER is the Multi-Fiber Arrangement (MFA) restricting textile exports from twenty-two countries (including Japan and developing countries) to the United States. The Uruguay Round of trade negotiations introduced a rule that explicitly forbids the use of VERs, so that VERs are not WTO-legal.

Because a VER is a quota that is administered by the exporting country (rather than by the importing country) the domestic government does not receive any rents while the foreign country does. The allocation of the rents between the foreign government and firms depends on the licensing system adopted by the government administering the quota.

Like any other type of quota, a VER reduces foreign exports and increases the domestic price of the good to which it applies. Because foreign exporters sell a smaller quantity at a higher price, they may obtain greater rents under the VER than in its absence. If this happens, both domestic and foreign producers will benefit at the expense of domestic consumers.

13.13.1. VERs as Facilitating Practices under Price Competition

A VER can be viewed as a collusive agreement to reduce production in order to sustain a higher price and thus raise domestic and foreign firms profits (Harris, 1985; Krishna, 1989). Therefore, VERs are truly voluntary. In this context, VERs have been called facilitating practices.

Krishna (1989) considers a model of two firms that produce differentiated goods and compete in prices in the domestic market. The quantitative restriction cannot be circumvented by increasing product quality. Consider a simultaneous-move Bertrand competition game in which a domestic and a foreign firm produce differentiated products. Assume that the home country imposes a VER set at the free trade level of imports. What is the effect of the VER on a duopoly equilibrium with price competition? Krishna (1989) shows that

1. if domestic and foreign goods are substitutes, there is a unique mixed equilibrium in which the domestic firm obtains the same profits as a Stackelberg leader,
2. if domestic and foreign goods are complements, the VER does not affect the equilibrium.

Substitute Goods
If domestic and foreign goods are substitutes, there is no equilibrium in which the domestic firm follows pure strategies. There is a unique mixed equilibrium in which the domestic firm randomizes and the foreign firm charges a single price. The reason is

that, if goods are substitutes, the domestic firm profit function under a VER will not be concave in its own price. For a given level of the foreign exporter's price, there will be two domestic firm's prices that maximize profits. Because both prices give equal profits, the domestic consumer is indifferent between them and is willing to randomize. It can be shown that the domestic firm has incentives to randomize strategies by charging a high price p_H with probability α and a low price p_L with probability $1 - \alpha$.

In contrast, the foreign firm's profit function is concave in its own price and there is a single profit maximizing price (given the price chosen by the domestic producer). The foreign exporter charges the unique price that clears the market at the level of the VER. This price will be higher than under free trade because the VER reduces the excessive competition that takes place under price competition, raising prices, and profits in equilibrium. The foreign firm sets prices to ensure that its exports are equal to the quantity allowed under the VER. If the VER is set at the quantity exported under free trade, the domestic firm gains from the VER because it gets the Stackelberg leader profits associated with a first mover advantage. The foreign exporter also gains because it can sell the same quantity as under free trade, but at a higher price. This is why the VER is voluntary.

Suppose that the domestic firm sets its price above the free trade level. If goods are substitutes, the demand for the foreign good increases and the VER constraint will become binding. The foreign exporter would like to expand sales but the VER does not permit it. This means that the presence of a VER reduces the elasticity of the domestic firm's demand function for price increases over the free trade level. The domestic firm can thus increase profits by raising its product price above the free trade level. Because the VER is binding, the quantity-constrained foreign exporter will also raise its price. These effects raise domestic and foreign profits. The VER can thus be a practice that is voluntarily accepted by exporters because it facilitates collusion.

Recapping, when firms compete in prices and goods are substitutes, strategic inter-actions under quotas and tariffs are fundamentally different. If the level of the quota is set at the free trade level (or close to it), there is no equilibrium in pure strategies but there is a unique equilibrium in mixed strategies. Notice that a quota on a foreign firm can be viewed as a capacity constraint on that firm. The nonexistence of a pure strategy equilibrium relates to the standard result that, in the presence of capacity constraints, there is no Bertrand equilibrium in pure strategies (Kreps and Scheinkman, 1983).

Complementary Goods
If domestic and foreign goods are complements, a VER set at the free trade level (or close to it) has no effect on the equilibrium. The VER on the foreign firm makes the domestic firm's demand function less elastic for price decreases. The reason is that a price decrease would make the restraint binding on the foreign firm. Because goods are complementary the foreign firm would like to increase sales but it is restrained not to expand sales. However, the domestic firm would not augment profits by lowering the product price and the presence of VER does not have a monopoly effect. Because the VER does not change the interaction between the duopolists, it is rendered ineffective

when goods are complementary. In other words, a restraint set at the free trade level of imports will not change the equilibrium when goods are complementary.

13.14. US VERs ON JAPANESE AUTOS

The auto industry is the largest manufacturing industry in the United States. For decades, high income levels, economies of scale arising from massive car production, continuing product innovation, low oil prices, and low gasoline taxes, encouraged the development of a gigantic market for cars, and particularly large cars. In the 1980s, the US auto industry fell into deep troubles. The 1974 and 1979 oil shocks led to high gasoline prices, reducing the demand for large cars. Foreign producers, particularly the Japanese, made huge inroads into the American market by satisfying the new demand for small high-quality cars. Surveys conducted in the 1980s indicated that American consumers thought that Japanese autos had better quality than American autos.

Political pressures for US auto industry protection entered the scene in the early 1980s. In May 1981, the US recurred to VERs to restrict Japanese automobile exports, limiting them to 1.68 million automobiles. In 1984, the upper limit was raised to 1.85 million automobiles. During 1985–92, Japanese automobile exports to the United States were restricted to no more that 2.3 million. In 1992, the VERs were scaled back to 1.65 million by President Bush's administration, and were finally lifted in 1994 during the Clinton administration.

The VERs on Japanese automobiles aimed to limit low-cost auto competition and permit US auto manufacturers to receive higher prices. Because the US market was the major export market for Japanese autos, the VERs hit hard and encouraged a multi-level strategic reaction from Japanese auto makers. These responses limited the VERs' effectiveness and their negative impact on Japanese producers.

One strategic reaction from Japanese firms was to substantially increase the quality of Japanese cars. By the late 1980s, a large segment of American consumers perceived Japanese autos as better in quality than comparable American cars. The quality impact of US VERs on Japanese auto exports has been thoroughly studied by Feenstra (1984, 1988), who utilizes methods that identify the component of the total price increase due to improved quality. The 1988 study uses data from 1979 to 1985 to document the quality-improving effect of the VERs on Japanese auto exports to the United States. Specifically, Japanese autos improved in terms of greater horsepower, larger vehicle size, and other characteristics. The data shown also indicate improvements in US auto quality.

A second strategic response of Japanese car producers was to foreign invest in the United States. In 1982, Honda established a plant in Marysville, Ohio. Honda's move was followed by Nissan, Toyota, Mazda, and Mitsubishi. The United States included, within the scope of the VERs, imported Japanese cars sold under the US brand, but VERs did not apply to cars actually produced in the United States. The idea behind the local production strategy, that is, the 'VERs jumping' strategy, is similar to a tariff jumping strategy to bypass trade restrictions.

What were the effects of the VERs on US auto prices? Feenstra (1988) detected US price increases, which were partly attributed to higher auto quality. The study by Berry *et al.* (1999) utilizes 1971–1990 data. They find that the VERs did not significantly raise prices initially, but were responsible for an increase in Japanese car prices in the late eighties. The authors find that US producers did not significantly raise prices but rather reacted by following aggressive selling strategies trying to get a greater market share (a higher demand intercept but weak strategic complementarity in prices).

Did the VERs benefit US producers at the expense of Japanese producers? The evidence suggests that US producers benefited but at the expense of US consumers rather than Japanese producers. Berry *et al.* (1999) estimate that, over the years for which they find the VERs to increase Japanese auto prices (1986–1990), the VERs increased US producers' profits about $10 billion (in current 1983 dollars). On the Japanese side, producers' profits were not significantly affected by the VERs during this period. The evidence on the net welfare effects in the US indicates that the welfare effects were negative, though small. This suggests that US consumers were the ultimate losers, especially the buyers of Japanese cars.

What were the effects of autos VERs on third parties (i.e., non-restricted suppliers)? In particular, what were the effects of US VERs on European producers and prices? Dinopoulos and Kreinin (1988) focused on Germany, Sweden and France, which accounted for about 93 percent of all US auto imports from Europe. Their "triangle" measures (based on the price increase that is not explained by the quality adjustment that took place at the time) produced welfare gains for Europe and welfare losses for the US. The estimated cost of a US job saved by the VER was over $180,000. Berry *et al.* (1995, 1999) find that the VER lowered European prices. Strategic complementarity can occur if the demand slope increases (greater price sensitivity) when the rival raises prices. During 1986–1990, European producers' annual profits in the US market increased between $59 million and $148 million (depending on the year).

The study by Goldberg (1995) develops a model of the US auto industry and utilizes an empirical methodology applying to imperfectly competitive markets to quantify the effects of VERs on market shares, prices and quality. A demand model is estimated using micro data, and supply is modeled as an oligopoly with differentiated products. Using data from 1983–87, the impact of the VER on US domestic production and employment is found to be limited, while the price effect is found to be substantial. In contrast to Berry *et al.* (1999), which find that VERs were not binding until 1986 and afterwards, Goldberg finds that the VERs' quota constraints were binding in the early years of their implementation (1983–1984). In those years, Japanese sales in the US were substantially reduced due to the VERs.

13.15. THE MULTI-FIBER ARRANGEMENT

The MFA is an international compact covering fibers made from cotton, wool, and synthetics. This quota agreement, negotiated with and administered by exporting countries, is the major instance of a long-standing VER. It was negotiated under GATT and allows signatory countries to apply quantitative restrictions on imports of textiles and apparel. These restrictions are established when a country deems them necessary to prevent market disruption and achieve orderly marketing. The MFA provides standards for determining whether or not there is market disruption, and requires importing countries to permit the growth of imports.

Even though negotiated under the GATT, the MFA is thought to be contrary to the spirit of GATT rules. It went into effect in January 1974 and was renegotiated on several occasions afterward. The Uruguay Round of trade negotiations, concluded in 1994, provided for the phase out of the MFA by 2005.

The MFA became one of the most important barriers to trade facing developing countries. It opened the door to a wide array of restraints on imports from low-wage countries. In the 1980s, over 80 percent of US imports of textile and apparel were covered by the restraints allowed by the MFA. The United States had negotiated bilateral quotas with twenty exporting countries and developed consultation mechanisms with another eleven countries. Exporting countries agreed to enter into restrictive bilateral agreements as a strategy to prevent the United States from carrying out the explicit or implicit threat of imposing quotas on a unilateral basis.

Throughout its history, the MFA has remained one of the most controversial elements of the international trade regime. On one hand, defenders argue that it reduces barriers and encourages trade in textile products. On the other hand, developing countries' advocates counter that the MFA has delayed economic takeoff by limiting developing countries' access to major export markets.

Krishna and Tan (1998) study the details of the implementation of the US textiles and apparel quotas established under the MFA. They focus on the implementation of the MFA in the 1980s by selected exporters to the United States (Hong Kong, Korea, Indonesia, India, and Mexico). Because exporting countries administer the quotas, in a perfectly competitive environment they would get the full license quota rents generated by the agreement. The license price will be equal to the difference between the price at which the level of imports is demanded and the supply price.

The division of quota rents depends on the degree of seller and buyer market power as well as on the rules of quota allocation. Trela and Whalley (1995) discuss quota allocation schemes in seventeen countries. Suppose that licenses to import are auctioned among importing country retailers or consumers. Krishna (1990) shows that, if quotas are close enough to the free trade import level, a foreign monopolist can appropriate rents by raising the product price to the maximum level that the importing country's market will take. The license price, the gap between the demand price in the importing country and the seller's supply price, falls down to zero. Because the monopolist strips the licenses of any value, the revenues from auctioning import licenses are nil.

Hong Kong has a transparent quota implementation process in which some licenses are given free and are nontransferable while others are based on past performance in using the quota and are traded in a relatively free market. Quota rents estimates based on the prices of quota licenses can be as high as 25 percent of the total clothing imports from Hong Kong. In fact, Hong Kong has a large number of producers negotiating with large importing companies that hold a degree of monopoly power. Krishna and

Tan find that there is rent sharing between the producers and the large importers and that most of the rent might be retained in the United States. Hong Kong might not be receiving its full quota rents under competitive conditions and pays a welfare cost in terms of lost trade.

The process of quota implementation initially represented a system of regulation guided by objectives. Over time, though, loopholes were discovered and the agreement evolved into a complex discretionary system that does not embody WTO/GATT spirit. The quotas have generated rent sharing between exporters and importers.

13.16. LOCAL CONTENT REQUIREMENTS

How do we distinguish between domestic and foreign products? Do Honda and Nissan cars produced in the United Kingdom have enough local content to be considered European Union cars? The local content of a good is the portion of production costs incurred locally. For instance, assembly plants that bring parts to be put together in a location have a relatively low local content consisting of the labor and other local inputs used to assemble the product. This is the case of Mexican maquiladoras that assemble products in Mexico for exportation into the United States.

Local content is at the forefront of trade policy discussions. First, the regionalization of the world economy into blocks raises a nationality issue for trade policy formulation because the application of policies to a particular product must determine if it will be treated as an import or as a domestic product. Specifically, a discriminatory tariff must depend on whether an imported good is produced by a favored trading partner, or has been produced by a partner that does not enjoy trade preferences but sells the good through a favored partner to gain access to the discriminating country.

Second, the practice of imposing local content requirements on foreign direct investors has generated a lot of heat. The Trade-Related Investment Measures (TRIMs) Agreement will make local content requirements illegal under WTO rules. For the time being, however, content requirements are well and alive.

13.16.1. Local Content Requirements and the Mode of Entry

A local content regulation is a nontax instrument forcing foreign firms to use domestic inputs by carrying out some activities domestically that perhaps could be done more profitably elsewhere. Local content requirements represent nontariff barriers to trade that can be used to offset the reduction of tariff barriers sponsored by the GATT/WTO and to support domestic interests. The required percentage of local inputs can be quite high and burdensome. Canadian domestic content requirements establish that Canadian performers must account for at least a minimum percentage of the records played in radio stations. The requirements artificially increase the earnings of domestic performers and their managers. Developing countries have utilized local content regulations for a long time as part of their industrialization strategies. These regulations intend to generate local employment and protect domestic producers of final goods and parts from foreign competition. In China, where sino-foreign joint ventures accounted for about 90 percent of domestically produced cars in the 1990s, local content requirements in the automobile industry reach the 80–90 percent mark. How do local content requirements on foreign investment affect the mode of entry into a country's markets? Qiu and Tao (2001) develop a trade model with heterogeneous multinationals to examine the determinants of the FDI vs export mode of entry in a setting with zero fixed entry costs. Content requirements increase production costs for multinational firms because locally made parts and components are of lower quality and higher cost than alternative sources.

How do protection through tariffs and local content affect the model of entry into a foreign market? Tariffs penalize the export mode of entry relative to FDI. By contrast, local content requirements penalize FDI relative to exportation. Moreover, local content requirements favor less efficient over more efficient multinationals. For instance, consider two firms that produce at costs of $1000 and $2000 per unit, respectively, in the absence of content requirements. Suppose that these firms foreign invest in a country where production using local input costs $2000 per unit. If the required local content requirement is 50 percent, the first firm's costs will rise to $1500 per unit ($500 in low cost inputs plus $1000 in local inputs) while the highest cost firm will be unaffected by the policy.

Suppose that the choice between exporting and FDI is endogenous. For any given local content requirement, a less efficient firm is more likely to choose the FDI mode of entry over the export mode than a more efficient multinational. The reason is that local content requirements cause a larger cost increase for a more efficient multinational than for a less efficient multinational. This implies that, for a parameter space range, more efficient firms might choose to export rather than foreign invest while less efficient firms might do the opposite.

What is the best local content requirements policy? The best policy is established by balancing opposite effects. On one hand, high content requirements discourage FDI relative to exportation and reduce local consumer surplus because they raise foreign investors' production costs. On the other hand, given that entry takes place through FDI, high content requirements allow the host country to capture the employment and technology-transfer benefits of FDI (although the improvement in the quality of locally made parts and components might be quite costly if the licensing fee reflects the technological gap).

13.17. POLICY-DRIVEN FDI: TARIFF-JUMPING FDI

FDI often takes place to bypass trade restrictions. This strategic response is called tariff jumping if it bypasses tariffs and antidumping jumping if it bypasses antidumping duties (i.e. temporary duties to offset low pricing by foreign exporters).

Multinationals have developed various strategies to increase local content as a mechanism to bypass or jump over tariff and quota barriers. Flam (1994) examines the export-foreign investment decision in relation to tariff policy. A common multi-nationals' strategy is to establish assembling and screwdriver operations (that finish and put nuts and bolts into a product largely produced abroad) in a host country. If local content is high enough, this mechanism serves to avoid tariffs and import quotas. Notice that the local content of goods produced by multinationals is difficult to measure accurately. For instance, it is difficult to price intrafirm traded inputs.

If Honda and Nissan cars produced in the United Kingdom are deemed to have enough European content, they can be sold in European countries free of tariffs. If they do not, then they must pay tariffs as imported cars. In 1990, France alleged that Nissan Bluebirds produced in the United Kingdom did not satisfy European local content requirements. The British government reacted angrily. The United Kingdom had been able to become a preferred location for foreign investment on the basis of relatively low wages, a policy environment favorable to foreign investment, and access to the large European market. The dispute was finally resolved when Nissan agreed to raise the local content of the cars it produced in the United Kingdom.

Multinationals have strong incentives to pass foreign goods for domestic goods in order to avoid being subject to tariffs. Recall that importing countries have incentives to discriminate in order to maximize rent extraction from foreign exporters that hold some degree of monopoly power (Gatsios, 1990). Because the optimal discriminating policy subjects more efficient foreign exporters to higher tariffs, there are strong incentives for them to foreign invest to introduce local content and avoid the tariff.

Smith (1987) and Motta (1992) develop partial equilibrium models to consider the choice between foreign direct investment (FDI) and trade as a function of market size, trade costs and the sequencing of moves in strategic games. Smith and Motta consider partial equilibrium models in which the incumbent's home market is protected from both foreign trade and foreign direct investment.

A reduction in trade costs might paradoxically induce firms to choose FDI rather than exports. In this case, the world as a whole experiences a welfare loss. The effect of trade costs on entry into foreign markets is generally ambiguous. Lower trade costs have cost-saving effects that can induce entry but make competition more aggressive and make entry less profitable. These effects work for both foreign investment and exports, and it is quite difficult to see which one is stronger. For instance, directing foreign investment into one particular location in order to supply foreign markets is made more profitable if trade costs decline. But exports are also made more profitable, ceteris paribus. It is difficult to determine the net effects with any kind of generality. In addition, the negative welfare results must be qualified, as they ignore key sources of positive effects from foreign investment such as the international transfer of technology due to foreign investment, the externalities on local labor, and others.

13.18. CONCLUSIONS

Arguments for protection are based on the presence of some market imperfection or externality. The optimal *restrictive* tariff is applied by a monopsonist importer in order to drive world prices down. The optimal *rent-extracting* tariff is applied by a possibly small importing country to extract rents from a foreign monopolist exporter. These forms of protection are optimal because they involve the exploitation of trade imperfections relating to domestic monopsony power in international markets and the regulation of foreign monopoly power arising in the course of trade.

Many protection mechanisms have ambiguous effects. For instance, subjecting multinationals to local content requirements aims to create local employment and induce technology transfer. However, these requirements can have the counterproductive effect of increasing production costs and discouraging foreign investment, particularly of efficient multinationals.

The establishment of protective tariffs aiming to promote infant industries is often advanced because protection can paradoxically serve as indirect export promotion or to buy time for technology adoption. But tariff protection and a wide array of trade policies that are based on a variety of externalities and imperfections that are not directly related to trade are embroiled in deep controversy. In the first best, externalities and market imperfections that are not sourced on trade distortions do not call for trade policies but rather for policies addressing the source of the distortion directly.

Dixit (1987b, 1989a, 1989b, 1990) uses the targeting approach to show that perfectly competitive free trade can be Pareto optimal given the informational constraints imposed by adverse selection, moral hazard and imperfectly observed outcomes of risky activities. Policy interventions have thus reason to distinguish between domestic and foreign goods (see chapter 11).

Initial historical conditions such as country size and income are key to national competitive advantages and influence the effects of trade liberalization. For instance, consumer demand in countries featuring higher per capita income and larger markets is able to support higher quality products supplied to domestic costumers. This point is stressed by Michael Porter (1990), who points out that consumers' sophistication encourages domestic firms to raise production quality, which in turn contributes to the ability to penetrate foreign markets.

Are countries producing lower quality goods likely to match or surpass higher quality producers when economies open their markets to international trade? Motta et al. (1997) utilize an oligopolistic vertical differentiation setup to show that large size differences tend to determine an initial and persistent quality hierarchy among nations, precluding leapfrogging through trade. When countries do not differ too much in terms of initial size and income, though, the open economy regime yields two Nash equilibria. In one equilibrium quality dominance persists. In the other there is a change in leadership (leapfrogging) and the smaller or poorer country becomes the new leader. The intuition for why leapfrogging is possible if differences in quality are sufficiently small is that, given that the low quality firm leapfrogs, it might not be worthwhile for the high quality firm to upgrade.

The appearance of multiple equilibria when countries are not too asymmetric raises an equilibrium selection problem. It can be shown that the risk dominance criterion for equilibrium selection of Harsanyi and Selten (1988) selects the persistence equilibrium as the unique Nash equilibrium. Unilateral R&D or production subsidies change the cost of providing quality and can induce leapfrogging. However, retaliation leading to bilateral subsidy competition nullifies the subsidy. In particular, if the rival government reacts by imposing an appropriate subsidy, no leapfrogging will take place (Helguera and Lutz, 1998).

14

Dumping, Market Access, and Sanctions

Exporters incur in dumping when they charge unfair or abnormally low prices abroad. Antidumping laws seek to eliminate these practices. If the targeted firms fail to increase prices or to reduce sales, the imposition of antidumping duties corrects the price distortion. Antidumping activity, the most important form of contingent protection and a major source of trade friction, proliferated in the 1980s and 1990s. The number of antidumping petitions filed by General Agreement Tariffs and Trade (GATT) members surged from about 100 cases in the 1960s to about 1600 in the 1980s and over 2200 in the 1990s.

The proliferation of antidumping investigations stems from their use as a protectionist tool in a world where traditional protection instruments have lost their force because tariff barriers are relatively low and quotas are on their way out. In contrast with traditional forms of protection, antidumping duties are temporary measures, selective in terms of target, discretionary in application, based on administrative decisions rather than legislation and are not transparent. These features also characterize other forms of contingent protection. These include countervailing duties intending to counter foreign subsidies and escape clauses allowing the imposition of temporary duties to protect domestic firms from fair but still disrupting market penetration by foreign firms.

Firms and governments do not remain passive entities before actual or threatened trade barriers. One set of responses aims to influence the determination of endogenous trade policies. Targeted agents address protection by stopping or modifying the offending behavior and by undertaking actions to generate goodwill in the protecting country. Targeted governments that subsidize exports can contain export subsidization in order to reduce the likelihood of facing antidumping actions. Targeted firms may contract exports to alleviate the pressures for protection abroad. Exports decline when prices in export markets are raised or exports are replaced by production in-site.

Because a firm carries the costs of its response to protection, but the benefits accrue to all firms, a free-riding problem arises, and policy coordination might be required. A government's response along these lines is to set policies reducing overall exports. An alternative policy response is to support foreign direct investment (FDI). This quid pro quo FDI policy aims to create employment abroad in exchange for ameliorating the resistance to exports in the importing country and reducing the probability and strength of antidumping actions.

A second set of responses seeks to bypass trade restrictions. An FDI strategy allows agents to avoid tariffs, antidumping duties, and other trade barriers. In trade jargon, foreign investment is undertaken to 'jump' over tariffs and other trade barriers. Notice the distinction between quid pro quo FDI, which is undertaken to defuse protection, and tariff-jumping or antidumping-jumping FDI, which is undertaken to circumvent protection.

Forward-looking firms attempt to minimize the losses from prospective restrictions. For instance, dumping taking place in anticipation of protection through quotas leads to increased exports prior to an antidumping action. Dumping is an appropriate strategy if higher current exports lead to greater allocation of quotas in the period following the antidumping action.

The threat of sanctions constitutes a key tool in negotiations aiming to extract trade concessions from foreign countries (Eaton and Engers, 1992, 1999). Trade concessions can have protectionist or market-opening goals. A protectionist concession aims to help domestic firms by limiting foreign competition. This goal can be achieved by negotiating Voluntary Export Restraints (VERs) specifying quantitative limits on the amounts exported by foreign countries into the protected market. A second type of trade concession opens foreign markets to domestic firms. Market opening is often achieved by negotiating Voluntary Import Expansions (VIEs) agreements seeking to expand foreign countries' purchases from domestic firms. Of course, a foreign country 'voluntarily' agrees to restrict its exports, or expand its imports, in order to avoid potential sanctions.

An extensive literature analyzes the effectiveness of sanctions as a tool for extracting trade concessions, inducing market opening, achieving security goals, and exerting political pressures. Hufbauer *et al.* (1990) find that the imposition of sanctions turns out to be effective in achieving the stated goals about a third of the time. There is also substantial empirical evidence illustrating the point that credible threats can extract concessions and induce market opening, even if sanctions are not actually imposed.

Section 14.1 reviews the economics of dumping. Section 14.2 presents the Brander and Krugman model of reciprocal dumping. Section 14.3 examines antidumping policies. Section 14.4 reviews recent empirical evidence bearing on the determinants and effects of antidumping and countervailing duty actions. Section 14.5 examines export policy as a channel to influence the likelihood of facing protection abroad. Section 14.6 examines the role of quid pro quo FDI aiming to defuse protection. Section 14.7 presents the theory and evidence on foreign investment as 'tariff-jumping' or 'antidumping-jumping'. Section 14.8 examines 'domino' dumping taking place in anticipation of future restrictions. Section 14.9 reviews the economics of section 301 trade sanctions and examines the analytical foundations of sanctions and threats. Finally, Section 14.10 reviews the theory of market access requirements, the performance of VIEs, and the use of threats to induce market opening, such as in the US–Japan auto parts dispute.

14.1. WHY DOES DUMPING TAKE PLACE?

Dumping is considered one of the major unfair trade practices. However, behavior classed as dumping can be shown to be consistent with perfect competition. Whether or not low prices represent a price distortion must thus be determined on a case-by-case basis.

A wide array of situations can give rise to dumping. These include price discrimination, divergent market structures at home and abroad, multimarket oligopolistic interaction, entry deterrence strategy, predatory behavior, cyclical fluctuations, competitive selection of most productive firms, anticipation of future restrictions, and other factors. Models of dumping assume that some form of market segmentation impedes goods arbitrage and prevents the law of one price from holding.

Three alternative definitions of dumping and the associated dumping margin are widely used. First, dumping is measured by the gap between the net-of-transport-costs price charged in the export market and the price charged to customers in the dumping firms' home market. Second, economists often measure the dumping margin by the extent to which export market prices fall below exporters' *marginal* costs. Third, regulators often use an alternative definition to set antidumping duties, focusing on the extent to which export prices fall below an appropriately defined *average* cost.

14.1.1. Price Discrimination in Segmented Markets

The classical theory of dumping is due to Viner (1923). He examined dumping arising from price discrimination across monopolized segmented markets featuring higher demand elasticity in the export market than in the home market.

If a monopolist can price discriminate across markets, it will charge higher prices in markets constituted by customers that react less to price changes (i.e. with inelastic demand) and lower prices in markets where customers highly react to price changes (i.e. with elastic demand). Specifically, a discriminating monopolist sets prices and allocates production to each market according to the condition that marginal revenue must equal marginal cost in each market. This optimization condition implies that the monopoly price in market i, p_i, is closer to marginal cost c the higher the elasticity of product demand $\varepsilon_i = -[dq_i/dp_i][p_i/q_i]$

$$\frac{p_i - c}{p_i} = \frac{1}{\varepsilon_i}.$$

Therefore, if demand abroad is more elastic than home country demand, a price discriminating monopolist will charge a lower price in the export market than in the home market. This price discrimination policy is classed as dumping.

14.1.2. Local Monopoly and Competition Abroad

Dumping can arise from differences in demand elasticities related to divergent market structures at home and abroad. Consider an exporter that holds a monopoly in the home market, say, sustained by protectionist measures or government-imposed restrictions to entry. If the local monopolist sells in competitive markets abroad it will be forced to charge a competitive price abroad. Dumping arises because, *ceteris paribus*, the competitive price will be lower than the monopoly price (Eichengreen and Van der Ven, 1984).

14.1.3. Reciprocal Dumping

Multimarket oligopolistic interaction can induce countries to dump goods on each other. Two-way dumping of the same goods can take place in two oligopolistic markets that are segmented on the demand side—so that sellers treat each country as a distinct market—but are interconnected through trade. Brander and Krugman (1983) show that exporters will have incentives to set low prices, net of transport costs, abroad. A setup in which mutual dumping takes place, known as the reciprocal dumping model or the cross-hauling model, is developed below.

What is the effect of market structure (i.e. the number of firms) on the propensity of firms to dump goods? Weinstein (1992) extends Brander and Krugman reciprocal dumping model to consider multiple firms in each of the two markets examined. He shows that firms operating in markets with a large number of domestic rivals are more likely to dump unilaterally (i.e. only the firms from one country dump) than firms in less competitive markets.

Weinstein's result provides a counterexample to the traditional notion that dumping is performed by firms operating in concentrated industries. The intuition is the following. Consider a given market supplied by several domestic firms and one foreign exporter. All firms are identical in terms of technologies. Because the exporter must incur production and transport costs, it bears higher costs than local firms. Now consider an exogenously given increase in the number of domestic firms. If the increase is large enough, the local price will fall below the sum of the exporter's production and transport costs. If this condition holds, the foreign exporter cannot subsist in the export market. Still, domestic producers will be able to dump goods abroad, (absorbing part of the transport costs).

14.1.4. Entry Deterrence and Predatory Pricing

An entry deterrence strategy is to sell at a price below marginal cost in order to discourage potential rivalry. In open economies, this limiting pricing strategy corresponds to dumping (Davies and McGuinness, 1982).

Predatory pricing by a foreign firm seeking to force exit of an export market rival can be implemented through dumping in oligopolistic segmented markets. Predatory behavior is defined as charging a price below that which would prevail in the absence of an exit inducement strategy. Hartigan (1994) develops a signaling dumping model with asymmetric information in which the export market rival must infer the exporter's costs through the latter's pricing behavior. Markets are segmented and the exporter is assumed to be a monopolist in its home market. In the first period of a two-period game, the foreign exporter sets a low export price to signal that it is a low-cost competitor. Under appropriate conditions, the dumping strategy induces the export market rival to exit in the second period.

14.1.5. Cyclical Dumping

In Ethier (1982*b*), dumping takes place as a response to cyclical fluctuations in demand. The model dispenses with the price discrimination rationale for dumping. Firms producing a homogeneous good interact in competitive markets and face price uncertainty coupled with inflexible labor contracts. In the presence of fixed costs, labor contracts and restrained layoffs, competitive firms facing a cyclical downturn at home find it optimal to sell abroad at a price falling below average total cost. As a result, trading partners are flooded with dumped goods. Firms engaging in dumping behavior during the cyclical downturn recover their profits by selling at prices above average costs during the upturn.

The rigidities imposed by excessive capacity in recession periods can provide an argument in favor of transitory dumping practices. Staiger and Wolak (1992) develop a model with a competitive domestic market and a monopolized foreign market that is segmented by a prohibitive tariff. The foreign monopolist (or cartel) faces stochastic demand in its home market and chooses capacity before demand is observed. Installed capacity generates a production inflexibility that is partially overcome through dumping. The foreign monopolist dumps goods on world markets when it experiences excess capacity due to slack demand at home. Cyclical dumping arises from transitory excess capacity due to demand fluctuations in a monopolized market.

14.1.6. Firm Selection through Dumping

Industry selection through firm entry and exit can generate dumping in competitive markets in which individual firms are price takers. Clarida (1993) develops a Ricardian two-sector, two-country, two-period international trade model in which the number of firms is endogenous and countries differ only in their initial stock of technological knowledge. Unobserved differences in firms' initial stock of knowledge are enough to give rise to dumping.

Firms are viewed as equally productive ex ante, as measured by the Ricardian input–output ratio, but learning shows them to differ ex post. Following Jovanovic (1982), firms can only learn about their own productivities by entering the market as producers. High-cost firms exit the market forced by a competitive selection process in which prices fall below the average costs of the least efficient firms. This setup generates a process of entry, learning, dumping, and exit of some technological newcomers (i.e. shakeout).

In contrast to cyclical theories in which dumping takes place when demand declines, the firm selection framework can explain dumping in situations in which there is an increase in the demand for the dumped products. A high level of demand (assumed to be invariant to entry and exit decisions) induces entry of firms seeking a share in the rents accruing to those that are found to be more efficient ex post. Sectorial outputs and the countries' terms of trade are endogenous and dependent upon firms' entry and exit decisions. For dumping to take place in this setup, the two countries must not be identical. If they are identical, goods will be sold at prices below average cost but the *export* of goods at prices below average cost—dumping—will not arise.

14.1.7. Domino Dumping

Dumping can take place in anticipation of a future voluntary export restraint. If the negotiation of a voluntary export restraint (VER) is likely, and licenses to export are allocated in proportion to firms' market shares prior to the VER, it is optimal to engage in dumping. In forward-looking competitive export markets, exporters engage in dumping to increase current market share, and thus secure the option of receiving greater export licenses in the future.

The rationale for dumping when a negotiated export restriction is based on past exports is called domino dumping because it generates domino effects. Suppose that the possibility of a future VER leads to dumping, which in turn justifies the future VER and might increase its likelihood. The VER could then give rise to the prospect of an additional VER imposed by the home country of the affected firms, giving rise to anticipatory dumping there, and so on. This domino process describes an interrelated series of dumping actions in several markets or countries (Anderson, 1992, 1993).

14.2. ECONOMICS OF RECIPROCAL DUMPING

Oligopolistic rivalry naturally gives rise to *reciprocal* dumping in which firms dump identical goods into each others' markets. Brander and Krugman (1983) develop a duopoly model in which reciprocal dumping takes place as an equilibrium phenomenon even if it generates pure waste in the form of unnecessary transport costs. A crucial element is that each firm perceives each country as a segmented market and makes distinct quantity decisions for each.

14.2.1. Reciprocal Dumping

Consider two identical countries, labeled domestic and foreign. Two firms, one in each country, produce a homogeneous commodity. Each firm regards each country as a separate market. Production levels are chosen noncooperatively à la Cournot in a one-shot game.

The domestic firm produces quantity q for its domestic market and x for export. The foreign firm produces output q^* for its domestic market and x^* for export. Firms' marginal production costs are assumed to be constant at level c, which allows maximizing profits for each market separately. Selling abroad entails iceberg-type transport costs in the sense that only a proportion g of each exported unit arrives and can be sold abroad. In other words, transport costs can be viewed as increasing marginal costs per unit sold abroad from c to c/g, $0 \leq g \leq 1$. Notice that a lower g factor corresponds to higher transport costs.

Domestic and foreign firms' profits π and π^* are

$$\pi(q, x) = qp(Q) + xp^*(Q^*) - c\left(q + \frac{x}{g}\right) - F,$$

$$\pi^*(q^*, x^*) = q^* p^*(Q^*) + x^* p(Q) - c\left(q^* + \frac{x^*}{g}\right) - F^*,$$

where $Q = q + x^*$ and $Q^* = q^* + x$. F and F^* denote fixed costs paid by the domestic and foreign firms. Firms are symmetric except for these fixed costs.

Maximizing profits with respect to local sales and exports yields two equations relating the domestic market price p and the foreign firm share of the domestic market, $\sigma = x^*/Q$ (see appendix)

$$p(\sigma) = \frac{c\varepsilon}{\sigma - 1 + \varepsilon}, \qquad p(\sigma) = \frac{c\varepsilon}{g(\varepsilon - \sigma)}, \qquad \sigma \equiv \frac{x^*}{Q}, \qquad \varepsilon = -\frac{dQ}{dp}\frac{p}{Q}.$$

The first equation indicates that the price that can be charged in the domestic market diminishes with the share of the foreign rival. The second equation indicates that a higher domestic price motivates greater market penetration. A positive price requires conditions $\varepsilon > 1 - \sigma$ and $\varepsilon > \sigma$. Adding up these conditions results in $2\varepsilon > 1$ or $\varepsilon > 1/2$.

Solving the two-equation system for the price p and the market share σ

$$p = \frac{c\varepsilon(1+g)}{g(2\varepsilon - 1)}, \qquad \sigma \equiv \frac{x^*}{Q} = \frac{1 - (1-g)\varepsilon}{1+g}. \tag{14.1}$$

If transport costs are zero, then $g = 1$ and $\sigma = 1/2$ independently of the value of ε. When transport costs are positive ($g < 1$), the inequality $\varepsilon > 1/2$ implies: $\sigma < [1 - (1-g)/2]/(1+g)$. Simplifying yields $\sigma < 1/2$, which means that if transport costs are positive each firm has a smaller market share in its export market than at home. Also, it can be shown that each firm sets a smaller markup over costs in its export market than at home.

The price equation provides a condition for dumping. Reciprocal dumping occurs when there exists a positive markup that sustains foreign sales in equilibrium ($\sigma > 0$). A positive markup, $p > c/g > 0$, implies the following cross-hauling inequality condition

$$p = \frac{c\varepsilon(1+g)}{g(2\varepsilon - 1)} > \frac{c}{g} \quad \rightarrow \quad \varepsilon < \frac{1}{1-g}, \tag{14.2}$$

which is consistent with a positive market share σ in (14.1). The cross-hauling condition $1/2 < \varepsilon < 1/(1+g)$ and the second order conditions of the profit maximization problem imply that there is a unique stable two-way trade equilibrium.

Model symmetry implies that equilibrium prices p and p^* must be the same. Therefore, the price received from home market sales must exceed the net-of-transport-cost price received from sales abroad. This feature implies that exporters fully absorb transport costs. In terms of trade jargon, the free on board (f.o.b.) price for exports is below the domestic price. Recall that the f.o.b. price is the export price net of transportation costs.

The reciprocal dumping equilibrium examined, involving two-way trade in identical products with the feature that exporters fully absorb transport costs, is surprising in several respects. First, reciprocal dumping does not arise from accidental cross-country differences in demand elasticities—as in Viner's price discrimination theory of dumping—or from differences in cost functions across firms. In fact, the model is symmetric in demand and cost functions. Second, intra-industry trade (IIT) in identical products deriving from reciprocal dumping is not due to a demand for variety and must be distinguished from IIT in similar but not identical products. Furthermore, the game's outcome involves the paradoxical generation of pure waste due to transport costs incurred by dumping products abroad while receiving identical products from abroad at a cost.

Reciprocal dumping arises for systematic reasons related to oligopolistic behavior in segmented markets. Because each firm treats each country as a separate market, it determines profit-maximizing supplies to each country on the basis of a different duopoly game in each country. Market segmentation sustains an equilibrium in which marginal costs (gross of transport costs) and marginal revenues are higher in export markets than at home. If marginal costs were not constant, there would be interdependence between markets on the cost side, but reciprocal dumping could still arise.

14.2.2. Welfare Effects of Reciprocal Dumping

The reciprocal dumping solution is not Pareto efficient. The reason is that it entails a degree of monopoly power as well as socially wasteful transportation costs incurred in cross hauling. The welfare consequences of a move from autarky to trade with reciprocal dumping are ambiguous as there is a trade off involving two effects working in opposite directions:

(1) trade generates wasteful transport costs due to cross hauling;
(2) trade introduces international competition that ameliorates the monopoly distortion under autarky and leads to lower prices.

Which effect dominates depends on the conditions giving rise to dumping. We proceed to show that free trade with cross hauling might or might not be superior to autarky under monopoly conditions.

Reductions in Transport Costs
Consider a reduction of transport costs from a prohibitive level to a lower level that makes trade profitable. Let the representative consumer's utility function be

$$U(Q) = u(Q) + K, \quad Q = q + x^*,$$

where K is the numeraire. The sum of the welfare of the two countries involved is given by (symmetry implies that $Q = Q^*$ and $x^* = x$)

$$W(Q, x; c, t, F, F^*) = 2[U(Q) - cQ - tx] - F - F^* + 2K,$$

where $c + t = c/g$ and $t = c(1 - g)g$ represents international transport costs per unit exported (rather than iceberg costs as previously represented by g).

What is the welfare change of the shift from autarky to free trade? A slight change in transport costs alters welfare by

$$dW = 2\left[(p - c)\frac{dQ}{dt} - x - t\frac{dx}{dt}\right]dt,$$

where $dU/dQ = p$.

The previous equation illustrates three distinct effects from a reduction in transport costs ($dt < 0$). The first term indicates the welfare gain from the increase in consumption due to a reduction of transport costs ($dt < 0$ and $dQ/dt < 0$). The gain is equal to the wedge between price and marginal costs times the increase in consumption due to a reduction in transport costs. The second term indicates the gain due to a unit reduction in transport costs ($dt < 0$) applicable to the current level of imports $x^* = x$. The third term indicates the loss from the increase in imports ($dt < 0$ and $dx/dt < 0$). This loss derives from the replacement of domestic production with imports that require transport costs.

The welfare effects of the shift from autarky towards free trade with dumping are unambiguous in two special cases:

1. If transport costs become negligible, there are gains from trade due to the procompetitive effect. In terms of the equation for the change in welfare, the third term representing the losses due to transport costs disappears because $t = 0$.
2. If transport costs are reduced just below the prohibitive level, so that $p \simeq c + t$, the decline in costs permits trade but reduces welfare. In this case, $x = 0$ initially and the equation for the welfare change becomes

$$dW = 2\left[t\left(\frac{dq}{dt} + \frac{dx}{dt}\right) - t\frac{dx}{dt}\right]dt = 2t\frac{dq}{dt}dt,$$

where symmetry implies that $Q \equiv q + x^* = q + x$. The welfare change due to a reduction of transport costs is negative because $dt < 0$ and $dq/dt > 0$, which implies that exports replace domestic production if transport costs go down.

If the transport cost reduction is small enough, welfare is greater under autarky than in the reciprocal dumping equilibrium. Trade opening causes losses because the increase in consumption is accomplished by the combination of a fall of domestic production and an increase in imports. An additional unit of imports does not add to social welfare because it is valued above marginal production costs precisely by the same amount as the transport cost it generates. Therefore, the net effect of opening is the replacement of domestic production with imports requiring transport costs, which entails a net social cost.

Trade Liberalization

Does free trade with dumping improve upon an autarkic economy sheltering a local monopoly by means of prohibitive trade restrictions? This comparison involves a trade off. Reciprocal dumping is procompetitive relative to autarky because the price p under reciprocal dumping (i.e. $\sigma > 0$) is lower than the autarkic monopoly price p^M (i.e. $\sigma = 0$)

$$p = \frac{c\varepsilon}{\sigma - 1 + \varepsilon} < p^M = \frac{c\varepsilon}{\varepsilon - 1}, \quad \sigma \equiv \frac{x^*}{Q}.$$

Notice that the cross-hauling condition (14.2) is equivalent to the condition that the monopoly price under autarky exceeds marginal costs under reciprocal dumping

$$\varepsilon < \frac{1}{1 - g} \quad \Leftrightarrow \quad p^M = \frac{c\varepsilon}{\varepsilon - 1} > \frac{c}{g}.$$

In Brander and Krugman's model with constant demand elasticity, $p = AQ^{-1/\varepsilon}$, the shift from autarky supported by trade restrictions to free trade with reciprocal dumping can be shown to be welfare-improving. In this particular case, the procompetitive effect of shifting from monopoly to duopoly and the associated expansion of consumption can be shown to dominate the wasteful transport costs.

14.3. ANTIDUMPING POLICY

Antidumping policy addresses dumping as a form of price discrimination in segmented markets. An antidumping duty—or a price increase realized to avoid paying the duty—operates to eliminate the dumping margin, that is, the gap between the domestic price and the export price net of transport costs.

This section focuses on formally defining what is an antidumping policy, examining its effects on firms and consumers, and modeling government incentives for applying antidumping policies. We are concerned with several major questions. First, why is it that negotiations for price increases often break down and firms end up paying antidumping duties? Second, what are the effects of antidumping policies? Third, are antidumping policies welfare-improving? Fourth, will countries follow welfare-improving antidumping policies in equilibrium?

14.3.1. Dumping Margin and Injury Margin

Antidumping duties are set in relation to the dumping margin indicating the price distortion due to unfair pricing. Margins are calculated as the difference between the local price and the *fair* or *normal* price of imports, which can be measured by the price charged by the exporter, exporter's marginal costs or exporter's average costs. Let us focus on the dumping margin measured in terms of prices. The dumping margin for good i, DM_i, is the difference between the exporter's home market price p_i^i and the price received in export market j net of transport costs t, $p_i^j - t$,

$$DM_i = p_i^i - (p_i^j - t) > 0 \quad \rightarrow \quad p_i^j < p_i^i + t.$$

An antidumping duty offsets the dumping margin. It prevents an exporting firm from selling good i in market j for less than the price charged in its home market plus transport costs. The antidumping policy enforces the following inequality

$$p_i^j \geq p_i^i + t,$$

where j represents the country facing dumping. In practice, firms can simply increase the price of their exports and avoid paying the duty.

The injury margin is used in Europe and Australia to set antidumping duties. The injury margin on good i, IM_i, is defined as the amount by which its price in the export market, net of transport costs, undercuts the price p_j^j of the import-competing good

$$IM_i = p_j^j - (p_i^j - t) > 0 \quad \rightarrow \quad p_i^j < p_j^j + t.$$

In a symmetric equilibrium, $p_i^i = p_j^j$ and the dumping and injury margins are equal.

14.3.2. *Antidumping Duties vs Price Undertakings*

At first sight, it would appear that antidumping duties should never be observed. Indeed, targeted firms have incentives to increase prices to avoid paying the duties. Why is it that negotiations for price increases often break down and firms end up paying antidumping duties? Panagariya and Gupta (1998) model the choice between antidumping duties and price undertakings. An undertaking is an agreement in which the targeted suppliers voluntarily agree to set a minimum price—give a price undertaking—or voluntarily agree to restrict exports—give a volume undertaking. Because protection rents arising from higher prices are appropriated by the exporter, price undertakings are 'softer' than the payment of antidumping duties to the importing country government.

Under complete information, disputing parties in a Cournot duopoly game can anticipate the result of the antidumping process. If the imposition of an antidumping duty is anticipated and firms face no constraint on setting prices, there are incentives to avoid the duty by means of a price undertaking. However, this result can break down if agents lack perfect foresight about the final result of the investigation.

Consider the case in which duties can have only two levels, which we call high and low. Suppose that the firm being investigated for dumping knows whether or not it will be acquitted while its export market rival knowledge is limited to the probability of acquittal and nonacquittal. This information structure reflects a situation in which the firm being investigated knows its costs, home and export market prices and can thus anticipate the result of the investigation while its export market rival is not fully informed. If the investigated firm knows that it will not be acquitted, it has incentives to negotiate a price increase and this price will be consistent with the expectations of the uninformed firm. If the informed firm knows that a zero duty would be set, however, negotiations can break down because the uninformed firm calculates an expected duty that is larger than the zero duty resulting from the investigation. In this case, an antidumping duty might result.

14.3.3. Modeling Antidumping Policy

Antidumping policies have three main effects. First, they benefit domestic firms because the foreign rival is forced to increase prices. Second, domestic consumers lose from the local and rival firms' price increases. Third, the rival's reaction to an antidumping duty is to increase its export price while reducing its home price. This price reaction benefits the exporting firm's home country consumers. In other words, a unilateral antidumping action has a positive externality on foreign countries that is not taken into account by the government formulating the policy. Recapping, unilateral antidumping hurts the consumers of the country imposing it while favoring local firms and foreign consumers.

Reciprocal antidumping policies might be welfare improving for the world as a whole because they eliminate price discrimination. They can improve the world's welfare because consumers benefit (each country's policy favors foreign consumers and this effect can be dominant) and these benefits might outweigh the reductions in firms profits (each policy hurts foreign firms to a greater extent than it benefits domestic firms). But governments limit themselves to comparing the benefits to local firms with the losses to home consumers. When the other country policy is taken as given, the net national benefit of antidumping law enforcement might be negative. Consequently, reciprocal antidumping will not arise in a noncooperative equilibrium even if it would improve world welfare due to the externalities conferred on foreign consumers.

Anderson *et al.* (1995) develop a two–country model with two differentiated traded products and two firms, one in each country. Each firm is specialized in a different product and transport costs are symmetric. Welfare W is defined as consumers' indirect utility $V(p_I, p_{II}, Y)$, a function of goods prices and income Y, plus firm profits. If production costs are assumed to be zero, firm profits are equal to revenues and

$$W = V(p_I, p_{II}, Y) + p_I q_I + (p_I^* - t)x_I$$
$$= V(p_I, p_{II}, Y) - p_I \frac{\partial V}{\partial p_I} - (p_{II} - t)\frac{\partial V}{\partial p_{II}},$$

where q is the quantity sold domestically, x represents exports and p_I and p_I^* are domestic and export market prices. The second equality derives from symmetry— which implies that $p_I^* = p_{II}$ and $V = V^*$—and Roy's rule with $\lambda = \partial V/\partial Y = 1$

$$q_I = -\frac{\partial V(p_I, p_{II}, Y)}{\partial p_I}, \qquad x_I = -\frac{\partial V^*}{\partial p_I^*} = -\frac{\partial V(p_I, p_{II}, Y)}{\partial p_{II}}.$$

Consider the quadratic indirect utility function

$$V(p_I, p_{II}, Y) = -\alpha(p_I + p_{II}) + \frac{\beta_I}{2}(p_I^2 + p_{II}^2) - \beta_{II}p_I p_{II} + Y$$

$$= -2\alpha\bar{p} + (\beta_I - \beta_{II})\bar{p}^2 + \frac{\beta_I + \beta_{II}}{4}(p_I - p_{II})^2 + Y,$$

where $\bar{p} = (p_I + p_{II})/2$ is the average price, $\alpha, \beta_I, \beta_{II} > 0$, and $\beta_I - \beta_{II} > 0$. For the low enough prices for which the quadratic indirect utility function makes sense, welfare declines with the average price and increases with the gap between the prices.

The demand and profit functions associated with the previous indirect utility functions are obtained using Roy's identity

$$q_i = \alpha - \beta_I p_i + \beta_{II}p_j, \quad j \neq i, \quad \beta_I > \beta_{II}, \quad i, j \in \{I, II\},$$

where demands do not depend on Y (residual income is spent on other goods) and

$$\pi_i = p_i q_i + (p_i^* - t)x_i$$
$$= p_i(\alpha - \beta_I p_i + \beta_{II}p_j) + (p_i^* - t)(\alpha - \beta_I p_i^* + \beta_{II}p_j^*).$$

The Bertrand price competition solution for the segmented markets case is

$$p_I = p_{II}^* = \frac{\alpha}{2\beta_I - \beta_{II}} + \frac{\beta_I \beta_{II}}{(2\beta_I - \beta_{II})(2\beta_I + \beta_{II})}t,$$

$$p_{II} = p_I^* = \frac{\alpha}{2\beta_I - \beta_{II}} + \frac{2\beta_I^2}{(2\beta_I - \beta_{II})(2\beta_I + \beta_{II})}t$$

$$\rightarrow p_{II} - p_I = p_I^* - p_{II}^* = \frac{\beta_I}{2\beta_I + \beta_{II}}t < t.$$

In this setting, the average price of good I and imported good II is

$$\bar{p} = \frac{p_I + p_{II}}{2} = \frac{2\alpha + \beta_I t}{2(2\beta_I - \beta_{II})}$$

can be shown to be the same under segmented and tied markets. The difference between segmented and tied markets is that tied markets entail a cost pass-on and imply

$$p_I^* = p_I + t = p_{II} = p_{II}^* + t,$$

where p_I^* and p_{II} carry transport costs while p_I and p_{II}^* do not, and

$$p_I^* = p_{II} < p_I + t = p_{II}^* + t$$

holds in segmented markets because dumping implies a degree of transport cost absorption.

The welfare maximization condition is

$$\frac{dW}{dp_I} = p_I \left(\frac{\partial^2 V}{\partial p_I \partial p_{II}} - \frac{\partial^2 V}{\partial p_I^2} \right) + (p_{II} - t) \left(\frac{\partial^2 V}{\partial p_{II}^2} - \frac{\partial^2 V}{\partial p_I \partial p_{II}} \right)$$

$$= (\beta_I + \beta_{II})(p_{II} - t - p_I).$$

In order to maintain the average price $\bar{p}$ constant, the condition $dp_I = -dp_{II}$ is imposed in the derivation. Because a reciprocal antidumping policy ties markets and enforces the equality $p_{II} = p_I + t$, overall welfare is maximized at the price resulting from that policy. In other words, overall welfare is higher with reciprocal antidumping policies imposing market integration than under market segmentation. The intuition is that, at the optimum, product prices should reflect marginal social costs. This is precisely what the equalization of p_{II} and $p_I + t$ accomplishes. In this case, transport costs represent the relevant marginal social costs.

Anderson, Schmitt, and Thisse show that welfare-maximizing governments acting noncooperatively in deciding whether or not to impose an antidumping law prefer not to enforce antidumping laws. This preference arises because dumping favors domestic consumers while antidumping hurts local consumers and diffuses the benefits among the local firm and foreign consumers. In other words, a unilateral antidumping policy would hurt local consumers and lower national welfare relative to free trade even if reciprocal antidumping would favor all consumers and raise world welfare. In this situation, there is a free-rider problem. Governments failing to enforce antidumping laws would prefer to free ride on the antidumping actions of the other government. The reason is that an active country's unilateral antidumping action benefits the consumers of the passive country because it alters the pricing of the passive country firm in favor of passive country consumers.

Recapping, in a noncooperative equilibrium, the bilateral use of antidumping does not arise even if it would be welfare-improving because the increase in consumer welfare would outweigh the fall in firms' profits. Reciprocal antidumping would have to emerge as the result of a cooperative agreement. These welfare properties and equilibrium results can be shown to hold under both Bertrand and Cournot competition.

14.4. ANTIDUMPING IN THE UNITED STATES AND EUROPE

Between 1980 and 1994, the United States led the list of countries reporting antidumping activity. There were over 700 antidumping filings. A quarter of them were settled. Among the remaining cases, half of the cases resulted in duties and half were rejected.

US antidumping investigations have two main phases:

1. Dumping determination. An affirmative determination of dumping is issued if it is found that foreign exporters are selling at an unfair price in US markets. This phase of the antidumping process is conducted by the International Trade Administration (ITA) of the Department of Commerce.

2. Injury determination. Determines whether or not dumped imports cause or threaten to cause *material injury* to the domestic industry (material injury test). This phase of the process is conducted by the International Trade Commission (ITC), created by the Trade Act of 1974 to regulate US trade.

According to Prusa (2001), about 95 percent of the US cases reported during 1980–94 were determined to involve dumping (e.g. price discrimination, below-cost pricing). Only 5 percent of the cases were rejected at the dumping determination stage. However, the ITC dismissed near 50 percent of the petitions at the injury test phase. A large number of antidumping cases tend to be rejected at the injury test phase because it is difficult to prove the existence or threat of injury. This means that petitioners face substantial uncertainty with respect to whether an affirmative decision about the existence of injury will be obtained.

The US antidumping duties are high. Blonigen (2002) finds that antidumping duties averaged 34 percent in the 1980s (the median rate was 20 percent). Prusa (2001) reports that the median duty was 16 percent and the average dumping margin was 40 percent in 1980–94 cases. This dumping margin is ten times the 4 percent average most-favored-nation (MFN) tariff level of industries seeking protection.

14.4.1. Trade Effects of Antidumping Investigations

Antidumping actions aim to contain market disruption due to low-price imports. In fact, Baldwin and Steagall (1994) find that import penetration is a significant factor explaining US affirmative antidumping decisions. In order to assess the impact of antidumping actions we must examine two related issues. First, are antidumping cases effective in restricting imports and raising the prices of imports? Second, what are the social costs and benefits of antidumping actions? One can distinguish between the trade effects of petitions, antidumping duties, negotiated solutions, and rejections. Antidumping cases—petitions and resolutions—exert trade effects by reducing the volume of imports, increasing their price or both.

Petitions and Resolutions: Import and Output Response
Staiger and Wolak (1994) assess the first-year response of imports and output to the filing and resolution of antidumping suits related to a manufacturing product during 1980–85. The results suggest that the indirect (i.e. nonduty) effects of antidumping laws are substantial in practice. There are substantial trade-restricting effects during investigations (known as investigation or harassment effects) and associated with the suspension of agreements (known as suspension effects). Suspension of investigations are associated with restricted imports and expanded import-competing domestic output. In the sample, the effects of suspension agreements are similar in magnitude to the effects of antidumping duties. Also, using a 1980–81 sample period, Prusa (1992) finds that the value of imports declined to 57 percent of its previous value for those products that had petitions withdrawn.

A recent study by Prusa (2001) uses US data for 1980–94 to quantify the effect of antidumping protection on the value of imports and estimate how this change is decomposed into changes in the quantity and unit price of imports. The analysis not only considers the first impact, as in Staiger and Wolak (1994), but also the effects over the three years following the filing.

The statistical model of import values, import quantities, and prices (unit values) for the countries named in the filings is

$$y_{it} = \delta y_{it-1} + x'_{it}\beta + u_{it}, \quad u_{it} = \mu_i + v_{it},$$

$$\mu_i \sim iid(0, \sigma_\mu^2), \quad v_{it} \sim iid(0, \sigma_v^2),$$

where y_{it} and y_{it-1} represent the dependent variable and its one-year lag, δ is a scalar, and x_{it} is a vector of K explanatory variables (x_{it} and β have rank $K \times 1$). The error u_{it} is specified as an error component model that includes an individual-specific component μ_i—which differs across cases but is constant across time for a given case—and a time-varying component v_{it}. The individual-specific component might reflect comparative advantages that lead to sustained high imports from a given source.

Expressing the model in terms of changes

$$\Delta y_{it} = \delta \Delta y_{it-1} + \Delta x'_{it}\beta + v_{it} - v_{it-1},$$

eliminates the μ_i component but generates correlation between regressor and error. The model is estimated by instrumental variables to correct for the correlation between regressor Δy_{it-1} and the error $v_{it} - v_{it-1}$. Time is centered around the year the petition is filed ($t = 0$) and imports are considered for three years prior and three years after the year a petition is filed ($t = -3, -2, -1, 0, 1, 2, 3$).

In one set of regressions, the explanatory variables in x_{it} include a dummy variable for each of the three years after a duty is levied, which allows estimating the dynamic effects of the duties. Another set of regressions include a dummy variable for each of the three years after an affirmative decision is reached, a negative decision is reached, or a settlement is agreed. These dummy variables allow estimating the dynamic effects of alternative investigation outcomes.

Antidumping cases are found to exert strong effects in import values, import quantities and prices (unit values). First, estimations suggest that import prices increase about 30 percent. Second, quantities imported from targeted countries decline by 70 percent on average. Third, antidumping duties cause the value of imports from affected countries to fall by 30–50 percent on average.

If antidumping investigations result in the imposition of antidumping duties, the volume of imports tends to decline by 50 percent in each of the three years following the resolution. If the case is settled, the volume of imports declines by 60 percent. The mere initiation of antidumping investigations distorts trade patterns. Estimations show that average import quantities decline by 20 percent in rejected cases.

The previous results suggest that antidumping investigations, whether leading to an antidumping duty or to a negotiated agreement, can be used as a vehicle for trade-restricting firm collusion. Antidumping legislation provides a strategic tool to obtain rents from duties or negotiated trade restrictions. These rents accrue to both local and foreign firms. Prusa (1992) develops a model of bargaining along these lines. Staiger and Wolak (1989) develop a model in which antidumping is strategically used to enforce tacit international collusion.

Effectiveness and Third Party Response

Excessively high duties make difficult preempting antidumping-jumping, that is, FDI by firms aiming to avoid high duties. One factor explaining why antidumping rates are often high and counterproductive in terms of their objectives is that they are not set strategically to maximize a concept of welfare. Instead, rates are based on often controversial technical calculations of antidumping margins, as discussed in Boltuck and Litan (1991). The tight association between duty rates and calculated dumping margins does not provide the flexibility needed to be able to set low duties.

What is the response of third parties? Because antidumping protection is country-specific, in the sense that it applies only to the countries mentioned in the antidumping petition, the response of third parties can crucially affect the effectiveness of protection. Prusa (2001) finds that, on average, US petitions cover about 40 percent of the import market and that policy effectiveness is substantially hampered by trade diversion towards nonnamed countries. Imports by nonnamed countries are found to increase for the three years following the case (but the statistical evidence of offsetting effects is weak because coefficients are not statistically significant). In a previous study, Prusa (1997) finds that increased imports from nonnamed countries offset the protective impact of US antidumping duties within a six-year period. Staiger and Wolak (1994) report evidence of trade diversion during the investigation period.

14.4.2. European Union: Contingent Protection and Undertakings

Antidumping legislation is the major instrument of contingent protection in the European Union. Antidumping actions, like other trade policy actions, are conducted at the Union level so that individual member countries cannot bring antidumping cases to the World Trade Organization (WTO). The steel and chemicals industries have accounted for the lion's share of EU antidumping actions. During 1980–87, chemicals accounted for 40 percent of antidumping actions. Paradoxically, chemicals were often subject to both antidumping and anticartel actions. Messerlin (1990) and Lloyd et al. (1998) present evidence for the chemical industry indicating that antidumping actions are often used to maintain prices exceeding world market prices.

Traditionally, the EC/EU antidumping process has tended to apply political and administrative discretion to a greater extent than the US process, which has relied more on rules. However, Messerlin and Reed (1995) find convergence since the 1980s in terms of aims, outcomes and legal details. Still, relevant differences remain. Most European cases are resolved by price undertakings, a procedure that differs from the administrative review allowed in the United States after duties are levied. The EU antidumping duties are not tightly linked to estimated dumping margins. The

European Union often invokes a less-than-dumping-margin clause that allows levying duties on the basis of the estimated injury margin rather than the estimated dumping margin (the US method). A detailed discussion of EC antidumping procedures is contained in Vermulst (1987).

Antidumping actions lead to lower protective barriers in the European Union than in the United States but there are nevertheless large reductions in imports and substantial import price increases. Messerlin and Reed (1995) report average dumping margins of 37 percent for chemicals, nonelectrical machinery, electrical equipment, and metals in the European Community during 1980–89. *Ad valorem* duties for the first three industries mentioned were 18 percent compared with average most-favored-nation (MFN) barriers of 8 percent. Notice that duties are not tightly tied to dumping margin determinations. Messerlin (1989) reports that import quantities fell by 36 percent in the third year after the initiation of an investigation and prices went up by 12 percent in the fifth year.

The effectiveness of antidumping policies is hampered if imports from targeted countries are replaced by imports from countries that are not named in the petitions. In Europe, trade diversion to third parties has been limited in comparison with widespread trade diversion in the United States. Vandenbussche *et al.* (1999) report limited trade diversion caused by 246 antidumping cases initiated between 1985 and 1990. The result, obtained using data at the 8-digit product level, holds even after controlling for selection bias in antidumping investigations. The authors attribute this feature to lower duty rates and a lower degree of policy transparency in Europe combined with frequent tariff-jumping by targeted Japanese firms. These factors limit the potential benefits of antidumping protection to nonnamed countries and restrict trade diversion responses.

14.5. EXPORTS AND ENDOGENOUS PROTECTION UNCERTAINTY

Consider an exporting country anticipating that increased exports will raise the likelihood of facing restrictive quotas abroad. Policy uncertainty is endogenous because importing country authorities are more likely to invoke contingent protection laws when they face greater market disruption due to greater imports.

What is the optimal exporting country policy response to endogenous policy uncertainty in the importing country? Bhagwati and Srinivasan (1976) examine the optimal policy to address endogenous policy uncertainty in a two-sector, two-country general equilibrium model of trade. They present a setup in which the optimal response to policy uncertainty is to discourage exports to alleviate protection pressures abroad.

Consider a standard static model extended to a dynamic two-period setting that incorporates an stochastic policy function. Specifically, the probability P of facing a given quota restricting next period's exports to the predetermined level X_0 is assumed to increase at an increasing rate with the level of exports X

$$P = P(X), \qquad \frac{dP}{dX} > 0, \qquad \frac{d^2P}{dX^2} > 0.$$

Notice that equilibrium policy uncertainty is endogenous and subject to influence by the foreign exporter.

Let us label the exportable good as good I, so that its consumption equals production minus exports: $D_I = q_I - X_I$. The consumption of good II equals production plus the good-II value of exports of good-I: $D_{II} = q_{II} + p_I X_I / p_{II}$, where good II serves as the numeraire. The maximal second-period utilities with and without a quota are labeled $\underline{U}$ and $\bar{U}$, where $\underline{U} < \bar{U}$ holds if the quota is binding. Whether or not the predetermined quota is imposed is known at the beginning of the second period, but not in the first period. Because there is no production linkage between periods and consumption is time separable, the possible second-period utility values can be taken as constant for the purposes of period-1 maximization.

Expected utility is given by

$$EU = U(D_I, D_{II}) + \frac{1}{1+r}[P(X_I)\underline{U} + (1 - P(X_I))\bar{U}]$$

$$= U\left(q_I - X_I, q_{II} + \frac{p_I}{p_{II}}X_I\right) + \frac{1}{1+r}[P(X_I)\underline{U} + (1 - P(X_I))\bar{U}],$$

where r is the discount rate.

The optimal policy is chosen by maximizing expected utility subject to the economy's production transformation constraint $F(q_I, q_{II}) = 0$,

$$\max_{q_I, q_{II}, X_I} EU(q_I, q_{II}, X_I) - \lambda F(q_I, q_{II}).$$

The first order conditions of the maximization problem are

$$\frac{\partial EU}{\partial q_I} = \frac{\partial U}{\partial D_I} - \lambda \frac{\partial F}{\partial q_I} = 0, \qquad \frac{\partial EU}{\partial q_{II}} = \frac{\partial U}{\partial D_{II}} - \lambda \frac{\partial F}{\partial q_{II}} = 0,$$

$$\frac{\partial EU}{\partial X_I} = -\frac{\partial U}{\partial D_I} + \frac{\partial U}{\partial D_{II}}\left(\frac{p_I}{p_{II}} + \frac{\partial(p_I/p_{II})}{\partial X_I}X_I\right) - \frac{\bar{U} - \underline{U}}{1+r}\frac{dP}{dX_I} = 0,$$

where we use the definition $D_I = q_I - X_I$.

The first two equations imply the standard condition that the marginal rate of substitution is equal to the marginal rate of transformation, that is, the tangency of the social indifference curve and the transformation curve at equilibrium. Simplifying the optimization condition for exports yields

$$\frac{\partial U}{\partial D_I} \Big/ \frac{\partial U}{\partial D_{II}} = \frac{p_I}{p_{II}} + \frac{\partial(p_I/p_{II})}{\partial X_I}X_I - \frac{1}{1+r}\frac{\bar{U} - \underline{U}}{\partial U/\partial D_{II}}\frac{dP}{dX_I}.$$

The left-hand side represents the marginal benefits from consuming good I, measured in terms of good II marginal utility. The right-hand side embodies the benefits and costs from exporting an additional unit of good I (expressed in terms of good II marginal utility). The first term is just the selling price obtained for an additional unit of exports. The second term reflects the feature that increasing exports entails a cost because it reduces the terms of trade p_I/p_{II}. The third term relates to the increase in the probability of facing restrictions arising from an additional unit of exports. The term represents the increase in the discounted expected value of the utility cost $\bar{U} - \underline{U}$ (measured in terms of good II marginal utility) caused by the imposition of a quota.

The previous maximization condition covers various special cases. First, if the probability of restrictions does not respond to the level of exports, and the small economy assumption holds so that the relative price is not affected by the level of exports, we obtain the equality of the marginal rate of substitution and the world relative price. Second, if the probability of restrictions is constant but a higher level of good I exports reduces p_I/p_{II}, the marginal rate of substitution should be set to fall below the relative price. This condition can be satisfied by imposing an optimum tariff on good II, which shifts consumption toward exportable good I and reduces the equilibrium marginal rate of substitution of good I for good II (as well as the level of exports).

Third, if the prospect of quantitative restrictions increases with the level of exports, we have an additional negative term that calls for an import tariff. In other words, the presence of endogenous uncertainty has been shown to lead to reduced period-1 exports compared with the case in which there are no quotas (or quotas are present but are exogenous and do not respond to the level of foreign exports).

Notice that period-1 exports of good I are reduced by imposing a tariff on the importable good in period 1. This is an implication of Lerner's symmetry theorem, which states that an import tariff is equivalent to an appropriately set export tax (Lerner, 1936). The reason is that, in the standard two-sector general competitive equilibrium small economy model, a tariff on the importable good and an export tax have the same resource allocation effects. Namely, both policies increase the relative price of imports relative to exportables faced by domestic residents, shifting production towards importables and home consumption toward exportables. If trade is balanced, both imports and exports decline.

The concept of a response to endogenous policy uncertainty fits neatly into strategic frameworks. Blonigen and Ohno (1998) present a strategic model in which one of the responses to antidumping is to lower the volume of exports in the period preceding the restriction in order to induce lower levels of protection.

14.6. QUID PRO QUO FOREIGN INVESTMENT

In the 1980s, Japanese automakers stepped up direct foreign investment in the United States. Honda began production operations in 1982, Nissan in 1983, Toyota in 1984 (joint venture with General Motors), Mazda in 1987, Toyota in 1988 (separate subsidiary) and Mitsubishi in 1988. In 1989, Fiji Heavy Industries and Isuzu Motors joined the pack. These investments took place along with parallel investments in other sectors. The striking fact is that US subsidiaries of Japanese multinationals experienced losses at the time. The rate of return on Japanese investment in motor vehicles, equipment and other manufacturing was negative during 1980–86 and in some years reached double-digit negative rates of return (Wong, 1989).

Why did unprofitable investments take place? One explanation is that foreign investment that is unprofitable in the short run is undertaken to defuse the threat of future US protection. Short run losses are viewed as the current cost of defusing future protection. This hypothesis applies to the environment of the 1980s, when US producers faced stiff competition from Japanese car imports, a shrinking market share and lower profits. These difficulties, combined with layoffs of workers during the early 1980s recession, generated strong demands for protection. The quid pro quo of the short-term losses of Japanese companies' US subsidiaries was an anticipated reduced threat of protection in the long run. Japanese investment in the United States seems to have catered to the supplier of protection—the government—rather than to the demanders of protection—labor. In fact, plants were established in Ohio and other locations away from the core of the Detroit auto labor movement.

Quid pro quo investment takes place when firms incur short-term losses that are subsequently offset by defused protection. As a result, exporters end up operating in markets that are more open or prone to be more open than they would have been in the absence of foreign investment.

Bhagwati *et al.* (1987) examine quid pro quo investment in a perfectly competitive, two-sector, two-country general equilibrium dynamic setup with two periods. They extend the endogenous policy uncertainty approach by assuming that greater foreign investment lowers the probability of future protection. Short-term losses from foreign investment are justified by the greater prospects of reduced protection. A free-riding problem arises because foreign investors incur losses that result in the benefit of all foreign exporters even if they abstain from foreign investing. Free-riding problems imply that the foreign government has incentives to coordinate an expansion of foreign investment abroad. From the viewpoint of a foreign country facing the hazard of protection, the promotion of foreign direct investment by exporting firms represents a policy to induce lower protection abroad.

14.6.1. Strategic Analysis of Quid Pro Quo FDI

Quid pro quo investment can be viewed as a strategy to defuse the threat of protection by creating incentives for agents to oppose rather than support protection. Production in-site creates employment abroad and replaces exports that are perceived as costing employment abroad. Pressures for protection are thus alleviated, which reduces the probability of protection, the magnitude of potential trade restrictions, or both.

Dinopoulos (1989) examines the joint determination of exports and foreign investment in a strategic setup with endogenous policy uncertainty. Consider a two-period partial equilibrium model with a single host country firm and a single source country firm. A homogeneous good is sold under duopoly conditions in the host country and under monopoly conditions in the source country. The source country firm must decide how much to export to the host country and how much to foreign invest in order to produce directly in the host country.

Home country sales D^H are equal to the sum of host country firm production q_H^H, source country exports X_S, and source country firm production in the host country q_S^H. In the source country, the homogeneous good is produced under monopoly conditions and total sales D^S are equal to source country firm production destined to its own market, q_S^S. Symbolically,

$$ D^H = q_H^H + X_S + q_S^H, \qquad D^S = q_S^S, $$

where total source country firm output is $Q_S = q_S^S + X_S + q_S^H$.

The probability that a predetermined quota or trade barrier is imposed in the second period is assumed to increase with source country exports X_S and to decline with the foreign direct investment facility output q_S^H

$$ P = P(X_S, q_S^H), \qquad \frac{dP}{dX_S} > 0, \qquad \frac{dP}{dq_S^H} < 0. $$

Expected profits $E\pi$ are equal to the discounted value of revenues R minus production costs C

$$ E\pi_H = R_H^H(q_H^H, X_S + q_S^H) - C_H^H(q_H^H) + \frac{1}{1+r}[P\underline{\pi}_H + (1-P)\bar{\pi}_H], $$

$$ E\pi_S = R_S^H(q_H^H, X_S + q_S^H) - C_S^H(q_S^H) - cX_S + R_S^S(q_S^S) - cq_S^S $$
$$ + \frac{1}{1+r}[P\underline{\pi}_S + (1-P)\bar{\pi}_S], $$

where source country sales in the host country consist of exports, X_S, and the output of the foreign investment facility, q_S^H. Both firms are assumed to be subject to increasing costs $C(\cdot)$ when they produce in the host country. Source country production takes place at constant marginal costs c independently of whether it is sold locally or exported to the host country. Profits $\bar{\pi}_i$ and $\underline{\pi}_i$, $i \in \{H, S\}$, denote second-period profits without and with protection. In this setup, time separability implies that the value of second-period profits is not affected by first-period decisions. Dinopoulos (1989) examines general conditions under which the inequality $\bar{\pi}_i > \underline{\pi}_i$ holds.

The source country firm maximizes profits with respect to exports X_S, host country production q_S^H and production sold in the source country q_S^S. The profit maximization conditions are $(Q_S^H = X_S + q_S^H)$

$$\frac{\partial E\pi_S}{\partial X_S} = \frac{\partial R_S^H}{\partial Q_S^H} - c - \frac{1}{1+r}(\bar{\pi}_S - \underline{\pi}_S)\frac{\partial P}{\partial X_S} = 0,$$

$$\frac{\partial E\pi_S}{\partial q_S^H} = \frac{\partial R_S^H}{\partial Q_S^H} - \frac{\partial C_S^H}{\partial q_S^H} - \frac{1}{1+r}(\bar{\pi}_S - \underline{\pi}_S)\frac{\partial P}{\partial q_S^H} = 0,$$

$$\frac{\partial E\pi_S}{\partial q_S^S} = \frac{\partial R_S^S}{\partial q_S^S} - c = 0.$$

If the probability of protection P does not respond to exports and foreign direct investment, the first order conditions reduce to the equality of marginal revenues and marginal costs in all markets. In this case, the export and FDI quid pro quo effects do not appear.

The first order Nash equilibrium condition for exports captures how exports are set in order to induce less protection ($\bar{\pi}_S - \underline{\pi}_S$ is assumed to be positive). If the probability of facing protection increases with the volume of exports, the marginal revenue from exporting to the host country must rise above the marginal cost of exports in equilibrium. If marginal revenues rise with lower sales (e.g. linear demand functions), the equilibrium level of exports is lower than it would have been if trade restrictions were exogenous. The reduction of exports in turn lowers the probability of protection.

Combining the first order conditions for exports and production through foreign investment yields

$$\frac{\partial C_S^H}{\partial q_S^H} = c + \frac{1}{1+r}(\bar{\pi}_S - \underline{\pi}_S)\left(\frac{\partial P}{\partial X_S} - \frac{\partial P}{\partial q_S^H}\right).$$

The previous equation captures the rationale for quid pro quo investment undertaken to induce less protection. If the probability of protection declines with the output of the FDI facility, q_S^H, this contributes to drive the equilibrium marginal costs of host country production above the constant marginal costs of source country production. Because the cost function C_S^H is increasing in output, equilibrium foreign investment rises as the firm moves up the marginal cost curve of home country production. The firm engages in inefficient foreign investment because it reduces the probability of future protection. Balancing short-term losses with future opening represents quid pro quo investment.

14.6.2. *Rigid Wage, Unemployment, and Lobbying for Protection*

Wong (1989) considers a two-period partial equilibrium model of a competitive industry with a rigid wage and varying employment. In the first period, a labor union lobbies the government for tariff protection to combat unemployment. The probability P of imposing a tariff in the second period is assumed to be an increasing function of the amount of money spent on lobbying for protection, L, and to depend negatively on the level of the requested tariff rate t

$$P = P(L, t).$$

The analysis considers both the case in which the requested tariff is exogenous and the case in which it is determined jointly with the probability of protection. Source country firms' second-period profits hinge on whether a tariff is actually levied.

Foreign investment is undertaken in the first period as a means of containing the threat of protection by inducing a reduction in the amount of money spent on lobbying, which in turn lowers the probability of future protection. Lobbying can be influenced because foreign investment raises industry employment and the union takes this effect into account when deciding how much to spend on lobbying. In order to avoid a free-rider problem, the foreign government is assumed to coordinate firms actions so that they contribute equal shares of foreign investment. In general, foreign investment does not drive the host economy to full employment so that a demand for protection continues to arise.

14.7. FDI AS ANTIDUMPING-JUMPING

A trade restriction-jumping strategy consists of bypassing tariffs, duties, quotas, VERs and other trade restrictions by foreign investing and producing in the investigating country. Firms facing antidumping investigations can avoid the negative effects of actual or potential duties by engaging in antidumping-jumping FDI. The possibility of tariff-jumping affects the form and strength of trade restrictions imposed by a government to protect its domestic industry against import competition. Ellingsen and Wärneryd (1998) show that the possibility of tariff-jumping discourages setting high protection barriers, precisely because high levels of protection lead to counterproductive tariff-jumping.

14.7.1. Reciprocal Antidumping

Can antidumping policies be counterproductive in terms of their goals? The optimality of unilateral intervention depends on whether or not unilateral antidumping leads to tariff-jumping and on the relative weight given to producers and consumers in the intervening government's welfare function (Haaland and Wooton, 1998).

If transport costs are low enough, a unilateral antidumping duty does not lead to tariff-jumping and benefits the firm whose home market is being protected while hurting the protected market consumer. If the weight given to producers in government welfare is high (low) enough, unilateral antidumping policies will be (will not) followed. In contrast, if transport costs are high enough, an antidumping duty leads to tariff-jumping. In this situation, the protected local firm is paradoxically hurt by antidumping protection while the protected market consumers benefit from greater competition. If the weight given to producers in government welfare is high enough, a policy designed to protect local industry would be counterproductive in terms of its objectives and would not be chosen in equilibrium. But, if consumer welfare dominates an antidumping policy will be enforced.

What is the equilibrium when both governments are active and can engage in anti-dumping policies? Suppose that the weight given to producers is small enough so that a country has incentives to engage in unilateral dumping under tariff-jumping. If the home country of the firm subject to an antidumping action is allowed to reciprocate with its own antidumping action, the model has two Nash equilibria depending on the relative weight governments give to domestic consumers and producers and trade costs. In one case, tariff-jumping does not arise and it is not optimal to reciprocate. The reason is that retaliation would result in lower consumer welfare because it precludes consumption benefits from dumping. This gives rise to an asymmetric situation in which one country intervenes and the other does not intervene. In another case, it is optimal to reciprocate and both firms engage in antidumping-jumping. What are the consequences of government choices that result in reciprocal antidumping policies? Because the shift from exporting to in-site production lowers the rival's profit, both firms end up with lower profits. From the firms' perspective, a prisoner's dilemma situation arises. However, consumers are better off. Firms would prefer to prohibit anti-dumping actions while consumers would prefer to keep active antidumping policies. If the welfare weight given to consumers is high enough, reciprocal antidumping will take place. Do antidumping policies generate incentives for retaliation leading to reciprocal antidumping that might push firms or countries towards prisoner's dilemma situations? The answer is positive from the perspective of the firms but not necessarily from an overall welfare perspective in this setting.

The result that reciprocal antidumping can harm firms while increasing overall welfare also appears in a similar setting in which dumping takes place but tariff-jumping is not allowed (Anderson *et al.*, 1995). However, the equilibrium policies are different. When there is no tariff-jumping, reciprocal antidumping that would be welfare-improving does not take place in equilibrium. If there is tariff-jumping, welfare-improving reciprocal antidumping arises as an equilibrium.

14.7.2. *Evidence on Antidumping-Jumping FDI*

Is foreign investing a common response to antidumping investigations? The answer is positive in the case of Japan. Using country-level data for 1980–91, Barrell and Pain (1999) examine the determinants of Japanese foreign investment in the United States and the EC. They find that—after controlling for relative costs, size, and other variables—antidumping actions initiated in the United States and the EC are positively correlated with Japanese foreign investment flows into the United States and EC countries. There is also industry-level evidence that VERs and other trade barriers promote foreign investment in US manufacturing (Pugel *et al.*, 1996) and the US electronics industry (Kogut and Chang, 1996).

Recent microeconomic studies of dumping examine behavior at the level of the firm and product categories. Belderbos (1997*b*) finds that the tariff-jumping effects of

Japanese firms are much stronger for the European Union than for the United States. An affirmative antidumping action is found to increase the probability of foreign investment from 20 to 72 percent in the EC and from 20 to 36 percent in the United States. A cancelled antidumping investigation increases the probability of foreign investment from 20 to 48 percent in the EC but there is no significant effect in the United States. The comparative study conducted by Blonigen (2002) shows that Japanese firms are the most frequent tariff-jumpers, followed by European firms, and that Canada and developing countries are not frequent tariff-jumpers.

14.7.3. Protection-Building Investment

Blonigen and Ohno (1998) examine a two-period, three-country duopoly model that gives rise to three types of unique subgame perfect equilibria embodying the following possible responses to an expected restrictive policy. First, both firms' exports may decline in anticipation of trade restrictions in order to alleviate the pressures for protection abroad and induce a lower endogenously set protection level. This strategy, which corresponds with the standard endogenous protection outcome, is chosen when the costs of foreign investment are high. Second, if foreign investment costs are low enough, both firms might not reduce exports and instead engage in tariff-jumping by foreign investing in order to bypass any restriction imposed in the second period. Third, a firm may both foreign invest and increase exports in anticipation of a restriction while the other foreign firm lowers its exports. The FDI has a tariff-jumping motive. The increase in exports is intended to increase future protection hitting a rival that does not foreign invest. This strategy package is called protection-building to indicate that it is intended to heighten the future protection faced by a rival. In other words, foreign investment accompanied by greater exports can have a protection-building effect if it encourages future protection that hurts those rivals abstaining from foreign investment.

Protection-Building Behavior

Protection-building behavior might be involved in cases of foreign firms that fail to participate in antidumping proceedings while investing in the investigating country. By not participating, a firm increases the expected antidumping duty that will hit rivals. For instance, Honda failed to cooperate with a 1980 US escape clause investigation. In contrast, Nissan and Toyota cooperated with it. The investigation led to VERs imposed against all Japanese auto makers in 1981, but Honda had already set up a plant in Ohio in 1978 and started production operations in 1982. In this case, all manufacturers increased their exports prior to the establishment of protection, which is consistent with the domino theory of the response to anticipated restrictions. This theory asserts that firms increase current sales in an attempt to secure more licenses to sell after quotas become effective. Honda's refusal to cooperate with the investigation can be understood in terms of the option to produce in the United States. The more cooperative Toyota and Nissan developed their US manufacturing capacities later in the 1980s.

Another example of behavior that has a protection-building effect is the 1986–87 US antidumping investigation of color picture tubes. In this case, the Japanese firm with the largest share of exports to the United States during the investigation period—Toshiba—failed to cooperate with an antidumping investigation. It was found to have the largest dumping margin while rivals cooperated and got lower estimated antidumping margins. Toshiba informed US investigators that it was not going to cooperate as it was planning to move production to the United States.

14.7.4. Evidence on Quid Pro Quo and Tariff-Jumping

Blonigen and Feenstra (1997) use 4-digit SIC industry-level data to show that Japanese FDI flows into the United States were positively correlated with measures of actual and threatened antidumping activity during 1980–88. The threat of protectionism is indicated by whether an industry's imports have become subject to an affirmative escape clause or antidumping decision.

A probit threat-of-protection regression is used to estimate the probability of protection and to test the hypothesis that FDI negatively affects the probability of protection. Foreign investment is decomposed into acquisition FDI (mergers and acquisitions) and nonacquisition FDI (greenfield investments). The empirical analysis of the determinants of the threat of protectionism helps to distinguish between tariff-jumping FDI—undertaken to circumvent protection—and quid pro quo FDI—undertaken to defuse protection.

Both acquisition and nonacquisition FDI respond strongly to the threat of antidumping protection. These results are consistent with both quid pro quo FDI and tariff-jumping. The importance of quid pro quo FDI is apparent from the estimates of the effect of different forms of protection on different forms of FDI. The threat of escape clause protection does not affect acquisition FDI significantly but leads to substantial and statistically significant effects on nonacquisition FDI. This result suggests that quid pro quo FDI works through nonacquisition FDI, which is presumed to be more likely to defuse protectionist threats than foreign acquisitions, which often accentuate protectionist attitudes.

14.8. DUMPING IN ANTICIPATION OF VERs

Threats of VERs generate expectations of future price increases. The combination of VERs and restrictions on firm entry is often utilized to sustain a cartel price. In the Multi-Fibre Arrangement (MFA), for instance, sales are subject to quotas and new firms are allowed to enter but are allocated a low market share.

Expectations of VERs and higher future prices induce firms to engage in dumping. The reason is that higher firm sales typically raise the expected number of licenses to export at the cartel price. Dumping takes place to increase quota allocations and thus expected profits from possible future export licenses. Dumping also increases the likelihood that the government will react by negotiating a VER and thus increase expected future profits.

14.8.1. Current Dumping and Prospective VERs

Why is it that dumping can coexist with a forward-looking competitive market? Anderson (1992) develops a two-period perfect competition model of dumping taking place in anticipation of VERs. Consider a competitive firm holding expectations of forming part of an export cartel implemented through a VER. The price received by members of the VER-implemented export cartel is denoted by $\bar{p}$. The small firm assumption implies that the firm takes the current competitive price p and the future cartel price $\bar{p} \geq p$ as exogenously given. The discounted probability that the VER will be arranged is exogenous and is equal to P_{VER}.

Current sales yield future claims to export licenses at the rate $\lambda, 0 < \lambda < 1$. This means that an additional unit of current output translates into λ units sold at the cartel price $\bar{p}$. A production level of q_I yields licenses to produce $q_{II} = \lambda q_I$ units under the VER arrangement. The profits from the licenses held are thus equal to $\bar{p}\lambda q_I - C(\lambda q_I)$. The value of λ is assumed to be constant.

Expected profits $E\Pi$ are given by current revenues minus current costs plus the expected value of future profits from licenses held. Each exporter maximizes expected profits with respect to its first period output q_I

$$\max_{q_I} E\Pi(q_I; p, \bar{p}) = pq_I - C(q_I) + P_{VER}[\bar{p}\lambda q_I - C(\lambda q_I)],$$

where $C(\cdot)$ is an increasing and strictly convex cost function of output. The rate of discount is incorporated into the discounted probability P_{VER}.

The first order condition $dE\Pi/dq_I = 0$ yields

$$\frac{dE\Pi}{dq_I} = p - \frac{dC(q_I)}{dq_I} + \lambda P_{VER}\bar{p} - P_{VER}\frac{dC(q_{II})}{dq_{II}}\frac{d\lambda q_I}{dq_I} = 0$$

$$\rightarrow \frac{dC(q_I)}{dq_I} - p = \lambda P_{VER}\left[\bar{p} - \frac{dC(q_{II})}{dq_{II}}\right], \tag{14.3}$$

where industry output is taken as given, $q_{II} = \lambda q_I$, and a constant λ implies $d\lambda q_I/dq_I = \lambda$.

Dumping can be interpreted as purchasing an option to sell at a cartel price. In equilibrium, the exporter equates the price of the option—defined as the loss from an additional unit of exports, $dC/dq_I - p > 0$—to the option value of an additional unit of current exports. The worth $v(q_I, \bar{p})$ of the license to sell an additional unit of exports at the cartel price $\bar{p}$, conditional on the VER being in place, is

$$v(q_I, \bar{p}) = \bar{p} - \frac{dC(q_{II})}{dq_{II}}.$$

The expected value $Ev(q_I, \bar{p})$ is equal to P_{VER} times the conditional value v. Because current exports yield future claims at the rate λ, the option value of an additional unit of current exports is equal to $\lambda Ev(q_I, \bar{p}) = \lambda P_{VER}v(q_I, \bar{p})$. Therefore

$$\frac{dC(q_I)}{dq_I} - p = \lambda Ev(q_I, \bar{p}) = \lambda P_{VER}\left[\bar{p} - \frac{dC(q_{II})}{dq_{II}}\right],$$

which is the first order condition (14.3). The left-hand side represents the cost of an option to sell at the cartel price and the right-hand side represents its worth.

The competitive equilibrium can be shown to entail anticipatory dumping

$$\frac{dC(q_I^C)}{dq_I} - p > 0. \tag{14.4}$$

The last inequality implies that, paradoxically, a perfectly competitive firm engages in dumping in the sense that it sells at a price below marginal costs.

14.8.2. Domino Dumping and Antidumping Practices

Do antidumping policies safeguard competition? Anderson (1993) presents a framework for analyzing anticipated antidumping policy. Suppose that foreign exporters sell a homogenous good in a competitive market that is segmented from the rest-of-the-world (say, due to transaction costs, different product standards, or regulation). Producers are likely to face VERs or antidumping duties (ADs) in the future. Domino dumping arises when exporters' forward-looking strategies entail dumping practices (i.e. firms set export prices below their true marginal costs) in the present with the intention of obtaining more export licenses in the future. Exporter's domino dumping practices: (1) induce protectionist pressures in the country facing dumped imports, and, (2) trigger the enforcement of export restrictions or antidumping policies that are seen as remedies to antidumping enforcement problems.

Increased efforts to enforce antidumping laws can perversely induce more dumping. The reason is that increased dumping raises the probability of imposing VERs as the remedy and the exporter seeks to extract benefits from the antidumping policy. The result is driven by the assumption that in case of adopting a VER, the quota $\bar{q}$ is set on the basis of the exporters' market share at period t (a variable chosen by exporters). Also, the larger the probability of a VER, the lower the probability of reestablishing free trade practices, and the larger the probability that other countries will also impose a VER (i.e. domino effect).

14.9. SECTION 301: THEORY AND EVIDENCE

Section 301 of the Trade Act of 1974, subsequently evolving into sections 301–309 of the 1988 Omnibus Trade and Competitiveness Act, is the main statute addressing unfair practices hurting US exports. This legislation provides for (i) the investigation of foreign practices and actions, (ii) mandatory retaliation (with some loopholes) against countries that are determined to *unjustifiably* burden or restrict US commerce or deny US rights under international agreements, and (iii) discretionary retaliation for practices or actions that *unfairly* hurt US trade, even though targeted countries might be complying with US trade treaties.

14.9.1. Invoking Section 301 as a Bargaining Tool

Supporters of section 301 argue that it should be viewed as a bargaining tool for market opening negotiations. Its success as a bargaining tool hinges on how it alters the relative bargaining power of targeting and targeted countries.

McMillan (1990) provides a game-theoretic guide to section 301 and the factors determining relative bargaining power. Consider two countries bargaining to divide a 'pie' of given size among themselves. Bargaining takes place under conditions of perfect information and both countries have a zero discount rate (i.e. are equally patient). Following Binmore *et al.* (1986), countries bargain on the basis of alternating offers. Country A is assumed to make the first offer. If country B accepts, the game ends. Countries receive shares s^A and s^B, and reap utilities rs^A and s^B. The constant r indicates A's benefit per unit bargained. Player B's per unit benefit is normalized to unity. If country B rejects A's offer, negotiations continue. However, there is a fixed probability P that negotiations will break down at each stage of the game, at which point bargainers are allocated predetermined utility levels U_0^A and U_0^B. The probability of breakdown creates incentives to end the game as soon as possible.

When the probability of negotiation breakdown approaches zero, the subgame perfect equilibrium of the negotiating parties' shares s^A and s^B approaches

$$s^A = \frac{1 + U_0^A - rU_0^B}{2}, \qquad s^B = \frac{1 + U_0^B - U_0^A/r}{2}.$$

McMillan (1990) contains a simple proof of this result.

The invocation of section 301 can be viewed as a credible device to lower the utility of the negotiating party in case negotiations break down (i.e. lower the value of U_0^B). If the United States makes the first offer, US bargaining power and utility will be greater (1) the greater the harm to the targeted country from restrictions on US market access (a lower U_0^B), (2) the smaller the potential harm from retaliation by the targeted country (a higher U_0^A), and (3) the greater the potential US benefit from the negotiations (a higher r). In addition, the US share will be larger the smaller the foreign country cost of complying with US demands (not explicitly indicated in the formula above).

What happens if countries do not have full information about each other? When countries act under less than full information, actions could be directed at the wrong targets. If that happens, section 301 actions can break down negotiations, encourage counter-retaliation and generate costly delays to an agreement.

14.9.2. Has Section 301 Trade Retaliation Worked?

What is the record of section 301 investigations? The controversial nature of these investigations raises several questions. First, has market opening been achieved? How often has retaliation ensued? Has retaliation induced counterretaliation? Finally, is the multilateral trading system undermined or propped up by the proliferation of section 301 cases?

The actual performance of section 301 has been systematically examined by Bayard and Elliot (1994). They consider 91 section 301 investigations and assess the outcome of 72 section 301 cases from 1975 to June 1994 (for various reasons, nineteen cases are not assessed).

A successful case is defined as one in which the US objective—market-opening, reduced export subsidization—is at least partially achieved. The authors avoid classifying a case as successful unless it is clearly so. For instance, the Japan–US Semiconductors Trade Agreement, signed in 1986, stipulated that foreign firms would get a 20 percent share of the semiconductor market by 1992. The agreement followed a trade dispute in which the US Semiconductor Industry Association filed a section 301 petition and Micron filed an antidumping suit. The Japanese government remained in charge of enforcing the agreement under the threat of sanctions if the terms of the agreement were violated. The agreement is often considered a relative success because the foreign market share jumped from less than 10–14 percent when the agreement expired in 1991. But Bayard and Elliot class it as a failure because the market share was well below the 20 percent negotiated target. Furthermore, the United States kept the retaliatory duties imposed in 1987 until a new agreement was signed in 1991.

Bayard and Elliot reach the conclusion that section 301 has been a reasonably effective market-opening tool. About half of the cases were found to be successful (thirty-five of seventy-two section 301 cases assessed). If cases targeting intellectual property rights are excluded, the success rate is 60 percent of the cases studied. Effectiveness was greater during 1985–88 and declined thereafter. The authors suggest that, 'contrary to conventional wisdom, the provisions of the 1988 Trade Act, including super 301, did not improve the chances of achieving a successful outcome relative to the administrative and attitudinal changes adopted in 1985'.

Using a wider definition of success, Sykes (1992) finds that 70 percent of the cases examined were successful (fifty-eight out of eighty-three). Using a stricter definition of success, Low (1993) reports a 35 percent success rate.

Does section 301 lead to retaliation against the target country? The US retaliated in fifteen out of ninety-one section 301 investigations examined by Bayard and Elliot—about 16 percent of the time. A well-publicized US retaliation followed US allegations that the Japanese had not fulfilled the market access obligations of the 1986 semiconductor agreement (a voluntary import expansion agreement). In April 1987, the US Trade Representative imposed duties on $165 million in imports from Japan. Moreover, counterretaliation rarely ensued retaliation. It took place only three times during 1975–94, one by Canada and two by the European Community.

Do findings that section 301 cases are moderately successful in opening markets, and that there is no substantial retaliation or counterretaliation, imply that section 301 is commendable? Not necessarily. Because section 301 outcomes reflect US strong bargaining power, there is the possibility that US demands are satisfied by diverting trade from other countries in favor of the United States. In this case, global market opening does not improve. Bayard and Elliot (1994) do not find systematic evidence of trade diversion and discrimination favoring the United States but they and other researchers cite episodic evidence. In the mid-1980s, South Korea published lists showing trade diversion from other suppliers to the United States.

14.10. MARKET ACCESS POLICIES

Market access policies intend to enhance market access in the face of visible trade barriers such as tariffs and quotas or invisible trade barriers such as impenetrable interfirm networks. In general, whether market access policies enhance competition (procompetitive) or reduce competition (anticompetitive) depends on the type of policy and the conditions of the game played. Paradoxically, requirements of greater access in final goods markets supported by sanctions turn out to be anticompetitive in the standard duopoly model examined. However, competition can increase when the market access requirement is implemented by threats affecting a related market.

We focus on four types of market access policies implemented in a two-stage duopoly game.

1. A procompetitive rules-oriented policy consisting of a government subsidy to the exports of the country seeking greater market access. The subsidy rate is set to implement the desired market share.
2. A procompetitive rules-oriented policy consisting of a lump sum subsidy to the export sector of the country seeking greater market access, contingent on achieving the target market share.
3. An anticompetitive results-oriented policy consisting of a market share requirement negotiated with a foreign country under the threat of sanctions. Market access requirements (MARs) are also called voluntary import expansions (VIEs) to indicate that the targeted country 'voluntarily' agrees to increase its imports from the country seeking expanded market access.
4. A procompetitive policy under which competition increases when a market access requirement is implemented by threats affecting an intermediate input market.

14.10.1. Unilateral Subsidy Rate to Achieve a Target Market Share

Figure 14.1 illustrates the effects of a rules-oriented policy consisting of unilateral subsidization aiming to achieve a predetermined market share. Consider a symmetric two-stage duopoly game in which the government sets the subsidy in the first stage and firms determine output in the second stage. A target market share is $\alpha = q/(q + q^*)$ represented by the line $q^* = (1 - \alpha)q/\alpha$, where q is the output of the country seeking greater market access and q^* represents its trading partner's output.

The free trade Cournot–Nash equilibrium is depicted by point a, which lies along the 45-degree line indicating equal market share. At stage 1, the domestic government sets a subsidy rate s chosen to induce the domestic firm to achieve the target market share $\alpha \in [1/2, 1]$ in the second stage of the game. The reaction function of the firm from the country seeking greater market access shifts upward because (a subsidized firm produces more for any given level of rival output). The reaction function of the

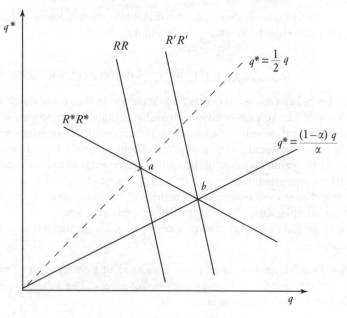

Figure 14.1. *Target market share*

targeted country firm remains unchanged. Equilibrium is depicted by point b, which is determined by the intersection of the market share line with the two reaction functions.

The subsidy equilibrium is procompetitive. Notice that the slope of the targeted country reaction function (i.e. the foreign country in Chapter 7) is less than 1 in absolute value. This means that q^* declines by a lesser amount than the increase in q. Therefore, total output $q + q^*$ is greater than in the no-subsidy case.

14.10.2. Unilateral Lump Sum Subsidy Contingent on a Target Market Share

Let us illustrate the effects of a rules-oriented policy consisting of a unilateral lump sum subsidy contingent on the attainment of a target market rate. The subsidy to the firm from the country seeking market share can be granted by the targeting government (say, the United States) or the targeted government (say, Japan). Targeting government welfare is higher when the targeted government pays the subsidy. In practice, targeted governments are responsible for implementing negotiated market share targets (VIEs) and they can choose to directly or indirectly subsidize the targeting country firm.

At stage 1, the government makes the following proposal to the firm of the country seeking greater market share. The government will grant a lump sum subsidy s if the firm is able to capture a larger market share than a prenegotiated level denoted by $\alpha \in [1/2, 1]$, which is chosen to exceed the market share achievable under free trade. At stage 2, the duopolists noncooperatively set their production levels, q and q^*. If the firm of the country seeking greater market access meets the market share requirement $q/(q + q^*) \geq \alpha$, or $q^* \leq (1 - \alpha)q/\alpha$, the government will grant the subsidy.

Targeting country firm's profits in the no-subsidization and subsidization cases are

$$\pi = (a - q - q^*)q - cq \quad \text{if } \frac{q}{q + q^*} < \alpha,$$

$$\pi(s) = (a - q - q^*)q - cq + s \quad \text{if } \frac{q}{q + q^*} \geq \alpha.$$

The profits of the targeted country firm are $\pi^* = (a - q - q^*)q^* - cq^*$.

Substituting $q \geq \alpha q^*/(1 - \alpha)$ (obtained from $q/(q + q^*) \geq \alpha$) into the targeted country firm reaction function yields (with demand given by $p = a - q$)

$$q^* = \frac{a - q - c}{2} \leq \frac{a - [\alpha q^*/(1 - \alpha)] - c}{2} = \frac{(1 - \alpha)(a - c) - \alpha q^*}{2(1 - \alpha)}.$$

Solving for q^* we have

$$q^* \leq \frac{(1 - \alpha)(a - c)}{2 - \alpha} = \bar{q},$$

where $\bar{q}$ declines with the required market share α. Substituting the restriction $q^* \leq \bar{q}$ into the targeting country firm reaction function implies

$$q = \frac{a - q^* - c}{2} \geq \frac{a - \bar{q} - c}{2} = \frac{a - c}{2(2 - \alpha)} = \underline{q},$$

where $q > \bar{q}$ if $\alpha > 1/2$.

Figure 14.2 illustrates a market share subsidy equilibrium with two symmetric firms. The Cournot–Nash equilibrium with no subsidy is depicted at point *a* on the 45-degree line, indicating that firms have the same market share, that is, $q/(q + q^*) = 1/2$ or $q = q^*$. The prenegotiated market share is implemented by a lump sum subsidy to the firm of the country seeking higher market share, contingent on achieving a target market share. If the output q of the targeting country firm satisfies the market share requirement, the subsidy equilibrium solution must lie below the 45-degree line, $q > q^*$ or $q/(q + q^*) > 1/2$. The binding market share requirement is represented by the line $q^* = (1 - \alpha)q/\alpha$.

Equilibrium with a lump sum subsidy contingent on a target market share is depicted by point *b* in Fig. 14.2, determined by the intersection of the market share line and two reaction functions. A lump sum subsidy to the targeting country firm does not modify the marginal decisions or the reaction function of its trading partner firm. The market share lump sum subsidy makes the targeting country firm reaction function discontinuous. When trading partner production q^* is high enough, it does not pay for a targeting country firm to increase market share because the lump sum subsidy requires a too large increase in output q. In that segment, the reaction curve remains the same as the no-subsidy reaction curve. If trading partner output q^* is below a critically

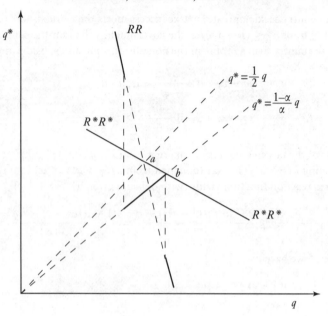

Figure 14.2. *Market share subsidy equilibrium*

low level, it is worthwhile to achieve the market share. The targeting country reaction curve coincides with the target market share line at (q, q^*). If q^* is low enough, the target market share is achieved by the output level indicated by the reaction function *RR*. The response with lump sum subsidy coincides with the no subsidy case.

The lump sum subsidy equilibrium entails the same output as the equilibrium with an appropriately chosen subsidy rate and thus is procompetitive in relation to nonintervention. Because the subsidized firm increases production in order to meet the market share requirement, and the rival's reaction function is downward sloping, the trading partner output level is smaller than the Cournot production level. However, it is easy to see that total production increases (and the market price declines) so that outcome is procompetitive. Recall that equilibria shift along the trading partner reaction function, the slope of which is equal to -0.5 (see Chapter 7). This means that q^* only declines by one-half the increase in q so that total output must increase.

Krishna *et al.* (1998) show that, if the timing of the subsidy game is such that firms play before the government sets the subsidy (i.e. the firms play first), a firm can manipulate government policy decision. With Bertrand competition, the effect of the MAR can be anticompetitive, yielding lower levels of production and larger prices than those achieved in the Cournot–Nash example. In other words, the outcome of trade policies intended to restrict market access is sensitive to the game staging. Why is it that, if the government grants a subsidy once the firms have set their prices, the effect of a market access requirement turns out to be anticompetitive? The reason is the following. First, the rival firm gets incentives to increase its price and induce the potentially subsidized firm to follow (recall that prices are strategic complements) and fail to accomplish the government requirement. Second, the targeting country firm has incentives to set larger prices in order to increase profits and compensate for the subsidies lost when the assigned market share target is not achieved.

14.10.3. Market Share Requirement with Sanctions

Consider now a results-oriented policy aiming to achieve a market share target supported by a threat. Specifically, the policy consists of a market share requirement negotiated with a targeted country under the threat of sanctions, which are assumed to be credible. This type of market access requirement can be represented by the pair (α, V), where α is the minimum market share target and V is the penalty cost imposed on the targeted country if the market share target is not achieved. In practice, if MAR negotiations end up in an agreement to guarantee a minimum market share, the targeted government remains in charge of enforcing it.

Equilibrium under a negotiated market access requirement and potential sanctions is represented by point c in Fig. 14.3. The requirement leaves unchanged the reaction function of the country seeking greater market access while creating a discontinuity in the rival firm reaction function. If the output levels q and q^* are high and low enough, respectively, so that the market share is achieved, the market share is not binding and the targeted country firm reaction curve corresponds with the no-requirement reaction curve. There is an intermediate range at which the market share requirement

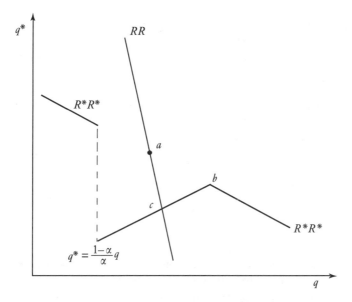

Figure 14.3. *Negotiated market access requirements with sanctions*

is binding and the targeted country firm reaction curve coincides with the line depicting a constant market share. If the production level q of the firm seeking greater market share is low enough, abiding by market share would force the trading partner to reduce output so much that it prefers to pay the penalty. There is a discontinuity and the targeted country reaction curve coincides with the reaction curve applying when there are no market requirements.

Paradoxically, the results–oriented market access requirement turns out to be anti-competitive in the sense that the market price is higher than in the Cournot–Nash equilibrium with no intervention. Because the movement from point a to point c takes place along the reaction curve RR, which has a slope of 2 in absolute value (see Chapter 7), the reduction in q^* must exceed the increase in q. Therefore, total output declines. The result-oriented policy achieves the same market share as the subsidy policy but with a lower level of total output and thus high prices. The reason is that the results-oriented policy does not affect the reaction curve of the firm seeking expanded access but works by inducing its rival to lower production in order to satisfy the market requirement. This is the basis of the common criticism that market share requirements on targeted country firms are inefficient. In addition, Greany (1996) shows that market access requirements on trading partners are anticompetitive when firms compete in prices and prices are strategic complements.

In short, what are the effects of market access requirements intending to open markets? The imposition of market share requirements can have procompetitive or anticompetitive effects depending on whether they are imposed on the right or the wrong set of firms. Specifically, a lump sum subsidy to the firm from the country seeking expanded access, contingent on achieving a predetermined market share, is procompetitive in situations in which a sanction-based market share requirement imposed on the targeted trading partner is anticompetitive. It can also be shown that a MAR affecting and potentially sanctioning an intermediate input can have indirect procompetitive effects on the related final good market. This happens because final good producers will expand production to make the constraint faced by intermediate inputs less binding (Krishna, Roy and Thursby, 2001).

Verdier (1998) surveys the literature on results-oriented policies. He discusses the extensions to market structures that are richer than the duopoly case, endogenous threats and penalties that can benefit the country imposing them, and imperfect information. Krishna and Morgan (1998) consider an oligopolistic setting with multiple firms and find that a results-oriented policy can have procompetitive effects when the number of exporting firms exceeds the number of domestic firms.

14.10.4. VIEs: Trade Promotion or Protection?

VIEs are agreements requiring a targeted country to increase its imports through market opening measures. The agreement can specify quantities of imports or guarantee a specified domestic market share to a given exporter or to foreign countries in general. Targeted countries face trade retaliation if they fail to achieve the specified import targets. Because VIEs are market opening measures negotiated under the threat of sanctions, they have been labeled export protectionism by Jagdish Bhagwati, who has stressed that this form of market opening entails market distortions. The United States has negotiated VIEs in which Japan agrees to expand imports of automobiles (1982), semiconductors (1986), and auto parts (1992, 1995).

The US sanctions were not directed to the auto parts market that was at the center of the dispute, but rather to luxury automobiles. Why did the United States threaten punitive tariffs on luxury autos to implement a market share target in auto parts? Krishna and Morgan (1998) develop a duopoly model of Cournot competition that applies to auto parts suppliers selling to a single auto producer, such as when one US firm and one Japanese firm sell to a Japanese auto producer. They show that credible threats of imposing tariffs in the auto market are sufficient to implement a market share requirement in the auto parts market. In other words, the game's Nash equilibrium is consistent with the market share requirement. This happens because the Japanese firm in the auto parts market (i.e. the upstream market) prefers to abide by the target rather than suffer the indirect effects of the tariffs in the related car market (i.e. the downstream market). A key condition is that the tariff should be high enough to hit the foreign auto parts supplier sufficiently to 'voluntarily' accept the target market share.

Levinsohn (1997) utilizes the empirical framework of Berry *et al.* (1995) paper to model what would have been the effects of the sanctions policy. He estimates that the 100 percent tariff on the landed cost of the car would correspond to a 65 percent *ad valorem* tariff based on the list price, which is substantially larger than the landed price. The model, estimated using annual data from 1975 to 1994, implies that the 100 percent tariff would have reduced Japanese luxury car sales in the United States by about 75 percent. In other words, enforcing the US threat would have hit Japanese firms hard. Furthermore, US producers would not have been harmed because the price received by Japanese producers would have declined by less than 10 percent (and would have risen in some cases). Therefore, consumer prices would have increased almost as much as the tariff.

Who would have benefited from the sanctions? Because producers' prices would not have changed significantly, most benefits would have gone to third parties. Levinsohn estimated that European firms' profits would have increased by about 15 percent due to the switch from Japanese and American cars to European cars (that were not subject to the luxury car tariff).

14.11. CONCLUSIONS

Antidumping actions and other forms of contingent protection cause international trade frictions. Antidumping and antisubsidy measures can be viewed as elements integrating trade policies with competition policies. From this perspective, appropriately formulated reciprocal policies can improve world welfare. Anderson *et al.* (1995) develop a setup in which welfare externalities imply that countries lack the incentives to engage in welfare-improving reciprocal antidumping policies.

The targets of antidumping actions often argue that, in practice, contingent protection represents more a politically correct method of protection than enforcement of fair trade legislation or provision of insurance against market disruption. The empirical analysis reviewed in this chapter provided evidence that allegations of protectionism are often right on the target. Antidumping activity has proliferated, has spread to developing countries and estimated welfare costs are substantial. The costly expansion of antidumping activity creates incentives for affected parties to respond by either seeking to influence policy or avoid trade restrictions.

This chapter has also focused on policies and strategies formulated to influence trade policies and minimize the cost of protection. The formulation and implementation of policies addressing unfair trade involve substantial strategic, negotiation, and political economy elements. The same point applies to processes resulting in export protectionism (e.g. voluntary import expansions), trade restrictions, subsidies, foreign investment promotion aiming to defuse the threat of protection, and other policies that impact on international trade.

A major government strategy *vis-à-vis* trade restrictions is to negotiate market access under the threat of retaliation. Firms and interest groups respond to protection by entering into the political arena to influence political choices and obtain beneficial rather than damaging trade restrictions. The politics concerning how interest groups act to benefit from trade restrictions is examined next.

14.12. APPENDIX

14.12.1. Reciprocal Dumping Model

Domestic and foreign firms' profits π and π^* are

$$\pi(q, x) = qp(Q) + xp^*(Q^*) - c\left(q + \frac{x}{g}\right) - F,$$

$$\pi^*(q^*, x^*) = q^*p^*(Q^*) + x^*p(Q) - c\left(q^* + \frac{x^*}{g}\right) - F^*,$$

where $Q = q + x^*$, $Q^* = q^* + x$, and F and F^* denote fixed costs. The profit maximization problem's first order conditions with regard to q and x^* are

$$\frac{\partial \pi(q, x)}{\partial q} = q\frac{dp(Q)}{dQ} + p(Q) - c = 0,$$

$$\frac{\partial \pi^*(q^*, x^*)}{\partial x^*} = x^*\frac{dp(Q)}{dQ} + p(Q) - \frac{c}{g} = 0.$$

Manipulating the expressions yields

$$p(Q)\left[\frac{q}{Q}\frac{Q}{p(Q)}\frac{dp(Q)}{dQ} + 1\right] = c \rightarrow p\left[(1-\sigma)\left(-\frac{1}{\varepsilon}\right) + 1\right] = c$$

$$\rightarrow p(\sigma) = \frac{c\varepsilon}{\sigma - 1 + \varepsilon},$$

$$p(Q)\left[\frac{x^*}{Q}\frac{Q}{p(Q)}\frac{dp(Q)}{dQ} + 1\right] = \frac{c}{g} \rightarrow p\left[\sigma\left(-\frac{1}{\varepsilon}\right) + 1\right] = \frac{c}{g}$$

$$\rightarrow p(\sigma) = \frac{c\varepsilon}{g(\varepsilon - \sigma)},$$

where $\sigma = x^*/Q$ and $1/\varepsilon = -Q\,dp(Q)/[p(Q)\,dQ]$. Equating both expressions for p obtains σ

$$\frac{c\varepsilon}{\sigma - 1 + \varepsilon} = \frac{c\varepsilon}{g(\varepsilon - \sigma)} \rightarrow g(\varepsilon - \sigma) = \sigma - 1 + \varepsilon \rightarrow \sigma = \frac{1 - \varepsilon + g\varepsilon}{g + 1}.$$

Finally,

$$p = \frac{c\varepsilon}{\sigma - 1 + \varepsilon} = \frac{c\varepsilon}{(1 - \varepsilon + g\varepsilon)/(g + 1) - 1 + \varepsilon} = \frac{c\varepsilon(g + 1)}{g(2\varepsilon - 1)}.$$

PART V

TRADE POLITICS AND REGIONALISM

15

Trade Politics

For a long time, economists stayed away from the political analysis of regulation and trade policies. The theories of regulation developed by Stigler (1971), Peltzman (1976), and Becker (1983) focus on the determinants of interest group demand for regulation and the supply of it by legislators and regulators. Interest groups spend resources on lobbying in order to increase their income net of political contributions paid out. Legislators and regulators receive contributions and supply regulation in return. The equilibrium structure of regulation results from the balance between politicians' concern for population welfare and their wish to extract contributions from competing interest groups.

What are the political determinants and consequences of trade policies? Interest groups affect trade policy decisions through direct voting, by making political contributions helping elect a congenial government in a representative democracy, and by directly influencing policy choices. Lobbying and other political activities absorb resources and create trade distortions causing negative welfare effects.

The endogeneity of trade policy by way of interest group pressure helps understand why governments opt for inefficient trade policies and maintain them over long periods. Tariffs on import-competing products make consumers pay higher than world market prices in order to protect low-productivity industries. The persistence of protection to a declining industry is a function of the political strength of the lobbies representing industry interests. Competing domestic lobbies also affect international economic policy by influencing the choice between protection and unilateral, regional or multilateral trade liberalization.

Section 15.1 reviews the trade politics literature. Sections 15.2–15.4 present the protection for sale approach to the political equilibrium determining lobbies' contribution schemes and trade policies. Section 15.5 presents empirical tests of endogenous trade policy models. Sections 15.6–15.8 examine the role of lobbies in the formulation of trade policies determined noncooperatively (trade wars) and cooperatively (trade talks). Section 15.9 uses electoral competition and all-pay auction models to discuss the trade policy effects of restrictions on political contributions. Section 15.10 focuses on dynamic policies.

15.1. RENT-SEEKING AND ENDOGENOUS POLICY

Bhagwati (1982) examines directly unproductive activities (DUP) comprising a wide array of policy-related resource spending that is unproductive from a social point of view, but generates rents and revenues to interest groups or particular agents. Revenue-seeking activities, such as lobbying for export subsidies and tariff protection, aim to increase industry revenues (Bhagwati and Srinivasan, 1980; Feenstra and Bhagwati, 1982). Rent-seeking, such as lobbying for quotas, induces political interventions that do not directly generate revenues but protect an industry from foreign competition and generate windfall profits to the successful lobbying industry. A main example of rent seeking is lobbying for quantitative restrictions on competing imports. European quotas on imports of a wide array of agricultural products generate rents to European farmers. Long-standing US restrictions on sugar imports protect the beet sugar industry. Voluntary export restrictions (VERs) containing Japanese auto exports are designed to protect US auto industry.

The assessment of trade policies should take into account the social costs of production and consumption distortions and the costs of resources spent on directly unproductive activities. Krueger (1974) examines the negative effects of rent-seeking activity. She shows that, in the perfect competition case in which quotas and equivalent tariffs generate the same trade distortion, the welfare loss associated with quotas is greater than the loss associated with an equivalent tariff. Recall that quota profits accrue only to those who succeed in getting quota licenses. As a result, competition for quota licenses generates rent-seeking costs that are not present in the case of tariffs. The welfare costs of a quota program include the distortions it generates, the costs of getting the quota program approved, and the cost of the resources spent to obtain quota licenses.

The regulation and rent-seeking literatures spun off a vast literature on endogenous trade policies. In order to provide some perspective, this section sketches and contrasts the main features of various nonstrategic and strategic political models of policy formation. Hillman (1989), Vousden (1990), Helpman (1997), and Grossman and Helpman (2001, 2002c) contain further in-depth discussions of trade politics.

15.1.1. Direct Democracy

The direct democracy approach is based on the notion that direct voting on specific issues, such as holding a referendum on a measure, can adequately reflect voters' preferences. Mayer (1984b) follows an electoral approach in which tariff formation is the outcome of majority voting over alternative tariff rates. Tariffs are determined by the preferences of the median voter—the voter on the fiftieth percentile—who determines the election outcome. A 2 good and 2 factor model—the 2×2 Heckscher–Ohlin (HO) general equilibrium setup—is used to generate voter preferences for alternative tariff policies.

In the HO framework, each factor owner has an optimal tariff rate. Voters that are relatively well endowed (poorly endowed) with the factor that is intensively used in the import good, will vote for a positive (negative) import tariff. If the import-competing good is capital-intensive, individuals with a capital-to-labor endowment ratio exceeding the economy's capital–labor ratio vote for an import tariff benefiting the capital-intensive good. Individuals with a capital–labor ratio below the ratio for the whole economy vote for an import subsidy.

The distribution of factors of production affects voting preferences and thus the level and the sign of the equilibrium tariff rate (i.e. whether the optimal policy involves a tariff, subsidy, or nonintervention). If the distribution of the capital–labor ratio K/L is unimodal, the equilibrium tariff t^{median} is the tariff preferred by the median voter. Formally,

$$sign(t^{median}) = sign\left(\left(\frac{K}{L}\right)^{median} - \frac{K}{L}\right)$$

$$= sign\left(\left(\frac{K}{L}\right)^{median} - \left(\frac{K}{L}\right)^{mean}\right),$$

where each voter is assumed to have the same endowment of labor so that the economy's capital–labor ratio is equal to the mean capital–labor ratio across individuals.

In the HO model, the equilibrium tariff depends on the asymmetry of the distribution of the capital–labor ratio. If the distribution of the capital–labor ratio is unimodal and symmetric, the median capital–labor ratio coincides with the mean and free trade ensues. If the distribution is skewed to the left, a majority of voters have a capital–labor ownership ratio that exceeds the economy's ratio. The median voter has an above-average capital–labor ratio and majority voting results in an import tariff on capital intensive imports (or an import subsidy on labor intensive imports). If the distribution is skewed to the right, as for most countries, the capital–labor ratio of the median voter is below the economy's ratio and labor interests dominate voting. Labor intensive imports receive tariffs while capital intensive imports receive subsidies.

Can a small group of firms obtain tariff protection through electoral means? A potential majority against a tariff increase can become a minority of actual voters once voting costs and the probability of voting are taken into account (Peltzman, 1976). If the probability of voting is positively related to the net gains from voting and the majority expects to receive relatively small gains from casting a ballot, then electoral abstention can give the election to the interested minority.

15.1.2. Electoral Competition

The electoral competition approach considers explicit political parties and a set of lobbies intending to influence election results (Hillman, 1989; Magee *et al.*, 1989; Riezman and Wilson, 1997). Lobbies pay political contributions because they increase the election probability of the candidate supporting their interests.

An electoral competition model of policy choice consists of a two–stage game between politicians and lobbies. In the first stage, rival candidates announce a particular policy (e.g. a trade policy) that they are committed to implement if they get elected. Political parties choose the policies maximizing the probability of winning the election. In the second stage, lobbies decide on the amount of political contributions granted to the candidate advancing their interests. Political contributions are strategic variables used to help a candidate obtain votes and thus get elected. The level of contributions is set to maximize expected net lobby benefits taking as given the trade policy profiles presented by political parties.

As an illustration, consider the following two-stage tariff determination game. In the first stage, political party D chooses and announces a tariff policy t that maximizes the probability of election $p_D^{Election}$, which is a function of t and political contributions $C_D(t)$. In the second stage, lobbyists determine contributions to maximize lobby welfare W^{Lobby} taking as given the policy commitment made by party D. Formally,

$$\max_t p_D^{Election} = p_D(t, C_D(t)),$$

$$\max_{C_D} W^{Lobby}(t, C_D) \quad \rightarrow \quad C_D = C_D(t).$$

In the political competition approach, interest groups make contributions to increase the election probabilities of political parties. Interest groups do not aim to directly modify policy choices t, which are taken as given when contributions are strategically allocated in the second stage. However, the formulation of a political platform is indirectly influenced by the prospects of receiving political contributions. Politicians take into account that the choice of t affects the level of contributions received and thus election probabilities.

15.1.3. Tariff-formation Function

Trade policy formation can be viewed as a game in which players compete in political contributions. The equilibrium tariff is determined through a tariff-formation function relating an industry tariff to the contributions received from rival interest groups. In the case of a pro-protection and an anti-protection lobby, the tariff t is a function of contributions C_I and C_{II}

$$t = t(C_I, C_{II}).$$

The tariff-formation function is increasing in the political contributions made by the pro-protection lobby and decreasing in the contributions made by the anti-protection lobby. The equilibrium tariff is determined by a noncooperative Nash equilibrium in lobby contributions.

In the two-group model developed by Findlay and Wellisz (1982), one group lobbies for a tariff and the other lobbies for an export subsidy. The tariff-lobbying group owns factors that are specific to an import-competing industry. In the specific factor model, a higher price and greater output of the import-competing industry go hand in hand with a higher specific factor reward. The group lobbying for an export subsidy owns factors specific to an export industry and thus lobbies against the tariff. The two groups devote labor resources to political activities intending to influence policy.

The tariff-formation function is often called a black-box or reduced form in the sense that the electoral or political process behind tariff determination is left unspecified.

Instead, the tariff rate is directly related to rival interest groups lobbying efforts. The tariff-formation approach is in principle consistent with both electoral and influence motives in representative democracies.

15.1.4. Political Support Maximization

The political support function approach focuses on an incumbent government (Hillman, 1982; Long and Vousden, 1991). Tariffs are determined by the maximization of a political support function *PS* that depends on the tariff rate. Formally,

$$\max_t PS(t) = PS[W^{Lobby}(t), W^P(t)].$$

Political support increases with (1) population welfare W^P, and (2) interest group income or welfare W^{Lobby}. Population welfare declines with a higher tariff level but lobby welfare increases with the tariff level. The government faces a trade off between the political support obtained from the population and from interest groups. The government-contributors strategic game does not acknowledge elections or candidates' positions explicitly. However, electoral competition in a representative democracy, and the role of contributions in keeping the government in power, are implicit elements of this approach.

15.1.5. Protection for Sale and Common Agency

The protection for sale approach combines an influence-driven contribution approach with a political support function. Lobbies move first. Their political strategy is to design contribution schedules that are contingent on government future policy and aim to manipulate government actions. In a later stage, the government determines policies on the basis of a political support function taking the contribution schedules as given.

Consider a two-stage game in which a single lobby manipulates government choices. In the first stage, the lobby designs a contribution schedule $C(t)$ setting contributions as a function of the tariff level chosen by the government. This schedule is designed to maximize net lobby welfare $W_{Net}^{Lobby}(t)$, defined as gross lobby welfare $W_{Gross}^{Lobby}(t)$ minus contributions made $C(t)$

$$\max_{C(t)} W_{Net}^{Lobby}(t) = W_{Gross}^{Lobby}(t) - C(t).$$

In the second stage, the government chooses the tariff level that maximizes its welfare $W^G(t)$, taking the contribution schedule $C(t)$ as given

$$\max_t W^G(t) = W^G(C(t), W^P(t)),$$

where $W^P(t)$ is population welfare. Notice that $W^G(t)$ can be interpreted as a political support function.

The contribution schedule formulation, specifying contribution levels as a function of the tariff rate, contrasts with the tariff-formation function specifying the tariff level as a function of contributions. It also differs from electoral competition approaches in which a candidate announces its policy first and lobbyists subsequently determine political contributions, taking policy as given, on the basis of electoral-outcome considerations about who gets elected.

The protection for sale framework is an instance of the common agency approach to political behavior. Agency models provide a framework to formalize the role of interest groups in a political equilibrium. The simplest agency relationship involves one principal and one agent acting on behalf of the principal. A more complex relationship is the single principal–multiple agent structure. For instance, in the employer–employee relationship, the employer is the single principal and the employees are agents.

Common agency is a multilateral relationship involving a single agent and several principals. For instance, the principals can be interest groups and voters who simultaneously try to influence the actions of an agent such as Congress or government officials. Dixit *et al.* (1997) develop a general model of common agency involving special interests that lobby the government for taxes, subsidies, and transfers.

15.1.6. The Free-riding Problem

Lobby influence is moderated by a free-rider problem and coordination costs. A free-rider problem arises from the public good nature of lobbying activity. An agent that lobbies for a tariff applying to a whole industry will find out that other industry members reap most benefits from its lobbying efforts. As a result, the Nash equilibrium lobbying effort is reduced. From the industry perspective, lobbying will be underprovided and the resulting tariff rate will be too low. In principle, the free-rider problem can be solved by coordinating efforts across the industry but this requires incurring fixed and variable coordination costs. The free-rider model implies that industries benefiting from a protective tariff are those facing smaller lobby coordination costs.

Rodrik (1986) examines free riding in an industry using capital as specific factor. The owners of capital benefit from a tariff level $t = t(L)$ that increases with the total amount of labor L spent on lobbying. This tariff formation function embodies a free-rider problem because an owner of capital will benefit from industry spending even if he or she does not spend at all.

Alternatively, owner i can lobby individually by pushing for a firm-specific production subsidy $s^i = s(L^i)$, which increases with i's labor resource spending rather than with industry spending. The specific subsidy solution avoids both the free-riding problem and the costs of coordination. Furthermore, production subsidies do not distort consumption and are thus preferable to tariffs from a welfare point of view. In practice, firm-specific subsidies such as loans to firms and regional assistance are quantitatively important. In the late 1970s, firm-specific subsidies accounted for about 50 percent of all subsidies in Sweden and Italy and 32 percent in Great Britain (Carlsson, 1983).

A model of protection must not only explain why governments bestow benefits to import-competing industries, but also why these benefits take the form of tariff protection rather than specific-subsidies. A political equilibrium might involve a tariff rather than a firm-specific production subsidy because the free-rider problem implies that the equilibrium tariff rate is low relative to the equilibrium firm-specific subsidy rate. The tariff and specific-subsidy regimes can be compared by using a social welfare function that treats all individuals equally. From the perspective of politicians (candidates or governments) a low tariff rate might entail smaller social costs than subsidization. Therefore, when free riding sufficiently undermines interest groups' lobbying efforts, the government has welfare incentives to precommit to tariff protection only.

15.2. TRADE POLICY WITH SPECIFIC FACTORS

The general equilibrium model based on the specific factor model of production (Mussa, 1974; Neary, 1978) underlies much of the work on political economy. In the simple model developed here, a specific factor reward increases with the domestic price of the commodity in which it is used. This feature implies that the interests of the owners of a specific factor are aligned with the interests of the employing industry. The politics resulting from the specific factor model are consistent with observed lobbying behavior, which explains the widespread use of this model in political analysis.

15.2.1. Consumer Problem

Individuals are assumed to display identical preferences but differ in their income. Individual i maximizes a quadratic utility function subject to a budget constraint

$$\max_{d_0, d_I, d_{II}} U^i(\cdot) = d_0 + u^i(d_I, d_{II}) = d_0 + (d_I + d_{II}) - \tfrac{1}{2}(d_I^2 + d_{II}^2) \tag{15.1}$$

$$\text{s.t } d_0 + p_I d_I + p_{II} d_{II} \leq y^i,$$

where d_0 is the numeraire (its price p_0 is set equal to 1), commodities D_I and D_{II} have domestic prices p_I and p_{II}, and the consumer has income y^i.

The direct demand functions associated with (15.1) are

$$d_0(p_I, p_{II}, y^i) = y^i - (p_I d_I + p_{II} d_{II}), \tag{15.2}$$

$$d_I(p_I) = 1 - p_I, \qquad d_{II}(p_{II}) = 1 - p_{II},$$

which display the simplifying feature that d_I and d_{II} depend only on their own price while residual income is spent on good 0.

The indirect utility function v^i is equal to individual spending y^i plus consumer surplus CS^i

$$v^i(p_I, p_{II}, y^i) = y^i + CS^i(p_I, p_{II})$$

$$= y^i + u^i(d_I(p_I), d_{II}(p_{II})) - p_I d_I(p_I) - p_{II} d_{II}(p_{II}),$$

where consumer surplus represents the excess of total utility over total spending. The numeraire cancels out from CS^i because its contribution to utility (d_0) equals spending on it ($p_0 d_0 = d_0$). As a result, CS^i depends only on the price vector (p_I, p_{II}) and has the same value for all individuals $i \in \{1, \ldots, N\}$ in the population.

Substituting the direct demand functions $d_I(p_I) = 1 - p_I$ and $d_{II}(p_{II}) = 1 - p_{II}$ in (15.2) into $v^i(p_I, p_{II}, y^i)$ yields (see appendix)

$$v^i(p_I, p_{II}, y^i) = y^i + \frac{(1 - p_I)^2 + (1 - p_{II})^2}{2}.$$

15.2.2. Factors, Rewards, and Output

Technologies display constant returns to scale. Numeraire production Q_0 is assumed to require a single labor input L_0 with an input–output coefficient equal to one. Production of goods I and II requires labor and an input that is specific to each industry. We assume that the production of good I requires physical capital K (but no human capital H) whereas good II utilizes human capital H (but no physical capital K). In other words, physical capital is specific to industry I while human capital is specific to industry II. Formally,

$$Q_0 = L_0, \qquad Q_I = AL_I^{1/2}\bar{K}^{1/2}, \qquad Q_{II} = AL_{II}^{1/2}\bar{H}^{1/2}.$$

All factors are supplied inelastically at levels $\bar{L} = L_0 + L_I + L_{II}, \bar{K}$ and $\bar{H}$.

In the specific factor model considered, the equilibrium rewards $r(p_I)$ and $w_H(p_{II})$ to physical capital and human capital are (see appendix)

$$r(p_I) = \left(\frac{p_I A}{2}\right)^2, \qquad w_H(p_{II}) = \left(\frac{p_{II} A}{2}\right)^2. \tag{15.3}$$

Specific factor rewards depend uniquely and positively on the domestic price of the commodity in which they are used. This feature implies that the interests of the owners of a specific factor are aligned with the interests of the industry that employs it.

Industry output is obtained from the relation indicating that output Q_I (or Q_{II}) is equal to the derivative of the aggregate specific factor reward $r\bar{K}$ (or $w_H\bar{H}$) with respect to the output price p_I (or p_{II}). Formally (see appendix),

$$Q_I = \frac{d(r(p_I)\bar{K})}{dp_I} = \frac{p_I A^2 \bar{K}}{2}, \qquad Q_{II} = \frac{d(w_H(p_{II})\bar{H})}{dp_{II}} = \frac{p_{II} A^2 \bar{H}}{2}. \tag{15.4}$$

In a competitive equilibrium with specific factors, an industry output depends positively on industry price and the endowment of the specific factor used in the industry. In contrast, when there are no specific factors, each industry's output might depend on all factor endowments in the economy.

15.2.3. Trade Instruments, Prices, and Transfers

Suppose that policy instruments are limited to *ad valorem* trade taxes and subsidies in any of the nonnumeraire goods. Trade policy influences domestic relative prices and can thus be used as a tool to redistribute rents among different sectors in society.

Let us clarify how trade policies affect domestic prices of final goods. An *ad valorem* trade tax or subsidy t_i opens a gap between the domestic price p_i and the exogenously given world price p_i^W,

$$p_i = (1 + t_i)p_i^W \rightarrow t_i = \frac{p_i - p_i^W}{p_i^W}, \quad i \in \{I, II\},$$

where t_i can be positive, negative or zero (i.e. free trade). The domestic and world prices of the numeraire, p_0 and p_0^W, are set equal to 1. Specifically,

$$\left.\begin{matrix} \text{import tariffs } (t_i > 0) \\ \text{export subsidies } (s_i > 0) \end{matrix}\right\} \implies p_i > p_i^W,$$

$$\left.\begin{matrix} \text{import subsidies } (t_i < 0) \\ \text{export taxes } (s_i < 0) \end{matrix}\right\} \implies p_i < p_i^W,$$

where an export subsidy $s_i > 0$ can be viewed as a negative tax $t_i < 0$ on a negative import $M_i < 0$.

Import tariffs and export subsidies benefit domestic producers by increasing domestic prices above world market prices. A subsidized exporter receives an export subsidy when it sells abroad but not when it sells in its home market. A higher domestic price must thus offset the export subsidy received when selling abroad. If higher domestic prices did not fully offset export subsidies, producers would not have incentives to sell in the domestic market. Helping domestic producers compete abroad by subsidizing their exports results in higher prices paid by domestic consumers.

Import subsidies and export taxes benefit domestic consumers by lowering domestic prices below world prices. For instance, export taxes impose additional costs to output sold abroad and thus reduce domestic prices below world levels. Developing countries often tax the exports of basic agricultural products to lower food prices paid by domestic consumers.

Tariffs (subsidies) generate positive (negative) government revenues. The government redistributes all taxes collected to the public and raises all subsidy financing by lump sum taxes. Assume that taxes are uniformly redistributed or imposed, meaning that all individuals receive or pay the same net transfer. The per capita government transfer to or from the population, $tr(p_I, p_{II})$, is equal to net per capita revenues from all *ad valorem* trade taxes and subsidies. Because per capita imports (exports correspond to negative imports) are defined as the sum of the gaps between each commodity's per capita consumption and production, $d_i - Q_i(p_i)/N$, per capita transfers are

$$tr = t_I p_I^W M_I + t_{II} p_{II}^W M_{II} = \frac{p_I - p_I^W}{p_I^W} p_I^W M_I + \frac{p_{II} - p_{II}^W}{p_{II}^W} p_{II}^W M_{II}$$

$$= (p_I - p_I^W)\left[d_I(p_I) - \frac{Q_I(p_I)}{N}\right] + (p_{II} - p_{II}^W)\left[d_{II}(p_{II}) - \frac{Q_{II}(p_{II})}{N}\right]$$

$$= (p_I - p_I^W)\left[1 - p_I - \frac{p_I A^2 \bar{K}}{2N}\right] + (p_{II} - p_{II}^W)\left[1 - p_{II} - \frac{p_{II} A^2 \bar{H}}{2N}\right],$$

$$(15.5)$$

where the population size is denoted by N and the latter equality is obtained using (15.2) and (15.4).

15.3. POLICY UNDER THE INFLUENCE

Specific factor owners pay out political contributions to influence policy design on their own behalf. Political contributions express a lobby's demand for protection by the government.

15.3.1. Contribution and Policy Stages

Trade policies are determined in a two-stage political equilibrium. Consider a game with a single lobby made up of the N_K owners of physical capital K, the specific factor operating in industry I. The lobby is a first mover that knows the government object-ive function and can influence trade policy decisions in the second stage. The model is solved by backward induction to produce a subgame perfect equilibrium. Because tariffs and subsidies are reflected in the gaps between domestic prices and exogen-ously given foreign prices, the contribution schedule and welfare can be expressed as functions of the domestic price vector $p = (p_I, p_{II})$.

In the first stage, the owners-of-capital lobby maximizes its members' net-of-contributions welfare W_{Net}^K by formulating a schedule of political contributions establishing the funds to be allocated to politicians as a function of trade policies. Lobby welfare coincides with the welfare of the owners of capital. Formally, the first-stage problem is

$$\max_{C^K(p)} W_{Net}^K(p) = W_{Gross}^K(p) - C^K(p),$$

$$= \sum_{k=1}^{N_K} \bar{l}^k + r(p_I)\bar{K} + \alpha_K N[tr(p) + CS^i(p)] - C^K(p), \quad (15.6)$$

where net-of-contribution welfare is defined as gross lobby welfare W_{Gross}^K minus polit-ical contributions C^K. The gross-of-contribution welfare level W_{Gross}^K is defined as

(1) the sum of the N_K lobby members' labor endowments $\bar{l}^k$ (the wage rate is normalized to one), (2) the reward on the endowment of physical capital, $r\bar{K}$, and (3) the share $\alpha_K = N_K/N$ of the sum of total transfers Ntr plus total consumer surplus NCS^i, where α_K is the fraction of the population affiliated to the lobby.

In the second stage, the government chooses the domestic price vector that maximizes the welfare or political support function $W^G(p)$, taking the whole contribution schedule $C^K(p)$ as given. Government welfare depends on (1) a given contribution schedule $C^K(p)$ designed by the capital owners' lobby and (2) voters' aggregate welfare $W^P(p)$, which can be interpreted as the welfare of the average voter.

The second stage problem is

$$\max_{p} W^G(p) = C^K(p) + \phi W^P(p), \quad \phi \geq 0, \tag{15.7}$$

where the parameter ϕ denotes the weight that the government places on population welfare relative to political contributions. If $\phi = 0$, then policy formation is driven by political contributions alone.

Population welfare comprises both organized lobby members and unorganized voters. The analysis assumes a well-defined class structure in the sense that no agent is allowed to have endowments of both human and physical capital. Moreover, the endowment of physical or human capital possessed by each individual is assumed to be nontransferable and indivisible. The aggregate welfare W^P of a population of size N is defined as total income received plus aggregate consumers' surplus

$$W^P(p) = \bar{L} + r(p_I)\bar{K} + w_H(p_{II})\bar{H} + Ntr(p_I, p_{II}) + CS(p_I, p_{II}), \tag{15.8}$$

where w is normalized to one ($w\bar{L} = \bar{L}$), and $CS = NCS^i$ is the sum of the N individuals' consumer surpluses.

15.3.2. Free Trade in the Absence of Lobbies

Consider a small competitive economy in which there are no lobbies making contributions to politicians. In the absence of contributions, the government problem consists of maximizing the population's aggregate welfare W^P, ignoring interest group preferences.

The government problem is

$$\max_{p} W^G = W^P = \bar{L} + r(p)\bar{K} + w_H(p)\bar{H} + Ntr(p) + NCS(p),$$

where $p = p(p_I, p_{II})$. The first order conditions yield (see appendix)

$$\frac{\partial W^G}{\partial p_I} = 0 \ \rightarrow \ (p_I - p_I^W)\left[-N - \frac{A^2\bar{K}}{2}\right] = 0 \ \rightarrow \ p_I^N = p_I^W,$$

$$\frac{\partial W^G}{\partial p_{II}} = 0 \ \rightarrow \ (p_{II} - p_{II}^W)\left[-N - \frac{A^2\bar{H}}{2}\right] = 0 \ \rightarrow \ p_{II}^N = p_{II}^W.$$

If there are no lobbies or contributions, then the equilibrium coincides with free trade. The first-best (i.e. the social optimum) is attained because lobby pressures do not impose any externality on society. The optimality of free trade results from the small country, perfect competition, and lack of externalities assumptions. Optimality breaks down if the country has monopoly power in some good, there is imperfect competition inducing strategic trade policy, or there are production externalities.

15.3.3. Political Equilibrium Concept

The concept of 'protection for sale' hinges on the notion that an incumbent government obtains political support by selling privileges that increase interest groups' welfare. The protection for sale approach differs in key aspects from the strategic trade policy approach. In the latter, the government plays first and maximizes population welfare by setting a subsidy function $s(Q)$ specifying the subsidy granted as a function of output (or exports). In the second stage, firms determine output given the subsidy function. In the political model, the government does not simply maximize social welfare, but rather social welfare plus political contributions. The lobby plays first and its political contribution schedule $C^K(p)$ is used to manipulate the government, which sets policy in the second stage of the game given the contribution schedule designed by the lobby.

A subgame perfect Nash equilibrium is defined by a contribution scheme and a government price rule embodying trade policy choices. The equilibrium contribution scheme $C^{K,N}(p)$ maximizes lobby welfare given the anticipated government decision rule $p^N(C^K(p))$. The equilibrium price vector p^N maximizes government welfare given the lobby's contribution scheme $C^{K,N}(p)$. The contribution scheme represents a commitment made by the lobby to induce the government to set the price vector maximizing lobby welfare.

Proposition 1 (Grossman and Helpman, 1994; Bernheim and Whinston, 1986a). The pair $\{C^{K,N}(p), p^N\}$, consisting of an equilibrium contribution function and an equilibrium domestic price vector, is a subgame perfect Nash equilibrium of the trade policy game if the following four conditions hold.

(i) Feasibility of contributions. The lobby contribution schedule must satisfy two conditions: (a) contributions must be nonnegative, and (b) contributions cannot exceed the total income Y^K available to the N_K lobby members. Formally,

$$0 \leq C^{K,N}(p) \leq Y^K.$$

(ii) The government chooses the price vector (and hence the optimal trade policy) that maximizes its welfare, taking as given the lobby's contribution schedule. Formally, the equilibrium price p^N is given by

$$p^N = (p_I^N, p_{II}^N) \in \arg\max_p W^G(p) = C^{K,N}(p) + \phi W^P(p). \tag{15.9}$$

Assuming that the contribution schedule is differentiable with respect to prices around the equilibrium, the first order conditions for the government maximization problem are

$$\frac{\partial W^G(p^N)}{\partial p_i} = \frac{\partial C^K(p^N)}{\partial p_i} + \phi \frac{\partial W^P(p^N)}{\partial p_i} = 0, \quad i \in \{I, II\}. \tag{15.10}$$

(iii) The equilibrium price vector p^N maximizes the sum of lobby and government welfare

$$p^N \in \arg\max_p W_{Net}^K(p) + W^G(p) = W_{Gross}^K(p) + \phi W^P(p), \tag{15.11}$$

where $W_{Net}^K = W_{Gross}^K(p) - C^K(p)$ is lobby welfare net of contributions paid. Contributions cancel out because they simply represent a reallocation of resources between the government and the lobby. The first order conditions associated with (15.11) are

$$\frac{\partial W_{Net}^K(p^N)}{\partial p_i} + \frac{\partial W^G(p^N)}{\partial p_i} = \frac{\partial W_{Gross}^K(p^N)}{\partial p_i} + \phi \frac{\partial W^P(p^N)}{\partial p_i} = 0. \tag{15.12}$$

Given the government welfare-maximizing condition $\partial W^G(p^N)/\partial p_I = \partial W^G(p^N)/\partial p_{II} = 0$ in (15.10), the coalition maximization condition (15.12) implies that the price maximizing net lobby welfare must be the same as the price maximizing joint lobby-government welfare. Notice that joint maximization coincides with separate maximization of lobby and government welfare because the government-lobby coalition does not generate any externalities and the joint welfare is simply the sum of the separate welfare levels.

The condition requiring the equilibrium price to maximize the joint welfare of the lobby and the government can be rationalized by viewing the government and the lobby as a coalition. It is optimal for them to maximize their joint welfare and then redistribute the welfare gains by means of contributions transferring funds from the lobby to the government. To see why, suppose that the government chooses a price p that does not maximize joint welfare. The lobby could then redefine the contribution schedule to pay the government an infinitesimal amount if the government would change the policy. The government increases its welfare due to the additional contribution, while the lobby gets the additional joint surplus, $W_{Net}^K(p^N) + W^G(p^N) - W_{Net}^K(p) - W^G(p)$, minus the additional contribution.

(iv) There exists a (nonequilibrium) price vector p^0 that maximizes the government objective function $W^G(p)$ and does not induce transfers to the government under the equilibrium contribution schedule (i.e. $C^{K,N}(p^0) = 0$ so that $W^G(p^0) = \phi W^P(p^0)$).

This condition requires the existence of a policy p^0 that does not induce lobby contributions and the government finds equally attractive as the equilibrium policy p^N. The policy p^0 does not represent an equilibrium because it does not maximize lobby welfare. In the single lobby case, free trade prices satisfy condition (iv). A single lobby that moves first has a monopoly position that permits extracting the whole joint lobby-government surplus generated by trade intervention relative to free trade. This surplus extraction property implies that free trade with no political contributions will produce the same welfare to the government as intervention. Of course, free trade will not be an equilibrium because the lobby will have incentives to make a contribution to induce the government to increase the domestic price of the organized industry.

Recapping, the previous analysis implies that, when there is trade intervention, a single lobby that moves first gets the whole surplus accruing to the lobby-politicians coalition, net of the contributions needed to induce the government to choose the political equilibrium policy. The required contribution is *smaller* than the increase in the joint lobby-politician welfare resulting from the implementation of the optimal price, so that the lobby reaps gains from forming a coalition with the politicians. Population welfare, however, goes down.

15.3.4. Government Participation Constraint

The lobby contribution function should satisfy a participation constraint ensuring that the government is willing to play the political contribution game. The participation constraint makes sure that government welfare in the presence of contributions is no less than the maximum level of population welfare attainable in the absence of contributions

$$W^G(p^N) = C^K(p^N) + \phi W^P(p^N) \geq \max_p [\phi W^P(p)] = \phi W^P(p^W). \qquad (15.13)$$

In the single lobby case, condition (15.13) is binding. The lobby to government transfer will be the minimum required to influence the policy outcome.

15.3.5. Truthful Contribution Schedules

Consider a political equilibrium implementing price vector p^N and assume that the contribution schedule $C^K(p^N)$ is differentiable around the equilibrium vector p^N. The effect of a small policy change on the contribution is equal to the impact of a small policy change on the lobby's gross welfare level

$$\frac{\partial C^K(p^N)}{\partial p_I} = \frac{\partial W^K_{Gross}(p^N)}{\partial p_I}, \qquad \frac{\partial C^K(p^N)}{\partial p_{II}} = \frac{\partial W^K_{Gross}(p^N)}{\partial p_{II}}. \qquad (15.14)$$

The previous equations are obtained using first order conditions (15.12) and (15.10). For instance, adding $\partial C^K(p^N)/\partial p_I - \partial C^K(p^N)/\partial p_I$ to the right-hand side of (15.12) and using (15.10) yields $\partial W^K_{Gross}(p^N)/\partial p_I - \partial C^K(p^N)/\partial p_I = 0$.

Contribution schemes satisfying condition (15.14) are known as *locally* truthful because each lobby sets its contribution schedule so that the *marginal* change in the contribution in response to changes in policy is equal to the *marginal* effect of the policy change on the lobby's gross welfare. The notion of local truthfulness means that the lobby's marginal preferences are reflected in the marginal contribution at the equilibrium point. In other words, the lobby finds it optimal to reveal, through its contribution schedule, its true marginal preferences regarding government trade policies.

A contribution schedule that indicates lobby preferences in the sense of the welfare level achieved *at each possible price* is called a truthful contribution schedule. It reveals preferences everywhere (i.e. at each price) rather than just revealing marginal preferences locally (i.e. at the equilibrium point). The truthful contribution function corresponds to the gap (if positive) between gross lobby welfare and a required base level of net lobby welfare B^K. Formally,

$$C^K(p, B^K) = \max\{W^K_{Gross}(p) - B^K, 0\}. \tag{15.15}$$

Notice that, given a constant B^K, if the nonnegativity constraint is not binding, the sum $C^K(p, B^K) + B^K$ measures gross lobby welfare corresponding to each possible price. Because $W^K_{Gross}(p)$ is assumed to be differentiable and B^K is a constant, the truthful contribution schedule must be differentiable except when it is equal to zero.

15.3.6. Truthful Nash Equilibria and Policy Choice

A Nash equilibrium supported by a truthful contribution schedule is known as a Truthful Nash Equilibrium (TNE). The equilibrium contribution scheme maximizes lobby welfare evaluated at the equilibrium government policy.

How should the lobby design the contribution function to effectively influence government decisions? The optimal contribution schedule maximizes base welfare $B^{K,TNE}$ subject to the restriction that the contribution schedule implements a price maximizing joint lobby-government welfare. The lobby aims to maximize B^K, and thus to minimize the contribution, without inducing the government to deviate from the equilibrium to an alternative price vector that harms the lobby.

Formally, the constant $B^{K,TNE}$ is obtained as the maximum value satisfying the constraint that the joint lobby-government welfare at equilibrium prices is greater than under any other alternative price vector

$$B^{K,TNE} = \max B^K$$

s.t.

$$\begin{aligned}
C^K\left(p^{TNE}, B^K\right) + \phi W^P\left(p^{TNE}\right) &= W^K_{Gross}\left(p^{TNE}\right) - B^K + \phi W^P\left(p^{TNE}\right) \\
&\geq W^K_{Gross}(p) - B^K + \phi W^P(p) \\
&= C^K(p, B^K) + \phi W^P(p)
\end{aligned}$$

If the lobby contribution function is truthful and the nonnegativity constraint is not binding in (15.15), then the equilibrium price p^{TNE} in (15.9) is given by

$$p^{TNE} = \arg\max_{p} \left[C^{K,TNE}(p) + \phi W^P(p) \right]$$

$$= \arg\max_{p} \left[W^K_{Gross}(p) - B^{K,TNE} + \phi W^P(p) \right]$$

$$= \arg\max_{p} \left[W^K_{Gross}(p) + \phi W^P(p) \right] - B^{K,TNE}. \qquad (15.16)$$

Because B^K is a constant and does not affect the maximization, the first order conditions are given by (15.12).

Expression (15.8) implies that population welfare W^P is the sum of the capitalist lobby gross-of-contribution welfare W^K_{Gross} and the level of welfare W^H achieved by owners of human capital (the specific factor in the unorganized sector),

$$W^P(p) \equiv W^K_{Gross}(p) + W^H(p).$$

The equilibrium condition (15.16) can thus be rewritten as

$$p^{TNE} = \arg\max_{p}(1 + \phi)W^K_{Gross}(p) + \phi W^H(p). \qquad (15.17)$$

In a truthful Nash equilibrium (i.e. under a TNE contribution scheme), the government chooses the optimal policy by maximizing a welfare function in which the weight $(1 + \phi)$ attached to lobby members exceeds the weight ϕ given to individuals who are not lobby members.

15.4. EQUILIBRIUM TRADE POLICIES AND LOBBIES

What is the role of competition among lobbies in the determination of trade policies? Consider equilibria with no lobbies, a single lobby and multiple lobbies. When there are no lobby contributions, free trade prevails.

When there is a single lobby, the organized sector always benefits from a higher domestic price, achieved by (1) protection through an import tariff if the sector is an importing sector, or (2) subsidization through an export subsidy if the sector is an exporting sector. The price of the unorganized sector in which the lobby is a net buyer is lowered through either (1) an export tax, or (2) an import subsidy. When there is a single lobby, the government keeps an infinitesimal surplus, relative to free trade, that is large enough to induce intervention.

When there are multiple lobbies, organized sectors receive trade benefits while unorganized sectors suffer from negative protection. In the extreme case in which all sectors have lobbies and all voters are active buyers of influence, all lobbies make positive contributions but lobby competition leads to free trade. Lobby competition allows the government to capture the entire surplus from intervention.

15.4.1. Trade Intervention as a Political Equilibrium

In the presence of political pressures, equilibrium trade policy consists of a pair of domestic prices $(p_I^{TNE}, p_{II}^{TNE})$ maximizing the joint welfare level of the lobby (net of contributions) and the government. Equivalently, the price pair maximizes the sum of gross lobby welfare and population welfare, as given by (15.16). The small country assumption ensures that trade policies are driven by political motives rather than by the attempt to exploit monopoly or terms of trade effects.

Grossman and Helpman (1994) show that the determination of an industry's price can be specified using the indicator function I_i telling whether industry i is organized or not. Specifically, $I_i = 1$ if i has a lobby and $I_i = 0$ if i does not have a lobby. The combination of trade taxes or subsidies that maximize joint lobby-government welfare can be summarized by the following formula specifying industry i price (see appendix)

$$\frac{p_i - p_i^W}{p_i} = \frac{\alpha_K - I_i}{p_i(\alpha_K + \phi)} \frac{Q_i}{\partial M_i / \partial p_i} = \frac{I_i - \alpha_K}{\alpha_K + \phi} \frac{Q_i}{M_i \varepsilon_i}, \qquad i \in \{I, II\}, \qquad (15.18)$$

where $\varepsilon_i = -[p_i/M_i][\partial M_i/\partial p_i]$ represents the elasticity of import demand or the elasticity of export supply. The superscripts indicating equilibrium are ignored for notational simplicity.

The product $M_i \varepsilon_i$ is always positive because the property $\partial M_i / \partial p_i < 0$ implies that (1) if $M_i > 0$ (i is an import-competing sector) the elasticity of imports ε_i is positive, and (2) if $M_i < 0$ (i is an export sector), the elasticity ε_i is negative. Because $M_i \varepsilon_i > 0$, we obtain

$$sign(p_i - p_i^W) = sign(I_i - \alpha_K).$$

An organized sector ($I_i = 1$ and $I_i - \alpha_K > 0$) benefits from a higher domestic price than the world price. Producers in an unorganized sector ($I_i = 0$ and $I_i - \alpha_K < 0$) receive a domestic price below the world price.

The structure of trade policies depends on whether the country exports or imports the good that uses capital as specific factor. Suppose that the domestic country imports the good that uses capital as a specific factor ($M_I > 0$) and exports the good that uses human capital as specific factor ($M_{II} < 0$). Let us use $p_i = (1 + t_i)p_i^W$ to translate prices into trade intervention instruments t_i. The equilibrium trade policy $t = (t_I, t_{II})$ satisfies

$$\frac{t_I}{1 + t_I} = \frac{1 - \alpha_K}{\phi + \alpha_K} \frac{Q_I}{M_I \varepsilon_I} \quad \rightarrow \quad t_I > 0,$$

$$\frac{t_{II}}{1 + t_{II}} = \frac{-\alpha_K}{\phi + \alpha_K} \frac{Q_{II}}{M_{II} \varepsilon_{II}} \quad \rightarrow \quad t_{II} < 0,$$

where $M_i \varepsilon_i > 0$.

At equilibrium, the lobby representing the interests of the owners of physical capital pays out contributions inducing authorities to establish an import tariff ($t_I > 0$). The tariff supports a higher price in the import-competing sector and increases the reward on capital. Moreover, authorities tax exports ($t_{II} < 0$) thus lowering the price of exportables, reducing the reward on human capital and benefiting the capitalist lobby, which is implicitly a net buyer of human capital.

Recapping, equilibrium policies can be interpreted as a political pressure index, in the sense that the structure of trade policies allows an observer to determine which sector is making political contributions. The sector using physical capital as specific input pays out contributions and benefits from an import tariff or an export subsidy whereas the unorganized human capital-intensive sector is slapped with a price-reducing export tax or import subsidy.

15.4.2. Predictive Content

The rate of protection in the organized physical capital sector is greater

(1) the lower the share α_K of lobby members in the total population. In order to illustrate this result notice that if α_K is near one, the surplus of the citizens belonging to the lobby coincides with population welfare, which encourages minimizing protection;

(2) the smaller the weight ϕ assigned to population's welfare. A smaller weight assigned to population welfare implies a lower weight given to economic distortions and greater willingness to grant distorting trade benefits;

   The unorganized sector tariff though, is higher the lower the unorganized sector's output-to-import ratio (the greater the import penetration ratio or the lower the absolute value of the output-to-export ratio (where $M_2 < 0$);

(3) the greater the organized sector's output-to-import ratio Q_I/M_I (the lower the import penetration ratio M_I/Q_I) or the greater the absolute value of the output-to-export ratio Q_I/M_I (where $M_I < 0$). First, higher protected sector output implies larger lobby gains from higher prices. Second, the lower the volume of imports, the smaller the economic losses from protection, which makes the government more willing to protect. Notice that this prediction stands in contradiction with the common idea that greater import penetration encourages stronger protection. The unorganized sector tariff, though, is higher the lower the unorganized sector's output-to-import ratio (the greater the import penetration ratio) or the lower the absolute value of the output-to-export ratio (where $M_{II} < 0$);

(4) the lower the import demand elasticity $\varepsilon_I = -[p_I/M_I][\partial M_I/\partial p_I] > 0$ and the lower the absolute value of the elasticity of the supply of exports $\varepsilon_I = -[p_I/M_I][\partial M_I/\partial p_I] < 0$. More inelastic imports and exports lead to greater protection. The intuition is that the deadweight losses from protection are smaller the lower the import or export elasticity, which makes the government more willing to grant protection.

The link between a lower import elasticity and a higher tariff illustrates a general principle in public finance. Welfare maximization implies that goods with more inelastic demand should be taxed at higher proportional taxes (known as Ramsey taxes in this context). Inelastic demands justify higher proportional tax rates because they lead to smaller changes in consumption and thus to lower welfare losses from taxes.

Multiple Lobbies
In the case of multiple lobbies, domestic prices are given by

$$\frac{p_i - p_i^W}{p_i} = \frac{I_i - \sum_j^J \alpha_j}{\phi + \sum_j^J \alpha_j} \frac{Q_i}{M_i \varepsilon_i},$$

where J is the number of sector-specific inputs and $\sum \alpha_j$ is the fraction of people owning sector-specific inputs.

Organized industries ($I_i = 1$) receive trade benefits while unorganized industries ($I_i = 0$) suffer from negative protection. Notice that in the multiple lobby case, protection to each organized industry i depends on the fraction of voters $\sum \alpha_j$ that belong to some lobby rather than on the fraction of voters belonging to the lobby of the industry under consideration. In the single lobby case, the rate of protection to organized sector i depends on the fraction of voters $\alpha_i = N_i/N$ having a stake in the i industry.

Competition among multiple lobbies allows the government to capture part of the surplus from intervention. Consider the extreme case in which (1) all individuals belong to a lobby ($\sum \alpha_j = 1$), and (2) all sectors have lobbies ($I_i = 1$ for all i). In this case, opposing lobbies compete for trade benefits but they neutralize each other and equilibrium involves free trade. Contributions are paid out in this free-trade equilibrium because each lobby contributes in order to avoid being harmed by other lobbies.

15.4.3. *Endogenous Lobby Formation*

Mitra (1999) endogenizes lobby formation in the protection for sale framework by introducing an initial stage in which owners of specific factors decide whether or not to finance a fixed and sunk cost of forming a lobby. In an endogenous lobby formation setup, the equilibrium trade benefits to the lobby are not necessarily negatively related to the weight ϕ that the government assigns to population welfare. A smaller ϕ leads to a larger number of lobbies. If this positive entry effect is strong enough, trade benefits to lobbies are paradoxically reduced.

15.5. PROTECTION FOR SALE: THE EVIDENCE

The protection for sale model represents a benchmark for empirical work on the determinants of protection. Empirical findings confirming several testable predictions of this model suggest that it captures relevant features of trade policy formation.

15.5.1. Is Protection for Sale?

Maggi and Goldberg (1999) test the predictions deriving from the protection for sale model. The government welfare function is

$$W^G(p) = (1 - \beta)C^K(p) + \beta W^P(p) = (1 - \beta)\left[C^K(p) + \frac{\beta}{1 - \beta}W^P(p)\right]$$

$$= (1 - \beta)[C^K(p) + \phi W^P(p)],$$

which represents a shift of the welfare function in (15.7) under the equivalences $\phi = \beta/(1 - \beta)$ and $\beta = \phi/(1 + \phi)$.

The trade protection empirical model is given by Grossman and Helpman protection for sale equation augmented to include an error term u_i

$$\frac{t_i \varepsilon_i}{1 + t_i} = \frac{I_i - \alpha_K}{\phi + \alpha_K}\frac{Q_i}{M_i} + u_i = -\frac{\alpha_K}{\phi + \alpha_K}\frac{Q_i}{M_i} + \frac{1}{\phi + \alpha_K}I_i\frac{Q_i}{M_i} + u_i$$

$$= \gamma\frac{Q_i}{M_i} + \delta I_i\frac{Q_i}{M_i} + u_i, \tag{15.19}$$

where $t_i, \varepsilon_i, Q_i/M_i$ and I_i represent the *ad valorem* tariff on good i, the import demand or export supply elasticity of good i, the inverse import penetration ratio, and a political organization dummy that takes a value of 1 if industry $i \in L$ and 0 if $i \notin L$, where L represents the sectors in which owners of specific factors are able to form a lobby.

The tested hypotheses are: (1) trade protection is higher in industries with a lower import elasticity (i.e. a lower ε_i implies a higher t_i), (2) in the group of unorganized sectors, protection should increase with greater import penetration (if $\gamma < 0$, then a lower Q_I/M_I implies a higher t_I), and (3) within the subset of organized industries, protection declines with greater import penetration (if $\delta > 0$ and $\gamma + \delta > 0$, then a lower Q_I/M_I implies a lower t_I).

Formally, the authors test the following hypotheses

$$\gamma = -\frac{\alpha_K}{\phi + \alpha_K} < 0, \qquad \delta = \frac{1}{\phi + \alpha_K} > 0, \qquad \gamma + \delta = \frac{1 - \alpha_K}{\phi + \alpha_K} > 0,$$

$$\tag{15.20}$$

which match the predictions of Grossman and Helpman's 'Protection for Sale' article. Estimated parameters $\hat{\gamma}$ and $\hat{\delta}$ are used to estimate the proportion of individuals belonging to an interest group, $\alpha_K = -\gamma/\delta$, the weight the government attaches to population welfare relative to contributions, $\phi = (1 + \gamma)/\delta$, and the welfare weight $\beta = \phi/(1 + \phi) = (1 + \gamma)/(1 + \gamma + \delta)$.

Following Trefler (1993*b*), trade protection is measured using the nontariff barrier coverage ratio (provided by UNCTAD) as a proxy for the extent of protection. The coverage ratio is the fraction of an industry's imports covered by one or more nontariff barriers such as antidumping and countervailing duties, quotas and voluntary export restraints, and threats of quality and quantity monitoring. The use of nontariff barriers instead of tariff levels is justified because: (1) the US tariff rates are very low, and (2) the correlation coefficient between tariff levels and nontariff barriers is 0.78.

The study utilizes cross-sectional US data for 1983, aggregated at the 3-digit SIC level. Import elasticities are taken from Shiells *et al.* (1986) and the dummies for political organization (I_i) are constructed using data on political action committee (PAC) campaign contributions for 1982 and 1983. Reported results use a threshold level of $100 million in 3-digit industry contributions.

Due to the difficulties in obtaining adequate proxies for the variables, the actual estimated model is an adaptation of the econometric model (15.19). The model is expressed in terms of the latent variable t_i^{latent}, which is thought of as the unobserved true level of protection. This latent variable is equal to a multiple μ of the coverage ratio t_i, that is, $t_i^{latent} = \mu t_i$. The unobserved μ, is set equal to 1, 2, and 3 in alternative estimations. The multiple μ is a scaling factor mapping the fractional coverage ratio used to measure protection into an equivalent tariff level that reflects the importance of protection.

Formally,

$$\frac{t_i^{latent} \varepsilon_i}{1 + t_i^{latent}} = \gamma \frac{Q_i}{M_i} + \delta I_i \frac{Q_i}{M_i} + u_i \tag{15.21}$$

with

$$\frac{Q_i}{M_i} = \zeta_{1i}' Z_{1i} + u_{1i},$$

$$t_i = \begin{cases} 0 & t_i^{latent} \leq 0 \\ \dfrac{1}{\mu} & t_i^{latent} \quad 0 < t_i^{latent} < \mu \\ 1 & t_i^{latent} \geq \mu \end{cases},$$

$$I_i = \begin{cases} 0 & I_i^{latent} = \zeta_2' Z_{2i} + u_{2i} \leq 0 \\ 1 & I_i^{latent} = \zeta_2' Z_{2i} + u_{2i} > 0 \end{cases},$$

where the errors u_i, u_{1i}, and u_{2i} are the normally distributed $N \sim (0, \sum)$ and ε_i is the import demand or export supply elasticity of good i. The inverse import penetration ratio Q_i/M_i and the latent variable I_i^{latent}, which accounts for whether or not the sector is organized, are assumed to be function of vectors Z_{1i} and Z_{1i} consisting of factor shares (physical capital, inventories, skilled workers, semi-skilled workers and others), seller and buyer concentration, seller and buyer number of firms, minimum efficient scale, capital stock, geographic concentration, unionization, and others.

Maximum likelihood estimation of the estimated trade protection model (15.21) setting μ equal to 3 is

$$\frac{t_i^{latent} \varepsilon_i}{1 + t_i^{latent}} = \hat{\gamma} \frac{Q_i}{M_i} + \hat{\delta} I_i \frac{Q_i}{M_i} + \hat{u}_i = -\underset{(0.0070)}{0.0155} \frac{Q_i}{M_i} + \underset{(0.0093)}{0.0186} I_i \frac{Q_i}{M_i} + \hat{u}_i,$$

$$\hat{\phi} = \frac{1 + \hat{\gamma}}{\hat{\delta}} = 53, \qquad \hat{\beta} = \frac{1 + \hat{\gamma}}{1 + \hat{\gamma} + \hat{\delta}} = 0.98, \qquad \hat{\alpha}_{Lobby} = -\frac{\hat{\gamma}}{\hat{\delta}} = 0.84.$$

The estimation results confirm the hypothesized signs in (15.20) and thus support the pattern of protection predicted by Helpman and Grossman (1994).

1. The levels of trade protection are different in organized and unorganized sectors ($\hat{\delta} > 0$ and statistically significant).
2. The hypothesis that there is a negative relationship between the inverse import penetration ratio and protection (and thus a positive relation between import penetration and protection) in the unorganized sectors is confirmed ($\hat{\gamma} < 0$ and statistically significant).
3. The hypothesis that there is a positive relationship between the inverse penetration ratio and protection levels (and thus a negative relation between import penetration and protection) in the organized sectors, is weakly supported by the data ($\hat{\gamma} + \hat{\delta} > 0$ but not statistically significant).

The result that import penetration might be negatively related to protection in the organized sector ($\hat{\gamma} + \hat{\delta} > 0$) is in apparent contradiction with previous empirical work. Baldwin (1985), Trefler (1993*b*), Lee and Swagel (1997), and others report that greater import penetration is associated with higher protection. Goldberg and Maggi argue that previous work does not constitute evidence against the model. From the perspective of the model, previous work is misspecified because it introduces import penetration and political variables additively on the right-hand side of the equation. In Grossman and Helpman model, import penetration Q_i/M_i and the political organization variable I_i enter multiplicatively. The additive specification imposes the restriction that the coefficient of Q_i/M_i is the same in organized sectors ($I_i = 1$) and unorganized sectors ($I_i = 0$). This implies that the expected estimate of the coefficient of Q_i/M_i in the additive form is an average of $\gamma < 0$ and $\gamma + \delta$. This average can be negative or positive even if $\gamma + \delta$ is positive.

The implicit estimate $\hat{\phi}$ of the weight assigned to population welfare by the US government in 1983 is fifty-three times the weight attached to contributions. The estimated degree of affiliation to an interest group, $\hat{\alpha}_{Lobby}$, is about 84 percent of the population. In alternative estimations, a lower μ is found to imply a lower equivalent tariff level, $t_i^{latent} = \mu t_i$, which in turn implies higher estimates of the weight assigned to population welfare $\hat{\phi}$ and the degree of lobby representation $\hat{\alpha}_{Lobby}$. For instance, if μ is equal to 2, the resulting estimates yield $\hat{\phi} = 64$ and $\hat{\alpha}_{Lobby} = 0.86$.

Finally, alternative econometric specifications provide evidence that industries providing greater total employment and sectors experiencing unemployment tend to get more protection.

15.5.2. *Protection for Sale with Intermediate Inputs*

Gawande and Bandyopadhyay (2000) extend the protection for sale model in two
directions. First, they consider an intermediate goods sector. In practice, lobbies in
the intermediate goods sector are often active in the trade policy formation process.
Second, the empirical analysis includes tests of models explaining protection, political
contributions and import penetration. The structural coefficients of the three-equation
model are estimated using 2SLS—two stage least squares estimators—due to the
nonlinearity of the econometric specifications for protection, political contributions,
and import penetration.

Let us focus on the protection equation. The cross-industry trade tax equation
incorporating the tariff t_X on intermediate inputs X is (see appendix of Gawande and
Bandyopadhyay, 2000)

$$
\frac{t_i}{1+t_i} = \frac{I_i - \alpha_L - \alpha_X}{\phi + \alpha_L + \alpha_X} \frac{Q_i}{M_i} \frac{1}{\varepsilon_i} + \frac{p_X^W}{\varepsilon_i M_i} \frac{\partial M_X}{\partial p_i} t_X + u_i
$$

$$
= \frac{-\alpha_L - \alpha_X}{\phi + \alpha_L + \alpha_X} \frac{Q_i}{\varepsilon_i M_i} + \frac{1}{\phi + \alpha_L + \alpha_X} \frac{Q_i}{\varepsilon_i M_i} I_i + \frac{p_X^W}{\varepsilon_i M_i} \frac{\partial M_X}{\partial p_i} t_X + u_i
$$

$$
= \alpha_0 + \alpha_1 \frac{Q_i}{10,000 M_i} \frac{1}{\varepsilon_i} + \alpha_2 \frac{Q_i}{10,000 M_i} \frac{1}{\varepsilon_i} I + \alpha_3 t_X + u_1,
$$

where α_L and α_X represent the share of the population belonging to final goods and
intermediate inputs lobbies and p_X^W is the world price of intermediate goods. The
response of intermediate goods imports M_X to the price of good i is taken to be
positive, $\partial M_X / \partial p_i > 0$, because an increase in the price of good i through protection
is related to an increase in domestic demand and thus in the demand for intermediate
goods.

The estimated equation relates nontariff barriers to the ratio of consumption to
imports C/M (i.e. a variant of the inverse import penetration ratio) rescaled up by
10,000, the interaction between the inverse import penetration ratio and an indicator I
of politically organized industries, average tariffs t_X on intermediate goods employed
in an industry, and average coverage ratios NTB_X of intermediate goods used in an
industry. The estimated model using data for 242 four-digit SIC US industries is

$$
\frac{NTB}{1+NTB} = \hat{\alpha}_0 + \hat{\alpha}_1 \frac{C}{10,000 M} \frac{1}{\varepsilon} + \hat{\alpha}_2 \frac{C}{10,000 M} \frac{1}{\varepsilon} I + \hat{\alpha}_3 t_X + \hat{\alpha}_4 NTB_X + \hat{u}_1
$$

$$
= \underset{(0.02)}{-0.04} - \underset{(1.5)}{3.09} \frac{C}{10,000 M} \frac{1}{\varepsilon} + \underset{(1.6)}{3.14} \frac{C}{10,000 M} \frac{1}{\varepsilon} I
$$

$$
+ \underset{(0.2)}{0.78} t_X + \underset{(0.06)}{0.36} NTB_X + \hat{u}_1.
$$

Industry import elasticities ε_i are 3-digit SIC elasticities taken from Shiells *et al.*
(1986), adjusted using the errors-in-variables correction proposed by Fuller (1987)
and replicated at the 4-digit level. Standard errors are reported in parenthesis.

The empirical results confirm Grossman and Helpman findings on the protection and lobbying side. Tariff protection is found to be negatively related to the inverse import penetration ratio in unorganized industries (i.e. $\hat{\alpha}_1 < 0$) and thus positively related to import penetration. Tariff protection is positively related to the inverse import penetration ratio in organized industries (i.e. $\hat{\alpha}_2 + \hat{\alpha}_1 > 0$) but the sum is not significantly different from zero. Also, industry protection is found to be an increasing function of the production of intermediate inputs.

The welfare weight $\hat{\phi} = (1 + (\hat{\alpha}_1/10,000))/(\hat{\alpha}_2/10,000) = 3184$ differs drastically from Goldberg and Maggi's $\hat{\phi} = 53$ estimate of the weight assigned to social welfare relative to contributions. The government welfare function can be expressed as the weighted average of contributions received and net-of-contributions population welfare

$$
W^G = \phi_C C^K + \phi_P (W^P - C^K) = (\phi_C - \phi_P) C^K + \phi_P W^P
$$

$$
= (\phi_C - \phi_P) \left[C^K + \frac{\phi_P}{\phi_C - \phi_P} W^P \right] = (\phi_C - \phi_P)[C^K + \phi W^P],
$$

where $\phi = \phi_P/(\phi_C - \phi_P)$ and $\phi_C > \phi_P$. This welfare function represents a shift of the equivalent welfare function in Grossman and Helpman (1994). Because $\phi(\phi_C - \phi_P) = \phi_P$, we have that $3184\phi_C = 3185\phi_P$, which implies that the government weights aggregate contributions almost equally as population welfare net of contributions.

15.6. A GLOBAL SPECIFIC-FACTOR TRADE MODEL

A key insight of international trade analysis is that large governments acting non-cooperatively have incentives to impose trade barriers to improve the terms of trade in their countries' favor and to subsidize exports to gain market share. Another key insight is that noncooperative intervention incentives are likely to lead into prisoners' dilemma situations in which all countries lose due to excessively high tariffs or export subsidies. Terms of trade analysis requires relaxing the small country assumption and extending the framework to a two-country setting.

15.6.1. Demand, Production, and Transfers

Individuals are assumed to display identical preferences but differ in their initial endowments. Foreign country demand and production functions are

$$
d_I^* = 1 - p_I^*, \qquad d_{II}^* = 1 - p_{II}^*, \qquad d_0^* = y^{*i} - (p_I^* d_I^* + p_{II}^* d_{II}^*),
$$

$$
Q_I^* = A^* L_I^{*1/2} \bar{K}^{*1/2}, \qquad Q_{II}^* = A^* L_{II}^{*1/2} \bar{H}^{*1/2}, \qquad Q_0^* = L_0^*,
$$

where the price of the foreign numeraire is $p_0^* = 1$ and y^{*i} denotes individual i spending. Technologies display constant returns to scale and are the same in both countries (i.e. $A^* = A$). Physical capital is specific to industry I, human capital to industry II, and $L_0^* + L_I^* + L_{II}^* = \bar{L}^*$.

Per capita transfers to or from the population, $tr^*(p_I^*, p_{II}^*)$, are defined as a function of the difference between each commodity's per capita consumption d_i^* and per capita production $Q^*(p^*)/N^*$,

$$tr^*(p_I, p_{II}) = \left(p_I^* - p_I^W\right)\left[d_I^*(p_I^*) - \frac{1}{N^*}Q_I^*(p_I^*)\right]$$
$$+ \left(p_{II}^* - p_{II}^W\right)\left[d_{II}^*(p_{II}^*) - \frac{1}{N^*}Q_{II}^*(p_{II}^*)\right],$$

where N^* is the foreign population.

Trade policy is used as a mechanism to redistribute rents among different sectors in the society. Foreign trade taxes and subsidies open a gap between foreign prices and world or 'offshore' prices

$$p_i^* = (1 + t_i^*)p_i^W \rightarrow t_i^* = \frac{p_i^* - p_i^W}{p_i^W}, \quad i \in \{I, II\}.$$

15.6.2. *Global Equilibrium*

The global market for product $i \in \{I, II\}$ clears when one country's imports equal the other country's exports

$$d_i(p_i) - Q_i(p_i) = -[d_i^*(p_i^*) - Q_i^*(p_i^*)],$$

where population size is normalized to one so that $Q_i/N = Q_i$ and $Q_i^*/N^* = Q_i^*$.

At equilibrium, domestic and foreign prices can be written as a function of domestic and foreign tariffs (or subsidies, or both)

$$p_i = p_i(t, t^*), \qquad p_i^* = p_i^*(t, t^*),$$

where $t = (t_I, t_{II})$ and $t^* = (t_I^*, t_{II}^*)$. World market prices can be rewritten as a function of the domestic and foreign trade policies, t and t^*

$$\begin{aligned}
p_i(t, t^*) &= (1 + t_i)p_i^W \rightarrow p_i^W(t, t^*) = (1 + t_i)^{-1}p_i(t, t^*), \\
p_i^*(t, t^*) &= (1 + t_i^*)p_i^W \rightarrow p_i^W(t, t^*) = (1 + t_i^*)^{-1}p_i^*(t^*, t).
\end{aligned} \tag{15.22}$$

Notice that the demand functions and the specific factor model used implies that a sector's prices depend only on that sector's tariffs: $p_I^W(t, t^*) = p_I^W(t_I, t_I^*) = p_I(t_I, t_I^*)$ $(1 + t_I)^{-1}$ and so on.

15.7. TRADE WARS: NONCOOPERATIVE POLICIES

This section examines an equilibrium in which governments formulate trade policies in a noncooperative fashion, in the sense that each government behaves unilaterally ignoring the impact of its actions on trading partner's political and economic agents. Each government receives rents from a single domestic lobby aiming to influence its own country's trade policy. It is assumed that lobbies do not try to influence foreign governments and foreign lobbies, and that the domestic contribution schedule is not observed abroad.

At stage 1, a domestic and a foreign lobby noncooperatively design contribution schemes relating political contributions to government trade policy choices. Contribution schedules are designed to maximize lobby welfare net of contributions, taking as given foreign trade policy and how the domestic government will react to the contribution scheme in setting domestic trade policy. At stage 2, the domestic and foreign governments formulate trade policies noncooperatively taking as given the trading partner's trade policy and the domestic lobby contribution schedule. Trade policies maximize government welfare including contributions received taking into account that the level of contributions varies with the specific policy chosen.

Domestic and foreign lobby and government welfares are

$$W_{Gross}^K = W_{Net}^K(t, t^*) - C^K(t, t^*), \qquad W^G = C^K(t, t^*) + \phi W^P(t, t^*),$$

$$W_{Gross}^{*K} = W_{Net}^{*K}(t, t^*) - C^{*K}(t, t^*), \qquad W^{*G} = C^K(t, t^*) + \phi^* W^{*P}(t^*, t),$$

where ϕ^* denotes the weight attached to foreign population welfare.

15.7.1. *Noncooperative Equilibrium*

Let us follow Bernheim and Whinston (1986a) and Grossman and Helpman (1995b) and apply the Nash noncooperative equilibrium concept to determine the two-country political trade policy equilibrium. A noncooperative trade policy equilibrium consists of sets of political contribution functions $C^{K,N}$ and $C^{*K,N}$ and a pair of trade policy vectors t^N and t^{*N} such that $\{C^{K,N}, t^N\}$ is an equilibrium response to t^{*N} and $\{C^{*K,N}, t^{*N}\}$ is an equilibrium response to t^N.

The pair $\{C^{K,N}, t^N\}$, consisting of feasible contributions and a trade policy vector, constitutes a best response to an arbitrary foreign trade policy t^* if two conditions hold:

1. The government chooses the policy vector that maximizes its welfare W^G, taking as given foreign actions and the domestic contribution schedule. First, a policy vector t^N and a contribution schedule $C^{K,N}$ satisfy

$$t^N \in \arg\max_t C^{K,N}(t, t^*) + \phi W^P(t, t^*),$$

where $t = \{t_I, t_{II}\}, t^* = \{t_I^*, t_{II}^*\}$ denote the domestic and foreign country's trade policy vectors. This condition means that the equilibrium trade policy response must maximize government's welfare for any given foreign policy and the equilibrium domestic contribution schedule.

2. The equilibrium contribution scheme $C^{K,N}$ maximizes lobby welfare. There does not exist any feasible contribution schedule $C^K(t, t^*)$ and trade policy vector t that yield higher welfare to the lobby than the equilibrium schedule

$$W_{Gross}^K(t, t^*) - C^K(t, t^*) > W_{Gross}^{K,N}(t^N, t^*) - C^{K,N}(t^N, t^*),$$

where foreign policy is taken as given. Recall that the specific factor model implies that lobby welfare depends on the trade policy applied to its industry but not on the trade policy applied to other industries. Similar conditions apply for the foreign government when choosing the optimal policy t^{*N}.

Following a similar procedure as in the small country case, the optimal trade policy can be shown to be a function of the welfare weight ϕ, the fraction of voters α_i and α_i^* having a stake in industry i (i.e. own the factor that is specific to the industry), industry production Q_i and Q_i^*, product world price p_i^W, and export supply elasticities ε_i and ε_i^*. Formally,

$$t_I^N = \frac{1 - \alpha_K}{\phi + \alpha_K} \frac{Q_I}{p_I^W M_I'} + \frac{1}{\varepsilon_I^*}, \qquad t_I^{*N} = \frac{1 - \alpha_K^*}{\phi^* + \alpha_K^*} \frac{Q_I^*}{p_I^W M_I^{*'}} + \frac{1}{\varepsilon_I},$$

$$t_{II}^N = -\frac{\alpha_K}{\phi + \alpha_K} \frac{Q_{II}}{p_{II}^W M_{II}'} + \frac{1}{\varepsilon_{II}^*}, \qquad t_{II}^{*N} = -\frac{\alpha_K^*}{\phi^* + \alpha_K^*} \frac{Q_{II}^*}{p_{II}^W M_{II}^{*'}} + \frac{1}{\varepsilon_{II}},$$

$$(15.23)$$

where

$$\varepsilon_i^* = \frac{\partial M_i^*}{\partial p_i^W (1 + t_i^*)} \frac{p_i^W (1 + t_i^*)}{M_i^*}, \qquad M_i^{*'} = \frac{\partial M_i^*}{\partial p_i^W (1 + t_i)} < 0,$$

and $\varepsilon_i^* > 0$ denotes the foreign country's export supply elasticity and $\varepsilon_i^* < 0$ is the foreign country's import demand elasticity.

15.7.2. Lobbies and the Terms of Trade

The trade policy expressions can be decomposed into two terms reflecting the roles of (1) political support by interest groups, and (2) the manipulation of the terms of trade. The first component coincides with the tariff imposed by a small country government. Because prices cannot be manipulated, the terms of trade do not play a role and this component of the tariff reflects lobby pressures. Ignoring terms of trade effects, the lobby in the industry utilizing physical capital is protected whereas the unorganized human capital sector receives negative protection. The second component is the well-known optimal tariff formula (Johnson, 1953) and captures the role of the terms of trade. A more elastic foreign country's export supply function ε_I^* (i.e. a higher ε_I^*) leads to a lower domestic country equilibrium tariff.

How does the political strength of lobbies affect domestic and foreign governments' trade policies? An increase in lobby influence relative to population welfare is modeled as a reduction of the population welfare weight ϕ. In this setup, tariffs and subsidies are instruments used to influence the terms of trade. Suppose that the foreign country's elasticity ε_I^* is positive and constant, meaning that the foreign country exports physical capital goods. In this case, the lobby will intensify efforts to obtain protection from its domestic government whereas the unorganized sector will suffer from higher trade taxes. From the trade policy equation, a reduction in ϕ implies a higher equilibrium tariff t_I^N (i.e. $\partial t_I^N / \partial \phi < 0$ for ε_I^* constant because $\partial M_i / \partial (p_i^W (1 + t_i)) < 0$). The equilibrium tax and price of home exports p_I^N increase, and the domestic country's terms of trade improve.

15.8. TRADE TALKS: COOPERATIVE TRADE POLICIES

If domestic and foreign governments are aware of the mutual costs generated by their trade policies, they have incentives to engage in trade talks and coordinate policies. A trade agreement represents an instrument to avoid the harmful terms of trade effects arising in prisoners' dilemma situations. We follow Grossman and Helpman (1995*b*) extension of the protection for sale model to examine how domestic lobbies affect the relations of a country with foreign trading partners when trade policies are chosen cooperatively (trade talks). Bagwell and Staiger (1999*a*) develop a related model of WTO negotiations in which terms of trade considerations create incentives for coordinating tariff policies (see chapter on WTO).

A cooperative equilibrium can be supported by international lump sum transfers tr^{Int} providing compensation to countries that would lose from the cooperative equilibrium. This transfer mechanism has been used within the European Union but not in NAFTA or by the WTO. The domestic and foreign government utility functions are

$$
\begin{aligned}
W^G &= C^K(t, t^*) + \phi[W^P(t, t^*) + tr^{Int}], \\
W^{*G} &= C^{*K}(t, t^*) + \phi^*[W^{*P}(t, t^*) - tr^{Int}].
\end{aligned}
\tag{15.24}
$$

15.8.1. Cooperative Trade Policies

Consider the following two–stage game. At stage 1, a domestic and foreign lobby set optimal contribution schemes in a noncooperative fashion. At stage 2, the domestic and foreign governments choose trade policies cooperatively, given the contribution schedules.

A cooperative Pareto efficiency solution requires governments to act as a single agent choosing trade policy vectors t and t^* that maximize a weighted sum of the governments' welfares, W^G and W^{*G}. Formally,

$$
\begin{aligned}
W^C &= \phi^* W^G + \phi W^{*G} \\
&= \phi^* (C^K(t, t^*) + \phi[W^P(t, t^*) + tr^{Int}]) \\
&\quad + \phi(C^{*K}(t, t^*) + \phi^*[W^{*P}(t, t^*) - tr^{Int}]) \\
&= \phi^* C^K(t, t^*) + \phi C^{*K}(t, t^*) + \phi\phi^*[W^P(t, t^*) + W^{*P}(t, t^*)]. \quad (15.25)
\end{aligned}
$$

The weight attached to each government's welfare corresponds to the weight the trading partner's government attaches to population welfare. Notice that weights ϕ^* and ϕ are chosen to simplify the treatment by allowing canceling intergovernmental transfers tr^{Int}.

A cooperative trade policy equilibrium consists of a set of political contribution schedules $C^{K,C}$ and $C^{*K,C}$ and a pair of trade policy vectors t^C and t^{*C} such that:

1. the pair $\{t^C, t^{*C}\}$ maximizes the joint weighted welfare levels of the foreign and domestic governments, that is, $\{t^C, t^{*C}\}$ maximizes (15.25);
2. for every organized domestic lobby there does not exist a feasible contribution function C^K and policy pair $\{t, t^*\}$ that maximize the joint welfare of the lobby and the government and yields a greater welfare to the lobby than the equilibrium welfare. A similar condition is required for the foreign country lobby.

The cooperative equilibrium can be represented in terms of international trade policy differentials

$$
t_I^C - t_I^{*C} = \left(-\frac{I_i - \alpha_K}{\phi + \alpha_K} \frac{Q_I}{p_I^W M_I'} \right) - \left(-\frac{I_i - \alpha_K^*}{\phi^* + \alpha_K^*} \frac{Q_I^*}{p_I^W M_I^{*'}} \right).
$$

where symbols are defined in (15.23), $M_I' < 0$ and $M_I^{*'} < 0$. Each sectorial equation can be interpreted as an international differential in domestic and foreign lobby political power indexes. The more powerful group is the one representing the industry with a greater output, lower fraction of the population lobbying for favorable policies, lower weight on population welfare, and inelastic import demand.

When governments cooperate in the presence of lobbies, whether or not an interest group receives protection depends exclusively on the strength of domestic and foreign interest group pressures. In contrast with the noncooperative setup discussed above, a country's trade policies do not depend on the trading partner's export supply or import demand elasticities. Indeed, the optimal tariff terms do not appear on the expression for the trade policy differential.

15.8.2. Lobbies, Terms of Trade and Cooperation

If sector I is organized while sector II is unorganized, we have

$$
\begin{aligned}
t_I^C - t_I^{*C} &= -\frac{1-\alpha_K}{\phi+\alpha_K} \frac{Q_I}{p_I^W M_I'} - \left(-\frac{1-\alpha_K^*}{\phi^*+\alpha_K^*} \frac{Q_I^*}{p_I^W M_I^{*\prime}}\right), \\
t_{II}^C - t_{II}^{*C} &= \frac{\alpha_K^*}{\phi+\alpha_K^*} \frac{Q_{II}}{p_{II}^W M_{II}'} - \frac{\alpha_K^*}{\phi^*+\alpha_K^*} \frac{Q_{II}^*}{p_{II}^W M_{II}^{*\prime}}.
\end{aligned}
\tag{15.26}
$$

If sector I is organized in both countries, the extent of protection depends on the relative political power index of domestic and foreign lobbies. From (15.26), an industry is more heavily protected in the domestic than in the foreign country if and only if the political power index in the domestic country is larger than the foreign country political power index

$$
-\frac{1-\alpha_K}{\phi+\alpha_K} \frac{Q_I}{p_I^W M_I'} > -\frac{1-\alpha_K^*}{\phi^*+\alpha_K^*} \frac{Q_I^*}{p_I^W M_I^{*\prime}} > 0.
$$

The domestic and foreign lobbies of a given industry have opposed interests in trade negotiations. Both of them want to be protected. The lobby with a larger relative political clout will succeed in getting heavier protection than the weaker lobby.

Notice that, if specific factor owners are organized at home but not abroad, then the organized group gains from government cooperation relative to free trade. Specifically, the industry represented by the lobby obtains protection through a tariff or export subsidy whereas the unorganized physical capital industry will suffer from an import subsidy or export tax.

15.9. CAPS ON LOBBYING AND ELECTIONS

The issue of campaign reform remains on the table. Candidates, elected legislators, and public officials devote large amounts of resources and time to raise funds from lobbies. For instance, Levitt (1995) reports that political action committees (PACs) accounted for half of all the money spent by incumbents in the 1992 US House of Representatives elections. In an effort to control political contributions, the 1971 Federal Election Campaign Act (FECA) was amended in 1974 to set caps on contributions by individuals, political parties, and PACs. However, increasing campaign spending continued unabated even though PAC contributions were limited to $5000 per elected candidate and per calendar year. The 2002 campaign reform bill increased the caps on individual 'hard money' contributions (i.e. funds raised and reported according to federal laws and regulations) and banned 'soft money' contributions (i.e. donations to political parties' committees in amounts and sources, such as corporations and labor unions, not allowed in federal elections). The previous law had failed to limit the amount of soft money raised by national political parties' committees, which was used for party strengthening activities but also for broadcast advertisement on behalf of specific political candidates. The 2002 campaign finance reform kept the limits on PAC contributions unchanged and maintained the policy of no restrictions on the number of contributors.

What are the trade policy effects of restrictions on political contributions? If the restrictions reduce lobbying activity, then trade barriers will decline. However caps on political lobbying can be ineffective or even counterproductive.

There are two broad types of contribution restrictions: a ceiling on the levels of contribution per contributor and a ceiling on the number of contributors. The contribution levels and the number of contributors are strategically chosen so that restrictions on one variable will affect the choice of the other. For instance, restrictions on contribution levels have two offsetting effects. First, contributions can be increased by augmenting the number of contributors. Riezman and Wilson (1997) show that this effect can cause the restrictions to be ineffective or even counterproductive. Second, Che and Gale (1998) show that contribution limits can create incentives for small contributors that are below the limits to increase their political contributions.

15.9.1. Trade Policy Effects of Contribution Limits

Riezman and Wilson (1997) examine the effects of restrictions on political contributions in an electoral competition model with pressure group politics. The strategic electoral competition setup involves two political candidates that play a Nash game in the choice of (1) the number of contributors accepted, and (2) the contribution levels required per contributor. Electoral results are uncertain, and the probability of being elected is determined by two types of voters: informed voters and uninformed voters (i.e. voters that lack information about the policies advocated by the candidates). Political contributions are assumed to influence the decisions of uninformed voters but not of informed voters. The latter are assumed to vote according to the benefits or costs derived from the known candidate policies.

What are the trade policy effects of limits on political contributions? The welfare effects of government-imposed restrictions depend crucially on the design of the intervention. If candidates are forced to lower the level of contributions accepted, or the number of contributors, by a small amount leading to small reductions in contributions, the restrictions are welfare improving.

Strong restrictions on the level of contributions (with no ceiling on the number of contributors) induce candidates to seek additional contributors and might be welfare worsening. The reason is that the number of industries affected by trade restrictions will increase. Furthermore, strong restrictions undertaken by imposing a low enough ceiling on the number of contributors (with no ceiling on the amounts contributed) might also worsen welfare. Candidates respond by seeking greater contributions, and thus grant greater tariff protection to contributors.

The paradoxical result is that political reform imposing strong but partial restrictions on political contributions of groups favoring protection might lead to an increase in protection. The results also show how partial restrictions allowing loopholes might reduce welfare relative to comprehensive restrictions or a situation with no restrictions at all.

15.9.2. Auctioning Political Favors

Fund raising can be seen as all-pay auctions in which lobbies bid for a political prize, by submitting nonnegative bids simultaneously. The political price is awarded to the highest bidder and bids are not returned to unsuccessful bidders. Politicians are the sellers and lobbies are the buyers of the object or political favor being auctioned.

Che and Gale (1998) show that caps on bids can attenuate one bidder's ability to preempt a rival bidder. As a result, bidding competition gets stronger. The reason is that contribution limits reduce the probability that the high-valuation bidder wins the auction. This creates incentives for small contributors that are below the limits to increase their political contributions. Caps that are effective on large bidders are thus offset by greater bids placed by small bidders, which can raise the fund-raiser's expected revenues.

15.10. THE DYNAMICS OF TRADE POLITICS

What are the economics of protection to declining industries? Why is it that some industries experience cycles in import protection and export promotion? In order to answer these questions, we should focus on the dynamics of protection and resource allocation. Dynamic models of lobbying can generate diverse patterns of protection and industry dynamics.

Brainard and Verdier (1994) present a model where an adverse trade shock leads to lobbying and protection that slows down industry decline as a response to an adverse shock. Endogenous policy means that current tariffs depend on past tariffs, which produces a smooth industrial decline (an industry collapse can only arise in special circumstances). In Sánchez (1998) protection dynamics in developing countries arise as a response to continuous innovation by developed trading partners. Protection cycles result from domestic lobbying for protection as a substitute for costly innovation. Tariff rates evolve in cycles of protection followed by trade liberalization, the reemergence of protection, a further round of liberalization, and so on.

15.10.1. Adverse Shocks and Declining Industries

Why does protection persist in the face of declining industries? Brainard and Verdier (1994) follow Grossman and Helpman (1994) in introducing a lobbying process in which an industry tariff rate is determined from the interaction between a politician and a lobby of specific factor owners. The resulting contribution schedule is

$$C(p_t, p^W) = \frac{\phi(p_t - p^W)^2}{2(1 - \phi)},$$

where ϕ is the weight given by the government to population welfare, $p_t - p^W = tp^W$, and t is the *ad valorem* tariff. The tariff response function is derived endogenously from lobbying activities.

Assume that the world price of a good is constant over time except that it experiences a discrete decline at some point in time (time 0). When the permanent adverse trade shock hits, the industry can respond by either undertaking a costly adjustment or lobbying for trade protection to mitigate the need for adjustment. In a continuous-time setup with an infinite horizon, tariff determination and industry adjustment are continuously decided over time. At each time, there are two stages. In the first stage, the firm simultaneously chooses the level of adjustment and a contribution schedule that takes into account the anticipated government response. In the second stage, the government sets an *ad valorem* industry tariff.

The tariff level can be shown to be an increasing function of past tariffs. In other words, current protection is an increasing function of past protection. The intuition is the following. Current protection reduces the need for current adjustment, which increases the effectiveness of future lobbying and raises future protection. Specifically, a higher initial domestic price leads to weaker industrial adjustment, greater future lobbying and a higher future tariff level.

The dynamics of protection affects the dynamics of resource allocation. Because current protection is an increasing function of past protection, an adverse trade shock leads to a smooth pattern of tariff reduction and industry decline. Employment is adjusted smoothly at a declining rate and converges to a level that is permanently above the efficient employment level. Protected declining industries contract less and more slowly over time than in the absence of protection. Also, the more responsive politicians are to lobbying, the more slowly the industry contracts over time. Sudden industry collapse such as that generated by Cassing and Hillman (1986) can only emerge under special assumptions.

15.10.2. Cycles of Protection and Trade Liberalization

Why are trade reforms often reversed in developing countries? Sánchez (1998) develops a quality ladder model of North–South trade in which the South imitates the innovation that takes place in the North. Tariffs arise endogenously in a political market in which import-competing firms lobby for a sequence of increasing tariffs that insulate domestic profits from a widening quality gap. Protection serves to postpone adjustment that would require costly product quality upgrades. However, protection implies that local firms fail to keep up with the innovation realized by foreign competitors. Protection must thus increase over time. Moreover, the contributions required by the government to increase protection grow with the size of the quality gap.

When the technological lag and the size of required contributions become large enough, the costs of protection undermine the effectiveness of the lobbying effort. The political incentives for protection break down and trade is liberalized. It becomes optimal to adjust quality and reduce the lobbying effort, which leads to liberalization and technological catch-up.

Trade liberalization creates benefits from greater protection and thus induces renewed lobbying activity in support of protection. The reason is that the equilibrium post-liberalization tariff rate is small and does not generate large social costs. Under these circumstances, a tariff is cheap from a lobby perspective. It pays to restart lobbying and promote the reestablishment of protection. Over time, cycles of protection and trade liberalization take place. The political will for trade liberalization eventually gains enough strength to reduce tariffs but liberalization is subsequently reversed.

15.10.3. Trade Policy Cycles in Uruguay: 1925–83

Rama (1994) examines import-protection and export-promotion cycles in Uruguay during 1925–83. Import substitution and export promotion policies are measured by the number of foreign trade regulations passed each year for the benefit of a single firm or industry. These measures indicate that Uruguay entered into an import-protection stage that lasted from the 1930s to the 1960s and was associated with protracted economic stagnation. A surge in export promotion during the seventies ended abruptly in the eighties. Rama treats the number of regulations as an endogenous variable and finds that endogenous regulations increase with discretionary policies, with adverse macroeconomic shocks, and under dictatorships. These regulations had a negative long run effect on output growth rates and export growth, but had a positive short run effect.

15.11. CONCLUSIONS

In addressing the interaction between politics and trade policy, we have moved beyond the realm of a welfare-maximizing social planner. Politicians and governments do have social welfare maximization in mind, but are also responsive to interest groups. Specifically, trade policy instruments can be used to generate a positive price differential between domestic and international prices in organized and unorganized sectors. The political economy-strategic approach to trade politics shades light on the process leading to the formulation of trade policies and the actual structure of trade protection and promotion policies.

A long-standing limitation of trade policy models remains a challenge. A general policy determination framework should be able to explain why governments bestow benefits to import-competing industries through tariff protection, quotas, production subsidies, tax benefits, or alternative forms of protection. A similar point applies to export industries. Political economy analyses have focused on the determinants of the extent of protection but have not tackled in earnest the politics of alternative forms of protection.

15.12. APPENDIX

15.12.1. Indirect Utility Function

The indirect utility $v^i(p, y^i)$ depends only on prices (p_I, p_{II}) and income y^i.

$$v^i(p, y^i) = y^i + (d_I + d_{II}) - \frac{1}{2}(d_I^2 + d_{II}^2) - p_I d_I(p_I, p_{II}) - p_{II} d_{II}(p_I, p_{II})$$

$$= y^i + (1 - p_I) + (1 - p_{II}) - \frac{1}{2}(1 - p_I)^2 - \frac{1}{2}(1 - p_{II})^2$$

$$- p_I(1 - p_I) - p_{II}(1 - p_{II})$$

$$= y^i + 1 - p_I - p_{II} + \frac{1}{2}p_I^2 + \frac{1}{2}p_{II}^2 = y^i + \frac{(1 - p_I)^2 + (1 - p_{II})^2}{2}.$$

15.12.2. Specific Factor Rewards and Supply of Goods

Firm i produces q_I with specific factor K and firm j produces q_{II} with specific factor H. Firms maximize profits π taking product prices as given

$$\max_{L_I, K} \pi_i(\cdot) = p_I q_I - L_I - rK = p_I A L_I^{1/2} K^{1/2} - L_I - rK,$$

$$\max_{L_{II}, H} \pi_j(\cdot) = p_{II} q_{II} - L_{II} - w_H H = p_{II} A L_{II}^{1/2} H^{1/2} - L_{II} - w_H H.$$

The first order conditions are

$$\frac{\partial \pi_i(\cdot)}{\partial L_I} = \frac{1}{2}p_I A L_I^{-1/2} K^{1/2} - 1 = 0, \qquad \frac{\partial \pi_i(\cdot)}{\partial K} = \frac{1}{2}p_I A L_I^{1/2} K^{-1/2} - r = 0,$$

$$\frac{\partial \pi_j(\cdot)}{\partial L_{II}} = \frac{1}{2}p_{II} A L_{II}^{-1/2} H^{1/2} - 1 = 0, \qquad \frac{\partial \pi_j(\cdot)}{\partial H} = \frac{1}{2}p_{II} A L_{II}^{1/2} H^{-1/2} - w_H = 0.$$

Multiplying the first condition by L_I and the second by K yields

$$\frac{1}{2}p_I A L_I^{1/2} K^{1/2} = L_I, \qquad \frac{1}{2}p_I A L_I^{1/2} K^{1/2} = rK. \tag{15.27}$$

The demand functions for L_I and K are obtained by solving (15.27) for L_I and K (using $q_I = A L_I^{1/2} K^{1/2}$)

$$L_I = \frac{1}{2}p_I q_I, \qquad K = \frac{1}{2r}p_I q_I. \tag{15.28}$$

Substituting (15.28) into $q_I = L^{1/2} K^{1/2}$ yields

$$q_I = A\left(\frac{1}{2}p_I q_I\right)^{1/2}\left(\frac{1}{2r}p_I q_I\right)^{1/2} = A\left(\frac{1}{2}p_I q_I\right)\left(\frac{1}{r}\right)^{1/2}.$$

The previous expression can be solved for the reward on physical capital r

$$r(p_I) = \left(\frac{p_I A}{2}\right)^2.$$

Substituting $r(p_I)$ into $K = p_I q_I / 2r$ in (15.28) for q_I and using the full employment condition yields

$$Q_I(p_I, \bar{K}) = \frac{p_I A^2 \bar{K}}{2}.$$

Following similar steps yields w_H and q_{II} in terms of price p_{II}

$$q_{II} = A\left(\frac{1}{2}p_{II}q_{II}\right)\left(\frac{1}{w_H}\right)^{1/2} \quad \rightarrow \quad w_H(p_{II}) = \left(\frac{p_{II}A}{2}\right)^2$$

$$\rightarrow \quad Q_{II}(p_{II}, \bar{H}) = \frac{p_{II}A^2\bar{H}}{2}.$$

The discussion in the text uses the fact that Q_I can also be computed as

$$Q_I = \frac{d(r\bar{K})}{dp_I} = \frac{d\left((p_I^2 A^2/4)\bar{K}\right)}{dp_I} = \frac{p_I A^2}{2}\bar{K},$$

and similarly for Q_{II}.

15.12.3. Equilibrium Policies in the Absence of Lobbies

In the absence of pressures, the government chooses the price vector maximizing population welfare

$$\max_{p} W^P = \bar{L} + r(p_I)\bar{K} + w_H(p_{II})\bar{H} + N[tr(p_I, p_{II}) + CS^i(p_I, p_{II})],$$

where $tr(p_I, p_{II})$ represents per capita transfers to the population and CS^i represents the consumer surplus of individual i.

The first order conditions are

$$\frac{\partial W^P}{\partial p_I} = Q_I(p_I) + N\left(\frac{\partial tr}{\partial p_I} + \frac{\partial CS^i}{\partial p_I}\right)$$

$$= Q_I(p_I) + N\left[d_I - \frac{1}{N}Q_I + (p_I - p_I^W)\left(\frac{d(d_I)}{dp_I} - \frac{1}{N}\frac{\partial Q_I}{\partial p_I}\right) - d_I\right]$$

$$= Q_I + Nd_I - Q_I + (p_I - p_I^W)\left(N\frac{d(d_I)}{dp_I} - \frac{\partial Q_I}{\partial p_I}\right) - Nd_I$$

$$= (p_I - p_I^W)\left(N\frac{d(d_I)}{dp_I} - \frac{\partial Q_I}{\partial p_I}\right) = (p_I - p_I^W)\frac{\partial M_I}{\partial p_I}$$

$$= (p_I - p_I^W)\left(-N - \frac{A^2\bar{K}}{2}\right) = 0,$$

where the second equality is derived using tr in (15.5) and $CS = u^i(d_I, d_{II}) - [p_Id_I + p_{II}d_{II}]$.

Similarly, for p_{II}

$$\frac{\partial W^P}{\partial p_{II}} = Q_{II} + N\left(\frac{\partial tr}{\partial p_{II}} + \frac{\partial CS^i}{\partial p_{II}}\right)$$

$$= Q_{II} + Nc_{II} - Q_{II}(p_{II}) + (p_{II} - p_{II}^W)\left(N\frac{d(d_{II})}{dp_{II}} - \frac{\partial Q_{II}}{\partial p_{II}}\right) - Nc_{II}$$

$$= (p_{II} - p_{II}^W)\left(N\frac{d(d_{II})}{dp_{II}} - \frac{\partial Q_{II}(p_{II})}{\partial p_{II}}\right) = (p_{II} - p_{II}^W)\frac{\partial M_{II}}{\partial p_{II}}$$

$$= (p_{II} - p_{II}^W)\left(-N - \frac{A^2\bar{H}}{2}\right) = 0.$$

15.12.4. Equilibrium Trade Policies with One Lobby

Substituting (15.14) into (15.10) yields (15.12), which correspond to the first order conditions associated to the *TNE* problem in (15.16)

$$\frac{\partial W^K_{Gross}(p^N)}{\partial p_I} + \phi\frac{\partial W^P(p^N)}{\partial p_I} = 0, \qquad \frac{\partial W^K_{Gross}(p^N)}{\partial p_{II}} + \phi\frac{\partial W^P(p^N)}{\partial p_{II}} = 0. \qquad (15.29)$$

Using

$$W^K_{Gross} = \sum_{k=1}^{N_K} l^k + r(p_I)\bar{K} + \alpha_K N(tr - CS^k),$$

where *tr* is defined in (15.5) and $CS^i = u^i(d_I, d_{II}) - [p_I d_I + p_{II} d_{II}]$, we get

$$\frac{\partial W^K_{Gross}}{\partial p_I} = Q_J + \alpha_K N \left[d_I - \frac{1}{N}Q_J + (p_I - p_I^W)\left(\frac{\partial d_I}{\partial p_I} - \frac{1}{N}\frac{\partial Q_J}{\partial p_I}\right) - d_I \right]$$

$$= (1 - \alpha_K)Q_J + \alpha_K(p_I - p_I^W)\left(N\frac{\partial d_I}{\partial p_I} - \frac{\partial Q_J}{\partial p_I}\right)$$

$$= (1 - \alpha_K)Q_J + \alpha_K(p_I - p_I^W)\frac{\partial M_I}{\partial p_I}$$

$$= (1 - \alpha_K)\left(\frac{p_I A}{2}\right)^2 + \alpha_K(p_I - p_I^W)\frac{\partial M_I}{\partial p_I},$$

where $\partial M_I/\partial p_I = N\partial d_I/\partial p_I - \partial Q_J/\partial p_I$ (since $M_I = Nd_I - Q_J$) and the last equality is obtained using (15.3). Similarly

$$\frac{\partial W^K_{Gross}}{\partial p_{II}} = Q_{II}(p_{II}) + \alpha_K(p_{II} - p_{II}^W)\frac{\partial M_{II}}{\partial p_{II}}$$

$$= (1 - \alpha_K)\left(\frac{p_{II} A}{2}\right)^2 + \alpha_K(p_{II} - p_{II}^W)\frac{\partial M_{II}}{\partial p_{II}}.$$

Recall that in the no-lobby case we obtained

$$\frac{\partial W^P}{\partial p_I} = (p_I - p_I^W)\frac{\partial M_I}{\partial p_I},$$

$$\frac{\partial W^P}{\partial p_{II}} = (p_{II} - p_{II}^W)\frac{\partial M}{\partial p_{II}}.$$

Substituting $\partial W^K_{Gross}/\partial p_I$ and $\partial W^P/\partial p_I$ into (15.29) yields

$$0 = (1 - \alpha_K)Q_J(p_I) + \alpha_K(p_I - p_I^W)\frac{\partial M_I}{\partial p_I} + \phi(p_I - p_I^W)\frac{\partial M_I}{\partial p_I}.$$

Rearranging terms,

$$(p_I - p_I^W)\frac{\partial M_I}{\partial p_I}(\alpha_K + \phi) = (\alpha_K - 1)Q_J(p_I).$$

Dividing the previous expression by p_I and the resulting right-hand side expression by M_I/M_I yields

$$\frac{p_I - p_I^W}{p_I} = \frac{(\alpha_K - 1)Q_J}{p_I(\alpha_K + \phi)(\partial M_I/\partial p_I)} = \frac{\alpha_K - 1}{\alpha_K + \phi}\frac{M_I Q_J}{p_I M_I(\partial M_I/\partial p_I)}$$

$$= \frac{1 - \alpha_K}{\alpha_K + \phi}\frac{Q_J}{M_I \varepsilon_I},$$

where $\varepsilon_I = -[p_I/M_I][\partial M_I/\partial p_I]$. A similar procedure applied to the unorganized sector II produces

$$\frac{p_{II} - p_{II}^W}{p_{II}} = \frac{\alpha_K Q_{II}}{p_{II}(\alpha_K + \phi)(\partial M_{II}/\partial p_{II})}$$

$$= \frac{-\alpha_K}{\alpha_K + \phi}(Q_{II}/M_{II})\frac{1}{-(p_{II}/M_{II})(\partial M_{II}/\partial p_{II})} = \frac{-\alpha_K}{\alpha_K + \phi}\frac{Q_{II}}{M_{II}\varepsilon_{II}}.$$

The previous formulas can be summarized using the indicator function I_i ($I_i = 1$ if i has a lobby and $I_i = 0$ if i does not have a lobby)

$$\frac{p_i - p_i^W}{p_i} = \frac{(I_i - \alpha_K)Q_i}{p_i(\alpha_K + \phi)(-\partial M_i/\partial p_i)} = \frac{I_i - \alpha_K}{\alpha_K + \phi}\frac{Q_i}{M_i}\frac{1}{-p_i/M_i(\partial M_i/\partial p_i)}$$

$$= \frac{I_i - \alpha_K}{\alpha_K + \phi}\frac{Q_i}{M_i\varepsilon_i},$$

where the first and last equalities correspond to the two equivalent expressions in Grossman and Helpman (1994). Finally, let us reexpress in terms of the *ad valorem* tariff $t_i = (p_i - p_i^W)/p_i^W$ and in terms of the tariff factor $\tau_i \equiv 1 + t_i$

$$\frac{p_i - p_i^W}{p_i} = \frac{(p_i - p_i^W)/p_i^W}{(p_i^W + p_i - p_i^W)/p_i^W} = \frac{(p_i - p_i^W)/p_i^W}{1 + ((p_i - p_i^W)/p_i^W)} = \frac{t_i}{1 + t_i} = \frac{\tau_i - 1}{\tau_i}.$$

Grossman and Helpman (1994) use the symbol t^0 to denote the *ad valorem* tariff (our t) and define t as 1 plus the *ad valorem* tariff rate (our τ).

16

Preferential Trade Arrangements

The proliferation of preferential trading arrangements (PTAs) since the 1980s represents a most significant development in global trade. A large share of world trade takes place within about sixty overlapping arrangements that reduce barriers to trade on a preferential basis. Thirty percent of world trade takes place within the two largest preferential trading areas: the European Union (EU) and the North American Free Trade Agreement (NAFTA). To a large extent, preferential arrangements represent regionalism in the sense of joining countries that are geographically close to each other.

This chapter examines the economics of PTAs. Section 16.1 describes the main types of PTAs. Section 16.2 reviews the rationales for PTAs while Section 16.3 examines their costs, benefits, and welfare effects. Section 16.4 asks why a small country might decide to join an existing free trade agreement and Section 16.5 examines the political viability of a free trade area. Section 16.6 discusses how the multilateral system can accommodate preferential agreements.

16.1. TYPES OF PREFERENTIAL AGREEMENTS

Between 1948 and 1994, 109 preferential agreements were notified to the GATT. Most of these arrangements involved European countries. In fact, the European Community and the European Free Trade Association (EFTA) were parties to 76 of these 109 notified agreements. The European Union is involved in most of the over sixty extant arrangements (Sapir, 1998). The number of regional agreements notified to the WTO had surged to 194 by 1999.

The major types of preferential arrangements are free trade areas, customs unions, common markets, and economic unions. Free trade areas and customs unions eliminate internal trade barriers. The distinction between these arrangements is that customs unions coordinate external policies by setting a common external tariff wall while each free trade area member is allowed to set its own external tariffs on imports from nonmembers. GATT Article XXIV:5 requires that the external duties and commercial regulations applied by free trade areas and customs unions to nonmembers must not exceed or be more restrictive than those applied before their creation.

The NAFTA negotiated between Canada, Mexico, and the United States, which became effective in January 1995, is currently the largest free trade area. The EFTA, is a free trade area formed in 1960 by Austria, Denmark, Norway, Portugal, Sweden, Switzerland, and the United Kingdom as a response to the formation of the European Economic Community (EEC) in 1957. Except Norway and Switzerland, all original members of the EFTA have become members of the European Union. Mercosur, established in March 1991, set up a partial customs union in 1995 among Argentina, Brazil, Uruguay, and Paraguay. Mercosur has set a dateline, 2005, for achieving free trade and setting a common external tariff structure. In 1996, Bolivia and Chile became associate members who kept their own external tariff structure.

A common market is a customs union that allows the free movement of capital and people. The EEC , created in 1957 by the Treaty of Rome, and its successor the European Community (EC), created in 1965, were customs unions that constituted a limited common market. The EEC and the EC were imperfect common markets because movements of capital and people were limited.

An economic union is a common market that unifies fiscal, tax, monetary, and other policies. By harmonizing policies, an economic union goes beyond free trade in goods, services, and factors of production. The European Union—the European Community changed its name to the European Union in 1994—is an example of an economic and monetary union.

16.2. RATIONALES FOR PREFERENTIAL AGREEMENTS

The proliferation of preferential trade arrangements raises two basic questions. First, why should governments enter into preferential trade agreements? Second, what explains the proliferation of regional trade agreements since the 1980s?

Let us review the rationales for preferential agreements and some counterarguments and caveats presented by advocates of the multilateral approach. The multiple rationales for preferential arrangements include the management of market power, raising incomes and growth, reaction against delays in multilateral negotiations, benefiting political interests, insurance against foreign protection, stimulus to reform, and enhanced security.

16.2.1. *Market Power, Terms of Trade, and Bargaining Rationales*

Paradoxically, preferential agreements can be formed by countries to obtain greater monopoly power in world markets or to avoid the deleterious effects of market power. In other words, these groupings can be made to work as a block for monopolization while impeding the exploitation of monopoly power among members.

On one hand, the exploitation of market power aims to achieve favorable terms of trade. However, Krugman (1991*a*), Richardson (1994), and Findlay and Panagariya (1996) present different setups in which the proliferation of this type of regionalism can be counterproductive and end up raising tariffs worldwide and reducing block and global welfare. Ceteris paribus, an import tariff in the presence of market power lowers the world price of the affected import relative to the price of exports. But this term of trade effect disappears if all countries impose import tariffs on each other's goods.

Larger size also confers greater bargaining power *vis-à-vis* third parties and serves as a coordination device for members. This rationale is often cited in the European Union.

On the other hand, preferential agreements can be used to avoid harmful terms of trade effects arising in prisoner's dilemma situations. In a prisoners' dilemma situation, large countries have incentives to establish trade barriers to improve their terms of trade at the expense of their trading partners. However, if all governments follow these incentives, trade shrinks and all parties lose. A preferential arrangement among countries facing a prisoners' dilemma establishes rules that can break a negative prisoner's dilemma outcome. However, Bagwell and Staiger (1999a) show that preferential agreements create market power and entail discriminatory distortions, concluding that multilateralism is in principle the best way to address terms of trade prisoners' dilemmas. For other models stressing terms of trade effects see Mayer (1981) and Grossman and Helpman (1995b).

16.2.2. Greater Trade, Incomes, and Growth Rates

Preferential agreements encourage trade between natural trading partners. Economic geography supports the idea that countries that are close to each other tend to trade more among themselves. The elimination of artificial trade barriers is welfare-improving, although it is not clear why the discriminatory elimination of barriers improves upon multilateral liberalization. Krugman (1991b), Frankel (1997), and the papers in Frankel (1998) examine the theory and empirical evidence relating to the economic geography rationale.

The larger market size achieved by grouping countries together can increase income per capita and accelerate economic growth. Market enlargement sustains greater product variety and permits cost reductions by allowing firms to spread fixed costs over larger sales and by allowing exploitation of economies of scale. The endogenous growth approach emphasizes the idea that economic integration creates larger markets that can induce a shift of resources toward inventive activities and produce growth effects (see Rivera-Batiz and Romer, 1991; Grossman and Helpman, 1991a). The notion that integration can lead to higher income per capita or faster growth rates was used to promote the formation of the European Union.

Advocates of multilateralism point out that the higher income and faster growth arguments for integration are usually cast in terms of multilateral liberalization and do not necessarily hold under preferential trade liberalization. The extent of the growth and income effects due to the creation of PTAs is still a subject of controversy.

16.2.3. Bypass Delays in Negotiations for Liberalization

Bilateral negotiations for trade liberalization often represent a faster and less costly negotiation channel compared with delayed multilateral liberalization. This approach stresses that the consensus requirement of the WTO/GATT and the complexity of multilateral negotiations lead to long delays in the completion of GATT negotiation rounds. In fact, it took almost a decade (1986–94) to complete the Uruguay Round of multilateral negotiations. When multilateral negotiations become cumbersome enough, countries negotiate preferential agreements directly as an alternative path to liberalization. Ethier (1998*a*) stresses that regionalism is a function of the benefits and costs of negotiation and can replace multilateralism if the latter runs out of steam.

The delay rationale for preferential agreements has given rise to counterarguments by advocates of the multilateral approach. First, because multilateral agreements cover more countries than bilateral agreements, they are likely to extend over a longer period. But this is just the nature of comprehensive and complex negotiations, not a disadvantage. Second, if it is true that the completion of the Uruguay Round was delayed by disagreements over the EU Common Agricultural Policy (CAP) and the protection of Japanese rice, it is also true that preferential agreements have been similarly delayed by disagreements over agriculture and other issues. In fact, preferential agreements typically leave agricultural liberalization out of their scope. The real issue concerns which approach best tackles disagreements and produces the best outcome. The answer to this question is not obvious at all.

16.2.4. Insurance, Economic Reform, and Credibility

The best way to obtain insurance against trading partners' protectionist measures is to join its trading system as an insider. Many observers argue that small countries enter into preferential agreements to obtain insurance against reversions toward protectionism by large trading partners (Whalley, 1998). Regional arrangements incorporate a legal framework and dispute settlement procedures that provide substantial insurance against member misbehavior such as slapping protectionist policies on each other. The safe haven motive is a major factor explaining why Mexico sought a free trade agreement with the United States and Canada. Mexico aggressively pursued the approval of NAFTA despite small tariff reduction benefits—United States and Canada's tariff levels were low to begin with—and small estimated welfare gains.

Joining a trading group can facilitate reform, secure foreign investment, and induce transfer of technology. In a globalized world in which firms foreign invest in those regions offering low wages and other benefits, developing countries have incentives to engage in regionalism to increase the likelihood of attracting foreign investment. Regionalism creates synergies involving trade, economic reform, foreign direct investment, and transfer of technology. These points are formalized in Ethier (1998*b*) and have been repeatedly mentioned in relation to Mexico's decision to form a free trade agreement (FTA) with the United States and Canada.

Abiding by rules embodied in preferential agreements enhance government credibility. The commitment to a preferential arrangement represents a credible mechanism to contain lobby protectionist pressures and avoid an inefficient allocation of resources in a political equilibrium with interest groups (Maggi and Rodríguez-Clare, 1998). The commitment effect does not depend on terms of trade effects and applies whether countries are small or large. Notice that this argument can also be used to advocate a comprehensive multilateral agreement and that political pressures do not disappear but are rather shifted from internal to external trade barriers. Fernandez and Portes (1998), Tornell and Esquivel (1997), and others point out that a preferential agreement affects the credibility of the commitment to ongoing reform policies, signals government intentions and goals, and provides other nontraditional benefits through mechanisms that are not necessarily available through unilateral liberalization (which can be reversed) or multilateral liberalization (which might be limited and late).

16.2.5. Political Rationals: Interest Groups and Security

The formation of a large protected market can be a response to interest group pressure. The interest group pressure approach takes a political economy perspective stressing that preferential agreements can serve to favor interest groups. The formation of preferential arrangements is viewed as a political equilibrium in the presence of interest groups favoring or opposing them (Grossman and Helpman, 1995*a*).

Trade is said to enhanced security. Greater trade interactions raise trust among peoples of different countries and enhance security levels. Because security is a public good, security effects are external to individuals and are not fully exploited. Preferential agreements and closer integration can be viewed as a trade subsidy granted to attain optimal security levels. In fact, the formation of the EC/European Union and the enlargement to incorporate Eastern European countries are considered as much a security as an economic arrangement. Observers have hailed the deepening of integration by establishing a single currency, the euro, in 2002 as a mechanism for maintaining peace and consolidating security.

Schiff and Winters (1998) accept the security argument at face value and proceed to argue that optimum trade preferences for security reasons have a transitory nature. As security improves over time, both the marginal value of security and the marginal impact of trade on security decline. Therefore, dynamic optimality calls for external liberalization to keep the value of the preferential arrangement. The gradual decline of EU external tariffs is consistent with this dynamic view. The authors point out that global free trade would also enhance interactions and that trade preferences have a special value only if political rapprochement cannot take place without a preferential agreement.

16.2.6. Who is Right?

Recapping, the rationales advanced in the literature rely on economic, political, and security elements. Economic elements include two opposing goals depending on specific circumstances: the exploitation of favorable terms of trade effects or the avoidance of adverse terms of trade effects. Preferential arrangements can also encourage trade among natural trading partners, allow the exploitation of economies of scale, generate product variety and growth effects, represent a response to delays of the WTO multilateral negotiation process, support reform efforts, enhance government credibility, attract foreign investment, and consolidate procompetitive policies though market opening. Political elements include two opposite rationales depending on specific circumstances: a response to pressures exerted by local lobbies or a mechanism to prevent local lobby control.

If a partial review of arguments for preferential arrangements produces a long check-list, the list of counterarguments and caveats is even longer (Bhagwati and Krueger, 1995; Panagariya, 1999, 2000*b*). It stands to reason that it is difficult to assess preferential arrangements by looking at individual arguments alone. Reaching a conclusion about the preferential arrangement vs multilateralism controversy requires an evaluation of the overall consequences of preferential arrangements. This means examining static and dynamic implications, alternative ways of reaching the same goals and relevant empirical evidence as it becomes available.

16.2.7. Dynamic Trade Effects of NAFTA and CUSFTA

A full assessment of the economic effects of preferential arrangements on members must go beyond static considerations to consider the dynamic implications of blocks on trade creation and diversion (Bhagwati, 1993).

Romalis (2002*b*) focuses on the dynamic trade effects of NAFTA and CUSFTA. His research strategy is to contrast where the United States and the European Union source their imports of about 5000 products. The dynamic analysis takes into account the timing of US tariff preferences favoring Canadian and Mexican products. The counterfactual analysis suggests that, without NAFTA, the growth of Mexican share in US trade since 1994 would have been less than the fast growth actually experienced. About one third of the increase of US imports from Mexico since 1994 can be attributed to NAFTA. Moreover, the Canadian share of US trade might not have increased without CUSFTA. In the 1980s, the Canadian share of US imports declined in all tariff classes but there was a rebound just as CUSFTA was being negotiated.

Many observers did not expect great trade effects from NAFTA. The argument was that US tariff rates were already low. The average elasticities of substitution estimated by Romalis, which fall between 4 and 7, can help explain why modest trade liberalization had pronounced trade effects. The worrisome result, however, is that the tariff preferences were granted in industries with large imports from outside North America. As a result, NAFTA had substantial trade diverting effects.

16.3. ESTIMATING THE WELFARE EFFECTS OF PTAs

Viner (1950) exposed the basic fallacy of identifying customs union formation with a move toward free trade: a customs union represents free trade between members but protection with respect to nonmembers. The same point applies to free trade areas. The net welfare effect of a preferential arrangement depends on the relative weight of its trade creation and trade diversion effects. In addition, the welfare effect of forming a customs union depends on its terms of trade effects and on the extent to which the market power associated to larger size and a coordinated external trade policy is exploited by setting a higher external tariff.

16.3.1. Trade Diversion and Creation

What are the net welfare-effects of preferential agreements? The answer given by Viner (1950) classic analysis of customs unions is that the net welfare effect is ambiguous in sign. The answer rests on the distinction between the trade creating and trade diverting effects of customs unions.

Viner focused on the trade effects of exogenously determined external tariff structures in a perfect competition model with constant returns to scale. Trade creation takes place when the imports and exports of members of a preferential arrangement expand due to the elimination of internal trade barriers. High-price products that are produced locally at relatively high costs can be imported from low-cost fellow members. Trade diversion occurs when trade shifts from outside trading partners to members of the preferential arrangement. A product that is available at a relatively low price from a more efficient outsider is produced at a higher cost and sold at a higher price within the arrangement. Trade diversion induces inefficient production within the arrangement and lowers consumer surplus. The balance between trade diversion and trade creation is one of the key elements determining the net welfare effects of preferential arrangements.

16.3.2. Ex Post and Ex Ante Modeling

What are the welfare effects of preferential arrangements in practice? The tools used by economists to assess the welfare effects of preferential arrangements fall into two categories: ex post and ex ante assessments.

Ex ante analyses are based on computable general equilibrium models and are used to predict the effects of a preferential arrangement before it is formed. Assessments of resource allocation effects and welfare changes are based on estimated parameters and data corresponding to the period preceding the formation of the preferential agreement.

Computable general equilibrium models (CGE), also called applied general equilibrium models (AGE), have been used for policy purposes by the US government, the European Commission, the World Bank, and other institutions. A detailed review of the initial efforts in general equilibrium trade policy modeling is offered by Shoven and Whalley (1984) and Srinivasan and Whalley (1986). Reviews of existing evidence on the welfare effects of preferential agreements include Srinivasan *et al.* (1993), who summarize ex post and ex ante studies of regional agreements conducted between the 1960s and 1989, and Baldwin and Venables (1995). Work on NAFTA is examined in Francois and Shiells (1994) and Kehoe and Kehoe (1994, 1995).

The evidence offered by general equilibrium exercises was used as supporting evidence during the process leading to the creation of the Single Market in Europe (1993) and NAFTA (1995). Most work using computable general equilibrium models reports positive but often small welfare gains from preferential agreements. The reported estimates range from near zero to about 10 percent of gross domestic product. Most static estimates fall below 3 percent of GDP. Generally, models that account for scale and growth effects yield higher estimates than static models.

Ex post analyses utilize data available after the preferential arrangement has been formed. These studies often focus on the effect of preferential arrangements on the trade shares of members and nonmembers. These analyses are limited because trade shares relate to welfare measures only indirectly through the measurement of trade diversion and trade creation effects.

16.3.3. Decomposing the Welfare Effects of Integration

Policy initiatives such as forming a preferential arrangement generate welfare effects through numerous channels. Baldwin and Venables (1995) present the following useful decomposition of welfare changes into components that capture major static and dynamic effects.

Consider the indirect utility function $V(p + t, n, E)$, where p, t and n are vectors of border prices, unit tariff rates (including the tariff equivalent of nontariff barriers) and the number of available varieties in each industry. E represents aggregate consumption expenditure and is equal to aggregate income minus aggregate investment I (the symbol $'$ indicates the row vectors formed by transposing column vectors)

$$E = wL + rK + [p' + t' - c'(w, r, q)]Q + t'Rm - I.$$

Aggregate income is equal to the sum of the aggregate wage bill wL, aggregate income from capital rK, firm profits $(p' + t' - c')Q$ and domestically accrued trade rents $t'Rm$ (see interpretation below), where $p' - t' - c'$ is a row vector of the gaps between prices inclusive of trade barriers and average costs while Q and m are column vectors of industry outputs and net imports (net exports correspond to $m < 0$). The vector $c(w, r, q)$ consists of the average cost in each industry and depends on the wage rate w, the return to capital r and the vector q of production per firm in each industry.

Totally differentiating $V(p+t, n, E)$ and dividing by the marginal utility of spending $V_E = \partial V / \partial E$ yields (see derivation in the appendix)

$$\frac{dV}{V_E} = t'Rdm - m'd(t - Rt) - m'dp + (p' + t' - c')dQ$$

$$- Q'c_q dq + \left[\frac{V_n}{V_E}\right]' dn + \left(\frac{\tilde{r}}{\rho} - 1\right) dI, \tag{16.1}$$

where d represents a differential. The column vectors n and q indicate the number of varieties per industry and output per firm in each industry.

The terms in the previous decomposition of welfare changes correspond to the following welfare effects of policies or preferential arrangements:

1. $t'Rdm$ measures the trade volume welfare effect . The matrix R is a diagonal matrix consisting of constant proportions $r_{ii} \in [0, 1]$ along the diagonal and zeros elsewhere. The diagonal elements measure the proportion of the wedges between

consumer and producer prices that create rents for domestic agents. The vector $t'R$ measures the trade barrier component that represents rents to domestic agents. If $r_{ii} = 1$ for all i, $t'R = t'$ and the rents from tariff and nontariff barriers in each sector i are fully captured by domestic agents. If $r_{ii} = 0$, $t'R = 0$ and domestic agents are not able to capture any rents from the applicable tariff and nontariff barriers. If $r_{ii} > 0$, the reduction in import volumes due to higher trade barriers ($dm < 0$) has a first-order negative effect on welfare.

The term $t'R\,dm$ is akin to the standard triangle measure of welfare losses from existing trade restrictions. If all elements of the diagonal of R are equal to $1/2$ ($r_{ii} = 1/2$ for all i), $t'R = t'/2$. In this case, $t'R\,dm$ specializes to the standard welfare triangle $(1/2)t_i\,dm_i$ for all industries. The welfare decomposition shows that changes in imports and exports do not matter by themselves but rather through their interactions with existing trade barriers.

2. $m'd(t - Rt)$ is the trade cost effect. The trade cost effect depends on the volume of net imports and the change in the vector $t - Rt$ representing the component of trade barriers lost to the economy.

3. $-m'\,dp$ measures the terms of trade effect. The welfare impact of a boost in a product's price is negative if the good is an importable, $m > 0$, and positive if the good is an exportable, $m < 0$.

4. $(p' + t' - c')\,dQ$ measures the output effect in the presence of imperfect competition. Imperfect competition prevails when the price plus the tariff paid to the government exceeds marginal costs. The welfare decomposition assumes that marginal costs are equal to average costs c. A higher output level has a positive welfare effect if and only if consumer prices are greater than average costs.

5. $-Q'c_q\,dq$ is the scale effect. The matrix $c_q = \partial c/\partial q$ consists of the derivatives of the average cost vector with respect to the output per firm vector. It indicates the effect of a greater output per firm on each industry's average cost. When output per firm increases, $dq > 0$, the cost per unit of output changes by c_q and the total change in average cost is $Q'c_q dq$. Notice that increasing returns imply that $\partial c_i/\partial q_i < 0$.

6. $[V_n/V_E]'\,dn$ is the variety effect. If there is a positive variety effect ($V_n > 0$), an increase in the number of firms in each industry, each assumed to specialize in a different variety, improves welfare.

7. $((\tilde{r}/\rho) - 1)dI$ is the accumulation effect. The variable $\tilde{r}$ is the social return to capital and ρ is the economy's rate of discount. Greater investment dI is assumed to generate a flow of welfare equal to the discounted value $\tilde{r}/\rho$ of the social rate of return $\tilde{r}$ and to entail current forgone consumption costs equal to the amount invested. If the discounted value of the social rate of return of additional investment is greater than the implied unit of forgone consumption, capital accumulation has a positive welfare effect. An implicit assumption is that it takes a unit of consumption to generate a unit of investment.

The welfare decomposition illustrates the difficulties faced when trying to evaluate the welfare effects of preferential arrangements. Researchers must measure existing trade restrictions and price markups at a disaggregated level. They must also estimate induced investment, and determine changes in net imports, terms of trade, output levels, output per firm, and product variety. Furthermore, the application of the previous welfare decomposition requires estimating the trade rent parameters in R, the cost parameters in c_q, and assessing the welfare effects of changes in industry prices, number of goods and expenditure (i.e. estimating V_p, V_n, and V_E).

16.4. WHY UNILATERALLY JOIN AN FTA?

Why would a government unilaterally decide to join an existing FTA? Maggi and Rodríguez-Clare (1998) show that an FTA serves to mitigate internal pressures from interest groups. Lobbies pressure the government to engage in trade intervention that sustains an increase of the domestic price of the organized industry. Lobbying activity induces an inefficient equilibrium allocation of resources. The shift of resources toward the organized industry leads to overextended production relative to the free trade output level. If the inefficiencies in the allocation of resources are large enough, the government might be worse off in the political equilibrium than if pre-committing to an FTA or free trade.

16.4.1. *Political Pressures in a Bargaining Game*

Consider a small economy that produces a numeraire good labeled 0 and a manufacturing good labeled I. Capital K is used in both sectors but land T is only used in the numeraire sector

$$q_0 = q_0(K_0, \bar{T}), \qquad q_I = q_I(K_I) = K_I,$$

where $p_0 = 1$ and $K_0 + K_I = \bar{K}$ (the bar represents economywide endowments). The linear manufacturing production function $q_I(K_I) = K_I$ implies the price of the manufacturing good p_I is also the value of the marginal product of capital $r_I = d(p_I q_I)/dK_I = p_I$.

Government welfare W^G depends on contributions and population welfare

$$W^G(p_I, K_I) = a^{K_I} C^{K_I}(p_I, K_I) + W^P(p_I, K_I).$$

The factor a^{K_I} represents the relative weight given to the lobby made up of the owners of capital in the manufacturing sector. Population welfare W^P is given by the income on capital in both sectors plus tariff revenues (or minus export subsidies) plus aggregate consumer surplus CS

$$W^P(p_I, K_I) = \frac{\partial q_0}{\partial T} T \frac{\partial q_0}{\partial K_0} K_0 + p_I K_I + (p_I - p_I^W)(D_I - K_I) + CS,$$

where imports of manufacturing goods are given by domestic consumption D_I minus production $q_I = K_I$. Because population is normalized to unity ($N = 1$ and

$D_i = Nd_i = d_i$), aggregate consumer surplus equals

$$CS(d_I, p_I) = u(d_0, d_I) - p_0 d_0 - p_I d_I$$
$$= d_0 + d_I - \tfrac{1}{2} d_I^2 - d_0 - p_I d_I$$
$$= d_I - \tfrac{1}{2} d_I^2 - p_I d_I,$$

where the demand for d_I is $d_I(p_I) = 1 - p_I$. Because d_0 enters linearly into the utility function, it does not generate consumer surplus.

A single lobby maximizes a welfare function W_{Net}^K given by the total income obtained by the owners of capital in the manufacturing sector net of total political contributions made, $r_I K_I - c^{K_I} K_I$ (c^{K_I} is the contribution per unit of capital)

$$W_{Net}^K(p, K_I) = W_{Gross}^K(p, K_I) - C^{K_I}(p, K_I) = r_I K_I - c^{K_I} K_I$$
$$= p_I K_I - c^{K_I} K_I,$$

where $p = (1, p_I)$. Owners of capital are true capitalists that do not earn any income from land. Furthermore, manufacturing capital is assumed to be extremely concentrated so that the number of capital owners in manufacturing N_{K_I} is negligible in relation to total population N ($N_{K_I}/N \approx 0$). Accordingly, lobby welfare ignores land rents as well as the share of the lobby in the redistribution of tariff revenues or in domestic consumer surplus.

In the first stage of the political game, owners of capital decide to which sector to devote their capital (i.e. determine $K_I = \bar{K} - K_0$). After the sectorial allocation decision is taken, capital becomes specific. In other words, capital is initially mobile across sectors but becomes immobile after the sectorial allocation takes place. In the second stage, the government and the lobby simultaneously bargain over the lobby contribution c^{K_I} and the domestic price of manufacturing p_I (that reflects the trade policy), taking as given the allocation of capital. The world price of manufacturing p_I^W is exogenously given. The existing free trade area corresponds to the rest of the world and there are no external tariffs against third countries.

The structure of the game implies that owners of capital, the government and the lobby do not make any commitments. The capital allocation decision is undertaken nonstrategically by decentralized owners of capital, meaning that (1) they do not exploit any strategic power against each other, and (2) they do not exploit the first mover advantage against the government and the lobby. Finally, there is no commitment or manipulation in the lobby-government interaction because they bargain simultaneously on the basis of exogenously-given bargaining power.

In the second stage, (1) the government sets a welfare-maximizing short term equilibrium price $p_I^E(K_I)$ embodying trade intervention, and (2) Nash bargaining between the government and the lobby determines the per unit of capital contribution function

$c^{K_I,E}(K_I)$. Welfare maximization yields the price function (see appendix)

$$p_I^E(K_I) = \arg\max_{p_I} W^G(p, K_I) = a^{K_I} C^{K_I,E}(p, K_I) + W^P(p, K_I)$$

$$\rightarrow p_I^E(K_I) = p_I^W + a^{K_I} K_I,$$

where p_I^W is the world price level. The equilibrium price exceeds the world price level and is higher (1) the greater the allocation of capital to the manufacturing sector K_I, which is the variable set in period 1 and is thus predetermined from the perspective of the second stage, and (2) the higher the weight given to contributions in the government welfare function.

The contribution function is the outcome of a Nash bargaining problem involving the maximization of the geometric average of government and lobby surplus with weights given by the bargaining power of each player. Formally,

$$W^B(c^{K_I,E}(K_I))$$

$$= \max_{c^{K_I}}[W^G(p_I^E(K_I), K_I) - W^G(p_I^W, K_I)]^\sigma \times [(p_I - c^{K_I})K_I - p_I^W K_I]^{(1-\sigma)}.$$

The first order maximization condition implies that the negotiated contribution function per unit if capital is (see appendix)

$$c^{K_I,E}(K_I) = (1-\sigma)\frac{W^P(p_I^W, K_I) - W^P(p_I^E(K_I), K_I)}{a^{K_I}K_I} + \sigma(p_I^W - p_I)$$

$$= \frac{1+\sigma}{2}a^{K_I}K_I.$$

The last equality is obtained by plugging $p_I^E(K) = p_I^W + a^{K_I}K_I$ into the equilibrium equation for c^{K_I} and using $W^G = a^{K_I}C^{K_I} + W^P$. Total contributions are determined as the contribution per weighted capital times the units of capital allocated to the manufacturing sector, $C^{K_I} = c^{K_I}K_I$.

The equilibrium contribution function is a weighted average of (1) the welfare gain from protection per weighted manufacturing capital (welfare under free trade minus welfare under trade intervention, all divided by $a^{K_I}K_I$), and (2) the lobby willingness to pay for protection per unit of manufacturing capital or output ($K_I = q_I$), which equals the increase in price achieved by protection. The equilibrium contribution increases with the relative bargaining power of the government, denoted by σ, the weight of contributions in government welfare and the value of predetermined capital.

We have solved for prices and contributions as a function of a given sectorial allocation of capital (i.e. short run). Given K_I, the equilibrium price and associated trade policy do not depend on bargaining power σ. However the bargaining power parameter σ affects the contributions, and thus the distribution of the surplus. If $\sigma = 0$, the government has no bargaining power and contributions $c^{K_I,E}(K_I) = a^{K_I}K_I/2$ are just enough to compensate the government for the reduction of population welfare caused by protection. If $\sigma = 1, c^{K_I,E}(K_I) = a^{K_I} K_I$, then the lobby has no bargaining power and the government extracts all the surplus derived from protection. The bargaining power parameter σ affects the contributions, and thus the distribution of the surplus, but does not affect trade policy. The reason is that, at the bargaining stage, the allocation of resources is given. Thus, the determination of trade policy and the determination of the distribution of the surplus can be separated.

Looking at lobby contributions and trade policy from the perspective of the first period, in which capital allocation is still a decision variable, bargaining power affects the allocation of capital and thus the domestic price and trade policy. In this situation, the determination of trade policy and the distribution of the surplus cannot be separated. In order to clarify these points one must focus on the whole game including the allocation of capital in the first stage.

In the first stage, investors allocate capital knowing that manufacturing will be protected. The returns on capital in manufacturing net of contributions must be equal to the return on capital invested in the numeraire good. Therefore, the equilibrium allocation of capital to manufacturing K_I^E satisfies

$$p_I^E(K_I) - c^{K_I,E}(K_I) = p_0 \frac{\partial q_0(K_0, \bar{T})}{\partial K_0} = \frac{\partial q_0(\bar{K} - K_I, \bar{T})}{\partial K_0}.$$

Substituting for $p_I^E(K_I)$ and $c^{K_I,E}(K_I)$, and simplifying terms yields

$$p_I^W + a^{K_I} \left(\frac{1 - \sigma}{2} \right) K_I^E = \frac{\partial q_0(\bar{K} - K_I^E, \bar{T})}{\partial K_0}.$$

Suppose that σ is strictly less than 1. The allocation of capital to manufacturing increases when the world price p_I^W is lower, the bargaining power of the government σ is greater, and the political weight of the lobby a^{K_I} is smaller. A greater bargaining power on the part of the government leads to a lower investment into the organized sector, which in turn translates into a lower domestic price (i.e. less protection). From the full game perspective (i.e. long run) greater government bargaining power leads to a smaller allocation of capital to manufacturing, which reduces the contributions and thus the share of the surplus that goes to the government. In other words, the government is compensated less in the long run than in the short run.

The equilibrium domestic price of manufactures, p_I^E, is obtained by substituting K_I^E back into the previously derived price function.

$$p_I^E(K_I^E) = p_I^W + a^{K_I} K_I^E \quad \rightarrow \quad K_I^E = \frac{p_I^E(K_I^E) - p_I^W}{a^{K_I}}.$$

The previous condition implies that trade intervention to increase the price of the manufacturing good above the world price must increase the allocation of capital to manufacturing above the free trade allocation. The associated distortion arises from an excessive amount of capital devoted to manufacturing relative to the numeraire good.

The equilibrium price of manufactures is (see previous contribution equation)

$$p_I^E(K_I^E) = \frac{\partial q_0(\bar{K} - K_I^E, \bar{T})}{\partial K_0} + c^{K,E}(K_I^E)$$

$$= \frac{\partial q_0(\bar{K} - K_I^E, \bar{T})}{\partial K_0} + \frac{1+\sigma}{2} a^K K_I^E.$$

Under free trade and no contributions, the world price prevails and the allocation of capital to manufacturing K_I^{FT} is obtained by equating the value of the marginal product of capital in both sectors

$$p_I^W(K_I^{FT}) = \frac{\partial q_0(\bar{K} - K_I^{FT}, \bar{T})}{\partial K_0}.$$

Because protection sustains an equilibrium price exceeding the world price, the amount of capital allocated to manufacturing is greater under protection than under free trade.

16.4.2. Deciding to Join a Free Trade Area

In a political game without commitment, the government must receive contributions that fully compensate (when the government has no bargaining power) or more than compensate (when the government has some bargaining power) the distortions caused by protecting the lobby. Otherwise, the government will not engage in protection and will move to free trade. Formally, in the political game trade intervention implies

$$W^G(p^E, K_I^E) \geq W^G(p^W, K_I^E). \tag{16.2}$$

The policy choice compares welfare under intervention and under free trade given the distorted level of capital allocation decided in the first period. K_I^E represents a distorted level of capital because, if capitalists know that the government will intervene in the second period in favor of capital in manufacturing, they will overinvest in the politically organized industry. In the political equilibrium, the government reservation level of utility is not undistorted free trade but rather free trade given the distorted allocation of capital. Welfare under free trade with a distorted resource allocation is lower than welfare $W^G(p^W, K_I^{UFT})$ under undistorted free trade (UFT)

$$W^G(p^W, K_I^{UFT}) > W^G(p^W, K_I^E). \tag{16.3}$$

Can a government choosing protection over free trade end up worse off than under a free trade agreement? The answer is positive. Consider a stage previous to the political game in which the government decides between precommitting to undistorted free trade and entering into the political game. Introducing the possibility of precommitment to free trade by joining an existing free trade area creates an environment in which there are no lobby contributions and no distortions in the allocation of capital.

A precommitment to free trade yields greater welfare than a political game with lobby contributions if

$$W^G(p^W, K_I^{FT}) > W^G(p^E, K_I^E).$$

If the previous condition holds, the government prefers to precommit to undistorted free trade at the start of the game and preclude lobby contributions.

Why is it that a government who would choose protection instead of free trade in the political game can still prefer to precommit to free trade? The explanation of this paradoxical result is that the government is not fully compensated for the distortions generated by intervention. On one hand, the government gets compensated for the second stage distortions generated by the tariff for a given allocation of capital. On the other hand, the government does not get compensated for the first stage distortion in the allocation of capital caused by prospects of trade intervention. If the capital allocation distortion is large enough, then the government is worse off under protection than unilaterally precommitting to a free trade agreement. The precommitment allows the government to credibly distance itself from interest group pressures and thus improve efficiency and welfare.

What are the parameter conditions under which unilateral free trade is appealing to a government? The conditions are:

1. The government has low bargaining power in relation to the lobby (σ is low enough). A weak bargaining position leads to a political equilibrium with low contributions and excessive benefits granted to the lobby (i.e. large distortions). In other words, the government derives low rents from the political process and lobbying induces large economic distortions. Therefore, the government will be better off by breaking the political equilibrium. This is realized by precommitting to a free trade agreement.
2. The weight a^{K_I} the government gives to lobby contributions in relation to population welfare is not too low or too high (assuming that the bargaining power of the government is low enough, which works in favor of the FTA). First, if the weight attached to the lobby is low enough, the government will not be willing to generate large distortions on behalf of the lobby. There will be a low level of protection and thus few incentives to precommit to free trade. Second, if the weight given to the lobby is large enough relative to social welfare, the government will generate large distortions on behalf of the lobby and will not be willing to forgo political contributions by precommitting to an FTA. Third, there is an intermediate region of lobby weight values in which there are incentives to enter into an FTA. Notice that if the government bargaining power is relatively low the relative weight given to the lobby has a nonmonotonic relationship with government incentives to join a free trade agreement.

We have focused on inefficiencies linked to lobbying activity that results in overextended production of the organized sector relative to the free trade production level. Other sources of inefficiencies involve keeping unviable firms in operation or slowing down their exit. Organized lobbying can maintain an inefficient unviable industry in operation. The industry survives international competition thanks to government protection. In this setup, the model has multiple equilibria, and free trade can work as a mechanism to eliminate bad equilibria. Alternatively, lobbying can induce protection of declining industries, slowing down the rate of firm exit. In an industry facing a negative shock, the reallocation of resources will be delayed or undertaken at lower speed than that applying to an unprotected industry in the same circumstances. We refer the reader to Maggi and Rodriguez-Clare (1998) for further details.

The analysis provides an explanation for why the Mexican government unilaterally decided to push for entering into an existing free trade agreement between the United States and Canada (CUSFTA). One major factor mentioned was the intent to eliminate once and for all the multiple inefficiencies due to extensive trade intervention in Mexico. It is also true that Mexico did not simply decide to join an existing free trade area. All sides negotiated special conditions strenuously as a requirement for the approval of NAFTA. This suggests the importance of analyzing bilateral decisions.

16.5. POLITICAL VIABILITY OF BILATERAL FTAs

What are the conditions under which FTAs arise as a political equilibrium? Free trade areas can arise by expanding an existing agreement or by forming a new agreement. The question of expansion asks why a country might unilaterally choose to join an existing free trade area (Maggi and Rodriguez-Clare, 1998). The question of formation examines the political viability of the formation of a new free trade area between two trade partners (Grossman and Helpman, 1995a).

In the protection for sale model developed by Grossman and Helpman (1994), political contributions explain why governments obtain greater welfare under protection than without protection. This suggests that, in the presence of lobbies, a government will not go for free trade unilaterally (an exception in which free trade prevails occurs when all individuals belong to lobbies and all sectors have lobbies that compete among themselves and offset each other). The potential lack of political support for free trade leaves open the question about the political basis of preferential trade arrangements. These arrangements (1) involve more than one country, and (2) combine free trade and protection (a country has free trade with some but not all trading partners).

How does the presence of domestic lobbies affect the viability of free trade negotiations between two governments? Which specific economic conditions are required for an FTA to be sustainable in the presence of interest groups? The presence of lobbies generates two types of interactions: foreign relations involving interactions between policymakers, and internal politics involving interactions between policymakers and domestic lobbies. In this context, external and internal politics become dependent on each other. On one hand, free trade negotiations between governments take into account the effect of the negotiations on domestic lobby politics. On the other hand, lobbies seeking domestic privileges recognize the implications of the parallel external negotiation process.

Consideration of the viability of free trade areas (FTAs) requires examination of the interaction between countries. The North American Free Trade Agreement (NAFTA) is not supported by compensation schemes between the members. Other preferential arrangements allow for international compensation. For instance, the European Common Market (i.e. the European Union) has established compensation schemes that provides a transfer of resources to lower income countries such as Greece, Portugal, and Spain.

16.5.1. Rules of Origin in Trade Agreements

A globalized production process means that goods are produced and assembled in many countries. Production sharing implies that there are many goods having multiple origins. In this context, it is arbitrary to impose the same tariff rate on goods produced 80 percent abroad and goods produced only 20 percent abroad.

Rules of origin are regulations imposed by a country or trading region to determine which goods are considered local and which are considered imported goods. These rules provide criteria to determine whether or not a good is subject to tariff and the tariff rate applied if a tariff must be paid. In a globalized world, all countries must formulate clear rules of origin in order to specify tariffs.

The WTO determines national origin on the basis of several considerations or criteria. The first is the country where an imported product experienced the last substantial transformation in the sense of being subject to a change in tariff classification. The second is the percentage of value added accounted for by the countries where production takes place. The third refers to the countries where particular manufacturing processes are located. In other words, national origin is determined on the basis of where a substantial product transformation occurred, a large percentage of value was added, and key manufacturing processes took place. Under NAFTA, the United States utilizes a 62.5 percent value added criterion for automobiles in order to preclude Japanese manufacturers from producing in Mexico to export to the United States. Mercosur utilizes a shift from the 4-digit level tariff classification or 60 percent regional value added as national origin criteria.

Free trade areas rely heavily on rules of origin. First, like all trading regions, free trade areas must specify the conditions under which a product is considered to have been produced inside or outside the area. Second, free trade areas rely on rules of origin to preclude arbitrage practices motivated by the coexistence of different consumer prices within an integrated market. Because free trade areas allow each country to impose its own tariffs against the rest of the world, consumers in different countries within the area pay different tariffs when importing from the rest of the world.

Consider a good that is imported from third countries by two members of a free trade area. Imported good i will have a different price in each importing member country depending on the *ad valorem* tariff rates t_i^L and t_i^H imposed by the low- and high-tariff countries. In terms of the the high-tariff and low-tariff factors $\tau_i^H = 1 + t_i^H$ and $\tau_i^L = 1 + t_i^L$,

$$p_i^H = \tau_i^H p_i^W = \tau_i^H \; > \; p_i^L = \tau_i^L p_i^W = \tau_i^L, \quad \tau_i = 1 + t_i,$$

where the world price $p_i^W = 1$, and p_i^H and p_i^L represent the high-tariff and the low-tariff country price. The coexistence of more than one price for the same imported good opens the door for arbitrage possibilities within the area. If a member does not have adequate rules of origin impeding tariff-free entry of goods that do not have enough local or free trade area content, arbitrageurs would import goods at the low-tariff in one member country and sell them at a profit at the high-tariff price in the other member country.

Notice that, because members of a customs union share a common external tariff wall, there are no intraunion arbitrage opportunities due to multiple external tariffs on the same good. Due to the need to identify nonnational products under production globalization, rules of origin are still important to customs unions. Their role, though, is not to prevent the possibility of arbitrage.

16.5.2. The Politics of FTAs

Grossman and Helpman (1995*a*) utilize the common agency approach to determine the political and economic conditions for the viability of an FTA between two small countries that are subject to pressures from lobbies. In the status quo, two small countries trade among themselves and with the rest of the world. The assumptions on the tariff structure are as follows.

1. Each member country has a different tariff structure, $\{\tau_1^A, \ldots, \tau_G^A\}$ and $\{\tau_1^B, \ldots, \tau_G^B\}$, where G is the number of goods, in which third country imports are taxed at the most-favored nation rate (i.e. tariff factors are unequal across countries, $\tau_i^A \neq \tau_i^B$, but for each country A and B they are independent of the country of origin of the import).
2. An FTA removes tariffs within the free trade area but countries can still maintain their own tariff structure against third countries. The MFN tariff factors τ_i are assumed to be the same in the *pre-FTA* and *post-FTA* stages, $\tau_i^{PreFTA} = \tau_i^{PostFTA}$. This can happen if the tariff structure is incorporated into a tariff law that cannot be changed when a preferential agreement is negotiated.

A government goes for an FTA if it increases its welfare including political contributions received. The viability of the preferential agreement depends on the strength of political support deriving from its trade creation and trade diversion effects. These trade effects determine lobby influence through political contributions. Each government welfare function is

$$W^G(p) = C^K(p) + aW^P(p),$$

which depends on lobby contributions, population welfare, and the weight $a \geq 0$ given to population welfare.

An interest group designs a contribution schedule $C^K(p)$ as a function of the most profitable policy scheme (FTA or status quo) in terms of its particular interests. A group that benefits from a free trade area will make contributions if the government chooses to be a member of an FTA, but will not contribute otherwise. If a group is harmed by a free trade area, it will contribute only if the government remains in the status quo and abstains from joining a free trade area.

The establishment of an FTA entailing complete liberalization among both member countries would be sustainable if (1) the population welfare gains are sufficiently large to make unprofitable the coordination of harmed lobbies aiming to block the agreement, or (2) exporters' gains are large enough to compensate for both importers' losses and social welfare losses.

The world price p_i^W is assumed to be exogenously given for all industries i so that the FTA neither relies on terms of trade effects nor generates them. Countries are assumed to apply the same tariffs to imports from the rest of the world before and after the formation of the FTA. The initial tariffs are politically determined as in the protection for sale framework.

Figure 16.1 helps to clarify the effects of an FTA between the high-tariff country and a low-tariff country in industry $i(\tau_i^H > \tau_i^L > 1)$. The world price p_i^W is normalized to one. The high-tariff country is assumed to remain an importer of good i after the FTA is signed while the low-tariff country becomes an exporter. The import schedule $M_i^H = D_i^H - q_i^H$ depicts the demand for imports of i by the country subjecting i to a high tariff. Schedules q_i^{Ls} and q_i^{Ll} depict two possible locations of the supply curves of the country that imposes a low tariff τ_i^L on industry i. Small and large suppliers (denoted by superscripts s and l) are characterized by small and high endowments of the specific factor used in the export industry.

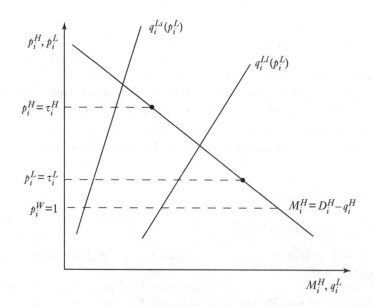

Figure 16.1. *The protection effects of a free trade area*

We proceed to show that:

1. If the low-tariff country's supply curve is small enough (q_i^{Ls}), the FTA will result in enhanced protection for the low-tariff member while there is no change in protection from the perspective of the high-tariff member.
2. If the low-tariff country's supply curve is large enough (q_i^{Ll}), the FTA will result in reduced protection for the high-tariff member while protection remains the same in the low-tariff member.

16.5.3. Enhanced Protection for Low-Tariff Member

If the low-tariff member's supply q_i^{Ls} is small enough, it will not be able to satisfy the high-tariff member demand for imports at price τ_i^H (the world price is normalized to one). The high-tariff member will continue to import from the rest of the world at τ_i^H. Therefore, high-tariff member consumers will continue to pay the price τ_i^H after the FTA is formed. The price τ_i^L will continue to prevail in the low-tariff member, who supplies the high-tariff member at the higher price τ_i^H. Formally,

$$ p_i^H = \tau_i^H p_i^W = \tau_i^H \ > \ p_i^L = \tau_i^L p_i^W = \tau_i^L, $$

where the world price $p_i^W = 1$, and p_i^H and p_i^L represent the high-tariff and low-tariff country prices. The possibility of arbitrage due to the coexistence of two different consumer prices is precluded by formulating and enforcing adequate rules of origin.

What is the effect of the FTA on the population welfares W^{PL} and W^{PH} of the low- and high-tariff members? The change in welfare is given by the sum of the change in tariff revenues, the change of producers profits, and the change of consumer surplus.

The overall population welfare of the low-tariff member unambiguously increases. The FTA enhances the protection received by producers, increases the tariff revenues of its government, and leaves consumers unaffected. Because the price τ_i^H prevailing in the high-tariff member is greater than the price τ_i^L, producers will shift all their sales to the high-tariff member. Therefore, producers in the low-tariff member capture the gains associated with protection of the high-tariff member. Their profits must increase $(\pi_i^L(\tau_i^H) - \pi_i^L(\tau_i^L) > 0)$ because the better price applying to all units sold compensates the higher marginal costs incurred.

The shift in production toward the high-tariff member forces low-tariff member consumers to import from the rest of the world the amount $q_i^L(\tau_i^L)$ they were purchasing from domestic producers. The increase in imports increases tariff revenues from zero to $\tau_i^L q_i^L(\tau_i^L)$. Consumers remain unaffected because there is no change in price and thus in consumption levels.

The population welfare of the high-tariff country is unambiguously reduced because its government loses tariff revenues. All previous imports from the rest of the world, bringing tariff revenues $\tau_i^H q_i^H(\tau_i^H)$, are replaced by imports from the free trade area (trade diversion effect). Because the price remains at the level τ_i^H, there are no effects on domestic producers or consumers.

Formally, the changes in the welfare levels of the population are

$$\Delta W^{PL} = \tau_i^L q_i^L(\tau_i^L) + \pi_i^L(\tau_i^H) - \pi_i^L(\tau_i^L) > 0,$$

$$\Delta W^{PH} = -\tau_i^H q_i^H(\tau_i^H) < 0,$$

where

$$\pi_i^L(\tau_i^H) - \pi_i^L(\tau_i^L)$$

$$= [\tau_i^H q_i^L(\tau_i^H) - C(q_i^L(\tau_i^H))] - [\tau_i^L q_i^L(\tau_i^L) - C(q_i^L(\tau_i^L))]$$

represents the change in producers' profits and C denotes costs.

The change in world welfare can be shown to be negative. It is given by the sum of the changes in member countries' welfare

$$\Delta W^W = \Delta W^{PL} + \Delta W^{PH} = C(q_i^L(\tau_i^L)) - C(q_i^L(\tau_i^H)) < 0,$$

where it is assumed that $q_i^L(\tau_i^H) > q_i^L(\tau_i^L)$ and that marginal costs increase with the level of production.

The negative change in world welfare is due to a trade diverting effect. Initially, the high-tariff country was importing from the rest of the world at tariff factor τ_i^H. With the FTA, this trade is diverted into imports from the low-tariff member. The social cost increase takes place because the low-tariff country firms produce at greater marginal cost than the price τ_i^L at which goods could be imported from the rest of the world in the absence of an FTA.

16.5.4. Reduced Protection for High-Tariff Member

If the low-tariff member country's supply is large enough, it will be able to satisfy the high-tariff member demand for good i at price τ_i^L. Therefore, the high-tariff member will stop importing from the rest of the world at τ_i^H and redirect trade to the low-tariff member at the lower price τ_i^L. The price prevailing in the initially high-tariff member declines to τ_i^L, which will prevail throughout the free trade area

$$p_i^H = p_i^L = \tau_i^L p_i^W = \tau_i^L, \quad p_i^W \equiv 1, \quad \tau_i^L \equiv 1 + t_i^L.$$

The low-tariff country welfare increases because producers in the low-tariff member receive the same protection as before, consumers face the same price and are thus unaffected by the FTA, and the government gathers greater tariff revenues.

The net effect on the high-tariff country welfare could be positive or negative depending on the economy's parameters. Because the low-tariff member becomes the source of all imports of good i, the high-tariff member loses tariff revenues. Furthermore, the reduction in price negatively affects the producers in the initially high-tariff country. However, the price reduction favors consumers. Thus, the net effect is ambiguous.

In short, an FTA reduces the protection received by the high-tariff member and leaves unaffected the low-tariff member protection.

16.5.5. Coalition-Proof Equilibria and FTAs

If international compensation through inter-country transfers is assumed away, an FTA agreement requires the unilateral support of both governments. The unilateral government decision can be reached in the absence of contributions and lobby pressures (unpressured stance in support of the FTA) but making the decision might require the pressure of domestic lobbies (pressured stance in support of the FTA).

There are cases where pressured stances and unpressured stances support different positions in relation to FTA formation. If this happens, we have multiple political equilibria. A refinement of the concept of Nash equilibrium, coalition-proof equilibrium (Bernheim and Whinston, 1986*b*) can be used to select between equilibria. The coalition-proof equilibrium allows players to communicate to propose the plays made by the coalition, but not to make binding agreements. Each coalition member follows the proposal only if it is beneficial to him or herself. In other words, a coalition-proof equilibrium must be self-enforcing for the members of the coalition.

Formally, the coalition-proof equilibrium concept rejects any outcome for which there exists a set of actions by some coalition of players such that

1. the proposed action of each coalition member is a best-response to the proposed or given actions of the other members of the coalition (self-enforcing requirement);
2. each member of the coalition attains a payoff as high or higher than in any other self-enforcing Nash equilibrium, given the actions of those players that are not members of the coalition.

In the single-lobby contribution game, the Nash equilibrium and the coalition-proof equilibrium concepts coincide, but this is not the case in the multiple lobby case. It is easy to see that, if the government would select different trade regimes in the absence of lobby pressures and in the pressured stance with multiple lobbies, the unpressured stance will not be a coalition-proof equilibrium. Suppose that several domestic industries setting their contributions noncooperatively are negatively affected by an unpressured stance to abstain from forming an FTA. Even if we disallow commitments between domestic industries, they could still communicate to propose that they join in a coalition and contribute enough to induce the government to accept the FTA (we assume there is no communication between domestic and foreign lobbies). If no member is asked to contribute more than what it would gain from the FTA, there are no incentives to deviate from the coalition proposal. In other words, commitments are not needed to sustain the coalition. In this case, the unpressured stance does not survive.

16.5.6. The Viability of an FTA

What are the conditions that make an FTA politically viable in the absence of international compensations? The analysis of the free trade area is particularly complex because the effects of the FTA on industries vary according to the relative position of demand and supply curves, which requires the analysis of alternative cases. Furthermore, a viable FTA requires support in both countries which in turn requires balance of costs and benefits across countries. For instance, in the enhanced protection case considered above, there is political support for an FTA in country A (with a low tariff in industry i) but not in country B (with a high tariff in that industry), which loses tariff revenues and experiences lower welfare. In order to obtain support for a free trade agreement, there must be industries j producing gains to country B. If the government welfare gains are not balanced across countries, a free trade agreement is not possible.

We follow Grossman and Helpman (1995a) in illustrating the balance condition in a simplified setting in which (1) the two countries trade only with each other so that nonmember demands and supplies are equal to zero, there are no tariff revenues from imports from the rest of the world, and external tariffs can be ignored, and (2) supplies are inelastic, so that producer surplus can be ignored.

Both countries are assumed to have industries that gain enhanced protection from an FTA, but the number of these industries differs across countries. All products i have the same inelastic world supply function: $q_i^W = \bar{q}^W$ for all i. Countries A and B differ in terms of the share $\theta > 1/2$ and $1 - \theta < 1/2$ of world supply. Parameter θ measures the imbalance in the output of any sector produced by the countries. Moreover, countries also differ in terms of the extent of the imbalance in the number of potential exporting industries.

In a fraction s of the industries, country A has the larger inelastic supply

$$\bar{q}^W = \theta \bar{q}_i^A + (1 - \theta)\bar{q}_i^B.$$

In a fraction $1 - s$ of the industries, country B has the larger inelastic supply

$$\bar{q}^W = \theta \bar{q}_i^B + (1 - \theta)\bar{q}_i^A.$$

Parameter s measures the extend of imbalance in the number of potential export industries in country A (due to a larger supply in some industries) compared with country B (due to a larger supply in other industries). For instance, $s = 1/2$ represents perfect balance in the sense that both countries have the same number of export industries. Without loss of generality we take $s \geq 1/2$.

Recall from Fig. 16.1 that if supply $\bar{q}_i$ is small enough in relation to the demand curve intercept a (i.e. $a/\bar{q}_i$ is sufficiently greater than one), all industries experienced enhance protection under the FTA. The share s of industries in which country A dominates, and the share $1 - s$ of industries in which country B dominates the supply, will become exporters after the FTA is formed.

Because the political support for a free trade area comes from exporters, an FTA will be politically viable only if the following conditions hold:

1. There must be enough exporters in both countries to generate sufficient contributions to induce the governments to accept the FTA.
2. The number of exporting industries must be nearly balanced ($s = 1/2$) between the countries. If the number of exporting industries is not balanced across the countries, the FTA is not viable. If $s = 0$, country A will always lose tariff revenues. Because there are no exporters, no agent will benefit from the trade agreement. A similar

phenomenon takes place if $s = 1$. The FTA is not viable because there will be no political support in country B. In contrast, consider $s = 1/2$. In this case, there will be exporters in both countries making political contributions to induce the approval of the FTA. If there are enough of these exporters, then the protection for sale argument operates because there is a welfare loss for the world as a whole but each country's exporters will influence their government through contributions to secure the FTA, which is beneficial to them.

The political analysis suggests that FTAs are the outcome of lobbying by exporters that seek enhanced protection. The result is worrisome because enhanced protection was shown to be unambiguously welfare-reducing to the world as a whole. The conditions that unambiguously make an-FTA politically viable (when tariffs against nonmembers are kept constant after the agreement is formed), are precisely those that make the FTA welfare-reducing.

16.6. ACCOMMODATING PREFERENTIAL ARRANGEMENTS

Taking as granted that PTAs are here to stay, it is useful to examine the best ways to accommodate such arrangements. The accommodation approach raises questions about what are the types of agreements to be encouraged and what are the means available for achieving a second-best block structure.

Deardorff and Stern (1994) argue that the World Trade Organization should encourage large PTAs between countries displaying dissimilar factor endowments. International trade causes countries to specialize and export the goods in which they enjoy a comparative advantage. The Heckscher–Ohlin trade model suggests that countries tend to enjoy a comparative advantage in those goods utilizing relatively more intensively the factors that are relatively abundant in the country. The comparative advantage perspective implies that, ceteris paribus, differences in relative factor endowments leads to gains from trade. Therefore, large PTAs including countries displaying wide differences in factor endowments tend to capture a significant portion of the gains from multilateral liberalization. In fact, a system of large blocks each composed of countries with wide differences in comparative advantages might be able to capture most of the gains from global free trade, as long as the blocks can be prevented from increasing trade barriers to each other's imports.

Can the global trading system accommodate the type of preferential arrangements that better exploit potential gains from trade? First, large PTAs incorporating many members including developing countries can emerge if PTAs are open to new members instead of behaving as closed trading clubs. For instance, the Asia Pacific Economic Cooperation (APEC) favors open regionalism and a policy of low barriers to trade *vis-à-vis* nonmembers. It sponsors free and open trade in the Asia Pacific region by 2020. The Free Trade Area of the Americas seeks free trade among the diverse American countries by 2005. The ongoing expansion of the European Union aims to incorporate central and eastern European countries with sharply lower income levels and different comparative advantages than current members. These initiatives entail the formation of large trading areas embodying internal free trade among countries with different factor endowments.

Second, a major problem created by the existence of larger PTAs is that members have greater incentives to increase tariffs against nonmembers, which might lead into prisoner's dilemma situations. A solution is to strengthen the enforcement of GATT's Article XXIV. This article incorporates the requirement that a PTA should not increase the level of protection against nonmembers of the PTA.

Third, larger groups acquire greater economic and political power to block multilateral agreements that hurt some of their members. Possible solutions include following the European Union policy of granting compensatory payments to adversely affected parties or negotiating multilateral liberalization on a reciprocity basis so that all members gain something. The economics of negotiations and agreement enforcement are examined in the chapter on cooperation.

Fourth, the wave of PTAs has been associated with reductions of actual or most-favored nation (MFN) tariffs. Cadot, de Melo and Olearraga (2001) construct a politically viable equilibrium with MFN tariff reductions after the formation of a free trade area. Country A exports electronics to B. Country B keeps this industry protected while reducing tariffs on textiles. Country B exports textiles to A. Country A keeps this industry protected while reducing tariffs on electronics. Producer prices in import-competing sectors in the two countries are maintained by rules of origin rules while the losses of tariff revenues are offset by efficiency gains that improve government welfare.

16.7. CONCLUSIONS

The double edge character of preferential arrangements has turned out to be highly controversial: preferential liberalization generally reduces one economic distortion while maintaining another. As a result, there are as many counterarguments as rationales for preferential agreements. On one hand, trade liberalization reduces economic distortions and represents a mechanism for economic integration among members of the arrangement. On the other hand, preferential liberalization gives rise to a distortion because it applies only to members of the arrangement and is thus discriminatory toward nonmembers. By their own nature, preferential arrangements are solidly placed in the always controversial territory of second-best economics. Their implications and welfare effects hinge on the delicate balance between liberalization for members, discrimination toward nonmembers and the effects on the multilateral system.

The popular natural trading partner theory (Frankel (1998) is challenged by Krishna (2003), who does not find support for it. The empirical tests examine the welfare effects of liberalization between the United States and over twenty partners during the 1964–95 period. The correlation between the overall welfare effect and distance is found to be statistically insignificant. Moreover, the null hypothesis that the bilateral volume of trade does not matter for welfare is not rejected. Opposed econometric findings indicate that the scientific controversy over the role of preferential agreements continues to rage.

16.8. APPENDIX

16.8.1. Baldwin and Venables Welfare Decomposition

Totally differentiating the indirect utility function $V(p + t, n, E)$ yields

$$
\begin{aligned}
dV(p + t, n, E) &= \left[\frac{\partial V(p + t, n, E)}{\partial (p + t)}\right]' d(p + t) \\
&+ \left[\frac{\partial V(p + t, n, E)}{\partial n}\right]' dn + \frac{\partial V(p + t, n, E)}{\partial E} dE \\
&\equiv [V_p]' d(p + t) + [V_n]' dn + V_E \, dE,
\end{aligned}
$$

where the superscript $'$ indicates a transpose of a column vector into a row vector.

Using the definition $E = wL + rK + [(p' + t' - c'(w, r, q)]Q + t'Rm - I$ and assuming that the labor supply L is fixed yields

$$
\begin{aligned}
dE &= L \, dw + K \, dr + r \, dK + (p' + t' - c') \, dQ + Q' d(p + t - c(w, r, q)) \\
&\quad + t'R \, dm + m' d(Rt) - dI \\
&= L \, dw + K \, dr + (p' + t' - c') \, dQ + Q' d(p + t) - Q'c_w \, dw \\
&\quad - Q'c_r \, dr - Q'c_q \, dq + t'R \, dm + m' \, d(Rt) + r \, dK - dI \\
&= (L - Q'c_w) \, dw + (K - Q'c_r) \, dr + (p' + t' - c') \, dQ + Q' \, d(p + t) \\
&\quad - Q'c_q \, dq + t'R \, dm + m' \, d(Rt) + r \, dK - dI \\
&= (p' + t' - c') \, dQ + Q' \, d(p + t) - Q'c_q \, dq \\
&\quad + t'R \, dm + m' \, d(Rt) + \left(\frac{\tilde{r}}{\rho} - 1\right) dI,
\end{aligned}
$$

where R is a diagonal matrix consisting of constant proportions $r_{ii} \in [0, 1]$ along the diagonal. Shepard's lemma implies that $L = Q'c_w$ and $K = Q'c_r$. To see why, recall from Chapter 1 that Shepard's lemma states that a firm's factor demand expressed as an input–output ratio, $a_i(\omega, q) \equiv a_i(w, r, q_i)$, is given by the partial derivative of the average cost function with respect to the input's rental price $\omega \in \{w, r\}$

$$
a_i(\omega, q_i) = \frac{\partial c_i(\omega, q)}{\partial \omega} \quad \rightarrow \quad L = Q' \frac{\partial c(w, r, q)}{\partial w}, \qquad K = Q' \frac{\partial c(w, r, q)}{\partial r}.
$$

The aggregate input demand equations are obtained by multiplying each industry's input–output ratio a_i by industry output q_i and summing over all industries. Assuming that dI generates a permanent change in the capital stock that yields a social rate of return $\tilde{r}$ and is discounted at ρ, we have $(\tilde{r}/\rho)dI = r \, dK$ or $r \, dK - dI = (\tilde{r}/\rho - 1) \, dI$.

The derivation below makes use of Roy's identity, which states that the demand function $D(p, E)$ is equal to the negative of the partial derivative of the indirect utility function V with respect to prices p divided by partial derivative of V with respect to expenditure E. Formally,

$$D(p, E) = -\frac{\partial V}{\partial p} \Big/ \frac{\partial V}{\partial E} = -\frac{V_p}{V_E},$$

where the demand and first derivative vectors are represented as column vectors. In an open economy, the demand vector is equal to the domestic production vector Q plus the import vector m. Hence, $D = Q + m = -V_p/V_E$ or $V_p/V_E + Q = -m$.

Dividing the welfare decomposition formula by V_E and observing that Roy's identity implies $[V_p/V_E]' + Q' = -m'$ so that $([V_p/V_E]' + Q')d(p + t) = -m'd(p + t) = -m'dp + -m'dt$, produces (16.1)

$$\frac{dV}{V_E} = \left[\frac{V_p}{V_E}\right]' d(p + t) + \left[\frac{V_n}{V_E}\right]' dn + dE$$

$$= \left(\left[\frac{V_p}{V_E}\right]' + Q'\right) d(p + t) + \left[\frac{V_n}{V_E}\right]' dn + (p + t - c)' dQ$$

$$- Q'c_q \, dq + t'R \, dm + m'd(Rt) + \left(\frac{\tilde{r}}{\rho} - 1\right) dI$$

$$= t'R \, dm - m'd(t - Rt) - m' \, dp + (p' + t' - c')dQ$$

$$- Q'c_q \, dq + \left[\frac{V_n}{V_E}\right]' dn + \left(\frac{\tilde{r}}{\rho} - 1\right) dI.$$

16.8.2. *Political Pressures in a Bargaining Game*

Consider the following maximization problem

$$\underset{p_I}{\arg\max} \; a^K C^{K_I, E}(p, K_I) + W^P(p, K_I).$$

First order conditions yield

$$a^K \frac{\partial C^{K_I, E}(p, K_I)}{\partial p_I} + \frac{\partial W^P(p, K_I)}{\partial p_I} = 0. \tag{16.4}$$

Recalling the discussion of the contribution function in the chapter on trade politics,

$$\frac{\partial C^{K_I, E}(p, K_I)}{\partial p_I} = \frac{\partial W^K(p, K_I)}{\partial p_I} = K_I, \tag{16.5}$$

given $W^{K_I}(p, K_I) = p_I K_I$. Moreover,

$$\frac{\partial W^P(p, K_I)}{\partial p_I} = K_I + 1 - 2p_I - K_I + p_I^W - d_I$$

$$= 1 - 2p_I + p_I^W - d_I = d_I - p_I + p_I^W - d_I$$

$$= -p_I + p_I^W, \tag{16.6}$$

since $W^P(p, K_I) = (\partial q_0/\partial K_0)K_0 + p_I K_I + (p_I - p_I^W)(D_I - K_I) + CS = (\partial q_0/\partial K_0)K_0 + p_I K_I + (p_I - p_I^W)(1 - p_I - K_I) + d_I - d_I/2 - p_I d_I$.

Substituting (16.5) and (16.6) into (16.4) yields

$$a^{K_I}K_I - p_I + p_I^W = 0 \rightarrow p_I^E = p_I^W + a^{K_I}K_I. \tag{16.7}$$

The Nash bargaining problem entails the maximization of the geometric average of government and lobby surplus with weights given by the bargaining power of each player. Formally

$$W^B(c^{K_I,E}(K_I)) = \max_{c^{K_I}}[W^G(p_I^E(K_I), K_I) - W^G(p_I^W, K_I)]^\sigma$$

$$[(p_I - c^{K_I})K_I - p_I^W K_I]^{(1-\sigma)},$$

where $W^G(p_I^W, K_I) = W^P(p_I^W(K_I), K_I)$ and $W^G(p_I^W, K_I)$
$$= a^{K_I}c^{K_I}K_I + W^P(p_I^E(K_I), K_I).$$

The first order condition $\partial W^B/\partial c^{K_I} = 0$ is

$$-K_I(1 - \sigma)[a^{K_I}c^{K_I}K_I + W^P(p_I^E(K_I), K_I) - W^P(p_I^W, K_I)]^\sigma$$

$$[(p_I - c^{K_I})K_I - p_I^W K_I]^{-\sigma} + a^{K_I}K_I\sigma[ac^{K_I}K_I + W^P(p_I^E(K_I), K_I)$$

$$- W^P(p_I^W, K_I)]^{(\sigma-1)}[(p_I - c^{K_I})K_I - p_I^W K_I]^{(1-\sigma)} = 0.$$

Simplifying terms yields

$$-(1 - \sigma)[a^{K_I}c^{K_I}K_I + W^P(p_I^E(K_I), K_I) - W^P(p_I^W, K_I)]$$

$$+ a^{K_I}\sigma[(p_I - c^{K_I})K_I - p_I^W K_I] = 0,$$

and solving for c^{K_I}

$$-(1 - \sigma)a^{K_I}c^{K_I}K_I - a^{K_I}\sigma c^{K_I}K_I$$

$$= (1 - \sigma)[W^P(p_I^E(K_I), K_I) - W^P(p_I^W, K_I)] - a^{K_I}\sigma(p_I - p_I^W)K_I$$

or

$$c^{K_I} = (1 - \sigma)\left[\frac{W^P(p_I^W, K_I) + a^{K_I}W^P(p_I^E(K_I), K_I)}{a^{K_I}K_I}\right] + \sigma(p_I^W - p_I).$$

17

International Economic Politics

General Agreement on Tariffs and Trade's (GATT) Article XXIV permits the formation of preferential agreements among World Trade Organization (WTO) members as long as free trade prevails within the blocks and barriers to trade with other members do not increase. Notwithstanding their legal compatibility, WTO agreements and preferential arrangements can be at odds with each other. WTO 'multilateralism' seeks nonpreferential treatment for all members, which is violated by all preferential trading arrangements, and all-inclusive trade negotiations. The so-called 'bilateralism' embodied in preferential arrangements represents a trend toward block formation and negotiations conducted parallel to the multilateral framework.

The 'new regionalism' that burgeoned in the 1980s is quite distinct from the 'old regionalism' of the 1950s and 1960s. Old regionalism, particularly in Europe and among developing countries, was largely a device to increase market size while protecting local industry behind high tariff walls. It was also accompanied by controls over foreign investment and substantial public sector intervention. The new regionalism has a different policy orientation. It is often accompanied by trade barriers reductions through simultaneous participation in several preferential arrangements and the GATT, openness toward foreign investment, and public sector reform including cuts in fiscal deficits and privatization. However, both developed and developing countries have expanded the use of a host of nontariff barriers to trade.

Bhagwati (1993), Frankel (1997), and other experts stress that assessing the economic effects of preferential arrangements requires an evaluation extending well beyond static effects and impact on members. A full assessment encompasses the still unfinished task of determining the dynamic implications of block policies, the impact on nonmembers and the consequences for the evolution of the multilateral system.

Do approaches to liberalization based on preferential trading (regionalism, bilateralism) compete or complement multilateral trade liberalization? This hotly contested issue raises a key dynamic question concerning whether preferential arrangements constitute building blocks or stumbling blocks to ongoing multilateral trade liberalization. A building block creates incentives for subsequent multilateral liberalization. A stumbling block discourages multilateral liberalization and thus undermines the multilateral system.

This chapter examines the bilateralism vs multilateralism controversy. Section 17.1 discusses the relation between preferential trading arrangements (PTAs) and global welfare when tariffs are endogenously set. Sections 17.2 and 17.3 look at PTAs as stumbling blocks or building blocks to multilateralism. Section 17.4 examines the economics of endogeneous regionalism and open membership. Section 17.5 endogenizes the choice between regional and multilateral negotiations. Section 17.6 examines the interaction between reform, foreign investment and technology transfer.

17.1. REGIONALISM AND GLOBAL WELFARE

Kemp and Wan (1976) and related work present a mechanism ensuring that the formation of a customs union is welfare-increasing for the world as a whole. The mechanism relies on appropriately adjusting the customs union's external tariff structure. If a customs union dismantles internal tariffs while maintaining the volume of trade with the rest-of-the-world, then the union will benefit from trade liberalization without hurting the rest-of-the-world. In other words, a condition ensuring that nonmembers are not hurt is that the union's external tariff policy maintains trade volumes with nonmembers constant. The lesson derived from Kemp and Wan analysis is that an appropriate external tariff policy can support greater intraregional trade without hurting nonmembers. Whether union members have incentives to follow such a policy is of course an entirely different matter.

17.1.1. Block Size, Endogenous Tariffs, and Welfare

What are the welfare effects of enlarging customs unions that set external tariffs to maximize block welfare? In the influential 1991 paper titled 'Is Bilateralism Bad'? Paul Krugman examines how the number of customs unions affects the level of external tariffs and block and global welfare. The process leading to the formation of customs unions and the determinants of the number of blocks B are not analyzed. The model rather focuses on determining how world welfare depends on B treated as an exogenous variable. World trade consists of pure exchange among endowment economies.

Consider a global economy constituted by N identical countries (i.e. countries are symmetric in the sense that they have the same demand functions and size). Each country is assumed to specialize in producing one unit of a single good, which is an imperfect substitute for the goods produced in other countries. The representative country has a constant elasticity of substitution (CES) utility function

$$U(c_1, \ldots, c_N) = \left[\sum_{i=1}^{N} c_i^{\theta} \right]^{1/\theta}, \tag{17.1}$$

where c_i is the consumption of the good produced by country $i \in \{1, \ldots, N\}$ and $0 < \theta < 1$. The utility function (17.1) implies that the elasticity of substitution between any two commodities i and j is constant and equal to

$$\sigma_{ij} \equiv \frac{\hat{c}_i - \hat{c}_j}{U'(c_j) - U'(c_i)} = \frac{\hat{c}_i - \hat{c}_j}{\widehat{p}_{ji}} = \frac{1}{1 - \theta} > 1,$$

where the 'hat' symbol indicates proportional change, U' represents marginal utility and p_{ij} is the relative price of good i in terms of good j.

Regionalization takes the form of $B < N$ identical customs unions. Each customs union sets its external tariff against nonmembers endogenously to exploit market power. The external tariff aims to reduce the world price of imports, improve the block's terms of trade and increase block welfare. The global effect is to increase tariffs above the optimal free trade level. However, because countries are symmetric, all goods are subject to the same external tariff and blocks are unable to affect their equilibrium terms of trade. A customs union's optimal tariff, assuming that the commercial policies of other blocks remain constant, is (see appendix)

$$t^{CU} = \frac{1}{(1 - s)(\sigma - 1)},$$

where $\sigma = 1/(1 - \theta)$ is the elasticity of substitution in consumption. The level of t^{CU} increases with block size as measured by the share $s = pm^*/y^*$ of block exports in rest-of-the-world spending and declines with the elasticity of substitution in consumption σ.

The value of s is given by

$$s = \frac{1}{(1 + t^{CU})^\sigma + B - 1}, \tag{17.2}$$

where s becomes smaller as the tariff rate t increases. Substituting (17.2) into t^{CU}, we obtain the optimal tariff in implicit form

$$t^{CU} = \frac{1}{\left(1 - \left(1/\left(1 + t^{CU}\right)^\sigma + B - 1\right)\right)(\sigma - 1)}$$

$$= \frac{(1 + t^{CU})^\sigma + B - 1}{((1 + t^{CU})^\sigma + B - 2)(\sigma - 1)}. \tag{17.3}$$

Condition $\sigma > 1$ ensures that the optimal tariff rate is positive.

For values of σ near one, the value of the numerator in (17.3) is greater than the value of the denominator, which implies that the optimal tariff is greater than one (i.e. greater than 100 percent). Numerical simulation shows that it is only when σ is near 10, which is an unrealistically high value, that we get a near-10 percent tariff rate. Therefore, the model fails to replicate real world tariffs and results should be viewed as suggestive rather than realistic.

Differentiating (17.3) with respect to the number of blocks shows that the optimal tariff declines with the number of blocks. This result reflects reduced block monopoly power as the number of blocks increases and suggests the conjecture that a consolidation of the world economy into a low number of blocks could reduce welfare due to the higher optimal tariff. This conjecture is partially correct. Solving for the consumption of block and nonblock goods as a function of the optimal tariff, substituting consumption into the utility function, and normalizing by making $N = 1$, yields a formula for the level of country (block, world) welfare U as a function of B, t^{CU}, and σ (see appendix)

$$
U = \left\{ \frac{1}{B} \left[\frac{B(1 + t^{CU})^\sigma}{[(1 + t^{CU})^\sigma + B - 1]} \right]^\theta + \frac{B-1}{B} \left[\frac{B}{[(1 + t^{CU})^\sigma + B - 1]} \right]^\theta \right\}^{1/\theta} .
$$

The equation for $U(B, t^{CU}, \sigma)$ and the formula for the optimal tariff rate as a function of the number of blocks B constitute a two-equation system that can be used to obtain utility as a function of the number of symmetric blocks. There is a U-shaped relation between the number of customs unions and welfare. If there is a single worldwide block with no internal tariffs (i.e. free trade), symmetric block welfare is maximized. Welfare declines with the number of blocks until it reaches a minimum and then rises back to the free trade level as the number of blocks becomes very large and perfect competition among multiple blocks is approached. In this setup, a world economy with a very large number of blocks is akin to free trade because each individual block lacks market power and does not have incentives to impose an external tariff.

The relation between the number of blocks and block welfare is the result of the balance between two effects. On one hand, as the number of blocks increases, block market power declines in the sense that the maximizing external tariff rate declines. The proliferation of trading blocks reduces block size and diminishes market power. This shrinking market power effect is welfare-increasing. On the other hand, as the number of blocks increase, the number of countries within a block decline. Because each country is specialized in producing a single differentiated good, the external tariff applies to more and more differentiated goods. The application of a given tariff to more differentiated goods is welfare-reducing. Notice that this effect is larger when the number of blocks increases from one to two because half of the previously unprotected goods are subject to tariffs. The U-curve emerges because the welfare-reducing cost of variety effect dominates when the number of blocks is small but is dominated by the welfare-increasing shrinking market power effect when the number of blocks is large enough.

What is the number of blocks that minimizes world welfare? Model simulation allows estimating the welfare effect of an exogenously given increase in the number of symmetric customs unions (and the associated reduction in the number of countries per customs union). For a wide range of values of the constant elasticity of substitution between any two goods in consumption, the following result is obtained. Welfare declines as the number of blocks increases from one worldwide block (i.e. free trade) to two and three blocks. With more than three blocks, global welfare increases monotonically with the number of blocks.

Numerical simulation confirms the conjecture that a reduction in the number of commercial blocks can lead to an increase of protectionism and a reduction of welfare. The striking result is that welfare is minimized by three blocks for various levels of the elasticity of substitution σ. Varying σ changes the level of block utility but leaves the welfare-minimizing number of blocks largely unaffected. The provocative result that a global economy composed of three symmetric blocks minimizes global welfare hits home. It suggests that the ongoing regionalization of the world trading system into three trading blocks, the American, European, and Asian blocks, might reduce global welfare. The exploitation of market power is shown to be consistent with high external trade barriers entailing suboptimally large trade creation among block members.

Is the world economy moving toward a welfare-minimizing situation? This suggestion that three-block regionalism minimizes welfare is based on a model that biases welfare calculations against regionalism. First, recall that the tariff rates calculated from the model are excessively high in relation to observed rates in industrial countries. Also, customs unions are assumed to set external tariffs noncooperatively to fully exploit market power as they unsuccessfully attempt to influence terms of trade in their favor. This motive can be moderated by trade cooperation, political elements, and other omitted factors. Second, the model is based on the Armington assumption that each country specializes in the production of a differentiated good so that all countries import and consume every other country's goods. Therefore, high tariffs are costly because they hit a broad spectrum of goods not produced within the customs unions. Third, because transport costs are zero, there is no natural advantage from regionalism.

Transport Costs

How do transport costs affect the welfare analysis of customs unions? Krugman (1991*a*,*b*) and Frankel *et al.* (1995, 1998) find that introducing transport costs into variants of Krugman's differentiated products model can reverse the initial negative finding on the welfare effects of consolidating the global economy into a small number of blocks.

Suppose that transport costs are high between two continents, say Europe and North America, and inexistent within continents. If countries are otherwise symmetric, intracontinental trade will be high relative to intercontinental trade in a tariff equilibrium. Let us compare a situation in which countries levy a common tariff to each other with a situation in which two customs unions are formed by countries in the same continent. Because there is little intercontinental trade due to high transport costs, the elimination of intracontinental tariffs does not generate much trade diversion. On the contrary, the formation of customs unions entails trade creation, corresponds to a move toward free trade, and is welfare-increasing. Specifically, the formation of 'natural blocks' eliminating tariffs between countries that trade a lot with each other at low transport costs tends to raise global welfare compared with a situation in which each country levies tariffs on all its trading partners or compared with the formation of 'unnatural blocks' by countries in different continents. The presence of transport costs offers a geographic concentration rationale for regionalism.

Supporters of multilateralism offer a counterargument based on the notion of comparative advantage. The symmetric country scenario with differentiated goods and transport goods ignores comparative advantage considerations that can very well motivate greater trade among distant than among neighboring regions. Furthermore,

Bhagwati and Panagariya (1996) show that trade diversion is not necessarily minimized by establishing PTAs among 'natural' trading partners in the sense that they are geographically near to each other or that pre-PTA trade volumes among members are large.

17.2. STUMBLING BLOCKS TO MULTILATERALISM

Can preferential agreements undermine the incentives and political support for multilateral trade liberalization? The proliferation of PTAs since the 1980s has raised concerns that it would constitute a threat to multilateralism. These concerns have been formalized in explicit sequential models that identify specific channels for the stumbling block effect.

17.2.1. Political Dead End and Gains from Variety

Levy (1997) examines how the approval of a free trade area can shift median voter preferences against subsequent multilateral liberalization and bring about a political dead end. A PTA results in a political dead end if it reduces, by a large enough margin, median voter gains from subsequent multilateral liberalization. Because a preferential agreement increases the number of available varieties, it also reduces the variety gains from subsequent multilateral trade liberalization. As a result, additional potential variety gains might not be large enough to offset the adverse factor price effects that multilateral liberalization can have on the median voter. Political support for multilateral liberalization is thus undermined even if multilateral liberalization would command majority support in the absence of a PTA.

Consider a model with an endogenous number of varieties in which the extent of product differentiation depends on the trade regime and trade liberalization results in greater consumption variety. Trade liberalization takes place in stages. Voters endowed with perfect foresight are given a sequential voting choice. First, they vote on whether or not to join a free trade area. Subsequently, they vote on participating vs abstaining to participate in a multilateral trade agreement. Because a simple majority of voters is required to pass a proposal, trade policy is determined by the preferences of the median voter. This means that, in order to get approval, multilateral trade liberalization must benefit at least half the voters.

Trade policy involves a potential trade off between variety gains and adverse factor price effects. Everybody gains from the greater variety afforded by free trade. Individuals, however, gain or lose depending on (1) the effect of trade policy on factor prices, and (2) individuals' holdings of capital and labor. The outcome of voting is determined by the effect of the agreement on the voter holding the median capital–labor ratio. If the median voter experiences large enough losses from factor price changes to offset the variety gains from multilateral liberalization, he or she will block the multilateral initiative.

A free trade area is more likely to command political support from a majority of voters when the partners have similar factor endowments. The reason is that, when factor endowments are similar, the free trade area does not generate adverse factor price effects. Therefore, the benefits from greater product variety are not offset by adverse factor income effects on the median voter. These considerations suggest that it is easier to gather political support for the formation of the European Union than for the Free Trade Area of the Americas ongoing initiative. The European Union enforces free trade among its members, which have similar factor endowments. By contrast, the Americas initiative incorporates countries with dramatically different factor endowments.

The approval of a free trade area alters the incentives to vote for multilateral liberalization. A free trade agreement (FTA) provides consumption variety gains to the median voter and thus raises its reservation level of utility with respect to a subsequent multilateral agreement. In other words, the variety gains generated by the free trade area reduce the marginal consumption gains obtained by the median voter under multilateral liberalization. This undermines political support for subsequent multilateral liberalization.

Because multilateral liberalization necessarily involves countries with different factor endowments, it generates changes in factor prices that cause losses in some sectors. If the median voter owns factors that experience adverse price effects, the reduced potential consumption gains from multilateral liberalization might not offset median voter losses due to adverse factor price effects. In this case, the FTA undermines the political support for subsequent multilateral trade liberalization leading to a dead-end precluding further liberalization. Paradoxically, the shift of median voter preferences implies that a multilateral liberalization that would have been approved if an FTA were not in place might not pass if the voting takes place after the FTA is formed.

17.2.2. *Reciprocal Dumping, Trade Diversion, and Exporter Opposition*

A PTA creates trade diversion that strengthens the opposition to multilateral liberalization of exporters protected by the preferential agreement. Krishna (1998) presents a model in which greater trade diversion leads to greater exporter support for the preferential arrangement and reduced incentives for multilateral liberalization. The political economy approach is used to tackle two questions. First, which conditions favor the formation of a free trade arrangement? The answer provided is that preferential arrangements resulting in trade diversion are more likely to be supported politically. Second, does the presence of a free trade area create incentives for subsequent liberalization with respect to a third country? The answer provided is that a trade diverting preferential arrangement can make infeasible multilateral liberalization that would have been politically feasible before the preferential arrangement was approved.

Consider an extension of Brander and Krugman (1983) reciprocal dumping model to a three-country (A, B, and C), two-good world economy. One good is a competitively produced numeraire good that is freely traded and is used to settle trade imbalances across countries. The other homogeneous good is subject to reciprocal dumping. Firms in each country produce this good and sell it in markets A, B, and C. These markets are oligopolistic and are perceived to be segmented in the sense that the price in each market is determined according to local demand and supply (even though each market has firms from A, B, and C). The segmented market hypothesis allows simultaneously importing and exporting a homogeneous good that can have different prices across countries even when tariffs are the same in all countries. Arbitrage is assumed to be infeasible.

The political framework has two sequential decisions: a bilateral arrangement decision and a subsequent multilateral arrangement decision. In the bilateral arrangement decision, countries A and B decide whether or not to form a preferential area, lowering intra-area tariffs to zero. In the multilateral arrangement decision, countries decide on a multilateral agreement that will set all tariff rates to zero, taking as given the existence of a preferential area between A and B. Finally, firms choose quantities produced. The decision model is sequential but the model is not solved as a sequential game. Instead, the decision about the formation of an FTA is reached without taking into consideration the implications for the subsequent multilateral decision.

Political support for a free trade area between two countries derives from rent-seeking producers who increase their profits by gaining preferential access to member countries' markets. Producers' gains from the arrangement arise from two sources. One source is the elimination of the preferences previously favoring other member countries' firms. The other source is the diversion of trade away from the rest-of-the-world and toward the arrangement. Trade diversion helps to gather political support for the FTA because it shifts market share toward member countries and away from rest-of-the-world firms. If there is no trade diversion from the rest-of-the-world, the arrangement becomes similar to a zero sum game from the perspective of member countries' firms. These firms gain access to other members' markets, but lose market share in their home country.

The trade diversion condition favoring the formation of an FTA discourages multilateral liberalization that would have been politically feasible in the absence of the FTA. The reason is that producer rents derived from trade diversion are tied to the preferences granted by the area. These rents would be lost if the preferences *vis-à-vis* the rest-of-the-world were eliminated. Further liberalization will be blocked if (1) governments give enough weight to domestic producers, and (2) further liberalization fails to generate enough consumer surplus or producer rents from access to larger markets to offset the losses from the elimination of preferences.

Trade diversion can undermine government support for protection. The reason is that liberalization diminishes the tariff base and a member country's revenues from tariffs. Trade diversion caused by free trade areas means that imports from outside the area are replaced by tariff-free imports from other area members. This replacement leads to smaller tariff revenues, which weakens government support for tariff protection (López-Córdova, 1999).

17.3. BUILDING BLOCKS TO MULTILATERALISM

Can preferential agreements encourage multilateral trade liberalization? Preferential liberalization can promote multilateral trade liberalization by weakening the position of import-competing lobbies, strengthening exporter lobbies, generating economies of size that increase outsiders' incentives to join, and inducing the reduction of free trade area members' external tariffs. Many observers argue that the formation or enlargement of a preferential arrangement have induced multilateral tariff reductions (Sapir, 1992; Winters, 1993; Bergsten, 1997). For instance, the formation of the European Economic Community (EEC) in 1957 is often viewed as a catalytic element inducing the initiation of the Dillon and Kennedy Rounds of multilateral liberalization. In these cases, preferential liberalization is consistent and can act as a building block to multilateral liberalization.

Preferential agreements might not be building or stumbling blocks to multilateralism but rather act as a complement to multilateral agreements. Ethier (1998*a,b*) argues that recent regionalism has emerged as a mechanism to deepen liberalization when successful multilateral liberalization exhausts the benefits from further multilateral liberalization. In addition, regionalism has served to facilitate developing country reform by securing foreign direct investment and transferring technology to reforming economies.

17.3.1. The Weakening of Import-Competing Lobbies

Wei and Frankel (1996) present a counterexample to the claim that FTAs discourage multilateral free trade. If the formation of a free trade area undermines anti-liberalization industries and benefits pro-liberalization industries, lobbying for further liberalization can be strengthened. The authors follow Destler (1995) in arguing that trade liberalizations succeed when the benefits of openness to exporters outweigh the benefits of protection to import-competing firms. For instance, free trade areas that convert former import-competing firms into exporters to other members of the area, reduce the political support for tariffs in the home country because the new exporters do not pay tariffs (Frankel and Wei, 1996; López-Córdova, 1999).

Consider the political effects of the formation of a free trade area. The contraction of less-competitive industries forming anti-liberalization lobbies undermines the support for protection. An extreme example of this effect occurs when the less-competitive industry altogether disappears after the formation of a free trade area. Furthermore, the free trade area can strengthen pro-liberalization exporters seeking access to larger markets. As a result, lobbying for further liberalization can become stronger than anti-protection lobbying, propping up political support for further liberalization.

17.3.2. Outsiders Incentives to Join: The Domino Effect

Baldwin (1995, 1997) examines the incentives facing the government of a nonmember country when deciding to join or not to join a pre-existing preferential arrangement. He develops a domino theory of regionalism showing that the expansion of a regional block creates incentives for nonmembers to join the block. Preferential agreements that lead to cost reductions and generate gains from larger size create a domino effect by increasing the incentives of nonmembers to join the arrangement. Nonmembers incentives lead to free trade by an indirect mechanism: increasing the size of preferential areas featuring internal free trade.

A nonmember government's decision to join a PTA is made by maximizing a political support function. Political support is a positive function of the level of industry donations, the level of social welfare net of donations, and a term that reflects the support of groups that oppose the membership on noneconomic grounds (i.e. nationalism and other factors). The political equilibrium emerges from the balance of anti-membership forces such as nationalists and pro-membership forces such as exporters to the regional block.

What are the incentives of nonmember countries to join a pre-existing arrangement? The formation of a preferential arrangement generates a domino effect that encourages the expansion of the area. The reason is that nonmember exporters can increase profits if their countries join the regional block and the larger the block the greater the benefits from being a member. A larger regional block means that nonmembers face a larger cost disadvantage relative to members (because nonmembers face restrictions in a larger number of markets). This increases outside exporters' incentives to lobby for membership. If the government was initially indifferent as to whether or not to join, the additional lobbying activity can shift the political balance toward joining the block. As a result, there is a block-enlarging domino effect.

The domino mechanism works smoothly in preferential areas that subscribe to open regionalism in the sense that the supply of membership on the part of the block is perfectly elastic. However, the block might not have incentives to accept any country requesting admission.

17.4. ENDOGENOUS REGIONALISM

How do PTAs evolve over time? Most of the literature assumes that the formation of a preferential arrangement is an exogenous event (Krugman, 1991*a*) or considers a stage game that does not allow the evolution of regionalism (Levy, 1997; Krishna, 1998). The impact on the multilateral system is examined taking as given the formation and structure of PTAs.

Is a symmetric block structure such as that examined in Krugman (1991*a*) stable? Bond and Syropoulos (1996*a*) utilize a version of Krugman's pure exchange trade model with N countries and N commodities to examine how relative customs union size affects block and world welfare. External tariffs are specified as the Nash-equilibrium tariffs that maximize block welfare. Consider the case in which one customs union increases its relative size by recruiting the same number of new members from each of the rival blocks, which thus remain symmetric. A large enough increase in the relative size of a block is shown to enhance its relative market power as measured by the chosen external tariff level and to drive the aggregate welfare of block members above the free trade welfare level.

Can the welfare benefits from forming a large block lead to the formation of a single global block (i.e. free trade)? The analysis suggests that symmetric customs unions are unstable in the sense that countries have incentives to join blocks that are large relative to other blocks. However, a large enough customs union lacks incentives to add new members to create a worldwide block that covers all countries (i.e. free trade). Because a large block's welfare exceeds members' welfare under free trade, the block loses if it becomes an all-encompassing global block.

17.4.1. Customs Unions with Open Membership

Open regionalism has been proposed as a mechanism to achieve compatibility between the proliferation of regional trading arrangements and the multilateral system. The Asia Pacific Economic Council (APEC) has adopted an open regionalism stance but the concept has not been clearly defined. Bergsten (1997) examines several concepts of open regionalism. Broader concepts include permitting open membership, granting unconditional most-favored-nation (MFN) treatment to members' trading partners, and engaging in global liberalization. Narrower concepts focus on granting conditional MFN treatment and trade facilitation beyond elimination of traditional trade barriers such as tariffs and quotas.

The concept of open membership in a preferential arrangement means that any country who wishes to join the arrangement and commits to abide by its preferential trading rules is allowed to do so. A second popular concept is unconditional MFN treatment automatically extending trade liberalization within the arrangement to all members' trading partners. Granting unconditional MFN treatment to trading partners irrespective of their trade policies, however, gives rise to the same type of free rider problem afflicting the MFN clause in the GATT. For instance, APEC has favored a policy of trade liberalization on an MFN basis. This stance has generated worries that the European block would free ride on liberalization while failing to reciprocate. Conditional MFN treatment refers to the notion of reciprocitarianism in the sense that MFN treatment is granted only to those economies offering a similar liberalization path. Bergsten (1997) proposes this approach because it provides a solution to the free rider problem associated with open regionalism.

Is open regionalism compatible with multilateral trade liberalization? Can customs union enlargement conducted under appropriate rules lead to free trade? In order to answer these questions we must adopt an explicit definition of open regionalism and endogenize customs union formation. Yi (1996) provides a theoretical rationale for the 'open membership' approach. Strategic analysis is used to examine the formation of preferential agreements as an endogenous process through a mechanism relying on terms of trade effects.

Consider N ex ante symmetric countries, each of which produces one differentiated good at constant marginal cost in terms of the numeraire good. Gains from intra-industry trade (IIT) derive from increased variety of goods and reduced market power of domestic industry. The model endogenously determines the number and size of customs unions and examines their stability. Customs unions are viewed as coalitions, and their formation and behavior is modeled as a two-stage game. In the first stage, countries form customs unions. In the second stage, optimal tariffs are set taking as given the structure of customs unions determined in the first stage. Firms are assumed to compete in quantities.

What are the welfare effects of expanding a customs union? In the setup examined, welfare-maximizing customs unions improve the welfare of new members as well as the aggregate welfare of existing and new members, but not necessarily the welfare of existing members. Furthermore, the expansion of a customs union always reduces the welfare of nonmember countries. Specifically, a customs union expansion lowers the exports of nonmembers to the expanded union and lowers the terms of trade of nonmembers with respect to the expanded customs union's members. Because the welfare effect of expanding one customs union is positive on new members, ambiguous on existing members and negative on nonmembers, the effect on global welfare is ambiguous. Notice that this global welfare result does not contradict the welfare theorem proved by Kemp and Wan (1976). Recall that this theorem states that an expanded customs union can set external tariffs at levels that result in higher union welfare without reducing nonmembers welfare. However, the theorem does not assert that a welfare-maximizing union has incentives to set tariffs in such a way as to protect nonmembers from welfare losses.

Can global free trade arise as an equilibrium of a customs union formation game? This depends on the rules of customs union formation. Open membership refers to a membership rule by which a union is open to all players willing to abide by its rules. No rule-abiding outsider can be excluded. If customs unions are formed under the 'open membership' rule, they can be seen as stepping stones toward global free trade in the sense that global free trade arises as a stable equilibrium outcome of the customs union game.

Why is it that the 'open membership rule' leads to free trade? The reason is that, for any given customs union structure, a member of a larger union enjoys a greater welfare level than a member of a small union. There are thus incentives to leave a small union to join a larger one. Under the 'open regionalism rule', customs unions can be seen as a building block toward global free trade.

An alternative customs union's membership rule is the 'unanimity rule' under which a coalition is formed if and only if all potential members agree to form the customs union coalition. Under the 'unanimous regionalism rule', customs unions can become a stumbling block against global free trade because the latter does not typically arise as a stable outcome of the customs union formation process.

The analyses by Bond and Syropoulos (1996a) and Yi (1996) show that symmetric customs unions are not stable because countries have incentives to form a large customs union that breaks the symmetric structure. However, unless an open membership rule is imposed exogenously, a large customs union does not have incentives to move all the way to free trade. Also, notice that analyses so far do not address the question of how to make customs unions stable in the broader sense of precluding violations of customs union rules. For instance, customs union members have incentives to raise trade barriers against fellow members while continuing to benefit from zero tariffs. Enforcement mechanisms precluding members from getting away with breaking union rules are examined in the chapter on international cooperation.

17.5. REGIONAL OR MULTILATERAL NEGOTIATIONS?

The so-called 'new regionalism' differs from the 'old regionalism' of the 1950s (i.e. the formation of the European Community). In the 1950s, regionalism represented a response to high tariffs and a nascent multilateral system. Trade diversion and trade creation thus played a key role in the analysis of regionalism. In contrast, multilateral tariff reductions are now largely completed across industrial countries.

What determines the choice between entering into regional or multilateral negotiations? The type of negotiation chosen is a function of the benefits and cost of negotiation. Because the number of countries engaging in multilateral negotiations increases over time and the marginal benefits of negotiations decline as negotiations broaden, the marginal costs of negotiating can eventually render further multilateral negotiations unprofitable. As a result, multilateral tariff cuts stop short of achieving free trade.

Regionalism is preferred to multilateralism in situations in which the costs of multilateral negotiations are large in relation to the benefits (Ethier, 1998a). Regional negotiations might be beneficial after multilateral negotiations run their course precisely because the former involves fewer partners. Regional negotiations can complement multilateral negotiations in the sense of deepening liberalization by supporting free trade among regional trading partners even if overall free trade is not achieved. A sequential process in which successful multilateral negotiations give way to regionalism roughly corresponds to the rise of the new regionalism in the 1980s, following successful rounds of multilateral negotiations under the GATT.

Consider a model of symmetric countries and regional groupings described by Ethier (1998a). Countries are grouped into N continents, each of which consists of n countries. There are two types of trade barriers: tariff rates and transaction costs, which increase with distance. Because the continents are assumed to be wider apart than the countries in each continent, transaction cost considerations bias trade toward the regional group (i.e. the continent to which a country belongs). The degree of regionalism, V_i/V_j, is measured by the ratio of the trade volume V_i between the negotiating country and its regional trading partners to the country's trade volume V_j with its nonregional trading partners.

What is the effect of tariff cuts on the extent of regionalism measured by the ratio of trade among regional partners to trade with nonregional partners? Given the assumed geography of trade, tariffs cuts tend to accentuate the extent of regionalism. Formally, $d(V_i/V_j)/dt < 0$. First, it is easy to see that tariff reductions negotiated among regional trading partners will bias trade towards those regional partners. Second, multilateral tariff reductions will also stimulate regionalism in a setting in which preferential arrangements are based on regional groupings determined by transaction costs related to the distance between trading partners. When tariffs rates are very high, tariff barriers represent the major trade barriers and thus heavily influence trade volumes across countries. As tariff rates become lower and lower, the role of transaction costs becomes relatively more important. The incentives to bias trade towards the geographical or natural region are accentuated. In short, both regional and multilateral negotiations tend to accentuate the degree of regionalism (biased trade) in the world economy.

Each government authority faces a binary choice between negotiating with $Nn - 1$ partners at the multilateral level or negotiating with $n - 1$ partners at the regional level. In each negotiation period, governments maximize an index of net negotiation benefits with respect to the choice between regional or multilateral negotiations. Benefits $b = 2l + \delta\pi$ increase with (1) the degree of liberalization l achieved by the negotiations, and (2) the number of negotiating partners $\pi \in \{Nn - 1, n - 1\}$, which depends on the type of negotiation.

The marginal benefit δ of negotiating with an additional partner is assumed to decline with the degree of trade regionalization V_i/V_j. Therefore,

$$\frac{d\delta}{dt} = \frac{d\delta\left(V_i/V_j\right)}{d(V_i/V_j)} \frac{d(V_i/V_j)}{dt} > 0, \quad \frac{d\delta\left(V_i/V_j\right)}{d(V_i/V_j)} < 0, \quad \frac{d(V_i/V_j)}{dt} < 0,$$

where, in consonance with the geographic scenario, V_i/V_j is a decreasing function of the level of barriers to trade t. In words, the marginal benefit of negotiating with an additional partner increases with the tariff level and thus declines as multilateral negotiations lead trading partners toward free trade.

The negotiation cost $c = l + \gamma\pi$ is a linear function that increases with the degree of liberalization l and the number of partners π. Notice that both the benefits and the costs of negotiations increase with the number of trading partners.

Formally, the government chooses between regional and multilateral negotiations

$$\max_{\pi}(b - c) = 2l + \delta\pi - (l + \gamma\pi) = l + (\delta - \gamma)\pi,$$

where $l + (\delta - \gamma)\pi > 0$ ensures that $b > c$. The gap between the benefits from regional and multilateral negotiations is

$$(b - c)^{regional} - (b - c)^{multi} = l + (\delta - \gamma)(n - 1) - l - (\delta - \gamma)(Nn - 1)$$
$$= n(\gamma - \delta)(N - 1),$$

where

$$sign\left[(b - c)^{regional} - (b - c)^{multi}\right] = sign(\gamma - \delta).$$

The negotiation choice hinges on the relation between the constant marginal cost γ and the marginal benefit δ attached to having an additional trading partner. Regional negotiations maximize the net benefits index if $\gamma > \delta$ and multilateral negotiations maximize net benefits if $\gamma < \delta$.

Assume that tariff negotiations start at $\delta = \delta_0 \geq \delta^{FT}$, where δ^{FT} is the marginal benefit under the degree of regionalization prevailing at free trade. Countries choose between regional and multilateral negotiations and negotiations continue until incentives for further negotiation stop. The time frame and dynamics are left unspecified.

If $\gamma > \delta_0$, then regional negotiations dominate. Furthermore, multilateral negotiations will never take place. The reason is that when countries engage in regional negotiations, the extent of regionalism is accentuated, the value of δ declines, and the gap $\gamma - \delta$ widens. Recall that $d\delta(V_i/V_j)/d(V_i/V_j) < 0$ indicates that the marginal negotiating benefits per trading partner decline with the volume of regional trade relative to trade with nonregional partners.

If $\gamma < \delta_0$, then multilateral negotiations dominate. There are two possible cases that lead to different equilibria. If $\gamma < \delta^{FT} < \delta_0$, then regional negotiations will not take place because multilateral tariff negotiations dominate and will continue until governments achieve free trade, that is, $\delta = \delta^{FT}$. If $\delta^{FT} < \gamma < \delta_0$, then multilateral negotiations dominate initially but they are subsequently replaced by regional negotiations. The replacement takes place when δ declines below the value of γ. In this case, multilateral negotiations do not result in free trade. Regional negotiations leading to free trade between trading partners eventually take over and in this sense complement multilateral negotiations. The equilibrium external tariff among symmetric regional groups is the tariff rate that solves the equation $\gamma = \delta(V_i(t)/V_j)$, which specifies the tariff rate at which further multilateral liberalization stops and regional tariff reductions take over.

What is the relation between regional arrangements and the process of multilateralization? The previous simplified example shows how regional negotiations can arise as an endogenous outcome of the success of multilateral negotiations in reducing tariffs and how regional negotiations can deepen the tariff reductions accomplished by multilateral negotiations. Regional negotiations are neither a stumbling block nor a building block to multilateral negotiations but rather act as a complement after multilateralism runs out of steam.

17.6. REFORM, FDI, AND TECHNOLOGY TRANSFER

Why do countries engage in regional negotiations that do not appear to produce large trade benefits? The new regionalism responds to motives that cannot be fully assessed by trade diversion vs trade creation, optimal tariff setting or terms of trade arguments. For instance, tariff reductions accomplished by means of a preferential agreement can represent a mechanism to attract foreign direct investment (FDI) from developed countries, induce transfer of technology, and facilitate economic reform. Allowing a role for these factors helps to understand the evolution from the Canada–US Free Trade Agreement (CUSFTA) of 1988 into the North American Free Trade Agreement (NAFTA) in 1994 as well as the ongoing expansion of the European Union to incorporate developing countries.

The role of regionalism, in the sense of selective market opening, as a development tool is examined by Ethier (1998b). He develops a specific factor, perfect competition model in which preferential arrangements between developed and developing countries arise endogenously in the context of a multilateral world. The analysis: (1) does not allow harmful trade diversion or beneficial trade creation and thus departs from the Vinerian trade-off between trade creation and trade diversion, (2) does not hinge on terms of trade changes, which are precluded by assumption, and (3) explicitly recognizes the political influence of the welfare of unskilled labor but does explicitly rely on pressure group politics.

17.6.1. *Equilibrium with Global Externalities*

Consider a world economy divided into N developed and M developing countries. Developed countries are symmetric in all aspects including the political weight given to special interests. Developing countries are symmetric except that they differ from each other in terms of the political weight given to special interests.

There are three types of inputs. Developed countries are endowed with unskilled labor U, skilled labor L and sophisticated human capital H. Developing countries are endowed only with U and L.

Developed country consumers spend their income in a traded and a nontraded good produced in amounts q and z. The domestic demand for the traded good is

$$d^j(p^j) = \frac{1}{N} \left(\frac{p_q^j}{p_z^j} \right)^{-\epsilon} = \frac{1}{N}(p^j)^{-\epsilon},$$

where p^j is the relative price of the traded good in terms of the nontraded good. The remaining domestic income is spent on nontraded good z.

Each developed country j,

(1) utilizes two types of labor, skilled labor L_z and unskilled labor U to produce homogeneous nontraded commodity z under a constant returns to scale production function

$$z^j = z\left(L_z^j, U^j \right),$$

where z^j is sold in competitive markets and is produced under constant returns to scale;

(2) produces a final traded good in the amount q utilizing a process involving two stages a and b. Specifically, the combination of intermediate input b and human capital used in a customization stage a produces q units of the final good

$$q^j = q(a^j, b^j) = q\left(H^j, k\left(L_b^j + F_b^j \right) \right),$$

$$a^j = H^j, \quad b^j = k\left(L_b^j + F_b^j \right).$$

From a firm's perspective, k has a constant value representing the marginal productivity of domestic and foreign skilled labor L and F in stage b.

The first stage a must be undertaken at home and utilizes local human capital H^j to produce input a under constant returns to scale: $a^j = H^j$. This stage can be viewed as a customization stage that requires sophisticated human capital and can only be realized in the developed country.

Second stage b can be undertaken at home or through foreign investment abroad. This stage utilizes domestic skilled labor L_b^j or foreign labor F_b^j to produce intermediate input b^j. The use of foreign skilled labor by country j, F_b^j, also serves to measure foreign direct investment in this setup.

The productivity coefficient $k = k\left(L_b^W\right)$, $dk\left(L_b^W\right)/dL_b^W > 0$, embodies a global externality in that labor productivity depends positively on the amount of skilled labor L_b^W used to produce b worldwide. These externalities are not internalized by producers of stage b, who make decisions taking the factor k as a constant even though condition $dk\left(L_b^W\right)/dL_b^W > 0$ means that stage b is produced under global increasing returns to scale

$$k = k\left(L_b^W\right) = k\left(\sum_{j=1}^N L_b^j + \sum_{j=1}^N F_b^j\right) = k\left(\sum_{j=1}^N L_b^j + \sum_{j=1}^M L_b^{*j}\right).$$

The global effect depends on the sum of:

1. The total amount of developed country skilled labor utilized to produce b, where L_b^j represents the amount used to produce b in developed country j.
2. The total amount of skilled labor utilized by developed country multinationals in developing countries, where F_b^j is the amount utilized by multinationals from developed country $j \in \{1, \ldots, N\}$. Observe that the total developing country labor employed by the N foreign investors is equal to the total amount of labor employed to produce b in the M developing countries, where L_b^{*j} represents the amount used to produce b in developing country j (the asterisk denotes a developing country). The amount of skilled labor F_b^j utilized by multinationals from developed country j in developing countries is included as part of L_b^W but its location abroad remains indeterminate. Depending on how foreign direct investment location decisions are made, this indeterminacy might force developing countries to either attract foreign investment or face a random allocation of it.

Skilled labor wages w_L, and thus the marginal productivity of skilled labor, are equalized across industries q and z. Intersectorial wage equality implies

$$w_L = p^j \frac{\partial q^j}{\partial L_b^j} = \frac{\partial z^j}{\partial L_z^j}, \quad \frac{\partial q^j}{\partial L_b^j} = \frac{\partial q^j}{\partial b^j}\frac{\partial b^j}{\partial L_b^j} = \frac{\partial q^j}{\partial b^j}k.$$

Observe that skilled labor productivity in the traded good sector is calculated taking k as a constant. Under free trade and symmetry, world demand for the traded product, given by $d^W = p^{-\epsilon}$, must equal world supply $\sum q^j$.

Market equilibrium requires: (1) full employment of human capital in each country j (the supply of human capital $\bar{H}^j$ must be equal to the amount used H^j), (2) full employment of unskilled labor ($\bar{U}^j = U^j$), and (3) full employment of skilled labor ($\bar{L}^j = L_z^j + L_b^j$). Recall that H and U are specific factors used in stage a and industry z, respectively.

17.6.2. Developing Countries

Developing countries (denoted by an asterisk) use skilled labor L^* as domestic input in the production of a good that is rudimentary in the sense that it requires only stage of production b and does not benefit from the customization stage a. This good can be either used for consumption purposes (d^*) or exported to be used as an intermediate input in developed countries (b^*).

A developing country's production function depends on whether it is autarkic or participates in the multilateral system. Production under an autarkic trade regime is

$$q_A^{*j} = k\left(L^{*j}\right) L^{*j} = d_A^{*j},$$

where A denotes autarky and the country j's labor supply L^{*j} is used entirely to produce the rudimentary good for consumption. Production under multilateralism is devoted to produce for consumption (d) and for exportation (b)

$$q^{*j} = k(L_b^W)(L_{d*}^{*j} + L_b^{*j}) = d^{*j} + b^{*j}, \quad L_b^W = \sum_{j=1}^{N} L_b^j + \sum_{j=1}^{M} L_b^{*j},$$

where L_b^W is the global amount of skilled labor used in stage b, L_{d*}^{*j} is used to produce the consumption amount d^* and L_b^{*j} is used in the part of stage b realized in the developing country. The value of k depends on domestic labor L^{*j} under autarky and on global skilled labor devoted to b, L_b^W, if the country belongs to the multilateral system.

Entry into the multilateral system allows developing countries to attract foreign investment and share in the productivity levels achieved by developed countries. Two key assumptions are that (1) technological transfer can take place only if the developing country forms part of the multilateral system, and (2) the productivity effect is a global externality that does not depend on the protection level selected by an individual developing country.

17.6.3. Noncooperative and Multilateral Tariffs

Developed countries trade policies are the result of maximizing a social welfare function with respect to the *ad valorem* tariff t. Each government's welfare function W^G is a linear combination of unskilled labor wage w_U and total population utility W^P

$$\max_t W^{Gj}(t) = rw_U^j(t) + (1 - r)W^{Pj}(t),$$

where r represents the weight given to unskilled labor wages. The unskilled wage term reflects the role of labor unions. The selected tariff applies to imports of goods produced abroad, including imports of stage b inputs produced in developing countries.

Revenues are distributed as lump sum payments to the population and are assumed to be spent on nontraded good z.

Unilateralism in trade policy means levying noncooperative Nash tariffs t^N determined taking as given other countries' tariffs. Multilateralism means that developed countries jointly select a common tariff t^M taking as given the tariff choice made by developing countries. When developed countries reduce tariffs through a multilateral agreement, skilled labor employment in the intermediate sector b expands and all countries benefit from the externality. Utilizing superscripts N and M to indicate the noncooperative Nash and multilateral regimes, we have

$$ t^M < t^N \quad \rightarrow \quad L_b^{WN} < L_b^{WM} \quad \rightarrow \quad k^N \left(L_b^{WN} \right) < k^M \left(L_b^{WM} \right). $$

The externality might encourage some or all developing countries to abandon autarky and begin producing and exporting the intermediate input b.

The equilibrium condition when (1) each developed country levies a common *ad valorem* tariff t on imports from the $N - 1$ developed trading partners, and (2) developing countries are autarkic, is

$$ Nq(H, k(NL_b)L_b) = \frac{1}{p^\epsilon} + (N-1)\frac{1}{p^\epsilon(1+t)^\epsilon}. $$

A reduction in t increases the production of the final good and thus the allocation of skilled labor to stage b in each developed country. The global production externality implies that the productivity parameter k increases. The key assumption is that this externality favors only those developing countries that are able to attract foreign direct investment by reducing tariffs below prohibitive levels.

The number of countries is assumed to be large enough to cause all countries to take world prices as given so that tariff changes do not have terms of trade effects. Tariffs are determined on a political basis rather than to manipulate terms of trade. Higher tariffs shift demand and resources toward nontraded good z thus increasing the wage w_U of unskilled labor, which is an specific factor used to produce z.

17.6.4. Lobbies, Reform, and Technology Transfer

The choices facing developing countries consist of implementing free trade reform or remaining autarkic thus maintaining local lobbies' rents. Developing countries are assumed to decide on reform taking as given the tariffs levied by developed countries. Reform alters global equilibrium and should induce changes in the tariffs levied by developed countries but these induced effects are not considered.

Trade reform is deemed successful if it attracts foreign direct investment to produce intermediate input b^{*j} used in the second stage of tradable good production q^j. The intermediate input is exported and the customization stage a^j is undertaken in the developed country.

Developing countries differ in terms of the propensity to favor special interests, as measured by the value r^{*j} assigned to local interests. Let us rank countries from lower to greater propensities to favor special interests. Higher values of j and r^{*j} represent greater propensities to favor local interests. The equilibrium number of reforming developing countries, M_R, is given by those having a lower ranking than a critical value $\bar{j}$ corresponding to critical propensity $r^{*\bar{j}}$

$$M_R(P, k) = \int_0^{\bar{j}(P,k)} M(j) \, dj,$$

where $M(j)$ denotes the number of developing countries with propensity r^{*j}. The critical propensity $r^{*\bar{j}}$ is shown below to increase with the probability P of attracting foreign investment P and with the productivity level k.

Assume that a unit of the rudimentary developing country good is a perfect substitute of α units of the sophisticated developed country good. The value of reform measured in terms of developed country tradable goods is equal to the value of reform measured in terms of developing country goods multiplied by α

$$R(k) = \alpha \left[k \left(L_b^W \right) (L_b^* + L_{d*}^*) - q_A^* \right],$$

where $k \left(L_b^W \right) (L_b^* + L_{d*}^*)$ is the level of developing country stage b and consumption d^* under multilateralism while q_A^* is the output of the rudimentary good under autarky. L_b^* is employed by developed countries multinationals.

The presence of foreign investment implies that the international externality extends to production allocated to consumption purposes, that is, global technology spills over to the total production of the rudimentary good. Moreover, in this setup, the externality does not depend on how much foreign investment is attracted as long as it is a positive amount.

Reform is undertaken when its expected value to the reforming country exceeds the welfare weight assigned to local interests

$$E[R(k)] = P(L_b^* > 0)R(k) \geq r^{*j} \quad \rightarrow \quad r^{*\bar{j}} = P(L_b^* > 0)R(k),$$

where P is the probability of attracting a positive amount of foreign direct investment. The critical value of the propensity to favor special interests, $r^{*\bar{j}}$, increases with P and k (as R increases with k). This relation in turn implies that the number of reforming countries increases with P and k.

If foreign investment is distributed equally among developing countries, P is equal to one because all countries will get foreign investment. In this case, the critical value is higher than when $P < 1$

$$P = 1 \quad \rightarrow \quad r^{*\bar{j}} = R(k).$$

What is the condition under which all developing countries remain autarkic when developed countries set tariffs noncooperatively at t^N but at least one developing country undertakes reform when tariffs are set cooperatively at t^M? Let us assume that the probability of attracting foreign investment is equal to one. Recall that the developing country assigning a lower weight r^* to interest groups will lead in reform and that $k^N < k^M$. If the following condition holds,

$$R\left(k^N\right) = \alpha \left[k^N L_b^{*N} - q_A^*\right] < r^* < R\left(k^M\right) = \alpha \left[k^M L_b^{*M} - q_A^*\right],$$

an increase in the value of the productivity parameter k due to the success of the multilateral system will induce reform in at least one developing country.

If the probability of attracting FDI is equal to one, the previous condition ensures that at least one developing country undertakes reform after multilateral negotiations achieve a reduction of developed countries tariff rates. Moreover, given this condition, no developing country would reform if developed countries selected noncooperative Nash equilibrium tariffs (i.e. unilateralism).

17.6.5. Regionalism as a Facilitator of Reform

What happens if the probability P of attracting foreign investment is less than one? Attracting foreign investment can be uncertain because the allocation of stage b production across developing countries is indeterminate. Because all developing countries are symmetric, the model does not provide any rationale for the location of foreign investment in a particular location. Let us then assume that foreign investment is allocated randomly across developing countries.

A reform is deemed successful if it attracts foreign direct investment. The probability of successful reform is thus given by the probability of attracting foreign investment

$$P(L_b^* > 0) = P(M_R^*, m) = \phi \left(\frac{Nm}{(M_R^* - 1)L^*}\right), \quad \phi'(\cdot) > 0,$$

where $\phi(\cdot)$ is an exogenously given density function reflecting the process through which foreign investment is allocated internationally. M_R^* is the number of developing countries undertaking reform (given P and k) and m denotes total employment of skilled labor by the foreign subsidiaries of each developed country. The numerator Nm represents global employment by multinationals' subsidiaries in developing countries. The denominator represents the total skilled labor endowments in all but one of the reforming developing economies.

Suppose that total employment generated by multinationals, Nm, is large enough to absorb the total labor endowments of all reforming economies except for one reformer, $(M_R^* - 1)L^*$. In that case, all reformers must receive some foreign investment and $P = 1$. If this condition does not hold, $P < 1$ and some countries might not get foreign investment. In this case, some countries abstain from reforming because they are not certain they will be able to attract foreign investment and $P(M_R^*, m)R(k) \geq r^{*j}$ might not hold even if $R(k) \geq r^{*j}$.

Regionalism can play a role in facilitating reform by ensuring that $P = 1$. For instance, a developing country can commit to eliminate *ad valorem* tariffs imposed on a developed country's imports. In exchange, the developed country agrees to marginally reduce the duties t_b applied to intermediate input b. This type of regionalism refers to largely one-sided arrangements between developing and developed countries in which a developing country lowers trade barriers and receives small tariff benefits from a developed country partner. This small tariff benefit, however, is enough to be able to shift the developed partner's foreign investment toward the regional group. Multinationals produce intermediate inputs in the developing country to supply developed partner's markets (P becomes equal to one). Regionalism implies that developing countries impose different tariffs to regional partners and nonpartners. However, the developing country regards all imported goods as perfect substitutes, which precludes harmful effects from trade diversion.

Consider a regional arrangement under which a developed country grants a small tariff preference to a developing country's exports of an input. The country receiving the tariff preference will become the single source of the input. This outcome induces other developing countries to form preferential arrangements with developed countries. In equilibrium, each developed country forms a regional arrangement with a developing country. Regionalism between developed and developing countries emerges as a response to successful multilateral liberalization undertaken by developed countries. This mechanism helps explain developing country partial liberalization through preferential agreements, although we must point out that countries like Chile and Mexico liberalized unilaterally before entering into FTAs.

The gain from engaging in reform supported by small tariff concessions from developed countries is that foreign direct investment is secured. Foreign investment entails transfers of technology and allows undertaking production in developing countries. Regionalism is not a mechanism for indirect protection, for delaying broad reform or for obtaining large tariff concessions. It rather represents a mechanism permitting developing economies to compete in attracting foreign investment, which in turn transfers technology and facilitates participation in the multilateral trading regime.

17.7. CONCLUSIONS

What are the criteria used to determine if PTAs are stumbling or building blocks to multilateralism? PTAs promote multilateralism if they reduce the size of import-competing sectors, the strength of their lobbies, and thus the political opposition for further multilateral liberalization. By the same token, an enlargement of the global exporter sector strengthens the lobbies for multilateralism. Also, the domino mechanism works smoothly in preferential areas that subscribe to open regionalism. However, the incentives for open regionalism might be exhausted before free trade is achieved.

PTAs can represent stumbling blocks if they augment the importance of exporters dependent on the protected market. Furthermore, PTAs can be especially pernicious if they eat up part of the variety trade gains from multilateralism while keeping the costs of reducing barriers among countries with heterogeneous endowments.

Finally, PTAs involving developing countries might complement rather than block or encourage the multilateral system. This can happen if developing countries need to participate in the multilateral regime to attract foreign investment and transfer of technology requires the presence of foreign direct investment. PTAs can also complement multilateral efforts because regional negotiations can take over after multilateral liberalization is almost completed.

Intra-regional exporter lobby for lower input tariffs (counter-lobbying) after PTAS are formed can lead to lower external tariffs. PTAs, such as NAFTA and Mercosur, generate counter-lobbying because they partially or completely eliminate the traditional reimbursement (rebates) or waiving (drawbacks) of imported input tariffs for the case of intra-regional exports. Cadot, de Melo and Olearraga (2003) model this political equilibrium and estimate that Mercosur tariffs would have been 3.5 percentage points higher if the drawbacks had not been eliminated.

17.8. APPENDIX

17.8.1. Welfare and Customs Union Size

The foreign offer curve also called the foreign (rest-of-the-word in the present context) reciprocal demand for imports, shows how the foreign demand for imports changes as exports supplied by foreigners change. The elasticity of the foreign reciprocal demand (FRD) for imports, ε^*_{FRD}, is given by

$$\varepsilon^*_{FRD} = \frac{dm^*}{dm}\frac{m}{m^*} > 0,$$

where we use the equality between foreign exports and domestic imports m (i.e. block imports in this context) and $dm^*/dm > 0$ (when m increases along the offer curve, m^* also increases). Observe that the offer curve is upward-sloping.

The block's optimal external tariff is chosen to drive the equilibrium to the position on the rest-of-the-world offer curve that maximizes the block's utility. Mathematically, the monopolist equates the domestic rate of substitution to the marginal rate of transformation as represented by the offer curve

$$\frac{p_d}{p_m} = \frac{p_d}{(1+t^{CU})p_d^*} = \frac{U'(d)}{U'(m)} = MRS_{dm} = MRT^*_{mm^*},$$

where d and m^* represent the demand for the block's goods by the block itself and by the rest-of-the-world, respectively, and m represents block imports of goods produced by the rest-of-the-world. The optimal tariff is denoted t^{CU}, and $(1+t^{CU})p$ represents internal prices of foreign goods, which are the prices facing block importers of rest-of-the world exports.

To explicitly determine the optimal external tariff, recall that the marginal rate of transformation as represented by the offer curve is related to the offer curve's slope, dm^*/dm. We have $(p = p_d/p_d^*)$

$$\frac{p}{1+t^{CU}} = \frac{dm}{dm^*} \quad \rightarrow \quad \left(1+t^{CU}\right) = \frac{dm^*}{dm}p$$

or, solving for t^{CU} (m/m^* refers to the offer curve),

$$t^{CU} = \frac{dm^*}{dm}p - 1 = \frac{dm^*}{dm}\frac{m}{m^*} - 1 = \varepsilon^*_{FRD} - 1,$$

where the price p before the tariff is equal to m/m^* ($pm^* = m$), and $\varepsilon^*_{FRD} = (dm^*/dm)(m/m^*) > 0$ is the elasticity of foreign (i.e. rest-of-the-world) reciprocal demand for imports. The previous condition can be expressed in terms of the foreign import demand elasticity (in the present context, the price elasticity of the rest-of-the-world's demand for the block's exports), $\varepsilon^* = -(dm^*/dp)(p/m^*) = -(\hat{m}^*/\hat{p}) > 0$, were p is the price of block's goods in terms of rest-of-the-world goods.

Recalling the balanced trade condition $pm^* = m$, we have

$$\varepsilon^*_{FRD} = \frac{dm^*}{dm}\frac{m}{m^*} = \frac{dm^*}{d(pm^*)}\frac{pm^*}{m^*} \;\rightarrow\; \varepsilon^*_{FRD}\frac{1}{p} = \frac{dm^*}{p\,dm^* + m^*dp}$$

$$\rightarrow \varepsilon^*_{FRD}\frac{1}{p}(pdm^* + m^*dp) = dm^*$$

$$\rightarrow \varepsilon^*_{FRD}\left(\frac{dm^*}{m^*}\frac{p}{dp} + 1\right) = \frac{dm^*}{m^*}\frac{p}{dp}$$

$$\rightarrow \varepsilon^*_{FRD} = \frac{-\varepsilon_{m^*}}{-\varepsilon_{m^*} + 1} = \frac{\varepsilon_{m^*}}{\varepsilon_{m^*} - 1},$$

or, $\varepsilon_{m^*} = \varepsilon^*_{FRD}/(\varepsilon^*_{FRD} - 1)$, where $\varepsilon^*_{FRD} \equiv [dm^*/dm][m/m^*]$. A member's optimal tariff, assuming that the commercial policies of other blocks remain constant, is

$$t^{CU} = \frac{1}{\varepsilon_{m^*} - 1}.$$

Let us now determine the value of ε_{m^*} in this model.

The elasticity of the demand for exports and the optimal tariff are determined as follows. The rest-of-the-world's budget constraint indicates the division of its spending between goods that they produce themselves, d^*, and imports from the remaining commercial block, pm^*,

$$d^* + pm^* = y^*, \tag{17.4}$$

where m^* are units of goods imported by the rest-of-the-world, and p is the world price of the commercial block's output relative to the rest-of-the-world's output. This means that the income of the rest-of-the-world is measured in terms of its own output.

Total differentiation of (17.4) yields

$$d(d^*) + m^*dp + pdm^* = dy^* = 0,$$

or, dividing by y^* and multiplying by $1 = d^*/d^* = p/p = m^*/m^*$,

$$\frac{d^*}{y^*}\frac{d(d^*)}{d^*} + \frac{pm^*}{y^*}\frac{dp}{p} + \frac{pm^*}{y^*}\frac{dm^*}{m^*} = \frac{dy^*}{y^*} = 0.$$

This equation can be expressed as

$$(1 - s)\hat{d}^* + s[\hat{p} + \hat{m}^*] = (1 - s)(\sigma\hat{p} + \hat{m}^*) + s[\hat{p} + \hat{m}^*]$$
$$= [(1 - s)\sigma + s]\hat{p} + \hat{m}^* = 0,$$

where $s = (pm^*)/y^*$ and $(1 - s) = [y^* - pm^*]/y^* = d^*/y^*$, and we use $\hat{d}^* = \sigma\hat{p} + \hat{m}^*$ (obtained from the definition of the elasticity of substitution in consumption, $\sigma = \sigma_{d^*m^*} = [\hat{d}^* - \hat{m}^*]/\hat{p}$.

The elasticity of the demand for the block's exports, $\varepsilon_{m^*} = -(dm^*/m^*)(p/dp) = -\hat{m}^*/\hat{p}$, is obtained by solving for $\hat{m}^*$ in the previous equation

$$\hat{m}^* = -[s + (1 - s)\sigma]\hat{p}$$

$$\rightarrow \varepsilon_{m^*} = -\frac{\hat{m}^*}{\hat{p}} = s + (1 - s)\sigma.$$

The optimal tariff is

$$t^{CU} = \frac{1}{\varepsilon_{m^*} - 1} = \frac{1}{(1 - s)(\sigma - 1)}, \tag{17.5}$$

where t^{CU} increases with $s = pm^*/y^*$. Because trade must balance, $pm^* = m$, block's exports as a proportion of nonmembers' income are

$$s = \frac{pm^*}{y^*} = \frac{m}{y^*} = \frac{m}{N(B - 1)/B}, \tag{17.6}$$

where y^* is determined as follows. There are N/B countries in each block, and thus $N(1 - 1/B)$ countries that do not belong to a given commercial block. The analysis assumes N/B could take any value, and does not explicitly restrict N/B to be an integer. Because it is assumed that each country produces one unit of a single good, the levels of block and rest-of-the-world production, y and y^*, are also given by N/B and $N(B - 1)/B$ (which are also equal to the number of commodities produced in the block and in the rest-of-the-world)

$$y = \frac{N}{B}, \qquad y^* = \frac{N(B - 1)}{B}. \tag{17.7}$$

Because imports from third countries (i.e. nonmembers) are subject to a tariff, and the elasticity of substitution σ between two commodities is constant, we have ($p = 1$)

$$\frac{m}{d} = (1 + t)^{-\sigma}(B - 1) = \frac{B - 1}{(1 + t)^{\sigma}} \rightarrow d = m\frac{(1 + t)^{\sigma}}{B - 1}. \tag{17.8}$$

Utilizing $m = y - d$ and substituting for d from (17.8) we obtain the imports of the block

$$m = y - m\frac{(1+t)^\sigma}{B-1} \quad \rightarrow \quad m = \frac{y}{(1+t)^\sigma/(B-1)+1}$$

$$= \frac{N/B}{(1+t)^\sigma/(B-1)+1} = \frac{N(B-1)/B}{(1+t)^\sigma + B - 1}. \tag{17.9}$$

with $y = N/B$ from (17.7). Substituting m into (17.6) yields

$$s = \frac{1}{(1+t)^\sigma + B - 1}. \tag{17.10}$$

Using (17.3) in the text and labeling $(1+t^{CU})^\sigma + B - 2 = D$, we have

$$\frac{\partial t^{CU}}{\partial B} = \frac{\partial(1+t^{CU})^\sigma/\partial B + 1}{D(\sigma-1)} - \frac{(1+t^{CU})^\sigma + B - 1}{\sigma - 1}\frac{\partial(1+t^{CU})^\sigma/\partial B + 1}{D^2}$$

$$= \frac{1}{D(\sigma-1)}\left[\frac{\partial(1+t^{CU})^\sigma}{\partial B} + 1 - \left(\frac{\partial(1+t^{CU})^\sigma}{\partial B} + 1\right)\right.$$

$$\left. \times \frac{(1+t^{CU})^\sigma + B - 1}{D}\right],$$

which is negative.

The number of commercial blocks and world's utility can now be determined. There are N/B commodities produced inside the block, and $N(B-1)/B = N - N/B$ goods produced outside any block. A country's utility function can be expressed as

$$U(c, c^*) = \left[\frac{N}{B}c^\theta + \left(N\frac{B-1}{B}\right)c^{*\theta}\right]^{1/\theta},$$

where c and c^* are the country levels of consumption of each good produced in the block and each good produced outside the block, respectively.

To find the level of country imports c^* of each nonblock good typically consumed in a country, notice that total block imports m can be represented as $m = c^*(N/B)N(B-1)/B$ (because there are N/B countries in a block, $N(B-1)/B$ imported goods, and country consumption of each good is c^*). Solving for c^*, yields

$$c^* = m\frac{B}{N}\frac{1}{N(B-1)/B} = \frac{N(B-1)}{B[(1+t)^\sigma + B - 1]}\frac{B}{N}\frac{1}{N(B-1)/B}$$

$$= \frac{B}{N[(1+t)^\sigma + B - 1]}. \tag{17.11}$$

The total block consumption d of goods produced inside the block is equal to $d = c(N/B)(N/B)$ (because there are N/B countries in a block, N/B different goods are produced in the block, and the country consumption of each good is c). Country consumption d of each good produced inside the block is

$$
c = d\left(\frac{B}{N}\right)\left(\frac{B}{N}\right) = \frac{(1+t)^\sigma N}{B[(1+t)^\sigma + B - 1]}\left(\frac{B}{N}\right)^2
$$
$$
= \frac{B(1+t)^\sigma}{N[(1+t)^\sigma + B - 1]},
\tag{17.12}
$$

where $d = (1+t)^\sigma N/[B(1+t)^\sigma + B - 1]$.

Substituting (17.9) into (17.8) yields

$$
\frac{m}{d} = \frac{N/B((B-1)/(1+t)^\sigma) + B - 1}{d} = \frac{B-1}{(1+t)^\sigma}
$$
$$
\rightarrow d = \frac{N(B-1)/B[(1+t)^\sigma + B - 1]}{B - 1/(1+t)^\sigma} = \frac{(1+t)^\sigma N}{B[(1+t)^\sigma + B - 1]}.
$$

Substituting (17.12) and (17.11) into the utility function

$$
U = \left\{\frac{N}{B}\left[\frac{B(1+t)^\sigma}{N[(1+t)^\sigma + B - 1]}\right]^\theta + N\frac{B-1}{B}\left[\frac{B}{N[(1+t)^\sigma + B - 1]}\right]^\theta\right\}^{1/\theta}.
$$

Normalizing by making $N = 1$ (or dividing by $N^{1/\theta}$ and abusing rotation by denoting the result U), we have

$$
U = \left\{\frac{1}{B}\left[\frac{B(1+t)^\sigma}{[(1+t)^\sigma + B - 1]}\right]^\theta + \frac{B-1}{B}\left[\frac{B}{[(1+t)^\sigma + B - 1]}\right]^\theta\right\}^{1/\theta}.
$$

Due to country and block symmetry, U indicates country, block and global welfare.

PART VI

WTO AND INTERNATIONAL COOPERATION

18

The Economics of the WTO

In 1947, twenty-three countries formed the first multilateral organization ever devoted to set principles for international trade and coordinate trade opening among members. Ironically, the creation of the General Agreement on Tariffs and Trade (GATT) resulted from the failed efforts to create a fully-fledged trade agency, the International Trade Organization (ITO), which was not approved by the US Congress. As a result, the GATT was born to play dual roles as a trade agreement and as a proxy institution for the ITO, which was never created. The GATT was envisioned as a provisional *ad hoc* contract among member parties. It did not require ratification by member countries' parliaments and focused on trade in goods because member countries refused to assign a broader agenda.

The GATT initiated a successful series of extended negotiations, also called rounds, for dismantling barriers to trade in goods. GATT-sponsored reductions in tariffs and nontariff barriers to trade (such as quotas) played a central role in shaping trade policies around the world. Each of the eight negotiation rounds sponsored by the GATT produced a binding trade liberalization agreement signed by all members.

The Uruguay Round (1986–94), launched in Punta del Este, the plush Uruguayan resort, has been by far the longest round of multilateral trade negotiations. Ironically, after being widely criticized and dismissed for almost a decade, the trade negotiations round turned out to be most successful. Perhaps its greatest accomplishment was the creation of a new multilateral trade agency that replaced the institutional structure of the GATT.

The birth of the World Trade Organization (WTO) on 1 January 1995, finally brought to life a fully-fledged multilateral trade organization with permanent character and with the same status as the International Monetary Fund and the World Bank. The GATT disappeared as an international agency. As an international agreement, consisting of a document establishing the rules for conducting international trade in goods, GATT 1947 went through a major revision. The refurbished GATT 1994 became the new rule book for trade in goods.

The WTO mandate expanded the scope of multilateral trade negotiations well beyond the original GATT focus on trade in goods. New multilateral agreements covered trade in services (GATS) and intellectual property rights (IPRS). Plurilateral agreements on civil aircraft and government procurement entered into force. A multilateral agreement is one signed by all members while a plurilateral agreement is approved by a subset of members. The civil aircraft agreement eliminated import duties on all nonmilitary aircraft, engines, flight simulators, and other products. The government procurement agreement aimed to make procurement more transparent and open it to international competition, eliminating existing discrimination against foreign products or suppliers. The Uruguay Round produced a timetable for dismantling long-standing protection of textiles and agriculture by industrial countries. Finally, dispute settlement procedures were strengthened by replacing the requirement of consensus among involved parties (which facilitates blocking adverse reports) with the automatic adoption of Appellate Body reports. Member disputes that are not resolved by consultation, arbitration or other means, are settled by setting up a panel of experts to produce a panel report that is subject to appeal before the Appellate Body. The procedure is completed when the Dispute Settlement Body adopts the appeals report.

The Geneve-based WTO is the world's preeminent international trade organization. Its 145 February 2003 members, plus observers such as the Russian Federation and Saudi Arabia, account for almost all world trade. The WTO represents more than a forum for trade negotiations and dispute settlement among members. It is a cooperative institution aiming to implement efficient trade arrangements. Its operation is based on a rules-oriented approach establishing common principles of international negotiations and trading behavior. These common principles should not be viewed as strict rules of behavior but rather as goals guiding trading relations towards desirable outcomes.

This chapter examines the economic basis of the WTO/GATT. It explores the following broad questions.

1. What is the role of the WTO/GATT? Is it ineffective in practice?
2. What are the economic bases of the rules and principles of the GATT?
3. Is multilateral cooperation in trade policy welfare-improving?

Section 18.1 examines the roles of reciprocity, consensus, and tariff bindings. Section 18.2 examines the two nondiscrimination principles: most-favored-nation (MFN) treatment and national treatment. Section 18.3 focuses on the free rider problem attached to the MFN clause. Section 18.4 reviews the do's and don'ts of export subsidies. Sections 18.5 and 18.6 develop a formal model of the GATT, trade negotiations and their efficiency properties. Sections 18.7 and 18.8 examine the debate over labor and environment standards and the potential role of the WTO in enforcing social standards.

18.1. RECIPROCITY, CONSENSUS, AND BINDINGS

What are the main principles of the WTO? The pillars of the multilateral trading system are the principles of consensus and reciprocity in trade negotiations, nondiscrimination, and tariff bindings. The reciprocity and nondiscrimination principles are crucial for ensuring mutual gains from negotiations of market access through an open trading system and fair competition (which forbids discrimination and unfair practices such as export subsidization and dumping). Consensus and tariff bindings aim to preclude basic disagreements and the reversion of negotiated trade concessions.

WTO principles and rules are embodied in the GATT's Articles of Agreement, several other Agreements focusing on specific sectors, and on market access commitments. Special principles agreed for specific sectors cover agriculture, financial services, telecommunications, investment measures, product standards, and rules of origin among others. Deardorff and Stern (1994), Hoekman and Kostecki (1996), Krueger (1998), Jackson (1997, 2000), and Bagwell and Staiger (2000*a*, 2003) offer detailed institutional, legal and economic analyses. Jackson and Sykes (1997) examine the implementation of the Uruguay Round agreements in selected countries. Vines (1998) compares the competencies, agendas and linkages of the WTO, the IMF and the World Bank.

18.1.1. Reciprocity and Balanced Concessions

The reciprocity principle establishes that WTO members have symmetric rights and obligations and should obtain mutually beneficial reductions of trade barriers. Bhagwati (1988) stresses that reciprocity in negotiations has been interpreted as a balanced reduction of tariffs (first-difference approach). In other words, the first-difference approach to negotiations interprets reciprocity in the marginal sense of balanced tariff reductions rather than in the absolute sense of establishing equal market access for all members.

In practice, reciprocity means that trade liberalization proceeds on a quid pro quo basis. Negotiating governments balance the concessions given to each other in the sense that a member proposing to reduce its trade barriers receives in return similar trade concessions from other members.

Krugman (1997) points out that negotiations through reciprocity appear to contradict the 'free trade is best' paradigm, which calls for unilateral rather than reciprocal tariff reductions. The requirement of reciprocity in trade negotiations can be understood in terms of mercantilist theories asserting that exports are good and imports are bad while equal increases in imports and exports are good because they keep the trade balance unchanged. This type of logic reflects the mercantilist fallacy that welfare increases when more domestic goods are given away in the form of exports and declines when more foreign goods are consumed as imports. The mercantilists aimed to accumulate wealth through trade and believed that trade deficits were bad while trade surpluses were good.

Notwithstanding its mercantilist flavor, GATT thinking paved the way for successful multilateral negotiations aiming to open markets worldwide and reduce inefficiencies associated with protectionism. Reciprocal trade concessions, meaning trade concessions that are matched by equivalent concessions abroad:

1. Generate political support on the part of exporters benefitting from required tariff reductions abroad. The support offered by domestic exporters to trade liberalization balances the opposition of domestic producers of import-competing goods.
2. Offset the adverse terms of trade effects of unilateral trade liberalization and thus internalize terms of trade externalities. Specifically, reciprocal concessions facilitate negotiations aiming to induce large countries to reduce tariffs and other barriers to trade. In a noncooperative setting, large countries do not have incentives to cut tariffs

or eliminate nontariff barriers unilaterally. In markets in which large countries are major traders, unilateral liberalization hurts them by raising the global demand and thus the world prices of imported goods facing lower trade barriers.

3. Help to break down the dominance of bargaining power in negotiations. The requirement of balanced concessions undermines multilateral negotiations in which concessions hinge on the relative bargaining power of the participants. Balance in bargaining power promotes participation of countries that would otherwise lose or obtain small benefits from multilateral trade liberalization based on relative power.

Let us examine the role of the WTO in the context of tariff reductions. Similar points apply to the elimination of nontariff barriers to trade.

Propping up Political Support from Exporters

When the benefits from tariff reductions partly accrue to foreign producers, political support for unilateral liberalization flounders. Domestic producers of import-competing goods and owners of adversely affected factors of production oppose trade liberalization on the grounds that they experience losses from its implementation. Domestic exporters might support unilateral liberalization only to the extent to which they benefit from lower tariffs on imported inputs. Furthermore, consumers are isolated from each other and do not represent a powerful interest group for liberalization. As a result, trade liberalization does not receive strong enough political support.

In the reciprocal concessions scenario, trade liberalization generates political support from domestic exporters. The reason is that reciprocity requires tariff reductions abroad. These reductions directly benefit domestic exporters thus generating support to balance opposition by owners of adversely affected factors of production and domestic producers of import-competing products.

Offsetting Adverse Terms of Trade Effects

Let us see how the principle of reciprocity can be justified as a mechanism to offset the adverse terms of trade implications of countries' unilateral trade liberalization policies. First of all, consider a country that is a large buyer in the world market for a particular imported product. What happens when the country unilaterally reduces the tariff on this product? The tariff cut increases the world demand for the product and thus its world price. As a result, the country's terms of trade deteriorate and foreign producers end up reaping part of the social benefits from the tariff cut. The liberalizing country does not get all the benefits from liberalization because it gives a positive terms of trade externality to foreign exporters. In this scenario, countries are reluctant to lower tariffs unilaterally. In general, when the benefits from dismantling protection are not fully internalized, governments oversupply trade restrictive policies and undersupply trade promotion policies.

Why is it that the reciprocity principle helps ensure that multilateral trade negotiations result in mutually beneficial trade liberalization? Reciprocity makes possible negotiating tariff reductions in situations in which countries that lower tariffs unilaterally are hurt by an increase in the world prices of the imported goods subject to tariff reductions. These countries would be willing to cut tariffs as long as their trading partners undertake compensating tariff reductions. The reciprocity principle brings about the required compensating tariff reductions (Bagwell and Staiger, 1999*a*).

Negotiations: Rules vs Bargaining Power

A rules approach requiring trade concessions to be exchanged on a quid pro quo basis ensures that negotiating partners benefit on a substantially equal basis. In other words, the requirement of reciprocity contributes to diminish the dominance of relative bargaining power in the distribution of the benefits from trade liberalization. As a consequence, the distribution of payoffs displays greater balance than if negotiations were conducted under a pure bargaining power approach.

There are several situations in which bargaining power influences the support for multilateral negotiations. First, small countries in a weak bargaining position lack incentives to cut tariffs if they can free ride on concessions negotiated by large countries dominating the bargaining process. Second, weak bargaining power can also mean that small countries end up reaping small benefits from a multilateral agreement based on large country bargaining power. Specifically, a highly specialized small country dependent on trade with a large country will be vulnerable to negotiating processes based on bargaining power. These countries might abstain from joining negotiations under a pure bargaining approach even if they would join under a rules approach.

McLaren (1997) develops a two–country model of the effects of anticipated future tariff negotiations when countries must make irreversible decisions that affect the outcome of the bargaining processes. He utilizes a modified version of the two–sector Ricardian comparative advantage framework. There is a single factor of production, labor, which for simplicity is viewed as a worker–entrepreneur.

The model has two periods. In the first period, the sectorial allocation of labor is made on the basis of comparative advantage. The small country's labor force is relatively more productive in sector *I* while the large country's labor is relatively more productive in sector *II*. Production requires irreversible decisions in the sense that labor chooses its sectorial allocation in the first period and remains immobile thereafter. Moreover, any investments made in the first period are irreversible and do not require incurring additional future costs, so that all costs are sunk.

In the second period, output becomes available, countries specify the Nash tariffs determining the threat point of the tariff negotiation process, and tariff bargaining and consumption take place. Because the inherited sectorial allocation of labor cannot be altered and all production costs are sunk costs, output can be viewed as the period–two endowment of an exchange economy. This model captures a situation in which tariff negotiations are conducted after factors of production have been allocated across sectors and cannot be allocated further.

Consider *ad valorem* tariff bargaining between the governments of a small and a large country (denoted by an asterisk*). The Nash bargaining solution is the tariff pair

(t, t^*) that maximizes welfare W specified as the product of utility levels in excess of the threat point utility attainable under Nash equilibrium tariffs

$$W(t, t^*) = [U(t, t^*) - U(t^N, t^{*N})][U^*(t, t^*) - U^*(t^N, t^{*N})].$$

Relative size is measured by the ratio $L/L^* < 1$, which is defined as the small country's labor endowment divided by the size of the large country's labor endowment. Suppose that, anticipating liberal trade, the small country makes an irreversible allocation of labor resources favoring its export sector (i.e. the one in which it enjoys relative comparative advantage). This irreversible allocation creates a dependency on trade with the large country and lowers the small country's bargaining power. Irreversible decisions alter the threat point to which parties move if negotiations break down and change the payoffs from bargaining.

As a country's relative size becomes infinitesimally small, $L/L^* \to 0$, it loses the incentive to protect itself because it loses the ability to affect its terms of trade. However, the Nash tariff t^{*N} maximizing large country benefits from protection does not vanish. Formally, McLaren shows that t^{*N} is higher the greater the ratio indicating small country specialization in its export good q_{II} relative to large country specialization in that good,

$$\lim_{L/L^* \to 0} (1 + t_I^{*N}) = \frac{q_I/q_{II}}{q_I^*/q_{II}^*}.$$

If the Nash equilibrium payoff of the threat point worsens by a large enough value due to past investments in the export sector, the net gains from subsequent negotiations might become negative. Therefore, countries might not participate in multilateral negotiations based on bargaining power. Even if participation is potentially worthwhile, ex ante investment decisions made in anticipation of negotiations reduce flexibility and can discourage participation ex post. Because negotiations based on reciprocity rules ensure greater balance in the distribution of the gains from bargaining, participation might take place even if it is not worthwhile under a pure bargaining power approach.

18.1.2. *Consensual Decisions and Tariff Bindings*

Consensus in deciding over multilateral rules and tariff bindings are two key multilateral negotiation principles. Consensus imposes a unanimity requirement. Unanimity ensures that all trading partners agree on the overall results of a negotiation round and have a stake on it. Tariff bindings aim to make costly reneging on previous trade concessions. Once a tariff reduction has been negotiated and accepted, it becomes 'bound' at the negotiated rate. A tariff cannot be subsequently increased above the bound rate without permitting affected partners to reciprocate by withdrawing 'substantially equivalent' trade concessions. The reciprocity rules surrounding tariff bindings (Article XXVIII of GATT 1947) aim to minimize the reversion of trade concessions by imposing costs on countries renegotiating previously bound tariffs.

A negotiation process based on consensual decisions leading to multiple bindings is difficult to complete and can be subject to long delays. The Uruguay Round of trade negotiations was afflicted by disagreements over the proposed treatment of cultural products, agricultural protection, and other issues. Tough positions delayed the approval of the proposed new agreement for years.

18.2. NONDISCRIMINATION PRINCIPLES

The enforcement of nondiscrimination principles intends to eliminate discriminatory behavior in international trade. The WTO/GATT rules out two major forms of discrimination against member countries. The national treatment rule aims to preclude discrimination against foreign goods after they enter a country. The most-favored-nation treatment (MFN) principle aims to extend trade concessions to all members and minimize trading relations favoring some nations over others.

18.2.1. National Treatment

One type of nondiscrimination principle is the national treatment rule requiring that, once foreign products enter into an importing country, they should be accorded the same treatment as similar national products for tax and other purposes (GATT 1947: Article *III*). National treatment ensures equal competitive opportunities between domestic and imported products once the latter cross national borders. Notice that national treatment does not imply equal opportunities for foreign products in the sense of zero import tariffs, but only equal treatment after foreign products have entered a country.

In practice, national treatment means that imports: (1) do not pay internal taxes in excess of those applied to domestic products, (2) are accorded the same treatment as that given to a similar domestic product in terms of sales, transportation, and others, and (3) are not subject to domestic content requirements, which typically require that a minimum fraction of domestic value added be included in goods sold on domestic markets. For instance, local content regulations often protect domestic producers of parts by inducing foreign firms to procure parts from local suppliers even if these parts could be obtained at a lower cost elsewhere.

18.2.2. Most-Favored-Nation Treatment

A second nondiscrimination principle establishes the MFN rule stating that all members should receive the same treatment as the member receiving the best treatment (GATT 1947: Article I). Tariffs set according to the MFN principle do not depend on the country of origin of imports. This means that the tariff rate on any given product should be uniform across trading partners (but tariffs do not have to be uniform across different imported goods). In the context of trade negotiations, the MFN rule requires extending to third countries all the concessions negotiated between any two members.

Specifically, a tariff rate reduction negotiated between two member countries should apply to all WTO members without exception.

18.2.3. *Is MFN Treatment Necessary for Efficient Agreements?*

Is the MFN nondiscrimination rule necessary to implement efficient multilateral trade agreements? The answer is yes, except in the case of customs unions, such as the European Union, conceived as a single country so that zero internal tariffs are not considered discrimination against outsiders. The MFN treatment clause eliminates inefficiencies arising when a country imposes different tariffs rates on the same good imported from different trading partners. Gatsios (1990) shows that in oligopolistic markets there are incentives to discriminate by setting a higher tariff to low-cost, high output foreign exporters in order to benefit from the higher tariff revenues due to a wider tax base. Moreover, customs unions among dissimilar countries and free trade areas impede the attainment of efficiency because they discriminate in favor of union or area members.

In a two-country world, tariff discrimination cannot take place because there is only one foreign country and thus one external tariff for each good. Bagwell and Staiger (1999a) develop a multicountry model in which countries have incentives to set tariffs and associated domestic prices in a discriminatory fashion to maximize rent extraction from trading partners. They find that the combination of the principle of nondiscrimination and the principle of reciprocity facilitates tariff reductions and can contribute to the implementation of an efficient multilateral trade agreement. First, reciprocity internalizes tariff externalities that lead to higher tariff rates and are transmitted through lower world prices. Second, nondiscrimination eliminates tariff externalities that are transmitted by differentially influencing domestic prices in different countries. Inefficiencies due to international divergences in domestic prices arise when importing countries impose higher tariffs on countries that provide greater rent extraction opportunities. Therefore, in the presence of reciprocal trade liberalization, efficiency requires nondiscrimination.

Article XXIV of GATT 1947 contains an exception permitting the type of discrimination created by preferential trade arrangements. Do preferential arrangements impede the implementation of an efficient trade system? Because preferential arrangements by their own nature violate the MFN rule, they do not support efficiency. The principle of reciprocity cannot be used to implement an efficient multilateral trade agreement in the absence of a nondiscrimination rule. Efficiency breaks down in the presence of free trade areas and customs unions among countries that are not 'natural' integration partners. Countries are said to be natural integration partners when they have similar income levels and their governments maximize similar welfare functions.

Customs unions between natural integration partners are consistent with efficiency in the sense that they do not violate the nondiscrimination rule. To see why, notice that members of a customs union between natural integration partners can be validly treated as regions of a single country surrounded by a common external tariff wall. However, because the 'natural integration partners' requirement is stringent, one might still conclude that most preferential agreements undermine the multilateral system. Moreover, countries discriminate against other countries in the same manner as any customs union. In fact, a country can be viewed as a customs union among regions united by a common political authority.

18.3. FREE RIDER PROBLEM OF THE MFN CLAUSE

There is an upside and a downside to the MFN rule. The upside is that its application eliminates inefficiencies arising from the imposition of different tariff rates on the same good imported from different trading partners. The downside is that the MFN obligation to apply negotiated tariff reductions to all members generates a free rider externality problem. Third countries benefit from tariff reductions negotiated by any two members even if third countries do not reciprocate by reducing tariffs. Reciprocal concessions avoid the externality that enables a WTO member to free ride on concessions made by other members. In practice, however, the reciprocity negotiation principle states a goal rather than an outcome. Concessions and negotiation outcomes are not necessarily balanced and free rider problems do arise.

18.3.1. Free Riding with Bilateral Bargaining

The consequences of the MFN clause depend on how negotiations are conducted, particularly on whether negotiations within the WTO are conducted on a multilateral or bilateral basis. In a multilateral negotiation framework, all WTO members participate in determining reductions in trade barriers and must make reciprocal concessions. In a bilateral trade negotiation framework, some countries meet to jointly determine reductions in their trade barriers. To the extent that other WTO members do not participate in this negotiation, they reap windfall gains from negotiated tariff reductions. The free-rider possibility arises due to the structure of bilateral negotiations and the MFN clause.

In practice, tariff reductions are often negotiated on a bilateral basis. A case in point concerns the strenuous negotiations between the United States and the European Union (i.e. France) on the liberalization of trade in agricultural and cultural products. WTO negotiations for the liberalization of trade in services are being conducted on a multilateral basis.

Caplin and Krishna (1988) present a model of simultaneous bilateral tariff bargaining with and without an MFN clause. Bilateral bargaining in the presence of an MFN clause generates a free rider problem because third countries benefit from negotiated tariff reductions even if they do not reciprocate by reducing tariffs. The free-riding problem leads to an equilibrium in which countries impose higher tariffs with the MFN clause than without the clause. Paradoxically, bilateral bargaining with an MFN clause produces higher tariffs and less efficient outcomes than unconstrained bilateral bargaining. These results suggest that the special form of multilateralism achieved by introducing an MFN clause into a bilateral bargaining framework can be counterproductive.

18.3.2. Free Riding with Multilateral Bargaining

Ludema (1991) considers negotiations among three countries to show that, if negotiations are conducted on a multilateral basis, the MFN clause does not have to generate free-riding problems. In each period, one country is randomly selected to make an offer to the other two countries. The offer consists of a tariff structure proposal (t_1, t_2, t_3) specifying the level of external tariffs for each country. The rate t_1 is the tariff applied by country 1 to countries 2 and 3, the rate t_2 is the rate country 2 applies to 1 and 3, and country 3 applies t_3 to 1 and 2. Notice that different countries are allowed to set a different tariff level but they must be levied on an MFN basis (i.e. tariffs cannot discriminate by the source of an imported product).

The proposing country's offer must be answered simultaneously by the other two countries. If both countries reject the proposal, the process is repeated next period. If both countries accept the proposal to reduce trade barriers, the game ends and the proposal is adopted. If one country rejects, the other country has the option of accepting the proposal as a bilateral agreement that implements the elements over which the accepting partners have control. Because the rejecting party will maximize its welfare subject to no tariff setting restriction, the bilateral partners obtain a lower utility level under a bilateral than under a multilateral agreement. The reason is that the rejecting country does not have to lower its tariffs while benefiting from bilateral partners' tariff reductions due to the MFN rule.

How does the proposing country formulate its proposal? The optimal tariff structure offer must (1) leave the other two countries indifferent between accepting the multilateral agreement and continuing negotiations, and (2) induce a country accepting the multilateral proposal to reject the bilateral alternative, which always yields less utility than the multilateral proposal to the proposing and accepting countries.

If the multilateral proposal is well-designed, a country rejecting it in an attempt to free ride on a bilateral negotiation will not achieve its goal. Free riding is precluded because the other country considering the offer will continue to negotiate rather than accept the bilateral alternative. The reason is that proposed tariffs are set such that the value of continuing negotiations is the same as the value of the multilateral proposal and greater than the value of a bilateral negotiation with free riding by a rejecting country. In this setting in which each country negotiates by proposing a complete tariff structure for all trading partners, the presence of the MFN clause does not generate free-rider externalities.

18.4. EXPORT SUBSIDIES AND THE WTO

Which types of export subsidies are WTO-legal? The WTO defines subsidies as any type of government financial contribution or mechanism sustaining prices or revenues aiming to provide an advantage to firms. This definition includes direct payments to exporters, export credits, tax and fiscal exemptions, and subsidized insurance of export credits. Drawbacks and temporary admissions are not considered subsidies and are permitted by the WTO.

The WTO distinguishes between three categories of domestic or export subsidies. Prohibited subsidies, such as those requiring recipients to meet export targets or to use domestic goods (i.e. impose a domestic content requirement), have to be removed. Actionable subsidies are permitted unless a complaining member proves that damage has been caused. Nonactionable subsidies—such as subsidies assisting disadvantaged regions and specific subsidies for industrial research or pre-competitive development activity—cannot be challenged within the WTO. In this context, 'specific' refers to a subsidy available only to an enterprise, industry or a group of them.

Observe that not all subsidies are banned by the WTO. The Agreement does not preclude the direct reimbursement of indirect taxes and those incentives aimed to equalize domestic and foreign competitors' positions. For instance, governments are allowed to grant export credits to ensure that domestic exporters have access to the international interest rates granted to international competitors.

The Agreement on Subsidies and Countervailing Measures (SCM Agreement), which is part of the WTO Agreements, broadly recognizes the role of export incentives in poor countries' development programs. Countries with a per capita gross national product (GNP) not exceeding $1000 are exempted from export incentive limitations. The application of the WTO Agreement is fully restored once developing country exports of a commodity—defined by its four digits according to the harmonized system—reaches a market share exceeding 3.25 percent of the world market in two consecutive years.

Article XIX.9, known as DeMinimis Clause, allows developing countries to (1) grant export subsidies if they represent less than 2 percent of the unit value of the exports, and (2) grant specific subsidies to goods in which the country has a small enough world market share. Also, the WTO allows the use of subsidies to encourage research and development, to assist less developed regions, to promote pre-competitive activities— obtaining information about foreign consumers' preferences, distribution channels, market studies, and others—and to facilitate the adoption of new environmental rules.

Member countries hurt by a foreign subsidy can use the WTO dispute settlement procedure to seek its withdrawal or the removal of its adverse effects. If the dispute settlement procedure confirms that a subsidy is prohibited or is actionable and causes injury, either the subsidy must be withdrawn or the complaining WTO member is allowed to take countermeasures. Specifically, the complaining country can investigate by itself and impose countervailing duties on subsidized imports that are found to hurt domestic producers. Countervailing duties (CVDs) target a foreign exporter and thus violate the WTO principles stating that tariffs should not be increased above bound (i.e. maximum) levels and that all members should be treated equally. The WTO escape clause allowing countervailing duties requires a detailed investigation showing that domestic industry is hurt before a member country is allowed to charge countervailing duties.

In order to prevent disputes over export incentives, countries have signed numerous bilateral agreements limiting the use of export subsidies in exchange for limitations on the application of compensatory measures on imports. The Uruguay Round of trade negotiations (1985–94) sponsored by the GATT—the WTO predecessor—took measures to limit the proliferation of these bilateral agreements. The round produced an agreement limiting the use of both export incentives and related compensatory measures.

Despite export subsidy restrictions by WTO agreements and by means of bilateral agreements, countries continue to display incentives to subsidize exports. Overt subsidization in violation of WTO subsidy agreements takes advantage of the fact the subsidy agreements are not directly enforceable by the WTO or in domestic courts. Hidden or indirect subsidies take advantage of multiple grey areas not yet clarified by the WTO. Well-publicized disputes continue to arise.

18.4.1. The Foreign Sales Corporation Dispute

The European Union and the United States have frequently clashed over export subsidies. The Foreign Sales Corporation (FSC) dispute is yet another episode of what has been called the transatlantic war over whether US tax incentives represent hidden export subsidies. The dispute can be traced back to the 1971 tax incentives for a new type of corporation that was called Domestic International Sales Corporations (DISC). The US trading partners complained that the tax incentives (a tax deferral) violated the GATT subsidy rule stating that member countries should not use tax benefits as hidden export subsidies.

The 1984 Foreign Sales Corporation Act introduced the FSC to replace the DISC and attempt to comply with GATT rules. An FSC must be incorporated in a qualified foreign country or US possession outside the customs territory of the United States under the specific requirements of Sections 921–7 of the US Internal Revenue Code. An FSC benefits from a tax exemption on its foreign trade income treated as foreign source income not effectively connected with a trade or business in the United States and thus not subject to US taxes. The exemption on foreign trade income has benefited US multinationals such as Boeing, Microsoft, and others by granting tax reductions of 15–30 percent if they export through foreign sales corporations established in Virgin Islands, Barbados, Guam, and other fiscal havens.

In 2000, the WTO backed European Union claims that the special FSC tax treatment represented WTO-illegal subsidies that violated both the Agreement on Subsidies and Countervailing Measures and the Agreement on Agriculture. The United States revised the program and claimed that it was compatible with global trading rules. However, an August 2001 decision by a Dispute Settlement Body panel declared US tax breaks incompatible with WTO rules. There was a violation of WTO agreements because, even if enterprises established outside the United States did not need to export to obtain a tax exemption, if they were established in the United States they had to export to obtain the exemption.

The special tax treatment of FSC was said to embody export subsidies that discriminated unfairly in favor of US products. The decision entitled the European Union to levy sanctions on the accumulated losses to its exporters, which the European Union estimated to mount to about $4–$5 billion per year. In order to avoid sanctions, the

United States would have to eliminate the program or change its operation. The transatlantic war continues.

18.5. MODELING THE WELFARE ROLE OF THE WTO

Countries holding a substantial share of the world demand for a particular imported product are not willing to engage in unilateral trade liberalization because a tariff cut would increase the imported product demand and thus its world price. As a result, terms of trade would deteriorate and foreign producers would end up reaping part of the social benefits from the tariff cut. However, large countries would be willing to reduce tariffs and move away from a noncooperative equilibrium if the world price of imported products could be kept unchanged. The reciprocity rule of the GATT can be viewed as a mechanism encouraging cooperation by offsetting the adverse terms of trade effects resulting from unilateral trade liberalization. Nondiscrimination is required for achieving efficiency through negotiations conducted under the reciprocity principle.

Bagwell and Staiger (1999a) formalize a theory of the GATT as an institution enabling trade liberalization among countries that are not willing to engage in unilateral trade liberalization. This section focuses on the inefficiencies of noncooperative equilibria and the conditions for efficiency. The analysis shows how tariff negotiations conducted according to the GATT reciprocity and nondiscrimination rules help to implement trade liberalization and examines conditions under which trade negotiations lead to a politically optimal equilibrium.

18.5.1. Welfare, Politics, and Free Trade

Consider a scenario with two large countries and two goods produced under competitive conditions. The home country exports good I and imports good II while the foreign country exports II and imports I. Values are expressed in terms of good I, which is taken to be the numeraire.

Trade balance implies that the value of home country imports in terms of good I, $p^W M_{II}$, is equal to its exports X_I, which in turn equals foreign country imports, M_I^*. Formally,

$$p^W M_{II}(p, p^W) = M_I^*(p^*, p^W), \quad p = \frac{p_{II}}{p_I}, \quad p^* = \frac{p_{II}^*}{p_I^*}, \quad p^W = \frac{p_{II}^*}{p_I}, \qquad (18.1)$$

where M represents quantities imported and imports are valued using the world relative price. The domestic importables price $p_{II} = p_{II}^*(1 + t)$ and the foreign importables price $p_I^* = (1 + t^*)p_I$ are local prices affected by applicable tariffs. World prices correspond to 'offshore' or exporting country prices p_{II}^* and p_I, which are not subject to tariffs.

The domestic and foreign governments maximize national welfare functions $W(p, \tilde{p}^W)$ and $W^*(p^*, \tilde{p}^W)$

$$\max_p W(p, \tilde{p}^W), \quad \max_{p^*} W^*(p^*, \tilde{p}^W),$$

where $\tilde{p}^W = \tilde{p}_{II}^* / \tilde{p}_I$ represents the equilibrium offshore price of good II relative to the offshore price of good I and

$$\frac{\partial W(p, \tilde{p}^W)}{\partial \tilde{p}^W} < 0, \quad \frac{\partial W^*(p^*, \tilde{p}^W)}{\partial \tilde{p}^W} > 0.$$

The welfare functions are assumed to satisfy the standard condition that a higher world relative price of good II worsens the welfare of the economy importing it and increases the welfare of the exporting economy.

Local relative prices are functions of the *ad valorem* tariff rates t and the equilibrium world price

$$p(\tau, \tilde{p}^W) = (1 + t)\tilde{p}^W = \tau\tilde{p}^W, \quad p^*(\tau^*, \tilde{p}^W) = \frac{\tilde{p}^W}{1 + t^*} = \frac{\tilde{p}^W}{\tau^*},$$

where $\tau = 1 + t$ and $\tau^* = 1 + t^*$. A higher tariff factor τ is associated with a higher local relative price p. Because the foreign tariff falls on numeraire good I, a higher tariff factor τ^* is associated with a lower relative price $p^* = p_{II}^*/p_I^*$.

The welfare functions $W(p, \tilde{p}^W)$ and $W^*(p^*, \tilde{p}^W)$ are assumed to be concave with respect to p and p^*, respectively. There is an intermediate local price level $p = p(\tau, \tilde{p}^W)$ and associated tariff factor τ at which welfare is maximized and $\partial W(p, \tilde{p}^W)/\partial p = 0$. A higher absolute value of the import subsidy rate $t < 0$ corresponds to a lower local price p. At low levels of p, lowering the absolute value $|t|$ of the subsidy rate raises the local price and increases welfare: $\partial W(p, \tilde{p}^W)/\partial p > 0$. A higher tariff corresponds to a higher price. At high levels of p, raising the tariff rate t increases the local price and reduces welfare: $\partial W(p, \tilde{p}^W)/\partial p < 0$. A similar analysis applies to $W^*(p^*, \tilde{p}^W)$.

Political and distributive goals are reflected in the functional relation between relative prices and welfare. Because the welfare functions W and W^* implicitly incorporate political and distributional motives, free trade is not necessarily optimal from the government's perspective. Government welfare as a function of the local price does not have to achieve a maximum at free trade. Formally, $\partial W(p, \tilde{p}^W)/\partial p$ and $\partial W^*(p^*, \tilde{p}^W)/\partial p^*$ do not have to be equal to zero at $p = \tilde{p}^W$ and $p^* = \tilde{p}^W$, respectively.

18.5.2. Noncooperative Nash Equilibrium

Governments choose the welfare-maximizing noncooperative tariff factors $\tau = 1 + t$ and $\tau^* = 1 + t^*$, where t and t^* represent *ad valorem* tariff rates. The Nash equilibrium or best-response tariff factors are given by

$$\tau^N \in \arg\max_\tau W(p(\tau, \tilde{p}^W), \tilde{p}^W), \quad \tau^{*N} \in \arg\max_{\tau^*} W^*(p^*(\tau^*, \tilde{p}^W), \tilde{p}^W),$$

where arg max means the argument that maximizes a function. Prices $p = p(\tau, \tilde{p}^W)$ and $p^* = p(\tau^*, \tilde{p}^W)$ are functions of the tariffs on goods II and I, respectively, and world prices. Notice that the equilibrium import tariff would correspond to an equivalent export tax. This result follows from Lerner's symmetry theorem in a two-good scenario. This theorem states that an import tariff is equivalent to an export tax that reduces exports and imports by the same amount as the import tariff.

The first order welfare maximization conditions determining Nash equilibrium tariff factors (τ^N, τ^{*N}) are

$$\frac{\partial W}{\partial p} \frac{dp}{d\tau} + \frac{\partial W}{\partial \tilde{p}^W} \frac{\partial \tilde{p}^W}{\partial \tau} = 0 \rightarrow \frac{\partial W}{\partial p} = -\lambda \frac{\partial W}{\partial \tilde{p}^W} < 0,$$

$$\frac{\partial W^*}{\partial p^*} \frac{dp^*}{d\tau^*} + \frac{\partial W^*}{\partial \tilde{p}^W} \frac{\partial \tilde{p}^W}{\partial \tau^*} = 0 \rightarrow \frac{\partial W^*}{\partial p^*} = -\lambda^* \frac{\partial W^*}{\partial \tilde{p}^W} > 0,$$

(18.2)

where $\lambda = (\partial \tilde{p}^W/\partial \tau)/(dp/d\tau) < 0$ because the numerator is negative and the denominator is positive. A higher tariff τ on imports of II leads to a reduction in the world relative price $\tilde{p}^W$ and an increase in the local relative price p. The factor $\lambda^* = (\partial \tilde{p}^W/\partial \tau^*)/(dp^*/d\tau^*) < 0$ because the numerator is positive and the denominator is negative. A higher tariff factor τ^* on imports of good I lowers its world relative price and thus increases $\tilde{p}^W = \tilde{p}^*_{II}/\tilde{p}_I$. The inequality $dp^*/d\tau^* < 0$ holds because $p^* = \tilde{p}^W(\tau, \tau^*)/\tau^*$ and the increase in $\tilde{p}^W$ is smaller than the increase in τ^*.

Tariff rates are set taking into account that a higher tariff (1) induces an increase of the local price, which has a negative welfare effect, and (2) induces a reduction in the world price, p_I or p_{II}, which has a positive welfare effect. If a country has a degree of monopoly power in world markets but local firms act competitively, there are incentives for trade intervention. The importer of good II can levy a tariff on the imports of good II to increase domestic welfare at the expense of foreign welfare. The second term in each maximization condition embodies the externality related to the ability to change the terms of trade (i.e. the world relative price $\tilde{p}^W$) in a country's favor. The terms of trade externality is a source of inefficiency because it motivates both countries to increase tariffs in order to attempt to lower the world relative price of the good they import.

If the world price could be kept constant, both countries would like to lower tariffs. To see why, examine the maximization condition (18.2). At the equilibrium tariff factor τ^N, the negative welfare effect of an increase in the local relative price p due to a higher tariff is exactly offset by the positive welfare effect of the tariff-induced reduction in the world relative price p^W. The equilibrium domestic price is such that domestic welfare at given world prices declines with domestic prices: $\partial W/\partial p < 0$, which creates incentives to lower tariffs if world prices are kept fixed. By the same token, the Nash tariff factor τ^{*N} balances (1) the positive welfare effect of a higher τ^* through a lower world price of good I and a higher $\tilde{p}^W = \tilde{p}^*_{II}/\tilde{p}_I : \partial W^*/\partial \tilde{p}^W > 0$, and (2) the negative welfare effect of a higher τ^* through a higher domestic relative price of I and a lower relative price $p^* = \tilde{p}^W/\tau^* = \tilde{p}^*_{II}/(\tilde{p}_I\tau^*) : \partial W^*/\partial p^* > 0$. Keeping the world price constant, there are incentives for tariff reductions.

18.5.3. Efficient Tariff Equilibria

Why do countries negotiate trade agreements? One motivating factor is to pull economies out of a suboptimal equilibrium characterized by unilateral tariff setting aiming to exploit terms of trade externalities. A trade agreement is attractive because it enables members to cooperate and replace the suboptimal Nash equilibrium tariffs with lower tariffs.

Efficiency is achieved when domestic and foreign governments internalize the terms of trade externalities by jointly determining their trade policies and implied prices. The cooperative welfare maximization problem entails choosing the domestic and foreign price levels that maximize welfare function W, subject to the foreign welfare level W^*. Formally,

$$\max_{\{p,p^*\}} W(p, \tilde{p}^W) \quad \text{s.t.} \quad W^*(p^*, \tilde{p}^W) \geq \overline{W}^{*EF} \equiv W^*(p^{*EF}, \tilde{p}^W),$$

where $\overline{W}^{*EF}$ is the foreign welfare level achieved under the efficient price levels $(p^{*EF}, \tilde{p}^W)$.

The pair of efficient tariff factors (τ^{EF}, τ^{*EF}) and efficient prices (p^{EF}, p^{*EF}) satisfy the first order condition (see appendix)

$$\left(1 - \frac{1 - \tau\lambda}{\partial W/\partial p + \lambda \partial W/\partial p^W} \frac{\partial W}{\partial p}\right)$$

$$\times \left(1 - \frac{1 - \lambda^*/\tau^*}{\partial W^*/\partial p^* + \lambda^* \partial W^*/\partial p^W} \frac{\partial W^*}{\partial p^*}\right) = 1, \tag{18.3}$$

where $\lambda = [\partial \tilde{p}^W/\partial \tau]/[dp/d\tau] < 0$ and $\lambda^* = [\partial \tilde{p}^W/\partial \tau^*]/[dp^*/d\tau^*] < 0$ measure the response of the world relative price to the tariffs.

The Nash equilibrium is not efficient. This property can be proved by substituting the Nash equilibrium condition $\partial W/\partial p + \lambda \partial W/\partial p^W = \partial W^*/\partial p^* + \lambda^* \partial W^*/\partial p^W = 0$ into the denominators of the fractional terms in efficiency condition (18.3). The efficiency condition is not satisfied because we obtain $+\infty \times -\infty \neq 1$.

18.5.4. Politically Optimal Tariffs

Politically optimal tariffs (τ^{PO}, τ^{*PO}) maximize government welfare subject to the condition that players do not attempt to exploit terms of trade externalities. Politically optimal tariffs imply local prices that simultaneously maximize governments welfare functions W and W^*, which incorporate the political motives of the governments, and keep the terms of trade constant. This definition of political optimality (Bagwell and Staiger, 1999a) identifies government behavior that eliminates inefficiencies due to countries attempt to exploit terms of trade externalities.

Consider the case in which governments act as if world prices do not respond to changes in tariffs rates and local prices. In this case, political motives are embodied in welfare functions but governments do not attempt to exploit the terms of trade externality when they unilaterally maximize welfare functions W and W^* with respect to prices. The resulting tariff rates are labeled politically optimal. The politically optimal equilibrium is efficient and can be shown to be unique in this setup.

The prices solving the domestic and foreign welfare maximization problems are:

$$\tilde{p} = \arg\max_{p} W(p, \tilde{p}^W), \quad s.t. \ \frac{\partial \tilde{p}^W}{\partial \tau} = 0,$$

$$\tilde{p}^* = \arg\max_{p^*} W^*(p^*, \tilde{p}^W), \quad s.t. \ \frac{\partial \tilde{p}^W}{\partial \tau^*} = 0. \tag{18.4}$$

Maximizing as if the world relative price does not respond to the tariff corresponds to welfare maximization as if $\lambda = \lambda^* = 0$, ignoring that $\lambda \neq 0$ and $\lambda^* \neq 0$.

The first order conditions for welfare maximization subject to $\partial \tilde{p}^W / \partial \tau = \partial \tilde{p}^W / \partial \tau^* = 0$ (i.e. world prices are taken as given) are

$$\frac{\partial W}{\partial p} \frac{dp}{d\tau} = 0 \rightarrow \frac{\partial W}{\partial p} = 0, \qquad \frac{\partial W^*}{\partial p^*} \frac{dp^*}{d\tau^*} = 0 \rightarrow \frac{\partial W^*}{\partial p^*} = 0,$$

given that $dp/d\tau > 0$ and $dp^*/d\tau^* < 0$. The politically optimal equilibrium is efficient. Substituting the first order maximization conditions $\partial W / \partial p = \partial W^* / \partial p^* = 0$ into (18.3) yields the equation $1 = 1$, which means that the efficiency condition is satisfied.

Recapping, noncooperative maximization of a country's welfare function produces an inefficient equilibrium in the presence of terms of trade externalities. Political optimality identifies government behavior that would lead to efficiency.

18.6. NEGOTIATING UNDER WTO RULES

This section presents a framework in which politically optimal tariffs are the only efficient tariff rates that can be implemented in negotiations conducted under the reciprocity and nondiscrimination principles of the GATT. When side payments are allowed, politically optimal tariffs can be achieved as long as countries are not too asymmetric. When side payments are not allowed or countries are too asymmetric, however, the politically optimal equilibrium is not achieved. Renegotiations of tariffs under the reciprocity principle and a rule that precludes forcing a country to import a greater amount than its proposal during the renegotiation stage, partially reallocate welfare toward the welfare allocation achieved in the politically optimal equilibrium. However, some tariffs remain too high and the equilibrium is inefficient.

18.6.1. Reciprocity Principle and the Terms of Trade

Let us focus on the reciprocity principle in a two-country world in which tariff discrimination cannot take place. The reciprocity principle allows tariff reductions because it neutralizes the terms of trade externalities underlying a suboptimal outcome in which countries hurt themselves by attempting to exploit terms of trade effects.

Mutual changes in trade policies realized according to the principle of reciprocity leave world prices unchanged and thus eliminate the incentives to manipulate world prices. Consider an initial tariff pair (τ_0, τ_0^*). Let us define reciprocity in tariff negotiations as mutual changes in trade policy $(\tau_1 - \tau_0, \tau_1^* - \tau_0^*)$ causing equal changes in import volumes across trading partners

$$\tilde{p}_0^W[M_{II}(p_1, \tilde{p}_1^W) - M_{II}(p_0, \tilde{p}_0^W)] = M_I^*(p_1^*, \tilde{p}_1^W) - M_I^*(p_0^*, \tilde{p}_0^W)$$

$$= \tilde{p}_1^W M_{II}(p_1, \tilde{p}_1^W) - \tilde{p}_0^W M_{II}(p_0, \tilde{p}_0^W),$$

where the second equality utilizes the trade balance equation (18.1), imports are evaluated at the initial relative price $\tilde{p}_0^W$, and the new equilibrium world price is $\tilde{p}_1^W = \tilde{p}^W(\tau_1, \tau_1^*)$. Canceling common terms in the previous equation yields

$$(\tilde{p}_1^W - \tilde{p}_0^W)M_{II}(p_1, \tilde{p}_1^W) = 0 \rightarrow \tilde{p}_1^W = \tilde{p}_0^W.$$

The previous argument has shown that the principle of reciprocity imposes the restriction that any renegotiated tariff must preserve the initial world relative price $\tilde{p}_0^W$. The reciprocity principle embodies the idea that concessions should be balanced at the margin in the sense that a country benefitting from tariff reductions should balance the concessions by reducing its tariffs, leaving import volumes and world prices unchanged.

18.6.2. Tariff Negotiations and Efficiency

Suppose that tariff negotiations begin from an initial Nash equilibrium. If a country lowers local prices unilaterally by reducing tariffs, the world price of the imported good subject to the tariff will increase and its welfare will decline. However, at given world prices, both countries gain by lowering local relative prices p and $1/p^*$ because $\partial W/\partial p < 0$ and $\partial W^*/\partial(1/p^*) < 0$ (i.e. $\partial W^*/\partial p^* > 0$). If a country could unilaterally reduce tariffs without being hit by an increase in the imported good's world price, it would proceed to lower tariff rates below the Nash equilibrium level. This world price neutralization effect is precisely what the reciprocity principle ensures. Reciprocity in tariff renegotiations requires keeping world prices unchanged thus opening the door to the implementation of mutually beneficial tariff reductions.

Will negotiations initiated from a Nash equilibrium lead to the politically optimal equilibrium? The general answer is 'no'. To see why, notice that as tariffs decline, the value of $\partial W/\partial p$ increases toward zero and the value of $\partial W^*/\partial p^*$ declines toward 0 (i.e. $\partial W^*/\partial(1/p^*)$ increases towards 0). Tariff cuts continue until either $\partial W/\partial p = 0$ or $\partial W^*/\partial p^* = 0$. If renegotiations involve two symmetric countries and tariff cuts are symmetric, $\partial W/\partial p = 0$ if and only if $\partial W^*/\partial p^* = 0$. In this case, negotiations must lead to the politically optimal equilibrium. However, if the negotiating countries are asymmetric, negotiations stop when $\partial W/\partial p = 0$ (or $\partial W^*/\partial p^* = 0$) but this does

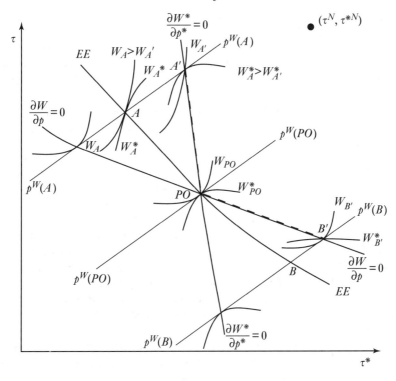

Figure 18.1. *Politically optimal equilibrium*

not imply that $\partial W^*/\partial p^* = 0$ (or $\partial W/\partial p = 0$). Therefore, the politically optimal equilibrium is not reached.

Figure 18.1 illustrates why tariff cut negotiations neither have to reach the politically optimal equilibrium nor any other efficient point. The figure depicts the following loci of tariff pairs.

1. The lines $p^W(PO), p^W(A)$, and $p^W(B)$ depict the set of tariff factors that preserve relative prices p_{PO}^W, p_A^W and p_B^W. Because a higher domestic tariff lowers a good's relative world price, preserving the world relative price requires raising the foreign tariff.

2. The set of tariff rates sustaining efficiency is labeled EE. Each point in EE is determined by maximizing a welfare function that incorporates political and distributional factors taking as given the welfare of the other country and keeping the relative world price fixed. In other words, each point in EE is determined by maximizing world welfare along a line that preserves the world relative price. Expression (18.3) implies that a higher domestic tariff requires a lower foreign tariff to maintain efficiency.

3. The curves $\partial W/\partial p = 0$ and $\partial W^*/\partial p^* = 0$ represent the loci of points at which, taking the world price as given, countries do not wish to alter tariffs. Points above these curves represent a preference for lowering tariff rates. These curves can only intersect at the politically optimal equilibrium (*PO*). The locus of efficient points *EE* passes through point *PO*, indicating that the politically optimal equilibrium is efficient.

4. W and W^* represent indifference curves between tariff rates. Domestic utility increases to the northwest ($W_{B'} < W_{PO} < W_{A'}$). Foreign utility increases to the southeast ($W^*_{A'} < W^*_{PO} < W^*_{B'}$).

If tariff negotiations according to the reciprocity principle lead to tariff cuts along the $p^W(PO)$ line, the process will stop at the politically optimal tariff pair. If negotiations proceed along any other price line, such as $p^W(A)$ or $p^W(B)$, the tariff cut process terminates at a point at which tariffs hit the upper envelope of the curves $\partial W/\partial p = 0$ and $\partial W^*/\partial p^* = 0$. This envelope is depicted by the broken line passing through points $A'POB'$. In this case, tariff cuts do not go far enough to reach efficient points such as A and B. At point A', the domestic economy would like to continue cutting tariffs along line $p^W(A)$ but the foreign economy is not willing to cut tariffs any further. At point B', the foreign economy would like to continue cutting tariffs along line $p^W(B)$ but the domestic economy is not willing to do so. Efficiency cannot be achieved unless the reciprocal tariff cuts proceed along line $p^W(PO)$.

What determines the equilibrium tariff point? The equilibrium point is determined by relative bargaining power. If the domestic economy is strong, it will maximize utility by pushing negotiations toward the price line $p^W(A)$, which yields a high domestic tariff and a low foreign tariff. If the foreign economy is strong, it will maximize utility by pushing negotiations toward the price line $p^W(B)$, which yields a high foreign tariff and a low domestic tariff. There is a distribution of bargaining power that can support the politically optimal equilibrium. If the distribution of bargaining power is such that negotiations do not start from the world relative price supporting the politically optimal equilibrium, tariffs cuts are accomplished but full efficiency is not obtained.

18.6.3. Renegotiation-proof Tariffs and Side Payments

If countries achieve the politically optimal equilibrium in the first stage, there are no incentives for tariff renegotiations. In the politically optimal equilibrium, no party has incentives to deviate from efficiency because neither country wishes to change local prices, that is, $\partial W/\partial p = \partial W^*/\partial p^* = 0$. In other words, the politically optimal outcome is renegotiation proof under the rules of the GATT.

Figure 18.1 illustrates why noncooperative tariff renegotiation subject to the reciprocity principle leads to inefficiency except if renegotiations start at the politically optimal equilibrium. Let us show that the efficient point A is not renegotiation proof under GATT rules. If renegotiations start from efficient point A, the home and foreign countries have opposite renegotiation incentives. The home country wishes to expand the volume of trade by lowering the tariff on imports of good *II* and the local relative

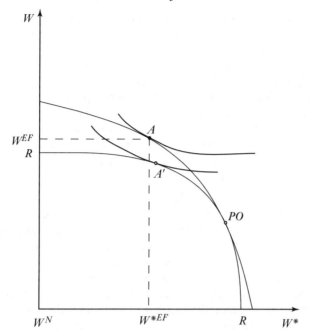

Figure 18.2. *Renegotiation under the GATT reciprocity principle*

price of II ($\partial W/\partial p < 0$ in (18.2)). In contrast, the foreign country wishes to contract the volume of trade by raising the tariff on imports of good I and raising the relative price of I ($\partial W^*/\partial\tau^* > 0, \partial W^*/\partial p^* > 0$).

Because parties do not agree about how to set tariff bindings in the renegotiation process, a rule requiring that a country cannot be forced to import a greater amount than it wishes to do in the renegotiation stage, serves to determine the equilibrium point. Specifically, the domestic country will not be able to force the foreign country to accept a set of tariffs that imply greater trade. Noncooperative tariff renegotiation according to the reciprocity principle (i.e. must move along the line representing an unchanged world relative price) and the import limit constraint (must move up along the line $p^W(A)p^W(A)$) ensures that the efficient tariff rates will be renegotiated away. Equilibrium settles at point A' where tariffs are higher and the volume of trade contracts relative to point A. The move from A to A' benefits the weaker foreign country and hurts the stronger domestic country, breaks bindings and triggers retaliation.

Figure 18.2 shows the efficient frontier of welfare levels ($W^{EF}W^{*EF}$) and the set of welfare levels that can be implemented when renegotiations under GATT reciprocity rule are allowed (RR). The origin is the Nash equilibrium welfare level W^N. Because renegotiations under the RR lead to inefficient outcomes except when the equilibrium tariff rates are politically efficient (point PO), the RR frontier lies inside the WW frontier except at point PO. The equilibrium welfare levels are determined by countries' relative bargaining power. In a cooperative solution without renegotiation, efficient point A is achieved. Under noncooperative renegotiation subject to the GATT reciprocity principle, equilibrium takes place at inefficient point A'. This point illustrates a situation favoring the foreign country relative to the domestic country. Renegotiation under the reciprocity rule (and an import limit constraint specifying that a country cannot be forced to import more than its initial import proposal) shifts the allocation of welfare toward the politically optimal solution. The shift from A to A' under renegotiation undermines the allocation of welfare resulting from a pure bargaining power approach (i.e. without renegotiations). The reallocation of welfare toward the weaker country encourages its participation in trade negotiations.

Side Payments and Political Optimality
In a two-country world, renegotiations under reciprocity produce an efficient outcome only if they start from a politically efficient equilibrium. Specifically, except for the politically optimal equilibrium point, efficient points are not renegotiation proof given the GATT reciprocity rules (Article XVIII). This result raises a question about the conditions under which politically optimal tariffs are achieved.

Politically optimal tariffs can be achieved when countries are not too asymmetric and side payments are allowed. This result is an application of Coase theorem (1960). Ronald Coase examined negotiations between partners that have symmetric information and do not face transaction costs. Negotiated side payments serve to correct externalities and lead to efficiency, allowing the realization of gains from trade.

Consider point A' in Fig. 18.1. The foreign country gains from a move to the politically optimal equilibrium, the domestic country loses from that move, and efficiency is not attained. The move to an efficient point can be implemented if the foreign country makes a side payment to the domestic country to compensate for the losses suffered. If countries are not too asymmetric, a shift to the politically optimal equilibrium can be induced through side payments from the country earning most to the country earning less from the shift. However, Kennan and Riezman (1988) show that if the size asymmetry between two countries is large enough, the larger country might gain from a trade war in which both countries set the individually optimum tariffs. In this case, the politically optimal equilibrium is not attained.

If side payments are not allowed, the weaker country will improve its lot by renegotiating an increase in tariffs that leads to an inefficient equilibrium. The renegotiation strategy reallocates welfare toward the allocation achieved in the politically optimal equilibrium and favors the weak country. These considerations suggest that the use of side payments within the multilateral system can but does not have to lead to improvements in economic efficiency.

18.6.4. Reciprocity and Nondiscrimination

The concept of discrimination requires considering multiple countries. Discrimination among trading partners cannot be analyzed in a two-country world in which each country has a single trading partner.

In a world with multiple countries, there will be many efficient points that entail discriminatory tariffs. Tariff discrimination is consistent with efficiency as long as it allows rent extraction but does not distort production and consumption choices (e.g. a perfectly discriminating monopolist). Nondistorting discrimination takes place if each demander pays a price that reflects its preference for a product and each producer receives a price that reflects its costs of production. Otherwise, discrimination will distort agent choices.

Bagwell and Staiger (1999*b*) show that the politically optimal tariffs are efficient if and only if they do not involve tariff discrimination. Furthermore, a multilateral agreement is renegotiation proof under the rules of the GATT if and only if it is supported by politically efficient tariffs and satisfies the principle of nondiscrimination. The intuition for this result is the following. Because externalities can be transmitted through world prices or through local prices, rules aiming to achieve efficiency must consider both channels. First, reciprocity internalizes tariff externalities that lead to higher tariff rates and are transmitted by lowering world prices. However, any given world price is consistent with inefficiencies arising from tariff discrimination. The reciprocity principle alone is unable to tackle inefficiencies that do not depend on the world price. Second, nondiscrimination eliminates tariff externalities that are transmitted through divergences in domestic prices in different countries. Because the remaining terms of trade externality travels through the world price, it can be addressed through reciprocity. Notice that the role of nondiscrimination is not to generate efficiency. Discrimination is consistent with efficiency. The role of nondiscrimination in this setting is to ensure that the reciprocity principle operates well in the sense that politically optimal tariffs are efficient in a multicountry world.

18.7. INTERNATIONAL ENVIRONMENTAL AGREEMENTS

When pollution diffuses across frontiers, a noncooperative equilibrium maximizes domestic welfare ignoring the externalities conferred to other countries. In this case, lower environmental taxes or standards have two positive effects: lowering the domestic firms' costs and reducing the positive externality conferred to other countries by the taxes and standards reducing domestic pollution. As a consequence, the noncooperative equilibrium will also entail lower environmental taxes than the optimal level from a global viewpoint. The reason is that domestic authorities do not have incentives to charge domestic firms on damages to third countries, or to limit licenses on account of the damages caused to third countries.

Consider a world made of small polluting countries that do not affect world market prices. They choose optimal taxes to address domestic pollution, considering foreign prices and environmental policies as given. Because they do not affect the policies of the rest of the world, there are no incentives for considering transboundary pollution when formulating domestic policies. As a result, there will be excessive world pollution even if policies are optimal from the limited viewpoint of each individual country.

Global environmental policies represent a strategic problem for the nations involved. The noncooperative solution is not optimal. Strategic policy intervention and transboundary pollution motivate inefficient behavior when countries act noncooperatively. A solution consists of inducing cooperation by means of international agreements. Because the optimal global solution requires cooperation, income transfers might be needed in order to induce reluctant countries to cooperate.

Are tariff cuts the best instrument to extract concessions on developing countries' environmental management? Abrego *et al.* (2001) compare the use of tariff cuts and side payments in a two-region model, North and South, trading heterogeneous products differentiated by production location à la Armington. The South is assumed to be endowed with environmental assets that are depleted faster when employed for export-related activities. Using developed country tariff cuts as a bargaining tool to reach environmental targets generates gains for the negotiating parties. However, developed country trade discipline (i.e. tariff cuts) turns out to be an inferior negotiating tool than direct transfers of cash among the parties.

18.7.1. The Environment in the WTO

Why is it that environmental protection has become embroiled in a dispute over whether the WTO should rule on environmental standards? There are several trade-related conditions that could justify including environmental issues in the WTO agenda.

1. Overly lax environmental standards used as a strategic tool for shifting market conditions in favor of local firms. Developed countries often blame developing countries for this form of abuse.
2. Tough environmental standards can effectively hurt foreign competitors or exclude them from local markets. Tariff liberalization and globalization have encouraged the use of this form of nontariff barrier and developing countries often accuse developed countries of this type of abuse.
3. When pollution diffuses across frontiers, a noncooperative pollution control equilibrium maximizes domestic welfare ignoring the externalities conferred to the rival country. The international externalities of environmental dumping are often generated by exporters. WTO involvement is justified on the grounds that polluting exporters effectively shift costs to other nations.

Are the claims made about the interaction between environmental regulation and trade valid? First, do countries use lax environmental standards to improve local firms competitiveness?

How does environmental regulation affect trade and competitiveness? Standards have often been found to have little effects on trade but Wilson *et al.* (2002) find that tougher regulations implied lower net exports of four out of five pollution-intensive industries in twenty-four countries during 1994–98. Rugman *et al.* (1999) report competitiveness effects on multinationals capturing regulations to use them as entry barriers.

The WTO deals with the trade implications of the cost of environmental improvements in Article 8 of the subsidies agreement. This Article permits countries to subsidize exporters in order to alleviate the financial costs of higher environmental standards. Environmental standards are also incorporated in the agenda for the Doha round of trade negotiations that was launched in 2001. The nontariff protection aspect of environmental policies falls within the WTO agenda of securing market access to exporters. The problem of transboundary pollution have been addressed in the Kyoto and other environmental agreements rather than within the WTO.

To what extent should the WTO get involved with environmental issues? Bagwell and Staiger (2001c) argue that the WTO can deal with environmental and labor standards without establishing 'core' standards. The key idea maintains the WTO principle that once a country has agreed to reduce tariffs it should not be allowed to reverse or undercut the negotiated reduction. This principle can be sustained in two different ways. First, countries could be forbidden from offering indirect protection to import-competing industries by lowering environmental and labor standards. If a government wishes to protect imports by lowering standards, it should renegotiate tariff levels to allow its trading partners to set a compensating higher tariff. Alternatively, countries can be allowed to raise tariffs to offset the competitiveness effect of higher standards. Under these procedures, there is no need to negotiate a fixed set of core labor or environmental standards as long as market access to foreign exporters is maintained.

18.8. LABOR STANDARDS

The policy debate over standards responds to the intensification of public concerns in developed countries over the use of weak labor standards in developing countries as a form of protection to local industries. A number of members of the World Trade Organization have proposed broadening the scope of trade agreements to cover domestic policies, such as the determination of core labor standards, not currently covered by the GATT and the WTO. Proponents of broadening the WTO scope have advanced the so-called social clause that would allow imposing restrictions on imports from countries that do not comply with minimum standards. The social clause would permit governments to increase tariffs applying to countries that adopt weak labor standards.

What do parties involved understand by labor standards? Labor standards alludes to a multifaceted concept. According to the OECD (1996), core labor standards include the prohibition of forced labor, freedom of association, right to negotiate and bargain collectively, elimination of child labor exploitation and nondiscrimination in employment. These core standards have been ratified by the United Nations, approved by the International Labour Organization (ILO) and are universally accepted. Other less universally accepted standards include practices, such as minimum wages, limited number of working hours, and health and safety conditions in the workplace, summarized under the label 'acceptable work conditions'.

Should labor standards be included into the WTO agreement? Is the social agenda in agreement or in conflict with the basic principles of the WTO? These questions have generated a heated debate among two groups with drastically opposed views. On one hand, developed countries argue that core labor standards should be recognized in the WTO, since weak standards constitute an unfair trade practice harming their interests. Developed countries allege that low labor standards are used by developing countries as a sort of protectionist device that launches a race to the bottom type of competition. The establishment of strong labor standards by developing countries would reestablish fair play and avoid a 'prisoners' dilemma' outcome. On the other hand, developing countries argue that the introduction of labor standards under the scope of a multilateral agreement would violate national sovereignty and would severely limit their flexibility to compete in the global economy.

Proposals to address potential losses of international competitiveness due to different domestic standards, point towards reforming GATT provisions to introduce the 'social clause' provision with a set of minimum enforceable international labor standards. The question is: should countries cede control over domestic policies on labor (and also on competition and environment standards) and assign achieving efficiency to a multilateral trade institution such as WTO? (Bagwell 2000*b*, 2001*b*; Brown 2001)

The opposition to broadening the scope of the WTO is strong in many quarters. Many countries complain that negotiations on labor and other standards will affect countries' political independence. Also, developing countries counter that the labor standards proposed by developed countries represent a mechanism to reduce the competitive advantages enjoyed by developing countries due to low labor costs. The issue has become one of the most controversial in the field of trade negotiations.

The controversy over the social agenda focusing on enforcing minimum labor standards resulted in demonstrations around the world and on the temporary removal of this dossier from the post-Doha agenda. In Seattle, demonstrators called for an extension of the social agenda to developing countries that delay social advancement to gain artificial comparative advantages against countries supporting a progressive social agenda. In India and other developing countries, demonstrators had quite different motives. They protested against the imposition of a social agenda that would destroy the comparative advantages of developing countries.

18.8.1. *Core Labor Standards and Competitiveness*

Do weak core labor standards improve domestic firms' competitive position *vis-à-vis* foreign rivals? Martin and Maskus (2001) present different theoretical frameworks to show that, contrary to the standard view, weak labor standards can work against a country's short and long run economic efficiency. If weak standards discriminate against export sector workers, they can ultimately increase firms' costs, lower production levels, and thus, harm the country's competitive advantages in the world economy.

Let us examine the introduction of labor standards in a simple perfectly competitive partial equilibrium setup in which wages and the amount of labor are at equilibrium in the status quo. Consider the imposition of a discriminatory lower-than-equilibrium wage rate $w < w^E$ that takes the form of, say, low wages for women or children in sector D. The discriminatory standard would result in a larger quantity of labor demanded and a lower quantity of labor supplied. This scheme could be sustained only if the excess demand for the discriminated group labor in the industry is eliminated because migration to other sectors drives other sectors wages down to w. Such solution configuration entails lower production and lower efficiency levels because wage w is inconsistent with firms' profit maximization condition $w^E = \partial F(K, L)/\partial L \equiv F_L(K, L)$. Similarly, the introduction of labor unions, able to negotiate as monopolists higher-than-equilibrium wages, yields a similar loss of competitiveness. In this case, $w > w^E \equiv F_L(K, L)$ and employment levels are lower than at equilibrium. Moreover, in the opposite case in which labor unions are weak but firms in the industry act as a monopsony, wages and employment levels in the domestic market will also be lower than at the competitive equilibrium.

The outcome of these different analyses implies that, as a long run equilibrium, higher than or lower than equilibrium wages can be sustained only by some sort of market imperfection (such as imperfect information or cultural idiosyncrasies) or by government regulations. There are thus, economic gains for firms and the government from removing such imperfections.

18.8.2. Domestic vs Worldwide Standards

Absence of coordination in labor standards may encourage a race to the bottom and a worldwide shopping for low standard production locations. In the environmental case, Bhagwati and Srinivasan (1996) conclude in favor of standards diversity under free trade. The result was drawn from the standard two–country, two–goods trade model.

Does this diversity result apply to labor standards? or should countries coordinate their labor standard policies to avoid a prisoners' dilemma type of result? And if so, what is the optimal level of harmonization? Brown *et al.* (1996) introduce labor standards into a model characterized by free trade. Several nonstrategic partial and general equilibrium models are presented to contrast the effects of country-specific standards and common standards imposed worldwide. They focus on labor standards that increase production costs. This assumption implies that weak labor standards result in lower wages (distorting the true price of labor) and in excessive use of labor relative to capital.

Consider a partial equilibrium model of a small country establishing labor standards to offset a local production externality. Consumers face exogenously given world prices and are thus unaffected by the standards, except in cases such as those involving social opposition to child labor. Domestic standards raise production costs and reduce producer surplus. However, overall welfare increases as long as standards are efficiently set to correct the externality. This happens when the levels of domestic standards are chosen to equate private costs and social costs inclusive of the externality. In this setup, appropriately chosen domestic standards are welfare increasing while trade policies such as higher tariffs are welfare reducing, given appropriately chosen domestic standards.

What is the effect of a common worldwide standard for a particular product? Once multilateral standards are introduced, terms of trade effects must also be considered. First, notice that common worldwide standards raise a product's world price to a lesser extent than the increase in production costs. To see why, notice that if the price increase would match the higher costs due to the standards, world supply would remain constant while world demand would decline. This excess supply would require a price reduction to equilibrate world markets.

Second, notice that the effects of common worldwide standards that raise a product's world price vary according to whether a country is an importer or an exporter. In general, an increase in a product's world price reduces the welfare of net importers and increases the welfare of net exporters. Importing countries lose because producer surplus is reduced and consumers do not share in the social benefits from labor standards set abroad while facing a higher world market price. In contrast, exporting countries gain even if consumers lose due to a higher world price and producer surplus declines when the increase in production costs is not matched by the increase in the world price. The source of exporting countries' welfare gain is the social benefit accruing from labor standards established to reduce a preexisting production distortion. This social benefit increases with the output levels of exporting countries.

Consider now the establishment of common labor standards in a two-good, two country Heckscher–Ohlin general equilibrium model. Stricter labor standards divert resources away from labor intensive sectors. A common labor standard raises labor costs and thus the world price of the good produced by labor intensive methods. Developing country producers use labor intensive methods and are negatively affected by the cost increase, which is not matched by the world price increase of labor intensive goods. The welfare of developed countries' consumers declines but developed country workers employed in labor intensive industries may experience an increase in welfare because they would be facing high standards anyway. Therefore, developed country unions may have incentives to push for common labor standards.

In the setups considered, externalities do not extend across borders and countries abstain from using domestic standards to exploit terms of trade effects, even if those effects are exploitable. Domestic standards are welfare increasing but common standards introduce distortions. World efficiency requires letting each country select its own standards according to the specific conditions and externalities faced.

The exploitation of terms of trade effects introduces an additional externality. Large exporting countries have incentives to set stricter than optimal labor standards in order to reduce supply and increase the world price of their exports. In contrast, importers have incentives to adopt weaker than optimal standards. Furthermore, exporting countries selecting high domestic standards have incentives to harmonize standards at the worldwide level so their high standards extend to exporters selecting lower standards. The harmonization of standards lowers world supply and raises the world price at the expense of lower standard exporters. Suboptimal policies and North–South conflicts emerge naturally under these conditions. The consideration of terms of trade effects gives room for negotiations intending to discourage countries from introducing distortions when they attempt to exploit terms of trade effects through labor standards.

18.9. CONCLUSIONS

The WTO and its predecessor the GATT represent remarkable instances of the successful operation of cooperative agreements at a global level. The WTO offers a coherent set of principles and rules for trade negotiations and international trade. The multilateral trading framework has been refined over time and continues to be developed. It is most remarkable that the GATT and its successor the WTO have been able to substantially dismantle barriers to trade through negotiations based on consensual decisions and reciprocity in the sense of negotiations characterized by a balanced concessions policy. By opening world markets and establishing predictable and stable trade rules, the multilateral trading system has helped to bolster trade-led growth.

In order to support a shift from a high tariff equilibrium to a low tariff equilibrium, trade concessions must yield mutual gains to countries relative to the level of welfare achieved in the unilateral Nash equilibrium. The GATT's reciprocity and discrimination principles support a negotiation process that reduces tariffs relative to the Nash equilibrium and facilitates achieving a politically optimal outcome. Reciprocity internalizes externalities that encourage setting higher tariffs and are transmitted through lower world prices. Nondiscrimination eliminates externalities that are transmitted through international divergences in domestic prices and induce importing countries to impose higher tariffs on countries providing greater rent extraction opportunities.

Effectiveness in cutting tariffs on a most-favored-nation basis through negotiation rounds is not the same as effectiveness in boosting trade and overall trade liberalization. The systematic empirical examination of the trade impact of the GATT/WTO has been launched by a series of papers in which Andrew Rose finds no evidence indicating that membership in the GATT/WTO is associated with greater trade or more liberal policies.

First, Rose (2002*a*) offers empirical evidence, covering 175 countries for the period 1950–200, suggesting that GATT/WTO membership is not associated with an increase in the volume of trade. By contrast, regional free trade deals, the generalized system of preferences (introduced in the 1960s to offer preferred market access to developing countries), membership in a currency union, and membership in the Organization for Economic Cooperation and Development (see Rose 2003), boost trade. The results, largely but not exclusively based on a gravity model of bilateral trade, indicate that trade-promoting factors include common language, short distance between trading partners, a common border, and historical colonial relations.

Second, Rose (2002*b*) reports that GATT/WTO members do not have a more liberal trade policy than nonmembers. This result follows from the utilization of sixty-eight measures of trade policy and trade liberalization indicating that almost no measure is associated with membership in the GATT/WTO.

What explains the paradoxical lack of association of GATT/WTO membership with both trade volumes and multiple measures of trade liberalization? Possible reasons include (1) the liberalization agenda of the GATT was largely limited to tariff cuts, (2) lower bound rates do not necessarily mean lower rates, (3) developing countries continue to face high tariffs and nontariff barriers restricting their exports to developed countries, and (4) member countries are not obliged to open markets. Indeed, many members, such as India (a WTO founding member) kept trade-restricting high protection levels for decades. Other countries, such as China prior to joining the WTO in 2001, opened their economies before becoming members of the WTO.

The WTO system of multilateral trade rules and negotiations operates alongside a parallel system of preferential trade arrangements. The interrelationships between multilateral and preferential trade agreements generate multiple tensions. We have already examined political economy and other approaches to preferential arrangements. The next chapter focuses on the role of cooperation and enforcement in preferential and multilateral agreements. Noncooperative approaches to negotiations and the sustainability of cooperation provide a noncooperative basis for multicountry groupings and the WTO. It is crucial to examine the ways to self-enforce international agreements, especially when there is no world institution acting as an international enforcer of agreements.

18.10. APPENDIX

18.10.1. Efficient Tariff Equilibria

Efficiency requires the tangency of indifference curves W and W^* on the (τ, τ^*) plane. Therefore, the tariffs arising from an efficient reciprocal trade agreement satisfy

$$\frac{d\tau}{d\tau^*}\bigg|_{dW=0} = \frac{d\tau}{d\tau^*}\bigg|_{dW^*=0},$$

where the slopes of the indifference curve are obtained by setting the total differential of the welfare functions equal to zero.

Setting the total differential of $W(\tau, \tau^*)$ equal to zero yields

$$dW = \frac{\partial W}{\partial \tau}d\tau + \frac{\partial W}{\partial \tau^*}d\tau^* = 0$$

$$\rightarrow \frac{d\tau}{d\tau^*}\bigg|_{dW=0} = -\frac{\partial W/\partial \tau^*}{\partial W/\partial \tau} = -\frac{\partial \tilde{p}^W/\partial \tau^* \left[\tau \partial W/\partial p + \partial W/\partial \tilde{p}^W\right]}{dp/d\tau \left[\partial W/\partial p + \lambda \partial W/\partial \tilde{p}^W\right]},$$

$$(18.5)$$

where

$$W(p, \tilde{p}^W) = W(p(\tau, \tilde{p}^W(\tau, \tau^*)), \tilde{p}^W(\tau, \tau^*))$$

implies (using $\partial p/\partial \tilde{p}^W = \tau$)

$$\frac{\partial W}{\partial \tau^*} = \frac{\partial W}{\partial p}\frac{\partial p}{\partial \tilde{p}^W}\frac{\partial \tilde{p}^W}{\partial \tau^*} + \frac{\partial W}{\partial \tilde{p}^W}\frac{\partial \tilde{p}^W}{\partial \tau^*} = \left[\tau \frac{\partial W}{\partial p} + \frac{\partial W}{\partial \tilde{p}^W}\right]\frac{\partial \tilde{p}^W}{\partial \tau^*},$$

$$\frac{\partial W}{\partial \tau} = \frac{\partial W}{\partial p}\frac{dp}{d\tau} + \frac{\partial W}{\partial \tilde{p}^W}\frac{\partial \tilde{p}^W}{\partial \tau} = \frac{dp}{d\tau}\left[\frac{\partial W}{\partial p} + \frac{\partial \tilde{p}^W/\partial \tau}{dp/d\tau}\frac{\partial W}{\partial \tilde{p}^W}\right]$$

$$= \frac{dp}{d\tau}\left[\frac{\partial W}{\partial p} + \lambda \frac{\partial W}{\partial \tilde{p}^W}\right].$$

Setting the total differential of $W^*(\tau, \tau^*)$ equal to zero yields

$$
dW^* = \frac{\partial W^*}{\partial \tau} d\tau + \frac{\partial W^*}{\partial \tau^*} d\tau^* = 0
$$

$$
\rightarrow \frac{d\tau}{d\tau^*} \Big|_{dW^*=0} = -\frac{\partial W^*/\partial \tau^*}{\partial W^*/\partial \tau}
$$

$$
= -\frac{dp^*}{d\tau^*} \left[\frac{\partial W^*}{\partial p^*} + \lambda^* \frac{\partial W^*}{\partial \tilde{p}^W} \right] \Big/ \frac{\partial \tilde{p}^W}{\partial \tau} \left[\frac{1}{\tau^*} \frac{\partial W^*}{\partial p^*} + \frac{\partial W^*}{\partial \tilde{p}^W} \right], \tag{18.6}
$$

where

$$
W^*(p^*, \tilde{p}^W) = W^*(p^*(\tau^*, \tilde{p}^W(\tau, \tau^*)), \tilde{p}^W(\tau, \tau^*))
$$

implies (using $\partial p^*/\partial \tilde{p}^W = 1/\tau^*$)

$$
\frac{\partial W^*}{\partial \tau} = \frac{\partial W^*}{\partial p^*} \frac{\partial p^*}{\partial \tilde{p}^W} \frac{\partial \tilde{p}^W}{\partial \tau} + \frac{\partial W^*}{\partial \tilde{p}^W} \frac{\partial \tilde{p}^W}{\partial \tau} = \left[\frac{1}{\tau^*} \frac{\partial W^*}{\partial p^*} + \frac{\partial W^*}{\partial \tilde{p}^W} \right] \frac{\partial \tilde{p}^W}{\partial \tau},
$$

$$
\frac{\partial W^*}{\partial \tau^*} = \frac{\partial W^*}{\partial p^*} \frac{dp^*}{d\tau^*} + \frac{\partial W^*}{\partial \tilde{p}^W} \frac{\partial \tilde{p}^W}{\partial \tau^*} = \frac{dp^*}{d\tau^*} \left[\frac{\partial W^*}{\partial p^*} + \frac{\frac{\partial \tilde{p}^W}{\partial \tau^*}}{\frac{dp^*}{d\tau^*}} \frac{\partial W^*}{\partial \tilde{p}^W} \right]
$$

$$
= \frac{dp^*}{d\tau^*} \left[\frac{\partial W^*}{\partial p^*} + \lambda^* \frac{\partial W^*}{\partial \tilde{p}^W} \right].
$$

Equating the slopes given by (18.5) and (18.6) yields

$$
\frac{d\tau}{d\tau^*} \Big|_{dW=0} = \frac{d\tau}{d\tau^*} \Big|_{dW^*=0} \rightarrow -\frac{\partial \tilde{p}^W/\partial \tau^*}{dp/d\tau} \frac{\tau \partial W/\partial p + \partial W/\partial \tilde{p}^W}{\partial W/\partial p + \lambda \partial W/\partial \tilde{p}^W}
$$

$$
= -\frac{dp^*/d\tau^*}{\partial \tilde{p}^W/\partial \tau} \frac{\partial W^*/\partial p^* + \lambda^* \partial W^*/\partial \tilde{p}^W}{1/\tau^* \partial W^*/\partial p^* + \partial W^*/\partial \tilde{p}^W}
$$

$$
\rightarrow -\frac{\partial \tilde{p}^W/\partial \tau}{dp/d\tau} \frac{\tau \partial W/\partial p + \partial W/\partial \tilde{p}^W}{\partial W/\partial p + \lambda \partial W/\partial \tilde{p}^W}
$$

$$
= \frac{dp^*/d\tau^*}{\partial \tilde{p}^W/\partial \tau^*} \frac{\partial W^*/\partial p^* + \lambda^* \partial W^*/\partial \tilde{p}^W}{1/\tau^* \partial W^*/\partial p^* + \partial W^*/\partial \tilde{p}^W}
$$

where the last expression is obtained by multiplying both sides by $\partial \tilde{p}^W/\partial \tau$ and dividing both sides by $\partial \tilde{p}^W/\partial \tau^*$. Defining $\lambda = [\partial \tilde{p}^W/\partial \tau]/[dp/d\tau]$ and $1/\lambda^* = [dp^*/d\tau^*]/[\partial \tilde{p}^W/\partial \tau^*]$ yields

$$
\lambda \frac{\tau \partial W/\partial p + \partial W/\partial \tilde{p}^W}{\partial W/\partial p + \lambda \partial W/\partial \tilde{p}^W} = \frac{1}{\lambda^*} \frac{\partial W^*/\partial p^* + \lambda^* \partial W^*/\partial \tilde{p}^W}{1/\tau^* \partial W^*/\partial p^* + \partial W^*/\partial \tilde{p}^W}.
$$

Adding $0 = \partial W/\partial p + \lambda \partial W/\partial \tilde{p}^W - [\partial W/\partial p + \lambda \partial W/\partial \tilde{p}^W]$ to the numerator of the expression on the left-hand side and $0 = \partial W^*/\partial p^* + \lambda^* \partial W^*/\partial \tilde{p}^W - [\partial W^*/\partial p^* + \lambda^* \partial W^*/\partial \tilde{p}^W]$ to the denominator of the expression on the right-hand side yields

$$\frac{\partial W/\partial p + \lambda \partial W/\partial \tilde{p}^W - \partial W/\partial p - \lambda \partial W/\partial \tilde{p}^W + \tau \lambda \partial W/\partial p + \lambda \partial W/\partial \tilde{p}^W}{\partial W/\partial p + \lambda \partial W/\partial \tilde{p}^W}$$

$$= \frac{\partial W^*/\partial p^* + \lambda^* \partial W^*/\partial \tilde{p}^W}{\partial W^*/\partial p^* + \lambda^* \partial W^*/\partial \tilde{p}^W - \partial W^*/\partial p^* - \lambda^* \partial W^*/\partial \tilde{p}^W + \frac{\lambda^*}{\tau^*}\partial W^*/\partial p^* + \lambda^* \partial W^*/\partial \tilde{p}^W}$$

Simplifying and rearranging terms produces

$$\frac{\partial W/\partial p + \lambda \partial W/\partial \tilde{p}^W - (1 - \tau \lambda)\partial W/\partial p}{\partial W/\partial p + \lambda \partial W/\partial \tilde{p}^W}$$

$$= \frac{\partial W^*/\partial p^* + \lambda^* \partial W^*/\partial \tilde{p}^W}{\partial W^*/\partial p^* + \lambda^* \partial W^*/\partial \tilde{p}^W - (1 - (\lambda^*/\tau^*))\partial W^*/\partial p^*}$$

$$\rightarrow 1 - \frac{1 - \lambda \tau}{\partial W/\partial p + \lambda \partial W/\partial \tilde{p}^W}\frac{\partial W}{\partial p}$$

$$= 1 \Big/ 1 - \left(\frac{1 - \lambda^*}{\tau^*} \Big/ \frac{\partial W^*}{\partial p^*} + \lambda^* \frac{\partial W^*}{\partial \tilde{p}^W}\right)\frac{\partial W^*}{\partial p^*}$$

$$\rightarrow \left(1 - \frac{1 - \tau \lambda}{\partial W/\partial p + \lambda \partial W/\partial \tilde{p}^W}\frac{\partial W}{\partial p}\right)$$

$$\times \left(1 - \frac{1 - \lambda^*/\tau^*}{\partial W^*/\partial p^* + \lambda^* \partial W^*/\partial \tilde{p}^W}\frac{\partial W^*}{\partial p^*}\right) = 1.$$

19

Cooperative Agreements

The need for devising mechanisms to facilitate international cooperation has been broadly recognized. However, sustaining cooperation among countries and regional groups that interact strategically with each other is a tough task. To begin with, there must be pre-negotiation incentives for opening negotiations. Second, the negotiation stage among potential partners might or might not end up in a satisfactory agreement, depending on how negotiations are conducted and the partners' negotiating positions. Third, the completed cooperation agreement must be either enforceable by an external agent or self-enforceable in the sense that the losses from breaking the agreement are greater than the benefits from breaking it. In the absence of a global enforcer, self-enforceability is key to agreements involving sovereign nations.

The literature on the mechanisms for sustaining international cooperation explores the following broad questions.

1. How can cooperation be enforced when there is no supranational enforcer? In particular, what are the incentives that can make multilateral cooperation self-enforceable?
2. What are the effects of the formation of preferential arrangements on the sustainability of a multilateral agreement? In particular, what are the optimal multilateral trade policies in the presence of preferential arrangements?

This chapter examines self-enforceable multilateral agreements. Multilateral cooperation is weakened when enforcement problems encourage agents to act noncooperatively or when countries form subcoalitions that undermine the stability of the multilateral agreement. The self-enforceable cooperation approach differs from approaches to cooperation that take for granted that agreements are binding contracts and are infinitely costly to violate.

The formation and sustenance of multilateral agreements can be approached from the perspectives of noncooperative and coalitional games. The noncooperative approach to cooperation and agreement enforceability came into itself as an analytical tool in the 1990s and is now widely used. It focuses on nonbinding agreements that can be violated at a cost and can only be enforced by current and anticipated retaliatory actions. This framework fits the WTO because its dispute settlement procedures do not have direct enforcement powers. Specifically, WTO rules are not enforceable in domestic or international courts but the WTO can permit members to impose sanctions when trade rules are violated.

The coalitional games approach views multilateral arrangements as grand coalitions and preferential arrangements as subcoalitions among member countries. A key question asked is whether multilateral agreements are stable in the sense that countries do not have incentives to defect from the grand coalition and form smaller coalitions. Countries asymmetries and domestic political influences might cause welfare-enhancing multilateral arrangements to be unstable. However, stability may be achieved by allowing compensation in the form of side payments to potential defectors.

Section 19.1 explains how agreements are self-enforced through retaliation against defectors. Section 19.2 focuses on cooperative tariff setting viewed as a commitment sustained by credible sanctions. Sections 19.3 and 19.4 examine the transition to a multilateral regime with free trade areas and customs unions. Section 19.5 deals with multilateral negotiations and enforcement through bilateral and multilateral sanctions. Section 19.6 offers explanations for the long delays observed in trade negotiations and examines the effects of lags in punishing deviators. Section 19.7 utilizes the core and Shapley value concepts to examine the role of country asymmetries, side payments, and political influence in the coalitional game approach to cooperation.

19.1. SELF-ENFORCEABLE COOPERATION

How can cooperation between noncooperative agents be sustained over time? Agreements between sovereign nations cannot be directly enforced through domestic courts or international dispute settlement procedures. Therefore, the sustenance of international cooperation must rely on self-enforcing mechanisms that create adequate compliance incentives. The key for achieving self-enforcing sustainable agreements is the presence of credible threats of punishment for violations of rules and agreements.

Enforcement of agreements can be modeled in the context of a repeated game involving the infinite repetition of a static game. The literature on self-enforcement mechanisms focuses on punishments that take the form of reversion to a welfare-reducing noncooperative solution. A credible punishment strategy, however, must be consistent with a subgame perfect equilibrium.

A harsh punishment for a one-period defection consists of reversion to autarky for the rest of the game. If a country defects from an agreement, trading partners will abstain from trading with the defector. Because it represents an extremely harsh punishment, a threat of reversion to autarky strongly supports cooperative behavior. However, reversion to autarky is costly to the party implementing the punishment and might not be credible.

A mild punishment consists of reversion to the static Nash equilibrium. A country defecting from a trade agreement would face higher tariffs and limited trade with some or all its trading partners for the rest of the game. Reversion to the Nash equilibrium is credible if, given defection of one country, the best response of its trading partners is to make good the threat and move to the Nash equilibrium tariff.

Consider an infinitely repeated game in which two symmetric countries, labeled A and B, choose whether to set cooperative tariff rates or set noncooperative Nash tariff levels. The cooperative two-good tariff structure consists of the tariff pair $(t_b^{A,C}, t_a^{B,C})$, where country A imposes a cooperative tariff $t_b^{A,C}$ on imports of good b from country B while country B imposes a cooperative tariff $t_a^{B,C}$ on imports of good a from country A. The noncooperative tariff structure consists of the Nash equilibrium tariff pair $(t_b^{A,N}, t_a^{B,N})$. The punishment to defecting for one period from the cooperative equilibrium is to move to the noncooperative Nash equilibrium for the rest of the game.

Let $W^j(t^C)$, $W^j(t^N)$, and $W^j(t^N, t^C)$ denote the one-period welfare of country $j \in \{A, B\}$ under cooperation, noncooperation, and unilateral defection from the cooperative to the Nash equilibrium tariff. Symmetry implies $t_b^{A,C} = t_a^{B,C} = t^C$ and $t_b^{A,N} = t_a^{B,N} = t^N$, which allows economizing on notation. Suppose that payoffs are exogenously given and that the one-period welfare obtained by a unilateral defector is larger than that obtained under cooperation, which in turn exceeds welfare under noncooperation

$$W^j(t^N, t^C) > W^j(t^C) > W^j(t^N).$$

This welfare ranking implies that countries have incentives to defect from cooperation if the one-period welfare gain from unilaterally defecting exceeds the welfare loss from defection.

What is the mechanism enabling cooperative tariffs (t^C, t^{*C}) to be the outcome of the infinitely repeated game? In a static game, the welfare obtained by a unilateral defector is larger than that obtained under cooperation. However, in a repeated game the defector will have to face punishment forever after defection. Reversion to the Nash equilibrium for an infinite period constitutes a punishment because it yields lower payoffs than under cooperation.

A cooperative solution is obtained by maximizing the joint welfare $W^A + W^B$ with respect to the tariff rates imposed by countries A and B. The maximization is performed subject to two no-defection constraints, one for each partner, indicating the conditions required for trading partners A and B to have enough incentives to cooperate. The no-defection constraints are also called sustainability, incentive or self-enforcement constraints. The no-defection constraints state that cooperation requires the one-period gain from noncooperation, $G^N(t^N, t^C) = W^j(t^N, t^C) - W^j(t^C)$ to be less than the discounted value $L^N(t^N, t^C)$ of the one-period losses from defection to Nash tariffs

$$G^N(t^N, t^C) = W^j(t^N, t^C) - W^j(t^C)$$

$$< L^N(t^N, t^C) = \sum_{t=1}^{\infty} \delta^t \left[W_t^j(t^C) - W_t^j(t^N) \right]$$

$$= \frac{\delta}{1-\delta} \left[W^j(t^C) - W^j(t^N) \right],$$

where $j \in \{A, B\}, \delta = 1/(1 + \beta) \leq 1$ is the discount factor, and β is the discount rate. Rearranging terms, we obtain

$$\frac{W^j(t^C)}{1-\delta} > W^j(t^N, t^C) + \frac{\delta W^j(t^N)}{1-\delta}$$

$$\rightarrow \delta = \frac{1}{1+\beta} > \frac{W^j(t^N, t^C) - W^j(t^C)}{W^j(t^N, t^C) - W^j(t^N)} > 0.$$

A cooperative solution $t^C = (t^C, t^C)$ is self-sustained if the following condition holds for all trading partners in a repeated game. The discounted welfare from cooperation, $W^j(t^C)/(1 - \delta), j \in \{A, B\}$, exceeds the sum of the instantaneous payoffs from unilateral defection $W^j(t^N, t^C)$ plus the discounted payoffs $\delta W^j(t^N)/(1 - \delta)$ obtained under punishment. Self-enforceability requires the discount factor δ to be high enough (i.e. a low enough discount rate β). If a potential defector has a low enough discount factor, future punishment is discounted heavily. As a consequence, the discouraging effect of future punishment is weak, defection takes place and cooperation breaks down.

19.1.1. Does the WTO Provide Effective Punishment?

The enforcement of multilateral agreements hinges on the severity of retaliation following the violation of rules. The World Trade Organization (WTO) dispute settlement mechanism is limited in two main aspects. First, the dispute settlement process is subject to lags. In practice, this means that countries can often deviate for several periods before a sanction is imposed. Second, WTO sanctions must be removed as soon as the offending member suspends the offending practices and goes back to cooperation. The primary goal of the multilateral sanctions mechanism is not to impose punishment or extract compensation from defectors, but rather to encourage returning to cooperation. However, this feature can undermine the enforcement process and can make it ineffective. Kovenock and Thursby (1992, 1997) and Mitchell (1997) discuss various aspects of this problem.

To see why enforcement can break down, assume that (1) there is a lag of L periods before a WTO finding is made, and (2) a defecting country follows the strategy of avoiding punishment by reverting to cooperation as soon as a negative finding is revealed. In this extreme case, the no-defection condition is not satisfied. Member countries can reap the gains from transitory noncooperative behavior while avoiding punishment

$$G^N(t^N, t^C) = \sum_{t=1}^{L} \delta^t \left[W_t^j(t^N, t^C) - W_t^j(t^C) \right]$$

$$= \frac{\delta(1 - \delta^L)}{1 - \delta} \left[W^j(t^N, t^C) - W^j(t^C) \right] > L^N \left(t^N, t^C \right) = 0.$$

If the costs of moving from defection to cooperation are zero, there are always gains from defection. A defecting country will enter into negotiations and revert back to cooperation as soon as a deviation is identified. In practice, however, punishment cannot be fully avoided.

There are various factors supporting multilateral cooperation even when sanctions are delayed and cannot be sustained over time. First, there are real costs of defecting for a period and then reverting back to cooperation. The costs arise if the defecting country makes investments that are not productive after a return to cooperation. For instance, export subsidies can encourage high production and large investments in plant and equipment. After the subsidies are eliminated, however, these investments represent excessive capacity. Another cost of transitory defection is the loss of goodwill among members of the WTO, such as the loss of reputation after violating an international obligation.

Second, WTO procedures allow the imposition of provisional retaliatory measures. In principle, the imposition of provisional retaliatory measures after defection is detected can restore the repeated game enforcement relation. This mechanism allows applying punishment while negotiations and the dispute settlement procedures are going on. In practice, however, provisional measures invite retaliation and countries shy away from them. As a result, enforcement lags remain.

Third, countries supplement WTO sanctions with their own sanctions. One notable example of retaliatory tool operating outside the WTO framework is the contingent protection mechanism embodied by Section 301 in US trade laws. Section 301 seeks export promotion and aims to protect domestic firms against unfair practices by foreign firms. The 1994 European Union Trade Barriers Regulation 3286/94, which superseded the New Commercial Policy Instrument (Regulation EC-2641/84) of September 1984, specifies procedures to respond to trade barriers causing injury or adverse trade effects to EU members. Retaliatory measures under this regulation must comply with the recommendation of the WTO Dispute Settlement Procedure.

Countries recur to retaliation outside the WTO framework when the multilateral process is viewed as long and uncertain. The need to impose costs on defectors helps to explain why countries do not eliminate the retaliatory measures immediately after the offending practices end. Of course, the permanence of contingent protection might just represent protectionism favoring local interest groups.

19.2. THE MOST-COOPERATIVE TARIFF RATE

Self-enforcement of multilateral tariff agreements can be illustrated by considering two governments both of which intervene to set import tariffs (i.e. bilateral intervention). The gains from cooperation and defection are functions of the tariff rates obtained in cooperative and noncooperative Nash equilibria, which are derived endogenously.

The analysis focuses on the most cooperative tariff, defined as the lowest tariff consistent with equilibrium in a repeated game. The most cooperative tariff is shown to coincide with free trade only if the discount factor is high enough (i.e. the discount rate is low enough). A high discount factor implies that cooperation does not face great enforcement difficulties and free trade can be self-enforced. A low enough discount factor (i.e. high discount rate) makes enforcing cooperation more difficult and precludes the self-enforceability of free trade. In this case, the agreement cannot achieve full efficiency.

19.2.1. Noncooperative Outcome in a Static Game

Two symmetric endowment economies, A and B, are assumed to trade G goods among themselves. Country A is endowed with two units of each of $G/2$ goods and will be an exporter of these goods while the foreign country is endowed with zero units of these goods and will import them. Country B is endowed with two units of the other $G/2$ goods while country A is endowed with zero units of and will import these goods.

Each country's demand function for good i is assumed to be linear: $Q(p_i) = \alpha - p_i$, where $\alpha > 0$ and p_i is the product price. The market clearing condition for good i is that global supply is equal to global demand, which is the sum of the demand in the exporting country $Q(p_i^x)$ and the demand in the importing country $Q(p_i^m)$. The price of good i in the importing country, $p_i^m = p_i^x + t_i$, is equal to the exporting country's price p_i^x plus the specific import tariff t_i. Algebraically,

$$2 = Q(p_i^x) + Q(p_i^m) = Q(p_i^x) + Q(p_i^x + t_i). \tag{19.1}$$

Industry symmetry allows dropping the i index.

The one-period welfare function of country $j \in \{A, B\}$ can be expressed as a linear function of the number of goods G and a quadratic function of domestic and foreign tariffs (see appendix)

$$W^j(G, t, t^*) = \frac{G}{2}\left(2\alpha - 1 + \frac{t}{2} - \frac{3t^2}{8} - \frac{t^*}{2} + \frac{t^{*2}}{8}\right), \tag{19.2}$$

where the asterisk represents the foreign country. Welfare under free trade ($t = t^* = 0$) is

$$W^j(G) = \frac{G}{2}(2\alpha - 1). \tag{19.3}$$

The Nash-equilibrium tariff t^N is obtained by noncooperative welfare maximization

$$\frac{\partial W^j(G, t, t^*)}{\partial t} = \frac{G}{2}\left(\frac{1}{2} - \frac{3}{4}t\right) = 0 \;\to\; t^N = \frac{2}{3} > 0. \tag{19.4}$$

In this model, the Nash tariff rate is independent of the number of goods G, the demand parameter α, and the conjectured foreign tariff t^*. The property that a country's best noncooperative tariff does not depend on the conjectured foreign tariff implies that the Nash tariff represents a strongly dominant strategy in this game. A strategy strongly dominates all other strategies of a given player if its payoff is strictly greater than the payoff to any other strategy regardless of the strategy chosen by the other players.

The bilateral intervention setting gives rise to a prisoners' dilemma situation. If both authorities set tariff rate t^N, welfare is (from (19.2) and (19.4))

$$W^j(G, t^N) = \frac{G}{2}\left(2\alpha - \frac{10}{9}\right),$$ (19.5)

which is lower than the free trade welfare level. There are thus incentives to initiate negotiations to lower tariffs.

19.2.2. *Multilateral Cooperation in a Repeated Game*

Let us analyze enforceability of tariff negotiations in the context of a repeated tariff determination game involving two countries that negotiate directly with each other. The welfare-maximizing cooperative tariff solution t^C can be self-enforced by the following rule. If a country deviates from the cooperative solution, its trading partner punishes it by permanently moving to the Nash equilibrium solution t^N, which entails a higher tariff rate. The noncooperative Nash equilibrium tariff rate determines the strength of the threat countries face if they defect from an existing cooperative agreement. If there is no defection, the cooperative static equilibrium with t^C is repeated each period ad infinitum.

A defecting country chooses the best-response tariff under the conjecture that the other country keeps the cooperative tariff rate t^C. The additive form of the welfare function (19.2) implies that the defector's best-response tariff coincides with the Nash equilibrium tariff $t^N = 2/3$. Also, given defection of one country to $t^N = 2/3$, the best response by the affected country is to make good the threat and match the defection with a move to the noncooperative tariff $t^N = 2/3$. Therefore, a punishment consisting of a shift to the Nash equilibrium tariff is credible. Given that both countries know they will be worse off if they defect, they will choose to cooperate in order to achieve a greater level of welfare.

The decision to defect embodies the following trade-off:

(1) The deviating country can obtain extra profits by choosing the optimal noncooperative tariff t^N, given that the other country follows the agreed-upon tariff t^C. The total gains from deviation are given by the welfare $W^j(G, t^N, t^C)$ obtained when the defector chooses the best-response tariff rate t^N for all the goods it produces (given that the other country sticks to the cooperative solution t^C) minus the welfare $W^j(G, t^C)$ obtained under cooperation.

The gain from defection is (see appendix)

$$W^j(G, t^N, t^C) - W^j(G, t^C) = \frac{G}{4}\left[\frac{1}{3} - t^C + \frac{3(t^C)^2}{4}\right].$$ (19.6)

(2) The one-period loss from defection corresponds to the one-period gain from cooperation minus the noncooperative welfare (see appendix)

$$W^j(G, t^C) - W^j(G, t^N) = \frac{G}{4}\left[\frac{2}{9} - \frac{(t^C)^2}{2}\right],$$

where both countries choose t^C under cooperation and t^N under noncooperation. Because the defector is punished for life, it loses the discounted value of the one-period loss from defection.

The balance between the gains and losses from defection is summarized in the no-defection condition stating that the one-period gain from unilateral defection to the Nash equilibrium, $G^N(G, t^N, t^C)$, is less than the discounted value of the losses experienced in all future periods due to sanctions, $L^N(G, t^N, t^C)$. Formally

$$G^N(G, t^N, t^C) = W^j(G, t^N, t^C) - W^j(G, t^C)$$

$$\leq L^N(G, t^N, t^C) = \frac{\delta}{1-\delta}\left[W^j(G, t^C) - W^j(G, t^N)\right],$$

$$\frac{G}{4}\left[\frac{1}{3} - t^C + \frac{3(t^C)^2}{4}\right] \leq \frac{\delta}{1-\delta}\frac{G}{4}\left[\frac{2}{9} - \frac{(t^C)^2}{2}\right], \tag{19.7}$$

where $j \in \{A, B\}, \delta \in (0, 1)$ is the one-period discount factor, $\delta/(1-\delta)$ is the present value factor of a constant flow (the one-period defection losses) beginning next period, and the value of the Nash tariff is already substituted into the equation.

The decision on whether or not to defect depends on two key parameters: the discount factor δ and the cooperative tariff rate t^C. A higher discount factor implies a greater discounted loss from defection and thus stronger enforcement of cooperation. The net effect of the tariff rate on enforcement is not immediately clear. On one hand, the loss from defection declines unambiguously with a higher tariff (i.e. a smaller volume of trade). On the other hand, the gain from defection is minimized at the Nash tariff rate. If t^C is less than the Nash tariff rate ($t^C < t^N = 2/3$), the value of defection declines with a higher tariff rate.

The cooperative solution is obtained by jointly maximizing welfare $W^A + W^B$ with respect to the tariff rates imposed by trading partners, subject to the sustainability constraints requiring that countries have no incentives to defect. The welfare-maximizing cooperative tariff corresponds to the minimum tariff sustaining cooperation (i.e. the 'most cooperative' tariff). Even if there are higher cooperative tariff rates that can also sustain cooperation, maximizing governments would choose the most cooperative tariff because it maximizes joint welfare.

The minimum tariff rate that sustains cooperation is the minimum rate that makes a country indifferent between defection and cooperation, that is, the rate that balances the gains from defection and the discounted gains from cooperation. There are two tariff rates t^C that equate both sides of (19.7): $t = 2(3 - 5\delta)/[3(3 - \delta)]$, which is the most cooperative tariff, and $t = t^N = 2/3$, which corresponds to the noncooperative Nash solution

$$t^{MostC} = \frac{2(3 - 5\delta)}{3(3 - \delta)} < \frac{2}{3} = t^N, \qquad \frac{dt^{MostC}}{d\delta} < 0. \tag{19.8}$$

As long as the future is discounted (i.e. $\delta > 0$), the most cooperative tariff is smaller than the noncooperative Nash tariff $t^N = 2/3$. Because a higher discount factor provides greater enforceability, the level of the most cooperative tariff declines with a higher discount factor. If the discount factor is high enough, $\delta \geq 3/5$, free trade becomes self-enforceable. Therefore, in many but not all circumstances, free trade can be sustained by a credible threat of reversion to the static Nash equilibrium (Dixit, 1987a).

Figure 19.1 illustrates the determination of the most cooperative tariff for various values of the discount factor ($0 < \delta_1 < \delta_2$). The quadratic function G represents the gains from defection. It reaches a minimum at the Nash equilibrium tariff and does not depend on the discount rate. A higher value of δ entails an upward shift of the curve $L(\delta)$ representing the discounted value of cooperation and thus sustains a lower most cooperative tariff.

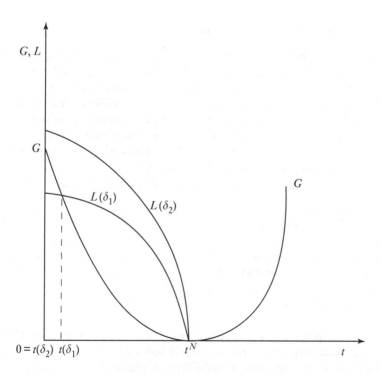

Figure 19.1. *The most-cooperative tariff*

If the discount factor is equal to zero, the loss from defection curve coincides with the horizontal axis, punishment is not effective and cooperation breaks down. If the discount rate is equal to δ_1, the discounted loss from noncooperation L (i.e. the value of cooperation) exceeds the gain from defection for any tariff rate in the range $t \in (t^{MostC}, t^N)$, where $t^{MostC} = t(\delta_1)$ when $\delta = \delta_1$. Free trade is not sustainable because the gain from defection exceeds the loss in the range $(0, t^{MostC})$. If the discount rate is equal to δ_2, any tariff rate below the Nash equilibrium rate can be sustained, the most cooperative tariff is equal to zero and free trade is self-enforceable.

19.3. TRADE DIVERSION AND TRANSITION TO A FREE TRADE AREA

This section focuses on the impact of the transition to new Free Trade Areas (FTA) on an existing multilateral cooperation agreement. The analysis provides a strategic rationalization of the notion that FTAs negotiations put multilateral agreements under fire. In the transitional phase in which new free trade areas are anticipated but have not yet taken place, multilateral enforcement is weakened. This creates pressures for raising multilateral tariffs during the transition. However, once the free trade areas are formed, tensions are relaxed and multilateral tariffs decline.

19.3.1. The Free Trade Area Game

A simple dynamic framework based on Bagwell and Staiger (1997*a*) is used to characterize tariff dynamics. Initially, all countries belong to a multilateral system without preferential arrangements. The analysis focuses on two endowment economies, A and B, who engage in negotiations leading to the formation of free trade areas between A and C and B and D. The free trade areas set internal tariffs to zero and are assumed to be trade diverting. The motives justifying their creation are not explicitly considered. The question asked concerns how multilateral tariffs between countries A and B change when these countries form competing free trade areas.

The formation of Free Trade Areas involves a dynamic multilateral tariff game:

1. At the initial multilateralism phase, countries A and B exchange G goods. Multilateral cooperation yields a common tariff t^C that is self-enforced as a repeated game equilibrium. The formation of free trade areas is not anticipated at this stage.
2. In the transition period, countries anticipate that countries A and C and countries B and D will form new free trade areas. At this stage, countries A and B still exchange G goods and no free trade agreement (FTA) has been set up yet. However, countries expect that a FTA will take place for sure in the next phase, with attendant trade diversion effects.
3. At the post free trade agreement phase, new free areas have been set up. The model assumes trade diversion, that is, the newly formed FTAs shift economic activity away from old trading partners. In the first two phases, countries A and B trade G goods among themselves and some undetermined number of goods with the rest of

the world. In the third phase, there is trade diversion and countries A and B trade only $G - F$ goods among themselves while trading F goods with their respective new Free Trade Area allies.

Let us compare the no-defection conditions for trade between countries A and B in the multilateral, transition, and post-Free Trade Area phases. The no-defection condition for a multilateral system without preferential agreements is given by (19.7)

$$G^N = W^j(G, t^N, t^C) - W^j(G, t^C)$$

$$\leq \frac{\delta}{1 - \delta}\left[W^j(G, t^C) - W^j(G, t^N)\right] = L^N$$

$$\rightarrow \frac{G}{4}\left[\frac{1}{3} - t^C + \frac{3(t^C)^2}{4}\right] \leq \frac{\delta}{1 - \delta}\frac{G}{4}\left[\frac{2}{9} - \frac{(t^C)^2}{2}\right].$$

The post free trade area no-defection condition is

$$G^{FTA} = W^j(G - F, t^N, t^{FTA}) - W^j(G - F, t^{FTA})$$

$$\leq L^{FTA} = \frac{\delta}{1 - \delta}[W^j(G - F, t^{FTA}) - W^j(G - F, t^N)]$$

$$\rightarrow \frac{G - F}{4}\left[\frac{1}{3} - t^{FTA} + \frac{3(t^{FTA})^2}{4}\right]$$

$$\leq \frac{\delta}{1 - \delta}\frac{G - F}{4}\left[\frac{2}{9} - \frac{(t^{FTA})^2}{2}\right].$$

The no-defection condition during the transition is

$$G^{Transition} = W^j(G, t^N, t^{Transition}) - W^j(G, t^{Transition})$$

$$\leq L^{Transition} = \frac{\delta}{1 - \delta}[W^j(G - F, t^{FTA}) - W^j(G - F, t^N)]$$

$$\rightarrow \frac{G}{4}\left[\frac{1}{3} - t^{Transition} + \frac{3(t^{Transition})^2}{4}\right]$$

$$\leq \frac{\delta(G - F)}{(1 - \delta)4}\left[\frac{2}{9} - \frac{(t^{FTA})^2}{2}\right],$$

where there is current trade in G goods and future trade in $G - F$ goods.

The most cooperative tariffs are independent of the number of goods exchanged among trading partners and are thus the same before and after the formation of the free trade areas. The relation between the tariff rates is

$$t^{MostC} = t^{FTA} = \frac{2(3 - 5\delta)}{3(3 - \delta)} < t^{Transition}. \tag{19.9}$$

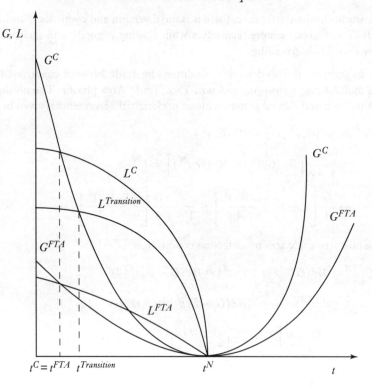

Figure 19.2. *Multilateral agreements with Free Trade Areas*

Figure 19.2 depicts the equilibria before, during the transition, and after the establishment of a multilateral regime with free trade areas. The nondefection conditions for multilateralism without preferential arrangements and the post-Free Trade Area period yield the same tariff rates. The reason is that the number of goods alters the level of gains and losses from defection but does not alter the balance between the gains and the losses from defection (both of them are proportional to the number of goods). In the period in which the Free Trade Areas are anticipated but have not yet been formed, the gains from defection remain unaltered while the losses from defection become smaller than under multilateralism without preferential arrangements. The anticipation of free trade agreements foretells future trade diversion, which reduces the discounted value of cooperation. As a result, the self-sustained tariff is higher during the transition period.

Equilibrium multilateral tariffs increase during the transition (i.e. $t^{MostC} < t^{Transition}$) because the discounted value of cooperation is smaller when new free trade agreements are anticipated than when they are not anticipated. The reason is that the one-period value of cooperation declines from the initial phase (when G goods are still traded) to the post-free trade area phase (when $G - F$ goods are traded). Therefore, the losses from defection in the pre-free trade area are smaller than under multilateralism and a higher most-cooperative tariff can be sustained. In this setup, multilateral tariffs are the same with and without free trade areas, so that tariffs go back to the most cooperative level after the free trade areas are operational.

Compared with multilateralism without preferential arrangements, a regime with free trade areas entails lower trade, and thus both lower gains and losses from defection. In principle, either effect can exert a dominant influence in tariff setting, depending on the specific scenario being considered. The setup considered above illustrates a case in which multilateral tariffs are the same with and without free trade areas, but increase during the transition to a regime with free trade areas.

19.4. MARKET POWER AND CU TRANSITION

What is the impact of the formation of customs unions (CUs) on multilateral tariff cooperation? Bagwell and Staiger (1997*b*) examine the formation of larger CU that hold greater market power but do not generate trade diversion. In the long term, the market power of larger CUs implies higher multilateral tariffs. Paradoxically, in the transition period prior to the formation of CUs self-enforceable tariffs become lower than multilateral tariffs, leading to a honeymoon effect that is ended when the CUs are formed.

The transition to CUs contrasts with the transition to a regime with free trade areas. The latter leads to higher transitional tariffs relative to multilateralism without free trade areas, but multilateral tariffs go down toward their pre-transition levels after the free trade areas are implemented.

Why is it that the expansion of the size of CUs with market power (but no trade diversion) generates opposite incentives to those related to the trade diversion effects associated with the formation of free trade areas? The reason is that the discounted costs of defection increase during the transition to larger CUs but decline during the transition to a regime with free trade areas.

The honeymoon effect of the transition to CUs arises from anticipated market power effects. First, CUs coordinate a common external tariff and thus enhance the monopoly power of its members. Because the market power of the members of new CU will increase in the future, they will be able to charge higher Nash equilibrium tariffs and thus inflict a greater punishment than individual countries or smaller CUs. This means that the discounted costs of defection increase during the transition period. *Ceteris paribus*, the incentives for cooperation increase. Second, notice that the gains from defection do not change during the transition from multilateralism to a regime with CUs. This result hinges on the property that, before the CUs are actually formed, the degree of market power of member countries remains unchanged. *Ceteris paribus*, the incentives to deviate from the multilateral arrangement remain unchanged.

In contrast, the formation of free trade areas does not enhance member countries' market power currently or in the future. Each member of a free trade area keeps the right to determine its own tariff structure *vis-à-vis* the rest of the world. Free trade areas do not harmonize or coordinate their external policies and cannot exploit the market power associated with larger economic size.

19.4.1. The Customs Union Game

The discussion stresses the role of market power and the features of the transition period in which the formation of larger CUs is anticipated for sure but has not been yet implemented. The deterministic partial equilibrium model used isolates the role of market power in the sense that it is constructed to preclude trade diversion. The analysis is based on Bagwell and Staiger (1997*b*), who examine a more complicated setup with a negotiation stage in which customs union formation is stochastic.

Consider a model with two goods and a world economy divided into two sets of K countries of equal sizes, labeled the domestic and the foreign sets of countries. Each set of K countries is endowed with two units of one good and none of the other good. The world endowment of each good is 2 units and each country is endowed with $2/K$ units.

Each set of K countries is divided into R symmetric regions that correspond to CUs. The global effects of CUs are examined by varying the number of regions while keeping fixed the number of countries. Symmetry implies that the R regions set the same external tariff rate. The key simplifying assumption is that domestic countries do not trade among themselves but rather trade only with foreign countries (and vice versa). This assumption precludes trade diversion due to customs union formation and allows focusing on the market power distinguishes CUs from free trade areas.

Domestic and foreign countries are organized in domestic and foreign CUs of equal size. The R CUs within each set of countries are made of competing suppliers of a common export good. The world market equilibrium condition for any given good is

$$2 = \alpha - \beta p^x + \sum_{r=1}^{R} \frac{1}{R}(\alpha - \beta p^{mr}),$$

where p^x is the price prevailing in the exporting set of countries and p^{mr} is the price prevailing in importing region r. The demand in the importing set of countries is divided by the number R of constituent regions, taking into account that each region (customs union) sets its own specific tariff rate t^{mr}.

The expansion of CUs is defined as a symmetric reduction in the number of regions in each set of countries. Larger CUs hold greater market power, which leads to higher Nash equilibrium tariffs. Formally, the symmetric Nash equilibrium tariff $t^N = t^{mr}, r \in \{1, \ldots, R\}$ as a function of the number of regions is given by

$$t^N(R) = \frac{2}{4R - 1},$$

where R is the number of regions. The previous formula implies that the punishment from defection is greater the smaller the number of regions in the world economy.

The customs union game studied is an infinite-period game in which countries pass through the following three phases. In the pure multilateralism phase, domestic, and foreign countries are not aware that they will organize CUs and will thus have greater market power in the near future. In the transition phase, countries anticipate the formation of CUs for sure next period. In the post CU phase, CUs start operations. In each phase, regions set subgame perfect tariff rates that maximize the welfare level of the regions' members subject to (1) the customs union restriction that all members of each region hold a common external tariff in each phase, and (2) no-defection conditions ensuring no unilateral deviations from multilateral cooperation.

Let us illustrate the honeymoon effect of the anticipation of the formation of larger CUs. Figure 19.3 shows the customs union tariff $t^{CU}(R)$ as a function of the number of regions R and the transitional phase tariff $t^{Transition}$. When the number of regions declines ($R' < R$), the curve G depicting the gain from defection shifts to the right. CUs hold greater market power than individual countries and can thus support greater Nash equilibrium tariffs when they deviate from cooperation, $t^N(R') > t^N(R)$. The cost of defection curve $L(R' < R)$ shifts upward when the number of CU decreases to R'. This shift reflects the fact that defectors are punished more heavily by larger CUs and thus higher Nash tariffs.

The most cooperative tariff rate as a function of the number of regions is

$$t^{CU}(R, \delta) = t^N \frac{(4R-1)^2(1-\delta) - 2\delta(4R^2-1)}{(4R-1)^2(1-\delta) + 2\delta(4R^2-1)} \leq t^N, \qquad \frac{\partial t^{CU}}{\partial \delta} < 0.$$

The sign of $\partial t^{CU}/\partial R$ is negative if δ is low and positive if δ is high enough. For instance, if $\delta = 0$, the cooperative tariff coincides with the Nash equilibrium tariff

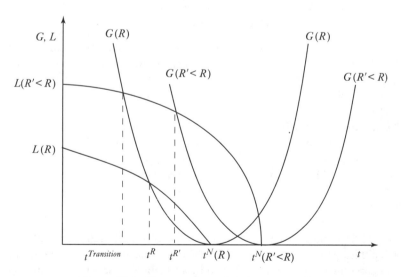

Figure 19.3. *Customs union and the honeymoon effect*

and declines with the number of regions. As δ increases, the gain from one-period defection remains constant while the discounted costs of defection increase. Given a value of R, a high enough value of the discount factor implies a smaller $t^{CU}(R)$.

After CUs actually expand, self-enforceable tariffs might or might not exceed the tariff levels prevailing under pure multilateralism. There are two opposing effects arising from the formation of CUs. First, potential defecting nonmembers know that their defection will induce reversion to the Nash equilibrium in the presence of larger CUs, which entails higher Nash tariffs than with smaller CUs. Therefore, customs union expansion increases nonmembers' costs of defection from a multilateral agreement. Second, nonmembers lose from the formation of larger CUs, which reduces the value of the multilateral relationship. If the first effect dominates, the larger costs of defection dominate the lower benefits from the multilateral agreement for nonmembers. Incentives for cooperation increase and induce a reduction in equilibrium tariffs in the long-run.

Summarizing, the formation of larger CUs does not generate tensions with a pre-existing multilateral agreement in the short run. On the contrary, it induces lower multilateral tariffs because larger CUs can extract heavier punishments. However, the honeymoon effect disappears as soon as the CUs are formed. When the new CUs are in place, and the members of the CUs harmonize the external tariff rate imposed to third parties in order to exploit market power, the sustainability of the multilateral tariff agreement becomes more troublesome. As a result, multilateral tariffs increase above those prevailing in the transition phase in order to reduce the incentives for defection. If post-customs union tariff levels exceed the initial multilateral tariff levels, the formation of larger CUs undermines multilateral liberalization in the long run.

19.5. MULTILATERAL SANCTIONS AND NEGOTIATIONS

The WTO provides an arena for negotiations over global trading rules and reductions in trade barriers. Cooperation to implement negotiated agreements relies heavily on bilateral self-enforcing mechanisms involving the parties embroiled in a conflict. The economics of bilateral enforcement is examined in Kovenock and Thursby (1992) and Bagwell and Staiger (1997a,b).

This section examines the economics of self-enforcement through multilateral trade sanctions involving third parties that are not directly involved in the violation of a negotiated agreement. In other words, violators of negotiated agreements are punished by both the affected party and the rest of the trading community. How effective are bilateral and multilateral enforcement mechanisms when there are power imbalances? By power imbalances we mean that some countries have greater bilateral enforcement power and can exact greater punishment by setting higher tariffs.

Maggi (1999b) shows that when there are power imbalances multilateral enforcement involving third party sanctions can strengthen enforcement relative to bilateral sanctions imposed by parties directly affected by a violation. More effective enforcement of agreements in turn leads to greater cooperation and greater joint welfare. However, multilateral enforcement mechanisms that can be implemented when all information is publicly observed are not feasible in the asymmetric information case in which third parties are not able to discern whether disputed violations are true violations. In this environment, monitoring and dissemination of information by the WTO serves to clarify the true nature of the violations.

The nature of agreement enforcement (i.e. bilateral or multilateral sanctions) should be distinguished from the type of bargaining leading to the agreements enforced (i.e. multilateral or bilateral bargaining). Multilateral bargaining over rules refers to a single bargaining game in which all member countries negotiate at the same time. By contrast, bilateral bargaining proceeds as a web of simultaneous bilateral Nash bargaining games in which each negotiating pair takes other countries' tariffs as given.

The notions of greater bargaining power and greater trading power are related but are not the same. A less powerful party (the weak party) is the one that has more to lose in a trade war, that is, by moving from the free trade zero-tariff rates to the static Nash-tariff rates. The notion of more or less powerful country is linked to each country endowments, and thus to their condition as a net exporter or net importer *vis-à-vis* the other party in the bilateral relation. A net importer is the more powerful member in the relation whereas the net exporter is the less powerful.

In this setup, a multilateral enforcement mechanism permits balancing all parties positions in the negotiation process in the sense that with third-parties participating in the sanctioning of a defection, the punishment is harsher, which discourages deviations by more powerful parties. Otherwise, the weak party would find it extremely difficult to inflict a sanction against a powerful party that deviates. It is in this sense that the strong party makes larger concessions in favor of weak parties if subject to a multilateral enforcement mechanism rather than to a bilateral mechanism. In general, a more powerful party should grant greater concessions a larger bargaining power in the division of gains from trade liberalization. Moreover, Maggi shows that the results hold even if both the weak and strong parties have the same weight (or bargaining power) in the welfare function.

Consider multilateral enforcement in a situation in which countries have the same bargaining power, in the sense that they are assigned the same welfare weight in the division of the gains from trade liberalization. Multilateral bargaining can Pareto-improve the results of bilateral bargaining if and only if there are bilateral power imbalances in trading relationships. Specifically, if there are bilateral trading power imbalances among countries, bilateral bargaining with multilateral sanctions is shown to be locally efficient but not globally efficient. By contrast, multilateral bargaining supported by multilateral sanctions is globally efficient and produces a Pareto-superior outcome relative to bilateral bargaining with multilateral sanctions.

19.5.1. *Noncooperative Tariffs and Bilateral Power*

Figure 19.4 illustrates the trading pattern of endowment economies A, B, and C. Each country is endowed with e_0 units of numeraire good 0. Country A is endowed with (e_{a_1}, e_{a_2}) units of differentiated tradeables (a_1, a_2), B is endowed with (e_{b_1}, e_{b_2}) units of

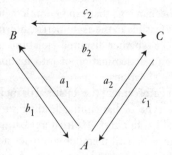

Figure 19.4. *Bilateral trade patterns*

goods (b_1, b_2), and C is endowed with (e_{c_1}, e_{c_2}) units of goods (c_1, c_2). Each country has two trading partners and exports only one of the endowment goods to each of them. For instance, country A exports product a_1 to B only and product a_2 to C only. Because all goods are assumed to be traded bilaterally, there is no possibility of trade diversion from one trading partner to the other or of trade creation when a preferential area is formed. Importing countries' governments are active in the sense that they are allowed to levy tariffs. Exporting countries' governments are assumed to be passive actors in the sense that export taxes and subsidies are not allowed.

The additive quadratic utility function of the representative consumer in country A is assumed to be

$$u^A(\cdot) = d_0 + u(d_{a_1}^A) + u(d_{a_2}^A) + u(d_{b_1}^A) + u(d_{c_1}^A)$$

$$= d_0 + \alpha \left[d_{a_1}^A + d_{a_2}^A + d_{b_1}^A + d_{c_1}^A \right] - \frac{1}{2} \left[(d_{a_1}^A)^2 + (d_{a_2}^A)^2 + (d_{b_1}^A)^2 + (d_{c_1}^A)^2 \right],$$

where d_i^A is the consumption of good i in country A. Country A consumes five goods: the numeraire, exportables a_1 and a_2 and importables b_1 and c_1. Country A is assumed not to consume goods b_2 and c_2, that is, $d_{b_2}^A = d_{c_2}^A = 0$. Similar expressions hold for countries B and C.

Country A's budget constraint impedes spending more than total income y^A

$$d_0 + p_{a_1}^x d_{a_1}^A + p_{a_2}^x d_{a_2}^A + p_{b_1}^m d_{b_1}^A + p_{c_1}^m d_{c_1}^A \le y^A,$$

$$d_0 + p_{a_1}^x d_{a_1}^A + p_{a_2}^x d_{a_2}^A + (p_{b_1}^x + t_{b_1}^A) d_{b_1}^A + (p_{c_1}^x + t_{c_1}^A) d_{c_1}^A \le y^A,$$

where $p_0 = 1$, p_i^x stands for the price of good i in the exporting country (offshore price), t_i is the specific tariff on good i, and $p_i^m = p_i^x + t_i$ stands for the local price of good i in the importing country. For instance, the specific import tariffs $t_{b_1}^A$ and $t_{c_1}^A$ imposed by country A on its imports, create gaps $t_{b_1}^A = p_{b_1}^m - p_{b_1}^x$ and $t_{c_1}^A = p_{c_1}^m - p_{c_1}^x$ between local and offshore prices.

Country A's demand function for good $i \in \{a_1, a_2, b_1, c_1\}$ is linear and depends only on the price of i, $d_i^j(p_i^j) = \alpha - p_i^j$, where $j \in \{x, m\}$ indicates whether the price is an offshore price or a local price. The market clearing condition for good i requires the sum of the internal demand in the exporting country and the demand in the foreign importing country to be equal to the endowment, that is, $d_i^x(p_i^x) + d_i^m(p_i^m) = e_i$. For instance,

$$d_{a_1}^x + d_{a_1}^m = \alpha - p_{a_1}^x + \alpha - p_{a_1}^m = 2\alpha - p_{a_1}^x - (p_{a_1}^x + t_{a_1}^B) = e_{a_1}^A,$$

$$\rightarrow p_{a_1}^x(t_{a_1}^B, e_{a_1}^A) = \alpha - \frac{t_{a_1}^B + e_{a_1}^A}{2}, \qquad p_{a_1}^m(t_{a_1}^B, e_{a_1}^A) = \alpha + \frac{t_{a_1}^B - e_{a_1}^A}{2}.$$

Notice that $\partial p_{a_1}^x/\partial t_{a_1}^B < 0$, $\partial p_{a_1}^x/\partial e_{a_1}^A < 0$, $\partial p_{a_1}^m/\partial t_{a_1}^B > 0$, and $\partial p_{a_1}^m/\partial e_{a_1}^A < 0$. Similar demand functions apply to other countries. Prices for other goods can be obtained following the same procedure.

The consumption of a_1 as a function of the tariff in country B and its endowment is

$$d_{a_1}^x(t_{a_1}^B, e_{a_1}^A) = \alpha - p_{a_1}^x(t_{a_1}^B, e_{a_1}^A) = \frac{t_{a_1}^B + e_{a_1}^A}{2},$$

$$d_{a_1}^m(t_{a_1}^B, e_{a_1}^A) = \alpha - p_{a_1}^m(t_{a_1}^B, e_{a_1}^A) = \frac{e_{a_1}^A - t_{a_1}^B}{2}.$$

Exporting country consumption (offshore demand $d_{a_1}^x$) increases with the tariff level and the endowment while importing country consumption (local demand) declines with the level of tariffs. The imposition of foreign tariff $t_{a_1}^B$ increases the local price abroad and reduces foreign demand. Equilibrium is achieved by a reduction in the offshore price (i.e. the price in country A), which generates enough demand to fully offset the reduced consumption abroad.

Each country's authority maximizes a welfare function consisting of the sum of the welfare derived from the consumption of exportables (a_1, a_2) and imports (b_1, c_1). Formally,

$$W^A = d_0 + W^x(t_{a_1}^B, e_{a_1}^A) + W^x(t_{a_2}^C, e_{a_2}^A) + W^m(t_{b_1}^A, e_{b_1}^B) + W^m(t_{c_1}^A, e_{c_1}^C),$$

where superscripts x and m denote exportables and importables, respectively. The welfare component $W^x(t_{a_1}^B, e_{a_1}^A)$ derived from domestic consumption of good a_1 includes: (1) the consumer surplus derived from its consumption, $CS_{a_1}^x = u(d_{a_1}^x) - p_{a_1}^x d_{a_1}^x$, and (2) the endowment owners' profits, $\pi_{a_1}^A = p_{a_1}^x(t_{a_1}^B, e_{a_1}^A)e_{a_1}^A$ evaluated at the offshore price. Formally,

$$W^x(t_{a_1}^B, e_{a_1}^A) = \left[u\left(d_{a_1}^x\left(t_{a_1}^B, e_{a_1}^A\right)\right) - p_{a_1}^x d_{a_1}^x\left(t_{a_1}^B, e_{a_1}^A\right) \right] + p_{a_1}^x\left(t_{a_1}^B, e_{a_1}^A\right) e_{a_1}^A.$$

A similar formula holds for a_2.

The welfare component $W^m(t_{b_1}^A, e_{b_1}^B)$ derived from imports of good b_1 includes: (1) the consumer surplus of the imported good, $CS_{b_1}^m = u(d_{b_1}^m) - p_{b_1}^m d_{b_1}^m$, and (2) import revenues, $t_{b_1}^A d_{b_1}^m(t_{b_1}^A, e_{b_1}^B)$. Formally,

$$W^m(t_{b_1}^A, e_{b_1}^B) = \left[u\left(d_{b_1}^m\left(t_{b_1}^A, e_{b_1}^B \right) \right) - p_{b_1}^m d_{b_1}^m\left(t_{b_1}^A, e_{b_1}^B \right) \right] + t_{b_1}^A d_{b_1}^m\left(t_{b_1}^A, e_{b_1}^B \right).$$

A similar formula holds for c_1.

The government sets the one-shot Nash equilibrium tariff level $t_{b_1}^{A,N}$ by maximizing country welfare W^A. Due to the separability of the welfare function, the government problem reduces to maximizing the welfare component $W^m(t_{b_1}^A, e_{b_1}^B)$ derived from imports of b_1

$$W^m(t_{b_1}^A, e_{b_1}^B) = CS(d_{b_1}^m) + t_{b_1}^A d_{b_1}^m(t_{b_1}^A, e_{b_1}^B)$$

$$= \frac{1}{2}\left(\frac{t_{b_1}^A - e_{b_1}^B}{2} \right)^2 + t_{b_1}^A \left(\frac{e_{b_1}^B - t_{b_1}^A}{2} \right)$$

$$= -\frac{3}{8}\left(t_{b_1}^A \right)^2 + \frac{1}{4}\left(t_{b_1}^A \right)\left(e_{b_1}^B \right) + \frac{1}{8}\left(e_{b_1}^B \right)^2,$$

where the consumer surplus associated to good b_1 is

$$CS(d_{b_1}^m) = u(d_{b_1}^m) - p_{b_1}^m d_{b_1}^m = \alpha d_{b_1}^m - \tfrac{1}{2}(d_{b_1}^m)^2 - p_{b_1}^m d_{b_1}^m$$

$$= \frac{1}{2}(\alpha - p_{b_1}^m)^2 = \frac{1}{2}\left(\frac{t_{b_1}^A - e_{b_1}^B}{2} \right)^2,$$

with $d_{b_1}^m = d_{b_1}^A = \alpha - p_{b_1}^m$ and $p_{b_1}^m = \alpha + (t_{b_1}^A - e_{b_1}^B)/2$.

The first order condition $\partial W^m(t_{b_1}^A, e_{b_1}^B)/\partial t_{b_1}^A = 0$ implies that the tariff imposed by country A on imports from country B is

$$-\frac{3}{4}t_{b_1}^A + \frac{1}{4}e_{b_1}^B = 0 \quad \rightarrow \quad t_{b_1}^{A,N} = \frac{e_{b_1}^B}{3},$$

where the equilibrium tariff level depends on the exporter's endowment $e_{b_1}^B$. The larger the exporter country's endowment, the higher the one-shot Nash tariff level faced by its exports. In other words, higher tariffs fall on the goods with a higher supply.

The selected tariff combines a rent-extracting tariff capturing part of the profits accruing to the monopolist exporter (country B) with an optimal tariff set by a monopsonistic importer (country A). The separability of markets in the specific case considered here implies that, strictly speaking, the tariff set by A lacks a strategic component as it does not depend on the tariff set by country B. We keep the Nash equilibrium notation because the general case results in Nash equilibrium tariffs that are selected taking into account the interactions among countries. When importer and exporter markets interact strategically, the tariff imposed by country A on imports from country B depends on the tariff selected by B. By the same token, the tariff imposed by country B on its imports from A depends on the tariff selected by A. Nash equilibrium tariffs are determined simultaneously using tariff reaction functions.

A similar analysis holds for other goods traded. For instance, country B levies a Nash tariff $t_{a_1}^{B,N} = e_{a_1}^A/3$ on its imports of good a_1 from country A. Observe that the tariff ratio is equal to the ratio of the endowments of the goods subject to tariff

$$\frac{t_{b_1}^{A,N}}{t_{a_1}^{B,N}} = \frac{e_{b_1}^B/3}{e_{a_1}^A/3} = \frac{e_{b_1}^B}{e_{a_1}^A}.$$

Let us define bilateral imbalances of power in terms of how much partners lose when they move from free trade to noncooperation. In any bilateral relationship, the more powerful country is the one that loses less if the two trading partners shift from free trade to the static Nash tariff structure. The relative strength of countries' powers in a bilateral relationship is related to goods' endowments and associated trade imbalances. Each country enters into one bilateral relationship in which it is a net exporter and one in which it is a net importer. If the endowment of the good exported abroad is smaller than the foreign endowment of the imported good, the domestic country is a net importer and the foreign country a net exporter in the bilateral relationship involving these two goods. The foreign country would be subjected to the greater tariff in a Nash equilibrium, would lose more from a shift to noncooperation and is the less powerful bilateral partner. In this setup, a net importer is more powerful than a net exporter in a bilateral relationship.

The feature that each nonnumeraire product demand depends exclusively on the own price implies that the numeraire good receives all residual spending. The demand for the numeraire thus depends on all product prices as well as on total income. Specifically, the country achieving a net surplus in the bilateral exchange of the two tradable goods spends the excess on the tradable numeraire produced by the deficit country. As a result, overall bilateral trade balances, including the numeraire and nonnumeraire products, are zero no matter the distribution of power.

In a noncooperative setting, countries have incentives to defect from free trade or low tariffs to the Nash equilibrium tariff solution. A tariff defector exploits monopoly power but causes a net global welfare loss. First, the income extracted from trading partner B represents a distributional effect that cancels out for the global economy. Second, the defecting country incurs a consumption loss in the form of lost consumer surplus from imports that is not compensated for by the additional consumption of the numeraire good. Recall that the numeraire does not generate a utility surplus in this setup: $CS(d_0) = u(d_0) - p_0 d_0 = d_0 - d_0 = 0$. Third, the tariff defection does not cause any loss on the production side because production distortions do not arise in an endowment economy. The net change in welfare is equal to the loss of consumer surplus. There are thus benefits from promoting cooperation to lower tariffs.

19.5.2. Bilateral Enforcement

Consider a repeated game in which each country chooses the same import tariffs all the time. Both bilateral and multilateral trade agreements are nonbinding in the sense that neither the WTO nor domestic courts can directly enforce international agreements. Cooperation in a repeated tariff game requires either a bilateral or a multilateral enforcement mechanism. Bilateral enforcement hinges on the sanctions imposed by the trading partner hurt by a tariff agreement violation. Multilateral enforcement requires additional sanctions imposed by third parties that are not directly affected by the violation.

Let us focus on bilateral punishment. The determination of the tariff structure sustainable under bilateral enforcement mechanisms can be formulated in terms of power imbalances in the bilateral relationships. Relative power strength determines the level of the Nash equilibrium tariffs that play the role of the 'stick' in the enforcement mechanism. The 'carrot' is the gain from low tariffs. Therefore, the country with greater enforcement power (1) can secure that its exports are subject to a lower tariff rate abroad, and (2) can impose a higher tariff on foreign goods.

The most-cooperative tariffs t^{MostC} with bilateral punishment maximize trading partners' welfare in the absence of third party punishment. Formally, tariffs ($t^A_{b_1} > 0, t^B_{a_1} > 0$) maximize the component of the joint welfare of A and B derived from their bilateral relationship

$$\max_{(t^A_{b_1}, t^B_{a_1})} \quad W^A_{b_1}(t^A_{b_1}, e^B_{b_1}) + W^B_{a_1}(t^B_{a_1}, e^A_{a_1}) \tag{19.10}$$

subject to bilateral enforcement constraints capturing bilateral punishments. The incentive constraints ensure that country A will not deviate from cooperation with B and that country B will not deviate from cooperation with A

$$G^A_{b_1}(t^A_{b_1}, e^B_{b_1}) = W^m(t^{A,N}_{b_1}, e^B_{b_1}) - W^m(t^A_{b_1}, e^B_{b_1}) \leq \frac{\delta L^A_{b_1}(t^A_{b_1}, t^B_{a_1}, e^A_{a_1}, e^B_{b_1})}{1 - \delta}$$

$$= \frac{\delta}{1 - \delta} \Big[W^m(t^A_{b_1}, e^B_{b_1}) + W^x(t^B_{a_1}, e^A_{a_1})$$

$$- W^m(t^{A,N}_{b_1}, e^B_{b_1}) - W^x(t^{B,N}_{a_1}, e^A_{a_1}) \Big], \tag{19.11}$$

and

$$G^B_{a_1}(t^B_{a_1}, e^A_{a_1}) = W^m(t^{B,N}_{a_1}, e^A_{a_1}) - W^m(t^B_{a_1}, e^A_{a_1}) \leq \frac{\delta L^B_{a_1}(t^A_{b_1}, t^B_{a_1}, e^A_{a_1}, e^B_{b_1})}{1 - \delta}$$

$$= \frac{\delta}{1 - \delta} \Big[W^m(t^B_{a_1}, e^A_{a_1}) + W^x(t^A_{b_1}, e^B_{b_1})$$

$$- W^m(t^{B,N}_{a_1}, e^A_{a_1}) - W^x(t^{A,N}_{b_1}, e^B_{b_1}) \Big], \tag{19.12}$$

where A is assumed to import b_1 from B and export a_1 to B. The incentive constraints are binding when countries are indifferent between defection and nondefection.

Country A defection gain $G_{b_1}^A$ is equal to the one-period benefit from unilaterally shifting to the Nash tariff on imports from B. The deviation loss $L_{b_1}^A$ is the discounted losses from (i) the (negative) loss from setting the Nash tariff on imports from B, and (ii) the punishment loss incurred when trading partner B sets a Nash equilibrium tariff on its imports of a_1 from A. The consumption surplus losses imply that countries lose when they simultaneously deviate to the Nash equilibrium. Therefore, the value of the negative loss in (i) is less than the value of the loss due to punishment in (ii). In other words, $L_{b_1}^A > 0$.

For the sake of simplicity, let us assume that endowments satisfy the following symmetry relation

$$e_{a_1}^A = e_{b_2}^B = e_{c_1}^C < e_{a_2}^A = e_{b_1}^B = e_{c_2}^C.$$

Country A is a net importer with respect to B and a net exporter with respect to C.

Representative governments A and B maximize the component of joint welfare derived from their bilateral relationship. Because the contributions of different bilateral relationships to countries' welfare are additive, and endowments are symmetric, the contribution of the bilateral relationship between A and B to the joint welfare is equal to the sum of the contributions of the imports from B and C to A's welfare. Therefore, the welfare maximization problem can be restated in terms of the component of A's welfare derived from its imports from B and C

$$\max_{(t_{b_1}^A, t_{a_1}^B)} W_{b_1}^A(t_{b_1}^A, e_{b_1}^B) + W_{a_1}^B(t_{a_1}^B, e_{a_1}^A)$$

$$\Longleftrightarrow \quad \max_{(t_{b_1}^A, t_{c_1}^A)} W_{b_1}^A(t_{b_1}^A, e_{b_1}^B) + W_{c_1}^A(t_{c_1}^A, e_{c_1}^C),$$

where the remaining components of A's welfare do not depend on tariffs $t_{b_1}^A$ and $t_{c_1}^A$

$$W^A = d_0 + W^x(t_{a_1}^B, e_{a_1}^A) + W^x(t_{a_2}^C, e_{a_2}^A) + W^m(t_{b_1}^A, e_{b_1}^B) + W^m(t_{c_1}^A, e_{c_1}^C).$$

Incentive constraint (19.12) is equivalent to

$$G_{c_1}^A = W^m(t_{c_1}^{A,N}, e_{c_1}^C) - W^m(t_{c_1}^A, e_{c_1}^C) \leq \frac{\delta}{1-\delta} L_{c_1}^A$$

$$= \frac{\delta}{1-\delta} \Big[W^m(t_{c_1}^A, e_{c_1}^C) + W^x(t_{b_1}^A, e_{b_1}^B)$$

$$- W^m(t_{c_1}^{A,N}, e_{c_1}^C) - W^x(t_{b_1}^{A,N}, e_{b_1}^B) \Big], \tag{19.13}$$

where $e_{c_1}^C = e_{a_1}^A < e_{b_1}^B = e_{a_2}^A$. Country A imports b_1 from B and c_1 from C. The incentive constraints require that country A does not deviate from cooperation with B and C.

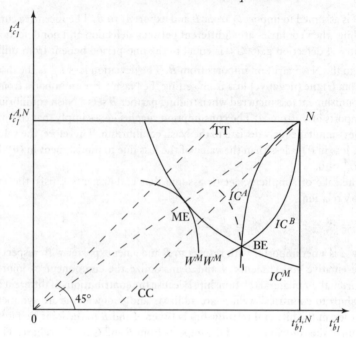

Figure 19.5. *Bilateral and multilateral enforcement*

If A, B, and C have the same consumption and production patterns, the welfare maximization problem can be expressed as follows. A representative country, say A, sets the import tariffs that maximize the sum of the welfare obtained from its imports from B and C subject to the self-enforcement constraints. The maximization problem yields the relation $t^A_{c_1} < t^A_{b_1}$. This relation can be understood by recalling that the highest tariff is inflicted on the weakest party and observing that $e^C_{c_1} < e^B_{b_1}$.

Figure 19.5 shows the bilateral equilibria under noncooperation and cooperation when power is unbalanced. Point N depicts the noncooperative Nash equilibrium. The equilibrium sustained by a bilateral enforcement mechanism is depicted by point BE. Country B has larger endowments than country A and is a net exporter *vis-à-vis A*. In contrast, country C is a net importer *vis-à-vis A*. Therefore, country B is the weak party and thus faces, in case of trade war, a higher non–cooperative tariff rate than the 'more powerful' country C, $t^A_{c_1} < t^A_{b_1}$, as illustrated in Fig. 19.5. Graphically, point N lies below the 45-degree line TT beginning at the origin, which depicts equal tariffs. The stronger country C is also able to extract a larger tariff concession from A than the weaker country B: $t^{A,N}_{c_1} - t^A_{c_1} > t^{A,N}_{b_1} - t^A_{b_1}$. Graphically, the bilateral enforcement tariff point BE is located below and to the right of the 45-degree line CC beginning at the noncooperative Nash equilibrium point N, which depicts equal concessions. IC means incentive constraint.

19.5.3. Multilateral Enforcement

Can multilateral enforcement lead to greater gains from cooperation than bilateral enforcement? The question is not trivial because, if power is balanced, bilateral and multilateral punishments are equally efficient in the sense that they sustain the same most cooperative tariffs. To see why, observe that multilateral punishment doubles both the losses and the gains from defection in comparison with the bilateral punishment case. The losses double due to third party participation in the punishment. The gains double because a defecting country would have incentives to defect against both partners simultaneously. As a result, the reinforcement of punishment does not sustain greater cooperation than bilateral enforcement.

Suppose that countries B and C have the same endowments $e = e^B_{b_1} = e^C_{c_1}$ and thus the same power in their bilateral relationship with A. Then $G = G^A_{b_1} = G^A_{c_1}$, $L = L^A_{b_1} = L^A_{c_1}$, and $t = t^A_{c_1} = t^A_{b_1}$. The maximization problem yielding the most-cooperative tariff is the same under the bilateral and the multilateral enforcement mechanisms

$$\max_{(t^A_{b_1}, t^A_{c_1})} W^A_{b_1}(t^A_{b_1}, e^B_{b_1}) + W^A_{c_1}(t^A_{c_1}, e^C_{c_1}) = \max_t 2W(t, e) \iff \max_t W(t, e),$$

s.t.

$$G^A_{b_1} + G^A_{c_1} = 2G(t, e) \le \frac{\delta(L^A_{b_1} + L^A_{c_1})}{1 - \delta} = \frac{2\delta L(t, e)}{1 - \delta} \iff G(t, e) \le \frac{\delta L(t, e)}{1 - \delta}.$$

A similar argument applies to countries B and C.

If power is balanced, the shift from bilateral to multilateral enforcement mechanisms does not alter the most-cooperative tariff. Multilateral enforcement creates incentives for multilateral deviations and thus increases both the gains and the losses from defection. Therefore, the relative effectiveness of bilateral and multilateral enforcement does not hinge simply on the fact that multilateral sanctions are stronger than bilateral sanctions.

Under power imbalances, joint welfare is higher with multilateral punishment than with bilateral punishment. The reason is that the third party acts as an enforcer of a bilateral trade relationship in which it is not directly involved. The resultant transfer of power across relationships partially offsets power imbalances allowing cooperation that would not be possible under bilateral punishment when the distribution of trading power is unbalanced. Under bilateral punishment, the weaker partner makes a larger concession to the stronger partner. Under multilateral punishment, a transfer of enforcement power is achieved and the stronger partner is forced to make a larger concession than the weaker country.

The optimal self-enforcing agreement requires countries with greater enforcement power to make larger concessions than weaker countries. This concession condition can be implemented under multilateral enforcement, but not under bilateral enforcement. For instance, consider a case in which country A imports only from B and exports only to C, $b_1 > 0, a_2 > 0$, and $a_1 = c_1 = 0$, so that it is strong against B and weak against C. Country A actually gains if it imposes a noncooperative tariff to B but loses if there is no cooperation with C. Under bilateral punishment, the weak party gains from cooperation are limited by the fact that it is not possible to effectively punish the strong party.

Let us focus on concessions under multilateral sanctions when trading power is not balanced. The most-cooperative tariff with multilateral enforcement maximizes joint welfare $W_{b_1}^A + W_{a_1}^B = W_{b_1}^A + W_{c_1}^A$ subject to nonnegativity constraints on tariffs and three sustainability constraints ruling out (1) defection with respect to B under multilateral enforcement, (2) defection with respect to C under multilateral enforcement, and (3) simultaneous defection with respect to B and C under multilateral enforcement. A multilateral punishment mechanism in a bilateral relationship means that defection by one country against another leads to the static Nash equilibrium in both bilateral relationships in which the defector is involved. Multilateral punishment generates an incentive to deviate simultaneously against both trading partners. The related multilateral sustainability constraint requires that there is no temptation to defect simultaneously against the two trading partners.

Country A maximizes the component of its welfare derived from imports from B and C

$$\max_{(t_{b_1}^A, t_{c_1}^A)} W_{b_1}^A(t_{b_1}^A, e_{b_1}^B) + W_{c_1}^A(t_{c_1}^A, e_{c_1}^C),$$

subject to multilateral enforcement constraints

(i) $G_{b_1}^A \le \dfrac{\delta}{1-\delta}(L_{b_1}^A + L_{c_1}^A),$

(ii) $G_{c_1}^A \le \dfrac{\delta}{1-\delta}(L_{b_1}^A + L_{c_1}^A),$

(iii) $G_{b_1}^A + G_{c_1}^A \le \dfrac{\delta}{1-\delta}(L_{b_1}^A + L_{c_1}^A).$

Observe that multilateral enforcement of single deviations differs from the bilateral incentive constraints $G_{b_1}^A \le \delta L_{b_1}^A/(1-\delta)$ and $G_{c_1}^A \le \delta L_{c_1}^A/(1-\delta)$. The multilateral constraint ruling out simultaneous deviations is obtained by adding up the bilateral constraints (i) and (ii) and eliminating redundant sanctions. If the bilateral deviation enforcement constraints (i) and (ii) are satisfied, simultaneous deviations might not be avoided and the simultaneous no–defection constraint (iii) is not necessarily satisfied. Together, the bilateral no–defection constraints are weaker than the simultaneous no–defection constraint.

Maximizing joint welfare with respect to tariffs $t_{b_1}^A$ and $t_{c_1}^A$ subject to the binding constraint ruling out simultaneous defection under multilateral enforcement implies that the bilateral relationship constraints under multilateral enforcement are automatically satisfied (they are not binding). The problem thus reduces to maximizing welfare subject to the multilateral enforcement constraint relating to simultaneous defection. The maximization implies that the ratio of the tariff imposed by country A on good b_1

to the tariff imposed by country A on c_1 is equal to the ratio of country B's endowment to country C's endowment. The appendix shows that

$$\frac{t_{b_1}^A}{t_{c_1}^A} = \frac{e_{b_1}^B}{e_{c_1}^C} = \frac{t_{b_1}^{A,N}}{t_{c_1}^{A,N}}, \tag{19.14}$$

where the multilateral enforcement tariff ratio is equal to the ratio of the noncooperative Nash equilibrium tariffs.

Multilateral enforcement sustains the most-cooperative tariff structure depicted at point ME in Fig. 19.5. This point represents the tangency of the incentive constraint ruling out simultaneous deviation and the iso welfare curve $W^M W^M$. The strongest trader grants a greater tariff concession than the weaker country, that is, point ME lies to the left and above the line CC depicting equal concession. Despite greater concessions, the stronger country sets a higher tariff than the weaker country. The tariff ratio that is sustainable under multilateral sanctions is the same as the tariff ratio prevailing under the noncooperative equilibrium. This reflects the fact that under multilateral sanctions the stronger country still has greater power than the weaker country. From the perspective of joint welfare maximization, multilateral enforcement achieves greater welfare than bilateral enforcement. In the figure, welfare increases as the iso welfare curves get closer to the zero–tariff origin and the iso joint welfare is closer to the origin at ME than at BE.

19.5.4. WTO and Sanctions under Asymmetric Information

Suppose that trading partners are able to verify violations to negotiated agreements directly affecting them but third parties do not directly observe these deviations. This information asymmetry can arise when deviations take the form of contingent protection and nontariff barriers that are not transparent to third parties, such as health and product standards. In this situation, sanctions can operate on a bilateral basis because trading partners monitor all the bilateral agreements they enter into and are thus able to retaliate against defectors. However, third party sanctions are ruled out due to lack of information. As a result, multilateral enforcement collapses.

What is the role of the WTO when there is asymmetric information? In the absence of the WTO, third countries remain unaware of trade norm violations involving any two countries and the possibility of multilateral enforcement collapses. By contrast, a strong WTO scenario entails enforcing cooperation through a multilateral reputation and punishment mechanism. Contested issues can be submitted to the WTO dispute settlement body, who launches an investigation to settle the main contested issues. The investigation provides the information required to either enable third parties to contribute to punish defectors or permit multilateral punishment threats. The possibility that otherwise uninformed third parties will be able to verify violations in bilateral disputes and the threat of multilateral sanctions sustain a multilateral reputation and punishment mechanism. Multilateral enforcement increases the costs of violations to the defecting country and sustains greater joint welfare when power is unbalanced.

Maggi (1999*b*) finds that a combination of full bilateral punishment (i.e. permanent reversion to Nash tariffs) and partial third party punishment (i.e. transitory reversion to Nash tariffs) achieves the optimal tariff structure, defined as the most-cooperative tariffs under the multilateral enforcement mechanism. The reason is that, if the multi-lateral sustainability constraint ruling out simultaneous defection is binding, the multilateral enforcement constraints ruling out bilateral deviation are not binding. Therefore, the strength of third-party punishment in these constraints can be partially relaxed.

Third-party punishments that are combined with full bilateral sanctions

(1) Should be selective and strong enough to preclude violations of the agreement that cannot be deterred by bilateral punishments. Third-party sanctions should focus on violations by strong parties against weak parties, which cannot be effectively deterred with bilateral sanctions alone;

(2) Should have minimal severity meaning that punishers impose the least severe third-party sanctions that, together with full bilateral sanctions, are able to sustain the most-cooperative tariff level under multilateral cooperation. Minimal third-party sanctions are found to be optimal when monitoring of trade policies is slightly imperfect and imposing sanctions is slightly more costly for third parties than for the second party. Minimal third-party sanctions can be modeled as temporary reversions to higher tariffs.

19.5.5. *Multilateral Trade Negotiations*

A key role of the WTO is to promote multilateral trade negotiations in place of a web of bilateral negotiations. Multilateral bargaining aims to produce self-enforcing agreements that improve upon a web of bilateral agreements. The concept of multilateral bargaining should be distinguished from the concept of multilateral sanctions, which can be applied to both bilateral and multilateral negotiations.

The economics of WTO-sponsored multilateral trade negotiations can be modeled in terms of Nash bargaining over the set of self-enforcing agreements (Maggi, 1999*b*). Governments select a tariff structure subject to the constraint that no participant has incentives to defect. The threat point of the bargaining game is given by the static Nash equilibrium payoff profile.

Multilateral bargaining corresponds to the maximization of surplus, defined as equilibrium joint welfare $W_{b_1}^A + W_{c_1}^A$ minus the joint welfare $W_{b_1}^{A,N} + W_{c_1}^{A,N}$ achievable at the bargaining game threat point N. Formally,

$$\max_{(t_{b_1}^A, t_{c_1}^A)} (W_{b_1}^A + W_{c_1}^A - W_{b_1}^{A,N} - W_{c_1}^{A,N})^3$$

$$\Longleftrightarrow \max_{(t_{b_1}^A, t_{c_1}^A)} W_{b_1}^A + W_{c_1}^A - W_{b_1}^{A,N} - W_{c_1}^{A,N}.$$

Bilateral bargaining corresponds to the maximization of the Nash criterion ($W_{b_1}^A -$ $W_{b_1}^{A,N})(W_{c_1}^A - W_{c_1}^{A,N})$. If countries endowments differ, the multilateral and bilateral bargaining problems have different solutions. Multilateral enforcement of a negotiated agreement requires the maximization to be subject to the incentive constraint ruling out simultaneous deviations.

Consider a scenario in which there are no international transfers. Each bilateral negotiation with multilateral enforcement can be shown to be locally efficient, in the sense of efficiency conditional on the outcome of other bilateral negotiations. However, bilateral bargaining is not globally efficient unless there are no power imbalances. These negotiations are globally inefficient because bilateral bargaining generates a bias in favor of the strong country in each bilateral relationship. This inefficiency is due to market segmentation. Bilateral trade negotiations can be viewed as segmented markets in which participants exchange trade concessions that do not internalize the effects of parallel bilateral negotiations.

If international transfers can be enforced and the discount factor is high enough, bilateral bargaining with multilateral sanctions produces a globally efficient outcome. When utility is transferable, efficiency concerns are separated from distribution concerns and balance of power considerations. Then, bilateral bargaining parties will choose the tariff structure that maximizes the joint surplus of the bilateral trading partners while transfers are used to redistribute the surplus. As a result, the outcome is globally efficient. If enforceable international transfers are allowed but the discount factor is low enough, bilateral bargaining with multilateral sanctions and transfers can mitigate but not remove the bargaining inefficiency.

Figure 19.6 shows the tariff equilibrium under bilateral and multilateral bargaining, assuming in both cases that sanctions are enforced multilaterally. Tariff equilibrium under multilateral bargaining takes place at MB, which corresponds to the tangency of incentive constraint IC^M and the iso–joint welfare curve. Tariff equilibrium under bilateral bargaining is depicted by point BB, which represents the tangency of the incentive constraint IC^M and the iso bilateral bargaining welfare function. From the perspective of joint welfare maximization, the multilateral bargaining equilibrium at MB is able to achieve greater welfare than bilateral bargaining equilibrium at BB. In the figure, the iso joint welfare function is greater (i.e. is closer to the zero tariff point) at MB than at BB.

Multilateral negotiations with multilateral enforcement are more effective than bilateral bargaining in the sense that they yield a Pareto-superior outcome relative to bilateral negotiations with multilateral enforcement if and only if there are bilateral power imbalances. If endowments are equal so that power is balanced, bilateral negotiations yield the same tariffs as multilateral negotiations and are efficient

$$\max_{(t_{b_1}^A, t_{c_1}^A)} W_{b_1}^A + W_{c_1}^A - W_{b_1}^{A,N} - W_{c_1}^{A,N} = 2\max_t(W^A - W^{A,N})$$

$$\Longleftrightarrow \max_{(t_{b_1}^A, t_{c_1}^A)} (W_{b_1}^A - W_{b_1}^{A,N})(W_{c_1}^A - W_{c_1}^{A,N}) = \max_t(W^A - W^{A,N})^2.$$

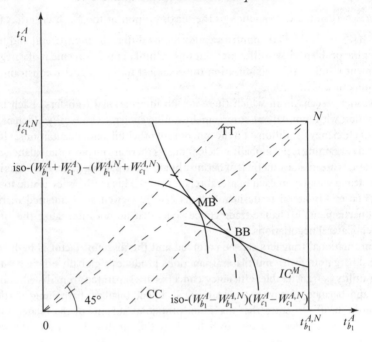

Figure 19.6. *Bilateral and multilateral bargaining*

Summarizing, multilateralism can take place at the level of trade negotiations and at the level of enforcement and sanctions. Bilateral negotiations are inefficient when supported by bilateral sanctions, and are locally but not globally efficient when supported with multilateral sanctions. Global efficiency can be achieved by (1) bilateral negotiations supported by multilateral sanctions and enforceable international transfers (if the discount factor is high enough), and (2) multilateral negotiations supported by multilateral sanctions (efficiency does not require international transfers or a high discount factor in this case).

19.6. NEGOTIATION, ENFORCEMENT, AND DELAYS

Trade liberalization is accomplished through trade negotiations aiming to achieve a sustainable outcome. Much theoretical work focuses either on the negotiation process (assuming that the required self-enforceability conditions hold) or on self-enforceability conditions (putting aside the negotiation process). Bac and Raff (1997) and Furusawa (1999) develop repeated game models in which governments explicitly negotiate over tariff rates subject to incentive constraints embodying self-enforcing conditions.

What explains the often long delays observed in trade negotiations? Bac and Raff (1997) develop a model in which countries enter into a war of attrition if they have a low discount factor and are optimistic enough. The authors extend Jensen and Thursby (1990) to consider a dynamic, infinitely repeated game with two-sided asymmetric information. Negotiations take place between a high tariff government that is reluctant to make concessions and a low tariff type that is willing to make concessions. Governments have the same discount factors but hold different prior beliefs about the other government's tariff preferences in terms of its willingness to cut tariff rates. A pessimistic prior means that there is a low prior probability that the other government is a low tariff type. An optimistic prior represents a high probability that the other government is a low tariff type.

In the perfect Bayesian equilibrium considered, concessions made are determined by the potential benefits derived from the agreement, the common discount rate and the prior distribution of the types. If the discount factor is large or trade volumes are small, priors do not play a role and reciprocal concessions are negotiated immediately. If the discount factor is low enough, the outcome can involve immediate reciprocal concessions, a unilateral concession by one country, or a war of attrition. If both countries are pessimistic about each other type, they will immediately grant reciprocal concessions. If one prior is optimistic and the other pessimistic, the pessimistic country immediately grants unilateral concessions. If both priors are optimistic, reaching an agreement can be delayed and countries engage in a war of attrition.

Furusawa (1999) utilizes a version of Rubinstein's bargaining model (1982) to examine how negotiations depend on countries' discount rates and the time lag between defection and punishment. The discount rate has two opposite effects in models with self-enforcement constraints. On one hand, the most patient country has greater bargaining power and captures a greater share of the pie. On the other hand, the most impatient country has greater incentives to defect and this reduces the discounted cost of defection. Because the patient party must prevent defection, the impatient country can exploit the self-enforcement constraint in the implementation phase. On that account, the impatient party is able to capture a larger piece of the negotiated pie.

Whether the bargaining effect dominates the punishment effect in the subgame perfect equilibrium considered by Furusawa depends on the time lag in the implementation phase. In the model considered, the most patient country gains more from the negotiation if the lag from defection to implementation is short. In contrast, the impatient country gains more if the implementation lag is long.

19.7. WTO, CORE, AND SHAPLEY VALUE

Cooperative games based on coalition formation provide a framework to analyze how individual countries or groups of countries deviate from a multilateral agreement. The range of potential deviations is wider than those typically considered in noncooperative approaches, such as single country deviation to Nash equilibrium or reversion to autarky. In coalitional games, free trade corresponds to a grand coalition while CUs and free trade areas correspond to subcoalitions within the grand coalition. Because the coalition structure is derived endogenously, coalitional games allow the endogenous formation of preferential agreements and permit examining the stability of these arrangements in the face of alternative potential coalitions or deviations.

Two popular coalitional game solution concepts are the core and the Shapley value. The core approach stresses the stability of a cooperative agreement in the face of the whole range of potential deviations from the agreement. Consider a set of N agents and define a coalition as a subset of the N agents. The core of a coalitional game is defined as the set of utility outcomes for which no coalition can improve the payoff of all its members. The utility levels implied by stable agreements must lie in the core. Otherwise, a coalition could on its own improve the welfare of its members.

The Shapley value is proposed as the basis for a fair or reasonable way to divide the gains from cooperation. In contrast to the core, this solution concept considers limited potential deviations from an agreement. Formally, the Shapley value of a coalitional game is a particular measure of the contribution of a member of a coalition to the other members of that coalition.

Riezman (1985) presents a theory of coalitional choice based on the core solution concept. He focuses on how country asymmetry affects the formation of CUs in a coalitional game in which transfers are not allowed. He shows that country symmetry does not necessarily lead to free trade because countries have incentives to block free trade and form a customs union in order to exploit monopoly power. Also, a customs union can be formed as a best response to a third country that can block free trade even if free trade would benefit customs union members.

Does the possibility of forming bilateral agreements impede or encourage free trade? The answer depends on countries' endowments. Riezman (1999) presents an example in which countries are asymmetric and free trade can be supported by the mere possibility of forming preferential agreements, even if these preferential arrangements are not stable (i.e. are not in the core). The possibility of forming preferential agreements enables smaller countries to block the exploitation of monopoly power by large countries.

What is the role of political factors in a coalitional game? Macho–Stadler *et al.* (1998) use the core solution concept in a symmetric game with no transfers to examine how political influences affect coalitional structures. The authors show that political influence can prevent the attainment of free trade, that is, can render free trade unstable and thus preclude it from being in the core.

Kowalczyk and Sjöström (1994) utilize the Shapley value approach to study the role of international income transfers in facilitating trade negotiations. Their results support the proposal to reform the WTO by allowing international transfers in exchange for trade concessions. The European Union has made use of international transfers to induce trade concessions and secure support for economic and monetary union.

19.7.1. CU and Core Solution Concepts

Consider a game with a set $N = \{1, \ldots, n\}$ of n players. Let $v(S)$ be a real-valued function that assigns a unique number to each subset S of players in N (i.e. coalition S).

The function $v(S)$ is called the characteristic function or the worth of a coalition. Formally, $v(S)$ is the maximal aggregate utility or payoff obtainable by a coalition $S \in \mathcal{S}(N)$, where $\mathcal{S}(N)$ is the set of all possible coalitions in a game, including coalitions made up of a single agent. The worth of a coalition with no members is zero: $v(\phi) = 0$, where ϕ represents the null set (a set with no elements). The function $v(S)$ specifies the total utility or 'size of the pie' to be divided among the members of coalition S. The total utility obtainable from a 'pie' to be divided among the n players of the game is denoted $v(N)$.

A coalitional game (N, v) entails the division of a 'pie' of size $v(N)$ among the n players in set N. Coalitional games can assume transferable utilities, meaning that transfers or side-payments are allowed, or nontransferable utilities.

The core of a coalitional game is defined as the set of feasible outcomes (i.e. utility vectors, utility allocations of the pie) satisfying the condition that no coalition can deviate and improve the payoffs of all the deviating coalition's members. In other words, an allocation of utilities or goods (i.e. payoff profile) is said to be in the core of a game if it cannot be blocked by any possible coalition.

Formally, let $x = (x_1, x_2, \ldots, x_i, \ldots, x_n)$ represent the payoff vector for agents $i \in \{1, \ldots, n\}$ belonging to a coalition. The core $C(N, v)$ of a coalitional game is given by

$$C(N, v) = \left\{ x \in \mathfrak{R}^n \mid x \text{ feasible}, \sum_{i \in S} x_i \geq v(S) \text{ for all } S \in \mathcal{S}(N) \right\},$$

where $v(S)$ is the worth of coalition S. A payoff profile x is an element of the core $C(N, v)$ if and only if no coalition can improve upon x.

Allocations within the core are said to be stable in the sense that it does not pay any member of a coalition to change the coalition structure (i.e. block the coalition structure). Formally, any stable payoff agreement x should satisfy the condition that the parties to the agreement should obtain at least the payoff they could obtain by themselves. Any vector x satisfying the condition $\sum_{i \in S} x_i < v(S)$ for some coalition $S \in \mathcal{S}(N)$, can be blocked by this coalition S. Because there are many allocations of goods that cannot be blocked by possible coalitions, the core solution concept assigns a set of outcomes to a coalitional game.

A key result of the literature utilizing the core solution concept is that, if countries differ enough in size, free trade is not in the core (Kennan and Riezman, 1988). Riezman (1985) examines the effect of country asymmetry on coalition structures (i.e. the number of coalitions and the number of members in each). The concept of the core is simplified by (1) restricting the amount of cooperation within possible coalitions to the formation of CU (i.e. free trade areas are not allowed), and (2) banning intra-coalition utility or income transfers (in general, the core allows utility transfers or side payments).

Consider a three country, three good coalitional game in an exchange world economy in which countries have identical preferences. Countries play a two stage game.

Table 19.1. *Endowments and payoffs*

Good\Country	A	B	C
Endowments			
1	0.3	0.1	0.1
2	0.1	0.3	0.1
3	0.1	0.1	0.3
Regime\Country	A	B	C
Payoff			
FT	2820	2820	2820
NC	2818	2818	2818
CU_{AB}	2821	2821	2814
CU_{AC}	2821	2814	2821
CU_{BC}	2814	2821	2821

Coalitions are formed in the first stage according to the core concept. Tariffs are set optimally in the second stage, conditional on the coalition structure established in the first stage. Country symmetry does not necessarily lead to free trade in this setting, because any two countries might have incentives to block free trade and form a customs union to exploit monopoly power. When countries are asymmetric, Riezman presents an example showing that a customs union can be formed even if the countries forming it will be worse off than under free trade. The customs union enables smaller countries to obtain a greater share of the pie in the presence of a larger country.

First, consider a coalitional game with nontransferable utility (i.e. transfers are not allowed) and three symmetric economies, denoted $A, B,$ and C. Table 19.1 shows the countries' endowment vectors and game payoffs. Free trade yields utility vector (2820, 2820, 2820). A customs union CU_{AB} between A and B yields (2821, 2821, 2814), a customs union CU_{AC} between A and C yields (2821, 2814, 2821) and a customs union CU_{BC} between B and C yields (2814, 2821, 2821). Coalitions $(A, B), (A, C)$ or (B, C) can block free trade and form a customs union in order to exploit market power at the expense of the country remaining outside the union. The reason is that the customs union will control most of the world supply of two out of the three goods. The core consists of a set that includes all possible CU but not free trade or the noncooperative solution NC.

Second, consider a coalitional game with nontransferable utility (i.e. transfers are not allowed), a large economy (say, country A) and two smaller economies (say, B and C). It is easy to see why a customs union between the two smaller countries can block free trade and be an equilibrium outcome even though both members of the custom union do worse than under free trade. Let us focus on the following illustrative utility outcomes for countries $A, B,$ and C: free trade yields (3001, 2921, 2921), noncooperation yields

(3004, 2902, 2902), and a customs union between B and C yields (3002, 2907, 2907). Free trade is blocked by country A, who benefits from noncooperation. A customs union between the two smaller countries is worse than free trade, but offers greater utility than the noncooperative solution (2907 vs 2902). The customs union is formed because it represents a best response to noncooperation by country A. Notice that, if transfers were allowed in a game with transferable utility, everybody would win by moving toward free trade. For instance, countries B and C could offer, say, 2 units of utility each to country A to induce it to move to free trade.

Does the possibility of forming bilateral agreements impede or encourage free trade? How does endowment size asymmetries affect whether or not free trade and CUs are in the core? Riezman (1999) examines coalitional games that allow the formation of both free trade areas and CUs. In this setting, allowing bilateral agreements results in greater protection when countries or trading blocks initially have similar sizes. Because countries or existing trading blocks have incentives to make good the threat of forming bilateral agreements, banning bilateral agreements is beneficial.

When there are size asymmetries, however, banning bilateral agreements can lead to more protection. Greater protectionism can emerge even if bilateral agreements would facilitate protection aiming to exploit terms of trade advantages. The paradoxical result indicating that the opportunity to use protection through bilateral agreements can lead to less protection than if bilateralism is banned derives from the logic of coalitional games. The possibility of forming bilateral agreements permits smaller countries or trading blocks to pose a credible threat of forming a coalition. This threat can be used to prevent larger countries or trading blocks from exploiting terms of trade advantages. In short, the possibility of bilateralism can support less protection because the ability of the large country or trading block to exploit monopoly power is offset by the possibility of a competing arrangement.

Macho-Stadler *et al.* (1998) develop a three-country symmetric model with a single commodity and nontransferable utility. Multilateral negotiations for tariff reductions (tariffs are required to be nonnegative) are modeled as a game in coalitional form. The tariff agreements that lie in the core of the game (called stable agreements) are those such that no country or coalition of countries expect to obtain a higher payoff by not participating in the agreements. Negotiations proceed on a most-favored-nation (MFN) basis, under which countries set the same tariffs to all other countries ratifying the agreement. The analysis focuses on the political economy of multilateral negotiations that are conducted by countries subject to lobby pressures. Political influence is reflected in the weights countries' welfare functions assign to (1) the sum of domestic consumers' surplus and firms' profits earned in domestic markets (which is normalized to 1), (2) profits of domestic firms in foreign markets, and (3) tariff revenues. The relative weight given to each factor in the social welfare function determines which agreements lie in the core of the game.

Political influence can prevent the attainment of free trade, that is, can render free trade unstable and thus preclude it from being in the core. A positive tariff equilibrium agreement can take place if the welfare weight of tariff revenues is large enough and the weight of firms' profits in foreign markets is low enough relative to the weight attached to the sum of consumer surplus and firm's profits in domestic markets. In this case, the symmetric efficient agreement will not generally coincide with free trade. In other words, free trade is not part of the agreement or agreements in the core.

There is also a large region in the parameter space in which the core is empty. This happens when the relative weights assigned by countries to tariff revenues are small enough and the weights assigned to exporters' profits are large enough. In these circumstances, two cooperating countries forming a coalition would tend to set low tariffs against the third country thus opening up opportunities for the third trading partner's exports. Instability arises because the third trading partner assigns a large weight to exports and attempts to promote exports while free riding on the low tariffs set by the cooperating countries. This partner can thus cater to exporter lobbies without having to renounce to revenues on tariffs set against goods produced abroad. Therefore, deviating might turn out to be profitable.

A situation in which two countries cooperate bilaterally (i.e. regionalism) while a third country remains outside the coalition is similar to a three country trading regime consisting of a free trade area and a country that does not cooperate and intervenes in trade. This situation illustrates a case in which there is no cooperative agreement to which all countries will subscribe (but two countries do reach an agreement). In other words, multilateral agreements might be subject to instability even if they would yield gains to all participants relative to setting trade policies unilaterally.

19.7.2. The Shapley Value

What coalitional structures result when inter-country side payments are allowed? Consider a coalitional game entailing the division of a 'pie' of size $v(N)$ among the n players in set $N = \{1, \ldots, n\}$. In the context of a coalitional game with transferable payoffs (i.e. permitting side payments), a 'value' is a function that assigns a unique feasible payoff profile (i.e. allocation of the pie) to every coalitional game. A payoff profile is feasible if the sum of its components is equal to the size of the pie $v(N)$, defined as either total utility (assumed to be transferable) or the total supply of some good produced by the n players.

The Shapley value is a popular tool used to determine a fair or reasonable way to divide the gains from cooperation. In a nutshell, the Shapley value of a coalitional game is the average value of the marginal contributions of a member of a coalition to other members of that coalition. The average is taken over the set of all possible orderings of predecessors that can be considered in computing the marginal contributions.

The key idea of the Shapley value is that a pie should be divided according to the contribution of each player to the coalition. Consider an amount or total utility $v(N)$ to be divided among a set of n players. These n players can be arranged in many possible orderings $\pi \in \Pi$, where Π is the set of all orderings. The number of all possible orderings is equal to $n! = n(n - 1) \ldots 1$. The Shapley value $Sh^i(N, v)$ is defined as player i's expected marginal contribution to the set of players preceding i, where the expectation is calculated as an average over all orderings of players preceding i.

Player ordering turns out to be key to the computation of a member's contribution to a coalition. Two sets with the same members are treated as different coalitions if the sets differ in the ordering of the members: $\{1, 2, 3\} \neq \{1, 3, 2\}$. The reason is that the marginal contribution of a given player depends on which players are already in the coalition (i.e. its predecessors) when the marginal contribution is computed. For instance, the contribution of the first member is not the same as that of the nth member. Because it is not possible to assign a constant place in the ordering to any given agent, the marginal contribution is averaged over all possible orderings of players. The computation of the average marginal contribution assumes that all possible orderings are equally likely.

Formally, the Shapley value of a coalitional game (N, v), denoted by $Sh^i(N, v)$, is

$$Sh^i(N, v) = \frac{1}{n!} \sum_{\pi \in \Pi} m(S(\pi, i), i),$$

where $S(\pi, i)$ represents the set of players preceding agent i in the ordering π and $m(S(\pi, i), i) = v(S(\pi, i) \cup i) - v(S)$ denotes the marginal contribution of agent i belonging to coalition S (given an ordering π of predecessors). The appendix contains an alternative way to obtain the Shapley value and an example explicitly computing it for a three-player game.

Mas-Colell *et al.* (1995) examine the basic properties of the Shapley value. The Shapley value solution concept assigns a single outcome to a coalitional game, restricts players' deviations, and generates a payoff profile that might or might not lie in the core. By contrast, the core solution concept assigns a set of outcomes to a game and, apart from imposing a feasibility constraint, does not impose any restriction whatsoever on a coalition's credible deviations. A shortcoming of the core solution concept is that the set of outcomes can be empty or comprise many outcomes.

19.7.3. *International Transfers to Bring GATT into the Core*

Kowalczyk and Sjöström (1994) develop a static coalitional game with transferable payoffs to examine international agreements that are self-enforcing in the sense that no country or group of countries have incentives to leave the agreement or cheat on it. Side payments facilitate trade negotiations. The Shapley value, which is shown to be in the core of the game studied, is used to (1) determine the trade policy prescription associated to the Shapley value payoff in the core of the coalitional game, and (2) compute the international income transfers required to sustain trade liberalization.

The trade policy prescription associated to the Shapley value requires (1) the formation of a grand coalition, and (2) a mechanism for international side payments that are a function of countries' tastes and costs differences. In order to establish a globally Pareto-optimal trading order, it might be necessary to tax those countries that have much to gain from the formation of the coalition, and subsidize those countries that do not. In other words, the supporting financial mechanism requires countries that might benefit more from coalition formation to compensate those members that might find the agreement less profitable.

Consider an n-country world in which each country counts with one firm producing a single good sold in n markets. Firm j sells d_j^i product units in countries $i \in \{1, \ldots, n\}$, where the subscript identifies both the producer and the good sold while the superscript identifies the market in which the good is consumed. The global market clearing condition for good j is: $q_j = D_j = d_j^1 + \cdots + d_j^n$, where q_j represents output and D_j is global demand.

The representative consumer in country i is endowed with $\bar{q}_0^i$ units of traded resource 0, which is chosen as numeraire. Resource 0 can be consumed, utilized as a productive input or used as a medium of international income transfer. Country i consumes d_0^i units of good 0 and uses l_{0i} units as an input into the production of good i according to cost function $l_{0i} = \beta_i q_i$, where $i \in \{1, \ldots, n\}$ represents both the good consumed or used as input and the producing country, β_i is the constant marginal cost of good i and q_i represents units of i. The market-clearing condition for resource 0 is

$$\bar{q}_0 = \sum_{i=1}^{n} \bar{q}_0^i = \sum_{i=1}^{n} d_0^i + \sum_{i=1}^{n} l_{0i} + \sum_{i=1}^{n} tr^i,$$

where $\bar{q}_0$ is the global supply of 0 and tr^i is the transfer received ($tr^i > 0$) or granted ($tr^i < 0$) by country i. The consumption demands for resource 0 in each country is a residual equal to total income Y^i minus the demand for all other goods: $d_0^i = Y^i - p_1^i d_1^i - \cdots - p_n^i d_n^i$.

The utility function of a representative consumer in country i is

$$u^i(d^i) = d_0^i + \sum_{j=1}^{n} \frac{(d_j^i)^{\theta_j^i}}{\theta_j^i} \quad \rightarrow \quad p_j^i = \frac{\beta_i}{\theta_i^j} > \beta_i,$$

where $i, j \in \{1, \ldots, n\}, 0 < \theta_i^j < 1$ is the taste parameter and β_i is the constant marginal cost of good i. The domestic price p_j^i of good j in country i represents a markup over marginal costs and is independent of other goods prices.

In this framework, the supply of each consumer good (except the numeraire) is controlled by a single firm holding a natural monopoly. Therefore, unless existing monopolies are broken up, free trade does not lead to a Pareto-optimal outcome. When a coalition is formed, governments are also assumed to implement price controls or antitrust policies to lower prices to a level equal to marginal cost β_i and preclude the exploitation of monopoly power.

The use of regulation to break up existing monopolies can be viewed as a proxy for a setup in which each country has monopoly in the good it produces but there are many local firms acting competitively. In this situation, monopoly power is not exploited unless firms collude or each government restricts trade as a means of exploiting monopoly power. For instance, in the absence of a coalition, an optimal tariff or nontariff barriers such as quotas or voluntary export restrictions (VERs) can be used to support

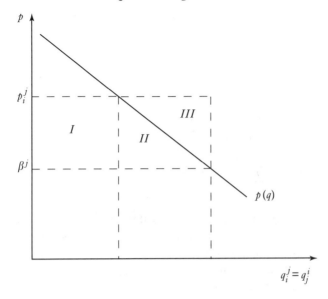

Figure 19.7. *Bilateral trade and welfare*

a monopoly price. If tariffs, quotas or VERs are dismantled, the monopoly unravels and the price falls to become equal to marginal costs.

Figure 19.7 illustrates the change in the welfare of the trading pair consisting of the firms from countries i and j. Suppose that firm i reduces its price in market j from p_i^j to marginal cost β_i. Define δ_i^j as the increase in consumer surplus in country j when firm i reduces its price to marginal cost (area $I + II$ in Fig. 19.7). Define $\pi_i^j = (p_i^j - \beta_i)q_i^j$ as the reduction in firm i profits in market j when the price charged declines to marginal cost β_i (area I). The net welfare increase for the trading pair (i,j) is equal to $\delta_i^j - \pi_i^j$ (area II). By the same token, the net welfare increase for trading pair (i,j) when firm j reduces its price to marginal cost in market i is equal to $\delta_j^i - \pi_j^i$. Adding these welfare gains yields $\delta_i^j - \pi_i^j + \delta_j^i - \pi_j^i$. The total increase in welfare for a coalition is obtained by adding these welfare gains over all pairs of coalition members.

Let us focus on the gains and losses from an individual country perspective. First, notice that $\delta_i^j - \pi_j^i$ is country j's net gain from joining the coalition. Country j's net gain is measured as j's welfare gain δ_i^j due to increased consumer surplus when i lowers the price charged minus the monopoly profits π_j^i the producer of good j would obtain in market i by charging the monopoly price p_j^i. Second, $\delta_j^i - \pi_i^j$ is country i's net gain from joining the coalition. This gain is measured as the welfare gain due to greater consumer surplus minus the welfare loss from charging the monopoly price p_i^j in country j. Countries' gains are the mirror image of the losses from leaving the coalition.

The Shapley value profile for the transferable utility GATT game is given by (see appendix)

$$Sh^i(N, v) = \bar{q}_0^j + \sum_{j=1}^{n} CS_i^j + \frac{1}{2} \sum_{j=1}^{n} \left[(\delta_i^j - \pi_i^j) - (\delta_j^i - \pi_j^i) \right]$$

$$= \bar{q}_0^i + \sum_{j=1}^{n} CS_j^i + \frac{1}{2} \sum_{j=1}^{n} \left[(\pi_j^i - \delta_j^i) - (\pi_i^j - \delta_i^j) \right]$$

$$= \bar{q}_0^i + \sum_{j=1}^{n} CS_j^i + tr^i(N, v),$$

and corresponds to the sum of country i's good 0 endowment $\bar{q}_0^i$, the consumer surplus CS_j^i accruing to i when each country j charges the marginal costs on its exports (area $I + II + III$ in Fig. 19.7) and the term $tr^i(N, v)$ representing the international transfers received by i from all countries in order to induce it to participate in the grand coalition.

The GATT can be brought into the core by implementing the vector $tr^i(N, v)$ of international payments to country i. Observe that the formula for $tr^i(N, v)$ implies that if the agreement yields a lower welfare gain or larger loss to country j than to country i, then j should receive positive transfers from i. Because the transfer mechanism gives some countries exactly what it takes out from others, it is balanced in the sense that the sum of receipts equals the sum of payments made.

The Shapley value implies that a country's share in the utility generated by a multilateral agreement is greater (1) the greater its endowment of good 0, (2) the greater the consumer surplus it accrues when all other countries move to marginal cost pricing, and (3) the smaller the gains reaped relative to those obtained by other coalition members.

The European Union has used international transfers to induce trade concessions and secure support for economic and monetary union. The creation of the European Economic Area (EEA), the free trade area between the European Union and the members of the European Free Trade Association (EFTA) that came into effect in 1994, also involved international transfers. Estimates of EFTA payments to the EU countries in connection with the formation of the EEA are less than 1 per cent of EFTA 1992 national income. This represents an instance in which small countries with a high income level, Austria, Finland, Norway, Sweden, and Iceland make transfers to larger countries in order to consolidate trade concessions.

19.8. CONCLUSIONS

Multilateral agreements can be rationalized as a device to generate welfare improving terms of trade effects and avoid the prisoners' dilemma attached to noncooperative tariff setting. The cooperative game-theoretic approach provides a useful perspective to examine the formation and sustainability of multilateral cooperation agreements as well as the interaction between different types of coexisting preferential agreements. The noncooperative approach to cooperation does not take for granted that binding agreements can be made and enforced by the WTO or that countries will actually act cooperatively.

Countries' incentives to defect or cheat in the post-negotiation stage mean that multilateral agreements raise serious enforceability and sustainability problems. This result is a leitmotif of the analysis of cooperation. In the absence of an international enforcer, multilateral trade agreements can be viewed as self-enforcing commitments sustained by the establishment of credible penalties such as retaliation by other members of the cooperative agreement. Because power imbalances undermine bilateral enforcement, efficient solutions cannot be achieved under multilateralism subject to bilateral enforcement. However, multilateral enforcement can always improve welfare when there are power imbalances. WTO investigations and findings expose violators of multilateral rules to losses of reputation and make third-party punishment possible.

Despite active work on cooperative agreements, many issues remain on the board. Work endogenizing the formation of preferential agreements remains scarce. Coalitional games approaches should in principle be able to endogenize coalition formation but in practice the coalitions allowed are restricted in order to simplify the analysis. The study of the internal operation of preferential arrangements also remains almost unexplored—Gatsios and Karp (1991) analysis of delegation in CUs is a notable exception. For instance, how do CUs reach an agreement on their external tariff structure? What type of tensions emerge within preferential arrangements? Empirical work on the interaction between free trade areas, CUs, and the multilateral system is still scarce. This is perhaps due to the fact that preferential arrangements proliferated relatively recently during the 1980s and 1990s. Given the long-standing controversy on multilateralism vs bilateralism, the systematic assessment of the actual performance of these preferential arrangements remains a major task to be completed.

19.9. APPENDIX

19.9.1. Derivation of the Welfare Function

Substituting the linear demand expressions into (19.1) yields

$$2 = (\alpha - p_i^x) + [\alpha - (p_i^x + t_i)] \rightarrow p_i^x = (\alpha - 1) - \frac{t_i}{2}. \tag{19.15}$$

Using $p_i^m = p_i^x + t_i$ and (19.15), the prices for imports are

$$p_i^m = p_i^x + t_i = (\alpha - 1) - \frac{t_i}{2} + t_i = (\alpha - 1) + \frac{t_i}{2} \rightarrow \frac{\partial p_i^m}{\partial t_i} = \frac{1}{2} > 0. \tag{19.16}$$

A unit increase in a domestic tariff translates into lower export prices (i.e. $\partial p_i^x / \partial t_i = -1/2 < 0$) and higher import prices. If tariffs increase by one unit, equilibrium export prices decline by one-half and equilibrium import prices increase by one-half.

The volume of imports M_i is (using (19.16))

$$M_i(t_i) = \alpha - p_i^m = \alpha - \left(\alpha - 1 + \frac{t_i}{2}\right) = 1 - \frac{t_i}{2} \quad \rightarrow \quad \frac{\partial M_i(t_i)}{\partial t_i} = -\frac{1}{2} < 0.$$

$$(19.17)$$

The volume of imports declines with the tariff rate.

Tariffs and Domestic Welfare

Trade policy decisions maximize a welfare function that depends on tariff rates. The level of welfare is obtained by adding up over all G goods (1) the consumers' surplus $CS(p_i^m(t_i))$ obtained from the $G/2$ imported goods, (2) the consumers' surplus $CS(p_i^x(t_i^*))$ obtained from domestic consumption of the $G/2$ exportables (evaluated at the international price), (3) the producers' surplus $PS(p_i^x(t_i^*))$ obtained from the $G/2$ domestically-produced goods, and (4) government revenues $R = t_i M_i(t_i)$ obtained from the tariffs imposed on the $G/2$ imported goods.

Because all goods have the same demand function and we are considering an endowment economy (so all goods have zero production costs) each importing country will choose the same tariff rate for all imported goods. Allowing tariff rates to differ across countries, the welfare function is

$$W(G, t, t^*) = \frac{G}{2}[CS(p^m(t)) + CS(p^x(t^*)) + PS(p^x(t^*)) + R]$$

$$= \frac{G}{2}\left[\int_{p^m(t)}^{\alpha} Q(p)dp + \int_{p^x(t^*)}^{\alpha} Q(p)dp + \int_0^{p^x(t^*)} 2dp + tM(t)\right].$$

$$(19.18)$$

The domestic tariff t affects both domestic consumers' surplus from imported goods and government revenues. The foreign tariff t^* affects the consumers' surplus and producers' surplus obtained from domestically-produced goods.

The welfare function (19.18) can be expressed as a linear function of the number of goods G and a quadratic function of domestic and foreign tariffs

$$W(G, t, t^*) = \frac{G}{2}\left(2\alpha - 1 + \frac{t}{2} - \frac{3t^2}{8} - \frac{t^*}{2} + \frac{t^{*2}}{8}\right),$$

$$(19.19)$$

where we use the demand functions defined above, domestic and foreign prices (p^m, p^x) in (19.15) and (19.16), and the volume of imports in (19.17). Welfare under free trade $(t = t^* = 0)$ is

$$W(G) = \frac{G}{2}(2\alpha - 1).$$

19.9.2. Trade Policy Cooperation and Self-Enforcement

Welfare $W(\cdot)$ is defined by

$$\frac{G}{2}\left[\int_{p_i^m(t)}^{\alpha} Q(p)dp + \int_{p_i^x(t^*)}^{\alpha} Q(p)dp + \int_0^{p_i^x(t^*)} 2dp + tM(t)\right]. \qquad (19.20)$$

Let us compute each component:

$$\int_{p_i^m(t)}^{\alpha} Q(p)dp = \int_{p_i^m(t)}^{\alpha}(\alpha - p)dp = \alpha p - \frac{p^2}{2}\Big|_{p_i^m(t)}^{\alpha}$$

$$= \alpha^2 - \frac{\alpha^2}{2} - \alpha p_i^m(t) + \frac{[p_i^x(t)]^2}{2}$$

$$= \alpha^2 - \frac{\alpha^2}{2} - \alpha\left[\alpha - 1 + \frac{t}{2}\right] + \frac{(\alpha - 1 + (t/2)^2)}{2}$$

$$= \frac{1}{2} + \frac{t^2}{8} - \frac{t}{2}.$$

$$\int_{p_x^i(t_m^{*i})}^{\alpha} Q(p)dp = \int_{p_x^i(t_m^{*i})}^{\alpha}[\alpha - p]dp = \alpha p - \frac{p^2}{2}\Big|_{p_x^i(t_m^{*i})}^{\alpha}$$

$$= \alpha^2 - \frac{\alpha^2}{2} - \alpha p_i^x(t^*) + \frac{[p_i^x(t^*)]^2}{2}$$

$$= \alpha^2 - \frac{\alpha^2}{2} - \alpha\left(\alpha - 1 - \frac{t^*}{2}\right) + \frac{(\alpha - 1 - (t^*/2)^2)}{2}$$

$$= \frac{1}{2} + \frac{(t^*)^2}{8} + \frac{t^*}{2}.$$

$$\int_0^{p_i^m(t^*)} 2dp = 2p\Big|_0^{p_i^m(t^*)} = 2p_i^m(t^*) = 2\left(\alpha - 1 - \frac{t^*}{2}\right)$$

$$= 2(\alpha - 1) - t^*; \quad tM(t) = t\left(1 - \frac{t}{2}\right).$$

Substituting each component into (19.20) and simplifying terms yields

$$W(\cdot) = \frac{G}{2}\left[\frac{1}{2} + \frac{t^2}{8} - \frac{t}{2} + \frac{1}{2} + \frac{(t^*)^2}{8} + \frac{t^*}{2} + 2(\alpha - 1) - t^* + t\left(1 - \frac{t}{2}\right)\right]$$

$$= \frac{G}{2}\left(2\alpha - 1 + \frac{t}{2} - \frac{3t^2}{8} - \frac{t^*}{2} + \frac{(t^*)^2}{8}\right). \qquad (19.21)$$

Differentiating (19.21) with respect to t yields the Nash-equilibrium subsidy

$$\frac{\partial W(\cdot)}{\partial t} = \frac{G}{2}\left(\frac{1}{2} - \frac{6t}{8}\right) = 0 \quad \rightarrow \quad t^N = \frac{2}{3} > 0. \tag{19.22}$$

From (19.21), if $t = t^* = t^C$

$$W(G, t^C) = \frac{G}{2}\left[2(\alpha - 1) - \frac{(t^C)^2}{4}\right]. \tag{19.23}$$

If $t = t^N$ and $t^* = t^C$

$$W(G, t = t^N, t^* = t^C)$$

$$= \frac{G}{2}\left(2\alpha - 1 + \frac{t^N}{2} - \frac{3(t^N)^2}{8} - \frac{t^C}{2} + \frac{(t^C)^2}{8}\right)$$

$$= \frac{G}{2}\left(2\alpha - 1 + \frac{2/3}{2} - \frac{3(2/3)^2}{8} - \frac{t^C}{2} + \frac{(t^C)^2}{8}\right)$$

$$= \frac{G}{2}\left(2\alpha - \frac{5}{6} - \frac{t^C}{2} + \frac{(t^C)^2}{8}\right), \tag{19.24}$$

obtained by substituting $t = t^N = 2/3$.

The difference between (19.24) and (19.23) is

$$G^N(G, t^N, t^C)$$

$$= W(G, t = t^N, t^* = t^C) - W(G, t = t^* = t^C)$$

$$= \frac{G}{2}\left(2\alpha - \frac{5}{6} - \frac{t^C}{2} + \frac{(t^C)^2}{8}\right) - \frac{G}{2}\left(2\alpha - 1 - \frac{(t^C)^2}{4}\right)$$

$$= \frac{G}{4}\left(\frac{1}{3} - t^C + \frac{3(t^C)^2}{4}\right). \tag{19.25}$$

Finally, let us compute $L^N(G, t^N, t^C)$. To do it we need first to compute $W(G, t = t^* = t^N)$, which is obtained from (19.21) when $t = t^* = t^N$ (instead of $t = t^* = t^C$) and (19.22)

$$W(G, t = t^* = t^N) = \frac{G}{4}\left(2\alpha - 1 - \frac{(t^N)^2}{4}\right) = \frac{G}{4}\left(2\alpha - \frac{10}{9}\right). \tag{19.26}$$

Therefore, the one period loss is (using (19.23) and (19.26))

$$W(G, t = t^* = t^C) - W(G, t = t^* = t^N)$$

$$= \frac{G}{2}\left(2\alpha - 1 - \frac{(t^C)^2}{4}\right) - \frac{G}{2}\left(2\alpha - \frac{10}{9}\right) = \frac{G}{4}\left(\frac{2}{9} - \frac{(t^C)^2}{2}\right). \qquad (19.27)$$

Using (19.25) and (19.27) the no-defection condition can be rewritten as

$$L^N(G, t^N, t^C) \leq \frac{\delta}{1 - \delta}\omega(G, t^N, t^C),$$

$$\frac{G}{4}\left(\frac{1}{3} - t^C + \frac{3(t^C)^2}{4}\right) \leq \frac{\delta}{1 - \delta}\frac{G}{4}\left(\frac{2}{9} - \frac{(t^C)^2}{2}\right), \qquad (19.28)$$

$$\left(\frac{1}{3} - t^C + \frac{3(t^C)^2}{4}\right) \leq \frac{\delta}{1 - \delta}\left(\frac{2}{9} - \frac{(t^C)^2}{2}\right).$$

19.9.3. Multilateral Enforcement

Country A maximizes welfare

$$W^A = d_0 + W^x(t^B_{a_1}, e^A_{a_1}) + W^x(t^C_{a_2}, e^A_{a_2}) + W^m(t^A_{b_1}, e^B_{b_1}) + W^m(t^A_{c_1}, e^C_{c_1}),$$

subject to the binding multilateral incentive constraint $G^A_{b_1} + G^A_{c_1} - \delta(L^A_{b_1} + L^A_{c_1})/(1 - \delta)$. This incentive constraint is obtained by adding up the incentive constraints (19.11) and (19.13). The incentive constraint can be rewritten by collecting all constant terms in K

$$G^A_{b_1} + G^A_{c_1} - \frac{\delta}{1 - \delta}(L^A_{b_1} + L^A_{c_1}) = -\frac{1}{1 - \delta}W^m(t^A_{b_1}, e^B_{b_1})$$

$$- \frac{1}{1 - \delta}W^m(t^A_{c_1}, e^C_{c_1}) + K.$$

The constrained maximization problem is

$$\max_{(t^A_{b_1}, t^A_{c_1})} \mathcal{L} = W^A - \lambda\left(\frac{1}{1 - \delta}W^m(t^A_{b_1}, e^B_{b_1}) + \frac{1}{1 - \delta}W^m(t^A_{c_1}, e^C_{c_1}) - K\right).$$

Assume that endowments satisfy the following symmetry relation

$$e^A_{a_1} = e^B_{b_2} = e^C_{c_1} < e^A_{a_2} = e^B_{b_1} = e^C_{c_2}$$

$$\rightarrow t^{B,N}_{a_1} = t^{C,N}_{b_2} = t^{A,N}_{c_1} < t^{C,N}_{a_2} = t^{A,N}_{b_1} = t^{B,N}_{c_2}.$$

The first order conditions $\partial \mathcal{L}/\partial t_{b_1}^A = 0$ and $\partial \mathcal{L}/\partial t_{c_1}^A = 0$ are

$$\frac{\partial W^m(t_{b_1}^A, e_{b_1}^B)}{\partial t_{b_1}^A} + \frac{\partial W^x(t_{b_1}^A, e_{b_1}^B)}{\partial t_{b_1}^A} - \frac{\lambda}{1-\delta}\frac{\partial W^m(t_{b_1}^A, e_{b_1}^B)}{\partial t_{b_1}^A} = 0,$$

$$\frac{\partial W^m(t_{c_1}^A, e_{c_1}^C)}{\partial t_{c_1}^A} + \frac{\partial W^x(t_{c_1}^A, e_{c_1}^C)}{\partial t_{c_1}^A} - \frac{\lambda}{1-\delta}\frac{\partial W^m(t_{c_1}^A, e_{c_1}^C)}{\partial t_{c_1}^A} = 0,$$

where λ is the Lagrange multiplier. Dividing both expressions to eliminate the multiplier yields

$$\left(\frac{\partial W^m(t_{b_1}^A, e_{b_1}^B)}{\partial t_{b_1}^A} + \frac{\partial W^x(t_{b_1}^A, e_{b_1}^B)}{\partial t_{b_1}^A}\right) \Big/ \left(\frac{\partial W^m(t_{c_1}^A, e_{c_1}^C)}{\partial t_{c_1}^A} + \frac{\partial W^x(t_{c_1}^A, e_{c_1}^C)}{\partial t_{c_1}^A}\right)$$

$$= \frac{\partial W^m(t_{b_1}^A, e_{b_1}^B)}{\partial t_{b_1}^A} \Big/ \frac{\partial W^m(t_{c_1}^A, e_{c_1}^C)}{\partial t_{c_1}^A},$$

which can be simplified to

$$\frac{\partial W^m(t_{b_1}^A, e_{b_1}^B)}{\partial t_{b_1}^A}\frac{\partial W^m(t_{c_1}^A, e_{c_1}^C)}{\partial t_{c_1}^A} + \frac{\partial W^x(t_{b_1}^A, e_{b_1}^B)}{\partial t_{b_1}^A}\frac{\partial W^m(t_{c_1}^A, e_{c_1}^C)}{\partial t_{c_1}^A}$$

$$= \frac{\partial W^m(t_{c_1}^A, e_{c_1}^C)}{\partial t_{c_1}^A}\frac{\partial W^m(t_{b_1}^A, e_{b_1}^B)}{\partial t_{b_1}^A} + \frac{\partial W^x(t_{c_1}^A, e_{c_1}^C)}{\partial t_{c_1}^A}\frac{\partial W^m(t_{b_1}^A, e_{b_1}^B)}{\partial t_{b_1}^A}$$

$$\rightarrow \frac{\partial W^x(t_{b_1}^A, e_{b_1}^B)}{\partial t_{b_1}^A}\frac{\partial W^m(t_{c_1}^A, e_{c_1}^C)}{\partial t_{c_1}^A} = \frac{\partial W^x(t_{c_1}^A, e_{c_1}^C)}{\partial t_{c_1}^A}\frac{\partial W^m(t_{b_1}^A, e_{b_1}^B)}{\partial t_{b_1}^A},$$

or,

$$\frac{\partial W^m(t_{b_1}^A, e_{b_1}^B)/(\partial t_{b_1}^A}{\partial W^x(t_{b_1}^A, e_{b_1}^B)/\partial t_{b_1}^A} = \frac{\partial W^x(t_{c_1}^A, e_{c_1}^C)/\partial t_{c_1}^A}{\partial W^m(t_{c_1}^A, e_{c_1}^C)/\partial t_{c_1}^A}.$$

Solving for the multilateral enforcement tariffs yields (19.14), which indicates that the tariff ratio is equal to the endowment ratio.

19.9.4. Shapley Value: Three Player Game

The ith component of the Shapley value profile can be expressed as a summation of marginal values (1) over all possible orderings $\pi \in \Pi$ of players preceding i, (2) over all coalitions S not containing player i, and (3) over all coalitions K that contain i.

Formally,

$$Sh^i(N, v) = \frac{1}{n!} \sum_{\pi \in \Pi} m(S(\pi, i), i) = \frac{1}{n!} \sum_{\pi \in \Pi} [v(S(\pi, i) \cup i) - v(S)]$$

$$= \sum_{S \in \mathcal{S}(N)} \frac{(n-s)!(s-1)!}{n!} [v(S \cup \{i\}) - v(S)]$$

$$= \sum_{K \in \mathcal{K}(N)} \frac{(n-k)!(k-1)!}{n!} [v(K) - v(K - \{i\})],$$

where n, s, and k denote the number of players in the grand coalition N, in coalition S ($i \notin S$) and coalition K ($i \in K$). $S(\pi, i)$ represents the set of players preceding agent i in the ordering π and $m(S(\pi, i), i) = v(S(\pi, i) \cup i) - v(S)$ denotes the marginal contribution of agent i belonging to coalition S. S is an element of the set of all coalitions $\mathcal{S}(N)$ of sets that do not contain player i and K is an element of the set of all coalitions $\mathcal{K}(N)$ of sets containing player i.

The summation of the components of the Shapley value profile can be shown to be equal to the value $v(N)$: $\sum Sh^i(N, v) = v(N)$.

Consider the following characteristic function $v(S)$ for a three-person cooperative game

$$v(\emptyset) = 0, \quad \begin{array}{ll} v(\{1\}) = 0, & v(\{1, 2\}) = 2, \\ v(\{2\}) = 1, & v(\{1, 3\}) = 3, \\ v(\{3\}) = 1, & v(\{2, 3\}) = 4, \end{array} \quad v(\{1, 2, 3\}) = 5,$$

where $v(\emptyset)$ is the value of the empty coalition. The Shapley value is the vector $\{Sh^1, Sh^2, Sh^3\} = \{5/6, 11/6, 14/6\}$, where $Sh^1 + Sh^2 + Sh^3 = v(\{1, 2, 3\}) = 5$, and the vectorial components are calculated as follows

$$Sh^1(3, v) = \frac{(3-1)!(1-1)!}{3!} [v(\{1\}) - v(\emptyset)]$$

$$+ \frac{(3-2)!(2-1)!}{3!} [v(\{1, 2\}) - v(\{2\})] + \frac{(3-2)!(2-1)!}{3!}$$

$$\times [v(\{1, 3\}) - v(\{3\})] + \frac{(3-3)!(3-1)!}{3!} [v(\{1, 2, 3\}) - v(\{2, 3\})].$$

The first term refers to the coalition formed by a single player (agent 1). The second and third terms refer to the 2-member coalitions in which player 1 participates, and the last term accounts for the 3-member coalition. Substituting for the payoffs described in the characteristic function v yields

$$Sh^1(3, v) = \frac{(3-2)!(2-1)!}{3!} (2-1) + \frac{(3-2)!(2-1)!}{3!} (3-1)$$

$$+ \frac{(3-3)!(3-1)!}{3!} (5-4) = \frac{1}{6} + \frac{1}{3} + \frac{1}{3} = \frac{5}{6}.$$

Similarly, for agent 2

$$Sh^2(3,v) = 0 + \frac{(3-1)!(1-1)!}{3!}[v(\{2\}) - v(\emptyset)] + \frac{(3-2)!(2-1)!}{3!}$$

$$\times [v(\{2,1\}) - v(\{1\})] + \frac{(3-2)!(2-1)!}{3!}[v(\{2,3\}) - v(\{3\})]$$

$$+ \frac{(3-3)!(3-1)!}{3!}[v(\{1,2,3\}) - v(\{1,3\})]$$

$$= \frac{(3-1)!(1-1)!}{3!}(1-0) + \frac{(3-2)!(2-1)!}{3!}(2-0)$$

$$+ \frac{(3-2)!(2-1)!}{3!}(4-1) + \frac{(3-3)!(3-1)!}{3!}(5-3)$$

$$= \tfrac{1}{3} + \tfrac{2}{6} + \tfrac{3}{6} + \tfrac{4}{6} = \tfrac{11}{6}.$$

Finally, agent 3's Shapley value is

$$Sh^3(3,v) = 0 + \frac{(3-1)!(1-1)!}{3!}[v(\{3\}) - v(\emptyset)] + \frac{(3-2)!(2-1)!}{3!}$$

$$\times [v(\{1,3\}) - v(\{1\})] + \frac{(3-2)!(2-1)!}{3!}[v(\{2,3\}) - v(\{2\})]$$

$$+ \frac{(3-3)!(3-1)!}{3!}[v(\{1,2,3\}) - v(\{1,2\})]$$

$$= \frac{(3-1)!(1-1)!}{3!}(1-0) + \frac{(3-2)!(2-1)!}{3!}(3-0)$$

$$+ \frac{(3-2)!(2-1)!}{3!}(4-1) + \frac{(3-3)!(3-1)!}{3!}(5-2)$$

$$= \tfrac{1}{3} + \tfrac{3}{6} + \tfrac{3}{6} + 1 = \tfrac{14}{6}.$$

The contribution of agent 3 to the Shapley value profile is higher than the value attached to agents 1 and 2. This relation reflects the fact that agent 3 adds more value to coalitions than agents 1 and 2.

19.9.5. Shapley Value: GATT Game

The marginal value of player $i \in \{1, \ldots, n\}$ in coalition K is given by (1) the utility $v(i)$ of a coalition consisting of single member i, plus (2) a summation term incorporating the net gains generated in the bilateral trading relations between i and other coalition members $j \in \{1, \ldots, i-1, i+1, n\}$

$$v(K \cup \{i\}) - v(K) = v(i) + \sum_{j \neq i} \left[\left(\delta_i^j - \pi_i^j\right) + \left(\delta_j^i - \pi_j^i\right) \right],$$

where the summation does not include i, which is not a member of coalition K. The Shapley value profile for Kowalczyk and Sjöström (1994) transferable utility GATT game is given by summing the marginal value of country i over all coalitions within the grand coalition N

$$
\begin{aligned}
Sh^i(N, v) &= \sum_{K \in \mathcal{K}(\mathcal{N})} \frac{(n-k)!(k-1)!}{n!}[v(K) - v(K - \{i\})] \\
&= \sum_{K \in \mathcal{K}(\mathcal{N})} \frac{(n-k)!(k-1)!}{n!} v(i) \\
&\quad + \sum_{\substack{j \neq i}}^{n}[(\delta_i^j - \pi_i^j) + (\delta_j^i - \pi_j^i)] \sum_{K \in \mathcal{K}(\mathcal{N})} \frac{(n-k)!(k-1)!}{n!} \\
&= v(i) + \frac{1}{2} \sum_{\substack{j \neq i}}^{n}[(\delta_i^j - \pi_i^j) + (\delta_j^i - \pi_j^i)],
\end{aligned}
$$

where the summation includes all n members of the grand coalition except i. We use the fact that the sum of the probabilities attached to each permutation sum to 1 when each permutation is assigned the same probability weight and a second relation proved in Kowalczyk and Sjöström (1994)

$$
\sum_{K \in \mathcal{K}(\mathcal{N})} \frac{(n-k)!(k-1)!}{n!} = \sum_{k=1}^{n} \frac{(n-k)!(k-1)!}{n!} = 1,
$$

$$
\sum_{k=1}^{n} \sum_{K \in \mathcal{K}(\mathcal{N})} \frac{(n-k)!(k-1)!}{n!} = \frac{1}{2}.
$$

The characteristic value $v(i)$ of a coalition consisting of single member i is

$$
v(i) = \bar{q}_0^i + \sum_{j=1}^{n} CS_j^i - \sum_{\substack{j \neq i}}^{n}(\delta_j^i - \pi_j^i),
$$

where the second summation includes all n members of the grand coalition except i. The first term of $v(i)$ is the endowment of good 0, the second term measures total surplus in country i if all n members of the grand coalition would price at marginal cost, and the last term includes the losses of consumer's surplus because all potential members except country i do not form part of the coalition considered. Substituting

$v(i)$ into the Shapley value yields

$$Sh^i(N,v) = \bar{q}_0^i + \sum_{j=1}^n CS_j^i - \sum_{j\neq i}(\delta_j^i - \pi_j^i) + \frac{1}{2}\sum_{j\neq i}[(\delta_i^j - \pi_i^j) + (\delta_j^i - \pi_j^i)]$$

$$= \bar{q}_0^i + \sum_{j=1}^n CS_j^i + \frac{1}{2}\sum_{j=1}^n[(\delta_i^j - \pi_i^j) - (\delta_j^i - \pi_j^i)]$$

$$= \bar{q}_0^i + \sum_{j=1}^n CS_j^i + tr^i(N,v),$$

where the second equality follows because, for $j = i$, $(\delta_i^j - \pi_i^j) - (\delta_j^i - \pi_j^i) = 0$. The endowment and consumer surplus terms represent what i would obtain if the grand coalition would be formed without side-payments. The term $tr^i(N,v)$ represents the international transfers received by i from all countries. Countries that gain more than i from i's membership make positive side-payments. Countries who gain less than i from i's membership receive positive side-payments from i. The net transfer received by i is equal to one-half of the gain from having i in the grand coalition over and above the gain reaped by i from belonging to the coalition.

The Shapley value can also be expressed as

$$Sh^i(N,v) = \bar{q}_0^i + \sum_{j=1}^n CS_j^i + \frac{1}{2}\sum_{j=1}^n[(\pi_j^i - \delta_j^i) - (\pi_i^j - \delta_i^j)].$$

References

Abrego, L., C. Perroni, J. Whalley, and R. M. Wigle (2001), 'Trade and the environment: bargaining outcomes from linked negotiations', *Review of International Economics*, 9(3), 414–28.

Acemoglu, D. (1998), 'Why do new technologies complement skills: directed technical change and wage inequality', *Quarterly Journal of Economics*, 113, 1055–89.

—— (1999), 'Changes in unemployment and wage inequality: an alternative theory and some evidence', *American Economic Review*, 89, 1259–78.

—— and J. Ventura (2002), 'The world income distribution', *Quarterly Journal of Economics*, 117(2), 659–94.

Aghion, P. and P. Howitt (1992), 'A model of growth through creative destruction', *Econometrica*, 60, 323–51.

—— (1998), *Endogenous Growth Theory*, MIT Press, Cambridge.

Aitken, B. J., G. Hanson, and A. E. Harrison (1997), 'Spillovers, foreign investment, and export behavior', *Journal of International Economics*, 43, 103–32.

—— and A. E. Harrison (1999), 'Do domestic firms benefit from direct foreign investment? Evidence from Venezuela', *American Economic Review*, 89, 605–18.

Al-Atrash, H. M. and T. Yousef (1999), 'Intra-Arab trade—is it too little?' IMF Working Paper WP/00/10.

Altonji, J. G. and D. Card (1991), 'The Effects of immigration on the labor market outcomes of less-skilled natives', in J. Abowd and R. Freeman (eds), *Immigration, Trade, and the Labor Market*, University of Chicago Press, Chicago.

Amiti, M. (1998a), 'Inter-industry trade in manufactures: does country size matter?' *Journal of International Economics*, 44(2), 231–55.

—— (1998b), 'New trade theory and industrial location in the EU: a survey of evidence', *Oxford Review of Economic Policy*, 14, 45–53.

Amsden, A. H. (1989), *Asia's New Giant: South Korea and Late Industrialization*, Oxford University Press, Oxford.

Anderson, J. E. (1979), 'A theoretical foundation for the gravity equation', *American Economic Review*, 69, 106–16.

—— (1992), 'Domino dumping, I: competitive exporters', *American Economic Review*, 82, 65–83.

—— (1993), 'Domino dumping, II: antidumping', *Journal of International Economics*, 35, 133–50.

—— and D. Marcouiller (2002), 'Insecurity and the pattern of trade: an empirical investigation', *Review of Economics and Statistics*, 84(2), 345–52.

—— and J. P. Neary (1994), 'Measuring the restrictiveness of trade policy', *World Bank Economic Review*, 8(2), 151–68.

—— (1996), 'A new approach to evaluating trade policy', *Review of Economic Studies*, 63, 107–25.

—— (2003), 'The Mercantilist index of trade policy', *International Economic Review*, forthcoming, May.

—— and L. Young (2002), 'Imperfect contract enforcement', NBER Working Paper No. 8847.

Anderson, S. P., N. Schmitt, and J.-F. Thisse (1995), 'Who benefits from antidumping legislation?' *Journal of International Economics*, 38, 321–37.

Antràs, P. (2003), *Firms, Contracts, and Trade Structure*, MIT, Mimeo.

Antweiler, W. and D. Trefler (2002), 'Increasing returns and all that: a view from trade', *American Economic Review*, 92(1), 93–119.

——B. R. Copeland, and M. Scott Taylor (2001), 'Is free trade good for the environment?' *American Economic Review*, 91(4), 877–908.

Armington, P. (1969), 'A theory of demand for products differentiated by place of production', *IMF Staff Papers*, 16, 159–76.

Arora, A., Fosfuri, A., and Gambardella, A. (2001), 'Specialized technology suppliers, international spillovers and investment: evidence from the chemical industry', *Journal of Development Economics* 65(1), 31–54.

Asilis, C. and L. A. Rivera-Batiz (2002), *Industry, Agriculture and the Environment: A General Interregional Equilibrium Model*, Columbia University, Mimeo.

Athey, S. (2001), 'Single crossing properties and the existence of pure strategy equilibria in games of incomplete information', *Econometrica*, 69(4), 861–90.

Aturupane, C., S. Djankov, and B. Hoekman (1997), 'Determinants of intra-industry trade between East and West Europe', World Bank Policy Research Working Paper 1750.

Bac, M. and H. Raff (1997), 'A theory of trade concessions', *Journal of International Economics*, 42, 483–504.

Bagwell, K. (1991), 'Optimal export policy for a new-product monopoly', *American Economic Review*, 81(5), 1156–69.

—— and R. W. Staiger (1989), 'The role for export subsidies when product quality is unknown', *Journal of International Economics*, 27, 69–89.

—— (1994), 'The sensitivity of strategic and corrective R&D policy in oligopolistic industries', *Journal of International Economics*, 36, 133–50.

—— (1997a), 'Multilateral tariff cooperation during the formation of regional free trade areas', *International Economic Review*, 38(2), 291–319.

—— (1997b), 'Multilateral tariff cooperation during the formation of customs unions', *Journal of International Economics*, 42, 91–123.

—— (1999a), 'An economic theory of GATT', *American Economic Review*, 89(1), 215–48.

—— (1999b), 'Regionalism and Multilateral tariff cooperation', in J. Piggott and A. Woodland (eds), *International Trade Policy and the Pacific Rim*, McMillan, London, England.

—— (2000a), 'GATT-think', NBER Working Paper No. 8005.

—— (2000b), 'The simple economics of labor standards and the GATT', in A. V. Deardorff and R. M. Stern (eds), *Social Dimensions of U.S. Trade Policy*, Michigan University Press, Ann Arbor.

—— (2001a), 'Strategic trade, competitive industries and agricultural trade disputes', *Economics and Politics*, 13(2), 113–28.

—— (2001b), 'Domestic policies, national sovereignty and international economic institutions', *Quarterly Journal of Economics*, 116(2), 519–62.

—— (2001c), 'The WTO as a mechanism for securing market access property rights. Implications for global labor and environmental issues', *Journal of Economic Perspectives*, 15(3), 69–88.

—— (2003), *The Economics of the World Trading System*, MIT Press, Cambridge, MA.

Balassa, B. (1965), 'Tariff protection in industrial countries: an evaluation', *Journal of Political Economy*, 73(6), 573–94.

Baldwin Snr., R. E. (1969), 'The case against infant-industry protection', *Journal of Political Economy*, 77, 295–305.

—— (1985), *The Political Economy of U.S. Import Policy*, MIT Press, Cambridge, MA.

—— T.-J. Chen, and D. Nelson (1995), *Political Economy of U.S.-Taiwan Trade*, Michigan University Press, Ann Arbor.

Baldwin Jnr., R. E. (1995), 'A Domino theory of regionalism', in R. Baldwin, P. Haarparanta, and J. Kianden (eds), *Expanding Membership of the European Union*, Cambridge University Press, Cambridge.

—— (1997), 'The causes of regionalism', *World Economy*, 20(7), 865–88.

—— (1999), 'The core-periphery model with forward-looking expectations', CEPR Discussion Paper 2085, Center for Economic Policy Research.

—— H. Braconier, and R. Forslid (2001), *Multinationals, Endogenous Growth and Technological Spillovers: Theory and Evidence*, Graduate Institute of International Studies, Geneve, Mimeo.

—— and H. Flam (1989), 'Strategic trade policy in the market for 30–40 seat commuter aircraft', *Weltwirtschaftlisches Archiv*, 125(3), 485–500.

—— and P. R. Krugman (1988a), 'Market access and international competition: a simulation study of 16k random access memories', in R. C. Feenstra (ed.), *Empirical Methods for International Trade*, MIT Press, Cambridge.

—— (1988b), 'Industrial policy and international competition in wide-bodied jet aircraft', in R. E. Baldwin (ed.), *Trade Policy Issues and Empirical Analysis*, University of Chicago Press, Chicago.

—— and G. I. P. Ottaviano (2001), 'Multiproduct multinationals and reciprocal FDI jumping', *Journal of International Economics*, 54, 429–48.

—— and J. W. Steagall (1994), 'An analysis of ITC decisions in antidumping, countervailing duty and safeguard cases', *Weltwirtschaftlisches Archiv*, 130(2), 290–308.

—— and A. Venables (1995), 'Regional economic integration', in G. Grossman and K. Rogoff (eds), *Handbook of International Economics*, North Holland, Amsterdam.

Ballard, C., J. Shoven, and J. Whalley (1985), 'General equilibrium computations of the marginal welfare costs of taxes in the United States', *American Economic Review*, 75(1), 128–38.

Barrell, R. and N. Pain (1999), 'Trade restraints and japanese direct investment flows', *European Economic Review*, 43(1), 29–45.

Barret, S. (1994), 'Strategic environmental policy and international trade', *Journal of Public Economics*, 54, 324–38.

Barreto, R. A. and K. Kobayashi (2001), *Economic Integration and Endogenous Growth Revisited: Procompetitive Gains from Trade in Goods and the Long Run Benefits to the Exchange of Ideas*, Adelaide University, Mimeo.

Barro, R. J. and X. Sala-i-Martin (1998), *Economic Growth*, MIT Press, Cambridge.

Barros, P. P. and L. Cabral (1994), 'Merger policy in open economies', *European Economic Review*, 38, 1041–55.

Bayard, T. O. and K. A. Elliot (1994), *Reciprocity and Retaliation in U.S. Trade Policy*, Institute for International Economics, Washington, DC.

Bayoumi, T., D. T. Coe, and E. Helpman (1999), 'R&D spillovers and global growth', *Journal of International Economics*, 47, 399–428.

Becker, G. S., (1964), *Human Capital: A Theoretical and Empirical Analysis, with Special Reference to Education*. 2nd ed, Columbia University Press, New York.

—— (1983), 'A theory of competition among pressure groups for political influence', *Quarterly Journal of Economics*, 98(3), 371–400.

Belderbos, E. A. (1997a), *Japanese Electronics Multinationals and Strategic Trade Policies*, Oxford University Press, Oxford and New York.

—— and L. Sleuwaegen (1996), 'Japanese firms and the decision to invest abroad: business groups and regional core networks', *Review of Economics and Statistics*, 78(2), 214–20.

—— (1998), 'Tariff jumping DFI and export substitution: Japanese electronics firms in Europe', *International Journal of Industrial Organisation*, 16(5), 601–38.

Ben-David, D. (1993), 'Equalizing exchange: trade liberalization and income convergence', *Quarterly Journal of Economics*, 108, 653–79.

—— (1996), 'Trade and convergence among countries', *Journal of International Economics*, 40, 279–98.

—— (2001), 'Trade liberalization and income convergence: a comment', *Journal of International Economics*, 55(1), 229–34.

Benkard, C. L. (2000), 'Learning and forgetting: the dynamics of aircraft production', *American Economic Review*, 90, 1034–54.

Bergsten, C. F. (1997), 'Open regionalism', Working Paper No. 97/3. Washington DC.: Institute for International Economics.

Bergstrand, J. H. (1985), 'The gravity equation in international trade: some microeconomic foundations and empirical evidence', *Review of Economics and Statistics*, 67, 474–81.

—— (1989), 'The generalized gravity equation, monopolistic competition and the factor-proportions theory in international trade', *Review of Economics and Statistics*, 71, 143–53.

Bernard, A. B., J. Eaton, J. B. Jensen, and S. Kortum (2000), 'Plants and productivity in international trade', NBER Working Paper No. 7688.

—— and J. B. Jensen (1995), 'Exporters, jobs, and wages in U.S. manufacturing: 1976–1987', *Brookings Papers on Economic Activity*, Microeconomics, 67–112.

—— (1999), 'Exceptional exporter performance: cause, effect, or both?' *Journal of International Economics*, 47, 1–25.

—— (2001a), 'Why some firms export', NBER Working Paper No. 8349.

—— (2001b), 'Exporting and productivity: the importance of reallocation', NBER Working Paper No. 7135.

Bernheim, D. B. and M. D. Whinston (1986a), 'Menu auctions, resource allocation, and economic influence', *Quarterly Journal of Economics*, 101, 1–31.

—— (1986b), 'Common agency', *Econometrica*, 54(4), 923–42.

Bernhofen, D. M. and J. C. Brown (2001), *A Direct Test of the Theory of Comparative Advantage: The Case of Japan*, Clark University, Mimeo.

Bernstein, J. I. and P. Mohnen (1998), 'International R&D spillovers between U.S. and Japanese R&D intensive sectors', *Journal of International Economics*, 44, 315–38.

Berry, S., J. Levinsohn, and A. Pakes (1995), 'Automobile prices in market equilibrium', *Econometrica*, 63(4), 841–90.

—— (1999), 'Voluntary export restraints in automobiles: evaluating a trade policy', *American Economic Review*, 89(3), 400–30.

Bhagwati, J. N. (1958), 'Immiserizing growth: a geometric note', *Review of Economic Studies*, 25, 201–05.

—— (1969), *Trade, Tariffs, and Growth*, MIT Press, Cambridge, MA.

—— (1971), 'The Generalized theory of distortions and welfare', in J. N. Bhagwati, R. W. Jones, R. A. Mundell, and J. Vanek (eds), *Trade, Balance of Payments, and Growth: Papers in International Economics in Honor of Charles P. Kindleberger*, North Holland, Amsterdam.

——(1982), 'Directly-Unproductive Profit-Seeking (DUP) activities', *Journal of Political Economy*, 90, 988–1002.

——(1988), *Protectionism*, MIT Press, Cambridge, MA.

——(1993), 'Regionalism and multilateralism: an overview', in J. de Melo and A. Panagariya (eds), *New Dimensions in Regional Integration*, Cambridge University Press, Cambridge.

——R. A. Brecher, E. Dinopoulos, and T. N. Srinivasan (1987), 'Quid Pro Quo foreign investment and welfare: a political-economy-theoretic model', *Journal of Development Economics*, 27, 127–38.

——P. Krishna, and A. Panagariya (eds) (1999), *Trading Blocks: Alternative Approaches to Analyzing Preferential Trade Agreements*, MIT Press, Cambridge, MA and London.

—— and A. O. Krueger (1995), *The Dangerous Drift to Preferential Trade Agreements*, American Enterprise Institute for Public Policy Research, Washington DC.

—— and A. Panagariya (1996), 'Preferential trading areas and multilateralism: strangers, friends or foes?' in J. N. Bhagwati and A. Panagariya (eds), *The Economics of Preferential Trading Agreements*, American Enterprise Institute Press, Washington DC.

—— and V. K. Ramaswami (1963), 'Domestic distortions, tariffs and the theory of optimum subsidy', *Journal of Political Economy*, 71, 44–50.

—— and C. Rodriguez (1975), 'Welfare-theoretical analyses of the brain drain', *Journal of Development Economics*, 2(3), 195–221.

—— and T. N. Srinivasan (1976), 'Optimal trade policy and compensation under endogenous uncertainty: the phenomenon of market disruption', *Journal of International Economics*, 6, 317–36.

——(1980), 'Revenue-seeking: a generalization of the theory of tariffs', *Journal of Political Economy*, 88, 1069–87.

Bhagwati, J. and T. N. Srinivasan. (1996), 'Trade and the environment: does environment diversity detract from the case for free trade?', in J. Bhagwati and R. E. Hudec (eds), *Fair Trade and Harmonization: Prerequisites for Free Trade?*, Vol. 1, Economic Analysis, MIT Press, Cambridge.

Binmore, K., A. Rubinstein, and A. Wolinsky (1986), 'The Nash bargaining solution in economic modeling', *Rand Journal of Economics*, 17, 176–88.

Boltuck, R. and R. Litan (eds) (1991), *Down in the Dumps: Administration of the Unfair Trade Laws*, Brookings Institution, Washington, DC.

Black, D. and V. Henderson (1999), 'A theory of urban growth', *Journal of Political Economy*, 107, 252–84.

Bliss, C. (1996), 'Trade and competition policy', in Jagdish N. Bhagwati and Robert E. Hudec (eds), *Fair Trade and Harmonization: Prerequisites for Free Trade?* vol. 1, MIT Press, Cambridge, MA.

Blomström, M. (1989), *Foreign Investment and Spillovers*, Routledge, London.

—— and A. Kokko (1998), 'Multinational Corporations and spillovers', *Journal of Economic Surveys*, 12, 247–77.

Blonigen, B. A. (2002), 'Tariff-jumping antidumping duties', *Journal of International Economics*, 57, 31–49.

—— and R. C. Feenstra (1997), 'Protectionist threats and foreign direct investment', in R. C. Feenstra (ed.), *Effects of U.S. Trade Protection and Promotion Policies*, University of Chicago Press, Chicago.

—— and Y. Ohno (1998), 'Endogenous protection, foreign direct investment and protection-building trade', *Journal of International Economics*, 46(2), 205–27.

Bond, E. W. and C. Syropoulos (1996a), 'The size of trading blocks, market power and world welfare effects', *Journal of International Economics*, 40(3–4), 411–37.

—— (1996b), 'Trading blocks and the sustainability of interregional cooperation', in M. B. Canzoneri, W. J. Ethier, and V. Grilli (eds), *The New Transatlantic Economy*, Cambridge University Press, Cambridge.

Borensztein, E., J. De Gregorio, and J.-W. Lee (1998), 'How does foreign direct investment affect economic growth?' *Journal of International Economics*, 45, 115–35.

Borjas, G. J. (1987), 'Self-selection and the earnings of immigrants', *American Economic Review*, 77(4), 531–53.

—— (1999), *Heaven's Door: Immigration Policy and the American Economy*, Princeton University Press, Princeton.

—— R. B. Freeman, and L. F. Katz (1996), 'Searching for the effect of immigration on the labor market', *American Economic Review*, 86(2), 246–51.

Bowen, H. P., A. Hollander, and J.-M. Viaene (1998), *Applied International Trade Analysis*, University of Michigan Press, Ann Arbor.

—— E. Leamer, and L. Sveikauskas (1987), 'Multicountry, multifactor tests of the factor abundance theory', *American Economic Review*, 77(5), 791–809.

Brainard, L. S. (1993), 'A simple theory of multinational corporations with a trade-off between proximity and concentration', NBER Working Paper No. 4269.

—— (1997), 'An empirical assessment of the proximity-concentration tradeoff between multinational sales and trade', *American Economic Review*, 87, 520–44.

—— and D. Martimort (1997), 'Strategic trade policy with incompletely informed policy-makers', *Journal of International Economics*, 42, 33–65.

—— and T. Verdier (1994), 'Lobbying and adjustment in declining industries', *European Economic Review*, 38(3), 586–95.

Brander, J. A. (1981), 'Intra-industry trade in identical commodities', *Journal of International Economics*, 11, 1–14.

—— and P. R. Krugman (1983), 'A reciprocal dumping model of international trade', *Journal of International Economics*, 15, 313–23.

—— and B. J. Spencer (1984a), 'Trade warfare: tariffs and cartels', *Journal of International Economics*, 16, 227–42.

—— (1984b), 'Tariff protection and imperfect competition', In H. Kierzkowski (ed.), *Monopolistic Competition and International Trade*, Oxford University Press, Oxford.

—— (1985), 'Exports subsidies and international market share rivalry', *Journal of International Economics*, 18, 83–100.

Branstetter, L. G. (2001), 'Are knowledge spillovers international or intranational in scope? Microeconometric evidence from the U.S. and Japan', *Journal of International Economics*, 53, 53–79.

Braunerhjelm, P., R. Faini, V. Norman, F. Ruane, and P. Seabright (2000), *Integration and the Regions of Europe: How the Right Policies Can Prevent Polarization*, CEPR, London.

Bresnaham, T. (1981), 'The relationship between price and marginal cost in the U.S. automobile industry', *Journal of Econometrics*, 17, 201–27.

Brezis, E. S., P. R. Krugman, and D. Tsiddon (1993), 'Leapfrogging in international competition: a theory of cycles in national technological leadership', *American Economic Review*, 83(5), 1211–19.

Brown, D. K. (2001), 'Labor standards: where do they belong on the international trade agenda?' *Journal of Economic Perspectives*, 15(3), 89–112.

—— A. V. Deardorff, and R. M. Stern (1996), 'International labor standards and trade: a theoretical analysis', in J. N. Bhagwati and R. E. Hudec (eds), *Fair Trade and Harmonization*, MIT Press, Cambridge, MA.

Browning L. D., and J. C. Shetler (2000), *Sematech. Saving the U.S. Semiconductor Industry*, Texas A&M University Press, Texas.

Brülhart, M. and J. Torstensson (1996), 'Regional integration, scale economies and industry location', CEPR Discussion Paper 1435, Center for Economic Policy Research.

Buckley, P. J. and M. Casson (1976), *The Future of the Multinational Enterprise*, Macmillan, London.

Buigues, P. and A. Jacquemin (1994), 'Foreign direct investment and exports to the European Community', in M. Mason and D. Encarnacion (eds), *Does Ownership Matter? Japanese Multinationals in Europe*, Oxford University Press, Oxford and New York.

Bulow, J. L., J. D. Geanakoplos, and P. D. Klemperer (1985), 'Multimarket oligopoly: strategic substitutes and complements', *Journal of Political Economy*, 93(3), 488–511.

Cadot, O. and D. Desruelle (1998), 'R&D: who does r, who does d?' *Journal of International Economics*, 46, 87–103.

—— J. de Melo and M. Olearraga (2001), 'Can Regionalism Easy the Pain of Multilateral Trade Liberalization?', *European Economic Review*, 45: 27–44.

——, ——, —— (2003), 'The Protectionist Bias of Duty Drawbacks: Evidence from Mercosur', *Journal of International Economics*, 59: 161–82.

Campa, J. and L. Goldberg (1997), 'The evolving external orientation of manufacturing industries: evidence from four countries', *Federal Reserve Bank of New York Economic Policy Review*, 4, 79–99.

Cantwell, J. and R. Mudambi (2001), *MNE Competence-Creating Subsidiary Mandates: An Empirical Investigation*, University of Reading, Mimeo.

Caplin, A. and K. Krishna (1988), 'Tariffs and the most-favored-nation clause: a game-theoretic approach', *Seoul Journal of Economics*, 1(3), 267–89.

Card, D. (2001), 'Immigrant flows, native outflows, and the local labor market impacts of higher immigration,' *Journal of Labor Economics*, 19(1), 22–64.

—— and J. DiNardo (2000), 'Immigrant inflows and the location decisions of the native-born: do immigrant inflows push the native-born out?' *American Economic Review*, 90(2), 360–67.

Carlsson, B. (1983), 'Industrial subsidies in Sweden: macroeconomic effects and an international comparison', *Journal of Industrial Economics*, XXXII(1), 1–23.

Carmichael, C. M. (1987), 'The control of export credit subsidies and its welfare consequences', *Journal of International Economics*, 23, 1–19.

—— (1991), 'The interdependence of firm and government behaviour: Boeing and Eximbank', *Applied Economics*, 23, 107–12.

Carraro, C. and M. Galeotti (1997), 'Economic growth, international competitiveness, and environmental policies: R&D and innovation strategies with the WARM model', *Energy Economics*, 19, 2–28.

Carrington, W. J. and E. Detragiache (1998), 'How big is the brain drain? IMF Working Paper WP/98/102.

Cassing, J. H. and A. L. Hillman (1986), 'Shifting comparative advantage and senescent industry collapse', *American Economic Review*, 76, 516–23.

Caves, R. E. (1996), *Multinational Enterprise and Economic Analysis*, 2nd edn, Cambridge University Press, Cambridge.

Che, Y.-K. and I. L. Gale (1998), 'Caps and political lobbying', *American Economic Review*, 88(3), 643–51.

Chiswick, B. (1978), 'The effect of Americanization on the earnings of foreign-born men', *Journal of Political Economy*, 86(5), 897–921.

—— (1999), 'Are immigrants favorably self-selected?' *American Economic Review*, 89, 181–5.

Cho, I. K. and D. M. Kreps (1987), 'Signalling games and stable equilibria', *Quarterly Journal of Economics*, 102, 179–221.

Choi, J. P. (1991), 'Dynamic R&D competition under hazard-rate uncertainty', *RAND Journal of Economics*, 22, 596–610.

Choi Y.-S. and Krishna, P. (2001), *The Factor Content of Trade: An Empirical Test*, Brown University, Mimeo.

Choksi, A. M. and D. Papageorgiou (eds) (1986), *Economic Liberalization in Developing Countries*, Basil Blackwell, Oxford.

Clarida, R. H. (1993), 'Entry, dumping, and shakeout', *American Economic Review*, 83(1), 181–202.

Clerides, S., S. Lach, and J. Tybout (1998), 'Is "Learning-by-Exporting" important? Micro-dynamic evidence from Colombia, Mexico and Morocco', *Quarterly Journal of Economics*, 113(3), 903–47.

Coase, R. (1960), 'The problem of social cost', *Journal of Law and Economics*, 3, 1–44.

Coe, D. and E. Helpman (1995), 'International R&D spillovers', *European Economic Review*, 39, 859–87.

Coe, D., E. Helpman, and A. W. Hoffmaister (1997), 'North-South R&D spillovers', *Economic Journal*, 107, 134–49.

—— and A. W. Hoffmaister (1999), 'Are there international R&D spillovers among randomly matched trade partners? A response to Keller', IMF Working Paper WP/99/18.

Combes, P.-P. and M. Lafourcade (2001), 'Transport cost decline and regional inequalities: evidence from France', *Discussion Paper No.* 2894, The Centre for Economic Policy Research (CEPR), London.

Copeland, B. R. and M. Scott Taylor (1994), 'North-South trade and the environment', *Quarterly Journal of Economics*, 109(3), 755–87.

—— (1995), 'Trade and transboundary pollution', *American Economic Review*, 85(4), 716–37.

Cordella, T. and J. J. Gabszewicz (1997), 'Comparative advantage under oligopoly', *Journal of International Economics*, 43, 333–46.

Corden, W. M. (1966), 'The structure of a tariff system and the effective protection rate', *Journal of Political Economy*, 74(3), 221–37.

—— (1997), *Trade Policy and Economic Welfare*. 2nd edn, Clarendon Press, Oxford.

Curry, D. J. and P. C. Riesz (1988), 'Prices and price/quality relationships: a longitudinal analysis', *Journal of Marketing*, 52, 36–51.

D'Aspremont, C. and A. Jacquemin (1988), 'Cooperative and non-cooperative R&D in duopoly with spillovers', *American Economic Review*, 78, 1133–7.

Davis, S. and A. McGuinness (1982), 'Dumping at less than marginal cost', *Journal of International Economics*, 12, 169–82.

Davis, D. R. (1995), 'Intra-industry trade: a Heckscher-Ohlin-Ricardo Approach', *Journal of International Economics*, 39, 201–26.

—— (1998), 'The home market, trade and industrial structure', *American Economic Review*, 88(5), 1264–76.

—— and D. E. Weinstein (1999), 'Economic geography and regional production structure: an empirical investigation', *European Economic Review*, 43, 379–407.

—— (2001), 'An account of global factor trade', *American Economic Review*, 91(5), 1423–53.

—— (2003a), 'Market access, economic geography, and comparative advantage: an empirical assessment', *Journal of International Economics*, 59(1).

—— (2002a), 'The mystery of the excess trade (Balances)', *American Economic Review*, 92(2), 170–4.

—— (2002b), Bones, Bombs, and Break Points: The Geography of Economic Activity. *American Economic Review*, 92(5): 1269–89.

—— (2002c), 'Technological superiority and the losses from migration', Working Paper, Columbia University.

—— (2003b), 'The factor content of trade', in K. Choi and J. Harrigan (eds), *Handbook of International Trade*, Basil Blackwell, New York.

—— S. C. Bradford, and K. Shimpo (1997), 'Using international and Japanese regional data to determine when the Factor Abundance theory of trade works', *American Economic Review*, 87(3), 421–46.

De Gregorio, J. (1992), 'Economic growth in Latin America', *Journal of Development Economics*, 39, 54–84.

Deardorff, A. V. (1979), 'Weak links in the chain of Comparative Advantage', *Journal of International Economics*, 9(2), 197–209.

—— (1980), 'General validity of the Law of Comparative Advantage', *Journal of Political Economy*, 88, 941–57.

—— (1998), 'Determinants of bilateral trade: does gravity work in a neoclassical world?' in J. A. Frankel (ed.), *The Regionalization of the World Economy*, University of Chicago Press, Chicago.

—— (2001), 'Fragmentation in simple trade models', *The North American Journal of Economics and Finance*, 12(2), 121–37.

—— and R. M. Stern (1994), 'Multilateral trade negotiations and preferential trading arrangements', in A. V. Deardorff and R. M. Stern (eds), *Analytical and Negotiating Issues in the Global Trading System*, University of Michigan Press, Ann Arbor, MI.

—— and R. M. Stern (1998), *Measurement of Nontariff Barriers*, University of Michigan, Ann Arbor.

Dekle, R. and J. Eaton (1999), 'Agglomeration and land rents: evidence from the prefectures', *Journal of Urban Economics*, 46(2), 200–14.

Destler, I. M. (1995), *American Trade Politics*, 3rd ed. Institute for International Economics, Washington, DC.

Dertouzos, M. L., Lester, R. K., and R. M. Solow (1989), *Made in America: Regaining the Productive Edge*, Harper Perennial, New York.

Dick, A. R. (1993), 'Strategic trade policy and welfare: the empirical consequences of cross-ownership', *Journal of International Economics*, 35, 227–49.

—— (1994), 'Does import protection act as export promotion? evidence from the United States', *Oxford Economic Papers*, 46, 83–101.

DiNardo, J., N. Fortin, and T. Lemieux (1996), 'Labor market institutions and the distribution of wages, 1973–1992: a semi-parametric approach', *Econometrica*, 64, 1001–44.

Dinopoulos, E. (1989), 'Quid Pro Quo foreign investment', *Economics and Politics*, I, 145–60.

—— and M. Kreinin (1988), 'Effects of the U.S.-Japan auto VER on European prices and on U.S. welfare', *The Review of Economics and Statistics*, 70(3), 484–91.

—— T. R. Lewis, and D. E. M. Sappington (1995), 'Optimal industrial targeting with unknown learning by doing', *Journal of International Economics*, 38, 275–95.

—— and P. Segerstrom (1999), 'The dynamic effects of contingent tariffs', *Journal of International Economics*, 47, 191–222.

—— (1984), 'International trade policies for oligopolistic industries', *Economic Journal*, 94 (Supplement), 1–16.

—— (1987*a*), 'Strategic aspects of trade policy', in T. Bewley (ed.), *Advances in Economic Theory. Fifth World Congress*, Cambridge University Press, New York.

—— (1987*b*), 'Trade and insurance with moral hazard', *Journal of International Economics*, 23(3–4), 201–20.

—— (1989*a*), 'Trade and insurance with adverse selection', *Review of Economic Studies*, 56(2), 235–48.

—— (1989*b*), 'Trade and insurance with imperfectly observed outcomes', *Quarterly Journal of Economics*, 54(1), 195–203.

—— (1990), 'Trade policy with imperfect information', in R. Jones and A. Krueger (eds), *The Political Economy of International Trade*, Basil Blackwell, Cambridge, MA.

—— and G. M. Grossman (1986), 'Targeted export promotion with several oligopolistic industries', *Journal of International Economics*, 21, 233–49.

—— G. M. Grossman, and E. Helpman (1997), 'Common agency and coordination: general theory and application to government policy making', *Journal of Political Economy*, 105(4), 752–69.

—— and V. Norman (1980), *Theory of International Trade*, Cambridge University Press, Cambridge.

—— and J. E. Stiglitz (1977), 'Monopolistic competition and optimum product diversity', *American Economic Review*, 67, 297–303.

Dollar, D. and A. Kraay (2002), 'Growth is good for the poor', *Journal of Economic growth*, 7(3), 193–225.

—— (2001), 'Trade, growth and poverty', World Bank Policy Research Working Paper No. 2615.

—— and K. Sokoloff (1990), 'Patterns of productivity growth in south Korean manufacturing industries, 1963–1979', *Journal of Development Economics*, 33, 309–27.

—— E. Wolff, and W. Baumol (1988), 'The Factor Price equalization model and industry labor productivity: an empirical test across countries', in, R. C. Feenstra (ed.), *Empirical Methods for International Trade*, MIT Press, Cambridge.

Dumais, G., G. Ellison and E. Glaeser (1997). 'Geographic concentration as a dynamic process', *Review of Economics and Statistics*, 84(2), 193–204.

Dornbusch, R., S. Fischer, and P. A. Samuelson (1977*a*), 'Comparative Advantage, trade, and payments in a Ricardian model with a continuum of goods', *American Economic Review*, 67, 823–39.

—— (1977*b*), 'Heckscher-Ohlin trade theory with a continuum of goods', *Quarterly Journal of Economics*, 95, 203–24.

Duleep, H. O. and M. C. Regets (1999), 'Immigrants and human capital investment', *American Economic Review*, 89(2), 186–91.

Dunning, J. (1977), 'Trade, location of economic activity and MNE: a search for an eclectic approach', in B. Ohlin, P.-O. Hesselborn, and P. M. Wijkman (eds), *The International Allocation of Economic Activity*, Macmillan, London.

Eaton, J. and Z. Eckstein (1997), 'Cities and growth: theory and evidence from France and Japan', *Regional Science and Urban Economics*, 27, 443–74.

—— and M. Engers (1992), 'Sanctions', *Journal of Political Economy*, 100(5), 899–928.

—— (1999), 'Sanctions: some simple analytics', *American Economic Review*, 89(2), 409–14.

—— and G. M. Grossman (1986), 'Optimal trade and industrial policy under oligopoly', *Quarterly Journal of Economics*, 101, 383–406.

—— and S. Kortum (1996), 'Trade in ideas: patenting and productivity in the OECD', *Journal of International Economics*, 40, 251–78.

—— (1999), 'International technology diffusion: theory and measurement', *International Economic Review*, 40(3), 537–70.

—— (2002), Technology, Geography, and Trade. *Econometrica*, 70(5), 1741–79.

Edwards, S. (1998), 'Openness, productivity and growth: what do we really know?' *Economic Journal*, 108(447), 383–98.

Eichengreen, B. and H. Van der Ven (1984), 'US antidumping policies: the case of steel', in R. Baldwin and A. Krueger (eds), *The Structure and Evolution of Recent US Trade Policy*, University of Chicago Press, Chicago.

Ellingsen, T. and K. Wärneryd (1998), 'Foreign direct investment and the political economy of protection', *International Economic Review*, 40(2), 357–79.

Engel, C. and J. H. Rogers (1996), 'How wide is the border?' *American Economic Review*, 86(5), 1112–25.

Ethier, W (1982a), 'National and international returns to scale in the Modern Theory of International Trade', *American Economic Review*, 72, 389–405.

—— (1982b), 'Dumping', *Journal of Political Economy*, 90(3), 487–506.

—— (1984), 'Higher dimensional issues in trade theory', in R. Jones and P. B. Kenen (eds), *Handbook of International Economics*, 1, North-Holland, Amsterdam.

—— (1986), 'The multinational firm', *Quarterly Journal of Economics*, 101, 805–33.

—— (1998a), 'The new regionalism', *Economic Journal*, 108, 1149–61.

—— (1998b), 'Regionalism in a multilateral world', *Journal of Political Economy*, 106(6), 1214–45.

—— and J. R. Markusen (1998), 'Multinational firms, technology diffusion and trade', *Journal of International Economics*, 41, 1–28.

Evenett, S. J. and W. Keller (2002), 'On theories explaining the success of the Gravity equation', *Journal of Political Economy*, 110(2), 281–316.

Falvey, R. (1981), 'Commercial policy and intra-industry trade', *Journal of International Economics*, 11, 495–511.

—— and H. Kierzkowski (1987), 'Product quality, intra-industry trade and (Im)perfect competition', in H. Kierzkowski (ed.), *Protection and Competition in International Trade*, Basil Blackwell, Oxford.

Farrell, J. and C. Shapiro (1990), 'Horizontal mergers: an equilibrium analysis', *American Economic Review*, 80(1), 107–26.

Feeney, J. and A. Hillman (2001), 'Privatization and the political economy of strategic trade policy', *International Economic Review*, 42(2), 535–56.

Feenstra, R. C. (1984), 'Voluntary export restraint in U.S. autos, 1980–81: quality, employment, and welfare effects', in R. E. Baldwin and A. O. Krueger (eds), *The Structure and Evolution of Recent U.S. Trade Policies*, University of Chicago Press, Chicago.

—— (1988), 'Quality change under trade restraints in Japanese autos', *Quarterly Journal of Economics*, 103(1), 131–46.

References

—— (1996), 'U.S. imports, 1972–1994: data and concordances', NBER Working Paper No. 5515.

—— (1998), 'Integration of trade and disintegration of production in the global economy', *Journal of Economic Perspectives*, 12, 31–50.

—— (2003), *Advanced International Trade: Theory and Evidence*, Princeton University Press, Princeton.

—— and J. N. Bhagwati (1982), 'Tariff seeking and the efficient tariff', in J. N. Bhagwati (ed.), *Import Competition and Response*, University of Chicago Press, Chicago and London.

—— and G. H. Hanson (2002), 'Global production sharing and rising inequality: a survey of trade and wages', in K. Choi and J. Harrigan (eds), *Handbook of International Trade*, Basil Blackwell, New York.

—— G. G. Hamilton, and D.-S. Huang (2001), 'The organization of the Taiwanese and south Korean economies: a comparative equilibrium analysis', in A. Casella and J. E. Rauch (eds), *Networks and Markets*, Russell Sage Foundation, New York.

—— and —— (2004), *Emerging Economies, Divergent Paths: Business Groups and Economic Organization in South Korea and Taiwan*, Cambridge University Press, Cambridge.

—— T.-H. Yang, and G. G. Hamilton (1999), 'Business groups and product variety in trade: evidence from South Korea, Taiwan and Japan', *Journal of International Economics*, 48(1), 71–100.

—— J. R. Markusen, and A. K. Rose (2001), 'Using the gravity equation to differentiate among alternative theories of trade', *Canadian Journal of Economics*, 34(2), 430–47.

—— and A. K. Rose (2000), 'Putting things in order: trade dynamics and product cycles', *Review of Economics and Statistics*, 82(3), 369–82.

Fernandez, R. and J. Portes (1998), 'Returns to regionalism: an analysis of nontraditional gains from regional trade agreements', *World Bank Economic Review*, 12(2), 197–220.

Findlay, R. (1995), *Factor Proportions, Trade, and Growth*, MIT Press, Cambridge, MA.

—— and S. Wellisz (1982), 'Endogenous tariffs, the political economy of trade restrictions, and welfare', in J. N. Bhagwati (ed.), *Import Competition and Response*, University of Chicago Press, Chicago and London.

Fink, C. and C. A. Primo Braga (1999), 'How stronger protection of intellectual property rights affects international trade flows?' World Bank Research Paper No. 2051.

Fitzgerald, B. and T. Monson (1989), 'Preferential credit and insurance as means to promote exports', *World Bank Research Observer*, 4, 89–114.

Flam, H. (1994), 'EC members fighting about surplus: VERs, FDI, and Japanese cars', *Journal of International Economics*, 36, 117–31.

—— and E. Helpman (1987), 'Vertical product differentiation and North-South trade', *American Economic Review*, 77, 810–22.

Fosfuri, A., M. Motta, and T. Ronde (2001), 'Foreign direct investment and spillovers through workers' mobility', *Journal of International Economics*, 53, 205–22.

Francois, J. F. and C. R. Shiells (1994), 'AGE models of north American free trade', in J. F. Francois and C. R. Shiells (eds), *Modeling Trade Policy: Applied General Equilibrium Assessments of North American Free Trade*, Cambridge University Press, Cambridge.

Frankel, J. A. (1997), *Regional Trading Blocks in the World Economic System*, Institute for International Economics, Washington, DC.

—— (1998), *The Regionalization of the World Economy*, Chicago-University Press, Chicago.

—— and D. Romer (1999), 'Does trade cause growth?' *American Economic Review*, 89(3), 379–99.

—— and A. K. Rose (2002), 'An estimate of the effect of common currencies on trade and income', *Quarterly Journal of Economics*, 117(2), 437–66.

—— E. Stein, and S. J. Wei (1995), 'Trading blocs and the Americas: the natural, the unnatural, and the super-natural', *Journal of Development Economics*, 47(1), 61–95.

—— (1998), 'Continental trading blocs: are they natural or supernatural', in J. E. Frankel (ed.), *The Regionalization of the World Economy*, Chicago University Press, Chicago.

Fudenberg, D. and J. Tirole (1984), 'The fat cat effect, the puppy dog ploy, and the lean and hungry look', *American Economic Review*, 74, 361–8.

Fujita, M. (1988), 'A Monopolistic competition model of spatial agglomeration: a differentiated product approach', *Regional Science and Urban Economics*, 18(1), 87–124.

—— P. R. Krugman, and A. J. Venables (1999), *The Spatial Economy: Cities, Regions, and International Trade*, MIT Press, Cambridge, MA.

—— and J.-F. Thisse (2002), *Economics of Agglomeration: Cities, Industrial Location and Regional Growth*, Cambridge University Press, Cambridge.

Fuller, W. (1987), *Measurement Error Models*, Wiley, New York.

Fung, K. C. (1991), 'Characteristics of Japanese industrial groups and their potential impact on U.S.-Japanese trade', in R. E. Baldwin (ed.), *Empirical Studies of Commercial Policy*, University of Chicago Press, Chicago.

Furusawa, T. (1999), 'The negotiation of sustainable tariffs', *Journal of International Economics*, 48, 321–45.

—— and E. L.-C. Lai (1999), 'Adjustment costs and gradual trade liberalization', *Journal of International Economics*, 49, 333–61.

Gabaix, X. (1999), 'Zipf's law for cities: an explanation', *Quarterly Journal of Economics*, 114, 739–67.

Gabor, A. and C. Granger (1965), 'The pricing of new products', *Scientific Business*, 3, 141–50.

Gang, I. N. and F. Rivera-Batiz (1994), 'Labor market effects of immigration in the United States and Europe: substitution vs. complementarity', *Journal of Population Economics*, 7, 157–75.

Gatsios, K. (1990), 'Preferential tariffs and the "Most favoured nation" principle', *Journal of International Economics*, 28, 365–73.

—— and L. Karp (1991), 'Delegation games in customs unions', *Review of Economic Studies*, 58(2), 391–7.

Gawande, K. and U. Bandyopadhyay (2000), 'Is protection for sale? Evidence on the Grossman-Helpman theory of endogenous protection', *Review of Economics and Statistics*, 82(1), 139–52.

Ginarte, J. C. and W. G. Park (1997), 'Determinants of patent rights: a cross-national study', *Research Policy*, 26, 283–301.

Glass, A. J. and K. Saggi (2002), 'Licensing versus direct investment: implications for economic growth', *Journal of International Economics*, 56, 131–53.

Glaeser, E. L., J. A. Scheinkman, and A. Schleifer (1995), 'Economic growth in a cross-section of cities', *Journal of Monetary Economics*, 36, 117–43.

—— H. D. Kallal, J. A. Scheinkman, and A. Schleifer (1992), 'Growth in cities', *Journal of Political Economy*, 100(6), 1126–52.

Glick, R. and A. K. Rose (2001), 'Does a currency union affect trade? The time series evidence', NBER Working Paper No. 8396.

Goldberg, P. K. (1995), 'Product differentiation and oligopoly in international markets: the case of the U.S. automobile industry', *Econometrica*, 63(4), 891–951.

—— and M. M. Knetter (1997), 'Goods price and exchange rates: what have we learned?' *Journal of Economic Literature*, 35(3), 1243–72.

—— and G. Maggi (1999), 'Protection for sale: an empirical investigation', *American Economic Review*, 89(1), 1135–55.

Goolsbee, A. (1998), 'Does government R&D policy mainly benefit scientists and engineers?', *American Economic Review*, 88(2), 298–302.

Gould, D. M. (1994), 'Immigrant links to the home country: empirical implications for U.S. Bilateral trade flows', *Review of Economics and Statistics*, 76, 302–16.

Greaney, T. (1996), 'Import now! an analysis of market-share Voluntary Import Expansions (VIEs)', *Journal of International Economics*, 40, 159–63.

Greenaway, D., R. C. Hine, and C. R. Milner (1994), 'Adjustment and the measurement of intra-industry trade,' *Weltwirtschaftliches Archiv*, 130, 418–27.

—— P. Lloyd, and C. Milner (1998), 'Intra-industry FDI and trade flows: new measures of globalization of production', GLM Research Paper 85(5), University of Nottingham.

Greif, A. (1994), 'Cultural beliefs and the organization of society: a historical and theoretical reflection on collectivist and individualist societies', *Journal of Political Economy*, 102(5), 912–50.

Gropp, R. and K. Kostial (2001), 'FDI and corporate tax revenue: tax harmonization or competition?' *Finance and Development*, 38(2) 10–13.

Grossman, G. M. (2002), *The Distribution of Talent and the Pattern and Consequences of International Trade*, Princeton University, Mimeo.

—— and E. Helpman (1990), 'Comparative advantage and long run growth', *American Economic Review*, 80(4), 796–815.

—— (1991a), *Innovation and Growth in the Global Economy*, MIT Press, Cambridge, MA.

—— (1991b), 'Quality ladders in the theory of growth', *Review of Economic Studies*, 58(1), 43–61.

—— (1991c), 'Endogenous product cycles', *Economic Journal*, 101(408), 1214–29.

—— (1991d), 'Quality ladder and product cycles', *Quarterly Journal of Economics*, 106(2), 557–86.

—— (1994), 'Protection for sale', *American Economic Review*, 84(4), 833–50.

—— (1995a), 'The politics of free trade agreements', *American Economic Review*, 85, 667–90.

—— (1995b), 'Trade wars and trade talks', *Journal of Political Economy*, 103(4), 675–708.

—— (2001), *Special Interest Politics*, MIT Press, Cambridge, MA and London.

—— (2002a), 'Integration versus outsourcing in industry equilibrium', *Quarterly Journal of Economics*, 117(1), 85–120.

—— and E. Helpman (2002b), 'Outsourcing in a global economy', NBER Working Paper No. 8728.

—— (2002c), *Interest Groups and Trade Policy*, Princeton University Press, Princeton and Oxford.

—— and H. Horn (1988), 'Infant-industry protection reconsidered: the case of informational barriers', *Quarterly Journal of Economics*, 103, 767–87.

—— and G. Maggi (1998), 'Free trade vs. strategic trade: a peak into Pandora's box', in R. Sato, R. V. Ramachandran, and K. Mino (eds), *Global Competition and Integration*, Kluwer Academic Publishers, Boston.

—— (2000), 'Diversity and trade', *American Economic Review*, 90(5), 1255–75.

Grossman, S. and M. Perry (1986), 'Perfect sequential equilibria', *Journal of Economic Theory*, 39, 97–119.

Grubel, P. and P. Lloyd (1975), *Intra-Industry Trade: The Theory and Measurement of International Trade in Differentiated Products*, McMillan, London.

Gruenspecht, H. K. (1988), 'Export subsidies for differentiated products', *Journal of International Economics*, 24, 331–44.

Haaland, J. I. and I. Wooton (1998), 'Antidumping jumping: reciprocal antidumping and industrial location', *Weltwirtschaftliches Archiv*, 134(2), 340–62.

—— H. J. Kind, K. H. M. Knarvik, and J. Torstensson (1999), 'What determines the economic geography of Europe?' CEPR Discussion Paper 2072, Center for Economic Policy Research.

Hadar, J. and W. R. Russell (1969), 'Rules for ordering uncertain prospects', *American Economic Review*, 59, 25–34.

Hanson, G. (1997), 'Increasing returns, trade and the regional structure of wages', *Economic Journal*, 107, 113–33.

—— (1998), 'Regional adjustment to trade liberalization', *Regional Science and Urban Economics*, 28, 419–44.

—— (2001), 'Scale economies and the geographic concentration of industry', *Journal of Economic Geography*, 1, 255–76.

—— and A. Spilimbergo (1999), 'Illegal immigration, border enforcement, and relative wages', *American Economic Review*, 89(5), 1337–57.

Harberger, A. C. (1959), 'Using the resources at hand more effectively', *American Economic Review*, 49, 134–46.

Harrigan, J. (1999), 'Estimation of cross-country differences in industry production functions,' *Journal of International Economics*, 47, 267–93.

—— (2003), 'Specialization and the volume of trade: do the data obey the laws?' in K. Choi and J. Harrigan (eds), *The Handbook of International Trade*, Basil Blackwell, New York.

Harris, R. G. (1985), 'Why voluntary export restraints are "voluntary"?' *Canadian Journal of Economics*, 4, 799–809.

Harsanyi, J. and R. Selten (1988), *A General Theory of Equilibrium Selection in Games*, MIT Press, Cambridge.

Hartigan, J. C. (1994), 'Dumping and signaling', *Journal of Economic Behavior and Organization*, 23, 69–81.

Haveman, J. and D. Hummels (2001), *Alternative Hypotheses and the Volume of Trade: The Gravity Equation and the Extent of Specialization*, Federal Trade Commission, Mimeo.

Head, K. (1994), 'Infant industry protection in the steel rail industry', *Journal of International Economics*, 37, 141–65.

—— and J. Ries (1998), 'Immigration and trade creation', *Canadian Journal of Economics*, 31(1), 47–62.

—— (1999), 'Rationalization effects of tariff reductions', *Journal of International Economics*, 47(2), 295–320.

—— (2001), 'Overseas investment and firm exports', *Review of International Economics*, 9(1), 108–22.

—— (2002), 'Offshore production and skill upgrading by Japanese manufacturing firms', *Journal of International Economics*, 58(1): 81–105.

Helguera, I. and S. Lutz (1998), 'Oligopoly and quality leapfrogging', *World Economy* 21(1), 75–94.

Helliwell, J. F. (1998), *How Much Do National Borders Matter?* Brookings Institution, Washington, DC.

Helpman, E. (1984a), 'The factor content of foreign trade', *Economic Journal*, 94, 84–94.

—— (1984b), 'A simple theory of trade with Multinational Corporations', *Journal of Political Economy*, 92, 451–71.

—— (1987), 'Imperfect competition and international trade: evidence from fourteen industrial countries', *Journal of the Japanese and International Economies*, 1, 62–81.

—— (1997), 'Politics and trade policy', in D. M. Kreps and K. F. Wallis (eds), *Advances in Economics and Econometrics*, vol. 1, Cambridge University Press, Cambridge.

—— (1998a), 'Explaining the structure of foreign trade: where do we stand?' *Weltwirtschaftliches Archiv*, 134(4), 573–89.

—— (1998b), 'The structure of foreign trade', *Journal of Economic Perspectives*, 13(2), 121–44.

—— and P. R. Krugman (1985), *Market Structure and Foreign Trade: Increasing Returns, Imperfect Competition, and the International Economy*, MIT Press, Cambridge, MA.

—— (1989), *Trade Policy and Market Structure*, MIT Press, Cambridge, MA.

——, M. J. Melitz and S. R. Yeaple (2002), *Export versus FDI*, Harvard University, Mimeo.

Henderson, J. V. (1974), 'The sizes and types of cities', *American Economic Review*, 64, 640–56.

—— (1988), *Urban Development: Theory, Fact, and Illusion*, Oxford University Press, New York.

Hillbery, R. and D. Hummels (2000), *Explaining Home Bias in Consumption: Production Location, Commodity Composition and Magnification*, Washington, DC, US International Trade Commission, Mimeo.

Hillman, A. (1982), 'Declining industries and political-support protectionist motives', *American Economic Review*, 72, 1180–7.

—— (1989), *The Political Economy of Protection*, Harwood, Chur.

Hoekman, B. M. and M. M. Kostecki (1996), *The New Political Economy of the World Trading System*, Oxford University Press, Oxford.

Horn, H. and L. Persson (2001), 'The equilibrium ownership of an international oligopoly', *Journal of International Economics*, 53, 307–33.

Horstmann, I. J. and J. R. Markusen (1986), 'Up the average cost curve: inefficient entry and the new protectionism', *Journal of International Economics*, 20, 225–47.

—— (1987), 'Licensing versus direct investment: a model of internalization by the Multinational Enterprise', *Canadian Journal of Economics*, 20, 464–81.

—— (1992), 'Endogenous market structures in international trade (Nature Facit Saltum)', *Journal of International Economics*, 32, 109–29.

—— (1996), 'Exploring new markets: direct investment, contractual relations and the Multinational Enrterprise', *International Economic Review*, 37(1), 1–19.

Hufbauer, G. C. and K. A. Elliot (1994), *Measuring the Costs of Protection in the United States*, Institute for International Economics, Washington, DC.

—— J. J. Schott, and K. A. Elliot (1990), *Economic Sanctions Reconsidered*, 2nd edn, Institute for International Economics, Washington, DC.

Hummels, D. J. (1999a), *Toward a Geography of Trade Costs*, University of Chicago, Mimeo.

—— (1999b), *Have International Transportation Costs Declined?* University of Chicago, Mimeo.

—— and P. J. Klenow (2002), 'The variety and quality of a nation's trade', NBER Working Paper No. 8712.

—— and J. Levinsohn (1995), 'Monopolistic competition and international trade: reconsidering the evidence', *Quarterly Journal of Economics*, 110, 799–835.

—— D. Rapoport, and K.-M. Yi (2001), 'The nature and growth of vertical specialization in world trade', *Journal of International Economics*, 54, 75–96.

Hunter, L. (1991), 'The contribution of nonhomothetic preferences to trade', *Journal of International Economics, 30*, 345–358.

—— and J. Markusen (1988), 'Per-capita income as a determinant of trade', in R. C. Feenstra, (ed.), *Empirical Methods for International Trade*, MIT Press, Cambridge.

Hwang, H. and C.-C. Mai (1991), 'Optimum discriminatory tariffs under oligopolistic competition', *Canadian Journal of Economics*, 24(3), 693–702.

Irwin, D. A. and P. J. Klenow (1994), 'Learning-by-doing spillovers in the semiconductor industry', *Journal of Political Economy*, 102(6), 1200–27.

—— (1996), 'High-tech R&D subsidies: estimating the effects of sematech', *Journal of International Economics*, 40, 323–44.

—— and N. Pavcnik (2001), 'Airbus versus Boeing revisited: international competition in the aircraft market', NBER Working Paper No. 8648.

Jackson, J. H. (1997), *The World Trading System: Law and Policy of International Economic Relations*, MIT Press, Cambridge, MA.

—— (2000), *The Jurisprudence of GATT & the WTO: Insights on Treaty Law and Economic Relations*, Cambridge University Press, Cambridge, UK.

—— and A. Sykes (1997), *Implementing the Uruguay Round*, Oxford University Press, Oxford.

Jensen, R. and M. Thursby (1990), 'Tariffs with private information and reputation', *Journal of International Economics*, 29, 43–67.

Johnson, H. G. (1953/54), 'Optimum tariffs and retaliation', *Review of Economic Studies*, 21, 142–53.

—— (1965), 'Optimal trade intervention in the presence of domestic distortions', in R. E. Caves, H. G. Johnson, and P. B. Kenen (eds), *Trade, Growth and the Balance of Payments: Essays in Honor of Gottfried Haberler*, North Holland, Amsterdam.

Jones, R. W. (1965), 'The structure of simple general equilibrium models', *Journal of Political Economy*, 73, 557–72.

Jovanovic, B. (1982), 'Selection and the evolution of industry', *Econometrica*, 50, 649–70.

Justman, M. (1994), 'The effects of local demand on industry location', *Review of Economics and Statistics*, 76, 742–53.

Kang, N.-H. and S. Johansson (2000), 'Cross-border mergers and acquisitions: their role in industrial globalization', STI Working Papers, 2000/1. Paris. OECD, Directorate for Science, Technology and Industry.

Katz, E. and O. Stark (1987), 'International migration under asymmetric information', *Economic Journal*, 97(387), 718–26.

Katz, L. F. and D. Autor (1999), 'Changes in the wage structure and earnings inequality', in O. Ashenfelter and D. Card (eds), *Handbook of Labor Economics*, 3, North Holland, Amsterdam.

Katrak, H. (1977), 'Multi-national monopolies and commercial policy', *Oxford Economic Papers*, 29, 283–91.

Kehoe, P. J. and T. J. Kehoe (1994), 'Capturing NAFTA's impact with applied general equilibrium models', *Federal Reserve Bank of Minneapolis Quarterly Review*, 18(1), 17–34. Reprinted, in P. J. Kehoe and T. J. Kehoe (eds), *Modelling North American Economic Integration*, (1995). Kluwer Academic Press, London and Boston.

—— (1995), *Modelling North American Economic Integration*, Kluwer Academic Press, London and Boston.

Keller, W. (1998), 'Are international R&D spillovers trade-related? Analyzing spillovers among randomly matched trade partners', *European Economic Review*, 42, 1469–81.

—— (2002), 'Geographic localization of international technology diffusion', *American Economic Review*, 92(1), 120–42.

Kemp, M. C. and H. Y. Wan Jr. (1976), 'An elementary proposition concerning the formation of customs unions', *Journal of International Economics*, 6, 95–7.

Kennan, J. and R. Riezman (1988), 'Do big countries win tariff wars?' *International Economic Review*, 29(1), 81–5.

Khan, M. S. and Iqbal, Z. (eds) (1998), *Trade Reforms and Regional Integration in Africa*, International Monetary Fund, Washington, DC.

Kim, S. (1995), 'Expansion of markets and the geographic distribution of economic activities: the trends in U.S. regional manufacturing structure, 1860–1987', *Quarterly Journal of Economics*, 110(4), 881–908.

—— (1999), 'Regions, resources, and economic geography: sources of U.S. regional comparative advantage, 1880–1987', *Regional Science and Urban Economics*, 29, 1–32.

Klemperer, P. D. and M. A. Meyer (1989), 'Supply function equilibria in oligopoly under uncertainty', *Econometrica*, 57, 1243–77.

Klepper, G. (1990), 'Entry into the market for large transport aircraft', *European Economic Review*, 34, 775–803.

Kluth, A. (2001), 'Survey: Asian business', *The Economist*, April 4, 359, 4.

Kogut, B. and S. J. Chang (1996), 'Platform investments and volatile exchange rates: Japanese direct investment in US electronic industries', *Review of Economics and Statistics*, 78(2), 221–31.

Kohli, U. (1991), *Technology, Duality, and Foreign Trade: The GNP Function Approach to Modeling Imports and Exports*, University of Michigan Press and Harvester Wheatsheaf, Ann Arbor and London.

Kolev, D. R. and T. J. Prusa (1999), 'Tariff policy for a monopolist under incomplete information', *Journal of International Economics*, 49, 51–76.

Kovenock, D. and M. Thursby (1992), 'GATT, dispute settlement and cooperation', *Economics and Politics*, 4(1), 151–70. Reprinted, in A. V. Deardoff and Robert M. Stern (eds), Analytical and Negotiating Issues in the Global Trading System, Michigan University Press, Ann Arbor.

—— (1997), 'GATT, dispute settlement and cooperation: a reply', *Economics and Politics*, 9(1), 95–8.

Kowalczyk, C. and T. Sjöström (1994), 'Bringing GATT into the core', *Economica*, 61, 301–17.

Kreinin, M. (1961), 'Effect of tariff changes on the prices and volume of imports', *American Economic Review*, 51(3), 310–24.

Kreps, D. M. and J. Scheinkman (1983), 'Quantity precommitment and Bertrand competition yield Cournot outcomes', *Bell Journal of Economics*, 14(2), 326–37.

Kreps, D. M. and J. Sobel (1994), 'Signaling', in R. J. Aumann and S. Hart (eds), *Handbook of Game Theory*, North Holland, Amsterdam.

——, —— and R. Wilson (1982), 'Sequential equilibria', *Econometrica*, 50, 863–94.

Krishna, K. (1989), 'Trade restrictions as facilitating practices', *Journal of International Economics*, 26, 251–70.

Krishna, K. (1990*a*), 'Protection and the product line: monopoly and product quality', *International Economic Review*, 31(1), 87–102.

—— (1990*b*), 'The case of the vanishing revenues: auction quotas with monopoly', *American Economic Review*, 80(4), 828–36.

—— and J. Morgan (1998), 'Implementing results-oriented trade policies: the case of the U.S.-Japanese auto parts dispute', *European Economic Review*, 42(8), 1443–67.

—— S. Roy, and M. C. Thursby (1998), 'Implementing market access', *Review of International Economics*, 6(4), 529–44.

—— and L. H. Tan (1998), *Rags and Riches: Implementing Apparel Quotas under the Multi-Fibre Arrangement*, University of Michigan Press, Ann Arbor.

—— and M. C. Thursby (1991), 'Optimal policies with strategic distortions', *Journal of International Economics*, 31, 291–308.

——, S. Roy and M. C. Thursby (2001), 'Can Subsidies for MARs Be Procompetitive?' *Canadian Journal of Economics* 34(1): 212–24.

Krishna, P. (1998), 'Regionalism and multilateralism: a political economy approach', *Quarterly Journal of Economics*, 113(1), 227–51.

—— (2003), 'Are regional trading partners "natural"?', *Journal of Political Economy*, 111(1), 202–26.

Krueger, A. O. (1974), 'The political economy of the rent-seeking society', *American Economic Review*, 64(3), 291–303.

—— (ed.) (1998), *The WTO as an International Organization*, University of Chicago Press, Chicago.

Krugman, P. R. (1979), 'Increasing returns, monopolistic competition, and international trade', *Journal of International Economics*, 9(4), 469–79.

—— (1980), 'Scale economies, product differentiation and the pattern of trade', *American Economic Review*, 70, 950–9.

—— (1984), 'Import protection as export promotion: international competition in the presence of oligopoly and economies of scale', in H. Kierzkowski (ed.), *Monopolistic Competition and International Trade*, Oxford University Press, Oxford.

—— (1991*a*), 'Is bilateralism bad?' in E. Helpman and A. Razin (eds), *International Trade and Trade Policy*, MIT Press, Cambridge, MA.

—— (1991*b*), 'The move toward free trade zones', *Economic Review*, 76, 5–25. Kansas City: Federal Reserve Bank of Kansas City. Reprinted in *Policy Implications of Trade and Currency Zones*. Kansas City: Federal Reserve Bank of Kansas City.

—— (1991*c*), *Geography and Trade*, MIT Press, Cambrige, MA.

—— (1991*d*), 'Increasing returns and economic geography', *Journal of Political Economy*, 99, 483–99.

—— (1996), 'Urban concentration: the role of increasing returns and transport costs', *International Regional Science Review*, 19, 5–30.

Krugman, P. R. (1997), 'What should trade negotiators negotiate about?' *Journal of Economic Literature*, 35, 113–20.

—— and A. J. Venables (1995), 'Globalization and the inequality of nations', *Quarterly Journal of Economics*, 110(4), 857–80.

Laffont, J. J. and J. Tirole (1996), 'A note on environmental innovation', *Journal of Public Economics*, 62, 128–40.

Laird, S. and A. J. Yeats (1990), *Quantitative Methods for Trade Barrier Analysis*, World Bank, Washington, DC.

Lancaster, K. (1979), *Variety, Equity and Efficiency*, Columbia University Press, New York.

—— (1984), 'Protection and production differentiation', in H. Kierzkowski (ed.), *Monopolistic Competition and International Trade*, Clarendon Press, Oxford.

Lawrence, R. Z. (1991), 'Efficient or exclusionist? The import behavior of Japanese corporate groups', *Brookings Papers on Economic Activity*, 1, 311–41.

Laussel, D. (1992), 'Strategic commercial policy revisited: a supply-function equilibrium model', *American Economic Review*, 82(1), 84–99.

Leahy, D. and J. P. Neary (1997), 'Public policy towards R&D in oligopolistic industries', *American Economic Review*, 87, 642–62.

—— (1999*a*), 'R&D spillovers and the case for industrial policy in an open economy', *Oxford Economic Papers*, 51(1), 40–59.

—— (1999*b*), 'Learning by doing, precommitment and infant-industry promotion', *Review of Economic Studies*, 66(2), 447–74.

Lee, J. W. and P. Swagel (1997), 'Trade barriers and trade flows across countries and industries', *Review of Economics and Statistics*, 79(3), 372–82.

Lee, J.-Y. and E. Mansfield (1996), 'Intellectial property protection and U.S. foreign direct investment', *Review of Economics and Statistics*, 78, 181–6.

Lee, S. (1990), 'International equity markets and trade policy', *Journal of International Economics*, 29, 173–84.

Leamer, E. E. (1987), 'Paths of development in the three-factor, n-good general equilibrium model', *Journal of Political Economy*, 95, 961–99.

—— (1995), 'The Heckscher–Ohlin model in theory and practice', *Princeton Studies in International Finance*, 77.

—— (2000), 'What's the use of factor contents?', *Journal of International Economics*, 50, 17–49.

—— and J. Levinsohn (1995), 'International trade theory. The evidence', in G. Grossman and K. Rogoff (eds), *Handbook of International Economics* 3, North Holland, Amsterdam.

Leontief, W. (1953), 'Domestic production and foreign trade: the American capital position re-examined', *Proceedings of the American Philosophical Society*, 97(4), 332–49.

Lerner, A. (1936), 'The symmetry between import and export taxes', *Economica*, 3, 306–13.

Levinsohn, J. (1997), 'CARWARS: trying to make sense of U.S.–Japan trade frictions in the automobile and automobile parts markets', in R. C. Feenstra (ed.), *The Effect of U.S. Trade Protection and Promotion*, University of Chicago Press, Chicago.

Levitt, S. D. (1995), 'Congressional campaign finance reform', *Journal of Economic Perspectives*, 9(1), 183–93.

Levy, P. I. (1997), 'A political-economic analysis of free-trade agreements', *American Economic Review*, 87(4), 506–19.

Lichtenberg, F. R. and B. van P. Potterie (1998), 'International R&D spillovers: a comment', *European Economic Review*, 42, 1483–91.

Linder, S. B. (1961), *An Essay on Trade and Transformation*, John Wiley, New York.

Lipsey, R. E., E. D. Ramstetter, and M. Blömstrom (2000), 'Outward FDI and parent exports and employment: Japan, the United States, and Sweden', NBER Working Paper No. 7623.

Lloyd, T., O. Morrissey, and G. Reed (1998), 'Estimating the impact of anti-dumping and anti-cartel actions using intervention analysis', *Economic Journal*, 108, 458–76.

References 693

Long, N. V. and N. Vousden (1991), 'Protectionist responses and declining industries', *Journal of International Economics*, 30, 87–103.

Long, N. V. and N. Vousden (1995), 'The effects of trade liberalization on cost-reducing horizontal mergers', *Review of International Economics*, 3, 141–55.

López-Córdova, J. E. (1999), The Impact of Free Trade Agreements on Endogenous Tariffs: A Common Agency Analysis, University of California, Berkeley, Mimeo.

Low, P. (1993), *Trading Free: The GATT and US Trade Policy*, The Twentieth Century Fund Press, New York.

Lucas, R. E. Jr. (1990), 'Why doesn't capital flows from rich to poor countries?' *American Economic Review*, 80(2), 92–6.

—— (1993), 'Making a miracle', *Econometrica*, 61, 251–72.

Ludema, R. (1991), 'International trade bargaining and the most-favored-nation clause', *Economics and Politics*, 3(1), 1–20.

Lundborg, P. and P. S. Segerstrom (2002), 'The growth and welfare effects of international mass migration', *Journal of International Economics*, 56, 177–204.

Macho-Stadler, I., D. Perez-Castrillo, and C. Ponsati (1998), 'Stable multilateral trade agreements', *Economica*, 65, 161–77.

Magee, S. P., W. A. Brock, and L. Young (1989), *Black Hole Tariffs and Endogenous Policy Theory*, Cambridge University Press, Cambridge.

Maggi, G. (1996), 'Strategic trade policies policy with endogenous mode of competition', *American Economic Review*, 86(1), 237–58.

—— (1999a), 'Strategic trade policy under incomplete information', *International Economic Review*, 40(3), 571–94.

—— (1999b), 'The role of multilateral institutions in international trade cooperation', *American Economic Review*, 89(1), 190–214.

—— and A. Rodriguez-Clare (1998), 'The value of trade agreements in the presence of political pressures', *Journal of Political Economy*, 106, 574–601.

Mansfield, E. and A. Romeo (1980), 'Technology transfer to overseas subsidiaries by U.S.-based Firms', *Quarterly Journal of Economics*, 95, 737–50.

Markusen, J. R. (1975), 'International externalities and optimal tax structures', *Journal of International Economics*, 5(1), 15–29.

—— (1984), 'Multinationals, multi-plant economies, and the gains from trade', *Journal of International Economics*, 16, 205–26.

—— (1995), 'The boundaries of Multinational Enterprises and the theory of international trade', *Journal of Economic Perspectives*, 9(2), 169–89.

—— (2002), *Multinational Firms and the Theory of International Trade*, MIT Press, Cambridge, MA.

—— and A. J. Venables (1998), 'Multinational firms and the new trade theory', *Journal of International Economics*, 46, 183–203.

—— (1999), 'Foreign direct investment as a catalyst for industrial development', *European Economic Review*, 43, 341–56.

Martin, W. J. and K. E. Maskus (2001), 'The economics of core labor standards: implications for global trade policy', *Review of International Economics*, 9(2), 317–28.

Mas-Colell, A., M. D. Whinston, and J. R. Green (1995), *Microeconomic Theory*, Oxford University Press, Oxford.

Marshall, A. (1920), *Principles of Economics*, McMillan, New York.

Maskus, K. E. (2000), *Intellectual Property Rights in the Global Economy*, Institute for International Economics, Washington, DC.

—— and M. Penubarti (1995), 'How trade-related are intellectual property rights?' *Journal of International Economics*, 39(3–4), 227–48.

Matsuyama, K. (1990), 'Perfect equilibria in a trade liberalization game', *American Economic Review*, 80(3), 480–92.

Mayer, T. and J.-L. Mucchielli (1998), 'Strategic location behaviour: the case of Japanese investments in Europe', *Journal of Transnational Management Development*, 3(3–4), 131–67.

Mayer, W. (1981), 'Theoretical considerations on negotiated tariff adjustments', *Oxford Economic Papers*, 33(1), 135–53.

—— (1984a), 'The infant-export industry argument', *Canadian Journal of Economics*, 17, 249–69.

—— (1984b), 'Endogenous tariff formation', *American Economic Review*, 74(5), 970–85.

McCallum, J. (1995), 'National borders matter: Canada-U.S. regional trade patterns', *American Economic Review*, 85, 615–23.

McLaren, J. (1997), 'Size, sunk costs, and Judge Bowker's objection to free trade', *American Economic Review*, 87(3), 400–20.

—— (1999), 'Supplier relations and the market context: a theory of handshakes', *Journal of International Economics*, 48, 121–38.

—— (2000), ' "Globalization" and vertical structure', *American Economic Review*, 90, 1239–54.

McMillan, J. (1990), 'The economics of Section 301: a game-theoretic guide', *Economics & Politics*, 2(1), 45–57.

Melitz, M. (2002), 'The impact of trade on intra-industry reallocations and aggregate industry productivity', NBER Working Paper No. 8881.

Messerling, P. A. (1989), 'The EC antidumping regulations: a first economic appraisal, 1980–1985', *Weltwirtschaftliches Archiv*, 125(3), 563–87. See 1980–85.

—— (1990), 'Anti-dumping regulations or pro-cartel law? The EC chemical cases', *World Economy*, 13(4), 465–92.

—— (2001), *Measuring the Costs of Protection in Europe: European Commercial Policy in the 2000s*, Institute for International Economics, Washington DC.

—— and G. Reed (1995), 'Antidumping policies in the United States and the European Community', *Economic Journal*, 105, 1565–75.

Meyer, J. and M. B. Ormiston (1989), 'Deterministic transformations of random variables and the comparative statics of risk', *Journal of Risk and Uncertainty*, 2, 179–88.

Mitchell, S. K. (1997), 'GATT, dispute settlement and cooperation: a note', *Economics and Politics*, 9(1), 87–93.

Mitra, D. (1999), 'Endogenous lobby formation and endogenous protection: a long-run model of trade policy determination', *American Economic Review*, 89(1), 1116–34.

Miyagiwa, K. and Y. Ono (1995), 'Closing the technology gap under protection', *American Economic Review*, 85(4), 755–70.

Moran, T. H. (1998), *Foreign Direct Investment and Development: The New Policy Agenda for Developing Countries and Economies in Transition*, Institute for International Economics, Washington, DC.

Motta, M. (1992), 'Multinational firms and the tariff-jumping argument', *European Economic Review*, 36, 1557–71.

——, J.-F. Thisse and A. Cabrales (1997), 'On the persistence of leadership or leapfrogging in trade', *International Economic Review*, 38(4), 809–24.

Mountford, A. (1997), 'Can a brain drain be good for growth in the source economy?' *Journal of Development Economics*, 53(2), 287–303.

Mundell, R. (1957), 'International trade and factor mobility', *American Economic Review*, 47(3), 321–35.

Murphy, K. M., A. Shleifer and R. W. Vishny (1991), 'The allocation of talent: implications for growth', *Quarterly Journal of Economics* 106(2), 503–30.

Mussa, M. (1974), 'Tariffs and the distribution of income: the importance of factor specificity, substitutability, and intensity in the short and long run', *Journal of Political Economy*, 82, 1191–203.

Mussa, M. (1986), 'The adjustment process and the timing of trade liberalization', in A. M. Choksi and D. Papageorgiou (eds), *Economic Liberalization in Developing Countries*, Basil Blackwell, New York.

Nagaoka, S. (2000), 'International trade aspects of competition policy', in T. Ito and A. O. Krueger (eds), *Deregulation and Interdependence in the Asia-Pacific Region*, University of Chicago Press, Chicago.

Neary, J. P. (1978), 'Short-run capital specificity and the Pure Theory of International Trade', *Economic Journal*, 88, 488–510.

——(1994), 'Cost asymmetries in international subsidy games: should governments help winners or losers?' *Journal of International Economics*, 37(3–4), 197–218.

——(2001), 'Of hype and hyperbolas: introducing the new economic geography', *Journal of Economic Literature*, 39, 536–61.

Neven, D. and P. Seabright (1995), 'European industrial policy: the Airbus case', *Economic Policy*, 21, 313–58.

Nogués, J. (1990), 'The experience of Latin America with export subsidies', *Weltwirtschaftliches Archiv*, 126, 97–115.

Norbäck, P.-J. (2001), 'Multinational firms, technology and location', *Journal of International Economics*, 54, 449–69.

OECD (1980), *The Measurement of Scientific and Technical Activities, Frascati Manual 1980*, OECD, Paris.

——(1996), *Trade, Employment and Labor Standards: A Study of Core Workers' Rights and International Trade*, Organization for Economic Cooperation and Development, Paris.

——(1999), *Trends in International Migration*, Organization for Economic Cooperation and Development (SOPEMI), Paris.

Office of Technology Assessment (1983), *International Competitiveness in Electronics*, Government Printing Office, Washington, DC.

Oliva, M.-A. (2001), 'Estimating trade protection in Middle Eastern and North African countries', in Z. Iqbal (ed.), *Macroeconomic Issues and Policies in the Middle East and North Africa*, International Monetary Fund, Washington, DC.

——and L. A. Rivera-Batiz (2002a), 'Political institutions, capital flows and developing country growth: an empirical investigation', *Review of Development Economics*, 9(2), 248–62.

——(2002b), *Multinationals, Technology Networks and International Takeovers*, McGill University, Mimeo.

Ohlin, B. G. (1933), *Interregional and International Trade*, Harvard University Press, Cambridge, MA.

Pack, H. (2000), 'Industrial policy: growth elixir or poison?' *World Bank Research Observer*, 15(1), 47–67.

—— and K. Saggi (2001), 'Vertical technology transfer via international outsourcing', *Journal of Development Economics*, 65(2), 389–415.

Panagariya, A. (1999), *Regionalism in Trade Policy: Essays on Preferential Trading*, World Scientific, London.

—— (2000*a*), 'Evaluating the case for export subsidies', World Bank Working Paper Series Industry, Competition, Science Parks No. 2276.

—— (2000*b*), 'Preferential trade liberalization: the traditional theory and new developments', *Journal of Economic Literature*, 38(2), 287–331.

—— and R. Findlay (1996), 'A political-economy analysis of free-trade areas and customs unions', in R. Feenstra, D. Irwin, and E. Grossman (eds), *The Political Economy of Trade Reform: Essays in Honor of Jagdish Bhagwati*, MIT Press, Cambridge, MA.

—— and P. Gupta (1998), 'Anti-dumping duty versus Price negotiations', *The World Economy*, 21(8), 1003–20.

Park, W. G. and J. C. Ginarte (1997), 'Determinants of patent rights: a cross-national study', *Research Policy*, 26(3), 283–301.

Pavcnik, N. (2002), 'Trade liberalization, exit, and productivity improvements: evidence from chilean plants', *Review of Economic Studies*, 69, 245–76.

Peltzman, S. (1976), 'Toward a more General Theory of Regulation', *Journal of Law and Economics*, 19(2), 211–40.

Porter, M. (1990), *The Competitive Advantage of Nations*, Free Press, New York.

—— H. Takeuchi, and M. Sakakibara (2000), *Can Japan Compete?* Basic Books, New York, NY.

Prusa, T. (1992), 'Why are so many antidumping petitions withdrawn?' *Journal of International Economics*, 33, 1–20.

—— (1997), 'The trade effects of antidumping actions', in R. C. Feenstra (ed.), *The Effects of U.S. Trade Protection and Promotion Policies*, University of Chicago Press, Chicago.

—— (2001), 'On the spread and impact of anti-dumpins', *Canadian Journal of Economics*, 34(3), 599–611.

Puga, D. (1999), 'The rise and fall of regional inequalities', *European Economic Review*, 43, 303–34.

—— and A. Venables (1997), 'Preferential trading arrangements and industrial location', *Journal of International Economics*, 43, 347–68.

—— (1998), 'Trading arrangements and industrial development', *World Bank Economic Review*, 12(2), 221–49.

Pugel, T. A., E. S. Kragas, and Y. Kimura (1996), 'Further evidence on Japanese direct investment in US manufacturing', *Review of Economics and Statistics*, 78(2), 208–13.

Qiu, L. D. (1994), 'Optimal strategic trade policy under asymmetric information', *Journal of International Economics*, 36, 333–54.

—— and Z. Tao (2001), 'Export, foreign direct investment, and local content requirement', *Journal of Development Economics*, 66(1), 101–25.

Raff, H. and Y.-H. Kim (1999), 'Optimal export policy in the presence of informational barriers to entry and imperfect competition', *Journal of International Economics*, 49, 99–123.

Rama, M. (1994), 'Endogenous trade policy: a Time-Series Approach', *Economics and Politics*, 6, 215–31.

Rapp, R. T. and R. P. Rozek (1990), 'Benefits and costs of intellectual protection on developing countries', *Journal of World Trade*, 24, 75–102.

Rauch, J. E. (1999), 'Networks versus markets in international trade', *Journal of International Economics*, 48(1), 7–35.

—— (2001), 'Business and social networks in international trade', *Journal of Economic Literature*, 39(4), 1177–203.

—— (2002), 'Ethnic Chinese networks in international trade', *Review of Economic and Statistics*, 84(1), 116–30.

—— and A. Casella (2003), Overcoming Informational Barriers to International Resource Allocation: Prices and Ties. *Economic Journal* 113, 21–42.

—— and V. Trindade (2000), 'Information and globalization: wage co-movements, labor demand elasticity, and conventional trade liberalization', NBER Working Paper No. 7671.

Repetto, A. and J. Ventura (1998), *The Leontief-Trefler Hypothesis and Factor Price Insensitivity*, MIT, Mimeo.

Rhee, J. W. and T. Belot (1989), *Export Catalysts in Low-Income Countries. Industry and Energy Department, Industry Series Paper No. 5*, The Work Bank, Washington DC.

Richardson, M. (1994), 'Why a free trade area? The tariff also rises', *Economics & Politics*, 6(1), 79–95.

Riezman, R. (1985), 'Custom Unions and the core', *Journal of International Economics*, 19, 355–65.

—— (1999), 'Can Bilateral trade agreements help to induce free trade?' *Canadian Journal of Economics*, 32(3), 751–66.

—— and J. D. Wilson (1997), 'Political reform and trade policy', *Journal of International Economics*, 42, 67–90.

Rivera-Batiz, F. L. (1982), 'Nontraded goods and the Pure Theory of International Trade with equal numbers of goods and factors', *International Economic Review*, 23(2), 401–9.

—— (1983), 'Trade theory, distribution of income, and immigration', *American Economic Review*, 73(2), 183–7.

—— (1988), 'Monopolistic competition, economies of scale and agglomeration economies in consumption and production', *Regional Science and Urban Economics*, 18(1), 125–54.

—— (1999), 'Undocumented workers in the labor market: an analysis of the earnings of legal and illegal Mexican immigrants in the United States', *Journal of Population Economics*, 12(1), 91–116.

—— and L. A. Rivera-Batiz (1990), 'The effects of direct foreign investment in the presence of increasing returns due to specialization', *Journal of Development Economics*, 34(1), 287–307.

Rivera-Batiz, L. A. and P. M. Romer (1991a), 'Economic integration and endogenous growth', *Quarterly Journal of Economics*, 106(2), 531–55.

—— (1991b), 'International trade with endogenous technological change', *European Economic Review*, 35(4), 971–1001.

Roberts, M. and J. Tybout (1997a), 'The decision to export in Colombia: an empirical model of entry with sunk costs', *American Economic Review*, 87(4), 545–64.

—— (1997b), *What Makes Exports Boom?* Oxford University Press, New York and Oxford.

Rodriguez, F. and Rodrik, D. (2001), 'Trade policy and economic growth: a skeptic's guide to the cross-national evidence', in B. Bernanke and K. S. Rogoff (eds), *Macroeconomics Annual 2000*, MIT Press, Cambridge.

Rodrik, D. (1986), 'Tariffs, subsidies, and welfare with endogenous policy', *Journal of International Economics*, 21(3–4), 285–99.

Rodrik, D. (1993), 'Industrial organization and product quality: evidence from South Korean and Taiwanese exports', in P. Krugman and A. Smith (eds), *Empirical Studies of Strategic Trade Policy*, University of Chicago Press, Chicago.

—— (1995*a*), 'Getting interventions right: how South Korea and Taiwan grew rich?' *Economic Policy*, 20, 55–107.

—— (1995*b*), 'Taking trade policy seriously: export subsidization as a case study in policy effectiveness', in J. Levinsohn, A. V. Deardorff, and R. M. Stern (eds), *New Directions in Trade Theory*, University of Michigan Press, Ann Arbor.

Romalis, J. (2002*a*), *Factor Proportions and the Structure of Commodity Trade*, University of Chicago, Mimeo.

—— (2002*b*), *NAFTA's and CUSFTA's Impact on North American Trade*, University of Chicago, Mimeo.

Romer, P. M. (1990), 'Endogenous technological change', *Journal of Political Economy*, 90(SS), 71–102.

—— (1993), 'Implementing a National Technology Strategy with self organizing industry investment boards', *Brookings Papers on Economic Activity: Microeconomics*, 2, 345–90.

—— (1994), 'New goods, old theory, and the welfare costs of trade restrictions', *Journal of Development Economics*, 43, 5–38.

—— (2000), 'Should the government subsidize supply or demand in the market for scientists and engineers?' NBER Working Paper No. 7723.

Rose, A. K. (2000), 'One money, one market: the effect of common currencies on trade', *Economic Policy*, 30, 9–45.

—— and E. van Wincoop (2001), 'National money as a barrier to international trade: the real case for currency union', *American Economic Review*, 91(2), 386–39.

—— (2002*a*), 'Do we really know that the WTO increases trade?' NBER Working Paper No. 9273.

—— (2002*b*), 'Is trade good or bad for the environment? Sorting out the causality', NBER Working Paper No. 9201.

—— (2002*c*). 'Do WTO members have more liberal trade policy?' NBER Working Paper No. 9347.

—— (2003), 'Which international institutions promote international trade', Working Paper DP 3764, The Centre for Economic Policy Research (CEPR), London.

Rossi, S. and P. Volpin (2001), *The Governance Motive in Cross-Border Mergers and Acquisitions*, London Business School, Mimeo.

Rubinstein, A. (1982), 'Perfect equilibrium in a bargaining model', *Econometrica*, 50, 97–110.

Rugman, A., J. Kirton, and J. Soloway (1999), *Environmental Regulations and Corporate Strategy: A NAFTA Perspective*, Oxford University Press, Oxford.

Rybczinski, T. M. (1955), 'Factor endowment and relative commodity prices', *Economica*, 22, 336–41.

Rysman, M. (2000), 'Competition policy as strategic trade', Industry Studies Project Working Paper No. 100, Boston University.

Sachs, J. D. and Warner, A. M. (1995), 'Economic reform and the process of global integration', *Brookings Papers on Economic Activity*, 1, 1–118.

Sazanami, Y., S. Urata, and H. Kawai (1995), *Measuring the Costs of Protection in Japan*, Institute for International Economics, Washington, DC.

Samuelson, P. A. (1948), 'International trade and the equalization of factor prices', *Economic Journal*, 58(230), 163–84.

—— (1949), 'International factor-price equalization once again', *Economic Journal*, 59, 181–97.

Sánchez, G. (1998), *Lobbying, Innovation and Protectionist Cycles*, Universitat Pompeu Fabra, Barcelona, Mimeo.

Sapir, A. (1992), 'Regional integration in Europe', *Economic Journal*, 102, 1491–506.

—— (1998), 'The political economy of EC regionalism', *European Economic Review*, 42(3–5), 717–32.

Saxonhouse, G. (1993), 'What does Japanese trade structure tell us about Japanese trade policy?', *Journal of Economic Perspectives*, 7, 21–43.

Schiff, M. and A. Winters (1998), 'Regional integration as diplomacy', *World Bank Economic Review*, 12(2), 271–95.

Schott, P. (2000), *One Size Fits All? Heckscher–Ohlin Specialization in Global Production*, Yale University, Mimeo.

Segerstrom, P. S., T. Anant, and E. Dinopoulos (1990), 'A Schumpeterian model of the product life cycle', *American Economic Review*, 80, 1077–92.

Sharer, R., P. Sorsa, N. Calika, P. Ross, C. Shiells, and T. Dorsey (1998), *Trade Liberalization in IMF-Supported Programs*, International Monetary Fund, Washington DC.

Shiells, C., R. Stern, and A. Deardoff (1986), 'Estimates of the elasticities of substitution between imports and home goods in the United States', *Weltwirtschaftliches Archiv*, 122, 497–519.

Shoven, J. B. and J. Whalley (1984), 'Applied general equilibrium models of taxation and international trade: an introduction and survey', *Journal of Economic Literature*, 22(3), 1007–51.

Shuguang, Z., Yansheng, Z., and W. Zhongxin (1998), *Measuring the Costs of Protection in China*, Institute for International Economics, Washington, DC.

Shy, O. (2000), 'Exporting as a signal for product quality', *Economica*, 67, 79–90.

Sjaastad, L. A. (1962), 'The costs and returns of human migration', *Journal of Political Economy*, 70 (Supplement), 80–93.

Slaughter, M. J. (2000), 'Production transfer within multinational enterprises and american wages', *Journal of International Economics*, 50(2), 449–72.

—— (2001), 'Trade liberalization and per capita income convergence: a difference-in-differences analysis', *Journal of International Economics*, 55(1), 203–28.

Smith, A. (1987), 'Strategic investment, multinational corporations, and trade policy', *European Economic Review*, 31, 89–96.

—— and A. Venables (1988), 'Completing the internal market in the European Community: some industry simulations', *European Economic Review*, 32(7), 1501–25.

—— (1999), 'Are weak patent rights a barrier to U.S. exports?' *Journal of International Economics*, 48, 151–77.

Spence, A. M. (1984), 'Cost reduction, competition and industrial performance', *Econometrica*, 52, 101–21.

Spencer, B. J. and J. A. Brander (1983), 'International R&D rivalry and industrial strategy', *Review of Economic Studies*, 50, 707–22.

—— and L. D. Qiu (2001), 'Keiretsu and relationship-specific investment: a barrier to trade?' *International Economic Review*, 42(4), 871–901.

Srinivasan, T. N. and J. Whalley (eds) (1986), *General Equilibrium Trade Modeling*, MIT Press, Cambridge.

Srinivasan, T. N., Whalley, J., and Wooton, I. (1993). 'Measuring the effects of regionalism on trade and welfare', in K. Anderson and R. Blackhurst (eds), *Regional Integration and the Global Trading System*, Harvester Wheatsheaf, London.

—— and A. Panagariya (1998), *Lectures on International Trade*, 2nd edn, MIT Press, Cambridge, MA.

—— and J. Bhagwati (1999), *Outward-Orientation and Development: Are Revisionists Right?* Yale University, Mimeo.

Staiger, R. W. (1995), 'A theory of gradual trade liberalization', in J. Levinsohn, A.V. Deardorff, and R. M. Stern (eds), *New Directions on Trade Theory*, University of Michigan Press, Ann Arbor.

—— and F. A. Wolak (1989), 'Strategic use of antidumping law to enforce tacit international collusion', NBER Working Paper No. 3016.

—— (1992), 'The effects of AD law in the presence of foreign monopoly', *Journal of International Economics*, 32, 265–87.

—— (1994), 'Measuring industry specific protection: antidumping in the United States', *Brookings Papers on Economics Activity, Microeconomics* 1, 51–103.

Stark, O., C. Helmenstein, and A. Prskewetz (1998), 'A brain gain with a brain drain', *Economics Letters*, 55, 227–34.

Stigler, G. (1971), 'The Theory of Economic Regulation', *Bell Journal of Economic Management and Science*, 2, 3–21.

Stokey, N. (1991), 'The volume and composition of trade between rich and poor countries', *Review of Economic Studies*, 58, 63–80.

Stolper, W. F. and P. A. Samuelson (1941), 'Protection and real wages', *Review of Economic Studies*, 9, 58–73.

Sundaram, R. K. (1996), *A First Course in Optimization Theory*, Cambridge University Press, Cambridge.

Svedverg, P. (1979), 'Optimal tariff policy on imports from multinationals', *Economic Record*, 55, 64–7.

Svensson, R. (1996), 'Effects of overseas production on home country exports: evidence based on Swedish Multinationals', *Weltwirtschaftliches Archiv*, 132(2), 304–29.

Sykes, A. O. (1992), 'Constructive unilateral threats in international commercial relations: the limit cases for section 301', *Law and Policy in International Business*, 23, 263–330.

Thomas, V. and J. Nash (1991), *Best Practices in Trade Policy Reform*, Oxford University Press, Oxford.

Topkis, D. M. (1978), 'Minimizing a submodular function on a lattice', *Operations Research*, 26, 305–21.

Tornell, A. and G. Esquivel (1997), 'Political economy of Mexico's entry into NAFTA', in T. Ito and A. O. Krueger (eds), *Regionalism versus Multilateral Trade Arrangements*, Chicago University Press, Chicago.

Trefler, D. (1993a), 'Factor price differences: Leontief was right', *Journal of Political Economy*, 101(6), 961–87.

—— (1993b), 'Trade liberalization and the theory of endogenous protection: an Econometric Study of U.S. import policy', *Journal of Political Economy*, 101(1), 138–60.

—— (1995), 'The case of the missing trade and other mysteries', *American Economic Review*, 85(5), 1029–46.

—— (2001), 'The long and short of the Canada-U.S. free trade agreement', NBER Working Paper No. 8418.

—— and S. C. Zhu (2000), 'Beyond the Algebra of explanation: HOV for the technology age', *American Economic Review*, 90(2), 145–9.

Trela, I. and J. Whalley (1995), 'Internal quota-allocation schemes and the costs of the MFA', *Review of International Economics*, 3(3), 284–306.

Tybout, J. R. and D. Westbrook (1995), 'Trade liberalization and the dimensions of efficiency change in Mexican manufacturing industries', *Journal of International Economics*, 39(1–2), 53–78.

Ulph, A. (1997), 'Environmental policy, strategic trade and innovation', in C. Carraro and D. Siniscalco (eds), *New Directions in the Economic Theory of the Environment*, Cambridge University Press, Cambridge.

—— and D. Ulph (1996), 'Trade, strategic innovation and strategic environmental policy—a general analysis', in C. Carraro, Y. Katsoulacos, and A. Xepapadeas (eds), *Environmental Policy and Market Structure*, Kluwer Academic Publishers, Dordrecht.

US Department of Commerce (1979), *A Report on the U.S. Semiconductor Industry*, Government Printing Office, Washington, DC.

Vandenbussche, H., J. Konings, and L. Springael (2002), 'Import diversion under European antidumping policy', *Journal of Industry, Competition and Trade*, 1(3), 283–299.

Vanek, J. (1968), 'The factor proportions theory: the N-Factor case', *Kyklos*, 21(4), 749–55.

Venables, A. (1996), 'Equilibrium locations of vertically linked industries', *International Economic Review*, 37, 341–60.

—— and A. Smith (1986), 'Trade and industrial policy under imperfect competition', *Economic Policy*, 3, 622–72. Reprinted, in D. B. Audretsch (ed.), *International Library of Critical Writings in Economics: Industrial Policy and Competitive Advantage*, Edward Elgar, London, UK.

Ventura, J. (1997), 'Growth and interdependence', *Quarterly Journal of Economics*, 112(1), 57–84.

Verdier, T. (1998), 'Results-oriented versus rules-oriented trade policies: a theoretical survey', *European Economic Review*, 42, 733–44.

Vermulst, E. A. (1987), *Antidumping Law and Practice in the United States and the European Communities: A Comparative Analysis*, North Holland, Amsterdam.

Vernon, R. (1966), 'International investment and international trade in the product cycle', *Quarterly Journal of Economics*, 80(2), 190–207.

Viner, J. (1923), *Dumping: A Problem in International Trade*, University of Chicago Press, Chicago.

Viner, J. (1950), *The Customs Union Issue*, Carnegie Endowment for International Peace, New York.

Vines, D. (1998), 'The WTO in relation to the fund and the bank: competencies, agendas and linkages', in A. O. Krueger (ed.), *The WTO as an International Organization*, University of Chicago Press, Chicago and London.

Vousden, N. (1990), *The Economics of Trade Protection*, Cambridge University Press, Cambridge.

Wade, R. (1988), *Taiwan, China's Duty Rebate System*, Mimeo, Trade Policy Division, Country Economics Department, World Bank, Washington, DC.

Wei, S.-J. and J. Frankel (1996), 'Can regional blocks be stepping stones to global free trade?' *International Review of Economics and Finance*, 5, 339–47.

Weinstein, D. E. (1992), 'Competition and unilateral dumping', *Journal of International Economics*, 32, 379–88.

Whalley, J. (1998), 'Why do countries seek regional trade agreements?' in J. Frankel (ed.), *The Regionalization of the World Economy*, Chicago University Press, Chicago.

White, H. (1980), 'A Heteroskedasticity-consistent covariance matrix estimator and a direct test for Heteroskedasticity', *Econometrics*, 48, 817–38.

Wilson, J. S., T. Otsuki, and M. Sewadeh (2002), 'Dirty exports and environmental regulation: do standards mattter?' World Bank Policy Research Working Paper No. 2806, World Bank, Washington DC.

Winters, L. A. (1993), 'The European Community: a case of successful integration?' in J. de Melo and A. Panagariya (eds), *New Dimensions in Regional Integration*, Cambridge University Press, Cambridge.

—— and W. Chang (2000), 'Regional integration and the prices of imports: an empirical investigation', *Journal of International Economics*, 51, 363–77.

—— (1999), 'How regional blocs affect excluded countries: the price effects of MERCOSUR', CEPR Discussion Paper 2179, Center for Economic Policy Research.

Wolf, H. C. (2000), 'Intranational home bias in trade', *Review of Economics and Statistics*, 2(4), 555–63.

Wong, K.-Y. (1989), 'Optimal threat of trade restriction and Quid Pro Quo foreign investment', *Economics and Politics*, 1(3), 277–300.

—— (1995), *International Trade in Goods and Factor Mobility*, MIT Press, Cambridge, MA.

Woodland, A. D. (1982), *International Trade and Resource Allocation*, North-Holland, Amsterdam.

Yam, J. C. K. (2001), 'The WTO: China's future and Hong Kong's opportunity', *Cato Journal*, 21(1), 1–11.

Yang, G. and K. Maskus (2000), 'Intellectual property rights, licensing, and innovation in an endogenous product-cycle model,' *Journal of International Economics*, 53(1), 169–87.

Yeats, A. J. (2001), 'Just how big is global production sharing?' in S. W. Arndt and H. Kierzkowski (eds), *Fragmentation: New Production Patterns in the World Economy*, Oxford University Press, Oxford.

Yi, K.-M. (2003), 'Can vertical specialization explain the growth of world trade?', *Journal of Political Economy*, 111(1), 52–102.

Yi, S. S. (1996), 'Endogenous formation of customs unions under imperfect competition: open regionalism is good', *Journal of International Economics*, 41, 153–77.

Young, A. (1991), 'Learning by doing and the dynamic effects of international trade', *Quarterly Journal of Economics*, 106(2), 369–405.

—— (1995), 'The tyrany of numbers: confronting the statistical realities of the East Asian growth experience', *Quarterly Journal of Economics*, 110, 641–80.

Index